Philosophy

History and Readings

EIGHTH EDITION

Samuel Enoch Stumpf

Late, of Vanderbilt University

James Fieser

University of Tennessee at Martin

The McGraw-Hill Companies

Connect
Learn
Succeed™

PHILOSOPHY, HISTORY AND READINGS, EIGHTH EDITION

Published by McGraw-Hill, a business unit of The McGraw-Hill Companies, Inc., 1221 Avenue of the Americas, New York, NY 10020. Copyright © 2012 by The McGraw-Hill Companies, Inc. All rights reserved. Previous editions © 2008, 2003 and 1994. No part of this publication may be reproduced or distributed in any form or by any means, or stored in a database or retrieval system, without the prior written consent of The McGraw-Hill Companies, Inc., including, but not limited to, in any network or other electronic storage or transmission, or broadcast for distance learning.

Some ancillaries, including electronic and print components, may not be available to customers outside the United States.

This book is printed on acid-free paper containing 10% postconsumer waste.

1 2 3 4 5 6 7 8 9 0 DOC/DOC 1 0 9 8 7 6 5 4 3 2 1

ISBN 978-0-07-353576-0
MHID 0-07-353576-1

Vice President & Editor-in-Chief: *Michael Ryan*
Vice President & Director of Specialized Publishing: *Janice M. Roerig-Blong*
Editorial Director: *Beth Mejia*
Sponsoring Editor: *Mark Georgiev*
Managing Developmental Editor: *Meghan Campbell*
Director of Marketing & Sales: *Jennifer J. Lewis*
Senior Project Manager: *Joyce Watters*
Design Coordinator: *Brenda A. Rolwes*
Cover Design: *Studio Montage, St. Louis, Missouri*
Cover Image: *© CORBIS/RF*
Buyer: *Nicole Baumgartner*
Compositor: *S4Carlisle Publishing Services*
Typeface: *10/12 Palatino LT Std*
Printer: *R. R. Donnelley*

All credits appearing on page or at the end of the book are considered to be an extension of the copyright page.

Library of Congress Cataloging-in-Publication Data

Stumpf, Samuel Enoch, 1918-
   Philosophy: history and problems / Samuel Enoch Stumpf, James Fieser. —8th ed.
      p. cm.
   ISBN-13: 978-0-07-353576-0
   ISBN-10: 0-07-353576-1
   1. Philosophy—History. 2. Philosophy. I. Fieser, James. II. Title.
   B72.S788 2012
   190—dc22

                                                                    2011003433

www.mhhe.com

About the Authors

SAMUEL ENOCH STUMPF received his Ph.D. from the University of Chicago. He was a Ford Fellow at Harvard University and a Rockefeller Fellow at Oxford University. For fifteen years he was chairman of the Philosophy Department at Vanderbilt University, served a term as president of Cornell College of Iowa, and returned to Vanderbilt as Professor of the Philosophy of Law in the School of Law and as Research Professor of Medical Philosophy in the School of Medicine. He participated in various national organizations and lectured widely in the fields of philosophy, medical ethics, and jurisprudence and was Emeritus Professor of Philosophy and Law at Vanderbilt University. Professor Stumpf died in 1998.

JAMES FIESER is Professor of Philosophy at the University of Tennessee at Martin. He received his B.A. from Berea College, and his M.A. and Ph.D. in philosophy from Purdue University. He is author, coauthor, or editor of ten text books, including *Socrates to Sartre and Beyond* (9/e 2011), *Ethical Theory: Classical and Contemporary Readings* (6/e 2010), *An Historical Introduction to Philosophy* (2003), and *Moral Philosophy through the Ages* (2001). He has edited and annotated the ten-volume *Early Responses to Hume* (2/e 2005) and the five-volume *Scottish Common Sense Philosophy* (2000). He is founder and general editor of the *Internet Encyclopedia of Philosophy* Web site (www.iep.utm.edu).

Dedication
To Jean Stumpf and Laura Roberts-Fieser

Contents
Socrates to Sartre and Beyond
A History of Philosophy

Part Three
EARLY MODERN PHILOSOPHY

Part Four
LATE MODERN AND NINETEENTH
CENTURY PHILOSOPHY

Part Five
TWENTIETH CENTURY
AND CONTEMPORARY PHILOSOPHY

APPENDIX

Contents
Classic Readings
in the History of Philosophy

Part One
ANCIENT GREEK PHILOSOPHY

Part Two
HELLENISTIC AND MEDIEVAL PHILOSOPHY

Part Three
EARLY MODERN PHILOSOPHY

Part Four
LATE MODERN AND NINETEENTH CENTURY

Part Five
TWENTIETH CENTURY AND CONTEMPORARY

APPENDIX

Preface to Socrates to Sartre and Beyond

The history of philosophy is in many ways like an epic novel. There are revered ancestors who, through great suffering, establish traditions for the betterment of their descendants. There are black sheep of the family who stir up trouble, embarrass their brothers and sisters, and sometimes even invite the wrath of political and religious authorities. There are bitter feuds between families that last generations, often with no clear victor ever emerging. As the saga passes from one era to another, there is some feeling of progress. Old-fashioned ways are discarded and replaced with new—although sometimes faddish—ones. Thus, the history of philosophy is an "adventure of ideas," to use the words of one great philosopher. This book attempts to describe a major thread of that drama.

This book was originally published in 1966 by Samuel Enoch Stumpf, and was quickly embraced as an authoritative, yet reader-friendly survey of the history of philosophy in the Western tradition. The work starts with the first philosophers of ancient Greece, proceeds through the Middle Ages, Renaissance, and modern periods, and culminates with the most important contemporary contributions. New editions of this book have appeared over the years in response to the ever-changing needs of college instructors and students. Chapters were rearranged, sections added, scholarship updated, and each sentence meticulously picked over to make the writing style accessible to newer generations of readers. This newly revised edition attempts to reflect the spirit of change that directed previous editions, and the major changes include these:

- New section on John Rawls's theory of justice as fairness
- New section on Robert Nozick's entitlement theory
- New section on Jeremy Bentham's critique of rights theory and social contract theory
- New discussion of Sextus Empiricus on skepticism and morality

Other minor changes and improvements have been made throughout.

This text comes in two different formats. One, titled *Socrates to Sartre and Beyond*, is a survey of Western philosophy. The other, titled *History and Readings,* contains the entirety of *Socrates to Sartre and Beyond*, plus an anthology titled *Classic Readings in the History of Philosophy*. The *Classic Readings* portion of the combined book has also gone through changes in this edition, which include the following:

- New chronological arrangement of readings, with optional topical table of contents
- Selections by Presocratic philosophers
- Additional selections by Aristotle on nature and the soul (from *Physics*, *Metaphysics*, and *On the Soul*)
- Additional selections by Augustine on skepticism and the two cities (from *On the Trinity* and *City of God*)
- Voltaire on the best of all possible worlds (from *Philosophical Dictionary*)
- Georg W.F. Hegel on lordship-bondage and world history (from *Phenomenology of Spirit* and *The Philosophy of Right*)
- Søren Kierkegaard on faith and paradox (from *Fear and Trembling*)
- Willard Van Orman Quine on empiricism (from "Two Dogmas of Empiricism")
- Daniel Dennett on human dignity and science (from "How to Protect Human Dignity from Science")
- Appendix on classic Eastern philosophy with primary texts from the Hindu, Buddhist, Confucian, and Daoist traditions

Regrettably, as new material is added to each new edition of the anthology, an equal amount of material must be removed. Those selections deleted were the least used in the anthology, as indicated by a survey of a sample of current book users.

I thank Mark Georgiev, Meghan Campbell, Lori Bradshaw, and the rest of the gifted editorial staff at McGraw-Hill for their expertise and good nature throughout the production of this new edition. I also thank the many reviewers of this book for their helpful suggestions for improvements.

James Fieser
April 26, 2010 (Hume's birthday)

PART ONE

Ancient Greek Philosophy

CHAPTER 1

Socrates's Predecessors

*H*uman beings have lived on this planet for hundreds of thousands of years. We, of course, cannot know all the experiences and thoughts of the earliest people. Still, it is reasonable to suppose that people then, as now, were driven by a desire to explain the world. Perhaps our earliest ancestors thought about how the world was formed, whether they were unique among the animals, and whether there was a world beyond the earthly one surrounding them. They may have also wondered whether there was a uniform standard of moral behavior or social order that applied to the various tribes they encountered. Whatever they may have thought about these subjects, their opinions are now irretrievably lost to time. It is only through the introduction of writing—a comparatively recent invention—that we know the precise speculations of any of our ancestors. When we look at the earliest writings from around the globe, we find that various regions had their own speculative traditions—such as those of East Asia, the Indian subcontinent, the Middle East, and Africa. This book is an account of one such tradition, namely, that which developed within Europe and was later exported to the Americas and elsewhere around the world. This tradition is often called "Western," designating its origin within the western part of the Eurasian landmass.

The story of Western philosophy begins in a series of Greek islands and colonies during the sixth century BCE (that is, Before the Common Era). Some original thinkers were driven by very specific puzzles, most notably, "What are things really like?" and "How can we explain the process of change in things?" The solutions they gave to these puzzles were shortly thereafter dubbed "philosophy"—the love of wisdom. What underlies these specula-tions was the gradual recognition that things are not exactly what they seem to be. Appearance often differs from reality. There are brute facts of birth, death, growth, and decay—coming into being and passing away. These facts raised sweeping questions of how things and people come into existence, can differ at different times, and pass out of existence only to be followed by other things and persons. Many of the answers given to these questions by the earliest philosophers are not as important as the fact that they focused upon these *specific* questions. They approached these problems with a fresh point of view that was in stark contrast to the more mythical approach taken by the great poets of the time.

The birthplace of Greek philosophy was the seaport of Miletus, located across the Aegean Sea from Athens, on the western shores of Ionia in Asia Minor. Because of their location, the first Greek philosophers are called either Milesians or Ionians. By the time the Milesian philosophers began their systematic work, in roughly 585 BCE, Miletus had been a crossroads for both seaborne commerce and cosmopolitan ideas. The wealth of the city allowed for leisure time, without which the life of art and philosophy could not develop. Further, the broadmindedness and inquisitiveness of its people created a congenial atmosphere for philosophical intellectual activity. Earlier, Ionia had produced Homer (ca. 700 BCE), author of the *Iliad* and *Odyssey*. In these timeless classics of epic poetry, Homer describes the scene of Mount Olympus, where the gods pursued lives very similar to those of their human counterparts on earth. This poetic view of the world also depicted ways in which the gods intruded into people's affairs. In particular, the Homeric gods would punish people for their lack of moderation and especially for their pride or insubordination, which the Greeks called *hubris*. It is not that Homer's gods were exceptionally moral beings. Instead, they were merely *stronger* than humans, and demanded obedience.

Although Homer depicts the gods with largely human features, he occasionally hints at a rigorous order in nature. Specifically, he suggests that there is a power called "fate," to which even the gods are subject and to which everyone and everything must be subordinate. Nevertheless, Homer's poetic imagination is dominated so thoroughly by human terms that his world is peopled everywhere with human types. Also, his conception of nature is that of capricious wills at work instead of the reign of physical natural laws. It was Hesiod (ca. 700 BCE), writing around the same time as Homer, who altered this concept of the gods and fate. He thus removed from the gods all capriciousness and instead ascribed to them a moral consistency. Although Hesiod retains the notion that the gods control nature, he balances this personal element in the nature of things with an emphasis on the impersonal operation of the moral law of the universe. The moral order, in Hesiod's view, is still the product of Zeus's commands. However, contrary to Homer, these commands are neither capricious nor calculated to gratify the gods, but instead are fashioned for the good of people. For Hesiod the universe is a moral order, and from this idea it is a short step to say, without *any* reference to the gods, that there is an impersonal force controlling the structure of the universe and regulating its process of changes.

This was the short step taken by three great Milesian philosophers, namely, Thales (ca. 585 BCE), Anaximander (ca. 610–546 BCE), and Anaximenes (585–528 BCE). Whereas Hesiod still thought in terms of traditional mythology with humanlike gods, philosophy among the Milesians began as an act of independent thought. To ask, as they did, "What are things really like?" and "How can we explain the process of change in things?" substantially departs from the poetry of Homer and Hesiod and moves toward a more scientific way of thinking. In point of fact, at this stage of history, science and philosophy were the same thing, and only later did various specific disciplines separate themselves from the field of philosophy. Medicine was the first to do so. Thus, we can rightly call the Milesians primitive scientists, as well as the first Greek philosophers. The important thing to keep in mind, though, is that Greek philosophy from the start was an *intellectual* activity. It was not a matter only of seeing or believing, but of *thinking*, and philosophy meant thinking about basic questions with an attitude of genuine and free inquiry.

WHAT IS PERMANENT IN EXISTENCE?

Thales

We do not know as much as we would like about Thales of Miletus, and what we do know is rather anecdotal in nature. He left no writings, and all that is available are fragmentary references to him by later writers who recorded memorable incidents in his career. He was a contemporary of Greek king Croesus and statesman Solon, and the years of his life are set between 624 and 546 BCE. During a military campaign against Persia, he apparently solved the difficult logistical problem of enabling the Lydian king's army to cross the wide Halys River. His solution was to dig a channel that diverted part of the flow, thereby making two narrower rivers over which bridges could be built. While traveling in Egypt, Thales worked out a way of measuring the height of the pyramids. His solution was to use the simple procedure of measuring a pyramid's shadow at that time of day when his own shadow was equal in length to his own height. It may have been during these Egyptian travels, too, that he became acquainted with the kinds of knowledge that enabled him to predict the eclipse of the sun on May 28, 585 BCE. In a practical vein, while in Miletus, he constructed an instrument for measuring the distance of ships sighted at sea. And, as an aid to navigation, he urged sailors to use the constellation Little Bear as the surest guide for determining the direction of the north.

It was probably inevitable that tradition would attach questionable tales to such an extraordinary person as Thales. For example, Plato (427–347 BCE) writes about "the joke which the clever witty Thracian handmaid is said to have made about Thales, when he fell into a well as he was looking up at the stars. She said that he was so eager to know what was going on in heaven that he could not see what was before his feet." Plato adds that "this is a jest which is equally applicable to all philosophers." Aristotle (384–322 BCE) describes another episode:

> There is . . . the story which is told of Thales of Miletus. It is a story about a scheme for making money, which is fathered on Thales owing to his reputation for wisdom. . . . He was criticized for his poverty, which was supposed to show the uselessness of philosophy. But observing from his knowledge of meteorology (as the story goes) that there was likely to be a heavy crop of olives [during the next summer], and having a small sum at his command, he paid down earnest-money, early in the year, for the hire of all the olive-presses in Miletus

and Chios. And he managed, in the absence of any higher offer, to secure them at a low rate. When the season came, and there was a sudden and simultaneous demand for a number of presses, he let out the stock he had collected at any rate he chose to fix; and making a considerable fortune, he succeeded in proving that it is easy for philosophers to become rich if they so desire, though it is not the business which they are really about.

However, Thales is famous, not for his general wisdom or his practical shrewd-ness, but because he opened up a new area of thought for which he has rightly earned the title of "First Philosopher" of Western civilization.

Thales's novel inquiry concerns the nature of things. What is everything made of, or what kind of "stuff" goes into the composition of things? With these questions Thales was trying to account for the fact that there are many different kinds of things, such as earth, clouds, and oceans. From time to time some of these things change into something else, and yet they still resemble each other in certain ways. Thales's unique contribution to thought was his notion that, in spite of the differences between various things, there is nevertheless a basic similarity between them all. *The many* are related to each other by *the One*. He assumed that some single element, some "stuff," a stuff that contained its own principle of action or change, lay at the foundation of all physical reality. For Thales this One, or this stuff, is *water*.

Although there is no record of how Thales came to the conclusion that water is the cause of all things, Aristotle writes that he might have derived it from observation of simple events, "perhaps from seeing that the nutriment of all things is moist, and that heat is generated from the moist and kept alive by it." Thales, Aristotle continues, "got his notion from this fact and from the fact that the seeds of all things have a moist nature, and water is the origin of the nature of moist things." Other phenomena such as evaporation and freezing also suggest that water takes on different forms. But the accuracy of Thales's analysis of the composition of things is far less important than the fact that he raised the question concerning the nature of the world. His question set the stage for a new kind of inquiry, one that could be debated on its merits and could be either confirmed or refuted by further analysis. Admittedly, Thales also said that "all things are full of gods." But this notion apparently had no theological significance for him. Thus, when he tried to explain the power in things, such as magnetic powers in stones, he shifted the discussion from a mythological base to a scientific one. From his starting point others were to follow with alternative solutions, but always with his problem before them.

Anaximander

Anaximander was a younger contemporary and a pupil of Thales. He agreed with his teacher that there is some single basic stuff out of which everything comes. Unlike Thales, however, Anaximander said that this basic stuff is nei-ther water nor any other specific element. Water and all other definite things, he argued, are only specific variations or offshoots of something that is more primary. It may well be, he thought, that we find water or moisture in various forms everywhere. Water is only one specific thing among many other elements, and all these specific things need some more elementary stuff to account for their origin. The primary substance out of which all these specific things come, Anaximander argued, is an *indefinite* or *boundless* realm. Thus, on the one hand, we find specific and determinate things in the world, like a rock or a puddle of water; yet, on the other hand, we find the origin of these things, which he calls the *indeterminate boundless*. Whereas actual things are specific, their source is indeterminate, and whereas things are finite, the original stuff is infinite or boundless.

Besides offering a new idea about the original substance of things, Anaximander advanced philosophy by attempting some explanation for his new idea. Thales had not dealt in any detail with the problem of explaining how the primary stuff became the many different things we see in the world. Anaximander, though, addressed this question precisely. Although his explanation may seem strange, it represents an advance in knowledge. Specifically, it deals with known facts from which hypotheses can be formulated, instead of explaining natural phenomena in mythical, nondebatable terms. His explanation is this: The indeterminate boundless is the unoriginated and indestructible primary substance of things, yet it also has eternal motion. As a consequence of this motion, the various specific elements came into being as they "separated off" from the original substance. Thus, "there was an eternal motion in which the heavens came to be." First *warm* and *cold* were separated off, and from these two came *moist;* then from these came *earth* and *air.*

Turning to the origin of human life, Anaximander said that all life comes from the sea and that, in the course of time, living things came out of the sea to dry land. He suggested that people evolved from creatures of a different kind. This, he argued, follows from the fact that other creatures are quickly self-supporting, whereas humans alone need prolonged nursing and that, therefore, we would not have survived if this had been our original form. Commenting on Anaximander's account of the origin of human beings, Plutarch writes that the Syrians

> actually revere the fish as being of similar race and nurturing. In this they philosophize more suitably than Anaximander. For he declares, not that fishes and men came into being in the same parents, but that originally men came into being inside fishes. Having been nurtured there—like sharks—and having become adequate to look after themselves, they then came forth and took to the land.

Returning to the vast cosmic scene, Anaximander thought that there were many worlds and many systems of universes existing all at the same time. All of them die out, and there is a constant alternation between their creation and destruction. This cyclical process, he believed, is a matter of rigorous necessity. Opposite forces in nature conflict and cause an "injustice"—poetically speaking— that requires their ultimate destruction. The only sentence that survives from Anaximander's writings makes this point, again somewhat poetically: "From what source things arise, to that they return of necessity when they are destroyed; for they suffer punishment and make reparation to one another for their injustice according to the order of time."

Anaximenes

The third and last of the Milesian philosophers was Anaximenes (ca. 585–528 BCE), who was a young associate of Anaximander. He considered Anaximander's answer to the question concerning the composition of natural things but was dissatisfied with it. The notion of the *boundless* as being the source of all things was simply too vague and intangible. He could understand why Anaximander chose this solution over Thales's notion that water is the cause of all things. The boundless could at least help explain the "infinite" background to the wide variety of finite and specific things. Still, the indeterminate boundless had no specific meaning for Anaximenes, and therefore he chose to focus on a definite substance just as Thales did. Yet, the same time, he tried to incorporate the advance achieved by Anaximander.

Attempting to mediate between the two views of his predecessors, Anaximenes designated *air* as the primary substance from which all things come. Like Thales's notion of water, air is a definite substance, and we can readily see it at the root of all things. For example, although air is invisible, we live only as long as we can breathe, and "just as our soul, being air, holds us together, so do breath and air encompass the whole world." Like Anaximander's boundless in continued motion, air is spread everywhere—although unlike the boundless it is a specific and tangible material substance that can be identified. Moreover, the air's motion is a far more specific process than Anaximander's "separating off." To explain how air is the origin of all things, Anaximenes argued that things are what they are by virtue of how condensed or expanded the air is that makes up those things. In making this point he introduced the important new idea that differences in *quality* are caused by differences in *quantity*. The expansion and contraction of air represent quantitative changes, and these changes occurring in a single substance account for the variety of things that we see in the world around us. Expansion of air causes warming and, at the extreme, fire, whereas contraction, or condensation, causes cooling and the transformation of air into solids by way of a gradual transition whereby, as Anaximenes says, "air that is condensed forms winds . . . if this process goes further, it gives water, still further earth, and the greatest condensation of all is found in stones."

Although these Milesian philosophers proceeded with scientific concerns and temperaments, they did not form their hypotheses the way modern scientists would, nor did they devise any experiments to test their theories. Their ideas have a dogmatic quality—an attitude of positive assertion rather than the tentativeness of true hypotheses. But we must remember that the critical questions concerning the nature and limits of human knowledge had not yet been raised. Nor did the Milesians refer in any way to the problem of the relation between spirit and body. Their reduction of all reality to a material origin certainly raises this question, but only later did philosophers recognize this as a problem. Whatever may be the usefulness of their specific ideas about *water*, the *boundless,* and *air* as the primary substance of things, the real significance of the Milesians is, again, that they for the first time raised the question about the ultimate nature of things and made the first halting but direct inquiry into what nature really consists of.

THE MATHEMATICAL BASIS OF ALL THINGS

Pythagoras

Across a span of water from Miletus, located in the Aegean Sea, was the small island of Samos, the birthplace of a truly extraordinary and wise man, Pythagoras (ca. 570–497 BCE). From the various scraps of information we have about him and his followers, an incomplete but still fascinating picture of his new philosophical reflections emerges. Apparently dissatisfied with conditions not only on Samos but generally in Ionia during the tyrannical rule of the rich Polycrates, Pythagoras migrated to southern Italy and settled there in the prosperous Greek city of Crotone. His active philosophical life there is usually dated from about 525 to 500 BCE. Aristotle tells us that the Pythagoreans "devoted themselves to mathematics, they were the first to advance this study, and having been brought up in it they thought its principles were the principles of all things." In contrast to the Milesians, the Pythagoreans said that things *consist of numbers*. Although this account of things sounds quite strange, it makes more sense when we consider why Pythagoras became interested in numbers and what his conception of numbers was.

Pythagoras became interested in mathematics for what appear to be religious reasons. His originality consists partly in his conviction that the study of mathematics is the best purifier of the soul. He is in fact the founder both of a religious sect and a school of mathematics. What gave rise to the Pythagorean sect was people's yearning for a deeply spiritual religion that could provide the means for purifying the soul and for guaranteeing its immortality. The Homeric gods were not gods in the theological sense, since they were as immoral as human beings. As such they could be neither the objects of worship nor the source of any spiritual power to overcome the pervading sense of moral uncleanliness and the anxiety that people had over the shortness of life and the finality of death. The religion of Dionysus had earlier stepped into this area of human concern and was widespread during the seventh and sixth centuries BCE. The worship of Dionysus satisfied to some extent those yearnings for cleansing and immortality. Organized into small, secret, and mystical societies, the devotees would worship Dionysus under various animal forms. Working themselves into a frenzy of wild dances and song, they would drink the blood of these animals, which they had torn apart in a state of intoxication. They would finally collapse in complete exhaustion, convinced that at the height of their frenzy, the spirit of Dionysus had entered their bodies, purifying them and conferring his own immortality upon their souls.

The Pythagoreans were also concerned with the mystical problems of purification and immortality. It was for this reason that they turned to science and mathematics, the study of which they considered the best purge for the soul. In scientific and mathematical thought they saw a type of life that was purer than any other kind. Thought and reflection represent a clear contrast to the life of vocational trade and competition for various honors. Pythagoras distinguished three different kinds of lives, and by implication the three divisions of the soul.

By way of illustration, there are, he said, three different kinds of people who go to the Olympian games. The lowest class is made up of those who go there to buy and sell, to make a profit. Next are those who go there to compete, to gain honors. Best of all, he thought, are those who come as spectators, who reflect upon and analyze what is happening. Of these three the spectator illustrates the activity of philosophers who are liberated from daily life and its imperfections. To "look on" is one of the meanings of the Greek word *theory*. Pythagoreans considered theoretical thinking, or pure science and pure mathematics, to be a purifier of the soul. Mathematical thought could liberate people from thinking about particular things and lead their thoughts to the permanent and ordered world of numbers. The final mystical triumph of the Pythagorean is liberation from "the wheel of birth," from the migration of the soul to animal and other forms in the constant progress of death and birth. In this way the spectator achieves a unity with god and shares his immortality.

To connect this religious concern with the philosophical aspects of the Pythagoreans, we should first mention their interest in music. They considered music highly therapeutic for certain nervous disorders. There was, they believed, some relation between the harmonies of music and the harmony of a person's interior life. But their true discovery in the field of music was that the musical intervals between the notes could be expressed numerically. They discovered that the length of the strings of a musical instrument is proportionate to the actual interval of the sounds they produce. Pluck a violin string, for example, and you will get a specific note. Divide that string in half, and you will get a pitch one octave higher, the ratio here being 2:1. All the other intervals could similarly be expressed in numerical ratios. Thus, for the Pythagoreans, music was a remarkable example of the pervasive relevance of numbers in all things. This led Aristotle to say that "they saw that the attributes and the ratios of the musical scales were expressible in numbers; all other things seemed in their whole nature to be modeled after numbers, and numbers seemed to be the first things in the whole of nature, and the whole heaven to be a musical scale and a number."

Pythagoreans had a special practice of counting and writing numbers, and this may have facilitated their view that all things *are* numbers. Apparently, they built numbers out of individual units, using pebbles to count. The number *one* was therefore a single pebble, and all other numbers were created by the addition of pebbles, somewhat like our present practice of representing numbers on dice by the use of dots. But the significant point is that the Pythagoreans discovered a relation between arithmetic and geometry. A single pebble represents *one* as a single point. But *two* is made up of two pebbles or two points, and these two points make a line. Three points, as in the corners of a triangle, create a plane or area, and four points can represent a solid. This suggested to Pythagoreans a close relationship between number and magnitude, and Pythagoras is credited with what we now call the Pythagorean theorem: The square of the hypotenuse is equal to the squares of the other two sides of a right-angled triangle. This correlation between numbers and magnitude provided immense consolation to those who sought evidence of a principle of structure and order in the universe. It is understandable how an interesting but possibly apocryphal story could have arisen. A Pythagorean named Hippasus, so the story goes, was drowned in the Hellespont for letting out the secret that this principle does not hold true in the case of the isosceles right-angled triangle. That is, in such cases the relation between hypotenuse and sides cannot be expressed by any numerical ratio, only by an irrational number.

The importance of the relation between number and magnitude was that numbers, for the Pythagoreans, meant certain figures, such as a triangle, square, and rectangle. The individual points were "boundary stones," which marked out "fields." Moreover, the Pythagoreans differentiated these "triangular numbers," "square numbers," "rectangular numbers," and "spherical numbers" as being odd and even, thereby giving themselves a new way of treating the phenomenon of the conflict of opposites. In all these forms numbers were, therefore, far more than abstractions; they were specific kinds of entities. To say, then, as the Pythagoreans did, that all things *are* numbers meant for them that there is a numerical basis for all things possessing shape and size. In this way they moved from arithmetic to geometry and then to the structure of reality. All things had numbers, and their odd and even values explained opposites in things, such as one and many, square and oblong, straight and curved, or rest and motion. Even light and dark are numerical opposites, as are male and female, and good and evil.

This way of understanding numbers led the Pythagoreans to formulate their most important philosophical notion, namely, the concept of *form*. The Milesians had conceived the idea of a primary *matter* or stuff out of which everything was constituted, but they had no coherent concept of how specific things are differentiated from this single matter. They all spoke of an unlimited stuff, whether it be water, air, or the indeterminate boundless, by which they all meant some primary *matter*. The Pythagoreans now came forth with the conception of *form*. For them form meant *limit*, and limit is understandable especially in numerical terms. The concept of limit, they believed, was best exemplified in music and medicine. For in both of these arts the central fact is harmony, and harmony is achieved by taking into account proportions and limits. In music there is a numerical ratio by which different notes must be separated in order to achieve concordant intervals. Harmony is the form that the limiting structure of numerical ratio imposes upon the unlimited possibilities for sounds possessed by the strings of a musical instrument. In medicine the Pythagoreans saw the same principle at work. Health is the harmony or balance or proper ratio of certain opposites, such as hot and cold, or wet and dry, and the volumetric balance of various specific elements later known as biochemicals. Indeed, the Pythagoreans looked upon the body as they would a musical instrument. Health, they said, is achieved when the body is "in tune," and disease is a consequence of undue tensions or the loss of proper tuning of the strings. In the literature of early medicine, the concept of number was frequently used in connection with health and disease, particularly when number was translated to mean "figure." The *true* number, or figure, therefore, refers to the proper balance of all the elements and functions of the body. Number, then, represents the application of *limit* (form) to the *unlimited* (matter), and the

Pythagoreans referred to music and medicine only as vivid illustrations of their larger concept, namely, that all things *are* numbers.

The brilliance of Pythagoras and his followers is measured to some extent by the great influence they had upon later philosophers, particularly Plato. There is much in Plato that first came to light in the teachings of Pythagoras, including the importance of the soul and its threefold division, and the importance of mathematics as related to the concept of form and the Forms.

ATTEMPTS TO EXPLAIN CHANGE

Heraclitus

Earlier philosophers attempted to describe the ultimate constituents of the world around us. Heraclitus (ca. 540–480 BCE), an aristocrat from Ephesus, shifted attention to a new problem, namely, the problem of *change*. His chief idea was that "all things are in flux," and he expressed this concept of constant change by saying that "you cannot step twice into the same river." The river changes because "fresh waters are ever flowing in upon you." This concept of *flux*, Heraclitus thought, must apply not only to rivers but to all things, including the human soul. Rivers and people exhibit the fascinating fact of becoming different and yet remaining the same. We return to the "same" river although fresh waters have flowed into it, and the adult is still the same person as the child. Things change and thereby take on many different forms; nevertheless, they contain something that continues to be the same throughout all the flux of change. There must be, Heraclitus argued, some basic *unity* between these many forms and the single continuing element, between the many and the one. He made his case with such imaginative skill that much of what he had to say found an important place in the later philosophies of Plato and the Stoics; in more recent centuries he was deeply admired by Hegel and Nietzsche.

Flux and Fire   To describe change as unity in diversity, Heraclitus assumed that there must be *something* that changes, and he argued that this something is *fire*. But he did not simply substitute the element of fire for Thales's water or Anaximenes' air. What led Heraclitus to fasten upon fire as the basic element in things was that fire behaves in such a way as to suggest how the process of change operates. Fire is simultaneously a deficiency and a surplus; it must constantly be fed, and it constantly gives off something either in the form of heat, smoke, or ashes. Fire is a process of transformation, then, whereby what is fed into it is transformed into something else. For Heraclitus it was not enough simply to point to some basic element, such as water, as the underlying nature of reality; this would not answer the question of how this basic stuff could change into different forms. When, therefore, Heraclitus fastened upon fire as the basic reality, he not only identified the *something* that changes but thought he had discovered the principle of change itself. To say that everything is in flux meant for Heraclitus that the world *is* an "ever-living Fire" whose constant movement is assured by "measures of it kindling and measures going out." These "measures" meant for Heraclitus a kind of balance between what kindles and what goes out of the fire. He describes this balance in terms of financial exchange, saying that "all things are an exchange for Fire, and Fire for all things, similar to merchandise for gold and gold for merchandise." With this explanation of exchange, Heraclitus maintained that nothing is really ever lost in the nature of things. If gold is exchanged for merchandise, both the gold and the merchandise continue to exist, although they are now in different hands. Similarly, all things continue to exist, although they exchange their form from time to time.

There is a stability in the universe because of the orderly and balanced process of change or flux. The same "measure" comes out as goes in, just as if reality were a huge fire that inhaled and exhaled equal amounts, thereby preserving an even inventory in the world. This inventory represents the widest array of things, and all of them are simply different forms of fire. Flux and change consist of the movements of fire, movements that Heraclitus called the "upward and downward paths." The downward path of fire explains the coming into being of the things that we experience. So, when fire is condensed it becomes moist, and this moisture under conditions of increased pressure becomes water; water, in turn, when congealed becomes earth. On the upward path this process is reversed, and the earth is transformed into liquid; from this water come the various forms of life. Nothing is ever lost in this process of transformation because, as Heraclitus says, "fire lives the death of earth, and air the death of fire; water lives the death of air, earth that of water." With this description of the constant transformation of things in fire, Heraclitus thought he had explained the rudiments of the unity between the *one* basic stuff and the *many* diverse things in the world. But there was another significant idea that Heraclitus added to his concept of Fire, namely, the idea of *reason* as the universal law.

Reason as the Universal Law   The process of change is not a haphazard movement but the product of God's universal Reason (*logos*). This idea of *Reason* came from Heraclitus's religious conviction that the most real thing of all is the soul, and the soul's most distinctive and important attribute is wisdom or thought. But when he speaks about God and the soul, he does not have in mind separate personal entities. For him there is only one basic reality, namely, Fire, and it is this material substance, Fire, that Heraclitus calls the One, or God. Inevitably, Heraclitus was a *pantheist*—a term meaning that God is identical with the totality of things in the universe. For Heraclitus all things are Fire/God. Since Fire/God is in everything, even the human soul is a part of Fire/God. As wisdom is Fire/God's most important attribute, wisdom or thought is human beings' chief activity. But inanimate things also contain the principle of reason, since they are also permeated with the fiery element. Because Fire/God *is* Reason and because Fire/God is the One, permeating all things, Heraclitus believed that Fire/God is the universal Reason. And, as such, Fire/God unifies all things and commands them to move and change in accordance with thought and rational principles. These rational principles constitute the essence of *law*— the universal law immanent in all things. All people share this universal law to the degree that they possess Fire/God in their own natures and thereby possess the capacity for thought.

Logically, this account of our rational nature would mean that all of our thoughts are God's thoughts, since there is a unity between the One and the many, between God and human beings. We all must share in a common stock of knowledge since we all have a similar relation to God. Even stones partake in that part of God's Reason, which makes them all equally behave according to the "law" of gravity. But people notoriously disagree and behave quite inconsistently. Recognizing this fact about human disagreement, Heraclitus says that "those awake have one ordered universe in common, but in sleep everyone turns away to one of his own." "Sleep," for Heraclitus, must mean to be thoughtless or even ignorant. Unfortunately, he does not explain how it is possible for people to be thoughtless if their souls and minds are part of God. In spite of its limitations, Heraclitus's theory had a profound impact on succeeding thinkers. This is particularly so concerning his conviction that there is a common universe available to all thoughtful people and that all people participate in God's universal Reason or universal law. In later centuries it was this concept that provided the basis for the Stoics' idea of cosmopolitanism—the idea that all people are equally citizens of the world precisely because they all share in the One, in God's Reason. According to the Stoics, we all contain in ourselves some portion of the Fire, that is, sparks of the divine. It was this concept, too, that formed the foundation for the classic theory of *natural law*. With some variations the natural law passed from Heraclitus, to the Stoics, to medieval theologians, and eventually became a dynamic force in the American Revolution. Even today natural law is a vital component of legal theory.

The Conflict of Opposites   Although human beings can know the eternal wisdom that directs all things, we do not pay attention to this wisdom. We therefore "prove to be uncomprehending" of the reasons for the way things happen to us. We are distressed by meaningless disorders in the world and overwhelmed by the presence of good and evil, and we long for the peace that means the end of strife. Heraclitus offers us little comfort here, since, for him, strife is the very essence of change itself. The conflict of opposites that we see in the world is not a calamity but simply the permanent condition of all things. According to Heraclitus, if we could visualize the whole process of change, we would see that "war is common and justice is strife and that all things happen by strife and necessity." From this perspective, he says, "what is in opposition is in concert, and from what differs comes the most beautiful harmony." Even death is no longer a calamity, for "after death things await people which they do not expect or imagine." Throughout his treatment of the problem of strife and disorder, Heraclitus emphasizes again and again that the many find their unity in the One. Thus, what appear to be disjointed events and contradictory forces are in reality intimately harmonized. For this reason, he says, people "do not know how what is at variance agrees with itself. It is an attunement of opposite tensions, like that of the bow and the lyre." Fire itself exhibits this tension of opposites and indeed depends on it. Fire *is* its many tensions of opposites. In the One the many find their unity. Thus, in the One "the way up and the way down is the same," "good and ill are one," and "it is the same thing in us that is quick and dead, awake and asleep, young and old." This solution of the conflict of opposites rests upon Heraclitus's major assumption that nothing is ever lost, but merely changes its form. Following the direction of Reason, the eternal Fire moves with a measured pace, and all change requires opposite and diverse things. Still, "to God all things are fair and good and right, but people hold some things wrong and some right." Heraclitus did not come to this conclusion because he believed that there was a personal God who judged that all things are good. Instead, he thought that "it is wise to agree that all things are one," that the One takes shape and appears in many forms.

Parmenides

A younger contemporary of Heraclitus, Parmenides was born about 510 BCE and lived most of his life in Elea, a colony founded by Greek refugees in the southwest of Italy. He flourished there in more than one capacity, giving the people of Elea laws and establishing a new school of philosophy whose followers became known as Eleatics. Dissatisfied with the philosophical views of his predecessors, Parmenides offered the quite startling theory that the entire universe consists of one thing, which never changes, has no parts, and can never be destroyed. He calls this single thing the *One*. Granted, it may *appear* as though things change in the world, such as when a large oak tree grows from a tiny acorn. It may also *appear* as though there are many different things in the world, such as rocks, trees, houses, and people. However, according to Parmenides, all such change and diversity is an illusion. In spite of appearances, there is only one single, unchanging, and eternal thing that exists. Why would Parmenides offer a theory that is so contrary to appearances? The answer is that he was more persuaded by logical reasoning than by what he saw with his own eyes.

The logic of Parmenides's theory begins with the simple statement that *something is, or something is not*. For example, cows exist, but unicorns do not exist. On further consideration, though, Parmenides realizes that we can assert only the first part of the above statement, that *something is*. The reason is that we can only conceptualize and speak about things that exist; we are unable to do this with things that do not exist. Can any of us form a mental picture of the nonexistent? Thus, according to Parmenides, we must reject any contention that implies that *something is not*. Parmenides then unpacks several implications from this observation. First, he argues that nothing ever changes. Heraclitus, we have seen, held that *everything* is in constant change; Parmenides holds the exact opposite view. We typically observe that things change by coming into existence and then going out of existence. A large oak tree, for example, comes into existence when it emerges from a tiny acorn; the tree then goes out of existence when it dies and decomposes. Although this is how things appear to our eyes, Parmenides argues that this alleged process of change is logically flawed.

We first say that the tree *is not*, then *it is*, then once again it *is not*. Here we begin and end with the impossible contention that *something is not*. Logically, then, we are forced to reject this alleged process of change, chalking it up to one big illusion. Thus, nothing ever changes.

Parmenides argues similarly that the world consists of one indivisible thing. Again, we typically observe that the world contains many different things. Suppose, for example, that I see a cat sitting on a carpet. My common perception of this is that the cat and the carpet are different things, and not simply one undifferentiated mass of stuff. But this common view of physical differentiation is logically flawed. I am, in essence, saying that beneath the cat's feet the cat *is not*, but from its feet through its head the cat *is*, and above the cat's head the cat *is not*. Thus, when I demarcate the physical borders of the cat, I begin and end with the impossible contention that *something is not*. I must then reject the alleged fact of physical differentiation and once again chalk it up to one big illusion. In short, only one indivisible thing exists.

Using similar logic, Parmenides argues that the One must be motionless: If it moved, then it would not exist where it was before, which involves illogically asserting that *something is not*. Also, Parmenides argues that the One must be a perfect sphere. If it were irregular in any way—such as a bowling ball with three holes drilled in it—this would involve a region within the ball where nothing existed. This too would wrongly assert that *something is not*.

Even if we grant the logical force of Parmenides's arguments, it is not easy for us to cast off our commonsense view that the world exhibits change and multiplicity. Everywhere we see things in flux, and to us this represents genuine change. But Parmenides rejected these commonsense notions and insisted on a distinction between appearance and reality. Change and multiplicity, he says, involve a confusion between appearance and reality. What lies behind this distinction between appearance and reality is Parmenides's equally important distinction between opinion and truth. Appearance cannot produce more than opinion, whereas reality is the basis of truth. Common sense tells us that things appear to be in flux and, therefore, in a continuous process of change. However, Parmenides says that this opinion based on sensation must yield to the activity of reason. Reason, in turn, is able to discern the truth about things, and reason tells us that if there is a single substance of which everything consists, then there can be no movement or change. To some extent Thales made a similar point when he said that everything derives from water. Thales thus implies that the appearance of things does not give us the true constitution or stuff of reality. But Parmenides explicitly emphasized these distinctions, which became crucial to Plato's philosophy. Plato took Parmenides's basic idea of the unchangeability of being and developed from this his distinction between the intelligible world of truth and the visible world of opinion.

At the age of 65, Parmenides went to Athens accompanied by his chief pupil Zeno, and according to tradition, on this visit he conversed with the young Socrates. Parmenides's radical views about change and multiplicity inevitably incited critical challenges and ridicule. It was left to Zeno to defend his master's position against his attackers.

Zeno

Born in Elea about 489 BCE, Zeno was over 40 years old when he visited Athens with Parmenides. In defending Parmenides, Zeno's main strategy was to show that the so-called commonsense view of the world led to conclusions even more ridiculous than Parmenides's. The Pythagoreans, for example, rejected the basic assumption Parmenides had accepted, namely, that reality is One. Instead, they believed in a plurality of things—that there exist a quantity of separate and distinct things—and that, therefore, motion and change are real. Their argument seemed to accord more closely with common sense and the testimony of the senses. But Parmenides's approach, which Zeno followed, required a distinction between appearance and reality. To philosophize, according to Parmenides and Zeno, we must not only look at the world but also think about it in order to understand it.

Zeno felt strongly that our senses give us no clue about reality but only about appearances. Accordingly, our senses do not give us reliable knowledge but only opinion. He demonstrates this using the example of a millet seed. If we take a millet seed and drop it to the ground, it will not make a sound. But if we take a half-bushel of millet seeds and let them fall to the ground, there will be a sound. From this difference Zeno concluded that our senses have deceived us: Either there is a sound when the single seed falls or there is not a sound when the many seeds fall. So, to get at the truth of things, it is more reliable to go by way of thought than by way of sensation.

Zeno's Four Paradoxes   In answering Parmenides's critics, Zeno fashioned his arguments in the form of paradoxes. The commonsense view of the world rests on two principal assumptions: (1) Changes occur throughout time, and (2) a diversity of objects are spread throughout space. Following Parmenides, Zeno, of course, rejects both of these assumptions. However, in arguing against the commonsense view of things, Zeno provisionally grants the above two assumptions and then notes paradoxes that follow from them. The consequences are in fact so absurd that the commonsense view of the world no longer seems so commonsensical. By contrast, then, Parmenides's view of the One seems to be the more reasonable account of the world. Zeno presents four principal paradoxes:

1. *The racecourse.* According to this paradox of motion, a runner crosses a series of units of distance from the beginning to the end of the racecourse. But, Zeno asks, just what takes place in this example? Is there really any motion? In order to traverse the racecourse, the runner, according to the Pythagorean hypothesis, would have to cross an infinite number of points, and do so in a finite number of moments. But the critical question is, how can one cross an infinite number of points in a finite amount of time? The runner cannot reach the end of the course until first reaching the halfway point; but the distance from the beginning to the halfway point can also be divided in half, and the runner must first reach that point, the one-quarter mark, before reaching the halfway point. Likewise, the distance between the beginning and the one-quarter point is divisible, and this process of division must go on to infinitude since there is always a remainder and

every such unit is divisible. If, then, the runner cannot reach any point without first reaching its previous midpoint, and if there are an infinite number of points, it is impossible to cross this infinite number of points in a finite amount of time. For this reason, Zeno concludes that motion does not exist.

2. *Achilles and the tortoise.* This paradox is similar to the racecourse illustration. Imagine a race between the swift Achilles and a tortoise. Because he is a good sport, Achilles gives the tortoise a head start and is thus in pursuit of the tortoise. Zeno argues that Achilles cannot ever overtake the tortoise because he must always reach the point that the tortoise has passed. The distance between Achilles and the tortoise will always be divisible and, as in the case of the racecourse, no point can be reached before the previous point has been reached. The effect is that there can be no motion at all, and Achilles, on these assumptions, can never overtake the tortoise. What Zeno thought he had demonstrated here was, again, that although the Pythagoreans claimed the reality of motion, their theory of the plurality of the world made it impossible to think of the idea of motion in a coherent way.

3. *The arrow.* Does an arrow move when the archer shoots it at the target? Here again, the Pythagoreans, who had argued for the reality of space and therefore of its divisibility, would have to say that the moving arrow must at every moment occupy a particular position in space. But if an arrow occupies a position in space equal to its length, this is precisely what is meant when we say that the arrow is at rest. Since the arrow must always occupy such a position in space equal to its length, the arrow must always be at rest. Moreover, any quantity, as we saw in the example of the racecourse, is infinitely divisible. Hence, the space occupied by the arrow is infinite, and as such it must coincide with everything else, in which case everything must be One instead of many. Motion, therefore, is an illusion.

4. *The relativity of motion.* Imagine three passenger cars of equal length on tracks parallel to each other, with each car having eight windows on a side. One car is stationary, and the other two are moving in opposite directions at the same speed. In Figure 1 car *A* is stationary, and cars *B* and *C* are moving in opposite directions at the same speed until they reach the positions shown in Figure 2. In order to reach the positions in Figure 2, the front of car *B* would go past four of car *A*'s windows while the front of car *C* would go past all eight of car *B*'s windows. Each window represents a unit of distance, and each such unit is passed in an equal unit of time. Now, car *B*

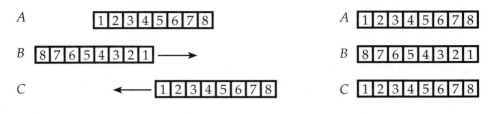

FIGURE 1   **FIGURE 2**

went past only four of A's windows while car C went past eight of B's windows. Since each window represents the same unit of time, it follows that four units of time are equal to eight units of time or that four units of distance equal eight units of distance, which is absurd. Whatever may be the inner complications of this argument, Zeno's chief point was that motion has no clear definition, and it is a relative concept.

In all of these arguments, Zeno was simply counterattacking the adversaries of Parmenides, taking seriously their assumption of a pluralistic world—a world where, for example, a line or time is divisible. By pushing these assumptions to their logical conclusions, Zeno attempted to demonstrate that the notion of a pluralistic world lands one in insoluble absurdities and paradoxes. He, therefore, reiterated Parmenides's thesis that change and motion are illusions and that there is only one being, continuous, material, and motionless. In spite of Zeno's valiant efforts, the commonsense view of the world persisted, which prompted succeeding philosophers to take a different approach to the problem of change and constancy.

Empedocles

Empedocles was an impressive figure in his native Agrigentum, Sicily, where he lived probably from 490 to 430 BCE. His interests and activities ranged from politics and medicine to religion and philosophy. Legend has it that, wishing to be remembered as a godlike figure, he ended his life by leaping into the crater of Mount Etna, hoping thereby to leave no trace of his body so that the people would think he had gone up to heaven. He wrote his philosophy in the form of poetry, of which only a small portion survives. From it we see not an original or new philosophy, but rather a new way of putting together what his predecessors had already said. Empedocles believed that the arguments both for and against motion and change had some merit. Instead of taking either side, however, he ingeniously merged both points of view in what was the first attempt at combining the major philosophical contributions of his predecessors. He thereby discovered a consistent way of saying that there is change and at the same time affirming that reality is fundamentally changeless.

Empedocles agreed with Parmenides that being is uncreated and indestructible, that it simply *is*. He writes that "from what in no wise exists, it is impossible for anything to come into being; and for being to perish completely is incapable of fulfillment and unthinkable; for it will always be there, wherever any one may place it on any occasion." But, unlike Parmenides, he did not agree that existence consists simply of the One. To accept the notion of the One requires us to deny the reality of motion, but to Empedocles the phenomenon of motion was both too obvious and too compelling to deny. He therefore rejected the idea of the One. However, agreeing with Parmenides that being is uncreated and indestructible, Empedocles argued that being is not One but many. It is *the many* that are changeless and eternal.

According to Empedocles, the objects that we see and experience do, in fact, come into being and are also destroyed. But such change and motion are possible because objects are composed of many material particles. Thus, although *objects* can change, as Heraclitus said, the *particles* of which they are composed are changeless, as Parmenides said about the One. But of what did these particles consist? Empedocles held that these particles are four eternal material elements, namely, earth, air, fire and water. He developed this idea by reinterpreting the philosophies of Thales and Anaximenes, who emphasized the primary elements of water and air, respectively. Following Greek tradition, which emphasized the four primary elements of earth, air, fire, and water, Empedocles expanded on Thales's and Anaximenes's theories. These four elements, he believed, are changeless and eternal, and can never be transformed into something else. What explains the changes in objects that we see around us is the *mixture* of the four elements, but not their transformation. There is, he writes, "only a mingling and interchange of what has been mingled." Earth, air, fire, and water, though they are unchangeable particles, mingle together to form objects and thereby make possible what in common experience we see as change.

Empedocles's account of earth, air, fire, and water constitutes only the first part of his theory. The second part is an account of the specific forces that animate the process of change. The Ionians assumed that the stuff of nature simply transformed itself into various objects. Only Anaximenes made any detailed attempt to analyze the process of change with his theory of condensed and expanded air. By contrast, Empedocles assumed that there are in nature two forces, which he called *Love* and *Hate* (alternatively, Harmony and Discord). These are the forces that cause the four elements to intermingle and later to separate. The force of Love causes elements to attract each other and build up into some particular form or person. The force of Hate causes the decomposition of things. The four elements, then, mix together or separate from each other depending on how much Love or Hate are present. In fact, Empedocles believed, there are cycles within nature that manifest Love and Strife in differing degrees at different times. Expressing this never-ending cycle in his poetic style, Empedocles writes that

> this process is clearly to be seen throughout the mass of mortal limbs: sometimes through love all the limbs which the body has as its lot come together into one, in the prime of flourishing life. At another time again, sundered by evil feuds, they wander severally by the breakers of the shore of life. Likewise too with shrub plants and fish in their watery dwelling, and beasts with mountain lairs and diver birds that travel on wings.

There are four stages to the cycle. In the first stage, Love is present and Hate is completely absent. Here the four elements are fully commingled and are held in Harmony by the governing principle of Love. In the second stage the force of Hate, lurking nearby, starts to invade things, but there is still more Love present than Hate. In the third stage Hate begins to predominate, and the particles fall into Discord and begin to separate. In the final stage only Hate is present, and all particles of earth, air, fire, and water separate into their own four groups. There the elements are ready to begin a new cycle as the force of Love returns to attract the elements into harmonious combinations. This process continues without end.

Anaxagoras

Anaxagoras (500–428 BCE) was from Clazomenae, a coastal town in what is now Turkey. He later moved to Athens, where he was in the company of the statesman Pericles. His major philosophical contribution was the concept of *mind* (*nous*), which he distinguished from matter. Anaxagoras agreed with Empedocles that all coming into and going out of being consists merely in the mixture and separation of already existing substances. But he rejected Empedocles' ambiguous and somewhat mythical notions of Love and Hate, by which various objects supposedly form. For Anaxagoras the world and all its objects were well-ordered and intricate structures; there must, then, be some being with knowledge and power that organizes the material world in this fashion. Such a rational principle is what Anaxagoras proposed in his concept of *Mind*, or *nous*.

According to Anaxagoras, the nature of reality is best understood as consisting of *Mind* and *matter*. Before Mind has influenced the shape and behavior of matter, matter exists, as a mixture of various kinds of material substances, all uncreated and imperishable. Even when this original mass of matter is divided into actual objects, each part contains portions of every other elemental "thing" (*spermata*, or seeds). Snow, for example, contains the opposites of black and white and is called white only because white predominates in it. In a sense, then, each part contains what is in the whole of reality, since each has a special "portion" of everything in it.

According to Anaxagoras, *separation* is the process by which this matter formed into various things, and such separation occurs through the power of Mind. Specifically, Mind produced a rotary motion, causing a vortex that spread out to encompass more and more of the original mass of matter. This forces a "separation" of various substances. This rotary motion originally caused a separation of matter into two major divisions—one mass that contained the warm, light, rare, and dry, and a second mass that contained the cold, dark, dense, and moist. This process of separation is continuous, and there is constant progress in the process of separation. Particular objects are always combinations of substances in which some particular substance predominates. For example, water predominates with the elemental stuff moistness but nevertheless has all other elemental things present. Describing this process in one of the preserved fragments of his last book, Anaxagoras writes that

> mind set in order all things that were to be and are now and that will be, and this revolution in which now revolve the stars and the sun and the moon and the air and the aether which are separated off. . . . The revolution itself caused the separating off, and the dense is separated off from the rare, the warm from the cold, the bright from the dark, and the dry from the moist. And there are many portions of many things.

Emphasizing the continued mixture of things, he says that "no thing is altogether separated off from anything else except Mind." Forces set in motion in the vortex account for the appearance of the thick and moist at the center and the thin and warm at the circumference—that is, of the earth and the atmosphere. The forces of rotation also caused red-hot masses of stones to be torn away from the earth and to be thrown into the ether, and this is the origin of the stars. The earth, originally mud, was dried by the sun and fertilized by germs contained in the air. Everything, even now, is animated by Mind, including life in plants and sense perception in human beings. Mind is everywhere, or as Anaxagoras says, Mind is "there where everything else is, in the surrounding mass."

Although Anaxagoras considered Mind the moving or controlling force in the cosmos and in human bodies, his account of the actual role of Mind was limited. For one thing the Mind was not the *creator* of matter, since he held that matter is eternal. Moreover, he did not see in Mind the source of any purpose to the natural world. Mind's role in the origin of particular things appears to be a mechanical explanation, principally through the process of "separation." Things are the products of material causes, and Mind appears to have no distinctive role apart from starting motion.

Aristotle, who later distinguished between different kinds of causes, offered a mixed evaluation of Anaxagoras's views. He contrasts Anaxagoras with his predecessors, who attributed the origin of things to spontaneity and chance. According to Aristotle, when Anaxagoras said that "reason was present—as in animals, so throughout nature—as the cause of order and of all arrangement, he seemed like a sober man in contrast with the random talk of his predecessors." But, adds Aristotle, Anaxagoras made use of his concept of Mind only "to a small extent." His criticism was that "Anaxagoras uses reason as a divine machine for making the world, and when he is at a loss to tell from what cause something necessarily is, then he drags reason in, but in all other cases ascribes events to anything rather than reason." Anaxagoras seemed to provide an explanation only of how matter acquired its rotary motion, leaving the rest of the order of nature to be a product of that motion.

Still, what Anaxagoras had to say about reason was of great consequence in the history of philosophy because he thereby introduced an abstract principle into the nature of things. He differentiated Mind and matter. While he may not have described Mind as completely immaterial, he nevertheless distinguished Mind from the matter it had to work with. He stated that Mind, unlike matter, "is mixed with nothing, but is alone, itself by itself." What makes Mind different from matter is that it is "the finest of all things and the purest, and it has all knowledge about everything and the greatest power." Thus, while matter is composite, Mind is simple. But Anaxagoras did not distinguish two different worlds—that of Mind and of matter—but saw these two as always interrelated. Thus, he writes, Mind is "there where everything else is." Although he had not worked out all the possibilities of his concept of Mind, this concept was nevertheless destined to have enormous influence in later Greek philosophy.

THE ATOMISTS

Leucippus and Democritus formulated a theory about the nature of things that bears an astonishing resemblance to some contemporary scientific views. However, it is difficult now to disentangle the contributions each individual made to this atomistic theory. Their writings are lost for the most part, but we at least know that Leucippus was the founder of the atomist school and that Democritus supplied much of the detailed elaboration of it. Leucippus was a contemporary of Empedocles (490–430 BCE), but we know little else of his life beyond that. Democritus, born in Abdera, Thrace, is reputed to have lived 100 years, from 460 to 360 BCE. Through his immense learning and painstaking attempt to state with clarity his abstract theory of atomism, Democritus inevitably overshadowed Leucippus. It is to Leucippus, though, that we must credit the central contention of atomism, namely, that everything is made up of atoms moving in empty space.

Atoms and the Void

According to Aristotle, the philosophy of atomism originated as an attempt to overcome the logical consequences of the Eleatic denial of space. Parmenides denied that there could be many independent things because everywhere there was *being*, in which case the total reality would be One. Specifically, he denied the existence of nonbeing or the void (empty space), because to say that there *is* the void is to say that the void *is something*. It is impossible, he thought, to say that there *is* nothing. Leucippus formulated his new theory precisely to reject this treatment of space or the void.

Leucippus affirmed the reality of space and thereby prepared the way for a coherent theory of motion and change. What had complicated Parmenides's concept of space was his thought that whatever exists must be *material*, and so space, if it existed, must also be material. Leucippus, on the other hand, thought it possible to affirm that space exists without having to say at the same time that it is material. Thus, he described space as something like a receptacle that could be empty in some places and full in others. As a receptacle, space, or the void, could be the place where objects move, and Leucippus apparently saw no reason for denying this characteristic of space. Without this concept of space, it would have been impossible for Leucippus and Democritus to develop their view that all things consist of atoms.

According to Leucippus and Democritus, the nature of things consists of an infinite number of particles or units called *atoms*. Leucippus and Democritus ascribed to these atoms the two chief characteristics that Parmenides had ascribed to the One, namely, indestructibility and eternity. Whereas Parmenides had said that reality consists of a single One, the atomists now said that there are an infinite number of atoms, each one being completely solid in itself. These atoms contain no empty spaces and therefore are completely hard and indivisible. They exist in space and differ from each other in shape and size, and because of their small size, they are invisible. Since these atoms are eternal, they did not have to be created. Nature consists, therefore, of two things only: *space*, which is a vacuum, and *atoms*. The atoms move about in space, and their motion leads them to form the objects we experience.

The atomists did not think it was necessary to account for how atoms first began moving in space. The original motion of these atoms, they thought, was similar to the motion of dust particles as they dart off in all directions in a sunbeam, even when there is no wind to impel them. Democritus said that there is no absolute "up" or "down," and since he did not ascribe weight to atoms, he thought that atoms could move in any direction. Things as we know them have their origin in the motion of the atoms. Moving in space, the atoms originally were single individual units. Inevitably, though, they began to collide with each other. In cases in which their shapes were such as to permit them to interlock, they began to form clusters. In this the atomists resembled the Pythagoreans, who said that all things are numbers. Things, like numbers, are made up of combinable units; for the atomists things are simply combinations of various kinds of atoms. Mathematical figures and physical figures are, therefore, similar.

In the beginning, then, there were atoms in space. Each atom is like the Parmenidean One, but though they are indestructible, they are in constant motion. The atomists described earth, air, fire, and water as different clusters of changeless atoms—the product of the movement of originally single atoms. These four elements were not the primeval roots of all other things, as earlier philosophers believed, but were themselves the product of the absolutely original stuff, the atoms.

The atomists produced a mechanical conception of the nature of things. For them everything was the product of the collision of atoms moving in space. Their theory had no place in it for the element of *purpose* or *design*, and their materialistic reduction of all reality to atoms left no place for a creator or designer. They saw no need to account either for the origin of the atoms or for the original motion impelling the atoms. The question of origins could always be asked, even about God; to ascribe eternal existence to the material atoms seemed as satisfactory as any other solution.

The theory of atomism envisioned by Leucippus and Democritus had a long and influential history. So formidable was this theory that, although it went into a decline during the Middle Ages, it was revived during the Renaissance and provided science with its working model for centuries to come. Isaac Newton (1642–1727) still thought in atomistic terms when he wrote his famous *Principia Mathematica*. In this work he deduced the motion of the planets, the comets, the moon, and the sea:

> I wish we could devise the rest of the phenomena of Nature by the same kind of reasoning from mechanical principles, for I am induced by many reasons to suspect that they may all depend upon certain forces by which the particles of bodies, by some causes hitherto unknown, are either mutually impelled towards one another and cohere in regular figures, or are repelled and recede from one another.

Although Newton assumed God had set things in motion, his physical analysis of nature was restricted to the mechanical principles of matter moving in space. After Newton atomism held sway until quantum theory and Einstein gave contemporary science a new conception of matter, which denied the attribute of indestructibility to the atoms.

Theory of Knowledge and Ethics

Besides describing the structure of nature, Democritus was concerned with two other philosophical problems: the problem of knowledge and the problem of human conduct. Being a thorough materialist, Democritus held that *thought* can be explained in the same way that any other phenomenon can, namely, as the movement of atoms. He distinguished between two different kinds of perception, one of the senses and one of the understanding, both of these being physical processes. When our eyes see something, this something is an "effluence" or the shedding of atoms by the object, forming an "image." These atomic images of things enter the eyes, and other organs of sense, and make an impact upon the soul, which is itself made up of atoms.

Democritus further distinguishes between two ways of knowing things: "there are two forms of knowledge, the trueborn and the illegitimate. To the illegitimate belong all these: sight, hearing, smell, taste, touch. The trueborn is quite apart from these." What distinguishes these two types of thought is that, whereas "trueborn" knowledge depends only on the object, "illegitimate" knowledge is affected by the particular conditions of the body of the person involved. For example, two people can agree that what they have tasted is an apple (trueborn). However, they can still disagree about the apple's taste (illegitimate knowledge), with one saying the apple is sweet and the other saying it is bitter. So, according to Democritus, "by the senses we know in truth nothing sure, but only something that changes according to the disposition of the body and of the things that enter into it or resist it." Still, Democritus had to say that both sensation and thought are the same type of mechanical process.

Concerning ethics, Democritus developed a very ambitious set of rules for human behavior. In general, he maintained that the most desirable goal of life is cheerfulness, and we best achieve this through moderation in all things along with the cultivation of culture. With the emergence of ethics as its primary concern, philosophy reached one of its major watersheds, closing out the first era, when the principal question had been about the natural physical order. Now people would ask more searching questions about how they should behave.

CHAPTER 2

The Sophists and Socrates

*T*he first Greek philosophers focused on nature; the Sophists and Socrates shifted the concerns of philosophy to the study of human beings. Instead of asking large cosmic questions about the ultimate principle of things, they instead asked questions that more directly related to moral behavior. This transition from predominantly scientific concerns to basic ethical questions is explained in part by the failure of the pre-Socratic philosophers to arrive at any uniform conception of the cosmos. They proposed inconsistent interpretations of nature, and there appeared to be no way of reconciling them. For example, Heraclitus said that nature consists of a plurality of substances and that everything is in a process of constant change. Parmenides took the opposite view, arguing that reality is a single, static substance—the One—and that motion and change are illusions cast on our senses by the appearances of things. Philosophy might have stopped at this point if these contradictory cosmologies had simply produced an intellectual fatigue resulting from the sheer difficulty of deciphering the secrets of nature. As it was, the controversy over the ultimate principle of things had generated an attitude of skepticism about the ability of human reason to discover the truth about nature. But this skepticism provided the impulse for a new direction for philosophy since skepticism itself became the subject of serious concern.

Instead of debating alternative theories of nature, philosophers now addressed the problem of human knowledge, asking whether it was possible to discover any universal truth. This question was further aggravated by cultural differences between various races and societies. Consequently, the question about truth became deeply entwined with the problem of goodness. Could there be a universal concept of goodness if people were incapable of knowing any universal truth? The principal parties to this new debate were the Sophists and Socrates.

THE SOPHISTS

The three most outstanding Sophists who emerged in Athens during the fifth century BCE were Protagoras, Gorgias, and Thrasymachus. They were part of

26

a group that came to Athens either as traveling teachers or, in the case of Hippias of Elis, as ambassadors. They specifically called themselves Sophists, or "intellectuals." Coming as they did from different cultures—Protagoras from Abdera in Thrace, Gorgias from Leontini in southern Sicily, and Thrasymachus from Chalcedon—they took a fresh look at Athenian thought and customs and asked searching questions about them. In particular, they forced Athenians to consider whether their ideas and customs were founded upon truth or simply upon conventional ways of behaving. Was the Athenian distinction between Greeks and barbarians, as well as that between masters and slaves, based on evidence or simply on prejudice? Not only had the Sophists lived in different countries with their different customs, but they had gathered a wide fund of information based on their observation of a multitude of cultural facts. Their encyclopedic knowledge of different cultures made them skeptical about the possibility of attaining any absolute truth by which society might order its life. They forced thoughtful Athenians to consider whether Hellenic culture was based on artificial rules (*nomos*) or on nature (*physis*). They had them question whether their religious and moral codes were *conventional*, and therefore changeable, or *natural*, and therefore permanent. In a decisive way the Sophists set the stage for a more deliberate consideration of human nature—specifically, how knowledge is acquired and how we might order our behavior.

The Sophists were primarily practical people, and especially competent in grammar, writing, and public discourse. These skills made them uniquely qualified to address a special social need within Athenian society. Under the leadership of the statesman Pericles (490–429 BCE), the old aristocracy of Athens had been replaced by a democracy. This, in turn, intensified political life by drawing free citizens into political discussion and making them eligible for leadership roles. But the older aristocratic educational system—based mainly on family tradition—did not prepare people for the new conditions of democratic life. There was no disciplined and theoretical training in the areas of religion, grammar, and the careful interpretation of the poets. The Sophists moved into this cultural vacuum, and their practical interest in teaching filled an urgent need. They became popular lecturers and were the chief source of new education. What made them particularly sought after was that they professed, above all, to teach the art of *rhetoric*, that is, persuasive speech. The power of persuasion was a political necessity in democratic Athens for anyone who hoped to rise to a position of leadership. The Sophists possessed the exact skills to facilitate this need.

The reputation of the Sophists was at first very favorable. They provided an immense service by training people to present their ideas clearly and forcefully. In a public assembly it would be disastrous to permit debate among unskilled speakers who could neither present their own ideas effectively nor discover the errors in their opponents' arguments. But rhetoric became somewhat like a knife, in that it could be employed for good or ill—to cut bread or to kill. On the one hand, those who possessed the power of persuasion could use that power to psychologically impel listeners to adopt a good idea. On the other hand, persuasive speakers could put over morally questionable ideas in which they had special interests. The inherent skepticism of the Sophists greatly facilitated a shift from the commendable use of rhetoric to its regrettable use. In time the Sophists' skepticism and relativism made them suspect. No one could criticize them for training lawyers to argue either side of a case—a technique called *anti-logic*. Surely the accused deserve to have their defense presented with as much skill as the prosecutor wields against them. As long as the art of persuasion was linked to the pursuit of truth, there could be no quarrel with the Sophists. But since they looked upon truth as a relative matter, they were eventually accused of teaching young citizens how to make a bad case look good or to make the unjust cause appear to be just. Furthermore, they developed the reputation of taking young people from good families and leading them in a critical and destructive analysis of their traditional religious and ethical views. As such, they moved youth away from an appreciation of tradition and toward a cynical egoism. To add to their ill repute, they departed from the earlier image of the philosopher as a disinterested thinker who engaged in philosophy with no concern for financial gain. The Sophists charged fees for their teaching, and they sought out the rich who were able to pay these fees. Socrates had studied under the Sophists but because of his poverty could only afford their "shorter courses." This practice of charging fees for their teaching prompted Plato to ridicule them as "shopkeepers with spiritual wares."

Protagoras

Among the Sophists who came to Athens, Protagoras of Abdera (ca. 490–420 BCE) was the oldest and, in many ways, the most influential. He is best known for his statement that "man is the measure of all things, of the things that are, that they are, and of the things that are not, that they are not." That is, each individual is the ultimate standard of all judgments that he or she makes. This means that whatever knowledge I might achieve about anything would be limited by my human capacities. Protagoras dismissed any discussion of theology, saying, "About the gods, I am not able to know whether they exist or do not exist, nor what they are like in form; for the factors preventing knowledge are many: the obscurity of the subject, and the shortness of human life." Knowledge, Protagoras said, is limited to our various perceptions, and these perceptions will differ with each person. If two people observe the same object, their sensations will be different, because each will occupy a different position in relation to it. Similarly, the same breeze blowing on two people might feel cool to one but warm to the other. Whether the breeze is or is not cold cannot be answered in a simple way. It is in fact cold for one person and warm for the other. To say that a person is the measure of all things is, therefore, to say that our knowledge is measured by what we perceive. If something within us makes us perceive things differently, there is then no standard for testing whether one person's perception is right and another person's is wrong. Protagoras thought that the objects we perceive by our various senses must possess all of the properties that different people perceive as belonging to them. For this reason it is impossible to discover what is the "true" nature of anything; a thing has as many characteristics as there are people perceiving it. Thus, there is no way to distinguish between the *appearance* of a thing and its *reality*. On this theory of knowledge, it would be impossible to attain any absolute scientific knowledge since there are built-in differences in observers that lead each of us to see things differently. Protagoras concluded, therefore, that knowledge is relative to each person.

When he turned to the subject of ethics, Protagoras held that moral judgments are relative. He was willing to admit that the idea of law reflects a general desire in each culture to establish a moral order among all people. But he denied that there was any uniform law of nature pertaining to human behavior that all people everywhere could discover. He distinguished between nature and custom and said that laws and moral rules are based on custom, not on nature. Each society has its own laws and its own moral rules, and there is no way of judging some to be right and others wrong. But Protagoras did not carry this moral relativism to the extreme view that every individual can decide what is moral for him- or herself. Instead, he took the conservative position that the state makes the laws, and everyone should accept these laws because they are as good as any that can be made. Other communities might have different laws, and individuals within a state might think of different laws, but in neither case are these better laws; they are only different. In the interest of a peaceful and orderly society, then, people should respect and uphold the customs, laws, and moral rules that their tradition has carefully nurtured. In matters of religion, Protagoras took a similar view: Just because we cannot with certainty know the existence and nature of the gods, this should not prevent us from participating in the worship of the gods. The interesting outcome of Protagoras's relativism was his conservative conclusion that the young should be educated to accept and support the traditions of their society, not because this tradition is true but because it makes possible a stable society. Still, there is no question that Protagoras's relativism seriously dislodged confidence in the possibility of discovering true knowledge. Indeed, his skepticism drew the heavy criticism of Socrates and Plato.

Gorgias

Gorgias (late fifth century BCE) came to Athens from Sicily as ambassador from his native city of Leontini in 427 BCE. He took such a radical view regarding truth that he eventually gave up philosophy and turned instead to the practice and teaching of rhetoric. His extreme view differed from Protagoras's in that, while Protagoras said that everything is true relative to the spectator, Gorgias denied that there is any truth at all. With hair-splitting keenness, and employing the type of reasoning used by the Eleatic philosophers Parmenides and Zeno, Gorgias propounded the extraordinary notions (1) that nothing exists, (2) that if anything exists it is incomprehensible, and (3) that even if it is comprehensible it cannot be communicated. Taking this third notion, for example, he argued that we communicate with words, but words are only symbols or signs, and no symbol can ever be the same as the thing it symbolizes. For this reason knowledge can never be communicated. By this type of reasoning, Gorgias thought he could prove all three of his propositions, or at least that his reasoning was as coherent as any used by those who disagreed with him. He was convinced, consequently, that there could be no reliable knowledge, and certainly no truth.

Abandoning philosophy, Gorgias turned to rhetoric and tried to perfect it as the art of persuasion. In this connection tradition relates that he developed the technique of deception, making use of psychology and the powers of suggestion. Having earlier concluded that there is no truth, he was willing to employ the art of persuasion for whatever practical ends he chose.

Thrasymachus

In Plato's *Republic* Thrasymachus (late fifth century BCE) is portrayed as the Sophist who asserted that injustice is to be preferred to the life of justice. He did not look upon injustice as a defect of character. On the contrary, Thrasymachus considered the unjust person as superior in character and intelligence. Indeed, he said that "injustice pays," not only at the meager level of the pick-pocket (although there is profit in that, too) but especially for those who carry injustice to perfection and make themselves masters of whole cities and nations. Justice, he said, is pursued by simpletons and leads to weakness. Thrasymachus held that people should aggressively pursue their own interests in a virtually unlimited form of self-assertion. He regarded justice as being the interest of the stronger and believed that "might is right." Laws, he said, are made by the ruling party for its own interest. These laws define what is right. In all countries alike the notion of "right" means the same thing, since "right" is simply the interest of the party established in power. So, Thrasymachus said, "the sound conclusion is that what is 'right' is the same everywhere: the interest of the stronger party."

Here, then, is the reduction of morality to power. This is an inevitable consequence of the Sophists' skepticism, which led them to a relativistic attitude toward truth and ethics. It was Socrates's chief concern to unravel the logical inconsistencies of the Sophists, to rebuild some notion of truth, and to establish some firm foundation for moral judgments.

SOCRATES

Many Athenians mistook Socrates for a Sophist. The fact is that Socrates was one of the Sophists' keenest critics. That Socrates should have been identified with them was due in part to his relentless analysis of any and every subject—a technique also employed by the Sophists. Nevertheless, there was a fundamental difference between the Sophists and Socrates. The Sophists split hairs to show that equally good arguments could be advanced on either side of any issue. They were skeptics who doubted that there could be any certain or reliable knowledge. Moreover, they concluded that since all knowledge is relative, moral standards are also relative. Socrates, on the other hand, had a different motivation for his constant argumentation. He was committed to the pursuit of truth and considered it his mission to seek out the basis for stable and certain knowledge. He was also attempting to discover the foundation of the good life. As he pursued his mission, Socrates devised a method for arriving at truth; he linked *knowing* and *doing*, so that to know the good is to do the good. In that sense "knowledge is virtue." Unlike the Sophists, then, Socrates engaged in argumentation, not to attain ends destructive of truth or to develop pragmatic skills among lawyers and politicians, but to achieve substantive concepts of truth and goodness.

Socrates's Life

Seldom has there been a time and place so rich in genius as the Athens into which Socrates was born in 470 BCE. By this time the playwright Aeschylus had written some of his great dramatic works. The playwrights Euripides and Sophocles were young boys who would go on to produce great tragedies that Socrates may well have attended. Pericles, who was to usher in a great age of democracy and the flowering of the arts, was still a young man. Socrates may have seen the Parthenon and the statues of Phidias completed during his life-time. By this time, too, Persia had been defeated, and Athens was becoming a naval power with control over much of the Aegean Sea. Athens had reached a level of unprecedented power and splendor. Although Socrates grew up in a golden age, his declining years were to see Athens defeated in war and his own life brought to an end in prison. In 399 BCE, at the age of 71, he drank hemlock poison in compliance with the death sentence issued by the court that tried him.

Socrates wrote nothing. Most of what we know about him has been preserved by three of his famous younger contemporaries—Aristophanes, Xenophon, and, most importantly, Plato. From these sources Socrates emerges as an intense genius who, along with extraordinary intellectual rigor, pos-sessed a personal warmth and a fondness for humor. He was a robust man with great powers of physical endurance. In his playful comedy *The Clouds*, Aristophanes depicts Socrates as a strutting waterfowl, poking fun at his habit of rolling his eyes and referring impishly to his "pupils" and "thinking shop." From Xenophon comes the portrait of a loyal soldier who had a passion for discussing the requirements of morality and who inevitably attracted younger people who sought his advice. Plato confirms this general portrait and in addi-tion pictures Socrates as a man with a deep sense of mission and absolute moral purity. In the *Symposium* Plato relates how Alcibiades, a fair youth, expected to win the amorous affections of Socrates, contriving in various ways to be alone with him. But, Alcibiades says, "nothing of the sort occurred at all: he would merely converse with me in his usual manner, and when he had spent the day with me he would leave me and go his way." In military campaigns Socrates could go without food longer than anyone else. Others wrapped themselves up with "unusual care" against the bitter cold of winter, using "felt and little fleeces" over their shoes. But Socrates, Alcibiades says, "walked out in that weather, dressed in a coat that he was always inclined to wear, and he made his way more easily over the ice without shoes than the rest of us did in our shoes."

Socrates was capable of intense and sustained concentration. On one occasion during a military campaign, he stood in deep contemplation for a day and night, "till dawn came and the sun rose; then walked away after offering a prayer to the sun." He frequently received messages or warnings from a mysterious "voice," or what he called his *daimon*. Although this "supernatural" sign invaded his thoughts from early childhood, it suggests more than anything else Socrates's "visionary" nature, particularly his sensitivity to the moral qualities of human actions that make life worth living. He must have been familiar with the natural science of the earlier Greek philosophers, although he does say in Plato's *Apology* that "the simple truth is, O Athenians, that I have nothing to do with physical speculations." For him such speculations gave way to the more urgent questions about human nature, truth, and goodness. The decisive event that confirmed his mission as a moral philosopher was the reply of the Delphic Oracle. As the story goes, one day a young religious zealot named Chaerophon went to the temple of Apollo near Delphi and asked whether there was any living person who was wiser than Socrates; the priestess replied that there was not. Socrates interpreted this reply to mean that he was the wisest because he realized and admitted his own ignorance. In this attitude Socrates set out on his quest for unshakable truth and wisdom.

Socrates as a Philosopher

Because Socrates left no writings of his own, there is today some disagreement over what philosophical ideas can be properly attributed to him. Our most extensive sources of his thought are the *Dialogues* of Plato, in which he is the leading character. But the persistent question is whether Plato is here reporting what Socrates actually taught or is expressing his own ideas through the figure of Socrates. Some argue that the Socrates found in Plato's dialogues is the historically correct Socrates. This would mean that Socrates must get all the credit for the novel philosophical activity these dialogues contain. On this view Plato would get credit only for the literary form he devised for preserving, elaborating on, and lending precision and color to Socrates's thought. On the other hand, Aristotle distinguished between the philosophical contributions made by Socrates and Plato. Aristotle gave Socrates credit for "inductive arguments and universal definitions," and to Plato he ascribed the development of the famous theory of Forms—the notion that universal archetypes exist independently of the particular things that embody them. In essence, the argument is over whether Socrates or Plato developed the theory of Forms. Since Aristotle was himself particularly interested in this subject and had discussed it at length with Plato in the Academy, it seems reasonable to suppose that his distinction between Socrates's and Plato's ideas is accurate. At the same time some of the early dialogues appear to represent Socrates's own thought, as in the case of the *Apology* and the *Euthyphro*. The most plausible solution to the problem, therefore, is to accept portions of both views. Thus, we can agree that much of the earlier dialogues are portrayals of Socrates's philosophic activity, while the later dialogues especially represent Plato's own philosophic development, including his formulation of the metaphysical theory of the Forms. On this basis we should see Socrates as an original philosopher who developed a new method of intellectual inquiry.

If Socrates was to be successful in overcoming the relativism and skepticism of the Sophists, he had to discover some immovable foundation upon which to build an edifice of knowledge. Socrates discovered this foundation within people, and not in the facts of the external world. The inner life, said Socrates, is the seat of a unique activity—the activity of knowing, which leads to the practical activity of doing. To describe this activity, Socrates developed the conception of the soul, or *psyche*. For him the soul was not any particular faculty, nor was it any special kind of substance. Instead, it was the capacity for intelligence and character; it was a person's conscious personality. Socrates further described what he meant by the soul as "that within us in virtue of which we are pronounced wise or foolish, good or bad." By describing it in these terms, Socrates identified the soul with the normal powers of intelligence and character, not as some ghostly substance. The soul was the structure of personality. However difficult it may have been for Socrates to describe exactly what the soul is, he was sure that the activity of the soul is to *know* and to influence or even direct and govern a person's daily conduct. Although for Socrates the soul was not a *thing*, he could say that our greatest concern should be the proper care of our souls so as to "make the soul as good as possible." We take best care of our souls when we understand the difference between fact and fancy, and thereby build our thought upon a knowledge of what human life is really like. Having attained such knowledge, those who have the proper care of their soul in mind will conduct their behavior in accordance with their knowledge of true moral values. In a nutshell Socrates was primarily concerned with *the good life*, and not with mere contemplation.

For Socrates the key point in this conception of the soul concerns our conscious awareness of what some words mean. To know that some things contradict others—for example, that justice cannot mean harming others—is a typical example of what the soul can discover simply by using its abilities to know. We thus do violence to our human nature when we act in defiance of this knowledge, such as when we harm someone while fully aware that such behavior is contrary to our knowledge of justice. Socrates was certain that people could attain sure and reliable knowledge, and that only such knowledge could be the proper basis of morality. His first major task, therefore, was to clarify for himself and his followers just *how* one attains reliable knowledge.

Socrates's Theory of Knowledge: Intellectual Midwifery

Socrates was convinced that the surest way to attain reliable knowledge was through the practice of disciplined conversation, with this conversation acting as an intellectual midwife. This method, which he called *dialectic*, is a deceptively simple technique. It always begins with a discussion of the most obvious aspects of any problem. Through the process of dialogue, in which all parties to the conversation are forced to clarify their ideas, the final outcome of the conversation is a clear statement of what is meant. Although the technique appeared simple, it was not long before anyone upon whom Socrates employed it could feel its intense rigor, as well as the discomfort of Socrates's irony. In the earliest dialogues in which this method is displayed, Socrates pretends to be ignorant about a subject and then tries to draw out from the other people their fullest possible knowledge about it. His assumption was that by progressively correcting incomplete or inaccurate notions, he could coax the truth out of anyone. He would often expose contradictions lurking beneath the other person's views—a technique called *elenchus*—and thereby force the person to abandon his or her misdirected opinion. If the human mind was incapable of knowing something, Socrates would want to demonstrate that, too. Accordingly, he believed that no unexamined *idea* is worth having any more than the unexamined *life* is worth living. Some dialogues therefore end inconclusively, since Socrates was concerned not with imposing a set of dogmatic ideas upon his listeners but with leading them through an orderly process of thought.

We find a good example of Socrates's method in Plato's dialogue *Euthyphro*. The scene is in front of the hall of King Archon, where Socrates is waiting in the hope of discovering who has brought suit against him for *impiety*, which was a capital offense. Young Euthyphro arrives on the scene and explains that he plans to bring charges of impiety against his own father. With devastating irony Socrates expresses relief at his good fortune in meeting him, for Euthyphro is making the identical charge against his father that has been made against Socrates. Sarcastically, Socrates says to Euthyphro that "not every one could rightly do what you are doing; only a man who is well advanced in wisdom." Only someone who knew exactly what impiety meant would charge anyone with such a serious offense. And to bring such a charge against one's *father* would only corroborate the assumption that the accuser knew what he was talking about. Socrates professes ignorance of the meaning of impiety and asks Euthyphro to explain what it means, since he has charged his father with this offense.

Euthyphro answers Socrates by defining piety as "prosecuting the wrongdoer" and impiety as not prosecuting him. To this Socrates replies, "I did not ask you to tell me one or two of all the many pious actions that there are; I want to know what is the *concept* of piety which makes all pious actions pious." Since his first definition was unsatisfactory, Euthyphro tries again, this time saying that "what is pleasing to the gods is pious." But Socrates points out that the gods quarrel among themselves, which shows that they disagree about what is better and worse. The same act, then, can be pleasing to some gods and not pleasing to others. So, Euthyphro's second definition is also inadequate. Trying to repair the damage, Euthyphro offers a new definition, saying that "piety is what *all* the gods love, and impiety is what they *all* hate." But, asks Socrates, "do the gods love an act because it is pious, or is it pious because the gods love it?" In short, what is the *essence* of piety? Trying again, Euthyphro says that piety is "that part of justice which has to do with the attention which is due to the gods." Again, Socrates presses for a clearer definition by asking what kind of attention is due to the gods. By this time Euthyphro is hopelessly adrift, and Socrates says, "It cannot be that you would ever have undertaken to prosecute your aged father . . . unless you had known exactly what is piety and impiety." And when Socrates presses him once more for a clearer definition, Euthyphro answers, "Another time . . . Socrates. I am in a hurry now, and it is time for me to be off."

The dialogue ends inconclusively as far as the subject of piety is concerned. Nevertheless, it is a vivid example of Socrates's method of dialectic and a portrayal of his conception of the philosophical life. More specifically, it illustrates Socrates's unique concern with *definition* as the instrument of clear thought.

The Importance of Definition   Nowhere is Socrates's approach to knowledge more clearly displayed than in his preoccupation with the process of definition. It is also in his emphasis on definition that Socrates most decisively combats the Sophists: Terms have definite meanings, and this undermines relativism. For him a definition is a clear and fixed concept. Although particular events or things varied in some respects or passed away, Socrates was impressed with the fact that something about them was the same—that is, never varied and never passed away. This was their definition, or their essential nature. It was this permanent meaning that Socrates wanted Euthyphro to give him when he asked for that "concept of Piety which makes all pious acts pious." In a similar way Socrates sought after the concept of *Justice* by which acts become just, and the concept of *Beauty* by which particular things are said to be beautiful, and the concept of *Goodness* by which we recognize human acts to be good. For example, no particular thing is perfectly beautiful; it is beautiful only because it partakes of the larger concept of Beauty. Moreover, when a beautiful thing passes away, the concept of Beauty remains. Socrates was struck by our ability to think about general ideas and not only about particular things.

He argued that in some way we think of two different kinds of objects whenever we think about anything. A beautiful flower is at once *this particular flower* and at the same time an examplar or partaker of the general or *universal meaning of Beauty*. Definition, for Socrates, involves a process by which our minds can distinguish or sort out these two objects of thought, namely, the particular (this beautiful flower) and the general or universal (the concept of Beauty of which this flower partakes so as to make it a beautiful flower). If Socrates asked, "What is a beautiful flower?" or "What is a pious act?" he would not be satisfied with your pointing to this flower or this act. For, although Beauty is in some way connected with a given thing, that thing does not either equal or exhaust the concept of Beauty. Moreover, although various beautiful things differ from each other, whether they are flowers or people, they are each called beautiful because, in spite of their differences, they share in common that element by which they are called beautiful. Only by the rigorous process of definition can we finally grasp the distinction between a particular thing (this beautiful flower) and the general fixed notion (Beauty or beautiful). The process of definition, as Socrates worked it out, is a process for arriving at clear and fixed concepts.

Through this technique of definition, Socrates showed that true knowledge is more than simply an inspection of facts. Knowledge has to do with our ability to discover in facts the abiding elements that remain after the facts disappear. Beauty remains after the rose fades. To the mind an imperfect triangle suggests *the* Triangle; imperfect circles are seen as approximations to the perfect Circle, the definition of which produces the clear and fixed notion of Circle. Facts can produce a variety of notions, for no two flowers are the same. By the same token no two people and no two cultures are the same. If we limited our knowledge simply to uninterpreted facts, we would conclude that everything is different, and there are no universal likenesses. The Sophists did just this, and from the facts they collected about other cultures, they argued that all notions of justice and goodness are relative. But Socrates would not accept this conclusion. To him the factual differences between people—for example, the differences in their height, strength, and mental ability—did not obscure the equally certain fact that they were all people. By his process of definition, he cut through the obvious factual differences about particular people and discovered what makes each person a person, in spite of the differences. His clear concept of *humanness* provided him with a firm basis for thinking about people. Similarly, though cultures differ, though their actual laws and moral rules differ, still, said Socrates, the notions of Law, Justice, and Goodness can be defined as rigorously as the notion of human being. Instead of leading to intellectual skepticism and moral relativism, Socrates believed that the variety of facts around us could yield clear and fixed concepts, so long as we employed the technique of analysis and definition.

Behind the world of facts, then, Socrates believed there was an order in things that we could discover. This led him to introduce into philosophy a way of looking at everything in the universe, namely, a *teleological* conception of things—the view that things have a function or purpose and tend toward the good. To say, for example, that a person has a definable nature is also to say that a special activity is appropriate to his or her nature. If people are rational beings, acting rationally is the behavior appropriate to human nature. From this it is a short step to saying that people *ought* to act rationally. By discovering the essential nature of everything, Socrates believed that he could thereby also discover the intelligible order in everything. On this view, not only do things have their own specific natures and functions, but these functions have some additional purpose in the whole scheme of things. There are many kinds of things in the universe, not because of some haphazard mixture, but because each thing does one thing best, and things acting together make up the orderly universe. Clearly, Socrates could distinguish between two levels of knowledge, one based upon the *inspection* of facts and the other based upon the *interpretation* of facts. Alternatively, one is based on particular things and the other on general or universal concepts.

The fact that universal concepts, such as Beauty, Straight, Triangle, and Human Being, are always used in discourse certainly suggests that there is some basis in reality for their use. The big question is whether these universal concepts refer to some *existing reality* in the same way that particular words do. If the word *John* refers to a person existing in a particular place, does the concept *Human Being* also refer to some reality someplace? Whether Socrates dealt with this problem of the metaphysical status of universals depends on whether we consider Plato or Socrates to be the author of the theory of the Forms. Plato certainly taught that these conceptual Forms, whatever they are, are the most real things there are and that they have a separate existence from the particular things we see, which partake of these Forms. Aristotle rejected this theory of the separate existence of Forms, arguing that in some way universal forms exist only in the actual things we experience. He showed, too, that Socrates had not "separated off" these Forms from things. If Socrates was not the author of the theory of Forms, found in the Platonic dialogues, he was, nevertheless, the one who fashioned the notion of an intelligible order lying behind the visible world.

Socrates's Moral Thought

For Socrates knowledge and virtue were the same thing. If virtue has to do with "making the soul as good as possible," it is first necessary to know what makes the soul good. Therefore, goodness and knowledge are closely related. But Socrates said more about morality than simply this. He in fact identified goodness and knowledge, saying that to know the good is to do the good, that knowledge is virtue. By identifying knowledge and virtue, Socrates meant also to say that vice, or evil, is the absence of knowledge. Just as knowledge is virtue, so, too, vice is ignorance. The outcome of this line of reasoning was Socrates's conviction that no one ever indulged in vice or committed an evil act knowingly. Wrongdoing, he said, is always involuntary, being the product of ignorance.

To equate virtue with knowledge and vice with ignorance may seem to contradict our most elementary human experiences. Common sense tells us that we frequently indulge in acts that we know to be wrong, so that wrongdoing for us is a deliberate and voluntary act. Socrates would have readily agreed that we commit acts that can be called evil. He denied, however, that people deliberately performed evil acts because they knew them to be evil. When people commit evil acts, said Socrates, they always do them thinking that they are good in some way.

When he equated virtue and knowledge, Socrates had in mind a particular conception of virtue. For him virtue meant fulfilling one's function. As a rational being, a person's function is to behave rationally. At the same time, every human being has the inescapable desire for happiness or the well-being of his or her soul. This inner well-being, this "making the soul as good as possible," can be achieved only by certain appropriate types of behavior. Because we have a desire for happiness, we choose our acts with the hope that they will bring us happiness. Which acts, or what behavior, will produce happiness? Socrates knew that some forms of behavior *appear* to produce happiness, but *in reality* do not. For this reason we frequently choose acts that may in themselves be questionable but that we nevertheless think will bring us happiness. Thieves may know that stealing as such is wrong, but they steal in the hope that it will bring them happiness. Similarly, we pursue power, physical pleasure, and property, which are the symbols of success and happiness, confusing these with the true ground of happiness.

The equating of vice with ignorance is not so contrary to common sense after all, since the ignorance Socrates speaks of refers to an act's ability to produce happiness, not to the act itself. It is ignorance about one's soul, about what it takes to "make the soul as good as possible." Wrongdoing is, therefore, a consequence of an inaccurate estimate of types of behavior. It is the inaccurate expectation that certain kinds of things or pleasures will produce happiness. Wrongdoing, then, is the product of ignorance simply because it is done with the hope that it will do what it cannot do. Ignorance consists in failing to see that certain behavior cannot produce happiness. It takes a true knowledge of human nature to know what is required to be happy. It also takes a true knowledge of things and types of behavior to know whether they can fulfill the human requirements for happiness. And it requires knowledge to be able to distinguish between what *appears* to give happiness and what *really* does.

To say, then, that vice is ignorance and is involuntary is to say that no one ever deliberately chooses to damage, disfigure, or destroy his or her human nature. Even when we choose pain, we do so with the expectation that this pain will lead to virtue and to the fulfillment of our human nature—a nature that seeks its own well-being. We always think we are acting rightly. But whether our actions are right depends on whether they harmonize with true human nature, and this is a matter of true knowledge. Moreover, because Socrates believed that the fundamental structure of human nature is constant, he also believed that virtuous behavior is constant as well. This was the basis for his great triumph over the Sophists' skepticism and relativism. Socrates set the direction that moral philosophy would take throughout the history of Western civilization. His thought was modified by Plato, Aristotle, and the Christian theologians, but it remained the dominant intellectual and moral tradition around which other variations developed.

Socrates's Trial and Death

Convinced that the care of the human soul should be our greatest concern, Socrates spent most of his time examining his own life, as well as the lives and thoughts of other Athenians. While Athens was a secure and powerful democracy under Pericles, Socrates could pursue his mission as a "gadfly" without serious opposition. He relentlessly looked for the stable and constant moral order underlying people's irregular behavior. This quest proved alternately irritating and amusing and gave him the reputation as an intellectual who dealt in paradoxes. Worse still, people believed that he thought too freely about sensitive issues that, according to many Athenians, shouldn't be questioned. Nevertheless, as long as Athens was in a position of economic and military strength, Socrates could question things as he pleased, without penalty. However, as Athens' social climate moved toward a condition of crisis and defeat, Socrates was no longer immune from sanction. His efforts to develop dialectical skill among young people from leading families had raised suspicions—particularly the skill of asking searching questions about customs in moral, religious, and political behavior. But his actions were not considered a clear and present danger until Athens was at war with Sparta.

A series of events connected with this war eventually led to the trial and sentence of Socrates. One event was the traitorous actions of Alcibiades, whom the Athenians knew was Socrates's pupil. Alcibiades actually went to Sparta and gave valuable advice to the Spartans in their war with Athens. Inevitably, many Athenians concluded that Socrates must in some way be responsible for what Alcibiades did. In addition, Socrates found himself in serious disagreement with the Committee of the Senate of Five Hundred, of which he was a member. The issue before them was the case of eight military commanders who were charged with negligence at a naval battle off the islands of Arginusae. The Athenians won this battle, but at the staggering cost of twenty-five ships and four thousand men. It was decided that the eight generals involved in this expensive campaign should be brought to trial. However, instead of determining the guilt of each general one by one, the Committee was instructed to take a single vote concerning the guilt of the whole group. At first the Committee resisted this move, holding it to be a violation of regular constitutional procedures. But when the prosecutors threatened to add the names of the Committee members to the list of generals, only Socrates stood his ground; the rest of the Committee capitulated. The generals were then found guilty, and the six of them who were in custody were immediately put to death. These events occurred in 406 BCE. In 404 BCE, with the fall of Athens, Socrates once again found himself in opposition to a formidable group. Under pressure from the Spartan victor, a Commission of Thirty was set up to fashion legislation for the new government of Athens. Instead, this group became a violent oligarchy, arbitrarily executing former supporters of Pericles's democratic order and seizing property for themselves. Within a year this oligarchy had been removed by force and a democratic order restored. Unfortunately for Socrates, however, some of the members of the revolutionary oligarchy had been his close friends, particularly Critias and Charmides. This was another occasion of guilt by association, as in the case of Alcibiades, whereby Socrates was put in the position of being a teacher of traitors. By this time, irritation had developed into distrust, and in 399 BCE, Socrates was brought to trial on the charge, as the Greek philosopher Diogenes Laertius recorded it, "(1) of not worshipping the gods whom the State worships, but introducing new and unfamiliar religious practices; (2) and, further, of corrupting the young. The prosecutor demands the death penalty."

Socrates could have gone into voluntary exile upon hearing the charges against him. Instead, he remained in Athens and defended himself before a court whose jury numbered about five hundred. His defense, as recorded in Plato's *Apology*, is a brilliant proof of his intellectual prowess. It is also a powerful exposure of his accusers' motives and the inadequacy of the grounds for their charges. He emphasized his lifelong devotion to Athens, including references to his military service and his actions in upholding constitutional procedures in the trial of the generals. His defense is a model of forceful argument, resting wholly on a recitation of facts and on the requirements of rational discourse. When he was found guilty, he was given the opportunity to suggest his own sentence. Being convinced not only of his innocence but of the value of his type of life and teachings to Athens, he proposed that Athens should reward him by giving him what he deserved. Comparing himself to someone "who has won victory at the Olympic games with his horse or chariots," Socrates said, "such a man only makes you seem happy, but I make you really happy." Therefore, he said, his reward should be "public maintenance in the prytaneum," an honor bestowed on eminent Athenians, generals, Olympians, and other outstanding people. Affronted by his arrogance, the jury sentenced him to death.

To the end his friends tried to make possible his escape, but Socrates would have none of it. Just as he refused to play on the emotions of the jury by calling attention to his wife and young children, so now he was not impressed by the plea of his student, Crito, that he should think of his children. How could he undo all he had taught others and unmake his conviction that he must never play fast and loose with the truth? Socrates was convinced that to escape would be to defy and thereby injure Athens and its procedures of law. That would be to strike at the wrong target. The laws were not responsible for his trial and sentence; it was his misguided accusers, Anytus and Meletus, who were at fault. Accordingly, he confirmed his respect for the laws and the procedures by complying with the court's sentence.

Describing Socrates's last moments after he drank the poisonous hemlock, Plato writes in his *Phaedo* that "Socrates felt himself, and said that when it came to his heart, he should be gone. He was already growing cold . . . and spoke for the last time. Crito, he said, I owe a cock to Asclepius; do not forget to pay it . . . Such was the end . . . of our friend, a man, I think, who was, of all the men of his time, the best, the wisest and the most just."

CHAPTER 3

Plato

*P*lato's comprehensive treatment of knowledge was so powerful that his philosophy became one of the most influential strands in the history of Western thought. Unlike his predecessors, who focused on single main problems, Plato brought together all the major concerns of human thought into a coherent body of knowledge. The earliest Greek philosophers, the Milesians, were concerned chiefly with the constitution of physical nature, not with the foundations of morality. Similarly, the Eleatic philosophers Parmenides and Zeno were interested chiefly in arguing that reality consists of a changeless, single reality, the One. Heraclitus and the Pythagoreans, on the other hand, described reality as always changing, full of flux, and consisting of a multitude of different things. Socrates and the Sophists showed less interest in physical nature and, instead, steered philosophy into the arena of morality. Plato's great influence stems from the manner in which he brought all these diverse philosophical concerns into a unified system of thought.

PLATO'S LIFE

Plato was born in Athens in 428/27 BCE, one year after the death of Pericles and when Socrates was about 42 years old. Athenian culture was flourishing, and as Plato's family was one of the most distinguished in Athens, his early training included the rich ingredients of that culture in the arts, politics, and philosophy. His father traced his lineage to the old kings of Athens and before them to the god Poseidon. His mother, Perictione, was the sister of Charmides and the cousin of Critias, both of whom were leading personalities in the short-lived oligarchy that arose following the fall of Athens in the Peloponnesian War. When his father died, early in Plato's childhood, his mother married Pyrilampes, who had been a close friend of Pericles. Such close ties with eminent public figures had long distinguished Plato's family. This was especially so on his mother's side; an early relative had been a friend of the great lawmaker

Solon, and another distant member of the family was the archon, or the highest magistrate, in 644 BCE.

In such a family atmosphere, Plato learned much about public life and developed at an early age a sense of responsibility for public political service. But Plato's attitude toward Athenian democracy was also influenced by what he witnessed during the last stages of the Peloponnesian War. He saw the inability of this democracy to produce great leaders and saw also the way it treated one of its greatest citizens, Socrates. Plato was present at Socrates's trial and was willing to guarantee payment of his fine. The collapse of Athens and the execution of his master, Socrates, could well have led Plato to despair of democracy and to begin formulating a new conception of political leadership in which authority and knowledge are appropriately combined. Plato concluded that as in the case of a ship, where the pilot's authority rests on knowledge of navigation, so also the ship of state should be piloted by someone who has adequate knowledge. He developed this theme at length in his book *Republic*.

Around 387 BCE, when he was about 40 years old, Plato founded the Academy at Athens. This was, in a sense, the first university to emerge in the history of Western Europe, and for twenty years, Plato administered its affairs as its director. The chief aim of the Academy was to pursue scientific knowledge through original research. Although Plato was particularly concerned with educating future leaders, he was convinced that their education must consist of rigorous intellectual activity, by which he meant scientific study, including mathematics, astronomy, and harmonics. The scientific emphasis at the Academy was in sharp contrast to the activities of Plato's contemporary Isocrates, who took a more practical approach to training young people for public life. Isocrates had little use for science, holding that pure research had no practical value or humanistic interest. But Plato put mathematics into the center of his curriculum, arguing that the best preparation for those who would wield political power was the disinterested pursuit of truth, the aim of scientific knowledge. A brilliant group of scholars associated with the Academy made significant advances over the mathematical knowledge of the older Pythagoreans, and this activity caused the famous mathematician Eudoxus to bring his own school from Cyzicus to unite with Plato's Academy in Athens.

The execution of Socrates deeply disillusioned Plato about politics, thus diverting him personally from an active life of public service. Plato nevertheless continued to teach that rigorous knowledge must be the proper training of the ruler. He gained a wide reputation for this view and was invited to Syracuse, a place he traveled to at least three times, to give instruction to a young tyrant, Dionysius II. His efforts did not meet with success since his student's education was started too late and his character was too weak. Plato continued to write in his later years, and while still active in the Academy, he died in 348/47 BCE at the age of 80.

Plato lectured at the Academy without the use of notes. Because his lectures were never written down, they were never published, although notes by his students were circulated. Aristotle, for example, who entered the Academy in 367 BCE when he was 18 years old, took notes of Plato's lectures. Nevertheless,

Plato did compose more than twenty philosophical dialogues, with the longest one running around two hundred pages. Scholars debate the exact chronology of these dialogues, but they are now commonly placed in three groups. The first is a group of early writings, usually called Socratic dialogues because of their preoccupation with ethics. These consist of the *Apology, Crito, Charmides, Laches, Euthyphro, Euthydemus, Cratylus, Protagoras*, and *Gorgias*. The second group, in which the theory of Forms and metaphysical theories are expounded, include the *Meno, Symposium, Phaedo, Republic*, and *Phaedrus*. Later in life, Plato wrote some more technical dialogues that often display an attitude of deepening religious conviction; these include the *Theaetetus, Parmenides, Sophist, Statesman, Philebus, Timaeus*, and *Laws*. There is no one work to which we can go to find a schematic arrangement of Plato's thought. Different dialogues address different issues, and many of his treatments shifted over time. Nevertheless, dominant themes emerge from the various dialogues, to which we will now turn.

THEORY OF KNOWLEDGE

The foundation of Plato's philosophy is his account of knowledge. The Sophists, we have seen, had skeptical views regarding our ability to acquire knowledge. Human knowledge, they believed, was grounded in social customs and the perceptions of individual people. Such "knowledge" fluctuated from one culture or person to another. Plato, though, staunchly rejected this view. He was convinced that there are unchanging and universal truths, which human reason is capable of grasping. In his dialogue, *The Republic*, he picturesquely makes his case with the Allegory of the Cave and the Metaphor of the Divided Line.

The Cave

Plato asks us to imagine some people living in a large cave in which from childhood they have been chained by their legs and necks so that they cannot move. Because they cannot even turn their heads, they can only see what is in front of them. Behind them is an elevation that rises abruptly from the level where they are shackled. On this elevation there are other persons walking back and forth carrying artificial objects, including the figures of animals and human beings made out of wood, stone, and various other materials. Behind these walking persons is a fire, and further back still is the entrance to the cave. The chained prisoners can look only forward toward the wall at the back of the cave; they can see neither each other nor the moving persons nor the fire behind them. All that they can ever see are the shadows on the wall in front of them, which are projected as people walk in front of the fire. They never see the objects or the people carrying them, nor are they aware that the shadows are shadows of other things. When they see a shadow and hear someone's voice echo in the cave, they assume that the sound is coming from the shadow, since they are not aware of the existence of anything else. The prisoners, then, recognize as reality only the shadows formed on the wall.

What would happen, asks Plato, if one of these prisoners were released from his chains and were forced to stand up, turn around, and walk with eyes lifted up toward the light of the fire? All of his movements would be exceedingly painful. Suppose he was forced to look at the objects being carried and the shadows of which he had become accustomed to seeing on the wall. Would he not find these actual objects less pleasing to his eyes, and less meaningful, than the shadows? And would not his eyes ache if he looked straight at the light from the fire itself? At this point he would undoubtedly try to escape from his liberator and turn back to the things he could see with clarity, being convinced that the shadows were clearer than the objects he was forced to look at in the firelight.

Suppose this prisoner could not turn back but was instead dragged forcibly up the steep and rough passage to the mouth of the cave and released only after he had been brought out into the sunlight. The impact of the radiance of the sun upon his eyes would be so painful that he would be unable to see any of the things that he was now told were real. It would take some time before his eyes became accustomed to the world outside the cave. He would first recognize some shadows and would feel at home with them. If it was the shadow of a person, he would have seen that shape before as it appeared on the wall of the cave. Next, he would see the reflections of people and things in the water, and this would represent a major advance in his knowledge. For what he once knew only as a solid dark blur would now be seen in more precise detail of line and color. A flower makes a shadow that gives very little, if any, indication of what the flower really looks like. But its image as reflected in the water provides our eyes with a clearer vision of each petal and its various colors. In time he would see the flower itself. As he lifted his eyes skyward, he would find it easier at first to look at the heavenly bodies at night, gazing at the moon and the stars instead of at the sun in daytime. Finally, he would look right at the sun in its natural positions in the sky and not at its reflection from or through anything else.

This extraordinary experience would gradually lead this liberated prisoner to conclude that the sun is what makes things visible. It is the sun, too, that accounts for the seasons of the year, and for that reason the sun is the cause of life in the spring. Now he would understand what he and his fellow prisoners saw on the wall—how shadows and reflections differ from things as they really are in the visible world, and how without the sun there would be no visible world. How would such a person feel about his previous life in the cave? He would recall what he and his fellow prisoners there took to be wisdom. He would recall how they gave prizes to the one who had the sharpest eye for the passing shadows and the best memory for the order in which they followed each other. Would the released prisoner still think such prizes were worth having, and would he envy the people who received honors in the cave? Instead of envy he would have only sorrow and pity for them.

If he went back to his former seat in the cave, he would at first have great difficulty, for going suddenly from daylight into the cave would fill his eyes with darkness. He could not, under these circumstances, compete very effectively with the other prisoners in making out the shadows on the wall. While his "cave vision" was still dim and unsteady, those who had their permanent residence in the darkness could win every round of competition with him. They would at first find this situation very amusing and would taunt him by saying that his sight was perfectly all right before he went up out of the cave but that now his sight was ruined. Their conclusion would be that it is not worth trying to go up out of the cave. Indeed, Plato says, "if they could grab hold of the person who was trying to set them free and lead them up, they would kill him."

This allegory suggests that most of us dwell in the darkness of the cave, that we have oriented our thoughts around the blurred world of shadows. It is the function of *education* to lead people out of the cave into the world of light. Education is not simply a matter of putting knowledge into a person's soul that does not possess it, any more than vision involves putting sight into blind eyes. Knowledge is like vision in that it requires an organ capable of receiving it. The prisoner had to turn his whole body around so that his eyes could see the light instead of the darkness. Similarly, it is necessary for us to turn completely away from the deceptive world of change and appetite that causes a kind of intellectual blindness. Education, then, is a matter of *conversion*—a complete turning around from the world of appearance to the world of reality. "The conversion of the soul," says Plato, is "not to put the power of sight in the soul's eye, which already has it, but to insure that, instead of looking in the wrong direction, it is turned the way it ought to be." But looking in the right direction does not come easily. Even the "noblest natures" do not always want to look that way, and so Plato says that the rulers must "bring compulsion to bear" upon them to ascend upward from darkness to light. Similarly, when those who have been liberated from the cave achieve the highest knowledge, they must not be allowed to remain in the higher world of contemplation. Instead, they return to the cave and take part in the life and labors of the prisoners.

Plato rejected the skepticism of the Sophists by arguing that there are these two worlds—the dark world of the cave and the bright world of light. For Plato knowledge was not only possible but virtually infallible. What makes knowledge infallible is that it is based upon what is most real. The dramatic contrast between the shadows and reflections and the actual objects parallels the different degrees to which human beings could be enlightened. The Sophists were skeptical about the possibility of true knowledge because they were impressed by the variety of change that we experience, which is relative to each person. Plato recognized that, if all we could know were the shadows, then indeed we could never have reliable knowledge. For these shadows would always change in size and shape depending on the, to us, unknown motions of the real objects. However, Plato was convinced that we could discover the real objects behind all the multitude of shadows, and thereby attain true knowledge.

The Divided Line

In his Metaphor of the Divided Line, Plato provides more detail about the levels of knowledge that we can obtain. In the process of discovering true knowledge, we move through four stages of development. At each stage there is a parallel between the kind of object presented to our minds and the kind of thought this object makes possible. These objects and their parallel types of thought can be diagramed as follows:

	Objects	y	Types of Thought	
Intelligible World	The Good, Forms		Intelligence	Knowledge
	Mathematical Objects		Thinking	
Visible World	Things		Belief	Opinion
	Images		Imagining	

x

In the above, the "line" itself appears vertically at the center of the diagram, linking y and x. It is broken into four segments, each representing different types of thought. The line is a continuous one, suggesting that there is some degree of knowledge at every point. But as the line passes through the lowest forms of reality to the highest, there is a parallel progression from the lowest degree of truth to the highest. The line is divided, first of all, into two unequal parts. The upper and larger part represents the intelligible world and the smaller, lower part the visible world. This unequal division symbolizes the lower degree of reality and truth found in the visible world as compared with the greater reality and truth in the intelligible world. Each of these parts is then subdivided in the same proportion as the whole line, producing four parts, each one representing a clearer and more certain type of thought than the one below. Recalling the Allegory of the Cave, we can think of this line as beginning in the dark and shadowy world at x and moving up to the bright light at y. Going from x to y represents a continuous process of our intellectual enlightenment. The objects presented to us at each level are not four different kinds of real objects; rather, they represent four different ways of looking at the same object.

Imagining   The most superficial form of mental activity is found at the lowest level of the line. Here we confront images, or the least amount of reality. The word *imagining* could, of course, mean the activity of penetrating beyond the mere appearances of things to their deeper reality. But here Plato means by *imagining* simply the sense experience of appearances wherein we take these appearances as true reality. An obvious example is a shadow, which can be mistaken for something real. Actually, the shadow *is* something real; it is a real shadow. But what makes imagining the lowest form of knowing is that at this stage we do not know that it *is* a shadow or an image that it has confronted. If a person knew that it was a shadow, she would not be in the state of imagining or illusion. The prisoners in the cave were trapped in the deepest ignorance because they were unaware that they were seeing shadows.

Besides shadows there are other kinds of images that Plato considered deceptive. These are the images fashioned by the artist and the poet. The artist presents images that are at least two steps removed from true reality. Suppose an artist paints a portrait of Socrates. Socrates represents a specific or concrete version of the ideal human. Moreover, the portrait represents only the artist's own view of Socrates. The three levels of reality here are, then, (1) the Form of Humanness, (2) the embodiment of this Form in Socrates, and (3) the image of Socrates as represented on canvas. Plato's criticism of art is that it produces images that, in turn, stimulate illusory ideas in the observer. Again, it is when the image is taken as a perfect version of something real that illusion is produced. For the most part we know that an artist puts on canvas his or her own way of seeing a subject. Still, artistic images do shape thoughts, and if people restrict their understanding of things to these images with all their distortions and exaggerations, they will certainly lack an understanding of things as they really are.

What concerned Plato most were the images fashioned by the art of using words. Poetry and rhetoric were for him the most serious sources of illusion. Words have the power of creating images in our minds, and the poet and rhetorician have great skill in using words to create such images. Plato was particularly critical of the Sophists, whose influence came from this very skill in the use of words. They could make either side of an argument *seem* as good as the other.

Belief   The next stage after imagining is belief. It may strike us as strange that Plato should use the word *believing* instead of *knowing* to describe the state of mind induced by seeing actual objects. We tend to feel a strong sense of certainty when we observe visible and tangible things. Still, for Plato, seeing constitutes only believing, because visible objects depend on their context for many of their characteristics. There is a degree of certainty that seeing gives us, but this is not absolute certainty. If the water of the Mediterranean looks blue from the shore but turns out to be clear when taken from the sea, our certainty about its color or composition is at least open to question. It may seem a certainty that all bodies have weight because we see them fall. But this testimony of our vision must also be adjusted to the fact of the weightlessness of bodies in space at certain altitudes. Plato, therefore, says that believing, even if it is based on seeing, is still in the stage of opinion. The state of mind produced by visible objects is clearly on a level higher than imagining, because it is based upon a higher form of reality. But although actual things possess greater reality than do their shadows, they do not by themselves give us all the knowledge that we want to have about them. Whether it be color, weight, or some other quality, we experience these properties of things under particular circumstances. For this reason our knowledge about them is limited to these particular circumstances. But we are unsatisfied with this kind of knowledge, knowing that its certainty could very well be shaken if the circumstances were altered. True scientists, therefore, do not confine their understanding to these particular cases, but instead look for principles behind the behavior of things.

Thinking   When we move from believing to thinking, we move from the visible world to the intelligible world and from the realm of opinion to the realm of knowledge. The state of mind that Plato calls *thinking* is particularly characteristic of the scientist. Scientists deal with visible things but not simply with their vision of them. For the scientist visible things are symbols of a reality that can be thought but not seen. Plato illustrates this kind of mental activity in reference to the mathematician. Mathematicians engage in the act of "abstraction," of drawing out from the visible thing what that thing symbolizes. When mathematicians see the diagram of a triangle, they think about *triangularity* or triangle-in-itself. They distinguish between the *visible* and the *intelligible* triangle. By using visible symbols, science provides a bridge from the visible to the intelligible world. Science forces us to think, because scientists are always searching for laws or principles. Although scientists may look at a particular object—a triangle or a brain—they go beyond this particular triangle or brain and think about *the* Triangle or *the* Brain. Science requires that we "let go" of our senses and rely instead on our intellects. Our minds know that two plus two equal four no matter two of what. Our minds also know that the angles of an equilateral triangle are all equal, regardless of the size of the triangle. Thinking, therefore, represents the ability of our minds to abstract from a visible object that property which is the same in all objects in that class even though each such actual object will have other variable properties. We can, in short, think the Form "Humanness" whether we observe small, large, dark, light, young, or old persons.

Thinking is characterized not only by its treatment of visible objects as symbols but also by reasoning from hypotheses. By *hypothesis* Plato meant a truth that is taken as self-evident but that depends on some higher truth: "You know," says Plato, "how students of subjects like geometry and arithmetic begin by postulating odd and even numbers, or the various figures and the three kinds of angle. . . . These data they take as known, and having adopted them as assumptions, they do not feel called upon to give any account of them to themselves or to anyone else but treat them as self-evident." Using hypotheses, or "starting from these assumptions, they go on until they arrive, by a series of consistent steps, at all the conclusions they set out to investigate." For Plato, then, a hypothesis did not mean what it means to us, namely, an assumption. Rather, he meant by it a firm truth but one that is related to a larger context. The sciences and mathematics treat their subjects as if they were independent truths. All Plato is saying here is that if we could view all things as they really are, we would discover that all things are related or connected. Thinking or reasoning from hypotheses gives us knowledge of the truth, but it bears this limitation: It isolates some truths from others, thereby leaving our minds still to ask *why* a certain truth is true.

Perfect Intelligence   We are never satisfied as long as we must still ask for a fuller explanation of things. But to have perfect knowledge would require that we grasp the relation of everything to everything else—that we see the unity of the whole of reality. With perfect intelligence we are completely released from the realm of sensible objects. At this level we deal directly with the *Forms*. The Forms are those intelligible objects, such as "Triangle" and "Human," that have been abstracted from the actual objects. We grasp these pure Forms without any interference from even the symbolic character of visible objects. Here, also, we no longer use hypotheses, which represent only limited and isolated truths. We approach this highest level of knowledge to the extent that we are able to move beyond the restrictions of hypotheses toward the unity of all Forms. It is through our intellectual capacity of *dialectic* that we move toward its highest goal, which involves the ability to see at once the relation of all divisions of knowledge to each other. Perfect intelligence, therefore, means the unified view of reality, and for Plato this implies the unity of knowledge.

Plato concludes his discussion of the Divided Line with this summary statement: "Now you may take, as corresponding to the four sections, these four states of mind: *intelligence* for the highest, *thinking* for the second, *belief* for the third and for the last *imagining*. These you may arrange as the terms in a proportion, assigning to each a degree of clearness and certainty, corresponding to the measure in which their objects possess truth and reality." The highest degree of reality, he argued, consists of the *Forms*, as compared with shadows, reflections, and even the visible objects. Just what he meant by the Forms we must now explore in greater detail.

Theory of the Forms

Plato's theory of the Forms is his most significant philosophical contribution. In a nutshell the *Forms* are those changeless, eternal, and nonmaterial essences or patterns of which the actual visible objects we see are only poor copies. There is the Form of *the* Triangle, and all the triangles we see are mere copies of that Form. There are at least five questions that we might ask about the Forms. And although they cannot be answered with precision, the replies to them that are found in his various dialogues will provide us with Plato's general theory of the Forms.

What Are the Forms?   We have already suggested Plato's answer to this question by saying that Forms are eternal patterns of which the objects we see are only copies. A beautiful person is a copy of Beauty. We can say about a person that she is beautiful because we know the Form of Beauty and recognize that this person shares more or less in this Form. In his *Symposium* Plato states that we normally grasp beauty first of all in a particular object or person. But having discovered beauty in this limited form, we soon "perceive that the beauty of one form is akin to another," and so we move from the beauty of a particular body to the recognition that beauty "in every form is one and the same." The effect of this discovery that all types of beauty have some similarity is to loosen our attachment to the beautiful object and to move from the beautiful physical object to the concept of Beauty. When a person discovers this general quality of Beauty, Plato says, "he will decrease his violent love of the one, which he will . . . consider a small thing and will become a lover of all beautiful forms. In the next stage he will consider that the beauty of the mind is more honorable than the beauty of outward form." Then, "drawing towards and contemplating the vast sea of beauty, he will create many fair and noble thoughts and notions in boundless love of wisdom; until on that shore he grows strong, and at last the vision is revealed to him of a single science, which is the science of beauty everywhere." That is, beautiful things in their multiplicity point toward a Beauty from which everything else derives its Beauty. But this Beauty is not merely a concept: Beauty has objective reality. Beauty is a Form. Things *become* beautiful, but Beauty always *is*. Accordingly, Beauty has a separate existence from those changing things that move in and out of Beauty.

In the *Republic* Plato shows that the true philosopher wants to know the essential nature of things. When he asks what is justice or beauty, he does not want examples of just and beautiful things. He wants to know what makes these things just and beautiful. The difference between opinion and knowledge is simply this: that those who are at the level of opinion can recognize a just act but cannot tell you why it is just. They do not know the essence of Justice, which the particular act shares. Knowledge does not involve simply the passing facts and appearances—that is, the realm of *becoming*. Knowledge seeks what truly *is;* its concern is with *Being*. What really is, what has Being, is the essential nature of things. These *essences* are eternal Forms, such as Beauty and Goodness, which make it possible for us to judge things as beautiful or good.

There are many other forms besides those of Beauty and Goodness. At one point Plato speaks of the Form of Bed, of which the beds we see are mere copies. But this raises the question of whether there are as many Forms as there are essences or essential natures. Although Plato is not sure that there are Forms of dog, water, and other things, he shows in the *Parmenides* that there are "certainly not" Forms of mud and dirt. Clearly, if there were Forms behind all classifications of things, there would have to be a duplicate world. These difficulties increase as we try to specify how many and which Forms there are. Nevertheless, what Plato means by the Forms is clear enough, for he considers them to be the essential archetypes of things, having an eternal existence, grasped by our minds and not our senses.

Where Do the Forms Exist?   If the Forms are truly real, it would seem that they must be somewhere. But how can the Forms, which are immaterial, have a location? We could hardly say that they are located in space. Plato's clearest suggestion on this problem is that the Forms are "separate" from concrete things, that they exist "apart from" the things we see. To be "separate" or "apart from" must mean simply that the Forms have an independent existence; they persist even though particular things perish. Forms have no dimension, but the question of their location comes up as a consequence of our language, which implies that Forms, being something, must be some place in space. It may be that nothing more can be said about their location than that the Forms have an independent existence. But there are three additional ways in which Plato emphasizes this. For one thing Plato argues that, before our souls were united with our bodies, our souls preexisted in a spiritual realm; and in that state our souls were acquainted with the Forms. Second, Plato argues that, in the process of creation, God used the Forms in fashioning particular things; this suggests that the Forms had an existence prior to their embodiment in things. Third, these Forms seem to have originally existed in the "mind of God" or in the supreme principle of rationality. In our treatment of Plato's Metaphor of the Divided Line, we showed how Plato traced the journey of the mind from the lowest level of images to the highest level, where the Form of the Good contained the perfect vision of *reality*.

Just as the sun in the Allegory of the Cave was at once the source of light and life, so also, says Plato, the Form of the Good is "the universal author of all things beautiful and right, parent of light and of the lord of light in this world, and the source of truth and reason in the other." Whether the Forms truly exist in the mind of God is a question, but that the Forms are the agency through which the principle of reason operates in the universe seems to be just what Plato means.

What Is the Relation of Forms to Things?   A Form can be related to a thing in three ways (which may actually just be three ways of saying the same thing). First, the Form is the *cause* of the essence of a thing. Next, a thing may be said to *participate* in a Form. And, finally, a thing may be said to imitate or *copy* a Form. In each case Plato implies that although the Form is separate from the thing— that the Form of Humanness is different from Socrates—still every concrete or actual thing in some way owes its existence to a Form. It in some degree participates in the perfect model of the class of which it is a member and in some measure is an imitation or copy of the Form. Later on, Aristotle would argue that form and matter are inseparable and that the only real good or beauty is found in actual things. But Plato allowed only participation and imitation as the explanation of the relation between things and their Forms. He accentuated this view by saying that it was the Forms through which order was brought into the chaos, indicating the separate reality of form and matter. Aristotle's criticism of Plato's view was formidable, since there seems to be no coherent way of accounting for the existence of the Forms apart from actual things. Still, Plato would ask him what makes it possible to form a judgment about the imperfection of something if our minds do not have access to anything more than the imperfect thing.

What Is the Relation of Forms to Each Other?   Plato says that "we can have discourse only through the weaving together of Forms." Thinking and discussion proceed for the most part on a level above particular things. We speak in terms of the essences or universals that things illustrate; thus, we speak of queens, dogs, and carpenters. These are definitions of things and as such are universals or Forms. To be sure, we also refer to specific things in our experiences, such as dark and beautiful and person, but our language reveals our practice of connecting Forms with Forms. There is the Form Animal, and within that there are also subclasses of Forms, such as Human and Horse. Forms are, therefore, related to each other as genus and species. In this way Forms tend to interlock even while retaining their own unity. The Form Animal seems to be present also in the Form Horse, so that one Form partakes of the other. There is, therefore, a hierarchy of Forms representing the structure of reality, of which the visible world is only a reflection. The "lower" we go in this hierarchy of Forms, the closer we come to visible things and, therefore, the *less* universal is our knowledge, as when we speak of "red apples." Conversely, the higher we go, or the more abstract the Form, as when we speak of Apple in general, the broader our knowledge. The discourse of science is the most abstract, and it is so precisely because it has achieved such independence from particular cases and particular things. For Plato it possesses the highest form of knowledge. The botanist who has proceeded in knowledge from *this rose* to Rose and to Flower has achieved the kind of abstraction or independence from particulars of which Plato was thinking. This does not mean, however, that Plato thought that all Forms could be related to each other. He only meant to say that every significant statement involves the use of some Forms and that knowledge consists of understanding the relations of the appropriate Forms to each other.

How Do We Know the Forms?   Plato mentions at least three different ways in which our minds discover the Forms. First, there is *recollection*. Before our souls were united with our bodies, our souls were acquainted with the Forms. People now recollect what their souls knew in their prior state of existence, and visible things remind them of the essences previously known. Education is actually a process of reminiscence. Second, people arrive at the knowledge of Forms through the activity of *dialectic*, which is the power of abstracting the essence of things and discovering the relations of all divisions of knowledge to each other. And third, there is the power of *desire, or* Love (*eros*), which leads people step by step, as Plato described in the *Symposium*, from the beautiful object, to the beautiful thought, and then to the very essence of Beauty itself.

Although the theory of the Forms solves many problems regarding human knowledge, it also leaves many questions unanswered. Plato's language gives the impression that there are two distinct worlds, but the relationship between these worlds is not easily conceived. Nor is the relation between Forms and their corresponding objects as clear as we would wish. Still, his argument is highly suggestive, particularly as he tries to account for our ability to make judgments of value. To say a thing is *better* or *worse* implies some standard, which obviously is not there as such in the thing being evaluated. The theory of the Forms also makes possible scientific knowledge, for clearly the scientist has "let go" of actual visible particulars and deals with essences or universals, that is, with "laws." The scientist formulates "laws," and these laws tell us something about *all* things, not just immediate and particular things. Although this whole theory of the Forms rests on Plato's metaphysical views—that ultimate reality is nonmaterial—it goes a long way toward explaining the more simple fact of how it is possible for us to have ordinary conversation. Any discourse between human beings, it seems, illustrates our independence from particular things. Conversation, Plato would say, is the clue that leads us to the Forms, for conversation involves more than seeing. Our eyes can see only the particular thing, but our thinking animates conversation and departs from specific things as our thoughts "see" the universal Form. There is, in the end, a stubborn lure in Plato's theory, even though it ends inconclusively.

MORAL PHILOSOPHY

There is a natural progression from Plato's theory of Forms to his ethical theory. If we can be deceived by appearances in the natural physical world, we can be equally deceived by appearances in the moral realm. There is a special kind of knowledge that helps us to distinguish between shadows, reflections, and real objects in the visible world. This is also the kind of knowledge that we need to discriminate between the shadows and reflections of the genuinely good life. Plato believed that there could be no science of physics if our knowledge were limited to visible things. Similarly, there could be no knowledge of a universal Form of Good if we were limited to the experiences we have of particular cultures. The well-known skepticism of the Sophists illustrated to both Socrates and Plato this connection between knowledge and morality. Believing that all knowledge is relative, the Sophists denied that people discover any stable and universal moral standards. The Sophists' skepticism led them to some inevitable conclusions regarding morality. First, they held that moral rules are fashioned deliberately by each community and have relevance and authority only for the people in that place. Second, the Sophists believed that moral rules are unnatural and that people obey them only because of the pressure of public opinion. If their acts could be done in private, they argued, even the "good" among us would not follow the rules of morality. Third, they argued that the essence of justice is power, or that "might is right." Fourth, in answer to the basic question "What is the good life?" the Sophists felt that it is the life of pleasure. Against this formidable teaching of the Sophists, Plato put forward the Socratic notion that "knowledge is virtue." Elaborating on Socrates's view of morality, Plato emphasized (1) the concept of the *soul* and (2) the concept of *virtue* as function.

The Concept of the Soul

In the *Republic* Plato describes the soul as having three parts, which he calls *reason, spirit*, and *appetite*. He based this three-part conception of the soul on the common experience of internal confusion and conflict that all humans share. When he analyzed the nature of this conflict, he discovered that there are three different kinds of activity going on in a person. First, there is an awareness of a goal or a value; this is the act of reason. Second, there is the drive toward action—the spirit—which is neutral at first but responds to the direction of reason. Last, there is the desire for the things of the body, the appetites. What made Plato ascribe these activities to the soul was his assumption that the soul is the principle of life and movement. The body by itself is inanimate, and, therefore, when it acts or moves, it must be moved by the principle of life, the soul. Our reason could suggest a goal for behavior only to be overcome by sensual appetite, and the power of the spirit could be pulled in either direction by these sensual desires. Plato illustrated this human condition in the *Phaedrus*, where he portrays the charioteer driving two horses. One horse, Plato says, is good and "needs no touch of the whip, but is guided by word and admonition only." The other is bad and is "the mate of insolence and pride . . . hardly yielding to whip and spur." Though the charioteer has a clear vision of where to go and the good horse is on course, the bad horse "plunges and runs away, giving all manner of trouble to his companion and the charioteer."

Plato vividly illustrates the breakdown of order with the image of horses moving in opposite directions and the charioteer standing helpless as his commands go unheeded. The charioteer, by being what he is—namely, the one who holds the reins—has the duty, the right, and the function to guide and control the horses. In the same way the rational part of the soul has the right to rule the spirited and appetitive parts. To be sure, the charioteer cannot get anywhere without the two horses, and for this reason these three are linked and must work together to achieve their goals. The rational part of the soul has this same sort of relation to its other parts, for the powers of appetite and spirit are indispensable to life itself. Reason works on spirit and appetite, and these two also move and affect reason. But the relation of reason to spirit and appetite is determined by what reason is, namely, a goal-seeking and measuring faculty. Of course, the passions also engage in goal seeking, for they constantly seek the goal of pleasure. Pleasure is a legitimate goal of life. However, the passions are simply drives toward the things that give pleasure. As such, the passions cannot distinguish between objects that provide higher or longer-lasting pleasure and those that only appear to provide these pleasures.

It is the function of the rational part of the soul to seek the true goal of human life, and it does this by evaluating things according to their true nature. The passions or appetites might lead us into a world of fantasy and deceive us into believing that certain kinds of pleasures will bring us happiness. It is, then, the unique role of reason to penetrate the world of fantasy and discover the true world, and thereby direct the passions to objects of love that are capable of producing true pleasure and true happiness. When we confuse appearance with reality, we become unhappy and experience a general disorder of the human soul. This confusion occurs chiefly when our passions override our reason. This is why Plato argued, as Socrates had before him, that moral evil is the result of *ignorance*. There can be order between the charioteer and the horses only if the charioteer is in control. Similarly, our human souls can achieve order and peace only if our rational part—our reason—is in control of our spirit and appetites.

Throughout his account of the moral experience of human beings, Plato alternates between an optimistic view of our capacity for virtue and a rather negative opinion about whether we will fulfill our potentiality for virtue. This double attitude rests upon Plato's theory of moral evil. We have already seen Socrates's view that evil or vice is caused by ignorance, that is, by false knowledge. False knowledge occurs when our passions influence our reason to think that what appears to bring happiness will do so, although in reality it cannot. When my appetites thus overcome my reason, the unity of my soul is adversely affected. While there is still a unity, this new unity of my soul is inverted, since now my reason is subordinated to my appetites and has thereby lost its rightful place. What makes it possible for this disordered unity to occur, or what makes false knowledge possible? In short, what is the cause of moral evil?

The Cause of Evil: Ignorance or Forgetfulness

We discover the cause of evil in the very nature of the soul and in the relation of the soul to the body. Before it enters the body, Plato says, the soul has a prior existence. As we have seen, the soul has two main parts, the rational and the irrational. This irrational part in turn is made up of two sections, the spirit and the appetites. Each of the two parts has a different origin. The rational part of the soul is created by the divine Craftsman (that is, the Demiurge); by contrast, the irrational part is created by the celestial gods, who also form the body. Thus, even before it enters the body, the soul is composed from two separate sources. In the soul's prior existence the rational part has a clear vision of the Forms and of truth. At the same time, though, the spirit and appetites, by their very nature, already have a tendency to descend. If we ask why the soul descends into a body, Plato says that it is simply the tendency of the irrational part—the part of the soul that is not perfect—to be unruly and to pull the soul toward the earth. Plato says that "when perfect and fully winged she [the soul] soars upward . . . whereas the imperfect soul, losing her wings and drooping in her flight at last settles on the solid ground—there, finding a home, she receives an earthly frame . . . and this composition of soul and body is called a living and mortal creation." Thus, the soul "falls," and that is how it comes to be in a body. But the point is that the soul has an unruly and evil nature in its irrational parts even before it enters the body. In one sense, then, the cause of evil is present even in the soul's preexistent state. It is in "heaven" that the soul alternates between seeing the Forms or the truth and "forgetting" this vision, whereupon its decline sets in. Evil, on this view, is not a positive thing but rather is a characteristic of the soul wherein the soul is "capable" of forgetfulness. It is those souls only that do forget the truth that in turn descend, being dragged down by the attraction for earthly things. The soul, then, is perfect in nature, but one aspect of its nature is this possibility to lapse into disorder, for the soul also contains the principle of imperfection, as do other parts of creation. Upon its entrance into the body, however, the difficulties of the soul are greatly increased.

Plato believed that the body stimulated the irrational part of the soul to overcome the rulership of reason. The soul's entrance into the body, therefore, is a further cause of disorder, or the breakdown of the harmony between the various parts of the soul. For one thing, when the soul leaves the realm of the Forms and enters the body, it moves from the realm of the One to the realm of the many. Now the soul is adrift in the bewildering sea of the multiplicity of things and subject to all sorts of errors because of the deceptive nature of these things. In addition, the body stimulates such activities in the irrational part of the soul as the indiscriminate search for pleasure, exaggerating such appetites as hunger, thirst, and the desire to procreate. This in turn can become lust. In the body the soul experiences desire, pleasure, and pain, as well as fear and anger. There is love, too, for a wide range of objects. This varies from the simplest morsel that can satisfy some taste to a love of truth or beauty that is pure and eternal. All this suggests that the body acts as a sluggish encumbrance to the soul and that the spirit and appetites of the soul are peculiarly susceptible to the workings of the body. In this way, then, our bodies disturb the harmony of our souls. For our bodies expose our souls to stimuli that deflect our reason from true knowledge or that prevent our reason from recalling the truth we once knew.

In the world of people, error is perpetuated whenever a society has the wrong values, causing individuals to accept as their own these wrong values.

Every society inevitably acts as a teacher of its members, and for this reason society's values become the values of individuals. Moreover, societies tend to perpetuate the evils and errors committed by earlier generations. Plato underscored this notion and suggested that, in addition to such a social trans-mission of evil, human souls would reappear through a transmigration and bring into a new body their earlier errors and judgments of value. It is the body, in the final analysis, that accounts for ignorance, rashness, and lust. For the body disturbs that clear working of reason, spirit, and appetites by exposing the soul to a cascade of sensations.

Looking back on Plato's account of the human moral condition, we can see that he begins with a conception of the soul as existing independently of the body. In this state the soul enjoys a basic harmony between its rational and irrational parts—a harmony wherein reason controls the spirit and appetites through its knowledge of the truth. But since the irrational part of the soul has the possibility of imperfection, it expresses this possibility by being attracted through its appetites to the lower regions, dragging with it the spirit and rea-son. Upon entering the body, the original harmony of the parts of the soul is further disrupted, former knowledge is forgotten, and the inertia of the body obstructs the recovery of this knowledge.

Recovering Lost Morality

For Plato morality consists in the recovery of our lost inner harmony. It means reversing the process by which our reason has been overcome by our appe-tites and the stimuli of our body. People always think that whatever they do will in some way give them pleasure and happiness. No one, Plato says, ever knowingly chooses an act that will be harmful to oneself. We may do "wrong" acts, such as murder or lying, and even admit the wrongness of these acts. But we always assume that some benefit will come from them. This is false knowledge—a kind of ignorance—which people must overcome in order to be moral. To say, then, that "knowledge is virtue" means that false knowledge must be replaced with an accurate appraisal of things or acts and their values.

Before we can go from false to true knowledge, we must somehow become aware that we are in a state of ignorance. It is as if we must be awakened from a "sleep of ignorance." We can be awakened by something that is happening within us or by something external to us or by someone else. Similarly, with regard to knowledge, and particularly moral knowledge, human awakening works in these three ways. Assuming, as Plato does, that knowledge is lodged deeply in our memory, this latent knowledge will from time to time come to the surface of consciousness. What the soul once knew is raised to present aware-ness by the process of *recollection*. Recollection begins first of all when our minds experience difficulties with the seeming contradictions of sense experience. As we try to make sense out of the multiplicity of things, we begin to go "beyond" the things themselves to ideas, and this action of our minds is set in motion by our experience of a problem that needs to be solved. Besides this internal source of awakening, Plato argues that this is also accomplished through a teacher. In his Allegory of the Cave, Plato depicted how people moved from darkness to light, from ignorance to knowledge. But in this allegory he portrays the attitude of self-satisfaction among the prisoners; they do not know that they are prisoners, that they are chained by false knowledge and dwell in the darkness of ignorance. Their awakening must come through some teacher. As Plato says, "their release from the chains and the healing of their unwisdom" is brought about by their being "forced suddenly to stand up, turn . . . and walk with eyes lifted to the light." That is, someone must break off the prisoner's chains and turn him around. Then, having been forcibly released, he can be led step by step out of the cave. Socrates, with the power of his irony and the persistence of his dialectic method, was one of history's most effective awakeners of people from their sleep of ignorance. But besides awakening us, or breaking our chains, the effective teacher must turn us around so that we shift our gaze from shadows to the real world.

Virtue as Fulfillment of Function

Throughout his discussions of morality, Plato viewed the good life as the life of inner harmony, well-being, and happiness. He frequently compared the good life to the efficient functioning of things. A knife is good, he said, when it cuts efficiently, that is, when it fulfills its function. We say of physicians that they are good when they fulfill the function of doctoring. Musicians are similarly good when they fulfill the function of their art. Plato then asks, "Has the soul a function that can be performed by nothing else?" Living, said Plato, is likewise an art, and the soul's unique function is the art of living. Comparing the art of music with the art of living, Plato saw a close parallel, for in both cases the art consists of recognizing and obeying the requirements of limit and measure. When musicians tune their instruments, they know that each string should be tightened just so much, no more and no less, for each string has its specific pitch. The musicians' art consists, therefore, in acknowledging the limit beyond which a string should not be tightened and, in playing their instruments, observing the "measure" between intervals. In a similar way sculptors must be ruled by a vivid awareness of measure and limit, for as they work with their mallets and chisels, they must regulate the force of each stroke according to the form they want to accomplish. Their strokes will be heavy as they begin to clear away the larger sections of marble. But as they work around the head of the statue, they must have a clear vision of the limits beyond which their chisels must not go, and their strokes must be gentle as they fashion the delicate features of the face.

Similarly, the art of living requires a knowledge of limits and of measure. The soul has various functions, but these functions must operate within the limits set by knowledge or intelligence. Because the soul has various parts, each part will have a special function. Since virtue is the fulfillment of function, there will be as many virtues as there are functions. Corresponding to the three parts of the soul are three virtues, which are achieved when those parts are respectively fulfilling their functions. The appetites need to be kept within limits and in their measure, avoiding excesses so that they do not usurp the position of the other parts of the soul. This moderation in pleasures and desires leads to the virtue of *temperance*. The energy of will, which issues from the spirited part of the soul, also needs to be kept within limits, avoiding rash or headlong action and becoming instead a trustworthy power in aggressive and defensive behavior. By doing this we achieve the virtue of *courage*. Reason achieves the virtue of *wisdom* when it remains undisturbed by the onrush of appetites and continues to see the true ideals in spite of the constant changes experienced in daily life. Between these three virtues there are interconnections, for temperance is the rational control of the appetites, and courage is the rational ordering of the spirit. At the same time, each part of the soul has its own function, and when each is in fact fulfilling its special function, a fourth virtue, *justice*, is attained, for justice means giving to each its own due. Justice, then, is the general virtue, which reflects a person's attainment of well-being and inner harmony, which in turn is achieved only when every part of the soul is fulfilling its proper function.

POLITICAL PHILOSOPHY

In Plato's thought political theory is closely connected with moral philosophy. In the *Republic* he says that different classes of the state are like different parts of an individual's soul. Likewise, the different types of states, with their characteristic virtues and vices, are analogous to different types of people, with their virtues and vices. In both cases we should analyze the health of the state or person in terms of whether the classes or parts are performing their functions well and have the proper relationships to one another. Indeed, Plato held that the state is like a giant person. As justice is the general virtue of the moral person, so also it is justice that characterizes the good society. In the *Republic* Plato argues that the best way to understand the just person is to analyze the nature of the state. "We should begin," he says, "by inquiring what justice means in a state. Then we can go on to look for its counterpart on a smaller scale in the individual."

The State as a Giant Person

For Plato, the state grows out of the nature of the individual, so that the individual comes logically prior to the state. The state is a natural institution—natural because it reflects the structure of human nature. The origin of the state is a reflection of people's economic needs, for, Plato says, "a state comes into existence because no individual is self-suffing; we all have many needs." Our many needs require many skills, and no one possesses all the skills needed to produce food, shelter, and clothing, as well as the various arts. Therefore, there must be a division of labor, for "more things will be produced and the work more easily and better done, when every person is set free from all other occupations to do, at the right time, the one thing for which he is naturally fitted." Our needs are not limited to our physical requirements, for our goal is not simply survival but a life higher than an animal's. Still, the healthy state soon becomes affected by a wide range of desires and "swollen up with a whole multitude of callings not ministering to any bare necessity." Now there will be "hunters and fishermen . . . artists in sculpture, painting and music; poets with their attendant train of professional reciters, actors, dancers, producers; and makers of all sorts of household gear, including everything for women's adornment. And we shall want more servants . . . lady's maids, barbers, cooks and confectioners."

This desire for more things will soon exhaust the resources of the community, and before long, Plato says, "we shall have to cut off a slice of our neighbor's territory . . . and they will want a slice of ours." Therefore, neighbors will inevitably be at war. Wars have their "origin in desires which are the most fruitful source of evils both to individuals and states." With the inevitability of war, it will now be necessary to have "a whole army to go out to battle with any invader, in defence of all this property and of the citizens." Thus emerge the guardians of the state, who at first represent the vigorous and powerful people who will repel the invader and preserve internal order. Now there are two distinct classes of people: those who fill all the crafts—farmers, artisans, and traders—and those who guard the community. From this latter class are then chosen the most highly trained guardians, who will become the rulers of the state and will represent a third and elite class.

The relation between the individual and the state now becomes plain: The three classes in the state are an extension of the three parts of the soul. The craftspeople or artisans represent as a class the lowest part of the soul, namely, the appetites. The guardians embody the spirited element of the soul. And the highest class, the rulers, represents the rational element. So far, this analysis seems quite plausible, since it does not strain our imagination to see the connection (1) between the individual's appetites and the class of workers who satisfy these appetites, (2) between the spirited element in people and the large-scale version of this dynamic force in the military establishment, and (3) between the rational element and the unique function of leadership in the ruler. But Plato was aware that it would not be easy to convince people to accept this system of classes in the state, particularly if they found themselves in a class that might not be the one they would choose if they had the chance.

The assignment of all people to their respective classes would come only after extensive training, and only those capable of doing so would progress to the higher levels. Although theoretically all people would have the opportunity to reach the highest level, they would in fact stop at the level of their natural aptitudes. To make all of them satisfied with their lot, Plato thought it would be necessary to employ a "convenient fiction . . . a single bold flight of invention." He writes, "I shall try to convince, first the Rulers and the soldiers, and then the whole community, that all that nurture and education which we gave them was only something they seemed to experience as it were in a dream. In reality they were the whole time down inside the earth, being molded . . . and fashioned . . . and at last when they were complete, the earth sent them up from her womb into the light of day."

This "noble lie" would also say that the god who fashioned all people "mixed gold in the composition" of those who were to rule and "put silver in the guardians, and iron and brass in the farmers and craftspeople." This implied that by nature some would be rulers and others craftspeople, and would provide the basis for a perfectly stratified society. But whereas later societies in Europe assumed that children born into such a stratified society would stay at the level at which they were born, Plato recognized that children would not always have the same quality as their parents. He said, therefore, that among the injunctions laid by heaven upon the rulers "there is none that needs to be so carefully watched as the mixture of metals in the souls of children. If a child of their own is born with an alloy of iron or brass, they must, without the smallest pity, assign him the station proper to his nature and thrust him out among the farmers and craftspeople." Similarly, if a child with gold or silver is born to craftspeople, "they will promote him according to his value." Most importantly, Plato thought that everyone should agree on who is to be the ruler and agree also on why the ruler should be obeyed.

The Philosopher-King

Plato believed that competence should be the qualification for authority. The ruler of the state should be the one who has the peculiar abilities to fulfill that function. Disorder in the state is caused by the same circumstances that produce disorder in the individual, namely, the attempt on the part of the lower elements to usurp the role of the higher faculties. In both the individual and the state, the uncontrolled drives of the appetites and spirited action lead to internal anarchy. At both levels the rational element must be in control. Who should be the captain of a ship—should it be a most "popular" person or the one who knows the art of navigation? Who should rule the state—should it be someone whose training is in war or in commerce? The ruler, said Plato, should be the one who has been fully educated and has come to understand the difference between the visible world and the intelligible world—between the realm of opinion and the realm of knowledge, between appearance and reality. In short, the philosopher-king is one whose education has led him, step by step, through the ascending degrees of knowledge of the Divided Line until at last he has a knowledge of the Good, that synoptic vision of the interrelation of all truths to each other.

To reach this point, the philosopher-king would have progressed through many stages of education. By the time he is 18 years old, he would have had training in literature, music, and elementary mathematics. His literature would be censored, for Plato accused certain poets of outright falsehood and of impious accounts of the behavior of the gods. Music also would be prescribed so that seductive music would be replaced by a more wholesome variety. For the next few years there would be extensive physical and military training, and at age 20 a few would be selected to pursue an advanced course in mathematics. At age 30 a five-year course in dialectic and moral philosophy would begin. The next fifteen years would be spent gathering practical experience through public service. Finally, at age 50, the ablest people would reach the highest level of knowledge, the vision of the Good, and would then be ready for the task of governing the state.

The Virtues in the State

Whether justice could ever be achieved in a state would depend, Plato thought, upon whether the philosophic element in society could attain dominance. He writes, "I was forced to say in praise of the correct philosophy that it affords a vantage-point from which we can distinguish in all cases what is just for communities and for individuals." He also believed that "the human race will not be free of evils until either the stock of those who rightly and truly follow philosophy acquire political authority, or the class who have power in the cities be led by some divine intervention to become real philosophers." But justice, as we have already seen, is a general virtue. It means that all parts are fulfilling their special functions and are achieving their respective virtues. Justice in the state can be attained only if the three classes fulfill their functions.

As the craftspeople embody the element of the appetites, they will also reflect the virtue of temperance. Temperance is not limited to the craftspeople but applies to all the classes since, when it is achieved, it shows the willingness of the lower to be ruled by the higher. Still, temperance applies in a special way to the craftspeople insofar as they are the lowest class and must be subordinate to the two higher levels.

The guardians, who defend the state, manifest the virtue of courage. To assure that these guardians will always fulfill their function, special training and provision are made for them. Unlike the craftspeople, who marry and own property, the guardians will have both property and wives in common. Plato considered these arrangements essential if the guardians were to attain true courage, for courage means knowing what to fear and what not to fear. The only real object of fear for the guardian should be fear of moral evil. He must never fear poverty or privation, and for this reason his type of life should be isolated from possessions. Although wives would be held in common, this did not imply a form of sexism. On the contrary, Plato believed that men and women were equal in respect to certain things; for example, "a man and a woman have the same nature if both have a talent for medicine." This being the case, they should both be assigned to the same task whenever they possess the appropriate talent. For this reason Plato believed that both men and women could be guardians.

In order to preserve the unity of the members of the class of guardians, the permanent individual family would be abolished, and the whole class would become a single family. Plato's reasoning here was that the guardians must be free not only from the temptation to acquire property but also from the temptation to prefer the advantages of one's family to those of the state. Moreover, he thought it was foolish to take such pains in breeding racing dogs and horses and at the same time rely on pure chance in producing the guardians and rulers of the state. For this reason sexual relations would be strictly controlled and would be limited to the special marriage festivals. These festivals would occur at stated times, and the partners, under the illusion that they had been paired by drawing lots, would, instead, be brought together through the careful manipulation of the rulers to ensure the highest eugenic possibilities. Plato does say that "young men who performed well in war and other duties, should be given, among other rewards and privileges, more liberal opportunities to sleep with a wife," but only for the practical purpose, that "with good excuse, as many as possible of the children may be born of such fathers." As soon as children were born to the guardians, they would be taken in charge by officers appointed for that purpose and reared in a nursery school in a special part of the city. Under these circumstances, Plato thought, the guardians would be most likely to fulfill their true function of defending the state without being deflected by other concerns and would thereby achieve their appropriate virtue of courage.

Justice in the state is therefore the same as justice in the individual. It is the product of people staying in their place and doing their special task. Justice is the harmony of the virtues of temperance, courage, and wisdom. Since the state is made up of individuals, it is also necessary for each of these virtues to be attained by each person. For example, even craftspeople must have the virtue of wisdom, not only to keep their appetites in check but also to know that they rightly belong where they are and must obey the rules. Similarly, as we have seen, the guardians must have sufficient wisdom to know what to fear and what not to fear so that they can develop genuine courage. Most importantly, the ruler must come as close as possible to a knowledge of the Good, for the well-being of the state depends on the ruler's knowledge and character.

The Decline of the Ideal State

Plato argued that, if the state were a giant person, then it would reflect the kind of people a community has become. What he had in mind was that although human nature is fixed, in that all people possess a tripartite soul, the kind of people they become will depend on the degree of internal harmony they achieve. The state will therefore reflect these variations in human character. For this reason Plato argued that "constitutions cannot come out of sticks and stones; they must result from the preponderance of certain characters which draw the rest of the community in their wake. So if there are five forms of government, there must be five kinds of mental constitution among individuals." And these five forms of government are aristocracy, timocracy, plutocracy, democracy, and despotism.

Plato considered the transition from aristocracy to despotism as a step-by-step decline in the quality of the state corresponding to a gradual deterioration of the moral character of rulers and citizens. His ideal state was an aristocracy, in which the rational element embodied in the philosopher-king was supreme and in which people's reason controlled their appetites. Plato emphasized that, although this was only an ideal, it was nevertheless a very significant target to aim at. He was deeply disenchanted with politics, particularly because of the way Athens had executed Socrates and had failed to produce consistently good leaders. "As I gazed upon the whirlpool of public life," he writes, "[I] saw clearly in regard to all States now existing that without exception their system of government is bad." Still, the norm for a state is *aristocracy*, since in that form we find the proper subordination of all classes.

Even if this ideal were achieved, however, there would be a possibility for change, since nothing is permanent, and aristocracy would decline first of all into a *timocracy*. This represents a degeneration, for timocracy represents the love of honor, and insofar as ambitious members of the ruling class love their own honor more than the common good, the spirited part of their soul has usurped the role of reason. Although this is only a small break in the structure of the soul, it does begin a process whereby the irrational part assumes a progressively larger role. It is a short step from love of honor to the desire for wealth, which means allowing the appetites to rule.

Even under a timocracy there would be the beginning of a system of private property, and this desire for riches paves the way for a system of government called *plutocracy*, in which power resides in the hands of people whose main concern is wealth. And, Plato says, "as the rich rise in social esteem, the virtuous sink." What is problematic about plutocracy, according to Plato, is that it breaks the unity of the state into two contending classes, the rich and the poor. Moreover, plutocrats are consumers of goods, and when they have used up their money, they become dangerous because they want more of what they have become accustomed to. The plutocrat is like the person who seeks constant pleasure. But the very nature of pleasure is that it is momentary and must therefore be repeated. There can never be a time of perfect satisfaction; the seeker of pleasure can never be satisfied any more than a leaky pail can be filled. Still, the plutocrat knows how to distinguish three sorts of appetites—the necessary, the unnecessary, and the lawless—and so is torn between many desires. "His better desires will usually keep the upper hand over the worse," and so the plutocrat, Plato says, "presents a more decent appearance than many."

Democracy is a further degeneration, Plato said, for its principles of equality and freedom reflect the degenerate human characters whose whole range of appetites are all pursued with equal freedom. To be sure, Plato's concept of democracy, and his criticism of it, were based on his firsthand experience with the special form that democracy took in the city-state of Athens. Here democracy was direct in that all citizens had the right to participate in the government. The Athenian Assembly consisted, theoretically at least, of all citizens over 18 years of age. Thus, Plato did not have in mind modern liberal and representative democracy. What he saw in his day was rather a type of direct popular government that clearly violated his notion that the rulership of a state should be in the hands of those with the special talent and training for it.

What produced this spirit of equality was the gradual legitimizing of all the appetites under the plutocracy, by the sons of the more restrained father-plutocrats, whereby the aim of life was to become as rich as possible. And, said Plato, "this insatiable craving would bring about the transition to democracy," for "a society cannot hold wealth in honor and at the same time establish self-control in its citizens." Even the dogs in a democracy exhibit equality and independence by refusing to move out of the way in the streets. It is, however, when the rich and poor find themselves in a contest under plutocracy that the turning point is reached, for "when the poor win, the result is a democracy." Then, "liberty and free speech are rife everywhere; anyone is allowed to do what he likes." Now, "you are not obliged to be in authority . . . or to submit to authority, if you do not like it." All this political equality and freedom stem from a soul whose order has been shattered. It is a soul whose appetites are now all equal and free and act as a "mob" of passions. The life of liberty and equality declares that "one appetite is as good as another and all must have their equal rights."

But the continuous indulgence of the appetites leads inevitably to the point at which a single master passion will finally enslave the soul. We cannot yield to every craving without finally having to yield to the strongest and most persistent passion. At this point we say that we are under the tyranny of our master passion. Likewise, in the state, the passion for money and pleasures leads the masses to plunder the rich. As the rich resist, the masses seek out a strong person who will be their champion. But this person demands and acquires absolute power and makes slaves of the people, and only later do the people realize to what depths of subjugation they have fallen. This is the unjust society, the enlargement of the unjust soul. The natural end of democracy is *despotism*.

VIEW OF THE COSMOS

Although Plato's most consistent and sustained thought centered around moral and political philosophy, he also turned his attention to science. His theory of nature, or physics, is found chiefly in the *Timaeus*—a dialogue that, according to some scholars, Plato wrote when he was about 70 years old. Plato had not deliberately postponed this subject, nor had he chosen to deal with moral matters instead of promoting the advancement of science. On the contrary, the science of his day had reached a blind alley, and there seemed to be no fruitful direction to take in this field. Earlier, according to Plato, Socrates had had "a prodigious desire to know that department of philosophy which is called the investigation of nature; to know the causes of things." However, Socrates was disillusioned by the conflicting answers and theories put forward by Anaximander, Anaximenes, Leucippus and Democritus, and others. Plato shared this disappointment. Moreover, as his own philosophy took shape, some of his theories about reality cast doubt on the possibility of a strictly accurate scientific knowledge. Physics, he thought, could never be more than "a likely story." It was particularly his theory of the Forms that rendered science as an exact type of knowledge impossible. The real world, he said, is the world of Forms, whereas the visible world is full of change and imperfection. Yet, it is about the visible world of things that science seeks to build its theories. How can we formulate accurate, reliable, and permanent knowledge about a subject matter that is itself imperfect and full of change? At the same time, though, Plato clearly felt that his theory of the Forms—as well as his notions of morality, evil, and truth—required a view of the cosmos in which all these elements of his thought could be brought together in a coherent way. Recognizing, then, that his account of the material world was only "a likely story," or at best probable knowledge, he nevertheless was convinced that what he had to say about the world was as accurate as the subject matter would allow.

Plato's first thought about the world was that, though it is full of change and imperfection, it nevertheless exhibits order and purpose. He rejected the explanation given by Democritus, who had argued that all things came into being through the accidental collision of atoms. When Plato considered, for example, the orbits of the planets, he observed that they were arranged according to a precise series of geometrical intervals, which, when appropriately calculated, produced the basis for the harmonic scale. Plato made much of Pythagorean mathematics in describing the world. However, instead of saying, as the Pythagoreans did, that things are numbers, he said that things *participate* in numbers and that they are capable of a mathematical explanation. This mathematical characteristic of things suggested to Plato that behind things there must be thought and purpose, and not merely chance and subsequent mechanism. The cosmos must therefore be the work of *intelligence*, since it is the mind that orders all things. Humanity and the world bear a likeness to each other, for both contain first an intelligible and eternal element, and second a sensible and perishable element. This dualism is expressed in people by the union of soul and body. Similarly, the world is a soul in which things as we know them are arranged.

Although Plato said that *mind* orders everything, he did not develop a theory of creation. Theories of creation typically hold, that things are created out of nothing. But Plato's explanation of the origin of the visible world bypasses this notion of creation. Granted, Plato does say that "that which becomes must necessarily become through the agency of some cause." However, this agent, which he calls the divine Craftsman or Demiurge, does not bring new things into being but rather confronts and orders what already exists in chaotic form. We have, then, a picture of the Craftsman with the material on which he will work. Thus, in explaining the generation of things as we know them in the visible world, Plato assumes the existence of all the ingredients of things, namely, that out of which things are made, the Demiurge who is the Craftsman, and the Forms or *patterns* after which things are made.

Plato departed from the materialists who thought that all things came from some original kind of matter, whether in the form of earth, air, fire, or water. Plato did not accept the notion that matter was the basic reality. Matter itself, Plato said, must be explained in more refined terms as the composition not of some finer forms of matter but of something other than matter. What we call matter, whether in the form of earth or water, is a reflection of a Form, and these Forms are expressed through a medium. Things are generated out of what Plato calls the *receptacle*, which he considered the "nurse of all becoming." The receptacle is a "matrix," or a medium that has no structure but that is capable of receiving the imposition of structure by the Demiurge. Another word Plato uses for the receptacle is *space*, which, he says, "is everlasting, not admitting destruction; providing a situation for all things that come into being, but itself grasped without the senses by a sort of illegitimate reasoning, and hardly an object of belief." There is no explanation of the origin of the receptacle, for in Plato's thought it is underived, as are the Forms and the Demiurge. The receptacle is where things appear and perish.

To an unreflective person earth and water may appear to be solid and permanent kinds of matter. But Plato said that they are constantly changing and therefore do not hold still long enough "to be described as 'this' or 'that' or by any phrase that exhibits them as having permanent being." What the senses consider "matter" or "substance" when they apprehend the elements of earth and water are only *qualities*. These qualities, then, appear through the medium of the receptacle "in which all of them are always coming to be, making their appearance and vanishing out of it." Material objects are composed of nonmaterial compounds. Here Plato is again influenced by the Pythagorean perspective when he argues that solid objects of matter are described and defined in geometric terms according to their surfaces. Any surface, he said, can be resolved by triangles, and any triangle in turn can be divided into right triangles. These shapes, these triangular surfaces, are irreducible and must therefore be the ingredients of the compound known as matter. The simplest solid, for example, would be a pyramid that consists of four triangular surfaces. Similarly, a cube could be made of six square surfaces, where each square surface is composed of two half squares, that is, two triangles. What we normally call "solid" never contains anything more than "surfaces," so that we can say that "body" or "molecules" are geometric figures. Indeed, the whole universe can be thought of in terms of its geometrical diagram—and can be defined simply as what is happening in space, or as space reflecting various forms. What Plato wanted particularly to establish was the notion that matter is only the appearance of something more basic.

If various kinds of triangles represent the basic constituents of all things, how can we account for the variations in things as well as their stability? What, in short, makes it possible to have the kind of world and universe that we know? Here again, Plato was forced to assume that all things must be ordered by mind, that the cosmos is the activity of the World Soul, namely, the soul of the living cosmos. The world of things is the world of *phenomena*, which is the Greek word for "appearances." What is presented to our perception is the multitude of appearances, which, when analyzed, are found to consist of geometric surfaces. These surfaces, again, are primary and irreducible and are found as "raw material" in the receptacle and require some organizing agency to arrange them first into triangles and then into phenomena. All this activity is achieved by the World Soul. The World Soul is eternal, though at times Plato appears to say that it is the creation of the Demiurge. Although the World Soul is eternal, the world of appearance is full of change, just as in humans the soul represents the eternal element whereas the body contains the principle of change. The world of matter and body changes because it is composite and always tends to return to its basic constituents, "going into" and "going out of" space. But insofar as the World Soul is eternal, there is, in spite of all the change in the world of our experience, an element of stability and permanence, a structure, a discernible universe.

There is evil in the world, Plato says, because there are obstacles in the way of the Demiurge. The world is not perfectly good even though the

Demiurge sought to make it as much like its pattern as possible. Although the Demiurge represents divine reason and the agency that fashioned the order of the universe, "the generation of this cosmos," Plato says, "was a mixed result of the combination of Necessity and Reason." Necessity in this context signifies unwillingness to change and, when applied to the "raw material" of the receptacle, it shows a recalcitrance as though impervious to the ordering of mind. In this sense *necessity* is one of the conditions of evil in the world, for evil is the breakdown of purpose, and purpose is characteristic of mind. Whatever, then, frustrates the working of mind contributes to the absence of order, which is the meaning of evil. This suggests that in human life, too, the circumstance of a recalcitrant body and lower parts of the soul produces evil insofar as mind is not in control. Necessity is expressed in various types, such as inertia and irreversibility, and reason, even God's reason, must cope with these obstacles while trying to order the world according to a definite purpose.

Finally, there is the question of *time*. According to Plato, time comes to be only after phenomena are produced. Not until there are things as we know them, as imperfect and changing, can there be time. Until then, by definition, whatever is, is eternal. The very meaning of time is change, and therefore, in the absence of change, there could be no time. Whereas the Forms are timeless, the various copies of them in the receptacle constantly "go in" and "go out," and this going in and out is the process of change, which is the cause of time. Still, time represents the double presence in the cosmos of time and eternity; since the cosmos is ordered by mind, it contains the element of eternity, and since the cosmos consists of temporary combinations of surfaces, it contains the element of change and time. And since change is not capricious but regular, the very process of change exhibits the presence of eternal mind. This regularity of change, as exhibited, for example, by the regular change or motion of the stars and planets, makes possible the measurement of change and makes it possible to "tell time."

Plato's "likely story" about the cosmos consisted, then, of an account of how the Demiurge fashioned things out of the receptacle, using the Forms as patterns. The World Soul is produced by the Demiurge and is the energizing activity in the receptacle, producing what to us appears to be substance or solid matter—though in reality is only qualities caused by the arrangement of geometric surfaces. Evil and time are, on this account, the product of imperfection and change. The world as we know it depends on an agency and "raw material" that are not found in the physical world as we know it, this agency being mind, and the raw material being explained chiefly in terms of mathematics.

At this point we would wish to engage in a sustained and critical appraisal of Plato's vast system of philosophy. But in a sense, the history of philosophy represents just such a large-scale dialogue, in which thinkers arise to agree and disagree with what he taught. So powerful was the mold into which he cast the enterprise of philosophy that for centuries to come his views dominated the intellectual scene. Indeed, Alfred North Whitehead once remarked that "the safest general characterization of the European philosophical tradition is that it consists of a series of footnotes to Plato." Many of these footnotes, it might be added, were written by Plato's prodigious successor, Aristotle, to whom we now turn.

CHAPTER 4

Aristotle

ARISTOTLE'S LIFE

Aristotle was born in 384 BCE in the small town of Stagira on the northeast coast of Thrace. His father was physician to the king of Macedonia. It could be that Aristotle's great interest in biology and science in general was nurtured in his early childhood. When he was 17 years old, Aristotle went to Athens to enroll in Plato's Academy, where he spent the next twenty years as a pupil and a member. At the Academy Aristotle had the reputation of being the "reader" and "the mind of the school." He was profoundly influenced by Plato's thought and personality even though eventually he broke away from Plato's philosophy in order to formulate his own version of certain philosophical problems. Still, while at the Academy, he wrote many dialogues in a Platonic style, which his contemporaries praised for the "golden stream" of their eloquence. In his *Eudemus* he even reaffirmed the very notion so central to Plato's thought, the theory of the Forms, which he later criticized so severely.

There is no way now to reconstruct with exactness just when Aristotle's thought diverged from Plato's. Plato's own thought, it must be remembered, was in the process of change while Aristotle was at the Academy. Indeed, scholars believe that Aristotle studied with Plato during Plato's "later" period, a time when Plato's interests had shifted toward mathematics, method, and natural science. During this time, also, specialists in various sciences, such as medicine, anthropology, and archeology, came to the Academy. This meant that Aristotle was exposed to a vast array of empirical facts, which, because of his outlook, he found useful for research and for formulation of scientific concepts. It may be, therefore, that the intellectual atmosphere of the Academy, marked by some of Plato's latest dominant concerns and the availability of collected data in special fields, provided Aristotle with a direction in philosophy that was congenial to his scientific disposition.

The direction Aristotle took did eventually cause him to depart from some of Plato's theories, though the degree of difference between Plato and Aristotle is still a matter of careful interpretation. But even when they were together at the Academy, certain temperamental differences must have been apparent. Aristotle, for example, was less interested in mathematics than Plato and more interested in empirical data. Moreover, as time went on, Aristotle's gaze seemed to be more firmly fixed on the concrete processes of nature, so that he considered his abstract scientific notions to have their real habitat in this living nature. By contrast, Plato separated the world of thought from the world of flux and things, ascribing true reality to the Forms, which, he asserted, had an existence separate from the things in nature. We can say, therefore, that Aristotle oriented his thought to the dynamic realm of *becoming*, whereas Plato's thought was fixed more upon the static realm of timeless *Being*. Whatever differences there were between these two great minds, the fact is that Aristotle did not break with Plato personally, as he remained at the Academy until Plato's death. Moreover, throughout Aristotle's later major treatises, we find unmistakable influences of Plato's thought in spite of Aristotle's unique interpretations and style. But his distinctly "Platonist" period came to an end with Plato's death. The direction of the Academy had then passed into the hands of Plato's nephew Speusippos, whose excessive emphasis on mathematics was uncongenial to Aristotle. For this and other reasons, Aristotle withdrew from the Academy and left Athens.

It was in 348/47 BCE that Aristotle left the Academy and accepted the invitation of Hermeias to come to Assos, near Troy. Hermeias had formerly been a student at the Academy and was now the ruler of Assos. Being somewhat of a philosopher-king, he gathered a small group of thinkers into his court, and here Aristotle was able for the next three years to write, teach, and carry on research. While at Hermeias's court, he married the ruler's niece and adopted daughter, Pythias, who bore him a daughter. Later, after they had returned to Athens, his wife died, and Aristotle then entered into a relationship with a woman named Herpyllis, which was never legalized. Nevertheless, it was a happy, permanent, and affectionate union from which there came a son, Nicomachus, after whom Aristotle's book the *Nicomachean Ethics* was named. After his three years in Assos, Aristotle moved to the neighboring island of Lesbos, settling for the time being in Mitylene, where he taught and continued his investigations in biology, studying especially the many forms of marine life. Here he also became known as an advocate of a united Greece, urging that such a union would be more successful than independent city-states in resisting the might of Persia. In 343/42 BCE, Philip of Macedon invited Aristotle to become the tutor of his son Alexander, who was then 13 years old. As a tutor to a future ruler, Aristotle's interests included politics, and it is possible that it was here that he conceived the idea of collecting and comparing various constitutions, a project he later carried out by collecting digests of the constitutions of 158 Greek city-states. When Alexander ascended the throne after his father Philip's death, Aristotle's duties as tutor came to an end, and after a brief stay in his hometown of Stagira, he returned to Athens.

Upon his return to Athens in 335/34 BCE, Aristotle began the most productive period of his life. Under the protection of the Macedonian statesman Antipater, Aristotle founded his own school. His school was known as the

Lyceum, named after the groves where Socrates was known to have gone to think and which were the sacred precincts of Apollo Lyceus. Here Aristotle and his pupils walked in the Peripatos, a tree-covered walk, and discussed philosophy, for which reason his school was called *peripatetic*—meaning "walking about." Besides these peripatetic discussions, there were also lectures, some technical for small audiences and others of a more popular nature for larger audiences. Tradition maintains that Aristotle also formed the first great library by collecting hundreds of manuscripts, maps, and specimens, which he used as illustrations during his lectures. Moreover, his school developed certain formal procedures whereby its leadership would alternate among members. Aristotle formulated the rules for these procedures, as he did for the special common meal and symposium once a month. On these occasions a member was selected to defend a philosophical position against the critical objections of the other members. For a dozen or so years Aristotle remained as the head of the Lyceum, teaching and lecturing. Above all, though, while there he formulated his main ideas about the classification of the sciences, fashioned a bold new science of logic, and wrote his advanced ideas in every major area of philosophy and science, exhibiting an extraordinary command of universal knowledge.

When Alexander died in 323 BCE, a wave of anti-Macedonian feeling arose, making Aristotle's position in Athens precarious because of his close connections with Macedonia. Like Socrates before him, Aristotle was charged with "impiety," but, as he is reported to have said, "lest the Athenians should sin twice against philosophy," he left the Lyceum and fled to Chalcis, where he died in 322 BCE of a digestive disease of long standing. In his will he expressed his humanity by providing amply for his relatives, preventing his slaves from being sold, and providing that some of the slaves should be emancipated. As with Socrates and Plato, Aristotle's thought was of such decisive force that it was to influence philosophy for centuries to come. From the vast range of his philosophy, we will consider here some aspects of his logic, metaphysics, ethics, politics, and aesthetics.

LOGIC

Aristotle invented formal logic. He also came up with the idea of the separate sciences. For him there was a close connection between logic and science, inasmuch as he considered logic to be the instrument (*organon*) with which to formulate language properly when analyzing what a science involves.

The Categories and the Starting Point of Reasoning

Before we can logically demonstrate or prove something, we must have a clear starting point for our reasoning process. For one thing we must specify the subject matter that we are discussing—the specific "kind" of thing we are dealing with. To this we must add the properties and causes that are related to that kind of thing. In this connection Aristotle developed his notion of the *categories*, which explains how we think about things. Whenever we think of some distinct thing, we think of a subject and its predicates—that is, of some *substance* and its accidents. We think the word *human* and also connect the word *human* with such predicates as *tall* and *able*. The word *human* is here a substance, and Aristotle proposed at least nine *categories* (that is, predicates) that can be connected with a substance, including *quantity* (such as, six feet tall), *quality* (such as, articulate), *relation* (such as, double), *place* (such as, at the school), *date* (such as, last week), *posture* (such as, standing), *possession* (such as, clothed), *action* (such as, serves), and *passivity* (such as, is served). We can consider *substance* itself as a category, since we say, for example, "he is a human," in which case *human* (a substance) is a *predicate*. These categories represented for Aristotle the classification of concepts that are used in scientific knowledge. They represent the specific ways in which whatever exists does exist or is realized. In our thinking we arrange things into these categories, classifying such categories into genera, species, and the individual thing. We see the individual as a member of the species and the species as related to the genus. Aristotle did not consider these categories or these classifications as artificial creations of the mind. He thought that they were actually in existence outside the mind and in things. Things, he thought, fell into various classifications by their very nature, and we think of them as members of a species or genus because they *are*. Thinking, as Aristotle saw it, was connected with the way things are, and this underlies the close relation between logic and metaphysics. Thinking is always about some specific individual thing, namely, a substance. But a thing never simply exists; it exists some*how* and has a reason *why*.

There are always predicates (categories) related to subjects (substances). Some predicates are intrinsic to a thing. Such predicates or categories belong to a thing simply because it is what it is. We think of a horse as having certain predicates *because* it is a horse; it has these predicates in common with all other horses. It also has other predicates, not so intrinsic but rather "accidental," such as color, place, size, and other determinations affecting its relation to other material objects. What Aristotle wants to underscore is that there is a sequence that leads to "science." This sequence is, first of all, the *existence* of things and their processes; second, our *thinking* about things and their behavior; and, finally, the transformation of our thought about things into *words*. Language is the instrument for formulating scientific thought. Logic, then, is the analysis of language, the process of reasoning, and the way language and reasoning are related to reality.

The Syllogism

Aristotle develops a system of logic, based on the *syllogism*, which he defines as a "discourse in which certain things being stated, something other than what is stated follows of necessity from their being so." The classic example of a syllogism is this:

Major premise. All humans are mortal.

Minor premise. Socrates is a human.

Conclusion. Therefore, Socrates is mortal.

The first two statements are premises, which serve as evidence for the third statement, which is the conclusion. How, then, can we be sure that a conclusion follows from its premises? The answer rests in the basic structure of valid syllogistic arguments, and Aristotle devised a set of rules that determine when conclusions are rightly inferred from their premises. Up until the nineteenth century, philosophers believed that Aristotle's account of the syllogism constituted everything there was to say about the subject of logic. Only in more recent decades have alternative systems of logic been offered that supercede Aristotle's account.

Although Aristotle's theory of the syllogism is an effective tool for determining valid relationships between premises and conclusions, his aim was to provide an instrument for scientific demonstration. For this reason, again, he emphasized the relation between logic and metaphysics—between our way of knowing and what things are and how they behave. That is, he thought that words and propositions are linked together because the things that language mirrors are also linked together. Accordingly, Aristotle recognized that it is entirely possible to employ the syllogism consistently without necessarily arriving at scientific truth. This would happen if the premises did not rest on true assumptions—that is, if they did not reflect reality. Aristotle distinguished between three kinds of reasoning, each of which might use the instrument of the syllogism, but with different results. These are (1) *dialectical* reasoning, which is reasoning from "opinions that are generally accepted"; (2) *eristic*, or contentious, reasoning, which begins with opinions that seem to be generally accepted but are really not; and (3) *demonstrative* reasoning, where the premises from which reasoning starts are true and primary.

Thus, the value of syllogistic reasoning depended for Aristotle on the accuracy of the premises. If true scientific knowledge is to be achieved, it is necessary that the premises be more than opinion or even probable truth. Demonstrative reasoning moves backward, as it were, from conclusions to those premises that constitute the necessary beginnings of the conclusion. When we say "all humans are mortal," we in effect move back to those causes and properties in animals that constitute their mortality. We then link humans with these properties by including them in the class of animals. Demonstrative reasoning must therefore lay hold of reliable premises, or what Aristotle calls *first principles* (*archai*)—that is, accurately defined properties of any thing, class, or distinctive area of subject matter. Valid reasoning, therefore, presupposes the discovery of true first principles from which conclusions can be drawn.

How do we arrive at these first principles? Aristotle answers that we learn these from observation and induction. When we observe certain facts many times, "the universal that is there," he says, "becomes plain." Whenever we observe any particular "that," we store it away in memory. After observing many similar "thats," we generate from all these particular "thats" a general term with a general meaning. We discover the universal within the particulars by the process of induction, which results in the discovery of additional meanings in the particular "thats" observed.

If we then ask the additional question of whether and how we can know that the first principles are true, Aristotle answers that we know they are true simply because our minds, working with certain facts, "recognize" or "see" their truth. These first principles are not in turn demonstrated. If it were necessary to demonstrate every premise, this would involve an infinite regress, since each prior premise would also have to be proved, in which case the enterprise of knowledge could never get started. Aristotle, referring again to first principles, says that "not all knowledge is demonstrative: on the contrary, knowledge of the immediate premises is independent of demonstration." Scientific knowledge, he says, rests on knowledge that is not itself subject to the same proof as scientific conclusions. So, "besides scientific knowledge there is its originative source which enables us to *recognize* the definitions."

Here Aristotle uses the word *recognize* to explain how we know certain truths; this is in contrast to Plato's use of the word *recollect* or *remember*. To "recognize" a truth is to have a direct intuitive grasp of it, as when we know that two plus two equal four. It may be that the occasion for "recognizing" this truth of arithmetic was the act of adding particular things such as bricks or stones. Still, from these specific factual cases we "see" or "recognize" the truth that certain things belong to a species or genus and that certain relations exist between them, such as two plus two equal four. Thus, Aristotle argued that science rests on primary premises, which we arrive at by intellectual intuition (*nous*). Once these primary premises and definitions of the essential natures of things are in hand, it is then possible for us to engage in demonstrative reasoning.

METAPHYSICS

In his work titled *Metaphysics*, Aristotle develops what he called the science of *first philosophy*. The term *metaphysics* has a somewhat cloudy origin, but in this context it seems at least in part to signify the position of this work among Aristotle's other writings, namely, that it is *beyond*, or comes *after*, his work on physics. Throughout *Metaphysics* he deals with a type of knowledge that he thought could be most rightly called *wisdom*. This work begins with the statement "All men by nature desire to know." This innate desire, Aristotle says, is not only a desire to know in order to do or make something. In addition to these pragmatic motives, there is in us a desire to know certain kinds of things simply for the sake of knowing. An indication of this, Aristotle says, is "the delight we take in our senses; for even apart from their usefulness they are loved for themselves" inasmuch as our seeing "makes us know and brings to light many differences between things."

There are different levels of knowledge. Some people know only what they experience through their senses, as, for example, when they know that fire is hot. But, Aristotle says, we do not regard what we know through the senses as wisdom. Instead, wisdom is similar to the knowledge possessed by scientists. They begin by looking at something, then repeat these sense experiences, and finally go beyond sense experience by thinking about the *causes* of the objects of their experiences. There are as many sciences as there are definable areas of investigation, and Aristotle deals with many of them, including physics, ethics, politics, and aesthetics. In addition to the specific sciences, though, there is another science, first philosophy, or what we now call *metaphysics*, which goes beyond the subject matter of the other sciences and is concerned with the knowledge of true reality.

The Problem of Metaphysics Defined

The various sciences seek to find the first principles and causes of specific kinds of things, such as material bodies, the human body, the state, or a poem. Unlike these sciences, which ask, "What is such-and-such a thing like and why?" metaphysics asks a far more general question—a question that each science must ultimately take into account, namely, "What does it mean to be anything whatsoever?" What, in short, does it mean *to be*? It was precisely this question that concerned Aristotle in his *Metaphysics*, making metaphysics for him "the science of any existent, as existent." The problem of metaphysics as he saw it was therefore the study of Being and its "principles" and "causes."

Aristotle's metaphysics was to a considerable extent an outgrowth of his views on logic and his interest in biology. From the viewpoint of his logic, "to be" meant for him to be *something* that could be accurately defined and that could therefore become the subject of discourse. From the point of view of his interest in biology, he was inclined to think of "to be" as something implicated in a dynamic process. "To be," as Aristotle saw the matter, always meant to be *something*. Hence, all existence is individual and has a specific nature. All the categories (or predicates) that Aristotle dealt with in his logical works—categories such as *quality, relation, posture,* and *place*—presuppose some subject to which these predicates can apply. This subject to which all the categories apply Aristotle called *substance (ousia)*. "To be," then, is to be a particular kind of substance. Also, "to be" means to be a substance as the product of a dynamic process. In this way metaphysics is concerned with *Being* (that is, existing substances) and its *causes* (that is, the processes by which substances come into being).

Substance as the Primary Essence of Things

Aristotle believed that the way we know a thing provides a major clue as to what we mean by "substance." Having in mind again the categories or predicates, Aristotle says that we know a thing better when we know *what it is* than when we know its color, size, or posture. We separate a thing from all its qualities, and we focus upon what a thing really is, upon its *essential nature*. To this end Aristotle distinguishes between *essential* and *accidental* properties of things. For example, to say that a person has red hair is to describe something accidental, since to be a human it is not necessary or essential that one have red hair—or even any hair for that matter. But it is essential to my being human that I am mortal. We similarly recognize that all humans are *human* in spite of their different sizes, colors, or ages. *Something* about each concretely different person makes him or her a person in spite of the unique characteristics that make him or her *this particular* person. At this point Aristotle would readily agree that these special characteristics (categories, predicates) also exist and have some kind of being. But the being of these characteristics is not the central object of metaphysical inquiry.

The central concern of metaphysics is the study of substance, that is, the essential nature of a thing. On this view substance means "that which is not asserted of a subject but of which everything else is asserted." Substance is what we know as basic about something, *after* which we can say other things about *it*. Whenever we define something, we get at its essence *before* we can say anything about it, as when we speak of a large table or a healthy person. Here we understand table and person in their "essence"—in what makes them a table or a person—before we understand them as large or healthy. It is true that we can know only specific and determinate things—actual individual tables or persons. At the same time, the essence, or substance, of a table or a person has its existence peculiarly separate from its categories or its qualities. This does not mean that a substance is ever in fact found existing separately from its qualities. Still, Aristotle believed that we can know the essence of a thing such as "tableness" as separated from its particular qualities of round, small, and brown. Thus, he says, there must be some universal essence that is found wherever we see a table. And this essence or substance must be independent of its particular qualities inasmuch as the essence is the same, even though in the case of each actual table the qualities are different. Aristotle's point is that a thing is more than the sum of its particular qualities. There is something "beneath" *(sub stance)* all the qualities; thus, any specific thing is a combination of qualities, on the one hand, and a substratum to which the qualities apply, on the other. With these distinctions in mind, Aristotle was led, like Plato before him, to consider just how this essence, or "universal," was related to the particular thing. What, in short, makes a substance a substance; is it *matter* as a substratum or is it *form*?

Matter and Form

Although Aristotle distinguished between *matter* and *form*, he nevertheless said that, in nature, we never find matter without form or form without matter. Everything that exists is some concrete individual thing, and every *thing* is a unity of matter and form. Substance, therefore, is always a composite of form and matter. Plato, you will recall, argued that Forms, such as Human or Table, have a separate existence. Particular things, such as the table in front of me, obtain their nature by *participating* in the Forms, such as the Form Tableness. Aristotle rejected Plato's explanation of the universal Forms—specifically, the contention that the Forms existed separately from individual things. Of course, Aristotle did agree that there are universals and that universals such as Human and Table are more than merely subjective notions. Indeed, Aristotle recognized that without the theory of universals, there could be no scientific knowledge, for then there would be no way of saying something about all members of a particular class.

What makes science effective is that it identifies classes of objects (for example, a certain form of human disease), so that whenever an individual falls into this class, we can also assume that other facts are relevant. These classes, then, are not merely mental fictions but do in fact have objective reality. But, Aristotle said, we simply find their reality in the individual things themselves. What purpose, he asked, could be served by assuming that the universal Forms exist separately? If anything, this would complicate matters, since everything would have to be replicated in the world of Forms—not only individual things but also their relationships. Moreover, Aristotle was not convinced that Plato's theory of the Forms could help us know things any better; "they help in no wise toward the knowledge of other things." Since presumably the Forms are motionless, Aristotle concluded that they could not help us understand things as we know them, as full of motion. Nor could they, being immaterial, explain objects of which we have sense impressions. Again, how could the immaterial Forms be related to any particular thing? It is not satisfactory to say, as Plato did, that things *participate* in the Forms: "to say that they are patterns and that other things share in them, is to use empty words and poetical metaphors."

When we use the words *matter* and *form* to describe any specific thing, we seem to have in mind the distinction between what something is made *of* and what it is made *into*. This, again, inclines us to assume that matter—what things are made of—exists in some primary and unformed state until it is made into a thing. But, again, Aristotle argues that we shall not find anywhere such a thing as "primary matter," that is, matter without form. Consider the sculptor who is about to make a statue of Venus out of marble. He or she will never find marble without some form. It will always be this marble or that, a square piece or an irregular one. But he or she will always work with a piece in which form and matter are already combined. That the sculptor will give it a different form is another question. The question here is, How does one thing become another thing? What, in short, is the nature of *change*?

The Process of Change: The Four Causes

In the world around us we see things constantly changing. Change is one of the basic facts of our experience. For Aristotle the word *change* meant many things, including motion, growth, decay, generation, and corruption. Some of these changes are *natural*, whereas others are the products of *human art*. Things are always taking on new form; new life is born and statues are made. Because change always involves taking on new form, we can ask several questions about the process of change. Of anything, Aristotle says, we can ask four questions, namely (1) What is it? (2) What is it made of? (3) By what is it made? and (4) For what end is it made? The four responses to these questions represent Aristotle's four *causes*. Although the word *cause* refers in modern use primarily to an event prior to an effect, for Aristotle it meant an *explanation*. His four causes, therefore, represent a broad pattern or framework for the total explanation of anything or everything. Taking an object of art, for example, the four causes might be (1) a statue (2) of marble (3) by a sculptor (4) for decoration.

Distinguished from objects produced by human art, there are also things that are caused *by nature*. Although nature does not, according to Aristotle, have "purposes" in the sense of "the reason for," it does always and everywhere have "ends" in the sense of having built-in ways of behaving. For this reason seeds sprout, and roots go down (not up!), and plants grow. In this process of change, plants move toward their "end," that is, their distinctive function or way of being. In nature change will involve these same four elements. Aristotle's four causes are therefore (1) the *formal* cause, which determines what a thing is, (2) the *material* cause, or that out of which it is made, (3) the *efficient* cause, by what a thing is made, and (4) the *final* cause, the "end" for which it is made.

Aristotle looked at life through the eyes of a biologist. For him nature was *life*. All things are in motion—in the process of becoming and dying away. The process of reproduction was for Aristotle a clear example of the power inherent in all living things to initiate change and to reproduce. Summarizing his causes, Aristotle said that "all things that come to be come to be by some agency and from something, and come to be something." From this biological viewpoint Aristotle elaborated the notion that form and matter never exist separately. In nature generation of new life involves first of all an individual who already possesses the specific form that the offspring will have (the male parent). After that there must be matter capable of being the vehicle for this form (this matter being contributed by the female parent). Finally, from this comes a new individual with the same specific form. In this example Aristotle shows that change does not involve bringing together formless matter with matterless form. On the contrary, change occurs always in and to something that is already a combination of form and matter and that is on its way to becoming something new or different.

Potentiality and Actuality

All things, said Aristotle, are involved in processes of change. Each thing possesses a power to become what its form has set as its end. There is in all things a dynamic power of striving toward their "end." Some of this striving is toward external objects, as when a person builds a house. But there is also the striving to achieve ends that pertain to a person's internal nature, as when we fulfill our nature as a human being by the act of thinking. This notion of a self-contained end led Aristotle to consider the distinction between *potentiality* and *actuality*. He used this distinction to explain the processes of change and development. If the *end* of an acorn is to be a tree, in some way the acorn is only potentially a tree but not actually so at this time. A fundamental type of change, then, is the change from potentiality to actuality. But the chief significance of this distinction is that Aristotle argues for the priority of actuality over potentiality. That is, although something actual emerges from the potential, there could be no movement from potential to actual if there were not first of all something actual. A child is potentially an adult, but before there can be a child with that potentiality, there has to be an actual adult.

As all things in nature are similar to the relation of a child to an adult, or an acorn to a tree, Aristotle was led to see in nature different levels of being. If everything were involved in change—in generation and corruption—everything would partake of potentiality. But, as we have seen, for there to be something potential, there must already be something actual. To explain the existence of the world of potential things, Aristotle thought it was necessary to assume the existence of some actuality at a level above potential or perishing things. This led to the notion of a Being that is pure actuality, without any potentiality, at the highest level of being. Since change is a kind of motion, Aristotle saw the visible world as one composed of things in motion. But motion, a type of change, involves potentiality. Things are potentially in motion but must be moved by something that is actually in motion.

The Unmoved Mover

For Aristotle the Unmoved Mover is the ultimate cause of all change in the natural world. However, this notion is not the same thing as a *first* mover, as though motion could be traced back to a *time* when motion began. Nor did he consider the Unmoved Mover to be a *creator* in the sense of later theology. From his previous distinction between potentiality and actuality, Aristotle concluded that the only way to explain how motion or change can occur is to assume that something actual is *logically* prior to whatever is potential. The fact of change implies the existence of something *purely* actual without any mixture of potentiality. This mover is not, according to Aristotle, an *efficient* cause in the sense of a mighty force exerting its power. Such acts would imply potentiality, as when we say that God intended to create the world. This would mean that *before* God created the world, he was potentially capable or intended to create it.

The heart of Aristotle's notion of the Unmoved Mover is that it is a way of explaining the fact of motion. All of nature is full of things that strive toward fulfilling their particular purposes. Each thing aims at perfecting its possibilities and its *end*, that is, at becoming the perfect tree, the perfectly good person, and so on. The aggregate of all these strivings constitutes the large-scale processes of the world order. All of reality, then, is in the process of change, moving from its potentialities and possibilities to the ultimate perfection of these potentialities. To explain this comprehensive or general motion, Aristotle referred to the Unmoved Mover as the "reason for" or the "principle of" motion. For this reason the Unmoved Mover stood for the actual and—because there is here no potentiality—the *eternal* principle of motion. Since this explanation of motion implies an eternal activity, then, there was never a "time" when there was not a world of things in process. For this reason, too, Aristotle denied that there was a "creation" in time.

To speak of an Unmoved Mover involved Aristotle in certain metaphorical language. In explaining how an Unmoved Mover can "cause" motion, he compared it to a beloved who "moves" the lover merely by being the object of love, by the power of attraction and not by force. In a more technical way Aristotle considered the Unmoved Mover as the *form* and the world as the substance. From the point of view of his four causes, Aristotle considered the Unmoved Mover as the *final* cause, in the same way that the *form* of the adult is in the child, directing the motion of change toward a *final* end—one that is fixed or appropriate. By being a final cause, the Unmoved Mover thereby becomes an *efficient* cause of the world. Through the power of attraction, it inspires things to strive toward their natural ends. Although Aristotle's Unmoved Mover functions as a scientific principle of motion and immanent form of the world, it nevertheless carries some religious overtones. Centuries later—especially at the hands of Aquinas in the thirteenth century—this notion was transformed into the philosophical description of the God of Christianity.

THE PLACE OF HUMANS: PHYSICS, BIOLOGY, AND PSYCHOLOGY

In the hierarchical nature of things, Aristotle placed people in a spot distinct from inanimate things and animals. In the order of nature there are, first of all, simple bodies, plants, and animals. Unlike artificially created objects, such as chairs and tables, natural objects are such that "each of them has *within* itself a principle of motion and of rest." This internal motion is the decisive aspect of things, for through this motion Aristotle explains the whole process of generation and corruption.

Physics

Limiting our concern to the question of how things come to be in the natural world, Aristotle begins with the notion of *prime matter*. We have already said that Aristotle rejected the position that either pure forms or pure matter could exist separately. There is no *primary matter* existing by itself anywhere. By *prime matter* Aristotle meant the substratum in things that is capable of changing, of becoming other substances or things, of assuming novel forms. The processes of nature, then, involve the continuous transformation of matter from one form to another. When the sculptor makes a statue, his or her material, let us say marble, already has some form, and he or she will then transform it. In this same sense Aristotle says that there are certain materials out of which *nature* makes things, and he calls these *simple bodies*, namely, air, fire, earth, and water. In one way or another, he says, all things are analyzable down to these. Still, when these bodies combine with one another, they form novel substances. Unlike the sculpture, however, the origin of these new forms is a product of nature itself, since these bodies have within themselves a "principle of motion and rest." For this reason fire tends to rise and become air, water to fall and become earth, the solid to become liquid, and the wet to become dry. In any case, to say that things *change* is to say that these basic simple bodies are constantly being transformed into things through their internal principle of motion and by the motion of other things.

Biology

What gives life to certain kinds of bodies? Aristotle accounts for the transition from inorganic to organic bodies by considering the nature of the *soul*. All bodies, he says, are a combination of the primary elements, but some have life and

others do not. By life Aristotle means "self-nutrition and growth (with its correl-
ative decay)." Matter as such is not the principle of life, since material substance
is only potentially alive. Matter is always potentiality, whereas form is actuality.
A body, then, that is actually alive has its life from the source of actuality,
namely, *form*. The soul, then, is the form of an organized body. Neither can exist
without the other, nor are they identical. And, Aristotle says, "That is why we
can wholly dismiss as unnecessary the question whether the soul and body are
one: it is as meaningless as to ask whether the wax and the shape given to it
by the stamp are one." The soul, as Aristotle defines it, is "the first grade of
actuality of a natural organized body." When a body is "organized," its parts
have set motions to perform. Thus, in a living plant "the leaf serves to shelter
the pericarp, the pericarp to shelter the fruit, while the roots of plants are analogous to the mouth of animals . . . serving for the absorption of food." The soul
is "the definitive formula of a thing's essence." The soul exists when there is a
particular kind of body, namely, "one having *in itself* the power of setting itself
in movement and arresting itself." Soul and body are not two separate things but
are rather the matter (body) and form (soul) of a single unity. And, "from this it
indubitably follows that the soul is inseparable from its body." Without the body
the soul could not exist, any more than there could be vision without an eye.

Aristotle distinguished between three types of soul in order to show the
three different ways a body can be organized. He called these the *vegetative, sensitive,* and *rational* souls. They represent various capacities of a body for activity,
the first being simply the act of living, the second both living and sensing, and
the third including living, sensing, and thinking.

Psychology

We find the sensitive soul at the animal level. Its chief characteristic lies in its
power to absorb qualities and *forms* of things without taking in their *matter*. This
is in contrast to the lower nutritive soul, which takes in the *matter* (such as, food)
but has no capacity to absorb its *form*. The basic sense is tactile, or touch, and
is capable of absorbing what all bodies have in common. For the other senses
Aristotle says that "each sense has one kind of object which it discerns, and
never errs in reporting that what is before it is color or sound." Again, the sensitive soul absorbs only the form and not the matter: "In the way in which a piece
of wax takes on the impress of a signet ring without the iron or gold . . . in a
similar way the sense is affected by what is colored or flavored or sounding, but
it is indifferent to what in each case the *substance* is."

Aristotle used the notion of *potentiality* to explain how the sensitive soul
senses things. The sense organs must be capable of sensing many different forms.
They must, therefore, be potentially capable of adjusting to any quality. The eye,
for example, must be composed of material that potentially can become blue
and that in fact does become blue when a certain kind of object is sensed. This
neutral material of the eye must potentially possess all colors and shapes. Our
various other senses have similar potentialities with respect to other qualities.
Moreover, the five senses have a way of combining their information into a

unified whole, reflecting the single object or world from which these "sensibles" come. The qualities we sense can continue even after we are no longer directly perceiving an object, and this Aristotle explains in terms of *memory* and also *imagination*. Much of what we remember retains its associations with other things, suggesting that neither sensation nor memory is a random act but rather tends to reproduce what in fact exists in the real world. From the power of memory and imagination comes finally the higher form of soul, the human or the rational soul.

Human Rationality   The human soul combines in itself all the lower forms of soul—the vegetative, nutritive, and sensitive—and has in addition to these a *rational soul*. The rational soul has the capacity of scientific thought. Our *reason* is capable of distinguishing between different kinds of things, which is the capacity of analysis, and it also understands the relationships of things to each other. Besides scientific thought the rational soul has the capacity of *deliberation*. Here we not only discover what truth is in the nature of things but also discover the guidelines for human behavior.

Again, for Aristotle, the soul is the definitive form of the body. Without the body the soul could neither be nor exercise its functions. Aristotle says that the body and soul together form one substance. This is in sharp contrast to Plato's explanation of the body as the prison house of the soul. Because he separated soul and body, Plato could speak of the preexistence of the soul. He could also describe knowledge or learning as the process of recollection of what the soul knew in its previous state. Moreover, Plato could speak of the immortality of the individual soul. Aristotle, on the other hand, tied soul and body so closely together that with the death of the body, the soul, its organizing principle, also dies.

The rational soul of people, like the sensitive soul, is characterized by potentiality. Just as the eye is capable of seeing a red object but will only see it when it actually confronts a red object, so, also, our rational soul is capable of understanding the true nature of things. But reason has its knowledge only potentially; it must reason out its conclusions. Human thought, in short, is a possibility and not a continuous actuality, for if it is *possible* for the human mind to attain knowledge, it is also possible for it *not* to attain knowledge. Human thought is, therefore, intermittent between *actually* and *potentially* knowing. Truth is never continuously present in the human intellect.

The continuity of truth is implied by the continuity of the world. What the human mind has as potential knowledge must therefore be perfect and continuous knowledge in some mind. Aristotle spoke of the Unmoved Mover as the mind (*nous*) of the world and its intelligible principle. In his *De Anima* he speaks of the Active Intellect, saying "*Mind* does not at one time function and at another not." Here he appears to compare the individual human intellect, which knows only intermittently, with the Active Intellect, which is in some sense independent of particular people and is eternal. If this intellect is indeed purely active, it possesses no potentiality. And this is what Aristotle described as the Unmoved Mover. The distinctive activity of the Unmoved Mover is pure act, which is an exercise of the mind in complete harmony with the truth about the whole of reality. The whole system of Forms taken as the intelligible structure of all things must therefore constitute the continuous knowledge of the Unmoved Mover, the Active Intellect. This Intellect is immortal, and to the extent that our passive and potential intellects know any truth, they have in them what the Active Intellect always knows. What is immortal when we die is what belongs to the Active Intellect, but as this is not a part of *us*, our own individual soul perishes with the matter for which it was the form. Only what is pure act is eternal, and our substance, being an admixture of potentiality, does not survive.

ETHICS

Aristotle's theory of morality centers around his belief that people, like everything else in nature, have a distinctive end to achieve and function to fulfill. He begins his *Nicomachean Ethics* by saying that "every art and every inquiry, and similarly every action and pursuit, is thought to aim at some good." If this is so, the question for ethics is, "What is the *good* at which human behavior aims?" Plato answered this question by saying that people aim at a knowledge of the Form of the Good. For him this supreme principle of Good is separate from the world of experience and from individuals; we arrive at it by ascending from the visible world to the intelligible world. For Aristotle, on the other hand, the principle of good and right was imbedded within each person. Moreover, this principle could be discovered by studying the human nature and could be attained through actual behavior in daily life. Aristotle warns his readers, however, not to expect more precision in a discussion of ethics than "the subject-matter will admit." Still, just because this subject is susceptible to "variation and error" does not mean that ideas of right and wrong "exist conventionally only, and not in the nature of things." With this in mind, Aristotle set out to discover the basis of morality in the structure of human nature.

Types of "Ends"

Aristotle sets the framework for his ethical theory with a preliminary illustration. Having said that all action aims toward an end, he now wants to distinguish between two major kinds of ends: (1) *instrumental* ends (acts that are done as *means* for other ends) and (2) *intrinsic* ends (acts that are done for their own sake). These two types of ends are illustrated, for example, in activities connected with war. When we consider step by step what is involved in the total activity of a war, we find, Aristotle says, that there is a series of special kinds of acts. There is, for one thing, the art of the bridle maker. When the bridle is finished, its maker has achieved his end as a bridle maker. But the bridle is a means for the horseman to guide his horse in battle. Also, a carpenter builds a barrack, and when it is completed, he has fulfilled his function as a carpenter. The barracks also fulfill their function when they provide shelter for the soldiers. But the ends here achieved by the carpenter and the building are not intrinsic ends in themselves but are only instrumental in housing soldiers until they move on to their next stage of action. Similarly, the function of the builder of ships is fulfilled when the ship is successfully launched, but again, this end is in turn a means for transporting the soldiers to the field of battle. The doctor fulfills his function to the extent that he keeps the soldiers in good health. But the "end" of health in this case becomes a "means" for effective fighting. The officer aims at victory in battle, but victory is the means to peace. Peace itself, though sometimes taken mistakenly as the final end of war, is the means for creating the conditions under which people can fulfill their function as human beings. When we discover what people aim at, not as bridle makers, carpenters, doctors, or generals but as *humans*, we will then arrive at action *for its own sake*, and for which all other activity is only a means. This, Aristotle says, "must be the Good of Humanity."

How should we understand the word *good*? Like Plato before him, Aristotle tied the word *good* to the special function of a thing. A hammer is good if it does what hammers are expected to do. A carpenter is good if he or she fulfills his or her function as a builder. This would be true of all the crafts and professions. But here Aristotle distinguishes between a person's craft or profession and a person's activity as a human. For example, Aristotle felt that being a good doctor did not mean the same thing as being a good person. Someone could be a good doctor without being a good person, and vice versa. There are two different functions here, the function of doctoring and the function of acting as a person. To discover the good at which a person should aim, Aristotle said we must discover the distinctive function of human nature. The good person, according to Aristotle, is the person who is fulfilling his or her function as a human being.

The Function of Human Beings

Aristotle asks, "Are we then to suppose that while carpenter and cobbler have certain works and courses of action, people as Human Beings have none, but are left by Nature without a work?" Or, if "the eye, hand, foot and in general each of the parts evidently has a function, may we lay it down that humans similarly have a function apart from all these?" Surely, people too have a distinctive type of activity, but what is it? Here Aristotle analyzes human nature in order to discover its unique activity, saying, first of all, that our human end "is not mere life," because that plainly is shared even by vegetables, and, Aristotle says, "we want what is peculiar to [human beings]." Next there is the life of sensation, "but this again manifestly is common to horses, oxen and every animal." There remains then "an active life of the element that has a rational principle." He contends further that "if the function of people is an activity of soul which follows or implies a rational principle . . . then the human good turns out to be activity of soul in accordance with virtue."

Since a person's function as a human being means the proper functioning of the soul, Aristotle sought to describe the nature of the soul. The human soul is the form of the human body. As such, the soul refers to the total person. Accordingly, Aristotle said that the soul has two parts: the irrational and the rational. The irrational part is composed of two subparts. First, as with plants, a vegetative component gives us the capacity to take in nutrition and sustain our biological lives. Second, as with animals, an appetitive component gives us the capacity to experience desires, which in turn prompts us to move around to fulfill those desires. Both of these irrational parts of soul tend to oppose and resist the rational part. The conflict between the rational and irrational elements in human beings is what raises the issue of morality.

Morality involves action. Thus, Aristotle says, "As at the Olympic games it is not the finest and strongest people who are crowned, but they who enter the lists, for out of these the prize-men are selected; so too in life, of the honorable and good, it is they who act who rightly win the prizes." The particular kind of action implied here is the rational control and guidance of the irrational parts of the soul. Moreover, the good person is not the one who does a good deed here or there, now and then. Instead, it is the person whose whole life is good, "for as it is not one swallow or one fine day that makes a spring, so it is not one day or a short time that makes a person happy."

Happiness as the End

Human action should aim at its proper end. Everywhere people seek pleasure, wealth, and honor. Although these ends have some type of value, they are not the chief good for which people should aim. To be an ultimate end, an act must be *self-sufficient* and *final*, "that which is always desirable in itself and never for the sake of something else," and it must be *attainable by people*. Aristotle is certain that all people will agree that *happiness* is the end that alone meets all the requirements for the ultimate end of human action. Indeed, we choose pleasure, wealth, and honor only because we think that "through their instrumentality we shall be happy." Happiness, it turns out, is another word or name for *good*, for like good, happiness is the fulfillment of our distinctive function. As Aristotle says, "Happiness . . . is a working of the soul in the way of excellence or virtue."

How does the soul attain happiness? The general rule of morality is "to act in accordance with Right Reason." What this means is that the rational part of the soul should control the irrational part. It is obvious that the irrational part requires guidance when we consider what it consists of and what its mechanism is. When looking at our appetites, we discover first that they are affected or influenced by things outside of the self, such as objects and people. Also, there are two basic ways in which the appetitive part of the soul reacts to these external factors—these ways being *love* (or the *concupiscent* passions) and *hate* (or the *irascible* passions). Love leads us to desire things and persons, whereas hate leads us to avoid or destroy them. It becomes quickly apparent that these passions for love and hate could easily "go wild" when pursued by themselves. In themselves they do not contain any principle of measure or selection. What should a person desire? How much? Under what circumstances? How should we relate ourselves to things, wealth, honor, and other persons?

We do not automatically act the right way in these matters. As Aristotle says, "None of the moral virtues arises in us by nature; for nothing that exists by nature can form a habit contrary to its nature." Morality has to do with developing habits—the habits of right thinking, right choice, and right behavior.

Virtue as the Golden Mean

Human passions are capable of inciting a wide range of action, from too little to too much. Consider our appetites for food. On the one hand, we can become dominated by an excessive desire to eat; on the other, we can have a deficiency in our appetite for food to the point of starvation. The proper course of action—that is, the *virtuous* course—is a middle ground or *mean* between excess and deficiency. We should seek out this middle ground with all of our passions, such as those of fear, confidence, lust, anger, compassion, pleasure, and pain. When we fail to achieve this middle ground, we expose ourselves to vices of excess or of deficiency. We control our passions through the rational power of the soul, and thereby form virtuous habits that lead us spontaneously to follow the middle course. The virtue of *courage*, for example, is the mean between two vices: cowardice (a deficiency) and rashness (an excess). Virtue, then, is a state of being, "a state apt to exercise deliberate choice, being in the relative mean, determined by reason, and as the person of practical wisdom would determine." Therefore, virtue is a habit of choosing in accordance with a mean.

The mean is not the same for every person, nor is there a mean for every act. Each mean is relative to each person to the degree that our personal circumstances vary. In the case of eating, the mean will obviously be different for an adult athlete and a toddler. But for each person there is nevertheless a proportionate or relative mean, which is the virtue of *temperance*. This stands between two extreme vices, namely, gluttony (excess) and starvation (deficiency). Similarly, when we give money, *liberality* is the virtuous mean between the vices of prodigality and stinginess. There is no fixed amount of money that constitutes the virtue of liberality; instead, the dollar figure is relative to our assets. Although a large number of virtues stand between two extreme vices, there are other actions that have no mean at all. Their very nature already implies badness, such as spite, envy, adultery, theft, and murder. These are bad in themselves and not in their excesses or deficiencies. We are thus always wrong in doing them.

Moral virtue, then, consists of cultivating habits that will spontaneously incline us to take the middle course of action—or simply avoid bad conduct in the case of acts like theft and murder. Plato listed four main virtues (later called "cardinal" virtues), which Aristotle also endorses, namely, courage, temperance, justice, and wisdom. In addition to these, Aristotle discusses the virtues of generosity, good temper, friendship, and self-respect.

Deliberation and Choice

There are two kinds of reasoning within the rational soul. The first is theoretical, giving us knowledge of fixed principles or philosophical wisdom. The other is practical, giving us a rational guide to our moral action under the particular circumstances in which we find ourselves; this is practical wisdom. What is important about the role of reason is that without this rational element we would not have any moral capacity. Again, Aristotle stressed that although we have a natural capacity for *right* behavior, we do not act rightly *by nature*. Our life consists of an unfixed number of possibilities. Goodness is in us all *potentially*. An oak tree will grow out of an acorn with almost mechanical certainty. With people, though, we must move from what is potential in us to its actuality by knowing what we must do, deliberating about it, and then choosing in fact to do it. Unlike Plato and Socrates, who thought that to know the good was sufficient to do the good, Aristotle saw that there must be deliberate choice in addition to knowledge. Thus, Aristotle said that "the origin of moral action—its efficient, not its final cause—is choice, and (the origin) of choice is desire and reasoning with a view to an end."

There is an important connection between free choice and human responsibility. Suppose, for example, that you have a brain tumor that triggers within you an irresistible impulse to violence. If your violent conduct is truly beyond your control, then you cannot be held morally responsible for your conduct. Aristotle—and many other moral philosophers—accordingly held that people are responsible for their conduct and, consequently, that moral behavior is voluntary. But not all our actions are voluntary. There are some exceptions, for Aristotle said that "praise and blame arise upon such as are voluntary, while for the involuntary allowance is made, and sometimes compassion is excited." The principal distinction for Aristotle between voluntary and involuntary acts is this: *Involuntary* acts are those for which a person is not responsible because they are (1) done out of ignorance of particular circumstances, (2) done as a result of external compulsion, or (3) done to avoid a greater evil. *Voluntary* acts are those for which a person is responsible because none of these three extenuating circumstances is in force.

Contemplation

Human nature consists for Aristotle not simply in rationality but in the full range covered by the vegetative, appetitive, and the rational souls. Virtue does not imply the negation or rejection of any of these natural capacities. The moral person employs all of his or her capacities, *physical* and *mental*. Corresponding to these two broad divisions in human nature are two functions of reason, the moral and intellectual, and each has its own virtues. We have already seen Aristotle's account of *moral virtues*, namely, the habits that help us follow the middle ground in response to the desires of our appetitive nature. The intellectual virtues, by contrast, focus on our intellectual rather than bodily nature; chief among these is philosophical wisdom (*sophia*), which includes scientific knowledge and the ability to grasp first principles.

Aristotle concludes his principal work on ethics with a discussion of philosophical wisdom and the act of contemplating intellectual truths. If happiness is the product of our acting according to our distinctive nature, it is reasonable to assume that we are most happy when acting according to our *highest* nature, which is contemplation. This activity is the best, Aristotle says, "since not only is reason the best thing in us, but the objects of reason are the best of knowable objects." Moreover, contemplation "is most continuous, since we can contemplate truth more continuously than we can *do* anything." Finally, "we think happiness has pleasure mingled with it, but the activity of philosophical wisdom is admittedly the pleasantest of virtuous activities."

POLITICS

In his *Politics*, as in his *Ethics*, Aristotle stresses the element of purpose. Just like human beings, the state is naturally endowed with a distinctive function. Combining these two ideas, Aristotle says, "It is evident that the State is a creature of nature, and that human beings are by nature political animals." Human nature and the state are so closely related that "he who is unable to live in society, or who has no need because he is sufficient for himself, must be either a beast or a god." Not only does human nature incline us to live in a state, but the state, like every other community, "is established with a view to some good" and exists for some end. The family exists primarily to preserve life. The state comes into existence in the first instance to preserve life for families and villages, which in the long run cannot survive on their own. But beyond this economic end, the function of the state is to ensure the supreme good of people, namely, our moral and intellectual life.

Unlike Plato, Aristotle did not create a blueprint for an ideal state. Even though Aristotle viewed the state as the agency for enabling people to achieve their ultimate goals as human beings, he nevertheless realized that any theory of the state must take note of several practical issues. For example, we must determine "what kind of government is adapted to particular states" even though the best of these is often unattainable. Also, we must determine "how a state may be constituted under any given condition" and how it may be preserved. For Aristotle "political writers, although they have excellent ideas, are often impractical." For these reasons he had little patience with Plato's most radical ideas. He ridicules Plato's arrangement for abolishing the family for the guardian class and providing a public nursery for their children. With this kind of arrangement, according to Aristotle, "there is no reason why the so-called father should care about the son, or the son about the father, or brothers about one another." The communal ownership of property would likewise destroy certain basic human pleasures as well as create inefficiency and endless disputes.

Types of States

Aristotle was willing to recognize that, under appropriate circumstances, a community can organize itself into at least three different kinds of government. The basic difference among them is primarily the number of rulers each has. A government can have as its rulers *one*, a *few*, or *many*. But each of these forms of government can have a true or a perverted form. When a government is functioning rightly, it governs for the common good of all the people. A government is perverted when its rulers govern for their own private gain or interests. The true forms of each type of government, according to Aristotle, are *monarchy* (one), *aristocracy* (few), and *polity* (many). The perverted forms are *tyranny* (one), *oligarchy* (few), and *democracy* (many). His own preference was aristocracy, chiefly because there are not enough people of exceptional excellence, in spite of our best efforts. In an aristocracy there is the rule of a group of people whose degree of excellence, achievement, and ownership of property makes them responsible, able, and capable of command.

Differences and Inequalities

Because he relied so heavily upon anecdotal observation of things, it was inevitable that Aristotle would make some mistakes. Nowhere is this truer than with his view of slavery. Observing that slaves invariably were strong and large, he concluded that slavery was a product of nature. "It is clear," Aristotle said, "that some men are by nature free, and others slaves, and that for these slavery is both expedient and right." To be sure, Aristotle took great care to distinguish between those who became slaves by nature, a type of slavery that he accepted, and those who became slaves by military conquest, a type he rejected. Aristotle rejected slavery by conquest on the highly defensible grounds that to overpower people does not mean that we are superior to them in nature. Moreover, the use of force may or may not be justified, in which case enslavement could very well be the product and extension of an unjust act. At the same time, speaking of the "proper treatment of slaves," he proposed that "it is advantageous that liberty should be always held out to them as the reward of their services." The fact is that in his own last will and testament Aristotle provided for the emancipation of some of his slaves.

Aristotle also believed in the inequality of citizenship. He held that the basic qualification for citizenship was a person's ability to share in ruling and being ruled in turn. A citizen had the right and the obligation to participate in the administration of justice. Since citizens would therefore have to sit in the assembly and in the law courts, they would have to have both ample time and an appropriate temperament and character. For this reason Aristotle did not believe that laborers should be citizens, as they had neither the time nor the appropriate mental development, nor could they benefit from the experience of sharing in the political process.

Good Government and Revolution

Over and over again Aristotle made the point that the state exists for the sake of everyone's moral and intellectual fulfillment. "A state," he noted, "exists for the sake of a good life, and not for the sake of life only"; similarly, "the state is the union of families and villages in a perfect and self-sufficing life, by which we mean a happy and honorable life." Finally, he said, "Our conclusion . . . is that political society exists for the sake of noble actions, and not mere companionship." Still, whether a state produces the good life depends upon how its rulers behave. We have already seen that Aristotle distinguished between perverted forms of government and true forms, and that the good rulers seek to achieve the good of all, whereas the perverted rulers seek their own private gain.

Whatever form government has, it will rest on some conception of justice and proportionate equality. But these conceptions of justice can bring disagreement and ultimately revolution. Democracy, as Aristotle knew it, arises out of the assumption that those who are equal in any respect are equal in all respects: "Because people are equally free, they claim to be absolutely equal." On the other hand, Aristotle said *oligarchy* is based upon the notion that "those who are unequal in one respect are in all respects unequal." Hence, "being unequal . . . in property, they suppose themselves to be unequal absolutely." For these reasons, whenever the democrats or oligarchs are in the minority and the philosophy of the incumbent government "does not accord with their preconceived ideas, [they] stir up revolution. . . . Here then . . . are opened up the very springs and fountains of revolution."

Aristotle concluded that "the universal and chief cause of this revolutionary feeling [is] the desire of equality, when men think they are equal to others who have more than themselves." He did not overlook other causes such as "insolence and avarice," as well as fear and contempt. Knowing these causes of revolution, Aristotle said that each form of government could take appropriate precautions against it. For example, a king must avoid despotic acts, an aristocracy should avoid the rule by a few rich men for the benefit of the wealthy class, and a polity should provide more time for its abler members to share in the government. Most importantly, Aristotle urged that "there is nothing which should be more jealously maintained than the spirit of obedience to law." In the end people will always criticize the state unless their conditions of living within it are such that they can achieve happiness in the form of what they consider the good life.

PHILOSOPHY OF ART

Aristotle had a far more sympathetic interest in art than did Plato. For Plato, as for Aristotle, art was essentially a matter of imitating nature. What made Plato so contemptuous of some forms of art was his notion that a work of art is at least three steps removed from truth. The true reality of human beings, let us say, is the eternal Form of Humanity. A poor copy of this Form would be any particular person—Socrates, for example. A statue or portrait of Socrates would then be a copy of a copy. Plato was particularly concerned with the cognitive aspect of art, feeling that it had the effect of distorting knowledge because it was several steps removed from reality. Aristotle, on the other hand, believing that the universal Forms exist only in particular things, felt that artists are dealing directly with the universal when they study things and translate them into art forms. For this reason Aristotle affirmed the cognitive value of art, saying that since art does imitate nature, it therefore communicates information about nature.

In his *Poetics* he stresses the cognitive aspect of poetry by contrasting poetry with history. Unlike the historian, who is concerned only with particular persons and events, the poet deals with basic human nature and, therefore, universal experience. The true difference between them is that history relates what has happened, whereas poetry considers what may happen. "Poetry, therefore, is a more philosophical and a higher thing than history: for poetry tends to express the universal, history the particular." By universality Aristotle means "how a person of a certain type will on occasion speak or act, according to the law of probability or necessity," and it is "this universality at which poetry aims."

In addition to its cognitive value, art has in Aristotle's view considerable psychological significance. For one thing, art reflects a deep facet of human nature by which people are differentiated from animals, this being their implanted instinct for imitation. Indeed, from earliest childhood learning takes place through imitation. In addition to this instinct, there is also the pleasure that people feel upon confronting art. Thus, "the reason people enjoy seeing a likeness is, that in contemplating it they find themselves learning or inferring, and saying perhaps, 'Ah, that is he.'"

Aristotle gave detailed analyses of *epic, tragic,* and *comic* poetry, showing what each consists of and what its function is. However, it was his remarks about tragedy that resonate most strongly in subsequent thought. He particularly emphasized the emotional aspect of tragedy, centering upon the notion of *catharsis*—a purging of unpleasant emotions. "A tragedy," Aristotle says,

> is the imitation of an action that is serious and also, as having magnitude, complete in itself; in language with pleasurable accessories, each kind brought in separately in the parts of the work; in a dramatic, not a narrative form; with incidents arousing pity and fear, wherewith to accomplish its catharsis of such emotions.

Does the term *catharsis* imply that through tragedy we "get rid of" our feelings? Or does it mean that we are given an occasion to express or give vent to our deepest emotions in a vicarious way? In either case, what Aristotle seems to be saying is that the artistic representation of deep suffering arouses in the audience genuine terror and pity, thereby purging and in a sense purifying each audience member's spirit. Thus, Aristotle says that "tragedy is an imitation of an action . . . through pity and fear effecting the proper purgation of these emotions."

PART TWO

Hellenistic and Medieval Philosophy

CHAPTER 5

Classical Philosophy after Aristotle

After Aristotle completed his great speculative system, philosophy moved in a new direction. Four groups of philosophers helped to shape this new direction, namely, the Epicureans, the Stoics, the Skeptics, and the Neoplatonists. They were, of course, greatly influenced by their predecessors. Thus, we find that Epicurus relied upon Democritus for his atomic theory of nature; the Stoics made use of Heraclitus's notion of a fiery substance permeating all things; the Skeptics built a method of inquiry upon the Socratic form of doubt; and Plotinus drew heavily on Plato. What made their philosophy different, however, was not so much its subject matter as its direction and its emphasis. Its emphasis was practical, and its direction was individually centered. Philosophy became more practical by emphasizing the art of living. To be sure, each of these new movements of thought did involve speculative descriptions of the structure of the universe. But instead of working out blueprints for the ideal society and fitting individuals into large social and political organizations, as Plato and Aristotle did, these philosophers led people to think primarily about themselves and how they as individuals in the larger scheme of nature could achieve the most satisfactory life.

These new directions in philosophy were brought about to a great extent by historical conditions. After the Peloponnesian War and with the fall of Athens, Greek civilization declined. With the breakdown of the small Greek city-state, individual citizens lost the sense of their own importance and their ability to control their social and political destiny. As they were absorbed into the growing Roman Empire, people increasingly felt this loss of personal control over their lives within the community. When Greece became a mere province of Rome, people lost interest in pursuing the speculative questions concerning the ideal society. What was needed was a practical philosophy to give life direction under changing conditions. And at a time when events overwhelmed people, it seemed futile to try to change history. But if history was beyond humanity's control, at least a person's own life could be managed with some success. Philosophy, therefore, shifted in the direction of increasing concern for the more immediate world of the individual.

The Epicureans focused on an ideal for living through what they called *ataraxia*, or tranquility of soul. The Stoics sought to control their reactions to inevitable events. The Skeptics sought to preserve personal freedom by refraining from any basic commitment to ideals whose truth was doubtful. Finally, Plotinus promised salvation in a mystical union with God. They all looked to philosophy for a source of meaning for human existence, and it is no wonder that their philosophy, particularly Stoicism, was later to compete with religion for allegiance. They sought to discover ways in which individuals could achieve happiness or contentment in a world that was not altogether friendly and filled with many pitfalls. In their efforts to find meaning, some philosophers of the time, called "eclectics," embraced elements from several of the distinct philosophical schools. Whether understood individually or collectively, each approach offers a remarkable insight into human nature.

EPICUREANISM

Epicurus was born about five or six years after Plato's death, when Aristotle was 42 years old. Born in 342 or 341 BCE on the island of Samos in the Aegean Sea, he was exposed in his teens to the writings of Democritus, whose ideas about nature had a permanent influence on his own philosophy. When the Athenians were driven out of Samos, Epicurus went to Asia Minor, where he became a teacher in several schools. About 306 BCE he moved to Athens and founded his own school, which met in his garden. In time this ranked with Plato's Academy, Aristotle's Lyceum, and Zeno's Stoa as one of the influential schools of ancient times. Here Epicurus attracted a close group of friends, who were attached to him by deep affection and reverence, and to each other by the love of cultivated conversation. In spite of the loss of the bulk of his prolific writings, there emerged from this school a definite approach to philosophy, which survived Epicurus's death in 270 BCE. The lasting impact of his teaching is shown by its continuous appearance in Athens and its spread to Rome, where the poet Lucretius (98–55 BCE) embodied the major thoughts of Epicurus in his memorable poem *On the Nature of Things (De Rerum Natura)*, which survives to this day.

Epicurus was a practical philosopher. He thought that ideas should have as much effect on the control of life as medicine has on the health of the body. Indeed, he considered philosophy as the medicine of the soul. He did deal with questions such as "What is the world made of?" and, influenced by Democritus, he maintained that everything is composed of tiny particles, called "atoms," in empty space. If that is what the world consists of, thought Epicurus, what consequences follow from that for human behavior?

To Epicurus the chief aim of human life is pleasure. But it is ironic that his name should be linked even today with the indulgent glutton, for nothing could be further from the teachings of Epicurus than the notion that pleasure consists in the triple formula of eat, drink, and be merry. Instead, he took great pains to distinguish between various types of pleasures. For example, some are intense but last only a short while, and others are not so intense but last longer. Also, some pleasures have a painful aftermath, and others give a sense of calm and repose. He tried to refine the principle of pleasure as the basis of conduct.

Physics and Ethics

What made Epicurus turn to the pleasure principle was the "science" or physics inherited from Democritus. This science had the effect of eliminating the notion that God created everything and that human behavior should be based on obedience to principles whose source is divine. Building on this "atomic theory," Epicurus concluded that everything that exists must be made up of eternal atoms—small, indestructible bits of hard matter. Apart from these clusters of atoms, nothing else exists. This would mean that if God or gods exist, they too must be material beings. Most importantly, God is not the source or the creator of anything but is himself the result of a purposeless and random event.

The origin of everything is explained by the notion that there is no beginning to the atoms. Atoms have always existed in space. Like raindrops they were at one time separately falling in space, and since they encountered no resistance, they always remained the same distance apart from each other. During this vertical drop, thought Epicurus, one atom instead of falling perfectly straight developed a slight easing to one side—that is, a lateral "swerve." In time this atom moved into the path of an oncoming atom, and the resulting impact forced both of these atoms into the paths of other atoms, thereby setting in motion a whole series of collisions until all the atoms had formed into clusters. These clusters or arrangements of atoms are the things we see even now, including rocks, flowers, animals, and human beings—in short, the world. Since there were an infinite number of atoms, there must now be an infinite number of worlds. In any case, human beings are not part of a created or purposeful order caused or ruled by God but rather the accidental product of the collision of atoms.

God and Death

With this explanation of the origin of human beings—and for that matter of all beings including "divine beings"—Epicurus thought that he had liberated people from the fear of God and of death. They no longer had to fear God because God did not control nature or human destiny and was, therefore, unable to intrude into people's lives. As for death, Epicurus said that this need not bother anyone, because only a living person has sensation either of pain or of pleasure. After death there is no sensation, since the atoms that make up bodies and minds come apart. Thus, there is no longer this particular body or mind but only a number of distinct atoms that return, as it were, to the primeval inventory of matter to continue the cycle of new formations. Only matter exists, and in human life all each individual knows is this body and this present moment of experience. The composition of human nature includes atoms of different sizes and shapes. The larger atoms make up bodies, and the smaller, smoother, and swifter atoms account for sensation and thinking. No other principle is needed to explain a person's nature—no God and, therefore, no afterlife. Liberation from the fear of God and of death sets the stage for a way of life completely under a person's own control.

This was a new direction in moral philosophy, for it focused on the individual and his or her immediate desires for bodily and mental pleasures instead of on abstract principles of right conduct or considerations of God's commands. Just as his physical theory made the individual atom the final basis of all existence, so also Epicurus singled out the individual person as the arena of the moral enterprise.

The Pleasure Principle

Epicurus portrayed the origin of all things in a mechanical way and placed humans into the scheme of things as just another small mechanism whose nature leads us to seek pleasure. Nevertheless, Epicurus reserved for humans both the power and the duty to regulate the traffic of our desires. Even though Epicurus had liberated people from the fear of God's providence, he had no intention, thereby, of opening the floodgates of passion and indulgence. He was certain that pleasure was the standard of goodness, but he was equally certain that not every kind of pleasure had the same value.

If asked how he knew that pleasure was the standard of *goodness*, Epicurus would answer simply that all people have an immediate feeling of the difference between pleasure and pain and of the desirability of pleasure. He writes, "We recognize pleasure as the first good innate in us, and from pleasure we begin every act of choice and avoidance, and to pleasure we return again." Feeling, Epicurus said, is as immediate a test of goodness or badness as sensation is a test of truth. To our senses pain is always bad and pleasure always good, just as seeing tells us whether something is in front of us or not.

Still, in order to guide people to the happiest life, Epicurus emphasized the distinction between various kinds of pleasures. Clearly, some desires are both natural and necessary, as in the case of food. Others are natural but not necessary, as in the case of some types of sexual pleasure. Still others are neither natural nor necessary, as, for example, any type of luxury or popularity. It was because he could make these clear distinctions that he concluded that

> when . . . we maintain that pleasure is the end, we do not mean the pleasures of profligates and those that consist of sensuality, as is supposed by some who are either ignorant or disagree with us or do not understand, but freedom from pain in the body and from trouble in the mind. For it is not continuous drinkings and revelings, nor the satisfaction of lusts, nor the enjoyment of fish and other luxuries of the wealthy table, which produce a pleasant life, but sober reasoning, searching out the motives for all choice and avoidance, and banishing mere opinions, to which are due the greatest disturbance of the spirit.

Epicurus did not mean to denounce the pleasures of the body. Instead, he meant only to emphasize that too great a concern with these pleasures was both unnatural and the surest way to unhappiness and pain. Certain kinds of bodily pleasures could never be fully satisfied. Further, if such pleasures required continuous indulgence it followed that people pursuing such pleasures would by definition always be unsatisfied and would, therefore, constantly suffer some pain. If, for example, they wanted more money, or more public acclaim, or more exotic foods, or a higher position, they would always be dissatisfied with their present situation and would suffer some internal pain. The wise person, on the other hand, is able to determine what is the minimum his or her nature requires, and is able easily and quickly to satisfy these needs. When these needs are satisfied, a person's constitution is in balance. The wise person's diet of bread and water is far more likely to bring happiness than the gourmet's surplus of fancy foods, for the wise person has learned not only to consume little but also—and this is the key—to *need* little.

The ultimate pleasure human nature seeks is *repose*, by which Epicurus means the absence of bodily pain and the gentle relaxation of the mind. This sense of repose can best be achieved by scaling down desires, overcoming useless fears, and, above all, turning to the pleasures of the mind, which have the highest degree of permanence. In a sense these pleasures of the mind are physical pleasures inasmuch as they have the effect of preventing overindulgence in matters of the flesh and, therefore, preventing their ensuing pain.

Pleasure and Social Justice

Epicurus builds on his account of individual pleasure and extends it to an explanation of social interaction and justice. Epicurus personally sought to detach himself from entanglements with other people, particularly poor people, whose needs and problems were many, just as he sought to detach himself from the tyranny of exotic foods. Nevertheless, our inevitable connection with other people has a real impact on our happiness, which cannot be ignored. First, the development of friendship is a key ingredient to our happiness, particularly when our friends are congenial and intellectually fascinating. Second, a major task of civil society is to deter those who might inflict pain on individuals. Epicurus's theory of physics ruled out a higher rational order of things, such as we find in Plato's theory of the Forms. Nevertheless, his notion of pursuing pleasure and avoiding pain contains a very firm basis for natural justice insofar as people agree to not injure one another. He writes, "There never was such a thing as absolute justice, but only an agreement made in mutual dealings among people in various places and times, which provides against the infliction or suffering of harm." While the specifics of the social agreement will vary from place to place, Epicurus argues, the usefulness of some such social agreement is so apparent that societies will invariably adopt it.

STOICISM

Stoicism as a school of philosophy includes some of the most distinguished intellectuals of antiquity. Founded by Zeno of Citium (334–262 BCE), who assembled his school on the stoa (Greek for "porch," hence the term *Stoic*), this philosophical movement attracted Cleanthes (303–233 BCE) and Aristo in Athens. Later it found such advocates in Rome as Cicero (106–43 BCE), Epictetus (60–117 CE), Seneca (ca. 4 BCE–65 CE), and Emperor Marcus Aurelius (121–180 CE). This influence helped to fix the overwhelming emphasis of Stoic philosophy upon ethics, although the Stoics addressed themselves to all three divisions of philosophy formulated by Aristotle's Lyceum, namely, logic, physics, and ethics.

Wisdom and Control versus Pleasure

In their moral philosophy the Stoics aimed at happiness, but unlike the Epicureans they did not expect to find it in pleasure. Instead, the Stoics sought happiness through wisdom, a wisdom by which to control what lay within human ability and to accept with dignified resignation what had to be. Zeno was inspired as a youth by the ethical teachings and the life of Socrates, who had faced death with serenity and courage. This example of superb control over the emotions in the face of the supreme threat to one's existence—the threat of death—provided the Stoics with an authentic model after which to pattern their lives. Centuries later the Stoic Epictetus said, "I cannot escape death, but cannot I escape the dread of it?" Developing this same theme in a more general way, he wrote, "Do not demand that events should happen as you wish; but wish them to happen as they do happen, and you will go on well." We cannot control all events, but we can control our attitude toward what happens. It is useless to fear future events, for they will happen in any case. But it is possible by an act of will to control our fear. We should not, therefore, fear events—in a real sense we have "nothing to fear but fear itself."

There is an elegant simplicity to this moral philosophy, and yet it was a philosophy for an intellectual elite. The goal was simple enough—to control our attitudes—but how did the Stoics arrive at it in a philosophical way? They did so by creating a mental picture of what the world must be like and how human beings fit into this world. The world, they said, is an orderly arrangement where people and physical things behave according to principles of *purpose*. They saw throughout all of nature the operation of *reason* and *law*. The Stoics relied on a special idea of God to explain this view of the world, for they thought of God as a rational substance existing not in some single location but in all of nature, in all things. It was this kind of God—a pervading substantial form of *reason* that controls and orders the whole structure of nature—that the Stoics said determines the course of events. Herein lay the basis for moral philosophy, but the direction in which Stoic thought moved on these matters was set by their theory of knowledge.

Stoic Theory of Knowledge

The Stoics explained in great detail how we can achieve knowledge. They did not entirely succeed in their account, but their theory of knowledge was nevertheless important for at least two reasons: (1) It laid the foundation for their materialistic theory of nature, and (2) it provided the basis for their conception of truth or certainty.

Both of these consequences of the Stoic theory of knowledge stem from their account of the origin of ideas. Words, they said, express thoughts, and thoughts result from the influence of objects on the mind. The mind is blank at birth and builds up its store of ideas as it is exposed to objects. These objects make impressions on our minds through the channel of the senses. A tree, for example, impresses its image on our mind through the sense of vision in the same way that a seal leaves its imprint in wax. Repeated exposure to the world of things increases the number of impressions, develops our memory, and enables us to form more general conceptions beyond the objects immediately before us.

The real problem the Stoics faced was how to explain this last point, that is, how to account for general ideas such as goodness and beauty. They had to show how our thinking is related to our sensations. It is one thing to prove that our idea of a tree comes from our vision of trees. But how can we account for general ideas—ideas that refer to things beyond our senses? The Stoics replied that all thought is in some way related to the senses, even thoughts that represent judgments and inferences. A judgment or an inference that something is good or true is the product of the mechanical process of impressions. Our thinking in all its forms starts with impressions, and some of our thinking is based on impressions that start from within us, as in the case of feelings. Feelings can, therefore, give us knowledge; they are the source of "irresistible perceptions," which, in turn, are the ground of our sense of certainty. As the Skeptics later pointed out, this explanation cannot stand up to all the critical questions we might raise against it. In any case, through this theory the Stoics not only found in it a basis for truth but also imposed a distinctive slant on their general philosophy. For to argue as they did that all thought derives from the impact of objects on the senses is to affirm that nothing real exists except things that possess some material form. Stoic logic had cast Stoic philosophy into a materialistic mold.

Matter as the Basis of All Reality

This materialism provided Stoicism with an ingenious conception of the physical world and human nature. The broad picture the Stoics drew of physical nature followed from their position that all that is real is material. Everything in the universe is, therefore, some form of matter. But the world is not just a pile of inert or passive matter—it is a dynamic, changing, structured, and ordered arrangement. Besides inert matter there is force or power, which represents the active shaping and ordering element in nature. This active power or force is not different from matter but is rather a different form of matter. It is a constantly moving, subtle thing, like an air current or breath. The Stoics said it was fire, and this fire spread to all things, providing them with vitality. This material fire had the attribute of rationality, and since this was the highest form of being, the Stoics understood this rational force to be God.

God in Everything

The pivotal idea of Stoicism was the notion that God is in everything. When we say that God is in everything—as fire, or force, or rationality—we imply that all of nature is filled with the principle of reason. In a detailed manner the Stoics spoke of the permeability of matter, by which they meant that different types of matter are mixed up together. The material substance of God, they said, was mixed with what would otherwise be motionless matter. Matter behaves the way it does because of the presence in it of the principle of reason. *Natural law* is the continued behavior of matter in accordance with this principle; it is the law or principle of a thing's nature. Thus, for the Stoics, nature has its origin in God—the warm, fiery matrix of all things—and all things immediately receive the impress of God's structuring reason. Because things continue to behave as they were arranged to behave, we can see how the Stoics developed their notions of fate and providence.

Fate and Providence

To the Stoics *providence* meant that events occur the way they do because all things and people are under the control of the Logos, or God. The order of the whole world is based on the unity of all its parts, and what unifies the whole structure of matter is the fiery substance that permeates everything. Nothing "rattles" in the universe, for nothing is loose. Ultimately, the Stoics fashioned their moral philosophy against this background of a totally controlled material universe.

Human Nature

The Stoics knew that to build a moral philosophy it is necessary to have a clear view of what human nature is like. They shaped their view of human nature by simply transferring to the study of human beings the very same ideas they had used in describing nature at large. Just as the world has a material order permeated by the fiery substance called reason or God, so also a person is a material being who is permeated by this very same fiery substance. The Stoics are famous for the saying that people contain a spark of the divine within them. By this they meant that, in a real sense, a person contains part of the substance of God. God is the soul of the world, and each person's soul is part of God. This spark of the divine is a very fine and pure material substance that permeates a person's body, causing it to move and to be capable of all sensations. This pure material soul is transmitted by parents to children in a physical way. The Stoics thought that the soul was centered in the heart and that it circulated specifically through the bloodstream. What the soul added to the body was the delicate mechanism of the five senses, as well as the powers of speech and reproduction. But since God is the rational Logos, the human soul is also rooted in reason, and consequently, human personality finds its unique expression in its rationality. For the Stoics, however, human rationality did not mean simply that people are able to think or to reason about things. Instead, human rationality means that a person's nature participates in the rational structure and order of the whole of nature. Human rationality represents our awareness of the actual order of things and our place in this order. It involves our awareness that all things obey law. To relate human behavior to this order of law was the chief concern of Stoic moral philosophy.

Ethics and the Human Drama

According to Epictetus, moral philosophy rests on a simple insight, wherein each person is an actor in a drama. What Epictetus meant when he used this image was that an actor does not choose a role; on the contrary, it is the author or director of the drama who selects people to play the various roles. In the drama of the world, it is God, or the principle of reason, who determines what each person will be and how he or she will be situated in history. Human wisdom, said the Stoics, consists in recognizing what our role in this drama is and then performing the part well. Some people have "bit parts," while others are cast into leading roles. Epictetus explains: "If it is [God's] pleasure that you should act a poor person, see that you act it well; or a handicapped person, or a ruler, or a private citizen. For it is your business to act well the given part." The actor develops a great indifference to those things over which he or she has no control—for example, the shape and form of the scenery, as well as the other players. The actor especially has no control over the story or its plot. But there is one thing that actors can control, and that is their attitudes and emotions. We can sulk because we have a bit part, or be consumed with jealousy because someone else is chosen to be the hero, or feel terribly insulted because the makeup artist has provided us with a particularly ugly nose. But neither sulking nor being jealous nor feeling insulted can in any way alter the fact that we have bit parts, are not heroes, and must wear an ugly nose. These feelings can only rob the actors of happiness. If we can remain free from these feelings, or develop what the Stoics called *apathy*, we will achieve a serenity and happiness that are the mark of a wise person. The wise person is the one who knows and accepts his or her role.

The Problem of Freedom

There is, however, a persistent problem in Stoic moral philosophy, and this concerns the nature of human freedom. We can easily understand the Stoic notion that nature is fixed and ordered by God's reason, especially when we think of this grand scheme as a cosmic drama. It may be true that actors do not choose their roles. But what is the difference between choosing your *role* in the drama, on the one hand, and choosing your *attitude*, on the other? If you are not free to choose one, how can you be free to choose the other? It could well be that God not only chose you to be a poor person but also cast you as a particularly disgruntled poor person. Do attitudes float around freely, waiting to be chosen by the passing parade of people, or are they as much a part of a person as, say, eye color?

   The Stoics stuck doggedly to their notion that attitudes are under our control and that by an act of will we can decide how we will react to events. But they never provided a satisfactory explanation for the fact that providence rules everything while at the same time providence does not rule our attitudes. The closest they came to an explanation was to imply that whereas everything in the universe behaves according to divine law, it is the special feature of human beings that they behave according to their knowledge of the law. For example, water evaporates from the heat of the sun and later condenses and returns in the form of rain. But one drop never says to the other, "Here we go again," as if to register disgust at being uprooted from the sea. We undergo a similar process of change when we begin to age and face death. However, in addition to the mechanical process of aging, we know what is happening to us. No amount of additional knowledge will change the fact that we are mortal. Nevertheless, the Stoics built their whole moral philosophy on the conviction that if we know the rigorous law and understand our role as inevitable, we will not strain against the inevitable but will move cheerfully with the pace of history. Happiness is not a product of choice; it is rather a quality of existence, which follows from agreeing to what has to be. Freedom, therefore, is not the power to alter our destiny but rather the absence of emotional disturbance.

Cosmopolitanism and Justice

The Stoics also developed a strong notion of *cosmopolitanism*—the idea that all people are citizens of the same human community. To look at the world process as a drama is to admit that everyone has a role in it. The Stoics viewed human relations as having the greatest significance, for human beings are the bearers of a divine spark. What relates people to each other is the fact that each person shares a common element. It is as though the Logos is a main telephone line and all people are on a conference call, thereby connecting God to all people and all people to each other. Or, as Cicero put it,

> since reason exists both in people and God, the first common possession of human beings and God is reason. But those who have reason in common must also have right reason in common. And since right reason is Law, we must believe that people have Law also in common with the Gods. Further, those who share Law must also share Justice, and those who share these are to be regarded as members of the same commonwealth.

Universal brotherhood and the theory of a universal natural law of justice were among the most impressive contributions made to Western thought by the Stoics. They injected basic themes into the stream of thought that was to have a decisive impact in the centuries to come, particularly in medieval philosophy.

Although Stoicism shared many of the characteristics of Epicurean philosophy, it made some radical innovations. Like the Epicureans the Stoics emphasized the practical concerns of ethics, regarded self-control as the center of ethics, viewed all of nature in materialistic terms, and sought happiness as the end. The most significant variation injected by the Stoics was that they viewed the world not as the product of chance but as the product of an ordering mind, or reason. This view involved the Stoics in a highly optimistic attitude regarding the possibilities of human wisdom. Yet it was against this claim to wisdom—a claim that we can know so much about the detailed operation of the world—that the critical philosophy of the Skeptics was developed.

SKEPTICISM

Today we refer to skeptics as those whose basic attitude is that of doubt. But the old Greek word, *skeptikoi*, from which *skeptics* is derived, meant something rather different, namely, "seekers" or "inquirers." The Skeptics certainly were doubters too. They doubted that Plato and Aristotle had succeeded in discovering the truth about the world, and they had these same doubts about the Epicureans and Stoics. But for all their doubt, they were nevertheless seekers after a method for achieving a tranquil life. Pyrrho of Elis (361–270 BCE) was the founder of a specific school of skepticism that had an especially profound impact on philosophy many centuries later. His particular approach is known as *Pyrrhonism*. At the same time that Pyrrho was attracting followers, a rival school of skepticism emerged within Plato's Academy, particularly through the leadership of Arcesilaus (ca. 316–241 BCE), who was head of the Academy a generation or so after Plato. Known as *Academics*, they rejected Plato's metaphysics and revived Socrates's technique of dialectic argument, which they used as a tool for suspending judgment. Pyrrho wrote nothing, and the principal views of the Academics survive mainly through secondhand histories and discussions. The principal surviving text of ancient Greek skepticism is by Sextus Empiricus (ca. 200 CE), a follower of the Pyrrhonian tradition. In the opening sections of his *Outlines of Pyrrhonism*, Sextus offers an illuminating account of the meaning and purposes of the viewpoint of Skepticism.

The Search for Mental Peace

What gave rise to Skepticism? Sextus says that Skepticism originated in the hope of attaining mental peace or calmness. People have been disturbed, he says, by the contradiction in things and plagued by doubt as to which alternative they should believe. One philosopher tells us one thing, and another tells us something quite the opposite. Accordingly, the Skeptics thought that if they could by investigation separate truth from falsehood they could then attain mental tranquility. The Skeptics were struck, however, by the different conceptions of truth that different philosophers had proposed. They also noticed that people who searched for truth could be placed into three groups: (1) those who think they have discovered the truth (and these the Skeptics called *Dogmatists*), (2) those who confess they have not found it and also assert that it cannot be found (and this they also considered a dogmatic position), and (3) those who persevere in the search for it. Unlike the first two groups, Sextus says, "the Skeptics keep on searching." Skepticism is not a denial of the possibility of finding truth, nor is it a denial of the basic facts of human experience. It is rather a continuous process of inquiry in which every explanation of experience is tested by a counterexperience. The fundamental principle of Skepticism, Sextus says, is that to every proposition an equal proposition is opposed. It is in consequence of this principle, he says, that "we end by ceasing to dogmatize."

The Skeptics were greatly impressed by the fact that the same "appearances" result in a wide variety of explanations from those who experience them. They discovered also, Sextus says, that arguments opposed to each other seem to have equal force. That is, alternative explanations seem to have an equal probability of being correct. Accordingly, the Skeptics were led to suspend judgment and to refrain from denying or affirming anything. From this suspension of judgment they hoped to achieve an undisturbed and calm mental state.

Evident versus Nonevident Matters

Clearly, the Skeptics did not give up the enterprise of vigorous thought and debate. Nor did they deny the evident facts about life—for example, that people become thirsty and hungry and that they are in peril when they come near a precipice. It was obvious to the Skeptics that people must be careful about their behavior. They had no doubt that they lived in a "real" world. They only wondered whether this world had been accurately described. No one, Sextus says, will dispute that objects have this or that appearance; the question is whether "the object is in reality such as it appears to be." Therefore, even though the Skeptics refused to live dogmatically, they did not deny the evident facts about experience. "We pay due regard to appearances," says Sextus. Daily life seemed to the Skeptics to require careful recognition of four items, which Sextus calls (1) the guidance of nature, (2) the constraint of the feelings, (3) the tradition of laws and customs, and (4) the instruction of the arts. Each of these contributes to successful and peaceful living, and not one of them requires any dogmatic interpretation or evaluation, only acceptance. Thus, it is by Nature's guidance that we are naturally capable of sensation and thought. Also, it is by the force of our feelings that hunger drives us to food, and thirst to drink. And it is the tradition of laws and customs that constrains us in everyday life to accept piety as good and impiety as evil. Finally, Sextus says, it is by virtue of the instruction in the arts that we engage in those arts in which we choose to participate.

There can be no doubt, therefore, that the Skeptics were far from denying the evident facts of sense perception. Indeed, Sextus says that those who claim that the Skeptics deny appearances "seem to me to be unacquainted with the statements of our School." They did not question appearances but only "the account given of appearances." As an example Sextus says that honey appears to be sweet, and "this we grant, for we perceive sweetness through the senses." But the real question is whether honey is really, in essence, sweet. Thus, the arguments of the Skeptics about appearances are expounded not with the intention of denying the reality of appearance but in order to point out the rashness of the "Dogmatists." The moral Sextus drew from this treatment of the objects of sense was that if human reason can be so easily deceived by appearances, "if reason is such a trickster as to all but snatch away the appearances from under our very eyes," should we not be particularly wary of following reason in the case of nonevident matters and thus avoid rashness?

Nonevident matters had a central place in the great philosophical systems of Plato, Aristotle, and the Stoics. Here the Skeptics found elaborate theories, especially about the nature of physical things. But how can any theory of physics—an inquiry that deals with nonevident matters—give us reliable truth? The Skeptics had a dual attitude toward the study of physics. On the one hand, they refused to theorize about physics as if to find "firm and confident opinions on any of the things in physical theory about which firm theories are held." Nevertheless, they did touch on physics "in order to have for every argument an equal argument to oppose it, and for the sake of mental tranquility." Their approaches to matters of ethics and logic were similar. In each case their pursuit of mental tranquility was not a negative approach, or a refusal to think, but rather an active approach. Their method of "the suspension of judgment" involved the activity of "setting things in opposition." As Sextus says, "We oppose appearances to appearances, or thoughts to thoughts, or appearances to thoughts."

Sextus, then, distinguished between two types of inquiry, namely, those dealing with evident matters and those dealing with nonevident matters. Evident matters, such as whether it is night or day, raise no serious problems of knowledge. In this category, too, are evident requirements for social and personal tranquility, for we know that customs and laws bind society together. But nonevident matters—for example, whether the stuff of nature is made of atoms or some fiery substance—do raise intellectual controversies. Whenever we go beyond the sphere of what is evident in human experience, our quest for knowledge should proceed under the influence of creative doubt. Thus, if we ask how we know what the universe is like, the Skeptics would answer that we do not yet know. It may be, they said, that people can attain the truth; it may also be that they are in error. But we cannot decide whether they have the truth or are in error because we do not yet have a reliable criterion for determining the truth in nonevident matters.

The Senses Are Deceptive   Sextus argued that if our knowledge comes from experience or sense impressions then there is all the more reason to doubt the adequacy of all knowledge. For the fact is that our senses give us different information about the same object at different times and under different circumstances. For example, from a distance a square building looks round. A landscape looks different at different times of the day. To some people honey is bitter. Painted scenery at a theater gives the impression of real doors and windows when only lines exist on a flat surface. That we do have impressions is certain, as, for example, when we "see" a bent oar in the water. But what we can never be certain about is whether in fact the oar is bent. Although we can take the oar out of the water and discover the error of perception, not every perception affords such an easy test for its accuracy and truth. Most of our knowledge is based on perceptions for which we have no criterion of truth. The Skeptic's conclusion is that we cannot be certain that our knowledge of the nature of things is true or not true.

Moral Rules Raise Doubts   Moral conceptions as well as physical objects are subject to doubt. People in different communities have different ideas of what is good and right. Customs and laws differ with each community and in the same community at different times. The Stoics said that there is a universal reason in which all people share, leading to a general consensus of all people regarding human rights. The Skeptics challenged both the theory and the fact, saying that there was no proof that all people have the capacity to agree on the truth of universal moral principles. Further, they argued, there is no evidence that people in fact exhibit this universal agreement. The fact is, people disagree. Moreover, those who disagree can all make equally strong cases for their own points of view. On matters of morality there is no absolute knowledge; there is only opinion. The Stoics had argued that on certain matters the test for truth was "irresistible perception." The Skeptics responded by saying that the sad fact is that, however strongly an opinion is held, it is, after all, still only an opinion, and we can with as much evidence support an opposite position. When people take a dogmatic stand, their conclusions always seem to them to be irresistible, but this is no guaranty that their conceptions are true.

Sextus makes his skeptical case regarding morality in an especially systematic way. He amasses example after example of how people and societies have conflicting attitudes on the most fundamental of moral values. Because of these conflicts, we should recognize that nothing is good or bad by nature, and, thus, suspend judgment about the natural moral character of a given social value. He groups these examples into five categories. First, there are personal codes of conduct that people adopt, such as the lifestyle of Diogenes the ancient Greek cynical philosopher. Second, there are laws, that is, written codes where the violator gets punished, such as laws regarding adultery. Third are social customs that involve commonly accepted practices where the violator does not necessarily get punished, such as the practice of homosexuality. Fourth are mythical beliefs about things that never took place, such as tales about conflicts between the gods. Fifth are dogmatic opinions consisting of theories by philosophers that are supported by arguments, such as the view that the soul is not immortal. According to Sextus, within each of these categories, our moral values conflict with each other. Regarding laws, he writes, "Among the Tauri in Scythia, it was a law to sacrifice strangers to Artemis, but with us it is illegal to kill a man near a temple." Regarding social customs, "People from India have sex with their women in public, but most of the other nations find that shameful." Regarding religious myths, "Some say that the soul is immortal, and others that it is mortal." Further, he argues that values in any one of these categories will conflict with values in the other categories: "among the Persians it is the custom to practice homosexuality, but among the Romans it is forbidden by law to do that." Similarly, our mythical beliefs about the gods committing adultery are inconsistent with our laws that forbid adultery. Also, some philosophers held the dogmatic view that incest was morally permissible, whereas the laws of various countries prohibit this. Thus, no matter how we envision moral values—as personal lifestyles, or laws, or customs, or religious myths, or philosophical dogmas—we will find conflict after conflict between our values. This shows that we cannot say that a given moral value "is naturally of this or that character, but instead all are matters of convention and relative." Ultimately, then, we must suspend our belief about the objective nature of moral values: "thus, seeing so great a diversity of practices, the skeptic suspends judgment as to the natural existence of anything good or bad, or generally to be done."

The consequence of this skeptical attitude toward our knowledge of the nature of things and our knowledge of moral truth is that we have a right to doubt the validity of such knowledge. Since we lack sure knowledge, it is best to withhold judgment about the true nature of morality. But ethics is a matter about which it is difficult for people to withhold judgment. When we face a problem of behavior, we want to know what is the right thing to do, and this requires knowledge of the right. Critics of Skepticism, then, would argue that the Skeptics had made ethics impossible and had removed from people any guidelines for behavior.

Morality Is Possible without Intellectual Certainty   The Skeptics argued, however, that it was not necessary to have knowledge in order to behave sensibly. It is enough, they said, to have reasonable assurance, or what they called *probability*. There could never be absolute certainty, but if there was a strong probability that our ideas would lead us to a life of happiness and peacefulness, we would be justified in following these ideas. We are able from daily experience to distinguish between notions that are not clear and those that have a high degree of clarity. When notions of right have a high degree of clarity, they create in us a strong belief that they are right, and this is all we need to lead us to action. For this reason customs, the laws of the land, and our basic appetites are for the most part reliable guides. But even here the Skeptic urges a caution, so that we do not mistake appearance for reality and, above all, that we avoid fanaticism and dogmatism. Although we are able to act enthusiastically even without a criterion of truth, our psychological safety requires that we leave open the channels of inquiry. The only safe attitude to take is one of doubt about the absolute truth of any idea, including moral convictions. And the person who can maintain a sense of imperturbability under this attitude of doubt has the best chance of achieving the happy life.

If we ask whether the Skeptics had a "system," Sextus answers, "No," if by a *system* we mean "an adherence to a number of dogmas which are dependent both on one another and on appearances" and where we take *dogma* to mean "assent to a non-evident proposition." But if by a *system* we mean "a procedure which, in accordance with appearance, follows a certain line of reasoning . . . indicating how it is possible to seem to live rightly," then the Skeptic did have a system. For, as Sextus says, "we follow a line of reasoning which . . . points us to a life conformable to the customs of our country and its laws and institutions, and to our own instinctive feeling."

PLOTINUS

At the culmination of classical philosophy stands the influential figure of Plotinus (ca. 204–270 CE). He lived at a time when there was no single compelling philosophical theory that could satisfy the special concerns of his age. The great variety of religious cults attested to the desperate attempt by people in the second and third centuries of the Roman Empire to lay hold of an explanation of life and destiny. It was an age of syncretism, when ideas were taken from several sources and put together as philosophies and religions. The cult of Isis combined Greek and Egyptian ideas of the gods; the Romans developed the Imperial Cult and worshiped their emperors, living and dead; devotees of the Mithraic cult worshiped the sun; and there was the Phrygian worship of the Great Mother of the Gods. Christianity was still considered a cult, even though some Christian thinkers already had emerged, such as Justin Martyr (100–165), Clement of Alexandria (ca. 150–220), Tertullian (ca. 160–230), and Origen (185–254), who sought to give the Christian faith a systematic character and an intellectual foundation. Origen tried to provide a Platonic and Stoic framework for Christianity. Earlier, Clement of Alexandria had also tried to join Christian thought with philosophic ideas. But Christian theology would not achieve its full strength until Augustine formulated his mixture of Christian and Platonic thought. The decisive bridge between classical philosophy and Augustine was the writings of Plotinus. But Plotinus nowhere mentions Christianity; his original contribution consisted of a fresh version of Plato's philosophy, and for this reason is known as Neoplatonism.

Plotinus's Life

Plotinus was born in Egypt about 204 CE. He was the pupil of Ammonius Saccas in Alexandria. Alexandria was at this time an intellectual crossroads of the ancient world, and here Plotinus immersed himself in classical philosophy, including the ideas of Pythagoras, Plato, Aristotle, Epicurus, and the Stoics. Out of all these strands he selected Platonism as the surest source of truth and indeed criticized the others by using his version of Plato's thoughts as his standard. At age 40 he traveled from Alexandria to Rome, which was experiencing considerable chaos in morality and religion, as well as social and political unrest. At Rome he opened his own school, to which he attracted some of that city's elite, including the emperor and his wife. For a while he planned to develop a city based on the theories of Plato's *Republic*, to be called Platonopolis, but this plan was never realized. He wrote fifty-four treatises with no particular order and in a style less eloquent than his speech. These treatises were assembled after Plotinus's death by his ablest pupil, Porphyry, who arranged them into six sets of nines, or, as they are now called, *Enneads*. Plotinus was a brilliant lecturer and at the same time a man of spiritual idealism. Indeed, it was his moral and spiritual force combined with his intellectual rigor that influenced not only his contemporaries but especially Augustine. Later, Augustine said that Plotinus would have to change "only a few words" to become a Christian. In any case, the thought of Plotinus became a major strand in most medieval philosophy.

What made Plotinus's philosophy distinctive was that he combined a speculative description of reality with a religious theory of salvation. He not only described the world but also gave an account of its source, of our place in it, and of how we overcome our moral and spiritual difficulties in it. In short, Plotinus developed a theory about God as the source of all things and as that to which people must return. In formulating his thought, Plotinus successively analyzed and rejected as inadequate the views of the Stoics, Epicureans, Pythagoreans, and Aristotelians. Among his objections to these schools of thought was his conviction that they did not understand the true nature of the soul. The Stoics described the soul as a material body—a physical "breath." But Plotinus argued that neither the Stoics nor the Epicureans, both materialists, understood the essential independence of the soul from the material body. Likewise, the Pythagoreans, who said that the soul is the "harmony" of the body, would have to admit that when the body is not in harmony, it has no soul. Finally, Plotinus rejected Aristotle's notion that the soul is the form of the body and as such cannot exist without a body. For Plotinus, if part of the body lost its form, to that extent the soul would also be deformed. This would make the body primary, whereas, Plotinus said, it is the soul that is primary and gives life to the body as a whole. Everything for Plotinus turned upon the accurate understanding of a person's essential nature.

To understand human nature, Plotinus pursued the line of thought Plato had set forth in his vivid myths and allegories. He was struck by Plato's comprehensive treatment of reality. There was Plato's account of the Demiurge fashioning matter into the world. There was also Plato's theory that the Form of the Good is like the rays of light emanating from the sun. Next there was Plato's notion that the soul has an existence before it enters the body, is a prisoner in the body, and struggles to escape from this captivity and return to its source. Finally, there was Plato's conviction that we find true reality in the spiritual world, and not in the material world. Plotinus took these basic ideas, emphasizing particularly the central Platonic theme that only the spirit is true reality, and reformulated Plato's ideas into a new kind of Platonism.

God as the One

The material world, with its multiplicity of things, cannot be the true reality, Plotinus thought, because it is always changing. The true changeless reality is God, about whom nothing specifically descriptive can be said except that he absolutely transcends or lies beyond everything in the world. For this reason God is not material, is not finite, and is not divisible. He has no specific form—either as matter, soul, or mind—each of which undergoes change. He cannot be confined to any idea or ideas of the intellect and for this reason cannot be expressed in any human language. He is accessible to none of the senses and can only be reached in a mystical ecstasy that is independent of any rational or sense experience. For this reason Plotinus spoke of God as the One, signifying thereby that in God there is absolutely no complexity and that, indeed, God is Absolute Unity. The One signifies, moreover, that God does not change. He is indivisible, has no variety, is uncreated, and is in every way unalterable.

Plotinus held that the One cannot be the sum of particular things because it is precisely these things whose finite existence requires explanation and a source. Thus, the One "cannot be any existing thing, but is prior to all existents."

There are no positive attributes that we can ascribe to the One because all our ideas of attributes are derived from finite physical things. It is not possible, therefore, to say that God is this and not that since this procedure would attach to God certain limits. To say, then, that God is One is to affirm that God *is* and that God transcends the world. It is to say that he is simple, without any duality, potentiality, or material limitation, and that he transcends all distinctions. In a sense, God cannot engage in any self-conscious activity since this would imply complexity through thinking *particular* thoughts *before* and *after*, thus implying change. God in no way resembles a human. He is indeed simply One, Absolute Unity.

The Metaphor of Emanation

If God is One, he cannot create, for creation is an act, and activity implies change. Then how can we account for the many things of the world? Striving to maintain a consistent view of the Unity of God, Plotinus explained the origin of things by saying that they come from God, not through a free act of creation but through necessity. To express what he meant by "necessity," Plotinus used several metaphors, especially the metaphor of *emanation*. Things emanate—they flow from God—the way light emanates from the sun or the way water flows from a spring. The sun is never exhausted, and it does not *do* anything; it just *is*. And being what it is, the sun necessarily emanates light. In this way God is the source of everything, and everything manifests God. But nothing is equal to God, any more than the rays of light are equal in any way to the sun. All of these emanations fall in a spectrum between pure being (that is, God himself) and complete nonexistence. Thus, Plotinus does not appear to be a strict pantheist—the view that God is identical with nature as a whole. Although the entire universe consists of God and his emanations, there is nevertheless a hierarchical arrangement in nature. Just as the light closest to the sun is the brightest, so also the highest form of being is the first emanation. Plotinus described this first emanation from the One as *mind (nous)*. It is most like the One but is not absolute and can therefore be said to have a specific attribute or character. This *nous* is *thought* or *universal intelligence* and signifies the underlying rationality of the world. It is the nature of rationality to have no spatial or temporal boundaries. But rationality does imply multiplicity in that thinking contains the ideas of all particular things.

The World Soul   Just as light emanates from the sun in ever-diminishing intensity, so also is there a decline in the degrees of perfection as emanations are farther from God. Moreover, each succeeding emanation is the cause of the next-lower emanation, as if there were a principle at work requiring that every nature bring into being that which is immediately subordinate to it. In this way the *nous* is in turn the source of the next emanation, which Plotinus calls the Soul. The Soul of the World has two aspects: Looking upward, as it were, toward *nous* or pure rationality, the Soul strives to contemplate the eternal ideas of all things; looking downward, it further emanates one thing at a time and provides the life principle to all of nature. It thus bridges the gap between the ideas of things (in *nous*) and the realm of the natural world. The activity of the Soul accounts for the phenomenon of *time*, since now there is the emergence of things. The relations of things to each other result in events, and events come *after* one another, and this relationship of events is what we mean by time. To be sure, the One, the *nous*, and the World Soul are all coeternal and are thus outside of time. Below the World Soul lies the realm of nature and of particular things, which reflects through time the changing eternal ideas.

The Human Soul   The human soul is an emanation from the World Soul. Like the World Soul, it also has two aspects. Again, looking upward, the human soul shares in the *nous* or universal reason. Looking downward, the human soul becomes connected with, but is not identical to, the body. Here Plotinus reaffirmed Plato's theory of the preexistence of the human soul, believing also that the union of the soul with the body is a product of a "fall." Moreover, after death the human soul survives the body and conceivably enters a sequence of transmigrations from one body to another. Being spiritual, and therefore truly real, the human soul will not be annihilated but will join all other souls again in the World Soul. While in the body, it is the human soul that provides the power of rationality, sensitivity, and vitality.

The World of Matter   At the lowest level in the hierarchy of being—that is, at the farthest remove from the One—is matter. There is a principle at work in emanation, which requires that the higher grades of being overflow in accordance with the next realm of possibilities. After ideas and souls, then, there is the world of material objects. It exhibits a mechanical order whose operation or movement is the work of reason, subjecting all objects to the laws or rules of cause and effect. Once again, the material world displays a higher and lower aspect. The higher component is its susceptibility to the laws of motion. However, the lower component, its bare material nature, is a dark world of gross matter that moves aimlessly, with sluggish discord, toward collision and extinction. Plotinus compared matter to the dimmest and farthest reach of light—the most extreme limit of light—which is darkness itself. Darkness, clearly, is the very opposite of light; similarly, matter is the opposite of spirit and, therefore, is the opposite of the One. Again, insofar as matter exists in conjunction with the soul, either the individual soul or the World Soul, to this extent matter is not complete darkness. But just as light tends to emanate finally to the point of utter darkness, so also matter stands at the boundary line of nothingness, where it tends to disappear into nonbeing.

The Causes of Evil   Through the theory of emanation, Plotinus argued that God necessarily overflows in order to share his perfection as much as possible. Since God could not reduplicate himself perfectly, he did so in the only possible way, namely, by representing all the possible degrees of perfection by means of the emanations. To represent *all* degrees of perfection, it was necessary to have not only the *nous* but also the lowest level of being, namely, matter. However, within this lowest level we find various evils: pain, the continuing warfare of the passions, and, finally, death and sorrow. How could the Perfect One, from whom everything ultimately emanates, permit this kind of imperfection to exist among human beings? Plotinus explained the problem of evil in various ways. For one thing, he said, evil in its own way occupies a place in the hierarchy of perfection, since without evil something would be lacking in the scheme of things. Evil is like the dark shadings of a portrait, which greatly enhance the beauty of the image. Moreover, all events occur with rigorous necessity, as the Stoics had argued. Thus, the good person does not look on them as evil, and the bad person can consider this to be just punishment. But Plotinus finds the best explanation of evil in his account of matter.

For Plotinus matter is the necessary and final reach of the emanation from the One. The very nature of emanation, as we have seen, is that the higher levels necessarily move toward the lower. The One generates the *nous*, and, finally, the individual soul generates a material body. Brute matter, however, continues the process of emanation, as if moving farther and farther from the One, the way the light grows dimmer and dimmer the farther it moves from the sun. There is, then, a tendency for matter to move beyond—or separate itself from—the activity of the soul and to engage in motion that is not rationally directed. Again, as matter faces upward, it encounters the soul or the principle of rationality. For objects in nature this accounts for the orderliness of their movements. For individual people it means that the body responds to the activity of the soul at the levels of rationality, sensitivity, appetite, and vitality. But the natural tendency of matter is to face downward because of the downward momentum of emanation. Because of its downward thrust, matter encounters darkness itself, and at this point matter is separated from rationality.

The clue to the problem of moral evil, then, is that the soul is now united with a material body. And in spite of the rational character of the soul, it must contend with the body, whose material nature disposes it to move downward and away from rational control. When the body reaches the level below rationality, it becomes subject to an indefinite number of possible ways of acting. It is the job of the passions to move the body to respond to all kinds of appetites. Evil, then, is the discrepancy between the soul's right intentions and its actual behavior. It is an imperfection in the soul-body arrangement, and much of the cause for this imperfection is ascribed to the final irrational movement of the material body.

Matter, or body, is the principle of evil in the sense that matter is at the fringe of emanation, where the absence of rationality results in formlessness and the least degree of perfection. But since matter comes from God in the sense that everything emanates from the One, it could be said that God is the source of evil. Still, evil, for Plotinus, is not a positive destructive force; it is not a "devil" or rival god contending with the good God. Nor, as some Zoroastrian philosophers thought, is it a contest between the coequal forces of light and darkness. Evil, for Plotinus, is simply the absence of something; it is the lack of perfection and the lack of form for the material body, which is not itself essentially evil. A person's moral struggle is, therefore, a struggle not against some outside force but against the tendency to be undone within, to become disordered, to lose control of the passions. Evil, again, is no *thing* but rather is the absence of order. The body *as such* is not evil. Evil is the formlessness of matter as darkness is the absence of light. Throughout his analysis Plotinus tries simultaneously to argue that the soul is responsible for its acts and that all events are determined. Just how these two views can be reconciled is not exactly clear. At the same time, much of Plotinus's appeal came from the promise of salvation, which he thought his philosophy could provide.

Salvation

Plotinus moved from his philosophical analysis of emanation to the religious and mystical plan of salvation. The mystery cults of his day offered a swift fulfillment of a person's desire to unite with God. By contrast, Plotinus described the soul's ascent to unity with God as a difficult and painful task. This ascent required that a person develop successively the moral and intellectual virtues. Since the body and the physical world were not considered evil per se, it was not necessary to reject them altogether. Plotinus's key insight was that the physical things of the world must not distract the soul from its higher aims. We should renounce the world as a means of facilitating the soul's ascent to intellectual activity, as in philosophy and science. We must discipline ourselves in rigorous and correct thinking. Such thinking lifts us out of our individuality, and with a broad knowledge of things, we tend to relate the self to the whole arrangement of the world. All the steps up this ladder of knowledge lead toward the final union of the self with the One in a state of ecstasy, where there is no longer any consciousness of the self's separation from God. This ecstasy is the final result of right conduct, correct thinking, and the proper disposition of the affections.

Plotinus felt that achieving this union could require many incarnations of each soul. Finally, the soul is refined and purified in its love and, as Plato said in his *Symposium*, is capable of the fullest self-surrender. At this point the process of emanation is fully reversed, and the self merges once again with the One. For many Plotinus's Neoplatonism had all the power of a religion and represented a compelling alternative to Christianity. Although its intricate intellectual scheme prevented it from becoming widely popular, Neoplatonism had a considerable impact on the emerging Christian theology of this era. Augustine saw in the *Enneads* of Plotinus a strikingly new explanation of evil and of salvation through orderly love. Through Augustine Neoplatonism became a decisive element in the intellectual expression of the Christian faith during the Middle Ages.

CHAPTER 6

Augustine

AUGUSTINE'S LIFE

A ugustine was intensely concerned with his personal destiny, and this provided the driving force for his philosophical activity. From his early youth he suffered from a deep moral turmoil, which sparked within him a lifelong quest for wisdom and spiritual peace. He was born in Tagaste in the African province of Numidia in 354 CE. Although his father was not Christian, his mother, Monica, was a devout believer in the new faith. At the age of 16, Augustine began the study of rhetoric in Carthage, a port city given to immoral ways. Though his mother instilled in him the traditions of Christian thought and behavior, he rejected this religious faith and morality, taking at this time a mistress by whom he had a son and with whom he lived for a decade. At the same time, his thirst for knowledge impelled him to rigorous study, and he became a successful student of rhetoric.

A series of personal experiences led him to his unique approach to philosophy. He was 19 years old when he read the *Hortensius* of Cicero, which was an exhortation to achieve philosophical wisdom. These words of Cicero kindled his passion for learning, but he was left with the problem of where to find intellectual certainty. His Christian ideas seemed unsatisfactory to him. He was particularly perplexed by the ever-present problem of moral evil. How can we explain the existence of evil in human experience? The Christians said that God is the Creator of all things and also that God is good. How, then, was it possible for evil to arise out of a world that a perfectly good God had created? Because Augustine could find no answers in the Christianity he learned as a youth, he turned to a group called the Manichaeans. The Manichaeans were sympathetic to much of Christianity but, boasting of their intellectual superiority, rejected the basic monotheism of the Old Testament and with it the view that the Creator and Redeemer of humanity are one and the same. Instead, the Manichaeans taught a theory of dualism, according to which there were two basic principles in the universe: the principle of light or goodness, on the one hand, and the principle of darkness or evil, on the other. They held these two principles to be equally eternal, but eternally in conflict with each other. This conflict, they believed, is reflected in human life in the conflict between the soul, composed of light, and the body, composed of darkness. At first this theory of dualism seemed to provide the perfect answer to the problem of evil: It overcame the contradiction between the presence of evil in a world created by a good God. Augustine could now attribute his sensual desires to the external power of darkness.

Although this dualism seemed to solve the contradiction of evil in a God-created world, it raised new problems. For one thing, how could we explain why there were two conflicting principles in nature? If no convincing reason could be given, was intellectual certitude possible? Far more serious was Augustine's awareness that it did not help to solve his moral turmoil to say that it was all caused by some external force. The presence of fierce passion was no less unsettling just because the "blame" for it had been shifted to something outside of himself. What had originally attracted him to the Manichaeans was their boast that they could provide him with truth that could be discussed and made plain, not requiring, as the Christians did, "faith before reason." He therefore broke with the Manichaeans, feeling that "those philosophers whom they call Academics [that is, Skeptics] were wiser than the rest in thinking that we ought to doubt everything, and that no truth can be comprehended by human beings." He was now attracted to Skepticism, though at the same time he retained some belief in God. He maintained a materialistic view of things and on this account doubted the existence of immaterial substances and the immortality of the soul.

Hoping for a more effective career in rhetoric, Augustine left Africa for Rome and shortly thereafter moved to Milan, where he became municipal professor of rhetoric in 384. Here he was profoundly influenced by Ambrose, who was then bishop of Milan. From Ambrose, Augustine derived not so much the techniques of rhetoric but, somewhat unexpectedly, a greater appreciation of Christianity. While in Milan, Augustine took another mistress, having left his first one in Africa. It was here also that Augustine came upon certain forms of Platonism, especially the Neoplatonism found in the *Enneads* of Plotinus. There was much in Neoplatonism that caught his attention. First, there was the Neoplatonist view that the immaterial world is totally separate from the material one. Second, there was the view that people possess a spiritual sense that enables them to know God and the immaterial world. Third, from Plotinus Augustine derived the conception that evil is not a positive reality but is rather a matter of privation—that is, the absence of good. Above all, Neoplatonism overcame Augustine's former skepticism, materialism, and dualism. Through Platonic thought he was able to understand that not all activity is physical, that there is a spiritual as well as a physical reality. He could now see the unity of the world without having to assume the existence of two principles behind soul and body. He thus followed Plotinus's picture of reality as a single graduated system in which matter is simply on a lower level.

Intellectually, Neoplatonism provided what Augustine had been looking for, but it left his moral problem unsolved. What he needed now was moral strength to match his intellectual insight. This he found in Ambrose's sermons. Neoplatonism had finally made Christianity reasonable to him, and now he was also able to exercise the act of faith and thereby derive the power of the spirit without feeling that he was lapsing into some form of superstition. His dramatic conversion occurred in 386, when he gave "real assent" to the prospect of abandoning his profession of rhetoric and giving his life totally to the pursuit of philosophy, which, for him, also meant knowledge of God. He now conceived of Platonism and Christianity as virtually one. Seeing in Neoplatonism the philosophical expression of Christianity, he states, "I am confident that among the Platonists I shall find what is not opposed to the teachings of our religion." He therefore set out on what he called "my whole plan" of achieving wisdom, saying that "from this moment forward, it is my resolve never to depart from the authority of Christ, for I find none that is stronger." Still, he emphasized that "I must follow after this with the greatest subtlety of reason."

Augustine was an incredibly prolific writer, and as he became a noted leader in the Catholic Church, he was continually involved in writing as a defender of the faith and an opponent of heresy. In 396 he became bishop of Hippo, the seaport near his native town of Tagaste. Among his many opponents was Pelagius, with whom he entered into a famous controversy. Pelagius taught that all people possess the natural ability to achieve a righteous life, thereby denying the notion of original sin—the view that human nature is inherently corrupt. According to Augustine, Pelagius misunderstood human nature by assuming that our human wills are capable of achieving salvation on their own, which thereby minimizes the function of God's grace.

This controversy illuminates Augustine's manner of thought perfectly, since it shows again his insistence that all knowledge in all subjects must take into account the revealed truth of Scripture along with the insights of philosophy. Since all knowledge is aimed at helping people understand God, this religious dimension clearly had a priority in his reflections. As Aquinas said about him later, "Whenever Augustine, who was imbued with the theories of the Platonists, found in their writings anything consistent with the faith, he adopted it; and whatever he found contrary to the faith, he amended." Still, it was Platonism that rescued Augustine from skepticism, made the Christian faith reasonable to him, and set off one of the great literary achievements in theology and philosophy. As if to symbolize his tempestuous life, Augustine died in 430 at the age of 75 in the posture of reciting the Penitential Psalms as the Vandals besieged Hippo.

HUMAN KNOWLEDGE

Faith and Reason

Augustine is intimately connected with a long-standing discussion throughout the Middle Ages regarding the connection between faith and reason. The central issue is determining whether important philosophical and religious beliefs are grounded in the authority of faith or of reason, or some combination of the two. Take, for example, the origin of the cosmos, a subject about which philosophers and theologians alike have offered different views since antiquity. Perhaps the world naturally emerged from a swirling vortex of primordial stuff; perhaps it resulted from the accidental collision of atoms; perhaps it was created by a divine being or beings. In attempting to sort through the possibilities, do we rely on faith or reason as our guide? The faith option involves an attitude of trust that is grounded in divine revelation; the reason option, by contrast, involves belief that is grounded in methodical demonstration.

When addressing the faith-reason issue, the early Christian theologian Tertullian came down decisively on the side of faith, which we see in two famous statements from him. First, he rhetorically asks, "What does Athens have to do with Jerusalem?"—his point being that reason (Athens) has nothing to do with faith (Jerusalem). Second, when facing contradictions regarding the Christian concept of the incarnation, Tertullian says, "I believe because it is absurd"—his point being that faith is so distinct from reason that faith is essentially *irrational*. Religious faith, he contends, is both contrary to and superior to reason. Augustine's position on the relation between faith and reason was considerably more moderate but still gives priority to faith. For him faith illuminated reason, and without faith there could be no understanding. Inspired by the Old Testament prophet Isaiah, who maintained, "Unless you believe, you will not understand," Augustine's view is encapsulated in the expression "faith seeking understanding" (*fides quaerens intellectum*).

For Augustine true philosophy was inconceivable without a joining of faith and reason in this way. To understand the concrete condition of human existence, we must first consider ourselves from the point of view of the Christian faith, and this in turn requires that the whole world be considered from the vantage point of faith. There could be, for Augustine, no distinction between theology and philosophy. Indeed, he believed that we cannot properly philosophize until our human wills are transformed, that clear thinking is possible only under the influence of God's grace. It is, therefore, not possible to discuss Augustine's philosophy without at the same time considering his theological viewpoint. Indeed, Augustine wrote no purely philosophical works in the contemporary sense of that term. In this way Augustine set the dominant direction and style of Christian wisdom of the Middle Ages.

Overcoming Skepticism

For a time Augustine took the Skeptics seriously—specifically, the skepticism of the Academy—and he agreed with them that "no truth can be comprehended by human beings." But after his conversion, his problem was no longer *whether* people can attain certainty but rather *how* they can attain it. Augustine therefore sought to answer the Skeptics, and he did this first of all by showing that human reason does indeed have certainty about various things. Specifically, human reason is absolutely certain of the principle of contradiction. We know that a thing cannot both be and not be at the same time. Using this principle, we can be certain, for example, that there is either one world or many worlds, and if there are many, their number is either finite or infinite. What we know here is simply that both alternatives cannot be true. This is not yet any substantive knowledge, but it meant for Augustine that we are not hopelessly lost in uncertainty. Not only do we know that both alternatives cannot be true simultaneously, we know also that this is always, eternally, the case. In addition, he said that even the Skeptics would have to admit that the act of doubting is itself a form of certainty, for a person who doubts is certain that he doubts. Here, then, is another certainty—the certainty that I exist. For if I doubt, I must exist. Whatever else I can have doubts about, I cannot doubt that I doubt. The Skeptics argued that a person could be asleep and only dreaming that he sees things or is aware of himself. But to Augustine this was not a formidable argument, for in reply he said, "Whether he be asleep or awake he lives." Any conscious person is certain that he exists, that he is alive, and that he can think. "For we are," says Augustine, "and we know we are, and we love our being and our knowledge of it. . . . These truths stand without fear in the face of the arguments of the [skeptical] Academics." In the seventeenth century, Descartes formulated a similar argument in his classic statement "I think, therefore I am" and then proceeded to use it as a foundation for his system of philosophy. Augustine, however, was content merely to refute the Skeptic's basic position. Instead of proving the existence of external objects as Descartes did, Augustine assumed the existence of these objects and referred to them chiefly to describe how we achieve knowledge in relation to things.

Knowledge and Sensation

When we sense objects, we derive some knowledge from the act of sensation. But according to Augustine, such sensory information is at the lowest level of knowing. Still, the senses do give us a kind of knowledge. What puts sensory knowledge at the lowest level is that it gives us the least amount of certainty. There are two reasons for this lack of certainty: (1) The objects of sense are always changing, and (2) the organs of sense change. Thus, sensation varies both from time to time and from person to person. Something can taste sweet to one person and bitter to another, warm to one and cold to another. Still, Augustine believed that the senses are always accurate as such. It is unjust, he said, to expect or demand more from the senses than they can provide. For example, there is nothing wrong with our senses when the oar in the water appears bent to us. On the contrary, there would be something wrong if the oar appeared straight, since under these circumstances the oar ought to seem bent. The problem arises when we have to make a judgment about the actual condition of the oar. We would be deceived if we assented to the notion that the oar was in fact bent. To avoid this error, Augustine says, "do not give assent to more than the fact of appearance, and you will not be deceived." In this way, Augustine affirmed the reliability of the senses while also recognizing their limitations. Just how the senses give us knowledge Augustine explained by analyzing the nature or mechanics of sensation.

What happens when we sense an object? To answer this question, Augustine relied upon his Platonic interpretation of human nature. A person is a union of body and soul. He even suggested that the body is the prison of the soul. But when he described how the soul attains knowledge, he departed from the Platonic theory of recollection. Knowledge is not an act of remembering. It is an act of the soul itself. When we see an object, the soul (mind) fashions out of its own substance an image of the object. Since the soul is spiritual and not material, the object cannot make a physical "impression" on the mind the way a signet ring leaves its mark in wax. Accordingly, it is the mind itself that produces the image. Moreover, when we sense an object, we not only sense an image but also make a judgment. Suppose I look at a person and say that she is beautiful. In this act of judgment, I not only see the person with my senses but also compare her with a standard to which my mind has access in some realm other than that in which I sense the person. Similarly, when I see seven children and three children, I know that they can be added to make ten children. As other things in nature are mutable, these ten children, being mortal, will eventually pass away. But I am able to separate the numbers from the children and discover that seven and three do not depend on the children or any other things, and it is necessarily true that they make ten when added together.

Sensation, then, gives us some knowledge, but its chief characteristic is that it necessarily points beyond its objects. From the sensation of an oar, we are moved to think about straightness and bentness; from the sensation of a specific beautiful person, we think about beauty in general; and from the sensation of children, we think about the eternal truths of mathematics. With each of these inferences, the issue of our human nature is once again raised, since the explanation of the mechanics of sensation leads to a distinction between body and soul. Sensation involves the body insofar as some physical organ is required to sense things. However, unlike animals people not only sense things but have some rational knowledge of them and make rational judgments about them. When rational people make such judgments, they are no longer dependent solely on the senses but have directed their minds to other objects, such as Beauty and the truths of mathematics. A careful analysis shows, therefore, that the act of human sensation involves at least four elements: (1) the object sensed, (2) the bodily organ on which sensation depends, (3) the activity of the mind in formulating an image of the object, and (4) the immaterial object (such as Beauty), which the mind uses in making a judgment about the sensed object. What emerges from this analysis is that there are two different kinds of objects that human beings encounter, namely, the objects of bodily sensation and the objects of the mind. With the physical eye people see things, and with the mind then grasp eternal truths. These different objects account for the different degrees of intellectual certainty. We will have less reliable knowledge when we direct our mutable sense organs toward changing physical objects. By contrast, knowledge will be more reliable when we contemplate eternal truths independently of the senses. Sensation is only the beginning of a path of knowledge that ultimately leads to an activity within people, and not to things outside of us. Knowledge moves from the level of sensed things to the higher level of general truth. The highest level of knowledge is for Augustine the knowledge of God. Sensation plays its part in attaining this knowledge in that it directs our minds upward. Hence,

Augustine says that we move toward God "from the exterior to the interior, and from the inferior to the superior."

The Theory of Illumination

In his account of the relation between sensation and knowledge, Augustine was left with the problem of how our minds can make judgments involving eternal and necessary truths. What makes it possible for us to know that seven and three—which at first we see in relation to things—always and necessarily make ten? Why, as a matter of fact, is there a problem here? The problem exists because so far in his account of human knowledge, all the elements involved are mutable or imperfect, and hence finite and not eternal. The sensed objects are mutable, and the bodily organs of sense are also subject to change. The mind itself is a creature and is therefore finite and not perfect. How, then, can these elements be deployed in a way that rises above their own imperfection and mutability and discovers eternal truths about which we have no doubts? Such eternal truths confront us with the coercive power of certitude and are so superior to what our minds could produce on their own that we must adjust or conform to them. Plato answered this question with his theory that knowledge is recollection, whereby the soul remembers what it once knew before it entered the body. Aristotle, on the other hand, argued that universal ideas are abstracted by the intellect from particular things. Augustine accepted neither one of these solutions. He did, though, follow another of Plato's insights, namely the analogy between (1) the sun in the visible world and (2) the Form of the Good in the intelligible world.

Augustine was not so much concerned with the *origin* of our ideas as with our *awareness of the certitude* of some of our ideas. Rejecting recollection and some form of innate ideas, he came closer to the notion of abstraction. Actually, Augustine says that people are constructed in such a way that when the eyes of our bodies see an object, we can form an image of it provided the object is bathed in light. Similarly, our minds are capable of "seeing" eternal objects provided that they too are bathed in their own appropriate light. As Augustine says, we ought to believe "that the nature of the intellectual mind was so made that, by being naturally subject to intelligible realities, according to the arrangement of the Creator, it sees these truths [such as mathematical truths] in a certain incorporeal light of a unique kind, just as the eyes of the body sees the things all around it in this corporeal light." The human mind, in short, requires illumination if it is to "see" eternal and necessary truths. We can no more "see" the intelligible objects or truths of the intellect without some illumination than we can see the things in the world without the light of the sun.

Augustine states his theory of *illumination* in succinct form when he says, "There is present in [us] . . . the light of eternal reason, in which light the immutable truths are seen." Just what he means by this theory is not altogether clear. What is clear is that for Augustine the illumination comes from God just as light is shed by the sun. If we take this analogy seriously, the divine light must illuminate something that is already there. By the light of the sun, we can see the trees and houses. If the divine light performs the same kind of function, this light must also illuminate something—our ideas. This light is not so much the source of our ideas as it is the condition under which we recognize the quality of truth and eternity in our ideas. In short, divine illumination is not a process by which the content of ideas is infused into our minds; it is, rather, the illumination of our judgment whereby we are able to discern that certain ideas contain necessary and eternal truths. God, the source of this light, is perfect and eternal, and the human intellect operates under the influence of God's eternal ideas. This does not mean that our human minds can know God. But it does mean that divine illumination allows us to overcome the limitations of knowledge caused by the mutability of physical objects and the finitude of our minds. With this theory, then, Augustine solved to his satisfaction the problem of how the human intellect is able to go beyond sense objects and make judgments about necessary and eternal truths.

GOD

Augustine was not interested in mere theoretical speculations about the existence of God. His philosophical reflections about God were the product of his intense personal pursuit of wisdom and spiritual peace. His deep involvement in sensual pleasures gave him dramatic evidence that the soul cannot find its peace among the bodily pleasures or sensation. Similarly, in his quest for certainty of knowledge, he discovered that the world of things was full of change and impermanence. His mind, too, he discovered, was imperfect, since it was capable of error. At the same time, he had the experience of knowing certain truths that were eternal. He was able to compare the experience of contemplating truth with the experience of having pleasure and sensations. Of these two experiences he found that the mental activities could provide more lasting and profound peace. He considered the technical question of how it was that his finite human mind was capable of attaining knowledge beyond the capacity of his mind. He concluded that this knowledge could not have come from finite things outside of him; nor could it be produced fully by his own mind. Since the knowledge available to him was eternal and could not come from his limited or finite mind, he was led to believe that immutable truth must have its source in God. What led to this conclusion was the similarity between the characteristics of some of his knowledge and the attributes of God, namely, that both are eternal and true. The existence of some eternal truths meant for Augustine the existence of *the* Eternal Truth, which God is. In this way Augustine moved through various levels of personal experience and spiritual quest to what amounted to a "proof" of the existence of God.

Since God is truth, God in some sense is within us, but since God is eternal, he also transcends us. But what else can a person say by way of describing God? Actually, like Plotinus, Augustine found it easier to say what God is not than to define what he is. Still, to say that God is superior to finite things was a major step. Taking the scriptural name for God given to Moses, namely,

"I Am That I Am," Augustine interpreted this to mean that God is *being itself*. As such God is the highest being. This is not the same thing as the beingless One of Plotinus. Instead, it is the "something than which nothing more excellent or more sublime exists"—a phrase that centuries later influenced Anselm to formulate his famous ontological argument. As the highest being God is perfect being, which means that he is self-existent, immutable, and eternal. As perfect he is also "simple," in that whatever attributes are assigned to him turn out to be identical. That is, his knowledge, wisdom, goodness, and power are all one and constitute his essence. Further, Augustine reasoned that the world of everyday things reflects the being and activity of God. Although the things we see are mutable in that they gradually cease to be, nevertheless, insofar as they exist they have a definite form, and this form is eternal and is a reflection of God. Indeed, Augustine sees God as the source of all being insofar as things possess any being at all.

But unlike the things of the world, God, as Augustine says, "is . . . in no interval or extension of place" and similarly "is in no interval or extension of time." In short, Augustine described God as pure or highest being, suggesting thereby that in God there is no change either from nonbeing to being or from being to nonbeing. God *is;* "I Am That I Am." Again, the principal force of this line of thought is its relevance in solving Augustine's spiritual problem—although Augustine was convinced that this reasoning had sufficient philosophical rigor. As the source of being and truth and the one eternal reality, God now becomes for Augustine the legitimate object both of thought and affection. From God there comes both enlightenment for the mind and strength for the will. Moreover, all other knowledge is possible because God is the standard for truth. His essence is to exist, and to exist is to act, and to act is to know. Being both eternal and all-knowing, God always knew all the possible ways in which he could be reflected in creation. For this reason the various forms in which the world is shaped were always in God as ideal models. All things, therefore, are finite reflections of God's eternal thought. If God's thought is "eternal," difficulties arise in our language when it is said that God "foresees" what will happen. What is important to Augustine, however, is that the world and God are intimately related, and that the world reflects God's eternal thought, even though God is not identical with the world but is instead beyond it. Because there is this relation between God and the world, to know one is to know something of the other. This is why Augustine was so convinced that the person who knew the most about God could understand most deeply the true nature of the world and especially human nature and human destiny.

THE CREATED WORLD

Augustine concluded that God is the most appropriate object of thought and affection, and that the physical world could not provide us with true knowledge or spiritual peace. In spite of his emphasis on the spiritual realm, Augustine nevertheless paid considerable attention to the material world. After all, we must live in the physical world, and we need to understand this world in order to relate ourselves appropriately to it. From what he already said about the nature of knowledge and about God, we can see that Augustine believed that the world is the creation of God. In his *Confessions* Augustine says that, wherever we look, all things say, "We did not make ourselves, but He that lives forever made us." That is, finite things demand that there should be some permanent being to explain how they could come into existence. Just how God is related to the world was explained by Augustine in his unique theory of creation.

Creation from Nothing

Augustine's distinctive theory was that God created all things *ex nihilo* (out of nothing). This was in contrast to Plato's account of the world, which was not "created" but came about when the Demiurge combined the Forms and the receptacle, which always existed independently. Augustine also departed from the Neoplatonic theory of Plotinus, which explained the world as an emanation from God. Plotinus said that there was a *natural necessity* in God to overflow, since the Good must necessarily diffuse itself. Moreover, Plotinus's theory held that there is a continuity between God and the world insofar as the world is merely an extension of God. Against all these notions Augustine stressed that the world is the product of God's free act, whereby he brings into being, out of nothing, all the things that make up the world. All things, then, owe their existence to God. There is, however, a sharp distinction between God and the things he created. Whereas Plotinus saw the world as the overflowing, and therefore continuation, of God, Augustine speaks of God as bringing into being what did not exist before. He could not have created the world out of an existing matter because matter, even in a primary form, would already be something. To speak of a formless matter is really to refer to nothing. Actually, according to Augustine, everything, including matter, is the product of God's creative act. Even if there were some formless matter that was capable of being formed, this would also have its origin in God and would have to be created by him out of nothing. Matter is essentially good in nature since God creates matter, and God cannot create anything evil. The essential goodness of matter plays an important role in Augustine's theory of morality, as we shall see.

The Seminal Principles

Augustine was struck by the fact that the various species in nature never produce new species. Horses produce horses, and flowers produce flowers; at the human level, human parents produce human children. What fascinated Augustine about all of this was its relevance to the general question of *causality*. Although in a sense parents are the cause of children, and older flowers the cause of new flowers, still, none of these things is able to introduce new forms into nature. In the created order existing things are able to animate only existing forms into completed beings. Augustine drew from this fact (for which he admittedly did not have decisive empirical support) the conclusion that the causality behind the formation of all things is God's intelligence. There is no original causal power in things capable of fashioning new forms. How, then, do things, animals, and people produce anything? Augustine's answer was that in the act of creation God implanted seminal principles (*rationes seminales*) into matter, thereby setting into nature the potentiality for all species to emerge. These seminal principles are the germs of things; they are invisible and have causal power. Thus, all species bear the invisible and potential power to become what they are not yet at the present time. When species begin to exist, their seminal principle—that is, their potentiality—is fulfilled. Actual seeds then transmit the continuation of the fixed species from potentiality to actuality. Originally, God, in a single act of complete creation, furnished the germinating principles of all species.

With this theory Augustine explained the origin of species, locating their cause in the mind of God, from which came the seminal principles. With this theory of seminal principles, Augustine thought he had also solved a problem in the Bible, where it says in the Book of Genesis that God created the world in six days. It seemed inconsistent with Augustine's view of God that God should have to create things step by step. There was some question, too, about what is meant here by "six days," especially since the sun was not "created" until the fourth day. The theory of seminal principles enabled Augustine to say that God created all things at once, meaning by this that he implanted the seminal principles of all species simultaneously. But, since these germs are principles of potentiality, they are the bearers of things that are to be but that have not yet "flowered." Accordingly, though all species were created at once, they did not all simultaneously exist in a fully formed state. They each fulfilled their potentiality in a sequence of points in time.

MORAL PHILOSOPHY

Every philosophical notion developed by Augustine pointed, in one way or another, to the problem of the human moral condition. For him, therefore, moral theory was not some special or isolated subject. Everything culminates in morality, which clarifies the sure road to happiness, which is the ultimate goal of human behavior. In fashioning his ideas about morality, then, Augustine brought to bear his major insights about the nature of human knowledge, the nature of God, and the theory of creation. From the vantage point of these ideas, he focused on human moral constitution.

Our human moral quest is the outcome of a specific and concrete condition. The condition is that we are made in such a way that we seek happiness. Although the ancient Greeks also considered happiness to be the culmination of the good life, Augustine's theory provided a novel estimate of what constitutes true happiness and just how it can be achieved. Other philosophers also held that happiness is our aim in life, such as Aristotle, who said that happiness is achieved when people fulfill their natural functions through a well-balanced life. Augustine, though, held that true happiness requires that we go beyond the natural to the supernatural. He expressed this view in both religious and philosophical language. In his *Confessions* he writes, "Oh God You have created us for Yourself so that our hearts are restless until they find their rest in You." In more philosophical language he makes this same point by saying that human nature is so made that "it cannot itself be the good by which it is made happy." There is, in short, no purely "natural" person. The reason there is no purely natural person, Augustine says, is that nature did not produce people; God did. Consequently, human nature always bears the mark of its creation, which means, among other things, that there are some permanent relations between people and God. It is not by accident that we *seek* happiness, but rather is a consequence of our incompleteness and finitude. It is no accident that we can find happiness only in God, since we were made by God to find happiness only in God. Augustine elaborates on this aspect of human nature through the theory of love.

The Role of Love

According to Augustine, we inevitably love. To love is to go beyond ourselves and to fasten our affection on an object of love. It is again our incompleteness that prompts us to love. There is a wide range of objects that we can choose to love, reflecting the variety of ways in which we are incomplete. We can love (1) physical objects, (2) other persons, or even (3) ourselves. All of these things will provide us with some measure of satisfaction and happiness. Further, in some sense, all of these things are legitimate objects of love since nothing is evil in itself—as we've seen, evil is not a positive thing but the absence of something. Our moral problem consists not so much in loving or even in the objects of our love. The real issue is the *manner* in which we attach ourselves to these objects of love and our *expectations* regarding the outcome of this love. Everyone expects to achieve happiness and fulfillment from love, yet we are miserable, unhappy, and restless. Why? Augustine lays the blame on "disordered" love—that is, the fact that we love specific things more than we should and, at the same time, fail to devote our ultimate love to God.

Evil and Disordered Love   Augustine believed that we have different human needs that prompt different acts of love. There is in fact some sort of correlation between various human needs and the objects that can satisfy them. Love is the act that harmonizes these needs and their objects. In addition to the worldly needs that prompt our love of objects, other people, and ourselves, we also have a spiritual need that should prompt our love of God. Augustine formulates this point in somewhat quantitative terms. Each object of love can give only so much satisfaction and no more. Each of the person's needs likewise has a measurable quantity. Clearly, satisfaction and happiness require that an object of love contain a sufficient amount of whatever it takes to fulfill or satisfy the particular need. Thus, we love food and we consume a quantity proportionate to our hunger. But our needs are not all physical in that primary sense. We love objects of art too for the aesthetic satisfaction that they give. At a higher level we have the need for love between persons. Indeed, this level of affection provides quantitatively and qualitatively more in the way of pleasure and happiness than love of mere physical things can. From this it becomes clear that certain human needs cannot be met by an interchange of objects. For example, our deep need for human companionship cannot be met in any other way than by a relationship with another person. Things can't be a substitute for a person because things do not contain within themselves the unique ingredients of a human personality.

Accordingly, although each thing is a legitimate object of love, we must not expect more from it than its unique nature can provide. But this is particularly the case with our spiritual need. People were made, says Augustine, to love God, and God is infinite. In some way, then, we were made so that only God, the infinite, can give us ultimate satisfaction or happiness. "When," says Augustine, "the will which is the intermediate good, cleaves to the immutable good . . . people find therein the blessed life," for "to live well is nothing else but to love God." To love God, then, is the indispensable requirement for happiness, because only God, who is infinite, can satisfy that peculiar need in us that is precisely the need for the infinite. If objects are not interchangeable—if, for example, things cannot substitute for a person—neither can any finite thing or person substitute for God. Yet we all confidently expect that we can achieve true happiness by confining our love to objects, other people, and ourselves. While these are all legitimate objects of love in a limited way, our love of them is disordered when we love them for the sake of ultimate happiness. Disordered love consists in expecting more from an object of love than it is capable of providing, and this produces all kinds of pathology in human behavior. Normal self-love becomes pride, and pride is the cardinal sin that affects all aspects of our conduct. The essence of pride is the assumption of self-sufficiency.

Yet the permanent fact about human nature is precisely that we are not self-sufficient, neither physically, emotionally, nor spiritually. Our pride, which turns us away from God, leads us to many forms of overindulgence, since we try to satisfy an infinite need with finite entities. We therefore love things more than we should in relation to what they can do for themselves. Our love for another person can become virtually destructive of the other person, since we try again to derive from that relationship more than it can possibly give. Appetites flourish, passions multiply, and there is a desperate attempt to achieve peace by satisfying all desires. We become seriously disordered and then exhibit envy, greed, jealousy, trickery, panic, and a pervading restlessness. It does not take long for disordered love to produce a disordered person, and disordered people produce a disordered community. No attempt to reconstruct an orderly, peaceful community or household is possible without reconstructing each human being. The rigorous and persistent fact is that personal reconstruction and salvation are possible only by reordering love, that is, by loving the proper things properly. Indeed, Augustine argued that we can love a person properly only if we love God first, for then we will not expect to derive from human love what can be derived only from our love of God. Similarly, we can love ourselves properly only as we subordinate ourselves to God, for there is no other way to overcome the destructive consequences of pride than by eliminating pride itself.

Free Will as the Cause of Evil

Augustine did not agree with Plato that the cause of evil is simply ignorance. There are indeed some circumstances in which we do not know the ultimate good, and thus are not aware of God. Still, Augustine says that "even the ungodly" have the capacity to "blame and rightly praise things in the conduct of people." The overriding fact is that in daily conduct we understand praise and blame only because we already understand that we have an obligation to do what is praiseworthy and to abstain from what is blameworthy. Under these circumstances our predicament is not that we are ignorant but that we stand in the presence of alternatives. We must choose to turn toward God or away from God. We are, in short, free. Whichever way we choose, it is with the hope of finding happiness. We are capable of directing our affections exclusively toward finite things, other people, or ourselves, and thereby away from God. Augustine says that "this turning away and this turning to are not forced but voluntary acts."

According to Augustine, evil, or sin, is a product of the will. It is not, as Plato said, ignorance, nor, as the Manichaeans said, the work of the principle of darkness permeating the body. In spite of the fact of original sin, we still possess freedom of the will. This freedom (*liberum*) of the will is not, however, the same as spiritual freedom (*libertas*), for true spiritual liberty is no longer possible in its fullness in this life. We now use free will to choose wrongly. But, Augustine argues, even when we choose rightly, we do not possess the spiritual power to do the good we have chosen. We must have the help of God's grace. Whereas evil is caused by an act of free will, virtue is the product not of our will but of God's grace. The moral law tells us what we must do, but in the end it really shows us what we can't do on our own. Hence, Augustine concludes that "the law was . . . given that grace might be sought; grace was given that the law might be fulfilled."

JUSTICE

For Augustine public or political life is under the same rule of moral law as is a person's individual or personal life. There is a single source of truth for both realms, and this truth he considered "entire, inviolate and not subject to changes in human life." All people recognize this truth and know it as natural law or natural justice. Augustine considered natural law to be our intellectual sharing in God's truth, that is, God's *eternal law*. Augustine's notion of *eternal law* had been anticipated by the Stoics when they spoke of the diffusion of the principle of reason throughout all of nature. As such, they ascribed to this reason the role and power of ruling everything. Their theory was that mind (*nous*), the principle of reason, constituted the laws of nature. Whereas the Stoics, then, considered the laws of nature to be the working of the *impersonal* force of rational principles in the universe, Augustine interpreted the eternal law as the reason and will of a personal God. He writes, "Eternal law is the divine reason and the will of God which commands the maintenance (observance) of the natural order of things and which forbids the disturbance of it." Since *eternal law* is God's reason commanding orderliness, our intellectual grasp of the eternal principles is called *natural law*. When a political state makes a law, Augustine said, such temporal laws must be in accord with the principle of natural law, which in turn is derived from eternal law.

Augustine's chief argument regarding law and justice was that the political state is not autonomous and that, in making laws, the state does not merely express its power to legislate. Thus, the state must also follow the requirements of justice. Justice is a standard, moreover, that precedes the state and is eternal. What made Augustine's argument unique was his novel interpretation of the meaning of justice. He accepted Plato's formula that "justice is a virtue distributing to every one his due." But, he asked, what is "due" to anyone? He rejected the notion that justice is a matter of custom that differs in each society. For him we discover justice in the structure of human nature with its relation to God. Hence, he said that justice is "the habit of the soul which imparts to every person the dignity due him. . . . Its origin proceeds from nature . . . and this notion of justice . . . is not the product of personal opinion, but something implanted by a certain innate power." To require the state to follow such a standard was obviously to place heavy moral limitations on political power. Indeed, Augustine argued that if the laws of the state were out of harmony with natural law and justice, they would not have the character of laws, nor would there be a state.

By relating justice to moral law, Augustine argued that justice is not limited merely to the relations between people. The primary relationship in justice is between a person and God: "If people do not serve God what justice can be thought to be in them?" Moreover, collective justice is impossible apart from this individual justice, for "if this justice is not found in one person, no more then can it be found in a whole multitude of such like people. Therefore, among such there is not that consent of law which makes a multitude of people just." To serve God is to love God, but this means also to love our fellow human. All of ethics, then, is based on our love for God and love for other people. Love is the basis of justice.

Augustine believed that, according to God's law, religion is in a position of superiority over political institutions. Nevertheless, he did concede to the state the right to use coercive force. Indeed, the state is the product of the sinful condition of human nature and, therefore, exists as a necessary agency of control. Even so, Augustine would never concede that the principle of force was higher than the principle of love. For he says that

> a society cannot be ideally founded unless upon the basis and by the hand of faith and strong concord, where the object of love is the universal good which in its highest and truest character is God Himself and where people love one another with complete sincerity in Him, and the ground of their love for one another is the love of Him from whose eyes they cannot conceal the spirit of love.

The earthly state has an important function, even though its force cannot match the creative power of love. Specifically, the state's action can at least mitigate some evils: "When the power to do harm is taken from the bad people, they will carry themselves in a more controlled manner."

HISTORY AND THE TWO CITIES

Augustine made the love of God the central principle of morality. He also accounted for evil by his theory of disordered love. From this he concluded that the human race can be divided between those who love God, on the one hand, and those who love themselves and the world, on the other. Since there are two basically different kinds of love, there are, then, two opposing societies. Those who love God Augustine called the *City of God*, and those who love self and the world he called the *City of the World*.

Augustine did not consider these two cities to be identical with church and state, respectively. Having stressed that the decisive element in the formation of a society is the dominant love of its members, he pointed out that those who love the world are found both in the state and in the church. It does not follow that the church contains the whole society called the City of God. Similarly, there are in the state those who love God. These two cities therefore cut across both church and state and have an independence of them in an invisible way. Hence, wherever those people are who love God, there will be the City of God, and wherever there are those who love the world, there will be the City of the World.

Within the conflict between the two cities, Augustine saw the clue to a philosophy of history. What he meant by a *philosophy* of history was that history has meaning. The early Greek historians saw no pattern in human events other than, perhaps, the fact that kingdoms rise and fall and that there are cycles of repetition. Aristotle, you will recall, argued that history is hardly capable of teaching people any important knowledge about human nature. Unlike drama, according to Aristotle, history deals with individual people, nations, and events, whereas drama deals with universal conditions and problems. But Augustine thought that the greatest drama of all is human history. This is in large part because the author of history is God. History begins with creation and is interspersed with important events, such as the fall of humanity and the incarnation of God. History is now involved in a tension between the City of God and the City of the World. Nothing happens without reference to God's ultimate providence. Augustine thought that this was particularly so with the political events of his own day.

When the barbarian Goths sacked Rome in 410, many non-Christians laid the blame on Christians, saying that their excessive emphasis on loving and serving God had the effect of diluting patriotism and weakening the defenses of the state. To answer such charges and many others, Augustine wrote his book *The City of God* in 413. In it he argued that the fall of Rome was due not to the subversive activities of the Christians but, on the contrary, to the rampant vice throughout the Empire, which the Christian faith and love of God could have prevented. The fall of Rome was for Augustine just another example of God's purposeful intrusion into history, whereby he sought to establish the City of God and restrain the City of the World. Augustine believed that we all can find relevance in the drama of history, since our human destinies are inevitably linked with the two cities and with the activity of God. There is an all-embracing destiny for human beings and the world, and it will be achieved in God's good time and when the love of God reigns. With these views Augustine took what he considered otherwise random people and events and supplied them with a comprehensive meaning, a "philosophy of history."

CHAPTER 7

Philosophy in the Early Middle Ages

The fall of the Roman Empire in 476 ushered in a period of intellectual darkness. The barbarians who destroyed the political might of Rome also shattered the institutions of culture in Western Europe. Learning almost came to a halt, as virtually the whole body of ancient literature was lost. For the next five or six centuries, philosophy was kept alive by Christian scholars who became the channels through which the works of the ancient Greeks were transmitted to the West. Three early and influential thinkers were Boethius, Pseudo-Dionysius, and John Scotus Erigena.

In the ninth century King Charlemagne of the Holy Roman Empire aggressively attempted to revive classical learning. And with the appearance of Erigena's large-scale and systematic work *The Division of Nature*, we might have expected philosophy to emerge from this intellectually suppressed period and flourish once again throughout Western Europe. This early promise of continued revival was delayed, however, by several historical events. After Charlemagne's death, the Empire splintered into feudal divisions. The papacy entered a period of moral and spiritual weakness, and the monasteries exerted no effective leadership in their special province of education and learning. Invasions by the Mongols, Saracens, and Norsemen added to these forces, making for cultural darkness. For almost a hundred years, during most of the 900s, very little philosophical activity was carried on. But philosophy did revive in the next century, and from about 1000 to 1200, it focused on the issues of universals, proofs for God's existence, and the relation between faith and reason. In the discussion of these issues, several sources of philosophy were tapped, joining together Greek, Christian, Jewish, and Muslim thought.

BOETHIUS

Boethius's Life

One of the most prominent philosophic figures in the early Middle Ages was Anicius Manlius Severinus Boethius (ca. 480–524), of Rome and Pavia, Italy. He grew up in the kingdom of Theodoric as a Christian. At an early age he was sent to Athens, where he mastered the Greek language and encountered Aristotelianism, Neoplatonism, and Stoicism. Later, in 510, he was elevated to the position of consul in the court of Theodoric and was eventually showered with honors. In spite of his fame and his impressive political status, he was suspected of high treason, stripped of his honors, subjected to a long imprisonment, and finally, in 524, executed. Boethius became the most important channel through which Greek thought, especially some of Aristotle's works, was transmitted to the West in the early Middle Ages. Being an accomplished student of the Greek language, Boethius originally intended to translate the works of Plato and Aristotle into Latin and to show how their apparent differences could be harmonized. Although he did not accomplish this ambitious project, he did leave a considerable legacy of philosophical writings, consisting of translations of some of Aristotle's works and commentaries on these works and others by Porphyry and Cicero. In addition to these he wrote theological works and treatises on each of four liberal arts, namely, arithmetic, geometry, astronomy, and music. To these four disciplines he gave the name *quadrivium* to distinguish them from the other three liberal arts, the *trivium*, consisting of grammar, logic, and rhetoric. In his original treatises Boethius drew on a wide variety of authors, showing his familiarity with Plato, Aristotle, the Stoics, Plotinus, Augustine, and others, though clearly the dominant influence was Aristotle. His works achieved the status of classics and were later used by leading philosophers, including Thomas Aquinas, as authoritative guides for interpreting ancient authors and basic philosophical problems.

The Consolation of Philosophy

During his imprisonment, in Pavia, Boethius wrote his famous work *The Consolation of Philosophy*, which was widely circulated in the Middle Ages and had such lasting influence that Chaucer translated it and patterned some of his *Canterbury Tales* on its contents. The work is a dialogue between himself and a personification of philosophy, ranging over the subjects of God, fortune, freedom, and evil. In the early pages of this book, Boethius offers an allegorical description of philosophy, which can still be seen carved on the facades of many cathedrals in Europe. What led him to see philosophy in these allegorical terms was his attempt to overcome his melancholy by writing poetry as he languished in prison. At this point he was struck by a new vision of philosophy, which he set down with considerable imaginative force. Philosophy came to him as a noblewoman with eyes of such keenness as to suggest that philosophy has powers higher than human nature. She gives the impression of having no specific age, indicating that philosophy is perennial. On her robe appear the Greek letters phi (Φ), symbolizing practical philosophy, and theta (θ), symbolizing theoretical philosophy, and a ladder between them shows the ascent on the steps to wisdom. Boethius is consoled by philosophy when he discovers from it that no earthly goods and pleasures can give him true happiness, that he must turn to the Supreme Good to which philosophy leads. But in addition to this allegorical interpretation, Boethius formulated a more technical definition of philosophy, calling it the "love of wisdom." The word *wisdom* carried the whole freight of his definition. To Boethius *wisdom* meant a reality, something that exists in itself. Wisdom is the living thought that causes all things. In loving wisdom, we love the thought and cause of all things. In the end the love of wisdom is the love of God. In his *Consolation* he makes no mention of Christianity but rather formulates a natural theology based on what unaided human reason can provide.

The Problem of Universals

The problem of universals, by no means a new one, struck medieval thinkers as fundamental, because in their judgment the enterprise of thought rested to a great extent on its solution. The central issue in this problem is how to relate the objects of human thought and the objects that exist outside the mind. Objects outside the mind are individual and many, whereas objects in the mind are single or universal. For example, in normal discourse we use words such as *tree* or *person*, but such words refer to the actual and particular trees and people that we observe with our senses. To *see* a tree is one thing; to *think* it is quite another. We see particulars but we think universals. When we see a particular thing, we place it into either a species or a genus. We never see *tree* or *person*, only "this oak" or "John." *Tree* stands in our language for all the actual trees—oak, elm, and so on—whereas *person* includes John, Jane, and every other specific person. What, then, is the relation between these general words and these specific trees and people? Is the word "tree" *only* a word, or does it refer to something that exists someplace? If the word *tree* refers to something in this specific oak that belongs to all trees, the word refers to something universal. The universal, then, is a general term, but the objects that exist outside of our minds are single or particular and specific. If the universal is merely an idea in our minds, what is the connection between the way we think, on the one hand, and the actual particular objects outside our minds, on the other? How does my mind go about forming a universal concept? Is there anything *outside* my mind corresponding to the universal idea *in* my mind?

Boethius translated Porphyry's *Introduction to Aristotle's Categories*. There he found a discussion of the problem of universals in terms of certain questions raised by Porphyry. These questions centered on the relation between generic and specific notions. What, in short, is the relation between genera and specific objects? Porphyry raised these three questions: (1) Do genera really exist in nature, or are they merely constructions of our minds? (2) If they are realities, are they material or immaterial? and (3) Do they exist apart from sensible things or somehow in them? While Porphyry did not answer his own questions, Boethius formulated a solution chiefly in terms of Aristotle's approach to the problem.

Boethius was aware of the immense difficulty of the problem. If the issue is to discover whether human thought conforms to realities outside our minds, we can quickly discover some ideas in our minds for which there is no corresponding external object. We can think of a centaur, but such a combination of human and horse does not exist. Or, again, we can think of a line, the way a geometer does. But we do not find this kind of line existing as such anywhere. What is the difference between the idea of the centaur and of the line? We can say about the concept of the centaur that it is *false*, whereas the concept of the line is *true*. What Boethius wants to illustrate here is that there are two fundamentally different ways in which we form concepts, namely, by *composition* (putting together horse and human) and by *abstraction* (drawing from a particular object some of its predicates). He wanted to say that universal ideas, such as genera, are abstracted by the mind from actual individual things and are, therefore, *true* ideas.

Saying that universals are abstracted from individuals led Boethius to conclude that genera exist *in* the individual things and that they become universals when we *think* of them. In this way universals are simultaneously in the object and in our minds—*subsisting* in the thing and *thought about* in our minds. Such universals include not only genera, to which Boethius limited his analysis, but also other qualities such as *just, good,* and *beautiful*. What makes two trees both trees is that, as objects, they resemble each other because they contain a universal foundation to their being. At the same time, we can *think* of them both as trees because our minds discover the same universal element in both of them. This, then, was Boethius's way of answering the first question, namely, whether universals exist in nature or only in our minds. For him they exist both in things and in our minds. To the second question—whether universals are material or immaterial—he could now say that they exist both concretely in things and immaterially or abstractly in our minds. Similarly, his reply to the third question—whether universals exist apart from individual objects or are realized in them—was that they exist both in things and apart from them in our minds.

PSEUDO-DIONYSIUS

Around 500 BCE a collection of Neoplatonic writings circulated in Western Europe, which were attributed to a first-century disciple of the Apostle Paul named Dionysius the Areopagite. However, since these writings embody ideas developed by a much later thinker, Proclus (ca. 410–485), scholars now believe that they were probably written in Syria close to 500 CE, and that the author used a pseudonym. Accordingly, these works are now associated with the name "Pseudo-Dionysius." The treatises of Pseudo-Dionysius attempt to relate Christian thought systematically to Neoplatonic philosophy. These works consist of *The Divine Names, The Celestial Hierarchy, The Ecclesiastical Hierarchy, The Mystical Theology,* and also ten letters. They were all translated into Latin frequently, and several commentaries were written on them. The influence of Dionysius was substantial throughout the Middle Ages, and philosophers and theologians concerned with quite different problems made considerable use of his writings. The mystics drew heavily on his elaborate theory of the hierarchy of beings, since it afforded a rich source for describing the ascent of the soul to God. Aquinas used his theories in accounting for the great chain of being and the analogical relation between human beings and God. Above all, Dionysius was one of the most powerful sources of Neoplatonism, influencing philosophical thought regarding the origin of the world, the knowledge of God, and the nature of evil.

Knowledge of God

Dionysius gave an account of the relation of the world to God in which he combined the Neoplatonic theory of *emanation* and the Christian doctrine of *creation*. He wanted to avoid the pantheism embedded in Neoplatonic theory, according to which all things are emanations from God. At the same time, he wanted to establish that whatever exists comes from God, though he apparently had no clear conception of God's creative act as an act of free will. Nevertheless, Dionysius argued that the world is the object of God's providence. God has placed between himself and human beings a virtual ladder or hierarchy of beings called *heavenly spirits*. From the lowest level of being to the highest, where God is at the peak, there are various degrees of being. Dionysius indeed came close to pantheism and monism because of this continuous scale or chain of being, which he sometimes described as a shaft of light. Still, he countered this with a pluralistic view of things. God is the goal of all created things. He attracts all things to himself by his goodness and the love he inspires.

Dionysius held that we can come to a knowledge of God in two ways: a *positive* way and a *negative* way. When we take the positive way, we ascribe to God all the perfect attributes discovered by a study of creatures. In this way we can give the *divine* such names as *goodness, light, being, unity, wisdom,* and *life*. Dionysius said that these names belong in their perfection to God and only in a derivative sense to human beings, depending upon the degree to which the creature participates in these perfections. Dionysius thought that these attributes existed in God in a very literal sense, since surely God *is* goodness, life, wisdom, and so on. By contrast, humans have these to a lesser degree. Still, God and human beings are more alike than God and, say, a stone, since we cannot about a stone that it is good, wise, and alive.

Although we do gain knowledge of God through this positive way, Dionysius held that the *negative* way was more important. Dionysius was aware that people unavoidably develop anthropomorphic conceptions of God, and for this reason he undertook to remove from God all the attributes of creatures. It was obvious to him that what characterized God was precisely that he did not have the attributes of finite creatures. Step by step he removed from the conception of God all the things we say about creatures. In the negative way we consider God's nature by denying of God whatever seems least compatible with him, such as "drunkenness and fury." Then, by a process of "remotion," we remove various categories of attributes from our conception of God. Since all we know is the world of creatures, the negative process of "remotion" leads us not to a clear conception of God but only to a "darkness of unknowing." The only positive aspect of this approach is that we are assured of knowing what God is *not* like. Because God is no object, he is beyond the knowable. This view had a great influence on later mystics, who believed that as people ascended closer to God, the ordinary forms of human knowledge were annihilated by the blindness caused by the excess of God's light.

In Neoplatonic terms Dionysius denied the positive existence of *evil*. If evil was something positive and had some substantial being, we would be forced to trace it back to God as its cause, since all being is from God. For Dionysius existence and goodness are identical terms, for whatever is, is good, and if something is good, it obviously must first exist. In God goodness and being are one, and therefore, whatever comes from God is good. The corollary of this, though, is not necessarily true, namely, that evil is synonymous with nonbeing. Still, the absence of being amounts to evil because it means the absence of good. Evil people are good in all the ways in which they possess positive being but are evil in whatever respect they are lacking some form of being, particularly in the operation of their wills. Ugliness and disease in physical nature are called evil for the same reason that acts in the province of morality are, namely, because they suffer deficiency in form or the absence of some being. Blindness is the absence of light and not the presence of some evil force.

ERIGENA

Erigena's Life

Three centuries passed from the time of Boethius and Pseudo-Dionysius before another philosopher of stature appeared in the West. He was a remarkable Irish monk, John Scotus Erigena, who produced the first full-scale philosophical system in the Middle Ages. Born in Ireland in 810, he studied in a monastery and was one of the few scholars of his day who mastered Greek. By any standard Erigena was an unusually able Greek scholar, and given the philosophical material at his disposal at that time, his systematic writing set him apart as the most impressive thinker of his century.

Erigena left Ireland and appeared in the court of Charles the Bald on the Continent around 851. His studies at this time were devoted chiefly to Latin authors, especially Augustine and Boethius, on whose *The Consolation of Philosophy* he wrote a commentary. At the request of Charles the Bald, Erigena translated the Greek texts of Pseudo-Dionysius into Latin in 858 and in addition wrote commentaries on these texts. He also translated works by the earlier theologians Maximus the Confessor and Gregory of Nyssa. After this work of translation, Erigena produced his celebrated treatise on *The Division of Nature*, a book written in dialogue form around 864. In this work Erigena undertook the complicated task of expressing Christian thought and Augustine's philosophical views in terms of the Neoplatonism of Pseudo-Dionysius. Although it became a landmark in medieval thought, it attracted little attention from Erigena's contemporaries. Various later writers appealed to this book to corroborate unorthodox theories, such as pantheism. This led Pope Honorius III to condemn Erigena's *The Division of Nature* on January 25, 1225, and order it to be burned. In spite of this, several manuscript copies have survived down to the present.

The Division of Nature

The complicated argument of Erigena's *The Division of Nature* revolves around his special understanding of the two key words in the title of his book. First, by

nature Erigena meant "everything there is." In this sense nature includes both
God and creatures. Second, when he talks about the *division* of nature, he has in
mind the ways in which the whole of reality—God and creatures—is divided.
In addition, the word *division* has a special meaning. Erigena says that there
are two ways of understanding the structure of reality—one by *division* and the
other by *analysis*. By *division* he means moving from the more universal to the
less universal, as when we divide *substance* into *corporeal* and *incorporeal*. In turn,
incorporeal can be divided into *living* and *inanimate,* and so on. On the other hand,
by *analysis* the process of division is reversed, and the elements divided off from
substance are worked back into the unity of substance. Underlying Erigena's
method of division and analysis was his conviction that our minds work in
accordance with metaphysical realities. Our minds are not simply dealing with
concepts when we "divide" and "analyze"; we are describing how things really
exist and behave. If God is the ultimate unity, then things and the world are
divisions of this basic unity, and analysis is the process by which things return
to God. The laws of thought, according to Erigena, parallel the laws of reality.

With these distinctions in mind, Erigena argued that there is only one true
reality and that all other things depend on it and return to it; this reality is God.
Within the total reality of nature, a fourfold division is possible: (1) nature that
creates and is not created, (2) nature that is created and creates, (3) nature that
is created and does not create, and (4) nature that neither creates nor is created.

Nature That Creates and Is Not Created   By this Erigena meant God, who
is the cause of all things but does not himself need to be caused. He brought
all creatures into existence out of nothing. Following the distinction made by
Pseudo-Dionysius, our knowledge of God is *negative*. This is because none of
the attributes we derive from objects in our experience apply in any proper
sense to God, who possesses all the perfections in his infinity. To make sure
that not even the likely attributes of wisdom and truth are ascribed to God
without qualification, Erigena adds the term *super* to them. We thus would say
about God that he is superwisdom and supertruth. None of Aristotle's predicates or categories applies to God, for these predicates assume some form of
substance—as, for example, "quantity" implies dimension—but God does not
exist in a definable place. Erigena discusses several issues along Augustinian
lines, such as God's nature and the notion of creation out of nothing. But as he
pursues the subject of the relation between God and creatures, his Neoplatonism
seems to become dominant, and it is difficult to avoid the conclusion that for
Erigena there is no sharp distinction between God and creatures. "When we
hear that God made all things," says Erigena, "we should understand nothing
else but that God is in all things." This follows because only God "truly is," and
therefore, whatever is in anything is God.

Nature That Is Created and Creates   This division refers to the divine Forms,
which become the prototypes of all created things. They are the *exemplary causes*
of all the created species. To say that they are *created* does not mean, according
to Erigena, that they come to be at some point in time. He has in mind a logical

and not a chronological sequence. In God there is the full knowledge of everything, including the primordial causes of all things. These primordial causes are the divine Forms and prototypes of things, and they *create* in the sense that all creatures "participate" in them. For example, human wisdom participates in superwisdom. Though he uses the word *creation* here, his Neoplatonism once again dominates, particularly since creation for Erigena does not occur in time but is an eternal relation between God's Forms and creatures.

Nature That Is Created and Does not Create   This is the world of things as we experience it. Technically, it refers to the collective external effects of the primordial causes. These effects, whether incorporeal (such as angels or intelligence) or corporeal (such as people and things), are *participations* in the divine Forms. Erigena emphasizes that these things—this full range or hierarchy of beings—contain God as their essence, even though specific things give the impression of being individual. He compares this apparent plurality of things to the many varied reflections of light on the feathers of a peacock. Each color is a real one, but it depends on the feathers, and therefore, in the end, the color is not an independent reality. In the created world each individual is real by virtue of its primordial cause, which is in God's mind. But God is, if anything, a unity, and to speak of Forms, prototypes, and archetypes in his mind is to speak metaphorically, since these all constitute a unity. For this reason the world is also a unity, like the peacock's feathers, and there is also more comprehensive unity between the world and God, since God is in everything. For Erigena, then, the divine *Forms* stand midway between God and creatures, as though they could look "up" toward God and "down" toward these externalized forms. But in the end his Neoplatonism leads him to erase the spaces between the *Forms* and God and creatures, fusing them all into a unity and eventually a pantheism.

Nature That Neither Creates nor Is Created   This last division refers to God again, this time as the goal or end of the created order. As all things proceed from God, they also all return to God. Using Aristotle's metaphor, Erigena compares God to a beloved who, without moving, attracts the lover. Whatever starts from a principle returns again to this same principle, and in this way the universal cause draws to itself the multitude of things that have risen from it. With this return there is an end to all evil, and people find their union with God.

NEW SOLUTIONS TO THE PROBLEM OF UNIVERSALS

As we have seen, the medieval problem of universals was first formulated by Porphyry and answered by Boethius. It came under discussion almost 500 years later and precipitated a vigorous debate for centuries to come. Although the issues were formulated in relatively restricted and seemingly unimportant terms, the participants saw serious theological as well as philosophical consequences hinging on the outcome of the debate. At least three major approaches were developed to this problem of universals: exaggerated realism, nominalism, and conceptualism.

Odo and Guillaume: Exaggerated Realism

The problem of universals eventually resolved itself into the simple question of whether a universal is a real *thing* or not. Those who said universals were in fact real things were known as *exaggerated realists*. These people said that genera exist in reality and that individual things *share* in these universals. However, they did not go as far as Plato, who said that the universals were Forms and existed separately from individual things. Rather, the realists said, for example, that *humanity* exists but that it exists in the plurality of human beings.

Why should this form of realism seem such an important matter? We find one answer in the works of Odo of Taurnai, a notable thinker who taught in the Cathedral School of Tours, founded the Abbey of St. Martin, was bishop of Cambrai, and died in the monastery at Anchin in 1113. For him realism was the foundation of certain traditional theological doctrines. For example, the doctrine of original sin, according to him, requires the realistic description of human nature. Realism says that there exists a universal substance, which is contained in every member of a species. If we are to understand the condition of human nature accurately, he said, we must realize that in the sin of Adam and Eve the universal substance of *humanity* was infected so that all subsequent generations have inherited the consequences of their acts. If we deny realism, then what Adam and Eve did would pertain only to themselves, in which case the force of the concept of original sin would be lost.

Another exaggerated realist was Guillaume de Champeaux (1070–1121), who formulated two different views. First, in his *identity* theory he held that the universal—say, *humanity*—is identical in all members, in this case in all people. The *whole* reality of the universal is contained in each person. What differentiates Jane and John is merely certain secondary or accidental modifications of their essence or substance. Abelard (1079–1142) ridiculed this line of reasoning by saying that if each person is the whole human species, then humanity exists in Socrates in Rome and in Plato in Athens. If Socrates is present wherever the human essence is found, and since it is in both Rome and Athens, Socrates must be at the same moment in Rome and in Athens. And this, said Abelard, not only is absurd but leads to pantheism. Guillaume was forced by this and other criticisms to adopt a second theory, that of *indifferentism*, an antirealist view. According to his new view, the individuals of a species are the same thing not through some common essence but because in certain respects they are not different; that is, they are *indifferent*.

Roscellinus: Nominalism

One of the most formidable critics of exaggerated realism was Roscellinus (or Roscelin), who was born in Compiègne and traveled to England, Rome, and Tours. He taught at Taches, Compiègne, and Besançon, and was a teacher of Abelard. His central argument was that only individuals exist in nature. Genera are not real things. A general term such as humanity does not refer to anything; it is only a word (*voces*), or a name (*nomen*), composed of letters and expressed as a *vocal emission*, and therefore only air. For this reason discussions about universals are about words and not real things. Roscellinus was willing to draw certain obvious conclusions from his argument, particularly that the three persons of the Trinity are three separate beings and that they have in common a word but nothing really essential; hence, they can be considered three Gods. For these views he was accused by the Council at Soissons (1092) of tritheism, and when he was threatened with excommunication, he denied this doctrine. In spite of this denial, Roscellinus served a decisive function in the history of the problem of universals. Specifically, he rejected exaggerated realism and the attempt to make universals into a thing.

Abelard: Conceptualism or Moderate Realism

Roscellinus seemed to be as extreme in his nominalism as others had been in their realism. Both, though, were exaggerated views. Avoiding both of these extremes was the position developed by Peter Abelard, who was born in Le Pallet in 1079 of a military family. During his tempestuous life he quarreled with his teachers, had a celebrated romance with Heloïse, was abbott of the monastery in Brittany, was a famous lecturer in Paris, was condemned for his heretical teachings by Innocent II, and finally retired to Cluny, where he died in 1142.

On the problem of universals, Abelard said that universality must be ascribed principally to words. A word is *universal* when it is applied to many individuals. The word *Socrates* is not universal because it applies only to one person, whereas the word *humanity* is universal because it can be applied to all people. The function of a universal term, Abelard says, is to denote individual things in a special way. The question, then, is how it comes about that we formulate these universal terms. To this Abelard answers that certain individual things, because of the *way* they exist, cause anyone observing them to *conceive* a likeness in all these individuals. This so-called likeness is not what the realists called an essence or substance. It consists simply in the way things agree in likeness. When we experience an individual, we *see* it but also *think* or *understand* it. Unlike the eye, which requires an object, the mind does not require a physical object since it can form *conceptions*. Thus, our minds are capable of doing two things, namely, forming concepts of individuals, such as Plato or Socrates, and forming concepts of universals, such as *humanity*. The conception of the individual is clear, whereas the conception of the universal is blurred. We cannot clearly focus on the precise meaning of the universal even though we do in fact know what it means. As conceptions of the mind, universals exist apart from the individual sensible bodies; but as words applied to those individuals, they exist only in these bodies. The same word can be applied commonly to several individuals because each individual already exists in such a way as to cause it to be conceived the way others like it are conceived. The universal is therefore abstracted from the individual. The process of abstraction tells us how we understand the universal but not how the universal subsists. We understand things properly insofar as we abstract from them those properties that they truly possess. Abelard concluded, therefore, that the universal is a word and concept representing some reality that supplies the ground for this concept. This ground is the way similar things exist and strike our minds. To this extent there is an objective ground for the universals, but this ground is not, as the realist held, something *real* in the sense of a *thing*. Nor would Abelard agree with the strict nominalist who would say that the universal is *only* a subjective idea or word for which there is no objective ground. Abelard's theory of universals carried the day, defeating the extremes of both realism and nominalism.

ANSELM'S ONTOLOGICAL ARGUMENT

Anselm is famous in the history of thought primarily for his proof of God's existence, which in recent centuries has been titled the "Ontological Argument." He was born in Piedmont in 1033, entered the Benedictine Order, and eventually became archbishop of Canterbury, where he died in 1109. For Anselm there was no clear line between philosophy and theology. Like Augustine before him, he was particularly concerned with providing rational support for the doctrines of Christianity, which he already accepted as a matter of faith. He was convinced that faith and reason lead to the same conclusions. Moreover, he believed that human reason can create a natural theology or metaphysics that is rationally coherent and does not depend on any authority other than rationality. This did not mean, however, that Anselm denied any connection between natural theology and faith. On the contrary, his view was that natural theology consists of giving a rational version of what is believed. In this he was thoroughly Augustinian, saying that he was not trying to *discover* the truth about God through reason alone but rather wanted to employ reason in order to *understand* what he was believing. His method, therefore, was *faith seeking understanding;* "I do not seek to understand in order that I may believe," he said, "but I believe in order that I may understand." He made it particularly clear that his enterprise of proving God's existence could not even have begun had he not already believed in God. Anselm conceded that his human mind could not penetrate the profundity of God. Nevertheless, from the rational proof of God's existence, Anselm had a limited expectation: "I desire only a little understanding of the truth which my heart believes and loves."

Anselm's Realism

Before he composed the Ontological Argument, which appears in his book titled *Proslogion*, Anselm formulated three other arguments in an earlier work called *Monologion*. These three arguments show his overall philosophical orientation, namely, his acceptance of *realism* and his rejection of *nominalism*. His realism comes out in his belief that words are not simply sounds or grammatical conventions but stand for real things outside of our minds. Stated briefly, his three early arguments are these. First, people seek to enjoy what they consider *good*. Since we can compare things with each other as being *more* or *less* good, these things must share in one and the same goodness. This goodness must be good-in-itself and as such is the supreme good. One could use the same argument as applied to *greatness*. There must, therefore, be something that is the best and greatest of all. Second, everything that exists, exists either through something or through nothing. Obviously, it cannot come out of nothing. The only alternative, then, is to say that a thing is caused either by something else or by itself. It cannot be caused by itself because before it is, it is nothing. To say that it is caused by something else could mean that things cause each other, which is also absurd. There must, therefore, be one thing that alone is from itself and that causes all other things to be, and this is God. Third, there are various *degrees* or *levels* of being, whereby animals have a higher being than plants, and people have a higher being than animals. Using a line of reasoning similar to the first argument, Anselm concluded that as we moved up through a number of levels, we must arrive at a *highest* and most perfect being, than which there is none more perfect.

All three of these arguments start from an existing finite thing and move up through a hierarchy until they reach the peak of the scale of being. Again, Anselm's realism is evident here, as is the influence of Plato and Augustine. He assumes throughout that when a finite thing shares in what our language calls *good, great, cause,* or *being,* these words refer to some existing reality. Finite things therefore share not only in a *word* but in *being,* which somewhere exists in maximum perfection. Like the exaggerated realists Odo and Guillaume, Anselm also felt that the issue of realism had important theological implications—particularly for the doctrine of the Trinity. If we denied that an identical substance exists in several members, then the Trinity would amount to tritheism, whereby each member is a totally separate and different being. According to Anselm, "He who does not understand how many men are specifically one only man cannot understand that several persons, each one of which is God, are one only God."

The Ontological Argument

Anselm was aware that his three arguments for God's existence did not have the clarity or power of a mathematical proof. Moreover, his fellow monks wondered whether he could simplify these arguments. Accordingly, after much thought on the matter, Anselm said that he had discovered a single, clear, and virtually flawless argument, which he published in the *Proslogion; or, Faith Seeking Understanding.* The first thing to notice about this proof is that Anselm's thought proceeds from within his mind, rather than starting with the assumption that each proof must begin with some empirical evidence from which the mind can then move logically to God. Anselm followed Augustine's doctrine of divine illumination, which gave him direct access to certain truths. Indeed, before beginning the ontological argument, Anselm asks the reader to "enter the inner chamber of your mind" and to "shut out all things save God and whatever may aid you in seeking God." Clearly, Anselm is assured of the existence of God before he begins, saying again that "unless I believe, I will not understand."

The argument itself moves swiftly. We believe, Anselm says, that God is "that than which nothing greater can be thought"—or, more simply, that God is the greatest conceivable being. The question, then, is whether the greatest conceivable being really exists. There are those who would deny God's existence. Anselm quotes Psalms 14:1, which says, "The fool has said in his heart: There is no God." What is meant by the word *fool* in this context? It means that a person who denies God's existence is involved in a flat contradiction. For when the fool hears the words "the greatest conceivable being," he understands what he hears, and what he understands can be said to be in his intellect. But it is one thing for something to be in the intellect; it is another to understand that something actually exists. A painter, for example, thinks in advance what she is about to portray. At this point, there is in her intellect an understanding of what she is about to make, though not an understanding that the portrait, which is still to be made, actually exists. But when she has finally painted it, she both has in her understanding and understands as existing the portrait she has finally made. What this proves, according to Anselm, is that something can be in our intellects even before we know it to exist. There is, then, in the fool's intellect an understanding of what is meant by the phrase "the greatest conceivable being," even though the fool does not yet necessarily understand that this being does in fact exist. It is in his intellect because when the fool hears this phrase, he understands it, and whatever we understand is thereby in our understanding. Hence, even the fool knows that there is at least in his intellect a greatest conceivable being.

This brings Anselm to the crux of his argument. We should ask ourselves which of these two conceptions is greater: (a) a "greatest conceivable being" that exists in reality or (b) a "greatest conceivable being" that exists only in our minds? The answer must be (a), since, according to Anselm, for any given being, real existence is greater than imaginary existence. Now, God is defined as "the greatest conceivable being." If God existed only in our minds, then he could be greater; that is, God would be "the greatest possible being that could be greater," and this is a contradiction in terms. Thus, to avoid contradiction, "the greatest conceivable being" must exist in reality. In a concluding prayer, Anselm thanks God "because through your divine illumination I now truly understand that which, through your generous gift, I formerly believed."

Gaunilon's Rebuttal

In the Abbey of Marmontier near Tours, another Benedictine monk, Gaunilon, came to the defense of the "fool." Gaunilon did not want to deny God's existence but only intended to argue that Anselm had not constructed an adequate proof. For one thing, Gaunilon argued that the first part of the "proof" is impossible to achieve. It requires that there be in the understanding an idea of God, that upon hearing this word the fool is expected to have a conception of "the greatest conceivable being." But, Gaunilon says, the fool cannot form a concept of such a being since there is nothing among other realities he experiences from which this concept can be formed. Indeed, Anselm himself already argued that there is no reality like God. Actually, if the human mind could form such a concept, no "proof" would be necessary, for we would then already connect existence with an aspect of a perfect being. Gaunilon's other major objection is that we often think of things that in fact do not exist. We can, for example, imagine "the greatest conceivable island," but there is no way to prove that such an island exists.

Anselm's Reply to Gaunilon

Anselm gave two replies. First, he said that we, along with the fool, are able to form a concept of "the greatest conceivable being." We do this whenever we compare different degrees of perfection in things and move upward to the maximum perfection, than which there is no more perfect. Second, he thought Gaunilon's reference to a perfect island showed that he had missed the point of the argument. The whole concept of a "greatest conceivable island" is conceptually flawed. This is because an "island" is by its very nature finite or limited; thus, it cannot exist in an infinite (or "greatest conceivable") manner. Only the concept of "being" can in fact rise above the limitations of finitude and thereby exist in the "greatest conceivable" manner. It is safe to say that Anselm is victorious on this point: There is no real parallel between inherently finite "islands" and potentially infinite "being." The Ontological Argument, then, survives Gaunilon's critique, and it was left to philosophers of later centuries to offer more convincing criticisms.

FAITH AND REASON IN MUSLIM AND JEWISH THOUGHT

Most of medieval thought is an attempt to reconcile the domains of philosophy and theology—that is, of reason and faith. The leading writers were Christians, who wrote philosophy mixing in theology. Their religious orientation stemmed from the mainstream of the Christian tradition and was therefore, for the most part, the same for all of them. Their philosophical orientations, however, were quite diverse, since at different times and at different places they were exposed to different philosophers. Even when they relied on the same philosopher—Aristotle, for example—they were exposed to different interpretations of his writings. Muslim philosophers were important in the Middle Ages since they produced influential commentaries on Aristotle, upon which many Christian writers depended for their understanding of that great philosopher. As it turned out, these Muslim interpretations of Aristotle were not only the source of much knowledge about Aristotle but also the cause of serious difficulties in harmonizing the domains of faith and reason.

Under the leadership of Muhammad (570–632), a vast Muslim Empire was established with cultural centers in Persia and Spain, where during the ninth through the twelfth centuries significant philosophical activity took place. During these centuries the Muslim world was far more advanced in its knowledge of Greek philosophy, science, and mathematics than was the Christian world. Moreover, the Muslim world had access to the chief works of Aristotle centuries before Western Europe finally received them. Many texts of the Greek philosophers had been translated into Arabic, from which later Latin translations were made in the West. By 833 philosophy was well established in Baghdad, where a school had been established for translating Greek manuscripts on philosophy and science, and for creative scholarship as well. A distinguished line of thinkers worked here, especially Avicenna (980–1037). The other focal point of Muslim culture was Cordova, Spain, where the other leading Muslim philosopher, Averroës (1126–1198), wrote much of his philosophy. Although Avicenna and Averroës wrote in Arabic and were Muslims, they were not Arabs. Avicenna was a Persian, and Averroës a Spaniard.

Avicenna and Averroës both wrote important commentaries on Aristotle's philosophy, and some Christian writers accepted these interpretations as the authentic views of Aristotle. Because these interpretations showed Aristotle to be at variance with Christian doctrine, some medieval writers, such as Bonaventura, thought it necessary to reject Aristotle to avoid errors. The significance of Muslim philosophers was therefore twofold in that they were transmitters of Aristotle and other Greek thinkers to the West and were also the authors of interpretations of Aristotle that became the basis of controversy in medieval philosophy.

Avicenna

Avicenna, born in Persia in 980, was a phenomenal scholar. He studied geometry, logic, jurisprudence, the Koran, physics, theology, and medicine, becoming a practicing physician at the age of 16. He was the author of many works, and although his thought centered on Aristotle, he shows some Neoplatonic influences as well as original formulations of problems.

Of particular importance was Avicenna's formulation of the doctrine of creation. Here he combined Aristotelian and Neoplatonic views and arrived at a theory that was hotly debated in the thirteenth century. Starting with a proof for God's existence, Avicenna maintains that whatever begins to exist (as is the case with everything that we experience) must have a cause. Things that require a cause are called *possible* beings. A cause that is also a *possible* being must be caused by a prior being. This too must have a cause, but there cannot be an infinite series of such causes. There must therefore be a First Cause, whose being is not simply *possible* but *necessary*, having its existence in itself and not from a cause, and this is God. Aquinas would later make much of this line of reasoning.

God is at the apex of Being, has no beginning, always is in act (that is, always expressing his full Being), and therefore has always created. According to Avicenna, then, creation is both necessary and eternal. This conclusion struck Bonaventura in the thirteenth century as a serious error and in conflict with the biblical notion of creation. According to Bonaventura, two chief features of creation are that it is a product of God's free will, not of necessity, and that creation occurred at a point in time, not from eternity.

If Avicenna's metaphysics caused Christian philosophers difficulties because of his doctrine of creation, his psychology caused even more serious concern. In his psychology, Avicenna wanted particularly to account for human intellectual activity. Central to his theory was the distinction between the *Possible Intellect* and the *Agent Intellect*. To account for this distinction, Avicenna employed his Neoplatonic view of the gradations of beings, placing people under the lowest level of angelic beings or Intelligences. That is, God creates a single effect, and this effect is called an *Intelligence*, the highest angel, but this Intelligence in turn creates a subordinate Intelligence. There are nine such Intelligences in descending order, each one creating (1) the one below it and (2) the soul of the successive sphere. The ninth Intelligence, then, creates the tenth and final Intelligence, and this is the Agent Intellect. It is the Agent Intellect that creates the four elements of the world and the individual souls of people. The Agent Intellect not only creates the souls or minds of people but also "radiates forms" to these created minds.

What Avicenna was saying is that since a person's mind has a beginning, it is a *possible* being; therefore, a person has a Possible Intellect. Here Avicenna made a sharp distinction between existence and essence, saying that there are two different things in creatures. That is, because my essence is distinct from my existence, my *essence* is not automatically fulfilled, and it is certainly not given existence by itself. The essence of the human mind is to know, but it does not always know. The intellect is capable of knowing, and its essence is to know; but its knowing is only *possible*. The intellect is actually created without any knowledge but with an essence or possibility for knowledge. The *existence* of knowledge in the human intellect requires two elements: (1) the bodily senses through which we perceive sensible objects externally and the powers of retaining images of objects in the memory or imagination internally, and (2) the ability to discover the essence or universal in individual things through the power of abstraction. But—and here was Avicenna's unique point—this abstraction is not performed by the human intellect but is the work of the Agent Intellect. The Agent Intellect illuminates our human minds to enable us to *know*, thereby adding existence to our minds' essence. Since the Agent Intellect is the creator of the souls of all people and, in addition, is the active power in human knowledge, there is, then, only one active intellect in all people, in which all people share.

Bonaventura also reacted against Avicenna's psychological theory on the ground that it threatened the notion of the discrete individuality of each person. Avicenna did not mean to imply this, for he actually had a doctrine of the immortality of each soul: Each returned to its source, the Agent Intellect. Still, Christian writers tended to see in the theory of the Agent Intellect the annihilation of the individual soul. They also criticized the theory for radically separating humans from God, since the Agent Intellect, and not God, confers enlightenment on the human intellect. Individual people exist only insofar as matter is formed into their bodies, and the soul is the form of the body. But, again, the active part of the intellect is not *theirs*. In these ways, then, Avicenna injected into medieval philosophy some very provocative themes, including (1) the eternity and necessity of creation, (2) the gradations and emanations of a hierarchy of beings, (3) the doctrine of the Agent Intellect who both creates the human soul and illuminates the Possible Intellect, and (4) the distinction between essence and existence as related to possible and necessary being.

Averroës

Like Avicenna before him, Averroës was a prodigious scholar. He was born in 1126 in Cordova, Spain, where he studied philosophy, mathematics, jurisprudence, medicine, and theology. After serving as a judge, as his father had, he became a physician, but he spent much of his time writing his famous commentaries, for which reason he became known in the Middle Ages as The Commentator. He spent his last days in Morocco, where he died in 1198 at the age of 72.

Averroës considered Aristotle the greatest of all philosophers, going so far as to say that nature had produced him as the model of human perfection. For this reason Averroës structured all his work around Aristotle's texts and ideas. At some points he disagreed with Avicenna. For one thing, whereas Avicenna argued that creation is eternal and necessary, Averroës denied altogether the idea of creation, saying that philosophy knows no such doctrine and that this is merely a teaching of religion. Averroës also rejected the distinction between essence and existence, saying that there is no *real* distinction between them (such as led Avicenna to distinguish between the possible and agent intellects); instead, there is only a *logical* distinction between essence and existence for purposes of analysis. Moreover, Averroës held that the form of a person is the soul, but that the soul is a material and not a spiritual form. As such, the material soul has the same mortality as the body, so that upon death nothing survives. What confers special status to human beings among animals is that, unlike the lower animals, humans are united through knowledge with the Agent Intellect. Avicenna, we have seen, said that each person has a Possible Intellect and a unique spiritual power, but for all people there is one and the same Agent Intellect. Averroës denied that people have separate *possible* intellects. He therefore explicitly located human knowledge in the universal Agent Intellect and denied the doctrine of immortality. It is no wonder that Christian thinkers thought his teachings impious. But his influence was immense, and Aquinas frequently quotes from his works. Still, Averroës had little respect for theology and went to great lengths to distinguish the domains of philosophy and theology, of faith and reason.

The most infamous part of Averroës', philosophy was later dubbed "the doctrine of double truth." In its most radical form this view is that two incompatible assertions may be true at the same time—such as incompatible religious and scientific assertions about the creation of the cosmos. While Averroës probably did not hold this extreme view, his name was nevertheless associated with it by his critics. His actual position begins innocently enough. Philosophy and theology each have a function, said Averroës, because there are different kinds of people whom they respectively serve. He envisioned three groups of people. The majority of people live by imagination and not by reason. They are kept virtuous through fear communicated by eloquent preachers. By contrast, the philosopher needs no threat but is motivated by his knowledge. Although religion and philosophy work generally for the same end, they communicate different contents and, in this sense, different truths. These truths do not necessarily contradict each other; they simply are different kinds. Hence, the first group is composed of those who are governed more by dramatic forms of thought than by reason. The second group is composed of theologians, who differ from the first group only in that, while they have the same religious beliefs, they attempt to devise intellectual supports for them as their justification. But, having prejudiced their thinking by resting it on inflexible assumptions, they cannot arrive at truth even though they have some notion of the power of reason. The third and superior group consists of the philosophers, who constitute a small minority. They are able to appreciate the truth for which religious people and rational theologians are seeking, but they see no reason for trying to see this truth *through* the unavoidably indirect perspective of religion. The philosophers know truth directly. Actually, Averroës thought that religious beliefs had a social function in that they made philosophical truths accessible to minds that were incapable of philosophical thought. He thought, however, that the theologians, as compared with the masses, should have known better than to employ the powers of sophisticated reasoning on a subject matter, religion, that is by nature a deviation from, though not necessarily contrary to, reason.

Moses Maimonides

Moses ben Maimonides was born in 1135 at Cordova and was a contemporary of Averroës, who was also born there. He was forced to leave Spain, and he went first to Morocco and then to Egypt, where he earned his livelihood by practicing medicine. He died in Cairo in 1204 at the age of 69. His principal work was his book *Guide of the Perplexed*. In it he set out to prove that the teachings of Judaism harmonize with philosophical thought and, in addition, that biblical thought offers certain valid insights that reason alone cannot discover. To accomplish this end, Maimonides drew on an astonishing amount of literature, dominated, however, by the works of Aristotle.

Apart from expressing many of Aristotle's views, which others had also learned and taught, Maimonides proposed certain distinctive notions, several of which we will list here. First, Maimonides believed that there can be no basic conflict between theology, philosophy, and science—between faith and reason. His *Guide of the Perplexed* was addressed principally to those believing Jews who had studied the sciences of the philosophers and had become perplexed by the literal meaning of the religious Law (*Torah*). Philosophy, he argued, is a form of knowledge distinct from the religious Law. Although the two do not conflict, their range and content are not the same. For this reason not every religious doctrine will have a rational or philosophical explanation.

Second, the doctrine of the creation of the world is a matter of religious belief. Although Aristotle's philosophy suggests that the world existed from eternity—that there was no creation in time—Maimonides points out that on this matter the philosophical, proof is not decisive. That is, philosophically, the arguments for and against the doctrine of creation have equal weight.

Third, Maimonides thought that conflicts between faith and reason were produced by two things, namely, the anthropomorphic language of religion and the disorderly way in which problems of faith are approached by the perplexed. We must proceed step by step, moving from mathematics and the natural sciences, to the study of the Law, and then to metaphysics or technical philosophical theology. With this kind of methodical training, it becomes easier to understand the allegorical nature of much biblical language. But to detect the anthropomorphic element in religious language, one must be trained in the categories of scientific and philosophical concepts.

Fourth, Maimonides agreed with Avicenna regarding the structure of human nature. Like Avicenna he accepted the theory of the Agent Intellect as the source of a person's substantive knowledge. Each person has only a *possible* or *passive* intellect, belonging uniquely to him or her. Each person *acquires* an active intellect, which *is* the Agent Intellect, or comes from the Agent Intellect in varying degrees, depending on his or her degree of merit. Upon death a person's soul, which is the form of the body, perishes, and the only element that survives is the active intellectual ingredient that came from the Agent Intellect and that now returns to it. If this is a doctrine of immortality, then it is one in which the unique characteristics of each individual have been greatly diminished.

Fifth, Maimonides devised several proofs for the existence of God. Using portions of Aristotle's *Metaphysics* and *Physics*, he proved the existence of a Prime Mover, the existence of a *necessary* Being, and the existence of a primary cause. Whether the world was created out of nothing or existed from eternity did not, Maimonides thought, affect the enterprise of natural theology. But having proved the existence of God, Maimonides rejected the possibility of saying *what* God is like. No positive attributes can be ascribed to God but only negative ones, by saying what God is *not* like.

Sixth, the goal of human life is to achieve appropriate human perfection. The philosophers, Maimonides says, have made it clear there are four kinds of perfections that a person can attain. There are, in ascending order, (1) the perfection of possessions, (2) the perfection of the bodily constitution and shape, (3) the perfection of the moral virtues, and, finally, (4) the highest, which is the acquisition of the rational virtues. By rational virtues, Maimonides says, "I refer to the conception of intelligibles, which teach true opinions concerning the divine things. That is in true reality the ultimate end; thus what gives the individual true perfection." This rational account of human perfection had its counterpart also in faith, for Maimonides concluded by saying that "the prophets too have explained the self-same notions—just as the philosophers have interpreted them." Faith and reason are in harmony.

CHAPTER 8

Aquinas and His Late Medieval Successors

*T*he great achievement of Thomas Aquinas (1225–1274) was that he brought together the insights of classical philosophy and Christian theology. Although he drew on classical philosophical themes from Plato and Stoicism, Aquinas's philosophy stands out for its reliance on Aristotle. Aquinas was also aware of the vast scope of thought produced by Christian writers, as well as the contributions of Muslim and Jewish philosophers. By the time he began his literary work, a large part of Plato's and Aristotle's writings had become available in Western Europe. Augustine had formulated an earlier blending of philosophy and theology by combining the Christian faith with elements of Plato's thought, which he had discovered in the writings of the Neoplatonist Plotinus. Shortly after Augustine, in the sixth century, Boethius had made a portion of Aristotle's works available in Latin for the first time and thereby stimulated philosophical speculation again. From about the seventh to the thirteenth century, there were several lines of development, leading toward differences and controversies between Platonists and Aristotelians.

This conflict continued after the thirteenth century as a controversy between Augustinians and Thomists (that is, followers of Thomas Aquinas), insofar as Augustine and Aquinas built their thoughts around Plato and Aristotle, respectively. In these formative centuries medieval thinkers wrestled with the problem of relating philosophy and theology, expressing this problem as the relation between faith and reason. There was also the problem of *universals*, which not only reflected the different viewpoints of Plato and Aristotle but also had important ramifications for the Christian faith. On all these matters Aquinas now exerted a decisive influence by clarifying the questions involved, acknowledging solutions offered by different authorities, and answering the major objections to his Aristotelian-Christian solutions. In this way Aquinas perfected the "scholastic method."

The term *scholasticism* in this context is derived from the intellectual activity carried on in the medieval cathedral *schools*, and its proponents were called *doctores scholastici*. Eventually, scholasticism came to refer to the dominant system of thought developed by the doctors in the schools and to the special method they utilized in teaching philosophy. Scholastic philosophy was an attempt to put together a coherent system of *traditional* thought rather than a pursuit of genuinely novel forms of insight. The content of this system was for the most part a fusion of Christian theology and Greek philosophy—Plato and especially Aristotle. Most distinctive in scholasticism was its *method*, a process relying chiefly on strict logical deduction, taking on the form of an intricate *system* and expressed in a *dialectical* or disputational form in which theology dominated philosophy. Again, Aquinas perfected what Boethius (480–524)—"the first scholastic"—established as the "scholarly" point of view regarding theological subjects. Boethius urged that "as far as you are able, join faith to reason," and Aquinas raised the conjunction of faith with reason to its highest form. While accepting revealed and traditional theological truths, he simultaneously tried to provide rational argumentation in order to make these revealed truths comprehensible.

AQUINAS'S LIFE

Aquinas was born in 1225 near Naples. His father was a count of Aquino who had hoped that his son would someday enjoy a high ecclesiastical position. For this reason Aquinas was placed in the Abbey of Monte Cassino as a boy of 5, and for the next nine years he pursued his studies in this Benedictine abbey. At the age of 14, he entered the University of Naples, but while in that city he was fascinated by the life of some Dominican friars at a nearby monastery and decided to enter their order. As the Dominicans were particularly dedicated to teaching, Aquinas had, upon entering their order, resolved to give himself to a religious and also a teaching vocation. Four years later, in 1245, he entered the University of Paris, where he came under the influence of a prodigious scholar whose enormous intellectual achievements had earned him the names "Albert the Great" (Albertus Magnus) and the "Universal Teacher." During his long and intimate association with Albert, in both Paris and Cologne, Aquinas's thought was shaped in decisive ways.

Albert recognized the significance of philosophy and science for grounding Christian faith and for developing the capacities of the human mind. While other theologians looked suspiciously at secular learning, Albert concluded that the Christian thinker must master philosophical and scientific learning in all its forms. He had respect for all intellectual activity, and his writings attest to his acquaintance with a vast amount and variety of learning. He knew virtually all the ancient, Christian, Jewish, and Muslim writers. But his mind was encyclopedic rather than creative. Still, it was Albert who recognized the fundamental difference between philosophy and theology, sharpening more accurately than his predecessors had the boundaries between them. Albert thought that such writers as Anselm and Abelard, for example, had ascribed too much competence to reason, not realizing that from a rigorous point of view much of what they ascribed to reason was in fact a matter of faith. Albert's particular objective was to make Aristotle clearly understandable to all of Europe, hoping to put into Latin all of Aristotle's works. He considered Aristotle the greatest of all philosophers, and much of the credit for the dominance of Aristotle's thought in the thirteenth century must be given to him. It was under these circumstances that his pupil Aquinas would also see in Aristotle the most significant philosophical support for Christian theology.

Unlike Albert, who did not change anything in the philosophers he quoted in his works, Aquinas used Aristotle more creatively and systematically, and with a more specific recognition of the harmony between Aristotelian thought and the Christian faith. After an interval of teaching under the auspices of the Papal Court from 1259 to 1268, Aquinas returned once again to Paris and became involved in a celebrated controversy with followers of Averroës. In 1274, Pope Gregory X called him to Lyons to participate in a council, and while on his way there, he died in a monastery between Naples and Rome, at the age of 49.

Aquinas left a huge written legacy, the vastness of which is all the more remarkable when we recall that it was all composed within a twenty-year span. Among his principal works are his commentaries on many of Aristotle's writings, careful arguments against the errors of the Greeks and the Averroists, a brilliant early work on essence and existence, and a political treatise on rulers. His most renowned literary achievements, though, are his two major theological works, the *Summa contra Gentiles* and *Summa Theologica*.

Bonaventura and the University of Paris

To understand the issues that drove Aquinas's philosophy, it is important to understand the context of the medieval university in which he wrote. The first universities grew out of what were called "cathedral schools." The University of Paris evolved from the Cathedral School of Notre Dame, its formal rules of organization and procedures being approved officially by the Papal representative in 1215. Originally, like all early universities, Paris consisted of masters and students without any special buildings or other features we now associate with universities, such as libraries and endowments. These were added in the fourteenth and fifteenth centuries. But the most important ingredients were there, namely, masters and students with a passion for learning. Being originally church institutions, universities shared a common theological position. This meant, too, that of the four faculties—theology, law, medicine, and arts— the theological faculty enjoyed undisputed supremacy.

Besides its theological orientation the University of Paris was receptive to universal knowledge. This accounts for the gradual acceptance and triumph of Aristotle's philosophy at Paris. It was apparent, however, that the invasion of Aristotelianism would raise problems of orthodoxy. There was not only the concern over the impact of Aristotle's philosophy on Christian thought but also serious questions over whether Aristotle was faithfully and accurately interpreted by Muslim philosophers. In addition, whereas Augustine and Platonism triumphed at Oxford, this type of thought, although not dominant in Paris, was nevertheless strongly represented there at this time by Bonaventura, a contemporary of Aquinas. Bonaventura was critical of Aristotle, holding that by denying the Platonic theory of Forms, Aristotle's thought would produce serious errors if incorporated into theology. For example, to deny the Platonic Forms would mean that God did not possess in himself the Forms of all things and would therefore be ignorant of the concrete and particular world. In turn, this would deny God's providence or his control over the universe. This would also mean that events occur either by chance or through mechanical necessity.

Even more serious was Bonaventura's charge that if God does not think the Forms of the world, he could not have created it. On this point Aquinas was later to have serious difficulties with the church authorities, for in following Aristotle, he could discover no decisive reason for denying that the world always existed, instead of being created at a point in time. But, said Bonaventura, if the world always existed, there must have existed an infinite number of human beings, in which case there must be either an infinite number of souls or, as Averroists argued, only one soul or intellect, which all human beings share. If this Averroist argument were accepted, it would annul the theory of personal immortality. This was strongly urged by the leading Averroist of the thirteenth century, Siger de Brabant, who said that there is only one eternal intellect and that, while individual people are born and die, this intellect or soul remains and always finds another human being in which to carry out its functions of organizing the body and the act of knowing. In short, there is only one intellect, which all people have in common.

Against Aristotelian philosophy, which Bonaventura considered dangerous to Christian faith because of all the errors it engendered, he offered the insights of Augustine and Platonism. Still, because Aristotle's thought was so formidable and so systematic, particularly concerning matters of nature and science, its forward march was irresistible, and its triumph virtually inevitable. If most parts of the University were to be oriented to Aristotle's thought, the theologians could not avoid coming to terms with this monumental thinker. If Aristotle was to be accepted, the specific task of the theologians was to harmonize his philosophy with Christianity, that is, to "Christianize" Aristotle. This is what Aquinas set out to do, contending at the same time against Bonaventura's Augustinianism and Siger de Brabant's Averroism.

PHILOSOPHY AND THEOLOGY

Aquinas thought and wrote as a Christian, and he was primarily a theologian. At the same time, he relied heavily on the philosophy of Aristotle in writing his theological works. That he brought together philosophy and theology does not mean that he confused these two disciplines. On the contrary, it was his view that philosophy and theology played complementary roles in our quest for truth. Like his teacher Albert the Great, Aquinas went to great pains to delineate the boundaries between faith and reason, indicating what philosophy and theology respectively could and could not provide. The dominant religious orientation of thirteenth-century thought concerned the importance of our knowledge of God; Aquinas combined the insights of both philosophy and theology to address this issue. What made the correct knowledge of God so essential was that any basic errors on this subject could affect the direction of a person's life—directing him or her either toward or away from God, who is the ultimate end. Philosophy proceeds from principles discovered by human reason, whereas theology is the rational ordering of principles received from authoritative revelation and held as a matter of faith. Aquinas's philosophy, then, consists for the most part in that portion of his theology that he considered rationally demonstrable—that is, *natural theology* as philosophers of later centuries used this term.

Faith and Reason

Aquinas saw specific differences between philosophy and theology—between reason and faith. For one thing, philosophy begins with the immediate objects of sense experience and reasons upward to more general conceptions. Eventually, as in Aristotle's case, we fasten upon the highest principles or first causes of being, ending in the conception of God. Theology, on the other hand, begins with a faith in God and interprets all things as creatures of God. There is here a basic difference in method, since philosophers draw their conclusions from their rational description of the essences of things. Theologians, by contrast, base their demonstrations on the authority of revealed knowledge. Again, theology and philosophy do not contradict each other, but not everything that philosophy discusses is significant for a person's religious end. Theology deals with what people need to know for their salvation, and to ensure this knowledge, it was made available through revelation. Some of the truths of revelation could never be discovered by natural reason. Other elements of revealed truth, though, could be known by reason alone but were revealed to ensure that we indeed become acquainted with such truths.

For this reason there is some overlap between philosophy and theology. For the most part, however, philosophy and theology are independent disciplines. Wherever reason is capable of knowing something, faith, strictly speaking, is unnecessary, and what faith uniquely knows through revelation cannot be known by natural reason alone. Both philosophy and theology deal with God, but the philosopher can only infer that God exists and cannot by reflecting on the objects of sensation understand God's essential nature. There is, nevertheless, a connection between the aims of philosophy and theology since they are both concerned with truth. Aristotle had considered the object of philosophy the study of first principles and causes, the study of being and its causes. This led to a First Mover, which he understood as the ground of truth in the universe. This is the philosophical way of saying what the theologian has set as his object of knowledge, namely, God's being and the truth this reveals about the created world. To discover the chief aspects of Aquinas's philosophy, then, we must take from his vast theological writings those portions of it in which he attempts to demonstrate truths in a purely rational way. His philosophical approach is particularly evident in his attempts to demonstrate the existence of God.

PROOFS OF GOD'S EXISTENCE

Aquinas formulated five *proofs* or ways of demonstrating the existence of God. The proofs are deceptively short, each being only a paragraph in length. Some important assumptions, though, lay behind their brevity. Most importantly, his approach was the opposite of Anselm's Ontological Argument. Anselm began his proof with the *idea* of the greatest conceivable being, from which he inferred the existence of that being. Aquinas, though, said that all knowledge must begin with our experience of sense objects. Instead of beginning with innate ideas of perfection, he rested all five of his proofs on the ideas derived from ordinary objects that we experience with our senses.

Proofs from Motion, Efficient Cause, and Necessary Being

The first three of his proofs share a similar strategy, and in later centuries were called "cosmological arguments." They begin with an observed fact in the world and then trace that fact back through all of the connecting links to its original source. It is clear that the chain of links cannot go back to infinity past; thus, there must be an initiator to the chain of connections, which we call God.

   The first proof is from *motion*. Aquinas argues that we are certain, because it is evident to our senses, that in the world some things are in motion. It is equally clear to us that whatever is in motion was moved by something else. If a thing is at rest, it will never move until something else moves it. When a thing is at rest, it is only potentially in motion. Motion occurs when something potentially in motion is moved and is then actually in motion; motion is the transformation of *potentiality* into *actuality*. Imagine a series of dominoes standing next to each other. When they are set up in a row, we can say that they are all potentially in motion, though actually at rest. Consider a particular domino. Its potentiality is that it will not move until it is knocked over by the one next to it. It will move only if it is moved by something actually moving. From this fact Aquinas drew the general conclusion that nothing can be transformed from a state of potentiality by something that is also in a mere state of potentiality. A domino cannot be knocked over by another domino that is standing still. Potentiality means the absence of something and is therefore *nothing*. For this reason potential motion in the neighboring domino cannot move the next one because it is *nothing*, and you cannot derive motion from nonmotion. As Aquinas says, "Nothing can be reduced from potentiality to actuality except by something in a state of actuality." Moreover, it is not possible for the same thing—for example, a domino—to be *at the same time* in actuality and in potentiality regarding motion. What is actually at rest cannot be simultaneously in motion. This means that the particular domino cannot be simultaneously the thing that is moved and also the mover. Something potentially in motion cannot move itself, and whatever is moved must be moved by another. The last domino to fall was potentially in motion, but so was the next to last. Each domino could become a *mover* only after it had been moved by the one prior to it. Here we come to Aquinas's decisive point: If we are to account for motion, we cannot do so by going back in an infinite regress. If we were to say about each mover in this series that it in turn was moved by a prior mover, we would never discover the source of motion, because every mover would then be only potentially in motion. Even if such a series went back infinitely, each one would still be only potential, and from that no actual motion could ever emerge. The fact is, however, that there *is* motion. There must therefore be a mover, which is able to move things but which does not itself have to be moved, and this, says Aquinas, "everyone understands to be God."

Two things need to be noted about this proof. First, Aquinas does not limit his concept of motion to things such as dominoes, that is, to locomotion. He has in mind the broadest meaning of motion, including the ideas of *generation* and *creation*. Second, for Aquinas the First Mover is not simply the first member of a long series of causes, as though such a mover were just like the others, its only distinction being that it is the first. Clearly, this could not be the case, for then this mover would also be only potentially in motion. The First Mover must therefore be pure actuality without potentiality and is therefore first not in the series but in actuality.

The second proof is from *efficient cause*. We experience various kinds of effects, and in each case we assign an efficient cause. The efficient cause of the statue is the sculptor. If we took away the activity of the sculptor, we would not have the effect, the statue. But there is an order of efficient causes; the parents of the sculptor are his or her efficient cause. Workers in the quarry are the efficient cause of this particular piece of marble's availability to the sculptor. There is, in short, an intricate order of efficient causes traceable in a series. Such a series of causes is demanded because no event can be its own cause; sculptors do not cause themselves, and statues do not cause themselves. A cause is prior to an effect. Nothing, then, can be prior to itself; hence, events demand a prior cause. Each prior cause must itself have its own cause, as parents must have their own parents. But it is impossible to go backward to infinity, because all the causes in the series depend on a first efficient cause that has made all the other causes actual causes. There must then be a first efficient cause "to which everyone gives the name of God."

The third proof is from *necessary being*. In nature we find that things are possible to be and not to be. Such things are *possible* or *contingent* because they do not always exist; they are *generated* and are *corrupted*. There was a time when a tree did not exist; it exists, and finally it goes out of existence. To say, then, that it is *possible* for the tree to exist must mean that it is also possible for it *not* to exist. The possibility for the tree *not* to exist must be taken two ways. First, it is possible for the tree *never* to come into existence, and second, once the tree is in existence, there is the possibility that it will go out of existence. To say, then, that something is *possible* must mean that at both ends of its being—that is, before it comes into being and after it goes out of being—it does not exist. *Possible* being has this fundamental characteristic, namely, that it can *not-be*. It can *not-be* not only *after* having existed but, more importantly, *before* being generated, caused, or moved. For this reason something that is possible, which can not-be, in fact "at some time is not."

All *possible* beings, therefore, at one time did not exist, will exist for a time, and will finally pass out of existence. Once possible things *do* come into existence, they can cause other, similar possible beings to be generated, as when parents beget children, and so on. But Aquinas is making this argument: Possible things do not have their existence in themselves, or from their own essence; and if *all* things in reality were only *possible*—that is, if about *everything* we could say that it could not-be *both* before it is and after it is—then at one time there was nothing in existence. But if there was a time when nothing existed, then nothing could start to be, and even now there would be nothing in existence, "because that which does not exist begins to exist only through something already existing." But since our experience clearly shows us that things do exist, this must mean that not all beings are *merely possible*. Aquinas concludes from this that "there must exist something the existence of which is necessary." We must therefore admit, he says, "the existence of some being having of itself its own necessity, and not receiving it from another, but rather causing in others this necessity. This all people speak of as God."

Proofs from Perfection and Order

The final two proofs rest on different strategies. Aquinas's fourth proof is based on the degrees of perfection that we see in things. In our experience we find that some things are more and some less good, true, and noble. But these and other ways of comparing things are possible only because things resemble in their different ways something that is the maximum. There must be something that is truest, noblest, and best. Similarly, we can say about things that they have more or less being, or a lower or higher form of being, as when we compare a stone with a rational creature. Thus, there must also be "something which is most being." Aquinas then argues that the maximum in any genus is the cause of everything in that genus, as fire, which is the maximum of heat, is the cause of all hot things. From this Aquinas concludes that "there must also be something which is to all beings the cause of their being, goodness, and every other perfection; and this we call God."

Finally, Aquinas constructs a proof for God based on the order that we see in the world. We see things such as parts of the natural world or parts of the human body, which do not possess intelligence but nevertheless behave in an orderly manner. They act in special and predictable ways to achieve certain ends or functions. But things that lack intelligence, such as an ear or a lung, cannot carry out functions unless they are directed by something that does have intelligence. This is just as an arrow is directed by an archer. Aquinas concludes that "some intelligent being exists by whom all natural things are directed to their ends; and this being we call God."

Assessment of the Proofs

Aquinas's five proofs are a substantial intellectual achievement and are among the most famous arguments in Western philosophy. Nevertheless, his proofs are only as strong as the assumptions on which they are based. The first three proofs are especially vulnerable in this regard. Since, contrary to Aquinas, there may be no logical problems with tracing an infinite chain of causes back through infinity. Another problem with the first three proofs is that, even if successful, they do not lead to the idea of a God who is conscious and personal. These are, however, proofs that Aquinas considered philosophical corroborations of the religious notion of God, and we must remember that they were composed in the context of his theological task. In spite of the problems with the first three proofs, his arguments nevertheless advanced beyond Avicenna's. Also, as philosophers in later centuries refined the causal argument for God, they relied on modified versions of Aquinas's arguments.

The fourth proof is also questionable because of its assumption that fire, for example, is the maximum of heat—a view initially developed by Aristotle. Science today would reject this contention. The final proof—based on natural purposes—is a different case. For centuries following Aquinas, philosophers believed that we could decisively prove God's existence based on the appearance of natural order in the world. In point of fact, they argued, the world exhibits design, and the most reasonable explanation for this is that a cosmic designer produced the natural design around us. The greatest challenge to this argument occurred during the nineteenth century with the theory of evolution. Darwin and other theorists offered an alternative and thoroughly natural explanation for the apparent design that we see in the world. At minimum, theologians could no longer argue that a cosmic designer was the only possible explanation of design.

KNOWLEDGE OF GOD'S NATURE

To prove *that* God exists does not tell us positively *what* God is. Traditional theologians commonly state that there is a vast gulf between the powers of human knowledge and the infinitude of God's nature. Aquinas was always aware of this virtually unbridgeable gulf, saying that "the divine reality surpasses all human conceptions of it." But each of the five proofs adds something to the conception of God. As First Mover, God is seen as unchangeable and, therefore, eternal. As First Cause, God is seen as all-powerful to create. To say that God is a necessary rather than a possible being is to say that God is pure actuality. As the ultimate truth and goodness, God is perfection itself. And as the orderer or designer of the universe, God is the supreme intelligence directing things.

The Negative Way (*Via Negativa*)

Although the five proofs give us some information about God, it is more indirect knowledge than it is direct. We know what we do about God only in a negative way, that is, by knowing what God is not. The proof shows only that God is *un*moved and that, therefore, he must be *un*changeable. This must mean that God is *not* in time and so is eternal. Similarly, to account for motion, it is necessary that there be something that does *not* have potentiality—it is matter in particular that has potentiality—and therefore, in God there is nothing material.

God is pure act and *immaterial*. Since there is neither matter nor potentiality in God, he is then *simple, without* any composition. This idea of God's *simplicity* is achieved not by our direct apprehension of it but by way of negation, whereby we *remove* from our conception of God such notions as compositeness and corporeality. Philosophically, God's simplicity means that unlike creatures that possess both potentiality and actuality, God is simply pure act. Whereas a creature *has* its being, God *is* his being. Whereas in creatures existence is one thing and essence another, God's essence is his existence. But even these positive-sounding attributes of God are in the end ways of saying what God is not, of saying that God is other than creatures.

Knowledge by Analogy

All human language is inevitably derived from our experience with things in our sensed world. For this reason, as Aquinas realized, the names that we apply to God are the same ones we use when describing humans and things. These names, such as *wise* or *loving*, certainly cannot mean the same thing when applied to finite people, on the one hand, and to the infinite God, on the other. If, then, these names and words mean different things to us when we use them respectively to describe creatures and God, the critical question is whether we can know anything at all about God based on our knowledge of creatures.

Aquinas distinguishes between three possible ways that our human vocabulary might relate to God. The first type of relation is *univocal*, in which case words, such as *wise*, used about God and human beings would mean exactly the same things and would imply that God and people are alike in nature. This clearly cannot be the case since God and people are not alike. God is infinite, and human beings are finite. A second possible type of relation is what Aquinas calls *equivocal*, whereby terms applied to both would mean totally different things for each, implying that God and people are totally unlike. In this case our knowledge of people would give us no knowledge whatsoever about God. Aquinas insists, however, that insofar as we are creatures of God, we must in some degree, even though imperfectly, reflect the nature of God. The third and final possibility is that people and God are neither totally alike nor totally unlike; rather, their relationship is *analogical*. It is, in a sense, midway between univocal and equivocal. When a word such as *wise* is used to describe both God and humans, it does not mean that God and humans are wise in exactly the same sense, nor does it mean that they are wise in completely different ways.

Analogy for Aquinas is an ontological term, that is, a term about the being or nature of a thing. The notion of "analogy" implies that what is in God is also in human beings. This is more than mere metaphor or simile. To say that there is an analogical relationship between God and us is to say that we resemble God. "Resemble" here means that we are in some degree what God uniquely is. For example, Aquinas says that people have a degree of being. God, on the other hand, *is* Being. What makes the relationship between God and us analogical is, therefore, the fact that we are linked to God by common attributes.

Human nature derives its very existence from God, and this fact accounts for the common elements in both God and people. When we use a word such as *wise*, we refer to (but do not fully comprehend) an attribute perfectly realized in God and only partially realized in humans. Wisdom is something that exists both in God and in us. What makes wisdom different in people is that our minds are located in our physical bodies and are dependent on our senses. When we think and speak, we do so discursively, saying and thinking a word or an idea at a time. God, being pure act with no material substance, knows all things simultaneously. Analogy would mean, then, that we know what God knows but not everything that God knows and not the way God knows it. Again, what makes this analogical relation possible is that God's creatures bear a likeness to God. Analogy means, then, that we are simultaneously like and unlike God. To know what people are like is to have *some* degree of knowledge about God. For this reason, names and terms that people formulate first of all about human beings have some meaning when applied to God, provided that the meanings in each case are adjusted to reflect the different degrees and types of being that differentiate God from people.

CREATION

Throughout his discussion of the proofs of God's existence and of God's nature, Aquinas assumes the notion of creation. According to the five proofs, the objects of our senses cannot derive their existence from themselves but must have it from the First Mover, First Cause, Necessary Being, Perfect Being, and Orderer of the Universe. However, Aquinas sees specific philosophical problems concerning the theory of creation.

Is the Created Order Eternal?

According to biblical revelation, creation occurred at a point in time. But how could philosophical reasoning support this doctrine of faith? Aquinas did not think that it is possible to decide in a philosophical manner whether the world has existed from eternity or whether it was created in time. That it was created must follow from the revealed nature of God. Being pure act and free, God willed to create. Aquinas distinguishes Creation, as a free act, from a *necessary* emanation, as taught by Plotinus. But since God is pure act, he could have acted to create the world from eternity. In short, there is no contradiction in saying that God created and that he created eternally. There might be a more serious question of contradiction if we argued that God created in time, since this could imply potentiality in God—that before he created things he was potentially a creator. Aquinas is somewhat inconclusive on this point, which raises questions about his orthodoxy. But he maintained that Aristotle, who argued that God had created from eternity, could not be refuted, in spite of Bonaventura's attempts to do so. In the end Aquinas settled the question by accepting the authority of revelation, concluding that philosophically either solution is possible.

Creation out of Nothing

What does it mean to say that God creates out of nothing, or *ex nihilo*? Again, Aquinas thought that if God is the source of all being, then there could not be any other source of being. There is, in short, no useful comparison between God and an artist at this point. An artist rearranges already existing materials, as when a sculptor fashions a statue. Prior to creation there is only God: God does not act upon any existing material since no such primary matter exists. Only God exists originally, and whatever comes to be derives its existence from God. Everything, then, is a creature of God, because it came ultimately from God, and there are no independent sources of being other than God.

Is This the Best Possible World?

Philosophers often speculate about whether the current world is indeed the best of all possible worlds that God could have created. To answer this question, according to Aquinas, we need to bear two things in mind. First, unlike God, who is infinite, we are finite, and our perfection will, therefore, be less than God's. Second, the universe cannot be any better than or any different from what creatures are capable of by their nature. Throughout this discussion Aquinas stresses that certain limitations must pervade the universe only because creating certain kinds of beings sets limits on others. The world is the best only in the sense that it contains the best arrangement possible of the kinds of things that have been created.

Evil as Privation

If God is all-powerful and good, why does suffering occur? This question is aggravated when we consider that everything that exists comes from God. Since there is evil in the world, it would appear that evil, too, comes from God. But Aquinas accepted Augustine's solution to the problem of evil, saying that evil is not anything positive. God is not the cause of evil because evil is not a thing. Natural evil—that is, the suffering caused by forces of nature—represents the absence (or privation) in something that is otherwise good in itself. For example, blindness consists of the absence of sight. Similarly, moral evil—that is, the suffering caused by willful human choices—involves an absence and is thus not a positive thing. In this sense absence consists of an inappropriate type of action, although the action as such is not evil. The act of the adulterer, Aquinas says, is evil not in its physical aspects but in that which makes it adultery, namely, the absence of correctness. Still, in the moral realm there appear to be those who choose to indulge in acts that are obviously wicked. Like Plato, Aquinas argues that people always will their acts with the hope that some good will come out of them, however diabolical the acts may seem. The adulterer never wills his or her act solely as an evil but rather for that aspect of the act that is good and affords pleasure.

The question remains, however, why God should permit defects both in physical nature and in people's moral behavior. Aquinas replies that the perfection of the universe required the existence of various kinds of beings. This includes corruptible as well as incorruptible beings, which consequently provides the possibility for defect and suffering. But having created corruptible things, there will be corruption. In the moral order the primary fact is that people possess freedom. Without freedom we could not love God; with freedom we possess the capacity to choose for or against God—right, just, and good. Evil is the possibility for wrong choice that accompanies a person's freedom. God did not will its actual occurrence, even though God willed that people should have freedom. The possibility of evil is the unavoidable corollary of the greater good that comes from our freedom to love and serve God. Aquinas therefore concludes that God is not the cause of evil even though by creating human beings with freedom he permitted the possibility of it. Moral evil, under these circumstances, is the product of the will whereby the essentially good element in the willed act lacks its true end.

The Range of Created Being: The Chain of Being

Aquinas describes the universe as consisting of a full range, or hierarchy, of different things—as if there existed a great *chain of being*. These beings differ in species and in the degree of their being. This full range of beings is needed so that God's perfection can be most adequately represented in the total created order. Because no single creature could ever reflect God's perfection suitably, God created many levels of being, which overlap in such a way that there are no gaps in the structure of being. Thus, below God is the hierarchy of angels. Aquinas calls these *intelligences* and says that they are immaterial. We can know of their existence both through reason and through revelation. Reason requires their existence in order to account for the full continuity of beings from the lowest to the highest, without any unaccounted-for spaces. Below these angels are human beings, whose nature includes both material and spiritual aspects. Then come animals, plants, and finally the four elements of air, earth, fire, and water. As to revelation, the Bible speaks of these intelligences in various terms, such as principles, powers, and seraphim.

Aquinas points out that there are no gaps between the various levels of beings: They interlock like links in a chain. For example, the lowest species of animals overlap with the highest forms of plants, the highest forms of animals correspond to the lowest form of human nature, and the highest element in people (intelligence) corresponds to what uniquely constitutes angels. What distinguishes the beings on all these levels is their particular composite nature, or the way their form and matter are related. In a person the soul is the form, and the body is the material substance. Angels have no material substance, and because they do not possess the kind of matter that designates the particular qualities of a specific individual, each angel is its own species. Each angel, then, occupies a separate grade in the hierarchy of being, differing from other angels in the degree or amount of its being. The highest angel is nearest God and the lowest nearest human beings, and below us are the animals, plants, and single elements, all representing the full range of created beings.

MORALITY AND NATURAL LAW

Moral Constitution

Aquinas built upon Aristotle's theory of ethics. Like Aristotle he considered ethics a quest for happiness. Moreover, following Aristotle's lead, Aquinas argued that happiness is connected closely with our end or purpose. To achieve happiness we must fulfill our purpose. But whereas Aristotle envisioned a *naturalistic* morality whereby people could achieve virtue and happiness by fulfilling their natural capacities or end, Aquinas added to this his concept of a person's *supernatural* end. As a Christian Aquinas viewed human nature as having both its source and ultimate end in God. For this reason human nature does not contain its own standards of fulfillment. It is not enough for us simply to be human and to exercise our natural functions and abilities in order to achieve perfect happiness. Aristotle thought such a naturalistic ethics was possible. Aquinas agreed with most of this claim, adding only that the Aristotelian ethics is incomplete. Aquinas therefore argued that there is a dual level to morality corresponding to our natural end and to our supernatural end.

The ingredients of our moral experience are provided by human nature. For one thing, the fact that we have bodies inclines us to certain kinds of acts. Our senses become the vehicle for appetites and passions. Our senses also provide a certain level of knowledge about sensible objects so that we are attracted to some objects, which we perceive as pleasurable and good (concupiscent appetite), and repelled by other objects, which we perceive as harmful, painful, or bad (irascible appetite). This attraction and rejection are the rudiments of our capacity for love and pleasure, and hate and fear.

In animals these irascible and concupiscent appetites immediately control and direct behavior. In a person, however, the will, in collaboration with the power of reason, consummates the human act. The will is the agency that inclines a person toward the achievement of good. That is, our full range of appetites seeks to be satisfied, and the process of satisfaction requires that we make choices between alternative objects. We must make this choice by our wills under the direction of reason. If we make right choices, then we achieve happiness. But not every choice is a correct one. For this reason the will by itself cannot always make the right move; the intellect must be the guide. Nor is the intellect the final source of knowledge, for our supernatural end requires God's grace and revealed truth. Still, the will represents our appetite for the good and right, whereas the intellect has the function and capacity for apprehending the general or universal meaning of what is good. The intellect is our highest faculty, and a natural end requires that the intellect, as well as all the other faculties, seek its appropriate object. The appropriate object of the intellect is truth, and truth in its fullness is God. When the intellect directs the will, then, it helps the will to choose the good. The intellect knows, however, that there is a hierarchy of goods and that some goods are limited and must not be mistaken for our most appropriate and ultimate good. Riches, pleasure, power, and knowledge are all goods and are legitimate objects of the appetites, but they cannot produce our deepest happiness because they do not possess the character of the universal good that our souls seek. The perfect happiness is found not in created things but in God, who is the supreme good.

Moral constitution consists, then, of sensuality, appetites, the will, and reason. What confers on a person the attributes of morality is that these elements are the ingredients of *free* acts. If I am moved to act by my appetites in a mechanical or rigorously determined way, then my acts will not be free and cannot be considered from a moral point of view. Not only is freedom a prerequisite for an act to be considered *moral*, but Aquinas adds that an act is *human* only if it is free. For freedom is possible only where there is knowledge of alternatives and the power of will to make choices. Virtue, or goodness, consists in making the right choices, the mean between extremes. Aquinas agreed with Aristotle that the virtues of the natural person are achieved when the appetites are duly controlled by the will and reason. The dominant or "cardinal" natural virtues are courage, temperance, justice, and prudence. In addition to these particular virtues, our natural end is further realized through our knowledge of the natural law, that is, the moral law.

Natural Law

Morality, as Aquinas viewed it, is not an arbitrary set of rules for behavior. Rather, the basis of moral obligation is found, first of all, in human nature itself. Built into our nature are various inclinations, such as the preservation of life, the propagation of species, and, because people are rational, the inclination toward the search for truth. The basic moral truth is simply to "do good and avoid evil." As rational beings, then, we are under a basic natural obligation to protect our lives and health, in which case suicide and carelessness are wrong. Second, the natural inclination to propagate the species forms the basis of the union of wife and husband, and any other basis for this relation would be wrong. And third, because we seek for truth, we can do this best by living in peace in society with all others who are also engaged in this quest. To ensure an ordered society, human laws are fashioned for the direction of the community's behavior. These activities of preserving life, propagating the species, forming an ordered society under human laws, and pursuing the quest for truth—all these, again, pertain to us at our natural level. The moral law is founded upon human nature, upon the natural inclinations toward specific types of behavior, and upon the reason's ability to discern the right course of conduct. Because human nature has certain fixed features, the rules for behavior that correspond to these features are called *natural law*.

Aristotle already developed much of this theory of natural law. In his *Ethics* Aristotle distinguished between natural justice and conventional justice. Some forms of behavior, he said, are wrong only after a law has been made to regulate such behavior. It is wrong, for example, to drive a vehicle at certain speeds only because a speed limit has been set, but there is nothing in nature that requires that vehicles travel at that speed. Such a law is, therefore, not natural but conventional, because before the law was passed, there was nothing wrong with traveling at speeds exceeding the new limit. On the other hand, there are some laws that are derived from nature, so that the behavior they regulate has always been wrong, as in the case of murder. But Aquinas did not limit his treatment of natural law to the simple notion that in some way human reason is able to discover the natural basis for human conduct. Instead, he reasoned that if human existence and nature can be fully understood only when seen in relation to God, then natural law must be described in metaphysical and theological terms, as the Stoics and Augustine had done.

Law, Aquinas says, has to do primarily with reason. Human reason is the standard of our actions because it belongs to reason to direct our whole activity toward our end. Law consists of these rules and measures of human acts and therefore is based on reason. But Aquinas argues that since God created all things, human nature and the natural law are best understood as the product of God's wisdom or reason. From this standpoint Aquinas distinguishes between *four* kinds of law.

Eternal Law   This law refers to the fact that "the whole community of the universe is governed by Divine Reason. Because of this, the very notion of the government of things in God the Ruler of the universe, has the nature of a law. And since the Divine Reason's conception of things is not subject to time but is eternal . . . therefore it is that this kind of law must be called eternal."

Natural Law   For Aquinas natural law consists of that portion of the eternal law that pertains particularly to people. His reasoning is that "all things share somewhat of the eternal law . . . from its being imprinted on them" and from this all things "derive their respective inclinations to their proper acts and ends." This is particularly true of people, because our rational capacity "has a share of the Eternal Reason, whereby it has a natural inclination to its proper act and end." And, Aquinas says, "this participation of the eternal law in the rational creature is called the natural law," and again, "the natural law is nothing else than the rational creature's participation in the eternal law." We have already noted the basic precepts of the natural law as being the preservation of life, propagation and education of offspring, and pursuit of truth and a peaceful society. Thus the natural law consists of broad general principles that reflect God's intentions for people in creation.

Human Law   This refers to the specific statutes of governments. These statutes or human laws are derived from the general precepts of natural law. Just as "we draw conclusions of the various sciences" from "naturally known indemonstrable principles," so also "from the precepts of the natural law . . . human reason needs to proceed to the more particular determination of certain matters." And "these particular determinations, devised by human reason, are called human laws." What was so far-reaching about this conception of human law was that it repudiated the notion that a law is a law only because it is decreed by a sovereign. Aquinas argued that what gives a rule the character of law is its moral dimension, its conformity with the precepts of natural law, and its agreement with the moral law. Taking Augustine's formula, namely, that "that which is not just seems to be no law at all," Aquinas said that "every human law has just so much of the nature of law, as it is derived from the law of nature." But, he adds, "if in any point it deflects from the law of nature, it is no longer a law but a perversion of law." Such laws no longer bind in conscience but are sometimes obeyed to prevent an even greater evil. Aquinas went further than simply denying the character of human law that violated the natural moral law; such a command, he said, should not be obeyed. Some laws, he said, "may be unjust through being opposed to the Divine Good: such are the laws of tyrants inducing to idolatry, or to anything else contrary to the Divine Law." He concluded that "laws of this kind must nowise be observed, because ... *we ought to obey God rather than human beings*" (emphasis added).

Divine Law   The function of law, Aquinas said, is to direct people to their proper end. Since we are ordained to an end of eternal happiness, in addition to our temporal happiness, there must be a kind of law that can direct us to that supernatural end. Here, in particular, Aquinas parted company with Aristotle, for Aristotle knew only about our natural purpose and end, and for this purpose the natural law known by human reason was considered a sufficient guide. But the eternal happiness to which people are ordained, said Aquinas, is "in proportion to a person's natural faculty." Therefore, "it was necessary that besides the natural and the human law, people should be directed to their end by a law given by God." The *divine law*, then, is available to us through revelation and is found in the Scriptures. It is not the product of human reason but is given to us through God's grace to ensure that we all know what we must do to fulfill both our natural and, especially, our supernatural ends. The difference between the natural law and divine law is this: The natural law represents our rational knowledge of the good by which the intellect directs our wills to control our appetites and passions. This, in turn, leads us to fulfill our natural end by achieving the cardinal virtues of justice, temperance, courage, and prudence. The divine law, on the other hand, comes directly from God through revelation and is a gift of God's grace. Through this we are directed to our supernatural ends and obtain the theological virtues of faith, hope, and love. These virtues are infused into human nature by God's grace and are not the result of our natural abilities. In this way Aquinas both completed and surpassed the naturalistic ethics of Aristotle. He showed how the natural human desire to know God can be assured and how revelation becomes the guide for reason. He also described the manner in which our highest nature is perfected through God's grace.

THE STATE

The state, Aquinas said, is a natural institution. It is derived from human nature. On this view Aquinas was following the political theory of Aristotle, from whom he took the phrase "people are by nature social animals." But insofar as Aquinas had a different view of human nature, he was bound to have a somewhat different political philosophy as well. The difference lay in the two conceptions of the role or task of the state. Aristotle supposed that the state could provide for all the needs of the people because he knew only about our natural human needs. Aquinas, on the other hand, believed that, in addition to our material or natural needs, we also have a supernatural end. The state is not equipped to deal with this more ultimate end. It is the church that directs us to this end. But Aquinas did not simply divide these two realms of human concern, giving one to the state and the other to the church. Instead, he looked on the state and explained its origin in terms of God's creation.

The state, on this view, is willed by God and has its God-given function, which addresses the social component of human nature. For Aquinas the state is not a product of people's sinfulness, as it was for Augustine. On the contrary, Aquinas says that even "in the condition of innocence people would have lived in society." But even then, "a common life could not exist, unless there were someone in control, to attend to the common good." The state's function is to secure the common good by keeping the peace, organizing the activities of the citizens into harmonious pursuits, providing for the resources to sustain life, and preventing, as far as possible, obstacles to the good life. This last item concerning threats to the good life not only gives to the state a function tied to our ultimate human end but also accounts for the state's position in relation to the church.

The state is subordinate to the church. This does not mean that Aquinas considered the church a "superstate." Aquinas saw no contradiction in saying that the state has a sphere in which it has a legitimate function and that at the same time it must subordinate itself to the church. Within its own sphere the state is autonomous. But, insofar as there are aspects of human life that bear on our supernatural end, the state must not enact arbitrary hindrances to our spiritual life. The church does not challenge the autonomy of the state; it only says that the state is not absolutely autonomous. Within its own sphere the state is what Aquinas calls a "perfect society," having its own end and the means for achieving it. But the state is like a person; neither the state nor a person has only a natural end. Our human spiritual end cannot be achieved, as Aquinas says, "by human power, but by divine power." Still, because our destiny is connected with spiritual happiness, the state must recognize this aspect of human affairs: In providing for the common good of the citizens, the sovereign must pursue the community's end with a consciousness of their spiritual end. Under these circumstances the state does not become the church, but the sovereign "should order those things which lead to heavenly beatitude and prohibit, as far as possible, their contraries." In this way Aquinas affirmed the legitimacy of the state and its autonomy in its own sphere. The state should be subordinate to the church only to ensure that our ultimate spiritual end be taken into account.

As the state rules the behavior of its citizens through law, the state is in turn limited by the requirements of just laws. Nowhere is Aquinas's rejection of the absolute autonomy of the state so clearly articulated as when he describes the standards for the making of human or positive law. We have already analyzed the different types of law: eternal, natural, human, and divine. The state is particularly the source of human law. Each government is faced with the task of fashioning specific statutes to regulate the behavior of its citizens under the particular circumstances of its own time and place. Lawmaking, however, must not be an arbitrary act but instead must be done under the influence of the natural law, which involves human participation in God's eternal law. Human-made laws must consist of particular rules derived from the general principles of natural law. Any human law that violates the natural law loses its character as law, as a "perversion of law," and loses its binding force in the consciences of humanity. The lawmaker has authority to legislate from God and is responsible to God. If the sovereign decrees an unjust law by violating God's divine law, then, according to Aquinas, such a law "must in no way be observed."

The political sovereign has this authority from God, and the purpose of this authority is to provide for the common good. Authority is never to be used as an end in itself or for selfish ends. Nor must the common good be interpreted in such a way that we lose sight of the individual within the collective whole. The common good must be the good of concrete people. Thus, Aquinas says that "the proper effect of law is to lead its subjects to their proper virtue . . . to make those to whom it is given good." The only "true ground" of the lawmaker is the intention to secure "the common good regulated according to divine justice," and thus it follows that "the effect of the law is to make people good." Thus, the phrase *common good* has no meaning for Aquinas except insofar as it results in the good of individuals. At the same time, Aquinas says that "the goodness of any part is considered in comparison with the whole. . . . Since then every person is a part of the state, it is impossible that a person be good unless he be well proportionate to the common good." The entire scheme of society and its laws is characterized by the rational elements in it. Law itself, Aquinas says, is "an ordinance of reason for the common good, made by the ruler who has care of the community, and promulgated." Thus, although the sovereign has authority and power, the laws must reflect this power not in an unrestrained manner but as domesticated by reason and aimed at the common good.

HUMAN NATURE AND KNOWLEDGE

Human Nature

Aquinas had a distinctive conception of human nature. Human nature, he said, is a physical substance. What made this a unique conception was that Aquinas insisted on the *unity* of human nature. Plato had talked about the soul as being imprisoned in the body. Similarly, Augustine considered the soul to be a spiritual substance. Aristotle held that the soul is the form of the body but did not see, as Aquinas did, that the soul of a person is as dependent upon the body as the body is upon the soul. To say, as Aquinas did, that a person is a physical substance underscored the substantial unity of human nature. Human beings *are* a unity of body and soul. Without the soul the body would have no form. Without the body the soul would not have its required organs of sense through which to gain its knowledge. As a physical substance we are a composite of soul and body. The angels are pure intelligence and have no body, but although people, too, are rational creatures, our special attribute is to exist and function as people only when unified as body and soul. Since the soul confers upon us bodily form, it is the soul that gives us life, understanding, and special physical features. The soul accounts also for our human capacity for sensation and the powers of intellect and will. Our highest human capacity is located in the intellect, making us rational animals and conferring on us the means by which to attain the contemplation of God.

Knowledge

Aquinas followed Aristotle's theory of knowledge. He was especially impressed with Aristotle's answer to those who doubted that our human minds can arrive at certainty on any subject. Some ancient philosophers argued that there could be no certainty since human knowledge is limited to sense perception, and objects in the sensible world are always in flux. Plato agreed with this estimate of sense knowledge, saying that it could give us no certainty. But Plato avoided intellectual pessimism by assuming the existence of a separate world, the intelligible world, contrasting it with the visible world. For Plato there are Forms that possess eternal being and provide the basis for knowledge. Augustine adapted this Platonic theory of Forms to Christian thought by saying that God possesses these Forms in his mind and that human beings are able to know the truth insofar as these Forms illumine our minds through the divine light. But Aquinas accepted Aristotle's approach, saying that the human mind knows what it does through its confrontation with actual concrete objects. Our minds are able to grasp what is permanent and stable within sensible things. When we sense things or people, we *know* their essence—for example, the essence of tree and human—even though they are in the process of change. These things indeed are in flux; we are not in doubt about what they are. Our intellects, then, *see* the universal *in* the particular things; we *abstract* the universal from the particular. Following Aristotle, Aquinas calls this mental capacity the *active intellect.*

Aquinas denied that universals exist apart from particular concrete objects. For example, there is no *humanity* distinct from individual people. There is only the abstracted concept—not an independently existing Form—which our active intellect grasps. For Aquinas, then, we can have no knowledge without sense experience, for nothing can be in the intellect that was not first in the senses (*nihil in intellectu quod prius non fuerit in sensu*).

For the most part Aquinas was a moderate realist regarding the problem of universals. Following both Avicenna and Abelard, he held that universals exist (1) outside of things (*ante rem*) but as such only as the divine concepts in God's mind, (2) in things (*in re*) as the concrete individual essence in all members of a species, and (3) in the mind (*post rem*) after abstracting the universal concept from the individual. The problem of universals had one more major treatment in the Middle Ages, and this time it was given a different solution by William of Ockham.

SCOTUS, OCKHAM, AND ECKHART

Aquinas's most important achievement was to fuse theology with philosophy. Over the next century the most significant reactions to his work were from those who tried to split theology and philosophy apart again. The key figures here are John Duns Scotus (1265–1308), William of Ockham (ca. 1280–1349), and Johannes Eckhart (ca. 1260–1327). These thinkers did not disagree with everything Aquinas taught. Indeed, on many matters they were in general accord. However, they each set out a basic criticism that had the effect of driving a wedge between philosophy and theology—between faith and reason. Against Aquinas's notion of the supremacy of reason, Scotus argued that God's *will* (rather than God's reason) is supreme; this became known as the theory of *voluntarism*. Against Aquinas's notion that universals have at least some kind of real existence, Ockham argued that universals are only words; this view became known as *terminism* or *nominalism*. And against Aquinas's highly rational and technical articulation of religious concepts, Eckhart felt that religion involves a more direct encounter with God through the spiritual exercise of *mysticism*.

Voluntarism

Why should these three developments have the effect of separating philosophy and theology? The problem becomes clear when we consider some of the implications of voluntarism. Aquinas argued that, with both human beings and God, the will is subordinate to the intellect; reason guides or determines the will. Scotus rejected this view. If God's will was subordinate to his reason or was limited by eternal truths, then God himself would be limited. In that situation God could not do whatever he wants since he would be bound or determined by some prior rational standard looming *above* him. So, if God is to be free in any meaningful way, he must have an absolutely free will. Consequently God's *will* is his dominant faculty, and not his reason. During the nineteenth century, this position was dubbed *voluntarism*, based on the Latin word *voluntas*, meaning "will."

There is an important moral consequence to saying that God's will is primary over his intellect: God's actions and moral commands are acts of will and as such are nonrational. God's moral law reflects not his adherence to the standards of rationality but rather his unconstrained will. Accordingly, God could have willed any kind of moral rules he chose. Both murder and adultery could, strictly speaking, become good actions if God willed them to be so. To put it bluntly, morality would seem to be the result of an arbitrary choice on God's part. And, if moral standards are arbitrary edicts from God, then it would be equally arbitrary for God to punish us or condemn us to hell for violating these edicts. If God is absolutely free, then he can reward or punish any behavior he chooses. For Scotus, then, morality is grounded not in reason but in will. Consequently, morality cannot be a subject of rational and philosophical inquiry, but only a matter of faith and acceptance.

A broader consequence of voluntarism is that there can be no *natural theology* by which human reason discovers any divine rational order to the universe.

That is, on this view we could not discover any rational connection between the world of experience and God. Proofs for God's existence are at best only *probable* demonstrations, and the existence of God becomes a matter of faith, not a matter of philosophical discovery. Rational knowledge is thus limited to the empirical world, and religious knowledge in general becomes a product of divine illumination or revelation. In this way the subject matter of philosophy is split off from that of theology.

The alternative to voluntarism is a position called *intellectualism*—that God's reason is primary over his will, and his choices are in fact directed by rational standards. Aquinas held this view when saying that we know moral principles through a *natural light*, which we habitually contain in our consciences. On this view morality is capable of an intellectual discipline insofar as the principles of good can be discovered rationally. And, from a broader perspective, the entire universe created by God in fact reflects God's rational mind and choices. As philosophers we can view the rational order in creation, and make logically valid inferences about God's existence and nature. For centuries following Scotus, most theologians and philosophers took some stand on the voluntarism-intellectualism dispute.

Nominalism

Like Scotus, Ockham was a voluntarist, and some of his more radical statements on the subject created problems for him within the Catholic Church hierarchy. Ockham, though, is perhaps best remembered for his theory of *nominalism*—the view that universal terms such as *humanity* are simply *signs* or *names* that designate mental concepts that we form when looking at particular things. Again, the central problem of universals is whether terms such as *humanity* refer to any reality other than particular humans—for example, James and John. Is there a *substance* in addition to these particular humans to which the *universal* term *humanity* refers? For Ockham only concrete individual things exist, and when we use universal terms, we are simply thinking in an orderly way about particular things. Universal terms such as *humanity* refer equally to James and John, but not because there is some real substance of "human-ness" in which both James and John *share* or *participate*. Rather, it is because the nature that is James is like the nature that is John. Human reason, then, is limited to the world of individual things. Ockham's view was genuinely empirical. Our minds, he said, do not know anything more than individual things and their qualities even though we are able to use universal terms. Such terms are nothing more than names for classes of individual things. Above all, universal terms do not refer to a realm of reality beyond the world of concrete individual things. One of Ockham's arguments for nominalism is based on a principle of simplicity known as Ockham's razor: "What can be explained on fewer principles is explained needlessly by more." In this case we should not postulate two realms of existence when one will do. The realist actually posits three realms of existence: (1) individual objects, (2) the independently existing attributes that they have in common, and (3) our mental concepts of these. On Ockham's account there are only two: (1) individual objects and (2) our verbalized mental concepts about those objects.

How did this view differ from Aquinas's treatment of the problem of universals? For the most part their views harmonize. Aquinas said that universals are found in particular things (*in re*) and are abstracted from things (*post rem*) after our experiences of them. However, Aquinas believed that universals exist in the mind of God (*ante rem*) and thus have a metaphysical status prior to individual things. If universals exist in the mind of God, then two people are alike because they share in this metaphysical reality in God's mind. Also, our human minds, when we think about universals, share in some way in God's thought. This is where Ockham parted company with Aquinas. He rejected the theory of divine ideas for the same reason Scotus had: God's will is supreme over God's reason. People are what they are because God chose to make them that way, not because they reflect an eternal pattern that exists in God's mind.

If our thoughts are restricted to individual things in experience, then our knowledge of these things does not lead to any reality beyond experience. Realists believed that universal terms pointed to something beyond individual things, and they accordingly felt that our use of such terms gives us reliable knowledge about reality beyond the empirical scene. And if we assume further that universals are ideas in God's mind, then we can conclude that philosophical reasoning about individual things could lead to various theological truths. There could thus be a natural theology. But Ockham's strict interpretation of universals had the effect of severing philosophy from metaphysics, making out of philosophy something more like science. Theology and religious truth could not be achieved by philosophy or science. Indeed, his position involves the theory of *double-truth:* that one kind of truth is available through science or philosophy, and another kind of truth is received through revelation. The first truth is the product of human reason, and the other is a matter of faith. One kind of truth, moreover, cannot influence the other kind. The ultimate consequence of the double-truth theory was that theological and philosophical truths are not only independent and not derivable from each other but that can even contradict each other. This was the explicit teaching held by followers of Averroës. For example, they argued that, while it is true in philosophy that there is no personal immortality, such a theory is false for theology. Ockham had not gone that far in separating faith and reason. He had, nevertheless, set the stage for an empirical and scientific way of thinking about the facts of experience. His nominalism had the effect of separating science from metaphysics. The study of natural things became more and more independent of both metaphysical and theological explanations.

Ockham also rejected Aquinas's impressive system of natural theology, which traced causal connections in the world around us back to a first cause. Ockham developed instead a strictly empirical and, in a sense, skeptical view regarding knowledge. He argued that "from the fact that one thing is known to exist, it cannot be inferred that another thing exists." To say that some things are caused by other things gives us no warrant to argue that God is the cause of the natural order. Ockham concluded from this that unaided reason cannot discover God. Instead, knowledge of God is a gift of grace and is assured by an act of faith.

Mysticism

Strongly influenced by Neoplatonism, Eckhart offered a mystical approach to theology, which shifted emphasis from reason to feeling. Whereas Aquinas built his demonstrations of God's existence upon our experience of finite things, Eckhart urged people to pass beyond sensory knowledge, which is after all limited to material objects. Though he considered in great detail many traditional theological questions concerning God's nature, creation, and human nature, he was primarily a mystic who wanted to share with others his rich experiences of unity with God. This union, he believed, cannot be reached except by liberating oneself from the objects of the world. But union with God, he believed, is not achieved by human effort. Instead, only through God's grace and illumination is union consummated, and only in the deepest reaches of our souls do we grasp God in his fullness. When this happens, Eckhart says, people become one with God, for "we are transformed totally into God and are converted into him in a similar manner as in the sacrament the bread is converted into the body of Christ." Our mystical union with God is an experience beyond rationality, and Eckhart feels forced to use such terms as *wilderness* and *darkness* to express this mystical union. God, he believes, is both beyond existing beings and beyond knowledge. As such, normal human concepts and categories do not apply to him, and thus, we must fall back on metaphorical descriptions of God and our experience of him.

Eckhart's mysticism did not supplant the more rational approach to theology espoused by Aquinas. However, he gave a new voice to the older Neoplatonic views of Pseudo-Dionysius and others and had a strong impact on the mystical tradition that followed him.

PART THREE

Early Modern Philosophy

CHAPTER 9

Philosophy during the Renaissance

THE CLOSING OF THE MIDDLE AGES

*F*or most philosophers in the Middle Ages, the sky hung low, suggesting a close bond between heaven and earth and, accordingly, between philosophy and theology. During that time philosophy was virtually the handmaiden of theology, supplying religious thought with a reasoned account of its various doctrines. Plato and Aristotle had previously been concerned with the question of how the daily affairs of people could and should be related to the permanent structures of reality and to God. But the blending of theology and philosophy in the Middle Ages was an unstable one. For one thing, there were serious questions about the compatibility of Aristotle's nontheistic philosophy and the belief in the personal God of Christianity. Moreover, much of Aristotle's thought was made available at this time through Muslim thinkers, who construed Aristotle in ways that could hardly be accepted by Christians. Aquinas tried to reinterpret and Christianize Aristotle to overcome this incompatibility. Yet philosophy now found itself to a great extent doing a task that it had not originally set out to do, namely, providing an intellectual and metaphysical foundation for revealed religion. Nor had philosophy been previously restrained by an institution the way it was by the church in the Middle Ages. It is true that even the earliest philosophers were in mortal jeopardy when their teachings threatened the status quo. Socrates, after all, was put to death for just this reason, and Aristotle left Athens to keep his townsfolk from "sinning against philosophy for a second time." Nevertheless, classical philosophy had been more or less free to move wherever the pursuit of truth led it. By confining itself simply to human reasoning, philosophy could dwell on the subjects of human nature, ethics, the cosmos, God, and political authority. The spirit of medieval philosophy was sharply different in that its starting point was fixed by the doctrines of Christian theology, and the whole cultural atmosphere was affected by the predominance of the church.

By the close of the Middle Ages, the medieval marriage between religion and philosophy had become strained, and during the Renaissance there was a decisive separation between the two. The Renaissance—literally meaning "rebirth"—was a revival of Greek learning that took place during the fifteenth and sixteenth centuries. The writings of many philosophers and other great authors of antiquity once again became available. Scholars in the the Middle Ages were often only indirectly acquainted with Greek thinkers such as Plato, whom they read about in works by Plotinus and Augustine. However, during the Renaissance Greek manuscripts were brought back from Athens to Italy, and these texts could now be directly accessed. For example, in Florence, Cosimo de' Medici founded an academy where Plato's philosophy was the chief subject of study. This academic influence, reinforced by similar academies in Naples and Rome, further diluted the preeminence of Aristotelian thought and scholastic methodology. Direct access to texts also created a deep fascination for language.

The discovery of ancient Greek and Roman literature had the effect of encouraging a new style of writing, which was less formal than the texts of medieval authors and had its expression increasingly in the vernacular. With the use of the vernacular, literature became more and more the property of the people. Wycliffe's rendering of the Bible into the vernacular would in time have widespread reverberations in religious thought as the masses gained direct access to the contents of the Scriptures. The extensive diffusion of culture was most effectively facilitated by Johann Gutenberg's invention of movable type in the mid-fifteenth century, which made books readily available, smaller and easier to handle, and cheaper to buy. Printing presses soon appeared in Paris, London, and Madrid, and in Italy at the monastery of Subiaco. The making of books and the use of the vernacular inevitably affected the manner of philosophical writing since the freedom connected with these activities led philosophers to engage more in original formulations, rather than simply write commentaries on authoritative thinkers. In time, the modern philosophers would compose their treatises in the language of their own people, and thus, Locke and Hume would write in English, Voltaire and Rousseau in French, and Kant in German.

As with the revived attention to Plato, interest in Epicureanism, Stoicism, and even Skepticism was rekindled. A new breed of philosophy also emerged— namely, humanism—which emphasized the study of classical authors and the central role of human reason in discovering truth and structuring the community. Humanist philosophers did not reject religion but only affirmed that areas of human nature could be fruitfully studied by methods and assumptions not directly derived from religion. Other intellectual changes occurred during the Renaissance that impacted philosophy. Many European countries launched a religious Reformation against the domination of the Roman Catholic Church. Scientists investigated the makeup of the physical world from a nonreligious perspective. In this chapter we will explore the philosophical themes of humanism, the Reformation, Skepticism, and the scientific revolution.

HUMANISM AND THE ITALIAN RENAISSANCE

The Renaissance began as an artistic movement within Italy. Art throughout the Middle Ages was filled with religious symbolism and often viewed principally as a tool for teaching biblical stories and doctrines to illiterate parishioners.

Paintings and sculptures were far from being photographic images of their subject matter. Conveying very little sense of reality, early medieval art instead attempted to evoke an other-worldly, spiritual quality. Late medieval art slowly moved more toward accurate depictions of the world, incorporating three-dimensional artistic techniques and a study of human anatomy. This facilitated a transition to Renaissance artwork, which exalted nature through the accurate depiction of landscapes and the human form. We see this in the works of two of the most famous Italian artists of the time. Michelangelo (1475–1564), even while serving the church with the genius of his art, gave strong expression to lifelike forms. His Sistine Chapel painting of Adam is a striking evocation of physical beauty and strength. Leonardo da Vinci (1452–1519) looked beyond surface beauty to the more minute ingredients of human anatomy, as we see in his *Mona Lisa*.

Like artwork Italian Renaissance literature paid special attention to human nature. A leading figure is the poet and historian Petrarch (1304–1374), who is often credited with founding the humanist movement. His poetical works emphasize the joys and sorrows that we routinely experience as human beings. As a champion of classical learning, his writings on history attempted to breathe life into the events of ancient Rome. In other works he attacked the medieval Aristotelian tradition and instead offered a Stoic perspective of life. His work *On the Remedies of Good and Bad Fortune* emphasizes the importance of moderation and the avoidance of senseless recreational activities, such as watching wrestling.

Pico

Perhaps the most vivid representative of Renaissance humanism is Pico della Mirandola (1463–1494). At an early age Pico was schooled in every imaginable area of classical study—Greek, Muslim, and Christian traditions, and even Jewish mysticism—and his philosophical writings combine all of these elements. His most famous piece is the *Oration on Human Dignity*, a brief speech that he composed in 1486. The philosophical context of this discussion is the classic theory of the "great chain of being." Philosophers from Aristotle on through the Middle Ages believed that there was a natural hierarchy of things in the world. At the very bottom of the chain are rocks and other nonliving material things. Above that are plants and then simple animal forms such as worms and bugs. After that there are small animals like mice and large animals like horses. Humans are next on the chain, followed by angels and then God. The medieval assumption behind this hierarchy was that all things are fixed in their unique places, and, as Aristotle argued, the purpose of a natural thing is defined in relation to where it resides on this scale.

Pico begins his *Oration* by asking what makes humanity so special. A typical answer to this question is that God placed us in a unique spot in the chain of being, just above animals and just below the angels. In this position we can experience things in the physical world around us, yet at the same time we can grasp the spiritual truths of the eternal heavenly realm. As lofty as this answer sounds, Pico finds it unsatisfactory. Offering an alternative theory, he speculates about God's intentions when creating the world: "He gave animated souls to the celestial spheres. He filled the dregs of the lower world with a variety of animals." God in fact filled every conceivable niche in the chain of being with some kind of creature. Then, when it came time to create humans, God saw that every slot was already occupied by some thing. God's solution was to allow people to select their own spot within the great chain. God tells Adam, "You can degenerate into the forms of the lower animals, or climb upward by your soul's reason, to a higher nature which is divine." What, then, makes humanity so special? The answer is that we have a unique ability to choose our own destiny, and, unlike the animals and even angels, we are not confined within any boundaries. Pico's observation is as true as it is insightful. People can in fact neglect their reason and civility and sink to the lowest level of animal existence, as we see all too often in criminal behavior. Yet people can also cultivate the highest levels of moral selflessness, as Gandhi did, or push scientific knowledge to its utmost limits. According to Pico, then, we are not rigidly locked into a predefined conception of human existence, as his medieval predecessors presumed. We should take pride in our ability to choose our human destiny, Pico argued, and make the most of it.

Machiavelli

Niccolò Machiavelli (1469–1527) was not technically speaking a humanist, but he was nevertheless a product of the Italian Renaissance. The son of an Italian lawyer, he was a young man in his twenties when the great preacher Savonarola was at the height of his influence in Florence. Savonarola had established a remarkably successful democratic government in that city, but in spite of his most virtuous efforts, he clashed with religious and political officials, and was ultimately executed. That such an influential man came to such a miserable end taught Machiavelli an early lesson about the relative power of good and evil forces in society. During his own career in government and diplomacy, he gave considerable thought to the rules or principles of effective political behavior, recording his thoughts in two books, *The Discourses* and *The Prince*, both composed in 1513 but published after his death. In *The Discourses* Machiavelli writes approvingly of the Roman Republic, expressing enthusiasm for self-government and liberty. In *The Prince*, however, his emphasis is on the need for an absolute monarch.

A clue to Machiavelli's thought lies in the reason for his apparent inconsistency in these two books. By expressing a preference for an absolute monarch in *The Prince*, he did not intend to reject the desirability of self-government about which he spoke so approvingly in *The Discourses*. Rather, he felt that the moral decay in Italy at that time did not allow for the kind of popular government exemplified in the Roman Republic. Machiavelli thought that it was all too obvious that people are evil. He found corruption at every level of political and religious government; even the popes of his day were of such bad repute that Machiavelli could write that "we Italians then owe to the Church of Rome and to her priests our having become irreligious and bad." A basically corrupt society requires a strong government. He believed that a monarchy—or rule by a single person—was the most preferable form of government since republics are rarely well ordered.

The lasting fame of *The Prince* rests on its recommendation that rulers should develop the art of deception and do whatever necessary—even abandon traditional moral virtues—for political survival. Only the shrewdest and craftiest individuals, he believed, could manage the precarious art of governing. Basing his thought on a close inspection of the actual behavior of his contemporaries, he quickly concluded that to think of political behavior in moral terms would be to expose oneself to all the dangers that clever opponents could create. For this reason he developed an indifference to the claims of morality. Christian morality emphasized humility and lowliness, whereas the morality of ancient Greek and Roman religion emphasized the "grandeur of soul" and "strength of body." His chief criticism of Christian ethics was that it had "made men feeble, and caused them to become an easy prey to evil-minded men." Machiavelli envisioned a double standard of behavior, one for rulers and the other for the people. The masses, he believed, need to follow Christian ethics as a necessary means of securing peace within society. Being concerned only with the social usefulness of religion, and not its truth, Machiavelli put forward a pragmatic view of religion that many political philosophers would adopt for centuries to come.

In contrast to the morality of the masses, rulers, he believed, must have the freedom to adjust their acts to the requirements of each occasion, without feeling bound to any objective moral rules. Machiavelli felt that the attitudes of the masses continually shifted, and this inconsistency must be matched by the ruler's shrewdness and swift adaptability. He writes, "People are ungrateful, fickle, false, cowards, covetous and as long as you succeed they are yours entirely," but when the ruler really needs help, "they turn against you." Machiavelli was, therefore, repelled by any notions that would require the ruler to be domesticated by morality. He recognized no higher law, such as Aquinas had propounded, but urged a thoroughly secular approach to politics. He valued cunningness higher than moral conviction; the ruler should choose only those means that could guarantee that the ends in fact be achieved. In the context of unscrupulous and egotistical people, morality must give way to sheer power if the ruler is to succeed. The ruler should be virtuous only if his best interests are served thereby. But even when he abandons traditional morals for the sake of survival, the ruler must "disguise this character well, and . . . be a great feigner and dissembler." Thus, while it is not necessary for the ruler to have all of the virtues, "it is very necessary to seem to have them." Even ruthlessness has its place, and Machiavelli provides an example. Caesar Borgia, a tyrant of the Romagna region of northern Italy, risked losing favor with his subjects because of unpopular policies enacted by his subordinate, Ramiro d'Orco. To overcome the damage, Borgia had him executed and left his body in the town square, with "the block and a bloody knife at his side." According to Machiavelli, "the barbarity of this spectacle caused the people to be at once satisfied and dismayed."

There is some question as to whether *The Prince* was in any sense intended to be a philosophy of politics. Since it grew out of the particular circumstances of Machiavelli's day, one might argue that it was mainly a practical plan of action for existing rulers. Still, there appears to be a more universal message in this work, namely, that the most useful course of action is in fact the right one. So influential were his views that the term "Machiavellianism" quickly became part of political vocabulary—referring to the view that leaders can justifiably use any means, however unscrupulous, to achieve political power.

THE REFORMATION

On October 31, 1517, a German priest named Martin Luther (1483–1546) launched the Protestant Reformation when nailing a document of protest to the door of Wittenberg Castle. Luther was offended at many Roman Catholic policies that had emerged during the Middle Ages and become mainstream by the time of the Renaissance. Papal authority, he believed, had gotten out of hand. To raise money, popes would routinely endorse the sale of certificates that promised the forgiveness of sins, which one could purchase for oneself or on behalf of a loved one who had died and gone to purgatory. Luther spent years diplomatically protesting such abuses. When these efforts failed, he led a movement within the German churches to completely sever ties with the Roman Catholic hierarchy. The movement spread to other European countries, and thus, a group of "Protestant" Christian churches emerged. The Reformation had a profound impact on philosophy, especially in these Protestant countries. In addition to rejecting Catholic Church authority, many Protestant philosophers abandoned the entire tradition of medieval thought, replacing it with both the revived theories of ancient Greece and new philosophies of their own devising.

Luther

Luther was deeply influenced by two great medieval philosophers—Augustine and Ockham. Augustine argued that sin rests in the bondage of the human will, not in ignorance or undeveloped reason. It is, therefore, faith, not reason, that overcomes our sinful predicament. In fact, Luther said, "it is the quality of faith that it wrings the neck of reason." Thus, things that seem impossible to reason are possible to faith. Ockham argued that we cannot discover God through the mere use of reason and so-called proofs for his existence. Rather, we gain knowledge of God through faith, which is a gift of grace from God himself. Luther adopted this position wholeheartedly. In addition to rejecting Aquinas's natural theology, he condemned the entire metaphysical system of Aristotle, saying of the great philosopher that "God sent him as a plague for our sins."

According to Luther, the problem with human reason is that, being finite, it tends to reduce everything to its own limited perspective. This is especially true when the natural reason contemplates the nature and capacities of God. Here human reason limits God to strictly human estimates of what God is and can do.

Luther was particularly struck by the intellectual difficulties faced by Abraham when God promised that from his barren wife Sarah he would give him off-spring. "There is no doubt," said Luther, that "faith and reason mightily fell out in Abraham's heart about this matter, yet at last did faith get the better, and overcame and strangled reason, that all-cruelest and most fatal enemy of God."

Luther's version of the Christian life had the effect of challenging not only the medieval system of scholastic theology but also those optimistic visions of individual and social perfection based on good works. Luther said, "All man-ner of works, even contemplation, meditation and all that the soul can do, avail nothing." Only one thing is necessary for righteousness, liberty, and the Chris-tian life, and "that one thing is the most holy word of God." If someone asks, "What then is this word of God, and how shall it be used, since there are so many words of God?" Luther answers, "The Apostle explains that in Romans 1:17 'The just shall live by faith.' . . . It is clear then that a Christian man has in his faith all that he needs, and needs no works to justify him."

Luther's emphasis on faith in religious matters had its counterpart in his political thought. Government, according to Luther, is ordained by God. For this reason government's key function is the "preservation of the peace." Our sinful nature makes us defiant, and this in turn requires a strong ruler: "God has subjected them to the sword, so that even though they would do so, they cannot practice their wickedness." For Luther obedience in the political realm in many ways parallels the function of faith in the religious realm. The individual must obey the ruler no matter what the ruler commands, since his comments are directed toward the preservation of peace and order. Without the power of the ruler, self-centered people would produce anarchy, "and thus the world would be reduced to chaos." What should we do, though, if we fall under the reign of a corrupt and brutal tyrant? Are we entitled to rebel? The answer, for Luther, is no. Life on earth is not our most important consideration; what counts most is the salvation of our souls. Whatever a ruler or sovereign does "cannot harm the soul but only the body and property." Even to God, "the temporal power is a very small thing," and, so, we too should not be bothered by rulers to the point that we consider disobeying them. For Luther "to suffer wrong destroys no one's soul, nay, it improves the soul, although it inflicts loss upon the body and property." This is a far cry from the medieval view that Aquinas formu-lated when he said that we need not obey the human laws of the state if they are perversions of natural law.

Erasmus

Desiderius Erasmus (1466–1536) was an important figure both as a humanist and for the Reformation. He was born in Rotterdam in 1466, the illegitimate son of a priest. Although a foe of scholastic medieval theology, he had no intention of rejecting the Christian faith. Through his humanistic learning, especially in the Greek language, he sought to uncover the pure and simple elements of Christianity that had been overlaid and obscured by the excessive rationalism of scholastic doctrine. His earliest training began in the school of the Brethren of the Common Life, from which he later entered the Augustinian monastery at Steyn. At the monastery life was miserable for Erasmus since he was unfit mentally, physically, and temperamentally for a regime that offered little physical comfort and virtually no intellectual freedom. Through good fortune he was invited by the bishop of Cambrai to become his Latin secretary. The bishop sent him to study for a while at the Collège Montaigue in Paris, where again he felt only contempt for scholastic methods of instruction. It was here, nevertheless, that his enthusiasm for classical literature was stimulated. It was here, too, that he began his first book, which would in time become one of his famous volumes, a book of proverbs titled *Adagiorum Chiliades*. In 1499 Erasmus visited England, where he soon came under the influence of John Colet, a biblical scholar, and Sir Thomas More. Erasmus thought it strange that Colet should lecture on the Bible without a knowledge of Greek. He therefore set out to become proficient in this language, eventually publishing a widely accepted Greek Testament with a new Latin translation. During a second visit to England in 1511, Erasmus became a member of the academic community of Cambridge, where he was appointed Lady Margaret Professor. He had little respect for his colleagues, whom he called "Cyprian bulls and dung-eaters," nor did he have any good words for the English beer or climate. After a few years he went to Basel, where he made his home until his death in 1536 at the age of 70.

Erasmus made several contributions to the spirit of the Renaissance. His enthusiasm for classical learning was a decisive influence at this time. He realized that the invention of printing now made it possible to popularize the classics by bringing inexpensive editions within the reach of large numbers of intelligent readers. These books opened up new worlds of classical learning that had not been available in the Middle Ages. But Erasmus was not simply an editor, even though his work in making available these classic Greek and Latin editions would have secured his reputation and significance in the history of thought. More important was his contribution to the development of a new style of literary expression. Erasmus loved words and spent much thought in selecting just the right word or phrase to express his insights. As painters would display genius in their use of colors, Erasmus, long a foe of lifeless scholastic discourse, found deep joy and freedom in fashioning a new and pure literary style marked by the elegance of each phrase.

Erasmus criticized scholastic jargon not only because of its lack of elegance but even more because it obscured the true teachings of the Gospels. It appeared to Erasmus that the ideas of the great classical writers were in basic harmony with the Gospels. In particular, he saw a close similarity between Plato's philosophy and the teachings of Jesus. He sensed a deep incongruity between the simple teachings of Jesus and the opulence and arrogance of the Papal Court. This moved him to write the satirical *Julius Exclusus*, in which Pope Julius II is forbidden by Saint Peter to enter the heavenly gates. His own earlier experience with life in the monasteries prompted him to write a criticism of the clergy in a book called *Praise of Folly*, which Luther made much use of in his decisive argument with the church. But Erasmus was neither a religious skeptic nor a Lutheran. His was a lover's quarrel with the Catholic Church, and he mainly wished to harmonize the church's teachings with the new humanistic learning.

Erasmus's *Praise of Folly* was both an ironic and a serious treatment of various kinds of folly within institutionalized religion and academia. He first lashed out against priests for their intricate calculations regarding the exact duration of a soul's residence in purgatory. He ridiculed the disputations of the theologians as they struggled with each other over the doctrines of the Incarnation, Trinity, and transubstantiation. His chief complaint was that the whole point of religion had been lost, that too much emphasis was being put on trivial and irrelevant details, especially in the monasteries where matters of dress and minutiae of discipline deflected men from the central aim of Christianity. Imagining how these priests would stand before the judgment seat seeking to enter heaven by calling attention to all their good works, Erasmus, going beyond good humor to invective, describes a priest who points to "so many bushels of prayers, another [who] brags of not having touched a penny without at least two pairs of gloves on." To all these Jesus answers, "I left you but one rule, of loving one another, which I do not hear anyone claim that he has faithfully carried out." Closely connected with this criticism of monastic life was Erasmus's abiding dislike of the hair-splitting logic of scholastic doctrine. In contrast to these follies of the clergy, which he condemned, he praised the so-called follies of simple faith. True religion, he felt, is a matter of the heart and not the head. This view was central for the Protestant reformers and was again expressed with great force by Pascal, who wrote that "the heart has reasons which the reason does not know."

While Luther became a passionate reformer, Erasmus remained only a critic. In his moderate book *Essay on Free Will*, Erasmus expressed the Renaissance view that we have a great capacity for moral improvement. In response to this book, Luther dismissed him as a "babbler," a "skeptic," and "some other hog from the Epicurean sty." In this debate Erasmus was the great exponent of the spirit of the Renaissance. With unfaltering optimism he continued to believe that education would eventually conquer stupidity and ignorance. His interest in classical literature and philosophy did not lead him to formulate a new scholasticism or to subordinate Christian faith to the philosophy of Plato. Rather, he used his knowledge of the classical languages to discover the real words of the Gospels, saying that "if there is any fresh Greek to be had, I had rather pawn my coat than not get it, especially if it is something Christian, as the Psalms in Greek or the Gospels."

If Erasmus looked back to antiquity for the treasure of the classics, the reformers, particularly Luther, looked back to the primitive community of Christians for the original spirit of Christianity. In this way the Renaissance and the Reformation both epitomized a revival of the past. Erasmus and Luther could agree on many points in their mutual attacks on the state of Christianity in the sixteenth century. However, whereas Erasmus could balance classical humanistic learning with a simplified Christian faith, Luther's exaltation of faith had the effect of throwing serious doubt on the capacity of human reason to lead humanity to salvation.

SKEPTICISM AND FAITH

One of the most important philosophical developments during the Renaissance was the revival of ancient Greek Skepticism, particularly the skeptical tradition of Pyrrho, which was refined and systematized by Sextus Empiricus (ca. 200 BCE). The writings of Sextus became widely available during the Renaissance, and many readers felt the allure of skeptical tranquility that he advocated. Others were horrified at Sextus's assault on human reason and felt compelled to attack his views. Thus, much of philosophy in the following centuries involved an intellectual tug-of-war between Skeptics and non-Skeptics.

Montaigne

In his celebrated *Essays* Michel de Montaigne (1533–1592) expressed a captivating version of classical Skepticism. Within the ancient writings of the Skeptics, Montaigne discovered a new way of viewing daily life. The word "skepticism" has over the centuries come to mean chiefly the attitude of doubt, which is often accompanied with indifference to the drift of life's events. But these were not the chief characteristics of classical Skepticism or of Montaigne's thought. Central to classical Skepticism was the atmosphere of inquiry coupled with a desire to live a thoroughly exemplary human life. This also was Montaigne's chief concern. He was particularly attracted to a way of life that permitted him constantly to discover new insights and at the same time enjoy all the powers he possessed as a human being. Montaigne wrote that "Pyrrho did not want to make himself into a stone; he wanted to make himself a living man, discoursing and reasoning, enjoying all pleasures and natural delights, using all of his physical and spiritual parts regularly and properly."

Montaigne saw himself as "an unpremeditated philosopher"—one who was not confined intellectually to some rigid set of ideas within which his thought and life must be expressed. His desire to live a happy life could not be fulfilled if he committed himself to doctrines about which perfectly reasonable objections could be raised. Many problems, he felt, had no clear solutions. This is the case with questions about the true nature of things, which so preoccupied the pre-Socratics. Montaigne accepted the judgment of the Skeptics, who said that there is "no more likelihood that this is true than that that is true." But, again, this formula was not intended to deny what common sense tells us is the case. Skepticism was a liberating force for Montaigne, freeing him from the rigid theories of other philosophical systems, and, quite paradoxically, freeing him from the theory of Skepticism itself! To be truly skeptical, we must doubt the very doubting process that we are engaged in, and thus avoid being swayed by its own theoretical force. We should never make any permanent commitment to any doctrines but instead assume a perpetual attitude of inquiry. Contentment, said Montaigne, is possible only when we achieve a tranquility of mind. What disturbs this tranquility is the attempt to go beyond our ordinary experiences and penetrate the inner nature of things. The saddest spectacle of all is to find people formulating final answers on questions that are far too subtle and variable for such treatment. The final folly of this attempt is the attitude of fanaticism and dogmatism.

Montaigne knew well the frightful outcome of fanaticism. In his lifetime he saw wars and fierce religious persecution. He wrote of his "neighborhood grown so old in riot" that he wondered whether his society could be held together. "I saw," he wrote, "common and general behavior so ferocious, above all in inhumanity and treachery, that I cannot think of it without blanching in horror." This he blamed on the fires of fanaticism. The loss of inner peace of mind would in time, he felt, be reflected in social turmoil. He genuinely believed that an attitude of constructive skepticism could prevent such outbursts of cruelty. With an attitude of true skepticism, human energies would be directed toward manageable subjects and purposes. Rather than struggling with riddles about the universe and its destiny, Montaigne would counsel people to start their philosophy of life by reflecting upon matters close at hand.

A good place to begin, said Montaigne, is with one's own personal experiences: "Every man carries within himself the whole condition of humanity." For this reason he was convinced that whatever proved useful to himself might also be useful for someone else. In the true spirit of the Renaissance, Montaigne sought an open and clear form of expression about the most natural and normal actions of men, rejecting the obscurity of technical jargon. "My assistant," he writes, "makes love and knows what he is doing. But read to him Leo Hebraeus or Ficino where they speak of the actions and thoughts of love, and he can't make head or tail of it." Montaigne complained that "I can't recognize most of my daily doings when they appear in Aristotle. They are decked out or hidden in another cloak for the benefit of schoolmen." What Montaigne thought was needed was to "do as much to make art natural as they do to make nature artificial." The art of life is to recognize what it means to be human, for "there is nothing so handsome as to play the man properly and well. Of all our diseases, the worst is to despise our own being." Nothing disfigures human nature more than a person's attempt to think more highly of himself than he should. Whenever this happens, Montaigne says, "I have always observed a singular accord between supercelestial ideas and subterranean behavior." Whenever men "would flee from themselves and escape from being men [they] engage in folly. Instead of transforming themselves into angels, they turn themselves into beasts."

For Montaigne Skepticism did not mean either pessimism as an attitude or a rule for behavior. On the contrary, he saw in Skepticism a source for a positive affirmation of all the facets of human life. Although he saw serious limits to the power of technical reason, he glorified the human capacity for critical judgment. To be a human being in the deepest sense, he thought, is to have fully conscious experiences—experiences in which we consciously weigh alternatives and control our behavior through an act of judgment. He expressed the insight of classical Skepticism with this formula: "I stop—I examine—I take for my guide the ways of the world and the experience of the senses." Our senses give us sufficiently reliable information about ourselves and the physical world, which ensures physical survival and genuine pleasure. The ways of the world also have value almost irrespective of their objective rightness or truth. Political laws and religion are fixed facts about the world, and to deny or reject them is virtually the same as saying that we are in no danger as we stand at the edge of a precipice. As to politics, good judgment requires us to accept the conditions and organization of our respective countries, and by looking around us, we can distinguish between appropriate and inappropriate restrictions upon our life. Skepticism should not lead us to revolutionary or anarchic behavior. Montaigne himself became a true political conservative who believed that social change must not be abrupt. Since there are no absolute truths, there are no specific ends toward which society must be forced to move. Custom acquires therefore a strong claim on people's political allegiance. In matters of religion also the person of good judgment will respect the authority of tradition, seeing in the stability of the organized religious community the condition for continued inquiry that anarchy would render impossible.

Thus, Montaigne sought to remind his generation that wisdom lies in accepting life as it is and realizing how difficult it is to know anything with certainty. He wanted particularly to direct people's attention to the richness of human life that respectful acceptance of human capacities could make possible. In this he was a true representative of the main current of the Renaissance.

Pascal

Blaise Pascal (1623–1662) was another thinker who was strongly influenced by the resurgence of Skepticism. Although officially distancing himself from the school of Skepticism, he nevertheless believed that human reason was incapable of obtaining the most important of life's truths. Pascal was renown as a mathematician and scientist. He laid the foundations of infinitesimal calculus and integral calculus. In 1639, at the age of 16, he wrote an essay on conic sections. Shortly thereafter, he invented an adding machine—a kind of mechanical computer. He also tried to prove the truth of Torricelli's experimental discovery of the vacuum.

When Pascal was 31 years old, he underwent a deep religious experience, which influenced the rest of his life as a thinker. Although he devoted himself to his deep faith in God, this did not lead him to abandon his scientific interests. Rather than considering scientific activities as too worldly and, therefore, of lesser significance than religion, he saw these two activities as working together, though not always at an equal level. The formula for his new way of thinking is found in his famous statement "The heart has its reasons which the reason does not understand." It would appear that, instead of reason or rigorous thinking, Pascal substituted the elements of feeling or emotion. Thus, for Pascal, the guide to truth is the heart. He does not give a precise definition of "the heart," but from the various ways in which he uses the term, it becomes clear that by "the heart" Pascal means the power of intuition. He was convinced that certain basic propositions in our thinking cannot be demonstrated; instead, we arrive at these principles through a special insight. Things are true or false according to the context or perspective from which we see them. Hence, "we know the truth not only by reason but also by the heart." It is by the heart that we know the difference between a dream and waking life. Here the term *heart* refers to "instinctive, immediate, unreasoned apprehension of a truth." In geometry we have an immediate awareness of principles. In ethics we have a spontaneous and direct apprehension of right and wrong. And in religion we have a loving apprehension of God, which in no way rests on the rational proofs of natural theology.

Whereas other philosophers set out to prove the existence of God by rational arguments, Pascal approached the existence of God by asking us instead to assume the point of view of the gambler. Every gambler, he says, takes a certain risk for an uncertain gain. If there are as many chances on one side as on the other, you are playing for the same odds. And in that case the certainty of what you are risking is equal to the uncertainty of what you may win. In life what you are wagering or what you are risking is your eternal life and happiness as compared with your finite life and unhappiness. To say that there is an eternal life is a way of affirming the existence of God. But how do we *know* that God exists? We simply do not *know*. The issue, then, is a matter of a wager. There are four possible outcomes to the wager, which have radically different consequences: (1) If God exists, and we believe in him, then our reward will be infinitely great; (2) if God exists, and we do not believe in him, then we will lose out on this reward; (3) if God does not exist, and we believe in him, then we have gained or lost nothing; or (4) if God does not exist, and we do not believe in him, then we have gained or lost nothing. By weighing these outcomes, Pascal thinks that we should be psychologically compelled to believe in God, since that promises the greater possibility of reward. Pascal does not feel that we can mathematically calculate our way to a conviction of religious belief. Instead, he feels that our calculation will at least prompt us to begin down the path of faith. We may start by mechanically suppressing our passions, adopting religious virtues and following religious customs. After immersing ourselves in religious traditions, he contends, a genuine faith commitment will naturally grow.

THE SCIENTIFIC REVOLUTION

A scientific revolution began in the Renaissance that had a sweeping and permanent impact on virtually all branches of knowledge. Unlike the medieval thinkers who proceeded for the most part by reading traditional texts, the early modern scientists laid greatest stress on observation and the formation of hypotheses. The method of observation implied two things. First, traditional explanations of the behavior of nature should be empirically demonstrated, since such explanations could very well be wrong. Second, new information might be available to scientists if they could penetrate beyond the superficial appearances of things. People now began to look at the heavenly bodies with a new attitude, hoping not solely to find the confirmation of biblical statements about the divine creation but also to discover the principles and laws that describe the movements of bodies. Observation was directed not only to the stars but also in the opposite direction, toward the minutest constituents of physical substance.

New Discoveries and New Methods

There are two distinct components to the scientific revolution: (1) the new scientific discoveries and (2) new methods of conducting scientific inquiry. As to new discoveries, to enhance the exactness of their observations, scientists invented various scientific instruments. In 1590 the first compound microscope was created. In 1608 the telescope was invented. The principle of the barometer was discovered by Evangelista Torricelli (1608–1647). Otto von Guericke (1602–1686) invented the air pump, which was so important in creating a vacuum for the experiment that proved that all bodies, regardless of their weight or size, fall at the same rate when there is no air resistance. With the use of instruments and imaginative hypotheses, fresh knowledge began to unfold. Galileo Galilei (1564–1642) discovered the moons around Jupiter, and Anton Leeuwenhoek (1632–1723) discovered spermatozoa, protozoa, and bacteria, and William Harvey (1578–1657) discovered the circulation of the blood. William Gilbert (1540–1603) wrote a major work on the magnet, and Robert Boyle (1627–1691), the father of chemistry, formulated his famous law concerning the relation of temperature, volume, and pressure of gases.

Among the more dramatic discoveries of the time were new conceptions of astronomy. Medieval astronomers believed that human beings were the focus of God's creative activity, and thus, God placed us quite literally in the center of the universe. Renaissance astronomers shattered this conception. The Polish astronomer Nicolaus Copernicus (1473–1543) formulated a new hypothesis in his *Revolutions of the Heavenly Spheres* (1543), which said that the sun is at the center of the universe and that the earth rotates daily and revolves around the sun annually. Copernicus was a faithful son of the church and had no thought of contradicting any traditional biblical doctrines. His work expressed rather his irrepressible desire to develop a theory of the heavens that would conform to the available evidence. Tycho Brahe (1546–1601) made additional and corrective observations, and his young associate Johannes Kepler (1571–1630) formulated three important laws of planetary motion in which he added mathematical equations to support mere observation. It was Galileo, though, who provided the greatest theoretical precision to the new astronomy and, in the course of this endeavor, formulated his important laws of acceleration and dynamics.

The second contribution of the scientific revolution involved the development of new scientific methods. Medieval approaches to science were grounded in Aristotle's system of deductive logic. Several Renaissance and early modern scientists proposed alternative systems, often quite different from each other. The scientific methods that we follow today, though, are in many respects the direct descendants of these early theories, particularly those of Francis Bacon (1561–1626), which stress the importance of observation and inductive reasoning. Scientific methodology made further progress as new fields of mathematics were opened. Copernicus had employed a twofold method: first, the observation of moving bodies, and, second, the mathematical calculation of the motion of bodies in space.

What Copernicus had begun was then considerably refined by Kepler and, particularly, Galileo. Galileo stressed the importance of direct observation and avoided secondhand information based simply on tradition and opposing conjectures contained in books. This led to his discovery of the satellites around the planet Jupiter. He writes, "To demonstrate to my opponents the truth of my conclusions, I have been forced to prove them by a variety of experiments." In a letter to Kepler, he reflects on the stubborn attitudes of old-school astronomers of his time: "My dear Kepler, what would you say of the learned here, who, filled with the stubborness of a venomous snake, have steadfastly refused to cast a glance through the telescope? What shall we make of all this? Shall we laugh or shall we cry?" In addition to his emphasis on observation, Galileo sought to give astronomy the precision of geometry. By using the model of geometry for his reasoning about astronomy, he assumed that he could demonstrate the accuracy of his conclusions if he could, as one does in geometry, produce basic axioms from which to deduce his conclusions. Moreover, he assumed that empirical facts correspond to geometric axioms, or that the axioms that the mind formulates correspond to the actual characteristics of observable moving bodies. To think in terms of geometry is to know how things actually behave. Specifically, Galileo formulated, for the first time, a geometric representation of the motion of bodies and their acceleration.

The mathematical component of scientific inquiry was developed further by Isaac Newton (1642–1727) and Gottfried Wilhelm Leibniz (1646–1716), who independently invented differential and integral calculus. In time the method of observation and mathematical calculation became the hallmarks of modern science. What most of these thinkers had in common was their belief that human knowledge about the nature of things is available to anyone who uses the appropriate method in its pursuit. Instead of looking back to tradition or to the testimony of ancient authorities, individuals can have direct access to the truth about nature, and this truth is most likely be discovered if one takes the information received through observation and organizes it into a system of axioms.

Modern Atomism

One of the growing assumptions among scientists and philosophers of the time was the view that the universe and all that it contained is composed of material substances. According to this conception, everything behaves in orderly and predictable ways. The heavens above and the smallest particles below all exhibit the same laws of motion, thus implying that everything conforms to a mechanical model. Pushing the issue further, philosophers attempted to explain human thought and behavior in mechanical terms, which earlier moralists described as the product of free will.

As early as the fifth century BCE, Democritus had reduced all things in the universe to atoms in motion—that is, to matter. Later, Lucretius (98–55 BCE) showed how deceptive appearances can be. He described how a person standing on one side of a valley might see on the other side something that looked like a white cloud, only to find upon going there that the "cloud" was a flock of sheep.

Similarly, Galileo stressed the distinction between appearance and reality, where appearance is made up of secondary qualities while reality consists of primary qualities. He believed that we cannot trust appearances as a reliable path to truth. For example, our notion based on appearances leads us to the erroneous conclusion that the sun moves around the earth. Similarly, a tree or a rock appears to be a single solid thing but in reality is composed of a multitude of atoms. The most accurate knowledge available to us is produced by the mathematical analysis of moving bodies, not only as in astronomy but also closer to hand as in physics.

Having in mind the distinction between primary and secondary qualities, Galileo certainly gave the impression that only those qualities that belong to bodies or matter have true reality. Primary qualities, such as size, position, motion, and density, are truly real because they can be dealt with mathematically. By contrast, secondary qualities, such as color, taste, emotions, and sounds, "reside only in consciousness; if the living creature were removed, all these qualities would be wiped away and annihilated." A human being can be defined as a body with physical organs. But when one is defined as a person, it turns out that most personal characteristics are represented by secondary qualities. This would mean either that these secondary qualities must be explained mathematically—as being aspects of the primary qualities of matter—or that the secondary qualities do not participate at all in the realm of reality. In either case the unique dignity, value, or special status of human beings in the nature of things is severely diminished.

Newton, accepting the view that nature is composed of "particles and bodies," expressed the wish that all the phenomena of nature could be explained "by the same kind of reasoning derived from mechanical principles, for I am induced by many reasons to suspect that they may all depend upon certain forces by which the particles or bodies . . . are either mutually impelled towards one another and cohere in regular figures, or are repelled and recede from one another." Accordingly, Newton refined the earlier formulations of the laws of motion in his great work *Principia Mathematica* (1687), a work that had enormous influence for generations to come. Although Newton still spoke of God as the one who created the machine of nature, it became increasingly unnecessary to refer to God when explaining the phenomena of nature. The whole drift of the new scientific method was toward a new conception of human kind, of nature, and of the whole mechanism of human knowledge.

As the universe was now viewed as a system of bodies in motion, so now all other aspects of nature were described as bodies in motion. Human nature and human thought also were soon to be viewed in mechanical terms. If all things consist of bodies in motion, this mechanical behavior, it was thought, must be capable of mathematical description. Thus, again, observation and the use of mathematics emerged in the Renaissance as the ingredients of the new method of scientific thought. With this method, it was assumed, new knowledge could be discovered. It was the view of Renaissance scientists that medieval thinkers had simply worked out explanatory systems for what they already knew but had provided no method for discovering new information. But the spirit of discovery, dramatized by Columbus's discovery of a new continent and by the discovery of new worlds in the arts, in literature, and in the unused faculties and capacities of humans, was now impelling scientists to open up new worlds in the structure of nature. And it was this new attitude of science that had the most immediate effect on the development of modern philosophy, especially on Francis Bacon and Thomas Hobbes, to whom we now turn.

BACON

Francis Bacon assigned himself the task of reforming the philosophy and science of his day. His central criticism was that learning had become stagnant. Science was identified with learning, and learning meant reading ancient texts. The study of medicine, for example, was chiefly literary and was practiced by poets, rhetoricians, and clergymen, whose sole qualification was their ability to quote Hippocrates and Galen. Philosophy was still dominated by Plato and Aristotle, whose teachings Bacon denounced as "shadows" and "phantoms." Although Bacon famously said, "Knowledge is power," he was particularly agitated by the "uselessness" of traditional learning. What made this learning inadequate was that science had become mixed up with "superstition," unguided speculation, and theology. Bacon challenged this approach to science, charging that it had no adequate method for discovering what nature and its workings are really like. The one ancient thinker for whom he did have respect was Democritus, whose materialism he adopted. But the teachings of the schoolmen of the Middle Ages he considered as "degenerate" versions of Aristotle. Instead of deriving substantial evidence from the actual nature of things, they worked on their own imaginations. They were like spiders that brought forth "cobwebs of learning, admirable for the fineness of thread and work, but of no substance or profit."

Bacon advocated wiping the slate of human knowledge clean and starting over, using a new method for assembling and explaining facts. He was convinced that he had discovered such a method, one that would unlock all the secrets of nature. He was aware of other attempts to correct the inadequacies of traditional learning—particularly attempts by Gilbert, Copernicus, and Galileo to amend Aristotle's physics. But what impressed him most was Galileo's construction and use of telescopes. He considered this event one of the most important in the history of astronomy because it made possible a true advancement of learning. For example, whereas the ancients did not know the composition of the Milky Way, the telescope made it evident that it is a collection of distant stars. Bacon likened the mind to a pane of glass or mirror that has been made rough and uneven both by natural tendencies of passions and by the errors of traditional learning. In such a condition, the mind cannot reflect truth accurately. Bacon's method, and his hope, was to make the mind's surface clean and smooth and to supply it with new and adequate instruments so that it could observe and understand the universe accurately. To achieve this, he would have to free science from entrenched and traditional learning. This meant separating scientific truth from revealed truths of theology and fashioning a new philosophy based on a new method of observation and a new interpretation of nature.

Bacon's Life

By birth and breeding, Francis Bacon was destined to live, work, and think in a style befitting one of high social rank. He was born in 1561, the son of Sir Nicholas Bacon, who was then Lord Keeper of the Great Seal. He entered Cambridge at the age of 12 and at the age of 16 was admitted at a relatively senior status to the legal world of Gray's Inn. Through the succeeding years, he was honored by Queen Elizabeth and King James I as a member of Parliament, the House of Lords, and in time became Solicitor-General, Lord Keeper, and finally Lord Chancellor. We can appreciate Bacon's philosophical brilliance all the more when we consider that he was engaged in a full legal and political career. His philosophical works are as significant as they are monumental. The best known of these are his *Advancement of Learning* and *New Organon*. He was aware that his political life had interfered with his primary objectives as a thinker, saying "I reckoned that I was by no means discharging my duty, when I was neglecting that by which I could of myself benefit man." To add further misery to his last years, shortly after being named Lord Chancellor, he was accused of accepting bribes and was thereupon fined, sentenced to a short imprisonment, and barred from public office forever. The end came in 1626 when, pursuing his zeal for experimentation, wondering whether the putrefaction of flesh could be halted by freezing, he went out in the cold and stuffed a chicken with snow. Getting badly chilled, he died a few days later, at the age of 65.

Bacon's principal objective was, as he said, "the total reconstruction of the sciences, arts and all human knowledge," and this he called his "great instauration," or restoration. But before he could proceed with his creative task, he leveled some fierce criticisms against Oxford, Cambridge, and universities in general, and also against the reigning schools of philosophy, denouncing them for their slavish attachment to the past. He thus sounded the call for a break with the lingering influence of Aristotle.

Distempers of Learning

Bacon attacked past ways of thinking, calling them "distempers of learning," to which he offered a cure. He named three of these: fantastical learning, contentious learning, and delicate learning. In fantastical learning people concern themselves with words, emphasizing texts, languages, and style, and "hunt more after words than matter, and more after choiceness of phrase . . . than after the weight of matter." Contentious learning is even worse, he said, because it begins with the fixed positions or points of view taken by earlier thinkers, and these views are used as the starting point in contentious argumentation. Finally, there is delicate learning, wherein earlier authors, who claim more knowledge than can be proved, are accepted by readers as knowing as much as they claim. This accounts for the acceptance of Aristotle, for example, as the "dictator" of science. These three diseases, he argued, must be cured in order to relieve the mind of the errors they create.

Idols of the Mind

Similarly, the human thinking is corrupted by Idols. Bacon refers to four Idols, which he metaphorically calls the Idols of the Tribe, the Cave, the Market Place, and the Theatre. These Idols, or "false phantoms," are distortions of the mind, like distortions of beams of light reflected from an uneven mirror: "For from the nature of a clear and equal glass, wherein the beams of things should reflect according to their true incidence, it is rather like an enchanted glass, full of superstition and imposture." The only way to correct this wayward type of thought is through observation and experimentation—that is, through the inductive method. These Idols, or "false opinions," "dogmas," "superstitions," and "errors," distort knowledge in different ways.

The Idols of the Tribe involve our preoccupation with opinions, following from "the false assertion that the sense of man is the measure of things." Here Bacon wanted to make the point that simply looking at things is no guarantee that we will see them as they really are. We all bring our hopes and fears, prejudices, and impatience to things and thereby affect our understanding of them. The Idols of the Cave were taken by Bacon from the Platonic allegory and again suggest the limitations of the untrained mind, which is shut in the cave of its own environment of customs and opinions, reflecting the kinds of books one reads, the ideas one considers significant, and the intellectual authorities to whom one defers.

The third class of Idols is aptly designated as the Idols of the Market Place, since it stands for the words people use in the commerce of daily life, words that are common coin in daily conversation. In spite of their usefulness, words can weaken knowledge because they are not created with care or precision but rather are framed so that the common person will understand their use. Even philosophers are diverted by these Idols, for they often give names to things that exist only in their imaginations. In addition, they fashion names for mere abstractions, such as "element" of fire, or the "qualities" of heaviness, rareness, or denseness. Finally, the Idols of the Theatre are the grand systematic dogmas of long philosophical treatises. These represent "worlds of their own creation after an unreal and scenic fashion." Bacon includes here not only whole systems but all principles or axioms in science that "by tradition, credibility and negligence have come to be received."

The Inductive Method

Having duly warned his generation that human understanding can be distorted by these Idols, Bacon described a new method for acquiring knowledge. In order to "penetrate into the inner and further recesses of nature," he said, we need to derive our notions from things "in a more sure and guarded way." This way includes ridding ourselves of prejudices and looking at things as they are: "We must lead men to the particulars themselves." To assist our observations, we need to correct our errors "not so much by instruments as by experiments. For the subtlety of experiments is far greater than that of sense itself." Bacon's concept of experiment and his method of observation rest on the notion of induction—that is, deriving "laws" from the simple observation of particulars and their series and order. The alternative view, which he harshly criticized, was Aristotle's deductive method. Aristotle's classic example of a deductive argument is this: (1) All humans are mortal; (2) Socrates is a human; (3) therefore, Socrates is mortal. The problem with this approach, according to Bacon, is that the conclusions we draw only perpetuate the errors that are already contained in the premises. Instead, we need an argumentative strategy that gives us *new* information from which we can draw *new* conclusions. Induction does just this.

Bacon knew the limitations of "induction by simple enumeration," for example, concluding that all horses are black because the first eighteen counted were black. The solution, Bacon believed, was to look for the underlying nature or "form," which we find represented in the particulars that we observe. The example he gives of his inductive method involves discovering the nature of heat. The first step is to draw up a list of all the instances in which we encounter heat, such as "the rays of the sun." This list he called the Table of Essence and Presence. Next, another list must be compiled to include items that resemble those on the first list but that do not have heat, such as "the rays of the moon and of stars." This second list he called the Table of Deviation. A third, the Table of Comparison, is a further attempt to discover the nature of heat by analyzing the different degrees of heat to be found in different things: "Ignited iron, for instance, is much hotter and more consuming than flame of spirit of wine."

The fourth step is the Process of Exclusion, whereby, setting "induction to work," we try to find some "nature" that is present whenever there is heat and absent when heat is absent. Is light the cause of heat? No, because the moon is bright but is not hot. This process of exclusion was central to Bacon's method of science; he called it "the foundation of true induction." He assumed that "the Form of a thing is to be found in each and all the instances, in which the thing itself is to be found." Applying this assumption to the problem of heat, Bacon concluded that "heat itself, its essence and quiddity, is motion and nothing else." The emphasis on "essence" has an Aristotelian sound and suggests that Bacon's break with Aristotle was not complete. Nevertheless, this final step does have a modern ring, for Bacon wanted to verify his conclusions by checking them against all the items listed in his tables.

The major weakness in Bacon's method is that he had no grasp of what modern scientists mean by a "hypothesis." Bacon assumed that if we simply looked at enough facts, a hypothesis would suggest itself. However, contemporary scientists know that it is necessary to have a hypothesis before they inspect facts. This hypothesis, then, serves as a guide in the selection of facts relevant to the experiment. Bacon also underestimated the importance of mathematics for science. Nevertheless, he permanently dislodged the grip of scholastic thought and provided the impetus for making philosophy scientific.

HOBBES

Hobbes's Life

The life of Thomas Hobbes spans ninety-one eventful years, from 1588 to 1679. He was born in Westport near Malmesbury, England, the son of a minister. His education at Oxford stirred in him a fascination for classical literature, whereas his exposure to Aristotelian logic left him bored. In 1608 he left Oxford and had the good fortune of becoming the tutor of the Earl of Devonshire, William Cavendish. This association with the Cavendish family was to influence Hobbes's development significantly, as it afforded him the opportunity to travel widely on the Continent and to meet many leading thinkers and personages of the day. In Italy he met Galileo, and in Paris he formed a lasting friendship with Descartes's admirer, Mersenne, and also Descartes's antagonist, Gassendi. There is some question whether he ever met Descartes in person, but his carefully reasoned objections to the *Meditations* show Hobbes's close familiarity with Descartes's philosophy. In England Hobbes was much admired by Bacon, who, as lord chancellor, enjoyed conversations with him and frequently dictated his thoughts to Hobbes during "delicious walks at Gorambery." Hobbes's early interest in the classics led him to translate Thucydides. In his early forties, his interests shifted to mathematics and analysis with his discovery of Euclid's *Elements*—a book that "made [him] in love with geometry." The next stage of his development, which was to persist for the rest of his life, witnessed the publication of his brilliant philosophical treatises, among which the most renowned is *Leviathan*.

Influence of Geometry upon Hobbes's Thought

Although *Leviathan* is primarily a book on social and political philosophy, Hobbes had not intended to restrict his attention to that subject. Caught up in the rising tide of scientific discovery, he was deeply impressed by the precision of science and, above all, by the certainty of scientific knowledge. The intellectual atmosphere of the sixteenth and seventeenth centuries had been undergoing a radical alteration as one area of inquiry after another yielded to the probing method of science. Hobbes caught the spirit of the times. His initial fascination with mathematics came from his encounter with Euclid. He joined that small but eloquent company of thinkers who saw in geometry the key to the study of nature. With a razor-sharp intellect and a fervor that caused him to exaggerate the possibilities of this method, Hobbes undertook to recast the whole gamut of knowledge in accordance with this single approach. He assumed that, no mattered what the object of study was, he could gain exact knowledge through the method of observation and deductive reasoning from axioms, formed from observation. He therefore set out an ambitious project, which was to recast the study of physical nature, human nature, and society, using the same method throughout. He published *De Cive* (*The Citizen*) in 1642, *De Corpore* (*Concerning Body*) in 1655, and *De Homine* (*Concerning Man*) in 1658. In the end it was his political philosophy that made him famous, for it was here that his application of rigorous logic and the scientific method produced startling new results.

As a political philosopher Hobbes is frequently, though not accurately, called the father of modern totalitarianism. His books *De Cive* and *Leviathan* read like grammars of obedience. He describes the relation between citizen and sovereign in such severe terms that it is no wonder he brought upon himself widespread criticism. Two considerations led Hobbes to formulate his unique theory of political obligation. The first was the political turbulence of his times, which saw English politician Oliver Cromwell preparing to lead his people in a savage civil war. This experience of violence, growing out of deep disagreements on political matters, contrasted sharply in Hobbes's mind with the relatively quick agreements people achieved in mathematical and scientific matters. Second, Hobbes looked at political philosophy as a variation of the science of physics. He assumed that from a thoroughly materialistic view of human nature, in which human behavior could be explained simply in terms of bodies in motion, he could formulate an accurate political philosophy. He hoped that if political theory could be formulated with logical precision, people would be more likely to achieve agreement among themselves and thereby arrive at what he longed for most of all, namely, peace and order. There is some question whether Hobbes was logically consistent in his systematic political philosophy, and there is even greater question about his assumption that people would become orderly in their relations to each other just because they had been provided a logical plan for harmonious behavior. In any case his theory of humanity and society took its novel turn mainly because he built it according to a mechanical model, the chief ingredients of which were bodies in motion. And because Hobbes's political theory depends so much upon his unique theory of knowledge and his mathematical model of reality, these aspects of his philosophy need to be considered in some detail as the background to his views on political community.

Bodies in Motion: The Object of Thought

Philosophy, according to Hobbes, is concerned chiefly with the causes and characteristics of bodies. There are three major types of bodies: physical bodies (such as stones), the human body, and the body politic. Philosophy is concerned with all three types, inquiring into their causes and characteristics. There is one principal characteristic that all bodies share and that alone makes it possible to understand how they came to be and do what they do, and that characteristic is motion. Motion is thus a key concept in Hobbes's thought. Equally important is the assumption Hobbes makes that only bodies exist, that knowable reality consists solely of bodies. He will not admit that anything such as spirit or God exists if these terms refer to beings that have no bodies, or are incorporeal. Of God's existence, Hobbes writes, "By the visible things in this world, and their admirable order, a man may conceive there is a cause of them, which men call God: and yet not have an idea or image of him in his mind." Hobbes was willing to concede that God exists but argued that people do not know what God is. Still, it made no sense to Hobbes that there could be something with an incorporeal substance, as the theologians characterized God. Substance, he argued, could be only corporeal, and for this reason God would possess some form of body. But Hobbes did not wish to pursue theological subtleties. He appears to have dealt with God's nature in this connection only to make the broader point that whatever exists is corporeal and that the scope of philosophy is limited to the study of bodies in motion.

Hobbes set out to explain both physical and mental events as nothing more than bodies in motion. "Motion," says Hobbes, "is a continual relinquishing of one place and acquiring of another." Anything that moves is changing its location, and similarly, whatever is caused to move changes its place. If something is at rest, it will always be at rest unless something moves it. Only a moving body can cause a resting body to move, for "by endeavoring to get into its place by motion [it] suffers it no longer to remain at rest." Similarly, a body in motion tends to stay in motion unless its movement is halted by some other body. This account of motion appears to be restricted to locomotion. For such concepts as *inertia, force, impetus, resistance,* and *endeavor*—terms that Hobbes uses to describe motion—all seem to apply to things in space that occupy or change their location. But since Hobbes started with the premise that only bodies exist, it was inevitable that he would have to explain all of reality and all processes in terms of moving bodies. Motion is, therefore, not only locomotion in the simple sense but also what we know as the process of change. Things become different because something in them has been moved by something else, and this refers not only to physical but also to mental change.

Hobbes refers to two kinds of motion that are peculiar to animals or people, namely, vital and voluntary motions. Vital motions begin with the process of birth, continue through life, and include such motions as pulse, nutrition, excretion, the course of the blood, and breathing, "to which motions there needs no help of imagination." Voluntary motions, such as going, speaking, and deliberately moving our limbs, are first of all movements in our minds, and "because going, speaking and the like voluntary motions, depend always upon a precedent thought of whither, which way, and what; it is evident that the imagination is the first internal beginning of all voluntary motion." Imagination is the cause of voluntary acts, but imagination itself and the human activity we call thought are also explained as being effects of prior causes—as being consequences of prior motions.

Mechanical View of Human Thought

The human mind works in various ways, ranging from perception, to imagination, to memory, to thinking. All these types of mental activity are fundamentally the same because they are all motions in our bodies. It was particularly obvious to Hobbes that perception, imagination, and memory are alike. Perception, by which he meant our ability to "sense" things, is our basic mental act, and the others are "derived from that original." The whole structure and process of human thought is explained in terms of bodies in motion, and the variations in mental activity are accounted for by designating the location of each type of mental act along a describable causal chain. Thus, the thought process begins when a body external to us moves and causes a motion inside of us, as when we see a tree—seeing the tree is perception or sensation. When we look at an object, we see what Hobbes called a *phantasm*. A phantasm is the image within us caused by an object outside of us. Perception is not the sensation of motion or the sensation of the exact qualities that an object actually possesses. We see the green tree, but green and tree are two phantasms—a quality and an object—and these represent the ways we experience the motion caused by the body external to us. The initial impact on us caused by an external object creates not only our immediate sensation but more lasting effects as well, just as on the ocean, though the wind ceases, "the waves give not over rolling for a long time after." And "so also it happens in that motion, which is made in the internal parts of man . . . for after the object is removed, or the eye shut, we still retain an image of the thing seen, though more obscure than when we see it." This retention of the image within us after the object is removed is what Hobbes means by *imagination*. Thus, imagination is simply a lingering— or what Hobbes called a decaying—sensation. When, later, we wish to express this decay and show that the sense is fading, we call this memory, "so that imagination and memory are but one thing, which for divers considerations hath divers names."

It would appear that thinking, as occurs when we have conversations, is something quite different from sensation and memory. In sensation the sequence of images in our mind is determined by what is happening outside of us, whereas in thinking we seem to put ideas together whichever way we wish. But, using his mechanical model, Hobbes explained thinking in exactly the same terms that he used in his account of sensation, so that thinking, for him, is a variation of sensation. Ideas follow each other in thought because they first followed each other in sensation. For "those motions that immediately succeeded one another in sense, continue also together after sense." Our ideas have a firm relationship to each other for the reason that in any form of continued motion—and thought is such a motion—"one part follows another by cohesion." But the mechanism of thought is not all that perfect, and people are always thinking in ways that do not mirror their past sensations exactly. Hobbes was aware of this, but he tried to explain even the broken sequences as the invasions of more dominant sensations into the stream of imagination and memory. For example, the thought of the civil war might remind him of a personal experience and thereby break the chain of events for which the civil war stood in his memory. He wanted to establish the view that nothing happens in thinking that cannot be accounted for by sensation and memory.

Still, there is a difference between the mind of an animal and the mind of a human being, even though both have sensation and memory. What distinguishes them is that we are able to form signs or names to mark our sensations. With these names we are able to recall our sensations. Moreover, science and philosophy are possible because of the human capacity to formulate words and sentences. Knowledge, then, takes on two different forms, one being knowledge of fact and the other knowledge of consequences. Knowledge of fact is simply memory of past events. Knowledge of consequences is hypothetical or conditional but is still based on experience. For it affirms that if A is true, B will also be true—or, using Hobbes's illustration, "If the figure shown be a circle, then any straight line through the center shall divide it into two equal parts." Scientific knowledge, or philosophy in the broad sense, is possible only because of the human capacity to use words and speech. Although Hobbes spoke of signs and names as words "taken at pleasure to serve for a mark," these words represent our experiences. Words and sentences point to the actual way things behave. Reasoning with words is, therefore, not the same as playing with words, for once the meaning of words is established, certain consequences follow for their use, mirroring the reality they help our imagination recall.

Thus, for two reasons it is a true proposition to say that a human is a living creature. First, the word *human* already includes the idea of living. Second, the word *human* is a mark for the sensation we have when we see an actual human being. The relation of words to each other is based on the relations between the events for which the words stand as representations. Reasoning, then, is "nothing but reckoning—that is adding and subtracting, of consequences of general names." And even if the word *human* does not refer to any general or universal reality but only to particular people, Hobbes still maintains that we have reliable knowledge, that although "experience concludes nothing universally," science, based on experience, does "conclude universally." This encapsulates Hobbes's *nominalism*, which led him to say that universal terms such as *human* are merely words and point to no general reality. This also exhibits his *empiricism*, which led him to argue that we can know things about all people because of what we know from our experience about some people.

Political Philosophy and Morality

When we turn directly to Hobbes's political philosophy, we find that he employed as much of his theory of motion and his logic—as well as the method of geometry—as this subject would permit. Just as he looked to the concept of bodies in motion to describe human nature—and particularly to describe human knowledge—so also he now analyzes the structure and nature of the state in terms of moving bodies. Moreover, his account of the state is the most impressive example of his conception of philosophy. For if philosophy is a matter of "reckoning, that is adding and subtracting of consequences of general names," it is preeminently in his political philosophy that he exhibits his skill and rigor with language.

What strikes us first about Hobbes's theory of state is that he approaches the subject not from a historical point of view but from the vantage point of logic and analysis. He does not ask, "When did civil societies emerge?" but rather, "How do you explain the emergence of society?" He hopes to discover the cause of civil society, and, in harmony with his general method, he sets out to explain the cause of the state by describing the motion of bodies. His thought about political philosophy resembles the method of geometry only in the sense that from axiomlike premises he deduces all the consequences or conclusions of his political theory, and most of these premises cluster around his conception of human nature.

The State of Nature

Hobbes describes people, first of all, as they appear in what he calls "the state of nature," which is the condition of people before there was any state or civil society. In this state of nature all humans are equal and equally have the right to whatever they consider necessary for their survival. *Equality* here means simply that people are capable of hurting their neighbors and taking what they judge they need for their own protection. Differences in strength can in time be overcome, and the weak can destroy the strong. The "right of all to all" that prevails in the state of nature does not mean that one person has a right whereas others have corresponding duties. The word *right* in the bare state of nature is a person's freedom "to do what he would, and against whom he thought fit, and to possess, use and enjoy all that he would, or could get." The driving force in a person is the will to survive, and the psychological attitude pervading all people is fear—the fear of death, and particularly violent death. In the state of nature all people are relentlessly pursuing whatever acts they think will secure their safety. The picture we get of this state of nature is of people moving against each other—bodies in motion—or the anarchic condition Hobbes called "the war of all against all."

Why do people behave this way? Hobbes analyzes human motivation by saying that everyone possesses a twofold drive, namely, appetite and aversion. These two drives account for our motions to and from other people or objects, and they have the same meanings as the words *love* and *hate*. People are attracted to what they think will help them survive, and they hate whatever they judge to be a threat to them. The words *good* and *evil* have whatever meaning each individual gives them, and people call good whatever they love and evil whatever they hate, "there being nothing simply and absolutely so." We are fundamentally egotistical in that we are concerned chiefly with our own survival, and we identify goodness with our own appetites. It would appear, therefore, that in the state of nature there is no obligation for people to respect others and there is no morality in the traditional sense of goodness and justice. Given this egotistical view of human nature, it would appear also that we do not possess the capacity to create an ordered and peaceful society.

But Hobbes argued that several logical conclusions or consequences can be deduced from our concern for our survival, among these being what he called *natural laws*. Even in the state of nature, people know these natural laws, which are logically consistent with our principal concern for our own safety. A natural law, says Hobbes, "is a precept, or general rule, found out by reason," telling what to do and what not to do. If the major premise is that I want to survive, I can logically deduce, even in the state of nature, certain rules of behavior that will help me survive. The first law of nature is, therefore, that everyone ought to "seek peace and follow it." Now this law that urges me to seek peace is natural because it is a logical extension of my concern for survival. It is obvious that

I have a better chance to survive if I help to create the conditions of peace. My desire for survival therefore impels me to seek peace. From this first and fundamental law of nature is derived the second law, which states that "a man be willing, when others are so too, as farforth as for peace, and defense of himself he shall think it necessary, to lay down his right to all things; and be contented with so much liberty against other men, as he would allow other men against himself." More simply, we should willingly give up our hostile rights toward other people if they are willing to give up their hostile rights toward us.

Obligation in the State of Nature

If we know these and other natural laws even in the state of nature, do we have an obligation to obey them? Hobbes answers that these laws are always binding, in the state of nature as well as in civil society. But he distinguishes between two ways in which these natural laws are applicable in the state of nature, saying that "the laws of nature oblige *in foro interno*; that is to say, they bind to a desire they should take place: but *in foro externo*; that is, to putting them in act, not always." Thus, it is not as if there were no obligations in the state of nature; it is just that the circumstances for living by these laws in the state of nature are not always present. People have a right to all things in the state of nature not because there is no obligation but because if a person was modest and tractable, and kept his promises "in such time and place where no man else should do so, [he] should but make himself a prey to others, and procure his own ruin, contrary to the ground of all laws of nature, which tend to nature's preservations." And even when we act to preserve ourselves, we are not free from rational natural laws, for even in the state of nature we ought to act in good faith: "If any man pretend somewhat to tend necessarily to his preservation, which yet he himself does not confidently believe so, he may offend against the laws of nature."

Hobbes was aware that anarchy is the logical outcome of egotistical individuals all deciding how best to survive. It would be a horrible condition in which there are "no arts; no letters; no society; and which is worst of all, continual fear, and danger of violent death; and the life of man solitary, poor, nasty, brutish, and short." We should thus avoid this condition of anarchy to the extent that it is in our power. The chief cause of this condition is the conflict of individual and egotistical judgments. By following the dictates of natural law, however, we can seek peace, renounce some of our rights or freedoms, and enter into a social contract. We will thereby create an artificial person—that great leviathan—called a *commonwealth*, or *state*.

The Social Contract

The contract by which we avoid the state of nature and enter civil society is an agreement between individuals, "as if every man should say to every man, I authorize and give up my right of governing myself, to this man, or to this assembly of men, on this condition, that you give up your right to him, and authorize all his actions in like manner." Two things stand out clearly in this contract. First, the parties to the contract are individuals who promise each other to hand over their right to govern themselves to the sovereign; it is not a contract between the sovereign and the citizens. The sovereign has absolute power to govern and is in no way subject to the citizens. Second, Hobbes clearly states that the sovereign can be either "this man" or "this assembly of men," suggesting that, in theory at least, his view of sovereignty was not identified with any particular form of government. It may be that he had a preference for a single ruler with absolute power, but he recognized the possible compatibility of his theory of sovereignty with democracy. But whatever form the sovereign took, it is clear that Hobbes saw the transfer of the right to rule from the people to the sovereign as both absolute and irrevocable.

Hobbes was particularly anxious to demonstrate with logical rigor that sovereign power is indivisible. Having shown that in the state of nature anarchy is the logical consequence of independent individual judgments, he concluded that the only way to overcome such anarchy is to make a single body out of the several bodies of the citizens. The only way to transform multiple wills into a single will is to agree that the sovereign's single will and judgment represent the will and judgment of all the citizens. In effect, this is what the contract says when people agree to hand over their right to govern themselves. The sovereign now acts not only on behalf of the citizens but as if he embodies the will of the citizens—thereby affirming an identity between the wills of the sovereign and citizens. Resistance to the sovereign by a citizen is therefore illogical on two counts. First, such resistance would amount to resistance to oneself; second, to resist is to revert to independent judgment, which is to revert to the state of nature or anarchy. The power of the sovereign must therefore be absolute in order to secure the conditions of order, peace, and law.

Civil Law versus Natural Law

Law begins only when there is a sovereign. This is a logical truism, for in the judicial or legal sense, a law is defined as a command of the sovereign. It follows that where there is no sovereign, there is no law. To be sure, Hobbes affirmed that even in the state of nature people have knowledge of the natural law, and in a special sense the natural law is binding even in the state of nature. But only after there is a sovereign can there be a legal order, because only then is there the apparatus of law in which the power of enforcement is central. Without the power to enforce, said Hobbes, covenants are "mere words." Hobbes identifies law with sovereign command, and he makes the additional point that "there can be no unjust law."

Nowhere does Hobbes's severe authoritarianism express itself in more startling form than when he argues that there can be no unjust law. It appears that justice and morality begin with the sovereign, that there are no principles of justice and morality that precede and limit the acts of the sovereign. Hobbes affirmed this in a notable passage: "To the care of the sovereign, belongs the making of good laws. But what is a good law? By good law, I mean not a just law: for no law can be unjust." Hobbes suggests two reasons no law can be unjust. First, because justice means obeying the law, justice comes into being only after a law has been made and cannot itself be the standard for law. Second, when a sovereign makes a law, it is as though the people were making the law, and what they agree on cannot be unjust. Indeed, the third natural law Hobbes speaks of is "that men perform their covenants made," and he says that this is the "fountain of justice." Hence, to keep the contract in which one agreed to obey the sovereign is the essence of Hobbesian justice.

It is evident that Hobbes forces his readers to take each word seriously and "reckon" all the "consequences" that can be deduced from it. If law means the sovereign's command and if justice means obeying the law, there can be no unjust law. But there can be a bad law. For Hobbes was enough of an Aristotelian to recognize that a sovereign has a definite purpose "for which he was trusted with the sovereign power, namely, the procuration of the safety of the people; to which he is obliged by the law of nature, and to render an account thereof to God." But even in such a case, in which the sovereign has commanded a "bad" law, the citizens are not the ones to judge it as such, nor does this justify their disobedience. The sovereign has the sole power to judge what is for the safety of the people. If the people disagree with him, they would revert to anarchy. If the sovereign engages in iniquitous acts, this is a matter between the sovereign and God, not between the citizens and the sovereign. And because he feared anarchy and disorder so deeply, Hobbes pushed his logic of obedience to the point of making religion and the church subordinate to the state. To the Christian who felt that the sovereign's command violated the law of God, Hobbes gave no comfort, but insisted that if such a person could not obey the sovereign, he must "go to Christ in martyrdom."

With these bold strokes Hobbes altered the course of philosophy. He was among the first to apply the methods of science to the study of human nature, providing novel explanations for human knowledge and moral behavior, departing also from the medieval notion of natural law, and arriving in the end at a highly authoritarian concept of sovereignty. Although Hobbes did not win widespread approval in his day, and even though there is much in his philosophy to question and criticize, his enduring influence was assured by the precision of his formulation of the problems of philosophy.

CHAPTER 10

Rationalism on the Continent

Although philosophy rarely alters its direction with radical suddenness, there are times when its new concerns and emphases clearly separate it from its immediate past. Such was the case with seventeenth-century Continental rationalism, whose founder was René Descartes and which initiated what is called *modern philosophy*. In a sense, much of what the Continental rationalists set out to do had already been attempted by the medieval philosophers and by Bacon and Hobbes. But Descartes, Baruch Spinoza, and Gottfried Leibniz fashioned a new vision for philosophy. Influenced by the progress of science, they attempted to provide philosophy with the exactness of mathematics. They set out to formulate clear, rational principles that could be organized into a system of truths from which accurate information about the world could be deduced. They emphasized the rational capacity of the human mind, which they now considered the source of truth about both human nature and the world. Although they did not reject the claims of religion, they did consider philosophical reasoning something independent of supernatural revelation. They saw little value in subjective feeling and enthusiasm as means for discovering truth. Instead, they believed that, by following the appropriate method, they could discover the nature of the universe. This was an optimistic view of human reason, one that ran counter to the recent attempts at reviving ancient Skepticism, particularly those by Montaigne. The rationalists assumed that what they could think clearly with their minds did in fact exist in the world outside their minds. Descartes and Leibniz even argued that certain ideas are innate in the human mind, and, given the proper occasion, experience would cause these innate truths to become self-evident. The highly optimistic plan of rationalism was not altogether successful, as shown by the differences in the views of the leading proponents. To be sure, the rationalists ascribed determinism to all physical events, interpreting the natural world according to the mechanical model of physics. But Descartes described reality as a dualism consisting of two basic substances, namely, thought and things extended into three dimensions. Spinoza proposed a monism, saying that there is only a single substance, namely, Nature. Leibniz was a pluralist, saying that there are different kinds of elemental substances which make up the world.

DESCARTES

Descartes's Life

René Descartes was born in Touraine in 1596. His father, Joachim Descartes, was a councillor of the Parliament of Brittany. From 1604 to 1612 young Descartes studied in the Jesuit college of La Flèche, where his curriculum included mathematics, logic, and philosophy. He was most impressed during these years with the certainty and precision of mathematics, as compared with traditional philosophy, which invariably produced doubts and disputes. For a time he was a soldier in the army of Maximilian of Bavaria. After traveling widely throughout Europe, he decided, in 1628, to settle in Holland, and it was here that Descartes wrote his principal philosophical works, including his *Discourse on Method* (1637), *Meditations on First Philosophy* (1641), *Principles of Philosophy* (1644), and *The Passions of the Soul* (1649). He went to Sweden in 1649 at the invitation of Queen Christina, who wanted Descartes to instruct her in his philosophy. As the queen could see him only at five o'clock in the morning, this unaccustomed encounter with the bitter cold at that hour made him easy prey to illness. Within a few months he suffered an attack of fever, and in February 1650, at the age of 54, he died.

The Quest for Certainty

Descartes was chiefly concerned with the problem of intellectual certainty. He had been educated, as he says, "at one of the most celebrated schools in Europe," and yet he found himself embarrassed with "many doubts and errors." Looking back on his studies, he saw that ancient literature provided him with charming fables that stimulated his mind. However, these could not guide his behavior since these fables portrayed types of human conduct that were simply beyond the power of human beings to perform. He spoke kindly of poetry, saying that the poet gives us knowledge with "imaginative force," even making truth "shine forth the more brightly" than could the philosophers. Still, poetry is a gift of the mind and not the fruit of study; therefore, it gives us no method for consciously discovering truth. Though he honored theology, he concluded that its "revealed truths" were quite above human intelligence, that to think successfully about them "it was necessary to have some extraordinary assistance from above, and to be more than a mere man." He did not want to deny these truths, for he apparently remained a pious Catholic to the end. Nevertheless, he did not find in theology a method by which these truths could be arrived at solely through the capacities of human reason. Nor was the philosophy he learned at college any more helpful in this regard, for "no single thing is to be found in it which is not subject of dispute, and in consequence which is not dubious."

His quest for certainty led Descartes to turn from his books to that "great book of the world" where through travel he met "men of diverse temperaments and conditions" and collected "varied experiences." He thought that by exposing himself to people of the world he would discover more exacting reasoning, since in practical life, as compared with scholarly activity, a mistake in reasoning has harmful consequences. But, he says, he found as much difference of opinion among practical people as among philosophers. From this experience with the book of the world, Descartes decided "to believe nothing too certainly of which I had only been convinced by example and custom." He resolved to continue his search for certainty, and on a memorable night, November 10, 1619, he had three dreams that convinced him to construct the system of true knowledge upon the capacities of human reason alone.

Descartes broke with the past and gave philosophy a fresh start. In particular, since his system of truth would have to be derived from his own rational capacities, he would no longer rely on previous philosophers for his ideas, nor would he accept any idea as true simply because it was expressed by someone with authority. Neither the authority of Aristotle's great reputation nor the authority of the church could suffice to produce the kind of certainty he sought. Descartes was determined to discover the basis of intellectual certainty in his own reason. He therefore gave philosophy a fresh start by using only those truths he could know through his own powers as the foundation for all other knowledge. He was well aware of his unique place in the history of philosophy; he writes, "Although all the truths which I class among my principles have been known from all time and by all men, there has been no one up to the present, who, so far as I know, has adopted them as the principles of philosophy . . . as the sources from which may be derived a knowledge of all things else which are in the world. This is why it here remains to me to prove that they are such."

His goal was to arrive at a system of thought whose various principles were not only true but connected in such a clear way that we could move easily from one true principle to another. But in order to achieve such an organically connected set of truths, Descartes felt that he must make these truths "conform to a rational scheme." With such a scheme he could not only organize present knowledge but "direct our reason in order to discover those truths of which we are ignorant." His first task, therefore, was to work out his "rational scheme"—that is, his *method*.

Descartes's Method

Descartes's method consists of harnessing the abilities of the mind with a special set of rules. He insisted on the *necessity* of method and on systematic and orderly thinking. He was appalled at scholars who sought aimlessly for truth, comparing them to people who, "burning with an unintelligent desire to find treasure, continuously roam the streets, seeking to find something that a passerby might have chanced to drop." He continues, "It is very certain that unregulated inquiries and confused reflections of this kind only confound the natural light and blind our mental powers." But by themselves our mental capacities can lead us astray unless they are carefully regulated. Method consists, therefore, in those rules by which our capacities of intuition and deduction are guided in an orderly way.

The Example of Mathematics   Descartes looked to mathematics for the best example of clear and precise thinking. "My method," he writes, "contains everything which gives certainty to the rule of arithmetic." Indeed, he wanted to make all knowledge a sort of "universal mathematics." He was convinced that mathematical certainty is the result of a special way of thinking. If he could discover this way, he would have a method for discovering true knowledge "of whatever lay within the compass of my powers." Mathematics is not itself the method, but merely exhibits the method Descartes was searching for. Geometry and arithmetic, he says, are only "examples" or "the outer covering" and not "the constituents" of his new method. What, then, is there about mathematics that led Descartes to find in it the basis of his own method?

In mathematics Descartes discovered something fundamental about mental operations. Specifically, he fastened on the mind's ability to apprehend directly and clearly certain basic truths. He was not so much concerned with explaining the mechanics of how we form ideas from experience. Instead, he wanted to affirm the fact that our minds are capable of knowing some ideas with absolute clarity and distinctness. Moreover, mathematical reasoning showed how we progress in an orderly way from what we do know to what we do not know. For example, in geometry we begin with concepts of lines and angles and discover from these more complex concepts, such as the degrees of an angle. Why can we not use this same method of reasoning in other fields as well? Descartes was convinced that we could, and he claimed that his method contained "the primary rudiments of human reason" and that with it he could elicit the "truths in every field whatsoever." From his perspective all the various sciences are merely different ways in which the same abilities of reasoning and the same method are used. In each case it is the orderly use of intuition and deduction.

Intuition and Deduction   Descartes placed the whole edifice of knowledge on the foundation of intuition and deduction, saying that "these two methods are the most certain routes to knowledge," adding that any other approach should be "rejected as suspect of error and dangerous." In a nutshell, intuition gives us foundational concepts, and deduction draws more information from our intuitions. Descartes describes intuition as an intellectual activity or vision of such clarity that it leaves no doubt in the mind. The fluctuating testimony of our senses and the imperfect creations of our imaginations leave us confused. Intuition, though, provides "the conception which an unclouded and attentive mind gives us so readily and distinctly that we are wholly freed from doubt about that which we understand." Intuition gives us clear notions but also some truths about reality, as, for example, that *I think*, that *I exist*, and that *a sphere has a single surface*—truths that are basic, simple, and irreducible. Moreover, it is by intuition that we grasp the connection between one truth and another—such as the formula "if A = B and C = B, then A = C."

Descartes describes deduction as "all necessary inference from facts that are known with certainty." What makes intuition and deduction similar is that both involve truth. By intuition we grasp a simple truth completely and immediately, whereas by deduction we arrive at a truth by a process, a "continuous and uninterrupted action of the mind." By linking deduction so closely with intuition, Descartes gave a new interpretation of deduction, which up to his time had been identified with a type of reasoning called the *syllogism*. Deduction, as he described it, is different from a syllogism. Whereas a syllogism involves the relationship of *concepts* to each other, deduction for Descartes involves the relation of *truths* to each other. It is one thing to go from a premise to a conclusion as one does in a syllogism. But it is another thing to move from an indubitable fact to a conclusion about that fact, as he says we must do by deduction. Descartes emphasized this difference between reasoning from a *fact* and from a *premise*, for the central point of his method was at stake here. His quarrel with earlier philosophy and theology was that conclusions were drawn syllogistically from premises that were either untrue or based only on authority. If we start with facts, though, we are guaranteed the truth of our conclusion through proper deduction. He wanted to rest knowledge on a starting point that had absolute certainty in the individual's own mind. Knowledge requires the use, therefore, of intuition and deduction, where "first principles are given by intuition alone while the remote conclusions . . . are furnished only by deduction." This, then, is, key component of Descartes's method. Another component of his method consists of rules to guide intuition and deduction.

Rules of Method   The chief point of Descartes's rules is to provide a clear and orderly procedure for the operation of the mind. It was his conviction that "method consists entirely in the order and disposition of the objects toward which our mental vision must be directed if we would find out any truth." We must begin with a simple and absolutely clear truth and must move step by step without losing clarity and certainty along the way. Descartes spent many years at the task of formulating concrete rules. Of the twenty-one rules found in his *Rules for the Direction of the Mind*, the following are among the most important:

> *Rule III:* When we propose to investigate a subject, "our inquiries should be directed, not to what others have thought, nor to what we ourselves conjecture, but to what we can clearly and perspicuously behold and with certainty deduce."

> *Rule IV:* This is a rule requiring that other rules be adhered to strictly, for "if a person observes them accurately, he shall never assume what is false as true, and will never spend his mental efforts to no purpose."

> *Rule V:* We shall comply with the method exactly if we "reduce involved and obscure propositions step by step to those that are simpler, and then starting with the intuitive apprehension of all those that are absolutely simple, attempt to ascend to the knowledge of all others by precisely similar steps."

Rule VIII: "If in the matters to be examined we come to a step in the series of which our understanding is not sufficiently well able to have an intuitive cognition, we must stop short there."

In a similar way Descartes formulated four precepts in his *Discourse on Method*, which he believed were perfectly sufficient, "provided I took the firm and unwavering resolution never in a single instance to fail in observing them." His own words, these are the rules:

> The *first* was never to accept anything for true which I did not clearly know to be such; . . . to comprise nothing more in my judgment than what was presented to my mind so clearly and distinctly as to exclude all ground of doubt. The *second*, to divide each of the difficulties under examination into as many parts as possible, and as might be necessary for its adequate solution. The *third*, to conduct my thoughts in such order that by commencing with objects the simplest and easiest to know, I might ascend by little and little, and, as it were, step by step, to the knowledge of the more complex. . . . And the *last*, in every case to make enumerations so complete, and reviews so general, that I might be assured that nothing was omitted.

Compared with Bacon and Hobbes, Descartes's method puts very little emphasis on sense experience and experiment in achieving knowledge. How is it that we know the essential qualities, for example, of a piece of wax, Descartes asks? At one time a piece of wax is hard and has a certain shape, color, size, and fragrance. But when we bring it close to the fire, its hardness melts, its fragrance vanishes, its shape and color are lost, and its size increases. What remains in the wax that permits us still to know it is wax? "It cannot," he says, "be anything that I observed by means of the senses, since everything in the field of taste, smell, sight, touch, and hearing is changed, and still the same wax nevertheless remains." It is "nothing but my understanding alone which does conceive it . . . solely an inspection by the mind," which enables me to know the true qualities of the wax. And, he says, "what I have said here about the wax can be applied to all other things external to me." He relies for the most part on the truths contained in the mind, "deriving them from [no] other source than certain germs of truth which exist naturally in our souls." Descartes assumed that we possess certain innate ideas, in the sense that we are "born with a certain disposition or propensity for contracting them." Because we can know these truths, we can be assured of a reliable foundation for our deductions. He was confident that he could start from the beginning and rethink and rebuild all of philosophy by having recourse solely to his own rational abilities and by directing them in accordance with his rules. He therefore set out to show that we can have certainty of knowledge not only about mathematical concepts but also about the nature of reality.

Methodic Doubt

Descartes used the method of doubt in order to find an absolutely certain starting point for building up our knowledge. Having set out in his *Rules* that we should never accept anything about which we can entertain any doubt, he now tries to doubt everything. He says, "Because I wished to give myself entirely to the search after truth, I thought it was necessary for me . . . to reject as absolutely false everything concerning which I could imagine the least ground of doubt." His intention is clear, for he wants to sweep away all his former opinions, "so that they might later on be replaced, either by others which were better, or by the same, when I had made them conform to the uniformity of a rational scheme."

By this method of doubt, Descartes shows how uncertain our knowledge is, even of what seems most obvious to us. What can be clearer than "that I am here, seated by the fire . . . holding this paper in my hands"? But when I am asleep, I dream that I am sitting by the fire, and this makes me realize that "there are no conclusive indications by which waking life can be distinguished from sleep." Nor can I be sure that *things* exist, for I cannot tell when I am imagining or really knowing: "I have learned that [my] senses sometimes mislead me." But surely arithmetic, geometry, or sciences that deal with things must contain some certainty, for "whether I am awake or asleep, two and three together will always make the number five." Here Descartes refers to his long-held belief that there is a God who can do anything. But, he asks, how can he be sure that God "has brought it about that there is no earth, no sky, no extended bodies"? In spite of how evident his impressions are of the world around him, there is a possibility—remote as it may be—that it is all a divinely implanted hallucination. Perhaps God is deceiving him with *everything* he is experiencing!

At this point Descartes says that "if I am fortunate enough to find a single truth which is certain and indubitable," that will suffice to reverse doubt and establish a philosophy. Like Archimedes, who demanded only an immovable fulcrum to move the earth from its orbit, Descartes searched for his one truth and found it in the very act of doubting. I may doubt that my body exists, or that I am awake, or, in short, that all is illusion or false. Nevertheless, one thing remains about which I can have no doubt at all, that *I am*. Descartes makes his point here, in one of the most famous passages in the history of philosophy:

> But I was persuaded that there was nothing in all the world, that there was no heaven, no earth, that there were no minds, nor any bodies: was I not then likewise persuaded that I did not exist? Not at all; of a surety I myself did exist since I persuaded myself of something. But there is some deceiver or other, very powerful and very cunning, who ever employs his ingenuity in deceiving me. Then without doubt I exist also if he deceives me, and let him deceive me as much as he will, he can never cause me to be nothing so long as I think that I am something.

According to Descartes, even if God is deceiving me in every possible way, I know that I exist since; in the very mental act of doubting, I am affirming my own existence. Descartes expresses this in the phrase "I think, therefore I am" (*cogito ergo sum*, in Latin).

At first, nothing more is proved by this truth—"I think, therefore I am"—than the existence of my thinking self. My doubts still remain about the existence of my own body and about anything else that is other than my thinking.

To say "I think, therefore I am" is to affirm *my* existence: "But what then am I? A thing which thinks. What is a thing which thinks? It is a thing which doubts, understands, affirms, denies, wills, refuses and which also imagines and feels." Throughout, Descartes assumes that because thinking is a fact there must also be a thinker, "a thing which thinks." This "thing" is not the body, for "I knew that I was a substance the whole nature of which is to think, and that for its existence there is no need of any place, nor does it depend on any material thing." This much, then, seems absolutely certain, namely, that I, an ego, exist, "for it is certain that no thought can exist apart from a thing which thinks." But so far, the thinker is alone, a Robinson Crusoe, enclosed in his ideas.

The Existence of God and External Things

To go beyond the certainty of his own existence as a thinking being, Descartes asks again how we know something to be true. "What," he asks, "is required in a proposition for it to be true and certain"? What is there about the proposition "I think, therefore I am" that makes it certain? "I came to the conclusion that I might assume as a general rule that the things which we conceive very *clearly* and *distinctly* are all true." In this context *clear* means "that which is present and apparent to an attentive mind," in the same way that objects are clear to our eyes. *Distinctness* refers to "that which is so precise and different from all other objects that it contains within itself nothing but what is clear." The reason, then, that the proposition "I think, therefore I am" is true is simply that it is clear and distinct to my mind. This is the reason, too, that mathematical propositions are true, for they are so clear and distinct that we cannot help accepting them. But to guarantee the truth of our clear and distinct ideas, Descartes had to prove that God exists and that he is not a deceiver who makes us think that false things are true.

Descartes cannot use Aquinas's proofs for the existence of God because those proofs are based on the very facts that are still subject to Descartes's doubt, namely, facts about the external world such as *motion* and *cause* among physical things. Instead, Descartes must prove God's existence solely in terms of his rational awareness of his own existence and internal thoughts. He therefore begins his proof by examining the various ideas that pass through his mind.

Two things strike him about these ideas: (1) that they are caused and (2) that according to their content they differ markedly from each other. Ideas are effects, and their causes must be discovered. Some of our ideas seem to be "born with me," some "invented" by me, whereas others "come from without." Our reason tells us that "something cannot be derived from nothing" and also that "the more perfect . . . cannot be a consequence of . . . the less perfect." Our ideas possess different degrees of reality, but "it is manifest by natural light that there must be at least as much reality in the efficient and total cause as in the effect." Some of our ideas, judging by the degree of their reality, could have their origin in ourselves. But the idea of God contains so much "objective reality" that I wonder whether I could have produced that idea by myself. For "by the name God I understand a substance which is infinite, independent, all-knowing, all-powerful and by

which I myself and everything else, if anything else exists, have been created."
How can I, a finite substance, produce the idea of an infinite substance? Indeed,
how could I know that I am finite unless I could compare myself with the idea of
a perfect being? The idea of perfection is so clear and distinct that I am convinced
that it could not proceed from my imperfect nature. Even if I were *potentially*
perfect, the idea of perfection could not come from that potentiality, for an actual
effect must proceed from a being that *actually* exists. Thus, Descartes holds that
(1) ideas have causes, (2) the cause must have at least as much reality as the effect,
and (3) he is finite and imperfect. From these three points he concludes that his
idea of a perfect and infinite Being comes from outside himself—from a perfect
Being who exists, from God. In addition, Descartes concludes that God cannot
be a deceiver, "since the light of nature teaches us that fraud and deception
necessarily proceed from some defect," which could hardly be attributed to a
perfect Being.

In addition to this argument from causation, by which he proved the existence of God, Descartes, following Anselm, offered his version of the Ontological
Argument. In this argument Descartes sought to demonstrate the existence
of God by exploring what the very idea of God implies. He says that if "all
which I know clearly and distinctly as pertaining to this object really does
belong to it, may I not derive from this an argument demonstrating the existence of God?" How is it possible to move from an analysis of an idea to the
certainty that God exists?

Some of our ideas, Descartes says, are so clear and distinct that we immediately perceive what they imply. We cannot, for example, think of a triangle
without at once thinking of its lines and angles. Although we cannot think
about a triangle without also thinking about its attributes of lines and angles,
it does not follow that to think about a triangle implies that it exists. But just
as the idea of a triangle implies certain attributes, so also the idea of God
implies attributes—specifically, the attribute of existence. The idea of God
signifies a perfect Being. But the very idea of perfection implies existence.
To speak of a nonexistent perfection is to engage in contradiction. We cannot coherently conceive of a Being who is supremely perfect in all respects
and at the same time is nonexistent. Just as we cannot think the idea of a
triangle without recognizing its attributes, so also we cannot think the idea
of God, Descartes says, without recognizing that this idea clearly implies
the attributes of existence. Descartes says, "That which we clearly and distinctly understand to belong to the true and immutable nature of anything,
its essence or form, can be truly affirmed of that thing. But after we have with
sufficient accuracy investigated the nature of God, we clearly and distinctly
understand that to exist belongs to his true nature. Therefore we can with
truth affirm of God that he exists." Against this line of reasoning, Descartes's
critic Gassendi said that perfection does not imply existence, since existence
is not a necessary attribute of perfection. To lack existence, he said, implies
no impairment of perfection, only the lack of reality. Kant, as we shall see,
went into considerably greater detail in his criticism of these attempts to
prove the existence of God.

From his own existence Descartes has proved God's existence. Along the way he has also established the criterion of truth and provided thereby the foundation for mathematical thought and for all rational activity. Now, Descartes takes another look at the physical world, at his own body, and other things, and asks whether he can be certain that they exist. To be a thinking thing does not of itself prove that my body exists, for my thinking self "is entirely and absolutely distinct from my body and can exist without it." How, then, can I know that my body and other physical things exist?

Descartes answers that we all have the clear and distinct experiences of changing our position and moving about, activities that imply a body, or what he calls "an extended substance." We also receive sense impressions—of sight, sound, and touch—frequently even against our will, and these lead us to believe that they come from bodies other than our own. This overwhelming inclination to believe that these impressions "are conveyed to me by physical objects" must come from God; otherwise, he could not "be defended from the accusation of deceit if these ideas were produced by causes other than physical objects. Hence we must allow that physical objects exist." For Descartes, then, knowledge of the self is prior to knowledge of God, and both the self and God are prior to our knowledge of the external world.

Mind and Body

Descartes has now reversed all his doubts and has satisfied himself absolutely that the self, things, and God exist. He has concluded that there are thinking things and things that are extended, that have dimension. Since a person has both a mind and a body, Descartes is left with the problem of determining how body and mind are related. The whole drift of his thought is in the direction of *dualism*—the notion that there are two different kinds of substances in nature. We know a substance by its attribute, and since we clearly and distinctly know two quite different attributes—namely, *thought* and *extension*—there must be two different substances, the spiritual and the physical, mind and body. Because Descartes defines a *substance* as "an existent thing which requires nothing but itself to exist," he considers each substance as thoroughly independent of the other. To know something about the mind, therefore, we need make no reference to the body, and similarly, the body can be thoroughly understood without any reference to the mind. One of the consequences of this dualism was that Descartes hereby separated theology and science and assumed that there need be no conflict between them. Science would study physical nature in isolation of any other discipline, since material substance possessed its own sphere of operation and could be understood in terms of its own laws.

If thought and extension are so distinct and separate, how can we account for living things? Descartes reasoned that because living bodies partake of extension, they are part of the material world. Consequently, living bodies operate according to the same mechanical and mathematical laws that govern other things in the material order. Speaking, for example, of animals, Descartes considered them to be automata, saying that "the greatest of all prejudices we have retained from infancy is that of believing that brutes think." We assume animals think, he says, only because we see them act as humans do on occasion, as when dogs do acrobatic tricks. Because humans have two principles of motion, one physical and the other mental, we assume that when animals perform humanlike acts, their physical movements are caused by their mental faculties. But Descartes saw no reason for attributing mental abilities to animals, because all of their motions, or actions, can be accounted for by mechanical considerations alone. For it is "nature which acts in them according to the disposition of their organs, just as a clock, which is only composed of wheels and weights." Thus, animals are machines or automata. But what about human beings?

Many activities of the human body, said Descartes, are as mechanical as those of animals. Such physical acts as respiration, circulation of the blood, and digestion are automatic. The workings of the human body could be reduced, he thought, to physics. Every physical event can be adequately accounted for by a consideration of mechanical or "efficient causes," as Aristotle called them; there is no need to consider a "final cause" when describing the physical processes of the body. Moreover, Descartes believed that the total quantity of motion in the universe is constant. This led him to conclude that the movements of the human body could not *originate* in the human mind or soul; the soul, he said, could only affect or alter the direction of the motion in certain elements and parts of the body. Just how the mind could do this was difficult to explain precisely, because thought and extension—mind and body—were for Descartes such different and separate substances. He argued that the soul does not move the various parts of the body directly. Instead, having "its principal seat in the brain," in the pineal gland, comes first of all in contact with the "vital spirits," and through these the soul interacts with the body. Clearly, Descartes tried to give the human body a mechanical explanation and at the same time preserve the possibility of the soul's influence on human behavior through the activity of the will. Humans, therefore, unlike animals, are capable of several kinds of activities. We can engage in pure thought, our minds can be influenced by physical sensations and perceptions, our bodies can be directed by our minds, and our bodies are moved by purely mechanical forces.

But Descartes's strict dualism made it difficult for him to describe how the mind and body could interact with each other. If each substance is completely independent, the mind must dwell in the body as a pearl in an oyster or, to use his own metaphor, as a pilot in a ship. Scholastic philosophy had described humans as a unity, in which mind is the form and body is the matter, and said that without one there could not be the other. Hobbes had reduced mind to bodies in motion and achieved human unity in that way. But Descartes aggravated the separation of mind and body by his novel definition of "thinking." For he included in the act of thinking some experiences that had traditionally been referred to the body, namely, the whole sphere of sense perceptions—for example, "feeling." When Descartes defines "what I am" as "a thing which thinks," he makes no mention of the body, for everything essential to him is included in "thinking." A thinking thing "is a thing which doubts, understands, affirms, denies, wills, refuses, and which also imagines and *feels*." Presumably, the self could feel heat without a body. But here Descartes cannot, apparently, fully accept his own dualism. He admits that "nature also teaches me by these sensations of pain, hunger, thirst, etc., that I am not lodged in my body as a pilot in a vessel, but that I am very closely united to it, and, so to speak, so intermingled with it that I seem to compose with it one whole." While he tried to locate the mind in the pineal gland, the technical problem of interaction remains. If there is interaction, there would have to be contact, and so mind would have to be extended. On this problem, his rules of method did not lead him to any clear and distinct conclusion.

SPINOZA

Spinoza's Life

Baruch Spinoza was among the greatest of Jewish philosophers. His originality of mind is suggested by his expulsion from the Synagogue of Amsterdam for his unorthodox views. His refusal to accept the chair of philosophy at Heidelberg was further evidence of his desire to preserve his freedom to pursue his ideas wherever the search for truth might lead him. Though he was content to live in simplicity, to earn a modest living grinding lenses, his fame as a thinker spread abroad and inspired both admiration and condemnation. Spinoza was born in Amsterdam in 1632 in a family of Portuguese Jews who had fled from persecution in Spain. He was trained in the study of the Old Testament and the Talmud and was familiar with the writings of the Jewish philosopher Maimonides. Forced to leave Amsterdam, in 1663 he went to The Hague, where he carried on his literary career, of which his *Ethics* is the crowning work. In 1677, at the age of 45, he died of consumption.

Spinoza was influenced by Descartes's rationalism, his method, and his choice of the major problems of philosophy. But their similarity of interest and even terminology does not mean that Spinoza was a follower of Descartes. At many points Spinoza brought something new to Continental rationalism, which Descartes had begun.

Spinoza's Method

In common with Descartes, Spinoza thought that we can achieve exact knowledge of reality by following the method of geometry. Descartes had worked out the basic form of this method for philosophy, starting with clear and distinct first principles and attempting from these to deduce the whole content of knowledge. What Spinoza added to Descartes's method was a highly systematic arrangement of principles and axioms. Whereas Descartes's method was simple, Spinoza set out almost literally to write a geometry of philosophy, that is, a complete set of axioms or theorems (about 250 altogether) that would explain the whole system of reality the way geometry explains the relations and movement of things. In geometry conclusions are demonstrated, and Spinoza believed that our theory of the nature of reality could also be demonstrated. Hobbes questioned whether Spinoza had accomplished anything by arranging his vast number of axioms and theorems into a system of knowledge. Hobbes argued that it is certainly possible to draw consistent conclusions from axioms but that, since these axioms consist of nothing more than arbitrary definitions, they do not tell us about reality. Spinoza would not agree that his definitions were arbitrary, for he believed, as did Descartes, that our rational faculties are capable of forming ideas that reflect the true nature of things. "Every definition or clear and distinct idea," says Spinoza, "is true." It must follow, therefore, that a complete and systematic arrangement of true ideas will give us a true picture of reality, for "the order and connection of ideas is the same as the order and connection of things."

The order of things also provides the pattern for the order in which the philosopher should arrange his subjects. It is of utmost importance to observe this order carefully if we are to understand the various aspects of nature accurately. If, for example, we say that things depend for their nature upon God, we must first know all that we can about God before we can understand things. For this reason Spinoza could find little value in Francis Bacon's method, which consisted of enumerating observations of visible events and drawing conclusions from these observations by induction. Nor would he use Aquinas's method of accounting for the existence of God by first analyzing the nature of our ordinary experience with things and persons. At this point, too, Spinoza rejects Descartes's approach. Descartes started with a clear and distinct idea of his *own* existence and, from the formula *I think, therefore I am*, proceeded to deduce the other parts of his philosophy. Because in the true nature of things God is prior to everything else, Spinoza believed that philosophy must formulate ideas about God first. These ideas of God, then, could appropriately affect the conclusions we draw about such matters as human nature, ways of behaving, and the relation between mind and body. And because Spinoza had such novel things to say about God, it was inevitable that he would say novel things about human nature as well. Spinoza, therefore, begins his philosophy with the problem of the nature and existence of God.

God: Substance and Attribute

Spinoza offered a strikingly unique conception of God, in which he identified God with the whole cosmos—a view that we now call *pantheism*. His famous formula was "God or Nature" (*Deus sive Natura*), as if to say that these two words are interchangeable. We might find hints of pantheism in biblical descriptions of God as he "in whom we live and move and have our being." However, Spinoza stripped the idea of God of earlier meanings by emphasizing not the *relation* between God and humans but a basic *unity* between them. "Whatever is," he says, "is in God, and nothing can exist or be conceived without God." The clue to Spinoza's unique conception of God is found in his definition: "God I understand to be a being absolutely infinite, that is, a substance consisting of infinite attributes, each of which expresses eternal and infinite essence." Spinoza's special thoughts revolve around the ideas of *substance* and its *attributes*.

Through an intricate sequence of arguments, Spinoza arrives at the conclusion that the ultimate nature of reality is a single substance. He defines *substance* as "that which is in itself and is conceived through itself: I mean that the conception of which does not depend on the conception of another thing from which it must be formed." Substance, then, has no eternal cause but has the cause of itself within itself. So far this is only a *conception*, an idea of a self-caused infinite substance. This idea, however, includes not only what this substance is like but also that it exists. The very idea of substance includes its existence, for "existence appertains to substance" and "therefore from its mere definition its existence can be concluded." This resembles Anselm's *ontological* argument and raises the same problems. Still, Spinoza was certain that we can go with assurance from our idea of this perfect substance to its existence, saying that "if anyone says that he has a clear and distinct, that is, a true idea of substance and nevertheless doubts whether such a substance exists, he is like one who says that he has a true idea and yet doubts whether it may not be false." That this substance is one and infinite follows from the previous definition Spinoza has given of substance. There is, therefore, a single substance with infinite attributes.

An *attribute*, Spinoza says, is "that which an intellect perceives as constituting the essence of substance." Since God is defined as a "substance consisting of infinite attributes," God thus possesses an infinite number of aspects to his essence. However, as we examine God from our limited human perspective, we can comprehend only two attributes of God's substance: thought and extension—that is, God's mind and God's body. Descartes thought that these two attributes showed the existence of two distinct substances, thereby leading him to affirm the dualism of mind and body. Spinoza, though, saw these two attributes as different ways of expressing the activity of a single substance. God is therefore substance perceived as infinite thought and infinite extension. Being infinite, God contains everything.

The World as Modes of God's Attributes

Spinoza does not contrast God and the world as if they were as different and distinct as cause and effect—as though God were the immaterial cause and the world the material effect. He has already established that there is only one substance and that the word *God* is interchangeable with *Nature*. But Spinoza does distinguish between two aspects of Nature, using for this purpose the two expressions "nature nurturing" and "nature nurtured" (in Latin, *natura naturans* and *natura naturata*). The first of these, nature nurturing, designates an active and living principle in God whereby he changes through the exercise of his attributes. The sister concept, nature nurtured, is a passive notion that designates what God has already created. It is this passive notion of God that contains all the "modes" or features of the world that exist—general laws of nature such as motion and rest, and singular things such as rocks, trees, and people.

As the *world* consists of the modes of God's attributes, everything in the world acts in accordance with necessity—that is, everything is determined. Thus, the modes in which thought and extension take form in the world are determined by God's substance. As Spinoza says, these modes represent "everything which follows from the necessity of the nature of God." Spinoza gives us a picture of a tight universe in which every event unfolds in the only possible way in which it can occur. He writes, "In the nature of things nothing contingent is granted, but all things are determined by the necessity of divine nature for existing and working in a certain way." In a special way God is free; while he had to create just what he did, he was not forced to do this by some external cause, only by his own nature. On the other hand, people are not even that free, for we are determined to exist and behave according to God's substance, of whose attributes humanity is a mode. All modes of God's attributes are fixed from eternity, for "things could not have been produced by God in any other manner or order than that in which they were produced." All the things we experience "are nothing else than modifications of the attributes of God's [Nature], or modes by which attributes are expressed in a certain and determined manner." Thus, everything is intimately connected, the infinite substance providing a continuity through all things. Particular things are simply modes or modifications of God's attributes.

Because everything is eternally as it must be, and because particular events are simply finite modifications of substance, there is no direction toward which things are moving. There is no *end*, no *purpose*, no final cause. From our human vantage point, we try to explain events as either fulfilling or frustrating some purpose of history. Ideas of purpose, Spinoza says, are derived from our tendency to act with an end in view. From this habit we tend to look at the universe as though it, too, had some goal. But this is a wrong way of looking at the universe and, indeed, at our own behavior. For neither the universe nor human beings are pursuing purposes; they are only doing what they must. This "truth might have lain hidden from the human race through all eternity, had not mathematics, which does not deal with final causes but with the essences of things, offered to people another standard of truth." And the truth is that all events are a continuous and necessary set of modifications of the eternal substance, which simply *is*. Thus, Spinoza reduced the biological to the mathematical.

Knowledge, Mind, and Body

How can Spinoza claim to know the ultimate nature of reality? He distinguishes between three levels of knowledge and describes how we can move from the lowest to the highest. We begin with the things most familiar to us, and, says Spinoza, "the more we understand individual things the more we understand God." By refining our knowledge of things, we can move from (1) *imagination*, to (2) *reason*, and finally to (3) *intuition*.

At the level of *imagination*, our ideas are derived from sensation, as when we see another person. Here our ideas are very concrete and specific, and the mind is passive. Though our ideas at this level are specific, they are vague and inadequate, for we know things only as they affect our senses. For example, I know that I *see* a person, but as yet I do not know simply by looking what this person's essential nature is. I can form a general idea, such as *human*, by seeing several people, and the ideas I form from experience are useful for daily life, but they do not give me true knowledge.

The second level of knowledge goes beyond imagination to *reason*. This is scientific knowledge. Everyone can participate in this kind of knowledge because it is made possible by a sharing in the attributes of substance, in God's thought and extension. There is in humanity what is in all things, and since one of these common properties is mind, the human mind shares in the mind that orders things. At this level a person's mind can rise above immediate and particular things and deal with abstract ideas, as it does in mathematics and physics. At this level knowledge is *adequate* and *true*. If we ask Spinoza how we know that these ideas of reason and science are true, he replies in effect that truth validates itself, for "he who has a true idea knows at the same time that he has a true idea, nor can he doubt concerning the truth of the thing."

The third and highest level of knowledge is *intuition*. Through intuition we can grasp the whole system of Nature. At this level we can understand the particular things we encountered on the first level in a new way, for at that first level we saw other bodies in a disconnected way, and now we see them as part of the whole scheme. This kind of knowing "proceeds from an adequate idea of the formal essence of certain attributes of God to the adequate knowledge of the essence of things." When we reach this level we become more and more conscious of God and hence "more perfect and blessed," for through this vision we grasp the whole system of Nature and see our place in it, giving us an intellectual fascination with the full order of Nature, of God.

Descartes was left with the difficult problem of explaining how the mind interacts with the body. This was for him virtually unsolvable because he assumed that mind and body represent two distinct substances. For Spinoza, however, this was no problem at all because he viewed mind and body as attributes of a single substance. There is only one order of Nature, to which both the body and mind belong. Humans constitute a single mode. It is only because we are able to consider humans (1) as a mode of extension that we speak of a body or (2) as a mode of thought that we speak of a mind. There can be no separation of mind and body because they are aspects of the same thing. For every body there is a corresponding idea, and, in general, Spinoza says, the mind is the idea of the body, which is his way of describing the relationship of the mind to the body. The structure within which the mind and body operate is the same. Thus, human beings are finite versions of God, for it is a mode of God's attributes of thought and extension. This interpretation of both humans and God set the stage for Spinoza's distinctive theory of ethics.

Ethics

The central feature of Spinoza's account of human behavior is that he treats people as an integral part of Nature. Spinoza says that he looks upon "human

actions and desires exactly as if I were dealing with lines, planes, and bodies."
His point is that human behavior can be explained just as precisely in terms of
causes, effects, and mathematics as any other natural phenomenon. Although
people think they are *free* and are able to make *choices*, they are victims of an illusion, for it is only human ignorance that permits us to think we possess freedom
of the will. People like to think that in some special way they stand outside the
rigorous forces of cause and effect—that though their wills can cause actions,
their wills are themselves not affected by prior causes. But Spinoza argued for
the unity of all Nature, with people as an intrinsic part of it. Spinoza therefore develops a naturalistic ethics whereby all human actions, both mental and
physical, are said to be determined by prior causes.

   All people possess as a part of their nature the drive to continue or persist
in their own being, and this drive Spinoza calls *conatus*, that is, innate striving.
When this *conatus* refers to the mind and body, it is called *appetite*, and insofar
as appetite is conscious, it is called *desire*. As we become conscious of higher
degrees of self-preservation and perfection, we experience pleasure, and with
a reduction of such perfection, we experience pain. Our ideas of good and evil
are related to our conceptions of pleasure and pain. As Spinoza says, "By good
I understand here all kinds of pleasure whatever conduces to it, and more especially that which satisfies our fervent desires, whatever they may be. By bad
I understand all kinds of pain, and especially that which frustrates our desires."
There is no intrinsic *good* or *bad*. We simply call something *good* if we desire it
and *bad* if we dislike it. Goodness and badness reflect a subjective evaluation.
But because our desires are determined, so are our judgments.

   If all our desires and actions are determined by external forces, how can there
be any occasion for morality? Here Spinoza resembles the Stoics, who also argued
that all events are determined. The Stoics called for resignation and acquiescence
to the drift of events, saying that though we cannot control events, we can control
our attitudes. In a similar way Spinoza tells us that through our knowledge of
God we can arrive at "the highest possible mental acquiescence." Morality, therefore, consists of improving our knowledge by moving from the level of confused
and inadequate ideas up to the third level of intuition, where we have clear and
distinct ideas of the perfect and eternal arrangement of all things in God. Only
knowledge can lead us to happiness, for only through knowledge can we be liberated from the bondage of our passions. We are enslaved by passions when our
desires are attached to perishable things and when we do not fully understand
our emotions. The more we understand our emotions, the less excessive will be
our appetites and desires. And "the mind has greater power over the emotions
and is less subject hereto, in so far as it understands all things as necessary."

   We must study not only our emotions but the whole order of Nature, for it
is only from the perspective of eternity that we can really understand our own
particular lives, for then we see all events through the idea of God as cause.
Spiritual unhealthiness, Spinoza says, can always be traced to our "excessive
love for something which is subject to many variations and which we can never
be masters of." But we possess by nature the desire and the capacity for higher
degrees of perfection, and we achieve levels of perfection through our intellectual

faculties. Passions enslave us only when we lack knowledge. But "from this kind of knowledge necessarily arises the intellectual love of God. From this kind of knowledge arises pleasure accompanied by the idea of God as cause, that is, the love of God; not in so far as we imagine Him as present, but in so far as we understand Him to be eternal; this is what I call the intellectual love of God." This love of God is, of course, not the love of a divine person. Instead, it is more akin to the mental pleasure we have when we understand a mathematical formula or a scientific operation. That the way to morality described here is "exceeding hard" Spinoza was willing to admit, adding that "all things excellent are as difficult as they are rare."

LEIBNIZ

Leibniz's Life

From his early youth, Gottfried Wilhelm Leibniz showed unmistakable signs of a brilliant mind. At the age of 13, he was reading difficult scholastic treatises with the same ease that others would be reading novels. He developed infinitesimal calculus and published his results three years before Sir Isaac Newton had released his manuscript to the printers, the latter claiming to have made the discovery first. He was a man of the world, courting the favor and receiving the patronage of eminent people. He was personally acquainted with Spinoza, whose philosophy impressed him, though he departed from Spinoza's ideas in decisive ways. Leibniz engaged in extensive correspondence with philosophers, theologians, and other people of letters. Among his grand projects were attempts to achieve a reconciliation between Protestantism and Catholicism, and an alliance between Christian states, which in his day would have meant a United States of Europe. He became the first president of the Society of the Sciences at Berlin, which was later to become the Prussian Academy.

Leibniz was born at Leipzig in 1646 and entered the university there at the age of 15. At Leipzig he studied philosophy, going next to Jena to study mathematics and then to Altdorf, where he completed the course in jurisprudence and received a doctorate in law at the age of 21. With extraordinary vigor he lived actively in the two worlds of action and thought. He was the author of several significant works. His *New Essays on Human Understanding* examines systematically Locke's *Essay*. His *Essays in Theodicy* deals with the problem of evil. He also wrote shorter philosophical works, including *Discourse on Metaphysics, The New System of Nature and the Interaction of Substances*, and *The Monadology*. He was in the service of the House of Hanover, but when George I became king of England, Leibniz was not invited to go with him, possibly because of his quarrel with Newton. His public influence declined, and in 1716 at the age of 70, neglected and unnoticed even by the learned society he founded, he died.

Substance

Leibniz was dissatisfied with the way Descartes and Spinoza had described the nature of substance, because he felt they had distorted our understanding of human nature, freedom, and the nature of God. To say, as Descartes did, that there are two independent substances—thought and extension—led to the impossible dilemma of trying to explain how those two substances could interact as body and mind either in human beings or in God. Spinoza had tried to solve the dilemma by saying that there is only one substance with two knowable attributes, thought and extension. But to reduce all reality to a single substance was to lose the distinction between the various elements in nature. To be sure, Spinoza spoke of the world as consisting of many modes, in which the attributes of thought and expression appear. Still, Spinoza's monism was a pantheism in which God was everything and everything was part of everything else. To Leibniz this conception of substance was inadequate because it blurred the distinctions among God, humans, and nature, each of which Leibniz wanted to keep separate.

Extension versus Force   Leibniz challenged the fundamental assumption upon which both Descartes and Spinoza had built their theory of substance, namely, that *extension* implies three-dimensional size and shape. Descartes assumed that *extension* refers to a material substance that is extended in space and is not divisible into something more primary. Spinoza, too, considered extension to be an irreducible material attribute of God or Nature. Leibniz disagreed. Observing that the bodies or things we see with our senses are divisible into smaller parts, why can we not assume, asked Leibniz, that all things are compounds or aggregates? "There must be," he said, "simple substances, since there are compound substances, for the compound is only a collection or *aggregatum* of simple substances."

Monads   There is nothing new in saying that things must be made of simple substances, for Democritus and Epicurus had argued centuries before that all things consist of atoms. But Leibniz rejected this notion of atoms, because Democritus had described these atoms as extended bodies, as irreducible bits of matter. Such a particle of matter would have to be considered lifeless or inert and would have to get its motion from something outside itself. Rejecting the idea of matter as primary, Leibniz argued that the truly simple substances are the *monads*, and these are "the true atoms of nature . . . the elements of things." The monads differ from atoms in that atoms were viewed as extended bodies, whereas Leibniz described the monad as being non-three-dimensional *force* or *energy*. Leibniz therefore said that matter is not the primary ingredient of things. Instead, monads with their element of force constitute the essential substance of things.

Leibniz wanted to emphasize that substance must contain life or a dynamic force. Whereas Democritus's material atom would have to be acted on from outside itself in order to move or become a part of a large cluster, Leibniz said that simple substance, the monad, is "capable of action." He added that "*compound* substance is the collection of *monads. Monas* is a Greek word which signifies unity, or that which is one. . . . Simple substances, lives, souls, spirits are unities. Consequently all nature is full of life."

Monads are unextended; they have no shape or size. A monad is a point, not a mathematical or a physical point but a metaphysically existent point. Each monad is independent of other monads, and monads do not have any causal relation to each other. It is difficult to imagine a *point* that has no shape or size, yet Leibniz wanted to say just this in order to differentiate the monad from a material atom. Actually, his thinking here resembles the modern notion that physical particles are reducible to energy, that particles are a special form of energy. Essentially, Leibniz was saying that monads are logically prior to any corporeal forms. True substances, then, are monads, and these Leibniz also calls *souls* to emphasize their nonmaterial nature. Each monad is different from the others, and each possesses its own principle of action and its own force. Leibniz says, "There is a certain sufficiency which makes them the source of their internal actions and, so to speak, incorporeal automata." Monads are not only independent and different. They also contain the source of their activity within themselves. Moreover, in order to emphasize that the rest of the universe does not affect their behavior, Leibniz says that the monads are *windowless*. But there must be some relation between all monads that make up the universe— some explanation for their orderly actions. This explanation Leibniz finds in his idea of a *preestablished harmony*.

Preestablished Harmony   Each monad behaves in accordance with its own created purpose. These *windowless* monads, each following its own purpose, form a unity of the ordered universe. Even though each is isolated from the other, their separate purposes form a large-scale harmony. It is as though several clocks all struck the same hour because they keep perfect time. Leibniz compares all these monads to "several different bands of musicians and choirs, playing their parts separately, and so placed that they do not see or even hear one another." Nevertheless, Leibniz continues, they "keep perfectly together, by each following their own notes, in such a way that he who hears them all finds in them a harmony that is wonderful, and much more surprising than if there had been any connection between them." Each monad, then, is a separate world, but all the activities of each monad occur in harmony with the activities of the others. In this way we can say that each monad mirrors the whole universe—but from a unique perspective. If anything "were taken away or supposed different, all things in the world would have been different" from what they are like at present. Such a harmony as this could not be the product of an accidental assortment of monads; instead, it must be the result of God's activity, whereby this harmony is preestablished.

God's Existence

To Leibniz this fact of a universal harmony of all things provided a "new proof of the existence of God." He had accepted, for the most part, the earlier attempts to prove God's existence. He says of these that "nearly all of the means which have been employed to prove the existence of God are good and might be of service, if we would perfect them." But he was particularly impressed by "this perfect harmony of so many substances which have no communication with each other." This harmony, he believed, pointed to the existence of God with "surprising clearness," because a harmony of many windowless substances "can only come from a common cause." This resembles the argument from design and from a first cause, although Leibniz modified the argument from cause with his principle of *sufficient reason*.

The Principle of Sufficient Reason Leibniz argued that any event can be explained by referring to a prior cause. But that prior cause must itself be explained by a still earlier cause. In theory, then, we might find a continual chain of finite causes, tracing back to infinity. So, when seeking the ultimate cause of any event, it will not help to single out any individual cause in this infinite chain, since there will always be another preceding it. The solution, according to Leibniz, is to recognize the existence of some cause outside the series of causes. That is, it must be outside the complex organization of the universe itself. This cause must be a substance whose own existence is necessary, whose existence requires no cause or further explanation, a Being "whose essence involves existence, for this is what is meant by a necessary Being." The sufficient reason for the ordinary things we experience in the world of fact lies, therefore, in a Being outside the series of obvious causes—in a Being whose very nature or essence is a sufficient reason for its own existence, requiring no prior cause, and this Being is God.

Evil and the Best of All Possible Worlds The harmony of the world led Leibniz to argue not only that God had preestablished it but also that in doing this God has created the best of all possible worlds. Whether this is the best or even a good world is open to question because of the disorder and evil in it. Indeed, nineteenth-century German philosopher Arthur Schopenhauer thought that this is, if anything, the worst of all possible worlds and that consequently we are not justified in concluding that God exists or that the world with all its evil is the creation of a good God. Leibniz was aware of the fact of evil and disorder but considered it compatible with the notion of a benevolent creator. In his perfect knowledge God could consider all the possible worlds he could create, but his choice must be in accord with the moral requirements that the world should contain the greatest possible amount of good. Such a world would not be without imperfection. On the contrary, the world of creation consists of limited and imperfect things, "for God could not give the creature all without making it God; therefore there must needs be . . . limitations also of every kind." The source of evil is not God but rather the very nature of things God creates, for as these things are finite or limited, they are imperfect. Evil, then, is not something substantial but merely the absence of perfection. Evil for Leibniz is privation. This is why Leibniz could say that "God wills *antecedently* the good and *consequently* the best," since the most that God can do, in spite of his goodness, is to create the best possible world. As a final consideration Leibniz agrees that we cannot rightly appraise evil if we consider only the particular evil thing or event. Some things that in themselves appear to be evil turn out to be the prerequisites for good, as when "sweet things become insipid if we eat nothing else; sharp, tart and even bitter things must be combined with them, so as to stimulate the taste." Again, events in our lives, taken by themselves, lose their true perspective. Leibniz asks, "If you look at a very beautiful picture, having covered up the whole of it except a very small part, what will it present to your sight, however thoroughly you examine it . . . but a confused mass of colors, laid on without selection and without art? Yet if you remove the covering, and look at the whole picture from the right point of view, you will find that what appeared to have been carelessly daubed on the canvas was really done by the painter with very great art."

Freedom   How can there be any freedom in the determined world Leibniz portrays, where God preestablishes an orderly arrangement by infusing specific purposes into the several monads? Each monad is involved in developing its built-in purpose, and "every present state of a simple substance is naturally a consequence of its preceding state, in such a way that its present is big with its future." Each person, whose identity centers around a dominant monad, his or her soul, must represent in this mechanical view an unfolding of a life that has been set from the beginning. Yet, since the basic nature of this person is thought, his or her development through life consists in overcoming confused thoughts and arriving at true ideas, which lie in all of us in the murky form of potentiality seeking to become actual. When our potentialities become actual, we see things as they really are, and this, Leibniz says, is what it means to be free. For him freedom does not mean volition—the power of choice—but rather self-development. So, although I am determined to act in specific ways, it is my own internal nature that determines my acts and not outside forces. Freedom in this sense means the ability to become what I am destined to be without obstructions. It also means a quality of existence whereby my knowledge has passed from confusion to clarity. I am free to the extent that I know why I do what I do. It was along these lines that Leibniz thought he had succeeded in reconciling his deterministic view of nature with freedom.

Whether Leibniz succeeded in reconciling his world of monads with the notion of freedom is certainly questionable. Although he does at one point speak of freedom in terms of "choice in our will" and say that "free and voluntary means the same thing," still his dominant emphasis appears to be on determinism—on the notion of a mechanical-like universe, or a spiritual machine. Actually, Leibniz does not use the mechanical model in describing the universe, for if he did, he would have to say that the various parts of the universe act on each other the way parts of a clock affect the movements of each other. In a sense Leibniz's explanation is even more rigorously deterministic than the mechanical model suggests. For his monads are all independent of each other, are not affected by each other, but behave in accordance with their original purpose, which they received from the beginning through God's creation. This kind of determinism is more rigorous because it does depends not on the vagaries of external causation but on the given and permanently fixed internal nature of each monad.

Knowledge and Nature

This deterministic view of nature is further supported by Leibniz's theory of knowledge. A person, for example, is for Leibniz similar to a "subject" in the grammatical sense. For any true sentence or proposition, the predicate is already contained in the subject. Thus, to know the subject is already to know certain predicates. "All men are mortal" is a true proposition because the predicate *mortal* is already contained in the notion of *men*. Leibniz therefore says that in any true proposition "I find that every predicate, necessary or contingent, past, present, or future, is comprised in the notion of the subject." Similarly, in the nature of things, all substances are, so to speak, subjects, and the things they do are their predicates. Just as grammatical subjects contain their predicates, so also existing substances already contain their future behavior. Thus, Leibniz concludes, "In saying that the individual notion of Adam involves all that will ever happen to him, I mean nothing else but what all philosophers mean when they say that the predicate is in the subject of a true proposition." Leibniz patterned his theory of substance or metaphysics after his theory of knowledge or logic. At the center of his argument is his special treatment of the notion of truth.

Leibniz distinguished between truths of reason and truths of fact. We know truths of reason purely by logic, whereas we know truths of fact by experience. The test of a truth of reason is the law of contradiction, and the test of a truth of fact is the law of sufficient reason. A truth of reason is a necessary truth in that to deny it is to be involved in a contradiction. Truths of fact, on the other hand, are contingent, and their opposite is possible. A truth of reason is a necessary truth because the very meaning of the terms used and the type of human understanding require that certain things be true. For example, that a triangle has three sides is true because to have three sides is what a triangle means. To say that a triangle has four sides is clearly to be involved in a contradiction. That 2 plus 2 equal 4, that A is A, that A is not not-A, that heat is not cold—all these propositions are true because to deny their truth would be contradictory. Truths of reason are tautologies, because in such propositions the predicate simply repeats what is already contained in the subject. Once the subject is clearly understood, there needs to be no further proof about the truth of the predicate. Truths of reason do not require or affirm that the subject of the proposition exists. It is true, for example, that a triangle has three sides even though we do not refer to any specific existing triangle. Truths of reason tell us what would be true in any case in which a subject, in this case triangle, is involved. They deal with the sphere of the possible. It is impossible and contradictory that a triangle should be a square, and therefore it cannot be true.

Mathematics is a striking example of the truths of reason, since its propositions are true when they pass the test of the law of contradiction. Thus, Leibniz says that "the great foundation of mathematics is the principle of contradiction . . . that is, that a proposition cannot be true and false at the same time." He concludes that "this single principle is sufficient to demonstrate every part of arithmetic and geometry." In short, truths of reason are self-evident truths.

They are *analytic* propositions, the predicate of which is contained already in the subject, and to deny the predicate is to be involved in a contradiction.

What about truths of fact? These truths are known through experience. They are not necessary propositions. Their opposites can be considered possible without contradiction, and for this reason their truth is contingent. The statement "Mary exists" is not a truth of reason; its truth is not *a priori*. There is nothing in the subject *Mary* that necessarily implies, or makes it possible for us to deduce, the predicate *exists*. We know the predicate that she exists only *a posteriori*—that is, after an experience. This truth of fact, as is the case with all truths of fact, is based on the law of sufficient reason, which says that "nothing happens without a reason why it should be so rather than otherwise." As it stands, the proposition "Mary exists" is contingent on some sufficient reason. In the absence of any sufficient reason, it would be just as true to say that "Mary does not exist." When a sufficient reason is present, other propositions have a basis of truth, so that we say, "If A, then B." This hypothetical character of A shows that although there may be a necessary connection between A and B, it is not absolutely necessary that A exist. The existence of A is contingent, that is, is *possible*. Whether it will in fact exist depends on whether there is or will be a sufficient reason for it to exist. For every truth of fact that we entertain, we can see that its opposite is possible, without contradiction.

When we consider all the possibilities that propositions about facts imply, a principle of limitation emerges. Whereas some events can be considered possible, simply as the opposite of others, they cannot be possible once other possibilities have become actual. That is, some possibilities are *compossible* with some events though not with others. Thus, Leibniz says that "not all possible species are compossible in the universe, great as it is, and that this holds not only in regard to things that exist contemporaneously but also in regard to the whole series of things."

The universe of facts, as we know it, is only a collection of certain kinds of compossibles, that is, the collection of all the *existent* possibles. There could be other combinations of possibles than the ones our actual universe contains. The relation of the various possibles to each other requires us to understand the sufficient reason that connects each event to another event. Physical science, unlike mathematics, cannot, however, be a deductive discipline. The truths of mathematics are analytic. But in propositions concerning facts, the subject does not contain the predicate. The law of sufficient reason, which governs truths of fact, requires that these truths be verified. But this verification is always partial, since each preceding event in the causal chain of events must also be verified. However, no human being is able to account for the infinite sequence of causes. If the cause of A is B, it is then necessary to account for the cause of B and to go back as far as the beginning. The first fact about the universe is like any other fact; it does not contain, so far as the power of human analysis is capable of discovering, any clearly necessary predicate. To know its truth requires that we discover the sufficient reason for its being what it is.

The final explanation of the world, Leibniz says, is that "the true cause why certain things exist rather than others is to be derived from the free decrees of the divine will." Things are as they are because God willed them to be that way. Having willed some things to be what they are, he limited the number of other possibilities and determined which events can be compossible. God could have willed other universes and other combinations of possibilities. But having willed this universe, there now exist certain necessary connections between specific events. Although from the perspective of human reason, propositions concerning the world of facts are *synthetic*, or require experience and verification, if we are to know their truth, these propositions are, from God's perspective, *analytic*. Only God can deduce all the predicates of any substance. And only our ignorance prevents us from being able to see in any particular person all the predicates connected with that person. In the end truths of fact are also analytic, according to Leibniz. A person does already contain his or her predicates, so that if we really comprehended the complete notion of a person, we could deduce these predicates, as, for example, "the quality of king, which belongs to Alexander the Great."

For Leibniz, then, logic is a key to metaphysics. From the grammar of propositions, he inferred conclusions about the real world. In the end he argued that all true propositions are analytic. For this reason substances and persons are for Leibniz equivalent to subjects of an analytic proposition; they really contain, he said, all their predicates. He also applies a *law of continuity* to his notion of substance in order to confirm his theory that each substance unfolds its predicates in an orderly and (from God's perspective) predictable way. The *law of continuity* states that "nature makes no leaps." Among created things, every possible position is occupied, so that all change is continuous. According to the law of continuity, rest and motion are aspects of each other, merging into each other through infinitesimal changes, "so much so that the rule of rest ought to be considered as a particular case of the rule of motion." The *windowless* monads, then, bear in themselves all their future behavior. And as this is true of each monad, all the combinations and possibilities of events already contained in the world also contain the whole future of the world, and the sufficient reason for this order is "the supreme reason, which does everything in the most perfect way." Although the human mind cannot know all reality as God knows it, still, Leibniz says, we know certain innate ideas, self-evident truths. A child does not know all these truths at once but must wait until maturity and for specific occasions in experience when these ideas are called forth. Such notions are *virtually* innate, since we know them only on specific occasions. Still, this doctrine of innate ideas, along with Leibniz's general treatment of the relation of logic to reality, bear the clear marks of the rationalist tradition. He optimistically appraised the capacity of reason to know reality and felt that we could deduce considerable knowledge from innate self-evident truths.

CHAPTER 11

Empiricism in Britain

Although the school of empiricism came on the scene in an unassuming way, it was destined to alter the course and concerns of modern philosophy. Whereas Bacon aimed at "the total reconstruction of . . . all human knowledge," John Locke, who was the founder of empiricism in Britain, aimed at the more modest objective of "clearing the ground a little, and removing some of the rubbish that lies in the way of knowledge." But in the process of "clearing" and "removing," Locke hit on a bold and original interpretation of how the mind works and, from this, described the kind and extent of knowledge we can expect from the human mind.

The scope of our knowledge, Locke said, is limited to our experience. This was not a new insight, for others before him had said much the same thing. Both Bacon and Hobbes had urged that knowledge should be built on observation, and to this extent they could be called *empiricists*. But neither Bacon nor Hobbes raised any critical question about the intellectual capacities of human beings. They both uncovered and rejected types of thought that they considered fruitless and erroneous. However, they accepted without challenge the general view that we can attain certain knowledge, so long as we use the proper method. Similarly, Descartes assumed that there was no problem that human reason could not solve if the correct method was employed. This was the assumption Locke that called into critical question, namely, the belief that the human mind has capabilities that enable it to discover the true nature of the universe. David Hume pushed this critical point even further and asked whether any secure knowledge at all is possible. In their separate ways the British empiricists—Locke, George Berkeley, and Hume—challenged not only their English predecessors but also the Continental rationalists, who had launched modern philosophy on an optimistic view of our rational abililities that the empiricists could not accept.

LOCKE

Locke's Life

John Locke was born in 1632 at Wrington, Somerset, and died seventy-two years later in 1704. He grew up in a Puritan home, trained in the virtues of hard work and the love of simplicity. After a thorough education in the classics at Westminster School, Locke became a student at Oxford University, where he took the bachelor's and master's degrees and was appointed senior student and later censor of moral philosophy. He spent thirty years of his life in the city of Oxford. Though he continued his studies of Aristotle's logic and metaphysics, he was gradually drawn toward the newly developing experimental sciences, being influenced in this direction particularly by Robert Boyle. His scientific interests led him to pursue the study of medicine, and in 1674 he obtained his medical degree and was licensed to practice. As he pondered what direction his career might take, there was added to the considerations of medicine and Oxford tutor an alternative: political diplomacy. He actually served in various capacities, eventually becoming the personal physician and confidential advisor to the Earl of Shaftesbury, one of the leading politicians of London. But earlier influences—among them his reading of Descartes's works while at Oxford—confirmed his desire to devote his creative abilities to working out a philosophical understanding of certain problems that perplexed his generation. He wrote on such diverse topics as *The Reasonableness of Christianity, An Essay concerning Toleration*, and *The Consequences of the Lowering of Interest and Raising the Value of Money*, indicating his active participation in the public affairs of his day.

In 1690, when he was 57 years old, Locke published two books that were to make him famous as a philosopher and as a political theorist: *An Essay concerning Human Understanding* and *Two Treatises on Civil Government*. Although other philosophers before him had written about human knowledge, Locke was the first to produce a full-length inquiry into the scope and limits of the human mind. Similarly, others had written important works on political theory, but Locke's second of the *Two Treatises* came at a time when it could shape the thoughts of an era and affect the course of future events. *Two Treatises* and *An Essay* show Locke's way of combining his practical and theoretical interests and abilities. *Two Treatises* was expressly formulated to justify the English revolution of 1688. Some of its ideas took such strong hold on succeeding generations that phrases contained in it—for example, that we are "all equal and independent" and possess the natural rights to "life, health, liberty and possessions,"—worked their way into the Declaration of Independence and affected the shaping of the American Constitution. Regarding his *Essay*, he tells us that it grew out of an experience that occurred about twenty years before this work was published. On that occasion five or six friends met to discuss a point in philosophy, and before long they were hopelessly snarled, "without coming any nearer a resolution of those doubts which perplexed us." Locke was convinced that the discussion had taken a wrong turn. Before we could address "the principles of morality and revealed religion," he said, we first needed to "examine our own abilities, and see what *objects* our understandings were, or were not, fitted to deal with." From this examination Locke eventually composed his *Essay concerning Human Understanding*, which became the foundation of empiricism in Britain.

Locke's Theory of Knowledge

Locke set out "to enquire into the origin, certainty, and extent of human knowledge." He assumed that if he could describe what knowledge consists of and how it is obtained, he could determine the limits of knowledge and decide what constitutes intellectual certainty. His conclusion was that knowledge is restricted to *ideas*—not the innate ideas of the rationalists but ideas that are generated by objects we experience. Without exception, according to Locke, all our ideas come to us through some kind of experience. This means that each person's mind is in the beginning like a blank sheet of paper upon which experience alone can subsequently write knowledge. Before he could elaborate these conclusions, Locke felt that he must lay to rest the persisting theory of innate ideas, the notion that in some way we all come into the world with a standard collection of ideas built into the mind.

No Innate Ideas   It is obvious that if Locke is going to say that all ideas come from experience, he must reject the theory of innateness. He points out that "it is an established opinion among some men, that there are in the understanding certain innate principles . . . stamped upon the mind of man, which the soul receives in its very first beginning, and brings into the world with it." Not only does Locke reject this as not true, but he considers this doctrine a dangerous tool in the hands of those who could misuse it. If a skillful ruler could convince people that certain principles are innate, this could "take them off from the use of their own reason and judgment, and put them on believing and taking them upon trust without further explanation." And, "in this posture of blind credulity, they might be more easily governed." But there were those whose interest in the theory of innate ideas was not so malignant.

This was so with Ralph Cudworth (1617–1688)—member of a school of thought called Cambridge Platonism, which, following Plato, maintained that reason was the ultimate criterion of knowledge. Cudworth published his *True Intellectual System of the Universe* in 1678, just at the time when Locke was trying to sort out his thoughts on these problems. Cudworth took the position that the demonstration of God's existence rested on the premise that certain principles are innate in the human mind. He contended further that the famous empiricist formula that "nothing exists in the intellect which was not first in the senses" leads to atheism. According to Cudworth, if knowledge consists solely of information supplied to the mind by objects external to it, the external world existed before there was knowledge. In that case knowledge could not have been the cause of the world. Locke disagreed with this view, saying that it was indeed possible to prove the existence of God without recourse to the notion of innate principles. He was particularly concerned to expose the groundless claim for innate ideas in order to keep clear the distinction between prejudice, enthusiasm, and opinion, on the one hand, and knowledge, on the other. He therefore set out a series of arguments against this claim to innate ideas.

Those who argued for the theory of innate ideas did so on the grounds that people universally accept the truth of various rational principles. Among these are the principles "What is, is," which is the principle of identity, and "It is impossible for the same thing to be, and not to be," which is the principle of noncontradiction. But are these innate? Locke denied that they are, though he does not question their certainty. These principles are certain not because they are innate, but because, once we reflect on the nature of things as they are, our minds will not let us think otherwise. And, even if these principles were accepted by everyone, this would not prove that they are innate, provided that an alternative explanation could be given for this universal consent. Moreover, he argued, there is some question whether there is universal knowledge of these principles. "Seldom," says Locke, are these general principles "mentioned in the huts of Indians, much less are they found in the thoughts of children." If it is argued that such principles can be apprehended only after the mind matures, then why call them *innate*? If they were truly innate, they must always be known, for "no proposition can be said to be in the mind, which it never yet knew which it never yet was conscious of." As Locke saw the matter, the doctrine of innate ideas was superfluous because it contained nothing that he could not explain in terms of his empirical account of the origin of ideas.

Simple and Complex Ideas Locke assumed that knowledge could be explained by discovering the raw materials out of which it was made. Of these ingredients he said, "Let us then suppose the mind to be, as we say, white paper, void of all characters, without any ideas:—How comes it to be furnished? . . . Whence has it all the *materials* of reason and knowledge? To this I answer, in one word, from *experience*." Experience gives us two sources of ideas: *sensation* and *reflection*. From the senses we receive in our minds several distinct perceptions and thereby become conversant about objects external to us. This is how we come to have the ideas of yellow, white, heat, cold, soft, hard, bitter, sweet, and all the other sensible qualities. Sensation is the "great source of most of the ideas we have." The other facet of experience is reflection, an activity of the mind that produces ideas by taking notice of previous ideas furnished by the senses. Reflection involves perception, thinking, doubting, believing, reasoning, knowing, willing, and all those activities of the mind that produce ideas as distinct as those we receive from external bodies affecting the senses. All the ideas we have can be traced either to sensation or to reflection, and these ideas in turn are either simple or complex.

Simple ideas constitute the chief source of the raw materials out of which our knowledge is made. These ideas are received passively by the mind through the senses. When we look at an object, ideas come into our minds in single file. This is so even when an object has several qualities blended together. For example, a white lily has the qualities of whiteness and sweetness without any separation. Our minds receive the ideas of *white* and *sweet* separately because each idea enters through a different sense, namely, the sense of sight and the sense of smell. Sometimes different qualities enter by the same sense, as when both the hardness and coldness of ice come through the sense of touch. In this case our minds sort out the difference between them because there are in fact two different qualities involved. Simple ideas originate first of all, then, in sensation. But some also originate in reflection. Just as the senses are affected by objects, so, too, are our minds *aware* of the ideas we have received. In relation to the ideas received through the senses, our minds can develop other simple ideas by reasoning and judging. Thus, a simple idea of reflection might be pleasure or pain, or the idea of causal power obtained from observing the effect natural bodies have on one another.

Complex ideas, on the other hand, are not received passively but rather are put together by our minds as a compound of simple ideas. Here the emphasis is on the activity of our minds, which takes three forms: The mind (1) *joins* ideas, (2) brings ideas together but holds them separate, (3) and *abstracts*. Thus, my mind joins the simple ideas of whiteness, hardness, and sweetness to form the complex idea of a lump of sugar. My mind also brings ideas together but holds them separate for the purpose of thinking of relationships, as when I say that the grass is greener than the tree. Finally, my mind can separate ideas "from all other ideas that accompany them in their real existence" as when I separate the idea of *man* from John and Peter. In this manner of abstraction, "all its general laws are made."

Primary and Secondary Qualities   To describe in even more detail how we get our ideas, Locke turned his attention to the problem of how ideas are related to the objects that produce them. Do our ideas reproduce exactly the objects we sense? If, for example, we consider a snowball, what is the relation between the ideas that the snowball engenders in our minds and the actual nature of the snowball? We have ideas such as round, moving, hard, white, and cold. To account for these ideas, Locke says that objects have *qualities*, and he defines a quality as "the power [in an object] to produce any idea in our mind." The snowball, then, has qualities that have the power to produce ideas in our minds.

Locke here makes an important distinction between two different kinds of qualities in order to answer the question of how ideas are related to objects. He terms these qualities *primary* and *secondary*. Primary qualities are those that "really do exist in the bodies themselves." Thus, our ideas, caused by primary qualities, resemble exactly those qualities that belong inseparably to the object. The snowball looks round and *is* round; it appears to be moving and *is* moving. Secondary qualities, on the other hand, produce ideas in our minds that have no exact counterpart in the object. We have the idea of *cold* when we touch the snowball and the idea of *white* when we see it. But there is no whiteness or coldness in the snowball. What *is* in the snowball is the quality, the power to create in us the ideas of cold and white. Primary qualities, then, refer to solidity, extension, figure, motion or rest, and number—or qualities that belong to the object. Secondary qualities, such as colors, sounds, tastes, and odors, do not belong to or constitute bodies except as powers to produce these ideas in us.

The importance of Locke's distinction between primary and secondary qualities is that through it he sought to distinguish between appearance and reality. Locke did not invent this distinction. Democritus had long ago suggested something similar when he said that colorless atoms are the basic reality and that colors, tastes, and odors are the results of particular organizations of these atoms. Descartes also separated secondary qualities from the basic substance he called *extension*. Locke's distinction reflected his interest in the new physics and the influence of the "judicious Mr. Newton's incomparable book" on his thought. Newton explained the appearance of *white* in terms of the motion of invisible minute particles. Reality, then, is found not in whiteness, which is only an effect, but in the motion of something, which is the cause. His discussion of primary and secondary qualities assumed throughout that there was *something* that could possess these qualities, and this he called *substance.*

Substance   Locke approached the question of substance from what he regarded as a commonsense point of view. How can we have ideas of qualities without supposing that there is something—some substance—in which these qualities subsist? If we ask what has shape or color, we answer something solid and extended. *Solid* and *extended* are primary qualities, and if we ask in what they subsist, Locke answers *substance*. However inevitable the idea of substance may be to common sense, Locke was unable to describe it with precision. He admitted that "if any one will examine himself concerning his notion of pure substance in general, he will find he has no other idea of it at all, but only a supposition of he knows not what support of such qualities which are capable of producing simple ideas in us." Still, Locke saw in the concept of substance the explanation of sensation, saying that sensation is caused by substance. Similarly, it is substance that contains the powers that give regularity and consistency to our ideas. Finally, it is substance, Locke held, that constitutes the object of sensitive knowledge.

Locke was impelled by the simple logic of the matter: If there is motion, there must be something that moves. Qualities simply cannot float around without something that holds them together. We have ideas of *matter* and of *thinking*, but "we shall never be able to know whether any mere material being thinks or no." But if there is thinking, there must be something that thinks. We also have an idea of God, which, like the idea of substance in general, is not clear and distinct. Yet, "if we examine the idea we have of the incomprehensible supreme being, we shall find that we come by it in the same way, and that the complex ideas we have both of God and separate spirits are made up of the simple ideas that we receive from reflection." The idea of God, like the idea of substance, is inferred from other simple ideas and is the product not of immediate observation but of demonstration. But the idea of substance, being "something we know not what," does raise for Locke the question of just how far our knowledge extends and how much validity it has.

The Degrees of Knowledge   How far our knowledge extends and how much validity it has depends, according to Locke, on the relations our ideas have to each other. Indeed, Locke finally defines *knowledge* as nothing more than "the perception of the connection of and agreement, or disagreement and repugnancy of any of our ideas." Our ideas enter single file into our minds, but once they are inside they can become related to each other in many ways. Some of the relations our ideas have to each other depend on the objects we experience. Other times our imagination can rearrange our simple and complex ideas to suit our fancy. Whether our knowledge is fanciful or valid depends on our *perception* of the relationships of our ideas to each other. There are three types of perception—namely, *intuitive, demonstrative,* and *sensitive*—and each one leads us to a different degree of knowledge regarding reality.

Intuitive knowledge is immediate, leaves no doubt, and is "the clearest and most certain that human frailty is capable of." Such knowledge "like sunshine forces itself immediately to be perceived as soon as ever the mind turns its view that way." Instantly, we know that a circle is not a square or that 6 is not 8 because we can perceive the repugnancy of these ideas to each other. But besides these formal or mathematical truths, intuition can lead us to a knowledge of what exists. From intuition we know that we exist: "Experience then convinces us, that we have intuitive knowledge of our own existence, and an internal infallible perception that we are."

Demonstrative knowledge occurs when our minds try to discover the agreement or disagreement of ideas by calling attention to still other ideas. Ideally, each step of the demonstration must have intuitive certainty. This is particularly the case in mathematics, but again, Locke thought that demonstration is a type of perception that leads the mind to knowledge of some form of existing reality. Thus, "man knows, by an intuitive certainty, that bare nothing can no more produce any real being than it can be equal to two right angles." From this starting point Locke argued that since there are in fact existing things that begin and end in time, and since a "nonentity cannot produce any real being, it is an evident demonstration, that from eternity there has been something." Reasoning in a similar way, he concludes that this eternal Being is "most knowing" and "most powerful" and that "it is plain to me we have a more certain knowledge of the existence of God, than of anything our senses have not immediately discovered to us."

Sensitive knowledge is not knowledge in the strict sense of the term; it only "passes under the name of knowledge." Locke did not doubt that things outside of us exist, for, otherwise, where did we get our simple ideas? But sensitive knowledge does not give us certainty, nor does it extend very far. We sense that we see another man and have no doubt that he exists, but when he leaves us, we are no longer sure of his existence. "For if I saw such a collection of simple ideas as is wont to be called *man*, existing together one minute since, and am now alone, I cannot be certain that the same man exists now, since there is no *necessary connection* of his existence a minute since with his existence now." And therefore, "while I am alone, writing this, I have not that knowledge of it which we strictly call knowledge; though the great likelihood of it puts me past doubt." Since experience simply makes us aware of qualities, we have no assurance of the connections between qualities. In particular, sensitive knowledge does not assure us that qualities that seem to be related are in fact *necessarily* connected. We simply sense things as they are, and as we never sense *substance*, we never know from sensation how things are *really* connected. Nevertheless, sensitive knowledge gives us *some* degree of knowledge but not certainty. Intuitive knowledge gives us certainty that we exist, demonstrative knowledge shows that God exists, and sensitive knowledge assures us that other selves and things exist but only as they are when we experience them.

Moral and Political Theory

Ethics and the Law   Locke placed our thoughts about morality into the category of demonstrative knowledge. To him morality could have the precision of mathematics. He writes, "I am bold to think that morality is capable of demonstration, as well as mathematics: since the precise real essence of the things moral words stand for can be perfectly known, and so the congruity and incongruity of the things themselves be perfectly discovered." The key word in ethics—namely, *good*—is perfectly understandable, for everybody knows what the word *good* stands for: "Things are good or evil only in reference to pleasure or pain. That we call good which is apt to cause or increase pleasure, or diminish pain in us." Certain kinds of behavior will bring us pleasure, whereas other kinds will bring us pain. Morality, then, has to do with choosing or willing the good.

As a further definition of *ethics*, Locke says that "moral good and evil, then, is only the conformity or disagreement of our voluntary actions to some law." He speaks of three kinds of laws: the *law of opinion*, the *civil law*, and the *divine law*. The real issue here is to ask how Locke knows that these laws exist and how he views the relation of them to each other. Bearing in mind that he saw no difficulty in demonstrating the existence of God, he now wants to draw further deductions from that demonstrative knowledge:

> The idea of a supreme being infinite in power, goodness and wisdom, whose workmanship we are and on whom we depend, and the idea of ourselves as understanding rational beings, being such as are clear in us, would, I suppose, if duly considered and pursued, afford such foundations of our duty and rules of actions, as might place morality amongst the sciences capable of demonstration: wherein I doubt not but from self-evident principles, by necessary consequences, as incontestable as those in mathematics, the measures of right and wrong might be made out to anyone that will apply himself with the same indifference and attention as he does to the other of those sciences.

Locke is here suggesting that by the light of nature, that is, by our reason, we can discover the moral rules that conform to God's law. He did not elaborate this plan into a system of ethics, but he did suggest what relation the different kinds of laws should have to each other. The law of opinion represents a community's judgment of what kind of behavior will lead to happiness. Conformity to this law is called *virtue*, though it must be noted that different communities have different ideas of what virtue consists of. The civil law is set by the commonwealth and enforced by the courts. This law tends to follow the first, for in most societies the courts enforce those laws that embody the opinion of the people. The divine law, which we can know through either their own reason or revelation, is the true rule for human behavior. He writes, "That God has given a rule whereby men should govern themselves, I think there is nobody so brutish as to deny." And "this is the only true touchstone of moral rectitude." In the long run, then, the law of opinion and also the civil law should be made to conform to the divine law, the "touchstone of moral rectitude." The reason there is a discrepancy between these three kinds of laws is that people everywhere tend to choose immediate pleasures instead of choosing those that have more lasting value. However ambiguous this moral theory may seem to us, Locke believed that these moral laws were eternally true, and upon the insights derived from the divine law he built his theory of natural rights.

The State of Nature   In his *Second Treatise of Government* Locke begins his political theory as Hobbes did, with a treatment of "the state of nature." But he describes this condition in a very different way, even making Hobbes the target of his remarks. For Locke the state of nature is not the same as Hobbes's "war of all against all." On the contrary, Locke says that "men living together according to reason, without a common superior on earth with authority to judge between them is properly the state of nature." According to Locke's theory of knowledge, men were able even in the state of nature to know the moral law. He said that "reason, which is that law, teaches all mankind who will but consult it, that, being all equal and independent, no one ought to harm another in his life, health, liberty or possessions." This natural moral law is not simply the egotistical law of self-preservation but the positive recognition of each individual's value as a person by virtue of his or her status as a creature of God. This natural law implied natural rights with corresponding duties, and among these rights Locke emphasized particularly the right of private property.

Private Property   For Hobbes there could be a right to property only after the legal order had been set up. Locke said that the right to private property precedes the civil law, for it is grounded in the natural moral law. The justification of private ownership is labor. According to Locke, since a man's labor is his own, whatever he transforms from its original condition by his own labor becomes his, for his labor is now mixed with those things. It is by mixing his labor with something that a man takes what was common property and makes it his private property. There is consequently also a limit to that amount of property one can accumulate, namely, "as much as anyone can make use of to any advantage of life before it spoils, so much he may by his labour fix a property in." Locke assumed also that as a matter of natural right a person could inherit property, for "every man is born with . . . a right, before any other man, to inherit with his brethren his father's goods."

Civil Government   If men have natural rights and also know the moral law, why do they desire to leave the state of nature? To this question Locke answered that "the great and chief end of men's uniting into commonwealths and putting themselves under government is the preservation of their property." By the term *property* Locke meant people's "lives, liberty and estates, which I call by the general name, property." It is true that people know the moral law in the state of nature, or rather, they are capable of knowing it if they turn their minds to it. But through indifference and neglect they do not always develop a knowledge of it. Moreover, when disputes arise, people tend to decide them in their own favor. It is desirable, therefore, to have both a set of written laws and an independent judge to decide disputes. To achieve those ends, people create a political society.

Locke put great emphasis on the inalienable character of human rights, and this led him to argue that political society must rest on people's *consent*, for "men being . . . by nature all free, equal and independent, no one can be put out of this estate and subjected to the political power of another without his consent." But to what do people consent? They consent to have the laws made and enforced by society, but since "no rational creature can be supposed to change his condition with an intention to be worse," these laws must be framed so as to confirm those rights that people have by nature. They consent also to be bound by the majority, since "it is necessary the body should move that way whither the greater force carries it, which is the consent of the majority." For this reason Locke considered absolute monarchy as "no form of civil government at all." Whether in fact there was a time when we entered a compact is considered by Locke to be of no great consequence, for the important thing is that logically our behavior shows that we have given our consent, and this Locke calls "tacit consent." For if we enjoy the privilege of citizenship, own and exchange property, rely on the police and the courts, we have in effect assumed also the responsibilities of citizenship and consented to the rule of the majority. The fact that a person stays in his country, for all he could leave and go to another one, confirms his act of consent.

Sovereignty   Locke gives us a different picture of the sovereign power in society from the one we find in Hobbes. Hobbes's sovereign was absolute. Locke agreed that there must be a "supreme power," but he carefully placed this in the hands of the legislature, for all intents the majority of the people. He emphasized the importance of the division of powers chiefly to ensure that those who execute or administer the laws do not also make them, for "they may exempt themselves from obedience to the laws they make, and suit the law, both in its making and execution, to their own private advantage." The executive is, therefore, "under the law." Even the legislature is not absolute, although it is "supreme," for legislative power is held as a *trust* and is, therefore, only a fiduciary power. Consequently, "there remains still in the people a supreme power to remove or alter the legislature when they find the legislative act contrary to the trust reposed in them." Locke would never agree that people had irrevocably transferred their rights to the sovereign. The right to rebellion is retained, though rebellion is justified only when the government is *dissolved*. For Locke government is dissolved not only when it is overthrown by an external enemy but also when internally there has been an alteration of the legislature. The legislative branch can be altered, for example, if the executive substitutes his law for the legislature's or neglects the execution of the official laws; in these cases rebellion is justified. Whereas Hobbes placed the sovereign under God's judgment, Locke stated that "the people shall judge."

BERKELEY

Berkeley's Life

George Berkeley was born in Ireland in 1685. At the age of 15, he entered Trinity College, Dublin, where he studied mathematics, logic, languages, and philosophy. He became a Fellow of the College a few years after he earned his B.A. degree and was also ordained a clergyman in the Church of England, becoming a bishop in 1734. Beginning his famous literary career in his early twenties, his most important philosophical works include his *Essay towards a New Theory of Vision* (1709), *A Treatise concerning the Principles of Human Knowledge* (1710), and *Three Dialogues between Hylas and Philonus* (1713). He traveled in France and Italy, and in London became friends with Richard Steele, Joseph Addison, and Jonathan Swift. While in London he sought to interest Parliament in his project of creating a college in Bermuda, whose purpose would be "the reformation of manners among the English in our western plantations, and the propagation of the Gospel among the American savages." With his new bride he sailed in 1728 for America and for three years stayed in Newport, Rhode Island, making plans for his college. As the money for his college was never raised, Berkeley returned to London, but he continued to influence American philosophy through frequent associations with Jonathan Edwards. Shortly thereafter, he returned to Ireland, where for eighteen years he was bishop of Cloyne. At the age of 67, he settled down in Oxford with his wife and family; a year later, in 1753, he died and was buried in Christ Church Chapel in Oxford.

The Nature of Existence

It is ironic that Locke's commonsense approach to philosophy should have influenced Berkeley to formulate a philosophical position that at first seems so much at variance with common sense. He became the object of severe criticism and ridicule for denying what seemed most obvious to anyone. Berkeley had set out to deny the existence of matter. Samuel Johnson must have expressed the reaction of many when he kicked a large stone and said about Berkeley, "I refute him thus."

Berkeley's startling and provocative formula was that "to be is to be perceived" *(esse est percipi)*. Clearly, this would mean that if something were not perceived, it would not exist. Berkeley was perfectly aware of the potential nonsense involved in this formula, for he says, "Let it not be said that I take away Existence. I only declare the meaning of the word so far as I comprehend it." Still, to say that the existence of something depends on its being perceived does raise for us the question whether it exists when it is not being perceived.

For Berkeley the whole problem turned on how we interpret or understand the word *exists:* "The table I write on I say exists; that is, I see and feel it: and if I were out of my study I should say it existed; meaning thereby that if I were in my study I might perceive it, or that some other spirit actually does perceive it." Here Berkeley is saying that the word *exists* has no other meaning than the one contained in his formula, for we can know no instance in which the term *exists* is used without at the same time assuming that a mind is perceiving something. To those who argued that material things have some kind of *absolute* existence without any relation to their being perceived, Berkeley replied, "That is to me unintelligible." To be sure, he said, "the horse is in the stable, the books in the study as before, even if I am not there. But since we know of no instance of anything's existing without being perceived, the table, horse, and books *exist* even when I do not perceive them because someone does perceive them."

How did Berkeley come upon this novel view? In his *New Theory of Vision* he argues that all our knowledge depends on actual vision and other sensory experiences. In particular he argues that we never sense *space* or *magnitude;* we only have different visions or perceptions of things when we see them from different perspectives. Nor do we *see* distance; the distance of objects is *suggested* by our experience. All that we ever see are the qualities of an object that our faculty of vision is capable of sensing. We do not see the *closeness* of an object; we only have a different vision of it when we move toward or away from it. The more Berkeley considered the workings of his own mind and wondered how his ideas were related to objects outside of his mind, the more certain he was that he could never discover any object independent of his ideas. "When we do our utmost to conceive the existence of external bodies," he says, "we are all the while contemplating our own ideas." Nothing seems easier for us than to imagine trees in a park or books in a closet without anyone's looking for them. But what is all this, Berkeley says, except "framing in your mind certain ideas which you call *books* and *trees.* . . . But do not *you* yourself perceive or think of them all the while?" It is impossible, he concluded, ever to think of *anything* except as related to a mind. We never experience something that exists outside of us and separate from us as our ideas of *close* and *far* might suggest. There is nothing *out there* of which we do not have some perception.

Matter and Substance

It was Locke's philosophy that had raised doubts in Berkeley's mind about the independent existence of things—about the reality of matter. Locke had failed to push his own theory of knowledge to conclusions that to Berkeley seemed inevitable. When Locke spoke of substance as "something we know not what," he was only a short step from saying that it was nothing, which Berkeley did say. Locke's treatment of the relation between ideas and things assumed that there is a real difference between primary and secondary qualities—between an object's size and shape, on the one hand, and its color, taste, and smell, on the other. He assumed that whereas color exists only as an idea in the mind, size has to do with an object's substance. And *substance*, for Locke, is the reality that exists "behind" or "under" secondary qualities such as color and is, therefore, independent of a mind.

Berkeley, however, argued that size, shape, and motion "abstracted from all qualities, are inconceivable." What, for example, is a cherry? It is soft, red, round, sweet, and fragrant. All these qualities are ideas in the mind that the cherry has the power to produce through the senses. And so we feel its softness, see its color, feel and see its roundness, taste its sweetness, and smell its fragrance. Again, the very existence of all these qualities consists in their being perceived. And, apart from these qualities, there is no sensed reality—in short, nothing else. The cherry, then, consists of all the qualities we perceive; the cherry (and all things) represents a complex of sensations. Suppose I insist that there are some primary qualities that are not perceived by the senses, such as size and shape. Berkeley would respond that it is impossible even to conceive of shape or size as independent of perception and, therefore, independent of secondary qualities. Is it possible, he asks, to separate primary and secondary qualities "even in thought"? He adds, "I might as easily divide a thing from itself. . . . In truth, the object and the sensation are the same thing, and cannot therefore be abstracted from each other." A thing *is*, therefore, the sum of its perceived qualities, and it is for this reason that Berkeley argued that to be is to be perceived. Since substance, or matter, is never perceived or sensed, it cannot be said to exist. If substance does not exist and if only sensed qualities are real, then only thinking or, as Berkeley says, *spiritual* beings exist.

Besides leading Locke's empirical philosophy to what he thought were obvious conclusions, Berkeley was also contending with a complex of problems. In his *Principles of Human Knowledge* he refers to these as "the chief causes of error and difficulty in the sciences, with the grounds of scepticism, atheism and Irreligion . . . inquired into." It was the notion of *matter* that caused all the difficulties. For if an inert material substance is admitted as really existing, where is there any place for spiritual or immaterial substances in such a universe? Also, would not scientific knowledge, based on general ideas drawn from the behavior of things, give us a complete philosophy without requiring the idea of God, leading to "the monstrous systems of atheists"? This is not to say that Berkeley arbitrarily denounced the idea of matter because of these theological consequences. Instead, he had additional reasons for pressing his views, which, he was convinced, were intrinsically right.

Matter a Meaningless Term   Locke had said that substance, or matter, *supports* or acts as a *substitute* for the qualities we sense. In Berkeley's *First Dialogue between Hylas and Philonus*, Hylas expresses Locke's view: "I find it necessary to suppose a material *substratum*, without which [qualities] cannot be conceived to exist." Philonus replies that the word *substratum* has no clear meaning for him and that he would want to "know any sense, literal or not literal, that you understand in it." But Hylas admits that he cannot assign any definite meaning to the term *substratum*, saying "I declare I know not what to say." From this the conclusion is drawn that "the *absolute* existence of unthinking things [matter] are words without meaning." This is not to say that sensible things do not possess reality but only that sensible things exist only insofar as they are perceived. This, of course, implies that only ideas exist, but Berkeley adds that "I hope that to call a thing 'idea' makes it no less real."

Aware that his idealism could be ridiculed, Berkeley writes, "What therefore becomes of the sun, moon, and stars? What must we think of houses, rivers, mountains, trees, stones; nay even of our own bodies? Are all these so many chimeras and illusions of fancy?" By his principles, he says, "we are not deprived of any one thing in nature. Whatever we see, feel, hear, or any wise conceive or understand, remains as secure as ever, and is as real as ever. There is a *rerum natura*, and the distinction between realities and chimeras retains its full force." If this is the case, why say that only *ideas*, instead of *things*, exist? In order, Berkeley says, to eliminate the useless concept of matter: "I do not argue against the existence of any one thing that we can apprehend, either by sense or reflection. . . . The only thing whose existence we deny, is that which philosophers call matter or corporeal substance. And in doing of this, there is no damage done to the rest of mankind, who, I dare say, will never miss it."

Science and Abstract Ideas   Since the science of his day, particularly physics, relied so heavily on the notion of matter, Berkeley had to come to terms with its assumptions and methods. Science had assumed that we can, and must, distinguish between appearance and reality. The sea appears blue but is really not. Berkeley challenged the scientist to show whether there is any other reality than the sensible world. In this analysis Berkeley was pursuing the principle of empiricism and trying to refine it. Physicists, he said, were obscuring science by including metaphysics in their theories. They used such words as *force, attraction*, and *gravity* and thought they referred to some real physical entity. Even to speak of minute particles, whose motions cause the quality of color, is to engage in a rational and not empirical analysis. What disturbed Berkeley most was that scientists used general or abstract terms as though these terms accurately referred to real entities, particularly to an underlying material substance in nature. Nowhere, Berkeley argues, do we ever come upon such a substance, for substance is an abstract idea. Only sensed qualities really exist, and the notion of substance is a misleading inference drawn from observed qualities: "As several of these [qualities] are observed to accompany each other, they come to be marked by one name, and so to be reputed as one *thing*. Thus, for example, a certain colour, taste, smell, figure and consistence having been observed to go together, are accounted one distinct thing, signified by the name apple; other collections of ideas constitute a stone, a tree, a book and the like sensible things." Similarly, when scientists observe the operations of things, they use such abstract terms as *force* or *gravity* as though these were things or had some real existence in things. But *force* is simply a word describing our sensation of the behavior of things and gives us no more knowledge than our senses and reflections give us.

Berkeley did not mean to destroy science any more than he wanted to deny the existence of the "nature of things." What he did want to do was to clarify what scientific language was all about. Terms such as *force, gravity*, and *causality* refer to nothing more than clusters of ideas which our minds derive from sensation. We experience that heat melts wax, but all we know from this experience is that what we call *melting wax* is always accompanied by what we call *heat*. We have no knowledge of any single thing for which the word *cause* stands. Indeed, the only knowledge we have is of particular experiences. But even though we do not have firsthand knowledge of the causes of all things, we do know the order of things. We experience order—that A is followed by B—even though we have no experience of *why* this occurs. Science gives us a description of physical behavior, and many mechanical principles can be accurately formulated from our observations that are useful for purposes of prediction. Thus, Berkeley would leave science intact but clarify its language so that nobody would think that science was giving us more knowledge than we can derive from the sensible world. And the sensible world shows us neither substance nor causality.

God and the Existence of Things   Since Berkeley did not deny the existence of things or their order in nature, it was necessary for him to explain how things external to our minds exist—even when *we* do not perceive them—and how they achieve their order. Thus, elaborating on his general thesis that to be is to be perceived, Berkeley says, "When I deny sensible things an existence out of the mind, I do not mean my mind in particular, but all minds. Now it is plain they have an existence exterior to my mind, since I find them by experience to be independent of it. There is therefore some other mind wherein they exist, during the intervals between the time of my perceiving them." And because all human minds are intermittently diverted from things, "there is an *omnipresent eternal Mind*, which knows and comprehends all things, and exhibits them to our view in such a manner and according to such rules as he himself has ordained, and are by us termed the *Laws of Nature*." The existence of things, therefore, depends on the existence of God, and God is the cause of the orderliness of things in nature.

Again, Berkeley did not want to deny, for example, that even if he left the room, the candle would still be there, and that when he returned after an interval, it would have burned down. But this meant for Berkeley only that experience has a certain regularity that makes it possible for us to predict what our future experiences will be. To say that candles burn even when *I* am not in the room still does not prove that material substance exists independently from a mind. It seemed a matter of common sense to Berkeley to say that I can know about the candle only because I actually experience a perception of it. In a similar way I know that I exist because I have an awareness of my mental operations.

If, then, I try to describe or interpret reality in terms of my experience, I first come to the conclusion that there are other people like myself who have minds. From this it can be assumed that, just as I have ideas, other people likewise have ideas. Apart from my finite mind and the finite minds of others, there is a greater Mind analogous to mine, and this is God's Mind. God's ideas constitute the regular order of nature. The ideas that exist in our minds are God's ideas, which he communicates to us, so that the objects or things that we perceive in daily experience are caused not by *matter* or *substance* but by God. It is God, too, who coordinates all experiences of finite minds, assuring regularity and dependability in experience, which in turn enables us to think in terms of the "laws of nature." Thus, the orderly arrangement of ideas in God's Mind is communicated to the finite minds or spirits of people, with allowance made for the differences in competence between the divine and finite minds. The ultimate reality, then, is spiritual (God) and not material, and the continued existence of objects when *we* are not perceiving them is explained by God's continuous perception of them.

To say, as Berkeley does, that people's ideas come from God implies a special interpretation of causation. Again, Berkeley did not deny that we have an insight into causation; he only insisted that our sense data do not disclose to us a unique causal power. We do not, for example, when considering how and why water freezes, discover any power in cold that forces water to become solid. We do, however, understand causal connections through our mental operations. We are, for example, aware of our volition: We can will to move our arm, or, what is more important here, we can produce imaginary ideas in our minds. Our power to produce such ideas suggests that perceived ideas are also caused by a mental power. But whereas imaginary ideas are produced by finite minds, perceived ideas are created and caused to be in us by an infinite mind.

Berkeley was confident that through his treatment of the formula *esse est percipi* he had effectively undermined the position of philosophical materialism and religious skepticism. Locke's empiricism inevitably implied skepticism insofar as he insisted that knowledge is based on sense experience and that substance, or the reality behind appearances, could never be known. Whether Berkeley's arguments for the reality of God and spiritual beings successfully refuted materialism and skepticism remains questionable, for his arguments contained some of the flaws he held against the materialists. His influence was nevertheless significant, but it was his empiricism and not his idealism that had a lasting influence. Building on Locke's empiricism, Berkeley made the decisive point that the human mind reasons only and always about particular sense experiences—that abstract ideas refer to no equivalent reality. Hume, who was to carry empiricism to its fullest expression, spoke of Berkeley as "a great philosopher [who] has disputed the received opinion in this particular, and has asserted that all general ideas are nothing but particular ones. . . . I look upon this to be one of the greatest and most valuable discoveries that has been made of late years in the republic of letters."

HUME

Hume's Life

David Hume took the genuinely empirical elements in the philosophy of Locke and Berkeley, removed some lingering metaphysics from their thought, and gave empiricism its clearest and most rigorous formulation. Born in Edinburgh in 1711 of Scottish parents, his early interest in literature soon showed to his family that he would not follow their plan for him to become a lawyer. Though he attended the University of Edinburgh, he did not graduate. He was a gentle man with a tough mind who regarded "every object as contemptible except the improvement of my talents in literature," feeling "an insurmountable aversion to everything but the pursuits of philosophy and general learning." He spent the years 1734–1737 in France, under conditions of "rigid frugality," composing his *Treatise of Human Nature*. When this book appeared in 1739, Hume was disappointed with its reception, remarking later that "never literary attempt was more unfortunate," for the book "fell deadborn from the press." His next book, *Essays Moral and Political*, published in 1741–1742, was more successful. Hume then revised key themes in his *Treatise* and published it under the title *An Enquiry concerning Human Understanding*. Besides his extensive books on the history of England, Hume wrote three other works that were to enhance his fame: *An Enquiry concerning the Principles of Morals (1751)*, *Political Discourses (1752)*, and the posthumous *Dialogues concerning Natural Religion (1779)*.

Hume played a part in public life, going to France in 1763 as secretary to the British ambassador. His books had given him a wide reputation on the Continent, and among his European friends was the philosopher Jean-Jacques Rousseau. From 1767 to 1769 he was under-secretary of state, and in 1769 he returned to Edinburgh, where his house became the center for the most distinguished people of that society. Being now "very opulent," he lived a quiet and contented life among friends and admirers, among them the economist Adam Smith. He died in Edinburgh in 1776.

Hume wanted to build a science of human nature by using the methods of physical science. His wide acquaintance with literature had shown him how often conflicting opinions are offered to readers on all subjects. He considered this conflict of opinions the symptom of a serious philosophical problem: How can we know the true nature of things? If artful authors can lead readers to accept conflicting ideas about morality, religion, and the true nature of physical reality, are these ideas equally true, or is there some method by which to discover the reason for this conflict of ideas? Hume shared the optimism of his day, which saw in the scientific method the means for solving all the problems of the world. He believed that such a method could lead us to a clear understanding of human nature and, in particular, the workings of the human mind.

As it turned out, Hume discovered that this optimism about the possibilities of using scientific methods to describe the mechanics of human thought could not be justified. His early faith in reason led, in the end, to skepticism. For as he traced the process by which ideas are formed in the mind, he was startled to discover how limited is the range of human thought. Both Locke and Berkeley had come to this same point, but neither one took his own account of the origin of ideas seriously enough to rest his theory of knowledge wholly upon it. They still had recourse to the "commonsense" beliefs of people, which they were not willing to give up entirely. Although they argued that all our ideas come from experience, they felt confident that experience can give us certainty of knowledge on many subjects. Hume, on the other hand, concluded that if we take seriously the premise that all our ideas come from experience, we must accept the limits of knowledge that this explanation of ideas forces upon us, no matter what our customary beliefs may suggest.

Hume's Theory of Knowledge

The only way, Hume says, to solve the problem of disagreements and speculations regarding "abstruse questions" is to "enquire seriously into the nature of human understanding, and show from an exact analysis of its powers and capacity, that it is by no means fitted for such remote and abstruse subjects." Accordingly, Hume carefully analyzed a series of topics that led him to his skeptical conclusion, beginning with an account of the contents of the mind.

Contents of the Mind   Nothing seems more unbounded, Hume says, than human thought. Although our bodies are confined to one planet, our minds can roam the most distant regions of the universe. Nor, it may seem, is the mind bound by the limits of nature or reality, for without difficulty the imagination can conceive the most unnatural and incongruous appearances, such as flying horses and gold mountains. But, though the mind seems to possess this wide freedom, it is, Hume says, "really confined within very narrow limits." In the final analysis the contents of the mind can be reduced to the materials given us by the senses and experience, and those materials Hume calls *perceptions*. The perceptions of the mind take two forms, which Hume distinguishes as *impressions* and *ideas*.

Impressions and *ideas* make up the total content of the mind. The original stuff of thought is an *impression* (a sensation or feeling), and an *idea* is merely a copy of an impression. According to Hume, the difference between an impression and an idea is only the degree of their vividness. The original perception is an impression, as when we hear, see, feel, love, hate, desire, or will. These impressions are "lively" and clear when we have them. When we reflect on these impressions, we have ideas of them, and those ideas are less lively versions of the original impressions. To feel pain is an impression, whereas the memory of this sensation is an idea. In every particular, impressions and their corresponding ideas are alike, differing only in their degree of vividness.

Besides distinguishing between impressions and ideas, Hume argues that without impressions there can be no ideas. For if an idea is simply a copy of an impression, it follows that for every idea there must be a prior impression. Not every idea, however, reflects an exact corresponding impression, for we have never seen a flying horse or a golden mountain even though we have ideas of them. But Hume explains such ideas as being the product of the mind's "faculty of compounding, transposing, or diminishing the materials afforded us by the senses and experience." When we think of a flying horse, our imagination joins two ideas, wings and horse, that we originally acquired as impressions through our senses. If we have any suspicion that a philosophical term is employed without any meaning or idea, we need, Hume says, "but enquire, *from what impression is that supposed idea derived?* And if it be impossible to assign any, this will serve to confirm our suspicion." Hume subjected even the idea of God to this test and concluded that it arises from reflecting on the operations of our own minds "augmenting without limit" the qualities of goodness and wisdom that we experience among human beings. But if all our ideas follow from impressions, how can we explain what we call *thinking*, or the patterns by which ideas group themselves in our minds?

Association of Ideas   It is not by mere chance that our ideas are related to each other. There must be, Hume says, "some bond of union, some associating quality, by which one idea naturally introduces another." Hume calls it "a gentle force, which commonly prevails . . . pointing out to every one those simple ideas, which are most proper to be united in a complex one." It is not a special faculty of the mind that associates one idea with another, for Hume has no impression of the structural equipment of the mind. But by observing the actual patterns of our thinking and analyzing the groupings of our ideas, Hume thought he had discovered an explanation for the association of ideas.

His explanation was that, whenever there are certain qualities in ideas, these ideas are associated with each other. These qualities are three in number: resemblance, contiguity in time or place, and cause and effect. Hume believed that the connections of all ideas to each other could be explained by these qualities and gave the following examples of how they work: "A picture naturally leads our thoughts to the original [*resemblance*]: the mention of one apartment in the building naturally introduces an enquiry . . . concerning the others [*contiguity*]: and if we think of a wound, we can scarcely forebear reflecting on the pain which follows it [*cause and effect*]." There are no operations of the mind that differ in principle from one of these three examples of the association of ideas. But of these, the notion of cause and effect was considered by Hume to be the central element in knowledge. He took the position that the causal principle is the foundation on which the validity of all knowledge depends. If there is any flaw in the causal principle, we can have no certainty of knowledge.

Causality   Hume's most original and influential ideas deal with the problem of causality. Neither Locke nor Berkeley challenged the basic principle of causality. Although Berkeley did say that we cannot discover efficient causes *in* things, his intention was to look for the cause of phenomena, and therefore the predictable order of nature, in God's activity.

For Hume the very idea of causality is suspect, and he approaches the problem by asking "What is the origin of the idea of causality?" Since ideas are copies of impressions, Hume asks what impression gives us the idea of causality. His answer is that there is no impression corresponding to this idea. How, then, does the idea of causality arise in the mind? It must be, says Hume, that the idea of causality arises in the mind when we experience certain relations between objects. When we speak of cause and effect, we mean to say that A causes B. But what kind of a relation does this show between A and B? Experience furnishes us with two relations: (1) *contiguity*, for A and B are always close together, and (2) *priority in time*, for A, the "cause," always precedes B, the "effect." But there is still another relation that the idea of causality suggests to common sense, namely, that between A and B there is a "necessary connection." But neither contiguity nor priority implies "necessary" connection between objects. There is no object, Hume says, that implies the existence of another when we consider objects individually. No amount of observation of oxygen can ever tell us that when mixed with hydrogen it will necessarily give us water. We know this only after we have seen the two together: "It is therefore by *experience* only that we can infer the existence of one object from another." While we do have impressions of contiguity in space and priority in time, we do *not* have any impression of *necessary connection*. Thus, causality is not a quality in the objects we observe but is rather a mental "habit of association" produced by the repetition of instances of A and B.

Insofar as Hume assumed that the causal principle is central to all kinds of knowledge, his attack on this principle undermined the validity of all knowledge. He saw no reason for accepting the principle that *whatever begins to exist must have a cause of existence* as either intuitive or capable of demonstration. In the end Hume considered thinking or reasoning "a species of sensation," and as such our thinking cannot extend beyond our immediate experiences.

What Exists External to Us?

Hume's extreme empiricism led him to argue that there is no rational justification for saying that bodies or things have a continued and independent existence external to us. Our ordinary experience suggests that things outside of us do exist. But if we take seriously the notion that our ideas are copies of impressions, the philosophical conclusion must be that all we know is impressions. Impressions are internal subjective states and are not clear proof of an external reality. To be sure, we always act as though there is a real external world of things, and Hume was willing to "take for granted in all our reasonings" that things do exist. But he wanted to inquire into the reason *why* we think there is an external world.

Our senses do not tell us that things exist independent of us, for how do we know that they continue to exist even when we interrupt our sensation of them? And even when we sense something, we are never given a double view of it whereby we can distinguish the thing from our impression of it; we have only the impression. There is no way for the mind to reach beyond impressions or the ideas they make possible: "Let us chase our imagination to the heavens, or to the utmost limits of the universe; we never advance a step beyond our selves, nor can we conceive any kind of existence, but those perceptions which have appeared in that narrow compass. This is the universe of imagination, nor have we any idea but what is there produced."

Constancy and Coherence   Our belief that things exist external to us, Hume argues, is the product of our imagination as it deals with two special characteristics of our impressions. From impressions our imagination becomes aware of both *constancy* and *coherence*. There is a constancy in the arrangement of things when, for example, I look out of my window: There are the mountain, the house, and the trees. If I shut my eyes or turn away and then later look at the same view again, the arrangement is the same, and it is this constancy in the contents of my impressions that leads my imagination to conclude that the mountain, house, and trees exist whether I think of them or not. Similarly, I put a log on the fire before I leave the room, and when I return it is almost in ashes. But even though a great change has taken place in the fire, I am accustomed to finding this kind of change under similar circumstances: "This coherence . . . in their changes is one of the characteristics of external objects." In the case of the mountain, there is a constancy of our impressions, whereas with respect to the fire, our impressions have a coherent relation to the processes of change. For these reasons the imagination leads us to believe that certain things continue to have an independent existence external to us. But this is a *belief* and not a rational proof, for the assumption that our impressions are connected with things is "without any foundation in reasoning." Hume extends this skeptical line of reasoning beyond objects or things to consider the existence of the *self*, *substance*, and *God*.

The Self   Hume denied that we have any idea of *self*. This may seem paradoxical, that *I* should say that I do not have an idea of myself. Yet here, again, Hume wants to test what we mean by a "self" by asking, "From what impression could this idea be derived?" Is there any continuous and identical reality that forms our ideas of the self? Do we have any one impression that is invariably associated with our idea of *self*? "When I enter most intimately into what I call *myself*," says Hume, "I always stumble on some particular perception or other, of heat or cold, love or hatred, pain or pleasure. I never can catch *myself* at any time without a perception and never can observe anything but the perception." Hume denies the existence of a continuous self-identity and says that the self is "nothing but a bundle or collection of different perceptions." How, then, do we account for what we think is the self? It is our power of memory that gives the impression of our continuous identity. Nevertheless, Hume argues, the mind is "a kind of theatre where several perceptions successively make their appearance" and then disappear.

Substance   What led Hume to deny the existence of a continuous self that in some way retains its identity through time was his thorough denial of the existence of any form of substance. Locke retained the idea of substance as that something, which has color or shape, and other qualities, though he spoke of it as "something we know not what." Berkeley denied the existence of substance underlying qualities but retained the idea of spiritual substances. Hume denied that substance in any form exists or has any coherent meaning. If what is meant by the self is some form of substance, Hume argued that no such substance can be derived from our impressions of sensation. If the idea of substance is conveyed to us by our senses, Hume asks, "Which of them; and after what manner? If it be perceived by the eyes, it must be a colour; if by the ears, a sound; if by the palate, a taste. . . . We have therefore no idea of substance, distinct from that of a collection of particular qualities."

God   It was inevitable that Hume's rigorous premises, that "our ideas reach no further than our experience," would lead him to raise skeptical questions about the existence of God. Most attempts to demonstrate the existence of God rely on some version of causality. Among these the argument from *design* has always had a powerful impact on religious believers. Hume is aware of the power of this argument, but he quickly sorts out the elements of the problem, leaving the argument with less than its usual force.

The argument from design begins with the observance of a beautiful order in nature. This order resembles the kind of order the human mind is able to impose on unthinking materials. From this preliminary observation we conclude that unthinkable materials do not contain the principle of orderliness within themselves: "Throw several pieces of steel together, without shape or form; they will never arrange themselves so as to compose a watch." Order, it is held, requires the activity of a mind, an orderer. Our experience tells us that neither a watch nor a house can come into being without a watchmaker or an architect. From this it is inferred that the natural order bears an analogy to the order fashioned by human effort and that, just as the watch requires an ordering cause, so the natural order of the universe requires one. But such an inference, Hume says, "is uncertain; because the subject lies entirely beyond the reach of human experience."

If the whole argument from design rests on the proposition that "the cause or causes of order in the universe probably bear some remote analogy to human intelligence," then, Hume says, the argument cannot prove as much as it claims. Hume's criticism of the idea of causality has particular force here. We derive the idea of cause from repeated observations of two things. How, then, can we assign a cause to the universe when we have never experienced the universe as related to anything we might consider a cause? The use of analogy does not solve the problem because the analogy between a watch and the universe is not exact. Why not consider the universe the product of a vegetative process instead of a rational designer? And even if the cause of the universe is something like an intelligence, how can moral characteristics be ascribed to such a being? Moreover, if analogies are to be used, which one should be selected? Houses and ships are frequently designed by a group of designers: Should we say there are many gods? Sometimes experimental models are built with no present knowledge of what the finished form will be like: Is the universe a trial model or the final design? By this line of probing, Hume wished to emphasize that the order of the universe is simply an empirical fact and that we cannot infer from it the existence of God. This does not necessarily lead to atheism—although Hume himself seems to have been one. He is simply testing our idea of God the way he tested our ideas of the *self* and *substance* by his rigorous principle of empiricism. He ends, to be sure, as a skeptic, but finally makes the telling point that "to whatever length any one may push his speculative principles of skepticism, he must act and live and converse like other men. . . . It is impossible for him to persevere in total skepticism, or make it appear in his conduct for a few hours."

Ethics

Hume's skepticism did not prevent him from taking ethics seriously. On the contrary, in the opening passage of the third book of his *Treatise of Human Nature*, Hume writes that "morality is a subject that interests us above all others." His interest in ethics was so strong that he hoped to do for that subject what Galileo and Newton had done for natural science. To that end he says in the first section of his *Enquiry concerning the Principles of Morals* that "moral philosophy is in the same condition as . . . astronomy before the time of Copernicus." Older science with its abstract general hypotheses had to give way to a more experimental method. So also the time had come, Hume writes, when philosophers "should attempt a like reformation in all moral disquisitions; and reject every system of ethics, however subtle or ingenious, which is not founded on fact and observation."

For Hume the central fact about ethics is that moral judgments are formed not by reason alone but through feelings. There is no doubt that reason plays a considerable role in our discussions about ethical decisions. But, Hume says, reason "is not sufficient alone to produce any moral blame or approbation." What limits the role of reason in ethics is that reason makes judgments concerning the truth of empirical "matters of fact" and analytical "relations of ideas." Moral assessments are not judgments about the truth and falsehood of anything. Instead, moral assessments are emotional reactions.

Why, for example, do we judge murder to be a crime? Or, to use Hume's words, "Where is that matter of fact which we here call *crime?*" Suppose that you describe the action, the exact time at which it occurred, and the weapon used—in short, that you assemble all the details about the event. The faculty of reason would still not isolate that fact to which the label of "crime" is attached. After all, this act cannot always and in all circumstances be considered a crime. The same action might be called self-defense or official execution. The judgment of good or evil is made *after* all the facts are known. The goodness or badness of an act is not a new fact discovered or deduced by reason. Nor is moral assessment similar to mathematical judgment. From a few facts about a triangle or circle, additional facts and relations can be inferred. But goodness, like beauty, is not an additional fact inferred or deduced by reason. "Euclid has fully explained all the qualities of the circle," says Hume, "but has not in any proposition said a word of its beauty. The reason is evident. The beauty is not a quality of the circle. It lies not in any part of the line, whose parts are equally distant from a common center. It is only the effect which that figure produces upon the mind, whose peculiar fabric of structure renders it susceptible to such sentiments."

Hume presses this point by asking us to "see if you can find that matter of fact, or real existence, which you call *vice*." He argues that "in whichever way you take it, you find only certain passions, motives, volitions and thoughts. There is no other matter of fact in the case. . . . You can never find it, till you turn your reflection into your own breast and find a sentiment of disapprobation which arises in you toward this action. Here is a matter of fact; but it is the object of feeling, not reason. It lies in yourself, not in the object."

For Hume moral assessments involve sympathetic feelings of pleasure and pain that we experience when observing the consequences of someone's action. For example, if my neighbor is robbed, I will feel sympathetic pain for her, and this pain constitutes my moral condemnation of the robber's action. If I see someone help an old woman cross the street, I will feel sympathetic pleasure for the woman, and this pleasure constitutes my moral approval of the person who helped her out. Hume realized that to build a system of ethics on the faculty of feeling is to run the risk of reducing ethics to a matter of taste, whereby moral judgments are subjective and relative. Moreover, to designate feeling or sentiment as the source of praise or blame is to imply that our moral judgments flow from a calculus of individual self-interest or self-love. Hume rejects these assumptions by affirming that moral sentiments are found in all people, that people praise or blame the same actions, and that praise or blame is not derived from a narrow self-love. Hume writes, "A generous, a brave, a noble deed, performed by an adversary, commands our approbation; while in its consequences it may be acknowledged prejudicial to our particular interest." Further, the sympathetic feelings that we experience are not restricted to events that we see before us. Instead, we have an instinctive capacity to "bestow praise on virtuous actions, performed in very distant ages and remote countries; where the utmost subtlety of imagination would not discover any appearance of self-interest, or had any connection of our present happiness and security with events so widely separated from us."

What exactly are the qualities in people that trigger our sympathetic feelings of moral approval? According to Hume, these qualities—or virtues—include "whatever mental action or quality gives to a spectator the pleasing sentiment of approbation; and vice the contrary." These include "discretion, caution, enterprise, industry, economy, good-sense, prudence and discernment." Also, he argues, there is virtually universal agreement, even among the most cynical of people, concerning "the merit of temperance, sobriety, patience, constancy, considerateness, presence of mind, quickness of conception and felicity of expression." What is there about these qualities that generates our praise? It is, Hume says, that these qualities are *useful* and *agreeable*. But useful for what? Hume replies, "For somebody's interest, surely. Whose interest then? Not our own only: For our approbation frequently extends farther. It must, therefore, be the interest of those, who are served by the character or action approved of."

Hume's approach here is thoroughly empirical. First, experience tells us that moral assessments involve feelings and are not judgments of reason. Second, experience tells us that we have sympathetic feelings of pleasure and pain in response to a range of virtuous qualities that people possess. Third, experience tells us that all of these virtuous qualities have this in common: They are useful or agreeable to those affected by our conduct. Amidst this empirical analysis of moral assessment, we find in Hume a clear criterion of moral judgment: Virtuous behavior is that which is useful or agreeable to people who are impacted by this conduct. In Hume's words, "personal merit consists altogether in the possession of mental qualities, useful or agreeable to the person himself, or to others."

Hume's empirical approach to morality had its vocal critics. Morality, many argued, needs to be fixed, permanent, and absolute, and Hume grounds the entire plan of morality in unstable human faculties and emotions. Further, critics argued, we find the role of God completely absent from Hume's account. Thus, his whole approach is both flimsy and atheistic. However, the features about Hume's theory that bothered its critics so much were precisely the features that attracted others to it. After reading Hume's moral theory, Jeremy Bentham wrote, "I felt as if scales had fallen from my eyes." Bentham himself was in search of a nonreligious approach to morality that was based in empirical fact and not in mysterious rational intuitions. Bentham homed in on Hume's contention that we assess actions based on their usefulness—or, as Hume also expressed it, their "utility." This became the basis of the ethical theory of utilitarianism, championed by Bentham and many others throughout the nineteenth century and on through the present day.

CHAPTER 12

Enlightenment Philosophy

*D*uring the eighteenth century Europe experienced an intellectual movement called the Enlightenment whose rallying cry was that reason should
guide all human efforts, including those in science, politics, religion, aesthetics, and philosophy. Sparked by dramatic advances in the sciences, Enlightenment thinkers were convinced that through the exercise of human reason they
could unravel the mysteries of the universe and set society off in a new and
highly advanced direction. Such confidence in reason was already present during the Renaissance, which witnessed the scientific revolution and a revived
interest in the nearly forgotten works of the ancient Greek thinkers. The great
rationalist philosophers of the seventeenth century—Descartes, Spinoza, and
Leibniz—also encouraged the use of reason in long-standing puzzles about
human nature and the world around us. However, the Enlightenment emphasis on reason was unique because of its boldly secular theories of ethics, governmental authority, and human psychology, which parted company with
traditional religious views of human nature. Locke did much to establish the
Enlightenment conception of human nature with his view that the mind is a
blank slate at birth and assembles ideas as experience rushes in through the
senses. Hume furthered the Enlightenment agenda with his skeptical attacks on
belief in God, miracles, and life after death. In this chapter we will explore other
key contributors to Enlightenment philosophy, namely, the deists, Jean-Jacques
Rousseau, and Thomas Reid.

DEISM AND ATHEISM

Deism is the view that God created the world but thereafter left it alone. On
this conception God does not intervene in the world through divine revelation: There are no special appearances, miracles, prophecies, or divinely composed scriptures. God is much like a watchmaker who creates an intricate and
self-sustaining machine; once the watch leaves the shop, the watchmaker stays
behind and tinkers with it no more. Our knowledge of God and our moral

responsibilities to each other are things that we discover on our own through the exercise of human reason. Some deists still believed in an afterlife in which God would reward or punish us for our conduct, but even this was something that we would discover through reason, not through revelation.

English Deism

The father of deism in Great Britain was Edward Herbert of Cherbury (1583–1648), a nobleman who was a soldier and diplomat by vocation. In his most famous work, *On Truth* (1624), Herbert lays out a philosophical system built on the theory that our minds contain instinctive "common notions" that are universally true. Some of these are responsible for how we perceive the world around us, and others for how we reason in scientific matters. A group of five such common notions, though, form the basis of religion: (1) There exists a supreme God, (2) we should worship him, (3) the best form of worship consists of proper moral behavior, (4) we should repent for our immoral conduct, and (5) we will be rewarded or punished in the afterlife for our conduct on earth. While this list contains nothing controversial in itself, it is nevertheless ground-breaking since Herbert maintains that these principles are the *sole* foundation of true religion. There is no divinely inspired scripture; the true message of God comes to all of us through natural reason in the form of these five principles. If we find any doctrines within a religion that go beyond these five, we should view those extraneous doctrines as fabrications constructed by religious leaders for their own advantage. Further, there is nothing inherently superior about Christianity as a religion since we find these five principles within other religious systems around the world.

In a later work titled *A Dialogue between a Tutor and His Pupil*, Herbert describes the challenges that we face when opposing the leaders of a dominant religion like Christianity. The pupil in the dialogue believes that religion should be a matter of reason, and not a matter of faith, and he is frustrated that "our divines would have me begin at faith, and afterwards come to reason." The tutor agrees and says that without a foundation in reason a religion based entirely on faith "will be but little worth, and perchance be thought no better than as a holy legend or allegorical history." Unfortunately, Herbert continues, religious leaders "everywhere tell us that we must reject all faiths but theirs, and so would have us, at one blow, cut off all [religious doctrine] which [they] themselves do not teach." This is clearly an unreasonable approach, says Herbert, especially since even the dominant religions contain many doubtful doctrines. Religious leaders are also quick to condemn members of other faiths to hell, but we should not be intimidated by these threats. If we pursue the issue from a strictly rational point of view, we will discover that true religion is grounded only in the five principles. Thus, if "divines in any country tell you that you must reject all other faiths and trust only to theirs," the tutor avers, the pupil should reply that this restriction is "tyrannical and unjust" since it prevents him from finding out the truth.

Our quest for religious truth, Herbert tells us, should involve seeking out the five principles as they appear in all faiths, setting aside any religious doctrines that go beyond them:

> You may do well to take notice of all pious doctrines among foreigners, as far as they are grounded on common reason, and concur with the precepts of a [morally] good life, taught in our church. Though about the miraculous manner of the delivery thereof, you may be doubtful. While if anything be added to the said doctrine, which is either inconsistent with piety and virtue, or may be suspected as forgery in the priest for his own advantage, I should wish you to lay it aside, till you are sufficiently instructed how to distinguish the true from the likely, the possible, and false.

Islam, according to Herbert, is a clear example of a foreign religion that reflects the five principles. There will be some religions, though, that are complete fabrications created by their religious leaders. Even so, Herbert explains, God did not abandon those people. Religious truth was instead disseminated to those cultures through their philosophers and lawmakers, who discovered the principles of religion within themselves and nature around them.

Other English writers followed Herbert's deistic view of religion and God, one of the most notorious being Matthew Tindal (1657–1733). While Herbert was cautious about directly attacking Christianity—or even mentioning Christianity by name—Tindal's approach was more forthright. The very title of his most famous book sets forth a challenge: *Christianity as Old as Creation, or the Gospel, a Republication of the Religion of Nature* (1730). Tindal argues in this work that all the key elements of Christianity are present in natural religion, which predates the Bible itself. While Herbert's approach to deism was grounded in innate ideas, Tindal followed the more empirical approach of Locke, drawing on human experience as a means of demonstrating the religion of nature. Tindal writes, "By 'natural religion,' I understand the belief of the existence of a God, and the sense and practice of those duties, which result from the knowledge we, by our reason, have (1) of him and his perfections, and (2) of ourselves, and our own imperfections, and (3) of the relation we stand in to him, and to our fellow-creatures. So that, the religion of nature takes in everything that is founded on the reason and nature of things." The aim of Christianity, according to Tindal, should be to rid religion of superstition and return to this pure and natural religion. To do this, reason should be our guide, and not scriptural authority.

French *Philosophes*

The radical religious views of the English deists carried over to France where they were embraced by a unique group of thinkers known as the *philosophes*. These were for the most part rebel voices who challenged the traditional forms of thought concerning religion, government, and morality. Believing that human reason provides the most reliable guide to human destiny, they held that "reason is to the *philosophe* what grace is to the Christian." This was the theme of the remarkable *Encyclopédie* (1751–1780), which contained the distinctive ideas of the philosophes. Under the editorship of Denis Diderot (1713–1784) and Jean Le Rond d'Alembert, by 1780 this epic work ran to thirty-five volumes. In his article "Encyclopedia," Diderot writes, "It could only belong to a philosophical age to attempt an encyclopedia," the reason being that "such a work constantly demands more intellectual daring than is commonly found in ages of cowardly liking. All things must be examined, debated, investigated without exception and without regard for anyone's feelings." Ancient but childish views must be pushed aside, and barriers to reason must be overturned. Diderot continues, "We have for quite some time needed a reasoning age when people would no longer seek the rules in classical authors but in nature." Much of the *Encyclopédie* consisted of "how to" articles on various crafts and trades. While such manuals are hardly unique today, at the time, divulging the zealously guarded secrets of tradespeople was an act of social revolution. Diderot writes, "There are special circumstances when craftspeople are so secretive about their techniques that the shortest way of learning about them would be to apprentice oneself to a master or to have some trustworthy person do this." Diderot believed that he had a duty to humanity at large to spread the secret knowledge of the mechanical arts, which would elevate people's lives around the globe.

While many of the philosophically skeptical elements of the *Encyclopédie* were diluted through battles with censors, the work nevertheless sets goals of combating superstition, intolerance, and dogmatism. Further, many of the articles express a materialistic and deterministic view of the world, themes that were developed more fully by contributors in their own published writings.

One of the more prominent contributors to the *Encyclopédie* was François-Marie Arout, better known by his chosen name Voltaire (1694–1778). In 1765 he published a work titled *Philosophical Dictionary*, which develops many of the moral and religious themes of the philosophes. One especially incendiary article in that work is "Atheism and Deism," which criticizes atheism and recommends deism. Voltaire acknowledges that atheists are for the most part people of learning, but, as they are only part-time philosophers, they have reasoned poorly about creation, the origin of evil, and other issues that led them to conclude that God does not exist. However, the final blame for the atheist's disbelief, Voltaire says, rests with religious believers themselves, "the mercenary tyrants of our souls, who, while disgusting us with their trickery, urge some weak minds to deny the Gods . . ." These believers try to persuade us "that an ass spoke; believe that a fish swallowed a man and threw him up after three days, safe and sound, on the shore; doubt not that the God of the Universe ordered one Jewish prophet to eat excrement." These views are so absurd and revolting, Voltaire asserts, that it is no wonder weak minds conclude that there is no God. But Voltaire believes that God indeed exists and that belief in God is in fact so crucial for a civil society that if God did not exist, it would be necessary to invent him. Fortunately, he argues, God's existence is clearly revealed in nature itself. While we should reject traditional systems of religion that are grounded in superstitious notions of revelation, we should embrace a deistic view. Voltaire writes that "the deist is a person firmly persuaded of the existence of a supreme being equally good and powerful, who has formed all extended, sentient and reflective existences; who perpetuates their species, who punishes crimes without cruelty, and rewards virtue with kindness." In essence, deism is "good sense not yet instructed by revelation; and other religions are good sense perverted by superstition."

Another important contributor to the *Encyclopédie* was Paul-Henri Dietrich, better known as Baron d'Holbach (1723–1789), who composed 376 articles for that work, mostly on scientific topics. In two of his books, *A System of Nature* (1770) and *Common Sense* (1772), he pushed French skeptical philosophy to its extreme. Unlike Voltaire, who advocated deism, Holbach completely denies God's existence and argues that the very idea of a divine being is incomprehensible: "Can we imagine ourselves sincerely convinced of the existence of a being, whose nature we know not; who is inaccessible to all our senses; whose attributes, we are assured, are incomprehensible to us?" Religion, he argues, originated in ancient times among savage and ignorant peoples and was reinforced through fear by leaders who saw it as a convenient way to control people. Religious beliefs were then transmitted from parent to child, generation after generation: "The human brain, especially in infancy, is like soft wax, fit to receive every impression that is made upon it." In this way the religious opinions of parents were cemented into their children's minds.

According to Holbach, the true system of nature, divorced from all religious superstition, is thoroughly materialistic: There are fixed laws of nature that direct the movement and configuration of material stuff. Human beings emerged in the natural course of events on this planet, and, while Holbach resists speculating about how this may have occurred, he maintains that humans have no privileged place in nature above other living things. All creatures live and reproduce according to the "energies" that are unique to their respective species. If we humans feel that we hold a uniquely honored place in nature, we are just being misguided by ignorance and self-love.

As products of nature, says Holbach, our physical bodies and mental functions are composed entirely of material stuff, and the concept of an immaterial human spirit is incomprehensible. He writes, "The doctrine of spirituality, such as it now exists, offers nothing but vague ideas; or rather is the absence of all ideas. What does it present to the mind, but a substance which possesses nothing of which our senses enable us to have any knowledge? Truly, can we imagine ourselves as immaterial beings that have no size or parts, which, nevertheless, act upon matter without having any point of contact, any kind of analogy with it?" Once we recognize that we are composed solely of material stuff, it quickly follows that all of our actions are determined. Every movement we make is the outcome of unchanging laws that nature imposes on everything within its domain. Every person "is born without his own consent. His structure in no way depends upon himself. His ideas come to him involuntarily. His habits are under the power of those who cause him to form them. He is continuously changed by causes, whether visible or concealed, over which he has no control, and which set the tone for his way of thinking and determine his manner of acting." Thus, according to Holbach, we are not free agents in any single instant of our lives, and the best way of seeing this is to examine the specific motive that prompted us to perform an action: We will always find that this motive is beyond our control. It is only because of the individual's limited ability "to decompose the complicated motion of his machine, that man believes himself a free agent."

ROUSSEAU

Rousseau's Life

With the most unlikely credentials Jean-Jacques Rousseau entered into the vigorous intellectual climate of the French philosophes. Despite little formal education he fashioned a set of ideas about human nature with such compelling power that his thought ultimately prevailed over the most impressive thinkers of his time.

Rousseau was born in Geneva in 1712. His mother died a few days after his birth, and his father, a watchmaker, left him at age 10 in the care of an aunt, who raised him. After two years in a boarding school where, he says in his autobiography *Confessions*, "we were to learn . . . all the insignificant trash that has obtained the name of education," he was recalled to his aunt's household, and thus, at the age of 12, his formal education came to an end. After a short apprenticeship to an engraver of watchcases, he left Geneva and roamed from place to place, meeting a series of people who alternately helped him make a meager living or referred him to other potential benefactors. Along the way he read books and developed his skills in music. Eventually, he wandered into France and there came under the care of a noblewoman, Madame de Warens, who sought to further his formal education, an attempt that failed, and to arrange for his employment. His most consistent work was copying music, though he was for a while tutor to the children of M. de Mably, who was Grand Provost of Lyons, and later secretary to the French ambassador to Venice. Rousseau was a precocious child who learned to read at an early age. In his twenties he read portions of the classic works of Plato, Virgil, Horace, Montaigne, Pascal, and Voltaire, which in their variety strongly influenced his imagination. From Lyons he went, armed with letters of introduction from the Mablys, to Paris, where he met some of the most influential persons of this capital city. Here he was struck by the contrasts between wealthy nobles and sweaty artisans, between the majesty of cathedrals and the fact of bishops reading the heretical ideas of Voltaire, between the gaiety of the salons and the tragic themes of Racine's plays. Although he met many notables, including Diderot, and moved increasingly in the upper circles of French society, he retained his childhood shyness, especially with women, and in 1746 eventually formed a lifelong relationship with an uneducated servant girl, Thérèse Levasseur, whom he finally married in 1768.

Rousseau's literary career began with his prize-winning *Discourse on the Arts and Sciences* (1750). With strong emotional power he argued that morals had been corrupted by the replacement of religion by science, by sensuality in art, by licentiousness in literature, and by the emphasis on logic at the expense of feeling. The essay instantly made Rousseau famous, leading Diderot to say that "never was there an instance of a like success." There followed in 1752 an operetta, *Le Devin du Village*, performed before the king and his court at Fontainebleau, and a comedy, *Narcisse*, performed by the Comédie-Française. Two important works appeared in 1755—his discourse *What Is the Origin of the Inequality among Men, and Is It Authorized by Natural Law?* and *Discourse on Political Economy*, which appeared in the *Encyclopédie*. In 1761 Rousseau published a love story, *Julie, ou La Nouvelle Héloïse*, which became the most celebrated novel of the eighteenth century. His book *Émile*, published in 1762, offered an elaborate proposal for a new approach to education and contained also a provocative section, "The Confession of Faith of a Savoyard Vicar," which was critical of institutional religion even while advocating the importance of religion to humankind. In the same year he published his most famous work, *The Social Contract*, in which he sought to describe the passage from the "state of nature" to the civil state and to explain why it is that laws governing men are legitimate.

Rousseau's last days were unhappy as he was in failing health and suffered from profound paranoia. Moreover, his books were severely criticized by the leaders of both church and state, and word went out that "J. J. Rousseau shall be apprehended and brought to the Concierge prison in the Palace [of Justice]." He became a fugitive, and at one point he accepted Hume's invitation to visit him in England, where he spent sixteen months. He returned to France convinced that his enemies were plotting to defame him. When he was told that Voltaire was dying, he said, "Our lives were linked to each other; I shall not survive him long." In July 1778, Rousseau died at the age of 66. His remarkably frank and detailed autobiography was published after his death as his *Confessions*.

The Paradox of Learning

When Rousseau read the announcement by the Academy of Dijon that a prize would be given for the best essay on the question of "Whether the restoration of the arts and sciences has had the effect of purifying or corrupting morals," he reacted with passionate excitement at the prospect of writing just such an essay. Looking back on that moment, he said, "I felt myself dazzled by a thousand sparkling lights. Crowds of vivid ideas thronged into my mind with a force and confusion that threw me into unspeakable agitation." He was already 38 years old; had read widely in classical and contemporary literature; had traveled in Switzerland, Italy, and France; had observed the ways of different cultures; and had spent enough time in the social circles of Paris to feel nothing but contempt for that sophisticated society. "If ever I could have written a quarter of what I saw and felt," he continued, "with what clarity I should have brought out all the contradictions of our social system." What he did set out to show was that "man is by nature good, and that only our institutions have made him bad." This turned out to be the underlying theme of Rousseau's future writings. But in this essay, the theme lacked precision and clarity, for, as Rousseau himself admitted, "though full of force and fire [this first *Discourse*] was absolutely wanting in logic and order . . . and it is the weakest in reasoning of all the works I ever wrote." For this reason Rousseau's *Discourse on the Arts and Sciences* was an easy target for critics. His readers had particular difficulty with his paradoxical arguments that civilization is the cause of unhappiness and that the corruption of society is caused by learning in the arts and sciences.

Rousseau begins his *Discourse* with high praise for the achievements of human reason, saying that "it is a noble and beautiful spectacle to see man raising himself . . . from nothing by his own exertions; dissipating by the light of reason all the thick clouds by which he was by nature enveloped." Only a few sentences later his essay becomes a slashing attack on the arts, literature, and sciences, which, he says, "fling garlands of flowers over the chains which weight men down" in their common life and "stifle in men's hearts that sense of original liberty for which they seem to have been born." Rousseau recognizes that human nature was not really any better in earlier times but suggests that the arts and sciences produced some significant changes making people worse. Before art and literature molded our behavior and taught our passions to speak an artificial language, our morals, says Rousseau, were rude but natural. Modern manners have made everyone conform in speech, dress, and attitude, always following the laws of fashion, never the promptings of our own nature, so that we no longer dare appear to be what we really are. The herd of humanity all act exactly alike, and so we never know even among our friends with whom we are dealing. Human relationships are now full of deceptions, whereas earlier people could easily see through one another, which prevented them from having many vices.

Rousseau also directed his attack against luxury and against political leaders who emphasized the economic aspects of politics. He reminded his contemporaries that "the politicians of the ancient world were always talking about morals and virtue; ours speak of nothing but commerce and money." His argument against luxury was that it could produce a brilliant but not a lasting society, for although money "buys everything else, it cannot buy morals and citizens." Artists and musicians pursuing luxury will lower their genius to the level of the times, composing mediocre works that will be immediately admired. This is the evil consequence of learning in the arts and sciences, when morals no longer have their rightful place and taste has been corrupted. One way to confront this matter is to acknowledge the role of women for, says Rousseau, "men will always be what women choose to make them. If you wish then they should be noble and virtuous, let women be taught what greatness of soul and virtue are." But, says Rousseau, the question is no longer whether a man is honest but whether he is clever, not whether a book is useful but whether it is well written. Rewards are lavished on ingenuity, but virtue is left unhonored.

Rousseau pointed to historical evidence for the notion that progress in the arts and sciences always leads to the corruption of morals and the decay of society. Egypt, he said, was "the mother of philosophy and the fine arts; soon she was conquered by Cambyses, and then successively by the Greeks, the Romans, the Arabs and finally the Turks." Similarly, Greece, once peopled by heroes, "always learned, always voluptuous, and always a slave, has experienced amid all its revolutions no more than a change of masters." It was for this reason that in Greece "not all the eloquence of Demosthenes could breathe life into a body which luxury and the arts had once enervated." Rome developed a great empire when she was a nation of barbarians and soldiers, but when she relaxed the stoic discipline and fell into epicurean indulgence, she was scorned by other nations and derided even by the barbarians. In this context Sparta, where patriotism was the supreme virtue and where arts, artists, science, and scholars were not tolerated, emerged as Rousseau's ideal state.

To see Rousseau praising ignorance during the height of the Enlightenment is an astonishing spectacle. But he did not mean to say that philosophy and science had no value. He quoted approvingly the words of Socrates, who also had praised ignorance. For Athens had its Sophists, poets, orators, and artists who made extravagant claims to knowledge while in fact they knew very little, whereas, said Socrates, "I am at least in no doubt of my ignorance." What Rousseau was concerned about was the danger to morality and to society caused by the confusion of contending theories or points of view. If everyone was allowed to pursue their own thoughts about moral values or even about scientific truth, inevitably, there would be serious differences of opinion. If differences of opinion were to be found everywhere, it would not be long before a deep skepticism spread throughout the population.

A stable society is based on a set of opinions or values that the majority accept as the rule for their thought and behavior. Rousseau believed that these firmly held opinions can be undermined by philosophy and science for several reasons. For one thing each society is unique, and its genius is its local set of values. But science and philosophy seek to discover universal truth. The very pursuit of such universal truth exposes the local opinion as less than the truth and thereby undermines its authority. To compound this problem, science emphasizes the requirement of proof and evidence, yet the dominant opinions about the most important subjects cannot be demonstrated beyond a doubt and, therefore, lose their binding force. Moreover, science requires an attitude of doubt that is contrary to the mood of ready acceptance of opinion. What keeps society together is faith, not knowledge. Both the scientist and the philosopher suspend faith during their pursuit of knowledge. So long as this suspension of faith is restricted to certain individuals, there is no great harm. What disturbed Rousseau was the damage done by the wide diffusion among the population of the spirit of doubt, which culminates in skepticism. The step from skepticism to the loosening of morality in turn inevitably causes a weakening of public virtue, which Rousseau understood chiefly as the virtue of patriotism. The very spirit of science undermines patriotism since the scientist tends to be a cosmopolitan, whereas the patriot has a strong attachment to his own society. To counteract these disintegrating trends in society, strong governments become necessary, and this, according to Rousseau, paves the way to despotism.

In the end Rousseau's quarrel was not so much with philosophy and science as with the attempt to popularize these disciplines. He had great respect for Bacon, Descartes, and Newton, whom he considered great teachers of humankind. But, he said, "it belongs only to a few to raise monuments to the glory of human learning," and it is proper to allow some individuals to apply themselves to the study of the arts and sciences. His attack was upon those who would distort knowledge by trying to make it popular, "those compilers who have indiscreetly broken open the door to the sciences and introduced into their sanctuary a populace unworthy to approach it." People need to know, says Rousseau, that "nature would have preserved them from science, as a mother snatches a dangerous weapon from the hands of her child." Ordinary people should build their happiness on the opinions that "we can find in our own hearts." Virtue, says Rousseau, is the "sublime science of simple minds," for the true philosophy is to "listen to the voice of conscience."

The Social Contract

Although Rousseau compares natural humans in the "state of nature" with humans as citizens of a civil society, he admits that he cannot give a specific account of how the transition from the earlier condition to the later one occurred. The purpose of his book *The Social Contract* is, therefore, not to describe the move from our natural state to subsequent membership in a political society but rather to provide an answer to the question of why people ought to obey the laws of government. Thus, Rousseau begins his book with the famous statement "Man is born free; and everywhere he is in chains." "How," he continues, "did this change come about? I do not know. What can make it legitimate? That question I think I can answer."

In the state of nature, people were happy, not because they were angels but because each person lived entirely for him- or herself and therefore possessed an absolute independence. Rousseau rejected the doctrine of original sin and instead argued that the origin of evil is found in the later stages of human development in society. In the state of nature, says Rousseau, people are motivated by "a natural sentiment which inclines every animal to watch over his own preservation, and which, directed in people by reason and pity, produces humanity and virtue." By contrast, as people develop social contacts, they also develop vices, for now they are motivated by "an artificial sentiment which is born in society and which leads every individual to make more of himself than every other," and "this inspires in people all the evils they perpetuate on each other," including intense competition for the few places of honor as well as envy, malice, vanity, pride, and contempt. Ultimately, it was impossible to live alone, for in all probability, says Rousseau, it was the steady growth in numbers that first brought people together into society. How, then, were people to reconcile the independence into which they were born with the inevitability that they would have to live together? The problem, says Rousseau, is "to find a form of association which will defend and protect with the whole common force the person and goods of each associate, and in which each, while uniting himself with all, may still obey himself alone." The solution to this problem is "the total alienation of each associate, together with all his rights, to the whole community." While this solution appears on the surface to be a prescription for despotism, Rousseau was convinced that it was the road to freedom.

The idea of a *social contract* seems to imply that such a contract was entered into at some point in the past. Rousseau did not view the contract in historical terms since he admitted that there is no way to discover evidence for such an event. For him the social contract is a living reality that will be found wherever there is a legitimate government. This living contract is the fundamental principle underlying a political association; this principle helps to overcome the lawlessness of absolute license and assures liberty, because people willingly adjust their conduct to harmonize with the legitimate freedom of others. What they lose by the social contract is their "natural liberty" and an unlimited right to everything; what they gain is "civil liberty" and a property right in what they possess. The essence of the social contract, says Rousseau, is that "each of us puts his person and all his power in common under the supreme direction of the general will, and, in our corporate capacity, we receive each member as an indivisible part of a whole." This contract tacitly assumes that whoever refuses to obey the *general will* shall be compelled to do so by the whole body; in short, "this means that he will be forced to be free."

What is the justification for saying that citizens can be "forced to be free"? The law is, after all, the product of the "general will." In turn, the general will is, says Rousseau, the will of the "sovereign." For Rousseau the sovereign consists of the total number of citizens of a given society. The general will of the sovereign is, therefore, the single will that reflects the sum of the wills of all the individual citizens. The many wills of the citizens can be considered one general will because all people who are parties to the social contract (as every citizen is) have agreed to direct their actions (to limit their actions) to achieving the common good. All citizens, by thinking of their own good, realize that they should refrain from any behavior that would cause others to turn on and injure them. In this way all citizens understand that their own good and their own freedom are connected with the common good. Ideally, therefore, each individual's will is identical with every other individual's since they are all directed to the same purpose, namely, the common good. Because in this ideal setting all the individual wills are identical or at least consistent, it can be said that there is only one will, the general will. For this reason it can also be said that if laws are the product of the sovereign general will, each individual is really the author of those laws; in this sense one obeys only oneself. The element of force or compulsion enters Rousseau's formula only when someone refuses to obey a law.

Rousseau distinguishes between the "general will" and the "will of all," saying that "there is often a great deal of difference between the will of all and the general will." What differentiates these two forms of the collective will is the purpose each attempts to achieve. If the "will of all" had the same purpose as the "general will," namely, the common good or justice, there would be no difference between them. But, says Rousseau, there is often a different purpose pursued by the "will of all," where "all" refers to the voters of a group, even if by chance they are in the majority. Such a deviant purpose reflects special or private interests as opposed to the common good. When this happens, society no longer has a general will; it now has as many wills as there are groups or "factions." If, therefore, the general will is to be able to express itself, there must not be factions or partial societies within the state. Rousseau was convinced that if the people were given adequate information and had the opportunity to deliberate, even if they had no communication with one another and simply thought their own thoughts, they would arrive at the general will. They would choose the path leading to the common good or justice. Only the common good would provide the setting for the greatest possible freedom for each citizen.

At this point there could be someone who chooses not to obey the law. If the law was made with the common good or justice in mind, as opposed to special interests, then the law truly expresses the general will. The person who votes against this law or chooses to disobey it is in error: "When therefore the opinion that is contrary to my own prevails, this proves neither more nor less than that I was mistaken, and that what I thought to be the general will was not so." When a law is proposed, the citizens are not asked to approve or reject the proposal; rather, they are asked to decide whether it is in conformity with the general will, that is, with the common good or justice. Only when the question is put this way can it be said that "the general will is found by counting the votes." Only under these circumstances is there any justification for forcing any-one to obey the law. In effect, such individuals are then being forced to behave in accordance with a law they would have been willing to obey if they had accu-rately understood the requirements of the common good, which alone provides them with the greatest amount of freedom. Only under these circumstances, says Rousseau, is it legitimate to say that they "will be forced to be free."

Rousseau was under no illusion that it would be easy to establish all the conditions for making just laws in the modern world. For one thing, much of his thought reflected the conditions in his native Geneva, a small city where participation by the citizens could be more direct. In addition, his vision included certain assumptions that would require considerable human virtue. If everyone were required to obey the laws, then everyone would be entitled to participate in deciding on those laws. When making the laws, those persons involved in the decisions would have to overcome special interests or the con-cerns of factions and think of the common good. Rousseau also believed that all the citizens should be equally involved in the making of the laws, that the laws should not be made even by representatives, for "the people cannot, even if it wishes, deprive itself of this incommunicable right." But as the modern state has continued to grow in size and complexity, a development that Rousseau had already seen happening in his own day, his assumptions and conditions for achieving the just society appeared to be more of an ideal than an immedi-ate possibility.

Taken as a whole, Rousseau's writings attacked the Enlightenment, gave impetus to the Romantic movement by emphasizing feeling, and provided a new direction for education. He also inspired the French Revolution and had a unique impact on political philosophy. The great German philosopher Imman-uel Kant was so impressed by Rousseau's insights that he hung a picture of him on the wall of his study, convinced that Rousseau was the Newton of the moral world.

REID

Reid's Life

Like Rousseau, Scottish philosopher Thomas Reid (1710–1796) was a product of Enlightenment philosophy while at the same time one of its harshest critics. He wrote at a time when many of Great Britain's most influential authors—philosophers, historians, poets, essayists—were from Scotland; so prolific were these writers that this period has been dubbed "the Scottish Enlightenment." Among Britain's philosophers Reid was second in influence only to his fellow Scotsman, David Hume, and the two carried on a friendly correspondence for many years. Reid himself was a professor at two of Scotland's great universities, and he developed his major writings from his classroom lectures. His philosophy has two dominant themes, the first of which is critical: Philosophy since the time of Descartes has become increasingly skeptical, even to the point that its dominant theories have become pure absurdities. The second theme is constructive: The proper approach to philosophy is one that draws from commonsense principles of reason that we are born with and that shape our mental conceptions of the world. Following publication of his first book, *An Inquiry into the Human Mind, On the Principles of Common Sense* (1767), Reid's fame was almost instant, and several other Scottish philosophers adopted his approach, thus creating a school of "Scottish commonsense philosophy."

Criticism of the Theory of Ideas

Reid viewed the history of modern philosophy as a story that gets worse and worse as it proceeds. It started with Descartes who, while on a quest for certainty, probed into the issue of personal identity. His unfortunate solution was to doubt his own existence and then attempt to resurrect it through the assertion "I think therefore I am." However, Reid argues, "A man that disbelieves his own existence, is surely as unfit to be reasoned with, as a man that believes he is made of glass." Clearly, Reid argues, Descartes could never seriously doubt his existence, and Descartes's whole strategy was ill-founded. Locke similarly attempted to dismantle the notion of personal identity by arguing that we maintain our identities over time through the mental faculty of remembrance. That is, I am the same person today as I was yesterday since I carry memories of yesterday's events. But, Reid argues, this means that I lose my personal identity every time I forget something. Berkeley dismantled the mind further by asserting that material objects do not exist and cannot be the source of our mental ideas of external things. Hume then pushed Berkeley's reasoning to its most extreme conclusion by denying that we have any concrete identities whatsoever that continue through time; our conscious minds, according to Hume, are merely fleeting perceptions. However, Reid notes, Hume himself concedes that he cannot live in the real world while denying his personal identity.

According to Reid, it is not simply a problem with theories of personal identity. Rather, all of the investigations into the human mind inspired by Descartes "necessarily plunge a man into this abyss of skepticism." Descartes himself "no sooner began to dig in this mine, than skepticism was ready to break in upon him." There is some inherent defect to Descartes's approach that has skepticism embedded in it. The source of the problem is what Reid calls "the theory of ideas," namely, an erroneous assumption that we do not perceive actual objects as they really are but have only mental images (ideas) of those objects. Suppose I look at a chair that is placed on the floor in front of me. According to the theory of ideas, I do not really see the actual chair, but only a mental copy. It is like a snapshot of the chair that appears before my mind's eye. The mental image may resemble the real chair, but according to the theory it is only a likeness of it, and I should not confuse the two. Reid maintains that every modern philosopher from Descartes onward adopted the theory of ideas; Hume, though, explicitly embraces it in his *Enquiry concerning Human Understanding* when he writes that "nothing can ever be present to the mind but an image or perception, and that the senses are only the inlets, through which these images are conveyed."

What is so bad about the theory of ideas? After all, is not that the best explanation of why two people perceive the same object differently? Suppose Bob and I both look at an apple, and, while it appears red to me, it appears blue to Bob. According to the theory of ideas, while the apple is the same, our mental images differ because our visual "cameras" are feeding us different "pictures" of it. As appealing as this explanation seems, according to Reid, it is precisely this assumption that sets us on an inevitable road toward skepticism. The reason is that it destroys all access to the external world: All that we will ever know are our mental images, but never the objects themselves. We are condemned to knowledge that is generated only by our visual cameras, with no hope of perceiving anything as it really is, whether it is an apple, a chair, or even our own personal identity. Thus, my entire reality consists only of a collection of mental snapshots, and all of my beliefs about the world derive from comparing different snapshots. It does not make any difference how many snapshots my visual or auditory camera takes of external things. It does not make any difference how much my mind assembles, disassembles, or associates these sensory images: I will not be able to say anything about the objects themselves. The reality that my mind constructs is like an enchanted castle with no link to the external world. I am left with complete skepticism.

Commonsense Beliefs and Direct Realism

Reid's main attack against the skeptical trend of philosophers of his time can be encapsulated in a single sentence: They oppose the truth of commonsense beliefs that are commanded by human nature. Reid writes:

> If there are certain principles, as I think there are, which the constitution of our nature leads us to believe, and which we are under a necessity to take for granted in the common concerns of life, without being able to give a reason for them; these are what we call the principles of common sense; and what is manifestly contrary to them, is what we call absurd.

Philosophy, according to Reid, needs to be consistent with the principles of common sense that are embedded in our thought processes. By defying these principles in philosophical theories, we not only subscribe to falsehoods but go down the path of philosophical skepticism, which commits us to absurd views such as denying the existence of the external world.

According to Reid, commonsense directs our beliefs in countless ways, such as with our convictions about sense perception, personal identity, God, free will, and morality. Reid is not saying that we each have a list of precisely defined instinctive beliefs that we can enumerate from memory. For example, we do not have tiny voices in our minds reciting lists of beliefs like "An external world exists," "Things that look red are red," and "God is the ultimate cause of the universe." Rather, our knowledge of commonsense beliefs is more subtle. Reid says that we should start by examining the words that we use in conversation since language reflects our ordinary ways of thinking. Thus, the main indicator that we have a commonsense belief is that it is embedded in our natural way of speaking. For example, all languages have words for the concepts of *hard, soft, heavy*, and *light*, and this suggests that these notions are fixed components within our human minds. It is not an absolute proof, but it is very strong evidence. Reid maintains that as we identify commonsense beliefs one after the other within our language, we will find that they are all compatible with each other. That is, if today I discover a commonsense belief indicating that "the external world exists," I will not discover one tomorrow that says "the external world does not exist."

For Reid one clear benefit of commonsense beliefs is that having then enables us to dismiss outrageous skeptical theories. Even if the reasoning process behind a skeptical theory seems plausible, we should nevertheless reject it if it runs contrary to commonsense. A second benefit of commonsense beliefs is that they form the backbone of how the human mind works and, thus, can help us solve philosophical puzzles that baffled modern philosophers from Descartes through Hume. This is precisely what Reid does with philosophical puzzles about how we perceive external objects. According to the erroneous theory of ideas advocated by Descartes and others, there are three components to sense perception. First, there is an external object, such as a tree. Second, there is the mental image, or "snapshot," that I have of the tree. Finally, there is my awareness of the snapshot. According to Reid, our commonsense understanding of perception has only two components: the actual tree and my awareness of the tree. That is, we perceive external objects directly, without the aid of mental images as middlemen. Thus, when I perceive the shape and color of a tree, I am aware of features within the actual tree. Accordingly, Reid's theory of perception is called *direct realism*.

While Reid is committed to the theory that we perceive external objects directly, he recognizes that we do not perceive things *exactly* as they are. For example, when I look at a tree and perceive the greenness of its leaves, common sense does not force me to conclude that the color of green actually resides in the leaves themselves. I know that my perception of color depends on light conditions and other factors. Nevertheless, common sense does impel me to believe that there is *some* property within the leaves that enables me to perceive them as green. My perception of green leaves, then, is really a direct awareness of the tree's property to cause my sensations of green.

PART FOUR

Late Modern and Nineteenth-Century Philosophy

CHAPTER 13

Kant

KANT'S LIFE

*I*mmanuel Kant lived all of his 80 years (1724–1804) in the small provincial town of Königsberg in East Prussia. His parents were of modest means, and their religious spirit, nurtured by a sect known as Pietists, was to have a permanent influence on Kant's thought and personal life. His education began at the local Collegium Fredericianum, whose director was also a Pietist, and in 1740 Kant entered the University of Königsberg, where he studied the classics, physics, and philosophy. The German universities were at this time dominated by the philosopher Christian von Wolff (1679–1754), who stimulated philosophical activity by developing a comprehensive system of philosophy along the lines of Leibniz's rationalism and metaphysics. Kant's professor at Königsberg, Martin Knutzen, had come under the influence of this Wolff-Leibnizian approach to philosophy, and inevitably, Kant's university training laid much emphasis on the power of human reason to move with certainty in the realm of metaphysics. Although Knutzen had thus slanted Kant's early thought toward the tradition of Continental rationalism, it was also Knutzen who stimulated Kant's interest in Newtonian physics, an interest that played a very important part in the development of Kant's original and critical philosophy. Upon completion of his university course, Kant spent about eight years as a family tutor, and in 1755 he became a lecturer at the university. In 1770 he was appointed to the chair of philosophy that had been held by Knutzen.

Although Kant's personal life contains no remarkable events, as he did not travel and developed no notable political or social connections, he was, nevertheless, immensely successful as a lecturer and was an interesting conversationalist and charming host. He is often pictured as an old bachelor whose every activity was scheduled with such precision that neighbors could set their watches by when he stepped out of his house each day at half past four to walk up and down his small avenue eight times. Without this discipline, however, he could hardly have produced such a striking succession of famous books as his monumental *Critique of Pure Reason* (1781), *Prolegomena to Any Future Metaphysics* (1783), *Principles of the Metaphysics of Morals* (1785), *Metaphysical First Principles of Natural Science* (1786), the second edition of the *Critique of Pure Reason* (1787), the *Critique of Practical Reason* (1788), the *Critique of Judgment* (1790), *Religion within the Limits of Pure Reason* (1793), and the small work *Perpetual Peace* (1795).

THE SHAPING OF KANT'S PROBLEM

Kant revolutionized modern philosophy. What prompted this revolution was his profound concern with a problem that the philosophy of his day could not deal with. The elements of his problem are suggested by his famous comment that "two things fill the mind with ever new and increasing admiration and awe . . . the starry heavens above and the moral law within." To him the starry heavens were a reminder that the world, as pictured earlier by Hobbes and Newton, is a system of bodies in motion, where every event has a specific and determinate cause. At the same time, all people experience the sense of moral duty, an experience implying that humans, unlike some other elements of nature, possess freedom in their behavior. The problem, then, was how to reconcile the two seemingly contradictory interpretations of events—one holding that all events are the product of *necessity*, and the other that in certain aspects of human behavior there is *freedom*.

As Kant viewed the drift of scientific thought, he saw in it an attempt to include *all* of reality, including human nature, in its mechanical model. This would mean that all events, being parts of a unified mechanism, could be explained in terms of cause and effect. Moreover, this scientific approach would eliminate from consideration any elements that could not fit into its method. His method emphasized limiting knowledge to the realm of actual sense experience and to generalizations that could be derived by induction from such experience. Pursuing this method, science would have no need for, nor could it account for, such notions as freedom and God.

Kant was impressed by the obvious success and the constant advance of scientific knowledge. What the success of Newtonian physics did for Kant was to raise some serious questions about the adequacy of the philosophy of his day. The two major traditions of his day were Continental rationalism and British empiricism, and Newtonian physics enjoyed an independence from both of these philosophical systems. Since Continental rationalism had been built on a mathematical model, this type of philosophizing emphasized the relation of *ideas* to each other and so had no clear connection with things as they really are. Rationalism could not produce the kind of knowledge Newtonian physics represented, and for this reason its metaphysical speculations about reality beyond experience were considered dogmatic. Kant was to say with some respect that Christian Wolff, whose Leibnizian metaphysics had influenced Kant's earlier thought, was "the greatest of all dogmatic philosophers." This contrast between rationalism and science raised for Kant the question of whether metaphysics can increase our knowledge the way science obviously can. The dogmatic character of metaphysics was made clear particularly by the variety of conclusions to which metaphysicians had come in their systems of thought, as shown by the differences between Descartes, Spinoza, and Leibniz. But the heart of the matter was that scientists were unraveling the nature of reality and were showing less and less concern about such metaphysical notions as freedom and God and the possibility of moral truth.

At the same time, science proceeded independently of the other major philosophical tradition of Kant's day, namely, British empiricism. Hume's most striking philosophical argument was an attack on the traditional notion of causality. Since all our knowledge comes from experience, and we do not experience causality, we cannot infer or predict any future event from our experience of the present. What we call *causality*, said Hume, is simply our habit of associating two events because we experience them together, but this does not justify the conclusion that these events have any necessary connection. Thus, Hume denied inductive inference. And yet, it is precisely on the notion of causality and inductive inference that science is built. For it assumes that our knowledge of particular events in the present gives us reliable knowledge about an indefinite number of similar events in the future. The logical outcome of Hume's empiricism was that there cannot be any scientific knowledge, and this leads to philosophical skepticism. Kant was left, therefore, with great admiration for science but with serious questions about philosophy because of the dogmatism of rationalism and the skepticism of empiricism.

Although Newtonian physics impressed Kant, science itself raised two major questions for him. The first we have already mentioned, namely, that as the scientific method was applied to the study of all of reality, notions of morality, freedom, and God were threatened by absorption into a mechanical universe. The second problem for Kant was how to explain, or to justify, scientific knowledge. That is, did the scientist give an adequate explanation of what makes his understanding of nature possible? As it turned out, these two problems were very closely related. As Kant discovered, scientific knowledge is similar to metaphysical knowledge. Thus, the justification or explanation of scientific thought on the one hand and metaphysical thought concerning freedom and morality on the other are the same. Kant, therefore, rescued metaphysics without attacking science. Both in science and in metaphysics, our minds start with some given fact, which gives rise to a judgment within our reason. He thus says, "The genuine method of metaphysics is fundamentally the same kind which Newton introduced into natural science and which was there so fruitful." With this interpretation of scientific and moral thought, Kant provided a new function and a new life for philosophy. This function is suggested by the title of his major work, the *Critique of Pure Reason*, for now the task of philosophy became the critical appraisal of the capacities of human reason. In pursuing this new critical function, he achieved what he called his Copernican revolution in philosophy.

KANT'S CRITICAL PHILOSOPHY AND HIS COPERNICAN REVOLUTION

The turning point in Kant's intellectual development was his encounter with Hume's empiricism. He tells us, "I openly confess, the suggestion of David Hume was the very thing, which many years ago first interrupted my dogmatic slumber and gave my investigations in the field of speculative philosophy quite a new direction." Hume had argued that all our knowledge is derived from experience and that, therefore, we cannot have knowledge of any reality beyond our experience. This argument struck at the very foundation of rationalism. Rationalists argued confidently that human reason can derive knowledge about realities beyond experience simply by moving from one idea to another as one does in mathematics. The rationalist proofs for the existence of God were a case in point, and Spinoza's and Leibniz's explanation of the structure of reality was another. Kant eventually turned his back on rationalist metaphysics, calling it "rotten dogmatism," but he did not accept Hume's entire argument, saying, "I was far from following him in the conclusions at which he arrived."

Kant refused to follow Hume all the way, not merely because this would lead to Skepticism, but because he felt that although Hume was on the right track, he had not completed the task of explaining how knowledge is acquired. Nor did Kant wish to give up some of the subjects that concerned the rationalist metaphysicians, such as freedom and God, about which it is impossible to be "indifferent," even though he was prepared to say that we cannot have demonstrative knowledge of objects beyond our experience. Kant, therefore, sought to build on what he thought was significant in both rationalism and empiricism and to reject what could not be defended in these systems. He did not simply combine the insights of his predecessors but rather embarked on a genuinely new approach, which he called *critical philosophy*.

The Way of Critical Philosophy

Kant's *critical philosophy* consists of an analysis of the components of human reason, by which he meant "a critical inquiry into the faculty of reason with reference to all the knowledge which it may strive to attain independently of all experience." The way of critical philosophy is, therefore, to ask the question "What and how much can understanding and reason know, apart from all experience?" Earlier metaphysicians engaged in disputes about the nature of the supreme being and other subjects that took them beyond the realm of immediate experience. Kant, though, asked the principal question whether human reason possessed the powers to undertake such inquiries. From this point of view he thought it foolish for metaphysicians to construct systems of knowledge even before they had determined whether, by pure reason alone, we can apprehend what is not given to us in experience. Critical philosophy for Kant was, therefore, not the negation of metaphysics but rather a preparation for it. If metaphysics has to do with knowledge as developed by reason alone—that is, prior to experience, or *a priori*—the crucial question is how such *a priori* knowledge is possible.

The Nature of *a Priori* Knowledge

Kant affirmed that we possess a faculty that is capable of giving us knowledge without an appeal to experience. He agreed with the empiricists that our knowledge starts with experience, but he added that "though our knowledge begins *with* experience, it does not follow that it all arises *out of* experience." This was the point that Hume had missed, for Hume had said that all our knowledge consists of a series of impressions, which we derive through our senses. Yet we clearly possess a kind of knowledge that does not come *out of* experience even though it begins *with* experience. Hume was right that we do not, for example, experience or sense causality. But Kant rejected his explanation that *causality* is simply a psychological habit of connecting two events that we call cause and effect. Instead, Kant believed that we have knowledge about causality and that we get this knowledge not from sense experience but directly from the mental faculty of rational judgment and, therefore, *a priori*.

What, more specifically, is *a priori* knowledge? Kant replies that "if one desires an example from the sciences, one needs only to look at any proposition in mathematics. If one desires an example from the commonest operations of the understanding, the proposition that every change must have a cause can serve one's purposes." What makes a proposition of mathematics or the proposition that every change must have a cause *a priori* knowledge? It is, Kant says, that this kind of knowledge cannot be derived from experience. Experience cannot show us that *every* change must have a cause since we have not yet experienced every change. Nor can experience show us that connections between events are *necessary;* the most experience can tell us is "that a thing is so and so, but not that it cannot be otherwise." Experience, then, cannot give us knowledge about *necessary* connections or about the *universality* of propositions. Yet we do in fact have this kind of knowledge about causality and universality, for these are the notions that characterize mathematics and scientific knowledge. We confidently say that all heavy objects will fall in space or that all instances of 5 added to 7 will equal 12. That there is such *a priori* knowledge is clear, but what concerned Kant was how such knowledge can be accounted for. How, in short, can Hume's skepticism be answered? But it was not simply a question of how *a priori* knowledge is possible, but how "synthetic judgments *a priori*" are possible. To answer this question, Kant had first to discover what constitutes a synthetic judgment *a priori*.

The Synthetic *a Priori*

Kant distinguishes between two kinds of judgments, the *analytic* and the *synthetic*. A *judgment*, he says, is an operation of thought whereby we connect a subject and predicate, where the predicate qualifies in some way the subject. When we say that "the building is tall," we make a judgment, for the mind is able to understand a connection between the subject and the predicate. Subjects and predicates are connected to each other in two different ways, thereby leading us to make two different kinds of judgments.

In *analytic judgments* the predicate is already contained in the concept of the subject. The judgment that all triangles have three angles is an analytic judgment. Because the predicate is already implicit in the subject of an analytic judgment, such a predicate does not give us any new knowledge about the subject. Again, the judgment that "all bodies are extended" is analytic, for the idea of extension is already contained in the idea of body. An analytic judgment is true only because of the logical relation of subject and predicate. To deny an analytic judgment would involve a logical contradiction.

A *synthetic judgment* differs from the analytic in that its predicate is not contained in the subject. Thus, in a synthetic judgment the predicate adds something new to our concept of the subject. To say that "the apple is red" joins two independent concepts, for the concept *apple* does not contain the idea of *redness*. Similarly, for Kant, "all bodies are heavy" is an example of a synthetic judgment, for the idea of heaviness is not contained in the concept of body; that is, the predicate is not contained in the subject.

At this point Kant makes a further distinction, this time between judgments that are *a priori* and judgments that are *a posteriori*. All analytic judgments are *a priori*: Their meaning does not depend on our experience of any particular cases or events since they are independent of any observations, as in the case of mathematics. As "necessity and strict universality are sure marks of *a priori* knowledge," Kant has no trouble showing that analytic judgments represent *a priori* knowledge. Synthetic judgments, on the other hand, are for the most part *a posteriori*—that is, they occur after an experience of observation. To say, for example, that all boys in school X are six feet tall is a synthetic judgment *a posteriori*, for this proposition regarding their height is contingently and not necessarily true of all the present or future members of that school. This judgment cannot be made without experience with the particular details of this school. Thus, while all analytic judgments are *a priori*, most synthetic judgments are *a posteriori*.

There is, however, still another kind of judgment besides the analytic *a priori* and the synthetic *a posteriori*, and this is the *synthetic a priori*. This is the kind of judgment Kant was most concerned about because he was certain that we make these judgments, yet there was the persistent question of how such judgments are possible. The question arises because by definition synthetic judgments are based on experience, but if that is the case, how can they be called *a priori*, since this implies independence of experience? Still, Kant showed that in mathematics, physics, ethics, and metaphysics we do make judgments that are not only *a priori* but also synthetic. For example, the judgment 7 plus 5 equal 12 is certainly *a priori* because it contains the marks of necessity and universality; that is, 7 plus 5 *has* to equal 12, and it *always* has to do so. At the same time, this judgment is synthetic and not analytic because 12 cannot be derived by a mere analysis of the numbers 7 and 5. The act of intuition is necessary in order to achieve a synthesis of the concepts 7, 5, and plus.

Kant shows that in propositions of geometry also the predicate is not contained in the subject even though there is a necessary and universal connection between subject and predicate. Thus, propositions of geometry are at once *a priori* and synthetic. For example, Kant says, "That a straight line between two points is the shortest, is a synthetic proposition. For my concept of *straight* contains no notion of quantity, but only of quality. The concept of *shortest* is thus wholly an addition, and it cannot be derived by any analysis from the concept of a straight line. Intuition must, therefore, lend its aid here, by means of which alone is this synthesis possible." In physics, too, we find synthetic *a priori* judgments; Kant says that "natural science contains within itself synthetic *a priori* judgments as principles." The proposition "In all changes of the material world the quantity of matter remains unchanged" is *a priori*, for we make this judgment before we have experienced every change. It is also synthetic, for the idea of permanence is not discoverable in the concept of matter. In metaphysics we assume that we are extending or increasing our knowledge. If this is so, the propositions of metaphysics, such as the judgment "human beings are free to choose," must be synthetic, for here the predicate adds new knowledge to the concept of the subject. At the same time, this metaphysical judgment is *a priori*, for the predicate *are free* is connected to our idea of all people even before we have experience of all people.

What Kant wanted to show by these illustrations is that it is not only in metaphysics but also in mathematics and physics that we make synthetic *a priori* judgments. If these judgments create difficulties in metaphysics, they create the same ones for mathematics and physics. Kant believed, therefore, that if synthetic *a priori* judgments could be explained or justified in mathematics and physics, they would, thereby, also be justified in metaphysics.

Kant's Copernican Revolution

Kant solved the problem of the synthetic *a priori* judgment by substituting a new hypothesis concerning the relation between the mind and its objects. It was clear to him that if we assume, as Hume did, that the mind, in forming its concepts, must conform to its objects, there could be no solution to the problem. Hume's theory would work for our ideas of things we have actually experienced, but these are *a posteriori* judgments. If I ask, "How do I know that the chair is brown?" my answer is that I can see it; and if my assertion is challenged, I refer to my experience. When I thus refer to my experience, that settles the question, because we all agree that experience gives us a kind of knowledge that conforms to the nature of things. But a synthetic *a priori* judgment cannot be validated by experience. If I say, for example, that every straight line is the shortest way between two points, I certainly cannot say that I have had experience of every possible straight line. What makes it possible for me to make judgments about events before they even occur—judgments that are universally true and can always be verified? If, as Hume believed, the mind is passive and simply receives its information from the objects, it follows that the mind would have information only about that particular object. But the mind makes judgments about all objects, even those that it has not yet experienced, and, in addition, objects do in fact behave in the future according to these judgments we make about them. This scientific knowledge gives us reliable information about the nature of things. But since this knowledge, which is both synthetic and *a priori*, could not be explained on the assumption that the mind conforms to its objects, Kant was forced to try a new hypothesis regarding the relation between the mind and its objects.

According to Kant's new hypothesis, it is the objects that conform to the operations of the mind, and not the other way around. He came to this hypothesis with a spirit of experimentation, consciously following the example of Copernicus, who, "failing of satisfactory progress in explaining the movements of the heavenly bodies on the supposition that they all revolved round the spectator, he tried whether he might not have better success if he made the spectator to revolve and the stars to remain at rest." Seeing an analogy here with his own problem, Kant says that,

> until now it has been assumed that all our knowledge must conform to objects. But all our attempts to extend our knowledge of objects by establishing something in regard to them *a priori* by means of concepts, have, on this assumption, ended in failure. We must, therefore, make trial whether we may not have more success in the tasks of metaphysics, if we suppose that objects must conform to our knowledge. . . . If intuition must conform to the constitution of the objects, I do not see how we could know anything of the latter *a priori*; but if the object (as object of the senses) must conform to the constitution of our faculty of intuition, I have no difficulty in conceiving such a possibility.

Kant did not mean that the mind creates objects, nor did he mean that the mind possesses innate ideas. His Copernican revolution consisted rather in his saying that the mind brings something to the objects it experiences. Kant agreed with Hume that our knowledge begins with experience, but unlike Hume, Kant saw the mind as an active agent doing something with the objects it experiences. The mind, Kant says, is structured in such a way that it imposes its way of knowing on its objects. By its very nature the mind actively organizes our experiences. That is, thinking involves not only receiving impressions through our senses but also making judgments about what we experience. Just as a person who wears colored glasses sees everything in that color, so every human being, having the faculty of thought, inevitably thinks about things in accordance with the natural structure of the mind.

THE STRUCTURE OF RATIONAL THOUGHT

Kant says that "there are two sources of human knowledge, which perhaps spring from a common but to us unknown root, namely, sensibility and understanding. Through the former objects are *given* to us; through the latter they are *thought*." Knowledge is, therefore, a cooperative affair between the knower and the thing known. But, although I am able to distinguish between myself as a knower and the thing I know, I can never know that thing as it is in itself, for the moment I know it, I know it as my structured mind permits me to know it. If colored glasses were permanently fixed to my eyes, I should always see things in that color and could never escape the limitations placed on my vision by those glasses. Similarly, my mind always brings certain ways of thinking to things, and this always affects my understanding of them. What does the mind bring to the *given* raw materials of our experience?

The Categories of Thought and the Forms of Intuition

The distinctive activity of the mind is to synthesize and to unify our experience. It achieves this synthesis first by imposing on our various experiences in the "sensible manifold" certain forms of intuition: space and time. We inevitably perceive things as being in *space* and *time*. But space and time are not ideas derived from the things we experience, nor are they concepts. Space and time are encountered immediately in intuition and are, at the same time, *a priori* or, to speak figuratively, lenses through which we always see objects of experience.

In addition to space and time, which deal particularly with the way we sense things, there are certain categories of thought that deal more specifically with the way the mind unifies or synthesizes our experience. The mind achieves this unifying act by making various kinds of judgments as we engage in the act of interpreting the world of sense. The variety of our experiences—or "the manifold of experience" as Kant calls it—is judged by us through certain fixed forms or concepts, such as *quantity, quality, relation*, and *modality*. When we assert *quantity*, we have in mind one or many; when we make a judgment of *quality*, we make either a positive or a negative statement; when we make a judgment of *relation*, we think of cause and effect, on the one hand, or of the relation of subject and predicate, on the other; and when we make a judgment of *modality*, we have in mind that something is either possible or impossible. All these ways of thinking are what constitute the act of synthesis through which the mind strives to make a consistent single world out of the manifold of sense experience.

The Self and the Unity of Experience

What makes it possible for us to have a unified grasp of the world about us? Based on his analysis of the way our minds work, Kant's answer is that it is the mind that transforms the raw data given to our senses into a coherent and related set of elements. But this leads Kant to say that the unity of our experience must imply a unity of the self, for unless there was a unity between the several operations of the mind, there could be no knowledge of experience. To have such knowledge involves, in various sequences, sensation, imagination, and memory, as well as the capacity of intuitive synthesis. Thus, it must be the same self that at once senses an object, remembers its characteristics, and imposes on it the forms of space and time and the category of cause and effect. All these activities must occur in some single subject. If it were otherwise, there could be no knowledge, for if one subject had only sensations, another only memory, and so on, the manifold of sense experience could never be unified.

Where and what is this single subject that accomplishes this unifying activity? Kant calls it the "transcendental unity of apperception"—what we call the *self*. He uses the term *transcendental* to show that we do not experience the self directly even though such a unity, or self, is implied by our actual experience. Thus, the idea of this self is *a priori* a necessary condition for the experience we do have of having knowledge of a unified world of nature. In the act of unifying all the elements of experience, we are conscious of our own unity, so that our consciousness of a unified world of experience and our own self-consciousness occur simultaneously. Our self-consciousness, however, is affected by the same faculties that affect our perception of external objects. I bring to the knowledge of myself the same apparatus and, therefore, impose on myself as an object of knowledge the same "lenses" through which I see everything. Just as I do not know things as they are apart from the perspective from which I see them, so also I do not know the nature of this "transcendental unity of apperception" except as I am aware of the knowledge I have of the unity of the field of experience. What I am sure of is that a unified self is implied by any knowledge of experience.

Phenomenal and Noumenal Reality

A major aspect of Kant's critical philosophy was his insistence that human knowledge is forever limited in its scope. This limitation takes two forms. First, knowledge is limited to the world of experience. Second, our knowledge is limited by the manner in which our faculties of perception and thinking organize the raw data of experience. Kant did not doubt that the world as it appears to us is not the ultimate reality. He distinguished between *phenomenal* reality, or the world as we experience it, and *noumenal* reality, which is purely intelligible, that is, nonsensual, reality. When we experience a thing, we inevitably perceive it through the "lenses" of our *a priori* categories of thought. But what is a thing like when it is not being perceived? What is a "thing-in-itself" (*Ding an sich*)? We can obviously never have an experience of a nonsensuous perception. All objects we know are sensed objects. Still, we know that the existence of our world of experience is not produced by the mind. The mind, rather, imposes its ideas on the manifold of experience, which is derived from the world of things-inthemselves. This means that there is a reality external to us that exists independently of us but that we can know only as it appears to us and is organized by us. The concept of a thing-in-itself does not, then, increase our knowledge but reminds us of the limits of knowledge.

Transcendental Ideas of Pure Reason as Regulative Concepts

Besides the general concept of the noumenal realm, there are three regulative ideas that we tend to think about, ideas that lead us beyond sense experiences but about which we cannot be indifferent because of our inevitable tendency to try to unify all our experience. There are the ideas of the *self*, of the *cosmos*, and of *God*. They are *transcendental* because they correspond to no object in our experience. They are produced not by intuition but by pure reason alone. They are, however, prompted by experience in the sense that we think those ideas in our attempts to achieve a coherent synthesis of all our experience. Kant says,

"The first [regulative] idea is the 'I' itself, viewed simply as thinking nature or soul . . . endeavoring to represent all determinations as existing in a single subject, all powers, so far as possible, as derived from a single fundamental power, all change as belonging to the states of one and the same permanent being, and all *appearances* in space as completely different from the actions of thought." In this way our pure reason tries to synthesize the various psychological activities we are aware of into a unity, and it does this by formulating the concept of the *self*. Similarly, pure reason tries to create a synthesis of the many events in experience by forming the concept of the *world*. Thus,

> the second regulative idea of merely speculative reason is the concept of the world in general. . . . The absolute totality of the series of conditions . . . an idea which can never be completely realized in the empirical employment of reason, but which yet serves as a rule that prescribes how we ought to proceed in dealing with such series. . . . The cosmological ideas are nothing but simply regulative principles, and are very far from positing . . . an actual totality of such series. . . . The third idea of pure reason, which contains a merely relative supposition of a being that is the sole and sufficient cause of all cosmological series, is the idea of *God*. We have not the slightest ground to assume in an absolute manner the object of this idea . . . . It becomes evident that the idea of such a being, like all speculative ideas, seems only to formulate the command of reason, that all connection in the world be viewed in accordance with the principles of a systematic unity—*as if* all such connection had its source in one single all-embracing being as the supreme and sufficient cause.

Kant's use of these regulative ideas exemplifies his way of mediating between dogmatic rationalism and skeptical empiricism. With the empiricists Kant agrees that we can have no knowledge of reality beyond experience. The ideas of the self, the cosmos, and God cannot give us any theoretical knowledge of realities corresponding to these ideas. The function of these ideas is simply and solely regulative. As regulative ideas they give us a reasonable way of dealing with the constantly recurring questions raised by metaphysics. To this extent Kant acknowledged the validity of the subject matter of rationalism. His critical analysis of the scope of human reason, however, led him to discover that earlier rationalists had made the error of treating *transcendental* ideas as though they are ideas about actual beings. Kant emphasizes that "there is a great difference between something given to my reason as an *object absolutely*, or merely as an *object in the idea*. In the former case our concepts are employed to determine the object [transcendent]; in the latter case there is in fact only a scheme for which no object, not even a hypothetical one, is directly given, and which only enables us to represent to ourselves other objects in an indirect manner, namely in their systematic unity, by means of their relation to this idea. Thus, I say, that the concept of a highest intelligence is a mere idea [transcendental]."

The Antinomies and the Limits of Reason

Because regulative ideas do not refer to any objective reality about which we can have knowledge, we must consider these ideas as being the products of our pure reason. As such we cannot bring to these ideas the *a priori* forms of time and space or the category of cause and effect since these are imposed by us only on the manifold of sense experience. Science is possible because all people, having the same structure of mind, will always and everywhere order the events of sense experience in the same way. That is, we all bring to the *given* of sense experience the same organizing faculties of understanding. But there can be no science of metaphysics because there is not the same kind of *given* when we consider the ideas of self, cosmos, and God as when we consider "the shortest distance between two points." What is given in metaphysics is the felt need to achieve a synthesis of the wide variety of events in experience at ever-higher levels and of discovering an ever-wider explanation of the realm of phenomenon.

There is a difference for Kant between *a priori* or theoretical scientific knowledge, on the one hand, and speculative metaphysics, on the other. The difference is that we can have scientific knowledge of phenomena but cannot have scientific knowledge of the noumenal realm, or the realm that transcends experience. Our attempts to achieve a "science" of metaphysics, Kant says, are doomed to failure. Whenever we try to discuss the self, the cosmos, or God as though they were objects of experience, the inability of the mind ever actually to do so is showed by what Kant calls the *antinomies* into which we fall. These four antinomies show us that when we discuss the nature of the world beyond experience, we can argue with equal force on opposite sides of various propositions. Specifically, (1) the world is limited in time and space, or it is unlimited; (2) every composite substance in the world is made up of simple parts, or no composite thing in the world is made up of simple parts since there nowhere exists in the world anything simple; (3) besides causality in accordance with the laws of nature there is also another causality, that of freedom, or there is no freedom since everything in the world takes place solely in accordance with the laws of nature; and, finally, (4) there exists an absolutely necessary being as part of the world or as its cause, or an absolutely necessary being nowhere exists.

These antinomies reflect the disagreements generated by dogmatic metaphysics. The disagreements occur only because they are based on "nonsense"— that is, on attempts to describe a reality about which we have no sense experience. Kant did, however, believe that these antinomies have positive value. Specifically, they provide an additional argument for saying that the world of space and time is phenomenal only and that in such a world freedom is a coherent idea. This follows because if the world were a thing-in-itself, it would have to be either finite or infinite in extent and divisibility. But the antinomies show that there can be no demonstrative proof that either alternative is true. Insofar, then, as the world is phenomenal only, we are justified in affirming moral freedom and human responsibility.

As regulative ideas, the concepts of the self, the world, and God have a legitimate function, for they help us to synthesize our experience. Also, to speak of a noumenal realm, or the realm of the thing-in-itself, is to respond to certain given experiences and tendencies of our thought. For this reason we can think of a person in two different ways: as a phenomenon and as a noumenon. As a phenomenon a person can be studied scientifically as a being in space and time and in the context of cause and effect. At the same time, our experience of moral obligation suggests that a person's noumenal nature, what he or she is like beyond our sense perception of him or her, is characterized by freedom. In this context the concept of freedom, as the idea of the self, or God, is a regulative idea. There can never be any demonstrative proof either that people are free or that God exists because these concepts refer us beyond sense experience, where the categories of the mind have no data on which to work.

Proofs of God's Existence

With this critical estimate of the capacities and scope of human reason, it was inevitable that Kant would reject the traditional proofs for the existence of God, namely, the *ontological, cosmological,* and *teleological* proofs. His argument against the *ontological* proof is that it is all a verbal exercise. The essence of this proof is the assertion that since we have the idea of a most perfect being, it would be contradictory to say that such a being does not exist. Such a denial would be contradictory because the concept of a perfect being necessarily includes the predicate of *existence.* A being, that is, that does not exist can hardly be considered a perfect being. But Kant argues that this line of reasoning is "taken from judgments, not from things and their existence," that the idea of God is made to have the predicate of existence by simply fashioning the concept in such a way that existence is included in the idea of a perfect being. This argument nowhere shows why it is necessary to have the subject *God.* There would be a contraindication if a perfect being did exist and we denied that such a being was omnipotent. But to say that we avoid a contradiction by agreeing that a supreme being is omnipotent does not by itself demonstrate that such a being exists. Moreover, to deny that God exists is not simply to deny a predicate but also to abandon the subject and thereby all the predicates that go with it. And "if we reject subject and predicate alike, there is no contradiction; for nothing is then left to be contradicted." Kant concluded, therefore, that "all the trouble and labor bestowed on the famous ontological or Cartesian proof of the existence of a supreme Being from concepts alone is trouble and labor wasted. A man might as well expect to become richer in knowledge by the aid of mere ideas as a merchant to increase his wealth by adding some noughts to his cash account."

Whereas the ontological proof begins with an idea (of a perfect being), the *cosmological* proof "takes its stand on experience." For, it says that "I exist, therefore, an absolutely necessary being exists" on the assumption that if anything exists an absolutely necessary being must also exist. The error of this argument, according to Kant, is that while it begins with experience it soon moves beyond experience. Within the realm of sense experience, it is legitimate to infer a cause for each event, but "the principle of causality has no meaning and no criterion for its application save only in the sensible world." Here is the direct application of Kant's critical method, for he argues that we cannot employ the *a priori* categories of the mind in trying to describe realities beyond sense experience. The cosmological argument cannot, therefore, securely lead us to a first cause of all things, for the most we can infer from our experience of things is a regulative idea of God. Whether there actually is such a being, a ground of all contingent things, raises the same question posed by the ontological proof, namely, whether we can successfully bridge the gap between our idea of a perfect being and demonstrative proof of its existence.

Similarly, the *teleological* proof begins with considerable persuasiveness, for it says that "in the world we everywhere find clear signs of an order in accordance with a determinate purpose. . . . The diverse things could not of themselves have cooperated, by so great a combination of diverse means, to the fulfillment of determinate final purposes, had they not been chosen and designed for these purposes by an ordering rational principle in conformity with underlying ideas." To this argument Kant replies that it may very well be that our experience of order in the universe suggests an orderer, but order in the world does not demonstrate that the material stuff of the world could not exist without an orderer. The most this argument from design can prove, Kant says, "is an *architect* of the world who is always very much hampered by the adaptability of the material in which he works, not a *creator* of the world to whose idea everything is subject." To prove the existence of a creator leads us back to the cosmological proof with its idea of causality. But since we cannot use the category of causality beyond the things in experience, we are left simply with an idea of a first cause or creator, and this takes us back to the ontological proof with its deficiencies. Kant's conclusion, therefore, is that we cannot use transcendental ideas or theoretical principles, which have no application beyond the field of sense experience, to demonstrate the existence of God.

It follows from Kant's critical remarks about the "proofs," however, that just as we cannot demonstrate God's existence, neither can we demonstrate that God does *not* exist. By pure reason alone we can neither prove nor disprove God's existence. If, therefore, the existence of God cannot be effectively dealt with by the theoretical reason, then some other aspect of reason must be considered as the source of the idea of God. Thus, the idea of God has importance in Kant's philosophy, as do other regulative ideas.

PRACTICAL REASON

Besides the "starry heavens above," it was also the "moral law within" that filled Kant with wonder. He was aware that human beings not only gaze on a world of things but also become participants in a world of action. Reason is, therefore, alternately concerned with theory about things and with *practical* behavior—that is, *moral* behavior. But there is "ultimately only one and the same reason which has to be distinguished in its application," says Kant, and of the objectives of reason, "the first is *theoretical*, the second *practical* rational knowledge." It was Kant's way of explaining the scope and powers of pure theoretical reason that made possible his account of the practical reason.

The tendency of scientific thought in Kant's day was to identify reality with what we can know from sense experience, from appearance. If this were a true account of reality, knowledge would consist only of a manifold of sense experience understood as things strictly related to each other by causality. Reality would then be viewed as a large mechanism whose only activity was the product of prior causes, and people would also be viewed as a part of this mechanical system. If this were the case, Kant says, "I could not . . . without palpable contradiction say of one and the same thing, for instance the human soul, that its will is free and yet is subject to natural necessity, that is, not free." Kant avoided this contradiction by saying that a person's phenomenal self, or the self we can observe, is subject to natural necessity or causality, whereas the noumenal self as a thing-in-itself possesses freedom. It is in a negative way, by limiting the scope of theoretical reason to the sensible manifold, that Kant made way for the positive use of practical reason: Insofar as "our Critique limits speculative reason, it is indeed *negative*, but since it thereby removes an obstacle which stands in the way of the employment of practical reason, nay threatens to destroy it, it has in reality a positive and very important use."

Morality becomes possible because even though we cannot know things-in-themselves, or objects in the noumenal realm, "we must yet be in a position at least to *think* them as things-in-themselves; otherwise we should be landed in the absurd conclusion that there can be appearance without anything that appears." But "if our Critique is not in error in teaching that the object [for example, a human being] is to be taken *in a twofold sense*, namely as appearance and as a thing-in-itself . . . then there is no contradiction in supposing that one and the same will is, in the appearance, that is, in visible acts, necessarily subject to the law of nature, and so far not free, while yet, as belonging to a thing-in-itself, is not subject to that law, and is, therefore *free*." To be sure, the soul cannot be *known* by speculative reason as being free, "but though I cannot *know*, I can yet *think* freedom." Kant has, therefore, provided the basis for moral and religious discourse. Specifically, he distinguishes between two kinds of reality—the phenomenal and the noumenal; he then limits science to the phenomenal, thereby justifying the use of practical reason in connection with the noumenal world.

The Basis of Moral Knowledge

The task of moral philosophy, according to Kant, is to discover how we are able to arrive at principles of behavior that are binding upon all people. He was sure that we cannot discover these principles simply by studying the actual behavior of people, for although such a study would give us interesting anthropological information about how people *do* behave, it would not tell us how they *ought* to behave. Still, we do make moral judgments when we say, for example, that we ought to tell the truth, and the question is how we arrive at such a rule of behavior. For Kant the moral judgment that "we ought to tell the truth" is in principle the same as the scientific judgment that "every change must have a cause." What makes them similar is that both of these judgments come from our reason and not from the objects we experience. Just as our theoretical reason brings the category of causality to visible objects, and thereby explains the process of change, so also the practical reason brings to any given moral situation the concept of duty, or "ought." Both in science and in moral philosophy, we use concepts that go beyond particular facts we experience at any one time. Experience in both cases is the occasion for triggering the mind to think in universal terms. When we experience a given example of change, our minds bring to this event the category of causality. This makes it possible to explain the relation of cause and effect not only in this case but in all cases of change. Similarly, in the context of human relations, the practical reason is able to determine not only how we should behave at this moment but also what should be the principle of our behavior at all times. Like scientific knowledge, moral knowledge is based on *a priori* judgments. Kant discovered earlier that scientific knowledge is possible because of the *a priori* categories that the mind brings to experience. He now says, similarly, that "the basis of obligation must not be sought in human nature or in the circumstances of the world in which [humanity] is placed, but *a priori* simply in the concepts of reason."

Morality for Kant is, therefore, an aspect of rationality and has to do with our consciousness of rules or "laws" of behavior, which we consider both universal and necessary. The qualities of *universality* and *necessity* are the marks of *a priori* judgments, and this further confirms Kant's view that the principles of behavior are derived by the practical reason *a priori*. Instead of searching for the quality of "goodness" in the effects of our actions, Kant focuses on the rational aspect of our behavior.

Morality and Rationality

As a rational being I not only ask the question "What shall I do?" but am also conscious of being under an obligation to act in particular ways, that I "ought" to do something. These rational activities reflect the powers of practical reason, and I can assume that all rational beings are aware of the same problems. When I consider what I must do, therefore, I am also considering what all rational beings must do, for if a moral law or rule is valid for me as a rational being, it must be valid for all rational beings. A major test of a morally good act is, therefore, whether its principle can be applied to all rational beings and applied consistently. Moral philosophy is the quest for these principles that apply to all rational beings and that lead to behavior that we call *good*.

"Good" Defined as the Good Will

Kant says, "Nothing can possibly be conceived in the world, or even out of it, which can be called 'good,' without qualification, except a good will." He would admit, of course, that other things can be considered good, such as moderation of the passions, "and yet one can hardly call them unreservedly good . . . for without the principles of a good will they may become evil indeed. The cold-bloodedness of a villain not only makes him far more dangerous, but also directly makes him seem more despicable to us than he would have seemed without it." Kant's chief point is that the essence of the morally good act is the principle that a person affirms when he wills an act: "The good will is good not because of what it causes or accomplishes, not because of its usefulness in the attainment of some set purpose, but alone because of the willing, that is to say, it is good of itself."

A rational being strives to do what he or she *ought* to do, and this Kant distinguishes from an act that a person does either from *inclination* or from *self-interest*. We can all compare the differences in these motives, for to act from either inclination or self-interest appears to us to be on a different level morally from acting out of *duty* to the moral law. Kant makes the rather startling statement that the "good will is good not because of what it accomplishes." He says this as a way of emphasizing the dominant role of the will in morality. It is not enough for the effects or consequences of our behavior to *agree with* the moral law; the truly moral act is done *for the sake of the moral law*, "for all these effects—even the promotion of the happiness of others—could have been also brought about by other causes, so that for this there would have been no need of the will of a rational being." The seat of moral worth is in the will, and the good will is one that acts out of a sense of duty. And "an action done from duty must wholly exclude the influence of inclination, and with it every object of the will, so that nothing remains which can determine the will except objectively the *law* and subjective *pure respect* for this practical law."

Duty implies that we are under some kind of obligation—a moral law. And Kant says that as rational beings we are aware of this obligation as it comes to us in the form of an *imperative*. Not all imperatives or commands are connected with morality, for they are not in every case directed to all people, and, therefore, they lack the quality of universality that a moral rule requires. There are, for example, *technical* imperatives or rules of skill, which command us to do certain things *if* we want to achieve certain ends. For example, *if* we want to build a bridge across the river, we *must* use materials of certain strength. But we do not absolutely have to build a bridge. We can also build a tunnel or use surface craft to get to the other side. Similarly, there are certain *prudential* imperatives, which say, for example, that if I want to be popular with certain people, I *must* say or do certain things. But again, it is not absolutely necessary that I achieve this popularity. The technical and prudential imperatives are, therefore, *hypothetical* imperatives because they command us only if we decide to enter their sphere of operation.

The Categorical Imperative

Unlike the technical and prudential imperatives, which are hypothetical in nature, the truly moral imperative is *categorical*. This categorical imperative applies to all people and commands "an action as necessary of itself without reference to another end, that is, as objectively necessary." It commands certain conduct immediately, without having any other purpose as a condition. Actually, the categorical imperative commands a law that forms the basis of particular actions. It is *categorical* because it instantly applies to all rational beings, and it is *imperative* because it is the principle on which we *ought to act*. The basic formulation of the categorical imperative is this: "Act only on that maxim whereby you can at the same time will that it should become a universal law." Kant had said that "everything in nature works according to laws. Rational beings alone have the faculty of acting according *to the conception* of laws." Now he wants to show that the categorical imperative is our conception of the law of nature as it pertains to human behavior, and, therefore, he expresses the imperative of duty in an alternate way, namely, "Act as if the maxim of your action were to become a universal law of nature."

It is clear that the categorical imperative does not give us specific rules of conduct, for it appears to be simply an abstract formula. Still, this was precisely what Kant thought moral philosophy should provide us in order to guide our moral behavior. For once we understand the fundamental principle of the moral law, we can then apply it to specific cases. To illustrate how the categorical imperative enables us to discover our moral duties, Kant gives the following example:

> [A man] finds himself forced by necessity to borrow money. He knows that he will not be able to repay it, but sees also that nothing will be lent to him unless he promises stoutly to repay it in a definite time. He desires to make this promise, but he has still so much conscience as to ask himself: Is it not unlawful and inconsistent with duty to get out of a difficulty in this way? Suppose, however, that he resolves to do so, then the maxim of his action would be expressed thus: When I think myself in want of money, I will borrow money and promise to repay it, although I know that I never can do so. Now this principle of self-love or of one's own advantage may perhaps be consistent with my whole future welfare; but the question now is, Is it right? I change then the suggestion of self-love into a universal law, and state the question thus: How would it be if my maxim were a universal law? Then I see at once that it could never hold as a universal law of nature, but would necessarily contradict itself. For supposing it to be a universal law that everyone when he thinks himself in a difficulty should be able to promise whatever he pleases, with the purpose of not keeping his promise, the promise itself would become impossible, as well as the end that one might have in view of it, since no one would consider that anything was promised to him, but would ridicule all such statements as vain pretenses.

If we were still to ask why he must tell the truth, or why he should avoid the contradiction involved in a false promise, Kant answers that there is something about human beings that makes us resist and resent being treated as *things* instead of as *persons*. What makes us human is our rationality, and to be a human, or a rational being, is, therefore, an end in itself. We become a thing when someone uses us as a means for some other end, as when someone tells us a lie. But however necessary such use of us may seem at times, we nevertheless consider ourselves as being of absolute intrinsic worth as persons. The individual human being as possessing absolute worth becomes the basis for the supreme principle of morality:

> The foundation of this principle is: *rational nature exists as an end in itself.* All men everywhere want to be considered persons instead of things for the same reason that I do, and this affirmation of the absolute worth of the individual leads to a second formulation of the categorical imperative which says: *So act as to treat humanity, whether in your own person or in that of any other, in every case as an end withal, never as a means only.*

There is a third formulation of the categorical imperative, which is already implied in the first two but which Kant wants to make explicit. It is that we should "always so act that the will could regard itself at the same time as making universal law through its own maxim." Here Kant speaks of the *autonomy* of the will, that each person through his or her own act of will legislates the moral law. He distinguishes autonomy from *heteronomy*, the determination (of a law or action) by someone or something other than the self. Thus, a heteronomous will is influenced or even determined by desires or inclination. An autonomous will, on the other hand, is free and independent, and as such is the "supreme principle of morality." Central to the concept of the autonomy of the will is the idea of *freedom*, the crucial regulative idea, which Kant employed to distinguish between the worlds of science and morality—the phenomenal and noumenal worlds. He says that "the *will* is a kind of causality belonging to living beings in so far as they are rational, and *freedom* would be this property of such causality that it can be efficient, independently of foreign causes determining it, just as *physical necessity* is the property that the causality of all irrational being has of being determined to activity by the influence of foreign causes." And again, "I affirm that we must attribute to every rational being which has a will that it has also the idea of freedom and acts entirely under this idea. For in such a being we conceive a reason that is practical, that is, has causality in reference to its objects." The categorical imperative, therefore, speaks of the universality of the moral law, affirms the supreme worth of each rational person, and assigns freedom or autonomy to the will. Our experience of the moral law suggested to Kant some further insights concerning the postulates of freedom, immortality, and God.

The Moral Postulates

Kant did not think it possible to prove or demonstrate that God exists or that the human will is free. Freedom is an idea that it is necessary to assume because of our experience of moral obligation—that is, "because I must, I can." Though we cannot demonstrate that our wills are free, we are intellectually compelled to assume such freedom, for freedom and morality "are so inseparably united that one might define practical freedom as independence of the will of anything but the moral law alone." How could people be responsible or have a duty if they were not able or free to fulfill their duty or respond to the moral command? Freedom must be assumed, and as such it is the first postulate of morality.

A second moral postulate for Kant is *immortality*. The line of reasoning by which Kant was led to postulate immortality begins with his conception of the highest good, or the *summum bonum*. Although virtue is the highest conceivable good, we as rational beings are fully satisfied only when there is a union between virtue and happiness. Though it does not always happen so, we all assume that virtue ought to produce happiness. Kant had rigorously maintained that the moral law commands us to act not so that we be happy, but so that our actions will be *right*. Still, the full realization of a rational being requires that we think of the supreme good as including both virtue and happiness. But our experience shows that there is no necessary connection between virtue and happiness. If we were to limit human experience to this world, it would then appear impossible to achieve the supreme good in its fullness. Still, the moral law does command us to strive for perfect good, and this implies an indefinite progress toward this ideal, "but this endless progress is possible only on the supposition of the unending duration of the existence and personality of the same rational being, which is called the immortality of the soul."

The moral universe also compels us to postulate the existence of God as the grounds for the necessary connection between virtue and happiness. If we mean by happiness "the state of a rational being in the world with whom in the totality of his experience *everything goes according to his wish and will*," then happiness implies a harmony between a person's will and physical nature. But a person is not the author of the world, nor is he or she capable of ordering nature so as to effect a necessary connection between virtue and happiness. But we do conclude from our conception of the supreme good that virtue and happiness must go together. Consequently, we must postulate "the existence of a cause of the whole of nature which is distinct from nature and which contains the ground of this connection, namely, of the exact harmony of happiness with morality." And thus, "it is morally necessary to assume the existence of God." This is not to say that there cannot be morality without religion, for Kant has already said that a person can recognize his moral duty without the idea of God and that he must obey the law simply out of respect for the law—"for duty's sake." But Kant does say that "through the idea of the supreme good as object and final end of the pure practical reason the moral law leads to religion, that is to the recognition of all duties as divine commands, not as sanctions, that is, as arbitrary commands of an alien will . . . but as essential laws of every free will in itself, which, however, must be looked on as commands of the supreme Being, because it is only from a morally perfect and at the same time all-powerful will . . . that we hope to attain the highest good, which the moral law makes it our duty to take as the object of our endeavor."

Whether Kant succeeded in reaching the objectives he set for his new critical philosophy, his achievement was monumental. It may very well be that his mistakes along the way were more important than most individuals' successes, but what is beyond question is that although it is not necessary to accept everything Kant said, it is nevertheless difficult to philosophize today without taking his views into account.

AESTHETICS: THE BEAUTIFUL

As we have seen, Kant developed a specific set of rules of morality by which one could determine whether an action can rightly be called "good." These rules apply to all people, so that the test for morally good behavior is a universal or objective standard. Similarly, Kant argued that the human mind can develop reliable scientific knowledge, that nature must be considered uniform throughout, and that scientific laws must be valid or "true" for everyone. However, when he turns to the problems of aesthetics, Kant says that "there can be no rule according to which anyone can be compelled to recognize anything as *beautiful*." There are, Kant says, no reasons or principles signifying that a dress, a house, or a flower is beautiful. Nevertheless, we do say about things that they are beautiful, and we like to think that what *we* call beautiful should also be called beautiful by others. In the end Kant shows that even though our judgment of the beautiful is based on our subjective feeling, the beautiful is defined as "that which pleases universally." Just how he moves from our subjective feeling of the beautiful to the conclusion that the beautiful is what pleases universally provides us with some of Kant's key insights into the nature of our aesthetic experience.

The Beautiful as Independent Pleasant Satisfaction

The first step in discovering the nature of our aesthetic judgment is to see it as a matter of subjective taste. When we express the judgment that an object is beautiful, this judgment is subjective because upon experiencing the object our imagination refers our sensation of the object to us as subjects, to our feeling of pleasure or displeasure. This feeling of pleasure or displeasure denotes nothing in the object but is simply the manner in which the object affects us. Kant's key point here is that the judgment of taste is not a logical matter involving a knowledge of concepts. If I want to say about an object that it is "good," I have to know what kind of thing the object is intended to be. That is, I must have a concept of it. But it is not necessary for me to have a concept of an object to enable me to see beauty in it. For example, "flowers, free patterns, lines aimlessly intertwining—technically termed foliage—have no signification, depend upon no definite concept, and yet please." My judgment of beauty, my taste, is simply *contemplative*, which means that I do not need to know anything more about the object other than how its character affects my feelings of pleasure or displeasure. An aesthetic judgment is not a cognitive judgment; that is, it rests upon neither theoretical nor practical knowledge.

Kant insists that for an aesthetic judgment to be "pure," it must be independent of any special interest; it must be "disinterested." To be disinterested is, of course, not the same as being uninteresting. It means that the judgment that an object is beautiful is not biased by a prejudice for or against an object. The judgment that a house is beautiful or not must be independent of my prejudice against either large or small houses or of my desire to own such a house. The pure aesthetic judgment affirms that the form of the object is pleasing without reference to any special interest I may have in it. Of course, it is possible that I can have an interest in or a desire for an object. But my judgment that it is beautiful is independent of that interest or desire. For this reason Kant defines the beautiful as follows: "*Taste* is the faculty of estimating an object or a type of representation by means of a delight or aversion *apart from any interest*. The object of such a delight is called *beautiful*."

The Beautiful as an Object of Universal Delight

If my judgment that an object is beautiful is independent of any private interest or prejudice of mine, then my judgment does not depend on, nor is it influenced by, any other interest. My judgment is "free" when (1) I express my view that an object is beautiful, and (2) I am conscious when I do this that I am neither depending on nor influenced by any other interest—whether an appetite, a desire, or a bias. Because no interest peculiar or private to me is influencing my judgment, I have every reason to believe that others, similarly free of their private interests, would arrive at the same judgment of the beautiful. The aesthetic judgment is universal.

Kant is aware that not all uses of the word *taste* refer to universal aesthetic judgments. It is possible to have good taste regarding things about which different people disagree. Someone will say, "Canary wine is agreeable," but a friend will remind him to say, "agreeable *to me.*" A violet color may impress someone as soft and lovely; to someone else it appears dull and faded. One person likes the sound of wind instruments, while another likes that of string instruments. On these matters, where something is or is not "agreeable" to us, it is true that "everyone has their own taste." But "agreeable" must not be confused with the beautiful. For if something is agreeable to or even pleases only one person, he or she must not call it beautiful. As Kant says, many things possess for us charm and agreeableness. But if we put something on a pedestal and call it beautiful, we imply that everyone should make the same judgment, that everyone should have the same delight in the object. Those who judge differently can be "blamed" and denied that they have taste. And to this extent, Kant says, "it is not open to men to say: Every one has his own taste. This would be equivalent to saying that there is no such thing at all as taste; that is, no aesthetic judgment capable of making a rightful claim upon the assent of all men."

The ambiguous use of the word *taste* is clarified by distinguishing between the taste of our senses and the taste of reflection or contemplation. It is the taste of the senses—for example, the taste of foods and drinks—which is frequently merely private. But taste, which involves a judgment of the beautiful, implies universal agreement. This aesthetic judgment is not based on logic because it does not involve our cognitive faculties; rather, it involves only the feelings of pleasure or displeasure in every subject. The judgment of the beautiful rests not on any concept but on feeling. Kant therefore defines the beautiful in yet another way: "The *beautiful* is that which, apart from a concept, pleases universally."

Finality versus Purpose in the Beautiful Object

There are two kinds of beauty: (1) free beauty and (2) beauty that is merely dependent. Free beauty presupposes no concept of what the object should be. By contrast, dependent beauty presupposes a concept of what that object should be, and that concept makes it possible for us to determine whether that object is perfect.

A flower is a free beauty of matter. Just by looking at it we can tell whether it is beautiful. We need no further knowledge about it. There is no other concept connected with the flower, such as its purpose, that would help us determine whether it is beautiful. The manner in which the flower presents itself to us is final. The flower's form as we see it represents its "finality," and this finality provides the basis for the judgment of its beauty. Surely something is going on in our consciousness and understanding when we make this judgment, but our feeling, and not our reasoning power, is in control here. Kant says, therefore, that "a judgment is called aesthetic precisely because its determining ground is not a concept but the feeling of that harmony in the play of the mental powers, so far as it can be experienced in feeling." To be sure, botanists can know many things about the flower, but their concepts have no bearing on the judgment whether the flower is beautiful. Similarly, in painting, sculpture, horticulture, and even music, the design is what is essential, so that what pleases by its form is the fundamental prerequisite for taste.

But the beauty of a man or woman or child, the beauty of a building such as a church or a summer house—all these presuppose a concept of the "end" or purpose that defines what each is supposed to be. We can say about each person or building that it is beautiful. But here our judgment of beauty takes into account the concepts of ends or purposes. Moreover, the judgment of beauty becomes dependent on the fulfillment or lack of fulfillment of the proper end or purpose of the object in question. Here we do not have a pure aesthetic judgment based solely on feeling. Instead, there is an admixture of conceptual knowledge concerning the nature and purpose of a person or the purpose or function of the building. For example, someone might judge that a building excites displeasure because its form (although exquisite) is inappropriate for a church. One person might be judged beautiful because he or she behaves in a moral manner, in which case the judgment of the beautiful becomes confused or at least combined with the judgment of the good—which is a cognitive judgment. If our judgment that a person or building is beautiful depends on the purpose of human nature or of the building, then our judgment is placed under a restriction and is no longer a free and pure judgment of taste. Accordingly, Kant defines the beautiful in a third way: "Beauty is the form of finality in an object, so far as perceived in it apart from the representation of an end (or purpose)."

Necessity, Common Sense, and the Beautiful

There is something about the beautiful that leads to "a necessary reference on its part to delight (pleasure)." This does not mean, Kant says, that I can know ahead of time "that every one *will in fact feel* this delight in the object that is called beautiful by me." The *necessity* that combines the judgment of the beautiful with delight is neither a theoretical nor a practical necessity. Even though I claim that my aesthetic judgment is universal, I cannot assume that everyone will actually agree with it. Indeed, because I am not even capable of clearly formulating a rule that defines the beautiful in terms of concepts, I am left with my own feeling of beauty, which also includes my delight or pleasure. That my delight is referred to in the judgment of beauty does not mean that the element of delight is logically deduced from the concept of beauty. The "necessity" that delight is involved in the experience of the beautiful is, says Kant, "a necessity of a special kind." The necessity that is thought in an aesthetic judgment "can only be termed *exemplary*." It is "a necessity of the assent of *all* to a judgment regarded as exemplifying a universal rule incapable of formulation." My judgment, in short, is an example of a universal rule regarding beauty.

If I cannot formulate the principle of beauty in a rational or cognitive form, how is it possible for me to communicate to others the necessary components of the judgment of the beautiful? Two times two necessarily equal four for everyone. How can it be that the judgment of the beautiful also contains the element of necessity? I must have, Kant says, "a subjective principle and one which determines what pleases or displeases, by means of feeling only and not through concepts, but yet with universal validity." For this reason the judgment of taste depends on our presupposing the existence of a common sense. Only under such a presupposition of a common sense can I lay down a judgment of taste. This does not mean that everyone will agree with my judgment; rather, everyone *ought* to agree with it. We can assume, when we communicate that 2 plus 2 equal 4, that others can or even must understand the universal truth of this judgment—even though in this case we are dealing with an objective principle. So also can we assume that there is a common sense in everyone to which we can communicate the subjective judgment of the beautiful. For this reason Kant gives as his fourth definition that "the Beautiful is that which, apart from a concept, is cognized as object of a *necessary* delight."

Kant was himself aware, as he points out in the preface to his *Critique of Judgment*, that "the difficulty of unraveling a problem so involved in its nature may serve as an excuse for a certain amount of hardly avoidable obscurity in its solution." In spite of this confession, Hegel found in Kant's theory of aesthetics "the first rational word concerning beauty."

CHAPTER 14

German Idealism

KANT'S IMPACT ON GERMAN THOUGHT

*F*ollowing closely upon Kant's *critical* philosophy was the movement of nineteenth-century German idealism. As a metaphysical theory idealism in general is the view that the universe is composed solely of mental—or spiritual—things; there is in reality no material stuff. For example, the eighteenth-century British empiricist George Berkeley held that only spiritual minds exist, and my perception of the so-called physical world is simply a stream of mental perceptions that God feeds into my spiritual mind. The German approach to idealism had Kantian philosophy as its starting point. Kant did not technically deny the existence of the physical world. However, he maintained that the true nature of things-in-themselves is permanently hidden from us. Our minds are structured in such a way that we are forever barred from going beyond the realm of sense experience, that is, the realm of *phenomena*. Further, our interpretation of the world of experience is permanently fixed by the categories that our minds impose on our experiences. Kant believed that these categories—such as cause and effect, existence and negation, and others—are concepts that our minds possess prior to experience and employ in relation to objects, and this is what makes knowledge possible.

Although we are locked into a view of the world that is limited to our sense experience and mental constructs, Kant still believed that there existed a *noumenal* realm of things-in-themselves, even though we can never access it. For example, we experience only the *appearance* of the red apple—sensory information arranged by our mental abilities of perception. But behind the redness of the apple, there must be something to which the color red is related or that can *have* the color red, namely, that apple in itself. For Kant, though, the fact remains that we cannot *know* anything about such things-in-themselves because our mental categories apply only to the phenomenal world.

Johann Gottlieb Fichte (1762–1814) was one of the first German idealists to recognize a glaring contradiction in Kant's argument. How is it possible to say that something exists but that we can know nothing about it? Do we not already know *something* about it when we say that it exists? Further, Kant asserted the existence of things-in-themselves in order to account for our experiences of sensation, saying in effect that the thing-in-itself is the *cause* of any given sensation. But he had clearly argued that the categories of the mind, such as cause and effect, could not be used to give us knowledge about the noumenal world. When Kant says, then, that the thing-in-itself is the cause of our sensations, he thereby contradicts his own rule for limiting the use of the categories to our judgments about the objects of sense experience.

Even to say that the thing-in-itself *exists* is to go beyond the limits that Kant set for knowledge. For *existence* is simply a category of the mind that helps organize our sense experience in a coherent manner. Indeed, Kant's strongest argument against the earlier metaphysicians was that they wrongly ascribed *existence* to alleged beings and realities beyond sense experience. Now with his doctrine of the thing-in-itself, it seems that Kant has retained just what his critical philosophy was supposed to eliminate. Not only is it impossible, in Kant's theory, to ascribe the category of existence to things-in-themselves, it is also a clear contradiction to say that something can exist if it is unknowable. We can, of course, distinguish between something that is at the moment unknown (but potentially knowable) and something that is permanently unknowable. But to say that something is permanently unknowable is contradictory, because such a statement implies that we already know that something *is*, and to that extent it is knowable. Thus, Kant's conception of the thing-in-itself collapsed.

Fichte put forward the opposite thesis, namely, that whatever is, is knowable. At the same time, Fichte had no intention of reverting to the kind of metaphysics that Kant had rejected. He believed that Kant had achieved genuine progress in philosophy, and he intended to carry forward what Kant had begun. What Fichte tried to do, therefore, was to use Kant's method—stripped of the concept of the unknowable thing-in-itself—and transform Kant's critical idealism into a metaphysical idealism. That is, Fichte took Kant's theory that the mind imposes its categories upon experience and transformed this into the theory that every object, and therefore the entire universe, is a product of mind.

Other German philosophers also joined in the enterprise of transforming Kant's critical philosophy into a metaphysical idealism—most notably, Georg Wilhelm Friedrich Hegel (1770–1831), Friedrich Wilhelm Joseph von Schelling (1775–1854), and Arthur Schopenhauer (1788–1860). Each of these philosophers approached this enterprise in his own and somewhat different way. What they did agree on, however, was that there can be no unknowable thing-in-itself as Kant had presumed. Further, Kant believed that things-in-themselves are the ultimate source of our sense experience. The idealists argued instead that our experiential knowledge is the product of mind. In this chapter we will look at the views of two German idealists—Hegel and Schopenhauer.

HEGEL

Hegel's Life

Hegel's historical significance lies in the fact that he accomplished with extraordinary and systematic thoroughness what Kant so recently said could not be done. Kant argued that metaphysics is impossible, that it is impossible for the human mind to achieve theoretical knowledge about all of reality. Hegel, on the other hand, set forth the general proposition that "what is rational is real and what is real is rational," and from this concluded that everything that is, is knowable. Here was an elaborate metaphysics, which provided a new basis for thinking about the very structure of reality and about its manifestations in morality, law, religion, art, history, and, above all, thought itself. It might be argued that the eventual decline of Hegelian philosophy was more a matter of abandonment than of studied attack—more like deserting a mansion than capturing a stronghold. But to imply that Hegel's successors merely decided to ignore his elaborate metaphysical system is to misjudge the impact and grip his ideas had on the generations that followed him. The impact of Hegel's thought can be measured by the fact that most modern philosophy represents ways of revising or rejecting aspects of his absolute idealism.

Georg Wilhelm Friedrich Hegel was born at Stuttgart in 1770 and lived through Germany's most brilliant intellectual period. This was the year when Beethoven was born and when the poet-scientist Goethe, that "complete civilization in himself," was 20 years old. Kant was 46 years old and had not yet written his classic philosophical works. The Englishman William Wordsworth was also born in this year, and his poetry in time formed a part of that romanticism that shared some of the attitudes of German idealism. At an early age Hegel was deeply impressed by ancient Greek writers, coming eventually to believe that Plato and Aristotle were not only the sources of philosophy but even now its life-giving roots. After being a rather ordinary pupil at school in Stuttgart, Hegel enrolled at age 18 in the theological school at the University of Tübingen. Here he became friends with Hölderin and Schelling and was caught up in lively discussions over the issues of the French Revolution. During his five years at Tübingen, his interest gradually turned to the relation between philosophy and theology. It was after he left the university that his interest in philosophy finally flowered. He became a family tutor for six years, in Berne and in Frankfurt, and during these years he wrote some minor works that nevertheless contained germs of the major problems he eventually made central in his philosophical works.

By this time German idealism had found two influential spokesmen in Fichte and Schelling. In 1801, when Hegel was appointed to the faculty of the University of Jena, he published his first work, on the *Difference between the Philosophical Systems of Fichte and Schelling*, in which he expressed a dislike for Fichte. While he was more sympathetic with Schelling in these early days, it was not long before his independent and original approach to philosophy was made public in his first major work, *The Phenomenology of Mind*, which, he says, he finished at midnight before the Battle of Jena in 1807. As this battle closed his university, Hegel supported himself and his wife, whom he married in 1811, by becoming rector of the secondary school at Nürnberg, where he remained until 1816. It was here that he wrote his influential *Science of Logic*, which brought him invitations from several universities. In 1816 he joined the faculty at Heidelberg, where in the following year he published his *Encyclopedia of the Philosophical Sciences in Outline*, the work in which he presents the grand structure of his philosophy in its threefold aspect, namely, logic, philosophy of nature, and philosophy of mind. Two years later he was given the chair of philosophy at the University of Berlin, where he remained until his death from cholera in 1831, at the age of 61. At Berlin Hegel's writing was massive, although most of it was published after his death. His works during this period included his *Philosophy of Right* and his posthumously published lectures on *Philosophy of History, Aesthetics, Philosophy of Religion*, and *History of Philosophy*.

Absolute Mind

As noted, the thrust of German idealism is that mind is ultimately the source and content of knowledge—not physical objects or some mysterious thing-initself. As Hegel expressed it, every reality is rational, and the rational is real. But what kind of "mind" actually produces our knowledge? We do experience a world of things external to us, which we recognize as existing independently of us and which we did not create. If all objects of our knowledge are the products of mind, but not *our* minds, it must be assumed that they are the products of an intelligence other than that of a finite individual. Hegel and other idealists concluded that all objects of knowledge, and therefore all objects, and indeed the whole universe, are the products of an absolute subject, an Absolute Mind.

For Kant the categories of the mind merely make knowledge possible. However, for Hegel the categories have a type of existence that is independent of any individual's mind. Again, for Kant, the categories represented the mental process of an individual and provided for him the explanation of the types and limits of human knowledge. The categories, he said, are concepts in the human mind—concepts that the mind brings to experience and by which the mind can understand the world of experience. Hegel, on the other hand, considered the categories not only as mental processes but as objective realities possessing existence independently of the thinking individual. More specifically, Hegel argued that the existence of the categories is grounded in the Absolute Mind. But, as we shall see, Hegel did not mean to say that there were categories, on the one hand, and things such as chairs and apples, on the other. Such a distinction would suggest that ideas and things have separate existences—just as Plato distinguished Forms from things. Hegel, unlike Plato, did not ascribe any independent existence to the categories. Instead, he said that they have *existence* and have their being independently of a person's mind or thought. Hegel wanted to say that the real world is more than the subjective conceptions of people's minds. At the same time, he was saying that reality is rationality, or Thought.

Take, for example, a chair. What is a chair, or what does it consist of? Hegel said that if we take seriously the conclusion that there can be no unknowable thing-in-itself, a chair must consist of the sum of the ideas we can have about it. On this basis a chair must consist of all the universals we find in it when we experience it. We say that the chair is hard, brown, round, and small. These are all universal ideas, and when they are related to each other in this way, they are a chair. These universals have their being in the chair; universals or categories never exist singly or independently. Since there is no unknowable aspect of the chair—that is, nothing in addition to the qualities we experience—it follows that the chair *is* what we know about it, and what we know about it is that it consists of a combination of universals or ideas. To say, then, that the categories and universals have objective status means that they have their being independent of the knowing subject. At the same time, as the example of the chair shows, Hegel says that the object of thought consists after all in thought itself. There is, he said, an identity between knowing and being. Knowing and being are simply two sides of the same coin. To be sure, Hegel recognized that there is a subject and an object, a person and the world. But the essence of his idealism consisted in his notion that the object of our consciousness—the *thing* we experience and think about—is itself *thought*. In the end Hegel arrived at the notion that reality is to be found in the Absolute Idea.

So far, two major points in Hegel's argument have been set forth; (1) We must reject the notion of an unknowable thing-in-itself, and (2) the nature of reality is thought, rationality, and ultimate reality is the Absolute Idea. To indicate some of the steps by which Hegel came to this conclusion that reality is Thought, we turn next to a few of the basic elements in his intricate system of philosophy.

The Nature of Reality

Hegel looked upon the world as an organic process. We have already seen that for him the truly real is what he called the Absolute. In theological terms this Absolute is called God. But Hegel wanted to show that he was not here referring to a Being separate from the world of nature or even from individual people. Whereas Plato made a sharp distinction between appearance and reality, Hegel argued in effect that appearance *is* reality. Nothing, said Hegel, is unrelated. For this reason, whatever we experience as separate things will, on careful reflection, lead us to other things to which they are related. Eventually, the process of dialectic thought will end in the knowledge of the Absolute. Still, the Absolute is not the unity of separate things. Hegel rejected materialism, which held that there are separate, finite particles of hard matter that, when arranged in different formations, make up the whole nature of things. Nor did Hegel accept the extreme alternative put forward in the ancient world by Parmenides and more recently by Spinoza, namely, that everything is One—a single substance with various types and attributes. Hegel described the Absolute as a dynamic process, as an organism having parts but nevertheless unified into a complex system. The Absolute is, therefore, not some entity separate from the world; rather, it *is* the world when viewed in a special way.

Hegel believed that the inner essence of the Absolute could be reached by human reason because the Absolute is revealed in Nature as well as in the working of the human mind. What connects these three—the Absolute, Nature, and the mind—is Thought itself. A person's way of thinking is, as it were, fixed by the structure of Nature, by the way things actually behave. Things behave as they do, however, because the Absolute is expressing itself through the structure of Nature. Thus, a person thinks about Nature the way the Absolute expresses itself in Nature. Just as the Absolute and also Nature are dynamic processes, so also human thought is a process—a dialectic process.

Logic and the Dialectic Process   Hegel laid great stress on logic. To be sure, he understood logic to mean virtually the same thing as metaphysics. This was particularly so because he believed that knowing and being coincide. Still, it was Hegel's view that we can know the essence of reality by moving logically, step by step, and avoiding all self-contradiction along the way. Descartes had advocated a similar method, whereby certainty in knowledge would follow from the movement from one clear idea to the next. Unlike Descartes, however, whose emphasis was on the relations of ideas to each other, Hegel argued that thought must follow the inner logic of reality itself. That is, since Hegel had identified the rational with the actual, he concluded that logic and logical connections must be discovered *in* the actual and not in some "empty ratiocination." He argued that "since philosophy is the exploration of the rational, it is for that very reason the apprehension of the present and the actual, not the erection of a beyond, supposed to exist, God knows where." Logic, then, is the process by which we deduce, from our experiences of the actual, the categories that describe the Absolute. This process of deduction is at the very heart of Hegel's dialectic philosophy.

Hegel's dialectic process exhibits a *triadic* movement. Usually, this triadic structure of the dialectic process is described as a movement from *thesis* to *antithesis* and finally to *synthesis*, after which the synthesis becomes a new thesis, and this process continues until it ends in the Absolute Idea. What Hegel emphasized in his dialectic logic was that thought *moves*. Contradiction does not bring knowledge to a halt but acts as a positive moving force in human reasoning.

To illustrate Hegel's dialectic method, we can take the first basic triad of his logic, namely, the triad of *Being, Nothing*, and *Becoming*. Hegel said that the mind must always move from the more general and abstract to the specific and concrete. The most general concept we can form about things is that they are. Although various things have specific and different qualities, they all have one thing in common, namely, their being. Being, then, is the most general concept that the mind can formulate. Also, Being must be logically prior to any specific thing, for things represent determinations or the shaping of what is originally without features. Thus, logic (and reality) begins with the indeterminate, with "the original featurelessness which precedes all definite character and is the very first of all. And this we call Being." Hegel's system begins, therefore, with the concept of Being, and this is the thesis. The question now is, how can thought move from such an abstract concept to any other concept? More important still is the question, how is it possible to *deduce* any other concept from such a universal idea as Being?

It was here that Hegel believed he had discovered something new about the nature of thought. Ever since the time of Aristotle, logicians thought that nothing could be deduced from a category that was not contained in that category. To deduce B from A requires that in some way B already be contained in A. Hegel accepted this. But what he rejected in Aristotelian logic was the assumption that nothing could be deduced from a *universal* term. For example, Aristotle argued that everything is a distinct thing and that logic, therefore, provides us only with specific universal terms from which no other universal terms could be deduced. Thus, for example, there is either *blue* or *not-blue;* there is no way to deduce any other color from blue. If blue is blue, you cannot at the same time say that it is something else, a not-blue. This principle of noncontradiction is very important in any formal logic. Still, Hegel believed that it is not true that a universal does not contain another concept. Returning, then, to the concept of Being, Hegel said that we have here an idea that contains none of the particular qualities or characteristics of the many things that have being. The idea of Being has no content, for the moment you give it some content, it would no longer be the concept of pure Being but the concept of something. Unlike Aristotle, however, Hegel believed that from this concept of Being it is possible to deduce another concept. He argued that because pure Being is mere abstraction, it is, therefore, absolutely negative. That is, since the concept of Being is wholly undefined, it passes into the concept of not-Being. Whenever we try to think of Being without any particular characteristics, the mind moves from Being to not-Being. This, of course, means that in some sense Being and not-Being are the same. Hegel is aware, as he says, that "the proposition that Being and Nothing are the same is so paradoxical to the imagination or understanding, that it is perhaps taken for a joke." Indeed, to understand Being and Nothing as the same, says Hegel, "is one of the hardest things thought expects itself to do." Still, Hegel's point is that Nothing is deduced from Being. At the same time, the concept of Nothing easily leads the mind back to the concept of Being. Of course, Hegel is not implying that we can say of particular things that they simultaneously are the same as nothing. His argument is limited to the concept of pure Being, which, he says, contains the idea of Nothing. He has, then, deduced the concept of Nothing from the concept of Being. The antithesis, Nothing, is contained in the thesis, Being. In Hegel's logic the antithesis is always deduced from the thesis, because it is already contained in the thesis.

The movement of the mind from Being to Nothing produces a third category, namely, *Becoming*. The concept of Becoming is formed by the mind when it understands that Being, for the reasons already mentioned, is the same as Nothing. Becoming, Hegel says, is "the unity of Being and Nothing"; it is "*one* idea." Becoming is, therefore, the *synthesis* of Being and Nothing. If we ask how something can both be and not be, Hegel would answer that it can both be and not be when it becomes.

Throughout his vast and intricate system, Hegel employs this same dialectic method of logic. At each step he sets forth a thesis from which is deduced its antithesis; this thesis and antithesis then find their unity in a higher synthesis. In the end Hegel arrives at the concept of the Absolute Idea, which he describes, in accordance with his dialectic method, as Becoming—as a process of self-development. Beginning, then, at the lowest level of knowledge, with the sensation of qualities and characteristics of particular things, Hegel sought to expand the scope of knowledge by discovering the ever-widening interrelationships of all things. In this way our minds move rigorously by way of deduction from one concept to the other, which we find as categories in actuality. Single facts, for Hegel, are irrational. Only when such single facts are seen as aspects of the whole do they become rational. Thinking is forced to move from one fact to another by the very nature of each concept that facts engender. For example, consider the parts of an engine. By itself a spark plug has no rational character; what confers rationality upon it is its relation to the other parts of the engine. To discover the essence of the spark plug is, thus, to discover the truth about the other parts and, eventually, the entire engine. The human mind, then, moves dialectically, constantly embracing an ever-increasing scope of reality, discovering the truth of anything only after discovering its relation to the whole—that is, its relation to the *Idea*.

The *Idea* of which Hegel speaks is deduced in his logic by the same method that yielded Becoming out of Being. The category of *subjectivity* is deduced from the fact that a person can have a notion of a thing, make a judgment about it, and be able to reason out logical connections. But from *subjectivity* we can deduce its opposite, namely, *objectivity*. That is, the notion of subjectivity already contains the idea of objectivity. To say that I am a self (subjectivity) implies that there is a not-self (objectivity). Subjectivity consists of thought in its formal sense. Objectivity, on the other hand, is thought that is, as it were, *outside* itself and *in* things. Describing the objective character of a person's notion, Hegel says that it consists of *mechanism, chemism*, and *teleology*. What a subject knows about nature as mechanical laws, for example, objects express in their behavior. The synthesis of the subjective and the objective, Hegel says, is their unity in the Idea. That is, in the Idea the subjective (formal) and the objective (material) are brought together in unity. The Idea, however, contains its own dialectic, namely, life, cognition, and the Absolute Idea. Thus, the Idea is the category of self-consciousness; it knows itself in its objects. The whole drift of Hegel's logic, therefore, has been to move from the initial concept of Being finally to the notion of the Idea. But this Idea must also be understood as being in a dynamic process, so that the Idea is itself in a continuous process of self-development toward self-perfection.

The Philosophy of Nature   From the Idea we derive the realm of Nature. As Hegel puts it, Nature represents the Idea "outside itself." This expression is somewhat misleading, because it implies that the Idea exists independently of the world. In addition, Hegel ascribes "absolute freedom" to the Idea as it "goes forth freely out of itself as Nature." Recalling, however, Hegel's premise that the real is rational, it must follow here that Nature is simply rationality, or the Idea, in *external* form, somewhat the way a watchmaker's idea is found outside of the self, in the watch. But Hegel's view is subtler than the relation of the watchmaker to the watch would suggest. For Hegel does not really refer to two separately existing things, Idea and Nature. Ultimate reality is a single organic and dynamic whole. Hegel's distinction between the logical Idea "behind" all things, on the one hand, and Nature, on the other, is his attempt simply to distinguish between the "inner" and "outer" aspects of the self-same reality.

Nature, in short, is the opposite (the antithesis) of the rational Idea (thesis). Our thought moves dialectically from the rational (Idea) to the nonrational (Nature). The concept of Nature leads our thought finally to a synthesis represented by the unity of Idea and Nature in the new concept of Spirit (*Geist*, translated as either "Spirit" or "Mind"). What drives our thought from Nature back to Spirit is the dialectic movement within the concept of Nature. Just as logic begins with the most abstract concept—namely, Being—so the philosophy of Nature begins with the most abstract thing, which is, Hegel says, space. Space is empty (just as Being is indeterminate). At one "end," then, Nature touches emptiness. At the other end, it passes over into Spirit. Between space and Spirit is the diversity of particular things, which is what Nature is. Nature exhibits the laws of mechanics, physics, and organics. Each of these aspects of Nature is in turn analyzed by Hegel into its dialectic terms.

Much of what Hegel says about Nature is superceded by the developments of science since his day. But it was not his intention to take over the work of the scientists. He was concerned, rather, to discover through the philosophy of Nature a rational structure and pattern in all of reality. At the same time, he tried to show the difference between *freedom* and *necessity*, saying that Nature is the realm of necessity whereas Spirit is freedom. Nature, Hegel says, "is to be considered as a system of stages, of which one proceeds necessarily from the other." Freedom, on the other hand, is the act of Spirit. There is, then, a dialectic opposition between Spirit and Nature, between freedom and necessity. Indeed, the "career" of reality, the teleological movement of history, represents the gradual and continuous unfolding of the Spirit, of the Idea of freedom.

The Philosophy of Spirit   The third part of Hegel's system, following his logical Idea and his philosophy of Nature, is the philosophy of Spirit or Mind. Here again, Hegel sets forth the elements of his dialectic in which the thesis is subjective spirit, the antithesis is objective spirit, and the synthesis is Absolute Spirit. He goes into considerable detail, piling triad upon triad to illustrate that the Absolute is Spirit and that this Spirit finds its manifestation in the minds of individuals; in the social institutions of family, civil society, and the state; and, finally, in art, religion, and philosophy. The subjective spirit refers to the inner workings of the human mind, whereas the objective spirit represents the mind in its external embodiment in the social and political institutions. At the apex of knowledge are art, religion, and philosophy, which are the achievement of Absolute Spirit.

Most of what made Hegel's philosophy famous was that portion of his thought that he developed around his concept of objective spirit. Here we come upon the unity of Hegel's thought as he attempts to connect his moral, social, and political thought with the rest of his system. The whole sphere of human behavior, both individual and collective, is described by him as part of the actual and, therefore, is essentially rational. Moreover, as part of the actual this objective side of the Spirit is seen as involved in the dialectic process. Human behavior and social and political organisms contain or embody the Spirit, just as Nature is the objective embodiment of the Absolute Idea. For this reason

Hegel viewed institutions not as human creations but as the product of the dialectic movement of history, of the objective manifestation of rational reality. Speaking, for example, about his book on the *Philosophy of Right*, Hegel says that "containing as it does the science of the state, [it] is to be nothing other than the endeavor to apprehend and portray the state as something inherently rational. As a work of philosophy, it must be poles apart from an attempt to construct a state as it ought to be." This identification of the actual state with the very grounds of reality is what caused Hegel's political theory to have such a captivating influence among those who wished to think about the state in totalitarian or at least nondemocratic terms. We turn, then, to some of the "moments" in the dialectic process by which Hegel seeks to show the natural movement from the individual's concept of right to the state's authority over society. The basic triadic movement here is from *right* (thesis), to *morality* (antithesis), and then to *social ethics* (synthesis).

Ethics and Politics

The Concept of Right   We must first of all understand human behavior as the actions of individual people. Individuals, Hegel says, are aware of freedom. We express our freedom most concretely by an act of will. Hegel looked upon will and reason as virtually synonymous, saying that "only as thinking intelligence, will is free will." We express freedom chiefly in relation to material things, appropriating them, using them, and exchanging them. "To appropriate," says Hegel, "is at bottom only to manifest the majesty of my will towards things, by demonstrating that they are not self-complete and have no purpose of their own." The basis of the right to property is for Hegel the free will of the individual in the act of appropriation. Free people, however, are able to "alienate" themselves from property, and this we do through "contract." A contract is the product of two free wills agreeing to exchange property. It also shows the development of a duty, which the terms of the contract now embody. Hegel's central point here is that, insofar as individual people act rationally, our free acts conform to the rationality of the universe. Our individual wills harmonize with the universal will. But among free people the harmony of wills is precarious. Thus, there is always the possibility of the opposite of right; the negation of right is exemplified in violence and fraud. "Wrong" consists in the breakdown of harmony between the individual will and the universal will. The dialectic relation between "right" and "wrong" produces the tension between the way the "wrong" will acts and the way the will should act in order to be universal, that is, rational. This tension or conflict between right and wrong is what gives rise to morality.

Morality, says Hegel, is fundamentally a matter of purpose and intention in the ethical life of humanity. There is more to "goodness," in other words, than merely obeying laws and keeping contracts. Morality has to do with those deeds for which people can themselves be held responsible. Only those consequences that a person intends and that constitute the purpose of his or her act can affect the goodness or badness of this act. It appears, then, that for Hegel the essence of morality is found internally in a person's intention and purpose. Moral responsibility, then, begins with those acts that can be assigned to a free will—a will that intends the act. But, Hegel argues, this subjective aspect of the act does not exhaust the full scope of morality. After all, human behavior always takes place in a context, especially in the context of other persons, and hence other wills. Moral duty or responsibility is, therefore, broader than the concerns or intentions of the individual. Moral duty derives from the requirement of identifying a person's individual will with the universal will. Although it is perfectly legitimate for people to be concerned with their own happiness and welfare, the principle of rationality requires that we exercise our own will in such a way that the wills of other people, also acting freely, can achieve their welfare as well. Morality is, therefore, an element in the dialectic process: The thesis is the abstract right of each individual, and the antithesis is morality, for morality represents the duties that the universal will raises as limitations to the individual will. The relation between these two wills is the relation between freedom and duty, subjectivity and objectivity. The dialectic process in this ethical sphere is constantly moving toward a greater harmony between the subjective and the objective, and in this regard Hegel described the *good* as "the realization of freedom, the absolute final purpose of the world." But the realization of freedom, for Hegel, had to occur within the limits of duty. In this sense the freest person is the one who most completely fulfills his or her duty. It was inevitable, then, that Hegel should discover the synthesis of the individual's freedom and right, on the one hand, and the universal will, on the other, in our concrete human institutions, particularly in the state.

The State   Between the individual and the state there are two dialectic steps, according to Hegel, namely, the *family* and *society*. The family is, as it were, the first stage of the objective will. In marriage two people give up their individual wills to some degree in order to become one person. Because the family is a single unit, its property becomes a common possession, even though, for legal reasons, the husband might be said to own it. Again, the family, united by a bond of feeling, or love, constitutes the logically first moment of the embodiment of the universal will. At the same time, the family contains its own antithesis, namely, individuals who will eventually grow up, leave the family, and enter into that larger context of similar individuals that is called *civil society*. These individuals now chart out their own lives and have their own purposes. We need to remember at this point that Hegel is here analyzing the dialectic development of the state and is not giving a historical account of its emergence. The state is the synthesis of the family and of civil society. The family, in this analysis, stands for the embodied universal, whereas civil society represents particularity insofar as each individual, unlike the members of a family, sets his or her own goals. These two elements, universality and particularity, cannot exist independently, for they are contained in each other; their unity, therefore, is found in the state, which is the synthesis of universality and particularity. The state is a unity in difference. This does not seem to be a genuine deduction, but Hegel does conclude that the synthesis of the universal and the particular consists in the individual. In this context the state is conceived as an individual, the true individual, an organic unity of partial individuals.

Hegel did not conceive of the state as an authority imposed from the outside on the individual. Nor did he consider the state to be the product of the general or majority will. The state, says Hegel, "is absolutely rational—substantial will," and again, "the state is the actuality of the ethical idea." Hegel conferred upon the state the characteristic of a person, saying that the state represents universal self-consciousness. A particular individual, he notes, is conscious of himself insofar as he is a part of this larger self. And, Hegel says, "since the state is mind objectified, it is only as one of its members that the individual himself has objectivity, genuine individuality, and an ethical life." A person's spiritual reality is also found in the state, for as Hegel says, a human being's "spiritual reality consists in this, that his own essence—Reason—is objectively present to him, that it has objective immediate existence for him." Recalling that Hegel was not interested in formulating a theory of the *ideal* state, his descriptions of the *actual* state are all the more striking. It was the actual living state about which he said that "the state is the embodiment of rational freedom" and, most striking of all, that "the State is the Divine Idea as it exists on earth."

All these highly exalting descriptions of the state would make it appear that Hegel had advocated the totalitarian state. He did insist, however, that the state preserves individual liberty, by which we are members of civil society. Neither the family nor civil society is destroyed by the state; they continue to exist within the state. The laws of the state and, in general, the legislative and executive arms of the state do not issue arbitrary commands. Laws are universal rules, which have their application in individual cases involving individual people. Moreover, laws must be rational and directed at rational people. The reason for laws is that men, in their ability to make free choices, are capable of choosing ends that harm others. Insofar as their acts harm others, their behavior is irrational. The function of law is therefore to bring rationality into behavior. What makes an act rational is that it at once achieves a person's private good and the public good. Only a person who acts rationally can be free, because only rational acts can be permitted in society, because only rational acts avoid social harm. Thus, the function of the state is not to compound personal harm or misery by issuing arbitrary and, therefore, irrational commands but rather to increase, through its laws, the aggregate of rational behavior. The state is thus an organism that is seeking to develop the Idea of freedom to its maximum and to achieve objective freedom only as its individual members do. In this way the laws of the state, rather than being arbitrary, are rational rules of behavior that individuals themselves would choose if they were acting rationally. The only limitation on the individual will that reason allows is the limitation required by the existence of other wills. The sovereign acts in the name of the universal will and reason and not arbitrarily. The state, then, "is the Idea of Spirit in the external manifestation of human Will and its Freedom."

When it comes to the relations between states, Hegel emphasizes the autonomy and absolute sovereignty of each state. The relation of one state to another is different for Hegel from the relation of one person to another in civil society.

When two people disagree, the state is the higher power that resolves the dispute. But if two states disagree, there is no higher power to resolve the conflict. Each nation, Hegel says, "is mind in its substantive rationality and immediate actuality and is therefore the absolute power on earth." For this reason "every state is sovereign and autonomous against its neighbors. It is a fundamental proposition of international law that obligations between states ought to be kept." But, Hegel says, "states are . . . in a state of nature in relation to each other," and for this reason there is no universal will binding upon them. The "rights of states are actualized only in their particular wills," insofar as there are no constitutional powers over them. There is no one to judge between states.

It is not clear why Hegel did not carry his dialectic movement to the next level, at which individual states would be united into a community of nations. He was, of course, aware that Kant had an idea of securing "perpetual peace" by a League of Nations that would adjust every dispute. But he says that such an arrangement could not work because it would still be necessary for each state to *will* to obey the international tribunal. But a state will always *will* its own welfare. Indeed, Hegel says, "welfare is the highest law governing the relation of one state to another." There can be no moral limitations on the state, for the state is "the ethical substance." It follows, Hegel says, that "if states disagree and their particular wills cannot be harmonized, the matter can only be settled by war."

World History   In Hegel's view the history of the world is the history of nations. The dynamic unfolding of history represents the "progress in the consciousness of freedom." This progress is not a matter of mere chance but is rather a rational process. "Reason," says Hegel, "dominates the world and . . . world history is thus a rational process." In a special way the state is the bearer of reason, and because of this that the state is "the Idea of Spirit" in external form and is "the Divine Idea as it exists on earth." But the dialectic of the historical process consists in the opposition between states. Each state expresses a national spirit and, indeed, the world spirit in its own collective consciousness. To be sure, only individual minds are capable of consciousness. Still, the minds of a particular people develop a spirit of unity, and for this reason it is possible to speak of a "national spirit." Each national spirit represents a moment in the development of the world spirit, and the interplay between national spirits represents the dialectic in history.

The conflict between nations is inevitable inasmuch as the historical process is the very stuff of reality and is the gradual working out of the *Idea of Freedom*. Nations are carried along by the wave of history, so that in each epoch a particular nation is "the dominant people in world history for this epoch." A nation cannot choose when it will be great, for "it is only once that it can make its hour strike." At decisive points in history, Hegel says, special world-historical people emerge as agents of the world spirit. These persons lift nations to a new level of development and perfection. Hegel thought that such individuals could hardly be judged in terms of a morality that belonged to the epoch out of which a nation is being led. Instead, the value of such people consists in their creative responsiveness to the unfolding Idea of Freedom.

For Hegel the time process of history was the logical process of the dialectic. History is moving toward a purposive end, namely, freedom. To illustrate the dialectic of history, Hegel used examples of various nations, which, he thought, showed the three *moments* in the development of freedom. Asians, he thought, knew nothing of freedom except that the potentate alone could do what he wished. Although the ancient Greeks and Romans knew the concept of citizenship, they limited this status to only a few and regarded others as being by nature slaves. It was the *Germanic* nations that, under the influence of Christianity, developed the insight that people are free. Thus, Hegel says, "The East knew and to the present day knows, only that *One* is free; the Greek and Roman world, that *some* are free; the German world knows that *All* are free." The highest freedom, we have seen, occurs, according to Hegel, when the individual acts according to the universal, rational will of the whole society.

Absolute Spirit

Hegel's philosophy has its culmination in our knowledge of the Absolute. In the process of dialectic, knowledge of the Absolute is the synthesis of subjective spirit and objective spirit. Because reality is rationality (Thought, Idea), it followed for Hegel that our knowledge of the Absolute is actually the Absolute knowing itself through the finite spirit of human beings. Just how this moment of self-consciousness of the Absolute occurs in the spirit of people is described by Hegel in a final dialectic.

Our consciousness of the Absolute, Hegel says, is achieved progressively as we move through the three stages from art, to religion, and finally to philosophy. Art provides "a sensuous semblance of the Idea" by providing us with an object of sense. In the object of art, the mind apprehends the Absolute as beauty. The object of art, moreover, is the creation of Spirit and, as such, contains some aspect of the Idea. There is an ever-deepening insight into the Absolute as we move from Asian symbolic art, to classical Greek art, and finally to romantic Christian art.

Art leads beyond itself to religion. What differentiates religion from art is that religion is an activity of thought, whereas an aesthetic experience is primarily a matter of feeling. Although art can direct consciousness toward the Absolute, religion comes closer to it precisely because the Absolute is Thought. At the same time, religious thought, Hegel says, is pictorial thought. In early religions this pictorial element looms large. "The Greek God," for example, "is the object of naive intuition and sensuous imagination. His shape is therefore the bodily shape of man." At the apex of religion is Christianity, which is the religion of the Spirit.

Hegel regarded Christianity as the pictorial representation of philosophy. He believed that religion and philosophy have basically the same subject matter, that both represent "knowledge of that which is eternal, of what God is, and what flows out of his nature," so that "religion and philosophy come to the same things." Philosophy leaves behind the pictorial forms of religion and rises to the level of pure thought. But philosophy does not offer the knowledge of the Absolute at any particular moment, for such knowledge is the product of the dialectic process. Philosophy itself has a history, a dialectic movement, in which the major periods and systems of philosophy are not mere haphazard developments. These systems in the history of philosophy represent the necessary succession of ideas required by the progressive unfolding of the Idea. The history of philosophy is for Hegel, therefore, the development of the Absolute's self-consciousness in the mind of people.

SCHOPENHAUER

A contemporary of Hegel, Schopenhauer refused to acknowledge that Hegel was an appropriate or adequate successor to Kant. So great was Schopenhauer's disrespect for Hegel that he said, "There is no philosophy in the period between Kant and myself; only mere University charlatanism." This criticism aimed at Hegel was in the same vein as Schopenhauer's comment that "out of every page of Hume's there is more to be learned than out of [all] of the philosophical works of Hegel." But Hegel was not the only target of Schopenhauer's withering criticism. He expressed his broader disdain in the judgment that "I should like to see the man who could boast of a more miserable set of contemporaries than mine." What appears as egotism to others was to Schopenhauer simply the recognition by him of his unique gifts, just as, he said, a person knows whether he is taller or shorter than the average person. He had no hesitation, therefore, in saying, "I have lifted the veil of truth higher than any mortal before me."

Schopenhauer's Life

Arthur Schopenhauer was born in Danzig in 1788. Although his family was of Dutch origin, it had for a long time been settled in this German city with its ancient traditions and its Hanseatic commercial connections. His ancestors enjoyed considerable prominence and wealth. When Russia's Peter the Great and Empress Catherine visited Danzig, Schopenhauer's great-grandfather's house was selected as the place where these distinguished visitors would stay. His father was a wealthy merchant and wanted Schopenhauer to follow in his footsteps. As a child Schopenhauer accompanied his parents on their many travels, which introduced him to a variety of cultures and customs and developed in him a distinctly cosmopolitan point of view. Although he gained much from these travels in France, Italy, England, Belgium, and Germany, his systematic early education was disrupted. But his capacity to learn was so great that he was able to make up for his lack of ordinary schooling very quickly.

His early schooling began in France at age 9; after two years he returned to Germany, where his education focused on the requirements for a career as a merchant, with little or no emphasis on the classics. But soon Schopenhauer showed a strong inclination toward philosophy, a development not at all pleasing to his father, who worried that such a career could lead only to poverty. After more travel and study in England and Switzerland, Schopenhauer returned to Danzig and entered a merchant's office as a clerk. Shortly thereafter, his father died, and at age 17 he was on his own, without even a close or helpful bond between his mother and himself. He and his mother had opposite temperaments, she being full of optimism and the love of pleasure while he, from an early age, was inclined toward pessimism. This difference between the two made it impossible for them to live in the same house. Later, when his mother moved to Weimar, she wrote to him about the battle of Jena and the occupation of Weimar, saying, "I could tell you things that would make your hair stand on end, but I refrain, for I know how you love to brood over human misery in any case."

By the age of 21, Schopenhauer had more than adequately repaired his sketchy earlier education. He became engaged in a deep study of the classics, while his considerable aptitude for languages led him comfortably through Greek, Latin, and history; and mathematics was not neglected along the way. He was now ready to set out on a career, and in 1809 he enrolled in the medical school at Göttingen University. But the following year he transferred from medicine to the faculty of philosophy, captivated by Plato "the divine" and "the marvelous Kant." In due course he completed his studies, and for his doctoral dissertation at the University of Jena, he wrote a book titled *On the Fourfold Root of the Principle of Sufficient Reason*, which was published in 1813. The poet Goethe had praise for this book; nevertheless, it attracted virtually no attention from readers and remained unsold.

At Goethe's suggestion Schopenhauer was encouraged to study the problem of light, which at this time was approached from different points of view by Goethe and Newton. From this study Schopenhauer produced a brief work titled *On Vision and Colours*, which tended to support Goethe's view.

Schopenhauer's masterpiece is his *The World as Will and Idea*, which he wrote during 1814 and 1818 while living quietly in Dresden and which he published in 1819. Once again, this book aroused little notice and generated few sales. It contains Schopenhauer's complete philosophical system. He was convinced that in this work he had made his most distinctive contribution and was further convinced that he had discovered the solution to many long-standing philosophical problems. As he wrote, "Subject to the limitation of human knowledge, my philosophy is the real solution of the enigma of the world." As if to prepare for shallow criticism or even a brutal disregard of his major book, he wrote, "Whoever has accomplished an immortal work will be as little hurt by its reception from the public or the opinions of critics, as a sane man in a madhouse is affected by the upbraidings of the insane."

From Dresden Schopenhauer went to Berlin and began to lecture at the University of Berlin with the hope of winning acceptance, or at least recognition, of his systematic philosophy. His attempt failed, partly because of the continued indifference toward his view among academics, but also because he overconfidently set the time of his lectures at exactly the hour when the giant Hegel gave his lectures. In 1831 Schopenhauer left Berlin, urged on by a cholera epidemic that included Hegel among its victims. He settled in Frankfurt-am-Main and wrote other works that further explored and confirmed the fundamental ideas in *The World as Will and Idea*. Among these was *On the Will in Nature* (1836), in which he sought to provide scientific knowledge to support his theory of metaphysics. In 1838 he won a prize given by a scientific society in Norway for his essay on "whether free will could be proved from the evidence of consciousness." A second essay on the source or foundation of morals followed the announcement of a prize competition by the Royal Danish Academy. But even though Schopenhauer was the only one to submit an essay, he did not win this prize. Nevertheless, these two essays were published in 1841 as *The Two Fundamental Problems of Ethics*. In 1851 he published another major book titled *Parerga and Paralipomena*, which was a collection of essays on a variety of subjects. It included "On Women," "On Religion," "On Ethics," "On Aesthetics," "On Suicide," "On the Suffering of the World," and "On the Vanity of Existence." This was the book that first brought him wide popularity.

We find the sources of Schopenhauer's philosophy in his concentrated learning and equally in his pessimistic personal temperament. At an early stage one of his teachers urged him to concentrate his study of philosophy on Plato and Kant, and we can see the influence of these two seminal philosophers throughout his major work. In addition, Schopenhauer discovered another powerful but unlikely source of insight for his theory of metaphysics, namely, the classic of India the *Upanishads*. This work was brought to his attention by an Asian scholar, Friedrick Mayer, author of *Brahma, or the Religion of the Hindus*. This strand of Asian philosophy supports Schopenhauer's combination of intellectual and temperamental conclusions that there is no more to experience than appearance. To the questions "Is this all?" and "Is this life?" the answer is a pessimistic "yes." Schopenhauer's pessimism was certainly a matter of temperament. However, he tried to distinguish between his pessimism, which he considered the product of his mature judgment based on "an objective recognition of folly," on the one hand, and "malevolence of the wicked," on the other. He called his pessimism "a noble displeasure that arises only out of a better nature revolting against unexpected wickedness." He added that such pessimism as his is not directed at particular individuals only; rather, "it concerns all, and each individual is merely an example." We might even say that Schopenhauer's metaphysical system is not simply another way of dealing with the problems of metaphysics but is an elaborate metaphysical justification for a pessimistic outlook on life and reality.

The Principle of Sufficient Reason

As is frequently the case with an original thinker, at an early age Schopenhauer arrived at his major philosophical insights. The foundation for his systematic thought was formulated at age 25 in his doctoral dissertation *On the Fourfold Root of the Principle of Sufficient Reason*. In this work he sets out to answer the questions "What can I know?" and "What is the nature of things?" If this sounds grandiose, he intended to give nothing less than a thorough account of the whole scope of reality, and to accomplish this he relied on the Principle of Sufficient Reason.

In its simplest form, the Principle of Sufficient Reason states that "nothing is without a reason" (or "cause" or "because"). The most obvious application of this principle is found in the field of science, where the behavior and the relationships of physical objects are explained in a manner that is sufficient to satisfy the demands of reason or rationality. But Schopenhauer discovered that there are other variations besides this scientific form of the Principle of Sufficient Reason. This is so, he said, because there are objects other than those with which the scientist deals, and these other objects require unique forms of this governing principle.

Altogether, Schopenhauer set forth four basic forms of the Principle of Sufficient Reason corresponding to the four different kinds of ideas comprised in the whole range of human thought. There are four types of objects that give rise to different kinds of ideas:

1. *Physical objects.* These exist and are causally related in space and time, which we know through our ordinary experience of things, and this provides the subject matter of the material sciences, such as, for example, physics. At this point Schopenhauer closely follows Kant's basic theory that knowledge begins with experience but is not limited, as Hume thought, to what is empirically given or presented to us. Instead, the elements of our experience are organized by our human minds, which brings to our experience *a priori* categories of space, time, and causality as though these categories are lenses through which we look at objects. In this realm of phenomena, the Principle of Sufficient Reason explains *becoming* or *change.*

2. *Abstract concepts.* These objects take the form of conclusions that we draw from other concepts, as when we apply the rules of inference or implication. The relationship between concepts and the conclusions they infer or imply is governed by the Principle of Sufficient Reason. This is the realm of logic, and here the Principle of Sufficient Reason is applied to the ways of *knowing.*

3. *Mathematical objects.* Here we encounter, for example, arithmetic and geometry as they are related to space and time. Geometry is grounded in the principle that governs the various positions of the parts of space. Arithmetic, on the other hand, involves the parts of time, for as Schopenhauer says, "on the connection of the parts of time rests all counting." He concludes that "the law according to which the parts of space and time . . . determine one another I call the principle of sufficient reason of *being.*"

4. *The self.* "How can the self be an object?" Schopenhauer says that the self is the subject that wills and that this willing subject is the "object for the knowing subject." This we can call *self-consciousness.* The principle that governs our knowledge of the relation between the self and its acts of will is "the principle of . . . sufficient reason of acting . . . more briefly, the *law of motivation.*"

From these four forms of the Principle of Sufficient Reason Schopenhauer draws the striking conclusion that *necessity* or *determinism* is present everywhere. He stresses the fact of necessity through the whole range of objects, whether they are physical objects, the abstract concepts of logic, mathematical objects, or the self as the object of a knowing subject. Thus, we encounter physical necessity, logical necessity, mathematical necessity, and moral necessity. This element of necessity in the very nature of things is what led Schopenhauer to hold that people behave in daily life by necessity. We simply react to the motives produced by our character, leaving aside the question of whether we are capable of altering their character. The pervasiveness of necessity produced in Schopenhauer a deep sense of pessimism, which permeates all his writings concerning human existence. His pessimism becomes clearly understandable when we consider his account of the place of human beings in the universe, an account that is the central concern of his major work.

The World as Will and Idea

Schopenhauer's famous book *The World as Will and Idea* opens with the astonishing sentence "The world is my idea." What makes this sentence astonishing is that each word of it, as is the case also with each word in the title of the book, is capable of conveying a strange impression if the word is given its ordinary everyday meaning. What Schopenhauer meant by the *world* and the definition and role he ascribed to *will*, as well as the account he provides of our *ideas*, gives these words unique meanings and constitutes the major insights of his theory of metaphysics.

The World   For Schopenhauer the term *world* has the widest possible meaning. It includes human beings, animals, trees, stars, the moon, the earth, planets, and indeed the whole universe. But why call it *my* idea? Why not simply say that the world is "out there." Earlier, British philosopher George Berkeley had formulated the proposition that to be is to be perceived. If something has to be perceived for it to be, what happens to that thing when you are not perceiving it? If you go out of your library, are the books still there? But Schopenhauer insists that anyone who reflects carefully about his experience of the world discovers that "what he knows is not a sun and an earth but only an eye that sees a sun, a hand that feels an earth; that the world which surrounds him is there only as idea." This means, he says, that "all that exists for knowledge, and therefore this whole world, is only object in relation to subject, perception of a perceiver, in a word, idea."

The World as Idea   The English word *idea* does not convey the meaning of the German word *vorstellung* used by Schopenhauer, and the difference between the two meanings helps to explain why the sentence "The world is my idea" strikes us as strange. As used by Schopenhauer, the word *vorstellung* means, literally, anything that is "set in front of" or "placed before," or that is a "presentation." This refers to everything that is placed before or presented to our consciousness or understanding, so that the "world as idea" or "my idea" refers not only to what we *think* about (that is, ideas in the narrow view) but equally to what we hear, feel, or perceive in various other ways. There is no other object out there besides what we perceive, or, as Schopenhauer says, "The whole actual, that is active world is determined as such through the understanding and apart from it is nothing." The world presents itself to us as an object to a subject, and we as subjects know only the world we perceive. Thus, "the whole world of objects is and remains idea, and therefore wholly and forever determined by the subject."

It may be that no person's idea of the world is perfect, that therefore "my idea" will not be the same as "your idea." But each person can say that "the world is my idea" for the simple reason that I do not know anything about the world other than what I perceive or what is placed before my understanding. Moreover, the "world" surely continues to exist even if I no longer exist. Nevertheless, I do not know a more real world than the one I perceive. Perceptions are the basis of knowledge. In addition to perceptions we are able to formulate abstract conceptions. These abstract conceptions—for example, the idea of "tree" and "house"—have a very practical function. As Schopenhauer writes, "by means of them the original material of knowledge is more easily handled, surveyed, and arranged." These abstract conceptions are therefore not simply flights of fancy. Indeed, Schopenhauer says, the value of abstract conceptions depends on whether they rely on or are "abstracted" from original perceptions— that is, from actual experience—for "conceptions and abstractions which do not ultimately refer to perceptions are like paths in the woods that end without leading out of it." To say, therefore, that "the world is my idea" does not suggest that my idea of the world is an abstract conception unless this conception is, as it is for Schopenhauer, firmly based on perceptions. Hence, the world is my idea because it is an objective or empirical presentation to me as an understanding subject.

The World as Will   Nowhere is it more important to clarify Schopenhauer's language than in his use of the term *will*. Ordinarily, we use the word *will* to signify a conscious and deliberate choice to behave in a certain way. We consider the will an attribute or faculty possessed by a rational person. There can be no question that the will is influenced by reason. But this account does not prepare us for Schopenhauer's use of the term *will*—a use so novel and significant as to constitute the central theme or essence of his systematic philosophy.

Schopenhauer's concept of the will represents his major disagreement with Kant's theory of the thing-in-itself. Kant had said that we can never know things as they are in themselves. We are always on the outside of things and can never penetrate their inner nature. But Schopenhauer thought he had found a "single narrow door to the truth." There is, he said, a major exception to the notion that we are forever on the outside of things. That exception is our experience or knowledge, "which each of us has of his own *willing*." Our bodily action is normally thought to be the product of willing, but for Schopenhauer willing and action are not two different things but rather one and the same thing. "The action of the body," he says, "is nothing but the act of the will objectified . . . it is only a reflection that to will and to act are different." What we know of ourselves within our consciousness is that "we are not merely a *knowing subject*, but, in another aspect, we ourselves also belong to the inner nature that is to be known." He concludes that "we ourselves are the thing in itself."

And the thing in itself is *will*, or as Schopenhauer says, "the act of will is . . . the closest and most distinct *manifestation* of the thing in itself." This, then, is that single narrow door to the truth, namely, the discovery that the will is the essence of each person. While we are forever on the outside of everything else, we ourselves belong to the inner nature that can be known. This leads Schopenhauer to conclude that this "way from within [ourselves] stands open for us to that inner nature belonging to things in themselves," so that "in this sense I teach that the inner nature of everything is *will*." Since "everything" is what constitutes the world, it follows in Schopenhauer's thought that we must view the world as will.

For Schopenhauer the will does not belong solely to rational people. The will is to be found in everything that is—in animals and even in inanimate things. There is, in fact, only one will, and each thing is a specific manifestation of that will. Schopenhauer attributes the working of will to all of reality, saying that "the will is the agent in all the inner and unconscious bodily functions, the organism being itself nothing but the will. In all natural forces the active impulse is identical with will. In all instances where we find any spontaneous movements or any primal forces, we must regard the innermost essence as will. The will reveals itself as completely in a single oak tree as in a million." There is, then, in the whole of nature a pervasive force, energy, or what Schopenhauer calls "a blind incessant impulse." Moreover, he speaks of will as "endless striving," and this impulse, working "without knowledge" through all nature, is finally "the will to live."

The Ground of Pessimism

Here we come upon the reason for Schopenhauer's pessimism. His concept of the will portrays the whole system of nature as moving in response to the driving force in all things. All things are like puppets "set in motion by internal clockwork." The lowliest being (for example, the amoeba) or the highest (that is, a human being) is driven by the same force, the will. The blind will that produces human behavior "is the same which makes the plants grow." Every individual bears the stamp of a "forced condition." Schopenhauer thus rejects the assumption that human beings are superior to animals because animals are controlled only by instincts whereas people are rational beings. The intellect, he says, is itself fashioned by the universal will so that the human intellect is on the same level as the instincts of animals. Moreover, intellect and will in human beings are not to be thought of as two separate faculties. Instead, the intellect is for Schopenhauer an attribute of the will; it is secondary or, in a philosophical sense, accidental. It can sustain intellectual effort only for short periods of time. It declines in strength and requires rest, and it is, finally, a function of the body. By contrast, the will continues without interruption to sustain and support life. During dreamless sleep the intellect does not function, whereas all the organic functions of the body continue. These organic functions are manifestations of the will. While other thinkers spoke of the freedom of the will, Schopenhauer says, "I prove its omnipotence."

The omnipotence of the will in all of nature has pessimistic implications for human beings. As Schopenhauer says, "men are only apparently drawn from in front; really, they are pushed from behind; it is not life that tempts them on, but necessity that drives them forward." The primal drive in all of nature is to produce life. The will to live has no other purpose than to continue the cycle of life. Schopenhauer portrays the realm of nature as a fierce struggle where the will to live inevitably produces conflict and destruction. This will to live for one element of nature requires the destruction of other elements or parties. No purpose or aim is violated during this conflict; the underlying drive of the will leaves no alternative outcome. Schopenhauer tells of a report of a place in Java where, for as far as the eye can see, the land is covered with skeletons, which gives the impression of a battlefield. These are skeletons of large turtles, five feet long, three feet wide, and three feet high. They come out of the sea to lay their eggs and are then attacked by wild dogs, which flip them on their backs, strip off their armor, and eat them alive. Now, Schopenhauer says, "all this misery repeats itself thousands and thousands of times, year out, year in. For this, those turtles were born . . . it is thus the will to live objectifies itself."

If we move from the animal world to the human race, Schopenhauer admits that the matter becomes more complicated, "but the fundamental character remains unaltered." Individual human beings do not have any value for nature because "it is not the individual but only the species that nature cares for." Human life turns out to be by no means a gift for enjoyment but is "a task, a drudgery to be performed." Millions of people are united into nations striving for the common good, but thousands fall as a sacrifice for it. "Now senseless delusions, not intriguing politics, incite them to wars with each other. . . . In peace industry and trade are active, inventions work miracles, seas are navigated, delicacies are collected from all ends of the world." But, asks Schopenhauer, what is the aim of all this striving? His answer is "To sustain ephemeral and tormented individuals through a short span of time."

Life, Schopenhauer says, is a bad bargain. The disproportion between human trouble, on the one hand, and reward, on the other, means that life involves the exertion of all our strength "for something that is of no value." There is nothing to look forward to except "the satisfaction of hunger and the sexual instinct, or in any case a little momentary comfort." His conclusion is that "life is a business, the proceeds of which are very far from covering the cost of it." There can be no true happiness because happiness is simply a temporary cessation of human pain. Pain in turn is caused by desire, and expression of need or want, most of which can never be fulfilled. Finally, human life "is a striving without aim or end." And "the life of every individual . . . is really always a tragedy, but gone through in detail, it has the character of a comedy."

Is There Any Escape from the "Will"?

How is it possible for a person to escape from the overpowering force of the "will" that pervades everything in nature? Schopenhauer suggests at least two avenues of escape, namely, through ethics and aesthetics. From a moral perspective we can deny passions and desire; from an aesthetic standpoint we can contemplate artistic beauty. There is, of course, the question of whether the power of the universal will is so strong that any escape from it can only be temporary.

What complicates a person's life and causes pain is the continuous will to live, which expresses itself in the form of endless desires. Desire produces aggressiveness, striving, destruction, and self-centeredness. If there could be some way to reduce the intensity of human desire, a person could achieve at least periodic moments of happiness. To be sure, Schopenhauer always reminds us that "man is at bottom a dreadful wild animal . . . in no way inferior to the tiger or hyena." Still, we are able from time to time to rise to a level of thought and consciousness that is above the realm of things. Problems arise when we desire things and other people, for these objects of desire stimulate our inner will to live at the level of both hunger and procreation. But when these biological functions are satisfied, there still remains the aim of physical survival against violence and conquest. Beyond even this level a person can, Schopenhauer says, understand the difference between the specific individual objects of his desire and certain general or universal objects. That is, we are capable of knowing not only the individuals John and Mary but also universal humanity. This should enable us to move from an intense desire for a person to a sense of sympathy for all humankind. To this extent desire can give way to an ethics of a more disinterested love. At this point we recognize that we all share the same nature, and this awareness can produce an ethics of gentleness. Or, as Schopenhauer says, "My true inner being exists in every living creature as immediately as in my own consciousness. It is this confession that breaks forth as pity, on which every unselfish virtue rests, and whose practical expression is every good deed. It is this conviction to which every appeal to gentleness, love and mercy is directed; for these remind us of the respect in which we are all the same being."

In a similar way aesthetic enjoyment can shift our attention away from those objects that stimulate our aggressive will to live and focus attention instead on objects of contemplation that are unrelated to passion and desire. When we contemplate a work of art, we become a pure knowing subject—as opposed to a willing subject. What we observe in art, whether in painting or even music, is the general or universal element. We see in a painting of a person not some specific person but a representation of some aspect of humanity that we all share. Here Schopenhauer expresses views very similar to Plato's concept of Forms and shows the strong influence of the philosophy of India. Here, too, Schopenhauer's ethics and aesthetics have a similar function, for they both attempt to raise our consciousness above earthly, passion-filled striving to a level beyond the activity of the will where the supreme act is restful contemplation.

In spite of these attempts through ethics and aesthetics to escape from the restricting and directing power of the universal will, Schopenhauer simply does not succeed in discovering a truly free individual will in human beings. His last word on the subject of human behavior is that "our individual actions are . . . in no way free . . . so that every individual . . . can absolutely never do anything other than precisely what he does at that particular moment."

CHAPTER 15

Utilitarianism and Positivism

The views of Kant, Hegel, and Schopenhauer represent one direction that nineteenth-century philosophy took in response to the earlier debate between rationalists and empiricists, namely, an idealist direction. According to Kant and his German counterparts, traditional rationalism ignored the obvious fact that sense impressions form the content of our ideas. However, traditional empiricism ignored our inherent mental structures that shape our experiences. Kant and the German idealists thus emphasized the central role that mind plays in organizing experiences; this role was in fact so central that the idealists held that mind was the *source* of our sense experiences as well as the *shaper* of those experiences. There were, however, other approaches to philosophy during the nineteenth century that did not take this idealist route. Some philosophers believed that the empiricists largely got the story correct, and the task of philosophy was to refine empirical methodology. In Great Britain two such leading figures were Jeremy Bentham (1748–1832) and John Stuart Mill (1806–1873). Bentham and Mill both rejected the role of rational intuition in our quest for knowledge; instead, they refined techniques for sorting and assessing sense experiences. Their most memorable contribution in this regard is in the field of ethics—specifically, the theory of *utilitarianism*. According to this theory, moral actions are those which produce the greatest good for the greatest number of people. In France Auguste Comte (1798–1857) made similar efforts at refining empiricism and founded the approach known as *positivism*. According to positivism, we should reject any investigation that does not rest on direct observation.

The moral and political views of Bentham and Mill dramatically influenced the direction of Western philosophy. Rarely has a way of thinking captured the imagination of generations of people so completely as did their theory of utilitarianism. What attracts people to it is its simplicity and its way of confirming what most of us already believe—that everyone desires pleasure and happiness. From this simple fact Bentham and Mill argued that moral goodness involves achieving the greatest amount of pleasure—and minimizing the greatest amount of pain—for the greatest number of people.

Such a swift account of moral goodness had not only the merit of simplicity but, according to Bentham and Mill, the additional virtue of scientific accuracy. Earlier theories of ethics understood moral goodness in terms of commands of God, or the dictates of reason, or the fulfillment of the purpose of human nature, or the duty to obey the categorical imperative. These all raise vexing questions as to just what these commands, dictates, purposes, and imperatives consist of. However, the principle of utility measures every act by a standard that everyone knows, namely, pleasure. To bypass the moral teachings of theology and the classical theories of Plato and Aristotle, as well as the recently formulated ethics of Kant, Bentham and Mill followed in the philosophical footsteps of their own countrymen, the British empiricists.

Hobbes had already tried to construct a science of human nature and turned his back on traditional moral thought, emphasizing instead people's selfish concern for their own pleasure. Hume had also rejected the intricacies of traditional philosophy and theology and instead built his system of thought around the individual, denying that people can know universal moral laws any more than they can know universal laws of physics. For Hume the whole enterprise of ethics had to do with our capacity for experiencing sympathetic pleasure, a capacity that all people share and by which we "touch a string to which all mankind have an accord." In moral philosophy Bentham and Mill were, therefore, not innovators, for their predecessors had already stated the principle of utilitarianism in its general form. What makes Bentham and Mill stand out as the most famous of the utilitarians is that they, more than others, succeeded in connecting the principle of utility with the many problems of their age. To this end they provided nineteenth-century England with a philosophical basis not only for moral thought but also for practical reform.

BENTHAM

Bentham's Life

Born in Red Lion Street, Houndsditch, London, in 1748, Jeremy Bentham showed early signs of unusual intellectual abilities. While only 4 years old, he was already studying Latin grammar, and at age 8 he was sent off to Westminster School, where, he said later, the instruction "was wretched." He entered Queen's College in Oxford when he was 12 years old. After three not particularly happy years—as he disapproved of the vice and laziness of his fellow students—he took his B.A. degree in 1763 and entered Lincoln's Inn, in accordance with his father's wish, to prepare for a career in the legal profession. That same year he returned to Oxford for one of the decisive experiences of his intellectual life, for he went to hear the lectures on law given by William Blackstone. What made this such a significant event was that, as he listened to these lectures with deep concentration, he says he "immediately detected Blackstone's fallacy respecting natural rights," and this experience crystallized his own theory of law, in which he rejected the theory of "natural rights" as "rhetorical nonsense—nonsense on stilts." He took his M.A. degree in 1766 and again returned to London, but he never developed any affection for the legal profession and decided against being a lawyer. Instead, he was drawn into a vigorous literary career in which he tried to bring order and moral defensibility into what he considered the deplorable state of both the law and the social realities that the law made possible.

Bentham was, therefore, chiefly a reformer. For the most part his philosophical orientation was grounded in British empiricism. Locke's enlightened and free thought gave Bentham a powerful weapon against ideas based on prejudice. Bentham read Hume's *Treatise on Human Nature* with such profit that he said it was "as if scales fell" from his eyes regarding moral philosophy. His first book, *A Fragment on Government*, which appeared in 1776, was an attack on Blackstone. This *Fragment* was also in sharp contrast to another document that appeared in that year, namely, the Declaration of Independence. Bentham viewed the Declaration as a confused and absurd jumble of words that groundlessly presupposed the concept of natural rights. Among his later writings were *A Defense of Usury* (1787), his famous *Introduction to the Principles of Morals and Legislation* (1789), *A Plea for the Constitution* (1803), and *Catechism of Parliamentary Reform* (1809). With these writings and his personal involvement in the social and political problems of his day, Bentham remained a powerful public figure for most of his long life, until his death in 1832 at the age of 84.

The Principle of Utility

Bentham begins his *Introduction to the Principles of Morals and Legislation* with this classic statement: "Nature has placed mankind under the governance of two sovereign masters, *pain* and *pleasure*. It is for them alone to point out what we ought to do, as well as to determine what we shall do." To be subject to pleasure and pain is a fact we all recognize, and it is also a fact that we desire pleasure and avoid pain. He then offers his *principle of utility*, namely, "that principle which approves or disapproves of every action whatsoever, according to the tendency which it appears to have to augment or diminish . . . happiness." Bentham was aware that he had not *proved* that happiness is the basis of "good" and "right," but this was not an oversight. It is rather the very nature of the principle of utility, he says, that one cannot demonstrate its validity: "Is it susceptible to any proof? It should seem not, for that which is used to prove everything else cannot itself be proved; a chain of proofs must have their commencement somewhere. To give such proof is as impossible as it is needless."

But if Bentham could not *prove* the validity of the principle of utility, he felt that he could at least reject so-called higher theories. For Bentham they were either reducible to the principle of utility or inferior to this principle because they had no clear meaning or could not be consistently followed. As an example Bentham takes social contract theory and its explanation for our obligation to obey the law. First, there is the difficulty of determining whether there ever was such a contract or agreement. Second, even the theory itself rests on the principle of utility, for it really says that the greatest happiness of the greatest number can be achieved only if we obey the law. The case is the same when others say that goodness is determined by our *moral sense,* or *understanding,* or *right reason,* or the *theological* principle of the will of God. All of these, Bentham says, are similar to each other and are reducible to the principle of utility. For example, "the principle of theology refers everything to God's pleasure. But what is God's pleasure? God does not, he confessedly does not now, either speak or write to us. How then are we to know what is his pleasure? By observing what is our own pleasure, and pronouncing it to be his." Only pleasures and pains, therefore, give us the real value of actions. In both private and public life, we are in the last analysis all concerned with maximizing happiness.

Sanctions   Just as pleasure and pain give the real values to acts, so do they also constitute the causes of our behavior. Bentham distinguishes four sources from which pleasures and pains can come, and he identifies these as causes of our behavior, calling them *sanctions.* A sanction is what gives binding force to a rule of conduct or to a law, and he terms these four sanctions the *physical,* the *political,* the *moral,* and the *religious.* He explains these here:

> A man's goods, or his person, are consumed by fire. If this happened to him by what is called an accident, it was a calamity; if by reason of his own imprudence (for instance, from his neglecting to put his candle out), it may be styled a punishment of the *physical* sanction; if it happened to him by the sentence of the political magistrate, a punishment belonging to the *political* sanction; that is, what is commonly called a punishment, if for want of any assistance which his *neighbor* withheld from him out of some dislike to his *moral* character, a punishment of the *moral* sanction; if by an immediate act of *God's* displeasure, manifested on account of some *sin* committed by him . . . a punishment of the *religious* sanction.

In all these areas, then, the cause of behavior is the threat of pain. In public life the legislator understands that people feel bound to perform certain acts only when such acts have some clear sanction connected with them. This sanction consists of some form of pain if the citizen violates the type of conduct prescribed by the legislator. The legislator's chief concern, therefore, is to decide what forms of behavior will tend to increase the happiness of society and what sanctions will be most likely to bring about such an increase. Bentham's concept of *sanction* thus gave concrete meaning to the word *obligation.* For obligation now meant not some undefined duty but, instead, a prospect of pain if one did not obey a moral or legal rule. Kant argued that the morality of an act depends on having the right motive and not on the consequences of the act. Bentham, though, takes the opposite position, saying that morality depends directly on the consequences. He admits that some motives are more likely than others to increase happiness. But it is still pleasure and not the motive that confers the quality of morality on the act. Moreover, Bentham took the position that, generally, the law can punish only those who have actually inflicted pain, whatever their motive may be. Bentham believed that moral and legal obligations were similar in this regard since, in both cases, the external consequences of the action were more important than the motives behind them.

The Pleasure-Pain Calculus   Each individual and each legislator is concerned with avoiding pain and achieving pleasure. But pleasures and pains differ from each other and therefore have different values. With an attempt at mathematical precision, Bentham speaks of units—or what he called *lots*—of pleasure or pain. He suggests that before we act we should calculate the values of these lots. Their value, taken by themselves, will be greater or less depending, Bentham says, on a pleasure's *intensity, duration, certainty*, and *propinquity* or nearness. When we consider not only the pleasure by itself but what consequences it can lead to, we must calculate other circumstances. These include a pleasure's *fecundity*, or its chances of being followed by more pleasure, and its *purity*, or the chances that it will be followed by some pain. The *seventh* circumstance is a pleasure's *extent*, that is, the number of persons to whom it *extends* or who are affected by the action.

According to Bentham, we "sum up all the values of all the *pleasures* on the one side, and those of all the pains on the other. The balance, if it be on the side of pleasure, will give the *good* tendency of the act . . . if on the side of pain, the *bad* tendency." This calculus shows that Bentham was interested chiefly in the quantitative aspects of pleasure; thus, all actions are equally good if they produce the same amount of pleasure. Whether we actually do engage in this kind of calculation was a question Bentham anticipated, and he has a reply:

> There are some, perhaps, who . . . may look upon the nicety employed in the adjustment of such rules as so much labor lost: for gross ignorance, they will say, never troubles itself about laws, and passion does not calculate. But the evil of ignorance admits of cure: and . . . when matters of such importance as pain and pleasure are at stake, and these in the highest degree . . . who is there that does not calculate? Men calculate, some with less exactness, indeed, and some with more: but all men calculate.

Law and Punishment

Bentham made an especially impressive use of the principle of utility in connection with law and punishment. Since it is the function of the legislator to discourage some acts and encourage others, how should we classify those that should be discouraged as against those that should be encouraged?

Against Social Contract and Natural Rights Theories   Bentham believed that utilitarianism should be the guiding rule of all social and political decision making. No matter what the political issue is, the right answer should be decided on the basis of a utilitarian evaluation. In Bentham's day, the dominant views of political authority and decision making were the social contract and natural rights theories. Where do these concepts fit into Bentham's vision of law and government? He argued that, as influential as these theories are, they are unfounded and frequently even harmful.

Regarding social contract theory, defenders of this view commonly make an assumption about the so-called contractual agreement made between rules and citizens, whereby rulers promise to govern properly and citizens promise obedience. In Bentham's words, the alleged contract is something like this: "The people, on their part, promised to the king a general obedience: the king, on his part, promised to govern the people in such a particular manner always, as should be subservient to their happiness." When a king takes his coronation oath, we might think that this is the moment that he makes such a contractual agreement with the citizens. Not so, Bentham argues. The king's obligation to properly govern the country is grounded in utility, not in some alleged contractual promise. To prove his point, Bentham holds that there are four possible situations that show that happiness is the basis of governmental obligation, and not a promise. First, acting perfectly well within his contractual authority, the king might enact a law that directly goes against the people's happiness. Second, even when following the laws that are in place, the king might find ways of making society unhappy. He writes, "a king may, to a great degree, impair the happiness of his people without violating the letter of any single law." Third, even if the king aims at happiness, he might do so by violating the law. And, fourth, a single violation by the king would not release citizens from their obedience to him. The bottom line, for Bentham, is that the king's promise to govern and the citizens promise to obey are all about the utility of governing properly and the utility of obeying the government.

As to natural rights, defenders of this theory commonly hold that natural rights are not created by governments but, instead, are conferred on every person from birth by God. They are the same for every person around the world, and, even though governments might violate the natural rights of their citizens, those governments cannot take away those rights. As noble as this position sounds, Bentham argues that so-called natural rights have no validity, and the only type of rights that are valid are legal rights, that is, the rights that governments themselves create for their citizens by enacting laws through a legislative process. By holding this position, Bentham is an early advocate of the theory of "positive law," that is, the view that government-created laws and rights are the only valid laws and rights that exist. His rationale for this view is that legal rights are grounded in concrete facts—the actions and thought processes of the legislators who make laws about rights. But so-called "natural rights" are not grounded in any such facts that we can inquire into or investigate. Claims about natural rights are nonsense, and, when we add to that superlatives like "God-given" natural rights or "imprescriptible" natural rights, "this is just" nonsense on stilts." Not only are natural rights nonsense, they are also dangerous, since, in essence, they give a person license to assert any right that he wants. When a person has no grounds for claiming that he has a legal right, he simply asserts that he has a natural right:

> [when] a man has been contending for a political right which he either never has possessed, or having in his possession, is fearful of losing, he will not quietly be beaten out of his claim; but in default of the political right, or as a support to the political right, he asserts he has a natural right. . . . beaten out of this ground, he says he has a natural right—a right given him by that kind goddess and governess Nature whose legitimacy who shall dispute?

When someone appeals to nature or God as the source of his so-called natural right, we can do little to refute it since there is nothing factual in his claim that we can investigate. Accordingly, "The assertion of such rights, absurd in logic, is pernicious in morals." Thus, Bentham concludes, "there are no other than legal rights,—no natural rights—no rights of man, anterior or superior to those created by the laws.

The Object of Law   Bentham's method of legislation was first of all to measure the "mischief of an act," and this mischief consisted in the consequences, that is, the pain or evil inflicted by the act; acts that produce evil must be discouraged. There are, Bentham says, both primary and secondary evils that concern the legislator. Robbers inflict an evil on their victims, who lose their money, and this is a case of primary evil. But robbery creates a secondary evil because successful robbery sends the message that theft is easy. This suggestion is evil because it weakens respect for property, and property becomes more insecure. From the point of view of the legislator, the secondary evils are frequently more important than the primary evils. For, taking the example of robbery again, the actual loss to the victim may be considerably less than the loss of stability and security to the community as a whole.

The law is concerned with augmenting the total happiness of the community, and it must do this by discouraging those acts that would produce evil consequences. A criminal act is by definition one that is clearly detrimental to the community's happiness. For the most part the government accomplishes its business of promoting the happiness of society by punishing people who commit offenses that the principle of utility has clearly measured as evil. Bentham felt that governments should only use the principle of utility in deciding which acts should be considered "offenses." And if they did this, then many illegal acts of his time would thereby become only matters of private morals. Utilitarianism had the effect, then, of requiring a reclassification of behavior to determine what is and is not appropriate for the government to regulate. In addition, the principle of utility provided Bentham with a new and simple theory of punishment—a theory that he thought could not only be justified more readily than the older theories but could achieve the purposes of punishment far more effectively.

Punishment   "All punishment," Bentham writes, "is in itself evil" because it inflicts suffering and pain. At the same time, the "object which all laws have in common, is to augment the total happiness of the community." If we are to justify punishment from a utilitarian point of view, we must show that the pain inflicted by punishment will in some way prevent some greater pain. Punishment must therefore be "useful" in achieving a greater totality of pleasure, and it has no justification if its effect is simply to add still more units or *lots* of pain to the community. The principle of utility would clearly call for the elimination of pure "retribution," or retaliation, since no useful purpose is served by adding still more pain to the sum total that society suffers. This is not to say that utilitarianism rejects punishment. It means only that the principle of utility, particularly in the hands of Bentham, called for a reopening of the question of why society should punish offenders.

According to Bentham, punishment should not be inflicted in four particular situations. First, it should not be inflicted when it is *groundless*. This would be so when, for example, there is an offense that admits of compensation and where there is virtual certainty that compensation is forthcoming. Second, punishment should not be inflicted when it is *inefficacious*. This is the case when punishment cannot prevent a mischievous act, such as when a law has already been made but not been announced. Punishment would be inefficacious also where an infant, an insane person, or a drunkard was involved. Third, punishment should not be inflicted when it is *unprofitable* or too *expensive*, "where the mischief it would produce would be greater than what it prevented." Finally, punishment should not be inflicted when it is *needless*, "where the mischief may be prevented, or cease of itself, without it: that is at a cheaper rate." This is particularly so in cases "which consist in the disseminating [of] pernicious principles in matters of duty," since in these cases persuasion is more efficacious than force.

Whether a given kind of behavior should be left to *private ethics* instead of becoming the object of *legislation* was a question Bentham answered simply by applying the principle of utility. The matter should be left to private ethics if it does more harm than good to involve the whole legislative process and the apparatus of punishment. He was convinced that attempts to regulate sexual immorality would be particularly unprofitable, since this would require intricate supervision. This is also the case for offenses such as "ingratitude or rudeness, where the definition is so vague that the judge could not safely be entrusted with the power to punish." Duties that we owe to ourselves could hardly be the concern of law and punishment, nor must we be coerced to be benevolent, though we can be liable on certain occasions for failing to help. But the main concern of law must be to encourage those acts that would lead to the greatest happiness of the community. There is, then, a justification for punishment, which is that through punishment the greatest good for the greatest number is most effectively secured.

Besides providing a rationale for punishment, the principle of utility also gives us some clues to what punishment should consist of. Bentham describes the desirable properties of each unit or *lot* of punishment, considering "the proportion between punishments and offenses." To this end he gives the following rules: (1) The punishment must be great enough to outweigh the profit that the offender might get from the offense. (2) The greater the offense, the greater the punishment: Where two offenses come in competition, the punishment for the greater offense must be sufficient to induce a person to prefer the less. (3) Punishments should be variable and adaptable to fit the particular circumstances, although each offender should get the same punishment for the same offense. (4) The amount of punishment should never be greater than the minimum required to make it effective. (5) The more uncertain that an offender will be caught, the greater should be the punishment. (6) If an offense is habitual, the punishment must outweigh the profit not only of the immediate offense but also of the undiscovered offenses. These rules led Bentham to conclude that punishment should be *variable* to fit the particular case. It should be *equable* so as to inflict equal pain for similar offenses. It should be *commensurable* in order that punishments for different classes of crimes be proportional. It should be *characteristic* so as to impress the imagination of potential offenders. It should be *frugal* so as not to be excessive. It should be *reformatory* in order to correct faulty behavior. It should be *disabling* in order to deter future offenders. It should be *compensatory* to the sufferer. In order not to create new problems, punishment should have *popular* acceptance and be capable of *remittance* for sufficient cause.

Bentham's Radicalism

Bentham quickly discovered elements in the law and the general social structure of England that did not fit the requirements set by the principle of utility. He wanted the legislative process to operate on the principle of utility with practically the same rigor with which the planets obey the principle of gravitation. That is, he wanted to add the notion of systematic action to that of systematic thought. He thus pressed for reforms wherever he found a discrepancy between the actual legal and social order, on the one hand, and the principle of utility, on the other. He traced most of the evils of the legal system to the judges who, he charged, "made the common law. Do you know how they make it? Just as a man makes laws for his dog. When your dog does anything you want to break him of, you wait till he does it and then beat him . . . this is the way judges make laws for you and me." Having exposed one monstrous evil after another, Bentham zealously attempted to reform these evils, and to that end, he became associated with a group of like-minded utilitarians known as *philosophical radicals.*

Bentham blamed the aristocratic society of his day for the breakdown of the principle of utility. Why should social evils and evils of the legal system persist even after he demonstrated that certain new types of behavior would produce the "greatest happiness of the greatest number"? The answer, he thought, was that those in power did not want the "greatest happiness of the greatest number." The rulers were more concerned with their own interests. However, from the utilitarian perspective, whenever those in power represent only a class or a small group, their self-interest will be in conflict with the proper end of government. The way to overcome this conflict is to put the government into the hands of the people. If there is an identity between the rulers and the ruled, their interests will be the same, and the greatest happiness of the greatest number will be assured. This identity of interest cannot, by definition, be achieved under a monarchy. The monarch acts in his or her own interests, or, at best, aims at the happiness of a special class grouped around him or her. It is in a democracy that the greatest happiness of the greatest number is most apt to be realized, for the rulers are the people, and representatives of the people are chosen precisely because they promise to serve the greatest good. For Bentham the application of the principle of utility clearly required the rejection of monarchy with all its corollaries. That is, his country would have to do away with the monarchy, the house of peers, and the established church. In their place the country would need to construct a democratic order after the model of the United States. Since "all government is in itself one vast evil," its only justification is to apply evil in order to prevent or exclude some greater evil.

JOHN STUART MILL

Mill's Life

John Stuart Mill was born in 1806, and between the ages of 3 and 14, he was the object of a rigorous "educational experiment" imposed on him by his father, James Mill. So intense was this personal tutoring in the classics, languages, and history, he said, that "through the training bestowed on me by my father, I started, I may fairly say, with an advantage of a quarter of a century over my contemporaries." But this intense learning, with its emphasis not only on memorizing but also on critical and analytical thinking, took its toll on young Mill, and at the age of 20 he fell into "a dull state of nerves." He attributed his breakdown to the overemphasis on analysis without a parallel emotional development. He believed that his larger social surrounding underrated expressions of feeling, and he points out that Bentham himself "used to say that 'all poetry is misrepresentation.'" But "the habit of analysis has a tendency to wear away the feelings . . . [and] I was thus, as I said to myself, left stranded at the commencement of my voyage, with a well equipped ship and a rudder, but no sail." He eventually turned to such writers as Coleridge, Carlyle, and Wordsworth, who affected his thought so deeply that he could later say that "the cultivation of the feelings became one of the cardinal points in my ethical and philosophical creed." He had a long romance with Harriet Taylor (1807–1858), an acclaimed philosopher in her own right, which began when he was 25 and which later led to their marriage. This further confirmed his high assessment of the role of feeling among human faculties. His literary achievements reflect his attempt to maintain a balance among the wide range of human faculties, starting with the rigorous *System of Logic* (1843) and including *Principles of Political Economy* (1848), the essay *On Liberty* (1859), *Considerations on Representative Government* (1861), the essay *Utilitarianism* (1861), and his *Autobiography* and *Three Essays on Religion*, which were published after he died in 1873 at the age of 67.

Mill was one of the ablest advocates of utilitarianism. His father was closely associated with Bentham's philosophical theory. Later, young Mill wrote in his *Autobiography* that "it was my father's opinions which gave the distinguishing character to the Benthamic or Utilitarian propagandism." His father's ideas flowed into the thought of early nineteenth-century England through various channels, of which, Mill says, "one was through me, the only mind directly formed by his instructions, and through whom considerable influence was exercised over various young men." Mill had not only shared his father's ideas but through him was exposed to the thinking of some of the leading men of the day. He had known and visited the political economist Ricardo, but "of Mr. Bentham I saw much more, owing to the close intimacy which existed between him and my father." Mill adds that "my father was the earliest Englishman of any great mark, who thoroughly understood, and in the main, adopted, Bentham's general views of ethics, government and law." When young Mill read Bentham's principal work on law and administration, *Introduction to the Principles of Morals and Legislation*, it was "one of the turning points in my mental history." What impressed him most was that Bentham's "greatest happiness principle" rendered unnecessary any attempts to deduce morality and legislation from concepts such as law of nature, right reason, the moral sense, or natural rectitude. As he read Bentham, Mill says that "the feeling rushed upon me, that all previous moralists were superseded, and that here indeed was the commencement of a new era of thought." Upon finishing Bentham's book, he became a different person, for "the 'principle of utility', understood as Bentham understood it . . . gave unity to my conceptions of things. I now had opinions, a creed, a doctrine, a philosophy; in one among the best senses of the word, a religion; the inculcation and diffusion of which could be made the principal outward purpose of a life." When Bentham died, Mill was 26 years old, but already he was developing certain convictions of his own about utilitarianism—convictions that were to distinguish his approach from Bentham's in a significant way.

Mill's Utilitarianism

Mill's purpose in writing his famous essay on *Utilitarianism* was to defend the *principle of utility*, which he learned from his father and Bentham. In the course of his defense, however, he made such important modifications to this theory that his version of utilitarianism turned out to be different from Bentham's in several ways. His definition of utility was perfectly consistent with what Bentham taught: Mill writes,

> The creed which accepts as the foundation of morals Utility, or the greatest Happiness Principle, holds that actions are right in proportion as they tend to promote happiness, wrong as they tend to produce the reverse of happiness. By 'happiness' is intended pleasure, and the absence of pain; by 'unhappiness,' pain, and the privation of pleasure.

But, even though he started with the same general ideas as Bentham, especially relating *happiness* with *pleasure*, Mill soon took a different approach.

Qualitative versus Quantitative Approach　Bentham said that pleasures differ only in their amount—that is, that different ways of behaving produce different *quantities* of pleasure. He also said that the game of "pushpin is as good as poetry," by which he meant that the only criterion for goodness is the amount of pleasure an act can produce. It necessarily follows on this calculation that all types of behavior that produce the same amount of pleasure would be equally good, whether such behavior be the game of "pushpin" or the enjoyment of poetry. Bentham was so committed to the simple quantitative measurement of pleasure as the chief test of the morality of an act that he even suggested that "there ought to be a moral thermometer." Just as a thermometer measures the different degrees of heat, so also a "moral thermometer" could measure the degrees of happiness or unhappiness. This analogy reveals Bentham's exclusive emphasis on quantity in his treatment of goodness and pleasure. For just as it is possible to achieve the same degree of heat whether one burns coal, wood, or oil, so also is it possible to achieve equal quantities of pleasure through games, poetry, or other types of behavior. Goodness, for Bentham, is not connected with any particular *kind* of behavior but only with the amounts of pleasure as measured by his "calculus." Inevitably, the utilitarians were accused of being moral relativists who rejected all moral absolutes in favor of each person's subjective opinion about what is good. Mill sought to defend utilitarianism against these charges, but in the course of his defense, he was drawn into the position of altering Bentham's quantitative approach to pleasure by substituting a qualitative approach.

Whereas Bentham said that "pushpin is as good as poetry," Mill says he would "rather be Socrates dissatisfied than a fool satisfied," or that "it is better to be a human being dissatisfied than a pig satisfied." Pleasures, Mill notes, differ from each other in kind and quality, not only in quantity. He took his stand with the ancient Epicureans, who were also attacked for their "degrading" emphasis on pleasure as the end of all behavior. The Epicureans replied to their accusers that it was in fact they who had a degrading conception of human nature, for *they* assumed that the only pleasures people are capable of are those of which only swine are capable. But this assumption is obviously false, says Mill, because "human beings have faculties more elevated than the animal appetites, and when once conscious of them, do not regard anything as happiness which does not include their gratification."

Pleasures of the intellect and imagination have a higher value than the pleasures of mere sensation. Though Mill initially developed the notion of higher pleasures as an answer to the critics of utilitarianism, his concern over higher pleasures led to a criticism of the very foundation of Bentham's view of utility. He says that "it would be absurd that . . . the estimation of pleasures should be supposed to depend on quantity alone." For Mill the mere quantity of pleasure produced by an act was of secondary importance when we have to make a choice between pleasures. Imagine, for example, that a person is acquainted with a specific intellectual pleasure and a specific pleasure of sensation. If she prefers the intellectual pleasure, then this shows its superiority. This is particularly the case even if she knows that the intellectual pleasure is "attended with a greater amount of discontent, and would not resign it for any quantity of the other pleasure which [human] nature is capable of, we are justified in ascribing to the preferred enjoyment a superiority in quality so far outweighing quantity as to render it, in comparison, of small account."

The qualitative aspect of pleasure, Mill thought, was as much an empirical fact as was the quantitative element on which Bentham placed his entire emphasis. Mill departed even further from Bentham by grounding the qualitative difference between pleasures in the structure of human nature, thereby focusing on certain human faculties whose full use were to be the criterion of true happiness and, therefore, of goodness. In this regard Mill says,

> Few human creatures would consent to be changed into any of the lower animals for a promise of the fullest allowance of a beast's pleasures; no intelligent human being would consent to be a fool, no instructed person would be an ignoramus, no person of feeling and conscience would be selfish and base, even though they should be persuaded that the fool, the dunce, or the rascal is better satisfied with his lot than they are with theirs.

Pleasures, according to Mill, have to be assessed not for their quantity but for their quality. However, Mill's view of qualitative pleasures raises an important problem with the whole notion of the pleasure principle: If we must assess pleasures for their quality, then pleasure itself is no longer the standard of morality. That is, if only the full use of our higher faculties can lead us to true happiness, the standard of goodness in behavior has to do not with pleasure but with fulfilling our human faculties. It is not clear whether Mill appreciated the full impact of this problem. Nevertheless, he attempted to go beyond mere quantitative hedonism to a qualitative hedonism, wherein the moral value of life is grounded in the higher pleasures of our higher faculties. Thus, if it is better to be Socrates dissatisfied than a pig satisfied, morality is proportionate to the happiness we find in being truly human and not in the amount of pleasure we experience. Higher happiness, then, is the aim of all human life, a life "exempt as far as possible from pain, and as rich as possible in enjoyments."

Mill's Departure from Bentham   Mill's version of utilitarianism differs from Bentham's in three key ways. First, by preferring the higher quality of happiness over a mere quantity of pleasure, Mill thereby rejects Bentham's central assumption that pleasures and pains can be calculated or measured. Bentham based his pleasure-pain calculus on simple quantitative considerations, saying that pleasures can be measured as to their duration, intensity, or extent. Mill, though, argues that there is no way to measure either the quantity or the quality of pleasures. Whenever we have to make a choice between two pleasures, we can express a preference wisely only if we have experienced both possibilities. Mill asks, "What means are there of determining which is the acutest of two pains, or the intensest of two pleasurable sensations, except the general [feeling] of those who are familiar with both? . . . What is there to decide whether a particular pleasure is worth purchasing at the cost of a particular pain, except the feelings and judgment of the experienced?" Instead of calculating, people simply express a preference, and apart from this attitude of preference, "there is no other tribunal."

A second difference in Mill's theory involves when we should actually consult the utilitarian guideline. Bentham seems to say that for each act we perform we should consider whether that act produces a greater balance of happiness versus unhappiness. This, though, can become quite tedious, and our lives would grind to a halt when we paused to calculate the outcome of our various actions. According to Mill, though, we rarely need to consider the consequences of our specific actions. Instead, we should go about our lives following general moral rules, such as rules against killing, stealing, and lying. We can trust these rules since, throughout human civilization, people have continually tested them to determine whether we facilitate general happiness when we follow them. Only occasionally do we run into problems following these tried and true moral rules. For example, if I am poor and my family is starving, I may want to steal a loaf of bread from the local store. Here I am torn between two moral rules: (1) Provide for your family, and (2) do not steal. In this case I resolve the conflict by determining which course of action would bring about the most happiness.

The third difference between Bentham and Mill involves their respective ways of dealing with human selfishness. Bentham simply assumed that we ought to choose those acts that produce for us the greatest quantity of pleasure. He also assumed that we should naturally help other people achieve happiness because in that way we should secure our own. Mill accepted this point but added that we may rely on a variety of social institutions to help broaden our level of concern for others:

> Utility would enjoin, first, that laws and social arrangements should place the happiness . . . or the interest of every individual, as nearly as possible in harmony with the interest of the whole; and secondly, that education and opinion, which have so vast a power over human character, should so use that power as to establish in the mind of every individual an indissolvable association between his own happiness and the good of the whole . . . so that a direct impulse to promote the general good may be in every individual one of the habitual motives of action.

Proving and Reinforcing Utilitarianism   Nowhere is Mill's difficulty with the problem of moral obligation and choice more apparent than when he raises the issue of "proving" utilitarianism. But how can we prove that happiness is the true and desirable end of human life and conduct? Mill answers that "the only proof capable of being given that an object is visible, is that people actually see it. The only proof that a sound is audible, is that people hear it; and so of the other sources of our experience. In like manner, I apprehend, the sole evidence it is possible to produce that anything is desirable, is that people do actually desire it." Thus, we can give no reason why general happiness is desirable except that "each person so far as he believes it to be attainable, desires his own happiness."

In addition to the issue of proving utilitarianism, Mill discusses how we might reinforce this moral conviction as well. He notes that there are both external "sanctions" or motivations and internal ones. External sanctions principally involve other people approving of us when we pursue general happiness and disapproving of us when we instead produce unhappiness. But the most important motivation, according to Mill, is *internal* and involves a feeling of guilt when we go against the sense of duty toward society as a whole. How do we develop this sense of duty? Mill argues that it forms initially through education, such as through the teachings of our parents, teachers, church, and peer groups. In Mill's words it is "derived from sympathy, from love and still more from fear; from all forms of religious feeling, from the recollections of childhood and all of our past life; from self-esteem, desire of the esteem of others, and occasionally even self-abasement." If cultivated properly, then, we will all carry with us a strong sense of duty toward others, which will be very difficult for us to resist.

Liberty

Mill was as much concerned with the problems of society as was Bentham. The greatest-happiness principle led all utilitarians to consider how the individual and the government should be related. Bentham put his faith in democracy as the great cure for social evils, since in democracies the people being ruled are also the rulers. But Mill did not have the same implicit faith in democracy. Although Mill agreed that democracy is the best form of government, in his essay *On Liberty* he exposes certain dangers inherent in the democracies. Principally, he warned that it is entirely possible for the will of the majority to oppress minorities. In addition, democracies have a kind of tyranny of opinion, which is as dangerous as oppression. Even in a democracy, therefore, it is necessary to set up safeguards against the forces that would deny individual freedom. In this respect Mill reflected Bentham's desire for reform to eliminate clear social evils. His particular focus is on preserving liberty by setting limits to the actions of government.

Mill argued that "the sole end for which mankind are warranted, individually or collectively, in interfering with the liberty of action of any of their number, is self-protection. That the only purpose for which power can be rightly exercised over any member of a civilized community, against his will, is to prevent harm to others." There is, of course, a legitimate role for government, but there are three conditions under which the government should not interfere with its subjects. First, governments should not interfere when private individuals can perform the action better. Second, governments should not interfere when, although the government could possibly perform the action better than private individuals, it is desirable for the individuals to do it for their development and education. Third, governments should not interfere when there is danger that too much power will unnecessarily accrue to the government. Mill's argument for liberty was, therefore, an argument for individualism. Let individuals pursue their happiness in their own way. Even in the realm of ideas, we must be free to express our thoughts and beliefs, because truth is most quickly discovered when opportunity is given to refute falsehoods. Mill took the position that "there is the greatest difference between presuming an opinion to be true because, with every opportunity for contesting it, it has not been refuted, and assuming its truth for the purpose of not permitting its refutation." He assumed, however, that it is important that the truth be known. As he considered the ideal goal of human existence, Mill asked, "What more or better can be said of any condition of human affairs than that it brings human beings themselves nearer to the best thing they can be? But is it the function of government to make human beings the best thing they can be?" He deeply disliked totalitarian government even though he lived too soon to see its ugliest manifestations in the twentieth century.

The most memorable part of Mill's position is what we now call Mill's Principle of Liberty:

> That the only purpose for which power can be rightfully exercised over any member of a civilized community, against his will, is to prevent harm to others. His own good, either physical or moral, is not a sufficient warrant. . . . The only part of the conduct of any one, for which he is amenable to society, is that which concerns others. In the part which merely concerns himself, his independence is, of right, absolute. Over himself, over his own body and mind, the individual is sovereign.

Mill says here that governments may rightly constrain us when our actions harm other people, but not when our actions only harm ourselves. Thus, we should be at liberty to engage in dangerous activities, even to the point that our own lives are at risk.

COMTE

Comte's Life and Times

Although Auguste Comte is called the founder of *positive philosophy*, he did not discover this theory, for, as John Stuart Mill said, positivism was "the general property of the age." Comte studied in an age and at a place that were characterized by intellectual confusion and social instability. Born in Montpellier in 1798, he was educated at the École Polytechnique and for some years was secretary to the noted socialist Saint-Simon. In his early twenties he published a series of books of which his *System of Positive Polity* (1824) is the best known. This, as it turned out, was an early sketch of his major work *Course in Positive Philosophy*, which was written in several volumes between 1830 and 1842. He admitted that there was this contrast between his earlier and later ideas, claiming that he was an Aristotle in the early period of his career—that is, more rational—and a Saint Paul in the late period—that is, more emotional. Some of his later ideas were somewhat peculiar and even resulted in ridicule. He blamed the severe specialization of university scholars for their refusal to provide him a post for teaching the history of the sciences. Living off voluntary contributions from the friends of positivism, he continued to work in Paris in a little house only a short distance from the place at the Sorbonne where there now stands a statue of him. From this meager setting emerged Comte's other major books—his second *System of Positive Polity* (1851–1854), *Catechism of Positive Religion* (1852), and the *Subjective Synthesis* (1856). Before he could complete his projected series on ethics, the system of positive industrial organization, and other philosophical works, his career ended in 1857, when he died at the age of 59.

Comte's chief objective was the total reorganization of society. But he was convinced that this practical objective first required the reconstruction, or at least reformation, of the intellectual orientation of his era. As he saw the situation, the scientific revolution, which had been unfolding since the discoveries of Galileo and Newton, had not been sufficiently assimilated in other fields, particularly in social, political, moral, and religious thought.

The achievements of science in France had been outstanding, including the work of Ampère and Fresnel in physics, Chevreul and Dumas in chemistry, Magendie in physiology, and Lamarck, Saint-Hilaire, and Cuvier in biology and zoology. What commanded so much respect for their work was that their discoveries could be employed in solving problems of everyday life. This led to new methods in medicine and surgery and made possible new industrial techniques and transportation. Gaining a sense of authority from its spectacular accomplishments, science challenged other ways of thinking. A series of related questions now took on a greater degree of intensity. Such questions included the relation between science and religion, the freedom of the will, the value of metaphysics, and the possibility of discovering objective moral standards.

This was an age, too, when the state of philosophy in France was being influenced by both internal political events and external systems of thought. The major internal event was the French Revolution, which for Saint-Simon, as well as for Comte, was a dramatic example of social anarchy. In the aftermath of the Revolution, French thinkers entertained differing theories of society. Some theories were strongly antirevolutionary, contending that the Revolution involved a contest of power whose effect was to destroy the legitimate power and authority both of the government and of the church. The effect could only be the further destruction of the institutions of the family and private property. Other theorists argued that society rests on the consent of the governed as expressed in a social contract. Added to these internal differences in thought was the gradual importation of philosophies from other countries. These dealt not only with social philosophy but also the theory of knowledge and metaphysics in a way that stimulated an atmosphere of vigorous debate. The French were now reading such varied authors as Kant, Hegel, Fichte, Schelling, Strauss, Feuerbach, and Goethe. Advocates of materialism, idealism, and new metaphysical systems entered the lists, and grandiose theories of human nature, the absolute, and progress were put forth.

To overcome both political anarchy and the anarchy of ideas, Comte attempted to reform society and philosophy by developing a science of society, namely, *positivism*. The issue for Comte was how to maintain social unity when theological beliefs were no longer accepted as supports for political authority. Comte believed that a dictatorship of brute force would result when beliefs are no longer held in common and when anarchy of ideas creates anarchy in society. None of the usual arguments against dictatorship seemed satisfactory to Comte. Against those who sought to reinstate the earlier balance of worldly and spiritual powers, Comte answered that it is not possible to reverse the course of historical progress. Against those who advocated the methods of democracy, he argued that their concepts of *equality* and *natural rights*— especially *sovereignty of the people*—were metaphysical abstractions and dogmas. Only the method of positivism, he declared, can guarantee social unity. His task of reorganizing society, therefore, required that he first of all bring about an intellectual reformation, which in turn led him to formulate his classic theory of positivism.

Positivism Defined

Positivism involves both a negative and a positive component. On the negative side it rejects the assumption that nature has some ultimate purpose, and it gives up any attempt to discover either the "essence" or the secret causes of things. On the positive side it attempts to study facts by observing the constant relations between things and by formulating the laws of science simply as the laws of constant relations among various phenomena. In this spirit Newton described the phenomena of physics without going beyond useful limits by asking questions about the essential nature of things. Before him Galileo had made great strides in understanding the movements and relations of stars without inquiring into their physical constitution. Fourier discovered mathematical laws of the diffusion of heat without any theoretical assumption concerning the essential nature of heat. The biologist Cuvier worked out some laws concerning the structure of living things without hypothesizing about the nature of life. A consequence of this spirit of research and inquiry was the assumption that knowledge derived from science can also be used in the social realm. This was positivism's great appeal. For on the one hand, it promised an effective means for dealing with physical reality, such as the disorders of the body, which concerned medicine. On the other hand, it also addressed the science of society, which concerned sociology.

The initial rigor of positivism is suggested by Comte's clear statement that "any proposition which does not admit of being ultimately reduced to a simple enunciation of fact, special or general, can have no real or intelligible sense." Counting himself a positivist and using much of Comte's own language, Mill described the general outlook of positivism in these terms:

> We have no knowledge of anything but Phenomena, and our knowledge of phenomena is relative, not absolute. We know not the essence, nor the real mode of production of any fact but only its relations to other facts in the way of succession or of similitude. These relations are constant; that is, always the same in the same circumstances. The constant resemblances which link phenomena together, and the constant sequences which unite them as antecedent and consequent, are termed their laws. The laws of phenomena are all we know respecting them. Their essential nature, and their ultimate causes, either efficient or final, are unknown and inscrutable to us.

This was the intellectual attitude that Comte and his followers brought to the study of society and religion, saying that in the end every subject must utilize the same approach to truth. Only in that way could we achieve unity in thought as well as social life. To be sure, this method had its own assumptions, the foremost of them being that there is an order in the nature of things whose laws we can discover. Comte also assumed that we can overcome the pitfalls of subjectivity by "transforming the human brain into a perfect mirror of the external order." His optimism about achieving his objectives came from his interpretation of the history of ideas and from his study of the development of the various sciences. These, he believed, clearly pointed to the inevitability and the validity of positivism.

The Law of the Three Stages

The history of ideas, said Comte, shows that there has been a clear movement of thought through three stages, each stage representing a different way of discovering truth. The first stage is *theological*, in which people explain phenomena in reference to divine causal forces. The second is *metaphysical*, which replaces human-centered concepts of divinity with impersonal and abstract forces. The third stage is *positivistic*, or scientific, in that only the constant relations between phenomena are considered and all attempts to explain things by references to beings beyond our experience are abandoned. He called this evolution from one stage to another the *law of the three stages*. He believed that this law is at work in the history of ideas, in science, and in the political realm. In fact, he argued, the structure of a society reflects the philosophical orientation of an epoch, and any major change in philosophical thought will bring about a change in the political order. For example, in both Greek mythology and traditional Christianity, we find frequent instances of the intervention of the gods or of God. This had its counterpart in political theory in the theory of the divine right of kings. But this theological approach is superseded by metaphysics, which speaks of a *necessary being* as the explanation for the existence of finite things. This concept of necessary being, Comte says, is abstract and impersonal, and although it goes beyond the idea of some capricious being acting upon the physical world, it does not overcome the uselessness of dogmatism. Its counterpart in political thought is the attempt to formulate abstract principles such as *natural rights* or the *sovereignty of the people*. Comte harshly rejected the political structures in both of these stages. The theological stage, he argued, results in slavery and military states. The metaphysical stage involves the assumptions of liberal democracy and unfounded dogmas such as the equality of all people. Comte believed that these views must give way to the clear scientific fact that people are unequal and have different capacities and must, therefore, have different functions in society. To deal effectively with such questions of political order required a carefully worked-out science of society, which Comte did not find already available and which he, therefore, set out to create, calling it *sociology*.

Comte's conception of sociology illustrates his account of the development of knowledge. For in his theory the movement of thought is from decreasing generality to increasing complexity and from the abstract to the concrete. He notes this particularly with the five major sciences. Mathematics came first; then, in order, came astronomy, physics, chemistry, and biology. In this sequence he saw the movement from generality and simplicity to complexity and concreteness. Specifically, mathematics deals with quantities of a general kind. To quantity astronomy adds the elements of mass and force and some principles of attraction. Physics differentiates between types of forces when it deals with gravity, light, and heat. Chemistry makes quantitative and qualitative analyses of materials. Biology then adds the structure of organic and animal life to the material order. A sixth science—sociology—deals with the relations of human beings to each other in society, and as such it is the necessary outcome of the previous stage of science. Comte dramatically describes how mathematics and astronomy came early in the ancient world, whereas physics as a true science had to wait for Isaac Newton in the seventeenth century. Chemistry then began with Lavoisier, and biology with Bichat. It was now Comte's own task to usher in the science of sociology. For him sociology was the queen of the sciences, the summit of knowledge, for it makes use of all previous information and coordinates it all for the sake of a peaceful and orderly society.

Comte's Sociology and "Religion of Humanity"

Comte stands in contrast to both revolutionary thinkers who called for a radical reconstruction of society and idealists who proposed utopian communities. His approach was to always describe things in reference to science and the actual conditions of history. Two things in particular dominate his sociological theory, namely, what he calls the *static* and the *dynamic* components of social existence. The static component consists of certain stable elements of society, such as the family, private property, language, and religion. Since these are virtually permanent, he did not advocate any revolutionary change in them. At the same time, he recognized a dynamic component, which he understood as the force of progress. His theory of "the law of the three stages" contains the technical elaboration of this dynamic force. Progress does not involve altering any of the basic social elements. Instead, it involves simply understanding how we should utilize these stable structures in an optimum way. The stars and constellations do not change as we move from the theological to the metaphysical and finally to the scientific way of accounting for their behavior. Neither, then, should the structures of society change as far as their basic elements are concerned. The family, for example, must remain, and indeed Comte believed that the family constitutes the fundamental building blocks of society. However, some aspects of the family should change, such as an improved status for women. Similarly, property should be utilized in such a way as to call forth the highest instincts of altruism instead of greed and envy. Comte believed that religion is the key to the whole system, but instead of the worship of a supernatural being, religion should consist of the cult of *humanity*. Positivism also calls for a political organization that utilizes both religious and nonreligious institutions in such a way that these two do not compete with but rather harmoniously complement each other.

Comte frequently refers to the Middle Ages as a time when the static and dynamic components of society were most adequately attuned to each other. In fact, he used the medieval community as his model for the new society. He would, of course, reject the theological aspects of this period. But what struck him about it was the intimate relation between religion and society—between a body of thought and the organization of the structures of society in medieval Europe. The family, property, and government—all of these elements had a justification in and derived their motivations from a set of beliefs held in common. The reorganization of nineteenth-century society would not involve the destruction of old structures and the creation of new ones. Instead, it would bring the permanent elements of society up to date. It would then overcome contemporary anarchy by reestablishing the connection between religion and the institutions of society. This connection between religion and society can only be reestablished through intellectual and technological progress. Much of the anarchy of this period, both intellectual and political, stemmed, as Comte saw it, from the breakdown of theological authority brought on by the rise of science. He believed that it was impossible to reestablish this earlier grip of theology on modern people. Further, the legacy of the Enlightenment, which was the exaltation of each person's own ideas and opinions, could not lead to any unity.

Only a new religion could create the unity between all people and between their thinking and their ways of living. The Middle Ages had the correct approach to social organization, but, Comte thought, they had the wrong intellectual orientation. On the other hand, contemporary Europe seemed to him to have the right philosophy in scientific positivism but not an adequate organization. Although science had seriously shaken the hold of theology, it had not yet completely eliminated it. The ensuing debates over the relation between science and religion also raised the specific question of the comparative roles of intellect and feeling. Comte's enormous task, therefore, was to reconceive the whole nature of religion in terms of science. He would have to bind the new religion to the structures of society and unify people's intellects with their feelings. He would thus infuse every person's act with a sense of purpose or direction. Proceeding with this task, Comte said, "Love, then, is our principle; Order our basis; and Progress our end."

What his new society would be like is shown first of all by what he did *not* want it to be. Although the theological stage had passed, new dogmas created by metaphysics still lingered, and these would have to be rejected. To achieve the new society, every old fiction would have to be given up, whether it be the theistic God or the metaphysical dogma of equality or popular sovereignty. Since the function of the mind now would be to *mirror* the true state of things, the contents of the new religion would have to be drawn from such an objectively real source, and this, Comte said, is *humanity* itself. It is, after all, from humanity that we all draw our material, intellectual, spiritual, and moral resources. But although he did not want to retain past dogmas, he nevertheless built his new *religion of humanity* as though it were a secularized version of Catholicism. Instead of God, Comte substituted humanity, which he called *Grand-Être*, the Supreme Being. He appointed himself as high priest and instituted a calendar of saints, mostly renowned scientists. He also created a catechism, at the end of which he said, "Humanity definitely occupies the place of God." He added that "she does not forget the services which the idea of God provisionally rendered." The sacraments become "social" and first include *baptism*, then *initiation* at age 14, then *admission* when at age 21 a person is authorized to serve humanity. *Destination*, or choice of career, takes place at 28, *marriage* for men at 28 and for women at 21, and *retirement* at age 63. Mill regretted Comte's attempt to found a secularized version of the Roman Catholic Church from which all supernatural elements had been removed. Regarding Comte's self-appointed role as high priest, Mill said that "an irresistible air of ridicule" surrounds Comte's religion and while "others may laugh . . . we could far rather weep at this melancholy decadence of a great intellect."

From the beginning of his systematic thought, Comte undoubtedly considered the goal of his positive science the creation of a "sound philosophy, capable of supplying the foundation of true religion." However, there is equally no doubt that his later writings were influenced by his emotional crisis following his intense love affair with Clotilde de Vaux, his "incomparable angel." Their involvement, which lasted two years, from 1844 to 1846, and ended with her tragic death, led him to recognize the role that affection must play in life. Having earlier emphasized the role of the intellect, he now argued for the supremacy of the affections, claiming that "greater distinctness . . . is given to the truth that the affective element predominates in our nature." In this regard he now stated,

> Where the moral excellence of true Religion is illustrated, feeling takes the first place. The disastrous revolt of Reason against Feeling will never be terminated till the new Western priesthood can fully satisfy the claims of the modern intellect. But this being done, moral requirements at once reassume the place that belongs to them, since in the construction of a really complete synthesis, Love is naturally the one universal principle.

In light of this supremacy of feeling, it was the function of positivism to fashion "a system which regulates the whole course of our private and public existence, by bringing Feeling, Reason and Activity into permanent harmony." As love was the supreme moral principle, all thought or acts of the intellect must become subordinate to it, thereby making scientists philosophers, and philosophers priests. All of life was "a continuous and intense act of worship," and the truly human moral standard was that we should "live for others." The scientists would organize and rule society, and the philosopher-priests would exercise their influence over society by the organization of public worship and by controlling education. In this way Comte tried to achieve a modern version of the medieval separation between religious and political authority. In this way, too, morals would be independent of politics but would nevertheless be a constructive influence on the political and economic order.

The civil order would also reflect the forces of dynamic progress, particularly as this process showed had the movement from a *military* to an *industrial* basis. Comte considered that the military phase of history had much to do with developing the industrial power and organization of the modern state. Specifically, it forced people to bring together otherwise isolated material resources and human labor for the sake of survival. But now the habits of industry and discipline must be used for the sake of peace and internal order and civilization. The central aim of all human effort, Comte argued, must be the amelioration of the order of nature. Science helps us to understand nature so that we can alter it. Our worship of Humanity, the new God, was not solemn inactivity, as religion was previously. Instead, it was a *positive religion*, and "the object of worship is a Being [Humanity] whose nature is relative, modifiable and perfectible." We achieve progress through such worship, and progress is "development of Order under the influence of Love." In place of the theological theory of providence—or divine guidance—Comte stressed human effort. He stated that "we must look to our own unremitting activity for the only providence by which the rigor of our destiny can be alleviated."

Comte argued that human providence has four main divisions: Women are the *moral providence*, the priesthood the *intellectual providence*, the capitalists the *material providence*, and the workers the *general providence*. "The people," said Comte, "represent the activity of the Supreme Being, as women represent its sympathy, and philosophers its intellect." Of the capitalists, Comte said that they are "the nutritive reservoirs, the social efficiency of which mainly depends on their being concentrated in few hands." He added that only the influence of moral persuasion can regulate "their foolish and immoral pride." Inevitably, Comte's society would require that each person fulfill a special function by staying in the place most suited to his or her powers. Above all, there must be the supremacy of the intellectual elite, since only specialists can understand the technical problems of administering a complex society. For this reason, Comte thought it was just as senseless to permit the masses to freely inquire about matters of social and political administration as to allow them to voice their opinions about some technical matter in chemistry. These are both fields in which the masses lack proper information, and, therefore, he called for the abolition of the "vagabond liberty of individual minds."

Again, the success of the *religion of humanity* would require the stability of the family and the spirit of altruism and love. Comte would not accept the earlier theological appraisal of the depravity of humanity or the notion that altruism is incompatible with human nature. To Comte altruistic instincts were a matter of scientific fact. To support this contention, he cited Franz Joseph Gall, the founder of phrenology, who argued that there is an "organ" of benevolence in the brain. In addition, women would exert their creative function in the family and would spontaneously consecrate their "rational and imaginative faculties to the service of feeling." For Comte the very symbol of humanity on the *flag of positivism* was a young mother with her infant son—a final analogy between Christianity and the religion of humanity.

The more Comte concerned himself with the creation of a new religion, the further he seemed to depart from the principles of positivism. In the end he seems to be indicating the goal toward which society *ought* to be moving instead of describing the course that history *is* in fact taking. Comte's influence was soon eclipsed by the politically more captivating theories of Karl Marx. Nevertheless, he remains a leading figure in that impressive line of thinkers that began with Bacon and Hobbes and was followed by the empiricists Locke, Berkeley, and Hume, who came before him.

CHAPTER 16

Kierkegaard, Marx, and Nietzsche

T hroughout the nineteenth century the views of Kant, Hegel, and other German idealists had a strong impact not only on philosophy but also on religion, aesthetics, and the new field of psychology. These philosophers devised elaborate systems of thought and introduced complex philosophical vocabulary. While many philosophers embraced their views, three philosophers reacted quite critically to this trend, namely, Søren Kierkegaard (1813–1855), Karl Marx (1818–1883), and Friedrich Nietzsche (1844–1900). Though somewhat obscure figures in their own day, they each had a profound impact on intellectual thought in the following century. Kierkegaard rejected the system-building approach of Hegel and argued instead that the quest for truth involves personal choice, grounded in religious faith. Marx rejected the idealist direction of German philosophy and the entire capitalist economic structure of his time. Instead, he argued that laws governing the material world will eventually replace capitalism with a communist social system. Nietzsche rejected both religious and rational value systems and proposed in their place a morality grounded in individual choice. These three philosophers differ from each other on critical points such as the existence of God. Nevertheless, they share the conviction that nineteenth-century European culture was terribly dysfunctional. Further, they all argued that we will come to a proper understanding of human existence and society only when we radically break from prevailing cultural attitudes.

KIERKEGAARD

Kierkegaard's Life

Born in Copenhagen in 1813, Sören Kierkegaard spent his short life in a brilliant literary career, producing an extraordinary number of books before his death in 1855 at the age of 42. Although his writings were soon forgotten after his death, they had an enormous impact upon their rediscovery by German scholars in the early decades of the twentieth century. At the University of Copenhagen,

Kierkegaard was trained in Hegel's philosophy but was not favorably impressed by it. When he heard Schelling's lectures at Berlin, which were critical of Hegel, Kierkegaard agreed with this attack on Germany's greatest speculative thinker. "If Hegel had written the whole of his Logic and then said . . . that it was merely an experiment in thought," Kierkegaard wrote, "then he could certainly have been the greatest thinker who ever lived. As it is, he is merely comic." What made Hegel comic for Kierkegaard was that this great philosopher tried to capture all of reality in his system of thought and, in the process, lost the most important element, namely, *existence*. Kierkegaard reserved the term *existence* for the individual human being. To exist, he said, implies being a certain kind of individual, an individual who strives, who considers alternatives, who chooses, who decides, and who, above all, makes a commitment. Virtually none of these acts were implied in Hegel's philosophy. Kierkegaard's whole career might well be considered a self-conscious revolt against abstract thought and an attempt on his part to live up to Feuerbach's admonition: "Do not wish to be a philosopher in contrast to being a man . . . do not think as a thinker . . . think as a living, real being . . . think in Existence."

Human Existence

To think in terms of existence meant for Kierkegaard to recognize that we face personal choices. For this reason our thinking ought to deal with our own personal situations and the crucial decisions that we invariably make. Hegel's philosophy falsified people's understanding of reality because it shifted attention away from the concrete individual to the concept of universals. It called upon individuals *to think* instead of *to be*—to think the Absolute Thought instead of being involved in decisions and commitments. Kierkegaard distinguished between the *spectator* and the *actor*, arguing that only the actor is involved in existence. To be sure, we can say that the spectator exists, but the term *existence* does not properly belong to inert or inactive things, whether these are spectators or stones. He illustrated this distinction by comparing two kinds of people in a wagon, one who holds the reins in his hand but is asleep and the other who is fully awake. In the first case the horse goes along the familiar road without any direction from the sleeping man, whereas in the other case the man is truly a driver. Surely, in one sense we can say that both men exist, but Kierkegaard insists that *existence* must refer to a quality in the individual, namely, his conscious participation in an act. Only the conscious driver exists, and so, too, only a person who is engaged in conscious activity of will and choice can be truly said to exist. Thus, while both the spectator and the actor exist in a sense, only the actor is involved in existence.

Kierkegaard's criticism of rational knowledge was severe. He revolted against the rational emphasis in classic Greek thought, which, he charged, permeated subsequent philosophy and Christian theology. His specific argument was that Greek philosophy was too greatly influenced by a high regard for mathematics. Although he did not want to reject either mathematics or science in their proper uses, he did reject the assumption that the type of thought characteristic of science could be successfully employed when trying to understand human nature. Mathematics and science have no place for the human individual; their value is only for the general and universal. Likewise, Plato's philosophy emphasized the universal, the Form, the True, the Good. Plato's whole assumption was that if we *knew* the Good we would do it. Kierkegaard thought that such an approach to ethics was a falsification of people's real predicament. Instead, Kierkegaard underscored that even when we have knowledge we are still in the predicament of having to make a decision. In the long run the grand formulations of philosophical systems are only prolonged detours that eventually come to nothing unless they lead attention back once again to the individual. Mathematics and science can undoubtedly solve some problems, as can ethics and metaphysics. But over against such universal or general problems stands life—each person's life—which makes demands upon us. At these critical moments abstract thought does not help.

Kierkegaard saw in the biblical story of Abraham the typical human condition: After trying for many years to conceive a child, Abraham and his wife, Sarah, finally produce Isaac, the fulfillment of their life's dreams. God, then, approaches Abraham and tells him to kill his son as a human sacrifice. What kind of knowledge can help Abraham decide whether to obey God? The most poignant moments in life are personal, when we become aware of ourselves as a subject. Rational thought obscures and even denies this subjective element since it only considers our objective characteristics—those characteristics that *all* people have in common. But subjectivity is what makes up each of our unique existences. For this reason objectivity cannot give the whole truth about our individual selves. That is why rational, mathematical, and scientific thought are incapable of guiding us to a genuine existence.

Truth as Subjectivity

Truth, Kierkegaard said, *is* subjectivity. By this strange notion he meant that there is no prefabricated truth "out there" for people who make choices. As American philosopher William James similarly said, "Truth is made" by an act of will. For Kierkegaard, what is "out there" is only "an objective uncertainty." Whatever may have been his criticism of Plato, he did nevertheless find in Socrates's claim to ignorance a good example of this notion of truth. Accordingly, he says that "the Socratic ignorance which Socrates held fast with the entire passion of his personal experience, was thus an expression of the principle that the eternal truth is related to the Existing individual." This suggests that mental cultivation is not the only important or decisive thing in life. Of more consequence is the development and maturity of our personalities.

In describing the human situation, Kierkegaard distinguished between what we now *are* and what we *ought to be*. That is, there is a movement from our *essence* to our *existence*. Developing this notion, he draws on the traditional theological notion that our sins separate us from God. Our essential human nature involves a relation to God, and our existential condition is a consequence of our alienation from God. If my sinful actions drive me even further from

God, then my alienation and despair are further compounded. Sensing our insecurity and finitude, we try to "do something" to overcome our finitude, and invariably what we do only aggravates our problem by adding guilt and despair to our anxiety. For example, we might try to find some meaning for our lives by losing ourselves in a crowd, whether it is a group of political affiliates or even a congregation in a church. In every case, Kierkegaard says, "a crowd in its very concept is the untruth, by reason of the fact that it renders the individual completely impenitent and irresponsible, or at least weakens his sense of responsibility by reducing it to a fraction." Being in a crowd only dilutes our selves and thereby undoes our nature. The real solution, for Kierkegaard, is to relate ourselves to God rather than to groups of people. Until we do this, our lives will be full of anxiety. Shifting our orientation toward God, though, is often a tricky process, which Kierkegaard describes in terms of "stages on life's way."

The Aesthetic Stage

Kierkegaard's analysis of the "three stages" stands in sharp contrast to Hegel's theory of the gradual development of a person's self-consciousness. Hegel expounded the dialectic movement of the mind as we move from one stage of intellectual awareness to another through the process of thinking. Kierkegaard, though, describes the movement of the self from one level of existence to another through an act of choice. Hegel's dialectic moved gradually toward a knowledge of the universal, whereas Kierkegaard's dialectic involves the progressive actualization of the individual. And whereas Hegel overcame the antithesis by a conceptual act, Kierkegaard overcomes it by the act of personal commitment.

The first stage in this dialectic process, Kierkegaard says, is the *aesthetic stage*. At this level I would behave according to my impulses and emotions. Although I am not simply sensual at this stage, I am for the most part governed by my senses. For this reason I would know nothing of any universal moral standards. I have no specific religious belief. My chief motivation is a desire to enjoy the widest variety of pleasures of the senses. My life has no principle of limitation except my own taste; I resent anything that would limit my vast freedom of choice. At this stage I can *exist* inasmuch as I deliberately choose to be an aesthetic person. But even though I can achieve some existence at this level, it is a rather poor quality of existence. Even though I may be fully consumed by my aesthetic way of life, I am still aware that my life ought to consist of more than this.

According to Kierkegaard we must distinguish between our capacity for *spirituality*, on the one hand, and *sensuousness,* on the other. Our spiritual capacity, he believed, builds on the sensuous. To be able to make this distinction about someone else is one thing. However, when we are aware of these two possibilities within ourselves, this triggers a dialectic movement within us. The antithesis of the sensual drive is the lure of the spirit. In experience this conflict produces anxiety and despair when we discover that we are in fact living in the "cellar" of sensuousness and that life at this level cannot possibly result in true existence. I am now face to face with an *either-or* decision: Either I remain at the aesthetic level with its fatal attractions and inherent limitations, or I move to the next stage. I cannot make this transition by thinking alone, Kierkegaard maintains, but must instead make a commitment through an act of will.

The Ethical Stage

The second level is the *ethical stage*. Unlike the aesthetic person, who has no universal standards but only his or her own taste, the ethical person does recognize and accept rules of conduct that reason formulates. On this level moral rules give my life the elements of form and consistency. Moreover, as an ethical person I accept the limitations that moral responsibility imposes on my life. Kierkegaard illustrates the contrast between the aesthetic person and the ethical person in their specific attitudes toward sexual behavior. Whereas the aesthetic person gives in to impulses wherever there is an attraction, the ethical person accepts the obligations of marriage as an expression of reason. If Don Juan exemplifies the aesthetic person, it is Socrates who typifies the ethical person or the reign of universal moral law.

As an ethical person I have the attitude of moral self-sufficiency. I take firm stands on moral questions, and, as Socrates argued, I assume that to know the good is to do the good. For the most part I consider moral evil to be a product either of ignorance or of weakness of will. But the time comes, Kierkegaard says, when the dialectic process begins to work in the consciousness of the ethical person. I then begin to realize that I am involved in something more profound than an inadequate knowledge of the moral law or insufficient strength of will. I am doing something more serious than merely making mistakes. I ultimately come to realize that I am in fact incapable of fulfilling the moral law, and I even deliberately violate that law. I thus become conscious of my guilt and sin. Guilt, Kierkegaard says, becomes a dialectic antithesis that places before me a new *either-or*. Now I must either remain at the ethical level and try to fulfill the moral law or respond to my new awareness. This specifically involves an awareness of my own finitude and estrangement from God to whom I belong and from whom I must derive my strength. Again, my movement from the ethical to the next stage can be achieved not by thinking alone but by an act of commitment—that is, by a leap of faith.

The Religious Stage

When we arrive at the third level—the *religious stage*—the difference between faith and reason is particularly striking. My movement from the aesthetic to the ethical level required an act of choice and commitment. It ushered me into the presence of reason insofar as the moral law is an expression of universal reason. But the movement from the ethical to the religious level is quite different. The leap of faith does not bring me into the presence of a God whom I can rationally and objectively describe as the Absolute and Knowable Truth. Instead, I am in the presence of a Subject. Accordingly, I cannot pursue God in an "objective way" or "bring God to light objectively." This, Kierkegaard says, "is in all eternity impossible because God is subject, and therefore exists only for subjectivity in inwardness." At the ethical level it is possible for me to give my life, as Socrates did, for the moral law that I rationally understand. But when it is a question of my relation to God, I have no rational or objective knowledge about this relationship.

The relationship between God and each individual is a unique and subjective experience. There is no way, prior to the actual relationship, to get any knowledge about it. Any attempt to get objective knowledge about it is entirely an *approximation process*. Only an act of faith can assure me of my personal relation to God. As I discover the inadequacy of my existence at the aesthetic and ethical levels, self-fulfillment in God becomes clear to me. Through despair and guilt I am brought to the decisive moment in life when I confront the final *either-or* of faith. I experience my self-alienation and thereby become aware that God exists. A paradox of faith arises when I see that God has revealed himself in a finite human being, namely, Jesus. It is in fact an extraordinary affront to human reason to say that God, the infinite, is revealed in Jesus, the finite. Kierkegaard writes that this paradox is "to the Jews a stumbling block and to the Greeks foolishness." Nevertheless, for Kierkegaard there is only one way to cross the span between human beings and God, which is an "infinite qualitative distinction between time and eternity." It is not through speculative reason— not even Hegel's. Instead, it is through faith, which is a subjective matter and a consequence of commitment, and this will always involve some risk.

Kierkegaard's philosophy can be summed up in his statement "Every human being must be assumed in essential possession of what essentially belongs to being a human." This being the case, "the task of the subjective thinker is to transform himself into an instrument that clearly and definitely expresses in existence whatever is essentially human." In short, each person possesses an essential self, which he or she *ought* to actualize. This essential self is fixed by the very fact that human beings must inescapably become related to God. To be sure, we can *exist* at any one of the three stages along life's way. But the experience of despair and guilt creates in us an awareness of qualitative differences in various types of existence. We also become aware that some types of human existence are more authentic than others. But arriving at authentic existence is not an intellectual matter. Instead, it is a matter of faith and commitment and a continuous process of choice in the presence of varieties of *either-or*.

MARX

Marxism provided the official philosophical point of view for at least one-third of the world's population in the second half of the twentieth century. When we consider that Marx spent a considerable portion of his adult life in relative obscurity, it is all the more remarkable that his views should have achieved such immense influence for several generations. He rarely spoke in public, and when he did, he displayed none of the attributes of the captivating orator. He was primarily a thinker, thoroughly absorbed in the task of elaborating the intricate details of a theory whose broad outlines he grasped as a young man while still in his twenties. He rarely mingled with the masses whose status occupied the center of his theoretical concern. Although he wrote an enormous amount, his writings were not read extensively during his lifetime. For example, we find no reference to Marx in the social and political writings of his famed contemporary John Stuart Mill. Nor was what Marx said entirely original. We can find much of his economic thought in Ricardo, some of his philosophical assumptions and apparatus in Hegel and Feuerbach, the view that history is shaped by the conflict between social classes in Saint-Simon, and the labor theory of value in Locke. What was original in Marx was that out of all these sources he distilled a unified scheme of thought, which he fashioned into a powerful instrument of social analysis and social revolution.

Marx's Life and Influences

Karl Heinrich Marx was born in Trier, Germany, in 1818, the oldest son of a Jewish lawyer and the descendant of a long line of rabbis. In spite of his Jewish lineage, he was brought up as a Protestant after his father became a Lutheran, for apparently practical reasons rather than religious convictions. The elder Marx had a strong influence on his son's intellectual development through his own rational and humanitarian inclinations. Young Marx was also influenced by Ludwig von Westphalen, a neighbor and distinguished Prussian government official and his future father-in-law. Westphalen stimulated his interest in literature and a lifelong respect for the Greek poets as well as Dante and Shakespeare. After high school in Trier, Marx went to the University of Bonn in 1835 and began the study of law at the age of 17. A year later he transferred to the University of Berlin, giving up the study of law and pursuing instead the study of philosophy. In 1841, at the age of 23, he received his doctoral degree from the University of Jena, for which he wrote a dissertation titled *On the Difference between the Democritean and Epicurean Philosophies of Nature*.

At the University of Berlin, the dominant intellectual influence was the philosophy of Hegel, and Marx was deeply impressed by Hegel's idealism and his dynamic view of history. He became a member of a group of young radical Hegelians who saw in Hegel's approach to philosophy the key to a new understanding of human nature, the world, and history. Hegel centered his thought around the notion of *Spirit* or *Mind*. To him, Absolute Spirit or Mind is God. God is the whole of reality. God is identical with all of nature, and therefore, God is found also in the configurations of culture and civilization. History consists in the gradual self-realization of God in the sequence of time. What makes Nature knowable is that its essence is Mind, and what produces history is the continuous struggle of Mind to realize itself in perfect form. Thus, God and the world are one. The basic reality is, therefore, Spirit or Mind. Moreover, Hegel argued, the political dimension of reality, the Idea, is in a continuous process of unfolding from lower to higher degrees of perfection, and this is the process we know as *history*. History is a dialectic process moving in a triadic pattern from *thesis* to *antithesis* and finally to *synthesis*.

Whether Marx ever accepted Hegel's idealism in all its fullness is not certain. But what did strike him with force was Hegel's method of identifying God and Nature or the world. Hegel said that "Spirit [God] is alone reality. It is the inner being of the world, that which essentially is and is *per se.*" Whatever there is, and whatever there is to know, exists as the world of nature. Besides the world and its history, there is nothing. This rejection of the older theology, which separated God and the world, is what struck Marx as being so novel and significant. Although Hegel did not intend his views to destroy the foundations of religion, a radical young group of Hegelians at the University of Berlin undertook a "higher criticism" of the Gospels. David Strauss wrote a critical *Life of Jesus* in which he argued that much of Jesus's teaching was a purely mythical invention, particularly those portions that referred to another world. Bruno Bauer went even further by denying the historical existence of Jesus. Following the Hegelian method of identifying God and the world, these radical writers shattered the literal interpretation of the language of the Gospels and considered its only value to lie in its pictorial power, not in its truth. The inevitable drift of Hegelianism was to identify God with human beings, since people, among all things in Nature, embody the element of Spirit or Mind in a unique way. It was then only another step to the position of philosophical atheism, which Hegel himself did not take, but which Marx and others did.

Three components of Hegel's philosophy had a direct impact on Marx. First is the notion that there is only one reality, and this can be discovered as the embodiment of rationality in the world. Second is the recognition that history is a process of development and change from less to more perfect forms in all of reality, including physical nature, social and political life, and human thought. Third is the assumption that the thoughts and behavior of people at any given time and place are caused by the operation in them of an identical spirit or mind, the spirit of the particular time or epoch. Although these were the general themes that Hegelianism seemed to stimulate in Marx's thinking, other influences caused him to reject or reinterpret portions of Hegel's philosophy. For example, shortly after Marx finished his doctoral dissertation, the appearance of Ludwig Feuerbach's writings had a decisive effect on the young radical Hegelians, and especially on Marx.

Feuerbach took the Hegelian viewpoint to its extreme conclusion and thereby criticized the very foundation of Hegelianism itself. He did this by rejecting Hegel's idealism, substituting the view that basic reality is material. In short, Feuerbach revived philosophical materialism, and Marx instantly felt that this explained human thought and behavior much better than did Hegel's idealism. Hegel saw the thought and behavior of a particular epoch as the working in all people of an identical spirit. Feuerbach now contended that, on the contrary, the generating influence of people's thoughts was the total sum of the material circumstances of any historical time.

Feuerbach thus rejected Hegel's assumption of the primacy of Spirit and substituted for it the primacy of the material order. He developed this with particular force in the *Essence of Christianity*, in which he argued that human beings and not God are the basic reality. When we analyze our ideas of God,

Feuerbach said, we find no ideas of God beyond our human feelings and wants. All so-called knowledge of God, he said, is only knowledge about people. God, therefore, is humanity. Our various ideas of God simply reflect types of human existence. Thus, God is the product of human thought and not the other way around. In this way Feuerbach inverted Hegel's idealism, and the resulting materialism struck a fire within Marx and provided him with one of the most decisive and characteristic elements in his own philosophy.

Marx now acknowledged that Feuerbach was the pivotal figure in philosophy. Most importantly, Feuerbach shifted the focal point of historical development from God to human beings. That is, whereas Hegel said that it was Spirit that was progressively realizing itself in history, Feuerbach said that it is really human beings who are struggling to realize themselves. People, and not God, are in some way alienated from themselves, and history has to do with our struggle to overcome self-alienation. Clearly, if this was in fact the human condition, Marx thought, the world should be changed in order to facilitate human self-realization. This is what led Marx to say that hitherto "the philosophers have only *interpreted* the world differently: the point is, however, to *change* it." Marx thus grounded his thought in two major insights: (1) Hegel's dialectic view of history and (2) Feuerbach's emphasis on the primacy of the material order. Now he was ready to forge these ideas into a full-scale instrument of social analysis and, most importantly, to lay out a vigorous and practical plan of action.

At the age of 25, Marx left Berlin and went to Paris, where he and some friends undertook the publication of the radical, periodical *Deutsch-Französiche Jahrbücher*. In Paris, Marx met many radicals, revolutionaries, and utopian thinkers and confronted the ideas of such people as Fourier, Proudhon, Saint-Simon, and Bakunin. Of lasting significance was his meeting with Friedrich Engels, the son of a German textile manufacturer, with whom Marx was to have a long and intimate association. Apart from his progressively deeper involvement in practical social action through his journalism, Marx was greatly preoccupied in Paris with the question of why the French Revolution had failed. He wanted to know whether it was possible to discover any reliable laws of history in order to avoid mistakes in future revolutionary activity. He read extensively on this subject and discovered several promising answers. He was particularly impressed by Saint-Simon's account of class conflict, which led Marx to focus on the classes not only as the parties to conflict but also as the bearers of the material and economic realities in which their lives are set. What Marx began to see was that revolutions do not succeed if they consist only in romantic ideas while overlooking the realities of the material order. But it was only a year after Marx arrived in Paris that he was expelled from the city, and for the next three years, from 1845 to 1848, Marx and his family settled in Brussels. Here he helped to organize a German Worker's Union. At a meeting in London in 1847, this group united with similar European organizations and formed an international Communist League. The first secretary was Engels. The league asked Marx to formulate a statement of principles. This appeared in 1848 under the title *Manifesto of the Communist Party*.

From Brussels he returned to Paris briefly to participate in some revolutionary activities but was again required to leave. This time, in the autumn of 1849, he went to London, where he would spend the rest of his life. England at this time was not ripe for revolutionary activity, since there was no widespread organization of the mass of workers. Marx himself became an isolated figure, prodigiously studying and writing. Each day he went to the reading room of the British Museum, working there from nine in the morning until seven at night with additional hours of work after he returned to his bleak two-room apartment in the cheap Soho district of London. His poverty was deeply humiliating. But he was driven with such single-mindedness to produce his massive books that he could not deviate from this objective to provide his family with more adequate facilities. In addition to his poverty, he was afflicted with a liver ailment and plagued with boils. In this environment his 6-year-old son died, and his beautiful wife's health failed. Some financial help came from Engels and from his writing regular articles on European affairs for the *New York Daily Tribune*.

Under these incredible circumstances Marx produced many notable works, including his first systematic work on economics, which he called the *Critique of Political Economy* (1859). The most important of these is his massive *The Capital (Das Kapital)*, whose first volume he published in 1867 and whose second and third volumes were assembled from his manuscripts after his death and published by Engels in 1885 and 1894. Although Marx supplied the theoretical basis for the Communist movement, he participated less and less in the practical activities that he urged. Still, he had a lively hope that the great revolution would come and that his prediction of the downfall of capitalism would become a fact. But in the last decade of his life, as his name became famous around the world, he became less productive. In 1883, two years after his wife died and only two months after his eldest daughter's death, Karl Marx died of pleurisy in London, at the age of 65.

Marx often protested that he was not a "Marxist," and not every idea or every strategy utilized by world communism can rightly be ascribed to him. There is, nevertheless, a central core of thought, which constitutes the essence of Marxist philosophy and which Marx formulated in the highly charged intellectual atmosphere of the mid-nineteenth-century Europe of which he was a part. This core of Marxist thought consists in the analysis of four basic elements; (1) the major epochs of history, (2) the causal power of the material order, (3) the alienation of labor, and (4) the source and role of ideas. We will look at each of these in turn.

The Epochs of History: Marx's Dialectic

In his *Communist Manifesto* Marx formulated his basic theory, which he considered in many ways original. "What I did that was new," he said, "was to prove (1) that the *existence of classes* is only bound up with particular historic phases in the development of production; (2) that the class struggle necessarily leads to the dictatorship of the proletariat; (3) that the dictatorship itself only constitutes the transition to the *abolition of all classes* and to a classless society." Later, while in London, he worked out his argument in painstaking detail, which he thought provided scientific support for the more general pronouncements in his *Manifesto*. Accordingly, he stated in the preface to *The Capital* that "it is the ultimate aim of this work to lay bare the economic law of motion of modern society." This law of motion became his theory of dialectical materialism.

The Five Epochs   Marx showed that class struggle is bound up with "particular historic phases." He distinguished five such phases or epochs: (1) primitive communal, (2) slave, (3) feudal, (4) capitalist, and, as a prediction of things to come, (5) socialist and communist. For the most part this was a conventional division of Western social history into its major periods. But what Marx wanted to do was to discover the "law of motion." These would explain not only *that* history produced these various epochs but the *reasons why* these particular epochs unfolded as they did. If he could discover history's law of motion, he could not only explain the past but predict the future. He assumed that the behavior of individuals and societies is subject to the same kind of analysis as are the objects of physical and biological science. He considered the commodity and value products of economics as being "of the same order as those [minute elements] dealt with in microscopic anatomy." When analyzing the structure of each historical epoch, he viewed these as the result of conflict between social classes. In time this conflict itself would have to be analyzed in more detail. Now he looked upon history as the product of conflict and relied heavily upon the Hegelian concept of *dialectic* to explain it.

Of course, Marx rejected Hegel's idealism, but he accepted the general theory of the dialectic movement of history, which Hegel proposed. Hegel argued that ideas develop in a dialectic way, through the action and reaction of thought. He described this dialectic process as a movement from *thesis* to *antithesis* and then to *synthesis*, where the synthesis becomes a new thesis, and the process goes on and on. In addition, Hegel said that the external social, political, and economic world is simply the embodiment of people's (and God's) ideas. The development or the movement of the external world is the result of the prior development of ideas. Marx, again, considered Hegel's notion of dialectic a crucial tool for understanding history. But, through the powerful influence of Feuerbach, Marx supplied a materialistic basis for the dialectic. Accordingly, Marx said that "my dialectic method is not only different from the Hegelian, but is its direct opposite. To Hegel, the process of thinking . . . is the [creator] of the real world." However, to Marx, "the ideal is nothing else than the material world reflected by the human mind, and translated into forms of thought." According to Marx, we are to see history as a movement caused by conflicts in the material order, and for this reason history is a *dialectical materialism*.

Change: Quantitative and Qualitative   History shows that social and economic orders are in an ongoing process of change. Marx's dialectical materialism maintains further that material order is primary, since matter is the basis of what is truly real. He rejected the notion that somewhere there are stable, permanent structures of reality or certain "eternal verities." Instead, everything is involved in the dialectic process of change. Nature, he argued, "from the smallest thing to the biggest, from a grain of sand to the sun . . . to man, is in . . . a ceaseless state of movement and change." History is the process of change from one epoch to another in accordance with the rigorous and inexorable laws of historical motion.

For Marx change is not the same thing as mere growth. A society does not simply mature the way a child becomes an adult. Nor does nature simply move in an eternally uniform and constantly repeated circle. It passes through a real history. Change means the emergence of new structures and novel forms. What causes change is simply alteration in the *quantity* of things, which leads to something *qualitatively* new. For example, as I increase the temperature of water, it not only becomes warmer but finally reaches the point at which this quantitative change changes it from a liquid into a vapor. Reversing the process, by gradually decreasing the temperature of water, I finally change it from a liquid to solid ice. Similarly, I can make a large pane of glass vibrate, the range of the vibrations increasing as the quantity of force applied to it is increased. But finally, a further addition of force will no longer add to the quantity of vibration but will, instead, cause a qualitative change—the shattering of the glass. Marx thought that history displays this kind of change, by which certain quantitative elements in the economic order finally force a qualitative change in the arrangements of society. This is the process that moved history from the primitive communal to the slave and in turn to the feudal and capitalist epochs.

Marx's prediction that the capitalist order would fall was based on this notion that the changes in the quantitative factors in capitalism would inevitably destroy capitalism. He describes the development of these epochs with the low-key style of someone describing how water will turn into steam as heat is increased. He writes in *The Capital* that "while there is a progressive diminution in the number of capitalist owners, there is of course a corresponding increase in the mass of poverty, enslavement, degeneration and exploitation, but at the same time a steady intensification of the role of the working class." Then "the centralization of the means of production and the socialization of labor reach a point where they prove incompatible with their capitalist husk. This bursts asunder. The knell of private property sounds. The expropriators are expropriated." This, on the social level, is what Marx describes as the *quantitative leap*, which is "the leap to a new aggregate state . . . where consequently quantity is transformed into quality."

Determinism or Inexorable Law   There is a basic difference between the transformation of water into steam in a laboratory experiment and the movement of society from capitalism to socialism. The difference is that I can *choose* to raise or not to raise the temperature of the water. But there are no such hypothetical qualifications surrounding history. Though I can say, "*if* the temperature is raised," I cannot say, "*if* the social order is thus and so." Marxism holds that there is a fundamental "contradiction within the very essence of things" causing the dialectic movement. Although there are ways to delay or accelerate this inner movement in the nature of things, there is no way to prevent its ultimate unfolding. All things are related to each other *causally;* nothing floats freely. For this reason there are no isolated events either in physical nature or in human behavior or, therefore, in history. That there is a definite and inexorable process of movement and change at work producing "history" is, for Marx, as certain as the plain fact that nature exists.

There is an important distinction that we should make when claiming, as Marx does, that all things behave in accordance with a principle of regularity and predictability. The laws of physics, for example, describe "mechanical determinism." History, on the other hand, displays a law of determinism but not in a strictly mechanical way. The movement of one billiard ball by another is the typical example of mechanical determinism. If we can locate an object in space and measure its distance from another object whose velocity can also be measured, it would then be possible to predict the time of the impact and the subsequent trajectories and rates of motion. This mechanical determinism is hardly applicable to such a complex phenomenon as a social order, which does not have the same kind of location in space and time. But society is nevertheless the result of necessary causation and determinism, and its new forms are capable of prediction just as submicroscopic particles are determined in quantum mechanics, even though there is only "probable" prediction regarding particular particles. Thus, although the specific history of a particular person cannot be predicted with any high degree of accuracy, we can plot the future state of a social order. From his analysis of the various epochs of history, Marx thought he had discovered the built-in law of change in nature—a kind of inexorable inner logic in events—causing history to move from one epoch to the next with a relentless determinism. From this basis he predicted that capitalism would inevitably be transformed by the wave of the future, giving way to the qualitatively different social order of socialism and communism.

The End of History   For Marx history will end with the emergence of socialism and, finally, communism. Here again, he followed Hegel's theory in an inverted way. For Hegel the dialectic process would come to an end when the idea of freedom was perfectly realized. By definition this would mean the end of all conflict and struggle. Marx, though, believed that the dialectic struggle of opposites was in the material order, particularly in the struggle between the classes. When the inner contradictions between the classes were resolved, the principal cause of movement and change would disappear. A classless society would then emerge where all the forces and interests would be in perfect balance, and this equilibrium would be perpetual. For this reason there could be no further development in history, inasmuch as there will no longer be any conflict to impel history on to any future epoch.

Marx's theory of the dialectic development of the five epochs of history rests, on a close relation between the order of material reality, on the one hand, and the order of human thought, on the other. Marx was convinced that the only way to achieve a realistic understanding of history, and therefore to avoid errors in the practical plan of revolutionary activity, was to assess properly the roles of the material order and the order of human thought. Accordingly, he made a sharp distinction between the *substructure* and the *superstructure* of society. The *substructure* is the material order, containing the energizing force that moves history, whereas the *superstructure* consists in people's ideas and simply reflects the configurations of the material order.

The Substructure: The Material Order

According to Marx, the material world consists of the sum total of the natural environment, and this included for him all of inorganic nature, the organic world, social life, and human consciousness. Unlike Democritus, who defined matter in terms of irreducible tiny atoms, Marx defines matter as "objective reality existing outside the human mind." Again, unlike Democritus, who considered atoms to be the "bricks of the universe," Marxist materialism does not take this approach of trying to discover a single form of matter in all things. The chief characteristic of Marxist materialism is that it recognizes a wide diversity in the material world without reducing it to any one form of matter. The material order contains everything in the natural world that exists outside of our minds. The notion that any spiritual reality—God, for example—exists outside our minds and as something other than nature is denied. That human beings possess minds means only that organic matter has developed to the point where the cerebral cortex has become the organ capable of the intricate process of reflex action called human thought. Moreover, the human mind has been conditioned by the labor activity of humans as social beings. For this reason, relying on the Darwinian notion of human evolution, Marxism affirms the primacy of the material order and regards mental activity as a secondary by-product of matter. The earliest forms of life were without mental activity until human ancestors developed the use of their forelimbs, learned to walk erect, and began to use natural objects as tools to procure food and to protect themselves. The big transformation from animal to human being came with the ability to fashion and use tools and to control forces such as fire. This in turn made possible a wider variety of food and the further development of the brain. Even now, the complex material order is the basic reality, whereas the mental realm is a derivative. In particular, the material order consists of (1) the *factors* of production and (2) the *relations* of production.

The Factors of Production   The basic fact of human life is that in order to live people must secure food, clothing, and shelter. To have these material things, people must produce them. Wherever we find any society of people, there is always at hand the factors of production—the raw materials, instruments, and the experienced labor skill—by which to sustain life. But these factors or forces of production represent chiefly the way people are related to these material things. Of greater importance is the way we are related to each other in the process of production. Marx emphasized that production always takes place as a social act, whereby people struggle against and utilize nature not as individuals but as groups and societies. For Marx, then, the static analysis of what goes into production was not as important as the dynamic relations of people to each other as a producing society. To be sure, Marx felt that the factors of production affected the relations of production. For example, the scarcity of raw materials could have a considerable effect on the way people related to each other in the process of production. In any case, Marx centered his analysis of the material order on the way that people engaged in the act of production—on the *relations of production*.

The Relations of Production   Marx believed that his explanation of the relations of production is the core of his social analysis. It was here that he thought he located the energizing force of the dialectic process. The key to the relations of production is the status of property or its ownership. That is, what determines how people are related to each other in the process of production is their relation to property. Under the slave system, for example, slave owners owned the means of production, even owning the slaves, whom they could purchase or sell. The institution of slavery was a necessary product of the dialectic process, since it arose at a time when advanced forms of tools made possible more stable and sustained agricultural activity and a division of labor. But in the slave epoch, as well as in the subsequent historical epochs, laborers are "exploited" in that they share in neither the ownership nor in the fruits of production. The basic struggle between the classes is seen already in the slave system. For the ownership of property divides society between those who have and those who do not. In the feudal system the feudal lord owns the means of production. The serfs rise above the level of the former slaves and have some share in the ownership of tools, but they still work for the feudal lord and, Marx says, feel exploited and struggle against their exploiter. In capitalism the workers are free as compared with the slaves and the serfs, but they do not own the means of production, and in order to survive, they must sell their labor to the capitalist.

The shift from slave to feudal to capitalist relations of production is not the result of rational design but is a product of the inner movement and logic of the material order. Specifically, the impelling force to survive leads to the creation of tools, and in turn, the kinds of tools created affect the way people relate to each other. Thus, whereas certain tools, such as the bow and arrow, permit independent existence, the plough logically implies a division of labor. Similarly, whereas a spinning wheel can be used in the home or in small shops, heavier machinery requires large factories and a new concentration of workers in a given locality. The process moves in a deterministic way, impelled by basic economic drives whose direction is set by the technological requirements of the moment. The thoughts and behavior of all people are determined by their relations to each other and to the means of production. Although in all periods there is a conflict and struggle between the different classes, the class struggle is particularly violent under capitalism.

There are at least three characteristics of class struggle under capitalism. First, the classes are reduced basically to two—the owners (*bourgeoisie*) and the workers (*proletariat*). Second, the relations of those classes to each other rest on a fundamental contradiction, namely, that although both classes participate in the act of production, the type of distribution of the fruits of production does not correspond to the contribution made by each class. The reason for this discrepancy is that the forces of supply and demand determine the price of labor in the capitalist system, and the large supply of workers tends to push wages down to a subsistence level. But the products created by labor can be sold for more than it costs to hire the labor force. Marx's analysis assumed the labor theory of value, namely, that the value of the product is created by the amount of labor put into it. From this point of view, since the product of labor could be sold for more than the cost of labor, the capitalist would then reap the difference, which Marx called *surplus value*. The existence of surplus value constituted a contradiction in the capitalistic system for Marx. For this reason, Marx argued that in the capitalistic system exploitation was not merely an isolated occurrence here or there, now or then. Instead, it existed always and everywhere because of the manner in which the iron law of wages operates. Still, Marx made no moral judgment of this condition, saying that as a matter of fact workers received what they were worth if the determination of the wage through the supply and demand of labor is the norm. "It is true," he said, "that the daily maintenance of labor power costs only half a day's labor, and that nevertheless the labor power can work for an entire working day, with the result that the value which its use creates during a working day is twice the value of a day's labor power. So much the better for the purchaser, but it is nowise an injustice to the seller [worker]."

In a sense Marx did not "blame" the capitalist for this arrangement. These are rather the consequences of the material forces of history. Labor became a coherent group only because large-scale machinery required large factories, and suddenly the multitude of workers who were required to run the machines found themselves living close together. That history produced the capitalist system was one thing, but that it rested on a contradiction was something else. For this reason Marx excused the capitalist. However, for scientific reasons he compelled to say that the class conflict caused by this contradiction of surplus value would force the dialectic movement to the next stage of history, namely, socialism and finally communism.

The third characteristic of this class struggle was the prediction that the condition of workers in capitalism would become progressively more wretched. The poor would become poorer and more numerous while the rich would become richer and fewer, until the masses would take over all the means of production. As long as the means of production remained in the hands of a few, the class struggle would continue inexorably until the contradiction was resolved, ending the dialectic movement. Meanwhile, the workers' lives would be terribly dehumanized by what Marx calls "the alienation of labor."

The Alienation of Labor

While still in his twenties, Marx produced a brief series of manuscripts called the *Economic and Philosophical Manuscripts of 1844*, first published in 1932. The key concept of these manuscripts is that of *alienation*, a theme that informs the whole system of Marx's thought. Although Marx was by no means the first to develop a theory of alienation, his views were unique because they were based on his particular economic and philosophical assumptions, which formed the basis of his criticism of capitalism.

If people are alienated—that is, estranged or separated—they must be alienated from something. In Christian theology people are alienated from God through sin and the fall of Adam. In a legal sense alienation means selling or giving something away, or as Kant says, "the transference of one's property to someone else is its alienation." In the course of time almost everything became a sellable object. Balzac said ironically that "even the Holy Spirit has its quotation on the Stock Exchange." For Marx there is something crucial within our human nature from which we can be alienated, namely, our work.

Marx describes four aspects of alienation. We are alienated (1) from *nature*, (2) from *ourselves*, (3) from our *species-being*, and (4) from *other people*. He begins with the fundamental relation between workers and the product of their labor. Originally, our relation to the product of our labor was quite intimate. We took things from the material world, shaped them, and made them our own. Capitalism, though, breaks this relationship by forcing us to forfeit the products of our labor in exchange for money. In the productive process our labor becomes as much an object as the physical material that is worked upon, since labor is now bought and sold. The more objects we produce, the fewer we can personally possess and therefore the greater is our loss. To the extent that we are embodied in my labor, we become alienated from the natural world in which we work. "The worker," says Marx, "puts his life into the object, and his life then belongs no longer to himself but to the object." The object is appropriated and owned by someone else. In this way the original relation between people and nature is destroyed.

We next become alienated from ourselves by participating in capitalist labor. This comes about because work is *external* to us and not part of our nature. Work is not voluntary but is imposed upon us. We have a feeling of misery instead of well-being. Rather than fulfilling ourselves, we must deny ourselves. We do not freely develop our physical and mental capacities but are instead physically exhausted and mentally debased. As a consequence, we feel like human beings only during our leisure hours. Most important of all, we are alienated from our work because it is not our own work but rather work for someone else. In this sense, as workers, we do not belong to themselves but to someone else, and we have more or less become prostitutes. The result is that a worker "feels himself to be freely active only in his animal functions—eating, drinking and procreating—or at most also in his dwelling and personal adornment—while in his human functions he is reduced to an animal." Although eating, drinking and procreating are genuine human functions, even these become animal functions when separated from our other human functions.

At still another level, we are alienated from our *species-being*—that is, from our truly human nature. The character of any species resides in the type of activity it expresses. The species-character of human beings is "free, conscious activity." By contrast, an animal cannot distinguish itself from its activity; the animal *is* its activity. But, Marx says, a person "makes his life activity itself an object of his will and consciousness." It is true that animals can produce nests and dwellings, as in the case of bees, ants, and beavers. But their production of these things is limited to what is strictly required for themselves or their young. We, on the other hand, produce universally—that is, in a manner that is applicable and understandable to all human beings. Also, whereas animals produce only under the compulsion of specific physical need, we produce our most distinctive products only when we are free from physical need. Animals reproduce only themselves, whereas we can produce a whole world, a world of art, science, and literature. Animals are limited in their activity to the standards of the species to which they belong. We, on the other hand, know how to produce in accordance with the standards of every species. For these reasons the whole object of our labor is to impose on the world of nature our species-life—our free, spontaneous, and creative activity. In this way we reproduce ourselves in the things we create, not only intellectually in the realm of ideas but also actively, seeing our own reflection in the physical world that we have created. This unique character of human species-life is lost when our labor is alienated. Just as we are removed from the object of our labor, so also are we stripped of our free and spontaneous activity and creativity. Our consciousness is now deflected from creativity and is focused to simply on the means to our individual existence.

This leads to our alienation from other people. The breakdown in our relations to other people is similar to our alienation from the objects of our labor. In an environment of alienated labor, we look upon other people from the point of view of workers. We see other workers as objects whose labor is bought and sold, and not as full members of the human species. To say, then, that our species-being species nature is alienated or estranged from ourselves means that we are estranged from other people.

Marx asks, "If the product of labor is alien to me . . . to whom does it belong?" In an earlier age, when temples were built in Egypt and India, people thought that the product belonged to the gods. But, Marx says, the alienated product of labor can belong only to some human being. If it does not belong to the worker, it must belong to a person other than the worker. Thus, as a result of alienated labor, workers produce a new relationship between themselves and another person, and this other person is the capitalist. The final product of alienated labor is private property. Private property, in the form of capitalist business, is both a product of alienated labor and the means by which labor is alienated. In the wage system entailed by private property, labor finds itself not as an end but as the servant of wages. Nor would a forced increase in wages restore to either the workers or to their work their human significance or value. As a statement of eventual liberation, Marx concludes that the freeing of society from private property involves the emancipation of the workers, which in turn will lead to the emancipation of humanity as a whole.

Marx was convinced that the dialectic process inevitably involves tragic conflicts. He saw in history the deep tension between forces that are incompatible, each exerting its power to overcome the other. The use of revolutionary force could hardly be avoided, but force could not bring into being simply any desired utopian system. Only the relations of production toward which the inner logic of the material order was driving in a determined way could be the objective of revolution. Even when a society is aware of its ultimate direction, this society "can neither clear by bold leaps, nor remove by legal enactments, the obstacles offered by the successive phases of its normal development." What, then, is the function of the revolutionary activities of the working classes? It is, Marx says, to "shorten and lessen the birth-pangs."

With this rigorous view of the nature of the class struggle, Marx clearly assigned to the material substructure the supreme significance in the dialectic process of history. What, then, is the status and role of human thought? Do ideas have power and consequences? For Marx ideas represent a mere reflection of the basic material reality, and so he described the enterprise of human thought as the *superstructure*.

The Superstructure: The Origin and Role of Ideas

Each epoch, said Marx, has its dominant ideas. People formulate ideas in the areas of religion, morality, and law. Hegel argued that people agree for the most part in their religious, moral, and legal thought because there is at work in them a universal Spirit, the Idea. Marx, on the contrary, said that the ideas of each epoch grow out of and reflect the actual material conditions of the historical period. For this reason thinking comes *after* the material order has affected people's minds. In Marx's words, "it is not the consciousness of people that determines their being, but, on the contrary, their social being that determines their consciousness."

The source of ideas is rooted in the material order. Ideas such as justice and goodness and even religious salvation are only various ways of rationalizing the existing order. Justice, for the most part, represents the will of the economically dominant class and its desire to "freeze" the relations of production as they are. Marx was impressed during his early years as a law student with the teachings of the jurist Savigny, who defined law as the "spirit" of each epoch. Savigny argued that law is like language and, therefore, is different for each society. Like Savigny, Marx rejected the notion of a universal and eternal norm of justice. In fact, he argued that if ideas simply reflect the inner order of the relations of production, each successive epoch will have its own set of ideas and its own dominant philosophy.

The conflict of ideas within a society at a given time is due to the dynamic nature of the economic order. The dialectic process, which is a struggle of opposites, has its material aspect but also its ideological side. Since members of a society are related to the dialectic process by belonging to different classes, their interests are different and, therefore, their ideas are opposed. Moreover, the greatest error, according to Marx, is to fail to realize that ideas that accurately reflected the material order at an earlier time no longer do so because, in the meantime, the substructure of reality has moved on. Those who hold onto old ideas wrongly believe that some reality still remains that corresponds to the old ideas. Their desire, then, to reverse the order of things to fit these ideas makes them "reactionaries." On the other hand, astute observers can discover the direction in which history is moving and adjust their thinking and behavior to it. The fact is, Marx says, that the dialectic process involves the disappearance of some things and the birth of others. That is why one epoch dies and another is born, and there is no way to stop the process. Those who assume the objective reality of eternal principles of justice, goodness, and righteousness do not realize that such notions cannot refer to reality since the material order, which is the only reality, is constantly changing. "The sum total of the productive relations," Marx says, "constitutes the economic structure of society—the real foundation on which rise legal and political superstructure . . . [and which] determines the general character of the social, political and spiritual processes of life."

Because he believed that ideas are chiefly a reflection of the material order, Marx attributed a limited role or function to them. Ideas are particularly useless when they bear no relationship to economic reality. Marx's impatience with reformers, do-gooders, and utopians was intense. He argued that ideas cannot determine the direction of history but can only hinder or accelerate the inexorable dialectic. For this reason Marx thought that his own ideas about capitalism did not constitute a moral condemnation. He did not say that capitalism was either wicked or due to human folly. It was simply caused by the "law of motion of society." In the end Marx assumed that he was proceeding in his analysis as a scientist, limiting his thought to objective reality, and abstracting from it the laws of motion.

NIETZSCHE

Nietzsche died on August 25, 1900, at the age of 55, leaving a legacy of brilliant writings whose impact and influence were delayed until the twentieth century. His life was full of sharp contrasts. The son and grandson of Lutheran ministers, he was nevertheless the herald of the judgment that "God is dead" and undertook a "campaign against morality." He was raised in an environment thoroughly dominated by females, yet his philosophy of the Superperson is anything but nurturing. He called for the fullest expression of human vitality in the name of the Will to Power, yet he believed that sublimation and control are the truly human characteristics. While his writings are lucid, he ended his days in hopeless insanity.

Nietzsche's Life

Named after the reigning king of Prussia, Friedrich Wilhelm Nietzsche was born in Röcken, in the province of Saxony, on October 15, 1844. His father died when he was 4 years old, and he grew up in a household consisting of his mother, sister, grandmother, and two maiden aunts. At age 14 he was sent to the famed boarding school at Pforta, where for six years he underwent a rigorous education, excelling particularly in the classics, religion, and German literature. It was here that he came under the spell of ancient Greek thought, discovering it especially in Aeschylus and Plato. In October 1864 he went to the University of Bonn but, unimpressed by the caliber of his fellow students, he stayed only one year. He decided to follow his excellent teacher of classics and philology,

Friedrich Ritschl, who accepted a chair at the University of Leipzig. While at Leipzig he came upon the main work of Schopenhauer, whose atheism and antirationalism deeply influenced Nietzsche for a while and confirmed his own rebellion against contemporary European culture, which he came to despise as decadent. It was here also that Nietzsche came under the spell of Richard Wagner's music. "I could not have stood my youth without Wagner's music," Nietzsche said later. "When one wants to rid oneself of an intolerable pressure, one needs hashish. Well, I needed Wagner."

When the University of Basel was looking for someone to fill the chair of philosophy, Nietzsche's name figured prominently. He had not yet completed his doctoral degree, but some of his published papers attracted notice for their exceptional scholarship. On the additional strength of his teacher's enthusiastic recommendation, Nietzsche was appointed a university professor at the age of 24. After the University of Basel confirmed his appointment, the University of Leipzig conferred the doctoral degree on Nietzsche without examination. In May 1869 he delivered his inaugural lecture on "Homer and Classical Philology." During his years at Basel, Nietzsche visited Wagner frequently at his villa on Lake Lucerne. While this friendship was not destined to last, Wagner did exert an influence on Nietzsche's thought in his first book, *The Birth of Tragedy from the Spirit of Music* (1872). Of longer duration was Nietzsche's friendship with his older colleague, the eminent historian Jacob Burckhardt, with whom he shared a fascination for ancient Greece and Renaissance Italy. Nietzsche's wretched health and his dislike of his duties at the university led him to resign his professorship in 1879 at the age of 34. For the next decade he wandered through Italy, Switzerland, and Germany searching for some place where his health might be restored. In spite of his poor health, he wrote several books during the six-year period from 1881 to 1887, including *The Dawn of Day, Joyful Wisdom*, the famous *Thus Spake Zarathustra, Beyond Good and Evil*, and *A Genealogy of Morals*.

In 1888, when he was 44, Nietzsche enjoyed a brief respite from his prolonged cycle of sickness and recovery. During a span of six months, he produced five books: *The Case of Wagner, The Twilight of the Idols, Antichrist, Ecce Homo*, and *Nietzsche contra Wagner*. Shortly thereafter, in January 1889, Nietzsche collapsed on a street in Turin. He was taken back to Basel to a clinic. From there he was sent to an asylum in Jena and finally to the care of his mother and sister. For the last eleven years of his life, Nietzsche was irretrievably insane as a result of an infection that affected his brain. He was thus unable to complete his projected major work, the *Revaluation of All Values*. Nietzsche's books have great vivacity of style and are written with a passionate intensity. Even though some of his later works show signs of impending difficulties, scholars generally agree that we should not discount his writings because of his subsequent mental collapse.

"God Is Dead"

Nietzsche wrote philosophy in a manner calculated more to provoke serious thought than to give formal answers to questions. In this regard he resembled Socrates and Plato more than Spinoza, Kant, or Hegel. He produced no formal system because system building, he thought, assumes that we have at hand self-evident truths on which to build. He also believed that building systems lacks integrity, since honest thought must challenge precisely these self-evident truths on which most systems are built. We must engage in dialectic and be willing at times to declare ourselves against our previous opinions. Moreover, most philosophic system builders, he thought, try to solve all problems at once by acting as the "unriddler of the universe." Nietzsche believed that philosophers must be less pretentious and pay more attention to questions of human values than to abstract systems. Philosophers should also focus on immediate human problems with an attitude of fresh experimentation and a freedom from the dominant values of their culture. Nietzsche took a variety of positions on important problems, and because of this it is easy to interpret his views in contradictory ways. Moreover, he expressed his views on issues with brief aphorisms instead of detailed analyses, leaving the impression of ambiguity and ambivalence. Still, Nietzsche formulated many distinctive views, which emerge from his writings with considerable clarity.

While others saw in nineteenth-century Europe the symbols of power and security, Nietzsche grasped with prophetic insight the imminent collapse of the traditional supports of the values to which modern people committed themselves. The Prussian army made Germany a great power on the Continent, and the astonishing advances in science further animated the feeling of optimism. Nevertheless, Nietzsche boldly prophesied that power politics and bloody wars were in store for the future. He sensed an approaching period of *nihilism*, the seeds of which had already been sown. He did not base this either on the military power of Germany or on the unfolding advances of science. Instead, he was influenced by the incontrovertible fact that belief in the Christian God had drastically declined to the point where he could confidently say that "God is dead."

Although Nietzsche was an atheist, he reflected on the "death" of God with mixed reactions. He was appalled at the consequences that would follow once everyone became fully aware of all the implications of the death of God. He thought about both the collapse of religious faith and the mounting belief in the Darwinian notion of a relentless evolution of the species. He could see in this combination the destruction of any basic distinction between human and animal. If this is what we are asked to believe he said, then we should not be surprised when the future brings us colossal wars such as we have never seen before on earth. At the same time, the death of God meant for Nietzsche the dawn of a new day—a day when the essentially life-denying ethics of Christianity could be replaced with a life-affirming philosophy. "At last," he said, "the sea, *our* sea, lies open before us. Perhaps there has never been so open a sea." His ambivalent reaction to the nihilistic consequences of the death of God turned Nietzsche to the central question of human values. In his search for a new foundation for values in a day when God could no longer be the goal and sanction of human conduct, Nietzsche believed that aesthetics was the most promising alternative to religion. Only as an aesthetic phenomenon, he said, are human existence and the world eternally justified. The Greeks, he believed, originally discovered the true meaning of human effort. He initially drew his fundamental insights about human nature from the Greek conceptions of Apollo and Dionysus.

The Apollonian versus Dionysian

Nietzsche believed that aesthetic value results from a fusion between two principles, which are respectively represented by the Greek gods Apollo and Dionysus. Dionysus symbolized the dynamic stream of life, which knows no restraints or barriers and defies all limitations. Worshipers of Dionysus would lapse into a drunken frenzy and thereby lose their own identity in the larger ocean of life. Apollo, on the other hand, was the symbol of order, restraint, and form. If the Dionysian attitude was best expressed in the feeling of abandonment in some types of music, then the Apollonian form-giving force found its highest expression in Greek sculpture. Thus, Dionysus symbolized humanity's unity with life whereby individuality is absorbed in the larger reality of the life force. Apollo, then, was the symbol of the "principle of individuation"—the power that controls and restrains the dynamic processes of life in order to create a formed work of art or a controlled personal character. From another point of view, the Dionysian represented the negative and destructive dark powers of the soul, which, when unchecked, culminate in "that disgusting mixture of voluptuousness and cruelty" typical of "the most savage beasts of nature." The Apollonian, by contrast, represented the power to deal with the powerful surge of vital energy, to harness destructive powers, and to transmute these into a creative act.

Greek tragedy, according to Nietzsche, is a great work of art. It represents the conquest of Dionysus by Apollo. But from this account Nietzsche drew the conclusion that people are not faced with a choice between the Dionysian and the Apollonian. To assume that we even have such a choice is to misunderstand the true nature of the human condition. The fact is that human life inevitably includes the dark and surging forces of passion. What Greek tragedy illustrates, according to Nietzsche, is that instead of abandoning oneself to the flood of impulse, instinct, and passion, the awareness of these driving forces becomes the occasion for producing a work of art. This would be so whether in our own character through moderation or in literature or the arts through the imposition of form upon a resisting material. Nietzsche saw the birth of tragedy—that is, the creation of art—as a response of the basically healthy element in a person, the Apollonian, to the challenge of the diseased frenzy of the Dionysian. On this view art could not occur without the stimulus of the Dionysian. At the same time, if the Dionysian were considered either the only element in human nature or the dominant element, we might very well despair and come finally to a negative attitude toward life. But for Nietzsche the supreme achievement of human nature occurred in Greek culture where the Dionysian and Apollonian elements were brought together. Nineteenth-century culture denied that the Dionysian element had a rightful place in life. For Nietzsche, though, this only postponed the inevitable explosion of vital forces, which cannot be permanently denied expression. To ask whether life should dominate knowledge or knowledge dominate life is to raise the question concerning which of these two is the higher and more decisive power. There is no doubt, Nietzsche argued, that life is the higher and dominating power, but raw vital power is finally life-defeating. For this reason Nietzsche looked to the Greek formula—the fusion of the Dionysian and Apollonian elements—by which human life is transformed into an aesthetic phenomenon. Such a formula, Nietzsche thought, could provide modern culture with a relevant and workable standard of behavior at a time when religious faith was unable to provide a compelling vision of human destiny. What disqualified religious faith, he believed, was the essentially life-denying negativity of Christian ethics.

Master Morality versus Slave Morality

Nietzsche rejected the notion that there is a universal and absolute system of morality that everyone must equally obey. People are different, and to conceive of morality in universal terms is to disregard basic differences between individuals. It is unrealistic to assume that there is only one kind of human nature, whose direction can be prescribed by one set of rules. Whenever we propose a universal moral rule, we invariably seek to deny the fullest expression of our elemental vital energies. In this respect Judaism and Christianity are the worst offenders. Judeo-Christian ethics, he argues, is so contrary to our basic nature that its antinatural morality debilitates humanity and produces only "botched and bungled" lives.

How did human beings ever produce such unnatural systems of ethics? There is, Nietzsche says, a "twofold early history of good and evil," which shows the development of two primary types of morality: the *master morality* and the *slave morality*. In the *master morality* "good" always meant "noble" in the sense of "with a soul of high calibre." "Evil," by contrast, meant "vulgar" or "plebeian." Noble people regard themselves as the creators and determiners of values. They do not look outside of themselves for any approval of their acts. They pass judgment upon themselves. Their morality is one of self-glorification. These noble individuals act out of a feeling of power, which seeks to overflow. It is not out of pity that they help the unfortunate, but rather from an impulse generated by an abundance of power. They honor power in all its forms and take pleasure in subjecting themselves to rigor and toughness. They also have reverence for all that is severe and hard. By contrast, the *slave morality* originates with the lowest elements of society: the abused, the oppressed, the slaves, and those who are uncertain of themselves. For the slave, "good" is the symbol for all those qualities that serve to alleviate the existence of sufferers, such as "sympathy, the kind helping hand, the warm heart, patience, diligence, humility and friendliness." This slave morality Nietzsche argues, is essentially the morality of utility, since moral goodness involves whatever is beneficial to those who are weak and powerless. With the slave morality the person who arouses fear is "evil," but with the master morality it is in fact the "good" person who is able to arouse fear.

This revenge took the form of translating the virtues of the noble aristocrat into evils. Nietzsche's great protest against the dominant Western morality was that it exalted the mediocre values of the "herd," which "knows nothing of the fine impulses of great accumulations of strength, as something high, or possibly as the standard of all things." Incredibly, the "herd mentality" in time overcame the master morality by succeeding in making all the noble qualities appear to be vices and all the weak qualities appear to be virtues. The positive affirmation of life in the master morality was made to seem "evil" and something for which one should have a sense of "guilt." The fact is, Nietzsche says, that

> men with a still natural nature, barbarians in every terrible sense of the word, men of prey, still in possession of unbroken strength of will and desire for power, threw themselves upon weaker, more moral, more peaceful races. . . . At the commencement, the noble caste was always the barbarian caste: their superiority did not consist first of all in their physical, but in their psychical power—they were *complete* men.

But the power of the master race was broken by the undermining of its psychological strength. Against the natural impulse to exert aggressive strength, the weak races erected elaborate psychic defenses. New values and new ideals, such as peace and equality, were put forward under the guise of "the fundamental principle of society." This, Nietzsche said, was a not-so-subtle desire on the part of the weak to undermine the power of the strong. The weak have created a negative psychological attitude toward the most natural human drives. This slave morality is, Nietzsche says, "a Will to the *denial* of life, a principle of dissolution and decay." But, he continues, a skillful psychological analysis of the herd's resentment and its desire to exact revenge against the strong will show what must be done. That is, we must "resist all sentimental weakness: life is essentially appropriation, injury, conquest of the strange and weak, suppression, severity, obtrusion of peculiar forms . . . and at the least, putting it mildest, exploitation."

The Will to Power

Exploitation, according to Nietzsche, is not some inherently degenerate human action. Instead, it belongs "to the nature of the living being as a primary function." Exploitation is "a consequence of the intrinsic Will to Power, which is precisely the Will to Life—a *fundamental fact* of all history." The Will to Power is a central drive within human nature to dominate one's environment. This is more than simply the will to survive. It is, rather, an inner impulse to vigorously affirm all of our individual powers. As Nietzsche says, "the strongest and highest Will to Life does not find expression in a miserable struggle for existence, but in a Will to War. A Will to Power, a Will to Overpower!"

European morality denied the central role of the Will to Power—and did so in a dishonest manner. Nietzsche put the blame for this on the slavish morality of Christianity. He writes, "I regard Christianity as the most fatal and seductive lie that has ever yet existed—as the greatest and most *impious lie*." He was appalled that Europe should be subjected to the morality of that small group of wretched outcasts who clustered around Jesus. Imagine, he said, "the *morality of paltry people* as the measure of all things." This he considered "the most repugnant kind of degeneracy that civilization has ever brought into existence." To Nietzsche it was incredible that in the New Testament "the least qualified people . . . have their say in its pages in regard to the greatest problems of existence." Christianity contradicts nature when it requires us to love our enemies, since nature's injunction is to *hate* our enemies. Moreover, Christianity denies the natural origin of morality since it requires us to first love God before we can love anything. By injecting God into our affections, we subvert the immediate and natural moral standard that involves affirming life. By diverting our thinking toward God, we dilute our strongest and most vital energies. Nietzsche admitted that the "spiritual" people of Christianity performed invaluable services in Europe by offering comfort and courage to the suffering. But at what price was Christian charity achieved? The price, Nietzsche writes, was "the deterioration of the European race." It was necessary "to *reverse* all estimates of value—*that* is what they had to do! And to shatter the strong, to spoil great hopes, to cast suspicion on the delight in beauty, to break down everything autonomous, manly, conquering, and imperious." Christianity thus succeeded in inverting "all love of the earthly and of supremacy over the earth into hatred of the earth and earthly things."

Nietzsche was willing for the weak herd to have their own morality, provided that they did not impose it on the higher ranks of humanity. Why should people of great creative abilities be reduced to the common level of mediocrity characteristic of the herd? Nietzsche spoke of rising "beyond good and evil," by which he meant rising above the dominant herd morality of his day. He envisioned a new day when, once again, the truly complete person would achieve new levels of creative activity and thereby become a higher type of person—the Superperson (*Übermensch*). This new person will not reject morality; he or she will reject only the negative morality of the herd. Again, Nietzsche argued that the morality based on the Will to Power is only an honest version of what the slave morality has carefully disguised. If the Superperson is "cruel," Nietzsche said, we must recognize that, actually, almost everything that we now call "higher culture" is simply a spiritualized intensification of cruelty. "This is my thesis," he said, that "the 'wild beast' has not been slain at all, it lives, it flourishes, it has only been—transfigured." For example, ancient Romans took pleasure in the gladiatorial contests. Christians experience ecstasies of the cross. Spaniards delight at the gory sight of the bullfight. French workers are homesick for a bloody revolution. These are all expressions of cruelty.

From the vantage point of the master morality, the word *cruelty* refers simply to the basic Will to Power, which is a natural expression of strength. People are differentiated into ranks, and it is only quantity of power that determines and distinguishes one's rank. Thus, ideals such as political and social equality are nonsensical. There can be no equality where there are in fact different degrees of power. Equality can only mean the leveling downward of everyone to the mediocrity of the herd. Nietzsche wanted to preserve the natural distinction between two types of people, namely, between that "type which represents ascending life and a type which represents decadence, decomposition, weakness." To be sure, a higher culture will always require a mediocre herd, but only to make possible the development and emergence of the Superperson. If the Superperson is to emerge, he or she must go beyond good and evil as conceived by the lower ranks.

Revaluation of All Morals

What does Nietzsche want to put in the place of traditional morality, which he clearly believed was dying? His positive recommendations are not so clear as his critical analysis. However, we can infer much of the content of his new values from his rejection of the slave morality. If the slave morality originated in resentment and revenge, there must again occur a *revaluation* of all values. By *revaluation* Nietzsche did not mean the creation of a new table of moral values. He meant rather to declare war on the presently accepted values, like Socrates "applying the knife vivisectionally to the very virtues of the time." Since traditional morality is a perversion of original natural morality, *revaluation* must consist in rejecting traditional morality in the name of honesty and accuracy. Revaluation implies that all the "stronger motives are still extant, but that now they appear under false names and false valuations, and have not yet become conscious of themselves." It is not necessary to legislate new values but only to reverse values once again. Just as "Christianity was a revaluation of all the values of antiquity," so today the dominant morality must be rejected in favor of our original and deepest nature. Thus, Nietzsche's plan of *revaluation* was essentially a critical analysis of modern human ideals. He showed that what modern people called "good" was not at all virtuous. Their so-called truth was disguised selfishness and weakness, and their religion was a skillful creation of psychological weapons with which moral pygmies domesticated natural giants. Once the disguise is removed from modern morality, then true values will emerge.

In the final analysis moral values must be built on our true human nature and our environment. Unlike Darwin, who stressed external circumstances when describing the evolution of the species, Nietzsche focused on the internal power within individuals, which is capable of shaping and creating events—"a power which *uses* and *exploits* the environment." Nietzsche's grand hypothesis was that everywhere and in everything the Will to Power seeks to express itself. "This world," he says, "is the Will to Power—and nothing else." Life itself is a multiplicity of forces, "a lasting form of processes of assertions of force." People's psychological makeup shows that our preoccupation with pleasure and pain reflects a striving toward an increase of power. Pain can be the spur for exerting power to overcome an obstacle, whereas pleasure can involve a feeling of increased power.

The Superperson

Nietzsche's notion of the Will to Power is most clearly represented in the attitudes and behavior of the Superperson. We have already seen that Nietzsche rejected the concept of equality. He also showed that morality must suit each rank. Even after the *revaluation* of all values, the "common herd" will not be intellectually capable of reaching the heights of the "free spirits." In short, there can be no "common good." Great things, Nietzsche says, remain for the great, "everything rare for the rare." The Superperson will be rare but is the next stage in human evolution. History is moving not toward some abstract developed "humanity" but toward the emergence of some exceptional people; the *Superperson* is the goal. But the Superperson will not be the product of a mechanical process of evolution. The next stage can be reached only when superior people have the courage to revalue all values and respond with freedom to their internal Will to Power. Human beings need to be surpassed, and it is the Superperson who represents the highest level of development and expression of physical, intellectual, and emotional strength. The Superperson will be the truly free person for whom nothing is forbidden except what obstructs the Will to Power. The Superperson will be the very embodiment of the spontaneous affirmation of life.

Nietzsche did not think that his Superperson would be a tyrant. To be sure, there would be much of the Dionysian element within the Superperson. But these passions would be controlled, thereby harmonizing the animal nature with the intellect, and giving style to his or her behavior. We should not confuse such a Superperson with a totalitarian bully. As a model Nietzsche had in mind his hero Goethe, as well as "the Roman Caesar with Christ's soul." As Nietzsche's thought matured, his ideal person would have to possess a balanced unity of the Dionysian and Apollonian elements. Earlier, when Wagner and Schopenhauer influenced his thought, Nietzsche criticized Socrates for having caused Western thought to take a wrong turn toward rationality. In later years he gained a greater appreciation for rationality. Even at the end, though, he believed that rationality must be used in the service of life and that life must not be sacrificed for knowledge. Still, Socrates was important historically precisely because he saved people from self-destruction. The lust for life, Nietzsche says, would then have led to wars of annihilation. The Dionysian element by itself leads to pessimism and destruction. So it was necessary to harness people's energies, which required the kind of influence that Socrates provided. Although the Apollonian element of rationality risks subverting the vital streams of life, Nietzsche nevertheless believed that we cannot engage in life without some rational form-giving guidance. Socrates became important for Nietzsche precisely because this ancient philosopher was the first to see the proper relation between thought and life. Socrates recognized that thought serves life, whereas for other philosophers, life served thought and knowledge. Here, then, was Nietzsche's ideal: the passionate person who has his or her passions under control.

PART FIVE

Twentieth-Century and Contemporary Philosophy

CHAPTER 17

Pragmatism and Process Philosophy

A major theme in nineteenth-century thought is that the world is continually changing. Hegel believed that human history and everything around us are part of an ever-developing Absolute Mind. Darwin argued that all biological life—and even human social institutions—evolve from simple to more complex forms. As philosophy rounded the corner from the nineteenth to the twentieth century, the notion of change remained an important part of intellectual thought. Two philosophical movements in particular focus on change, namely pragmatism and process philosophy. Both approaches deny that there are fixed and unchanging truths; instead, we should understand things in terms of changing experiences and metaphysical processes.

Pragmatism emerged at the end of the nineteenth century as the most original contribution of American thought to the enterprise of philosophy. This movement received its initial theoretical formulation by Charles S. Peirce (1839–1914). It enjoyed wide and popular circulation through the brilliant and lucid essays of William James (1842–1910). It was then methodically implemented into the daily affairs of American institutions by John Dewey (1859–1952). The central message of these three philosophers is that there is little value in philosophical theories that do not somehow make a difference in daily life. Pragmatism was more of a method of solving problems than it was a metaphysical system of the world. Process philosophy, though, did offer a specific vision of the nature of things. Many writers, including some later pragmatists, are associated with process philosophy. The two leading proponents, though, are French philosopher Henri-Louis Bergson (1859–1941) and British philosopher Alfred North Whitehead (1861–1947).

PRAGMATISM

As a movement in philosophy, pragmatism was founded for the purpose of mediating between two divergent tendencies in nineteenth-century thought. On the one hand, there was the cumulative impact of empiricism, utilitarianism, and science, to which Darwin's theory of evolution gave the most recent and striking claim to authoritative thought about human nature. The drift of this tradition was that human nature and the world were simply parts of a mechanical and biological process. On the other hand, there was a more human-centered tradition, stemming from Descartes's rationalistic philosophy and moving through Kant, Hegel, and other German idealists. Between these two traditions there was an ever-widening gulf. Empirical philosophers and scientists rejected much rationalistic and idealistic philosophy because it lacked objective evidence. From the rational and idealistic points of view, science threatened moral and religious convictions and a general sense of human purpose.

Pragmatism mediated between these traditions, combining what was most significant in each of them. Like the empiricists the pragmatists thought that we have no conception of the whole of reality. We know things from many perspectives, and we must settle for a multifaceted approach to knowledge. Like the rationalists and idealists they saw morality, religion, and human purpose as constituting a significant aspect of our experience. Peirce, James, and Dewey each expressed a different aspect of pragmatism. Peirce was initially interested in logic and science, James wrote about psychology and religion, and Dewey was absorbed with the problems of ethics and social thought. They were all contemporaries, they all came from New England, and they were highly skilled academicians.

PEIRCE

Peirce's Life

Charles Sanders Peirce (pronounced *purse*) was born in Cambridge, Massachusetts, in 1839, where his father was a noted Harvard professor of mathematics. He was educated in mathematics, science, and philosophy both at home under his father's discipline and at Harvard College, where between the ages of 16 and 20 he was a student. After receiving an M.A. in mathematics and chemistry, he worked for three years at the Harvard Observatory and published his photometric researches in 1878. For thirty years, from 1861 to 1891, he was associated with the U.S. Coastal and Geodetic Survey. He was also for a short period a lecturer in logic at Johns Hopkins University. But Peirce was never a full-time member of a university faculty, presumably because his brilliance was overshadowed by personal eccentricities. Without an academic position he encountered resistance and indifference from publishers, so that very little of his total literary output appeared during his lifetime, and he received virtually none of the fame to which his abilities entitled him. Decades after his death, his works were collected and organized into several volumes, which stand as a prodigious achievement of creative thought. In his declining years Peirce faced financial difficulties, failing health, and virtual social rejection. His loyal friend throughout these difficulties was William James, who not only assisted him but became the channel through which Peirce's original thoughts about pragmatism found their way into the thought of a whole generation throughout the world.

A Theory of Meaning

At the heart of Peirce's pragmatism is a new explanation of how words acquire their meanings. He coined the word *pragmatism* from the Greek word *pragma* (meaning "act" or "deed") in order to emphasize the fact that words derive their meanings from actions of some sort. Our ideas are clear and distinct only when we are able to translate them into some type of operation. For example, the adjectives *hard* and *heavy* have meaning only because we are able to conceive of some specific effects that are associated with these terms. Thus, *hard* means that which cannot be scratched by many other substances, and *heavy* means that which will fall if we let go of it. Underscoring the decisive role of *effects* in the meanings of words, Peirce argued that there would be absolutely no difference between a hard thing and a soft thing as long as they did not test differently. From such simple examples Peirce generalized about the nature of meaning and knowledge. His basic point was that "our idea of anything *is* our idea of its sensible effects." That is, if words are to have any meaning, we must be able to use the operational formula, which says, "If A then B." That is, when specific objects are present, we can expect specific effects to follow. Thus, a word has no meaning if it refers to an object about which no practical effects can be conceived.

Peirce was highly influenced by the language of science, since it is particularly scientific language that satisfies this pragmatic test for meaning. He was arguing against rationalist theories, which held that validity is based solely on the consistency between ideas themselves, with no reference to outside things. Earlier empiricists tried to show the shortcomings of rationalism, but Peirce found the assumptions of rationalism still very much alive. Descartes, for example, believed that intellectual certainty consisted in "clear and distinct" ideas, which we grasp by intuition. As such, our minds are purely theoretical instruments that can operate successfully in isolation from environmental circumstances. Against all of these assumptions, Peirce argued that thinking always occurs in a context, not in isolation from it. We derive meanings not through intuition but by experience or experiment. Thus, meanings are not individual or private but social and public. Again, if there is no way of testing ideas by their effects or public consequences, such ideas are meaningless. He believed that it was most important to distinguish between meaningful and meaningless contentions, particularly when we are torn between opposing systems of thought.

The Role of Belief

Peirce argued that belief occupies a middle position between thought and action. Beliefs guide our desires and shape our actions. But beliefs are "unfixed" by doubts. It is when the "irritation of doubt" causes a struggle to attain belief that the enterprise of thought begins. Through thought we try to fix our beliefs so that we have a guide for action. There are several ways in which we can fix our beliefs, according to Peirce. There is the method of *tenacity*, whereby people cling to beliefs, refusing to entertain doubts about them or to consider arguments or evidence for another view. Another method is to invoke *authority*, as when people in authority require the acceptance of certain ideas under threat of punishment. Still another method is that of the metaphysician or philosopher such as Plato, Descartes, or Hegel, who, according to Peirce, settle questions of belief by asking whether an idea was "agreeable to *reason*." Peirce found himself in disagreement with all of these methods precisely because they could not achieve their intent, namely, to fix or settle belief. What they all lacked was some connection with experience and behavior.

Peirce therefore offered a fourth method, the method of *science*, whose chief virtue was its realistic basis in experience. The above-mentioned methods of *tenacity, authority*, and *reason* all rest on what we possess within our own minds as a consequence solely of our thinking. The method of science, by contrast, is built on the assumption that there are real things, things that are entirely independent of our opinions about them. Moreover, because these real things affect our senses according to regular laws, we can assume that they will affect each observer the same way. Beliefs that are grounded in real things can, therefore, be verified, and their "fixation" can be a public act rather than a private one. There is in fact no way to agree or disagree with a conclusion arrived at by means of the first three methods. All three attempts refer to nothing whose consequences or real existences can be tested. The method of tenacity is clearly irrational. The method of authority precludes argument. The method of *a priori* reasoning, because it occurs in isolation from facts, permits the affirmation of several different explanations of things, as was the case with the alternative metaphysical systems proposed by the Continental rationalists.

The Elements of Method

As a means of resolving conflicts between alternative beliefs, Peirce recommended the scientific method, which he felt combats personal prejudice. For one thing, the method of science requires that we state not only what truth we believe but also how we arrived at it. The procedures followed should be available to anyone who cares to retrace the same steps to test whether the same results will occur. Peirce continually emphasizes this public or community character of the method of science. Second, the method of science is highly self-critical. It subjects its conclusions to strict tests, and wherever shown, the conclusions of a theory are adjusted to fit the new evidence and insights. This, Peirce says, ought also to be our attitude toward all our beliefs. Third, Peirce felt that science requires a high degree of cooperation among all members of the scientific community. Such cooperation prevents any individual or group from shaping truth to fit its own interests. Conclusions of science, then, must be conclusions that all scientists can draw. Similarly, in questions of belief and truth, it should be possible for anyone to come to the same conclusions. This method of empirical inquiry means that there must be some practical consequence of any legitimate idea.

JAMES

James's Life

The rich flavor of William James's writings reflects the equally rich quality and breadth of his life. Born in New York City in 1842, he grew up in a cultured family, which produced not only the outstanding American philosopher but also his brother Henry James, the gifted novelist. William James studied at Harvard and traveled to universities throughout Europe, acquiring a broad outlook both culturally and intellectually. He received his M.D. from the Harvard Medical School in 1869 and was appointed to its faculty in 1872 as an instructor in physiology. From medicine James moved to psychology and philosophy, producing in 1890 his famous *Principles of Psychology*. He was a member of the Harvard philosophy department, which included George Santayana and Josiah Royce. Although he did not write any philosophical treatises comparable in scope to his famous book on psychology, he published a great many definitive essays, which singly and collected in book form were read throughout the world. By the time of his death in 1910 at the age of 68, James had fashioned a new approach to philosophy and managed to communicate his pragmatic principles to an unusually wide audience. Starting from the work already done by Peirce, he took a fresh look at pragmatism and developed it along novel lines. Among the important topics to which James turned his attention, we will examine four: (1) the pragmatic method, (2) the pragmatic theory of truth, (3) the problem of free will, and (4) the function of the human will in the belief process.

Pragmatism as a Method

James thought that "the whole function of philosophy ought to be to find out what definite difference it will make to you and me, at definite instants of our life, if this world-formula or that world-formula be the true one." He emphasized concrete concerns of life—specifically, facts and actions as they affect our lives now and the future. But pragmatism as such contained no substance or content and no special information about human purpose or destiny. As a philosophy pragmatism did not have its own creed. It did not, as such, offer a world formula.

"Pragmatism," James writes, "is a method only." Still, as a method, pragmatism assumed that human life has a purpose and that rival theories about human nature and the world need to be tested against this purpose. According to James, there is in fact no single definition of human purpose. Instead, our understanding of human purpose is part of the activity of thinking. Philosophical thinking arises when we want to understand things and the setting in which they live; purpose derives its meaning from a sense of being at home in the universe. James rejected rationalism chiefly because it was dogmatic and presumed to give conclusive answers about the world in terms that frequently left the issues of life untouched. By contrast, pragmatism "has no dogmas and no doctrines save its method." As a method pragmatism takes its cue from the newly discovered facts of life. We should not accept as final any formulations in science, theology, or philosophy, but instead see them as only approximations. The value of any theory rests in its capacity to solve problems, and not in its internal verbal consistency. Instead of mere consistency, James writes, we "must bring out of each word its practical cash value"—that is, we must focus on *results*. When we find a theory that does not make a difference one way or another for practical life, then the theory is meaningless, and we should abandon it.

The Pragmatic Theory of Truth

Establishing the meaning of a concept is one thing, and establishing its truth is another. For example, it may be meaningful for me to hold to the view that the CIA is watching every move I make. From a pragmatic standpoint this contention is meaningful if it produces some kind of consequence—such as various activities among CIA agents and even some impact on how I conduct my private life. However, this does not mean that the CIA is truly watching me. A test for truth is pickier than a test for mere meaning. Even here, though, pragmatism offers a method. James first rejects standard theories of truth, such as what is now called the *correspondence theory of truth*: An idea is true if it corresponds to reality. This theory assumes that an idea "copies" *reality*, and an idea is, therefore, true if it copies what is "out there" accurately. According to James, though, on this theory "truth means essentially an inert static relation. When you've got your true idea of anything, there's an end of the matter. You're in possession; you *know*." But truth, according to James, is less fixed than this. Similar to the theory of meaning, truth involves asking, "What concrete difference will its being true make in anyone's actual life?"

As an example of the pragmatic theory of truth, James asks us to consider a clock on the wall. We consider it to be a clock not because we have a "copy-view" of it. The so-called reality of the clock consists of its internal mechanism, which we cannot see. Our idea of the clock consists mainly of its face and hands, which in no way matches "reality." Still, our limited idea of the clock passes for true because we *use* this conception as a clock, and as such it *works*. Some practical consequences of this idea are that we can go to work "on time" and catch the train. We could scientifically verify aspects of our idea, such as inspecting the internal components of the clock. In point of fact, though, we rarely do this. What more would be added to the truth of our idea that the object before us is a clock than we already have in the successful regulation of our behavior? James writes, "For one truth-process completed there are a million in our lives that function in this state of nascency." Truth, then, lives "on a credit system."

Ideas become true insofar as they help us to make successful connections among various parts of our experience. Truth is, therefore, part of the process of living. As part of a process, successful experiences *make* truth, and this constitutes the verification process. Advocates of the correspondence theory believe that truths are absolute in the sense that there is a real clock on the wall whether anyone sees it or not. For James, though, questions about the "truth" of the clock arise only in actual life when we live "as if" that thing on the wall is a clock. Our successful behavior *makes* the truth of the clock. There is, then, no single absolute truth, but instead as many truths as there are concrete successful actions. James distinguished between what he called *tough-minded* and *tender-minded* approaches to truth. A tough-minded pragmatist would look only at more scientific kinds of successful behavior in the truth process. For example, my concept of the clock is true because I show up to events at the proper time, and I can check my notion of the clock against the time indicated by other clocks. A tender-minded pragmatist, though, would consider less scientific behavior in the truth process. For example, without scientifically analyzing things, my concept of the clock is true if it serves its principal function in organizing my daily routine. James believed that both the tough- and tender-minded approaches to truth were valid in their own ways. We cannot all be scientists. But this does not mean that truth is whimsical. Even with the tender-minded approach, a true belief must work beneficially, just as an untrue one will work destructively. For example, an imaginary clock will not do a good job of organizing my daily schedule and will in fact adversely affect my routine.

If we ask the pragmatist why anyone *ought* to seek the truth, James answers that "our obligation to seek the truth is part of our general obligation to do what pays," just as we ought to seek health because it pays to be healthy. Above all, James thought that the pragmatic theory of truth could bring a desperately needed service to philosophy by providing a means for settling disputes. Some disputes cannot be resolved if each party simply affirms that his or her views are true. James would ask, Which theory fits the facts of real life? One such dispute, which has exercised philosophers through the ages, is the question of freedom versus determinism.

Free Will

James was convinced that we cannot rationally prove that human will is either free or determined. We will only find equally good arguments for each side of the dispute. He was nevertheless convinced that the pragmatic method would shed new light on the problem. The crucial practical question here is, What difference does it make in actual life to accept one or the other side of a dispute? The issue is worth investigating since it involves something important about life: Either we are mechanically driven by physical forces or we have the power to shape at least some of our life events as we see fit. For James this was not simply an interesting puzzle. His whole philosophical orientation revolved around this problem of the role and status of the will. He was greatly concerned about human action and choosing those ideas and types of behavior with the highest value. Accordingly, he saw philosophy in terms of human striving, and this, he was convinced, indicated a certain kind of universe.

According to James, the issue of free will "relates solely to the existence of possibilities," of things that may, but need not, be. The determinist says that there are no ambiguous or uncertain possibilities, that what will be will be. On this view "those parts of the universe already laid down absolutely appoint and decree what the other parts shall be. The future has no ambiguous possibilities in its womb." On the other hand, the indeterminist says that there is some "loose play" in the universe and that the present arrangement of things does not necessarily determine what the future will be. Here, then, are two contradictory points of view. What divides us into *possibility* people and *antipossibility* people? The answer is differing claims of rationality. For some it seems more rational to say that all events are set down from eternity, whereas for others it seems more rational to assume that people can engage in genuine choice. If both of these points of view seem equally rational to their respective proponents, how can the dispute be resolved?

To solve the problem, according to James, we simply ask the pragmatic question, What does a deterministic world imply? That is, what kind of universe are we living in if all events without exception are rigorously determined from the beginning of time so that they could not have happened in any other way? We could only answer that such a universe is like a machine, in which each part fits tightly and all the gears are interlocked, so that the slightest motion of one part causes a motion of every other part. There is no loose play in the machine. But James feels that we are not just mechanical parts in a huge machine. What makes us different is our consciousness. For one thing, we are capable of judgments of regret. For example, someone may regret caving into peer pressure during high school, failing to study during college, or doing a poor job at work. But how can we regret anything if events were rigidly fixed and we could not have done otherwise?

Not only do we make judgments of regret, but we make moral judgments of approval and disapproval. We persuade others to perform some actions and avoid others. We also punish or reward people for their actions. All these forms of judgment imply that we constantly face genuine choices. A forced or determined act is simply not a choice. In actual practical life we see others and ourselves as vulnerable. People are capable of lying, stealing, and killing. We judge these acts to be wrong not only in retrospect but because we feel that they were not inevitable when they were done. People doing these things "could have" done otherwise. The determinist must explain away all of these judgments and instead define the world as a place where what "ought to be" is impossible. James concludes that this problem is a "personal" one and that he cannot conceive of the universe as a place where murder *must* happen. Instead, it is a place where murder *can* happen and *ought* not. For James, then, there are very practical implications to the free will issue; the free will option is pragmatically more true because it better accommodates judgments of regret and morality. If this reflects only his "instinct" concerning the kind of universe this is, then, James says, "there are *some* instinctive reactions which I, for one, will not tamper with."

The Will to Believe

The tough-minded scientist might think that our individual hopes should have no impact on the truth that we are investigating. In fact, a scientist might argue that we should abstain from belief in situations in which there is no clear evidence. For example, religious questions have a way of running ahead of evidence. Thus, in the absence of any clear evidence for the existence of God, a scientist might recommend agnosticism—neither believing nor disbelieving in God. In his essay "The Will to Believe," James combats this scientific view and argues that, when reason is truly neutral on an urgent issue, we may rightfully believe based solely on our feelings. However, we cannot will to believe just anything under any and all circumstances. This right to believe as we feel applies to only special situations. Right off, according to James, our reason must be completely neutral on the issue. For example, I am not justified in believing that Abraham Lincoln is still alive, since there are quite a number of compelling reasons to believe that he is dead. With other issues, though, reason seems to be genuinely neutral, such as the question of God's existence. According to James, proofs and disproofs for God are equally shaky. Beyond the stipulation of reason's neutrality, James lists three other conditions that determine when emotionally based beliefs are justified.

First, the belief must be a *live* option—as opposed to a dead one. That is, it must be a conception that we are psychologically capable of believing. For example, if a traditional Christian were asked to believe in the Muslim savior Mahdi, he or she would not be psychologically capable of making that shift. Belief in Mahdi, then, would be a dead option for such Christian believers. Second, the choice must be *forced* in the sense that we must either accept or reject a conception, with nothing in between. For example, I must either accept or not accept the contention that the Christian God exists. Third, the issue must be *momentous*, that is, of major concern rather than trivial. Belief in God seems to be a matter of some urgency. When all three of these conditions are fulfilled, we have what James calls a "genuine option." He then states his thesis:

> Our passional nature not only lawfully may, but must, decide an option between propositions, whenever it is a genuine option that cannot by its nature be decided on intellectual grounds; for to say, under such circumstances, "Do not decide, but leave the question open," is itself a passional decision,—just like deciding yes or no,—and is attended with the same risk of losing the truth.

In short, James holds that, when reason is neutral in matters that are genuine options, we can decide the issue based on our hopes and feelings.

According to James, we often receive real benefits when we proactively believe things that we cannot rationally demonstrate. This involves some intellectual risk, but it is a risk worth taking. Suppose a young man wants to know whether a certain young woman loves him. Let us also suppose that in fact she does love him but he does not *know* it. If he assumes that she does not, then his doubt will prevent him from saying or doing what would cause her to reveal her love. In this case he would "lose the truth." His will to believe would not necessarily create her love. That is already there. But belief has the effect of making what is already there come full circle. If the young man requires evidence before he can know the truth, he will never know it, because the evidence he is looking for will become available only after he acts on his belief. Similarly, in the realm of religious experience, we might not discover religious truth until we actually become religious believers—even in the absence of evidence for our belief. Again, our proactive religious belief would not make our religious experiences true, but it would provide us with the only means of discovering their truth.

Occasionally, nonrational proactive beliefs can even *create* facts, and not just *discover* them. For example, I may get a job promotion chiefly because I believed that I could achieve it and acted resolutely on that belief. Assuming the truth of my abilities, I incorporate this into my life and take a risk for the sake of it. My faith *creates* its own verification. Similarly, in a political campaign a candidate's optimistic will to believe can generate enough enthusiasm among constituents to win a majority vote. James illustrates this point with an example of a train robbery. All of the passengers on a train may be individually brave, but each one is afraid that in resisting the robbers he or she will be shot. However, if they optimistically believed that the others would rise up, resistance could begin. But if one passenger actually rose up, that could influence the others and would help create a unified resistance.

DEWEY

Dewey's Life

William James's lively writing style was unsurpassable, but in the final analysis John Dewey was the most influential of the pragmatists. By the time of his death at the age of 92, Dewey had brought about a reconstruction of philosophy and influenced many American institutions, particularly school systems and some political processes. His influence extended beyond the boundaries of the United States, especially into Japan and China, where his lectures made a lasting impression. Born in Burlington, Vermont, in 1859, Dewey was educated at the University of Vermont and at Johns Hopkins University, where he received his Ph.D. in philosophy in 1884. For the next ten years, except for one year when he was at Minnesota, he taught at the University of Michigan, and for the decade after that at the University of Chicago, where he gained renown for his pragmatic concepts of education. As director of the Laboratory School for children at the University of Chicago, he experimented with a more permissive and creative atmosphere for learning. He set aside the more traditional and formal method of learning—that is, listening and taking notes—and instead encouraged students to become directly involved with educational projects. From 1904 to 1929 he was a member of the faculty at Columbia University. He produced an enormous number of writings even after his retirement in 1929. His interests covered a wide range, and he wrote on logic, metaphysics, and the theory of knowledge. But as Dewey's chief expression of pragmatism was in the social rather than individual realm, his most influential works related to education, democracy, ethics, religion, and art.

The Spectator versus Experience

Dewey's chief quarrel with earlier philosophy was that it confused the true nature and function of knowledge. For the most part, he said, the empiricists assumed that thinking refers to fixed things in nature—that for each idea there is a corresponding something in reality. It is as though knowing is modeled after what is supposed to happen when we look at something. Thus, to see something is to have an idea of it. This he called a "spectator theory of knowledge." But rationalists argued that the reverse was true, namely, that when we have a clear idea we are guaranteed that the object of our thought exists in reality. In either case, empiricists and rationalists both viewed the human mind as an instrument for considering what is fixed and certain in nature. Nature is one thing and the mind another, and knowing is the relatively simple activity of looking, as a spectator does, at what is there.

Dewey believed that this view of knowledge is both too static and too mechanical. Influenced by Darwin's theories, Dewey looked on human beings as biological organisms. As such we can best be understood in relation to our environment. Like any other biological organism, human beings struggle for survival. Although Dewey gave up his early Hegelian orientation, he still believed that human beings were enmeshed in a dialectic process—specifically, a conflict in the material or natural environment. Dewey's grand concept was, therefore, *experience*, a concept he employed for the purpose of connecting people as dynamic biological entities with their precarious environments. If I and my environment are both dynamic, it is clear that a simple spectator-type theory of knowledge will not work. My mind is not a fixed substance, and knowledge is not a set of static concepts. Human intelligence is the ability within us to cope with our environment. Thinking is not an individual act carried on in private or in isolation from practical problems. Instead, thinking, or active intelligence, arises in "problem situations"; thinking and doing are intimately related.

All thinking, Dewey says, has two aspects, namely, "a perplexed, troubled, or confused situation at the beginning and a cleared-up, unified, resolved situation at the close." He named his theory *instrumentalism*, emphasizing that thinking is always instrumental in solving problems. Whereas empiricism and rationalism separate thinking and doing, instrumentalism holds that reflective thought is always involved in transforming a practical situation. My mind does not know simply individual things, but instead mediates between myself as an organism and my environment. My mind spreads itself over a range of things as these bear upon my desires, doubts, and dangers. Knowing may very well consist of a "cognitive act"—of an activity in my mind—but the full description of knowing must include the environmental origin of the problem or situation that calls forth the cognitive act. In this way instrumentalism differs from empiricism and rationalism.

Thinking, therefore, is not a quest for the "truth," as though the truth were a static and eternal quality in things. Thinking, rather, is the act of trying to achieve an adjustment between individuals and their environments. The best test of the value of any philosophy, Dewey says, is to ask, "Does it end in conclusions which, when referred back to ordinary life-experiences and their predicaments, render them more significant, more luminous to us and make our dealings with them more fruitful?" In this sense his instrumentalism is a problem-solving theory of knowledge.

Habit, Intelligence, and Learning

Dewey built his theory of instrumentalism around a special view of human nature. Even though he believed that people are strongly influenced by education and social surroundings, he nevertheless held that we have certain instincts. These instincts are not a fixed inheritance, he argued, but instead are "highly flexible" and will work differently under different social conditions. He writes that "any impulse may become organized into almost any disposition according to the way it interacts with surroundings." For example, *fear* may become cowardice, or reverence for superiors, or the reason for accepting superstitions. Just what an impulse will result in depends on the way the impulse is interwoven with other impulses, as well as with outlets supplied by our environment. Dewey thus rejected the simple, mechanical stimulus-response account of behavior. Even when an impulse always reflects itself in the same way, this is not a mechanical necessity but only the product of *habit*. But habit is only *one* way of responding to the stimuli of one's impulses, and there is no *necessary* connection between a person's natural impulses and any *particular* response. All responses, Dewey argues, are learned through the interaction between human nature and culture. Habits, then, do not represent fixed forms of human behavior. We can even test them for their usefulness based on whether they support life and generally facilitate the successful adaptation of a person to the environment.

Perhaps the most important implication of Dewey's analysis concerns the nature of social and human "evil." Evil is not the product of some permanent instinct or impulse in human nature that cannot be altered. Instead, evil is the product of the special ways a culture has shaped and conditioned people's impulses. On this view evil is the product of the "inertness of established habit." *Intelligence* itself is a habit by which we adjust our relation to its environment. Habits therefore include not only ways of reacting to certain stimuli but also ways of thinking about the environment. Since all habits are only *established* but not *necessary* types of behavior, the clue to overcoming personal and social evil is to alter a society's habits—its habits of response and its habits of thought.

Nothing is more important than *education* in remolding a society. If we are creatures of habit, then education provides the conditions for developing the most useful and creative habits. Dewey regretted that progress in the past had been achieved only when some catastrophe or major social upheaval broke the spell of long-standing habits. He preferred a more controlled approach to change, and nothing, he thought, provides us with more power to control than knowledge. Instead of revolution, therefore, we should bring about change through the skillful alteration of habits through education. He was convinced that "the chief means of continuous, graded, economical improvement and social rectification lies in utilizing the opportunities of educating the young to modify prevailing types of thought and desire." The spirit of education should be *experimental*, because our minds are fundamentally problem-solving instruments. It is, therefore, more important to try alternative means for successfully solving problems than to pursue neat theoretical formulations.

Dewey's instrumentalism was governed by the presuppositions of science. Like science, education should recognize the intimate connection between action and thought—between experiment and reflection. Achieving knowledge is a continuous process. It is a struggle to fashion theory in the context of experiment and thought. But if education is the key to social improvement, and if experimentation is the best way to discover the instrumental *means* for solving problems, the crucial questions concern the problem of *ends*. Improvement assumes a scale of values, and means are employed toward ends. How does society discover its ends or the foundations of its values? Dewey specifically examined this difficult problem of relating facts to value, and science to morality, and in the process fashioned a new theory of value.

Value in a World of Fact

Dewey's theory of value followed his general theory of knowledge. We discover values the same way that we discover facts, namely, through experience. Values do not exist as eternal entities to be discovered by the theoretical mind. Every person experiences the problem of choosing between two or more possibilities. The question about values arises in these experiences in which choices have to be made. We most often make choices about means for achieving ends. Where an end is already clear, we can pursue the means with scientific rigor. For Dewey the act that will bring about the end most successfully is by definition the most "valuable" act. Suppose that the roof on my house leaks. This at once raises the questions of both *ends* and *means*—the goal of stopping the leak and the ways of accomplishing this. I quickly realize that a leaky roof calls for action. Before I begin any action, I try to intelligently sort out the various possibilities for stopping the leak, drawing on past experience or experiment. According to Dewey, to deal effectively with this problem, I do not need to draw on elaborate value theories. He thus rejected any theory of values grounded in so-called essences of things or transcendent eternal truth. There is, Dewey says, "only relative, not absolute, impermeability and fixity of structure." Since the quest for values rests on a scientific methodology, all that we need to do is intelligently sort out the best means to achieve our aims.

Since intelligence is the agency for bridging the gap between *any* problem and its solution, Dewey believed that this same experimental and instrumental approach could successfully resolve the problems of individual and social destiny. This is so for value theories pertaining to morality, social policy, politics, and economics. His optimism rested on the spectacular successes of the sciences. If we were to ask Dewey where we could discover values in the absence of traditional moral and religious standards, he would answer, for the most part "from the findings of the natural sciences." There is some resemblance between Dewey's theory and utilitarianism—the view that right actions are those that produce the best consequences for society. However, Dewey sought to go beyond the theory of utilitarianism. Our moral choices begin by designating what we in fact desire, such as a fixed roof or a reformed school system.

We then submit these desires to the inspection of our intelligence, which in turn offers a satisfactory solution to the problem.

Unfortunately, we cannot devise a neat formula for determining how any given act will terminate and what the best means might be for attaining an end. Life is simply too dynamic and the circumstances of behavior too diverse to permit the making of any *list* of rules. The best values are those that produce satisfactory consequences, relative to the aim that we hope to achieve. It is through experience that we discover ends toward which life and behavior should move. According to Dewey, each generation should formulate its own ends in the context of democracy. Democracy itself represented Dewey's *faith* in the capacities of human intelligence. He believed that apart from "pooled and cooperative experience" there is no reliable source of knowledge, wisdom, or guidance for collective action.

PROCESS PHILOSOPHY

Just when modern science was reaching its most impressive heights of achievement, two bold speculative philosophers called into question the basic assumptions of scientific thought. Neither Henri Bergson nor Alfred North Whitehead wished to deny that the scientific method gave people considerable control over nature and, to that extent, was a brilliantly successful enterprise. What concerned them primarily was a philosophical question, namely, whether reality was what science assumed it to be. As late as the second half of the nineteenth century and the early decades of the twentieth, the major assumption of science was that nature consists of material objects located in space. On this view matter is the final, irreducible stuff out of which all things are formed. The model for thinking about the contents and behavior of nature was that of a machine. All the particular things in nature were thought to be parts of a large mechanism. This meant that the behavior of each part could in time be described with mathematical exactness, since material objects moved in space in accordance with precise rules or laws. Moreover, as parts of a mechanism, things were related to each other in a tight sequence of cause and effect. Human nature was also viewed in these material and mechanical terms. As parts of a tightly organized cosmic machine, people were no longer thought of as being "free," as possessing freedom of the will.

Each of these assumptions raised serious philosophical problems for Bergson and Whitehead. They wondered whether nature really does consist of inert material objects located in space. They also wondered whether the human intellect is capable of discovering "out there" such an orderly and mechanical arrangement of things as the logical and mathematical reasoning of science portrays. How, moreover, can there be any genuine novelty in nature if the basic reality is material and its various parts are organized in a tight mechanism? Can a world made of material things ever become anything more than these same objects simply rearranged from time to time? How, in short, can inert matter overcome its static status and evolve? How can we explain the concrete experience of life in terms of a lifeless nature? And how can human freedom be explained in a thoroughly mechanical universe? Science itself had recently developed new concepts—for example, the theory of evolution—that made the mechanical model of nature less and less plausible.

Whitehead pointed out that late in the nineteenth century the people of science "were quite unaware that the ideas they were introducing, one after the other, were finally to accumulate into a body of thought inconsistent with the Newtonian ideas dominating their thoughts and shaping their types of expression." Whitehead moved, as it were, from within science to his metaphysics, drawing out many of the implications of the emerging new physics. Similarly, Bergson had no intention of rejecting science, but thought instead that metaphysics and science could enrich each other. What Bergson and Whitehead did challenge in science, however, was the assumption that the scientific type of thought could be the sole comprehensive source of knowledge. Accordingly, they sought to show just what the limits of science are and what unique insights could be provided by discovering the metaphysical processes that form reality.

BERGSON

Bergson's Life

Henri Bergson was born in Paris in 1859, the brilliant son of a Polish father and an English mother. This same year saw the publication of Darwin's *On the Origin of Species by Means of Natural Selection* and the birth of John Dewey. Bergson's rise in the academic world was rapid. At age 22 he became professor of philosophy at the Angers Lycée, and in 1900 he was appointed to the distinguished chair of modern philosophy at the Collège de France. With uncommon lucidity and a captivating style, Bergson wrote a series of works that won wide attention and stimulated considerable discussion, including *Time and Free Will* (1889), *Matter and Memory* (1897), *An Introduction to Metaphysics* (1903), *Creative Evolution* (1907), and *The Two Sources of Morality and Religion* (1932). These last three works gained particular fame and contain his most distinctive ideas. Their publication assured him of a worldwide reputation and attracted people from many countries to hear his lectures in Paris, where he lived until his death in 1941 at the age of 82.

Going Around versus Entering Into

At the center of Bergson's philosophy was his conviction that there are "two profoundly different ways of knowing a thing." The first way, he says, "implies that we move around the object," and the second, that "we enter into it." Knowledge derived in the first way depends on the vantage point from which we observe an object, and therefore this type of knowledge will be different for each observer and, on that account, *relative*. Moreover, knowledge derived by observation is expressed in symbols, where the symbols used can refer not only to this specific object but to any and all similar objects. The second kind of knowledge, however, is *absolute*, Bergson says, because in this case, by "entering" the object, we overcome the limitations of any particular perspective and grasp the object as it really is.

Bergson illustrates these two types of knowing with several examples. First, there is the example of the movement of an object in space. My observation of this object, he says, will vary with the point of view from which I observe it, particularly whether I myself am moving or stationary. When I try to describe this motion, my expression of it will vary with the points of reference to which I relate it. Both in observing and in describing the moving object, I am placed outside of it. In describing the object's motion, I think of a line that is divided into units, and I express this through the symbol of a graph with its axes, a series of points through which the object is thought to move. By contrast to this attempt to plot and chart movement in terms of discrete units of space, there is, Bergson says, the true movement, a continuous flow, whereby there are in reality no points being crossed. Suppose, Bergson says, that you were inside the object as it moved. You would then know the object as it really is and moves, and not merely as translated into the symbolic language of points and units of distance. For, "what I experience will depend neither on the point of view I may take up in regard to the object, since I am inside the object itself, nor on the symbols by which I may translate the motion, since I have rejected all translations in order to possess the original." Instead of trying to grasp the movement from where I stand in my static position, I must try to grasp the object's motion from where *it* is, from within, as the motion is in the object itself. When I raise my own arm, I have a simple and single perception of the movement I have created; I have an "absolute" knowledge of this movement. But, Bergson says, for the spectator watching me raise my arm from the outside,

> your arm passes through one point, then through another, and between these points there will be still other points. . . . Viewed from the inside, then, an absolute is a simple thing; but looked at from the outside, that is to say, relatively to other things, it becomes, in relation to these signs which express it, the gold coin for which we never seem able to finish giving small change.

The case is the same when we take a character in a novel. The author labors to describe his traits and to make him engage in action and dialogue. But, Bergson says, "all this can never be equivalent to the simple and indivisible feeling which I should experience if I were able for an instant to identify myself with the person of the hero himself." The reason descriptive traits do not help me know this particular hero is that such traits are merely symbols, "which can make him known to me only by so many comparisons with persons or things I know already." Such symbols take me outside of him, and "they give me only what he has in common with others and not what belongs to him alone." It is not possible, Bergson says, to perceive what constitutes a person's "essence" from without, because by definition his essence is internal and, therefore, cannot be expressed by symbols. Description and analysis require the use of symbols, but symbols are always "imperfect in comparison with the object of which a view has been taken, or which the symbols seek to express." Not all the photographs of Paris, taken from every conceivable point of view, and not even motion pictures, would ever be equivalent to the solid Paris in which we live and move. Not all translations of a poem could render the inner meaning of the original. In every example there is, first of all, the original, which we can know absolutely only by entering into it. There is, second of all, the "translation," or copy, which we know only relatively, depending on our vantage point and the symbols we use for expression.

What, more precisely, does it mean to "go around" an object and to "enter into it"? To go around an object is what Bergson means by that special activity of the intellect that he calls *analysis*. By contrast, to enter into an object is what is implied by his use of the term *intuition*. By intuition Bergson means "the kind of *intellectual sympathy* by which one places oneself within an object in order to coincide with what is unique in it and consequently inexpressible." The basic contrast between science and metaphysics turns on the difference between *analysis* and *intuition*.

The Scientific Way of Analysis

Bergson believed that in the end scientific meaning, insofar as it is based on analysis, misrepresents the nature of whatever object it analyzes. This follows, he said, from the fact that analysis "is the operation which reduces the object to elements already known, that is, to elements common both to it and other objects." Therefore, "to analyze . . . is to express a thing as a function of something other than itself." For example, to analyze a rose is to take it apart and discover its constituents. From such an analysis we do in fact derive knowledge of the rose, but in such a state of analysis, the rose is no longer the living thing it was in the garden. Similarly, the science of medicine discovers much knowledge of human anatomy by dissecting the body.

In every case, Bergson says, the analytic intellect learns, ironically, by destroying the object's essence. Its essence is its dynamic, thriving, pulsing, living, continuing existence—its duration. Analysis, however, interrupts this essential duration. It stops life and movement. It separates into several independent and static parts what in true life is a unified, organic, and dynamic reality.

The language of analytic science tends, moreover, to exaggerate even further this static and disjointed conception of things through its use of symbols. Each new object is described by science using as many symbols as there are ways of looking at a thing. And, Bergson says, the content of each such perception is abstracted, that is, drawn or lifted out from the object. Thus, the intellect forms a series of concepts about a thing, "cutting out of reality according to the lines that must be followed in order to act conveniently upon it." Since we think in terms of our language—that is, in terms of single concepts—we tend to analyze things into as many concepts as there are ways of looking at and moving around an object. This is the ordinary function of scientific analysis, namely, to work with symbols. Even the sciences concerned with life "confine themselves to the visible form of living beings, their organs and anatomical elements. They make comparisons between these forms; they reduce the more complex to the more simple; in short, they study the workings of life in what is, so to speak, only its visual symbol." There seem to be, Bergson says, a "symmetry, concord and agreement" between our intellect and matter, as though our intellect were made to analyze and utilize matter. Indeed, he says, "our intelligence is the prolongation of our senses." Even before there was either science or philosophy, "the role of intelligence was already that of manufacturing instruments and guiding the action of our body on surrounding bodies."

If, then, the intellect has been made to utilize matter, "its structure has no doubt been modeled upon that matter." But it is precisely for this reason that the intellect has a limited function. Its very structure and function fit it for analysis—for separating what is unified into its parts. Even when it comes to the study of the most concrete reality—namely, the *self*—the intellect, proceeding analytically, is never capable of discovering the true self. Like all other sciences, psychology analyzes the self into separate states such as sensations, feelings, and ideas, which it studies separately. According to Bergson, to study the self by studying separately the various psychical states is like trying to know Paris by studying various sketches, all of which are labeled *Paris*. The psychologists claim to find the "ego" in the various psychical states, not realizing that "this diversity of states has itself only been obtained . . . by transporting oneself outside the ego altogether." And "however much they place the states side by side, multiplying points of contact and exploring the intervals, the ego always escapes them."

The Metaphysical Way of Intuition

But, Bergson says, there is another way of knowing the self, and that is by *intuition*. As he says, "there is one reality, at least, which we all seize from within, by intuition and not by simple analysis. It is our own personality through time—our self which endures." Just as Descartes did, Bergson founded his philosophy on the immediate knowledge of the self. But whereas Descartes built a system of rationalism on his self-knowledge, Bergson set forth the method of intuition, which was in sharp contrast to rationalism. Intuition, Bergson argued, is a kind of intellectual sympathy. It enables our consciousness to become identified with an object. Intuition "signifies . . . immediate consciousness, a vision which is scarcely distinguishable from the object seen, a knowledge which is contact or even coincidence."

Most importantly, Bergson says, "to think intuitively is to think in *duration*." This is the difference between analytic and intuitive thought. Analysis begins with the static and reconstructs movement as best it can with immobilities in juxtaposition. By contrast, "intuition starts from movement, posits it, or rather perceives it as reality itself, and sees in immobility only an abstract moment, a snapshot taken by our mind." Ordinarily, analytic thought pictures the new as a novel arrangement of what already exists; although nothing is ever lost, neither is anything ever created. But "intuition, bound up to a duration which is growth, perceives in it an uninterrupted continuity of unforeseeable novelty; it sees, it knows that the mind draws from itself more than it has, that spirituality consists in just that, and that reality, impregnated with spirit, is creation." Intuition, then, discovers that the self is in enduring and continuous flux.

Bergson compares the inner life of the self to a continually rolled up thread on a ball: "For our past follows us, it swells incessantly with the present that it picks up on its way; and consciousness means memory." An even better way of thinking about the self, he says, is to imagine an infinitely small elastic body, which is gradually drawn out in such a manner that from that original body comes a constantly lengthening line. While even this image is not satisfactory to him, Bergson does see in it an analogy to human personality. The drawing out of the elastic body is a continuous action representing the duration of the ego, which is the pure mobility of the self. But whatever images are used to describe it, "the inner life is all this at once: variety of qualities, continuity of progress, and unity of direction. It cannot be represented by images. . . . No image can replace the intuition of duration."

The Process of Duration

Bergson focused on the process in all things that he called *duration*, that is, becoming. Duration, he argued, constitutes the continuous stream of experience in which we live. His criticism of classical schools of philosophy was that they failed to take duration seriously. For the most part, philosophers such as Plato, Descartes, and Kant sought to interpret the world through fixed structures of thought. This was particularly the case with Plato, whose notion of the Forms provides us with a static structure of reality. Even the empiricists, in spite of their preoccupation with experience, analyzed experience into static components. This was so for Hume, who described knowledge in terms of individual impressions. Neither the rationalists nor the empiricists, Bergson charged, took the matter of mobility, development, becoming, and duration seriously. He was not entirely clear about how this metaphysical notion of duration could be employed in scientific knowledge. But he was certain that to "think in duration" is to have a true grasp of reality. Such thought also gives us a more accurate notion of time—real and continuous time—as compared with the "spatialized" time created by the intellect.

Only when we think of time and motion in such "spatialized" terms do we encounter the logical paradoxes that Zeno spoke of. Zeno, you will remember, said that a flying arrow really does not move, because at each instant the arrow occupies a single point in space, which would mean that at each instant the arrow is at rest. Bergson says that Zeno's argument would be irrefutable if his assumptions about space and time were correct. But he argues that Zeno was in error in assuming that there are real positions in space and discrete units of time. Bergson suggests that these so-called positions are merely *suppositions* of the intellect. The units of time are only the artificial segments into which the analytic intellect slices what in reality is a continuous flow. What Zeno's paradoxes show us is that it is impossible to construct mobility out of static positions, or true time out of instants. Although our intellects are capable of comprehending static parts, we are incapable of grasping movement or duration. Only intuition can grasp duration. And reality is duration. Reality, Bergson says, does not consist of *things*, but only of "things in the making, not self-maintaining *states*, but only changing states." Rest is only apparent, for all reality "is tendency, if we agree to mean by tendency an incipient change of direction."

Evolution and the Vital Impulse

Is not the theory of evolution an example of how science can successfully understand duration and becoming? After examining the major conceptions of evolution, Bergson concludes that none of these scientific theories are adequate, and thus, he offers a theory of his own. The particular inadequacy he found in the other theories was their inability to give a convincing account of how the transition is made through the gap that separates one level from a higher level. Darwin speaks of variations among members of a species, and other biologists speak of mutations as the conditions leading some members to possess variations favorable for survival. But these accounts do not explain how such variations in a species could occur. They merely hold that either slowly or suddenly a change occurs, presumably in some part of the organism. This overlooks the functional unity of an organism, which requires that any variation in one part must be accompanied by variations throughout the organism. Again, it does not explain just how this can occur. This leaves unanswered the question of how there can be a continuity of function in spite of successive changes of form. The neo-Lamarckian theory attributed evolution to the special "effort" employed by certain organisms, causing them to develop capacities favorable to survival. But can such acquired characteristics be transmitted from one generation to the next? Bergson insisted that although "effort" had some promising implications, it was too haphazard a notion to explain the overall process of development.

Evolution, Bergson concluded, is best explained in terms of a vital impulse (*élan vital*), which drives all organisms toward constantly more complicated and higher types of organization. The vital impulse is the essential interior element of all living things, and it is the creative power that moves in unbroken continuity through all things. Since the intellect can grasp only static things, it is not capable of grasping the vital impulse, because this is the essence of duration and of movement, and "all change, all movement, [is] . . . absolutely indivisible." Bergson argued that knowing is a secondary activity. Living, though, is more basic and, therefore, is primary. Intuition and consciousness, not analytic intellect, grasp this primary life and discover it to be a continuous and undivided process of which all things are expressions and not parts. All things are motivated by this vital impulse, and it is the fundamental reality. We discover it first through the immediate awareness of our own continuous self: We discover that we *endure*.

Here, finally, is where intuition must challenge intellect. For intellect, as we have seen, views movement as static states. Intuition, though, discovers that movement is continuous, that it cannot be reduced to parts, and that the creative process caused by the vital impulse is irreversible. Bergson writes that "to get a notion of this irreducibility and irreversibility, we must do violence to the mind, go counter to the natural bent of the intellect. But that is just the function of philosophy."

The intellect would describe evolution as a single and steady line moving upward through measurable levels. Intuition, though, suggests differing tendencies at work. According to Bergson, the vital impulse moved in three discernible directions, producing (1) vegetative beings, (2) anthropods, and (3) vertebrates (including, finally, human beings). Distinguishing intellect and intuition, he says that the emergence of intellect and matter occurred together, and these were intended to work together. He writes, "Our intellect in the narrow sense of the word, is intended to secure the perfect fitting of our body to its environment, to represent the relations of external things among themselves—in short, to think matter." Moreover, "matter is weighted with geometry." But neither matter nor geometrical figures represent ultimate reality. The vital impulse must itself resemble consciousness, from whence emerged life and all its creative possibilities. Evolution is creative precisely because the future is open. There is no preordained "final" goal; duration constantly endures, producing always genuinely novel events, like an artist who never knows precisely what she will create until she has created her work. Bergson finally refers to the creative effort of the vital impulse as being "of God, if it is not God himself."

Morality and Religion

Bergson argues that there are two sources of morality. The first is the sheer feeling of the necessity for social solidarity, and to achieve such solidarity, a society formulates certain rules of obligation. The second source lies in a deeper seat of feeling, which is sparked by the example of great moral people whose emotional appeal transcends particular cultural groups. These two sources—the pressure of social necessity and the aspiration toward higher types of life—reflect the differences between intellect and intuition. The intellect thinks in particular terms, directing specific rules to specific people to achieve specific ends. To this extent, the intellect tends to restrict morality to a closed society. Bergson was aware that the intellectually oriented Stoics believed that reason is a source of universal morality. But even when the intellect formulates laws for all people, we still need intuition to develop a genuine morality that extends to a wider group. Intuition opens up richer sources of emotional power, at once inducing aspiration and providing creative power to embrace new types of life. Such moral progress occurs only when obscure moral heroes appear. These mystics and saints raise humanity to a new destiny and "see in their mind's eye a new social atmosphere, an environment in which life would be more worth living." In this way morality moves constantly from a consideration of ourselves and our society to the larger field of humanity.

The difference between intellect and intuition is reflected also in two types of religion, which Bergson calls *static* and *dynamic*. Since we find that all people are religious in one way or another, religion must be due to some inherent aspect of human structure. Moreover, since the intellect is formed to aid us in survival, the intellect must be the source of religion, inasmuch as religion presumes to answer certain basic demands of life. Religious concepts seek to provide security, confidence, and a defense against fear. But these concepts soon become institutionalized and are converted into belief to protect them against critical reason. They are often surrounded by ceremonies and disciplines and tend to become embedded in the social structure. This is static religion, the religion of social conformity. Dynamic religion, on the other hand, is more in the nature of mysticism. Bergson's definition of *mysticism* closely follows his notion of intuition when he says that "the ultimate end of mysticism is the establishment of a contact, consequently of a partial coincidence, with the creative effort which life itself manifests." Just as intuition grasps reality more completely than intellect does, so does dynamic religion discover God more vividly. For, Bergson says, we must consider static religion "as the crystallization, brought about by a scientific process of cooling, of what mysticism had poured, white hot, into the soul of man."

WHITEHEAD

Whitehead reacted, as Bergson did, against the analytic type of thought, which assumed that facts exist in isolation from other facts. His main theme was that "connectedness is the essence of all things." What science tends to separate, philosophy must try to see as an organic unity. Thus, "the red glow of the sunset should be as much a part of nature as are the molecules and electric waves by which men of science would explain the phenomenon." The function of natural philosophy, he thought, is "to analyze how these various elements of nature are connected." Describing Wordsworth's romantic reaction against the scientific mentality, Whitehead says that "Wordsworth was not bothered by any intellectual antagonism. What moved him was moral repulsion." He was repulsed by the fact that scientific analysis left something out, "that what had been left out comprised everything that was most important," namely, moral intuitions and life itself. Agreeing with Wordsworth, Whitehead went on to say that "neither physical nature nor life can be understood unless we fuse them together as essential factors in the composition of really real things whose interconnections and individual characters constitute the universe." And, he says, "it is important therefore to ask what Wordsworth found in nature that failed to receive expression in science. I ask this question in the interest of science itself." Whitehead was convinced that "the status of life in nature . . . is the modern problem of philosophy and science." Although he shared these same problems with Bergson, Whitehead brought a different intellectual background to their solution and, therefore, produced a different and novel speculative metaphysics.

Whitehead's Life

Alfred North Whitehead had three careers, two in England and one in America. Born in the village of Kent in 1861, he was educated at Sherborn School and at Trinity College in Cambridge. For twenty-five years he taught mathematics at

Trinity. It was here, too, that Whitehead collaborated with Bertrand Russell on their famed *Principia Mathematica*, which went to press in 1910. From Trinity he moved to London, eventually becoming associated with the University of London as a member of its faculty of science and later as dean of faculty. During these thirteen years in London, he also developed a strong interest in the problems of higher education, being concerned particularly with the impact of modern industrial civilization on the enterprise of learning. But his major writings while in London represented an attempt to replace Isaac Newton's concept of nature with his own empirically grounded theory. These works on the philosophy of science include his *Enquiry concerning the Principles of Natural Science* (1919), *The Concept of Nature* (1920), and *The Principle of Relativity* (1922).

When Whitehead was 63 years old and nearing retirement, he was appointed professor of philosophy at Harvard University, and he embarked on the third and, in many ways, most important of his careers. To his achievements as a logician, mathematician, and philosopher of science he added his works as a metaphysician. His major works of this period are his *Science and the Modern World* (1925), *Process and Reality* (1929), and *Adventures of Ideas* (1933). What motivated Whitehead to write these books was his conviction that scientific knowledge had arrived at a point in its history that called for a new scheme of ideas to reflect more adequately the new developments in science. Since scientific thought always relies on some scheme of ideas, he said, the importance of philosophy is to make such schemes explicit so that they can be criticized and improved. Though his chief speculative work, *Process and Reality*, is a massive and intricate statement, Whitehead acknowledges in the preface that "there remains the final reflection, how shallow, puny, and imperfect are efforts to sound the depths in the nature of things. In philosophical discussion, the merest hint of dogmatic certainty as to finality of statement is an exhibition of folly." Thus, his metaphysical writings combine bold and creative speculations tempered with a sensitive humility. In 1937 Whitehead retired but continued to live near Harvard Yard until his death in 1947 at the age of 87.

The Error of Simple Location

Whitehead was convinced that Newtonian physics is based on a fallacy—what he called the *fallacy of misplaced concreteness*. Newton followed Democritus in assuming that the nature of things consists of individual bits of matter existing in space. What is fallacious about this? Whitehead says that

> to say that a bit of matter has *simple location* means that, in expressing its spatio-temporal relations, it is adequate to state that it is where it is in a definite region of space and throughout a definite duration of time, apart from any essential reference of the relations of that bit of matter to other regions of space and to other durations of time.

Against this view Whitehead argues that "among the primary elements of nature as apprehended in our immediate experience, there is no element whatsoever which possesses this character of simple location." The concept of an isolated atom, he says, is the product of intellectual abstraction. He admits that by a process of abstraction we can "arrive at abstractions which are the simply-located bits of material." But these abstractions, by definition, represent the lifting out of a thing from its concrete environment. To mistake the abstraction for the concrete is the error that Whitehead calls the *fallacy of misplaced concreteness*. Such things as instants of time, points in space, or independent particles of matter are certainly helpful concepts for scientific thought. However, when we take them as descriptions of ultimate reality, they are distortions of concrete reality.

When it came to giving his own account of concrete reality, Whitehead developed a novel form of *atomism*. He sought to draw out the implications of the recent developments in quantum physics, the theory of relativity, and evolution. His units of reality differed from the atoms of Democritus and Newton in two ways: (1) in their *content* and (2) in their *relations* to each other. Whitehead discarded the word *atom* because historically this term meant that the content of an atom is hard, lifeless matter and that, being hard, atoms never penetrate each other. Hence their relations to each other are always external. In place of the term *atoms*, Whitehead therefore substituted the term *actual entities* or its equivalent *actual occasions*. Unlike lifeless atoms Whitehead's actual entities are "chunks in the life of nature." As such, they never exist in isolation but are intimately related to the whole field of life that throbs around them. Whereas atomistic materialism gives us a mechanical view of nature, Whitehead's notion of actual occasions permits us to view nature as a living *organism*. Thus, whether we speak of God or "the most trivial puff of existence," there is the same principle of life in all things, for "actual entities are the final real things of which the world is made up."

Self-Consciousness

Whitehead saw in our own self-consciousness a good example of an actual occasion. He felt that the "direct evidence as to the connectedness of [my] immediate present occasion of experience with [my] immediately past occasions, can be validly used to suggest . . . the connectedness of all occasions in nature." Because an actual occasion is not a material thing, it is best understood as an experience. These occasions do not exist; they happen. The difference is that merely to exist implies no change, whereas to happen suggests a dynamic alteration. Whitehead's actual occasions represent continually changing entities, a change that comes about through the input of entities on each other. Consider what occurs when a person has an experience. We usually think that in this case there is, on the one hand, a permanent subject and then, or the other, something "out there" that the subject experiences. Whitehead argues that the subject and the object are both in a continual process of change and that every experience the subject has affects the subject. If it is true, as Heraclitus said, that we cannot step into the same river twice, it is also true that no person can think the same way twice, because after each experience he or she is a different person. And this is true of all of nature as it consists of actual occasions or aggregates of actual occasions. Thus, if all of reality is made up of actual occasions—drops of experience—nature is a throbbing organism undergoing constant change throughout. Says Whitehead, "The universe is thus a creative advance into novelty. The alternative to this theory is a static morphological universe."

Whitehead drew on his theory of actual occasions to account for the relation of body and mind and also to account for the presence of feeling and purpose in the universe. He believed that Democritus had not satisfactorily described how it is possible to have sensation, feeling, thinking, purpose, and life in a universe consisting solely of lifeless material atoms. Nor could Descartes ever join together his two substances—thought and extension. Leibniz did recognize that from lifeless matter it was impossible to derive life, and so he described nature as consisting of monads. Though they resembled the atoms of Democritus in some ways, Leibniz thought they were individual "souls," or centers of energy. Although the Leibnizian monad was a somewhat more satisfactory concept than the atom of Democritus, Whitehead considered it inadequate. Specifically, although Leibniz believed that monads undergo change, this change did not involve any truly novel process—no evolution, no creativity—but only the running of its predetermined course. By contrast, Whitehead's actual entities have no permanent identity or history. They are always in the process of becoming. They feel the impact of other actual occasions and absorb them internally. In this process actual occasions come into being, take on a determinate form or character, and, having become actual occasions, perish. To "perish" signifies that the creativity of the universe moves on to the next birth and that in this process an actual occasion loses its unique character but is preserved in the flow of the process. Perishing, Whitehead says, is what we mean by memory or causality—that with the passage of time something of the past is preserved in the present.

Prehension

We do not ever experience a single isolated actual entity, but only aggregates of these entities. He calls an aggregate of actual entities either a *society* or a *nexus* (plural *nexūs*) in which the entities are united by their *prehensions*. These are some of the novel words Whitehead invented to explain his novel ideas. He writes, "In the three notions—actual entity, prehension, nexus—an endeavor has been made to base philosophical thought upon the most concrete elements in our experience. . . . The final facts are, all alike, actual entities; and these actual entities are drops of experience, complex and interdependent." Whitehead visualized reality as a continual process in which actual entities are constantly becoming—a process in which *what* an actual entity becomes depends on *how* it becomes. His emphasis is on the notion of *creativity* as the fundamental characteristic of the process of nature. Creativity is the ultimate principle by which the many enter into complex unity. If we took each actual entity separately, we should have a disjoined universe, but the creative unity of the many constitutes the conjoined universe.

Whitehead uses the term *prehension* to describe how the elements of actual entities are related to each other and how these entities are further related to other entities. Nothing in the world is unrelated. In a sense every actual occasion absorbs, or is related to, the whole universe. Actual entities are brought together by the creative process into sets, or societies, or nexūs. In this process of becoming, actual entities are formed through prehension. Every prehension, Whitehead says, consists of three factors: (1) the "subject" that is prehending, (2) the "datum which is prehended," and (3) the "subjective form," which is *how* the subject prehends the datum. There are various species of prehensions: *positive prehensions*, which are termed *feelings*, and *negative prehensions*, which "eliminate from feeling." The subjective forms, or the ways data are prehended, are of many species, including emotions, valuations, purposes, and consciousness. Thus, for Whitehead, emotional feeling is the basic characteristic of concrete experience. Even in the language of physics it is appropriate to speak of *feelings*, for *physical feelings* are the physicist's idea that energy is transferred. Both physical feelings and conceptual feelings are positive prehensions, or internal relations of the elements of actual entities.

The distinction between physical and conceptual feelings does not imply the older dualism of body and mind. It is, of course, still meaningful to use the terms *body* and *mind*. But Whitehead insists that to assume that these terms imply a basic metaphysical difference, as Descartes said existed between his terms *thought* and *extension*, is to commit again the fallacy of misplaced concreteness. This fallacy, you will recall, is committed when one mistakes an abstraction for the concrete. Both body and mind are, for Whitehead, societies, or nexūs—they are sets of actual entities. The only concrete reality is an actual entity, but actual entities can be organized into different kinds of societies, such as body and mind. But in each case the actual entities possess the same characteristics, namely, the capacity for prehension, for feeling, for internal relations. Body and mind are both abstractions in the sense that their reality depends on the peculiar organization of the actual entities. Hence, body and mind are not permanently or ultimately different. To speak of the body as an abstraction is similar to speaking of a political body as an abstraction where only the individual citizens are the concrete reality. Whitehead insists that "the final facts are, all alike, actual entities," and all of these are capable of being interconnected in a stream of experience.

Eternal Objects

We might ask at this point just how Whitehead accounts for the underlying process of reality. That is, what is the process of creativity that brings actual entities into being and organizes them into societies and preserves what to our experience appears as the endurance of things? Here Whitehead's thought displays a strong Platonic influence. What makes an actual entity what it is, he says, is that the entity has been stamped with a definiteness of character by certain *eternal objects*. These *eternal objects*, resembling Plato's Forms, are uncreated and eternal. They are patterns and qualities, such as roundness or squareness, greenness or blueness, or courage or cowardice. An actual occasion acquires a definite character (and not other possible characters) because it selects *these* eternal objects and rejects *those*. Hence, an actual event is constituted by the togetherness of various eternal objects in some particular pattern.

Eternal objects, Whitehead says, are *possibilities*, which, like the Platonic Forms, retain their identity independent of the flux of things. He describes the relation between the eternal object and an actual entity as *ingression*, which means that once the actual entity has selected an eternal object, the latter *ingresses*, that is, stamps its character on the actual entity. Thus, "the functioning of an eternal object in the self-creation of an actual entity is the 'ingression' of the eternal object in the actual entity." Simple eternal objects stamp their character on actual entities, whereas complex eternal objects give definiteness, or the status of fact, to societies or nexūs.

To speak of eternal objects as *possibilities* required that Whitehead describe how and where these possibilities exist and how they become relevant to actual occasions. Since only actual occasions exist, what is the status of eternal objects? Whitehead designated one actual entity as being timeless, and this entity he called God. For him God is not a creator; he is "not *before* all creation, but *with* all creation." God's nature is to grasp conceptually all the possibilities that constitute the realm of eternal objects. This realm of eternal objects differs from Plato's system of Forms. For, whereas Plato visualized one perfect order for all things, Whitehead's God grasps virtually unlimited possibilities, "all possibilities of order, possibilities at once incompatible and unlimited with a fecundity beyond imagination." What makes the creative process of the world orderly and purposive is the availability of eternal objects, of possibilities. These possibilities exist in God as his primordial nature. God, moreover, is the active mediator between the eternal objects and the actual occasions. It is God who selects the relevant possibilities from the realm of eternal objects.

God does not impose the eternal objects on actual entities. Rather, God presents these possibilities as *lures* of what might be. Persuasion, not compulsion, characterizes God's creative activity. That God always presents relevant possibilities is no guarantee that actual entities will select them. When God's persuasive lure is accepted, the result is order, harmony, and novel advance. When it is rejected, the result is discord and evil. God is the ultimate principle striving toward actualizing all relevant possibilities. What we experience as the stable order in the world and in our intuition of the permanent rightness of things shows forth God's "consequent nature." "God's role," Whitehead says, "lies in the patient operation of the overpowering rationality of his conceptual harmonization. He does not create the world, he saves it: or, more accurately, he is the poet of the world, with tender patience leading it by his vision of truth, beauty and goodness."

CHAPTER 18

Analytic Philosophy

*D*uring a large part of the twentieth century, the dominant philosophical movement in the English-speaking world was known as *analytic philosophy*. Analytic philosophers differed widely in their stands on traditional philosophical issues and also in their methods for addressing these issues. What unifies them, though, is their agreement concerning the central task of philosophy, namely, to clarify notions through an analysis of language. For example, Ludwig Wittgenstein (1889–1951) said that "the object of philosophy is the logical clarification of thoughts" so that "the result of philosophy is not a number of philosophical propositions, but to make propositions clear." There is both a negative and positive side to this new approach to philosophy.

On the negative side, to say that the philosopher does not formulate "philosophical propositions" meant for the early analysts that there must be a self-imposed limit on the scope of philosophical activity. Practitioners of nineteenth-century idealism, especially Hegelians, constructed complete systems of thought regarding the whole universe. Analytic philosophers now undertook the more modest task of working on individual problems. Not only would these problems be single and manageable, but they would all fit into a single class: They would all be problems revolving around the meanings and usages of language. For this reason it would no longer be the task of the philosopher to investigate the nature of reality, to build complete systems that seek to explain the universe, or to fashion moral, political, and religious philosophies of behavior. Philosophy, in this new vein, "is not a doctrine but an activity," and as such, it can produce "no ethical propositions," Wittgenstein said. Philosophers are no longer to consider themselves capable of discovering unique forms of information about the world and human nature. The discovery of facts is the task of the scientist. There are no facts left over for the philosophers after all the scientists have done their work.

On the positive side, the new assumption was that philosophers can render a genuine service by carefully unraveling complex problems whose origin rests in the imprecise use of language. Scientists discussed their findings in language that was often misleading and in certain ways confusing. That is, scientific language contained ambiguities of logic, which required clarification. Analytic philosophers also assumed that rigorous linguistic analysis could *prevent* the use or abuse of language in ways that would cause us "to draw false inferences, or ask spurious questions, or make nonsensical assumptions," as Alfred Jules Ayer (1910–1989) said. For example, we often use propositions about nations as though nations were people. We talk about material things as though we believed in a physical world "beneath" or "behind" visible phenomena. We use the word *is* in relation to things whose existence we could not possibly want to infer. And we call on philosophy to remove these dangers from our use of language, Ayer said. In this way analytic philosophy is closely related to the enterprises of science. It is not a rival discipline offering propositions of what reality is like. Instead, philosophy functions as the "proofreader" of the scientists' expressions, checking the literature of science for its clarity and logical meaningfulness. It is not the philosopher's function to either propound vast systems of thought after the manner of Plato, Aristotle, and Hegel or to tell people how they ought to behave. Instead, the philosopher analyzes statements or propositions to discover the causes of ambiguities and the foundations of meaning in language.

RUSSELL

Russell's Mission

What caused this dramatic shift in the enterprise of philosophy? In the early decades of the twentieth century, several Hegelian philosophers still engaged in the idealist task of system building—most notably F. H. Bradley (1846–1924), Bernard Bosanquet (1848–1923), and J. E. McTaggart (1866–1925). At Cambridge University, Bertrand Russell (1872–1970) and George Edward Moore (1873–1958) reacted against this idealist trend. They questioned the extravagance of the metaphysical language these Hegelians used and wondered just what could be meant by these interpretations of the whole universe. Although Moore did not necessarily want to give up metaphysics, he was especially disturbed by the contrast between metaphysical language and so-called common sense. For example, McTaggart's famous notion, that "time is unreal," seemed to Moore to be "perfectly monstrous." This inspired Moore to analyze language—particularly to clarify ordinary language from a commonsense point of view. Bertrand Russell, on the other hand, was a brilliant mathematician, trained in precise thought, and in comparison with the language of mathematics, metaphysical language seemed to him loose and obscure. He did not want to reject metaphysics, any more than Moore did, but he did want to tighten up the language of metaphysics. While Moore set out to analyze commonsense language, Russell tried to analyze "facts" for the purpose of inventing a new language, namely, *logical atomism*. This would have the exactness and rigor of mathematics because this new language would be made to correspond exactly to the "facts." Neither Moore nor Russell gave up the attempt to understand reality.

Nevertheless, the way they went about their task emphasized the fact that philosophy is concerned not with discovery but with clarification and, therefore, in a sense, not with truth but with meaning.

Logical Atomism

Bertrand Russell's point of departure in philosophy was his admiration for the precision of mathematics. Accordingly, he announced that "the kind of philosophy that I wish to advocate, which I call logical atomism, is one which has forced itself upon me in the course of thinking about the philosophy of mathematics." He wanted to set forth "a certain kind of logical doctrine and on the basis of this a certain kind of metaphysics." Russell thought that it was possible to construct a logic by which the whole of mathematics could be derived from a small number of logical axioms. He did this with Alfred North Whitehead (1861–1947) in their coauthored work *Principia Mathematica* (1910–1913). Russell also considered that logic could form the basis of a language that could accurately express everything that could be clearly stated. Through his *logical atomism*, then, the world would correspond to his specially constructed logical language. The vocabulary of the new logic would, for the most part, correspond to particular objects in the world. To accomplish this task of creating a new language, Russell set out first to analyze certain "facts," which he differentiated from "things."

"The things in the world," Russell says, "have various properties, and stand in various relations to each other. That they have these properties and relations are *facts*." Facts constitute the complexity of the relations of things to each other, and therefore," it is with the analysis of *facts* that one's consideration of the problem of complexity must begin." Russell's basic assumption was that "facts, since they have components, must be in some sense complex, and hence must be susceptible to analysis." The complexity of facts is matched by the complexity of language. For this reason the aim of analysis is to make sure that every statement represents an adequate picture of its corresponding reality.

Language, according to Russell, consists of a unique arrangement of words, and the meaningfulness of language is determined by the accuracy with which these words represent facts. Words, in turn, are formulated into propositions. "In a logically perfect language," Russell says, "the words in a proposition would correspond one by one with the components of the corresponding facts." By analysis certain *simple* words are discovered. These are words that cannot be further analyzed into something more primary and, therefore, can be understood only by knowing what they symbolize. The word *red*, for example, is not capable of further analysis and so is understood as a simple *predicate*. Other words, similarly simple, refer to particular things, and as symbols of these things they are *proper names*. Language consists in part, then, of words, which in their simplest form refer to a particular thing and its predicate, as, for example, a *red rose*. A proposition states a fact. When a fact is of the simplest kind, it is called an *atomic fact*. Propositions that state atomic facts are called *atomic propositions*. If our language consisted only of such atomic propositions, it would amount only to a series of reports regarding atomic facts.

The underlying logical structure of language becomes more apparent when we assign symbols to our atomic propositions. For example, I can use the letter *p* to stand for the atomic proposition "I am tired," and the letter *q* to stand for "I am hungry." I can then link these two atomic propositions together with logical connectives such as *and* or *or*. The result will be a *molecular proposition*, such as "I am tired and I am hungry," which I can symbolize with the expression *p and q*. According to Russell, there is no single atomic fact corresponding to the entire proposition "I am tired and I am hungry." How can we test the truth or falsity, then, of molecular propositions such as this? The truth of this statement rests on the truth of the component atomic propositions. For example, if it is true that I am tired and it is also true that I am hungry, then the molecular proposition is also true, that "I am tired and I am hungry." In short, we make statements about the world in molecular propositions, which in turn are composed of atomic propositions, which in turn correspond to atomic facts. This ideal language expresses all there is to say about the world.

Problems with Logical Atomism

Russell's theory has problems when we try to account for universal statements such as "All horses have hooves." It is one thing to say, "This horse has hooves," where we check truth or falsity by connecting the *words* "horse" and "hooves" with the atomic *facts* of this particular horse and these hooves. It is another thing to say, "All horses have hooves." How would we test the truth or falsity of such a statement? According to logical atomism, we should analyze this statement into its atomic propositions and test *their* truth or falsity. However, there is no atomic fact corresponding to "all horses," for this means more than just this horse and that horse; it means, all horses, and this is a *general* fact.

Another problem with logical atomism is that it cannot adequately explain its own theory. Propositions can be stated meaningfully only when they are ultimately based, on some atomic fact. However, Russell did more than simply state atomic facts; he tried to say things *about* facts. That is, he attempted to describe the relation between words and facts, as though their description was somehow immune from logical atomist theory itself. If only propositions that state facts are meaningful, then language *about* facts is meaningless. This, then, would make logical atomism, and most of philosophy, meaningless. Wittgenstein recognized this problem in his own theory of logical atomism and concluded that "my propositions are elucidatory in this way: he who understands me finally recognizes them as senseless, when he has used them to climb out beyond them. (He must so to speak throw away the ladder, after he has climbed up on it)." What we need to throw away is the central assumption of logical atomism: that there really are atomic facts, and that these facts exist in some metaphysical way. The next movement in analytic philosophy—logical positivism—attempted to rid philosophy of metaphysical entities once and for all.

LOGICAL POSITIVISM

While Russell championed the cause of analytic philosophy in England, across the English Channel a handful of mathematicians, scientists, and philosophers formed a group in Vienna in the 1920s, known as the Vienna Circle. This group included, Rudolph Carnap, Herbert Feigl, Kurt Gödel, Otto Neurath, Moritz Schlick, and Friedrich Waismann. The Vienna Circle thought of themselves as the twentieth-century heirs to Hume's empirical tradition and were inspired by Hume's strict criterion of meaning that we find at the close of his *Enquiry concerning Human Understanding* (1748):

> When we run over libraries, persuaded of these principles, what havoc we must make? If we take in our hand any volume; of divinity or school metaphysics, for instance; let us ask, Does it contain any abstract reasoning concerning quantity or number? No. Does it contain any experimental reasoning concerning matter of fact and existence? No. Commit it then to the flames: for it can contain nothing but sophistry and illusion.

Also inspired by Comte and other nineteenth-century positivists, they were disposed to reject metaphysics as outdated by science. Unlike Hume and Comte, though, the Vienna Circle had a new weapon against metaphysics: the logical character of language. Members of the Vienna Circle called themselves *logical positivists*—or sometimes *logical empiricists*—to differentiate themselves from the earlier Comtean positivists and Humean empiricists. The Vienna Circle eventually dissolved in the 1930s when its members went off to teach at British and American universities. For the English-speaking world, A. J. Ayer's book *Language, Truth, and Logic* (1936) did "something to popularize what may be called the classic position of the Vienna Circle," as Ayer later said with considerable understatement.

The Principle of Verification

Logical positivists charged that metaphysical statements are meaningless. This charge, though, required some criterion to determine whether a given sentence did or did not express a genuine factual proposition. Accordingly, the logical positivists formulated the verification principle. If a statement passes the stringent requirements of the verification principle, then it is meaningful, and if a statement fails to do so, then it is meaningless. Ayer describes the verification principle as follows:

> The principle of verification is supposed to furnish a criterion by which it can be determined whether or not a sentence is literally meaningful. A simple way to formulate it would be to say that a sentence had literal meaning if and only if the proposition it expressed was either analytic or empirically verifiable.

The verification principle offers a two-pronged test. A statement is meaningful only if it is either (1) analytic—that is, true by definition—or (2) empirically verifiable. Both of these points need some explanation. Many philosophers in the eighteenth and nineteenth centuries drew rigid distinctions between analytic and empirical statements. Analytic statements derive their meaningfulness from the definitions of their words or symbols. To say that "all bachelors are unmarried men" has literal significance because the word *bachelor* is defined in such a way as to include the idea of *men*. As Kant argued, in analytic statements the subject already contains the predicate, and if we deny the predicate, then we get a contradiction, such as "bachelors are married men." The meaning of analytic statements depends not on experience but only on the consistent use of their clearly defined terms. Analytic statements, then, are necessarily true based the definitions of the words in the statements. Thus, the first prong of the verification principle is that analytically true statements are meaningful. They have a *formal* meaning, since their meaning is derived not from empirical facts but from the logical implications of words and ideas, particularly in mathematics and logic.

The second prong of the verification principle designates that empirically verifiable statements are also meaningful. An empirical statement is one whose truth rests on some kind of empirical observation, such as "The sun will rise tomorrow." In this example the notion of "rising tomorrow" is not already contained in the notion of the "sun." Further, we could deny the predicate of this statement and not have a contradiction, as in "The sun will not rise tomorrow." We certainly expect the sun to rise tomorrow, but this expectation is not based on the definition of the word "sun." Throughout our lives we see the sun rise in the morning and set in the evening, and this experience confirms or "verifies" the statement "The sun will rise tomorrow." Logical positivists did not believe that we actually had to verify empirical statements before they would be meaningful. Instead, we only need to have a possible procedure by which we could empirically verify the truth or falsehood of a given statement. For example, the statement "There are flowers growing on Pluto" is empirically verifiable since we could in theory build a space ship to Pluto and then explore the planet for flowers. In this case we most likely would not find any flowers and would thus disconfirm the statement. Regardless of the statement's actual truth or falsehood, it is still meaningful because it allows for some possible empirical inspection. The problem, then, with metaphysical statements is that they are not true by definition, nor do they allow for some possible empirical inspection.

Carnap's Logical Analysis

Among the foremost members of the Vienna Circle was the eminent positivist Rudolph Carnap (1891–1970). Born in Germany in 1891, he taught in Vienna and Prague from 1926 to 1935. After arriving in the United States in 1936, he taught for many years at the University of Chicago, and from 1954 until his death in 1970 he was associated with the University of California at Los Angeles. "The only proper task of Philosophy," Carnap writes in his *Philosophy and Logical Syntax*, "is Logical Analysis." It is the function of logical analysis, he said, to analyze all knowledge, all assertions of science and of everyday life, in order to make clear the sense of each assertion and the connections between them. The purpose of logical analysis is to discover how we can become certain of the truth or falsehood of any proposition. One of the principal tasks of the logical analysis of a given proposition is, therefore, to discover the method of verification of that proposition.

For Carnap the method of a proposition's verification is either direct or indirect. If a proposition asserts something about a perception I am having—for example, that I see a house—this proposition is effectively tested or verified by my present perception. On the other hand, there are propositions that cannot be verified so directly. To say, for example, "This key is made of iron" requires an indirect method of verification. One way to verify the assertion that the key is made of iron is to place it near a magnet, which enables me to perceive that the key is attracted. It now becomes possible to arrange a series of propositions in a tight logical sequence leading to verification as follows: A verified physical law holds that "if an iron thing is placed near a magnet it is attracted"; another verified proposition asserts that "this metal bar is a magnet"; it is verified through direct observation that "the key is placed near the bar." When the magnet finally attracts the key, the verification is complete. Thus, when we cannot directly verify a proposition, we must indirectly do so by verifying propositions deduced from the original one and linking these with more general propositions that have already been empirically verified. If a proposition is phrased as a prediction, as in the proposition "The magnet will attract the key," its verification requires observation of the completed attraction. If the magnet attracts the key, there is a considerable degree of certainty about the truth of the description of the key. Statements of predictions, however, are only *hypotheses* since there is always the possibility of finding in the future a negative instance. For this reason, even though the degree of certainty is sufficient for most practical purposes, the original proposition will never be completely verified so as to produce *absolute* certainty.

These two forms of verification—direct and indirect—are central to the scientific method. Carnap argues that in the field of science every proposition asserts something about either present perceptions or future perceptions. In both cases verification is either through direct perception or by the logical connection of already verified propositions. Thus, if a scientist made an assertion from which no proposition verified by perception could be deduced, it would be no assertion at all. For example, we could not verify the claim that there is a levitational force just as there is a gravitational force. While propositions concerning gravity can be verified by observing its effects on bodies, there are no observable effects or laws describing levitation. According to Carnap, assertions about levitation are no assertions at all because they do not speak about anything. They are nothing but a series of empty words—expressions with no sense.

When logical analysis is applied to metaphysics, Carnap concludes that metaphysical propositions are not verifiable, or, if an attempt at verification is made, the results are always negative. Take, for example, the proposition propounded by Thales that "the principle of the World is Water." We cannot deduce any propositions asserting any perceptions whatever that may be expected in the future. Such a proposition, therefore, asserts nothing at all.

Metaphysicians cannot avoid making their propositions nonverifiable because if they made them verifiable they would belong to the realm of empirical science, since their truth or falsehood would depend on experience. Carnap therefore rejects metaphysics, as he writes in his *Philosophy and Logical Syntax:*

> Metaphysical propositions are neither true nor false, because they assert nothing, they contain neither knowledge nor error, they lie completely outside the field of knowledge, of theory, outside the discussion of truth or falsehood. But they are, like laughing, lyrics, and music, expressive. They express not so much temporary feelings as permanent emotional or volitional dispositions. . . . The danger lies in the *deceptive* character of metaphysics; it gives the illusion of knowledge without actually giving any knowledge. This is the reason why we reject it.

According to Carnap, ethics and value judgments in general belong to the realm of metaphysics. When he applies his method of logical analysis to the propositions of ethics, these propositions predictably turn out to be meaningless. There can, he argues, be a science of ethics in the form of psychological or sociological or other empirical investigations into the actions of human beings and their effects on other people. But the philosophy of moral values does not rest on any facts since its purpose is to state norms for human action. The value statement "Killing is evil" has the grammatical form of an assertive proposition. But, Carnap says, "a value statement is nothing else than a command in a misleading grammatical form. It may have effects upon the actions of men, and these effects may be in accordance with our wishes or not; but it is neither true nor false. It does not assert anything and can neither be proved nor disproved."

Carnap held that the propositions of psychology belong to the region of empirical science in just the same way as do the propositions of biology and chemistry. He was aware that many people would consider it an offensive presumption to place psychology, "hitherto robed in majesty as the theory of spiritual events," into the domain of the physical sciences. Yet that is what he proceeded to do. In his essay "Psychology and Physical Language," he writes "Every sentence of psychology may be formulated in physical language." What he meant by this was that "all sentences of psychology describe physical occurrences, namely, the physical behavior of humans and other animals." This is part of the general theory of physicalism, which Carnap described as the view that "physical language is a universal language, that is, a language into which every sentence may be translated." In effect, Carnap would make psychology an aspect of physics since all science would become physics and the various domains of science would become parts of a unified science. In this manner we are to test propositions in psychology by translating them into physical language. Thus, the statement "John is in pain" is translated into a statement describing the observable state S of John's body. This process of translation requires only that there be a scientific law stating that someone is in pain if and only if his bodily condition is in a particular state S. It is then meaningful to say that "John is in pain" and "John's body is in state S" since, while not equivalent, these are interchangeable translations. Only those statements that can be directly verified or translated into verifiable statements have meaning. Neither metaphysics, some aspects of psychology, theories of "reality," nor the philosophy of normative values could satisfy the criterion of verifiability, and Carnap therefore rejected them as meaningless.

In time there were objections to Carnap's early formulation of the criterion of verifiability. In response, Carnap shifted his ground from verification to *confirmation*. He agreed that if verification is taken to mean a complete and definitive establishment of the truth, then the laws of science could never be verified. The number of instances to which the laws of biology or physics apply is infinite. If strict verification required personal observation of every instance, then obviously there could not be verification as so defined. Though we cannot verify the universal scientific law, we can nevertheless verify its universal application—that is, single instances in the form of particular sentences derived from the law and from other sentences previously established. In this manner *verification* in the strict sense gives way to the gradually increasing *confirmation* of scientific laws.

As a further aid to logical clarity, in his book *The Logical Syntax of Language*, Carnap distinguished between what he called the *material* and the *formal* modes of language. He argued that the *material* mode, commonly used in philosophy, frequently leads to the ambiguities and errors of metaphysicians and in general is the source of meaningless philosophical controversy. To overcome these dangers, Carnap felt it was necessary to translate sentences from the material idiom into the more accurate *formal* idiom. He gives the following example: The sentence "The moon is a thing" is in the material mode. It can be translated into the formal mode in this sentence: "The word 'moon' is a thing-designation." Every sentence that states, "Such and such is a *thing*," belongs in the material mode. Carnap holds that many other words, such as *quality, relation, number*, and *event*, also function the same way as the word *thing*. As another example, the sentence "7 is not a thing but a number" is in the material mode; its formal mode translation is "The sign 7 is not a thing sign but a numerical sign." The way to avoid the "dangerous material mode," Carnap says, is to avoid the word *thing* and use instead the syntactical term *thing-designation*. Similarly, instead of using the word *number*, we should use the term *numerical-designation;* instead of *quality, quality-designation;* instead of *event, event-designation;* and so forth. Other examples would include "He lectured about Babylon" translated into "The word *Babylon* occurred in his lecture."

By this method of translating sentences into the formal mode, Carnap hoped that we would free "logical analysis from all reference to extra-linguistic objects themselves." Analysis would then be concerned principally with the form of linguistic expressions—with *syntax*. In spite of this emphasis on syntactical form, Carnap believed that we must not forget the objects themselves to which our words refer. He writes, "There is no question of eliminating reference to objects themselves from object-sciences. On the contrary, these sciences are really concerned with objects themselves, with things, not merely with thing-designations."

Problems with Logical Positivism

The theory of logical positivism was not warmly received by many philosophers. Some were appalled at the incredible claim that moral language is meaningless. Others noted inherent defects with the verification principle, which the logical positivists themselves soon recognized. Among the difficulties encountered was, first of all, that the verification principle was not itself verifiable. Consider this sentence: "Meaningful statements are either analytic or empirically verifiable." But is this statement itself meaningful based on its own criteria? This sentence is not true by definition, nor can it be verified through experience. Thus, this statement of the verification principle fails its own test, and so is meaningless. Logical positivists recognized this problem and said that their principle was more like a recommendation than a meaningful scientific contention. The question still remains, though, why a metaphysician would want to adopt a recommendation like this if it rendered meaningless everything the metaphysician said.

A second problem arose in the very area where this principle was presumed to have its greatest relevance, namely, the sciences. Scientific knowledge is frequently expressed in the form of universal laws. These "laws" are the basis for scientific *prediction*. But the problem the logical positivists faced was whether to consider scientific statements meaningful. How can a statement that makes a prediction be verified? Can my present experience, or experiment, tell me anything about the future? Obviously, literal significance or meaning is one thing when we verify the statement "There is a black cow in Smith's barn." It is quite another thing when the scientist says, for example, that "when a moving body is not acted on by external forces, its direction will remain constant." The first case is specific and verifiable. The second involves an indefinite number of cases, and any single case in the future can falsify that statement. Since there is no single fact that can *now* verify the future truth of a general scientific statement, such a statement, by a rigorous application of the verification principle, would be meaningless. Logical positivists solved this problem by offering a weaker version of the verification principle: that a statement need only be "verifiable in principle," or *capable* of verification, that is, confirmed in some degree by the observation of something physical.

A third problem involves the crucial question of what constitutes *verification*. To answer "sense experience" raised the further question "Whose experience?" The problem begins with the central assumption behind the verification principle— that our empirical utterances need to be translated into more foundational statements. Scientific language would ultimately be reducible to *observational statements*. But what is the fact that an observation statement reports? Is it a subjective experience about a physical object, or is it a pure picture of that object? The technical problem concerns whether it is ever possible to translate a person's internal experience into a statement about a physical object, or vice versa. This is the problem of *solipsism*, the view that the self is the only object of real knowledge and, therefore, that the experiences of one person cannot be the same as those of another. Each person's experience is different, and all of our experiences are different from the objectively real world. If this is the case, what does the verification principle amount to in the end? Verification statements would mean one thing to one person and something else to others.

A fourth and more general problem with the verification principle is why it places such a high premium on sense experience. That is, why rule out the meaningfulness of statements that are grounded only in our intuitions, hopes, or gut feelings? Logical positivists did not answer this question in any formal way. It may be that for them empirical verification was central to the distinction between scientific procedures, on the one hand, and metaphysical speculation, on the other. Being oriented chiefly toward science, the logical positivists assumed that only language that referred to physical objects and their interrelationships could have cognitive meaning. By coupling all statements to physical facts, they hoped to achieve the *unity of science*; such a unified knowledge would give sciences a common language and tell us all there is to say.

Because of all these problems, logical positivists toned down the intensity of their views. The blanket rejection of metaphysics and morals was reversed, and analysts began to focus on these traditional areas of philosophy. Ayer described this new temper by saying, "The metaphysician is treated no longer as a criminal but as a patient: there may be good reasons why he says the strange things he does." Ethics, for example, is no longer nonsense but is a discipline whose language is analyzed both for its relation to fact and for its value in pointing to a problem. Although logical positivism in its classical form collapsed from the weight of its inner difficulties, its impact continues in the analytic movement, which is still concerned overwhelmingly with the usages and analysis of language.

Quine's Critique of Empiricism

By the mid-twentieth century logical positivism as a movement was largely a thing of the past. Nevertheless, fears of violating the verification principle still lingered in the minds of metaphysicians and moralists, many of whom avoided straying too far from empirical facts. But logical positivism was only the most recent effort to put forth an empiricist agenda. The empirical trend in philosophy is much older, dating as far back as Francis Bacon, and for several centuries after was a driving force in philosophical discussions. In 1951 Willard Van Orman Quine (1908–2000) attempted to expose a more fundamental problem with empiricism that applied not only to logical positivism but to all traditional accounts of empiricism. He addresses this in his 1951 essay "Two Dogmas of Empiricism." The first dogma of empiricism is the long-standing assumption that statements neatly divide between those that are *analytic* and those that are *synthetic* (that is, empirical). He writes, "A boundary between analytic and synthetic statements simply has not been drawn. That there is such a distinction to be drawn at all is an unempirical dogma of empiricists, a metaphysical article of faith." The other dogma is that of *reductionism*, which holds that every meaningful statement can be translated into a statement about immediate experience.

Quine was aware that to reject these dogmas would mean abandoning, or at least "blurring[,] the supposed boundary between speculative metaphysics and natural science." Nevertheless, this is what he tries to do. As to the first dogma, he argues that the notion of "analyticity" is very difficult to clarify, apart from a few limited logical statements. Even logical statements, presumably true "no matter what," can be altered in the interests of new conceptions of physics. Quine asks, "What difference is there in principle between such a shift [in logic] and the shift whereby Kepler superseded Ptolemy, or Einstein, Newton, or Darwin, Aristotle?" Synthetic statements, he argues, do not live up to their empirical verifiability as clearly as they are supposed to. Quine scrutinizes various ways that philosophers tried to establish the truth of both analytic and synthetic statements; he concludes that "no statement is immune to revision." This would mean that both analytic and synthetic propositions contain only contingent truth and, to that extent, do not differ.

What would science be like without the dogmas of empiricism? As an empiricist himself, Quine believed that science and logic are important conceptual schemes and useful tools. Indeed, the total range of our knowledge, he says, "is a man-made fabric which impinges upon experience only along the edges." Any conflict between a statement that we hold to be true and a new experience at variance with it requires an adjustment. We must alter not only our initial statement but, ultimately, all the interconnected concepts. Certainty seems greatest in the physical realm, but Quine argues that physical bodies are themselves only a convenient conceptual tool. Indeed, he says that physical objects are simply "irreducible posits," comparing them to the gods of Homer. As an empiricist he thinks that it would be erroneous to believe in Homer's gods rather than physical objects. "But," he says, "in point of epistemological footing the physical objects and the gods differ only in degree and not in kind." To argue in this manner clearly undercuts the distinction both between analytic and synthetic statements and between metaphysics and science. In the end Quine settles for a strongly pragmatic conception of truth, saying, "Each man is given a scientific heritage plus a continuing barrage of sensory stimulation; and the considerations which guide him in warping his scientific heritage to fit his continuing sensory promptings are, where rational, pragmatic."

WITTGENSTEIN

Wittgenstein's Road to Philosophy

Ludwig Wittgenstein was born on April 26, 1889, the youngest of eight children of one of the wealthiest and highest-placed families in the Austro-Hungarian Empire. His father, Karl Wittgenstein, built an immense fortune during the 1890s as a leader in the heavy metals industry. As he neared retirement, he understandably wanted his children to find their place in his vast company. But for the most part, his children followed their own interests. Under his sister Gretl's influence, Ludwig read some philosophy, but at the same time he could not altogether turn a deaf ear to his father's wishes for him to study engineering to prepare for his entry into the family's company.

Wittgenstein left Europe and went to Manchester to study aeronautics. But he could not deny the powerful inner drive to pursue his interest in philosophy.

Even when he was involved in the problems of engineering, his great interest lay in the philosophy of mathematics. This caused him to suffer the strains of deciding between the two professions of philosophy and engineering. But he still needed some confirmation that he had sufficient talent in philosophy to pursue it as a career. He took a sample of his work to the eminent philosopher Gottlob Frege in Jena, author of *The Foundation of Mathematics*. Wittgenstein felt that his interview went well enough, since Frege encouraged him to travel to Cambridge to study under Bertrand Russell.

After meeting Wittgenstein, Bertrand Russell said that "my German friend threatens to be an infliction, he came back with me after my lecture and argued till dinner time—obstinate and perverse, but I think not stupid." Again, "my German engineer very argumentative and tiresome. He would not admit that it was certain that there was not a rhinoceros in the room. . . . [He] came back and argued all the time I was dressing." Finally, "my German engineer, I think, is a fool. He thinks nothing empirical is knowable—I asked him to admit that there was not a rhinoceros in the room, but he wouldn't." In time these conversations became more relaxed, so that Russell "learned more about Wittgenstein than his all-consuming interest in philosophical problems, as for example, that he was Austrian and not German, and also that he was very literary, very musical, pleasant mannered . . . and I think really intelligent." When Wittgenstein returned to Cambridge in January 1912, he showed Russell a manuscript he had written during the vacation. This changed Russell's opinion of Wittgenstein to a very positive appreciation of his abilities. Russell called the manuscript "very good, much better than my English pupils do," adding, "I shall certainly encourage him. Perhaps he will do great things." During the next term Wittgenstein worked so hard at mathematical logic that Russell believed that Wittgenstein had surpassed him, saying that he had learned all he had to teach and, indeed, had gone further. "Yes, Wittgenstein has been a great event in my life—whatever may become of it." In fact, Russell now looked upon Wittgenstein as the one who could solve the problems that were raised by his own work. "I am too old" said Russell, "to solve all kinds of problems raised by my work, but want a fresh mind and the vigor of youth. He is *the* young man one hopes for." As a matter of fact, Russell was so impressed with Wittgenstein's abilities that he considered Wittgenstein his "protégé."

In addition, Wittgenstein developed a bond with G. E. Moore, whose lectures he began to attend. In spite of the praise of these philosophical leaders, Wittgenstein did not pursue a straight line in his philosophical development. There were certain peculiarities in his personality that deflected him from his course from time to time. His intense desire for solitude led him to withdraw to a rural setting in Norway, where he built a cottage and devoted himself entirely to his analysis of the problems of logic, which he thought would be his unique philosophical contribution. But he suffered from physical and emotional isolation. In time Wittgenstein inherited considerable wealth, which, without explanation, he gave away, leaving him without sufficient funds. With Europe drifting toward war, Wittgenstein enrolled in the Austrian army, taking with him his manuscript. By the time he completed his military duties, he was able to return to Cambridge with a virtually finished manuscript and a position as a lecturer at the university. But he was not happy in that teaching position, and, strangely enough, he urged the young scholars who were influenced by his teaching not to go into teaching themselves. Instead, he urged them to undertake some physical or manual work. Although his brilliance was recognized by his peers, Wittgenstein was not a happy scholar, and he made choices that undermined his clear commitment both to his work and to his friendships. In the end he lost the friendship and support of Bertrand Russell, who gave him such strong encouragement at the beginning of his career.

The only book of Wittgenstein's published during his lifetime is his early *Tractatus Logico-Philosophicus* (1919), which develops a theory of logical atomism similar to that of Russell's. Although Wittgenstein was not a member of the Vienna Circle, he conversed with them, and they considered his *Tractatus* to express their philosophical point of view with great accuracy. Not only did Wittgenstein say that "whatever can be said at all can be said clearly," he concluded his book by saying that "whereof one cannot speak, thereof one must be silent." After Wittgenstein's death in 1951, a number of books by him appeared based on manuscripts and lecture notes of students. Principal among these are his *Philosophical Investigations* (1953). These works reflect a completely different turn of thought from the *Tractatus*, and it is his later views that have brought him fame within the field of philosophy.

The New Wittgenstein

Shortly after his *Tractatus* appeared, Wittgenstein repudiated much of that work. He now believed that his former views were based on the erroneous assumption that language has only one function, namely, to state facts. The *Tractatus* further assumed that sentences for the most part derive their meanings from stating facts. Finally, Wittgenstein assumed, as did Carnap, that the skeleton behind all language is a logical one. What struck Wittgenstein now was the somewhat obvious point that language has *many* functions besides simply "picturing" objects. Language always functions in a *context* and, therefore, has as many purposes as there are contexts. Words, he said, are like "tools in a toolbox; there is a hammer, pliers, a saw, a screwdriver, a rule, a glue-pot, glue, nails, and screws. The function of words is as diverse as the functions of these objects."

What made Wittgenstein think initially that language had only one function? He says that he was held captive by the view that language gives names to things, just as Adam in the Bible gave names to animals. He writes that we are all the victims of "the bewitchment of our intelligence by means of language." Our incorrect picture of language is "produced by grammatical illusions." Analyzing grammar might lead us to discover some logical structure of language. But would that justify the conclusion that all language has essentially the same rules, functions, and meanings? It occurred to Wittgenstein that the assumption that all language states facts and contains a logical skeleton was derived not from observation but from thought. We simply assume that all language, in spite of certain superficial differences, is alike. He uncovered the flaw in this analogy by taking the case of games and asking,

> What is common to them all?—Don't say: There *must* be something common, or they would not be called 'games'—but *look and see* whether there is anything common at all.—For if you look at them you will not see something that is common to *all*, but similarities, relationships, and a whole series of them at that. To repeat: don't think, but look.

Wittgenstein therefore shifted his plan of analysis from a preoccupation with logic and the construction of a "perfect" language to the study of the ordinary usages of language. He moved away from what Russell and Carnap were doing and turned instead in the direction of G. E. Moore's analysis of ordinary language, testing it by the criterion of common sense.

Wittgenstein now felt that language does not contain one single pattern alone but is as variable as life itself. He writes, "To imagine a language means to imagine a form of life." Analysis, then, should consist not in the definition of language or its meanings but rather in a careful description of its uses: "We must do away with an explanation, and *description alone* must take its place." We must, says Wittgenstein, "stick to the subjects of everyday thinking, and not go astray and imagine that we have to describe extreme subtleties." Confusions arise not when our language is "doing work," but only when it is "like an engine idling."

Language Games and Following Rules

A central concept in Wittgenstein's philosophy is the notion of rule-following. Throughout our daily routines we engage in a variety of tasks that involve rules of some kind. We often copy the behavior of other people when, for example, we try to learn a dance routine. We often participate in ceremonies such as graduation, in which we wear special clothes, walk in a line with fellow graduates, and receive a diploma. Similar rule-following underlies all language. We say certain things in certain contexts, and we follow specific grammatical rules when we organize our words. Not just our spoken words but our entire thinking activity involves rule-following. Wittgenstein suggests that the rules of language are like rules of different games—language games—that vary in different contexts. When a student asks questions in a biology class, she follows the rules of various language games, such as the language game of an inquiring student in a formal classroom and the language game of the discipline of biology. He writes,

> But how many kinds of sentence are there? Say assertion, question, and command?—There are *countless* kinds: countless different kinds of uses of what we call "symbols," "words," and "sentences." And this multiplicity is not something fixed, given once for all; but new types of language, new language-games, as we may say, come into existence, and others become obsolete and get forgotten. . . . Here the term "language-game" is meant to bring into prominence the fact that the *speaking* of language is part of an activity, or of a form of life.

Because philosophical problems grow out of language, it is necessary to acquire a basic familiarity with the uses of the language out of which each problem arises. As there are many kinds of games, there are many sets of rules of the games. Similarly, as there are many kinds of languages (that is, the many forms of ordinary language of work, play, worship, science, and so forth), there are many *usages*. Under these circumstances "the work of the philosopher consists of *assembling reminders* for a particular purpose."

Clarifying Metaphysical Language

How does Wittgenstein deal with metaphysical language? Unlike the positivists he did not reject the statements of metaphysics outright. Instead, he considered the metaphysician as a patient instead of a criminal, and the function of philosophy as therapeutic. Metaphysical language can indeed create confusion, and the central concern of philosophy is to deal with problems that baffle and confuse us because of the lack of clarity. Philosophy is a "battle against the bewitchment of our intelligence by means of language." Bewitchment causes confusion, and so "a philosophical problem has the form: 'I don't know my way about.'" Philosophy helps us to find our way, to survey the scene; it brings "words back from their metaphysical to their everyday usage."

Philosophy does not provide us with new or more information, but instead adds clarity by a careful description of language. It is as though I can see all the pieces of a jigsaw puzzle but am baffled by how to put it together. I am actually looking at everything I need to solve the problem. Philosophical puzzlement is similar and can be removed by a careful description of language as we ordinarily use it. What confuses us is when language is used in new and unordinary ways. Hence, "the results of philosophy are the uncovering of one or another piece of plain nonsense." If metaphysics displays resistance or a prejudice that obscures the ordinary usage of words, he concedes that this is "not a *stupid* prejudice." The confusions of metaphysics is part of the human condition:

> The problems arising through a misinterpretation of our forms of language have the character of *depth*. They are deep disquietudes; their roots are as deep in us as the forms of our language and their significance is as great as the importance of our language.

True philosophy does not consist in giving crisp, abstract answers to questions. A person who has lost his or her way wants a map of the terrain, and this is supplied by the selection and arrangement of concrete examples of the actual use of language in ordinary experience.

But it is not enough simply to look at these examples of usage, any more than it is sufficient simply to look at the pieces of the jigsaw puzzle. We frequently "fail to be struck by what, once seen, is *most* striking and most powerful." The most important things are hidden "because of their simplicity and familiarity." But what does it mean to "fail to be struck"? There is no sure method according to Wittgenstein to guarantee that we will "be struck" and thereby find our way. In any case what Wittgenstein sought to do was to shift philosophy's concern away from meanings—from the assumption that words carry in them as so much freight "pictures" of objects in the world. Instead, he directed attention, through the assembling, selecting, and arranging of relevant examples, to the actual uses of words. Because most *philosophical* problems were assumed to arise from puzzlements about words, the scrupulous description of their ordinary uses would eliminate this puzzlement.

AUSTIN

Austin's Unique Approach

Another philosopher concerned with the ordinary use of language was Oxford scholar John Austin (1911–1960). He did not publish extensively, partly because of his untimely death at age 49. He once said that he had to decide early on whether he was going to write books or teach people to do philosophy in a way that he found so useful and satisfying in his own work and life. Austin had a unique approach to philosophy. In his essay "A Plea for Excuses," he tells the reader that philosophy provided for him what it is so often lacking, namely, "the fun of discovery, the pleasure of cooperation and the satisfaction of reaching agreement." With relief and humor, he tells how his research enabled him to consider various words and idioms "without remembering what Kant thought" and to move by degrees to discuss "deliberation without for once remembering Aristotle or self-control without Plato." In contrast to heavy and grim philosophizing, Austin exhibited a deceptive simplicity. In the opening sentence of *How to Do Things with Words*, he writes, "What I shall have to say here is neither difficult nor contentious: the only merit I should like to claim for it is that of being true, at least in parts."

Austin was aware that the use of such phrases as "the analysis of language," or "analytic philosophy," or even "ordinary language" could lead to the misunderstanding that philosophical analysis was *only* and *solely* concerned with words. Austin was concerned not only with words but also with "the realities we use the words to talk about." He writes, "We are using a sharpened awareness of words to sharpen our perception of, though not the final arbiter of, the phenomena." He even wondered in passing whether his approach to philosophy might not more usefully be called "linguistic phenomenology," a notion he gave up as being "rather a mouthful." Austin had little interest in criticizing the methods of other philosophers or putting excessive emphasis on his own style. He developed a technique for studying the nature of language and found it successful in dealing with various philosophical problems.

The Notion of "Excuses"

In his essay "A Plea for Excuses," we find some flavor of Austin's fruitful analysis of ordinary language. He elaborates in some detail just how and why he philosophizes about words. For one thing, he felt that philosophy can be "done" in a wide variety of ways. Unlike any one of the sciences, whose subject matter and methods are highly organized, philosophy functions in those spheres where no one is sure just what is the best way to resolve a particular problem. He thus selects some area of discourse that he thinks is of interest to philosophers. For him the word *excuses* provided a rich field for the study of language and human behavior. Through the analysis of this word, Austin discovers distinctions of various degrees between words closely connected with *excuses*. Moreover, his analysis yields interesting insights into human behavior as suggested by the distinctions among a web of interrelated words.

At the outset the word *excuses* turns out to be a term surrounded by other significant words, such as *defiance, justification,* or *plea.* It is necessary, Austin argues, to give a complete and clear account and to consider the largest possible number of cases of the use of the chosen word. In general, excuses involve a situation in which people are *accused* of having done something wrong, or "bad," or "inept," and either they try to defend their conduct or establish their innocence. They can admit that they *did* what they are accused of doing and then argue that under the prevailing circumstances it was either the right or the acceptable or at least the understandable thing to do. This would be to "justify" the action. A quite different way to proceed would be for the accused to admit that the act was a bad one but that it would be unfair to say without qualification that they *did* it. It could be that their action was unintentional or accidental or was precipitated by some other event. The word "responsibility" becomes significantly related to "they did it" and to "excuses." And the distinction between an "excuse" for an action and a "justification" of it turns out to be an important one. Moreover, if the charge happens to be murder, a plea for the accused could rest on the justification of self-defense or be excused as accidental. Words with finer degrees of distinction could be employed here, including "mitigation" and "extenuation." And what about the language of a defendant who says, "I didn't do it—something in me made me do it." An act can also be the result of a "fit of anger" as distinguished from a "deliberate act."

Why go through this analysis of "excuses" or any other term of discourse? Apart from the fact that the fashioning of excuses has occupied such an important role in human affairs and is on that account worthy of careful study, Austin believed that moral philosophy could benefit from this analysis for two reasons. First, such an analysis could facilitate development of a more accurate and up-to-date version of human conduct. Second, as a corollary, it could contribute toward the correction of older and prematurely settled theories. Since moral philosophy is the study of the rightness and wrongness of conduct or the doing of actions, it becomes crucial to understand what it means to "do something" before we can properly say about it that it is either right or wrong.

"Doing an action," Austin says, is a very abstract expression. Do we mean by it "to think something," "to say something," or "to try to do something"? It is just as inaccurate to think that all our actions are of the same nature as it is to think that all "things" are of the same kind—that winning a war, as an action, is the same as sneezing or that a horse as a thing is equal to a bed as a thing. Do we *do* an action when we breathe or see? For what, then, is the phrase "doing an action" an appropriate substitute? What rules are there for the proper word signifying "the" action for which a person is responsible or for which he or she manufactures excuses? Can human actions be divided in order to attribute one part to the actor and the remainder to someone or something else? Moreover, is an action a simple event? Austin emphasizes rather the complex nature of a human act. This even includes the mere motion of the body, which could involve intentions, motives, responses to information, the reflection upon rules, a studied control of the motion of a limb, or a shove from someone else.

Austin believed that the questions just raised and the problems posed can be illuminated by an analysis of the word *excuses*. For one thing, an excuse implies that a certain type of behavior went wrong in some way. To determine the nature of the wrongness involves a clarification of the "right." The abnormal frequently clarifies the normal. The careful study of excuses provides the opportunity to determine when excuses are appropriate, what actions can be classified as excusable, what particular abnormalities of behavior are truly "actions," and, in a more intricate manner, what constitutes the very structure or mechanism of human behavior. The study of excuses can also resolve some traditional mistakes or inconclusive arguments in moral philosophy. High on the list is the problem of freedom. Here Austin compares the words *freedom* and *truth*, pointing out that just as "truth" is not a name characterizing assertions, neither is "freedom" a name characterizing actions. Freedom, Austin says, is "the name of the dimension in which action is assessed." He then says, "In examining all the ways in which each action may not be 'free', i.e., the cases in which it will not do to say simply 'X did A,' we may hope to dispose of the problem of freedom."

The Benefits of Ordinary Language

Besides throwing light on moral philosophy, the study of excuses provides Austin with a concrete application for his philosophical method. He begins with "ordinary language," through which he expects to discover "what we should say when" and, therefore, "why and what we should mean by it." This, he believed, can clear up the uses and misuses of words and in that manner avoid the traps in which we can be caught through imprecise language. The analysis of ordinary language also emphasizes the differences between words and things and enables us to remove the words from the realities we use words to talk about, and in that way get a fresh look at those realities. Most of all, Austin believed that "our common stock of words embodies all the distinctions men have found worth drawing, and the connections they have found worth making, in the lifetimes of many generations." This stock of words in ordinary language must, he felt, be sounder and subtler than any we could think up for the purpose of philosophizing, for they have stood up to the test of time and the competition of other possible words. Moreover, ordinary language provides the philosopher "a good site for fieldwork." It makes possible a different climate of philosophical discourse by disengaging individuals from frozen and rigid philosophical positions. How much easier it is to agree on the uses of words or even on how to reach agreement. Austin hoped that this method could someday be applied to the turbulent field of aesthetics, saying, "If only we could forget for awhile about the beautiful and get down to the dainty and the dumpy."

Austin was aware that ordinary language, as a basis for analysis, could present certain problems. For one thing, there is a certain "looseness" in ordinary language so that one person's usage may not be the same as another's. To this Austin replies that there is not as much disagreement in the use of words as we might think. Surface differences tend to disappear when, through analysis, we discover that it was not really the *same* situation about which different people have been speaking: "The more we imagine the situation in detail," says Austin, "the less we find we disagree about what we should say." Sometimes, however, there are disagreements in the use of words. But even here, he says, "we can find *why* we disagree," and "the explanation can hardly fail to be illuminating." Besides its looseness, another question about ordinary language is whether it should be construed as the "last word" on matters. While ordinary language does not claim to be the last word, it is significant that it embodies the inherited experience and insights of many generations. And although these insights have been focused particularly on the practical affairs of people, that fact further strengthens the claim for its accuracy. For if the distinctions of words work well in ordinary life, "then there is something in it." Scholars may well have interests other than those whose language pertains to ordinary life. And there is no reason to believe that error and superstition cannot survive for long periods of time in a language. To this extent, he readily concedes that "ordinary language is *not* the last word: in principle it can everywhere be supplemented and improved upon and even superseded." But, he believed, it is the first word in his plan of analysis.

Austin recommended three resources that we can use in undertaking a full-scale analysis of the word *excuses*. Similar resources and methods would presumably be available for the analysis of other words as well. First, he advocated using the dictionary. A concise one would do, and he suggested reading through it entirely and listing all relevant words, remarking that it would not take as long as we might suppose. Or we could make a list of obviously relevant words first and consult the dictionary to discover their various meanings—a process that would then lead to other germane words until the relevant list was complete. A second source for this purpose is the law. Here we would be provided with a vast number of cases along with a wide variety of pleas for excuses and many analyses of the circumstances of the particular conduct in question. The third source is psychology. The use of psychology is an interesting example of how ordinary language is supplemented and even superseded. For psychology classifies some varieties of behavior or gives explanations of ways of acting that may not have been noticed by laypeople or captured by ordinary language. Given these resources, "and with the aid of imagination," Austin was confident that the meanings of a vast number of expressions would emerge and that a large number of human actions could be understood and classified, thereby achieving one of the central purposes of this whole process, namely, "explanatory definition."

CHAPTER 19

Phenomenology and Existentialism

*T*hroughout much of the twentieth century, the analytic approach to philosophy launched by Bertrand Russell dominated philosophical thought in the United States, Great Britain, and other English-speaking countries. However, on the Continent—particularly in Germany and France—philosophy had a different emphasis, which emerged in the movements of phenomenology and existentialism. Phenomenology set aside questions about the so-called objective nature of things; it recommended instead that we explore phenomena more subjectively, from within our human experience. Existentialism adopted phenomenology's subjective approach and further developed practical issues of human experience, such as making choices and personal commitments. Phenomenology was launched by Edmund Husserl (1859–1938) and modified by Martin Heidegger (1889–1976). Shortly after there followed a group of writers often called "religious existentialists," including Karl Jaspers (1883–1969) and Gabriel Marcel (1889–1973). Existentialism received its definitive expression through Jean-Paul Sartre (1905–1980) and Maurice Merleau-Ponty (1908–1961).

HUSSERL

Husserl's Life and Influence

Edmund Husserl was born of Jewish parents in the Moravian province of Prossnitz in 1859, the same year in which Bergson and Dewey were born. After his early education in that province, he went to the University of Leipzig, where, from 1876 to 1878, he studied physics, astronomy, and mathematics and found time to attend lectures by the philosopher Wilhelm Wundt. Husserl continued his studies at the Friederich Wilhelm University in Berlin. In 1881 he went to the University of Vienna where, in 1883, he earned his Ph.D. for his dissertation on "Contributions to the Theory of the Calculus of Variations." From 1884 to 1886, he attended the lectures of Franz Brentano (1838–1917), who became a most significant influence on Husserl's philosophical development, especially through his lectures on Hume and John Stuart Mill, and his treatment of problems in ethics, psychology, and logic. On Brentano's advice, Husserl went to the University of Halle, where in 1886 he became an assistant to Carl Stumpf (1848–1936), the eminent psychologist under whose direction he wrote his first book, *Philosophy of Arithmetic* (1891). His *Logical Investigations* appeared in 1900, and in the same year he was invited to join the philosophy faculty at the University of Göttingen. It was here that Husserl spent sixteen productive years, authoring a series of books developing his concept of phenomenology. Because of his Jewish origins, Husserl was forbidden to participate in academic activities after 1933. Although he was offered a professorship by the University of Southern California, he declined the offer, and in 1938, after several months of suffering, he died of pleurisy at the age of 79 at Freiburg in Breisgau.

Husserl's philosophy evolved gradually through several phases. His early interest was in logic and mathematics. Next, he developed an early version of phenomenology that focused chiefly on a theory of knowledge. Then he moved on to a view of phenomenology as a universal foundation for philosophy and science. Finally, he entered a phase in which the conception of the life-world (*Levenswelt*) became a more dominant theme in his phenomenology. It is no wonder, then, that Husserl's philosophy should have had a variety of influences on different scholars at various times. For example, Martin Heidegger, who became Husserl's assistant at Freiburg in 1920, was familiar during his student days with Husserl's work in logic and his earlier writings on phenomenology. As his assistant from 1920 to 1923, Heidegger worked closely with Husserl. Together they prepared an article on phenomenology for the *Encyclopaedia Britannica*. Heidegger also prepared some of Husserl's earlier lectures for publication. Even after Heidegger left in 1923 to become a professor at Marburg, he continued his close association with Husserl. As time passed, however, Heidegger found it difficult to share Husserl's novel developments, especially those dealing with transcendental phenomenology. In his major work, *Being and Time*, Heidegger was critical of Husserl's method and his distinctive view of the ego. By the time Heidegger succeeded to Husserl's chair at Freiburg in the fall of 1928, their relationship had begun to weaken, and it eventually came to an end.

Similarly, although Sartre was influenced by Husserl's writings when he studied phenomenology at Freiburg, he eventually came to believe that Heidegger's modification of Husserl's view was philosophically more significant. Nevertheless, upon his return to Paris from Germany in 1934, Sartre called Merleau-Ponty's attention to Husserl's book *The Idea of Phenomenology* (1906–1907) and urged him to study it carefully. Merleau-Ponty was impressed by several distinctive elements in Husserl's phenomenology and was inspired to work further in Husserl's writings. He was particularly influenced by Husserl's *Crisis of European Sciences* (1936). Although Merleau-Ponty was thoroughly familiar with Husserl's ideas as interpreted by Heidegger and Sartre, he made his own extensive study of the original documents. He even went to Louvain where he had access to the Husserl archives. These archives, which contain over 40,000 pages of Husserl's manuscripts written in shorthand, are gradually becoming available through transcriptions and translations. What we find, then, without analyzing all the details, is that Husserl exerted a strong influence on Heidegger, Merleau-Ponty, and Sartre, the leading exponents of phenomenology and existentialism. And even though they rejected many of Husserl's key ideas, their finished works bear the imprint of his phenomenology.

The Crisis of European Science

Before answering the question "What is phenomenology?" it is helpful to ask, "What prompted Husserl to develop phenomenology in the first place?" His philosophy grew out of his deep conviction that Western culture had lost its true direction and purpose. His attitude is reflected in the title of his last major philosophical work, *Crisis of European Sciences* (1936). The "crisis" consists of philosophy's departure from its true goal, which is to provide the best possible answers to human concerns, to deal rigorously with our quest for the highest values, and, in short, to develop the unique, broad-range capacities of human reason. He described the "crisis" as the "seeming collapse of rationalism," and he set his lifetime objective as "saving human reason." What human reason has to be saved from, according to Husserl, provides the background for his phenomenology.

The key to the crisis of modern thought is the enterprise of "natural science." Husserl was impressed by the brilliant successes of the sciences. In fact, his ultimate objective was to save human reason by developing philosophy into a rigorous science. His criticism was, therefore, not directed at science as such but rather at the assumptions and methods of the natural sciences. Husserl believed that the natural sciences had over the years developed a faulty attitude about human beings and about what the world is like and how best to know it. According to Husserl, the natural sciences rest on the fatal prejudice that nature is basically physical. On this view, the realm of spirit—that is, human culture—is causally based on physical things, which ultimately threatens our conceptions of knowing, valuing, and judging. The natural scientist rejects the possibility of formulating a self-contained science of the spirit. This rejection, Husserl argues, is quite naive and explains to a large degree the crisis of modern people. What makes this scientific rationalism naive is its blind reliance on *naturalism*, which is the view that physical nature envelops everything there is. It also means that knowledge and truth are "objective" in the sense that they are based on a reality beyond our individual selves. The problem started when philosophers and scientists departed from the original philosophical attitude developed in ancient Greece.

Before the days of Socrates, Plato, and Aristotle, people lived very practical lives, seeing to their basic needs for food, clothing, and shelter. They developed mythologies and early religions that supported the practical concerns of individuals and larger groups. In this condition there was no culture of ideas in the sense of concepts that reached beyond the immediate boundaries of local experience and practical interests. Greek philosophers then entered the picture with a new kind of outlook, namely, a universal critique of all life and its goals. The positive side of this critique was its aim of elevating people through universal reason toward a new humanity, rising above the limited horizons of custom, geography, and social groups. What made this possible was a new conception of truth. This truth was independent of tradition, universally valid, and capable of infinite refinement. Here, then, is the origin of the spiritual life and the culture of Europe. The systematic formulation of this attitude is what the Greeks called *philosophy*. Correctly understood, Husserl writes, this philosophy "bespeaks nothing but universal science, science of the world as a whole, of the universal unity of all being." Philosophy had a comprehensive grasp of all nature, which included the cultural as well as the physical—ideas as well as objects. In time, though, this one science—philosophy—began to splinter into several separate sciences. The dominant step in this splintering was the discovery of how the world of perceived nature can be changed into a mathematical world. This discovery eventually led to the development of the mathematical natural sciences. Ultimately, the success of the sciences resulted in the gradual scientific rejection of the spirit.

Democritus had much earlier offered a similar view that reduced everything in the world to material stuff and physical laws. Socrates rejected this view since he felt that spiritual life existed within the context of society. Plato and Aristotle also held this Socratic view of the spiritual dimension. For, while human beings belong to the universe of objective facts, we nevertheless have goals and aims. But with the later success of the mathematical natural sciences, the scientific methods soon enveloped knowledge of the spirit. A person's spirit was now conceived as an objective fact founded on physical stuff. So, the same causal explanations that apply to the physical world also apply to the spiritual. Husserl argues that, from the attitude of natural science,

> there can be no pure self-contained search for an explanation of the spiritual, no purely inner-oriented psychology or theory of spirit beginning with the ego in psychical-self-experience and extending to the other psyche. The way that must be traveled is the external one, the path of physics and chemistry.

He concluded that we cannot improve our understanding of our true human purposes so long as naturalistic objectivism studies spirit according to the methodology of the natural sciences. He thus formulated his transcendental phenomenology as a way of grasping the essential nature of the spirit and thereby overcoming naturalistic objectivism.

Descartes and Intentionality

Having explored Husserl's motivations for developing phenomenology, it will be helpful to look at one of the inspirations for his method, namely, Descartes. Husserl says that "phenomenology must honor Descartes as its genuine patriarch." There were other influences on Husserl's thought—notably, the empiricism of Locke, the skepticism of Hume, the Copernican revolution of Kant, and the pragmatism of James. In every case Husserl went beyond these and others whose insights shaped his own ideas. Nevertheless, Descartes's influence was decisive, for it led Husserl to begin where Descartes began, with the thinking self. However, whereas Descartes sought through systematic doubt to achieve an absolutely certain foundation for knowledge, Husserl formulated the distinctive atmosphere of phenomenology by accepting only one part of Descartes's starting point. Husserl writes, "We thus begin, everyone for himself and in himself with the decision to disregard all our present knowledge. We do not give up Descartes's guiding goal of an absolute foundation for knowledge. At the beginning, however, to presuppose even the possibility of that goal would be prejudice." Husserl thus takes an even more radical approach than Descartes did, for he tries to build a philosophy without *any* presuppositions, looking solely to "things and facts themselves, as these are given in actual experience and intuition." Husserl made it a cardinal rule "to judge only by the evidence" and not according to any preconceived notions or presuppositions. He sought to recapture humanity's prescientific life, which was filled with "immediate and mediate evidences." Thus, whereas Descartes employed systematic doubt, Husserl simply withheld any judgment about his experiences, seeking instead to describe his experiences as fully as possible in terms of the evidence of experience itself.

Experience obviously revolves around the self—the ego—and for Husserl as well as Descartes, the source of all knowledge is the self. But while for Descartes the self becomes the first axiom in a logical sequence, which enables him to deduce, as one would in mathematics, a series of conclusions about reality, Husserl saw the self simply as the matrix of experience. Husserl therefore put primary emphasis on experience instead of logic. His concern was to discover and describe *the given* in experience as it is presented in its pure form and found as the immediate data of consciousness. He criticized Descartes for moving beyond the conscious self to the notion of extended substance, a body, which ties the subject to an objective reality producing thereby mind-body dualism. Instead, Husserl believed that "pure subjectivity" more accurately describes the actual facts of human experience. Moreover, whereas Descartes emphasized the two terms in his famous "I think" (*ego cogito*), Husserl believed that a more accurate description of experience is expressed in the three terms "I think something" (*ego cogito cogitatum*). This is the philosophical concept of *intentionality*—consciousness is always consciousness *of* something.

The clearest fact about consciousness is that its essence is to point toward, or to intend, some object. Our perception of things consists of our projection toward intended objects. Thus, Husserl believed that the essence of consciousness is intentionality. By *intentionality* Husserl means that any object of my consciousness—a house, a pleasure, a number, another person—is something meant, constructed, constituted, that is, intended by me. Pure consciousness has no segments; rather, it is a continuous stream. Our primitive perception consists of the undifferentiated world. The separate objects of perception are those parts of the stream of consciousness that we as subjects constitute by intending them. Kant described how the mind organizes experience by imposing such categories as time, space, and causality on sensory experience. Similarly, Bergson said that "in the continuity of sensible qualities we mark off the boundaries of bodies."

For Husserl, too, intentionality is the active involvement of the self in creating our experience. Indeed, for Husserl, intentionality is both the structure of consciousness itself and the fundamental category of existence. This means that, in the process of discovering reality, we should look for reality in things, since things are what we intend them to be. For example, when I look at someone, I perceive him from a limited perspective, such as seeing only his profile. I also see him in a given setting, such as shopping in a store. These perceptions are only fragments of reality, and from these our consciousness "intends" *the* person in question. This process of intentionality is typically not conscious but rather automatic. The self's constitution of the world is what he calls a *passive genesis*.

Phenomena and Phenomenological Bracketing

The term *phenomenology* rests on Husserl's refusal to go beyond the only evidence available to consciousness—namely, phenomena—which is derived from appearances. Most theories of knowledge distinguish between a knowing mind, on the one hand, and the object of knowledge, on the other. Husserl, though, sees virtually no distinction between consciousness and the phenomenon. In fact, he argues that phenomena are ultimately contained in the very subjective act of experiencing something. This stands in sharp contrast to the more natural attitude, which assumes that there is an objective world of phenomena irrespective of our consciousness of it. For Husserl, knowing something is not like the act of a camera taking pictures of things. By focusing on the phenomena of a thing available to our consciousness, we actually have a more enlarged description of it. For it now includes the real object, our actual perception of it, the object as we mean it, and the act of intentionality. This moves beyond the description of the superficial aspects of a thing's appearances to the intricate activity of consciousness. Husserl writes, "Consciousness makes possible and necessary the fact that such an 'existing' and 'thus determined' Object is intended in it, occurs in it as such a sense." In short, we can best understand the elements of our experience by discovering the active role of consciousness in intending and creating phenomena.

Can we say anything about the external things themselves that we are experiencing? Husserl answers that we must put aside—or bracket—any assumptions about external things. He calls this process *phenomenological epoché*—where the term *epoché* is Greek for "bracketing." He writes that this method involves "detachment from any point of view regarding the objective world." Descartes began by doubting everything, including all phenomena except his thinking self. By contrast, Husserl "brackets" all phenomena, all the elements of experience, by refusing to assert whether the world does or does not exist. He abstains from entertaining any belief about experience. Thus, Husserl brackets the whole stream of experienced life, including objects, other people, and cultural situations. To bracket all these phenomena means only to look upon them without judging whether they are realities or appearances and to abstain from rendering any opinions, judgments, or valuations about the world.

We stand back from the phenomena of experience and rid our minds of all prejudices, especially the presuppositions of the natural sciences. When we do this, it makes little difference whether we deny or affirm the existence of the world. For phenomenological bracketing "discloses the greatest and most magnificent of facts: I and my life remain—in my sense of reality—untouched by whichever way we decide the issue of whether the world is or is not."

Phenomenological bracketing ultimately leads us back to the center of reality, namely, the conscious self. We discover that we ourselves are the life of consciousness through which the objective world exists in its entirety. Husserl writes, "I have discovered my true self. I have discovered that I alone am the pure ego, with pure existence. . . . Through this ego alone does the *being of the world*, and, for that matter, any being whatsoever, make sense to me and have possible validity." Unlike Descartes, who deduced the objective world from the fact that he exists, Husserl argues that the self *contains* the world. In his *Paris Lectures*, He says:

> For me the world is nothing other than what I am aware of and what appears valid in such *cogitationes* (my acts of thought). The whole meaning and reality of the world rests exclusively on such *cogitationes*. My entire worldly life takes its course within these. I cannot live, experience, think, value and act in any world which is not in some sense in me, and derives its meaning and truth from me.

Thus, the structure of thinking itself determines the appearance of all objects. He designates this immediate phenomenal world of experience as the *transcendental realm*, and rejects any philosophical theory that attempts to go beyond that realm. He thus rejects Kant's distinction between the *phenomenal* (experience) and the *noumenal* (the thing-in-itself).

The Life-World

We have seen that Husserl urges us to bracket all presuppositions and essentially go back to a prescientific viewpoint, which he believes reflects the original form of human experience. This is the realm of our daily world—our life-world (*Lebenswelt*). The life-world consists of all those experiences in which we are typically involved, including perception, response, interpretation, and the organization of the many facets of everyday affairs. This life-world is the source from which the sciences abstract their objects. To that extent the sciences provide only a partial grasp of reality. Much of the rich and meaningful elements of experience remains after the sciences have abstracted the elements of their concern. In fact, the very nature of being a scientist is unaccounted for by science itself. Only a rigorous analysis of the way in which the life-world functions in people's unsophisticated experience, as well as in science, will provide an adequate basis for philosophy. In the final analysis the basic justification or confirmation of truth is to be found in the type of evidence that derives from events of the life-world. The totality of these events of the life-world is what Husserl calls "our world-experiencing life."

Through this notion of the life-world, Husserl sought to liberate the philosopher—the phenomenologist—from a point of view dominated by the various natural sciences. For the purpose of an even more useful type of science, but especially in order to liberate the spirit, he fashioned a way of discovering what the world is like before it is interpreted by the scientific outlook. Through bracketing, the life-world emerges as a fresh terrain for the enterprise of description, opening a new way of experiencing, thinking, and even theorizing. Husserl thought he discovered that the "world" is what we as subjects know it to be.

HEIDEGGER

Heidegger's Life

Even before Martin Heidegger published anything, his reputation as an extraordinary thinker had spread among students in the German universities. What was unusual about Heidegger as a teacher was that he did not develop a "set of ideas" or a "system" of philosophy. He produced nothing in the way of a neat structure of academic ideas that a student could quickly understand and memorize. He was not interested so much in objects of scholarship as in matters of thinking. He shifted attention away from the traditional concerns about theories and books and focused instead on the concerns of thinking individuals. We are born in the world and respond to all of our experiences by thinking. What Heidegger set out to explore was the deepest nature of our thinking when we are thinking as existing human beings.

Born in 1889 in Germany's Black Forest region, Heidegger received his preparatory schooling in Constance and Freiburg. He was introduced to philosophy at the age of 17 when the pastor of his church gave him Franz Brentano's book *On the Manifold Meaning of Being according to Aristotle.* This book, though difficult, made such an impression on the young Heidegger that it launched him on his lifelong quest for the meaning of Being, or "the meaning that reigns in everything that is." Along the way Heidegger was also influenced by Kierkegaard, Dostoyevsky, and Nietzsche, from whom he discovered that some concerns of philosophy are most creatively clarified by paying attention to concrete and historically relevant problems. At the University of Freiburg he began his studies in theology, but after four semesters he came under the influence of Husserl and changed his major to philosophy. Upon completing his dissertation and some further advanced studies, Heidegger became Husserl's assistant until he was appointed in 1922 as an associate professor at the University of Marburg. Here, he pursued his studies in Aristotle, formulated a fresh interpretation of phenomenology, and was hard at work on a manuscript that was to become his most famous book. To facilitate his promotion, his dean at Marburg urged him to publish this manuscript, and in 1927, deliberately leaving it incomplete, Heidegger hurriedly published his book with the title *Being and Time.* One year later, in 1928, Heidigger was chosen to be Husserl's successor to the chair of philosophy at Freiburg.

He was elected rector of the University in 1933, and for a brief period he was a member of the Nazi party. In less than a year, in 1934, he resigned as rector and, for the next ten years, taught courses critical of the Nazi interpretation of philosophy. He was drafted into the "People's Militia," having been declared in 1944 the "most expendable" member of the Freiburg faculty. The French occupying forces did not permit him to return to his teaching post until 1951, one year before his retirement. Even after his retirement, he published several essays and interpretations of the history of philosophy, including a two-volume study on Nietzsche (1961) and his last work, *The Matter of Thinking* (1969). Heidegger died in 1976 in Freiburg at the age of 86.

Dasein as Being-in-the-World

Husserl, we have seen, argued that we understand the phenomena of the world only as they present themselves to our conscious selves. Heidegger takes a similar approach in *Being and Time* and attempts to understand Being in general by first understanding human beings. The notion of "human being" can be deceptive. This is particularly so since, throughout the history of philosophy, definitions of "human being" have tended to resemble the definition of things. Inspired by Husserl's phenomenology, Heidegger avoids defining people in terms of properties or attributes that divide them from the world. Phenomenology focuses rather on the full range of experienced phenomena without separating them into distinct parts. Heidegger took seriously the meaning of the Greek word *phenomenon* as "that which reveals itself." It is our human existence that reveals itself, and this is a quite different conception of "human being" than we find in traditional philosophy. To clearly separate his view of human beings from traditional theories, he coined the German term *Dasein*, meaning simply "being there." People—Dasein—are best described as a unique type of being rather than defined as an object. As Heidegger points out, "because we cannot define Dasein's essence by citing a 'what' of the kind that pertains to [an object] . . . we have chosen to designate this entity [person] as 'Dasien,' a term which is purely an expression of its being." If, then, we ask what the essence of human nature is, the answer lies not in some attributes or properties but rather in how people exist. That is, what do our basic human experiences tell us about who we are?

Our basic state of human existence is our *being-in-the-world*. Consider, first, our ordinary daily experiences, what Heidegger calls "average everydayness." To be in the world as Dasein is not the same as one thing being in another thing, as water is in a glass or as clothes are in a closet. Dasein is in the world in the sense of "dwelling on," or "being familiar with," or "I look after something." Here the emphasis is not on one object related in space to another object, but rather on a type of understanding. To say, for example, that "she is *in* love" does not refer to her location but rather to her type of being. Similarly, to say that people are in the world is not only to place them in space but to describe the structure of their existence that makes it possible for them to think meaningfully about the world.

The central feature of our being-in-the-world is that we encounter things as "gear," as what they are for. That is, we see things as utensils. Take, for example, a hammer. Our first encounter with a hammer is how we use it. We use it as a utensil to accomplish some purpose. The more I hammer, the less I am aware of the hammer as an object. There seems to be no distance between me and the hammer. I also see the hammer as part of a project, fulfilling its purpose within a context of various purposes included in the project. If the hammer breaks, I see it in a different way—as a thing or an object. According to Heidegger, we have a special kind of insight, called "circumspection," which reveals the purpose of the item. We do not choose a tool or utensil by inspecting its properties first and then inferring its purpose from those properties. Instead, we see its purpose first. This means that it is not the *properties* of a thing that determine whether it is a utensil, on the one hand, or a mere object, on the other. Rather, we *project* the context within which any item assumes its unique role that explains our different views of that item. Moreover, an item, such as a hammer, has a purpose only in relation to a task that involves several other purposes. No item possesses any properties that throw light on other purposes in the undertaking; for example, no properties in the hammer show that a ladder will also be needed to hammer nails on the roof. Any particular item has meaning only as it is related to other purposes. It is this networked relation of purposes that is revealed prior to our encounter with things as utensils and that gives us the understanding of items as being utensils. It is part of our nature to develop this network or context of purposes. There can be different worlds even composed of the same things because of the different ways individuals project "their" world.

Dasein possesses a threefold structure that makes possible the way that we project the world. First is our *understanding*, by which we project contexts and purposes to things. It is through these projected interrelationships that things derive meaning. Second is our *mood* or *approach*, which affects how we encounter our environment. In a despairing or joyful mood, our task will open up as either despairing or joyful. These are not merely attitudes; instead, they describe our manner of existence and the way the world exists for us. Third is our *discourse*. Only something that can be formulated in speech can be understood and become subject to our moods.

Dasein as Concern

For Heidegger, Dasein's "being-in-the-world" is our most primitive and basic view of things. But this is not the whole story. More important is the fact that we become preoccupied with things that we encounter. In a sense we are consumed by things, tasks, and relationships. We have a practical concern for the tools and tasks in our environment. We have a personal concern for the community of people that surrounds us. This is so central to our identities that *concern* is our fundamental attribute. To understand Dasein, then, we must understand the underlying nature of this concern. Heidegger argues that there are three components of concern, each of which generates a substantial amount of anxiety within us. First, we all have simply been thrown into the world. I did not ask to be born, but here I am nonetheless. This feature of our past he calls *facticity*. Second, we have freedom of choice. We are responsible for transforming our lives, and we must constantly become our true selves by making appropriate decisions. This involves our future and is a feature that he calls *existentiality*. Third, we are fallen, in the sense that we lose our "authentic" character. My authentic existence requires me to recognize and affirm my unique self and my responsibility for my every action. As facticity and existentiality involved my past and future, respectively, *fallenness* involves my present situation.

My drift into an inauthentic existence is subtle, but in every case it involves a tendency to escape from myself by finding shelter in a public self and an impersonal identity. I become an impersonal "one," behaving as one is expected, rather than a concrete "I," behaving as I ought to. I suppress any urge to be unique and excel, and thereby bring myself down to the level of an average person. I gossip, which reflects my shallow interpretation of other people. I seek novelty for the sake of distraction, and I have an overall sense of ambiguity for failing to know my own purpose. However, I cannot indefinitely avoid confronting my true self. Anxiety intrudes. For Heidegger anxiety is not simply a psychological state but rather a type of human existence. Nor is anxiety similar to fear. Fear has an object, such as a snake or an enemy against which it is possible to defend ourselves. But anxiety refers to nothing—precisely, to *no-thing*. Instead, anxiety reveals the presence of "nothingness" in my being. There is no way to alter the presence of nothingness in the center of my being— the inevitability that I will die. Time itself becomes an element of anxiety for me. I know time principally because I know that I am going to die. Each moment of my life is bound up with the fact that I will die, and it is impossible to separate my life from my death. I attempt to deny my temporality and to evade the inevitability of my limited existence. In the end I must affirm my authentic self and thereby see transparently what and who I am. I will then discover that, in my inauthentic existence, I have been trying to do the impossible, namely, to hide the fact of my limitations and my temporality.

RELIGIOUS EXISTENTIALISM

Like Heidegger, other writers were also struck by the phenomenological method that placed human existence at the center of our investigation of reality. Several philosophical theologians saw interesting parallels between the existential descriptions of human nature and religious conceptions of our relation to divine reality. For example, several existentialist theologians saw a parallel between the fall of Adam in the Garden of Eden and Heidegger's conception of inauthentic existence. Just as divine salvation is the solution to original sin, so, too, is authentic life the solution to inauthenticity. It is not just that these notions parallel each other. Instead, according to some theologians, the biblical themes of sin and salvation are simply mythological ways of expressing the distinction between inauthentic and authentic life. Foremost among the religious existentialists were Karl Barth (1886–1968), Emil Brunner (1889–1966), Martin Buber (1878–1965), Rudolf Bultmann (1884–1976), Gabriel Marcel (1889–1973), Karl Jaspers (1883–1969), and Paul Tillich (1886–1965). We will look at the contributions of Jaspers and Marcel.

Jaspers's Existence Philosophy

Karl Jaspers (1883–1969) was a professor in Heidelberg and, after World War II, in Basel. He wrote in several areas, including psychology, theology, and political thought. He was influenced by Kierkegaard, Nietzsche, and Husserl, and his philosophical works develop phenomenological and existentialist themes. His main publication in existentialist thought is the three-volume *Philosophie* (1932). The human condition, he argues in this work, has deteriorated with the development of technology, the emergence of mass movements, and the loosening of the bonds of religion. Each of the sciences has carved out a special area for its subject matter, and each science has developed its own method. Just as each science functions within strict subject-matter limits, so, too, the aggregate of all the sciences is characterized by a limitation of coverage. Thus, each of the sciences is ill-equipped for dealing with the broader issue of total reality. We could not explain total reality any better if we attempted to bring together all of the sciences with their various perspectives. For the central approach to science is to access objective data, and total reality is not limited to objective data.

Jaspers's quest is for the reality that underlies human life—a reality that he simply calls *Existence* (*Existenz*). We discover this component of our existence through philosophy, not through science. There are indeed various human sciences, such as psychology, sociology, and anthropology, but these deal with human nature on an incomplete and superficial level, viewing us only as objects. He writes, "Sociology, psychology and anthropology teach that man is to be regarded as an object concerning which something can be learnt that will make it possible to modify this object by deliberate organization." Jaspers does recognize the value and usefulness of each of these sciences in the context of their respective narrow goals. His argument, though, is that the task of philosophy is not the same as that of science. Thus, when studying Existence, philosophers must not mimic the sciences by treating Existence as an *object* of thought; this would simply turn Existence into one among many beings. Thus, although Jaspers does not reject the technical knowledge of science, he insists that the "practice of life" requires that we bring to this knowledge some additional reality. All the principles and laws of science, he insists, are of no avail "unless individual human beings fulfill them with an effective and valuable reality." The piling up of knowledge cannot by itself assure any particular outcome for us. He writes, "Decisive is a man's inward attitude, the way in which he contemplates his world and grows aware of it, the essential value of his satisfactions—these things are the origin of what he does." Philosophy, therefore, must be *existence philosophy*.

The main task of existence philosophy, then, is to deal with Existence, and to do this philosophers must consider their own immediate inner and personal experiences. Under these assumptions philosophical thinking cannot set out "to raise philosophy to a science," as Hegel had. Instead, philosophy must reaffirm that "truth is subjectivity" and that philosophizing means communicating not about objects or objective knowledge but about the content of personal awareness produced by the individual's *inner constitution*. Existential thinking, Jaspers says, is "the philosophic practice of life."

Jaspers does not offer any systematic definition of existence philosophy. Nevertheless, he gives some of its characteristics. Primarily, existence philosophy is the manner of thought through which we seek to become ourselves. It is a way of thought that does not restrict itself to knowing objects but rather "elucidates and makes actual the being of the thinker." It does not discover solutions in analytic reflection but rather "becomes real" in the dialogue that proceeds from one person to another in genuine communication. Existence philosophy does not assume that human existence is a settled piece of knowledge, since that would make it not philosophy but, once again, anthropology, psychology, or sociology. There is the danger that existence philosophy may lapse into pure subjectivity, into a restrictive preoccupation with one's own ego, into a justification for shamelessness. But Jaspers considers these possibilities as aberrations. Where it remains genuine, existence philosophy is uniquely effective in promoting all that makes us genuinely human. Each person is "completely irreplaceable. We are not merely cases of universal Being." The concept of Being, for existence philosophy, arises only in the consciousness of each concrete human being.

If existence philosophy can be said to have a "function," it is to make our minds receptive to what Jaspers calls the *Transcendent*. The human situation involves three stages. First, I gain knowledge of objects. Second, I recognize in myself the foundations of existence. Third, I become conscious of striving toward my genuine self. At this last stage I discover my finitude. There are certain "limiting situations" that I face, such as the possibility of my own death. However, when I become aware of my own finitude, I simultaneously become aware of the opposite, namely, Being as the Transcendent. This awareness of the Transcendent, which traditional theology calls God, is a purely personal experience incapable of specific delineation or proof. It is simply an awareness that everything, including myself and all objects, is grounded in Being. Central to my awareness of the Transcendent is my concurrent awareness of my own freedom. In my striving to fulfill my genuine self, I am free to affirm or deny my relationship to the Transcendent. Authentic existence, however, requires that I affirm it. I stand in the presence of a choice—an either-or—without the help of any scientific proof or even knowledge, only an awareness. In the end I must express a *philosophical faith*, which signifies a union with the depths of life.

Marcel's Existentialism

Like Jaspers, Gabriel Marcel (1889–1973) centered his existentialist philosophy on the problem of Being, particularly the human question "What am I?" The central notion of Marcel's thought is his distinction between a *problem* and a *mystery*. He argues that it is not possible to answer the question "What am I?"

by reducing it to a problem, analyzing its parts, and then producing a solution. A problem implies that we lack some information or knowledge and that all we need to do is look for it, engage in "research," and thereby overcome our temporary ignorance. A problem usually revolves around an object or a relationship between objects. Information regarding objects and their relationships can be gathered and calculated. But the question "What am I?" cannot be reduced to a problem, because the *I* is not an object or an *it*. Although I am some sort of object, since I do have a body, my being is a combination of subject and object. Because the subjective part of myself can never be eliminated, I cannot be reduced to a mere object, and therefore, the question about my existence is not merely a problem: It is a mystery. *Mysteries*, then, are certain kinds of experiences that are permanently incapable of being translated into objects "out there." These experiences *always* include the subject and are, therefore, matters of mystery. Marcel believed that the element of mystery is virtually irreducible precisely because human existence is a combination of "being and having." When we *have* things and ideas, we can express these in objective terms—for example, "I have a new car." However, *being* is always a subjective matter.

In the end human existence derives its deepest meaning from the subjective affirmation of Being through fidelity. Marcel writes that "the essence of man is to be in a situation." He means by this that a person's relation to Being is different from a stone's. For one thing, we are the only beings "who can make promises," a phrase of Nietzsche's that Marcel wanted to underscore. To be able to make a promise places us in a unique relationship with another person, a kind of relationship that could not possibly exist between two objects. This moral aspect of existence led Marcel to believe that the ultimate character of a person's relationships involves the element of fidelity. Fidelity offers a clue to the nature of our existence, since it is through fidelity that we continue to shape our lives. We discover fidelity through friendship and love, which gives us the power to overcome the "objectivity" of other people and to produce a new level of intimacy. We commit ourselves to them, such as we do with our spouses. Making commitments, though, creates a new problem. The future is always uncertain, and we do not know for sure what other people might do. Our spouses, for example, might just pack up and leave some day. Should we then just naively go into these relationships? The way out of this problem is to put a higher and more absolute faith in a divine and mysterious order. This has a kind of trickle-down effect and supports our more routine faith commitments between people. Although Marcel was in no sense a traditional theologian, he nevertheless found in the Christian faith the basic spirit of his philosophy, and he converted to Roman Catholicism at the age of 39.

SARTRE

Sartre's Life

Born in 1905, Jean-Paul Sartre was the son of Jean-Batiste, a naval officer, and Anne-Marie Schweitzer, a first cousin of the famous theologian and jungle doctor Albert Schweitzer. Sartre was educated at the École Normale Supérieure in

Paris, exhibiting at an early age his precocious gift for literary expression. While at the École Normale, he was attracted to philosophy by Henri Bergson, whose *Time and Free Will* (1889) left him "bowled over," feeling that "philosophy is absolutely terrific, you can learn the truth through it." He spent the years 1934 and 1935 at the Institut Français in Berlin, where he studied Husserl's phenomenology. Sartre wrote his *Transcendental Ego* (1936) in Germany while at the institut, and, as he says, "I wrote it actually under the direct influence of Husserl." It was in Berlin also that he worked on his novel *Nausea*, which he considered his best work even at the end of his career. In that novel Sartre deals with the pathological feeling we have upon experiencing through intuition the accidental and absurd nature of existence, the feeling that human existence is "contingent" and without explicit purpose. Because he could not find words adequate to describe this philosophical insight to the reader, "I had to garb it in a more romantic form, turn it into an adventure."

During World War II, Sartre was active in the French Resistance movement and became a German prisoner of war. While in the prisoner-of-war camp, he read Heidegger and "three times a week I explained to my priest friends Heidegger's philosophy." The notes he took on Heidegger at this time influenced Sartre very strongly and were, he says, "full of observations which later found their way into *Being and Nothingness*." For a brief period he taught at the lycée at Havre, the lycée Henry IV, and the lycée Cordorcet, afterwards resigning to devote himself exclusively to his writings, which ultimately numbered over thirty volumes. As a sequel to *Being and Nothingness* (1943), Sartre wrote another major work titled *Critique of Dialectical Reason* (1960). His last book was a three-volume work on Flaubert (*The Idiot of the Family*, 1971–1972). Although Sartre was influenced by Marxism and continued to be politically active, he was never a member of the Communist Party. While some commentators sought to moralize about Marxism, they were not very successful, Sartre says, "because it was pretty hard to find much in Marxism to moralize about." His own criticism of Marxism was that it provided no explicit role for morality and freedom. Nor should we consider, Sartre says, "that morality is a simple superstructure, but rather that it exists at the very level of what is called infrastructure." Because of his activism, he resisted personal acclaim, and when he was awarded the Nobel Prize in literature in 1964, he refused to accept it on the grounds that he did not want to be "transformed into an institution."

While a student at the elite École Normale Supérieure, he met a fellow student, Simone de Beauvoir, with whom he enjoyed a lifelong companionship. This was no ordinary relationship. Both were brilliant students. Although she was of immense assistance to Sartre in his prolific literary work, Beauvoir herself achieved great fame as a writer. Sartre never published anything without having Beauvoir read it critically and approve it. While Sartre was honored by the Nobel Prize Committee, Beauvoir similarly moved to first place among women of letters. At the time of Sartre's death, she was considered France's most celebrated living writer. Her novel *The Mandarins* won the Prix Goncourt. Her book *The Second Sex*, in which she wrote the often quoted words "one is not born a woman but becomes one," won her recognition as a feminist. Her literary works gave her money, fame, and independence. Although Sartre and Beauvoir never married during their fifty-one years together, they had a strong relationship of loyalty and love. There were, however, complications along the way. In one of her memoirs, Beauvoir says, "I was vexed with Sartre for having created the situation with Olga." This event became the theme of Beauvoir's first novel, *She Came to Stay*, about the fictional character's relation with another woman. This made Beauvoir say about her own situation, "From now on we will be a trio instead of a couple." Sartre said earlier that Beauvoir was his "privileged," but not his only, female companion. Sartre once said philosophically that "one can always be free"; Beauvoir asked, "What is the freedom of the women in a harem?" They were a rare couple—she was tall and strikingly beautiful while Sartre was short and homely. Together their fame reached around the world.

Sartre lived simply and with few possessions, finding fulfillment in political involvement and travel, and needing only a small apartment on the Left Bank in Paris. In declining health and virtually blind, he died on April 15, 1980, at the age of 74.

Existence Precedes Essence

Sartre's name became identified with existentialism primarily because of the lucid, accessible manner in which he wrote. What appeared first in the heavy language of Husserl and Heidegger now came forth from Sartre's pen in the open, captivating style of novels and short stories. His principal contribution to existentialism is undoubtedly his lengthy *Being and Nothingness*. However, for some time his views were best known from his brief lecture *Existentialism Is a Humanism*, published in 1946. Sartre later rejected this piece and defined existentialism in somewhat different terms. Nevertheless, in this lecture he presents his classic formulation of the basic principle of existentialism: *Existence precedes essence*.

What does it mean to say that existence precedes essence, and how does this formula bear on our understanding of human nature? Sartre argues that we cannot explain human nature in the same way that we describe a manufactured article. When we consider, for example, a knife, we know that it has been made by someone who had in his mind a conception of it, including what it would be used for and how it would be made. Thus, even before the knife is made, the knife maker already conceives it as having a definite purpose and as being the product of a definite process. If by the *essence* of the knife we mean the procedure by which it was made and the purposes for which it was produced, we can say that the knife's essence precedes its existence. To look on a knife is to understand exactly what its useful purpose is. When we think about human nature, we tend to describe ourselves also as the product of a maker, of a creator, of God. We think of God most of the time, Sartre says, as a heavenly artisan, implying that when God creates, he knows precisely what he is creating. This would mean that in the mind of God the conception of human nature is comparable to the conception of the knife in the mind of the artisan. Each individual, on this view, is the fulfillment of a definite conception, which resides in God's understanding.

Some philosophers of the eighteenth century, including Diderot, Voltaire, and Kant, either were atheists or suppressed the idea of God. Nevertheless, they retained the notion that people possess a "human nature"—a nature that is found in every person. Each person, they said, is a particular example of the universal conception of Humanity. Whether someone is a primitive native, in the state of nature, or in a highly civilized society, we all have the same fundamental qualities and are, therefore, all contained in the same definition or conception of Humanity. In short, we all possess the same essence, and our essence precedes our individual concrete or historical existence.

Sartre turned all this around by taking atheism seriously. He believed that if there is no God, then there is no *given* human nature precisely because there is no God to have a conception of it. Human nature cannot be defined in advance because it is not completely thought out in advance. People as such merely exist, and only later do we become our essential selves. To say that existence precedes essence means, Sartre says, that people exist, confront themselves, emerge in the world, and define themselves afterward. First, we simply are, and then we are simply that which we make of ourselves.

Perhaps our initial reaction to this formulation of Sartre's first principle of existentialism is that it is highly subjective—that we can presumably set out to make of ourselves anything we wish. However, his main point here is that a person has greater dignity than a stone or a table. What gives me dignity is possession of a subjective life, meaning I am something that moves myself toward a future and am conscious that I am doing so. The most important consequence of placing existence before essence in human nature is not only that we create ourselves but that responsibility for existence rests squarely on each individual. A stone cannot be responsible. And if human nature was already given and fixed, we could not be responsible for what we are.

Freedom and Responsibility

What began in Sartre's analysis as an amoral subjectivism now turns out to be an ethics of strict accountability based on individual responsibility. If, that is, we are what we make of ourselves, we have no one to blame for what we are except ourselves. Moreover, when I *choose* in the process of making myself, I choose not only for myself but for all people. I am, therefore, responsible not only for my own individuality but, Sartre says, for all people. This last point seems to contradict the line of reasoning that Sartre has so far been developing. For, before I can choose a course of action, I must ask what would happen if everyone else acted so; this assumes a general human essence that makes *my* type of action relevant to *all* people. Sartre does in fact say that, even though we create our own values and thereby create ourselves, we nevertheless create at the same time an image of our human nature as we believe it ought to be. When we choose this or that way of acting, we affirm the value of what we have chosen, and nothing can be better for any one of us unless it is better for all. This all sounds very much like Kant's categorical imperative. But Sartre does not wish to invoke any universal law to guide moral choice. Instead, he is calling attention to one of the clearest experiences of human beings. That is, all people must choose and make decisions, and although we have no authoritative guide, we must still choose and at the same time ask whether we would be willing for others to choose the same action. We cannot escape the disturbing thought that we would not want others to act as we do. To say that others will not so act is a case of self-deception. The act of choice, then, is one that all of us must accomplish with a deep sense of *anguish*, for in this act we are responsible not only for ourselves but also for each other. If I evade my responsibility through self-deception, I will not, Sartre argues, be at ease in my conscience.

Although Sartre's moral language sounds at times very much like traditional moral discourse, his intent is to spell out the rigorous implications of atheism. He accepts Nietzsche's announcement that "God is dead" and takes seriously Dostoyevsky's notion that "if God did not exist, everything would be permitted." In a Godless world our psychological condition is one of *abandonment*, a word Sartre takes from Heidegger. Abandonment means for Sartre that with the dismissal of God there also disappears every possibility of finding values in some sort of intelligible heaven. Again, there cannot now be any "good" prior to our choice since there is no infinite or perfect consciousness to think it. Our sense of abandonment is a curious consequence of the fact that everything is indeed permitted, and as a result we are forlorn, for we cannot find anything on which we can rely, either within or outside ourselves. We are without any excuses. Our existence precedes our essence. Apart from our existence there is nothingness. There is only the present. In his *Nausea* Sartre writes that the true nature of the present is revealed as what exists, that what is not present does not exist. Things are entirely what they appear to be, and apart from them there is nothing.

To say there is nothing besides the existing individual means for Sartre that there is no God, no objective system of values, no built-in essence, and, most importantly, *no determinism*. An individual, Sartre says, is free; a person is freedom. In a classic phrase he says that people are *condemned* to be free. We are condemned because we find ourselves thrown into the world, yet free because as soon as we are conscious of ourselves, we are responsible for everything we do. Sartre rejects the notion that we are swept up by a torrent of passion and that such passion could be regarded as an excuse for our actions. He also rejects Freud's view that human behavior is mechanically determined by unconscious and irrational desires; this provides us with an excuse to avoid responsibility. For Sartre we are responsible even for our passions, because even our feelings are formed by our deeds. Kierkegaard said that freedom is *dizzying*, and Sartre similarly says that freedom is *appalling*. This is precisely because there is nothing forcing us to behave in any given way, nor is there a precise pattern luring us into the future. Each of us is the only thing that exists. We are all free, Sartre says, so we must choose, that is, *invent*, because no rule of general morality can show us what we ought to do. There are no guidelines guaranteed to us in this world.

Nothingness and Bad Faith

There is an element of despair in human existence, which comes, Sartre says, from the realization that we are limited to what is within the scope of our own wills. We cannot expect more from our existence than the finite probabilities it possesses. Here Sartre believes that he is touching on the genuine theme of personal existence by emphasizing our finitude and our relation to nothingness. "Nothingness," he says, "lies coiled in the heart of being, like a worm." Heidegger located the cause of human anxiety in our awareness of our finitude when, for example, we confront death—not death in general but *our own* death. It is not only people who face nothingness, Heidegger says; all Being has this relation to nothingness. Human finitude is, therefore, not simply a matter of temporary ignorance or some shortcoming or even error. Finitude is the very structure of the human mind, and words such as *guilt, loneliness,* and *despair* describe the consequences of human finitude. The ultimate principle of Being, Heidegger says, is *will.* Sartre concurs by saying that only in action is there any reality. We are only a sum of our actions and purposes; besides our actual daily lives we are nothing. If I am a coward, I *make* myself a coward. It is not the result of my cowardly heart or lungs or cerebrum. I am a coward because I made myself into a coward by my actions.

Although there is no prior essence in all people, no human *nature*, there is nevertheless, Sartre says, a universal human *condition*. By discovering myself in the act of conscious thought, I discover the condition of all people. We are in a world of *intersubjectivity.* This is the kind of world in which I must live, choose, and decide. For this reason no purpose that I choose is ever wholly foreign to another person. This does not mean that every purpose defines me forever but only that we all may be striving against the same limitations in the same way. For this reason Sartre would not agree that it does not matter what we do or how we choose. I am always obliged to act in a *situation*—that is, in relation to other people—and consequently, my actions must not be capricious, since I must take responsibility for all my actions. Moreover, to say that I must make my essence, or invent my values, does not mean that I cannot *judge* human actions. It is still possible to say that my action was based on either error or self-deception, for if I hide behind the excuse of following my passions or espousing some theory of determinism, I deceive myself.

To invent values, Sartre says, means only that there is no meaning or sense in life prior to acts of will. Life cannot be anything until it is lived, but each individual must make sense of it. The value of life is nothing else but the sense each person fashions in it. To argue that we are the victims of fate, of mysterious forces within us, of some grand passion, or heredity, is to be guilty of bad faith (*mauvaise foi*) or self-deception, of *inauthenticity.* Suppose, Sartre says, that a woman who consents to go out with a particular man knows very well what the man's cherished intentions are, and she knows that sooner or later she will have to make a decision. She does not want to admit the urgency of the matter, preferring to interpret all his actions as discreet and respectful. She is, Sartre says, in self-deception; her actions are inauthentic. All human beings are guilty, in principle, of similar inauthenticity—of acting in bad faith, of playing roles, and of trying to disguise their actual personality behind a facade. The conclusion of Sartre's existentialism is, therefore, that if I express my genuine humanity in all my behavior, I will never deceive myself, and honesty will then become not my ideal but my very being.

Human Consciousness

Underlying Sartre's popular formulation of existentialism is his technical analysis of existence. He argues that there are different ways of existing. First, there is *being-in-itself (l'en-soi)*, which is the way that a stone is: It merely exists. In one respect: I am no different from any other kind of existing reality. I exist, just the same way anything else *is*, as simply *being there*. Second, there is *being-for-itself (le pour-soi)*, which involves existing as a *conscious subject*, which is what people do and things like rocks cannot do. As a conscious subject I can relate to both the world of things and people in a variety of ways. At one level I am conscious of "the world," which is everything that is beyond or other than myself and which, therefore, transcends me. At this level I experience the world simply as a solid, massive, undifferentiated, single something that is not yet separated into individual things. Sartre describes this type of consciousness in *Nausea* where the character Roquentin is sitting on a park bench. He looks at all the things before him in the park, and all at once he *sees* everything differently, everything as a single thing—"Suddenly existence had unveiled itself." Words vanished, and the points of reference that people use to give meaning to things also vanished. What Roquentin saw was existence as "the very paste of things": "The root [of the tree], the park gates, the bench, the sparse grass, all that had vanished: the diversity of things, their individuality, were only an appearance, a veneer. This veneer had melted, leaving soft, monstrous masses, all in disorder—naked." Only later, when we reflect, does the world become our familiar one. But, Sartre says, "The world of explanations and reasons is not the world of existence." At the level of Roquentin's experience, the world is the unity of all the objects of consciousness.

Sartre agrees with Husserl that all consciousness is consciousness of *something*, which means that there is no consciousness without affirming the existence of an object that exists beyond, that is, transcends, our consciousness. As we have seen, the object of consciousness can be "the world" as simply "being there." But in addition to the world as a single solid mass, we speak of specific objects like trees, benches, and tables. Whenever we identify a specific object, we do this by saying what it is not—we differentiate a thing from its background. When a chair appears as a chair, we give it that meaning by blacking out the background. What we call a chair is fashioned or drawn out of the solid context of the world by the activity of consciousness. The world of things appears as an intelligible system of separate and interrelated things only to consciousness. Without consciousness the world simply is, and as such it is without meaning. Consciousness constitutes the meaning of things in the world, though it does not constitute their being.

When we view the world as being-in-itself, as simply being there, Sartre says that "the essential point is contingency. I mean that by definition existence is not necessity. To exist is simply to be there." Contingency means that when something exists, it does so by chance and not because it necessarily follows from something else: "Existences appear . . . but you cannot deduce them." The world we experience is "uncreated, without reason for being, without any relation to another being; being-in-itself is gratuitous for all eternity." The meaning anything will have in the world will depend, Sartre says, on the choices people make. Even a table will have alternative meanings depending on what a particular person chooses to use it for—for example, to serve dinner or to write a letter. A mountain valley will mean one thing to a farmer and something else to a camper. Here consciousness shifts us from being-in-itself (simply being there) to being-for-itself, where consciousness dramatically differentiates the objects of the world from the conscious self as subject.

The activity of consciousness is at this point twofold. First, consciousness defines specific things in the world and invests them with meaning. Second, consciousness puts a distance between itself and objects and, in that way, attains freedom from those objects. Because the conscious self has this freedom from the things in the world, it is within the power of consciousness to confer different or alternative meanings on things. The activity of consciousness is what is usually called "choice." We choose to undertake this project or that project, and the meaning of things in the world will depend to a considerable extent on what project we choose. If I choose to be a farmer, then the mountains, the valley, and the impending storm will have special meanings for me. If I choose to be a camper in that valley, the surroundings and the storm will present different meanings.

Marxism and Freedom Revisited

Although Sartre believed that Marxism was the philosophy of his time, he was aware of a striking contradiction between his existentialism and Marxist dialectical materialism. Sartre's existentialism strongly espouses human freedom. By contrast, Marxist dialectical materialism emphasizes that all the structures and organizations of society and the behavior and thinking of human beings are determined by prior events. On this view freedom of choice is an illusion, and we are simply vehicles through which the forces of history realize themselves. Whereas Sartre argued that it is human consciousness that "makes history" and confers meaning on the world, Marxism holds that the social and economic structures of history direct its own development. Rather than conferring meaning on the world, our minds, the Marxist says, discover this meaning within the historical context as a matter of scientific knowledge. One reason Sartre never became a member of the Communist Party is, he says, because "I would have had to turn my back on *Being and Nothingness*" and its emphasis on human freedom.

In his earlier writings Sartre focused primarily on the individual and freedom. Later, in his *Critique of Dialectical Reason*, he focused more specifically on the historical and social context in which people find themselves and that has an effect on their behavior. He thought that Marx succeeded more than anyone else in describing how social and economic structures develop and how they bear on human decisions. Sartre accepted increasingly the limitations on human choice—the limitations of birth, status in society, and family background. Earlier, he sought to describe how individuals are capable of deceiving themselves by making excuses for their behavior, as if they were not free to have behaved otherwise—a form of self-deception. He never did depart from this emphasis on the freedom of the individual. But he did adjust his thinking under the influence of Marxism by facing the fact of people's social existence, or their relationship to other people, especially as a member of a group—for example, a labor union. Acknowledging the influence of group structures on human behavior and consciousness, resulting particularly in labor's sense of alienation, he revised his optimistic view of human freedom to some extent.

In 1945 Sartre wrote that "no matter what the situation might be, one is always free." As an example he states that "a worker is always free to join a union or not, as he is free to choose the kind of battle he wants to join, or not." Recalling this statement some years later, in 1972, Sartre says that this "all strikes me as absurd today." And he admits, "There is no question that there is some basic change in [my] concept of freedom." In his lengthy work on Flaubert, he concludes that although Flaubert was free to become uniquely Flaubert, his family background and his status in society meant that "he did not have all that many possibilities of becoming something else . . . he had the possibility of becoming a mediocre doctor . . . and the possibility of being Flaubert." This means, Sartre says, that social conditioning exists every minute of our lives. Nevertheless, he concludes that "I am still faithful to the notion of freedom." It is true, he says, that "you become what you are in the context of what others have made of you"; nevertheless, within these limitations a person is still free and responsible. This is Sartre's way of reconciling the fact that historical conditions affect human behavior with his intuitive certainty that human beings are also capable of shaping history. In doing this, Sartre sought to overcome with his existentialism what he considered the major flaw of Marxist philosophy, namely, its failure to recognize the individual as a "real person."

MERLEAU-PONTY

Merleau-Ponty's Life

Maurice Merleau-Ponty was born in 1908, and from 1926 to 1930, he studied at the École Normale Supérieure. The philosophy curriculum at that time was steeped in both rationalism and idealism. Merleau-Ponty says of his teacher, Leon Brunschvicg, that he "passed on to us the idealist heritage. . . . This philosophy consisted largely in reflexive effort . . . [which] sought to grasp external perception or scientific constructions as a result of mental activity." Merleau-Ponty was one year behind Sartre, who also attended that school. An interesting interview between Sartre and Simone de Beauvoir describes the relation between the two at that time. Beauvoir: "You were standoffish with people you did not like. Merleau-Ponty, for example. You were on very bad terms with him, weren't you?" Sartre: "Yes, but even so I once protected him from some men who wanted to beat him up." Beauvoir: "You were singing obscene songs; and being pious, he wanted to stop you?" Sartre: "He went out. Some fellows ran after him—there were two of them—and they were going to beat him up because they were furious. So I went out, too. I had a sort of liking for Merleau-Ponty. . . . [I said] Leave him alone, and let him go. So they didn't do anything; they went off."

In 1929 Merleau-Ponty came under the influence of Gustave Rodrigues, director of the Lycée Janson-de-Sailly where Merleau-Ponty was fulfilling his student teaching assignment. Merleau-Ponty, the young Catholic, found Rodrigues, an atheist, to have an "extraordinary character," leading Merleau-Ponty to say that "an atheist resembles other men." In 1936 he broke with Catholicism as he worked through his version of phenomenology in his first work, *The Structure of Behavior*. He saw active duty during World War II, in 1939 and 1940. He taught at the Lycée Carnot in Paris during the German occupation and at this time composed his greatest philosophical work, *The Phenomenology of Perception*.

From their early days at École Normale Supérieure, the lives and careers of Sartre and Merleau-Ponty unfolded as a stormy relationship during which they would be alternately friends and enemies. With the help of Merleau-Ponty, Sartre organized a resistance network in the winter of 1941, called "Socialism and Liberty." Their goal was to bring about a form of political society based on a harmony between a socialist economy and freedom for the individual. In a collaboration that lasted from 1945 to 1952, Sartre and Merleau-Ponty published *Les Temps Moderne*, a journal aimed at political commentary. While engaged in the journal, Merleau-Ponty taught at the University of Lyon and then the Sorbonne, and in 1952 he was appointed chair of philosophy at the Collège de France, a position that he held until his death.

Merleau-Ponty's political views were progressively becoming less sympathetic toward the former Soviet Union. In 1950 he wrote an editorial denouncing the labor camps there:

> If there are ten million concentration camp inmates while at the other end of the Soviet hierarchy salaries and standard of living are fifteen to twenty times higher than those of the free workers—then . . . the whole system swerves and changes meaning; and in spite of the nationalization of the means of production, and even though private exploitation of man by man and unemployment are impossible in the U.S.S.R., we wonder what reasons we still have to speak of socialism in relation to it.

These labor camps, Merleau-Ponty said, were "still more criminal because they betray the revolution." Around 1952, while Sartre was moving toward closer ties with the Communists, Merleau-Ponty left the editorship of *Les Temps Moderne*.

A few years later, Merleau-Ponty wrote a book, *Adventures of the Dialectic*, in which he included a chapter analyzing in detail Sartre's relationship with communism. The chapter "Sartre and Ultrabolshevism" ends with this critical sentence: "One cannot at the same time be both a free writer and a communist." Actually, both Sartre and Merleau-Ponty ultimately became disenchanted with communism. As we saw earlier, Sartre never became a member of the Communist Party because that would have forced him to give up his strongly held position that people are free. With his philosophical work still far from complete, and at the height of his creativity, Merleau-Ponty died on May 4, 1961, at the age of 53.

The Primacy of Perception

In *The Phenomenology of Perception* Merleau-Ponty offers a theory of perception in reaction against both dualist and realist theories. Intellectualists (or dualists), such as Descartes, argued that not only are our minds distinct from our bodies but our mental concepts and processes have priority over the sensory data that we get from our bodies. Our minds interpret sensory information, fill in the gaps, and make it meaningful. Descartes vividly espouses this view here:

> When looking from a window and saying I see men who pass in the street, I really do not see them, but infer that what I see is men. . . . And yet what do I see from the window but hats and coats which may cover automatic machines? Yet I judge these to be men. And similarly solely by the faculty of judgment which rests in my mind, I comprehend that which I believed I saw with my eyes.

Realists took the opposite view that we receive perceptions of the world exactly as it is and that our minds do not organize our perceptions any further. Merleau-Ponty strikes a middle ground: The perceptual nature of our bodies constructs and shapes sensory data; our higher mental functions play no such role. In fact, even our higher intellectual thought processes are grounded in the perceptual framework of our bodies. He writes, "All consciousness is perceptual, even the consciousness of ourselves." The main theme of this theory, then, is the *primacy of perception:*

> By the words, the 'primacy of perception,' we mean that the experience of perception is our presence at the moment when things, truths, values are constituted for us. . . . It is not a question of reducing human knowledge to sensation, but of assisting at the birth of this knowledge, to make it as sensible as the sensible, to recover the consciousness of rationality.

Merleau-Ponty was particularly influenced by the early-twentieth-century theory of Gestalt psychology, which held that our perceptual experiences are shaped by inherent forms and structures that give sense, meaning, and value to our experiences. For Merleau-Ponty these structures are embedded in bodily perception.

Merleau-Ponty encapsulates his position in the notion that "I am my body," thus denying that I can somehow separate myself as a mental subject from myself as a bodily object. The two components of myself are united in my lived experience through my body. By identifying the self as a body, Merleau-Ponty is not espousing the materialist views in the tradition of Democritus and the atomists. According to traditional materialism, I am essentially a physical machine, and the mental components of my life are more or less explained away by the machinery of my body. Instead, for Merleau-Ponty, the mental aspects of me are embedded in my body; I am a body-subject, rather than a thoughtless and mechanical body.

The Relativity of Knowledge

Merleau-Ponty says that "in the final analysis every perception takes place within a certain horizon and ultimately in the 'world.'" This follows from the fact that perception results from a person's bodily presence in the world. A bodily presence already means that as a subject each of us is situated in the world at a certain time and with a unique perspective. The ideas we ultimately have reflect this partial view and our experience in time so that "the ideas to which we recur are valid for only a period of our lives." The thing we perceive is not a complete thing or ideal unity possessed by the intellect, like a geometrical notion; "it is rather a totality open to a horizon of an indefinite number of perspectival views." This means further that "the things which I see are things for me only under the condition that they always recede beyond their immediate given aspects." For example, we never see all sides of a cube or a lamp or any other thing. Similarly, other observers will see things from *their* perspectives. Moreover, our perceptions occur during the ticking away of time, even though we are not aware of this sequence of the segments of time. At this point, Merleau-Ponty asks,

> Can I seriously say that I will always hold the ideas I do at present—and mean it? Do I not know that in six months, in a year, even if I use more or less the same formulas to express my thoughts, they will have changed their meaning slightly? Do I not know that there is a life of ideas, as there is meaning of everything I experience, and that every one of my most convincing thoughts will need additions and then will be, not destroyed, but at least integrated into a new unity?

He concludes that "this is the only conception of knowledge that is scientific and not mythological." It means, moreover, that "the idea of going straight to the essence of things is an inconsistent idea if one thinks about it." The most we can get from our perception of the world is "a route, an experience which gradually clarifies itself, which gradually rectifies itself and proceeds by dialogue with itself and others."

A dialogue with "others" assumes that everyone can in some way share a similar experience of the world. But can Merleau-Ponty's theory, which concentrates on each subject's internal experience of the world, explain how two people can have a coherent conversation? Perceptions are relative to each person as a result of our unique perspectives, since "our body . . . is our *point of view of the world.*" Merleau-Ponty tries to solve this problem by using the concept of an "a priori of the species." As members of a single species, all human beings perceive certain forms in a like manner. He says that "as Gestalttheorie has shown there are for me preferred forms that are also preferred for all other persons." I will, of course, "never know how you see red and you will never know how I see it. But our first reaction to this separation of our consciousnesses is to "believe in an undivided being between us." As I perceive another person, "I find myself in relation with another 'myself,' who is, in principle, open to the same truths as I am." Even though there are two of us looking at the world, it is not the case that because of our different perspectives there are "two numerically distinct worlds." There is, Merleau-Ponty says, a demand that "what I see be seen by [you] also."

Perception and Politics

We might think that Merleau-Ponty's account of the relativity of perceptual knowledge would not be well suited to deal with the problems of political, social, and economic order. After all, these subjects call for permanent and stable notions of "justice" and "freedom," which Plato's or Kant's theories might better explain. This would contradict the existentialist notion that there are no essential and timeless values, that there is no essential human nature to be fully realized, and that people must create their own values. Merleau-Ponty has an answer to this. Right off, he rejects the lofty claims of abstract theories of politics, justice, and morality. Although Plato and others claimed that such values are based on "timeless" notions of the human good, these values in fact are simply reflections of the present circumstances of a particular culture. So-called universal political values were imposed on us by people who themselves had not participated in creating those systems of government; as such, such values are not a blessing but represent the heavy hand of oppression. Invariably, the so-called universal values turned out to be to the advantage of special groups. This was one reason Merleau-Ponty found in Marxism a congenial type of thought. Marxism, while abstract up to a point, was nevertheless embodied in an actual system, the communism of the former Soviet Union.

Further, Merleau-Ponty argues that "things" are not all that we encounter through perception. Values are just as specifically perceived and have the same status as other aspects of the world. Values are significant, Merleau-Ponty says, "because they are apprehended with a certainty which, from the phenomenological viewpoint, is a final argument." In addition, perception provides us with the important element of *meaning*. This is particularly significant when our perceptions encounter the actual ways people live among each other. From these actual living and working arrangements, Merleau-Ponty says, we can discover certain background meanings that reveal the changes and movements of specific groups of people. These changes are not simply facts, but they reveal the direction of history. This is another reason why Merleau-Ponty was attracted to communism, for here was a system and theory that could be observed concretely as the bearer of meaning located in the aspirations of the whole class of workers. Thus, in the absence of any viable abstract theories of justice, Merleau-Ponty looked to the only sure source of political knowledge, namely, perception. Here he felt that he discovered not the universality of an idea but the universality of the proletariat, which is the bearer of the meaning of history.

Both Sartre and Merleau-Ponty were drawn to communism after World War II for similar reasons. It represented the chief alternative to the status quo, and the turbulent events of the time called for a new philosophical basis for political action, which they felt existentialism and phenomenology could provide. But they did not always agree with Marxism or with each other's views of Marxism. Their prolonged and heated disagreements ultimately led in 1952 to the termination of their friendship and affected their views on communism. As Sartre wrote in 1961, "Each of us was conditioned, but in opposite directions. Our slowly accumulated disgust made the one [Merleau-Ponty] discover, in an instant, the horror of Stalinism, and the other [Sartre] that of his own [bourgeois] class."

Merleau-Ponty held that it is possible to perceive in actual society the developing consciousness of the working class. He saw a relationship here between the individual, the institutions of society, a scale of values, and reality. Most importantly, he thought he perceived that the developing consciousness of this class was the bearer of a rather specific meaning, a meaning that was growing steadily stronger and was shaping the direction of history. At the center of this overall perception was the urge on the part of this class to resolve the contradictions of the workers' conditions and to organize a humane appropriation of nature. It also meant "as a universal class . . . to transcend national and social conflicts as well as the struggle between man and man." This was the heart of the promise of communism, which Merleau-Ponty originally thought was corroborated by his own perceptions. But he was willing to admit that Marxism would be refuted if the proletariat could not overcome the strong structure of capitalism, if it could not eliminate violence, and if it could not bring about humane relationships among people. "It would mean," Merleau-Ponty says, "that there is no history—if history means the advent of humanity and the mutual recognition of men as men."

CHAPTER 20

Recent Philosophy

*P*hilosophy has undergone dramatic changes since the mid-twentieth century. Foremost is the booming number of people writing in the field. Part of this owes to the remarkable increase in philosophy professors at colleges and universities around the world, which reflects both a spike in world population growth and a continually increasing percentage of people attending college. Not only are there more academically trained philosophers, but there also are increased expectations in universities for philosophers to write—publish or perish as the famous motto goes. Thus, perhaps five times as many philosophy books and journal articles appeared in the year 2000 as in 1950. A consequence of this literary productivity is that philosophy is now highly specialized. It is impossible for a single philosopher to have a full grasp of all the innovative ideas emerging in the different areas of philosophy. When philosophical output was more manageable, we might expect a great figure like Kant to single-handedly alter the direction of metaphysics, epistemology, ethics, aesthetics, and the philosophy of religion. Now, the most creative philosophers focus on only one or two of these areas. An influential writer in one area of philosophy may be a completely unknown figure to a specialist in another area. Paralleling other academic disciplines, philosophy now is driven less by the thoughts of great individual minds and more so by great issues and movements within the discipline. Some individual names certainly rise to the forefront in specific areas of philosophy, but the time may have passed to produce giants like Descartes, Hume, and Kant.

Philosophy is also more multicultural now than it has ever been. In past centuries leading philosophers in the Western world were white men who perpetuated a European tradition of thought. Most notable now is the presence of women in the discipline, who, in the United States, accounted for one-quarter of the academic philosophers by the beginning of the twenty-first century. This rising number of female philosophers sparked an interest in philosophical issues that directly address the concerns of women. Some of these discussions have a politically revolutionary tone and draw attention to the ways that male-centered culture has oppressed women. Other discussions explore how uniquely female ways of thinking impact traditional problems of philosophy, such as theories of knowledge, ethics, and aesthetics. Philosophy is also more multicultural in that it now recognizes the philosophical contributions of non-Western cultures. This is particularly so with Asian philosophy, which has a history of philosophical writings as old as the Greek tradition is in the West. As specialized and culturally diverse as philosophy is today, at best only a sample of key issues and figures can be presented here.

THE MIND-BODY PROBLEM

The mind-body problem is one of the oldest and most explored areas of philosophy. We have seen that Democritus and other atomists attempted to reduce all human mental processes to the operations of material stuff, which strictly follow physical laws. Plato, by contrast, believed that our souls (and thereby our rational minds) are distinct from our bodies and cannot be reduced to material constituents. Developing Plato's view, Descartes attempted to explain how our spiritual minds interact with our physical bodies. His solution was that messages pass between our spirits and bodies by way of the pineal gland within our brains—which acts as a type of metaphysical switchboard. Although Descartes's specific theory created more problems than it solved, the tendency in philosophy after Descartes was nevertheless to accept his radical split between our spiritual minds and physical bodies. As biologists learned more about the human brain in the nineteenth and twentieth centuries, Descartes's mind-body dualism became more untenable—at least to a scientific way of thinking. For scientists the original contention held by the atomists seemed more correct, namely, that mental events are simply the result of physical brain activity. This position—most generally called *materialism*—is now the standard philosophical solution to the mind-body problem. Some philosophers within religious traditions still defend the spirit-body dualism of Descartes, but the majority of the writers on this subject are from nonreligious universities and have set Descartes's solution aside. The dominant issue is not one of how our spiritual minds interact with our physical brains. Instead, the concern is with how our mental experiences can be best explained in terms of brain activity. Assuming that I lack an immaterial spirit, it is difficult to see how my mental experiences are simply the result of biological machinery in my brain.

Ryle's Ghost in the Machine

The inspiration for most discussions of the mind-body problem today is the book *Concept of Mind* (1949) by British philosopher Gilbert Ryle (1900–1976), who began teaching at Oxford University in 1924. Ryle contends that the "official doctrine" of mind is unsound and contradicts virtually everything we know about human mentality. In its simplest form the official doctrine holds that every human being has both a mind and a body, that these two are coordinated, but that upon the death of the body the mind may continue both to exist and exert its powers. Not only is this basic theory of mind-body incorrect, Ryle says, but it also leads to many other serious errors as we elaborate on the implications of the theory. One erroneous consequence of this theory is its implied view that each person has two parallel histories, one consisting of the events of the body and the other consisting of what transpires in the mind. Whereas human bodies are in space and are governed by mechanical physical laws, minds do not exist in space and are not subject to such laws. A person's bodily life is publicly observable, while the activities of the mind are not accessible to external observers and so are private. This requires us to say that the workings of the body are external whereas the workings of the mind are internal. It is then a short step to say that the mind is *in* the body. This language describing the place of the mind may be metaphorical, since minds do not occupy space and thus could hardly be in any particular place. Nevertheless, Ryle argues, we often do take quite literally this contrast between the outer and inner realms. Psychologists, for example, assume that sensory stimuli come from *outside* and from far distances and generate mental responses *inside* the skull. All of this suggests some type of transaction between mind and body. However, no laboratory experiment can discover this relationship. This also suggests that what goes on inside my mind is a secret activity, which people on the outside do not have access to. For example, my mental acts of knowing, hoping, dreading, and intending are private events.

Because this traditional theory completely isolates the mind from the body, Ryle calls this view the "dogma of the Ghost in the Machine." What Ryle finds wrong with this dogma is not that some details here and there are ambiguous but that the very principle on which the theory rests is false. It is not even a series of particular mistakes. It is, Ryle says, one big mistake of a unique kind, and this he calls a "category-mistake." The big mistake consists of representing the facts of mental life as if they belong to one and the same logical category when in fact they belong to quite different and separate ones. The official theory is, therefore, a "myth," and it is necessary to "rectify the logic of mental-conduct concepts."

To illustrate this category-mistake, Ryle describes the imaginary visit of a foreigner to Oxford University for the first time. The visitor is shown the museums, scientific laboratories, and some of the colleges. Having seen these various places, the visitor asks, "But where is the university?" The question assumes that the university is yet another institution, or a counterpart to the colleges and laboratories, or another entity that can be seen in the same way as the others. Actually, the "university" is simply how all of these components are coordinated. Thus, the visitor's mistake consists of the assumption that we can correctly speak of Oxford's library, museum, and various other components, *and* the university as if the university was the same kind of member in the class to which the others belong. In short, the visitor mistakenly placed the university into the wrong category—a category in which it does not belong. In a similar illustration Ryle speaks of the mistake that a child makes when watching a military parade in which a division is marching by. Having been told that he is seeing battalions, batteries, and squadrons, the child wants to know when the division is going to appear. Again, the child assumes that the division is another unit similar to the others, not realizing that in seeing the battalions, batteries, and squadrons he has already seen the division. The mistake is in thinking it correct to speak of battalions, batteries, squadrons, *and* a division. He placed the division in the wrong category. These category-mistakes show an inability to use certain elements in the English language correctly. What is more significant, Ryle says, is that people who are perfectly capable of applying concepts are nevertheless liable in their abstract thinking to allocate these concepts to logical categories to which they do not belong.

Ryle believes that the Ghost in the Machine dogma makes a similar error and that "a family of radical category-mistakes is the source of the double-life theory." Advocates of the dogma hold that a person's feelings, thinking, and purposive activities cannot be described solely in terms of physics; because of this they conclude that mental activity must be described in a set of counterpart idioms. Moreover, because mental conduct differs so from bodily activities, advocates of the dogma hold that the mind has its own metaphysical status, made of a different stuff and having a different structure and its own complex organization. And so they hold that body and mind are separate fields of causes and effects, with the body being mechanical and the mind nonmechanical.

How did this category-mistake originate? Although Ryle designates Descartes as the major culprit, the mind-body dualism has a history extending much further back than the seventeenth century. Descartes's specific version was inspired by the view that scientific methods are capable of providing a mechanical theory that applies to every occupant in space. From a strictly scientific point of view, Descartes was impressed with the mechanical description of nature. However, as a religious and moral person, he was reluctant to agree with the claim that human nature in its mental aspects differs only in degree of complexity from a machine. Consequently, Descartes and subsequent philosophers wrongly construed mental-conduct words to signify nonmechanical processes and concluded that nonmechanical laws must explain the nonspatial workings of minds. But what this explanation retained was the assumption that mind, though different from body, is nevertheless a member of the categories of "thing," "stuff," "state," "process," "cause," and "effect." Thus, just as the visitor expected Oxford University to be another, extra unit, so Descartes and his heirs treated minds as additional, though special, centers of the causal process. From these conclusions a host of theoretical difficulties arose. How are the mind and body related? How do they bring about effects in each other? If the mind is governed by strict laws analogous to the laws governing the body, does this not imply determinism, in which case such notions as responsibility, choice, merit, and freedom make no sense? Worst of all, only negative terms could be used to speak of the mind: Minds are *not* in space, have *no* motions, are *not* aspects of matter, and are *not* observable. For these and other reasons Ryle concludes that the entire argument of the Ghost in the Machine is "broken-backed."

How, then, should we understand mental events such as acts of knowing, exercising intelligence, understanding, willing, feeling, and imagining? Ryle's alternative to the Ghost in the Machine dogma is a view now called *logical behaviorism,* the theory that talk of mental events should be translated into talk about observable behavior. Virtually every assertion about the mind involves some relevant facts about bodily behavior: "When we characterize people by mental predicates, we are not making untestable inferences to any ghostly processes occurring in streams of consciousness which we are debarred from visiting; we are describing the ways in which those people conduct parts of their predominantly public behavior." Mental terms, then, refer to the way that people do things, and not to private spiritual states. Ultimately, all of our mental states can be analyzed through our behavior, and Ryle denies that our mental states reflect anything more than a predictable way of acting. For instance, when I speak of human emotions, I do not infer the working of some interior and obscure mental forces. In favorable circumstances, Ryle says, "I find out your inclinations and your moods more directly than this. I hear and understand your conversational avowals, your interjections and your tones of voice; I see and understand your gestures and facial expressions."

Identity Theory and Functionalism

Ryle's theory of logical behaviorism has its critics. Even if we accept his critique of Cartesian dualism, there are problems with his solution that reduces mind to observable behavior. Ryle's behaviorism presumes that we can explain everything there is about mental events by looking solely at sensory input and behavioral output. For example, I see a lion (input) and I exhibit fearful behaviors, such as trembling (output). For Ryle these inputs and outputs explain all that there is about my fear. This, however, seems simplistic. Hoping to avoid committing a category-mistake himself, Ryle ignores everything that takes place *between* the input and the output. But what about the most obvious source of my fear, namely, my brain? Even Descartes recognized that the human brain plays an important role in processing sensory data. And, for the past few decades, many physicians have defined death in terms of the cessation of brain activity. Addressing this problem, *identity theory* is the view that mental states are identical to brain activity. For example, if I wish to know something about my emotions when I see a lion, I need to look at the type of activity that takes place within my brain. My experience of fear, then, is explained by a series of neurological events, which occur in different parts of my brain. Identity theory attempts to bring the whole issue of human consciousness under the umbrella of science—specifically, neuroscience. Gone are the days when soothsayers, exorcists, theologians, or even metaphysicians could contribute anything meaningful to the subject by speculating about the nature of an immaterial human spirit.

The effort to identify human consciousness with brain activity is not unique. As noted, Democritus and other atomists suggested this view, and, more recently, in the eighteenth and nineteenth centuries, some biologists offered somewhat crude theories of how brain functions elicit conscious thought. As theories of brain functions have become more sophisticated in recent decades, so, too, have theories of mind-brain identity. Two philosophers, J. J. C. Smart and David Armstrong, are associated with the current version of this theory. Perhaps the most common criticism of identity theory is that it fails a principle called *Leibniz's law*. Leibniz argued that if two things are truly identical, then properties asserted about the one thing must also be asserted about the other. Thus, according to Leibniz's law, if mental events and brain activity are really identical—as Smart and Armstrong contend—then all properties about mental events apply to brain activity, and vice versa. However, as the criticism goes, there are some things that we can say about mental events that do not seem to apply to brain activity, and vice versa. First, brain activities are localizable in space, and mental events do not seem to be. We can, for instance, point to a particular region of my brain in which neurons are firing. However, we cannot point to a part of my brain and say, "My idea of a tree is right there." Second, brain activities are objectively observable in the sense that we can monitor them with scientific equipment, and mental events cannot be observed in that way. Finally, mental events have the distinct feature that they are directed *at* something—that is, they exhibit intentionality. For example, I have an idea *of* a tree, I wish *for* a new car, and I think *about* political turmoil around the world. By contrast, brain activities are not *about* anything. They simply are physical events.

Die-hard identity theorists are not bothered by any of these problems. In fact, they feel that the more we learn about brain activity, the more comfortable we will become with pointing to parts of a brain and saying "an intentional thought is occurring right there." Nevertheless, identity theory faces another and somewhat different criticism. Specifically, it presumes that mental events, such as thoughts and emotions, *must* be activities of a biological brain. Why, though, cannot thoughts occur in nonbiological systems, such as silicon chips? According to a rival theory called *functionalism*, mental events depend primarily on the networks, pathways, and interconnections of mental processes, and not on the material stuff that the brain is composed of. Functionalists do not deny that human mental processes are a function of human brain activity. They simply throw open the criteria of mental activity to include computers, robots, or other human-made devices that exhibit the relevant processes.

The field of *artificial intelligence* attempts to realize the functionalist theory and duplicate human cognitive mental states in computing machinery. For some time scientists have tried to replicate human thought processes in some kind of mechanical form. The 1939 New York World's Fair displayed a human-looking robot that mimicked some human activities. At the time the visual effect was convincing, and many spectators believed that scientists had produced a truly humanlike creature. However, at that stage of technology, the robot was little more than a wind-up toy, and it exhibited none of the internal processes that functionalists would associate with thinking. Computer technology of recent decades has provided the first viable opportunity for at least attempting to replicate human thought processes. In some ways the goal of artificial intelligence today is modest. Rather than attempting to replicate all human mental processes in machine form—such as emotions, willful activity, and artistic sensibility—advocates of artificial intelligence focus only on the thinking process—analyzing sensory data and making judgments about it. The claims of artificial intelligence advocates are as varied as are their techniques. Two approaches, though, are commonly distinguished. A *weak* version of artificial intelligence holds that suitably programmed machines can simulate human cognition. *Strong* artificial intelligence, by contrast, holds that suitably programmed machines are actually capable of cognitive mental states. The weak claim presents no serious philosophical problem, since a machine that merely simulates human cognition does not need to actually possess conscious mental states. The strong claim, though, is more philosophically controversial since it holds that a computer can have humanlike thoughts.

Searle's Chinese Room Argument

The most well known attack on strong artificial intelligence is by John Searle, a former student of John Austin's at Oxford University and later professor at the University of California, Berkeley. Searle was bothered by grandiose claims of computer scientists that a computer program could interpret stories the way humans do. That is, the computer could read between the lines and draw inferences about events in the story that we as humans draw from our life experience. Proponents of strong artificial intelligence claimed that the program in question both understands stories and explains our human ability to understand stories—that is, it provides the sufficient conditions for "understanding." Searle counters this view with a picturesque thought experiment. Suppose that I, or some other non-Chinese speaking person, am put in a room and given three sets of Chinese characters: (1) a large batch of Chinese writing constituting the structure of that language, (2) a story, and (3) questions about the story. I also receive a set of rules in English—kind of like a computer program—that allow me to correlate the three sets of characters with each other. Although I do not know the meaning of the Chinese symbols, I may get so good at manipulating the symbols that, from the outside, I answer all the questions correctly, and no one can tell if I am Chinese or not. According to Searle, it is quite obvious that "I do not understand a word of the Chinese stories. I have inputs and outputs that are indistinguishable from those of the native Chinese speaker, and I can have any formal program you like, but I still understand nothing." For Searle this scenario goes against both of the above claims of strong artificial intelligence. That is, I do not understand the Chinese stories, and the process I am following does not fully explain the notion of "understanding." In short, even if a computer program appears to meaningfully interpret nuances of a story, the program does not really understand the story.

Searle himself anticipated a variety of objections to his Chinese room argument. What if a computer program was embedded within a robot that acquired data by interacting with the real world, rather than simply being supplied with that data? The robot might ably interact by means of a video camera and motorized arms and legs. However, Searle argues, this would still only produce data very much like the data already embedded in the computer, and nothing significantly new would change in how the computer processes the information. But what if a computer program simulated a pattern of neurons firing, rather than simply the interrelations between words? Searle replies that we still only have a simulation, and not the real thing. According to Searle, then, a computer program—no matter how elaborate—is not capable of cognitive mental states. This is a feature reserved for biological and organic brains. Although Searle denies the extravagant claims of functionalists and advocates of artificial intelligence, he does not want to concede victory to either the pure identity theorist or the olden-day Cartesian dualists. He instead tries to forge a middle ground between the latter two theories, which he calls *biological naturalism*. Like the identity theorist, he believes that mental events are really biological in nature, specifically involving higher-level brain functions. So, when we investigate the nature of the human mind, we investigate the brain, and there is no mysterious spiritual component to our mental events. Like the dualist, though, Searle is swayed by Leibniz's law and insists that our descriptions about brain activity (such as neurons firing) are fundamentally different from descriptions about mental events (for example, I wish *for* a new car). Accordingly, philosophical descriptions of human thinking will never be replaced with scientific descriptions of brain activity. Each is valid within its own territory.

RORTY

Ever since Plato, traditional philosophers have tried to discover the foundations of knowledge. They wanted to know exactly what is "out there"—outside the mind—to distinguish between mind and body and between appearance and reality, and to provide a grounding for absolutely certain truth. By contrast, analytic philosophers scaled down the enterprise of philosophy to the more modest objective of discovering the foundations of meaningful language. Sentences or propositions would be considered meaningful only if they corresponded to objective and verifiable facts. In this way philosophy would resemble the rigor of scientific knowledge. But did this shift in the concerns of philosophy represent a major revolution? To be sure, linguistic analysis clarified some philosophical problems by demonstrating the frequent misuse of language. More dramatically, several traditional issues were simply eliminated from the agenda of philosophy when analytic philosophers insisted that language must accurately represent facts. What "facts" could be "represented" by language when talking about the "good" or the "beautiful" or the "just" or "God"? If there were no such facts, philosophy could no longer speak meaningfully about ethics, aesthetics, religion, justice, and metaphysics. Surely, we might think, this represents a revolutionary departure from the traditional concerns of philosophy.

Rorty's Analytic Philosophy

However, according to American philosopher Richard Rorty, analytic philosophy did not usher in a major change in the assumptions of philosophy. In *Philosophy and the Mirror of Nature* (1979), Rorty argues that analytic philosophy is not something new but rather a variation of what Descartes and Kant did, namely, provide a "foundation" for knowledge. What is new in analytic philosophy, Rorty says, is the conviction that knowledge is represented by what is linguistic and not by what is mental. But to say this is to leave unchanged the assumption that as human beings we possess by our very nature some framework within which the activity of inquiry takes place. We still have in analytic philosophy, (1) a "knowing subject," (2) a "reality out there," and (3) a "theory of representation" that describes how reality is represented to the knowing subject. The old account of how we know is still the same, namely, that the mind is like a great mirror containing representations of nature, some accurate and some inaccurate, which we then study by pure "rational" methods. Analytic philosophy does not remove the assumption that the mind is like a mirror. It simply tries to increase the accuracy of the representations captured by the mind, as Rorty says, by "inspecting, repairing and polishing the mirror." Moreover, to engage in repairing and polishing the mirror implies the presence of another old assumption, namely, that there is some reality that is eternally "out there" but that for some reason is inaccurately represented to the mind. For these reasons Rorty believes that a truly revolutionary move in philosophy would require the final rejection of several assumptions. We must first abandon the traditional mirror imagery—the assumption that human beings are equipped with a structural framework that dictates how our inquiries must proceed. We must also abandon the assumption that even before there is thinking or history there is an "essence" to reality, which to know is to know the truth.

Rorty was himself an analytic philosopher as a young professor at Princeton University. He was born in 1931 and raised in New York City as an only child whose parents were freelance journalists and whose maternal grandfather, Walter Raschenbusch, was an eminent liberal Protestant theologian. At age 14 Rorty entered the University of Chicago and later completed his graduate studies in philosophy at Yale University. After a brief teaching assignment at Wellesley College, he joined the faculty at Princeton, whose philosophy department at that time was strongly oriented toward analytic philosophy. For a few years Rorty immersed himself in "doing" analytic philosophy but finally grew dissatisfied with the piecemeal task of unraveling linguistic and logical puzzles. After a brief period of professional crisis during the early 1970s and to the considerable surprise of his colleagues, Rorty chose a new direction for his studies, toward the pragmatism of John Dewey.

The Influence of Pragmatism

In 1909, on the fiftieth anniversary of the publication of Darwin's *On the Origin of Species* (1859), Dewey delivered a lecture titled "The Influence of Darwinism on Philosophy." The influence it had, Dewey said, was that it introduced a new type of thinking—a type that influenced Dewey himself. The theory of biological evolution, Dewey said, emphasized that change is fundamental to everything that exists. This change represents not only simple rearrangements of bits of matter but the presence of "organic systems" and their creativity with respect to the environment. This meant that knowledge could no longer aim at realities lying behind any notion of the mathematical order of nature or any vestige of Platonic "eternality." There is no "givenness" about the world. Philosophy would no longer enquire about absolute origins and absolute final ends, as in Hegel's gradual realization of the idea of freedom or Marx's final phase of human society. Philosophy would no longer seek to prove that our lives necessarily must have certain qualities or values as a result of an earlier cause, such as creation, or a specific goal. The world, on this view, is not described as reflecting an eternal pattern, out there, abstractly.

Instead, according to Dewey, philosophical thinking should begin with our immediate, concrete life experiences. We would then see human life as Aristotle did. That is, although we are a part of nature and behave in certain mechanical ways as described by science, we are nevertheless *human*. And although we have some characteristics of other animals, we are nevertheless unique. What makes us unique is that we are aware of the processes of nature and we can know how we *function*. We know where some forms of behavior lead and what values or ends they support or frustrate. Experience tells us what things are "necessary for," or "better for," or "worse for" other things. We can evaluate things not in terms of some remote and abstract standards but in terms of some more obvious "ends" built into the very natural functions of organisms. Human life on this view reveals a close relationship between the functions of human nature and the various simultaneous functions of the larger natural environment, which provides wide choices of ends and values. It is easy to see how the new Darwinian approach to knowledge influenced Dewey in the direction of pragmatism. Instead of pursuing a single ultimate truth about reality, his emphasis shifted to a pluralism of truths, many truths, and the characteristic that these ideas or notions are true because they "work."

Rorty was drawn to Dewey's pragmatism for these and several other reasons. For one thing, it gave him an avenue of escape from the severe limitations that linguistic analysis placed on the scope of his philosophical activity. Pragmatism provided him with a basis for finally rejecting the traditional view that the mind is a reliable mirror reflecting reality, a notion that assumed that only those thoughts and language are true which faithfully represent the real world. Since there is no way to be absolutely certain that a thought or statement accurately corresponds to reality, it is, he thought, better to think that a statement is true if it leads to successful behavior—that is, if it "works." We should look upon statements as "tools" whose truth is based on their usefulness. Since there are several types of statements, there are correspondingly several kinds of truths. To view truth in this manner is to bring back to philosophy the subject matter of many fields. From this point of view, science has no special claim on truth since it is only one among many areas of practical human concern, along with politics, ethics, art, literature, history, and religion. Scientific methods cannot, therefore, provide the sole criterion for truth since there are several particular kinds of truth.

What especially attracted Rorty to pragmatism was that its pluralistic view of truth opened up wide areas of legitimate philosophical discussion. In addition to the analysis of language, it now became philosophically useful to study novels and poetry to find insights into human problems that philosophy virtually abandoned. Moreover, Anglo-American philosophers could more comfortably engage in discourse with their counterparts in Continental Europe, where the darker themes of dread, *angst*, and solitude permeate the works of Kierkegaard, Nietzsche, and Heidegger. Rorty discovered that while analytic philosophy isolated itself from some of the deepest concerns of life, it is possible to overcome this isolation by expanding the range and type of literature considered worthy of study. Following this insight, Rorty left the Department of Philosophy at Princeton and, in 1983, became university professor of humanities at the University of Virginia. Here, his approach to philosophy relied heavily on literary and cultural criticism and acknowledged the morally illuminating power of novelists and poets. Rorty had no interest in, nor did he think it useful to engage in, "systematic" philosophy. More and more, he believed, the emphasis would be on "edifying" philosophy, whose practitioners would be concerned with culture and self-transformation.

The Contingency of Language

If there is one theme that captures Rorty's philosophical point of view, it is his conviction that there are no eternal "essences." For example, there is no "human nature," "true nature of the self," or "universal moral law," discoverable by human reason. Instead of a timeless and stable structure in reality, what we find, Rorty says, is that everywhere we are confronted with "contingency," by the ever-presence of "chance." If everything is "contingent," how can there be any meaning to life? If there is no timeless truth, how can we know whether our lives fall short of their intended purpose or value? Rorty is aware of these consequences of his pragmatism. But instead of being intimidated by this bewildering world of chance, he sees in it opportunities for overcoming contingency by constant self-transformation or self-creation. Still, he insists that it is philosophically important to recognize that contingency and chance characterize such fundamental aspects of our experience as our *language*, our idea of our *selfhood*, and our conception of human society or *community*.

We normally think of language as a means by which our vocabulary represents reality to our minds. How can a vocabulary represent or be the medium of something "out there"? One way is to use the metaphor of a jigsaw puzzle. By the use of words, it is assumed that we can describe various pieces of the puzzle so that as the vocabulary changes and evolves, our language will come closer and closer to what exists out there. But this assumes that out there are to be found fixed and stable realities capable of being described.

Take, for example, the language of science. Galileo created a new vocabulary when he described the behavior of the earth and the sun in relation to each other. What does this history of the change in scientific language illustrate? Does it show that Galileo's new description represents a deeper insight into the intrinsic nature of the natural world? Rorty does not think so. "We must," he says, "resist the temptation to think that the re-descriptions of reality offered by contemporary physical or biological sciences are somehow closer to 'the things themselves.'" It is not as though the new language has filled in more of the jigsaw puzzle. Rather, we should use the metaphor of language as a "tool" so that the new vocabulary of science will simply enable those who create the new language to accomplish new objectives. There is no necessary line of development in language any more than there is a necessary line of evolution in nature. We cannot return to the way nature and its purposes were thought about before the time of Darwin. Contingency and chance—that is, the more or less random behavior of things—explain the changes in nature and in language. Physical evolution did not have to occur precisely as it did. Was it necessary or only by chance that orchids came upon the scene? And did not Mendel "let us see mind as something which just happened rather than as something which was the whole point of the process"? To say the opposite—namely, that the world has an intrinsic nature that the physicist or poet has glimpsed—is, Rorty says, "a remnant of the idea that the world is a divine creation, the work of someone who had something in mind, who Himself spoke some language in which He described His own project."

Because our language is the product of random choices made by those who sought to describe the world, there is no reason now to be bound by that inherited language. The language of the past certainly has influenced the way we think. However, we should create our own new vocabulary if that would be more useful in solving our problems. "It is essential to my view," Rorty writes, "that we have no pre-linguistic consciousness to which language needs to be adequate, no deep sense of how things are which it is the duty of philosophers to spell out in language." Truth, Rorty says, is no more than what Nietzsche called "a mobile army of metaphors."

The Contingency of Selfhood

Plato gave us the metaphor of two worlds: (1) the world of time, appearance, and change and (2) the world of enduring, changeless truth. Our lives involve an attempt to escape from the distractions of the flesh and the dominant opinions of a particular time and place in order to enter the real world of reason and contemplation. With this vocabulary Plato created a language designed to describe the essence of human nature, implying that there is only one true description of our human situation. As we face the contingent events of our lives, we are to control our affections by the use and power of our reason and thereby achieve moral and intellectual virtue. Theologians offered basically this same metaphor, urging human beings to strive toward our "true nature." Similarly, Kant described the difference between our daily experiences with their local influences on our choices, on the one hand, and our internal moral consciousness, which reveals for all human beings our timeless and universal moral laws, on the other. These versions of the two worlds that we encounter represent the true world as compared with the deceptive world that we must try to escape.

Rorty believed that Plato, the theologians, and Kant imposed labels and descriptions of "the self" on our consciousness as if these were absolutely true descriptions. There are, after all, alternative ways of defining the self. If, for example, Nietzsche says that "God is dead," he implies that there is nothing more to reality than the flow of events, and the flux of chance. Nor is there any universal moral law or "true self." This skepticism leaves the question of how to provide a meaning for human life. There is no other choice, Nietzsche said, to which Rorty agrees, than for each of us to give meaning to our own life by writing our own language and describing our own objectives. In a real sense, each of us must be involved in transforming our "self," not by seeking the truth but by overcoming the old self and by choosing and willing a new self. According to Rorty, "we create ourselves by telling our own story."

Plato tried to describe human nature in specific detail when he spoke of the tripartite aspect of the self, including the physical body, the passions and affections, and, highest of all, the mind. He assumed that our minds had a clear shot at the truth and could overcome the contingent events encountered in daily life. But Rorty finds that quite different descriptions of consciousness have been offered without assuming a realm of eternal truth. On the contrary, he finds in the writings of Freud a tripartite description of the self as nothing but the product of contingent events. The sense of guilt is explained not by an innate knowledge of the moral law. Rather, as Freud says, "a regressive degrading of the libido takes place, the super-ego becomes exceptionally severe and unkind, and the ego, in obedience to the super-ego, produces strong reaction-formations in the shape of conscientiousness, pity and cleanliness." It may be that the metaphor of the two worlds has been too powerful to overcome. But Freud replies that,

> if one considers chance to be unworthy of determining our fate, it is simply a relapse into the pious view of the universe which Leonardo himself was on the way of overcoming when he wrote that the sun does not move . . . we are all too ready to forget that in fact everything to do with our life is chance, from our origin out of the meeting of spermatozoon and ovum onwards. . . . Everyone of us human beings corresponds to one of the countless experiments in which [the countless causes] of nature force their way into experience.

The Contingency of Community

How can human beings live together? That is, how can human beings achieve solidarity and community? Here, again, Plato drew a tight connection between "the essential human nature" and the social and political arrangement of the community. Plato thought that the three classes of society were necessary extensions of the three parts of the human soul or self. The artisans embody the physical element of the person, the guardians express the spirited passions, and the rulers are the incarnation of the mind, or reason. Plato also argued that there must first be a harmony among the three parts of the private individual if the collective harmony of the community is to be achieved. All the elements of the self must be subject to and governed by the highest faculty, that is, by reason. Similarly, all the classes of society must be subordinate to the ruler. This whole arrangement is dictated by the structure of human nature.

Rorty disagrees with this notion that our public life must be based on the antecedent facts of human nature. Theologians have also offered their versions of the Platonic account of the origin and justification of political authority, especially in their theory of the divine rights of kings, while Marx drew from his description of history, and from the relation of human beings to the material order of nature, a theory of a classless society. These various vocabularies or languages describing the good society are contingent on the special perspectives of each author. Each account focuses on a different concept of "ultimate reality" and a different view of essential human nature. It is not surprising, then, Rorty says, that there can be no single concept of community that is required by some true description of human nature.

For his part Rorty holds that since there is no absolutely true account available of human nature, there is no point in looking in that direction for some moral basis of society. The contingency of language and the contingency of the self mean that there is no reliable objective information that can lead to the *right* kind of community. There is no theory of knowledge that can guarantee the just society—neither "rationality, the love of God, [nor] the love of truth." Instead, Rorty agrees with the insights of Dewey as reflected by John Rawls in his Dewey Lectures:

> What justifies a conception of justice is not its being true to an order antecedent and given to us, but its congruence with our deeper understanding of ourselves and our aspirations, and our realization that, given our history and the traditions embedded in our public life, it is the most reasonable theory for us.

The central values on which to build a community are the values of freedom and equality, which are the ideals of liberal democracy. It is not helpful, Rorty says, to ask at this point, "How do you *know* that freedom is the chief goal of social organization?" any more than it is to ask, "How do you *know* that Jones is worthy of your friendship?" The preference for freedom and equality and the desire to eliminate suffering are discovered not by reason but by chance. These values were not always obvious, nor were they always chosen. They were not always options, for example, for the Egyptians, nor can they be defended rationally against those who refuse to accept them. The social glue that holds a liberal society together consists in a consensus, Rorty says, in which everybody has an opportunity at self-creation to the extent of their abilities. From the point of view of his pragmatism, Rorty says that what matters most is the widely shared conviction that "what we call 'good' or 'true' [is] whatever is the outcome of free discussion," for if we take care of political freedom, "truth and goodness will take care of themselves."

VIRTUE THEORY REVISITED

For much of the nineteenth and twentieth centuries, moral philosophers were waging a war between two camps. On the one side were empiricists who believed that morality is determined solely by looking at the consequences of our conduct. If an action produces a greater balance of happiness or benefit, then it is morally good. If it produces a greater balance of unhappiness or dis-benefit, then it is morally bad. A representative from this camp is the utilitarian Jeremy Bentham, who argued that we can very mechanically calculate the balance of happiness and unhappiness that results from our actions. On the other side of the dispute were rationalists who believed that humans are naturally implanted with moral intuitions, similar to other rational concepts, such as the principle of cause and effect. On this view, an act is morally good if we can rationally assess that it is consistent with our moral intuitions. If inconsistent, then it is morally bad. Kant is a representative of this camp. Moral empiricists argued that, contrary to the rationalists, we simply have no rational moral intuitions, and the rationalist approach is wishful thinking aimed at discovering a universal and unchanging standard of morality. Moral rationalists, on the other hand, charged that the empirical approach ignores our truly rational nature and reduces morality to the whims of social groups. Defenders of each side continually modified and strengthened their theories in response to attacks from their opponents. In recent decades, though, several philosophers have argued that the entire dispute between these two camps is misguided. On this view, moral philosophy went astray in the eighteenth century when it set aside the central notion of ethics, namely, virtue, especially as developed by Aristotle. Virtues, for Aristotle, are habits that regulate our more animalistic desires. When we cultivate these virtuous habits, our actions reflect our natural purpose as rational and social creatures. The first such recent defense of virtue theory was by British philosopher Elizabeth Anscombe (1919–2001).

Anscombe's Defense

Anscombe was a student of Ludwig Wittgenstein, and, inspired by her teacher's views of the philosophy of mind, she made considerable contributions to that field as well. Her conception of virtue theory appears in her essay "Modern Moral Philosophy" (1958). Anscombe notes here that we commonly use several ethically loaded words in our moral vocabulary. I say that you *ought, must,* or are *obligated* to do certain things. These terms express a kind of moral edict or command. For example, if I say that "you ought not steal," then I imply that thieves violate some universal moral law and are accordingly morally guilty and punishable. Where does this notion of moral edict come from? She argues that Christian philosophers in the Middle Ages introduced it. Preoccupied with the concept of divine law, medieval philosophers believed that God was the ultimate authority behind proper conduct. Actions such as stealing are sinful, and God demands that we avoid these actions. Ultimately, for medieval philosophers, all morality involved obedience to God's laws or edicts. In more recent centuries philosophers such as Hume and Kant offered secular accounts of the origin of morality. Hume in particular was committed to offering a theory of morality that made no reference to divine authority, but instead was grounded in feelings and other psychological features of human nature. The problem, though, is that Hume and others retained the medieval notions of *ought* and *moral law* while at the same time casting off the idea of God as moral lawgiver. Put most simply, according to Anscombe, the notion of "law" requires a lawgiver, and it makes no sense to keep talking about obligations to moral laws once we abandon the notion of God as moral lawgiver. However—and this is Anscombe's key concern—philosophers from Hume until the present day discuss notions of *ought* and *moral law* anyway. Anscombe writes, "It is as if the notion 'criminal' were to remain when criminal law and criminal courts had been abolished and forgotten." Some philosophers offer questionable explanations of the foundation of moral obligation, and others concede that the concept of *ought* has no real content. Nevertheless, the concepts of *ought* and *moral law* are central to current ethical theories. In fact, such moral edicts are so embedded in contemporary moral theories that the theories would collapse without them.

There is more at stake here than simply a theoretical dispute among academic philosophers about the notions of *ought* or *moral law* and the groundless edicts that emerge from contemporary moral theories. According to Anscombe, some of the moral theories after Hume have contributed to a dangerous kind of moral reasoning in real life. One such theory is *consequentialism*—a revision of utilitarianism that Anscombe associates with nineteenth-century British moral philosopher Henry Sidgwick. On this theory right actions are those that bring about the best consequences that we can foresee. For Anscombe the problem with this approach is that it fails to distinguish between two completely different types of consequences. First, there are consequences that involve intrinsic goods, such as telling the truth and not killing. Second, there are more indirect consequences in which we might say that the ends justify the means—such as stealing a loaf of bread to feed one's starving family. True morality, according to Anscombe, should focus on intrinsic goods, without attempting to counterbalance these against the second and more indirect type of consequences. In another essay she provides a vivid example of how people sometimes blur these two consequences with disastrous results. According to Anscombe, at the close of World War II, President Harry Truman used consequentialist reasoning when deciding to drop atomic bombs on the Japanese cities of Hiroshima and Nagasaki. On one side of the balance, Truman placed the negative consequence of killing tens of thousands of innocent Japanese civilians; Anscombe contends that avoiding such killing would have been a fundamentally good thing to do. On the other side of the balance, Truman considered that the bombs would bring a quick end to the war, and thus serve as a useful means to an end. Believing that the latter reasoning was more weighty, he decided to drop the bombs—a decision that Anscombe believes was murderous. Thus, consequentialism is not only flawed but even hazardous when applied to decisions like this. And, in turn, the misguided force of consequentialism rests on the misguided conception of moral edicts embedded in concepts like *ought* and *moral law*.

What is the solution to this problem surrounding moral edicts? Anscombe herself is a secular moral theorist and would not recommend reviving medieval Christian conceptions of divine law. That is, she would not advise reinstating God as giver of the moral law. Instead, she recommends that we simply reject all talk about moral law and obligation and look to Aristotle for inspiration. Aristotle did not speak of divine legislators or moral edicts. Instead, he described virtues—habits that regulate our behavior in response to our animalistic appetites. People are bad, not because they violate moral laws, but because they fail to acquire virtues and instead develop vices such as cowardice, untruthfulness, unchasteness, or unjustness. If we adopt Aristotle's approach, not only will we abandon the notions of *ought* and *moral law*, but we will also abandon all the notions in moral psychology that philosophers since Hume have relied on, such as "action," "intention," "pleasure," and "wanting." This amounts to "laying aside" the whole discipline of moral philosophy until we have more adequate notions of moral psychology that are consistent with Aristotle's notion of virtue. In the decades after the appearance of her essay, several philosophers took Anscombe's challenge to heart by rejecting consequentialism and other traditional conceptions of moral obligation that involved moral edicts. These new virtue theorists also explore the psychological underpinnings of moral virtues, attempting to supplement Aristotle's discussion with more current accounts of human nature.

Noddings's Defense

One recent defender of virtue theory is Nel Noddings, who in her essay "Ethics from the Standpoint of Women" (1990) sees virtues as a way of articulating a uniquely female conception of morality. Noddings and other feminist writers argue that much of our intellectual heritage was not only formed by men but reflects a male way of looking at the world. There is some controversy surrounding possible differences between male and female ways of thinking. Male approaches, though, tend to emphasize following rules, devising strict laws, and finding subtle logical distinctions according to which we can categorize people and things. Female ways of thinking, by contrast, emphasize a capacity for nurturing and caring for others. We see this distinction when comparing vocations that tend to be male-dominated—such as engineering and mathematics—with those that are female-dominated—such as social work and education. Much of philosophy has been driven by male ways of thinking and, perhaps in some ways, contaminated by it. Ethics, Noddings argues, is a case in point. Kant, for example, argued that morality is grounded in cold rational duty, even to the point that "acts done out of love do not qualify as moral acts." Nietzsche's model of morality is that of a warrior who casts aside traditional values and forges new ones. His theory is "overtly and proudly masculine, and much of it depends directly on the devaluation of women and all that is associated with the feminine." Some of these moral philosophers even blatantly make sexist statements, devaluing the rational capacity of women and belittling female sentimentalism.

According to Noddings, the solution to the problem caused by male-oriented ethical theories is to replace them with ones that are female-oriented. Why, though, not just make ethics gender-neutral? After all, moral theories aim at universalization, that is, applying to all people. Focusing on only one gender undermines this. For Noddings, though, "to construct an ethic free of gendered views may be impossible in a thoroughly gendered society." At minimum, female-oriented theories need to be proposed to counterbalance male theories, and perhaps at some future time we can transcend them both with gender-neutral approaches. A critic might still argue that the traditional activities and attitudes of women have nothing to do with ethics and cannot serve as a basis for developing any meaningful moral theory. Examples of tasks commonly imposed on women are child rearing, cooking, cleaning, and homemaking. These all tend to be menial, and even exploitive when imposed on women at the expense of more meaningful and challenging life activities. Not only do men avoid these tasks and the effeminacy associated with them, but many contemporary women also denounce them as oppressive. Nevertheless, Noddings believes that even within these traditional women's activities we can find a foundation for female ethics. The theme that underlies all of these activities is *care*, or the capacity to nurture other people. Even if contemporary women abandon these tasks completely, the most oppressive of these activities still reflects an orientation toward caring for others.

Noddings believes that the ethical emphasis on care fits neatly into virtue theory. The caring attitude itself is a habit that we cultivate, similar to other virtues such as courage and temperance. Further, virtue theory and the caring attitude are both resistant to the harsh rules of traditional moral theories. There is a spontaneity to both virtuous and caring conduct that involves unique responses to unique situations. This, though, does not mean that we should simply adopt Aristotle's theory of virtue just as it is. Aristotle's account rests on an elitist and male-dominated conception of society in which the lifestyles of women and slaves were of no concern:

> Aristotle's identification of virtues depended almost entirely on the establishment of exclusive classes and the activities appropriate to each. The virtues of women and of slaves were not those of educated citizens. He made no attempt to identify virtues in one class that might be cultivated in others by extending the range of privilege or sharing the array of common tasks. If he had made such an attempt, it would surely have moved in only one direction. One might try to inculcate the virtues of the highest class into lower classes, but one would never try to develop, say, feminine virtues in men.

We must, then, expand Aristotle's list of virtues by adding ones that reflect the lifestyles of exploited groups, particularly women.

Feminists might still question whether women should identify themselves so boldly with a caring attitude. Just as nurturing women in the past were exploited, perhaps caring women today may make themselves vulnerable to the same kind of oppression. They may find themselves "dependent on men or on welfare in order to care for their children, and are sometimes physically abused." Noddings agrees that if only women adopted the ethics of caring then, indeed, oppression toward women would continue. What, though, if the attitude of caring was instilled in men, too? This would force us to recognize that all humans are interdependent, regardless of gender. With the right kind of moral education, we could instill in people a virtue of care that contains proper limits and prevents people from taking advantage of nurturers.

Virtue Epistemology

While interest in virtue theory has been revived in the area of ethics, it has also expanded into a different, seemingly unlikely arena of philosophy, namely, epistemology. *Epistemology*—the study of knowledge—focuses on the ways that we acquire knowledge and the standards that we use for maintaining that we know things, such as when I say, "I know that the car in front of me is white." The typical way of investigating knowledge claims is to examine the critical properties of a belief, such as the evidence supporting my belief that there is a white car in front of me. *Virtue epistemology*, though, shifts the emphasis from the properties of my belief to the properties of me the person. What are the specific mental qualities or "virtues" that are behind my knowledge claims such as this one about the white car? One group of virtue epistemologists, known as *virtue reliabilists*, maintains that genuine knowledge is grounded in special mental faculties that allow us to arrive at the truth of things in a reliable way. These epistemologically virtuous faculties include perception, memory, introspection, and logical reasoning. For example, for me to reliably know that the car in front of me is white, I need to have a good perceptual faculty of vision when I look at the car and a good memory about what the color "white" looks like. Ernest Sosa, one of the early leaders of virtue reliabilism, describes epistemological virtues as stable and reliable mental faculties that are "bound to help maximize one's surplus of truth over error."

But a bolder version of virtue epistemology, known as *virtue responsibilism*, maintains that the mental abilities that are truly important for knowledge are good intellectual *character traits*, such as inquisitiveness, thoroughness, fairmindedness, open-mindedness, carefulness, and tenacity. Not only are these traits central to our gaining knowledge, but they are character traits that a *responsible* knower should possess. Inquisitiveness, for example, is a good thing for responsible inquirers to have, since it prompts us to expand our knowledge of the world. Thoroughness is good since it has us pursue explanations of phenomena further than we would otherwise. Open-mindedness is good since it has us consider alternative explanations of things that we might otherwise initially reject. By possessing these virtues of inquisitiveness, thoroughness, and open-mindedness, I might not be satisfied with the explanation that mice simply spontaneously generate from old rags in my barn. Accordingly, I might set up an experiment in which I closely monitor a pile of rags and see if a plump adult female mouse shows up and delivers babies.

This conception of epistemological virtues parallels more closely the traditional notion of moral virtues forged by Aristotle. First, just as Aristotle maintained about moral virtues, these epistemological virtues are acquired through practice and eventually become habits of thinking. Linda Zagzebski, a leading proponent of this approach, writes that "the stages of learning the intellectual virtues are exactly parallel to the stages of learning the moral virtues as described by Aristotle. They begin with the imitation of virtuous persons, [and] require practice which develops certain habits of feeling and acting." Second, each of these intellectual virtues has a distinctly underlying moral component. Zagzebski writes,

> When people call others shortsighted or pigheaded, their criticism is as much like moral criticism as when they call them offensive or obnoxious; in fact, what is obnoxious about a person can sometimes be limited to a certain pattern of thinking. The same point can be made, in differing degrees, of a variety of other names people are called for defects that are mostly cognitive: mulish, stiff-necked, pertinacious, recalcitrant, or obstinate, wrongheaded, vacuous, shallow, witless, dull, muddleheaded, thickskulled, or obtuse.

According to Zagzebski, two features are present when we act upon epistemological virtues. One is our virtuous motivation: Other intellectually virtuous people would perform the same act in similar circumstances. The other feature is reliable success: Through our virtuous conduct we arrive at truth.

There is a major difference between how virtue reliabilists and virtue responsibilists envision the task of epistemological virtues. For reliabilists such as Sosa, epistemological virtues are cognitive faculties that humans typically possess naturally. However, for responsibilists such as Zagzebski, we must work hard at acquiring intellectual character traits, just as we do moral character traits. More importantly, reliabilists and responsibilists differ regarding the general task of gaining knowledge. By focusing on cognitive faculties like perception and memory, reliabilists emphasize knowledge of our immediate surroundings, such as knowledge that a car is white. However, if we wish to push the bounds of knowledge in more interesting ways, such as discovering new scientific or historical truths, we need to possess the intellectual character traits that responsibilists list. For example, Galileo's great scientific achievements in astronomy were the result of more than just having good eyesight, memory, or even logical reasoning. He needed open-mindedness to consider options that were taboo at the time and tenacity to invent new ways of exploring the possibilities.

CONTINENTAL PHILOSOPHY

By the mid-twentieth century, a rift had developed between Anglo-American philosophers of the analytic tradition and Continental European philosophers of the phenomenological and existentialist tradition. The two groups differed in methodology, with analytic philosophers emphasizing logic and language, and Continental philosophers emphasizing ontological concerns of human nature and action. They also sought inspiration from different major philosophers— Hume, Russell, and Wittgenstein for analytic philosophers, and Nietzsche, Husserl, Heidegger, and Sartre for Continental ones. In recent decades the gulf between the two has narrowed. Analytic philosophy is now taught in European universities, and Continental philosophy has made its way into British and American educational institutions, particularly within English and literature departments. Recent Continental philosophy is associated with several "isms" that overlap each other, including structuralism, post-structuralism, and post-modernism. We will look at these.

Structuralism

Structuralism began in the early 1900s as a theory explaining the nature of language. Its champion, Swiss linguist Ferdinand de Saussure (1857–1913), was bothered by standard nineteenth-century linguistic theories that presumed to find some commonality between various foreign languages. As tempting as this approach might seem, Saussure believed it was fundamentally mistaken. Each language, he argued, is a closed formal system—an entity unto itself—with no significant connection to other languages or even to the physical objects to which the words presumably refer. A given language, such as English, consists of an arbitrary system of words whose meanings are based solely on conventional structures or patterns of use. A single word is like the thread of a fabric, whose function is determined only in relation to the surrounding weave of threads; by itself the thread has no function. For example, a toddler just learning how to pronounce words might be hungry and say "muck"; by itself this word means nothing and certainly is not what an adult means by it. An astute parent, though, will understand the larger context of the toddler's language abilities and behavior, and recognize that the toddler means "milk." Language, in short, is an arbitrary social institution, and all the pieces of a language derive their meaning from that larger system of social structures.

Saussure realized that his theory had implications beyond language and in fact could apply to other systems of social convention. Following his lead, several writers pushed the structuralist agenda into the fields of anthropology, psychology, intellectual history, and political theory. The unifying theme of this movement was that any cultural object or concept gets its meaning from its surrounding cultural structures. French anthropologist Claude Lévi-Strauss (b. 1908) argued further that the surrounding cultural structures will typically involve a pair of opposites, such as male/female, odd/even, or light/dark. These paired opposites give systems a stable logical structure. For example, the Hindu caste system involves a hierarchy of social classes that are based on the paired opposites of purity and impurity: The higher castes are more pure and the lower castes are more impure. The two key components of the structuralist movement, then, are (1) the meaning of a thing is defined by its surrounding cultural structures, and (2) the system has a coherent structure that is reflected in paired opposites. Suppose, I want to understand the meaning of a wedding ring. It would be futile for me to investigate my own wedding ring in isolation from everything else in my culture. Instead, I should try to understand the internal structures of various wedding rings, such as whether they are flashy or modest (paired opposites), and the meanings that these features convey in our culture. I should also try to understand how wedding rings play a role in the larger system of cultural structures, such as what signals wedding rings send to others and how wearing a wedding ring might differ from wearing a high school ring.

Although structuralism was not initially developed as a philosophy per se, its philosophical implications soon became apparent, and it quickly emerged in reaction against Sartre's existentialism. Sartre believed that individual people create their own natures through free choices, and people are not predefined by their social surroundings. Lévi-Strauss and other structuralists rejected this emphasis on individual people and the subjectivism that existentialism implies. Just as wedding rings are defined by larger social structures, so, too, are people, and we cannot view ourselves as free, independent agents stripped of our social context. We must always use other people as a basis for understanding ourselves. By the 1960s structuralism overshadowed existentialism as France's most popular philosophy.

Post-Structuralism

Post-structuralism—which appeared in the 1970s—is both an expansion on and refutation of structuralism. Like structuralism, post-structuralism has branched out into several disciplines, perhaps most notably in the field of literary criticism. Consider, for example, what structuralists might say about interpreting a novel such as *Gone with the Wind*. We might be tempted to see this book as a somewhat historical discussion of the U.S. Civil War. However, structuralists would argue that the meaning of particular passages in the book rests mainly on the structures within the book itself, which is a closed system. Further, the structures in the book involve paired opposites of war/peace, wealth/poverty, and love/strife. Post-structuralism pushes the matter further. First, if *Gone with the Wind* is truly a closed system, then I must exclude any fact or consideration outside of that novel, such as what I might find in a history book on the Civil War. I must even set aside the author's intentions, which also rest outside of the novel, such as what I might find in a biography of the author. Whatever meaning the book has depends on what I the reader think about the book as I enter into that closed system. Since each reader will likely have a different interpretation of the book, the book will have *no* definitive meaning. Second, post-structuralists will argue that if we look carefully for so-called paired opposites within *Gone with the Wind*, we will find this to be an oversimplification. For example, although the book does contain elements of love and strife, we also see indifference: "Frankly, my dear, I don't give a damn," as Clark Gable expresses it in the movie. Similarly, we don't see only wealth and poverty, but middle-level income as well. Structuralists believed that paired opposites provided logical coherence to closed systems. But once we reject this notion of paired opposites—as post-structuralists recommend—then we are left without any internal logical structure of the book. Each reader, then, will play with the book, bringing his or her own meaning to it.

In philosophy, post-structuralism is most associated with French philosopher Jacques Derrida (b. 1930). Unlike other post-structuralists who focus on literary criticism, Derrida targets philosophy books. He argues that throughout the history of Western thought philosophers have built their theories around key opposing concepts, such as appearance/reality, opinion/knowledge, spirit/matter, and truth/falsehood. On face value these opposing concepts might support the structuralist theory that philosophical systems have a coherent structure, which is reflected in paired opposites. However, just as we should reject paired opposites in novels, Derrida believes that these philosophical concepts are also suspect. Through a technique that he calls *deconstruction*, he attempts to show that all of these paired opposites in philosophy are in fact self-refuting. For example, Husserl emphasizes a distinction between what is *present* to our consciousness (phenomena) and what is *absent* from it (whether the world exists). But when Husserl himself explores what is actually present to our consciousness, he finds that the "present" principally includes memories of what happened in the past and anticipation of what will occur in the future. The problem now is that neither the past nor the future are really "present" to our consciousness. Thus, Husserl's initial distinction between presence and absence collapses: The two concepts are in fact intertwined. Derrida believes that we can similarly deconstruct all of the standard paired opposites in philosophy. For example, with the appearance/reality dichotomy, when attempting to describe reality, my descriptions seem to be based solely on appearances, such as what appears to my senses. Similarly, with the matter/spirit dichotomy, when attempting to say something about spirits—my own spirit or a divine being—my descriptions are all grounded in some material reality. Because the internal logic of such philosophical systems is flawed, no such system offers an adequate description of the world.

According to Derrida, one of the more central dichotomies underlying philosophical discourse is that between speech and writing. Rousseau drew this distinction most clearly. Speech, Rousseau argued, is our natural form of communicating feelings, and as such it conveys what is real and certain. Writing, by contrast, is a degraded copy of speech. Because writing only indirectly conveys our feelings, it relies on a series of conventional devices that ultimately distort truth and are the source of illusion. However, Derrida argues, both speech and writing involve basic elements of language, such as conventional use of symbols and strict rules of grammar. In fact, we might argue that writing is a better vehicle of language than speech because established conventions are so central to language, and, on Rousseau's reasoning, writing relies on conventions more than speech.

Postmodernism

Post-structuralism and the specific technique of deconstruction make quite skeptical pronouncements about the success of traditional philosophical systems. Post-structuralists also cast doubt on the possibility of finding meaning to the world beyond what we as individual observers impose on things. It seems that the whole historical enterprise of finding a unified meaning of things is fatally flawed. In Western civilization the problem started during the Renaissance and Enlightenment periods—the sixteenth through eighteenth centuries—when scientists and philosophers ushered in a new and modern way of viewing the world. Scientists hoped to find a unified system of physical laws that govern the natural world around us. As an addendum to this scientific plan, philosophers described the mechanisms of human thought, thereby explaining how human beings and human culture fit into the larger natural machinery. The philosophical theories of humanism, rationalism, empiricism, and idealism all reflect the basic assumption that the world is one and a single explanatory system governs everything. All beliefs and values that we form are grounded in this unifying system. This modern conception of things was passed on through the nineteenth and twentieth centuries, right down to the present time. The modern notion of a unified world system is a nice fairy tale, but a fairy tale nonetheless. We need to step beyond this modern conception of things into a *postmodern* frame of mind.

Postmodernism is not a single philosophical theory; to be so would be self-defeating. Instead, it is an umbrella movement that covers a variety of critiques of the modern conception of things. Post-structuralism is perhaps the most dominant of these, and for this reason the terms *postmodern* and *post-structural* are often used interchangeably. However, much of recent philosophy targets modernism and thus would also count as postmodern. Rorty rejected the standard conception that there are "essences" to things, such as human nature. Anscombe challenged the "lawgiver" assumption behind modern moral theories. Feminist philosophers reject the largely male-oriented manner of imposing rigid schemes on things. We even find hints of postmodernist attitudes in earlier times, such as with Nietzsche, who rejected traditional value structures of the masses. Even American pragmatists such as Dewey rejected fixed solutions to standard philosophical issues and argued that there is no "givenness" about the world. Much of postmodernist discussion extends well beyond the discipline of philosophy, which is only one manifestation of modern culture. Literature, music, art, theater, film, and architecture are also under the sway of modernist attitudes of unified order, symmetry, and harmony. Postmodernist writers, musicians, and artists thus attempt to break the traditional molds of their respective genres.

POLITICAL PHILOSOPHY

Some major developments within recent political philosophy have involved enlarging on well established theories of the past, rather than the construction of all-new theories. Two cases in point are the theories of John Rawls (1921–2002) and Robert Nozick (1938–2002), whose views are both firmly grounded in traditional social contract theory, while, at the same time, pushing the concept in diametrically opposite directions.

Rawls: Justice as Fairness

Rawls was a philosophy professor at Harvard University for nearly 40 years, and among his various writings, the most influential is *A Theory of Justice* (1971). In this work he argues that social policies should be grounded in the notion of fairness. We create a fair set of guidelines through a process whereby we ignore our actual economic position within society and thus make decisions impartially. The guidelines we arrive at will guarantee equal rights and duties for all, and also regulate wealth in a way that would benefit both rich and poor. This view permits governments to restrict an individual's accumulation of property for the betterment of others. The heart of Rawls's view is a version of social contract theory that he devised as an answer to what he saw as inadequacies with utilitarian social theory. The key problem with utilitarianism, for Rawls, is that an individual's rights may be violated if the consequences of doing so benefit society as a whole. For example, we could conceive of a situation in which enslaving a minority group of people would bring about the greatest good for the greatest number of people. Rawls believes a theory of justice that is grounded in fairness avoids this problem, since the rules of justice would be agreed to in an initial contractual situation which is fair for all people involved, including the minority group in question. He titles his view "justice as fairness."

For Rawls, the starting point of forming a just society is what he calls "the original position," which is a hypothetical community of people who are rational, equal, and self-interested. These people are not trying to start a new social system, but, instead, seeking to establish a mutually beneficial set of principles that will reform and regulate all rights and duties within their system. They are, he argues, "the principles that free and rational persons concerned to further their own interests would accept in an initial position of equality as defining the fundamental terms of their association." In establishing this foundational guideline, the people see themselves behind a *veil of ignorance*. That is, they assume to be ignorant about their actual position in society, such as how rich or powerful they are. He writes, "I shall even assume that the parties do not know their conceptions of the good or their special psychological propensities." This assures that they will not create a foundational guideline that gives them special benefits.

The original position, then, is a state of impartiality and equality. It is impartial since, behind the veil of ignorance, there is no special consideration given to one's natural assets, such as one's personal education and wealth. "For example, if someone knew that he was wealthy, he might find it rational to advance the principle that various taxes for welfare measures be counted unjust. On the other hand, if he knew that he was poor, he would most likely propose the contrary principle. To represent the desired restrictions, one imagines a situation in which everyone is deprived of this sort of information." It is also a state of equality, since all have the same right in determining the foundational principle of justice. These, then, are the basic parameters of the original position, and it should be left up to the negotiators themselves to stipulate more specifically what things they should presume to be ignorant about. For example, Rawls feels that our society has already reached agreement about religious tolerance and racial injustice, so we may not need to place these behind the veil of ignorance. However, "we have much less assurance as to what is the correct distribution of wealth and authority," and, thus, knowledge of our actual wealth and power is something that we would place behind the veil of ignorance.

The aim of the original position is to arrive at precise rules of justice that are most acceptable to everyone. As we set up the parameters of the original position—exactly what we should place behind the veil of ignorance—we will be able to evaluate proposed principles of justice according to our common moral intuitions. We can then adjust the circumstances of the original position so that it gives rise to the notion of justice that conforms with our intuitions. This "going back and forth" from the original position to one's actual intuitions on justice is called *reflective equilibrium*. However, Rawls argues that this does not involve an appeal to self-evident moral truths about justice as intuitionist philosophers in the past have done. Rather, "its justification is a matter of the mutual support of many considerations, of everything fitting together into one coherent view."

Behind the veil of ignorance, Rawls argues, the negotiators would adopt two specific rules of justice: one that assures equal rights and duties for all, and a second that regulates power and wealth. They are these:

- Each person is to have an equal right to the most extensive basic liberty compatible with a similar liberty for others.
- Social and economic inequalities are to be arranged so that they are both (a) reasonably expected to be to everyone's advantage, and (b) attached to positions and offices open to all.

The first principle generates specific rights and duties, such as those regarding speech, assembly, conscience, thought, property, arbitrary arrest, and political liberties of voting and holding office. Every rational and self-interested person would want these to the fullest extent possible. The second principle regulates the fair distribution of wealth and power. To understand how these principles work, Rawls suggests that we start with the assumption that all rights, duties, wealth, and power should be equally distributed among all members of society. But, if certain inequalities would then make everyone better off, then these inequalities are permissible according to the second rule above. For example, it is cumbersome for each citizen to have equal political control. Everyone benefits if political power is concentrated in the hands of a few, as with representative democracies. Thus, "the general conception of justice imposes no restrictions on what sort of inequalities are permissible; it only requires that everyone's position be improved." Any equality may be permitted, perhaps even slavery, so long as each person benefits from that inequality, including the slave. According to Rawls, this is the point that makes his theory of "justice as fairness" superior to utilitarianism. For, under utilitarianism, an individual slave's unhappiness does not matter, so long as general happiness is served by that inequality. "Injustice, then, is simply inequalities that are not to the benefit of all."

Rawls recognizes that Part A of the second principle is the most controversial aspect of his account. He calls this the "difference principle," and it has two implications. First, people with fewer natural assets, such as education and wealth, deserve special considerations. Differences in natural assets are the result of what is sometimes called the natural lottery. The natural lottery is arbitrary, and therefore the principle of redress dictates that we should compensate those with fewer natural assets. For example, he suggests, "greater resources might be spent on the education of the less rather than the more intelligent, at least over a certain time of life, say the earlier years of school." It would be unrealistic to attempt to eliminate such natural distinctions altogether, but there are ways of structuring society so that these differences work for the good of the less fortunate as well as for the more fortunate. Second, Rawls argues that even rich people should agree to give up some wealth for the poor, since in the end they gain simply by being in a society of mutual cooperation. For, "it is clear that the well-being of each depends on a scheme of social cooperation without which no one could have a satisfactory life."

On the political spectrum from conservative to liberal, Rawls's theory falls on the liberal side, and is often classified as "welfare liberalism." What makes it liberal in character is that wealthier people in society need to give up some of their wealth to the less fortunate members to help redress the unfairness of the natural lottery. Behind the veil of ignorance, we would recognize this as the fair thing to do. Further, behind the veil of ignorance, I would want to enact such liberal social policies as a kind of insurance policy to protect me personally since, once the veil of ignorance is removed, it may turn out that I am one of society's less fortunate people who could benefit from a redistribution of society's wealth.

Nozick: Minimalist Government

Shortly after the appearance of Rawls's *Theory of Justice*, Harvard University philosophy professor Robert Nozick published his book *Anarchy, State, and Utopia* (1974), which was quickly seen as a conservative answer to Rawls. Nozick argued that the role of governments should be minimal and limited to securing our rights—especially the right to property. Governments are not justified in taking away private property against our wills, even when it is for a good cause such as helping needy people. Nozick's theory is often classified as "libertarian" in the sense that it aims to preserve as much of our individual liberty as possible—especially economic liberty, even if that means that there will be a wide gap in society between the wealthy and the poor.

For Nozick, only a government with very minimal responsibilities is justified, and anything beyond that would violate our rights. There are some anarchist political philosophers who believe that no government is justifiable since they all are coercive and restrictive by their very nature. But Nozick does not go quite that far. There is a natural justification for minimalist governments with a very narrowly defined role of protecting its citizens. In the state of nature, he argues, each person is entitled to protect himself against others. Being on guard to protect one's home twenty-four hours a day is a daunting task, and the first significant development beyond private attempts at self-defense would be the creation of mutual-protection associations. To make our lives more manageable, "groups of individuals may form mutual-protection associations: all will answer the call of any member for defense or for the enforcement of his rights." These would be something like private security companies, which would protect their members' property and punish violators. While different protection associations might develop different mechanisms for resolving conflicts, "most persons will want to join associations that follow some procedure to find out which claimant is correct."

Once I become a member of a mutual-protection association, the association would limit my right to individual retaliation, thus eliminating the confusion that would arise from one vigilante retaliating against another, and then another against another, and so on. To make the protection process more efficient, each protection association would develop procedures for handling conflicts with clients of other protection associations. Conflicts between different associations would soon lead to the development of a common system that judges between competing claims. In time, it would be natural for smaller associations to join together and create a dominant protective association, and, in turn, these would eventually develop into minimal states. From the formation of tiny, private protection associations to bare-bones minimal states, each stage in its advancement is justified and unavoidable: "Out of anarchy, pressed by spontaneous groupings, mutual-protection associations, division of labor, market pressures, economies of scale, and rational self-interest there arises something very much resembling a minimal state or a group of geographically distinct minimal states."

Nozick argues that "The minimal state is the most extensive state that can be justified. Any state more extensive violates people's rights." It is reasonable for governments to acquire the power to protect and punish offenders, but it is not justifiable when governments force us to give up some of our property to pay for other projects, such as welfare programs. The philosophical term for the reallocation of society's resources is called *distributive justice*, and Nozick argues that the term itself is a biased one since it presumes that the redistribution of private wealth should even take place. Thus, distributive justice is not justice at all, and, Nozick says, the only theory of property ownership that is consistent with the concept of a minimal state is the theory of *entitlement*. Entitlement has two main components. The first is the principle of justice in acquisition whereby we initially acquire property by just means, such as making an object from raw materials that no one owns. The second is the principle of justice in transfer whereby we voluntarily transfer that property to another person by just means, such as through a gift or sales contract. If the world were completely just, the following three points would "exhaustively cover the subject of justice in holdings":

1. A person who acquires a holding in accordance with the principle of justice in acquisition is entitled to that holding.
2. A person who acquires a holding in accordance with the principle of justice in transfer from someone else entitled to the holding, is entitled to the holding.
3. No one is entitled to a holding except by (repeated) applications of 1 and 2.

Any other mechanism for reassigning property will violate our rights. When, for example, the government taxes us to improve the conditions of the poor, this is really just forced labor since I will be working for the benefit of others without any choice or reward.

Nozick says that his entitlement theory follows what he calls an *historic* principle for distributing wealth, that is, it considers how we came to acquire our property. While this, he argues, is the only just way of considering the distribution of wealth, other theories disregard historical ownership. They focus instead on only the current distribution of ownership as it appears right now in the current-time-slice. For example, utilitarianism holds to a current-time-slice position since it advocates distributing wealth based on the greatest good for the greatest number right now, without considering how we arrived at our wealth. Similarly, governmental welfare programs consider only the current-time-slice by focusing on how much money people have right now, and then take from the wealthy to help the poor. What is wrong with current-time-slice approaches is that they consider only some *end result*—such as utility, or social welfare, or the elimination of poverty—and not the historical back story. For Nozick, most people reject current-time-slice approaches since "they think it relevant in assessing the justice of a situation to consider not only the distribution it embodies, but also how that distribution came about."

In addition to offering a conservative libertarian vision of social justice that is distinct from Rawls's welfare liberalism, Nozick also criticizes specific components of Rawls's view. In particular he questions the rules of justice that Rawls derives from the original position since, Nozick believes, they unfairly benefit the poor at the expense of the rich. Nozick theoretically grants Rawls's account of the original position—many critics of Rawls would not grant even that much. His objection is that people in the original position will not accept Rawls's second rule of justice that requires that the rich make sacrifices for the poor. We have seen that, according to Rawls, the rich sacrifice something to benefit the poor, but, in exchange, the rich also receive a greater gain by being in a society of mutual cooperation. This is sometimes called the minimax principle: a minimum loss produces a maximum gain. Nozick objects, though, that it is not clear how much the rich gain from mutual cooperation. The rich might prefer a principle of justice that would cost them much less, even if it has less cooperative benefit. Further, Nozick considers these to rival proposals from the poor and rich respectively:

> "Look, better endowed: you gain by cooperating with us. If you want our cooperation you'll have to accept reasonable terms. We suggest these terms: We'll cooperate with you only if we get *as much as possible.* . ."

> "Look, worse endowed: you gain by cooperating with *us*. If you want our cooperation you'll have to accept reasonable terms. We propose these terms: We'll cooperate with you so long as *we* get as much as possible. . ."

Based on how Rawls develops the original position, it is no more outrageous to establish an agreement that produces a higher benefit for the rich, than one that produces a higher benefit for the poor. Thus, for Nozick, Rawls's endorsement of the difference principle is arbitrary.

Nozick also criticizes Rawls for ignoring the manner in which natural assets are acquired. We noted above that, for Rawls, all natural assets are arbitrary, such as people who become rich through inheritance. But Nozick responds that people are entitled to their natural assets if they were acquired legitimately. Consider, for example, that a group of students take an exam, do not know how they did, and must decide on a procedure for assigning grades. They consider several procedures. An equity principle would have the result that all students receive the same grade. An historical entitlement principle would have the result that grades would be based on the number of correct answers given, and this, in turn, would hinge on how much a student studied. A strange reverse entitlement position would have the result that the highest historical entitlement scores are swapped with the lowest historical entitlement scores. Even stranger is that, in the eyes of the students, the historical entitlement and reverse entitlement principles might be on equal footing, since the students do not yet know how they performed on the test. Nozick's point is that Rawls's veil of ignorance locks us into a position where we can only consider a principle of wealth distribution if it is *not* based on historical entitlement—how we came by it. That is, the veil of ignorance will only allow for end-result principles of distribution, such as equality, that are not historically linked to how we came by our wealth. The problem, according to Nozick, is that we should accept end-result (nonhistorical) explanations only if all historical entitlement principles fail first. True entitlement assumes that the past history of the property owner is central to the legitimacy of his claim to ownership. The veil of ignorance, though, strips us of any knowledge of our history, and, thus, the principles of distributive justice that we arrive at will rest on end-result principles.

Introduction to Classic Readings in the History of Philosophy

There are two principal approaches to the study of philosophy. On the one hand we might approach it chronologically, starting with the very first philosophers several thousand years ago and working forward through time to the present day, one philosopher after another. This has the advantage of revealing theories in their proper historical contexts and showing how some ideas and people influenced others over time. We can, for example, see how Socrates influenced Plato, and how Plato in turn influenced Aristotle. On the other hand, we might look at key issues and topics that philosophy has wrestled with throughout its long history, such as questions about human knowledge, God's existence, or ethics. This approach allows us to stay focused on a single philosophical problem and perhaps find some satisfactory resolution to the various puzzles. For example, we might at one sitting examine the arguments for God's existence and decide whether any such proof is possible.

While this collection of classic readings in philosophy is structured historically, its contents can also be arranged topically. And for those wishing to approach the subject in this way, following is a topical layout of its contents, followed by a brief introduction to philosophy's main topics.

OPTIONAL TOPICAL TABLE OF CONTENTS

Epistemology

Plato: Knowledge (from *The Republic*)

Sextus Empiricus: The Goals and Methods of Skepticism (from *Outlines of Pyrrhonism*)

Augustine: On Skepticism (from *On the Trinity*)

René Descartes: Certainty (from *Meditations*)

John Locke: The Origin of All Our Ideas in Experience (from *Essay concerning Human Understanding*)

David Hume: Experience (from *Enquiry*)

Immanuel Kant: Pure Reason (from *The Critique of Pure Reason*)

William James: Pragmatism (from *Pragmatism*)

Arthur Eddington: Commonsense Knowledge and Scientific Knowledge (from *The Nature of the Physical World*)

Bertrand Russell: Appearance and Reality (from *Problems of Philosophy*)

Willard Van Orman Quine: Two Dogmas of Empiricism (from "Two Dogmas of Empiricism")

Metaphysics

Presocratic Philosophy: Ultimate Reality (from *Fragments*)

Aristotle: Nature (from *Physics, Metaphysics*)

George Berkeley: Consciousness, Not Matter, the True Reality (from *Three Dialogues*)

Georg W.F. Hegel: Lordship-Bondage and World History (from *Phenomenology of Spirit* and *The Philosophy of Right*)

Philosophy of Religion

Plato: Does God Create Morality? (from *Euthyphro*, complete)

Anselm: The Ontological Argument (from *Proslogium*)

Thomas Aquinas: God's Existence

Blaise Pascal: Wagering on Belief in God (from *Thoughts*)

David Hume: Miracles and God's Existence (from *Enquiry* and *Dialogues concerning Natural Religion*)

Voltaire: On the Best of All Possible Worlds (from *Philosophical Dictionary*)

William Paley: The Design Argument from Analogy Defended (from *Natural Theology*)

Søren Kierkegaard: Faith and Paradox (from *Fear and Trembling*)

Philosophy of Mind

Plato: Immortality of the Soul (from *Phaedo*)

Aristotle: The Soul (from *On the Soul*)

Lucretius: The Mind as Body (from *On the Nature of Things*)

René Descartes: The Mind (from *The Passions of the Soul*)

Anne Conway: Blurring the Distinction between Mind and Body (from *Principles*)

David Hume: The Self (from *Treatise*)

Thomas Nagel: What Is It Like to Be a Bat? (from "What Is It Like to Be a Bat?")

Free Will

Epictetus: Resigning Oneself to Fate (from *Handbook*)

David Hume: Determinism (from *Enquiry*)

Thomas Reid: The Argument for Free Will from Commonsense Beliefs (from *Essays on the Active Powers of Man*)

William James: Free Will (from *The Dilemma of Determinism*)

Ethics

Aristotle: Morality (from *Ethics*)

Epicurus: Pleasure and Life's Aim (from *Letter to Menoeceus*, complete)

Augustine: Our Primary Good (from *Of the Morals of the Catholic Church*)

Immanuel Kant: The Categorical Imperative (from *Groundwork of the Metaphysics of Morals*)

John Stuart Mill: Utilitarianism (from *Utilitarianism*)

Friedrich Nietzsche: Turning Values Upside Down (from *Beyond Good and Evil*, *The Twilight of the Idols*, and *The Will to Power*)

Carol Gilligan: Is There a Characteristically Feminine Voice Defining Morality? (from "In a Different Voice")

James Rachels: The Challenge of Cultural Relativism (from *Elements of Moral Philosophy*)

Political Philosophy

Plato: Obedience to the State (from *Crito*, complete)

Aristotle: Society (from *Politics*)

Augustine: The Two Cities (from *The City of God*)

Thomas Aquinas: Natural Law (from *Summa Theologica*)

Thomas Hobbes: The Social Contract (from *De Cive*)

Mary Wollstonecraft: The Rights of Women (from *A Vindication of the Rights of Woman*)

John Stuart Mill: Liberty (from *On Liberty*)

Karl Marx: The Clash of Class Interests (from *Manifesto of the Communist Party*)

John Rawls: Justice as Fairness (from "Justice as Fairness")

PHILOSOPHY'S MAIN TOPICS

The Meaning of Life

A theme that ties together most branches of philosophy is a concern with the overall value of human life, which German philosophers sometimes call *Lebensphilosophie*, or the philosophy of life. What is life's purpose or meaning? Whether there is a meaning to any person's life might depend on whether the universe itself has some overall purpose. We sometimes feel that as our scientific knowledge of the immense galaxies in space increases, the significance of individual people becomes ever more diminished. When we look down at the earth from an airplane, we appear to be infinitesimal. It is thus natural to wonder why we take ourselves so seriously, are full of anxiety about our futures, and search earnestly for the meaning of life.

The infinitude of interstellar space is matched by the equally impressive infinitude that we find in the microworld of molecular biology and particle physics. This puts human beings between twin infinities so that what is lost to human significance when viewed from vast outer space is restored when compared with the depth of microscopic reality. Moreover, the overriding fact is that our human minds are capable of grasping the structures of these two worlds so that human calculations can successfully place man and machine on the moon and also successfully manipulate the world of microbiology. This means that, while there is no overwhelming evidence of a purpose to the universe, neither is it surprising that our human minds can raise questions about the meaning of existence.

As seen throughout this book, many philosophers have offered broad visions of human existence that have clear implications for the question of life's meaning. For example, for Aristotle (384–322 BCE), the concept of purpose is fundamental to our meaning. Everything, he says, strives to fulfill its purpose, and it is not difficult to discover what that purpose is. Purpose and function are closely related. Each part of our bodies has a function: the eyes to see, the heart to circulate the blood, and the lungs to supply oxygen. Aristotle asks whether it makes sense to say, on the one hand, that every organ of the body has a purpose, but that on the other hand, when all these organs are united into a complete person, such a unified person has no specific function or purpose. Surely, he says, our human purpose is to fulfill all our natural functions, which include not only our physical capacities but also our passions and ultimately our intellectual powers. To Aristotle's natural philosophy, Thomas Aquinas (1224–1274) added the dimension of religion, which connects our natural functions and purpose to an eternal destiny of life with God. But the optimism of these philosophical and theological definitions of the meaning of life was ultimately challenged by science and skepticism. David Hume (1711–1776) in particular rejected the notion of cause and effect on which earlier thinkers had relied to prove that the universe has a source of order, purpose, and meaning. While Hume ended his philosophical investigations as a skeptic, he makes the significant comment that "to whatever length one may push his speculative principles, he must act and live and converse like other men. . . . It is impossible for him to persevere in total skepticism, or make it appear in his conduct for a few hours."

Aside from the general picture of life's meaning that we can derive from various philosophical systems, many of civilization's great philosophers addressed the issue head on, and samples of their views on the subject are included in this collection.

Epistemology

Epistemology, or theory of knowledge, focuses on the fundamental question "What can I know?" What occurs when we perceive something, say, an apple? Do we know that it is an apple? What does it mean to know anything? What does it mean to say that something is? Suppose I say, "I know that it is an apple because I recognize its shape and color." There can be no question that when I perceive an apple I in fact have the psychological experience of shape and color. But is that experience what we call "knowledge"? Does it follow, for example, when I perceive a certain shape and color—which appear identical to the apple I ate yesterday—that the present object will taste the same or even be an apple? Perhaps, unlike the apple I ate yesterday, the present object is something made of wax or paper or clay. If the object I perceive turns out differently from what I thought it was, then I did not have true knowledge about the object. True knowledge assumes that we know what reality is. But the problem philosophers have tried to solve is whether there is any reliable way to distinguish between appearance and reality. Many philosophers insist that we can, and they offer compelling arguments for their views; more skeptically minded philosophers, though, doubt this. This collection includes views on both sides.

Metaphysics

From earliest times philosophers have reflected on the question "What is there?" Sometimes they rephrased the question to ask, "What is real?" or "What really is?" They were puzzled by the fact that things come and go—they come into being, exist, and then cease to be. They were fascinated to discover that things are not what they appear to be. Answers to these questions involve the subject of *metaphysics*, or the study of the fundamental nature of reality. The origin of the term metaphysics is unclear, but it rests on two Greek words: *meta* (beyond) and *phusis* (nature). It may be helpful to see it as the study of things that exist—apart from or beyond what is immediately apparent in the physical world around us. Part of the job of metaphysics is to take an inventory of all the kinds of things that exist, and philosophers disagree widely about how many kinds of things there are. *Monism* is the view that there is one fundamental type of thing. Even here, though, there are disputes about what this one thing might be. Monistic *materialism* is the view that everything in the universe is made of material stuff. We might think that some sorts of nonmaterial spirits exist—such as human or divine spirits. However, materialists deny this and suggest that even whatever human or divine elements we consider must ultimately be made of material stuff. Monistic *idealism*, by contrast, is the view that everything in the universe is made of spiritual stuff, and nothing is actually material in nature. The term idealism is based on the word idea, insofar as ideas are thought to be spiritual in nature. Both types of monism have a simple conclusion: Says the materialist, "Never mind"; says the idealist, "No matter."

Against both of these types of materialism, the theory of *dualism* is the view that there are two basic types of stuff that exist in the world, namely, matter and spirit. Dualism acknowledges what appears to be obvious to at least some philosophers, namely, that there is both a physical component to the world and a realm of spiritual things, such as human minds and divine spirits. Yet another position, called *pluralism*, holds that there are *many* different types of things that exist. On this view both monism and dualism are far too simplistic, and pluralists argue that we should recognize that many things—and perhaps even everything out there—differ from other things in some major respect.

When philosophers investigate the issues of monism, dualism, and pluralism, they typically cast their eyes on one of two fields: (1) the broad makeup of things in the universe, or, (2) the more narrow makeup of human existence. The broader issue often focuses on the possible existence of a spiritual realm, the nature of God, and the way God interrelates with things in the universe. This is a special metaphysical subject called *the philosophy of religion*. The narrower issue of metaphysics is called *the philosophy of mind*. Both of these we turn to next.

Philosophy of Religion

Of the many subjects commanding the attention of philosophers of religion, few have received more careful treatment than the questions of the existence of God and the nature of God. Throughout the centuries theologians and philosophers have attempted to prove the existence of God in a variety of ways, as reflected in several selections in this collection. Aside from demonstrating the existence of a divine being, another question immediately arises about the nature or attributes of that being. First and foremost, theologians argue that God is the all-powerful creator of things. He is also all-knowing and all-good, and a personal being who acts with a purpose. Religious critics have argued that there is an incompatibility between this traditional conception of

God and the presence of suffering in the world. Some suffering is caused by the forces of nature—floods, tornados, diseases—and other suffering by the hands of humans, such as murderers, rapists, and thieves. In either case, it seems that an all-good, all-knowing, and all-powerful God would prevent such suffering. This is called *the problem of evil*.

Philosophy of Mind

As noted, the narrower view of metaphysics is called *the philosophy of mind*, and it attempts to discover whether human beings are composed of one, two, or many types of things. Even here, though, issues in the philosophy of mind often interweave with the broader metaphysical concerns about the makeup of the universe as a whole. Central to the philosophy of mind is the relation between the human mind and the human body, which today we call *the mind-body problem*. The dualistic presumption is that the human mind is spiritual in nature and that the body is physical. Monistic materialists, though, argue that the human mind is ultimately grounded in physical brain activity and that there is nothing spiritual about our thinking process. Idealists, on the other hand, deny that humans really have any physical bodies at all; instead, they hold that perceptions of our physical selves are sort of like a divinely imposed hallucination.

Free Will

One metaphysical issue in the philosophy of mind that has commanded the attention of philosophers from the earliest times to the present day is whether the human will is free. Why should this be a problem? Our commonsense intuitions tell us that we constantly face choices and that our wills are free to move in different directions. To say that you made a mistake means not only that you should have but also that you could have chosen to behave in a different way. However, the problem is not that simple. Many ways of thinking have been programmed by our genetics, our families, and our culture; this suggests that much of our life and behavior is determined and could be no other way. The question is: how much is determined? The determinist argues that *everything*—that is, every event and every aspect of nature—is determined and could be no other way. This view is mostly influenced by the notion that every event has a cause, and that scientific laws of nature define how all things work and are interrelated. For the determinist, all of reality functions as a machine; consider how your car or computer operates according to strict laws of nature. Human existence as well can be explained according to this rigid mechanical model. We are faced, then, with two opposite points of view regarding the human will. The determinist argues that in no way is the will free, and the indeterminist argues that human experience is incomprehensible without the assumption that the will is free. Some philosophers attempt to take a middle position between these two views—a position often called *soft determinism* or *compatibilism*. On this view, depending on how we define "free will" and "determinism," there may be some way to consistently espouse both of these positions at the same time.

Ethics

In countless ways, virtually every day, we are all faced with the simple ethical question "What should I do?" Though this question is a simple one, the answer is not so simple. If, for example, the question takes the form "Should I tell the truth?" even the most rigorous moral philosopher might say "yes" but agree that there could be exceptional cases. To distinguish between when we should and should not tell the truth involves further analysis of what really constitutes an ethical or moral situation and what our obligations might be in such situations. Philosophical discussions of ethics focus largely on two issues. The first, which is metaethical in nature, involves discovering the source of our moral obligation. Is morality grounded in human instinct, social convention, the will of God, or the rational order of the universe itself? The second issue, which is normative in nature, involves discovering a method for determining whether a given act is right or wrong. Do we judge the rightness of an action based on selfish considerations, the best interests of society, an intuitive list of moral duties, or an ideal conception of morally good character traits? Philosophers have defended each of these positions.

Political Philosophy

One of the most complicated problems facing modern society is how to bring into harmony the elements of authority, human rights, and freedom. The concept of authority, in particular, has been a matter of constant perplexity. Who has the authority to tell another person what he or she may or may not do in society? Does the government have the right to override the wishes of a citizen? Is a law, as a command of the government, just or right simply because that law has been officially promulgated? Or must a law, in order to be just, conform to some higher standard of justice? And finally, what should individuals do if they conclude that a law is unjust: Should they obey it, or do they have a right to disobey it? Answering these questions is the task of political philosophy.

PART ONE

Ancient Greek Philosophy

Presocratic Philosophy: Ultimate Reality

From *Fragments*

The first philosophers of Western civilization appeared in ancient Greece prior to Socrates, and, thus, are referred to as Presocratic philosophers. All were brilliant and inquisitive thinkers, and many were prolific writers. Regrettably, though, none of their writings have survived intact, and all that remain are stray sentences—or "fragments"—from their works that were quoted by later writers who were lucky enough to read the original texts while they still existed. The surviving fragments are sketchy, and, at times, frustrating to decipher. Nevertheless, they offer daring explanations of ultimate reality that set aside many of the religious assumptions of their time. They speculated that water, or air, or fire, or numbers might be the ultimate stuff or unifying force of everything that is. While many of their explanations do not stand up to modern scientific scrutiny, others have come very near the mark, and they all reveal the kind of creativity and intellectual rigor that it takes to advance beyond mythology. The selections below are among the more famous of the surviving quotations by thirteen prominent Presocratic philosophers.

MILESIANS

Thales

Of the first philosophers, most thought that the principles which pertained to the qualities of matter were the only principles of all things. . . . Yet they did not all agree as to the number and the nature of these principles. Thales, the founder of this type of philosophy, said the principle is water (for which reason he declared that the earth rests on water). Perhaps he got this notion from seeing that the

Source: collected fragments of Presocratic philosophers, tr. John Burnet.

11

nutrition of all things is moist, and that heat itself is generated from the moist and kept alive by it (and that from which they come to be is a principle of all things). Perhaps he also got his notion from the fact that the seeds of all things have a moist nature, and that water is the origin of the nature of moist things.

Anaximander

He held that that the principle and primary element of all things was the unbounded, giving no exact definition as to whether he meant air or water, or anything else. He said that while the parts were susceptible of change, the whole was unchangeable.

   Anaximander of Miletus, son of Praxiades, a fellow-citizen and associate of Thales, said that the material cause and first element of things was the Infinite, he being the first to introduce this name of the material cause. He says it is neither water nor any other of the so-called elements, but a substance different from them which is infinite, from which arise all the heavens and the worlds within them.

   [According to Anaximander,] there is a body distinct from the elements, the infinite, which is not air or water, in order that the other things may not be destroyed by their infinity. The elements are in opposition to each other: air is cold, water moist, and fire hot. Therefore, if any one of them were infinite, the rest would have ceased to be by this time. Accordingly he said that what is infinite is something other than the elements, and from it the elements arise.

Anaximenes

Anaximenes of Miletus, who had been an associate of Anaximander, said, like him, that the underlying substance was one and infinite. He did not, however, say it was indeterminate, like Anaximander, but determinate; for he said it was Air. It differs in different substances in virtue of its rarefaction and condensation. In its thinnest state it comes to be; being condensed it becomes wind, then cloud, and when still further condensed it becomes water, then earth, then stones, and the rest of things comes to be out of these.

IONIANS

Heraclitus

Cold things become warm, and what is warm cools; what is wet dries, and the parched is moistened.

   You cannot step twice into the same rivers; for fresh waters are ever flowing in upon you. It scatters and it gathers; it advances and retires.

   It is wise to listen, not to me, but to the Logos, and to agree that all things are one.

   Though this Logos is true always, yet people are as unable to understand it both when they hear it for the first time and when they have heard it at all again. For, though all things come into being in accordance with the

Logos, people seem as if they had no experience of it, when they make meet with words and actions that I establish, dividing each thing according to its kind and showing how it truly is. As for the rest of the people, they do not know what they are doing when awake, just as they forget what they do once asleep.

The ordered universe, which is the same for all, was not made by one of the gods or by humans. Rather, always was, is now, and forever will be an ever-living fire, ignited in measure, and extinguished in measure.

Pythagoras

Pythagoras declared that the soul is immortal, then that it changes into other kinds of animals. In addition, the things that happen recur at certain intervals, and nothing is absolutely new. Also, all things that come to be alive must be thought akin. Pythagoras seems to have been the first to introduce these opinions into Greece.

Do not stir the fire with a knife. Rub out the mark of a pot in the ashes. Do not wear a ring. Do not have swallows in the house. Spit on your nail parings and hair trimmings. Abstain from eating beans. Abstain from eating living things. Roll up your bedclothes on rising and smooth out the imprint of the body. Do not urinate facing the sun.

The tetractys is a certain number, which being composed of the four first numbers produces the most perfect number, ten. For one and two and three and four come to ten. This number is the first tetractys, and is called the source of ever flowing nature. This is because, according to them, the entire cosmos is organized according to harmony, and harmony is a system of three concords: the fourth, the fifth, and the octave. And the proportions of these three concords are found in the aforementioned four numbers.

ELEATICS

Parmenides

There are only two ways of inquiry that can be thought of. The first, namely, that *it is* (and that it is impossible for it not to be), is the way of belief, for truth is its companion. The other way of inquiry, namely, that *it is not* (and cannot be), is a path that none can learn at all. For you cannot know what is not, nor can you express it. It is the same thing that can be thought and that can be. What can be spoken and thought must be; for it is possible for it to be, but impossible for nothing to be. . . . One path only is left for us to speak of, namely, that *it is*. In this path are very many signs that "what is" is uncreated and indestructible; it is complete, immovable, and without end. . . .

[The One] is not divisible, since it is all alike, and there is no more of it in one place than in another, to hinder it from holding together, nor less of it, but everything is full of what is. For this reason it is wholly continuous; for what is, is in contact with what is.

Moreover, it is immovable in the bonds of mighty chains, without beginning and without end; since coming into being and passing away have been driven afar, and true belief has cast them away. It is the same, and it rests in the self-same place, abiding in itself. And thus it remains constant in its place; for hard necessity keeps it in the bonds of the limit that holds it fast on every side. For this reason it is not permitted to what is to be infinite; for it is in need of nothing; while, if it were infinite, it would stand in need of everything.

Zeno

The motive of my book was to protect Parmenides against ridicule by showing that the hypothesis of the existence of the many involved greater absurdities than the hypothesis of the one. The book was a youthful composition of mine, which was stolen from me, and therefore I had no choice about the publication.

Zeno's arguments about motion, which cause so much annoyance to those who try to solve the problems that they present, are four in number.

The first asserts the non-existence of motion on the ground that that which is in motion must arrive at the half-way stage before it arrives at the goal. This we have discussed above. [i.e., "It is always necessary to traverse half the distance, but these are infinite, and it is impossible to get through things that are infinite."]

The second is the so-called "Achilles," and it amounts to this, that in a race the quickest runner can never overtake the slowest, since the pursuer must first reach the point whence the pursued started, so that the slower must always hold a lead. . . .

The third is that already given above, to the effect that the flying arrow is at rest [i.e., "If everything when it occupies an equal space is at rest, and if that which is in locomotion is always occupying such a space at any moment, the flying arrow is therefore motionless."]

The fourth argument is that concerning the two rows of bodies, each row being composed of an equal number of bodies of equal size, passing each other on a race-course as they proceed with equal velocity in opposite directions, the one row originally occupying the space between the goal and the middle point of the course and the other that between the middle point and the starting-post. This, he thinks, involves the conclusion that half a given time is equal to double that time.

If place is something that exists, where will it be? The difficulty raised by Zeno requires some answer. For if everything that exists has a place, it is clear that place too will have a place, and so on without limit.

"Tell me, Protagoras," [Zeno said] "does a single millet seed, or the ten thousandth part of a seed, make a noise when they fall?" When Protagoras said they did not, he said: "Does the bushel then make a noise when it falls or not?" When Protagoras said this did, Zeno said: "Is there not then some ratio of the bushel to one seed, and to a ten-thousandth of a seed?" When Protagoras said there was, Zeno said: "But then must not the respective noises stand to one another in the same ratios? For as the sounding bodies are to one another, so must be the sounds they make. This being so, if the bushel of millet makes a noise, then the single millet seed must also make a noise, and so must the ten thousandth of a millet seed.

PLURALISTS

Empedocles

I will tell you of a twofold process. At one time it [i.e., the cosmos] grew together to be one only out of many, at another it parted to pieces so as to be many instead of one. Fire and Water and Earth and the mighty height of Air. And also, apart from these, dreaded Strife of equal weight to each, and Love in their midst, equal in length and breadth. . . . All these elements are equal and of the same age in their creation. But each presides over its own area, and each has its own character, and they dominate in turn in the course of time.

When Strife had fallen to the lowest depth of the vortex, and Love had reached to the center of the whirl, all things came together in it so as to be one only. This did not happen all at once, but they came together at their will each from different quarters. As they mingled, strife began to pass out to the furthest limit. Yet many things remained unmixed, alternating with the things that were being mixed, namely, all that Strife not fallen yet retained; for it had not yet altogether retired perfectly from them to the outermost boundaries of the circle. Some of it still remained within, and some had passed out from the limbs of the All. But in proportion as it kept rushing out, a soft, immortal stream of blameless Love kept running in, and immediately those things became mortal which had been immortal before, those things were mixed that had before been unmixed, each changing its path. As they mingled, countless tribes of mortal creatures were scattered abroad endowed with all manner of forms, a wonder to observe.

Many creatures with faces and breasts looking in different directions were born. Some offspring of oxen had faces of people, while others, again, arose as offspring of people with the heads of oxen. There were creatures in whom the nature of women and men was mingled, furnished with sterile parts.

Anaxagoras

Nor is there a least of what is small, but there is always a smaller; for it cannot be that what is should cease to be by being cut. But there is also always something, greater than what is great, and it is equal to the small in amount, and, compared with itself, each thing is both great and small.

And since the portions of the great and of the small are equal in amount, for this reason, too, all things will be in everything. Nor is it possible for them to be apart, but all things have a portion of everything. Since it is impossible for there to be a least thing, they cannot be separated, nor come to be by themselves; but they must be now, just as they were in the beginning, all together. And in all things many things are contained, and an equal number both in the greater and in the smaller of the things that are separated off.

All other things partake in a portion of everything, while Mind is infinite and self-ruled, and is mixed with nothing, but is alone, itself by itself. If it were not by itself, but were mixed with anything else, it would partake in all things if it were mixed with any. For in everything there is a portion of everything, as I said earlier, and the things mixed with it would hinder it, so that it would have power over nothing in the same way that it has now being alone by itself. It is the thinnest of all things and the purest, and it has all knowledge about everything and the greatest strength. Mind has power over all things, both greater and smaller, that have life. Mind had power over the whole revolution, so that it began to revolve in the beginning. It began to revolve first from a small beginning; but the revolution now extends over a larger space, and will extend over a larger still. All the things that are mingled together and separated off and distinguished are all known by Mind.

ATOMISTS

Leucippus and Democritus

Substances are unlimited in multitude and atomic . . . and scattered in the void. When they approach one another or collide or become entangled, the compounds appear as water or fire or as a plant or a human. But all things are atoms, which he calls forms; there is nothing else.

[Leucippus and Democritus] attributed sight to certain image-flakes, of the same shape as the object, which were continually streaming off from the objects of sight and impinging on the eye.

Democritus says that certain image-flakes of atoms approach humans, and of them some cause good and others evil . . . These are large and immense, and difficult to destroy though not indestructible. They indicate the future in advance to people when they are seen to emit voices. As a result people of ancient times, upon perceiving the appearances of these things, supposed that they are a god, though there is no other god aside from these having an indestructible nature.

SOPHISTS

Protagoras

Protagoras made the weaker and stronger arguments, and taught his students to blame and praise the same person.

A human being is the measure of all things—of things that are, that they are, and of things that are not, that they are not.

Concerning the gods, I am unable to know either that they are or that they are not, or what their appearance is like. For many are the things that hinder knowledge: the obscurity of the matter and the shortness of human life.

Gorgias

Gorgias declares that nothing exists; and if anything exists it is unknowable; and if it exists and is knowable, yet it cannot be communicated to others.

To prove that nothing exists. . . . Gorgias declares that if anything is, it must either be ungenerated or else have come to be. If it is ungenerated, it is unlimited, and he declares that the unlimited cannot exist anywhere. . . . Nor, again, has it come to be; for, surely, he argues, nothing could come to be out of either Being or Not-being. For if Being were to change, it would no longer be Being, just as also, if Not-being were to come to be, it would no longer be Not-being. . . . So if anything that is, necessarily either is ungenerated or else has come to be, and these are impossibilities, it is impossible for anything to be. . . .

He next goes on to prove that if anything exists, it is unknowable. For otherwise, he argues, all objects of thought must exist, and what does not exist (if it really does not exist) could not be thought. But were this so, nothing could be false, not even if one should say that chariots are racing on the sea. For all things would be just the same. For the objects of sight and hearing exist for the reason that they are in each case thought of. . . .

But even if they are knowable by us, how, Gorgias asks, could anyone communicate them to another? For how could anyone communicate by word of mouth that which he has seen? And how could that which has been seen be communicated to a listener if he has not seen it? For just as the sight does not recognize sounds, so the hearing does not hear colors but sounds. And he who speaks, speaks, but does not speak a color or a thing. When, therefore, one has not a thing in the mind, how will he get it there from another person by word or any other token of the thing except by seeing it, if it is a color, or hearing it, if it is a noise ? For he who speaks does not speak a noise at all, or a color, but a word. And so it is not possible to conceive a color, but only to see it, nor a noise, but only to hear it. . . .

READING 2

Plato: Does God Create Morality?
From Euthyphro (complete)

Born in Athens, Plato (427–347 BCE) is one of the founders of Western civilization's philosophical tradition, and even today is considered among history's most important philosophers. In his dialogue Euthyphro, Plato discusses the question concerning the relation between morality and the will of the gods. The key characters in the dialogue are Euthyphro, a young and especially religious man, and Plato's teacher Socrates (469–399 BCE). The two are outside the king's court regarding their own legal matters,

Source: Plato, *Euthyphro,* tr. Benjamin Jowett.

Socrates for his upcoming trial, and Euthyphro for bringing murder charges against his father. While Euthyphro believes that he is doing the right thing, he is neverthe- less defying his obligation of loyalty to his father. Socrates seizes this opportunity to investigate what true religious piety is. They debate whether true piety is simply what is congenial to the gods, or whether piety consists of tending to the gods, or whether piety is a sacrifice to the gods. In the process of discussing various defini- tions of piety, Socrates raises this fundamental question: "whether the pious or holy is beloved by the gods because it is holy, or holy because it is beloved of the gods." That is, he is asking whether the gods themselves adhere to universal standards of morality that are external to them, or instead, whether the gods themselves create the standards of morality.

EUTHYPHRO PROSECUTING HIS FATHER

EUTHYPHRO: Why have you left the Lyceum, Socrates? and what are you doing in the Porch of the King Archon? Surely you cannot be concerned in a suit before the King, like myself?

SOCRATES: Not in a suit, Euthyphro; impeachment is the word which the Athenians use.

EUTHYPHRO: What! I suppose that someone has been prosecuting you, for I cannot believe that you are the prosecutor of another.

SOCRATES: Certainly not.

EUTHYPHRO: Then someone else has been prosecuting you?

SOCRATES: Yes.

EUTHYPHRO: And who is he?

SOCRATES: A young man who is little known, Euthyphro; and I hardly know him: his name is Meletus, and he is of the deme of Pitthis. Perhaps you may remember his appearance; he has a beak, and long straight hair, and a beard which is ill grown.

EUTHYPHRO: No, I do not remember him, Socrates. But what is the charge which he brings against you?

SOCRATES: What is the charge? Well, a very serious charge, which shows a good deal of character in the young man, and for which he is certainly not to be despised. He says he knows how the youth are corrupted and who are their corruptors. I fancy that he must be a wise man, and seeing that I am the reverse of a wise man, he has found me out, and is going to accuse me of corrupting his young friends. And of this our mother the state is to be the judge. Of all our political men he is the only one who seems to me to begin in the right way, with the cultivation of virtue in youth; like a good husbandman, he makes the young shoots his first care, and clears away us who are the destroyers of them. This is only the first step; he will afterwards attend to the elder branches; and if he goes on as he has begun, he will be a very great public benefactor.

EUTHYPHRO: I hope that he may; but I rather fear, Socrates, that the opposite will turn out to be the truth. My opinion is that in attacking you he is simply aiming a blow at the foundation of the state. But in what way does he say that you corrupt the young?

SOCRATES: He brings a wonderful accusation against me, which at first hearing excites surprise: he says that I am a poet or maker of gods, and that I invent new gods and deny the existence of old ones; this is the ground of his indictment.

EUTHYPHRO: I understand, Socrates; he means to attack you about the familiar sign which occasionally, as you say, comes to you. He thinks that you are a neologian, and he is going to have you up before the court for this. He knows that such a charge is readily received by the world, as I myself know too well; for when I speak in the assembly about divine things, and foretell the future to them, they laugh at me and think me a madman. Yet every word that I say is true. But they are jealous of us all; and we must be brave and go at them.

SOCRATES: Their laughter, friend Euthyphro, is not a matter of much consequence. For a man may be thought wise; but the Athenians, I suspect, do not much trouble themselves about him until he begins to impart his wisdom to others, and then for some reason or other, perhaps, as you say, from jealousy, they are angry.

EUTHYPHRO: I am never likely to try their temper in this way.

SOCRATES: I dare say not, for you are reserved in your behavior, and seldom impart your wisdom. But I have a benevolent habit of pouring out myself to everybody, and would even pay for a listener, and I am afraid that the Athenians may think me too talkative. Now if, as I was saying, they would only laugh at me, as you say that they laugh at you, the time might pass gaily enough in the court; but perhaps they may be in earnest, and then what the end will be you soothsayers only can predict.

EUTHYPHRO: I dare say that the affair will end in nothing, Socrates, and that you will win your case; and I think that I shall win my own.

SOCRATES: And what is your suit, Euthyphro? are you the pursuer or the defendant?

EUTHYPHRO: I am the pursuer.

SOCRATES: Of whom?

EUTHYPHRO: You will think me mad when I tell you.

SOCRATES: Why, has the fugitive wings?

EUTHYPHRO: Nay, he is not very volatile at his time of life.

SOCRATES: Who is he?

EUTHYPHRO: My father.

SOCRATES: Your father! my good man?

EUTHYPHRO: Yes.

SOCRATES: And of what is he accused?

EUTHYPHRO: Of murder, Socrates.

SOCRATES: By the powers, Euthyphro! how little does the common herd know of the nature of right and truth. A man must be an extraordinary man, and have made great strides in wisdom, before he could have seen his way to bring such an action.

EUTHYPHRO: Indeed, Socrates, he must.

SOCRATES: I suppose that the man whom your father murdered was one of your relatives—clearly he was; for if he had been a stranger you would never have thought of prosecuting him.

EUTHYPHRO: I am amused, Socrates, at your making a distinction between one who is a relation and one who is not a relation; for surely the pollution is the same in either case, if you knowingly associate with the murderer when you ought to clear yourself and him by proceeding against him. The real question is whether the murdered man has been justly slain. If justly, then your duty is to let the matter alone; but if unjustly, then even if the murderer lives under the same roof with you and eats at the same table, proceed against him. Now the man who is dead was a poor dependant of mine who worked for us as a field laborer on our farm in Naxos, and one day in a fit of drunken passion he got into a quarrel with one of our domestic servants and slew him. My father bound him hand and foot and threw him into a ditch, and then sent to Athens to ask of a diviner what he should do with him. Meanwhile he never attended to him and took no care about him, for he regarded him as a murderer; and thought that no great harm would be done even if he did die. Now this was just what happened. For such was the effect of cold and hunger and chains upon him, that before the messenger returned from the diviner, he was dead. And my father and family are angry with me for taking the part of the murderer and prosecuting my father. They say that he did not kill him, and that if he did, the dead man was but a murderer, and I ought not to take any notice, for that a son is impious who prosecutes a father. Which shows, Socrates, how little they know what the gods think about piety and impiety.

SOCRATES: Good heavens, Euthyphro! and is your knowledge of religion and of things pious and impious so very exact, that, supposing the circumstances to be as you state them, you are not afraid lest you too may be doing an impious thing in bringing an action against your father?

EUTHYPHRO: The best of Euthyphro, and that which distinguishes him, Socrates, from other men, is his exact knowledge of all such matters. What should I be good for without it?

SOCRATES: Rare friend! I think that I cannot do better than be your disciple. Then before the trial with Meletus comes on I shall challenge him, and say that I have always had a great interest in religious questions, and now, as he charges me with rash imaginations and innovations in religion, I have become your disciple. You, Meletus, as I shall say to him, acknowledge Euthyphro to be a great theologian, and sound in his opinions; and if you approve of him you ought to approve of me, and not have me into court; but if you disapprove, you should begin by indicting him who is my teacher, and who will be the ruin, not of the young, but of the old; that is to say, of myself whom he instructs, and of his old father whom he admonishes and chastises. And if Meletus refuses to listen to me, but will go on, and will not shift the indictment from me to you, I cannot do better than repeat this challenge in the court.

EUTHYPHRO: Yes, indeed, Socrates; and if he attempts to indict me I am mistaken if I do not find a flaw in him; the court shall have a great deal more to say to him than to me.

SOCRATES: And I, my dear friend, knowing this, am desirous of becoming your disciple. For I observe that no one appears to notice you—not even this Meletus; but his sharp eyes have found me out at once, and he has indicted me for impiety. And therefore, I adjure you to tell me the nature of piety and impiety, which you said that you knew so well, and of murder, and of other offences against the gods. What are they? Is not piety in every action always the same? and impiety, again—is it not always the opposite of piety, and also the same with itself, having, as impiety, one notion which includes whatever is impious?

EUTHYPHRO: To be sure, Socrates.

EUTHYPHRO'S FIRST DEFINITION OF PIETY

SOCRATES: And what is piety, and what is impiety?

EUTHYPHRO: Piety is doing as I am doing; that is to say, prosecuting anyone who is guilty of murder, sacrilege, or of any similar crime—whether he be your father or mother, or whoever he may be—that makes no difference; and not to prosecute them is impiety. And please to consider, Socrates, what a notable proof I will give you of the truth of my words, a proof which I have already given to others:—of the principle, I mean, that the impious, whoever he may be, ought not to go unpunished. For do not men regard Zeus as the best and most righteous of the gods?—and yet they admit that he bound his father (Cronos) because he wickedly devoured his sons, and that he too had punished his own father (Uranus) for a similar reason, in a nameless manner. And yet when I proceed against my father, they are angry with me. So inconsistent are they in their way of talking when the gods are concerned, and when I am concerned.

SOCRATES: May not this be the reason, Euthyphro, why I am charged with impiety—that I cannot get away with these stories about the gods? and therefore I suppose that people think me wrong. But, as you who are well informed about them approve of them, I cannot do better than assent to your superior wisdom. What else can I say, confessing as I do, that I know nothing about them? Tell me, for the love of Zeus, whether you really believe that they are true.

EUTHYPHRO: Yes, Socrates; and things more wonderful still, of which the world is in ignorance.

SOCRATES: And do you really believe that the gods fought with one another, and had dire quarrels, battles, and the like, as the poets say, and as you may see represented in the works of great artists? The temples are full of them; and notably the robe of Athena, which is carried up to the Acropolis at the great Panathenaea, is embroidered with them. Are all these tales of the gods true, Euthyphro?

EUTHYPHRO: Yes, Socrates; and, as I was saying, I can tell you, if you would like to
    hear them, many other things about the gods which would quite amaze you.
SOCRATES: I dare say; and you shall tell me them at some other time when
    I have leisure. But just at present I would rather hear from you a more
    precise answer, which you have not as yet given, my friend, to the question,
    What is "piety"? When asked, you only replied, Doing as you do, charging
    your father with murder.
EUTHYPHRO: And what I said was true, Socrates.
SOCRATES: No doubt, Euthyphro; but you would admit that there are many
    other pious acts?
EUTHYPHRO: There are.
SOCRATES: Remember that I did not ask you to give me two or three examples
    of piety, but to explain the general idea which makes all pious things to be
    pious. Do you not recollect that there was one idea which made the impious
    impious, and the pious pious?
EUTHYPHRO: I remember.
SOCRATES: Tell me what is the nature of this idea, and then I shall have a stan-
    dard to which I may look, and by which I may measure actions, whether
    yours or those of anyone else, and then I shall be able to say that such and
    such an action is pious, such another impious.
EUTHYPHRO: I will tell you, if you like.
SOCRATES: I should very much like.

EUTHYPHRO'S SECOND DEFINITION: PIETY IS THAT WHICH IS DEAR TO THE GODS

EUTHYPHRO: Piety, then, is that which is dear to the gods, and impiety is that
    which is not dear to them.
SOCRATES: Very good, Euthyphro; you have now given me the sort of answer
    which I wanted. But whether what you say is true or not I cannot as yet tell,
    although I make no doubt that you will prove the truth of your words.
EUTHYPHRO: Of course.
SOCRATES: Come, then, and let us examine what we are saying. That thing or
    person which is dear to the gods is pious, and that thing or person which is
    hateful to the gods is impious, these two being the extreme opposites of one
    another. Was not that said?
EUTHYPHRO: It was.
SOCRATES: And well said?
EUTHYPHRO: Yes, Socrates, I thought so; it was certainly said.
SOCRATES: And further, Euthyphro, the gods were admitted to have enmities
    and hatreds and differences?
EUTHYPHRO: Yes, that was also said.
SOCRATES: And what sort of difference creates enmity and anger? Suppose
    for example that you and I, my good friend, differ about a number;
    do differences of this sort make us enemies and set us at variance with

one another? Do we not go at once to arithmetic, and put an end to them by a sum?

EUTHYPHRO: True.

SOCRATES: Or suppose that we differ about magnitudes, do we not quickly end the differences by measuring?

EUTHYPHRO: Very true.

SOCRATES: And we end a controversy about heavy and light by resorting to a weighing machine?

EUTHYPHRO: To be sure.

SOCRATES: But what differences are there which cannot be thus decided, and which therefore make us angry and set us at enmity with one another? I dare say the answer does not occur to you at the moment, and therefore I will suggest that these enmities arise when the matters of difference are the just and unjust, good and evil, honorable and dishonorable. Are not these the points about which men differ, and about which when we are unable satisfactorily to decide our differences, you and I and all of us quarrel, when we do quarrel?

EUTHYPHRO: Yes, Socrates, the nature of the differences about which we quarrel is such as you describe.

SOCRATES: And the quarrels of the gods, noble Euthyphro, when they occur, are of a like nature?

EUTHYPHRO: Certainly they are.

SOCRATES: They have differences of opinion, as you say, about good and evil, just and unjust, honorable and dishonorable: there would have been no quarrels among them, if there had been no such differences—would there now?

EUTHYPHRO: You are quite right.

SOCRATES: Does not every man love that which he deems noble and just and good, and hate the opposite of them?

EUTHYPHRO: Very true.

SOCRATES: But, as you say, people regard the same things, some as just and others as unjust,—about these they dispute; and so there arise wars and fightings among them.

EUTHYPHRO: Very true.

SOCRATES: Then the same things are hated by the gods and loved by the gods, and are both hateful and dear to them?

EUTHYPHRO: True.

SOCRATES: And upon this view the same things, Euthyphro, will be pious and also impious?

EUTHYPHRO: So I should suppose.

SOCRATES: Then, my friend, I remark with surprise that you have not answered the question which I asked. For I certainly did not ask you to tell me what action is both pious and impious: but now it would seem that what is loved by the gods is also hated by them. And therefore, Euthyphro, in thus chastising your father you may very likely be doing what is agreeable to Zeus but disagreeable to Cronos or Uranus, and what is acceptable to Hephaestus but unacceptable to Hera, and there may be other gods who have similar differences of opinion.

EUTHYPHRO: But I believe, Socrates, that all the gods would be agreed as to the propriety of punishing a murderer: there would be no difference of opinion about that.

SOCRATES: Well, but speaking of men, Euthyphro, did you ever hear any one arguing that a murderer or any sort of evil-doer ought to be let off?

EUTHYPHRO: I should rather say that these are the questions which they are always arguing, especially in courts of law: they commit all sorts of crimes, and there is nothing which they will not do or say in their own defense.

SOCRATES: But do they admit their guilt, Euthyphro, and yet say that they ought not to be punished?

EUTHYPHRO: No; they do not.

SOCRATES: Then there are some things which they do not venture to say and do: for they do not venture to argue that the guilty are to be unpunished, but they deny their guilt, do they not?

EUTHYPHRO: Yes.

SOCRATES: Then they do not argue that the evil-doer should not be punished, but they argue about the fact of who the evil-doer is, and what he did and when?

EUTHYPHRO: True.

SOCRATES: And the gods are in the same case, if as you assert they quarrel about just and unjust, and some of them say while others deny that injustice is done among them. For surely neither God nor man will ever venture to say that the doer of injustice is not to be punished?

EUTHYPHRO: That is true, Socrates, in the main.

SOCRATES: But they join issue about the particulars—gods and men alike; and, if they dispute at all, they dispute about some act which is called in question, and which by some is affirmed to be just, by others to be unjust. Is not that true?

EUTHYPHRO: Quite true.

SOCRATES: Well then, my dear friend Euthyphro, do tell me, for my better instruction and information, what proof have you that in the opinion of all the gods a servant who is guilty of murder, and is put in chains by the master of the dead man, and dies because he is put in chains before he who bound him can learn from the interpreters of the gods what he ought to do with him, dies unjustly; and that on behalf of such a one a son ought to proceed against his father and accuse him of murder. How would you show that all the gods absolutely agree in approving of his act? Prove to me that they do, and I will applaud your wisdom as long as I live.

EUTHYPHRO: It will be a difficult task; but I could make the matter very clear indeed to you.

SOCRATES: I understand; you mean to say that I am not so quick of apprehension as the judges: for to them you will be sure to prove that the act is unjust, and hateful to the gods.

EUTHYPHRO: Yes indeed, Socrates; at least if they will listen to me.

SOCRATES AMENDS AND CRITICIZES EUTHYPHRO'S DEFINITION

SOCRATES: But they will be sure to listen if they find that you are a good speaker. There was a notion that came into my mind while you were speaking; I said to myself: "Well, and what if Euthyphro does prove to me that all the gods regarded the death of the serf as unjust, how do I know anything more of the nature of piety and impiety? for granting that this action may be hateful to the gods, still piety and impiety are not adequately defined by these distinctions, for that which is hateful to the gods has been shown to be also pleasing and dear to them." And therefore, Euthyphro, I do not ask you to prove this; I will suppose, if you like, that all the gods condemn and abominate such an action. But I will amend the definition so far as to say that what all the gods hate is impious, and what they love pious or holy; and what some of them love and others hate is both or neither. Shall this be our definition of piety and impiety?

EUTHYPHRO: Why not, Socrates?

SOCRATES: Why not! certainly, as far as I am concerned, Euthyphro, there is no reason why not. But whether this admission will greatly assist you in the task of instructing me as you promised, is a matter for you to consider.

EUTHYPHRO: Yes, I should say that what all the gods love is pious and holy, and the opposite which they all hate, impious.

SOCRATES: Ought we to enquire into the truth of this, Euthyphro, or simply to accept the mere statement on our own authority and that of others? What do you say?

EUTHYPHRO: We should enquire; and I believe that the statement will stand the test of enquiry.

SOCRATES: We shall know better, my good friend, in a little while. The point which I should first wish to understand is whether the pious or holy is beloved by the gods because it is holy, or holy because it is beloved of the gods.

EUTHYPHRO: I do not understand your meaning, Socrates.

SOCRATES: I will endeavor to explain: we speak of carrying and we speak of being carried, of leading and being led, seeing and being seen. You know that in all such cases there is a difference, and you know also in what the difference lies?

EUTHYPHRO: I think that I understand.

SOCRATES: And is not that which is beloved distinct from that which loves?

EUTHYPHRO: Certainly.

SOCRATES: Well; and now tell me, is that which is carried in this state of carrying because it is carried, or for some other reason?

EUTHYPHRO: No; that is the reason.

SOCRATES: And the same is true of what is led and of what is seen?

EUTHYPHRO: True.

SOCRATES: And a thing is not seen because it is visible, but conversely, visible because it is seen; nor is a thing led because it is in the state of being led, or carried because it is in the state of being carried, but the converse of this.

And now I think, Euthyphro, that my meaning will be intelligible; and my meaning is, that any state of action or passion implies previous action or passion. It does not become because it is becoming, but it is in a state of becoming because it becomes; neither does it suffer because it is in a state of suffering, but it is in a state of suffering because it suffers. Do you not agree?

EUTHYPHRO: Yes.

SOCRATES: Is not that which is loved in some state either of becoming or suffering?

EUTHYPHRO: Yes.

SOCRATES: And the same holds as in the previous instances; the state of being loved follows the act of being loved, and not the act the state.

EUTHYPHRO: Certainly.

SOCRATES: And what do you say of piety, Euthyphro: is not piety, according to your definition, loved by all the gods?

EUTHYPHRO: Yes.

SOCRATES: Because it is pious or holy, or for some other reason?

EUTHYPHRO: No, that is the reason.

SOCRATES: It is loved because it is holy, not holy because it is loved?

EUTHYPHRO: Yes.

SOCRATES: And that which is dear to the gods is loved by them, and is in a state to be loved of them because it is loved of them?

EUTHYPHRO: Certainly.

SOCRATES: Then that which is dear to the gods, Euthyphro, is not holy, nor is that which is holy loved of God, as you affirm; but they are two different things.

EUTHYPHRO: How do you mean, Socrates?

SOCRATES: I mean to say that the holy has been acknowledged by us to be loved of God because it is holy, not to be holy because it is loved.

EUTHYPHRO: Yes.

SOCRATES: But that which is dear to the gods is dear to them because it is loved by them, not loved by them because it is dear to them.

EUTHYPHRO: True.

SOCRATES: But, friend Euthyphro, if that which is holy is the same with that which is dear to God, and is loved because it is holy, then that which is dear to God would have been loved as being dear to God; but if that which is dear to God is dear to him because loved by him, then that which is holy would have been holy because loved by him. But now you see that the reverse is the case, and that they are quite different from one another. For one (*theophiles*) is of a kind to be loved cause it is loved, and the other (*osion*) is loved because it is of a kind to be loved. Thus you appear to me, Euthyphro, when I ask you what is the essence of holiness, to offer an attribute only, and not the essence—the attribute of being loved by all the gods. But you still refuse to explain to me the nature of holiness. And therefore, if you please, I will ask you not to hide your treasure, but to tell me once more what holiness or piety really is, whether dear to the gods or not (for that is a matter about which we will not quarrel); and what is impiety?

EUTHYPHRO: I really do not know, Socrates, how to express what I mean. For somehow or other our arguments, on whatever ground we rest them, seem to turn round and walk away from us.

SOCRATES: Your words, Euthyphro, are like the handiwork of my ancestor Daedalus; and if I were the sayer or propounder of them, you might say that my arguments walk away and will not remain fixed where they are placed because I am a descendant of his. But now, since these notions are your own, you must find some other gibe, for they certainly, as you yourself allow, show an inclination to be on the move.

EUTHYPHRO: Nay, Socrates, I shall still say that you are the Daedalus who sets arguments in motion; not I, certainly, but you make them move or go round, for they would never have stirred, as far as I am concerned.

SOCRATES: Then I must be greater than Daedalus: for whereas he only made his own inventions to move, I move those of other people as well. And the beauty of it is, that I would rather not. For I would give the wisdom of Daedalus, and the wealth of Tantalus, to be able to detain them and keep them fixed. But enough of this. As I perceive that you are lazy, I will myself endeavor to show you how you might instruct me in the nature of piety; and I hope that you will not grudge your labor. Tell me, then—Is not that which is pious necessarily just?

EUTHYPHRO: Yes.

SOCRATES: And is, then, all which is just pious? or, is that which is pious all just, but that which is just, only in part and not all, pious?

EUTHYPHRO: I do not understand you, Socrates.

SOCRATES: And yet I know that you are as much wiser than I am, as you are younger. But, as I was saying, revered friend, the abundance of your wisdom makes you lazy. Please to exert yourself, for there is no real difficulty in understanding me. What I mean I may explain by an illustration of what I do not mean. The poet (Stasinus) sings—

> "Of Zeus, the author and creator of all these things,
> You will not tell: for where there is fear there is also reverence."

Now I disagree with this poet. Shall I tell you in what respect?

EUTHYPHRO: By all means.

SOCRATES: I should not say that where there is fear there is also reverence; for I am sure that many persons fear poverty and disease, and the like evils, but I do not perceive that they reverence the objects of their fear.

EUTHYPHRO: Very true.

SOCRATES: But where reverence is, there is fear; for he who has a feeling of reverence and shame about the commission of any action, fears and is afraid of an ill reputation.

EUTHYPHRO: No doubt.

SOCRATES: Then we are wrong in saying that where there is fear there is also reverence; and we should say, where there is reverence there is also fear. But there is not always reverence where there is fear; for fear is a more extended notion, and reverence is a part of fear, just as the odd is a part of number, and number is a more extended notion than the odd. I suppose that you follow me now?

EUTHYPHRO: Quite well.

SOCRATES: That was the sort of question which I meant to raise when I asked whether the just is always the pious, or the pious always the just; and whether there may not be justice where there is not piety; for justice is the more extended notion of which piety is only a part. Do you dissent?

EUTHYPHRO: No, I think that you are quite right.

A THIRD DEFINITION: PIETY IS PART OF JUSTICE

SOCRATES: Then, if piety is a part of justice, I suppose that we should enquire what part? If you had pursued the enquiry in the previous cases; for instance, if you had asked me what is an even number, and what part of number the even is, I should have had no difficulty in replying, a number which represents a figure having two equal sides. Do you not agree?

EUTHYPHRO: Yes, I quite agree.

SOCRATES: In like manner, I want you to tell me what part of justice is piety or holiness, that I may be able to tell Meletus not to do me injustice, or indict me for impiety, as I am now adequately instructed by you in the nature of piety or holiness, and their opposites.

EUTHYPHRO: Piety or holiness, Socrates, appears to me to be that part of justice which attends to the gods, as there is the other part of justice which attends to men.

SOCRATES: That is good, Euthyphro; yet still there is a little point about which I should like to have further information, What is the meaning of "attention"? For attention can hardly be used in the same sense when applied to the gods as when applied to other things. For instance, horses are said to require attention, and not every person is able to attend to them, but only a person skilled in horsemanship. Is it not so?

EUTHYPHRO: Certainly.

SOCRATES: I should suppose that the art of horsemanship is the art of attending to horses?

EUTHYPHRO: Yes.

SOCRATES: Nor is every one qualified to attend to dogs, but only the huntsman?

EUTHYPHRO: True.

SOCRATES: And I should also conceive that the art of the huntsman is the art of attending to dogs?

EUTHYPHRO: Yes.

SOCRATES: As the art of the oxherd is the art of attending to oxen?

EUTHYPHRO: Very true.

SOCRATES: In like manner holiness or piety is the art of attending to the gods?— that would be your meaning, Euthyphro?

EUTHYPHRO: Yes.

SOCRATES: And is not attention always designed for the good or benefit of that to which the attention is given? As in the case of horses, you may observe that when attended to by the horseman's art they are benefited and improved, are they not?

EUTHYPHRO: True.

SOCRATES: As the dogs are benefited by the huntsman's art, and the oxen by the art of the oxherd, and all other things are tended or attended for their good and not for their hurt?

EUTHYPHRO: Certainly, not for their hurt.

SOCRATES: But for their good?

EUTHYPHRO: Of course.

SOCRATES: And does piety or holiness, which has been defined to be the art of attending to the gods, benefit or improve them? Would you say that when you do a holy act you make any of the gods better?

EUTHYPHRO: No, no; that was certainly not what I meant.

SOCRATES: And I, Euthyphro, never supposed that you did. I asked you the question about the nature of the attention, because I thought that you did not.

EUTHYPHRO: You do me justice, Socrates; that is not the sort of attention which I mean.

SOCRATES: Good: but I must still ask what is this attention to the gods which is called piety?

EUTHYPHRO: It is such, Socrates, as servants show to their masters.

SOCRATES: I understand—a sort of ministration to the gods.

EUTHYPHRO: Exactly.

SOCRATES: Medicine is also a sort of ministration or service, having in view the attainment of some object—would you not say of health?

EUTHYPHRO: I should.

SOCRATES: Again, there is an art which ministers to the ship-builder with a view to the attainment of some result?

EUTHYPHRO: Yes, Socrates, with a view to the building of a ship.

SOCRATES: As there is an art which ministers to the house-builder with a view to the building of a house?

EUTHYPHRO: Yes.

SOCRATES: And now tell me, my good friend, about the art which ministers to the gods: what work does that help to accomplish? For you must surely know if, as you say, you are of all men living the one who is best instructed in religion.

EUTHYPHRO: And I speak the truth, Socrates.

SOCRATES: Tell me then, oh tell me—what is that fair work which the gods do by the help of our ministrations?

EUTHYPHRO: Many and fair, Socrates, are the works which they do.

SOCRATES: Why, my friend, and so are those of a general. But the chief of them is easily told. Would you not say that victory in war is the chief of them?

EUTHYPHRO: Certainly.

SOCRATES: Many and fair, too, are the works of the husbandman, if I am not mistaken; but his chief work is the production of food from the earth?

EUTHYPHRO: Exactly.

SOCRATES: And of the many and fair things done by the gods, which is the chief or principal one?

EUTHYPHRO: I have told you already, Socrates, that to learn all these things accurately will be very tiresome. Let me simply say that piety or holiness is learning how to please the gods in word and deed, by prayers and sacrifices. Such piety is the salvation of families and states, just as the impious, which is unpleasing to the gods, is their ruin and destruction.

SOCRATES: I think that you could have answered in much fewer words the chief question which I asked, Euthyphro, if you had chosen. But I see plainly that you are not disposed to instruct me—clearly not: else why, when we reached the point, did you turn aside? Had you only answered me I should have truly learned of you by this time the nature of piety. Now, as the asker of a question is necessarily dependent on the answerer, whither he leads I must follow; and can only ask again, what is the pious, and what is piety? Do you mean that they are a sort of science of praying and sacrificing?

EUTHYPHRO: Yes, I do.

SOCRATES: And sacrificing is giving to the gods, and prayer is asking of the gods?

EUTHYPHRO: Yes, Socrates.

SOCRATES: Upon this view, then, piety is a science of asking and giving?

EUTHYPHRO: You understand me capitally, Socrates.

SOCRATES: Yes, my friend; the reason is that I am a votary of your science, and give my mind to it, and therefore nothing which you say will be thrown away upon me. Please then to tell me, what is the nature of this service to the gods? Do you mean that we prefer requests and give gifts to them?

EUTHYPHRO: Yes, I do.

SOCRATES: Is not the right way of asking to ask of them what we want?

EUTHYPHRO: Certainly.

SOCRATES: And the right way of giving is to give to them in return what they want of us. There would be no meaning in an art which gives to any one that which he does not want.

EUTHYPHRO: Very true, Socrates.

SOCRATES: Then piety, Euthyphro, is an art which gods and men have of doing business with one another?

EUTHYPHRO: That is an expression which you may use, if you like.

SOCRATES: But I have no particular liking for anything but the truth. I wish, however, that you would tell me what benefit accrues to the gods from our gifts. There is no doubt about what they give to us; for there is no good thing which they do not give; but how we can give any good thing to them in return is far from being equally clear. If they give everything and we give nothing, that must be an affair of business in which we have very greatly the advantage of them.

EUTHYPHRO: And do you imagine, Socrates, that any benefit accrues to the gods from our gifts?

SOCRATES: But if not, Euthyphro, what is the meaning of gifts which are conferred by us upon the gods?

EUTHYPHRO: What else, but tributes of honor; and, as I was just now saying, what pleases them?

SOCRATES: Piety, then, is pleasing to the gods, but not beneficial or dear to them?

EUTHYPHRO: I should say that nothing could be dearer.

SOCRATES: Then once more the assertion is repeated that piety is dear to the gods?

EUTHYPHRO: Certainly.

SOCRATES: And when you say this, can you wonder at your words not standing firm, but walking away? Will you accuse me of being the Daedalus who makes them walk away, not perceiving that there is another and far greater artist than Daedalus who makes them go round in a circle, and he is yourself; for the argument, as you will perceive, comes round to the same point. Were we not saying that the holy or pious was not the same with that which is loved of the gods? Have you forgotten?

EUTHYPHRO: I quite remember.

SOCRATES: And are you not saying that what is loved of the gods is holy; and is not this the same as what is dear to them—do you see?

EUTHYPHRO: True.

SOCRATES: Then either we were wrong in our former assertion; or, if we were right then, we are wrong now.

EUTHYPHRO: One of the two must be true.

SOCRATES: Then we must begin again and ask, What is piety? That is an inquiry which I shall never be weary of pursuing as far as in me lies; and I entreat you not to scorn me, but to apply your mind to the utmost, and tell me the truth. For, if any man knows, you are he; and therefore I must detain you, like Proteus, until you tell. If you had not certainly known the nature of piety and impiety, I am confident that you would never, on behalf of a serf, have charged your aged father with murder. You would not have run such a risk of doing wrong in the sight of the gods, and you would have had too much respect for the opinions of men. I am sure, therefore, that you know the nature of piety and impiety. Speak out then, my dear Euthyphro, and do not hide your knowledge.

EUTHYPHRO: Another time, Socrates; for I am in a hurry, and must go now.

SOCRATES: Alas! my companion, and will you leave me in despair? I was hoping that you would instruct me in the nature of piety and impiety; and then I might have cleared myself of Meletus and his indictment. I would have told him that I had been enlightened by Euthyphro, and had given up rash innovations and speculations, in which I indulged only through ignorance, and that now I am about to lead a better life.

Plato: A Life Worth Living
From *The Apology* (complete)

In The Apology, Plato discusses the trial of his teacher Socrates. In one of the more dramatic pieces of world literature, Socrates is put on trial for promoting atheism and corrupting the youth of Athens, and during his defense he makes the famous statement that "an unexamined life is not worth living." It could be that Socrates was brought to trial as a result of his constant use of his Socratic method—persistently questioning and answering his Athenian colleagues, often quite impolitely. Through this method he challenged traditional ideas and showed that most people did not know what they pretended to know. According to many of his contemporaries, philosophers such as Socrates undermined the foundations of society by casting doubt on traditional ideas. The heart of Socrates's defense was that his method of philosophy was not a threat to Athens, but was instead of the greatest value to that city; he was in effect a nagging but useful pest on the body politic through his constant personal and fearless pursuit of truth. Athenian legal tradition permitted a defendant to speak at the end of a trial and suggest his own sentence. In view of his role as an important provocateur, Socrates claimed that, as an alternative to the death sentence rendered by the court, he should instead be given lifelong privileges in the Prytaneum. The Prytaneum was an institution set up in Athens to honor famous people, athletes, generals, and public benefactors. Socrates asserts, "There is no reward, Athenians, so suitable for me as receiving meals in the Prytaneum. It is a much more suitable reward for [me] than for any of you who has won a victory at the Olympic games with his horse or his chariots. Such a man only makes you seem happy, but I make you really happy."

SOCRATES'S OLD ACCUSERS

How you, O Athenians, have been affected by my accusers, I cannot tell; but I know that they almost made me forget who I was—so persuasively did they speak; and yet they have hardly uttered a word of truth. But of the many falsehoods told by them, there was one which quite amazed me;—I mean when they said that you should be upon your guard and not allow yourselves to be deceived by the force of my eloquence. To say this, when they were certain to be detected as soon as I opened my lips and proved myself to be anything but a great speaker, did indeed appear to me most shameless—unless by the force of eloquence they mean the force of truth; for if such is their meaning, I admit that I am eloquent. But in how different a way from theirs! Well, as I was saying, they have scarcely spoken the truth at all; but from me you shall hear the whole truth: not, however, delivered after their manner in a

Source: Plato, *The Apology*.

set oration duly ornamented with words and phrases. No, by heaven! but I shall use the words and arguments which occur to me at the moment; for I am confident in the justice of my cause (or, I am certain that I am right in taking this course): at my time of life I ought not to be appearing before you, O men of Athens, in the character of a juvenile orator—let no one expect it of me. And I must beg of you to grant me a favor:—If I defend myself in my accustomed manner, and you hear me using the words which I have been in the habit of using in the agora, at the tables of the money-changers, or anywhere else, I would ask you not to be surprised, and not to interrupt me on this account. For I am more than seventy years of age, and appearing now for the first time in a court of law, I am quite a stranger to the language of the place; and therefore I would have you regard me as if I were really a stranger, whom you would excuse if he spoke in his native tongue, and after the fashion of his country:—Am I making an unfair request of you? Never mind the manner, which may or may not be good; but think only of the truth of my words, and give heed to that: let the speaker speak truly and the judge decide justly.

And first, I have to reply to the older charges and to my first accusers, and then I will go on to the later ones. For of old I have had many accusers, who have accused me falsely to you during many years; and I am more afraid of them than of Anytus and his associates, who are dangerous, too, in their own way. But far more dangerous are the others, who began when you were children, and took possession of your minds with their falsehoods, telling of one Socrates, a wise man, who speculated about the heaven above, and searched into the earth beneath, and made the worse appear the better cause. The disseminators of this tale are the accusers whom I dread; for their hearers are apt to fancy that such enquirers do not believe in the existence of the gods. And they are many, and their charges against me are of ancient date, and they were made by them in the days when you were more impressible than you are now—in childhood, or it may have been in youth—and the cause when heard went by default, for there was none to answer. And hardest of all, I do not know and cannot tell the names of my accusers; unless in the chance case of a Comic poet. All who from envy and malice have persuaded you—some of them having first convinced themselves—all this class of men are most difficult to deal with; for I cannot have them up here, and cross-examine them, and therefore I must simply fight with shadows in my own defense, and argue when there is no one who answers. I will ask you then to assume with me, as I was saying, that my opponents are of two kinds; one recent, the other ancient: and I hope that you will see the propriety of my answering the latter first, for these accusations you heard long before the others, and much oftener.

Well, then, I must make my defense, and endeavor to clear away in a short time, a slander which has lasted a long time. May I succeed, if to succeed be for my good and yours, or likely to avail me in my cause! The task is not an easy one; I quite understand the nature of it. And so leaving the event with God, in obedience to the law I will now make my defense.

I will begin at the beginning, and ask what is the accusation which has given rise to the slander of me, and in fact has encouraged Meletus to proof this charge against me. Well, what do the slanderers say? They shall be my prosecutors, and

I will sum up their words in an affidavit: "Socrates is an evil-doer, and a curious person, who searches into things under the earth and in heaven, and he makes the worse appear the better cause; and he teaches the aforesaid doctrines to others." Such is the nature of the accusation: it is just what you have yourselves seen in the comedy of Aristophanes [in *Clouds*], who has introduced a man whom he calls Socrates, going about and saying that he walks in air, and talking a deal of nonsense concerning matters of which I do not pretend to know either much or little—not that I mean to speak disparagingly of anyone who is a student of natural philosophy. I should be very sorry if Meletus could bring so grave a charge against me. But the simple truth is, O Athenians, that I have nothing to do with physical speculations. Very many of those here present are witnesses to the truth of this, and to them I appeal. Speak then, you who have heard me, and tell your neighbors whether any of you have ever known me [to] hold forth in few words or in many upon such matters . . .You hear their answer. And from what they say of this part of the charge you will be able to judge of the truth of the rest.

As little foundation is there for the report that I am a teacher, and take money; this accusation has no more truth in it than the other. Although, if a man were really able to instruct mankind, to receive money for giving instruction would, in my opinion, be an honor to him. There is Gorgias of Leontium, and Prodicus of Ceos, and Hippias of Elis, who go the round of the cities, and are able to persuade the young men to leave their own citizens by whom they might be taught for nothing, and come to them whom they not only pay, but are thankful if they may be allowed to pay them. There is at this time a Parian philosopher residing in Athens, of whom I have heard; and I came to hear of him in this way:—I came across a man who has spent a world of money on the Sophists, Callias, the son of Hipponicus, and knowing that he had sons, I asked him: "Callias," I said, "if your two sons were foals or calves, there would be no difficulty in finding some one to put over them; we should hire a trainer of horses, or a farmer probably, who would improve and perfect them in their own proper virtue and excellence; but as they are human beings, whom are you thinking of placing over them? Is there any one who understands human and political virtue? You must have thought about the matter, for you have sons; is there any one?" "There is," he said. "Who is he?" said I; "and of what country? and what does he charge?" "Evenus the Parian," he replied; "he is the man, and his charge is five minae." Happy is Evenus, I said to myself, if he really has this wisdom, and teaches at such a moderate charge. Had I the same, I should have been very proud and conceited; but the truth is that I have no knowledge of the kind.

THE ORACLE OF DELPHI

I dare say, Athenians, that someone among you will reply, "Yes, Socrates, but what is the origin of these accusations which are brought against you; there must have been something strange which you have been doing? All these rumors and this talk about you would never have arisen if you had been like other men: tell us, then, what is the cause of them, for we should be sorry to judge hastily of you." Now I regard this as a fair challenge, and I will endeavor to explain to you the reason why I am called wise and have such an evil fame. Please to attend then. And although some of you may think that I am joking, I declare that I will tell you the entire truth. Men of Athens, this reputation of mine has come of a certain sort of wisdom which I possess. If you ask me what kind of wisdom, I reply, wisdom such as may perhaps be attained by man, for to that extent I am inclined to believe that I am wise; whereas the persons of whom I was speaking have a superhuman wisdom which I may fail to describe, because I have it not myself; and he who says that I have, speaks falsely, and is taking away my character. And here, O men of Athens, I must beg you not to interrupt me, even if I seem to say something extravagant. For the word which I will speak is not mine. I will refer you to a witness who is worthy of credit; that witness shall be the God of Delphi—he will tell you about my wisdom, if I have any, and of what sort it is. You must have known Chaerephon; he was early a friend of mine, and also a friend of yours, for he shared in the recent exile of the people, and returned with you. Well, Chaerephon, as you know, was very impetuous in all his doings, and he went to Delphi and boldly asked the oracle to tell him whether—as I was saying, I must beg you not to interrupt—he asked the oracle to tell him whether anyone was wiser than I was, and the Pythian prophetess answered, that there was no man wiser. Chaerephon is dead himself; but his brother, who is in court, will confirm the truth of what I am saying.

Why do I mention this? Because I am going to explain to you why I have such an evil name. When I heard the answer, I said to myself, What can the god mean? and what is the interpretation of his riddle? for I know that I have no wisdom, small or great. What then can he mean when he says that I am the wisest of men? And yet he is a god, and cannot lie; that would be against his nature. After long consideration, I thought of a method of trying the question. I reflected that if I could only find a man wiser than myself, then I might go to the god with a refutation in my hand. I should say to him, "Here is a man who is wiser than I am; but you said that I was the wisest." Accordingly I went to one who had the reputation of wisdom, and observed him—his name I need not mention; he was a politician whom I selected for examination—and the result was as follows: When I began to talk with him, I could not help thinking that he was not really wise, although he was thought wise by many, and still wiser by himself; and thereupon I tried to explain to him that he thought himself wise, but was not really wise; and the consequence was that he hated me, and his enmity was shared by several who were present and heard me. So I left him, saying to myself, as I went away: Well, although I do not suppose that either of us knows anything really beautiful and good, I am better off than he is,—for he knows nothing, and thinks that he knows; I neither know nor think that I know. In this latter particular, then, I seem to have slightly the advantage of him. Then I went to another who had still higher pretensions to wisdom, and my conclusion was exactly the same. Whereupon I made another enemy of him, and of many others besides him.

Then I went to one man after another, being not unconscious of the enmity which I provoked, and I lamented and feared this: but necessity was laid upon me,—the word of God, I thought, ought to be considered first. And I said to myself, Go I must to all who appear to know, and find out the meaning of the oracle. And I swear to you, Athenians, by the dog I swear!—for I must tell you the truth—the result of my mission was just this: I found that the men most in repute were all but the most foolish; and that others less esteemed were really wiser and better. I will tell you the tale of my wanderings and of the "Herculean" labors, as I may call them, which I endured only to find at last the oracle irrefutable. After the politicians, I went to the poets; tragic, dithyrambic, and all sorts. And there, I said to myself, you will be instantly detected; now you will find out that you are more ignorant than they are. Accordingly, I took them some of the most elaborate passages in their own writings, and asked what was the meaning of them—thinking that they would teach me something. Will you believe me? I am almost ashamed to confess the truth, but I must say that there is hardly a person present who would not have talked better about their poetry than they did themselves. Then I knew that not by wisdom do poets write poetry, but by a sort of genius and inspiration; they are like diviners or soothsayers who also say many fine things, but do not understand the meaning of them. The poets appeared to me to be much in the same case; and I further observed that upon the strength of their poetry they believed themselves to be the wisest of men in other things in which they were not wise. So I departed, conceiving myself to be superior to them for the same reason that I was superior to the politicians.

At last I went to the artisans. I was conscious that I knew nothing at all, as I may say, and I was sure that they knew many fine things; and here I was not mistaken, for they did know many things of which I was ignorant, and in this they certainly were wiser than I was. But I observed that even the good artisans fell into the same error as the poets;—because they were good workmen they thought that they also knew all sorts of high matters, and this defect in them overshadowed their wisdom; and therefore I asked myself on behalf of the oracle, whether I would like to be as I was, neither having their knowledge nor their ignorance, or like them in both; and I made answer to myself and to the oracle that I was better off as I was.

This inquisition has led to my having many enemies of the worst and most dangerous kind, and has given occasion also to many calumnies. And I am called wise, for my hearers always imagine that I myself possess the wisdom which I find wanting in others: but the truth is, O men of Athens, that God only is wise; and by his answer he intends to show that the wisdom of men is worth little or nothing; he is not speaking of Socrates, he is only using my name by way of illustration, as if he said, He, O men, is the wisest, who, like Socrates, knows that his wisdom is in truth worth nothing. And so I go about the world, obedient to the god, and search and make enquiry into the wisdom of any one, whether citizen or stranger, who appears to be wise; and if he is not wise, then in vindication of the oracle I show him that he is not wise; and my occupation quite absorbs me, and I have no time to give either to any public matter of interest or to any concern of my own, but I am in utter poverty by reason of my devotion to the god.

There is another thing:—young men of the richer classes, who have not much to do, come about me of their own accord; they like to hear the pretenders examined, and they often imitate me, and proceed to examine others; there are plenty of persons, as they quickly discover, who think that they know something, but really know little or nothing; and then those who are examined by them instead of being angry with themselves are angry with me: This confounded Socrates, they say; this villainous misleader of youth!—and then if somebody asks them, Why, what evil does he practice or teach? they do not know, and cannot tell; but in order that they may not appear to be at a loss, they repeat the ready-made charges which are used against all philosophers about teaching things up in the clouds and under the earth, and having no gods, and making the worse appear the better cause; for they do not like to confess that their pretence of knowledge has been detected—which is the truth; and as they are numerous and ambitious and energetic, and are drawn up in battle array and have persuasive tongues, they have filled your ears with their loud and inveterate calumnies. And this is the reason why my three accusers, Meletus and Anytus and Lycon, have set upon me; Meletus, who has a quarrel with me on behalf of the poets; Anytus, on behalf of the craftsmen and politicians; Lycon, on behalf of the rhetoricians: and as I said at the beginning, I cannot expect to get rid of such a mass of calumny all in a moment. And this, O men of Athens, is the truth and the whole truth; I have concealed nothing, I have dissembled nothing. And yet, I know that my plainness of speech makes them hate me, and what is their hatred but a proof that I am speaking the truth?—Hence has arisen the prejudice against me; and this is the reason of it, as you will find out either in this or in any future inquiry.

MELETUS AND THE NEW ACCUSERS

I have said enough in my defense against the first class of my accusers; I turn to the second class. They are headed by Meletus, that good man and true lover of his country, as he calls himself. Against these, too, I must try to make a defense:—Let their affidavit be read: it contains something of this kind: It says that Socrates is a doer of evil, who corrupts the youth; and who does not believe in the gods of the state, but has other new divinities of his own. Such is the charge; and now let us examine the particular counts. He says that I am a doer of evil, and corrupt the youth; but I say, O men of Athens, that Meletus is a doer of evil, in that he pretends to be in earnest when he is only in jest, and is so eager to bring men to trial from a pretended zeal and interest about matters in which he really never had the smallest interest. And the truth of this I will endeavor to prove to you.

Come hither, Meletus, and let me ask a question of you. You think a great deal about the improvement of youth?

MELETUS: Yes, I do.

SOCRATES: Tell the judges, then, who is their improver; for you must know, as you have taken the pains to discover their corrupter, and are citing and accusing me before them. Speak, then, and tell the judges who their improver is. Observe, Meletus, that you are silent, and have nothing to say. But is not this rather disgraceful, and a very considerable proof of what I was saying, that you have no interest in the matter? Speak up, friend, and tell us who their improver is.

MELETUS: The laws.

SOCRATES: But that, my good sir, is not my meaning. I want to know who the person is, who, in the first place, knows the laws.

MELETUS: The judges, Socrates, who are present in court.

SOCRATES: What do you mean to say, Meletus, that they are able to instruct and improve youth?

MELETUS: Certainly they are.

SOCRATES: What, all of them, or some only and not others?

MELETUS: All of them.

SOCRATES: By the goddess Hera, that is good news! There are plenty of improvers, then. And what do you say of the audience,—do they improve them?

MELETUS: Yes, they do.

SOCRATES: And the senators?

MELETUS: Yes, the senators improve them.

SOCRATES: But perhaps the members of the citizen assembly corrupt them?—or do they too improve them?

MELETUS: They improve them.

SOCRATES: Then every Athenian improves and elevates them; all with the exception of myself; and I alone am their corrupter? Is that what you affirm?

MELETUS: That is what I stoutly affirm.

SOCRATES: I am very unfortunate if that is true. But suppose I ask you a question: Would you say that this also holds true in the case of horses? Does one man do them harm and all the world good? Is not the exact opposite of this true? One man is able to do them good, or at least not many;—the trainer of horses, that is to say, does them good, and others who have to do with them rather injure them? Is not that true, Meletus, of horses, or any other animals? Whether you and Anytus say yes or no, that is no matter. Happy indeed would be the condition of youth if they had one corrupter only, and all the rest of the world were their improvers. And you, Meletus, have sufficiently shown that you never had a thought about the young: your carelessness is seen in your not caring about matters spoken of in this very indictment. And now, Meletus, I must ask you another question: Which is better, to live among bad citizens, or among good ones? Answer, friend, I say; for that is a question which may be easily answered. Do not the good do their neighbors good, and the bad do them evil?

MELETUS: Certainly.

MELETUS: And is there anyone who would rather be injured than benefited by those who live with him? Answer, my good friend; the law requires you to answer—does anyone like to be injured?

MELETUS: Certainly not.

SOCRATES: And when you accuse me of corrupting and deteriorating the youth, do you allege that I corrupt them intentionally or unintentionally?

MELETUS: Intentionally, I say.

SOCRATES: But you have just admitted that the good do their neighbors good, and the evil do them evil. Now is that a truth which your superior wisdom has recognized thus early in life, and am I, at my age, in such darkness and ignorance as not to know that if a man with whom I have to live is corrupted by me, I am very likely to be harmed by him, and yet I corrupt him, and intentionally, too;—that is what you are saying, and of that you will never persuade me or any other human being. But either I do not corrupt them, or I corrupt them unintentionally, so that on either view of the case you lie. If my offense is unintentional, the law has no cognizance of unintentional offenses: you ought to have taken me privately, and warned and admonished me; for if I had been better advised, I should have left off doing what I only did unintentionally—no doubt I should; whereas you hated to converse with me or teach me, but you indicted me in this court, which is a place not of instruction, but of punishment. I have shown, Athenians, as I was saying, that Meletus has no care at all, great or small, about the matter. But still I should like to know, Meletus, in what I am affirmed to corrupt the young. I suppose you mean, as I infer from your indictment, that I teach them not to acknowledge the gods which the state acknowledges, but some other new divinities or spiritual agencies in their stead. These are the lessons which corrupt the youth, as you say.

MELETUS: Yes, that I say emphatically.

SOCRATES: Then, by the gods, Meletus, of whom we are speaking, tell me and the court, in somewhat plainer terms, what you mean! for I do not as yet understand whether you affirm that I teach others to acknowledge some gods, and therefore do believe in gods and am not an entire atheist—this you do not lay to my charge; but only that they are not the same gods which the city recognizes—the charge is that they are different gods. Or, do you mean to say that I am an atheist simply, and a teacher of atheism?

MELETUS: I mean the latter—that you are a complete atheist.

SOCRATES: That is an extraordinary statement, Meletus. Why do you say that? Do you mean that I do not believe in the godhead of the sun or moon, which is the common creed of all men?

MELETUS: I assure you, judges, that he does not believe in them; for he says that the sun is stone, and the moon earth.

SOCRATES: Friend Meletus, you think that you are accusing Anaxagoras; and you have but a bad opinion of the judges, if you fancy them ignorant to such a degree as not to know that those doctrines are found in the books of Anaxagoras the Clazomenian, who is full of them. And these are the doctrines which the youth are said to learn of Socrates, when there are not infrequently exhibitions of them at the theater (price of admission one drachma at the most); and they might cheaply purchase them, and laugh at Socrates if he pretends to father such eccentricities. And so, Meletus, you really think that I do not believe in any god?

MELETUS: I swear by Zeus that you believe absolutely in none at all.

SOCRATES: You are a liar, Meletus, not believed even by yourself. For I cannot help thinking, O men of Athens, that Meletus is reckless and impudent, and that he has written this indictment in a spirit of mere wantonness and youthful bravado. Has he not compounded a riddle, thinking to try me? He said to himself:—I shall see whether this wise Socrates will discover my ingenious contradiction, or whether I shall be able to deceive him and the rest of them. For he certainly does appear to me to contradict himself in the indictment as much as if he said that Socrates is guilty of not believing in the gods, and yet of believing in them—but this surely is a piece of fun. I should like you, O men of Athens, to join me in examining what I conceive to be his inconsistency; and do you, Meletus, answer. And I must remind you that you are not to interrupt me if I speak in my accustomed manner. Did ever man, Meletus, believe in the existence of human things, and not of human beings? . . . I wish, men of Athens, that he would answer, and not be always trying to get up an interruption. Did ever any man believe in horsemanship, and not in horses? or in flute-playing, and not in flute-players? No, my friend; I will answer to you and to the court, as you refuse to answer for yourself. There is no man who ever did. But now please to answer the next question: Can a man believe in spiritual and divine agencies, and not in spirits or demigods?

MELETUS: He cannot.

SOCRATES: I am glad that I have extracted that answer, by the assistance of the court; nevertheless you swear in the indictment that I teach and believe in divine or spiritual agencies (new or old, no matter for that); at any rate, I believe in spiritual agencies, as you say and swear in the affidavit; but if I believe in divine beings, I must believe in spirits or demigods;—is not that true? Yes, that is true, for I may assume that your silence gives assent to that. Now what are spirits or demigods? are they not either gods or the sons of gods? Is that true?

MELETUS: Yes, that is true.

SOCRATES: But this is just the ingenious riddle of which I was speaking: the demigods or spirits are gods, and you say first that I don't believe in gods, and then again that I do believe in gods; that is, if I believe in demigods. For if the demigods are the illegitimate sons of gods, whether by the Nymphs or by any other mothers, as is thought, that, as all men will allow, necessarily implies the existence of their parents. You might as well affirm the existence of mules, and deny that of horses and asses. Such nonsense, Meletus, could only have been intended by you as a trial of me. You have put this into the indictment because you had nothing real of which to accuse me. But no one who has a particle of understanding will ever be convinced by you that the same man can believe in divine and superhuman things, and yet not believe that there are gods and demigods and heroes.

SOCRATES DEFENDS HIS COURSE OF LIFE

I have said enough in answer to the charge of Meletus: any elaborate defense is unnecessary, but I know only too well how many are the enmities which I have incurred, and this is what will be my destruction if I am destroyed;—not Meletus, nor yet Anytus, but the envy and detraction of the world, which has been the death of many good men, and will probably be the death of many more; there is no danger of my being the last of them.

Some one will say: And are you not ashamed, Socrates, of a course of life which is likely to bring you to an untimely end? To him I may fairly answer: There you are mistaken: a man who is good for anything ought not to calculate the chance of living or dying; he ought only to consider whether in doing anything he is doing right or wrong—acting the part of a good man or of a bad. Whereas, upon your view, the heroes who fell at Troy were not good for much, and the son of Thetis above all, who altogether despised danger in comparison with disgrace; and when he was so eager to slay Hector, his goddess mother said to him, that if he avenged his companion Patroclus, and slew Hector, he would die himself— "Fate," she said, in these or the like words, "waits for you next after Hector"; he, receiving this warning, utterly despised danger and death, and instead of fearing them, feared rather to live in dishonor, and not to avenge his friend. "Let me die forthwith," he replies, "and be avenged of my enemy, rather than abide here by the beaked ships, a laughing-stock and a burden of the earth." Had Achilles any thought of death and danger? For wherever a man's place is, whether the place which he has chosen or that in which he has been placed by a commander, there he ought to remain in the hour of danger; he should not think of death or of anything but of disgrace. And this, O men of Athens, is a true saying.

Strange, indeed, would be my conduct, O men of Athens, if I who, when I was ordered by the generals whom you chose to command me at Potidaea and Amphipolis and Delium, remained where they placed me, like any other man, facing death—if now, when, as I conceive and imagine, God orders me to fulfill the philosopher's mission of searching into myself and other men, I were to desert my post through fear of death, or any other fear; that would indeed be strange, and I might justly be arraigned in court for denying the existence of the gods, if I disobeyed the oracle because I was afraid of death, fancying that I was wise when I was not wise. For the fear of death is indeed the pretence of wisdom, and not real wisdom, being a pretence of knowing the unknown; and no one knows whether death, which men in their fear apprehend to be the greatest evil, may not be the greatest good. Is not this ignorance of a disgraceful sort, the ignorance which is the conceit that a man knows what he does not know? And in this respect only I believe myself to differ from men in general, and may perhaps claim to be wiser than they are:—that whereas I know but little of the world below, I do not suppose that I know: but I do know that injustice and disobedience to a better, whether God or man, is evil and dishonorable, and I will never fear or avoid a possible good rather than a certain evil. And therefore if you let me go now, and are not convinced by Anytus, who said that since I had been prosecuted I must be put to death; (or if not that I ought never to have been prosecuted at all); and that if I escape now, your sons will all be utterly ruined by listening to my words—if you say to me, Socrates, this time we will not mind Anytus, and you shall be let off, but upon one condition, that you are not to enquire and speculate in this way anymore, and that if you are caught doing so again you shall die;—if this was the condition on which you let me go, I should reply: men of Athens, I honor and love you; but I shall obey God rather than you, and while I have life and strength I shall never cease from the practice and citizen of the great and mighty and wise city of Athens,—are you not ashamed of heaping up the greatest amount of money and honor and repu- tation, and caring so little about wisdom and truth and the greatest improve- ment of the soul, which you never regard or heed at all? And if the person with whom I am arguing, says: Yes, but I do care; then I do not leave him or let him go at once; but I proceed to interrogate and examine and cross-examine him, and if I think that he has no virtue in him, but only says that he has, I reproach him with undervaluing the greater, and overvaluing the less. And I shall repeat the same words to everyone whom I meet, young and old, citizen and alien, but especially to the citizens, inasmuch as they are my brethren. For know that this is the command of God; and I believe that no greater good has ever happened in the state than my service to the God. For I do nothing but go about persuading you all, old and young alike, not to take thought for your persons or your prop- erties, but first and chiefly to care about the greatest improvement of the soul. I tell you that virtue is not given by money, but that from virtue comes money and every other good of man, public as well as private. This is my teaching, and if this is the doctrine which corrupts the youth, I am a mischievous person. But if any one says that this is not my teaching, he is speaking an untruth. Where- fore, O men of Athens, I say to you, do as Anytus bids or not as Anytus bids, and either acquit me or not; but whichever you do, understand that I shall never alter my ways, not even if I have to die many times.

Men of Athens, do not interrupt, but hear me; there was an understanding between us that you should hear me to the end: I have something more to say, at which you may be inclined to cry out; but I believe that to hear me will be good for you, and therefore I beg that you will not cry out. I would have you know, that if you kill such an one as I am, you will injure yourselves more than you will injure me. Nothing will injure me, not Meletus nor yet Anytus—they cannot, for a bad man is not permitted to injure a better than himself. I do not deny that Anytus may, perhaps, kill him, or drive him into exile, or deprive him of civil rights; and he may imagine, and others may imagine, that he is inflicting a great injury upon him: but there I do not agree. For the evil of doing as he is doing—the evil of unjustly taking away the life of another—is greater far.

And now, Athenians, I am not going to argue for my own sake, as you may think, but for yours, that you may not sin against the God by condemning me, who am his gift to you. For if you kill me you will not easily find a successor to me, who, if I may use such a ludicrous figure of speech, am a sort of gadfly, given to the state by God; and the state is a great and noble steed who is tardy in his motions owing to his very size, and requires to be stirred into life. I am that gadfly which God has attached to the state, and all day long and in all places am always fastening upon you, arousing and persuading and reproaching you. You will not easily find another like me, and therefore I would advise you to spare me. I dare say that you may feel out of temper (like a person who is suddenly awakened from sleep), and you think that you might easily strike me dead as Anytus advises, and then you would sleep on for the remainder of your lives, unless God in his care of you sent you another gadfly. When I say that I am given to you by God, the proof of my mission is this:—if I had been like other men, I should not have neglected all my own concerns or patiently seen the neglect of them during all these years, and have been doing yours, coming to you individually like a father or elder brother, exhorting you to regard virtue; such conduct, I say, would be unlike human nature. If I had gained anything, or if my exhortations had been paid, there would have been some sense in my doing so; but now, as you will perceive, not even the impudence of my accusers dares to say that I have ever exacted or sought pay of any one; of that they have no witness. And I have a sufficient witness to the truth of what I say—my poverty.

Some one may wonder why I go about in private giving advice and busying myself with the concerns of others, but do not venture to come forward in public and advise the state. I will tell you why. You have heard me speak at sundry times and in divers places of an oracle or sign which comes to me, and is the divinity which Meletus ridicules in the indictment. This sign, which is a kind of voice, first began to come to me when I was a child; it always forbids but never commands me to do anything which I am going to do. This is what deters me from being a politician. And rightly, as I think. For I am certain, O men of Athens, that if I had engaged in politics, I should have perished long ago, and done no good either to you or to myself. And do not be offended at my telling you the truth: for the truth is, that no man who goes to war with you or any other multitude, honestly striving against the many lawless and unrighteous deeds which are done in a state, will save his life; he who will fight for the right, if he would live even for a brief space, must have a private station and not a public one.

I can give you convincing evidence of what I say, not words only, but what you value far more—actions. Let me relate to you a passage of my own life which will prove to you that I should never have yielded to injustice from any fear of death, and that "as I should have refused to yield" I must have died at once. I will tell you a tale of the courts, not very interesting perhaps, but nevertheless true. The only office of state which I ever held, O men of Athens, was that of senator: the tribe Antiochis, which is my tribe, had the presidency at the trial of the generals who had not taken up the bodies of the slain after the battle of Arginusae; and you proposed to try them in a body, contrary to law, as you all thought afterwards; but at the time I was the only one of the Prytanes who was opposed to the illegality, and I gave my vote against you; and when the orators threatened to impeach and arrest me, and you called and shouted, I made up my mind that I would run the risk, having law and justice with me, rather than take part in your injustice because I feared imprisonment and death. This happened in the days of the democracy. But when the oligarchy of the Thirty was in power, they sent for me and four others into the rotunda, and bade us bring Leon the Salaminian from Salamis, as they wanted to put him to death. This was a specimen of the sort of commands which they were always giving with the view of implicating as many as possible in their crimes; and then I showed, not in word only but in deed, that, if I may be allowed to use such an expression, I cared not a straw for death, and that my great and only care was lest I should do an unrighteous or unholy thing. For the strong arm of that oppressive power did not frighten me into doing wrong; and when we came out of the rotunda the other four went to Salamis and fetched Leon, but I went quietly home. For which I might have lost my life, had not the power of the Thirty shortly afterwards come to an end. And many will witness to my words.

Now do you really imagine that I could have survived all these years, if I had led a public life, supposing that like a good man I had always maintained the right and had made justice, as I ought, the first thing? No indeed, men of Athens, neither I nor any other man. But I have been always the same in all my actions, public as well as private, and never have I yielded any base compliance to those who are slanderously termed my disciples, or to any other. Not that I have any regular disciples. But if any one likes to come and hear me while I am pursuing my mission, whether he be young or old, he is not excluded. Nor do I converse only with those who pay; but any one, whether he be rich or poor, may ask and answer me and listen to my words; and whether he turns out to be a bad man or a good one, neither result can be justly imputed to me; for I never taught or professed to teach him anything. And if any one says that he has ever learned or heard anything from me in private which all the world has not heard, let me tell you that he is lying.

But I shall be asked, Why do people delight in continually conversing with you? I have told you already, Athenians, the whole truth about this matter: they like to hear the cross-examination of the pretenders to wisdom; there is amusement in it. Now this duty of cross-examining other men has been imposed upon me by God; and has been signified to me by oracles, visions, and in every way in which the will of divine power was ever intimated to any one. This is true, O Athenians, or, if not true, would be soon refuted. If I am or have been corrupting the youth, those of them who are now grown up and have become sensible that I gave them bad advice in the days of their youth should come forward as accusers, and take their revenge; or if they do not like to come themselves, some of their relatives, fathers, brothers, or other kinsmen, should say what evil their families have suffered at my hands. Now is their time. Many of them I see in the court. There is Crito, who is of the same age and of the same deme with myself, and there is Critobulus his son, whom I also see. Then again there is Lysanias of Sphettus, who is the father of Aeschines—he is present; and also there is Antiphon of Cephisus, who is the father of Epigenes; and there are the brothers of several who have associated with me. There is Nicostratus the son of Theosdotides, and the brother of Theodotus (now Theodotus himself is dead, and therefore he, at any rate, will not seek to stop him); and there is Paralus the son of Demodocus, who had a brother Theages; and Adeimantus the son of Ariston, whose brother Plato is present; and Aeantodorus, who is the brother of Apollodorus, whom I also see. I might mention a great many others, some of whom Meletus should have produced as witnesses in the course of his speech; and let him still produce them, if he has forgotten—I will make way for him. And let him say, if he has any testimony of the sort which he can produce. Nay, Athenians, the very opposite is the truth. For all these are ready to witness on behalf of the corrupter, of the injurer of their kindred, as Meletus and Anytus call me; not the corrupted youth only—there might have been a motive for that—but their uncorrupted elder relatives. Why should they too support me with their testimony? Why, indeed, except for the sake of truth and justice, and because they know that I am speaking the truth, and that Meletus is a liar.

Well, Athenians, this and the like of this is all the defense which I have to offer. Yet a word more. Perhaps there may be someone who is offended at me, when he calls to mind how he himself on a similar, or even a less serious occasion, prayed and entreated the judges with many tears, and how he produced his children in court, which was a moving spectacle, together with a host of relations and friends; whereas I, who am probably in danger of my life, will do none of these things. The contrast may occur to his mind, and he may be set against me, and vote in anger because he is displeased at me on this account. Now if there be such a person among you,—mind, I do not say that there is,— to him I may fairly reply: My friend, I am a man, and like other men, a creature of flesh and blood, and not "of wood or stone," as Homer says; and I have a family, yes, and sons, O Athenians, three in number, one almost a man, and two others who are still young; and yet I will not bring any of them hither in order to petition you for an acquittal. And why not? Not from any self-assertion or want of respect for you. Whether I am or am not afraid of death is another question, of which I will not now speak. But, having regard to public opinion, I feel that such conduct would be discreditable to myself, and to you, and to the whole state. One who has reached my years, and who has a name for wisdom, ought not to demean himself. Whether this opinion of me be deserved or not, at any rate the world has decided that Socrates is in some way superior to other men. And if those among you who are said to be superior in wisdom and courage, and any other virtue, demean themselves in this way, how shameful is their conduct! I have seen men of reputation, when they have been condemned, behaving in the strangest manner: they seemed to fancy that they were going to suffer something dreadful if they died, and that they could be immortal if you only allowed them to live; and I think that such are a dishonor to the state, and that any stranger coming in would have said of them that the most eminent men of Athens, to whom the Athenians themselves give honor and command, are no better than women. And I say that these things ought not to be done by those of us who have a reputation; and if they are done, you ought not to permit them; you ought rather to show that you are far more disposed to condemn the man who gets up a doleful scene and makes the city ridiculous, than him who holds his peace.

But, setting aside the question of public opinion, there seems to be something wrong in asking a favor of a judge, and thus procuring an acquittal, instead of informing and convincing him. For his duty is, not to make a present of justice, but to give judgment; and he has sworn that he will judge according to the laws, and not according to his own good pleasure; and we ought not to encourage you, nor should you allow yourselves to be encouraged, in this habit of perjury—there can be no piety in that. Do not then require me to do what I consider dishonorable and impious and wrong, especially now, when I am being tried for impiety on the indictment of Meletus. For if, O men of Athens, by force of persuasion and entreaty I could overpower your oaths, then I should be teaching you to believe that there are no gods, and in defending should simply convict myself of the charge of not believing in them. But that is not so—far otherwise. For I do believe that there are gods, and in a sense higher than that in which any of my accusers believe in them. And to you and to God I commit my cause, to be determined by you as is best for you and me.

SOCRATES RESPONDS TO THE GUILTY VERDICT

There are many reasons why I am not grieved, O men of Athens, at the vote of condemnation. I expected it, and am only surprised that the votes are so nearly equal; for I had thought that the majority against me would have been far larger; but now, had thirty votes gone over to the other side, I should have been acquitted. And I may say, I think, that I have escaped Meletus. I may say more; for without the assistance of Anytus and Lycon, any one may see that he would not have had a fifth part of the votes, as the law requires, in which case he would have incurred a fine of a thousand drachmae.

And so he proposes death as the penalty. And what shall I propose on my part, O men of Athens? Clearly that which is my due. And what is my due? What return shall be made to the man who has never had the wit to be idle during his whole life; but has been careless of what the many care for—wealth, and family interests, and military offices, and speaking in the assembly, and magistracies, and plots, and parties. Reflecting that I was really too honest a man to be a politician and live, I did not go where I could do no good to you or to myself; but where I could do the greatest good privately to every one of you, thither I went, and sought to persuade every man among you that he must look to himself, and seek virtue and wisdom before he looks to his private interests, and look to the state before he looks to the interests of the state; and that this should be the order which he observes in all his actions. What shall be done to such an one? Doubtless some good thing, O men of Athens, if he has his reward; and the good should be of a kind suitable to him. What would be a reward suitable to a poor man who is your benefactor, and who desires leisure that he may instruct you? There can be no reward so fitting as maintenance in the Prytaneum, O men of Athens, a reward which he deserves far more than the citizen who has won the prize at Olympia in the horse or chariot race, whether the chariots were drawn by two horses or by many. For I am in want, and he has enough; and he only gives you the appearance of happiness, and I give you the reality. And if I am to estimate the penalty fairly, I should say that maintenance in the Prytaneum is the just return.

Perhaps you think that I am braving you in what I am saying now, as in what I said before about the tears and prayers. But this is not so. I speak rather because I am convinced that I never intentionally wronged any one, although I cannot convince you—the time has been too short; if there were a law at Athens, as there is in other cities, that a capital cause should not be decided in one day, then I believe that I should have convinced you. But I cannot in a moment refute great slanders; and, as I am convinced that I never wronged another, I will assuredly not wrong myself. I will not say of myself that I deserve any evil, or propose any penalty. Why should I? because I am afraid of the penalty of death which Meletus proposes? When I do not know whether death is a good or an evil, why should I propose a penalty which would certainly be an evil? Shall I say imprisonment? And why should I live in prison, and be the slave of the magistrates of the year—of the Eleven? Or shall the penalty be a fine, and imprisonment until the fine is paid? There is the same objection. I should have to lie in prison, for money I have none, and cannot pay. And if I say exile (and this may possibly be the penalty which you will affix), I must indeed be blinded by the love of life, if I am so irrational as to expect that when you, who are my own citizens, cannot endure my discourses and words, and have found them so grievous and odious that you will have no more of them, others are likely to endure me. No indeed, men of Athens, that is not very likely. And what a life should I lead, at my age, wandering from city to city, ever changing my place of exile, and always being driven out! For I am quite sure that wherever I go, there, as here, the young men will flock to me; and if I drive them away, their elders will drive me out at their request; and if I let them come, their fathers and friends will drive me out for their sakes.

Some one will say: Yes, Socrates, but cannot you hold your tongue, and then you may go into a foreign city, and no one will interfere with you? Now I have great difficulty in making you understand my answer to this. For if I tell you that to do as you say would be a disobedience to the God, and therefore that I cannot hold my tongue, you will not believe that I am serious; and if I say again that daily to discourse about virtue, and of those other things about which you hear me examining myself and others, is the greatest good of man, and that the unexamined life is not worth living, you are still less likely to believe me. Yet I say what is true, although a thing of which it is hard for me to persuade you. Also, I have never been accustomed to think that I deserve to suffer any harm. Had I money I might have estimated the offense at what I was able to pay, and not have been much the worse. But I have none, and therefore I must ask you to proportion the fine to my means. Well, perhaps I could afford a mina, and therefore I propose that penalty: Plato, Crito, Critobulus, and Apollodorus, my friends here, bid me say thirty minae, and they will be the sureties. Let thirty minae be the penalty; for which sum they will be ample security to you.

SOCRATES CONSOLES HIS FRIENDS

Not much time will be gained, O Athenians, in return for the evil name which you will get from the detractors of the city, who will say that you killed Socrates, a wise man; for they will call me wise, even although I am not wise, when they want to reproach you. If you had waited a little while, your desire would have been fulfilled in the course of nature. For I am far advanced in years, as you may perceive, and not far from death. I am speaking now not to all of you, but only to those who have condemned me to death. And I have another thing to say to them: you think that I was convicted because I had no words of the sort which would have procured my acquittal—I mean, if I had thought fit to leave nothing undone or unsaid. Not so; the deficiency which led to my conviction was not of words—certainly not. But I had not the boldness or impudence or inclination to address you as you would have liked me to do, weeping and wailing and lamenting, and saying and doing many things which you have been accustomed to hear from others, and which, as I maintain, are unworthy of me. I thought at the time that I ought not to do anything common or mean when in danger: nor do I now repent of the style of my defense; I would rather die having spoken after my manner, than speak in your manner and live. For neither in war nor yet at law ought I or any man to use every way of escaping death. Often in battle there can be no doubt that if a man will throw away his arms, and fall on his knees before his pursuers, he may escape death; and in other dangers there are other ways of escaping death, if a man is willing to say and do anything. The difficulty, my friends, is not to avoid death, but to avoid unrighteousness; for that runs faster than death. I am old and move slowly, and the slower runner has overtaken me, and my accusers are keen and quick, and the faster runner, who is unrighteousness, has overtaken them. And now I depart hence condemned by you to suffer the penalty of death,—they too go their ways condemned by the truth to suffer the penalty of villainy and wrong; and I must abide by my award—let them abide by theirs. I suppose that these things may be regarded as fated,—and I think that they are well.

And now, O men who have condemned me, I would fain prophesy to you; for I am about to die, and in the hour of death men are gifted with prophetic power. And I prophesy to you who are my murderers, that immediately after my departure punishment far heavier than you have inflicted on me will surely await you. Me you have killed because you wanted to escape the accuser, and not to give an account of your lives. But that will not be as you suppose: far otherwise. For I say that there will be more accusers of you than there are now; accusers whom hitherto I have restrained: and as they are younger they will be more inconsiderate with you, and you will be more offended at them. If you think that by killing men you can prevent someone from censuring your evil lives, you are mistaken; that is not a way of escape which is either possible or honorable; the easiest and the noblest way is not to be disabling others, but to be improving yourselves. This is the prophecy which I utter before my departure to the judges who have condemned me.

Friends, who would have acquitted me, I would like also to talk with you about the thing which has come to pass, while the magistrates are busy, and before I go to the place at which I must die. Stay then a little, for we may as well talk with one another while there is time. You are my friends, and I should like to show you the meaning of this event which has happened to me. O my judges—for you I may truly call judges—I should like to tell you of a wonderful circumstance. Hitherto the divine faculty of which the internal oracle is the source has constantly been in the habit of opposing me even about trifles, if I was going to make a slip or error in any matter; and now as you see there has come upon me that which may be thought, and is generally believed to be, the last and worst evil. But the oracle made no sign of opposition, either when I was leaving my house in the morning, or when I was on my way to the court, or while I was speaking, at anything which I was going to say; and yet I have often been stopped in the middle of a speech, but now in nothing I either said or did touching the matter in hand has the oracle opposed me. What do I take to be the explanation of this silence? I will tell you. It is an intimation that what has happened to me is a good, and that those of us who think that death is an evil are in error. For the customary sign would surely have opposed me had I been going to evil and not to good.

Let us reflect in another way, and we shall see that there is great reason to hope that death is a good; for one of two things—either death is a state of nothingness and utter unconsciousness, or, as men say, there is a change and migration of the soul from this world to another. Now if you suppose that there is no consciousness, but a sleep like the sleep of him who is undisturbed even by dreams, death will be an unspeakable gain. For if a person were to select the night in which his sleep was undisturbed even by dreams, and were to compare with this the other days and nights of his life, and then were to tell us how many days and nights he had passed in the course of his life better and more pleasantly than this one, I think that any man, I will not say a private man, but even the great king will not find many such days or nights, when compared with the others. Now if death be of such a nature, I say that to die is gain; for eternity is then only a single night. But if death is the journey to another place, and there, as men say, all the dead abide, what good, O my friends and judges, can be greater than this? If indeed when the pilgrim arrives in the world below, he is delivered from the professors of justice in this world, and finds the true judges who are said to give judgment there, Minos and Rhadamanthus and Aeacus and Triptolemus, and other sons of God who were righteous in their own life, that pilgrimage will be worth making. What would not a man give if he might converse with Orpheus and Musaeus and Hesiod and Homer? Nay, if this be true, let me die again and again. I myself, too, shall have a wonderful interest in there meeting and conversing with Palamedes, and Ajax the son of Telamon, and any other ancient hero who has suffered death through an unjust judgment; and there will be no small pleasure, as I think, in comparing my own sufferings with theirs. Above all, I shall then be able to continue my search into true and false knowledge; as in this world, so also in the next; and I shall find out who is wise, and who pretends to be wise, and is not. What would not a man give, O judges, to be able to examine the leader of the great Trojan expedition; or Odysseus or Sisyphus, or numberless others, men and women too! What infinite delight would there be in conversing with them and asking them questions! In another world they do not put a man to death for asking questions: assuredly not. For besides being happier than we are, they will be immortal, if what is said is true.

Wherefore, O judges, be of good cheer about death, and know of a certainty, that no evil can happen to a good man, either in life or after death. He and his are not neglected by the gods; nor has my own approaching end happened by mere chance. But I see clearly that the time had arrived when it was better for me to die and be released from trouble; wherefore the oracle gave no sign. For which reason, also, I am not angry with my condemners, or with my accusers; they have done me no harm, although they did not mean to do me any good; and for this I may gently blame them.

Still I have a favor to ask of them. When my sons are grown up, I would ask you, O my friends, to punish them; and I would have you trouble them, as I have troubled you, if they seem to care about riches, or anything, more than about virtue; or if they pretend to be something when they are really nothing,— then reprove them, as I have reproved you, for not caring about that for which they ought to care, and thinking that they are something when they are really nothing. And if you do this, both I and my sons will have received justice at your hands.

The hour of departure has arrived, and we go our ways—I to die, and you to live. Which is better God only knows.

READING 4

Plato: Obedience to the State
From *Crito* (complete)

One of the oldest and greatest works of political philosophy, which addresses several of these questions, is the Crito by Plato (427–347 BCE). The dialogue is set in the aftermath of Plato's Apology. Socrates was found guilty of atheism and of corrupting the youth of Athens and was sentenced to death by an Athenian jury. Socrates is in his final hours before his execution, and his young friend and student Crito makes one last attempt to get Socrates to escape and save his life. Crito offers a string of reasons why Socrates should disobey the jury's decision. However, Socrates insists that he should abide by their decision, regardless of the fatal consequences. Socrates feels that he must obey the laws of Athens both because he owes his government a debt of gratitude and also because he sees himself contractually bound to the Athenian government.

WHETHER SOCRATES SHOULD ESCAPE

SOCRATES: Why have you come at this hour, Crito? it must be quite early.
CRITO: Yes, certainly.
SOCRATES: What is the exact time?
CRITO: The dawn is breaking.

Source: Plato, *Crito.*

SOCRATES: I wonder that the keeper of the prison would let you in.

CRITO: He knows me because I often come, Socrates; moreover. I have done him a kindness.

SOCRATES: Have you only just arrived?

CRITO: No, I came some time ago.

SOCRATES: Then why did you sit and say nothing, instead of awakening me immediately?

CRITO: I should not have liked myself to be in such great trouble and unrest as you are—indeed I should not: I have been watching with amazement your peaceful slumbers; and for that reason I did not awake you, because I wished to minimize the pain. I have always thought you to be of a happy disposition; but never did I see anything like the easy, tranquil manner in which you bear this calamity.

SOCRATES: Why, Crito, when a man has reached my age he should not to be worrying about the approach of death.

CRITO: Yet other old men find themselves in similar misfortunes, and age does not prevent them from worrying.

SOCRATES: That is true. But you have not told me why you come at this early hour.

CRITO: I come to bring you a message which is sad and painful; not, as I believe, to yourself, but to all of us who are your friends, and saddest of all to me.

SOCRATES: What? Has the ship come from Delos, on the arrival of which I am to die?

CRITO: No, the ship has not actually arrived, but it will probably be here today, as persons who have come from Sunium tell me that they have left her there. Thus, tomorrow, Socrates, will be the last day of your life.

SOCRATES: Very well, Crito. If that is the will of God, I am willing. But my belief is that there will be a delay of a day.

CRITO: Why do you think so?

SOCRATES: I will tell you. Am I to die on the day after the arrival of the ship?

CRITO: Yes; that is what the authorities say.

SOCRATES: But I do not think that the ship will be here until tomorrow. This I infer from a vision which I had last night, or rather only just now, when you fortunately allowed me to sleep.

CRITO: And what was the nature of the vision?

SOCRATES: There appeared to me the image of an attractive woman, clothed in bright attire, who called to me and said: O Socrates, "The third day from now to fertile Phthia shall you go." [Homer, *Iliad*]

CRITO: What a remarkable dream, Socrates!

SOCRATES: There can be no doubt about the meaning, Crito, I think.

CRITO: Yes; the meaning is only too clear. But, oh! My beloved Socrates, let me beg you once more to take my advice and escape. For if you die I shall not only lose a friend who can never be replaced, but there is another evil: people who do not know you and me will believe that I might have saved you if I had been willing to give money, but that I did not care. Now, can there be a worse disgrace than this—that I should be thought to value money more than the life of a friend? For the many will not be persuaded that I wanted you to escape, and that you refused.

SOCRATES: But why, my dear Crito, should we care about the opinion of the many? Good men, and they are the only persons who are worth considering, will think of these things truly as they occurred.

CRITO: But you see, Socrates, that the opinion of the many must be regarded, for what is now happening shows that they can do the greatest evil to anyone who has lost their good opinion.

SOCRATES: I only wish it were so, Crito; and that the many could do the greatest evil; for then they would also be able to do the greatest good—and what a fine thing this would be! But in reality they can do neither; for they cannot make a man either wise or foolish; and whatever they do is the result of chance.

CRITO: Well, I will not dispute with you; but please tell me, Socrates, whether you are not acting out of regard to me and your other friends: are you not afraid that if you escape from prison we may get into trouble with the informers for having stolen you away, and lose either the whole or a great part of our property; or that even a worse evil may happen to us? Now, if you fear on our account, be at ease. For in order to save you, we ought surely to run this, or even a greater risk. Be persuaded, then, and do as I say.

SOCRATES: Yes, Crito, that is one fear which you mention, but by no means the only one.

CRITO: Fear not—there are persons who are willing to get you out of prison at no great cost; and as for the informers they are far from being exorbitant in their demands—a little money will satisfy them. My means, which are certainly ample, are at your service, and if you have a scruple about spending all mine, here are strangers who will give you the use of theirs; and one of them, Simmias the Theban, has brought a large sum of money for this very purpose; and Cebes and many others are prepared to spend their money in helping you to escape. I say, therefore, do not hesitate on our account, and do not say, as you did in the court, that you will have a difficulty in knowing what to do with yourself anywhere else. For men will love you in other places to which you may go, and not in Athens only; there are friends of mine in Thessaly, if you like to go to them, who will value and protect you, and no Thessalian will give you any trouble. Nor can I think that you are at all justified, Socrates, in betraying your own life when you might be saved. In acting in that way you are playing into the hands of your enemies, who are hurrying on your destruction. And further I should say that you are deserting your own children; for you might bring them up and educate them; instead of which you go away and leave them, and they will have to take their chance; and if they do not meet with the usual fate of orphans, there will be small thanks to you. No man should bring children into the world who is unwilling to persevere to the end in their nurture and education. But you appear to be choosing the easier part, not the better and manlier, which would have been more becoming in one who professes to care for virtue in all his actions, like yourself. And indeed, I am ashamed not only of you, but of us who are your friends, when I reflect that the whole business will be attributed entirely to our lack of courage. The trial need never have come on, or might have been managed differently. This last act, or crowning folly, will seem to have occurred through our negligence and cowardice, who might have saved you, if we had been good for anything; and you might have saved yourself, for there was no difficulty at all. See now, Socrates, how sad and discreditable are the consequences, both to us and you. Make up your mind then, or rather have your mind already made up, for the time of deliberation is over, and there is only one thing to be done, which must be done this very night, and if we delay at all will be no longer practical or possible. I implore you therefore, Socrates, be persuaded by me, and do as I say.

ONLY THE GOOD AND JUST LIFE IS WORTH HAVING

SOCRATES: Dear Crito, your zeal is invaluable, if a right one; but if wrong, the greater the zeal the greater the danger; and therefore we ought to consider whether I shall or shall not do as you say. For I am and always have been one of those natures who must be guided by reason, whatever the reason may be which upon reflection appears to me to be the best; and now that this chance has befallen me, I cannot repudiate my own words: the principles which I have until now honored and revered I still honor, and unless we can at once find other and better principles, I am certain not to agree with you; no, not even if the power of the multitude could inflict many more imprisonments, confiscations, deaths, frightening us like children with hobgoblin terrors. What will be the fairest way of considering the question? Shall I return to your old argument about the opinions of men? We were saying that some of them are to be regarded, and others not. Now were we right in maintaining this before I was condemned? Has the argument which was once good now proved to be talk for the sake of talking—mere childish nonsense? That is what I want to consider with your help, Crito, whether, under my present circumstances, the argument appears to be in any way different or not; and is to be allowed by me or disallowed. That argument, which, as I believe, is maintained by many persons of authority, was to the effect, as I was saying, that the opinions of some men are to be regarded, and of other men not to be regarded. Now you, Crito, are not going to die tomorrow—at least, there is no human probability of this, and therefore you are disinterested and not liable to be deceived by the circumstances in which you are placed. Tell me then, whether I am right in saying that some opinions, and the opinions of some men only, are to be valued, and that other opinions, and the opinions of other men, are not to be valued. I ask you whether I was right in maintaining this?

CRITO: Certainly.

SOCRATES: The good are to be regarded, and not the bad?

CRITO: Yes.

SOCRATES: And the opinions of the wise are good, and the opinions of the unwise are evil?

CRITO: Certainly.

SOCRATES: And what was said about another matter? Is the pupil who devotes himself to the practice of gymnastics supposed to attend to the praise and blame and opinion of every man, or of one man only—his physician or trainer, whoever he may be?

CRITO: Of one man only.

SOCRATES: And he ought to fear the criticism and welcome the praise of that one only, and not of the many?

CRITO: Clearly so.

SOCRATES: And he ought to act and train, and eat and drink in the way which seems good to his single master who has understanding, rather than according to the opinion of all other men put together?

CRITO: True.

SOCRATES: And if he disobeys and disregards the opinion and approval of the one, and regards the opinion of the many who have no understanding, will he not suffer evil?

CRITO: Certainly he will.

SOCRATES: And what will the evil be, whither tending and what affecting, in the disobedient person?

CRITO: Clearly, affecting the body; that is what is destroyed by the evil.

SOCRATES: Very good; and is not this true, Crito, of other things which we need not separately enumerate? In questions of just and unjust, fair and foul, good and evil, which are the subjects of our present consultation, ought we to follow the opinion of the many and to fear them or, instead, the opinion of the one man who has understanding? Ought we not to fear and reverence him more than all the rest of the world? And if we desert him shall we not destroy and injure that principle in us which may be assumed to be improved by justice and deteriorated by injustice. Is there such a principle?

CRITO: Certainly there is, Socrates.

SOCRATES: Take a parallel instance: If, acting under the advice of those who have no understanding, we destroy that which is improved by health and is deteriorated by disease, would life be worth having? And that which has been destroyed is the body?

CRITO: Yes.

SOCRATES: Could we live, having an evil and corrupted body?

CRITO: Certainly not.

SOCRATES: And will life be worth having, if that higher part of man be destroyed, which is improved by justice and depraved by injustice? Do we suppose that principle, whatever it may be in man, which has to do with justice and injustice, to be inferior to the body?

CRITO: Certainly not.

SOCRATES: Is it more honorable than the body?

CRITO: Far more.

SOCRATES: Then, my friend, we must not regard what the many say of us: but what he, the one man who has understanding of just and unjust, will say, and what the truth will say. And therefore you begin in error when you advise that we should regard the opinion of the many about just and unjust, good and evil, honorable and dishonorable. "Well," someone will say, "but the many can kill us:

CRITO: Yes, Socrates; that will clearly be the answer.

SOCRATES: And it is true. But still I find with surprise that the old argument is unshaken as ever. And I should like to know whether I may say the same of another proposition—that not life, but a good life, is to be chiefly valued?

CRITO: Yes, that also remains unshaken.

SOCRATES: And a good life is equivalent to a just and honorable one. That holds also?

CRITO: Yes, it does.

SOCRATES: From these premises I proceed to argue the question whether I ought or ought not to try and escape without the consent of the Athenians: and if I am clearly right in escaping, then I will make the attempt. But if not, I will abstain. The other considerations which you mention, of money and loss of character and the duty of educating one's children, are, I fear, only the doctrines of the multitude, who would be as ready to restore people to life, if they were able, as they are to put them to death—and with as little reason. But now, since the argument has thus far prevailed, the only question which remains to be considered is, whether we shall do rightly either in escaping or in suffering others to aid in our escape and paying them in money and thanks, or whether in reality we shall not do rightly. If it's the latter, then death or any other calamity which may result on my remaining here must not be allowed to enter into the calculation.

CRITO: I think that you are right, Socrates. How then shall we proceed?

SOCRATES: Let us consider the matter together, and do you either refute me if you can, and I will be convinced; or else cease, my dear friend, from repeating to me that I ought to escape against the wishes of the Athenians: for I highly value your attempts to persuade me to do so, but I may not be persuaded against my own better judgment. And now please consider my first position, and try how you can best answer me.

CRITO: I will.

SOCRATES: Are we to say that we are never intentionally to do wrong, or that in one way we ought and in another way we ought not to do wrong, or is doing wrong always evil and dishonorable, as I was just now saying, and as has been already acknowledged by us? Are all our former admissions which were made within a few days to be thrown away? And have we, at our age, been earnestly discoursing with one another all our life long only to discover that we are no better than children? Or, in spite of the opinion of the many, and in spite of consequences whether better or worse, shall we insist on the truth of what was then said, that injustice is always an evil and dishonor to him who acts unjustly? Shall we say so or not?

CRITO: Yes.

SOCRATES: Then we must do no wrong?

CRITO: Certainly not.

SOCRATES: Nor when injured injure in return, as the many imagine; for we must injure no one at all?

CRITO: Clearly not.

SOCRATES: Again, Crito, may we do evil?

CRITO: Surely not, Socrates.

SOCRATES: And what of doing evil in return for evil, which is the morality of the many—is that just or not?

CRITO: Not just.

SOCRATES: For doing evil to another is the same as injuring him?

CRITO: Very true.

SOCRATES: Then we ought not to retaliate or render evil for evil to anyone, whatever evil we may have suffered from him. But I would have you consider, Crito, whether you really mean what you are saying. For this opinion has never been held, and never will be held, by any considerable number of persons. Those who are agreed and those who are not agreed upon this point have no common ground, and can only despise one another when they see how widely they differ. Tell me, then, whether you agree with and assent to my first principle, that neither injury nor retaliation nor warding off evil by evil is ever right. And shall that be the premise of our argument? Or do you decline and dissent from this? For so I have ever thought, and continue to think; but, if you are of another opinion, let me hear what you have to say. If, however, you remain of the same mind as before, I will proceed to the next step.

CRITO: You may proceed, for I have not changed my mind.

SOCRATES: Then I will go on to the next point, which may be put in the form of a question:—Ought a man to do what he admits to be right, or ought he to betray the right?

CRITO: He ought to do what he thinks right.

SOCRATES: But if this is true, what is the application? In leaving the prison against the will of the Athenians, do I wrong any? Or rather do I not wrong those whom I ought least to wrong? Do I not desert the principles which were acknowledged by us to be just? What do you say?

CRITO: I cannot tell, Socrates, for I do not know.

GRATITUDE AND CIVIL OBEDIENCE

SOCRATES: Then consider the matter in this way. Imagine that I am about to skip town (you may call it by any name which you like), and the laws and the government come and interrogate me. "Tell us, Socrates," they say; "what are you doing? Are you not going by an act of yours to overturn us—the laws—and the whole state, as far as you can? Do you imagine that a state can subsist and not be overthrown when the decisions of law have no power, but are set aside and trampled upon by individuals?" What will be our answer, Crito, to these and similar words? Anyone, and especially a rhetorician, will have a good deal to say on behalf of the law which requires a sentence to be carried out. He will argue that this law should not be set aside; and shall we reply, "Yes; but the state has injured us and given an unjust sentence." Suppose I say that?

CRITO: Very good, Socrates.

SOCRATES: The law would answer, "Was that our agreement with you, or were you to abide by the sentence of the state?" If I were to express my astonishment at their words, the law would probably add: "Answer, Socrates, instead of opening your eyes; you are in the habit of asking and answering questions. Tell us: what complaint have you to make against us which justifies you in attempting to destroy us and the state? In the first place did we not bring you into existence? Your father married your mother by our aid and gave birth to you. Say whether you have any objection to urge against those of us who regulate marriage?" None, I should reply. "Or against those of us who after birth regulate the nurture and education of children, in which you also were trained? Were not the laws, which have the charge of education, right in commanding your father to train you in music and gymnastic?" Right, I should reply. "Well then, since you were brought into the world and nurtured and educated by us, can you deny in the first place that you are our child and slave, as your fathers were before you? And if this is true you are not on equal terms with us; nor can you think that you have a right to do to us what we are doing to you. Would you have any right to strike or insult or do any other evil to your father or your master, if you had one, because you have been struck or insulted by him, or received some other evil at his hands? You would not say this. And because we think it right to destroy you, do you think that you have any right to destroy us in return, and your country as far as in you lies? Will you, O professor of true virtue, pretend that you are justified in this? Has a philosopher like you failed to discover that our country is more to be valued and is higher and far more holy than mother or father or any ancestor, and more to be regarded in the eyes of the gods and of men of understanding? Also to be soothed, and gently and reverently pleaded to when angry, even more than a father, and either to be persuaded, or if not persuaded, to be obeyed? When we are punished by her, whether with imprisonment or stripes, the punishment is to be endured in silence. If she leads us to wounds or death in battle, there we follow as is right. Neither may anyone yield or retreat or leave his rank. Whether in battle or in a court of law, or in any other place, he must do what his city and his country order him. Otherwise he must change their view of what is just: and, if he may, he must do no violence to his father or mother, much less may he do violence to his country." What answer shall we make to this, Crito? Do the laws speak truly, or do they not?

CRITO: I think that they do.

THE SOCIAL CONTRACT AND CIVIL OBEDIENCE

SOCRATES: Then the laws will say: "Consider, Socrates, if we are speaking truly that in your present attempt you are going to do us an injury. For, having brought you into the world, and nurtured and educated you, and given you and every other citizen a share in every good which we had to give, we further proclaim to any Athenian by the liberty which we allow him, that if he does not like us when he has become of age and has seen the ways of the city, and made our acquaintance, he may go where he pleases and take his goods with him. None of us laws will forbid him or interfere with him. Anyone who does not like us and the city, and who wants to emigrate to a colony or to any other city, may go where he likes, retaining his property. But he who has experience of the manner in which we order justice and administer the state, and still remains, has entered into an implied contract that he will do as we command him. And he who disobeys us is, as we maintain, thrice wrong: first, because in disobeying us he is disobeying his parents; secondly, because we are the authors of his education; thirdly, because he has made an agreement with us that he will duly obey our commands; and he neither obeys them nor convinces us that our commands are unjust; and we do not rudely impose them, but give him the alternative of obeying or convincing us;—that is what we offer, and he does neither. These are the sort of accusations to which, as we were saying, you, Socrates, will be exposed if you accomplish your intentions; you, above all other Athenians."

Suppose now I ask, why me rather than anybody else? They will justly reply to me that I, more than all other men, have acknowledged the agreement. "There is clear proof," they will say, "Socrates, that we and the city were not displeasing to you. Of all Athenians you have been the most constant resident in the city, which we may suppose that you love since you never leave it. For you never went out of the city either to see the games, except once when you went to the Isthmus, or to any other place unless when you were on military service. Nor did you travel as other men do. Nor had you any curiosity to know other states or their laws: your affections did not go beyond us and our state. We were your especial favorites, and you accepted our governing of you. Right here in this city you had your children, which is a proof of your satisfaction. Moreover, during your trial, if you had liked, you might have fixed the penalty at banishment. The state which refuses to let you go now would have let you go then. But you pretended that you preferred death to exile, and that you were not unwilling to die. And now you have forgotten these fine sentiments, and pay no respect to us the laws, of whom you are the destroyer. You are doing what only a miserable slave would do, running away and turning your back upon the compacts and agreements which you made as a citizen. Now answer this specific question: Are we right in saying that you agreed to be governed according to us in your actions, and not merely in your words? Is that true or not?" How shall we answer, Crito? Must we not assent?

CRITO: We cannot help it, Socrates.

SOCRATES: Then will they not say: "You, Socrates, are breaking the covenants and agreements which you made with us at your leisure, but not in any haste or under any compulsion or deception. Rather, it is after you have had seventy years to think of them, during which time you were at liberty to leave the city, if we were not to your liking, or if our covenants appeared to you to be unfair. You had your choice, and might have gone either to Lacedaemon or Crete, both which states you often praised for their good government, or to some other Greek or foreign state. Because you, above all other Athenians, seemed to be so fond of the state, or, in other words, of us her laws (and who would care about a state which has no laws?), that you never stirred out of her. The lame, the blind, the maimed were not more stationary in her than you were. But now you run away and forsake your agreements. Not so, Socrates, if you will take our advice; do not make yourself ridiculous by escaping out of the city."

PROSPECTS FOR SOCRATES IF HE FLEES

SOCRATES: "For just consider, if you transgress and err in this sort of way, what good will you do either to yourself or to your friends? It is reasonably certain that your friends will be driven into exile and deprived of citizenship, or will lose their property. And you yourself, if you flee to one of the neighboring cities, as, for example, Thebes or Megara, both of which are well governed, will come to them as an enemy, Socrates, and their government will be against you, and all patriotic citizens will cast an evil eye upon you as a subverter of the laws, and you will confirm in the minds of the judges the justice of their own condemnation of you. For he who is a corrupter of the laws is more than likely to be a corrupter of the young and foolish portion of mankind. Will you then flee from well-ordered cities and virtuous men? and is existence worth having on these terms? Or will you go to them without shame, and talk to them, Socrates? And what will you say to them? What you say here about virtue and justice and institutions and laws being the best things among men? Would that be decent of you? Surely not. But if you go away from well-governed states to Crito's friends in Thessaly, where there is great disorder and license, they will be charmed to hear the tale of your escape from prison, set off with ludicrous particulars of the manner in which you were wrapped in a goatskin or some other disguise, and metamorphosed as the manner is of runaways. But will there be no one to remind you that in your old age you were not ashamed to violate the most sacred laws from a miserable desire of a little more life? Perhaps not, if you keep them in a good temper. But if they are out of temper you will hear many degrading things; you will live, but how? As the flatterer of all men, and the servant of all men? And doing what: Eating and drinking in Thessaly, having gone abroad in order that you may get a dinner? And where will be your fine sentiments about justice and virtue? Say that you wish to live for the sake of your children—you want to bring them up and educate them—will you take them into Thessaly and deprive them of Athenian citizenship? Is this the benefit which you will confer upon them? Or are you under the impression that they will be better cared for and educated here if you are still alive, although absent from them; for your friends will take care of them? Do you fancy that if you are an inhabitant of Thessaly they will take care of them, and if you are an inhabitant of the other world that they will not take care of them? No; but if they who call themselves friends are good for anything, they will—to be sure they will.

"Listen, then, Socrates, to us who have brought you up. Think not of life and children first, and of justice afterwards, but of justice first, that you may be justified before the princes of the world below. For neither will you nor any that belong to you be happier or holier or juster in this life, or happier in another, if you do as Crito proposes. Now you depart in innocence, a sufferer and not a doer of evil; a victim, not of the laws, but of men. But if you go forth, returning evil for evil, and injury for injury, breaking the covenants and agreements which you have made with us, and wronging those whom you ought least of all to wrong, that is to say, yourself, your friends, your country, and us, we shall be angry with you while you live, and our brethren, the laws in the world below, will receive you as an enemy; for they will know that you have done your best to destroy us. Listen, then, to us and not to Crito."

This, dear Crito, is the voice which I seem to hear murmuring in my ears, like the sound of the flute in the ears of the mystic; that voice, I say, is humming in my ears, and prevents me from hearing any other. And I know that anything more which you may say will be vain. Yet speak, if you have anything to say.

CRITO: I have nothing to say, Socrates.

SOCRATES: Leave me then, Crito, to fulfill the will of God, and to follow where he leads.

READING 5

Plato: Knowledge and Immortality of the Soul

From *The Republic* and *Phaedo*

In his masterpiece, The Republic, *Plato illustrates the contrast between appearance and reality by using two vivid illustrations, namely, the divided line and the cave. These two illustrations describe how Plato viewed the steps the mind takes on its way to true knowledge. The imaginary line is divided into two major parts; the lower part refers to the "visible" world, and the upper part to the "intelligible" world. In the visible world we encounter things that are constantly changing; in the intelligible*

Source: Plato, *The Republic*, Books 6 and 7, and *Phaedo*.

world we recognize ideas and ideals that Plato calls "real." Each of these two major parts is divided yet again, thus totaling four divisions, designated as A, B, C, D:

	VISIBLE			INTELLIGIBLE	
	A	B		C	D
	shadows	objects		lower forms	the Good
	(*imagination*)	(*belief*)		(*intelligence*)	(*knowledge*)

The two portions of the visible world consist of first shadows, then physical objects; the two portions of the intelligible world consist of lower forms and the Good. Corresponding to each of these divisions are four main kinds of human cognition; the weakest of these involves our imagination and belief, while the strongest involves our intelligence and knowledge. Plato's allegory of the cave further develops these four hierarchies of reality. The cave illustration describes how individuals who dwell in the cave have a very distorted idea of what they are experiencing. Not until they come up out of the cave do they discover, step by step, how limited their knowledge was in the cave. These two illustrations of the divided line and the cave are meant by Plato to say the same thing, namely, that there is a basic difference between appearance and reality. In his dialogue Phaedo, Plato explores the nature of the human soul, and offers the classic dualistic position that the soul and body are distinct entities where our immortal souls survive the death of our physical bodies.

THE DIVIDED LINE

SOCRATES: Now take a line which has been cut into two unequal parts, and divide each of them again in the same proportion, and suppose the two main divisions to answer, one to the visible and the other to the intelligible, and then compare the subdivisions in respect of their clearness and want of clearness, and you will find that the first section in the sphere of the visible consists of images. And by images I mean, in the first place, shadows, and in the second place, reflections in water and in solid, smooth and polished bodies and the like: Do you understand?

GLAUCON: Yes, I understand.

SOCRATES: You have to imagine, then, that there are two ruling powers, and that one of them is set over the intellectual world, the other over the visible. I do not say heaven, lest you should fancy that I am making a play on words. May I suppose that you have this distinction of the visible and intelligible fixed in your mind?

GLAUCON: I have.

SOCRATES: Imagine, now, the other section (B), of which this is only the resemblance, to include the animals which we see, and everything that grows or is made.

GLAUCON: Very good.

SOCRATES: Would you not admit that both the sections of this division have different degrees of truth, and that the copy is to the original as the sphere of opinion is to the sphere of knowledge?

GLAUCON: Most undoubtedly.

SOCRATES: Next proceed to consider the manner in which the sphere of the intellectual is to be divided.

GLAUCON: In what manner?

SOCRATES: Thus, there are two subdivisions. In the lower of the two (C), the soul uses the figures given by the former division as images; the inquiry can only be hypothetical, and instead of going upwards to a principle descends to the other end. In the higher of the two (D), the soul passes out of hypotheses, and goes up to a principle which is above hypotheses, making no use of images as in the former case, but proceeding only in and through the ideas themselves.

GLAUCON: I do not quite understand your meaning. . . .

SOCRATES: Then I will try again. (C) You will understand me better when I have made some preliminary remarks. You are aware that students of geometry, arithmetic, and the kindred sciences assume the odd and the even and the figures and three kinds of angles and the like in their several branches of science; these are their hypotheses, which they and everybody are supposed to know, and therefore they do not deign to give any account of them either to themselves or others; but they begin with them, and go on until they arrive at last, and in a consistent manner, at their conclusion?

GLAUCON: Yes . . . I know.

SOCRATES: And do you not know also that although they make use of the visible forms and reason about them, they are thinking not of these, but of the ideals which they resemble; not of the figures which they draw, but of the absolute square and the absolute diameter, and so on—the forms which they draw or make, and which have shadows and reflections in water of their own, are converted by them into images, but they are really seeking to behold the things themselves, which can only be seen with the eye of the mind?

GLAUCON: That is true.

SOCRATES: And of this kind I spoke as the intelligible, although in the search after it the soul is compelled to use hypotheses; not ascending to a first principle, because she is unable to rise above the region of hypothesis, but employing the objects of which the shadows below are resemblances in their turn as images, they having in relation to the shadows and reflections of them a greater distinctness, and therefore a higher value.

GLAUCON: I understand . . . that you are speaking of the province of geometry and the sister arts.

SOCRATES: And when I speak of the other division (D) of the intelligible, you will understand me to speak of that other sort of knowledge which reason herself attains by the power of dialectic, using the hypotheses not as first principles, but only as hypotheses—that is to say, as steps and points of departure into a world which is above hypotheses, in order that she may soar beyond them to the first principle of the whole; and clinging to this and then to that which depends on this, by successive steps she descends again without the aid of any sensible object, from ideas, through ideas, and in ideas she ends.

GLAUCON: I understand you . . .; not perfectly, for you seem to me to be describing a task which is really tremendous; but, at any rate, I understand you to say that knowledge and being, which the science of dialectic contemplates, are clearer than the notions of the arts, as they are termed, which proceed from hypotheses only: these are also contemplated by the understanding, and not by the senses: yet, because they start from hypotheses and do not ascend to a principle, those who contemplate them appear to you not to exercise the higher reason upon them, although when a first principle is added to them they are cognizable by the higher reason. And the habit which is concerned with geometry and the cognate sciences I suppose that you would term understanding and not reason, as being intermediate between opinion and reason.

SOCRATES: You have quite conceived my meaning. . . . And now, corresponding to these four divisions, let there be four faculties in the soul—reason answering to the highest, understanding to the second, faith (or conviction) to the third, and perception of shadows to the last—and let there be a scale of them, and let us suppose that the several faculties have clearness in the same degree that their objects have truth.

GLAUCON: I understand . . . and give my assent, and accept your arrangement.

THE ALLEGORY OF THE CAVE

SOCRATES: And now . . . let me show in a figure how far our nature is enlightened or unenlightened:—Behold! human beings living in a underground den, which has a mouth open towards the light and reaching all along the den; here they have been from their childhood, and have their legs and necks chained so that they cannot move, and can only see before them, being prevented by the chains from turning round their heads. Above and behind them a fire is blazing at a distance, and between the fire and the prisoners there is a raised way; and you will see, if you look, a low wall built along the way, like the screen which marionette players have in front of them, over which they show the puppets.

GLAUCON: I see.

SOCRATES: And do you see . . . men passing along the wall carrying all sorts of vessels, and statues and figures of animals made of wood and stone and various materials, which appear over the wall? Some of them are talking, others silent.

GLAUCON: You have shown me a strange image, and they are strange prisoners.

SOCRATES: Like ourselves, I replied; and they see only their own shadows, or the shadows of one another, which the fire throws on the opposite wall of the cave?

GLAUCON: True . . .; how could they see anything but the shadows if they were never allowed to move their heads?

SOCRATES: And of the objects which are being carried in like manner they would only see the shadows?

GLAUCON: Yes . . .

SOCRATES: And if they were able to converse with one another, would they not suppose that they were naming what was actually before them?

GLAUCON: Very true.

SOCRATES: And suppose further that the prison had an echo which came from the other side, would they not be sure to fancy when one of the passers-by spoke that the voice which they heard came from the passing shadow?

GLAUCON: No question. . .

SOCRATES: To them . . . the truth would be literally nothing but the shadows of the images.

GLAUCON: That is certain.

SOCRATES: And now look again, and see what will naturally follow if the prisoners are released and disabused of their error. At first, when any of them is liberated and compelled suddenly to stand up and turn his neck round and walk and look towards the light, he will suffer sharp pains; the glare will distress him, and he will be unable to see the realities of which in his former state he had seen the shadows; and then conceive some one saying to him, that what he saw before was an illusion, but that now, when he is approaching nearer to being and his eye is turned towards more real existence, he has a clearer vision,—what will be his reply? And you may further imagine that his instructor is pointing to the objects as they pass and requiring him to name them,—will he not be perplexed? Will he not fancy that the shadows which he formerly saw are truer than the objects which are now shown to him?

GLAUCON: Far truer.

SOCRATES: And if he is compelled to look straight at the light, will he not have a pain in his eyes which will make him turn away and take in the objects of vision which he can see, and which he will conceive to be in reality clearer than the things which are now being shown to him?

GLAUCON: True . . .

SOCRATES: And suppose once more, that he is reluctantly dragged up a steep and rugged ascent, and held fast until he's forced into the presence of the sun himself, is he not likely to be pained and irritated? When he approaches the light his eyes will be dazzled, and he will not be able to see anything at all of what are now called realities.

GLAUCON: Not all in a moment . . .

SOCRATES: He will require to grow accustomed to the sight of the upper world. And first he will see the shadows best, next the reflections of men and other objects in the water, and then the objects themselves; then he will gaze upon the light of the moon and the stars and the spangled heaven; and he will see the sky and the stars by night better than the sun or the light of the sun by day?

GLAUCON: Certainly.

SOCRATES: Last of he will be able to see the sun, and not mere reflections of him in the water, but he will see him in his own proper place, and not in another; and he will contemplate him as he is.

GLAUCON: Certainly.

SOCRATES: He will then proceed to argue that this is he who gives the season and the years, and is the guardian of all that is in the visible world, and in a certain way the cause of all things which he and his fellows have been accustomed to behold?

GLAUCON: Clearly, . . . he would first see the sun and then reason about him.

SOCRATES: And when he remembered his old habitation, and the wisdom of the den and his fellow-prisoners, do you not suppose that he would felicitate himself on the change, and pity them?

GLAUCON: Certainly, he would.

SOCRATES: And if they were in the habit of conferring honors among themselves on those who were quickest to observe the passing shadows and to remark which of them went before, and which followed after, and which were together; and who were therefore best able to draw conclusions as to the future, do you think that he would care for such honors and glories, or envy the possessors of them? Would he not say with Homer, "Better to be the poor servant of a poor master," and to endure anything, rather than think as they do and live after their manner?

GLAUCON: Yes, . . . I think that he would rather suffer anything than entertain these false notions and live in this miserable manner.

SOCRATES: Imagine once more . . . such an one coming suddenly out of the sun to be replaced in his old situation; would he not be certain to have his eyes full of darkness?

GLAUCON: To be sure . . .

SOCRATES: And if there were a contest, and he had to compete in measuring the shadows with the prisoners who had never moved out of the den, while his sight was still weak, and before his eyes had become steady (and the time which would be needed to acquire this new habit of sight might be very considerable) would he not be ridiculous? Men would say of him that up he went and down he came without his eyes; and that it was better not even to think of ascending; and if anyone tried to loose another and lead him up to the light, let them only catch the offender, and they would put him to death.

GLAUCON: No question . . .

SOCRATES: This entire allegory . . . you may now append, dear Glaucon, to the previous argument; the prison-house is the world of sight, the light of the fire is the sun, and you will not misapprehend me if you interpret the journey upwards to be the ascent of the soul into the intellectual world according to my poor belief, which, at your desire, I have expressed whether rightly or wrongly God knows. But, whether true or false, my opinion is that in the world of knowledge the idea of good appears last of all, and is seen only with an effort; and, when seen, is also inferred to be the universal author of all things beautiful and right, parent of light and of the lord of light in this visible world, and the immediate source of reason and truth in the intellectual; and that this is the power upon which he who would act rationally, either in public or private life must have his eye fixed.

GLAUCON: I agree . . . as far as I am able to understand you.

SOCRATES: Moreover, . . . you must not wonder that those who attain to this beatific vision are unwilling to descend to human affairs; for their souls are ever hastening into the upper world where they desire to dwell; which desire of theirs is very natural, if our allegory may be trusted.

GLAUCON: Yes, very natural.

SOCRATES: And is there anything surprising in one who passes from divine contemplations to the evil state of man, misbehaving himself in a ridiculous manner; if, while his eyes are blinking and before he has become accustomed to the surrounding darkness, he is compelled to fight in courts of law, or in other places, about the images or the shadows of images of justice, and is endeavoring to meet the conceptions of those who have never yet seen absolute justice?

GLAUCON: Anything but surprising . . .

IMMORTALITY OF THE SOUL

SOCRATES: I desire to prove to you that the real philosopher has reason to be of good cheer when he is about to die, and that after death he may hope to obtain the greatest good in the other world. And how this may be, Simmias and Cebes, I will endeavor to explain. For I deem that the true votary of philosophy is likely to be misunderstood by other men; they do not perceive that he is always pursuing death and dying; and if this be so, and he has had the desire of death all his life long, why when his time comes should he repine at that which he has been always pursuing and desiring?

SIMMIAS: . . . Though not in a laughing humor, you have made me laugh, Socrates; for I cannot help thinking that the many when they hear your words will say how truly you have described philosophers, and our people at home will likewise say that the life which philosophers desire is in reality death, and that they have found them out to be deserving of the death which they desire.

SOCRATES: And they are right, Simmias, in thinking so, with the exception of the words "they have found them out"; for they have not found out either what is the nature of that death which the true philosopher deserves, or how he deserves or desires death. But enough of them:—let us discuss the matter among ourselves: Do we believe that there is such a thing as death?

SIMMIAS: To be sure . . .

SOCRATES: Is it not the separation of soul and body? And to be dead is the completion of this; when the soul exists in herself, and is released from the body and the body is released from the soul, what is this but death?

SIMMIAS: Just so . . .

SOCRATES: There is another question, which will probably throw light on our present inquiry if you and I can agree about it:—Ought the philosopher to care about the pleasures—if they are to be called pleasures—of eating and drinking?

SIMMIAS: Certainly not . . .

SOCRATES: And what about the pleasures of love—should he care for them?

SIMMIAS: By no means.

SOCRATES: And will he think much of the other ways of indulging the body, for example, the acquisition of costly raiment, or sandals, or other adornments of the body? Instead of caring about them, does he not rather despise anything more than nature needs? What do you say?

SIMMIAS: I should say that the true philosopher would despise them.

SOCRATES: Would you not say that he is entirely concerned with the soul and not with the body? He would like, as far as he can, to get away from the body and to turn to the soul.

SIMMIAS: Quite true.

SOCRATES: In matters of this sort philosophers, above all other men, may be observed in every sort of way to dissever the soul from the communion of the body.

SIMMIAS: Very true.

SOCRATES: Whereas, Simmias, the rest of the world are of the opinion that to him who has no sense of pleasure and no part in bodily pleasure, life is not worth having; and that he who is indifferent about them is as good as dead.

SIMMIAS: That is also true.

SOCRATES: What again shall we say of the actual acquirement of knowledge?— is the body, if invited to share in the enquiry, a hinderer or a helper? I mean to say, have sight and hearing any truth in them? Are they not, as the poets are always telling us, inaccurate witnesses? and yet, if even they are inaccurate and indistinct, what is to be said of the other senses?—for you will allow that they are the best of them?

SIMMIAS: Certainly . . .

SOCRATES: Then when does the soul attain truth?—for in attempting to consider anything in company with the body she is obviously deceived.

SIMMIAS: True.

SOCRATES: Then must not true existence be revealed to her in thought, if at all?

SIMMIAS: Yes.

SOCRATES: And thought is best when the mind is gathered into herself and none of these things trouble her—neither sounds nor sights nor pain nor any pleasure,—when she takes leave of the body, and has as little as possible to do with it, when she has no bodily sense or desire, but is aspiring after true being?

SIMMIAS: Certainly.

SOCRATES: And in this the philosopher dishonors the body; his soul runs away from his body and desires to be alone and by herself?

SIMMIAS: That is true.

SOCRATES: Well, but there is another thing, Simmias: Is there or is there not an absolute justice?

SIMMIAS: Assuredly there is.

SOCRATES: And an absolute beauty and absolute good?

SIMMIAS: Of course.

SOCRATES: But did you ever behold any of them with your eyes?

SIMMIAS: Certainly not.

SOCRATES: Or did you ever reach them with any other bodily sense?—and I speak not of these alone, but of absolute greatness, and health, and strength, and of the essence or true nature of everything. Has the reality of them ever been perceived by you through the bodily organs? or rather, is not the nearest approach to the knowledge of their several natures made by him who so orders his intellectual vision as to have the most exact conception of the essence of each thing which he considers?

SIMMIAS: Certainly.

SOCRATES: And he attains to the purest knowledge of them who goes to each with the mind alone, not introducing or intruding in the act of thought sight or any other sense together with reason, but with the very light of the mind in her own clearness searches into the very truth of each; he who has got rid, as far as he can, of eyes and ears and, so to speak, of the whole body, these being in his opinion distracting elements which when they infect the soul hinder her from acquiring truth and knowledge—who, if not he, is likely to attain the knowledge of true being?

SIMMIAS: What you say has a wonderful truth in it, Socrates . . .

SOCRATES: And when real philosophers consider all these things, will they not be led to make a reflection which they will express in words something like the following? "Have we not found," they will say, "a path of thought which seems to bring us and our argument to the conclusion, that while we are in the body, and while the soul is infected with the evils of the body, our desire will not be satisfied? and our desire is of the truth. For the body is a source of endless trouble to us by reason of the mere requirement of food; and is liable also to diseases which overtake and impede us in the search after true being: it fills us full of loves, and lusts, and fears, and fancies of all kinds, and endless foolery, and in fact, as men say, takes away from us the power of thinking at all. Whence come wars, and fightings, and factions? whence but from the body and the lusts of the body? Wars are occasioned by the love of money, and money has to be acquired for the sake and in the service of the body; and by reason of all these impediments we have no time to give to philosophy; and, last and worst of all, even if we are at leisure and betake ourselves to some speculation, the body is always breaking in upon us, causing turmoil and confusion in our enquiries, and so amazing us that we are prevented from seeing the truth. It has been proved to us by experience that if we would have pure knowledge of anything we must be quit of the body—the soul in herself must behold things in themselves: and then we shall attain the wisdom which we desire, and of which we say that we are lovers, not while we live, but after death; for if while in company with the body, the soul cannot have pure knowledge, one of two things follows—either knowledge is not to be attained at all, or, if at all, after death. For then, and not till then, the soul will be parted from the body and exist in herself alone. In this present life, I reckon that we make the nearest approach to knowledge when we have the least possible intercourse or communion with the body, and are not surfeited with the bodily nature, but keep ourselves pure until the hour when God himself is pleased to release us. And thus having got rid of the foolishness of the body we shall be pure and hold converse with the pure, and know of ourselves the clear light everywhere, which is no other than the light of truth." For the impure are not permitted to approach the pure. These are the sort of words, Simmias, which the true lovers of knowledge cannot help saying to one another, and thinking. You would agree; would you not?

SIMMIAS: Undoubtedly, Socrates.

SOCRATES: But, O my friend, if this is true, there is great reason to hope that, going whither I go, when I have come to the end of my journey, I shall attain that which has been the pursuit of my life. And therefore I go on my way rejoicing, and not I only, but every other man who believes that his mind has been made ready and that he is in a manner purified.

SIMMIAS: Certainly . . .

SOCRATES: And what is purification but the separation of the soul from the body, as I was saying before; the habit of the soul gathering and collecting herself into herself from all sides out of the body; the dwelling in her own place alone, as in another life, so also in this, as far as she can;—the release of the soul from the chains of the body?

SIMMIAS: Very true . . .

SOCRATES: And this separation and release of the soul from the body is termed death?

SIMMIAS: To be sure . . .

SOCRATES: And the true philosophers, and they only, are ever seeking to release the soul. Is not the separation and release of the soul from the body their especial study?

SIMMIAS: That is true.

SOCRATES: And, as I was saying at first, there would be a ridiculous contradiction in men studying to live as nearly as they can in a state of death, and yet repining when it comes upon them.

SIMMIAS: Clearly.

SOCRATES: And the true philosophers, Simmias, are always occupied in the practice of dying, wherefore also to them least of all men is death terrible. Look at the matter thus:—if they have been in every way the enemies of the body, and are wanting to be alone with the soul, when this desire of theirs is granted, how inconsistent would they be if they trembled and repined, instead of rejoicing at their departure to that place where, when they arrive, they hope to gain that which in life they desired—and this was wisdom— and at the same time to be rid of the company of their enemy. Many a man has been willing to go to the world below animated by the hope of seeing there an earthly love, or wife, or son, and conversing with them. And will he who is a true lover of wisdom, and is strongly persuaded in like manner that only in the world below he can worthily enjoy her, still repine at death? Will he not depart with joy? Surely he will, O my friend, if he be a true philosopher. For he will have a firm conviction that there and there only, he can find wisdom in her purity. And if this be true, he would be very absurd, as I was saying, if he were afraid of death.

READING 6

Aristotle: Nature, The Soul, Moral Virtue, and Society

From *Physics, Metaphysics, On the Soul, Nicomachean Ethics,* and *Politics*

Aristotle (384–322 BCE) was Plato's pupil, and, like his teacher, lived and taught in Athens, and influenced virtually every area of philosophy for centuries to come. Below are some of the more famous discussions from Aristotle's writings on a variety of philosophical topics. A central feature of his thought is the notion of purpose, or teleology. All natural things, such as trees or animals, have an inherent purpose and function. Such natural objects have what he calls an innate impulse towards change and stability. By contrast, artificial objects, which are human-made things such as houses, have no innate impulse towards change and stability. The purpose they have is one that we assign to them. Within the natural world, he argues, there are also four types of causes: (1) an efficient cause, which is the force behind a cause, (2) a material cause, the stuff from which something is made, (3) a formal cause, the form or shape of a thing, and (4) a final cause, the purpose that the thing serves. Aristotle also famously distinguishes between substances and accidents, where substance is the reality that underlies an object's qualities, and accidents are changes that take place within substances, yet do not alter the basic nature or identity of that object. Next is his notion of the unmoved movers, that is, gods within the heavens who are responsible for the movement of the sun, moon, planets, stars, and, in turn, all motion on earth. His view of the human soul is that body and soul are inseparably interrelated insofar as the body is the material from which a person is made, and the soul is its form.

Aristotle's view of ethics is based on the concept of morally good character traits or virtues that people should acquire. The most important thing about moral behavior is that it should be habitual and arise spontaneously from good qualities that we have acquired. The starting point of his theory is the element of purpose or function: a thing is good if it fulfills its unique function, as when we speak of a good hand, a good heart, or a good eye. Aristotle asks, if every organ has a purpose or function, what about the total person—does a person, as person, have a unique function? He finds this unique function in human reason, so that the good person is one who behaves in accordance with reason. And, when we follow our reason, we will develop virtuous character traits. He discusses a range of virtues, including courage, temperance, generosity, self-respect, good temper, and modesty. Each of these, he argues, occupies a middle ground between two extreme vices. Courage, for example, rests somewhere between the vice of cowardice (too little courage) and rashness (too much fearlessness). Aristotle's view of politics is based on the idea that the state is a creation of nature and that humans are by nature political animals. We cannot survive on our own, and we are naturally inclined to form societies for our survival and well being.

Source: Aristotle, *Physics*, Books 1 and 2; *Metaphysics*, Books 5 and 12; *On the Soul* Book 2; *Nicomachean Ethics*, Books 1 and 2; *Politics*, Books 1, 3, and 7.

NATURE

Natural and Artificial Objects (*Physics* 1.4)

Of things that exist, some exist by nature, and some from other causes. "By nature" the animals and their parts exist, and also the plants and the simple bodies (earth, fire, air, water). For, we say that these and the like exist "by nature". All the things mentioned present a feature in which they differ from things which are not constituted by nature. Each of them has within itself a principle of motion and of stability (in respect of place, or of growth and decrease, or by way of alteration). On the other hand, [artificial objects, such as] a bed and a coat and anything else of that sort, as receiving these designations (that is, in so far as they are products of art) have no innate impulse to change. But in so far as they happen to be composed of stone or of earth or of a mixture of the two, they do have such an impulse. And they have that impulse to that extent which seems to indicate that nature is a source or cause of being moved and of being at rest in that to which it belongs primarily, in virtue of itself and not in virtue of a connected attribute. . . .

Some identify the nature or substance of a natural object with that immediate constituent of it which taken by itself is without arrangement, e.g., the wood is the "nature" of the bed, and the bronze the "nature" of the statue. As an indication of this Antiphon points out that if you planted a bed and the rotting wood acquired the power of sending up a shoot, it would not be a bed that would come up, but wood—which shows that the arrangement in accordance with the rules of the art is merely an incidental attribute, whereas the real nature is the other, which, further, persists continuously through the process of making.

But if the material of each of these objects has itself the same relation to something else, say bronze (or gold) to water, bones (or wood) to earth and so on, that (they say) would be their nature and essence. Consequently some assert earth, others fire or air or water or some or all of these, to be the nature of the things that are. For whatever any one of them supposed to have this character—whether one thing or more than one thing—this or these he declared to be the whole of substance, all else being its affections, states, or dispositions. Every such thing they held to be eternal (for it could not pass into anything else), but other things to come into being and cease to be times without number. This then is one account of "nature", namely that it is the immediate material substratum of things which have in themselves a principle of motion or change.

Another account is that "nature" is the shape or form which is specified in the definition of the thing. For the word "nature" is applied to what is according to nature and the natural in the same way as "art" is applied to what is artistic or a work of art. We should not say in the latter case that there is anything artistic about a thing, if it is a bed only potentially, not yet having the form of a bed; nor should we call it a work of art. The same is true of natural compounds. What is potentially flesh or bone has not yet its own "nature", and does not exist until it receives the form specified in the definition, which we name in defining what flesh or bone is. Thus in the second sense of "nature" it would be the shape or form (not separable except in statement) of things which have in themselves a source of motion. (The combination of the two, e.g., man, is not "nature" but "by nature" or "natural".)

The form indeed is "nature" rather than the matter; for a thing is more properly said to be what it is when it has attained to fulfillment than when it exists potentially. Again man is born from man, but not bed from bed. That is why people say that the figure is not the nature of a bed, but the wood is—if the bed sprouted not a bed but wood would come up. But even if the figure is art, then on the same principle the shape of man is his nature. For man is born from man.

We also speak of a thing's nature as being exhibited in the process of growth by which its nature is attained. The "nature" in this sense is not like "doctoring", which leads not to the art of doctoring but to health. Doctoring must start from the art, not lead to it. But it is not in this way that nature (in the one sense) is related to nature (in the other). What grows qua growing grows from something into something. Into what then does it grow? Not into that from which it arose but into that to which it tends. The shape then is nature. "Shape" and "nature", it should be added, are in two senses. For the privation too is in a way form. But whether in unqualified coming to be there is privation, i.e., a contrary to what comes to be, we must consider later.

Four Causes (*Physics*)

2.3. We must proceed to consider causes, their character and number. Knowledge is the object of our inquiry, and men do not think they know a thing till they have grasped the "why" of (which is to grasp its primary cause). So clearly we too must do this as regards both coming to be and passing away and every kind of physical change, in order that, knowing their principles, we may try to refer each of our problems to these principles.

In one sense, then, (1) that out of which a thing comes to be and which persists, is called "cause". This is so, for example, regarding the bronze of the statue, the silver of the bowl, and the genera of which the bronze and the silver are species.

In another sense (2) the form or the pattern (the definition of the essence), and its genera, are called "causes". This is so, for example, regarding the octave the relation of 2:1, and numbers generally, and the parts in the definition.

Again, (3) [a causes is] the primary source of the change or coming to rest. For example, the man who gave advice is a cause, the father is cause of the child, and generally what makes of what is made and what causes change of what is changed.

Again, (4) [something is a cause] in the sense of end or "that for the sake of which" a thing is done. For example, health is the cause of walking about. If asked "Why is he walking about?" we say, "To be healthy". Having said that, we think we have assigned the cause. The same is true also of all the intermediate steps which are brought about through the action of something else as means towards the end. For example, reduction of flesh, purging, drugs, or surgical instruments are means towards health. All these things are "for the sake of" the end, though they differ from one another in that some are activities, others instruments.

This then perhaps exhausts the number of ways in which the term "cause" is used.

Substance and Accident (*Metaphysics*)

5.8. We call "substance" (1) the simple bodies, that is, earth and fire and water and everything of the sort, and in general bodies and the things composed of them, both animals and divine beings, and the parts of these. All these are called substance because they are not predicated of a subject but everything else is predicated of them. [We also call "substance"] (2) that which, being present in such things as are not predicated of a subject, is the cause of their being, as the soul is of the being of an animal. . . .

5.30. "Accident" means (1) that which attaches to something and can be truly asserted, but neither of necessity nor usually. For example, if someone in digging a hole for a plant has found treasure. This (the finding of treasure) is an accident for the man who dug the hole, since neither does the one come of necessity from the other (or after the other), nor does he usually find treasure if he digs to plant something. A musician might be pale; but since this does not happen of necessity nor usually, we call it an accident. There are, then, attributes and they attach to subjects, and some of them attach to these only in a particular place and at a particular time. Thus, something will be an accident whenever it attaches to a subject, but not because it was this subject, or the time this time, or the place this place. Therefore, too, there is no definite cause for an accident, but a chance cause, that is, an indefinite one. Going to Aegina was an accident for a man, if he went not in order to get there, but because he was carried out of his way by a storm or captured by pirates. The accident has happened or exists, not in virtue of the subject's nature, however, but of something else. For, the storm was the cause of his coming to a place for which he was not sailing, and this was Aegina.

Unmoved Mover (*Metaphysics*)

12.7.8. The first heaven [i.e., the outer sphere of the universe] must be eternal. There is therefore also something which moves it. And since that which moves and is moved is intermediate, there is something which moves without being moved, being eternal, substance, and actuality. And the object of desire and the object of thought move in this way; they move without being moved. . . . The final cause, then, produces motion as being loved, but all other things move by being moved. . . . On such a principle, then, depend the heavens and the world of nature. . . .

It is clear then from what has been said that there is a substance which is eternal and unmovable and separate from sensible things. It has been shown also that this substance cannot have any magnitude, but is without parts and indivisible (for it produces movement through infinite time, but nothing finite has infinite power; and, while every magnitude is either infinite or finite, it cannot, for the above reason, have finite magnitude, and it cannot have infinite magnitude because there is no infinite magnitude at all). But it has also been shown that it is impassive and unalterable; for all the other changes are posterior to change of place. . . .

Since we see that besides the simple spatial movement of the universe, which we say the first and unmovable substance produces, there are other spatial movements—those of the planets—which are eternal. Each of these movements also must be caused by a substance both unmovable in itself and eternal. . . . Evidently, then, there must be substances which are of the same number as the movements of the stars, and in their nature eternal, and in themselves unmovable, and without magnitude, for the reason before mentioned. That the movers are substances, then, and that one of these is first and another second according to the same order as the movements of the stars, is evident. . . . the number of all the spheres—both those which move the planets and those which counteract these—will be fifty-five. Let this, then, be taken as the number of the spheres, so that the unmovable substances and principles also may probably be taken as just so many.

THE SOUL

Soul and Body (*On the Soul*)

2.1. We are in the habit of recognizing, as one determinate kind of what is, substance, and that in several senses, (a) in the sense of matter or that which in itself is not "a this," and (b) in the sense of form or essence, which is that precisely in virtue of which a thing is called "a this," and thirdly (c) in the sense of that which is compounded of both (a) and (b). . . . Every natural body which has life in it is a substance in the sense of a composite. But since it is also a body of such and such a kind, viz., having life, the body cannot be soul; the body is the subject or matter, not what is attributed to it. Hence the soul must be a substance in the sense of the form of a natural body having life potentially within it. . . .

Suppose that the eye were an animal: sight would have been its soul (for sight is the substance or essence of the eye which corresponds to the formula, the eye being merely the matter of seeing). When seeing is removed, the eye is no longer an eye, except in name. It is no more a real eye than the eye of a statue or of a painted figure. . . . As the pupil plus the power of sight constitutes the eye, so the soul plus the body constitutes the animal. From this it indubitably follows that the soul is inseparable from its body. . .

2.2. The soul does not exist without a body and yet is not itself a kind of body. For it is not a body, but something which belongs to a body, and for this reason exists in a body, and in a body of such-and-such a kind.

What has soul in it differs from what lacks it, in that the former displays life. Now the word "living" has more than one sense; if any one alone of these is found in a thing we say that thing is living. "Living" may mean thinking or perception or local movement and rest, or movement in the sense of nutrition, decay and growth. Hence we think of plants also as living, for they are observed to possess in themselves an originative power through which they increase or decrease in all spatial directions; they grow up and down, and everything that grows increases its bulk alike in both directions or indeed in all, and continues to live so long as it can absorb nutriment. . . . Certain kinds of animals possess in addition the power of locomotion, and still another order of animate beings, i.e., man and possibly another order like man or superior to him, the power of thinking, i.e., mind.

2.3. Hence we must ask in the case of each order of living things, What is its soul, i.e., What is the soul of plant, animal, man? Why the terms are related in this serial way must form the subject of later examination. But the facts are that the power of perception is never found apart from the power of self-nutrition, while (in plants) the latter is found isolated from the former. Again, no sense is found apart from that of touch, while touch is found by itself; many animals have neither sight, hearing, nor smell. Again, among living things that possess sense some have the power of locomotion, some not. Lastly, a small minority of certain living beings possess calculation and thought, for (among mortal beings) those which possess calculation have all the other powers above mentioned, while the converse does not hold—indeed some live by imagination alone, while others have not even imagination. The mind that knows with immediate intuition presents a different problem.

MORAL VIRTUES

Virtue and the Divisions of the Soul

Happiness is something which is both precious and final. This seems to be so because it is a first principle or ultimate starting point. For, it is for the sake of happiness that we do everything else, and we regard the cause of all good things to be precious and divine. Moreover, since happiness is an activity of the soul in accordance with complete or perfect virtue, it is necessary to consider virtue, as this will be the best way of studying happiness.

It appears that virtue is the object upon which the true statesman has expended the largest amount of trouble, as it is his wish to make the citizens virtuous and obedient to the laws. We have instances of such statesmen in the legislators of Crete and Lacedaemon and such other legislators as have resembled them. But if this inquiry is proper to political science, it will clearly accord with our original purpose to pursue it. But it is clear that it is human virtue which we have to consider; for the good of which we are in search is, as we said, human good, and the happiness, human happiness. By human virtue or excellence we mean not that of the body, but that of the soul, and by happiness we mean an activity of the soul.

If this is so, it is clearly necessary for statesmen to have some knowledge of the nature of the soul in the same way as it is necessary for one who is to treat the eye or any part of the body, to have some knowledge of it, and all the more as political science is better and more honorable than medical science. Clever doctors take a great deal of trouble to understand the body, and similarly the statesman must make a study of the soul. But he must study it with a view to his particular object and so far only as his object requires; for to elaborate the study of it further would, I think, be to aggravate unduly the labor of our present undertaking.

There are some facts concerning the soul which are adequately stated in the popular or exoterical discourses, and these we may rightly adopt. It is stated, e.g., that the soul has two parts, one irrational and the other possessing reason. But whether these parts are distinguished like the parts of the body and like everything that is itself divisible, or whether they are theoretically distinct, but in fact inseparable, as convex and concave in the circumference of a circle, is of no importance to the present inquiry.

Again, it seems that of the irrational part of the soul one part is common, *i.e., shared by man with all living things,* and vegetative; I mean the part which is the cause of nutrition and increase. For we may assume such a faculty of the soul to exist in all things that receive nutrition, even in embryos, and the same faculty to exist in things that are full grown, as it is more reasonable to suppose that it is the same faculty than that it is different. It is clear then that the virtue or excellence of this faculty is not distinctively human but is shared by man with all living things; for it seems that this part and this faculty are especially active in sleep, whereas good and bad people are never so little distinguishable as in sleep—from which we get the saying that there is no difference between the happy and the miserable during half their lifetime. And this is only natural; for sleep is an inactivity of the soul in respect of its virtue or vice, except in so far as certain impulses affect it to a slight extent, and make the visions of the virtuous better than those of ordinary people. But enough has been said on this point, and we must now leave the principle of nutrition, as it possesses no natural share in human virtue.

It seems that there is another natural principle of the soul which is irrational and yet in a sense partakes of reason. For in a continent or incontinent person we praise the reason, and that part of the soul which possesses reason, as it exhorts men rightly and exhorts them to the best conduct. But it is clear that there is in them another principle which is naturally different from reason and fights and contends against reason. For just as the paralyzed parts of the body, when we intend to move them to the right, are drawn away in a contrary direction to the left, so it is with the soul; the impulses of incontinent people run counter to reason. But there is this difference, however, that while in the body we see the part which is drawn astray, in the soul we do not see it. But it is probably right to suppose with equal certainty that there is in the soul too something different from reason, which opposes and thwarts it, although the sense in which it is distinct from reason is immaterial. But it appears that this part too partakes of reason, as we said; at all events in a continent person it obeys reason, while in a temperate or courageous person it is probably still more obedient, as being absolutely harmonious with reason.

It appears then that the irrational part of the soul is itself twofold; for the vegetative faculty does not participate at all in reason, but the faculty of desire or general concupiscence participates in it more or less, in so far as it is submissive and obedient to reason. But *it is obedient* in the sense in which we speak of "paying attention to a father" or "to friends," but not in the sense in which we speak of "paying attention to mathematics." All correction, rebuke and exhortation is a witness that the irrational part of the soul is in a sense subject to the influence of reason. But if we are to say that this part too possesses reason, then the part which possesses reason will have two divisions, one possessing reason absolutely and in itself, the other listening to it as a child listens to its father.

Virtue or excellence again, admits of a distinction which depends on this difference. For we speak of some virtues as intellectual and of others as moral, wisdom, intelligence and prudence, being intellectual, liberality and temperance being moral, virtues. For when we describe a person's character, we do not say that he is wise or intelligent but that he is gentle or temperate. Yet we praise a wise man too in respect of his mental state, and such mental states as deserve to be praised we call virtuous.

Virtues Are Acquired

Virtue or excellence being twofold, partly intellectual and partly moral, intellectual virtue is both originated and fostered mainly by teaching; it therefore demands experience and time. Moral virtue on the other hand is the outcome of habit, and accordingly its name is derived by a slight deflection of habit. From this fact it is clear that no moral virtue is implanted in us by nature; a law of nature cannot be altered by habituation. Thus, a stone naturally tends to fall downwards, and it cannot be habituated or trained to rise upwards, even if we were to habituate it by throwing it upwards ten thousand times; nor again can fire be trained to sink downwards, nor anything else that follows one natural law be habituated or trained to follow another. It is neither by nature then nor capacity is perfected by habit.

Again, if we take the various natural powers which belong to us, we first acquire the proper faculties and afterwards display the activities. It is clearly so with the senses. It was not by seeing frequently or hearing frequently that we acquired the senses of seeing or hearing; on the contrary it was because we possessed the senses that we made use of them, not by making use of them that we obtained them. But the virtues we acquire by first exercising them, as is the case with all the arts, for it is by doing what we ought to do when we have learnt the arts that we learn the arts themselves; we become, e.g., builders by building and harpists by playing the harp. Similarly it is by doing just acts that we become just, by doing temperate acts that we become temperate, by doing courageous acts that we become courageous. The experience of states is a witness to this truth, for it is by training the habits that legislators make the citizens good. This is the object which all legislators have at heart; if a legislator does not succeed in it, he fails of his purpose, and it constitutes the distinction between a good polity and a bad one.

Again, the causes and means by which any virtue is produced and by which it is destroyed are the same; and it is equally so with any art; for it is by playing the harp that both good and bad harpists are produced and the case of builders and all other artisans is similar, as it is by building well that they will be good builders and by building badly that they will be bad builders. If it were not so, there would be no need of anybody to teach them; they would all be born good or bad in their several trades. The case of the virtues is the same. It is by acting in such transactions as take place between man and man that we become either just or unjust. It is by acting in the face of danger and by habituating ourselves to fear or courage that we become either cowardly or courageous. It is much the same with our desires and angry passions. Some people become temperate and gentle, others become licentious and passionate according as they conduct themselves in one way or another way in particular circumstances. In a word character traits are the results of activities corresponding to the character traits themselves. It is our duty therefore to give a certain character to the activities, as the character traits depend upon the differences of the activities. Accordingly the difference between one training of the habits and another from early days is not a light matter, but is serious or rather all-important.

The Study of Virtue

Our present study is not, like other studies, purely speculative in its intention; for the object of our inquiry is not to know the nature of virtue but to become ourselves virtuous, as that is the sole benefit which it conveys. It is necessary therefore to consider the right way of performing actions, for it is actions as we have said that determine the character of the resulting character traits.

That we should act in accordance with right reason is a common general principle, which may here be taken for granted. The nature of right reason, and its relation to the virtues generally, will be subjects of discussion hereafter. But it must be admitted at the outset that all reasoning upon practical matters must be like a sketch in outline, it cannot be scientifically exact. We began by laying down the principle that the kind of reasoning demanded in any subject must be such as the subject matter itself allows; and questions of practice and expediency no more admit of invariable rules than questions of health.

But if this is true of general reasoning upon ethics, still more true is it that scientific exactitude is impossible in reasoning upon particular ethical cases. They do not fall under any art or any law, but the agents themselves are always bound to pay regard to the circumstances of the moment as much as in medicine or navigation.

Still, although such is the nature of the present argument, we must try to make the best of it.

The first point to be observed then is that in such matters as we are considering deficiency and excess are equally fatal. It is so, as we observe, in regard to health and strength; for we must judge of what we cannot see by the evidence of what we do see. Excess or deficiency of gymnastic exercise is fatal to strength. Similarly an excess or deficiency of meat and drink is fatal to health, whereas a suitable amount produces, augments and sustains it. It is the same then with temperance, courage, and the other virtues. A person who avoids and is afraid of everything and faces nothing becomes a coward; a person who is not afraid of anything but is ready to face everything becomes foolhardy. Similarly, he who enjoys every pleasure and never abstains from any pleasure is licentious; he who eschews all pleasures like a boor is an insensible sort of person. For temperance and courage are destroyed by excess and deficiency but preserved by the mean state.

Again, not only are the causes and the agencies of production, increase and destruction in the character traits the same, but the sphere of their activity will be proved to be the same also. It is so in other instances which are more conspicuous, e.g., in strength; for strength is produced by taking a great deal of food and undergoing a great deal of labor, and it is the strong man who is able to take most food and to undergo most labor. The same is the case with the virtues. It is by abstinence from pleasures that we become temperate, and, when we have become temperate, we are best able to abstain from them. So too with courage; it is by habituating ourselves to despise and face alarms that we become courageous, and, when we have become courteous, we shall be best able to face them.

Virtues Are Character Traits

We have next to consider the nature of virtue.

Now, as the qualities of the soul are three, viz., emotions, faculties and character traits, it follows that virtue must be one of the three. By the emotions I mean desire, anger, fear, courage, envy, joy, love, hatred, regret, emulation, pity, in a word whatever is attended by pleasure or pain. I call those faculties in respect of which we are said to be capable of experiencing these emotions, e.g., capable of getting angry or being pained or feeling pity. And I call those character traits in respect of which we are well or ill disposed towards the emotions, ill-disposed, e.g., towards the passion of anger, if our anger be too violent or too feeble, and well-disposed, if it be duly moderated, and similarly towards the other emotions.

Now neither the virtues nor the vices are emotions; for we are not called good or evil in respect of our emotions but in respect of our virtues or vices. Again, we are not praised or blamed in respect of our emotions; a person is not praised for being angry in an absolute sense, but only for being angry in a certain way; but we are praised or blamed in respect of our virtues or vices. Again, whereas we are angry or afraid without deliberate purpose, the virtues are in some sense deliberate purposes, or do not exist in the absence of deliberate purpose. It may be added that while we are said to be moved in respect of our emotions, in respect of our virtues or vices we are not said to be moved but to have a certain disposition.

These reasons also prove that the virtues are not faculties. For we are not called either good or bad, nor are we praised or blamed, as having an abstract capacity for emotion. Also while Nature gives us our faculties, it is not Nature that makes us good or bad, but this is a point which we have already discussed. If then the virtues are neither emotions nor faculties, it remains that they must be moral states.

The nature of virtue has been now generically described. But it is not enough to state merely that virtue is a moral state, we must also describe the character of that moral state.

It must be laid down then that every virtue or excellence has the effect of producing a good condition of that of which it is a virtue or excellence, and of enabling it to perform its function well. Thus the excellence of the eye makes the eye good and its function good, as it is by the excellence of the eye that we see well. Similarly, the excellence of the horse makes a horse excellent and good at racing, at carrying its rider and at facing the enemy.

If then this is universally true, the virtue or excellence of man will be such a moral state as makes a man good and able to perform his proper function well. We have already explained how this will be the case, but another way of making it clear will be to study the nature or character of this virtue.

The Virtuous Mean between Extremes

Now in everything, whether it be continuous or discrete, it is possible to take a greater, a smaller, or an equal amount, and this either absolutely or in relation to ourselves, the equal being a mean between excess and deficiency. By the mean in respect of the thing itself, or the absolute mean, I understand that which is equally distinct from both extremes and this is one and the same thing for everybody. By the mean considered relatively to ourselves I understand that which is neither too much nor too little; but this is not one thing, nor is it the same for everybody. Thus if 10 be too much and 2 too little we take 6 as a mean in respect of the thing itself; for 6 is as much greater than 2 as it is less than 10, and this is a mean in arithmetical proportion. But the mean considered relatively to ourselves must not be ascertained in this way. It does not follow that if 10 pounds *of meat* be too much and 2 be too little for a man to eat, a trainer will order him 6 pounds, as this may itself be too much or too little for the person who is to take it; it will be too little, e.g., for Milo, but too much for a beginner in gymnastics. It will be the same with running and wrestling; *the right amount will vary with the individual.* This being so, everybody who understands his business avoids alike excess and deficiency; he seeks and chooses the mean, not the absolute mean, but the mean considered relatively to ourselves.

Every science then performs its function well, if it regards the mean and refers the works which it produces to the mean. This is the reason why it is usually said of successful works that it is impossible to take anything from them or to add anything to them, which implies that excess or deficiency is fatal to excellence but that the mean state ensures it. Good artists too, as we say, have an eye to the mean in their works. But virtue, like Nature herself, is more accurate and better than any art; virtue therefore will aim at the mean; I speak of moral virtue, as it is moral virtue which is concerned with emotions and actions, and it is these which admit of excess and deficiency and the mean. Thus it is possible to go too far, or not to go far enough, in respect of fear, courage, desire, anger, pity, and pleasure and pain generally, and the excess and the deficiency are alike wrong; but to experience these emotions at the right times and on the right occasions and towards the right persons and for the right causes and in the right manner is the mean or the supreme good, which is characteristic of virtue. Similarly there may be excess, deficiency, or the mean, in regard to actions. But virtue is concerned with emotions and actions, and here excess is an error and deficiency a fault, whereas the mean is successful and laudable, and success and merit are both characteristics of virtue.

It appears then that virtue is a mean state, so far at least as it aims at the mean.

Again, there are many different ways of going wrong; for evil is in its nature infinite, to use the Pythagorean figure, but good is finite. But there is only one possible way of going right. Accordingly the former is easy and the latter difficult; it is easy to miss the mark but difficult to hit it. This again is a reason why excess and deficiency are characteristics of vice and the mean state a characteristic of virtue: "For good is simple, evil manifold." Virtue then is a state of deliberate moral purpose consisting in a mean that is relative to ourselves, the mean being determined by reason, or as a prudent man would determine it.

It is a mean state *firstly as lying* between two vices, the vice of excess on the one hand, and the vice of deficiency on the other, and secondly because, whereas the vices either fall short of or go beyond what is proper in the emotions and actions, virtue not only discovers but embraces the mean.

Accordingly, virtue, if regarded in its essence or theoretical conception, is a mean state, but, if regarded from the point of view of the highest good, or of excellence, it is an extreme.

But it is not every action or every emotion that admits of a mean state. There are some whose very name implies wickedness, as, e.g., malice, shamelessness, and envy, among emotions, or adultery, theft, and murder, among actions. All these, and others like them, are censured as being intrinsically wicked, not merely the excesses or deficiencies of them. It is never possible then to be right in respect of them; they are always sinful. Right or wrong in such actions as adultery does not depend on our committing therewith the right person, at the right time or in the right manner; on the contrary it is sinful to do anything of the kind at all. It would be equally wrong then to suppose that there can be a mean state or an excess or deficiency in unjust, cowardly or licentious conduct; for, if it were so, there would be a mean state of an excess or of a deficiency, an excess of an excess and a deficiency of a deficiency. But as in temperance and courage there can be no excess or deficiency because the mean is, in a sense, an extreme, so too in these cases there cannot be a mean or an excess or deficiency, but, however the acts may be done, they are wrong. For it is a general rule that an excess or deficiency does not admit of a mean state, nor a mean state of an excess or deficiency.

But it is not enough to lay down this as a general rule; it is necessary to apply it to particular cases, as in reasonings upon actions general statements, although they are broader, are less exact than particular statements. For all action refers to particulars, and it is essential that our theories should harmonize with the particular cases to which they apply.

Examples of Virtues and Vices

We must take particular virtues then from the catalogue of virtues. In regard to feelings of fear and confidence courage is a mean state. On the side of excess, he whose fearlessness is excessive has no name, as often happens, but he whose confidence is excessive is foolhardy, while he whose timidity is excessive and whose confidence is deficient is a coward.

In respect of pleasures and pains, although not indeed of all pleasures and pains, and to a less extent in respect of pains than of pleasures, the mean state is temperance, the excess is licentiousness. We never find people who are deficient in regard to pleasures; accordingly such people again have not received a name, but we may call them insensible.

As regards the giving and taking of money, the mean state is liberality, the excess and deficiency are prodigality and illiberality. Here the excess and deficiency take opposite forms; for while the prodigal man is excessive in spending and deficient in taking, the illiberal man is excessive in taking and deficient in spending.

In respect of money there are other dispositions as well. There is the mean state which is magnificence; for the magnificent man, as having to do with large sums of money, differs from the liberal man who has to do only with small sums; and the excess *corresponding to it* is bad taste or vulgarity, the deficiency is meanness. These are different from the excess and deficiency of liberality; what the difference is will be explained hereafter.

In respect of honor and dishonor the mean state is highmindedness, the excess is what is called vanity, the deficiency littlemindedness. Corresponding to liberality, which, as we said, differs from magnificence as having to do not with great but with small sums of money, there is a moral state which has to do with petty honor and is related to highmindedness which has to do with great honor; for it is possible to aspire to honor in the right way, or in a way which is excessive or insufficient, and if a person's aspirations are excessive, he is called ambitious, if they are deficient, he is called unambitious, while if they are between the two, he has no name. The dispositions too are nameless, except that the disposition of the ambitious person is called ambition. The consequence is that the extremes lay claim to the mean or intermediate place. We ourselves speak of one who observes the mean sometimes as ambitious, and at other times as unambitious; we sometimes praise an ambitious, and at other times an unambitious person. The reason for our doing so will be stated in due course, but let us now discuss the other virtues in accordance with the method which we have followed hitherto.

Anger, like other emotions, has its excess, its deficiency, and its mean state. It may be said that they have no names, but as we call one who observes the mean gentle, we will call the mean state gentleness. Among the extremes, if a person errs on the side of excess, he may be called passionate and his vice passionateness, if on that of deficiency, he may be called impassive and his deficiency impassivity.

There are also three other mean states with a certain resemblance to each other, and yet with a difference. For while they are all concerned with intercourse in speech and action, they are different in that one of them is concerned with truth in such intercourse, and the others with pleasantness, one with pleasantness in amusement and the other with pleasantness in the various circumstances of life. We must therefore discuss these states in order to make it clear that in all cases it is the mean state which is an object of praise, and the extremes are neither right nor laudable but censurable. It is true that these mean and extreme states are generally nameless, but we must do our best here as elsewhere to give them a name, so that our argument may be clear and easy to follow.

In the matter of truth then, he who observes the mean may be called truthful, and the mean state truthfulness. Pretence, if it takes the form of exaggeration, is boastfulness, and one who is guilty of pretence is a boaster; but if it takes the form of depreciation it is irony, and he who is guilty of it is ironical.

As regards pleasantness in amusement, he who observes the mean is witty, and his disposition wittiness; the excess is buffoonery, and he who is guilty of it a buffoon, whereas he who is deficient in wit may be called a boor and his moral state boorishness.

As to the other kind of pleasantness, viz., pleasantness in life, he who is pleasant in a proper way is friendly, and his mean state friendliness; but he who goes too far, if he has no ulterior object in view, is obsequious, while if his object is self interest, he is a flatterer, and he who does not go far enough and always makes himself unpleasant is a quarrelsome and morose sort of person.

There are also mean states in the emotions and in the expression of the emotions. For although modesty is not a virtue, yet a modest person is praised as if he were virtuous; for here too one person is said to observe the mean and another to exceed it, as, e.g., the bashful man who is never anything but modest, whereas a person who has insufficient modesty or no modesty at all is called shameless, and one who observes the mean modest.

Righteous indignation, again, is a mean state between envy and malice. They are all concerned with the pain and pleasure which we feel at the fortunes of our neighbors. A person who is righteously indignant is pained at the prosperity of the undeserving; but the envious person goes further and is pained at anybody's prosperity, and the malicious person is so far from being pained that he actually rejoices at misfortunes.

The Difficulty of the Virtuous Life

It has now been sufficiently shown that moral virtue is a mean state, and in what sense it is a mean state; it is a mean state as lying between two vices, a vice of excess on the one side and a vice of deficiency on the other, and as aiming at the mean in the emotions and actions.

That is the reason why it is so hard to be virtuous; for it is always hard work to find the mean in anything, e.g., it is not everybody, but only a man of science, who can find the mean or center of a circle. So too anybody can get angry—that is an easy matter—and anybody can give or spend money, but to give it to the right persons, to give the right amount of it and to give it at the right time and for the right cause and in the right way, this is not what anybody can do, nor is it easy. That is the reason why it is rare and laudable and noble to do well. Accordingly one who aims at the mean must begin by departing from that extreme which is the more contrary to the mean; he must act in the spirit of Calypso's advice, "Far from this smoke and swell you keep your bark," for of the two extremes one is more sinful than the other. As it is difficult then to hit the mean exactly, we must take the second best course, as the saying is, and choose the lesser of two evils, and this we shall best do in the way that we have described, i.e., by steering clear of the evil which is further from the mean. We must also observe the things to which we are ourselves particularly prone, as different natures have different inclinations, and we may ascertain what these are by a consideration of our feelings of pleasure and pain. And then we must drag ourselves in the direction opposite to them; for it is by removing ourselves as far as possible from what is wrong that we shall arrive at the mean, as we do, when we pull a crooked stick straight.

But in all cases we must especially be on our guard against what is pleasant and against pleasure, as we are not impartial judges of pleasure. Hence our attitude towards pleasure must be like that of the elders of the people in the *Iliad* towards Helen, and we must never be afraid of applying the words they use; for if we dismiss pleasure as they dismissed Helen, we shall be less likely to go wrong. It is by action of this kind, to put it summarily, that we shall best succeed in hitting the mean.

It may be admitted that this is a difficult task, especially in particular cases. It is not easy to determine, e.g., the right manner, objects, occasions, and duration of anger. There are times when we ourselves praise people who are deficient in anger, and call them gentle, and there are other times when we speak of people who exhibit a savage temper as spirited. It is not however one who deviates a little from what is right, but one who deviates a great deal, whether on the side of excess or of deficiency, that is censured; for he is sure to be found out. Again, it is not easy to decide theoretically how far and to what extent a man may go before he becomes censurable, but neither is it easy to define theoretically anything else within the region of perception; such things fall under the head of particulars, and our judgment of them depends upon our perception.

So much then is plain, that the mean state is everywhere laudable, but that we ought to incline at one time towards the excess and at another towards the deficiency; for this will be our easiest manner of hitting the mean, or in other words of attaining excellence.

THE NATURAL BASIS OF SOCIETY

Definition and Structure of the State

1.1. Every state is a community of some kind, and every community is established with a view to some good; for mankind always act in order to obtain that which they think good. But, if all communities aim at some good, the state or political community, which is the highest of all, and which embraces all the rest, aims at good in a greater degree than any other, and at the highest good.

Some people think that the qualifications of a statesman, king, householder, and master are the same, and that they differ, not in kind, but only in the number of their subjects. For example, the ruler over a few is called a master; over more, the manager of a household; over a still larger number, a statesman or king, as if there were no difference between a great household and a small state. The distinction which is made between the king and the statesman is as follows: When the government is personal, the ruler is a king; when, according to the rules of the political science, the citizens rule and are ruled in turn, then he is called a statesman.

But all this is a mistake; for governments differ in kind, as will be evident to any one who considers the matter according to the method which has hitherto guided us. As in other departments of science, so in politics, the compound should always be resolved into the simple elements or least parts of the whole. We must therefore look at the elements of which the state is composed, in order that we may see in what the different kinds of rule differ from one another, and whether any scientific result can be attained about each one of them.

1.2. He who thus considers things in their first growth and origin, whether a state or anything else, will obtain the clearest view of them. In the first place there must be a union of those who cannot exist without each other; namely, of male and female, that the race may continue (and this is a union which is formed, not of deliberate purpose, but because, in common with other animals and with plants, mankind have a natural desire to leave behind them an image of themselves), and of natural ruler and subject, that both may be preserved. For that which can foresee by the exercise of mind is by nature intended to be lord and master, and that which can with its body give effect to such foresight is a subject, and by nature a slave; hence master and slave have the same interest. Now nature has distinguished between the female and the slave. For she is not niggardly, like the smith who fashions the Delphian knife for many uses; she makes each thing for a single use, and every instrument is best made when intended for one and not for many uses. But among barbarians no distinction is made between women and slaves, because there is no natural ruler among them: they are a community of slaves, male and female. Wherefore the poets say, "It is meet that Hellenes should rule over barbarians;—as if they thought that the barbarian and the slave were by nature one." Out of these two relationships between man and woman, master and slave, the first thing to arise is the family, and Hesiod is right when he says, "First house and wife and an ox for the plough," for the ox is the poor man's slave. The family is the association established by nature for the supply of men's everyday wants, and the members of it are called by Charondas "companions of the cupboard," and by Epimenides the Cretan, "companions of the manger." But when several families are united, and the association aims at something more than the supply of daily needs, the first society to be formed is the village. And the most natural form of the village appears to be that of a colony from the family, composed of the children and grandchildren, who are said to be suckled "with the same milk." And this is the reason why Hellenic states were originally governed by kings; because the Hellenes were under royal rule before they came together, as the barbarians still are. Every family is ruled by the eldest, and therefore in the colonies of the family the kingly form of government prevailed because they were of the same blood. As Homer says: "Each one gives law to his children and to his wives." For they lived dispersedly, as was the manner in ancient times. Wherefore men say that the Gods have a king, because they themselves either are or were in ancient times under the rule of a king. For they imagine, not only the forms of the Gods, but their ways of life to be like their own.

When several villages are united in a single complete community, large enough to be nearly or quite self-sufficing, the state comes into existence, originating in the bare needs of life, and continuing in existence for the sake of a good life. And therefore, if the earlier forms of society are natural, so is the state, for it is the end of them, and the nature of a thing is its end. For what each thing is when fully developed, we call its nature, whether we are speaking of a man, a horse, or a family. Besides, the final cause and end of a thing is the best, and to be self-sufficing is the end and the best.

Hence it is evident that the state is a creation of nature, and that man is by nature a political animal. And he who by nature and not by mere accident is without a state, is either a bad man or above humanity; he is like the "tribeless, lawless, hearthless one," whom Homer denounces—the natural outcast is forthwith a lover of war; he may be compared to an isolated piece at draughts.

Now, that man is more of a political animal than bees or any other gregarious animals is evident. Nature, as we often say, makes nothing in vain, and man is the only animal whom she has endowed with the gift of speech. And whereas mere voice is but an indication of pleasure or pain, and is therefore found in other animals (for their nature attains to the perception of pleasure and pain and the intimation of them to one another, and no further), the power of speech is intended to set forth the expedient and inexpedient, and therefore likewise the just and the unjust. And it is a characteristic of man that he alone has any sense of good and evil, of just and unjust, and the like, and the association of living beings who have this sense makes a family and a state.

Further, the state is by nature clearly prior to the family and to the individual, since the whole is of necessity prior to the part; for example, if the whole body be destroyed, there will be no foot or hand, except in an equivocal sense, as we might speak of a stone hand; for when destroyed the hand will be no better than that. But things are defined by their working and power; and we ought not to say that they are the same when they no longer have their proper quality, but only that they have the same name. The proof that the state is a creation of nature and prior to the individual is that the individual, when isolated, is not self-sufficing; and therefore he is like a part in relation to the whole. But he who is unable to live in society, or who has no need because he is sufficient for himself, must be either a beast or a god: he is no part of a state. A social instinct is implanted in all men by nature, and yet he who first founded the state was the greatest of benefactors. For man, when perfected, is the best of animals, but, when separated from law and justice, he is the worst of all; since armed injustice is the more dangerous, and he is equipped at birth with arms, meant to be used by intelligence and virtue, which he may use for the worst ends. Wherefore, if he have not virtue, he is the most unholy and the most savage of animals, and the most full of lust and gluttony. But justice is the bond of men in states, for the administration of justice, which is the determination of what is just, is the principle of order in political society. . . .

The True Aim of the State Is Virtue

3.9. . . . But a state exists for the sake of a good life, and not for the sake of life only: if life only were the object, slaves and brute animals might form a state, but they cannot, for they have no share in happiness or in a life of free choice. Nor does a state exist for the sake of alliance and security from injustice, nor yet for the sake of exchange and mutual intercourse; for then the Tyrrhenians and the Carthaginians, and all who have commercial treaties with one another, would be the citizens of one state. True, they have agreements about imports, and engagements that they will do no wrong to one another, and written articles of alliance. But there are no magistrates common to the contracting parties who will enforce their engagements; different states have each their own magistracies. Nor does one state take care that the citizens of the other are such as they ought to be, nor see that those who come under the terms of the treaty do no wrong or wickedness at all, but only that they do no injustice to one another. Whereas, those who care for good government take into consideration virtue and vice in states. Whence it may be further inferred that virtue must be the care of a state which is truly so called, and not merely enjoys the name: for without this end the community becomes a mere alliance which differs only in place from alliances of which the members live apart; and law is only a convention, "a surety to one another of justice," as the sophist Lycophron says, and has no real power to make the citizens.

    This is obvious; for suppose distinct places, such as Corinth and Megara, to be brought together so that their walls touched, still they would not be one city, not even if the citizens had the right to intermarry, which is one of the rights peculiarly characteristic of states. Again, if men dwelt at a distance from one another, but not so far off as to have no intercourse, and there were laws among them that they should not wrong each other in their exchanges, neither would this be a state. Let us suppose that one man is a carpenter, another a husbandman, another a shoemaker, and so on, and that their number is ten thousand: nevertheless, if they have nothing in common but exchange, alliance, and the like, that would not constitute a state. Why is this? Surely not because they are at a distance from one another: for even supposing that such a community were to meet in one place, but that each man had a house of his own, which was in a manner his state, and that they made alliance with one another, but only against evil-doers; still an accurate thinker would not deem this to be a state, if their intercourse with one another was of the same character after as before their union. It is clear then that a state is not a mere society, having a common place, established for the prevention of mutual crime and for the sake of exchange. These are conditions without which a state cannot exist; but all of them together do not constitute a state, which is a community of families and aggregations of families in well-being, for the sake of a perfect and self-sufficing life. Such a community can only be established among those who live in the same place and intermarry. Hence arise in cities family connections, brotherhoods, common sacrifices, amusements which draw men together. But these are created by friendship, for the will to live together is friendship. The end of the state is the good life, and these are the means towards it. And the state is the union of families and villages in a perfect and self-sufficing life, by which we mean a happy and honorable life.

Our conclusion, then, is that political society exists for the sake of noble actions, and not of mere companionship. Hence they who contribute most to such a society have a greater share in it than those who have the same or a greater freedom or nobility of birth but are inferior to them in political virtue; or than those who exceed them in wealth but are surpassed by them in virtue. . . .

The Good Ruler

7.14. Since every political society is composed of rulers and subjects let us consider whether the relations of one to the other should interchange or be permanent. For the education of the citizens will necessarily vary with the answer given to this question. Now, if some men excelled others in the same degree in which gods and heroes are supposed to excel mankind in general (having in the first place a great advantage even in their bodies, and secondly in their minds), so that the superiority of the governors was undisputed and patent to their subjects, it would clearly be better that once for all the one class should rule and the other serve. But since this is unattainable, and kings have no marked superiority over their subjects, such as Scylax affirms to be found among the Indians, it is obviously necessary on many grounds that all the citizens alike should take their turn of governing and being governed. Equality consists in the same treatment of similar persons, and no government can stand which is not founded upon justice. For if the government be unjust everyone in the country unites with the governed in the desire to have a revolution, and it is an impossibility that the members of the government can be so numerous as to be stronger than all their enemies put together. Yet that governors should excel their subjects is undeniable. How all this is to be effected, and in what way they will respectively share in the government, the legislator has to consider. The subject has been already mentioned. Nature herself has provided the distinction when she made a difference between old and young within the same species, of whom she fitted the one to govern and the other to be governed. No one takes offense at being governed when he is young, nor does he think himself better than his governors, especially if he will enjoy the same privilege when he reaches the required age.

We conclude that from one point of view governors and governed are identical, and from another different. And therefore their education must be the same and also different. For he who would learn to command well must, as men say, first of all learn to obey. As I observed in the first part of this treatise, there is one rule which is for the sake of the rulers and another rule which is for the sake of the ruled; the former is a despotic, the latter a free government. Some commands differ not in the thing commanded, but in the intention with which they are imposed. Wherefore, many apparently menial offices are an honor to the free youth by whom they are performed; for actions do not differ as honorable or dishonorable in themselves so much as in the end and intention of them. But since we say that the virtue of the citizen and ruler is the same as that of the good man, and that the same person must first be a subject and then a ruler, the legislator has to see that they become good men, and by what means this may be accomplished, and what is the end of the perfect life.

PART TWO

Hellenistic and Medieval Philosophy

Epicurus: Pleasure and Life's Aim
From *Letter to Menoeceus* (complete)

Born on the Greek island of Samos, Epicurus (341–271 BCE) developed a view of ethics that has been echoed by a variety of moral philosophers down through the centuries to the present. According to Epicurus, the standard of right and wrong conduct is plea-sure and the absence of pain. In his words, "We recognize pleasure as the first good, being natural to us, and it is from pleasure that we begin every choice and avoidance. It is also to pleasure that we return, using it as the standard by which we judge every good." The selection below, one of the few remaining writings of his, discusses the emotional and physical pains we have, including fear of the gods and death, and how we can combat these pains by pursuing desires that are both natural and necessary. His recommendation is that we should seek pleasure through moderation.

DO NOT FEAR THE GODS OR DEATH

Let no one delay studying philosophy while he is young, and when he is old let him not become weary of the study; for no person can ever find the time unsuitable or too late to study the health of his mind. He who asserts either that it is not yet time to philosophize, or that the hour is passed, is like a man who should say that the time is not yet come to be happy, or that it is too late. Both young and old should study philosophy, so that when old one may be young in good things through the pleas-ing recollection of the past, and when young one may be both young and old at the same time because of one's absence of fear for the future. It is right then for a person to consider the things which produce happiness, since, if happiness is present, we have everything, and when it is absent, we do everything with a view to possess it.

Source: Epicurus, *Letter to Menoeceus*, in Diogenes Laertius, *Lives of Eminent Philosophers.*

I would have you do and practice these things that I have constantly recommended to you, considering them to be the elements of the good life. First of all, believe that God is a being that is eternal and happy, as the common opinion of the world says about God. Do not attach to your idea of him anything which is inconsistent with eternality or with happiness. Understand that he possesses everything that is able to preserve this happiness in him, in to eternality. We know there are Gods, since we have distinct knowledge of them. But they are not of the nature that people in general attribute to them, and they do not respect them in a way that agrees with the ideas that they entertain of them. A person is not irreverent for rejecting the Gods believed in by the masses, but, rather, is irreverent for applying to the Gods the opinions entertained of them by the masses. The views of the masses about the Gods are not grounded in sensation, but rather in false opinions—particularly the false view that the Gods are responsible for the greatest evils which happen to wicked people, and the benefits which are conferred on the good. They connect all their ideas of the Gods with human virtues, and everything that is different from human qualities they then regard as incompatible with the divine nature.

Accustom yourself to think that death is a matter that should not concern us. For all good and all evil depend on sensation, and death is only the removal of sensation. Accordingly, the correct view of the fact that death is no concern of ours makes the mortality of life pleasant to us, not because it gives us limitless time, but because it relieves us of the longing for immortality. There is nothing terrible in living to a person who rightly understands that there is nothing terrible in ceasing to live. Only a foolish person says that he fears death, not because it will cause him pain when it occurs, but because it pains him while he anticipates it. It is quite absurd if something that is not distressful when present should distress a person when it is only expected. Therefore, death, the most dreadful of all evils, is nothing to us since, when we exist, death is not present to us; and when death is present we have no existence. It is no concern then either of the living or of the dead, since, to the living, death has no existence, and the dead have no existence themselves. Sometimes people flee from death as the greatest of evils, yet other times they wish for it as a rest from the evils in life. But the wise person neither desires to end life nor fears the end of life. Just as he chooses food, not preferring the greatest amount, but the most enjoyable, so too, he enjoys his time, not measuring it as to whether it is of the greatest length, but as to whether it is most enjoyable.

He is foolish who instructs a young person to live well, and an old person to die well, not only because of the constantly delightful nature of life itself, but also because the care to live well is identical with the care to die well. Still worse is the person who says "It is best to experience life, but then when born to pass quickly into the shades below." For if this really is his opinion why did he not just end his life since it was easily in his power to do so? But if he was joking, then he was talking foolishly about a situation when he should not have done so. We must remember that the future is not our own, nor, on the other hand, is it wholly not our own. That is, we can never altogether await the future with a feeling of certainty that it will be, nor altogether despair of it as what will never be.

THE NATURE OF PLEASURE

We must recognize that some of our desires are natural, and some empty. Of the natural desires some are necessary, and some merely natural. Of the necessary desires, some are necessary for happiness, others for the removal of bodily troubles, and still others for living itself. A proper view of these things will refer all choice and avoidance to the health of the body and the freedom from uneasiness of the mind. This is the goal of the good life. It is for the sake of this that we do everything, wishing to avoid grief and fear. Once we accomplish this, the storm of the mind is put to an end, and the living creature will not need to keep searching to fill a deficiency or seek something different from that by which will perfect the good of the mind and body. We have need of pleasure when we feel pain, because pleasure is not present; but when we do not feel pain, then we have no need of pleasure.

Thus, we affirm that pleasure is the beginning and end of the good life. We recognize pleasure as the first good, being natural to us, and it is from pleasure that we begin every choice and avoidance. It is also to pleasure that we return, using it as the standard by which we judge every good.

While pleasure is the first good and natural with us, we do not choose every pleasure, but at times we pass over many pleasures when any difficulty is likely to result from them. Also we think many pains are better than pleasures, when a greater pleasure will follow pains by enduring them for a time. Though every pleasure is a good on account of its own nature, it does not follow that every pleasure is worthy of being chosen. Similarly while every pain is an evil, every pain must not be avoided. It is best to measure these things by comparing the advantages with the disadvantages. At times we may feel the good as an evil, and at times, on the contrary, we may feel the evil as good.

We think that contentment is a good thing. This is not so that we may only have a little, but so that if we do not have much we may make use of a little. We are thus persuaded that the people who enjoy luxury most completely are the ones best able to do without them. Everything natural is easily provided, and what is useless is difficult to obtain. Simple flavors give as much pleasure as costly ones when we remove everything that can give painful feelings of need. Bread and water give the most extreme pleasure when anyone in need eats them. To accustom oneself to a simple and inexpensive diet is a great ingredient in the perfecting of health, and makes a person free from hesitation with respect to the necessary activities of life. On certain occasions when we come by more luxurious things, it puts us in a better disposition towards them, and makes us fearless of fortune.

When we say that pleasure is the chief good, we are not speaking of the pleasures of the degenerate person, or those which involve sensual enjoyment—as some think who are ignorant or oppose our opinions, or else distort them. Rather, we mean the freedom of pain from the body and turmoil from the mind. Life is not made pleasant through continued drinking and partying, or sexual encounters, or feasts of fish and other such things as a costly banquet offers. It is sober contemplation which examines into the reasons for all choice and avoidance, and which chases away vain opinions from which the greater part of the confusion arises which troubles the mind.

The beginning and the greatest good of all these things is prudence, and so prudence is something more valuable than even philosophy. All the other virtues spring from prudence, teaching us that it is not possible to live pleasantly unless one also lives prudently, and honorably, and justly. One cannot live prudently, and honestly, and justly, without living pleasantly since the virtues are associated with living agreeably, and living agreeably is inseparable from the virtues. Who do you think is better than the prudent person that has proper opinions respecting the Gods, and is utterly fearless with respect to death, and has properly contemplated the end of nature? The prudent person understands that the chief good is easily perfected and easily provided. He knows that the greatest evil lasts but a short period, and causes but brief pain.

The prudent person also has no belief in necessity or fate, which is set up by some as the mistress of all things. Rather, the prudent person ascribes some things to fortune and some to ourselves, since necessity is an irresponsible power and unstable, while our own will is free. In our case, this freedom constitutes a responsibility which makes us meet with blame and praise. It would be better to follow the fables about the Gods than to be a slave to the necessity of the natural philosopher. Fables, at least, give us a sketch of how we can prevent the wrath of God by paying him honor; but the other presents us with a necessity that is unalterable. The prudent person does not think that necessity is a goddess, as the generality esteem her, for nothing is done at random by a God. Nor does he think that necessity is an erratic cause, or that good and evil are given to us to make us live happily, but that the principles of great goods or great evils are supplied by her; it is better to be unsuccessful when acting with reason, than to be successful but acting unreasonably; for those actions that are judged to be the best, are properly done through reason.

Study these precepts, and those which are similar to them, by all means day and night, pondering on them by yourself, and discussing them with anyone like yourself. You will never be disturbed either when sleeping or awake, but you will live like a God among humans. For a person living with immortal blessings is in no respect like a mortal being.

Lucretius: The Mind as Body
From On the Nature of Things

Roman philosopher Lucretius (ca. 94–55 BCE) is the author of a philosophical poem titled On the Nature of Things, *which is an elaboration of earlier ideas of nature, especially the theory taught by Democritus. Defending the view that we now call "monistic materialism," Lucretius begins by describing how our senses deceive us*

Source: Lucretius, *On the Nature of Things*, Books 1–3.

when we see a solid white mass on a distant hill: "Often the fleecy flock cropping the glad pasture on a hill creep on whither each is called and tempted by the grass bejeweled with fresh dew, and the lambs fed full gambol and butt playfully; yet all this seems blurred to us afar, and to lie like a white mass on a green hill." What appears to be a solid white mass from a distance turns out to be a flock of sheep. Lucretius uses this analogy of the flock of sheep to argue that everything in nature is similarly composed of small particles. Like Democritus, Lucretius held that everything is composed of tiny bits of solid matter, called "atoms." These tiny atoms are, he said, invisible, eternal, and indestructible, and come in different sizes and shapes. Everything can be explained by the movement and arrangement of these atoms. Atoms not only account for the nature of physical things but also explain the operation of our senses and feelings, as well as the functioning of our minds. Although Democritus and Lucretius offered no scientific proof of this atomic theory, which they arrived at intuitively, in time renowned scientists such as Isaac Newton accepted this theory as the basis of the science of physics. Contemporary scientists have modified this atomic theory, but they have nevertheless preserved it in principle.

BODIES AND THE VOID

All nature then, as it exists by itself, is founded on two things; there are bodies and there is void in which these bodies are placed and through which they move about. For that body exists by itself the general feeling of mankind declares; and unless at the very first belief in this be firmly grounded, there will be nothing to which we can appeal on hidden things in order to prove anything by reasoning of mind. Then again, if room and space which we call void did not exist, bodies could not be placed anywhere nor move about at all to any side; . . . Therefore beside void and bodies no third nature taken by itself can be left in the number of things, either such as to fall at any time under the ken of our senses or such as anyone can grasp by the reason of his mind. . . .

First of all then since there has been found to exist a two-fold and widely dissimilar nature of two things, that is to say of body and of place in which things severally go on, each of the two must exist for and by itself and quite un-mixed. For wherever there is empty space which we call void, there body is not; wherever again body maintains itself, there empty void no wise exists. First bodies therefore are solid and without void . . . These can neither be broken in pieces by the stroke of blows from without nor have their texture undone by aught piercing to their core nor give way before any other kind of assault; as we have proved to you a little before. For without void nothing seems to admit of being crushed in or broken up or split in two by cutting, or of taking in wet or permeating cold or penetrating fire, by which all things are destroyed. And the more anything contains within it of void, the more thoroughly it gives way to the assault of these things. Therefore if first bodies are as I have shown solid and without void, they must be everlasting. Again unless matter had been eternal, all things before this would have utterly returned to nothing and whatever things we see would have been born anew from nothing. But since I have proved above that nothing can be produced from nothing, and that what is begotten cannot be recalled to nothing, first-beginnings must be of an imperishable body into which all things can be dissolved at their last hour, that there may be a supply of matter for the reproduction of things. Therefore first-beginnings are of solid singleness, and in no other way can they have been preserved through ages during infinite time past in order to reproduce things.

But since I have taught that most solid bodies of matter fly about forever unvanquished through all time, mark now, let us unfold whether there is or is not any limit to their sum; likewise let us clearly see whether that which has been found to be void, or room and space, in which things severally go on, is all of it altogether finite or stretches without limits and to an unfathomable depth.

Well then the existing universe is bounded in none of its dimensions; for then it must have had an outside. Again it is seen that there can be an outside of nothing, unless there be something beyond to bound it, so that that is seen, farther than which the nature of this our sense does not follow the thing. Now since we must admit that there is nothing outside the sum, it has no outside, and therefore is without end and limit. And it matters not in which of its regions you take your stand; so invariably, whatever position any one has taken up, he leaves the universe just as infinite as before in all directions. Again if for the moment all existing space be held to be bounded, supposing a man runs forward to its outside borders, and stands on the utmost verge and then throws a winged javelin, do you choose that when hurled with vigorous force it, shall advance to the point to which it has been sent and fly to a distance, or do you decide that something can get in its way and stop it? For you must admit and adopt one of the two suppositions; either of which shuts you out from all escape and compels you to grant that the universe stretches without end.

THE "SWERVE" AS ATOMS MOVE IN SPACE: THE RANDOM CAUSE OF ALL THINGS

This point too herein we wish you to apprehend: when bodies are borne downwards sheer through void by their own weights, at quite uncertain times and uncertain spots they push themselves a little from their course: you just and only just can call it a change of inclination. If they were not used to swerve, they would all fall down, like drops of rain, through the deep void, and no clashing would have been begotten nor blow produced among the first-beginnings: thus nature never would have produced anything.

But if haply any one believes that heavier bodies, as they are carried more quickly sheer through space, can fall from above on the lighter and so beget blows able to produce begetting motions, he goes most widely astray from true reason. For whenever bodies fall through water and thin air, they must quicken their descents in proportion to their weights, because the body of water and subtle nature of air cannot retard everything in equal degree, but more readily give way, overpowered by the heavier: on the other hand empty void cannot offer resistance to anything in any direction at any time, but must, as its nature craves, continually give way; and for this reason all things must be moved and borne along with equal velocity though of unequal weights through the unresisting void. Therefore heavier things will never be able to fall from above on lighter nor of themselves to beget blows sufficient to produce the varied motions by which nature carries on things. Wherefore again and again I say bodies must swerve a little; and yet not more than the least possible—lest we be found to be imagining oblique motions and this the reality should refute. For this we see to be plain and evident, that weights, so far as in them is, cannot travel obliquely, when they fall from above, at least so far as you can perceive; but that nothing swerves in any case from the straight course, who is there that can perceive? . . .

And herein you need not wonder at this, that though the first-beginnings of things are all in motion, yet the sum is seen to rest in supreme repose, unless where a thing exhibits motions with its individual body. For all the nature of first things lies far away from our senses beneath their ken; and therefore since they are themselves beyond what you can see, they must withdraw from sight their motion as well; and the more so that the things which we can see, do yet often conceal their motions when a great distance off. Thus often the woolly flocks as they crop the glad pastures on a hill, creep on whither the grass jewelled with fresh dew summons and invites each, and the lambs fed to the full gambol and playfully butt; all which objects appear to us from a distance to be blended together and to rest like a white spot on a green hill. . . .

Now mark and next in order apprehend of what kind and how widely differing in their forms are the beginnings of all things, how varied by manifold diversities of shape; not that a scanty number are possessed of a like form, but because as a rule they do not all resemble one the other. . . . Again things which look to us hard and dense must consist of particles more hooked together, and be held in union because welded all through with branch-like elements. In this class first of all diamond stones stand in foremost line inured to despise blows, and stout blocks of basalt and the strength of hard iron and brass bolts which scream out as they hold fast to their staples. . . .

MATTER: THE ORIGIN OF SENSATION AND THOUGHT

Then again what is that which strikes your mind, affects that mind and constrains it to give utterance to many different thoughts, to save you from believing that the sensible is begotten out of senseless things? Sure enough it is because stones and wood and earth however mixed together are yet unable to produce vital sense. This therefore it will be well to remember herein, that I do not assert that the sensible and sensations are forthwith begotten out of all elements without exception which produce things; but that it is of great moment first how minute the particles are which make up the sensible thing and then what shape they possess and what in short they are in their motions, arrangements and positions. . . .

Above all senses cannot exist in any body before the nature itself of the living thing has been begotten, because sure enough the matter remains scattered about in air, rivers, earth, and things produced from earth, and has not met together and combined in appropriate fashion the vital motions by which the all-discerning senses are kindled into action in each living thing.

Again a blow more severe than its nature can endure, prostrates at once any living thing and goes on to stun all the senses of body and mind. For the positions of the first-beginnings are broken up and the vital motions entirely stopped, until the matter, disordered by the shock through the whole frame, unties from the body the vital fastenings of the soul and scatters it abroad and forces it out through all the pores. For what more can we suppose the infliction of a blow can do, than shake from their place and break up the union of the several elements?

In the first place we see that round in all directions, about, above, and underneath, throughout the universe there is no bound. . . .

Again when much matter is at hand, when room is there and there is no thing, no cause to hinder, things sure enough must go on and be completed. Well then if on the one hand there is so great a store of seeds as the whole life of living creatures cannot reckon up, and if the same force and nature abide in them and have the power to throw the seeds of things together into their several places in the same way as they are thrown together into our world, you must admit that in other parts of space there are other earths and various races of men and kinds of wild beasts.

And now since I have shown what-like the beginnings of all things are and how diverse with varied shapes as they fly spontaneously driven on in everlasting motion, and how all things can be severally produced out of these, next after these questions the nature of the mind and soul should I think be cleared up by my verses.

THE NATURE OF THE HUMAN MIND

First then I say that the mind which we often call the understanding, in which dwells the directing and governing principle of life, is no less part of the man, than hand and foot and eyes are parts of the whole living creature. . . . Now that you may know that the soul as well is in the limbs and that the body is not wont to have sense by any harmony, this is a main proof: when much of the body has been taken away, still life often stays in the limbs. . . .

Now I assert that the mind and the soul are kept together in close union and make up a single nature, but that the directing principle which we call mind and understanding, is the head so to speak and reigns paramount in the whole body. It has a fixed seat in the middle region of the breast: here throb fear and apprehension, about these spots dwell soothing joys; therefore here is the understanding or mind. All the rest of the soul disseminated through the whole body obeys and moves at the will and inclination of the mind. It by itself alone knows for itself, rejoices for itself, at times when the impression does not move either soul or body together with it. And as when some part of us, the head or the eye, suffers from an attack of pain, we do not feel the anguish at the same time over the whole body, thus the mind sometimes suffers pain by itself or is inspirited with joy, when all the rest of the soul throughout the limbs and frame is stirred by no novel sensation. . . .

This same principle teaches that the nature of the mind and soul is bodily; for when it is seen to push the limbs, rouse the body from sleep, and alter the countenance and guide and turn about the whole man, and when we see that none of these effects can take place without touch nor touch without body, must we not admit that the mind and the soul are of a bodily nature? . . .

I will now go on to explain in my verses of what kind of body the mind consists and out of what it is formed. First of all I say that it is extremely fine and formed of exceedingly minute bodies. That this is so you may, if you please to attend, clearly perceive from what follows: nothing that is seen takes place with a velocity equal to that of the mind when it starts some suggestion and actually sets it going; the mind therefore is stirred with greater rapidity than any of the things whose nature stands out visible to sight. . . . Since then the nature of the mind has been found to be eminently easy to move, it must consist of bodies exceedingly small, smooth, and round. The knowledge of which fact, my good friend, will on many accounts prove useful and be serviceable to you. The following fact too likewise demonstrates how fine the texture is of which its nature is composed, and how small the room is in which it can be contained, could it only be collected into one mass: soon as the untroubled sleep of death has gotten hold of a man and the nature of the mind and soul has withdrawn, you can perceive then no diminution of the entire body either in appearance or weight: death makes all good save the vital sense and heat. Therefore the whole soul must consist of very small seeds and be inwoven through veins and flesh and sinews; inasmuch as, after it has all withdrawn from the whole body, the exterior contour of the limbs preserves itself entire and not a tittle of the weight is lost. Just in the same way when the flavor of wine is gone or when the delicious aroma of a perfume has been dispersed into the air or when the savor has left some body, yet the thing itself does not therefore look smaller to the eye. . . .

Again we perceive that the mind is begotten along with the body and grows up together with it and becomes old along with it. For even as children go about with a tottering and weakly body, so slender sagacity of mind follows along with it; then when their life has reached the maturity of confirmed strength, the judgment too is greater and the Power of the mind more developed. Afterwards when the body has been shattered by the mastering might of time and the frame has drooped with its forces dulled, then the intellect halts, the tongue dotes, the mind gives way, all faculties fail and are found wanting at the same time. It naturally follows then that the whole nature of the soul is dissolved, like smoke, into the high air; since we see it is begotten along with the body and grows up along with it and, as I have shown, breaks down at the same time worn out with age.

Epictetus: Resigning Oneself to Fate
From *Handbook*

Born as a slave in what is now the country of Turkey, Epictetus (ca. 60–120 CE) was a prominent teacher of Stoic philosophy in the early days of the Roman Empire. According to the Stoics, all events that take place in the universe are determined by a larger cosmic force, which they variously referred to as fate, destiny, God, or Logos. Accordingly, much of what happens in our personal lives is also determined by fate, and perhaps the only thing that we have control over is whether we gracefully accept what is fated for us. Epictetus makes this point in his Handbook, *and argues that human unhappiness owes to our vain attempts to control things beyond our power. If we have any hope of being happy in life, we must resign ourselves to fate. Epictetus recognizes that it is a difficult task for any of us to abandon notions of human freedom. To psychologically help us accept our respective fates, he offers a series of potent and sometimes shocking metaphors.*

1. Some things are in our control and others not. Things in our control are opinion, pursuit, desire, aversion, and, in a word, whatever are our own actions. Things not in our control are body, property, reputation, command, and, in one word, whatever are not our own actions.

   The things in our control are by nature free, unrestrained, unhindered; but those not in our control are weak, slavish, restrained, belonging to others. Remember, then, that if you suppose that things which are slavish by nature are also free, and that what belongs to others is your own, then you will be hindered. You will lament, you will be disturbed, and you will find fault both with gods and men. But if you suppose that only to be your own which *is* your own, and what belongs to others such as it really is, then no one will ever compel you or restrain you. Further, you will find fault with no one or accuse no one. You will do nothing against your will. No one will hurt you, you will have no enemies, and you will not be harmed.

   Aiming therefore at such great things, remember that you must not allow yourself to be carried, even with a slight tendency, towards the attainment of lesser things. Instead, you must entirely quit some things and for the present postpone the rest. But if you would both have these great things, along with power and riches, then you will not gain even the latter, because you aim at the former too: but you will absolutely fail of the former, by which alone happiness and freedom are achieved.

   Work, therefore to be able to say to every harsh appearance, "You are but an appearance, and not absolutely the thing you appear to be." And then examine it by those rules which you have, and first, and chiefly, by this: whether it concerns the things which are in our own control, or those

Source: Epictetus, *The Enchiridion* (ca. 135 CE), Sections 1–15.

which are not; and, if it concerns anything not in our control, be prepared to say that it is nothing to you.

2. Remember that following desire promises the attainment of that of which you are desirous; and aversion promises the avoiding of that to which you are averse. However, he who fails to obtain the object of his desire is disappointed, and he who incurs the object of his aversion wretched. If, then, you confine your aversion to those objects only which are contrary to the natural use of your faculties, which you have in your own control, you will never incur anything to which you are averse. But if you are averse to sickness, or death, or poverty, you will be wretched. Remove aversion, then, from all things that are not in our control, and transfer it to things contrary to the nature of what is in our control. But, for the present, totally suppress desire: for, if you desire any of the things which are not in your own control, you must necessarily be disappointed; and of those which are, and which it would be laudable to desire, nothing is yet in your possession. Use only the appropriate actions of pursuit and avoidance; and even these lightly, and with gentleness and reservation.

3. With regard to whatever objects give you delight, are useful, or are deeply loved, remember to tell yourself of *what general nature they are,* beginning from the most insignificant things. If, for example, you are fond of a specific ceramic cup, remind yourself that it is only ceramic cups in general of which you are fond. Then, if it breaks, you will not be disturbed. If you kiss your child, or your wife, say that you only kiss things which are human, and thus you will not be disturbed if either of them dies.

4. When you are going about any action, remind yourself what nature the action is. If you are going to bathe, picture to yourself the things which usually happen in the bath: some people splash the water, some push, some use abusive language, and others steal. Thus you will more safely go about this action if you say to yourself, "I will now go bathe, and keep my own mind in a state conformable to nature." And in the same manner with regard to every other action. For thus, if any hindrance arises in bathing, you will have it ready to say, "It was not only to bathe that I desired, but to keep my mind in a state conformable to nature; and I will not keep it if I am bothered at things that happen."

5. Men are disturbed, not by things, but by the principles and notions which they form concerning things. Death, for instance, is not terrible, else it would have appeared so to Socrates. But the terror consists in our notion of death that it is terrible. When therefore we are hindered, or disturbed, or grieved, let us never attribute it to others, but to ourselves; that is, to our own principles. An uninstructed person will lay the fault of his own bad condition upon others. Someone just starting instruction will lay the fault on himself. Some[one] who is perfectly instructed will place blame neither on others nor on himself.

6. Don't be prideful with any excellence that is not your own. If a horse should be prideful and say, "I am handsome," it would be supportable. But when you are prideful, and say, "I have a handsome horse," know that you are proud of what is, in fact, only the good of the horse. What, then, is your

own? Only your reaction to the appearances of things. Thus, when you behave conformably to nature in reaction to how things appear, you will be proud with reason; for you will take pride in some good of your own.

7. Consider when, on a voyage, your ship is anchored; if you go on shore to get water you may along the way amuse yourself with picking up a shell-fish, or an onion. However, your thoughts and continual attention ought to be bent towards the ship, waiting for the captain to call on board; you must then immediately leave all these things, otherwise you will be thrown into the ship, bound neck and feet like a sheep. So it is with life. If, instead of an onion or a shellfish, you are given a wife or child, that is fine. But if the captain calls, you must run to the ship, leaving them, and regarding none of them. But if you are old, never go far from the ship: lest, when you are called, you should be unable to come in time.

8. Don't demand that things happen as you wish, but wish that they happen as they *do* happen, and you will go on well.

9. Sickness is a hindrance to the body, but not to your ability to choose, unless that is your choice. Lameness is a hindrance to the leg, but not to your ability to choose. Say this to yourself with regard to everything that happens, then you will see such obstacles as hindrances to something else, but not to yourself.

10. With every accident, ask yourself what abilities you have for making a proper use of it. If you see an attractive person, you will find that self-restraint is the ability you have against your desire. If you are in pain, you will find fortitude. If you hear unpleasant language, you will find patience. And thus habituated, the appearances of things will not hurry you away along with them.

11. Never say of anything, "I have lost it"; but, "I have returned it." Is your child dead? It is returned. Is your wife dead? She is returned. Is your estate taken away? Well, and is not that likewise returned? "But he who took it away is a bad man." What difference is it to you who the giver assigns to take it back? While he gives it to you to possess, take care of it; but don't view it as your own, just as travelers view a hotel.

12. If you want to improve, reject such reasonings as these: "If I neglect my affairs, I'll have no income; if I don't correct my servant, he will be bad." For it is better to die with hunger, exempt from grief and fear, than to live in affluence with perturbation; and it is better your servant should be bad, than you unhappy.

    Begin therefore from little things. Is a little oil spilt? A little wine stolen? Say to yourself, "This is the price paid for being without passion, for tranquility, and nothing is to be had for nothing." When you call your servant, it is possible that he may not come; or, if he does, he may not do what you want. But he is by no means of such importance that it should be in his power to give you any disturbance.

13. If you want to improve, be content to be thought foolish and stupid with regard to external things. Don't wish to be thought to know anything; and even if you appear to be somebody important to others, distrust yourself. For, it is difficult to both keep your faculty of choice in a state conformable

to nature, and at the same time acquire external things. But while you are careful about the one, you must of necessity neglect the other.

14. If you wish your children, and your wife, and your friends to live forever, you are stupid; for you wish to be in control of things which you cannot, you wish for things that belong to others to be your own. So likewise, if you wish your servant to be without fault, you are a fool; for you wish vice not to be vice, but something else. But, if you wish to have your desires undisappointed, this is in your own control. Exercise, therefore, what is in your control. He is the master of every other person who is able to confer or remove whatever that person wishes either to have or to avoid. Whoever, then, would be free, let him wish nothing, let him decline nothing, which depends on others else he must necessarily be a slave.

15. Remember that you must behave in life as at a dinner party. Is anything brought around to you? Put out your hand and take your share with moderation. Does it pass by you? Don't stop it. Is it not yet come? Don't stretch your desire towards it, but wait till it reaches you. Do this with regard to children, to a wife, to public posts, to riches, and you will eventually be a worthy partner of the feasts of the gods. And if you don't even take the things which are set before you, but are able even to reject them, then you will not only be a partner at the feasts of the gods, but also of their empire. For, by doing this, Diogenes, Heraclitus and others like them, deservedly became, and were called, divine.

READING 4

Sextus Empiricus: The Goals and Methods of Skepticism
From Outlines of Pyrrhonism

Sextus Empiricus (ca. 200 CE) was a physician and philosopher during the Roman Empire, whose writings are the most complete surviving representation of the ancient Greek skeptical tradition, which emphasizes our inability to know anything. In his Outlines of Pyrrhonism, *Sextus Empiricus explains that skeptics do not doubt just for the sake of doubting. Instead, the goal is to achieve a kind of psychological tranquility when we set aside our dogmatic views of everything—including metaphysics, religion, and morality. He explains a skeptical method of argumentation called the "ten methods of skepticism," by which we can come to doubt every subject of inquiry. The underlying reasoning for most of the ten methods is that there are vastly different ways of perceiving things, and we cannot prefer any one of these ways to another.*

Source: Sextus Empiricus, *Outlines of Pyrrhonism*, Book 1.

DEFINITION AND MEANING OF SKEPTICISM

The Principal Differences between Philosophers

1. It is probable that those who seek after anything whatever, will either find it as they continue the search, will deny that it can be found and confess it to be out of reach, or will go on seeking it. Accordingly, some have said regarding the things sought in philosophy that they have found the truth, while others have declared it impossible to find, and still others continue to seek it. Those who think that they have found it are those who are especially called Dogmatists, as for example, the Schools of Aristotle and Epicurus, the Stoics and some others. Those who have declared it impossible to find are Clitomachus, Carneades, with their respective followers, and other Academicians. Those who still seek it are the Skeptics. Therefore, it appears reasonable to conclude that the three principal kinds of philosophy are the Dogmatic, the Academic, and the Skeptic. Other writers may suitably examine the first two Schools, but I will here give an outline of the Skeptical School. I must comment in advance, though, that I will not declare absolutely with anything I say that it is exactly as I describe it. Rather, I will state things empirically as they appear to me now.

Ways of Examining Skepticism

2. One way of examining the Skeptical philosophy is called general, and the other particular. The general method is that by which we set forth the character of Skepticism, declaring what its idea is, what its principles are, its method of reasoning, its criterion, and its aim. It also presents the method of doubt, and the way in which we should understand the Skeptical formula, and the distinction between Skepticism and the related Schools of philosophy. The particular method, on the contrary, is that by which we speak against each part of so-called philosophy. Let us then treat Skepticism at first in the general way, beginning our delineation with the terminology of the Skeptical School.

The Definition of the Skeptical School

3. The Skeptical School is also called the "Seeking School," from its spirit of research and examination; the "Suspending School," from the condition of mind in which one is left after the search, in regard to the things that one has examined; and the "Doubting School," either because, as some say, the Skeptics doubt and are seeking in regard to everything, or because they never know whether to deny or affirm. It is also called the Pyrrhonean School, because Pyrrho appears to us the best representative of Skepticism, and is more prominent than all who before him occupied themselves with it.

What Is Skepticism?

4. Skepticism is *an ability to place appearances in opposition to judgments in any way whatever. By balancing reasons that are opposed to each other, we first reach the state*

of suspension of judgment, and afterwards that of tranquility. To clarify, I do not use the word "ability" in any unusual sense, but simply mean that we are able to do something. By "appearances" I mean the things that we sense, as opposed to our judgments about them. The phrase "in any way whatever" may refer either to the word "ability" in its simple sense as I have said, or it may refer to the "placing of appearances in opposition to judgments." For we place appearances in opposition to each other in a variety of ways: appearances to appearances, and judgments to judgments, or appearances to judgments. Also, the phrase "in any way whatever" may refer to "appearances and judgments," so that we need not ask how appearances appear, or how thoughts are judged; rather, we should understand these things in a simple sense. By "reasons opposed to each other," I do not in any way mean that they deny or affirm anything, but simply that they offset each other. By "balancing" I mean equally likely and equally unlikely, so that the opposing reasons do not surpass each other in likelihood. "Suspension of judgment" means holding back opinion so that we neither deny nor affirm anything. "Tranquility" is repose and calmness of mind. I will later explain how tranquility accompanies suspension of judgment when I speak about the aim of skepticism.

The Skeptic

5. The notion of a "Pyrrhonean philosopher" follows from the above definition of the Skeptical School. He is the one who possesses the ability that I have described.

The Primary Principle of Skepticism

6. Skepticism arose in the beginning from the hope of attaining tranquility. People of the greatest intelligence were perplexed by the contradiction of various things, and being at a loss what to believe, they began to question what things are true, and what false. They then hoped to attain tranquility through some solution. The primary principle of Skepticism, then, is to oppose every argument by one of equal weight, and in this way we finally reach the position where we have no dogmas.

Does the Skeptic Dogmatize?

7. I say that the Skeptic does not dogmatize. I do not say this with regard to the popular meaning of the word "dogma," namely, that it is a dogma to assert to anything rather than another. For even the Skeptic assents to feelings that are a necessary result of sensation; for example, when he is warm or cold, he cannot say that he thinks he is not warm or cold. Rather, when I say that the Skeptic does not dogmatize, I take the word "dogma" to mean the acceptance of any opinion in regard to the undetectable things investigated by science. For the Pyrrhonean assents to nothing that is undetectable.

Furthermore, the Skeptic does not dogmatize even when he utters the skeptical formula in regard to things that are undetectable, such as "Nothing is truer than another thing," or "I decide nothing," or any of the others which I will speak about later. For the dogmatist maintains that the things about which he dogmatizes actually exist in themselves. The Skeptic, however, does not regard these Skeptical formulas in any absolute sense, for he assumes that the saying "All is false" includes its own falsehood. Similarly, the saying "Nothing is true" and "Nothing is truer than another thing" implies that they are no truer than other things, and thus they cancel themselves out. We say the same also in regard to the other Skeptical expressions. In short, if he who dogmatizes assumes the truth about that which he dogmatizes, the Skeptic, on the contrary, expresses his sayings in a way that applies to the utterances themselves. Thus, we cannot say that the Skeptic dogmatizes in saying these things. The principal thing in uttering these formulas is that he says what appears to him, and communicates his own feelings in an unprejudiced way, without asserting anything in regard to external objects.

Is Skepticism a System?

8. I respond in a similar way if I am asked whether Skepticism is a sect or not. If the word "system" is defined as meaning a body of persons who hold dogmas which are in conformity with each other, and also with appearances, and dogma means an assent to anything that is undetectable, then I reply that we have no sect. If, however, one means by sect, a school which follows a certain line of reasoning based on appearances, and that reasoning shows how it is possible to apparently live rightly (not understanding "rightly" as referring to virtue only, but in a broader sense); if, also, it leads one to be able to suspend judgment, then I reply that we have a system. For we follow a certain kind of reasoning which is based upon appearances, and which shows us how to live according to the habits, laws, and teachings of our country, and our own feelings.

Does the Skeptic Study Natural Science?

9. I reply similarly to the question whether the Skeptic should study natural science. For we do not study natural science in order to express ourselves with confidence regarding any of the dogmas that it teaches, but we take it up in order to be able to meet every argument by one of equal weight, and also for the sake of tranquility. In the same way we study the logical and ethical part of so-called philosophy.

Do the Skeptics Deny Appearances?

10. Those who say that the Skeptics deny appearances are ignorant of our teachings. For as I said before, we do not deny the sensations which we think we have, and which lead us to assent involuntarily to them; we accept that we have appearances. When we ask whether the object is such as it appears to be, we concede that it appears so and so; however, while we do not question the phenomenon, we do question what is asserted about the phenomenon, and that

is different from doubting the phenomenon itself. For example, it appears to us that honey is sweet. This we concede, for we experience sweetness through sensation. We doubt, however, whether it is sweet by reason of its essence, which is not a question of the phenomenon, but of that which is asserted of the phenomenon. Should we, however, argue directly against appearances, it is not with the intention of denying their existence, but only to show the rashness of the Dogmatists. For if reasoning is such a deceiver that it snatches away genuine appearances from before our eyes, we should distrust it all the more in regard to things that are undetectable, and thus avoid rashly following it.

The Criterion of Skepticism

11. From what I say about the criterion of the Skeptical School it is evident that we pay careful attention to appearances. The word "criterion" is used in two ways. First, it is understood as a proof of existence or non-existence, in regard to which I will criticize later. Second, when it refers to action, it means the criterion that we follow in life by doing some things and refraining from doing others. It is about this that I will now speak. I say that the criterion of the Skeptical School is appearance, and in calling it so, I mean the image of what appears. This cannot be doubted, since it arises from receptiveness to an involuntary feeling. Hence virtually no one doubts that an object appears to be such and such; but we do question whether it is as it appears.

So, we cannot be entirely inactive with the observances of daily life since we live by following appearances, and in an unprejudiced way. Observance of daily life is of four different kinds. Sometimes it is directed by the guidance of nature, sometimes by the necessity of feelings, sometimes by the tradition of laws and of customs, and sometimes by the teaching of skills. It is directed by the guidance of nature, for by nature we are capable of sensation and thought. It is directed by the necessity of feelings, since hunger leads us to food, and thirst to drink. It is directed by the traditions of laws and customs, since according to them we consider piety a good in daily life, and impiety an evil. It is directed by the teaching of skills, for we are not inactive in the skills we undertake. I say all these things, however, without expressing a decided opinion.

What Is the Aim of Skepticism?

12. It is natural to examine next the aim of the Skeptical School. An aim is the end for which we do anything or think anything. It depends on nothing, or in other words, it is the ultimate objective of things to be desired. We say, then, that the aim of the Skeptic is tranquility in those things which pertain to the opinion, and moderation in the things that life requires of us. In order to attain tranquility, the Skeptic begins to philosophize about the ideas and to understand which are true and which are false. He then faces contradictions of equal weight, and, being unable to judge, he withholds his opinion. As if by fate, while his judgment is in suspension he attains tranquility in regard to matters of opinion. For a person will always be troubled if he holds the opinion that anything is

either good or bad by nature. For when he does not possess those things that seem good to him, he feels tortured by the things which are by nature bad, and pursues those that he thinks to be good. But once he acquires them, he becomes even unhappier through his irrational and excessive excitement, which makes him fear losing them and inclines him to do everything in his power to retain the things that seem good to him. On the other hand, if a person is undecided about things that are good and bad by nature, he will neither seek nor avoid anything eagerly, and is therefore in a state of tranquility.

A story is told about Apelles the painter that applies to the Skeptic. It is said that Apelles was once painting a horse and wished to depict foam in the horse's mouth. When he failed to do so, he gave up and threw a sponge at the picture with which he had wiped the colors from the painting. However, as soon as the sponge touched the picture, it produced an excellent representation of foam. Similarly, Skeptics initially hope to gain tranquility by making judgments about the irregularity between appearances and their thoughts about them. When they are unable to do this, they suspend their judgment. As if by fate, while their judgment is in suspension, tranquility follows, just as a shadow follows a body.

Nevertheless, I do not maintain that the Skeptic is completely undisturbed, since he is disturbed by some things that are inevitable. I confess that sometimes he is cold and thirsty, and that he suffers in these ways. However, in similar circumstances, the ignorant suffer in two ways: first from the feelings themselves, and, second, from the fact that they think these conditions are bad by nature. The Skeptic, by contrast, escapes more easily since he rejects the opinion that anything is in itself bad by nature. Therefore we say that the aim of the Skeptic is tranquility in matters of opinion, and moderation of feeling in those things that are inevitable. Some notable Skeptics have added also suspension of judgment in investigation.

METHODS OF SKEPTICISM

The General Methods of Suspending Judgment

13. Since, as I have said, tranquility follows the suspension of judgment in regard to everything, it is important for me to explain how this suspension of judgment takes place. Generally speaking, it occurs by placing things in opposition to each other. We either place appearances in opposition to appearances, or thoughts in opposition to thoughts, or some combination of these. For example, we place appearances in opposition to appearances when we say that this tower appears round from a distance but square when nearby. Thoughts are in opposition to thoughts when, for example, we take the view that providence exists because of the order in the heavens and oppose it to the fact that there is no providence since good people often suffer while evil people prosper. Thought is placed in opposition to appearances, when, for example, Anaxagoras opposed the fact that snow is white, by saying that snow is frozen water, and, as water is black, snow must also be black.

Likewise we sometimes place the present in opposition to the present, with reasoning similar to the above-mentioned cases. We sometimes also place the present in opposition to the past or the future. For example, when someone proposes an argument to us that we cannot refute, we say to him, "Before the founder of the School to which you belong was born, the argument which you propose had not appeared as a valid argument, but was dormant in nature; so in the same way it is possible that its refutation also exists in nature, but has not yet appeared to us, so that it is not at all necessary for us to agree with an argument that currently seems to be strong." In order to make it clearer to us what we mean by these oppositions, I will proceed to give the Methods through which suspension of judgment is produced. I will not say anything about their validity or their number, because they may be unsound and there may be more than I will enumerate.

The Ten Methods

14. Certain Methods were commonly handed down by the older Skeptics, by means of which suspension of judgment seems to take place. They are ten in number, and are synonymously called "arguments" and "points." They are these: the first is based upon the differences in animals; the second upon the differences in men; the third upon the difference in the constitution of the organs of sense; the fourth upon circumstances; the fifth upon position, distance, and place; the sixth upon mixtures; the seventh upon the quantity and constitution of objects; the eighth upon relation; the ninth upon frequency or rarity of occurrences; the tenth upon systems, customs, laws, mythical beliefs, and dogmatic opinions. I have made this order myself.

These Methods come under three general heads: the standpoint of the judge, the standpoint of the thing judged, and the standpoint of both together. Under the standpoint of the judge come the first four, for the judge is either an animal, or a man, or a sense, and exists under certain circumstances. Under the standpoint of that which is judged, come the seventh and the tenth. Under the one composed of both together, come the fifth and the sixth, the eighth and the ninth. Again, these three divisions are included under the Method of Relation, because that is the most general one. It includes the three special divisions, and these in turn include the ten. We say these things in regard to their probable number . . .

The first Method, I said, is the one based upon the differences in animals, and according to this Method, different animals do not get the same ideas of the same objects through the senses. This we conclude from the different origin of the animals, and also from the difference in the constitutions of their bodies.

In regard to the difference in origin, some animals originate without mixture of the sexes, while others originate through sexual intercourse. Of those which originate without intercourse of the sexes, some come from fire, as the little animals which appear in chimneys, others from stagnant water, as mosquitoes, others from fermented wine, as the stinging ants, others from the earth, others from the mud, like frogs, others from slime, as worms, others from donkeys, as beetles, others from cabbage, as caterpillars, others from fruit, as the gall insect from the wild figs, others from putrefied animals, as bees from bulls, and wasps from horses. Again, of those originating from intercourse of the sexes, some come from animals of the same kind, as in most cases, and others from those of different kinds, as mules. Again, of animals in general, some are born alive, as humans, others from eggs, as birds, and others are born a lump of flesh, as bears. It is probable therefore, that the inequalities and differences in origin cause great opposition in the animals, and the result is incompatibility, discord, and conflict between the sensations of the different animals.

Again, the differences in the principal parts of the body, especially in those fixed by nature to judge and to perceive, may cause the greatest differences in their ideas of objects, according to the differences in the animals themselves. For example, those who are jaundiced call that yellow which appears to us white, and those who have bloodshot eyes call it blood-red. Accordingly, as some animals have yellow eyes, and others bloodshot ones, and still others whitish ones, and others eyes of other colors, it is probable that they have a different perception of colors. Furthermore, when we look steadily at the sun for a long time, and then look down at a book, the letters seem to us gold colored, and dance around. Now, some animals have by nature a luster in their eyes, and these emit a fine and sparkling light so that they see at night, and we may reasonably suppose that external things do not appear the same to them as to us.

Jugglers by lightly rubbing the wick of the lamp with metal rust, or with the dark yellow fluid of the sepia, make those who are present appear now copper-colored and now black, according to the amount of the mixture used. If this is so, it is reasonable to suppose that because of the mixture of different fluids in the eyes of animals, their ideas of objects would be different. Furthermore, when we press the eye on the side, the figures, forms and sizes of things seen appear elongated and narrow. It is therefore probable that animals which have the pupil oblique and long, as goats, cats, and similar animals, have ideas different from those of the animals which have a round pupil. Mirrors, according to their different construction, sometimes show the external object smaller than reality, as concave ones, and sometimes long and narrow, as the convex ones do; others show the head of the one looking into it down, and the feet up. As some of the vessels around the eye fall entirely outside the eye, on account of their protuberance, while others are more sunken, and still others are placed in an even surface, it is probable that for this reason also the ideas vary, and dogs, fishes, lions, men, and grasshoppers do not see the same things, either of the same size, or of similar form, but according to the impression on the organ of sight of each animal respectively.

The same thing is true in regard to the other senses. For how can it be said that shellfish, birds of prey, animals covered with spines, those with feathers and those with scales would be affected in the same way by the sense of touch? And how can the sense of hearing perceive alike in animals which have the narrowest auditory passages, and in those that are furnished with the widest, or in those with hairy ears and those with smooth ones? For even humans bear differently when we partially stop up the ears, from what we do when we use them naturally. The sense of smell also varies according to differences in animals, since even our sense of smell is affected when we catch a cold and the phlegm is too abundant, and also when parts around our head are flooded with too much blood, for we then avoid odors that seem agreeable to others, and feel as if we were injured by them. Since also some of the animals are moist by nature and full of secretions, and others are very full of blood, and still others have either yellow or black bile prevalent and abundant, it is reasonable to think that odorous things appear different to each one of them.

It is the same with regard to things of taste, since some animals have the tongue rough and dry and others very moist. We too, when we have a dry tongue in fever, think that whatever we take is gritty, bad tasting, or bitter; and this we experience because of the varying degrees of the humors that are said to be in us. Since, then, different animals have different organs for taste, and a greater or less amount of the various humors, it may well be that they form different ideas of the same objects as regards their taste.

It is natural to suppose that external objects are regarded differently according to the different constitution of the animals which perceive them. This is similar to how the same food on being absorbed becomes in some places veins, in other places arteries, and in other places bones, nerves, or other tissues, showing different power according to the difference of the parts receiving it. This is just as the same water absorbed by the trees becomes in some places bark, in other places branches, and in other places fruit, perhaps a fig or a pomegranate, or something else. This is also just as the breath of the musician when blown into the flute becomes sometimes a high tone and sometimes a low one, or the same pressure of the hand upon the lyre sometimes causes a deep tone and sometimes a high tone.

We may see this more clearly in the things that are sought for and avoided by animals. For example, myrrh appears very agreeable to people and intolerable to beetles and bees. Oil also, which is useful to people, destroys wasps and bees if sprinkled on them; and seawater, while it is unpleasant and poisonous to men if they drink it, is most agreeable and sweet to fish. Swine also prefer to wash in vile filth rather than in pure clean water. Furthermore, some animals eat grass and some eat herbs; some live in the woods, others eat seeds; some are carnivorous, and others lactivorous; some enjoy putrefied food, and others fresh food; some raw food, and others that which is prepared by cooking; and in general that which is agreeable to some is disagreeable and fatal to others, and should be avoided by them. Thus hemlock makes the quail fat, and henbane the hogs, and these, as it is known, enjoy eating lizards; deer also eat poisonous animals, and swallows the cantharid. Moreover, ants and flying ants, when swallowed by men, cause discomfort and colic, but the bear, on the contrary, whatever sickness he may have, becomes stronger by devouring them. The viper is benumbed if one twig of the oak touches it, as is also the bat by a leaf of the plane-tree. The elephant flees before the ram, and the lion before the cock, and seals from the rattling of beans that are being pounded, and the tiger from the sound of the drum. Many other examples could be given, but that we may not seem to dwell longer than is necessary on this subject, we conclude by saying that since the same things are pleasant to some and unpleasant to others, and the pleasure and displeasure depend on the ideas, it must be that different animals have different ideas of objects.

Since the same things appear differently according to the difference in the animals, it will be possible for us to say how the external object appears to us, but as to how it is in reality we shall suspend our judgment. For we cannot ourselves judge between our own ideas and those of other animals, being ourselves involved in the difference, and therefore much more in need of being judged than being ourselves able to judge. Furthermore, we cannot give preference to our own mental representations over those of other animals, either without evidence or with evidence, for besides the fact that perhaps there is no evidence, as I will show, the evidence so called will be either manifest to us or not. If it is not manifest to us, then we cannot accept it with conviction. If it is manifest to us (since the question is in regard to what is manifest to animals, and we use as evidence that which is manifest to us who are animals), then it is to be questioned if it is true as it is manifest to us. It is absurd, however, to try to base the questionable on the questionable, because the same thing is to be believed and not to be believed, which is certainly impossible. The evidence is to be believed insofar as it will furnish a proof, and disbelieved insofar as it is itself to be proved. We therefore have no evidence according to which we can give preference to our own ideas over those of so-called irrational animals. Since ideas differ according to the difference in animals, and it is impossible to judge them, it is necessary to suspend the judgment in regard to external objects.

READING 5

Augustine: On Skepticism, The Two Cities, and Our Primary Good

From On the Trinity, City of God, and Of the Morals of the Catholic Church

Born in what is now Algeria, Augustine (354–430) was a bishop in the early Christian Church and one of its most influential theologians and philosophers. Augustine was a strong critic of philosophical skepticism, especially the more radical views of skeptics who claimed that we are deceived about reality and everything might even be a dream. His response is that even if we are deceived, we still can rely on the truth that we exist and are alive. Augustine argued that we should view society as consisting of two cities, an earthly one and a heavenly one. The earthly city is grounded in self-love, as represented by the Roman Empire and its drive for glory. The heavenly city, by contrast, consists of believers who strive after an eternal good that God provides. Members of

Source: Augustine, *On the Trinity*, 15; *City of God*, 14, *Of the Morals of the Catholic Church*.

the heavenly city still must reside within the earthly city and follow its basic rules. However, they are like travelers whose true desires rest with God. Augustine also developed a theological basis for ethics. Happiness, he argues, is attained through the enjoyment of the primary good of the human soul. Goodness, in turn, is based on loving all things in their appropriate manner. The primary good of the human soul is loving God supremely.

ON SKEPTICISM

The Academic philosophy has so succeeded as to be still more wretchedly insane by doubting all things;—passing by, then, those things that come into the mind by the bodily senses, how large a proportion is left of things which we know in such manner as we know that we live? In regard to this, indeed, we are absolutely without any fear lest perchance we are being deceived by some resemblance of the truth; since it is certain, that he who is deceived, yet lives. And this again is not reckoned among those objects of sight that are presented from without, so that the eye may be deceived in it; in such way as it is when an oar in the water looks bent, and towers seem to move as you sail past them, and a thousand other things that are otherwise than they seem to be: for this is not a thing that is discerned by the eye of the flesh.

The knowledge by which we know that we live is the most inward of all knowledge, of which even the Academic cannot insinuate: Perhaps you are asleep, and do not know it, and you see things in your sleep. For who does not know that what people see in dreams is precisely like what they see when awake? But he who is certain of the knowledge of his own life, does not therein say, I know I am awake, but, I know I am alive; therefore, whether he be asleep or awake, he is alive. Nor can he be deceived in that knowledge by dreams; since it belongs to a living man both to sleep and to see in sleep. Nor can the Academic again say, in confutation of this knowledge: "Perhaps you are mad, and do not know it: for what madmen see is precisely like what they also see who are sane" But he who is mad is alive. Nor does he answer the Academic by saying, "I know I am not mad," but instead, "I know I am alive." Therefore he who says he knows he is alive, can neither be deceived nor lie. Let a thousand kinds, then, of deceitful objects of sight be presented to him who says, I know I am alive; yet he will fear none of them, for he who is deceived yet is alive. . . .

For whereas there are two kinds of knowable things,—one, of those things which the mind perceives by the bodily senses; the other, of those which it perceives by itself,—these philosophers have babbled much against the bodily senses, but have never been able to throw doubt upon those most certain perceptions of things true, which the mind knows by itself, such as is that which I have mentioned, I know that I am alive. But far be it from us to doubt the truth of what we have learned by the bodily senses; since by them we have learned to know the heaven and the earth, and those things in them which are known to us, so far as He who created both us and them has willed them to be within our knowledge. Far be it from us too to deny, that we know what we have learned by the testimony of others: otherwise we know not that there is an ocean; we know not that the lands and cities exist which most copious report commends to us; we know not that those men were, and their works, which we have learned by reading history; we know not the news that is daily brought us from this quarter or that, and confirmed by consistent and conspiring evidence; lastly, we know not at what place or from whom we have been born: since in all these things we have believed the testimony of others. And if it is most absurd to say this, then we must confess, that not only our own senses, but those of other persons also, have added very much indeed to our knowledge.

THE TWO CITIES

Differences between the Two Cities

14.1. We have already stated in the preceding books that God desired that the human race might be able by their similarity of nature to associate with one another. He also desired that they might be bound together in harmony and peace by the ties of relationship. Accordingly, he happily created all people from one individual, and gave humans such a nature that the members of the race should not have died, had not the two first (of whom the one was created out of nothing, and the other out of him) deserved this by their disobedience. For they committed such a great sin that human nature was altered by it for the worse, and this was passed on to their offspring, namely, the capacity to sin and to die. The kingdom of death reigned so much over people that the deserved penalty of sin would have hurled all headlong even into a second and eternal death, if it had not been for the undeserved grace of God which saved some people from it. It has come about that there are very many and great nations all over the earth, whose rituals, customs, speech, and dress, are distinguished by clear differences. Nevertheless, there are no more than two kinds of human societies, which we may justly call two cities, according to the language of our Scriptures. The one consists of those who wish to live after the body, the other of those who wish to live after the spirit. When they respectively achieve what they wish, they live in peace, each after their kind.

Two Cities Formed by Two Loves

14.28. Accordingly, two cities have been formed by two loves: the earthly by the love of self (even to the point of contempt for God); the heavenly by the love of God (even to the point of contempt for self). The former, in a word, praises itself, the latter the Lord. The one seeks praise from men; but the other seeks the greatest praise which from is God, the witness of conscience. The one lifts up its head in its own glory; the other says to God, "You are my glory, and the lifter up of my head." In the one, the princes and the nations it subdues are ruled by the love of ruling; in the other, the princes and the subjects serve one another in love, the latter obeying, while the former show consideration for all. The one delights in its own strength, represented in the persons of its rulers; the other says to its God, "I will love You, O Lord, my strength." Therefore the wise men of the one city, living according to man, have sought for profit to their own bodies or souls, or both. Those of them who had once known God "did not glorify him as God; they were unthankful, became proud in their thoughts, and their foolish hearts were darkened as they professed themselves to be wise." That is, praising their own wisdom, and being possessed with pride—"they became fools, and exchanged the praise of the immortal God for images made like mortal man, birds, animals, and reptiles." For they were either leaders or followers of the people in worshiping images, "and worshipped and served the creature more than the Creator, who is blessed forever" (Romans 1:21–25). But in the other city there is no human wisdom, but only godliness, which offers proper worship of the true God, and looks for its reward in the society of the saints, of holy angels as well as holy men, "that God may be all in all."

LOVE OF GOD AS OUR PRIMARY GOOD

Happiness Is in the Enjoyment of Our Primary Human Good

4. How, rationally speaking, should people live? Certainly, we all desire to live happily, and everyone agrees with this statement almost before it is made. But, in my opinion, the term "happy" cannot belong either to the person who lacks what he loves (whatever it may be), or to the person who has what he loves if it is harmful, or to a person who does not love what he has even though it is perfectly good. For a person who seeks what he cannot obtain experiences torture, and a person who has what is undesirable is cheated, and a person who fails to seek for what is worth seeking for is diseased. Now in all these cases the person will certainly be unhappy, and happiness and unhappiness cannot reside in one person at the same time. So in none of these cases can the person be happy. But I find a fourth situation where the happy life exists: when a person both loves and possesses that which is our primary human good. For what do we call enjoyment but having at hand the objects of love? And no one can be happy who does not enjoy what is our primary good, nor is there anyone who enjoys this who is not happy. We must then have our primary good within reach if we think of living happily.

5. We must now inquire into what is our primary human good, which of course cannot be anything inferior to human nature itself. For whoever follows after what is inferior to himself, becomes himself inferior. But every person is bound to follow what is best. For that reason, our primary human good is not inferior to human beings. Is it then something similar to human nature itself? It must be so, if there is nothing above humans which we are capable of enjoying. But if we find something which is both superior to human beings, and can be possessed by the person who loves it, who can doubt that in seeking for happiness we should try to reach that which is more excellent than the being who makes the effort. For if happiness consists in the enjoyment of a good than which there is nothing better, which we call the primary good, how can a person be properly called "happy" who has not yet attained to his primary good?

Or how can that be the primary good beyond which something better remains for us to arrive at? Insofar as it is the primary good, it must be something that cannot be lost against the will. For no one can feel confident regarding a good which he knows can be taken from him, although he wishes to keep and cherish it. But if a person feels no confidence regarding the good which he enjoys, how can he be happy while in such fear of losing it?

Human Beings as Body and Soul

6. Let us then see what is better than human nature. This will certainly be hard to discover, unless we first examine what human beings are. I do not now need to give a definition of "human being." It seems to me that the question here is that we are made up of soul and body. Almost everyone agrees with this—or at least, which is enough, the group I have now to do with [that is, the Manichean religious believers] agree with my opinion. What, then, is a human being? Is it both of these, or is it just the body or just the soul? While the soul and body are two things, neither of these could be called "human" without the other: for the body would not be human without the soul, nor similarly would the soul be human if there were not a body animated by it. Still it is possible that one of these may be considered "human nature" and may be called such. What then do we call human beings? Are we soul and body, as like a double harness or a centaur? Perhaps we mean the body only, as being in the service of the soul which rules it. For example, it might be like how the word "lamp" refers only to the container (and not to both the light and the container) even though it is because of the light that the lamp gets its name. Perhaps instead we mean the mind only insofar as the mind rules the body. For example, it might be like how the term "horseperson" refers only to the person who rules the horse, and not to the person and the horse together. This dispute is not easy to settle, or, if the proof is plain, presenting it requires time. But this is an expenditure of effort and time that we need not take on. For whether the term "human being" refers to both, or only to the soul, our primary human good is not the main good of the body. Instead, our primary human good is the main good of either the soul and body combined, or the soul by itself.

Our Primary Good Is the Good of the Soul

7. Now if we ask, "What is the primary good of the body?" reason requires us to admit that it is that by means of which the body comes to be in its best state. But of all the things which invigorate the body, there is nothing better or greater than the soul. The primary good of the body, then, is not bodily pleasure, not absence of pain, not strength, not beauty, not swiftness, or whatever else is usually considered among the goods of the body, but simply the soul. For all the things mentioned the soul supplies to the body by its presence, and, what is above them all, life. Hence I conclude that the soul is not the primary human good, whether we give the name of man to soul and body together, or to the soul alone. For, rationally speaking, the primary good of the body is that which is better than the

body, and from which the body receives strength and life. So whether the soul itself is human nature, or soul and body both, we must discover whether there is anything which goes before the soul itself (whereby in following that thing the soul comes to the perfection of good of which it is capable in its own manner). If such a thing can be found, all uncertainty must be at an end, and we must pronounce this to be really and truly the primary human good.

8. If, again, the body is human nature, it must be admitted that the soul is the primary human good. But clearly, when we deal with morals (the inquiry into what kind of life we must follow in order to obtain happiness) it is not the body to which moral precepts are addressed; it is not bodily discipline that we discuss. In short, the observance of good guidelines belongs to that part of us that inquires and learns, which is the domain of the soul. So, when we speak of attaining virtue, the question does not regard the body. It thus follows that the body (which is ruled over by a soul possessed of virtue) is ruled both better and more honorably, and is in its greatest perfection because of the perfection of the soul which rightfully governs it. Accordingly, that which gives perfection to the soul will be our primary human good, even though we call the body "human." Suppose that my coachman, obeying my wishes, feeds and drives the horses he has charge of in the most satisfactory manner; he himself will receive more reward from me in proportion to his good conduct. Can anyone then deny that the good condition of the horses, as well as that of the coachman, is due to me? So the question seems to me to be not whether human beings are soul and body together, or the soul only, or the body only. Instead, it is a question of what gives perfection to the soul. For when this is obtained, a person cannot but be perfect, or at least will be much better than when lacking this one thing. . . .

God Is the Primary Good, Whom We Must Love Supremely

13. Let us see how the Lord himself in the gospel has taught us to live, and so too Paul the apostle (for the Manicheans would not dare reject these scriptures). Let us hear, O Christ, what primary end you establish for us; and that is evidently the primary end after which we are told to strive with supreme love. He says, "You shall love the Lord your God." Tell me also, I pray to you, what must be the amount of love? For I fear that the desire burning in my heart might either exceed or fall short in commitment. "With all your heart" he says. Nor is that enough: "With all your soul." Nor is it enough yet: "With all your mind" (Matthew 22:37). What do you wish more? I might, perhaps, wish more if I could see the possibility of more. What does Paul say on this? He says, "We know that all things result in good to them that love God." Let him, too, say what is the amount of love. He says, "Who then, shall separate us from the love of Christ? Shall tribulation, or distress, or persecution, or famine, or nakedness, or peril, or the sword?" (Romans 8:28, 35). We have heard, then, what and how much we must love. This is what we must strive after, and to this we must submit all our plans. The perfection of all our good things and our perfect good is God. We must neither come short of this nor go beyond it: the one is dangerous, the other impossible.

Anselm: The Ontological Argument
From *Proslogium*

Born in northern Italy, Anselm (1033–1109) was Archbishop of Canterbury, England, and, as a philosopher, developed one of the first systematic arguments for God's existence. The proof he formulated is now known as the "ontological argument." Anselm begins with the concept of "that than which nothing greater can be conceived"—or more simply, the greatest possible being. What type of qualities must this being possess? By definition the greatest possible being must possess every great-making quality. Anselm then argues that existence is a great-making attribute: If a being lacked existence, then it would have been greater if it actually possessed existence. Thus, the greatest possible being must possess the attribute of existence since, if it lacked existence, it would not be the greatest possible being. Shortly after, a monk named Gaunilon challenged Anselm's reasoning. Suppose, he argued, that we replace the notion of "the greatest possible being" with "the greatest possible island." Anselm's argument would then show that the greatest possible island actually exists, which is of course absurd. Thus, Anselm's logic is somewhere flawed. Responding to Gaunilon, Anselm contends that the ontological argument only works with the notion of the greatest possible being, since only "being" (and not islands) can have infinitely great qualities, without lapsing into logical contradiction. The principal difference is that an island is only a contingent being, whereas the notion of God is that of a necessary being.

THE ARGUMENT

Truly There Is a God

2. And so, Lord, do you, who gives understanding to faith, give me, so far as you know it to be profitable, to understand that you are as we believe; and that you are that which we believe. And indeed, we believe that you are a being than which nothing greater can be conceived. Or is there no such nature, since the fool hath said in his heart, there is no God? (Psalms 14:1). But, at any rate, this very fool, when he hears of this being of which I speak—a being than which nothing greater can be conceived—understands what he hears, and what he understands is in his understanding; although he does not understand it to exist.

For, it is one thing for an object to be in the understanding, and another to understand that the object exists. When a painter first conceives of what he will afterwards perform, he has it in his understanding, but he does not yet understand it to be, because he has not yet performed it. But after he has made the painting, he both has it in his understanding, and he understands that it exists, because he has made it.

Source: Anselm, *Proslogium*.

Hence, even the fool is convinced that something exists in the understanding, at least, than which nothing greater can be conceived. For, when he hears of this, he understands it. And whatever is understood, exists in the understanding. And assuredly that, than which nothing greater can be conceived, cannot exist in the understanding alone. For, suppose it exists in the understanding alone: then it can be conceived to exist in reality; which is greater.

Therefore, if that, than which nothing greater can be conceived, exists in the understanding alone, the very being, than which nothing greater can be conceived, is one, than which a greater can be conceived. But obviously this is impossible. Hence, there is no doubt that there exists a being, than which nothing greater can be conceived, and it exists both in the understanding and in reality.

God Cannot Be Conceived Not to Exist

3. And it assuredly exists so truly, that it cannot be conceived not to exist. For, it is possible to conceive of a being which cannot be conceived not to exist; and this is greater than one which can be conceived not to exist. Hence, if that, than which nothing greater can be conceived, can be conceived not to exist, it is not that, than which nothing greater can be conceived. But this is an irreconcilable contradiction. There is, then, so truly a being than which nothing greater can be conceived to exist, that it cannot even be conceived not to exist; and this being you are, O Lord, our God.

So truly, therefore, do you exist, O Lord, my God, that you cannot be conceived not to exist; and rightly. For, if a mind could conceive of a being better than you, the creature would rise above the Creator; and this is most absurd. And, indeed, whatever else there is, except you alone, can be conceived not to exist. To you alone, therefore, it belongs to exist more truly than all other beings, and hence in a higher degree than all others. For, whatever else exists does not exist so truly, and hence in a less degree it belongs to it to exist. Why, then, has the fool said in his heart, there is no God (Psalms 14:1), since it is so evident, to a rational mind, that you do exist in the highest degree of all? Why, except that he is dull and a fool?

How the Fool Has Said in His Heart
What Cannot Be Conceived

But how has the fool said in his heart what he could not conceive; or how is it that he could not conceive what he said in his heart? since it is the same to say in the heart, and to conceive.

But, if really, nay, since really, he both conceived, because he said in his heart; and did not say in his heart, because he could not conceive; there is more than one way in which a thing is said in the heart or conceived. For, in one sense, an object is conceived, when the word signifying it is conceived; and in another, when the very entity, which the object is, is understood.

In the former sense, then, God can be conceived not to exist; but in the latter, not at all. For no one who understands what fire and water are can conceive fire to be water, in accordance with the nature of the facts themselves, although this is possible according to the words. So, then, no one who understands what God is can conceive that God does not exist; although he says these words in his heart, either without any or with some foreign, signification. For, God is that than which a greater cannot be conceived. And he who thoroughly understands this, assuredly understands that this being so truly exists, that not even in concept can it be non-existent. Therefore, he who understands that God so exists, cannot conceive that he does not exist.

I thank you, gracious Lord, I thank you; because what I formerly believed by your bounty, I now so understand by your illumination, that if I were unwilling to believe that you do exist, I should not be able not to understand this to be true.

CHAPTER 5: GOD IS WHATEVER IT IS BETTER TO BE THAN NOT TO BE

5. What are you, then, Lord God, than whom nothing greater can be conceived? But what are you, except that which, as the highest of all beings, alone exists through itself, and creates all other things from nothing? For, whatever is not this is less than a thing which can be conceived of. But this cannot be conceived of you. What good, therefore, does the supreme Good lack, through which every good is? Therefore, you are just, truthful, blessed, and whatever it is better to be than not to be. For it is better to be just than not just; better to be blessed than not blessed.

CRITICISM AND RESPONSE

Gaunilon's Answer to Anselm's Argument

For example: it is said that somewhere in the ocean is an island, which, because of the difficulty, or rather the impossibility, of discovering what does not exist, is called the lost island. And they say that this island has an inestimable wealth of all manner of riches and delicacies in greater abundance than is told of the Islands of the Blest; and that having no owner or inhabitant, it is more excellent than all other countries, which are inhabited by mankind, in the abundance with which it is stored.

Now if someone should tell me that there is such an island, I should easily understand his words, in which there is no difficulty. But suppose that he went on to say, as if by a logical inference: "You can no longer doubt that this island which is more excellent than all lands exists somewhere, since you have no doubt that it is in your understanding. And since it is more excellent not to be in the understanding alone, but to exist both in the understanding and in reality, for this reason it must exist. For if it does not exist, any land which really exists will be more excellent than it; and so the island already understood by you to be more excellent will not be more excellent."

If a man should try to prove to me by such reasoning that this island truly exists, and that its existence should no longer be doubted, either I should believe that he was jesting, or I know not which I ought to regard as the greater fool: myself, supposing that I should allow this proof; or him, if he should suppose that he had established with any certainty the existence of this island. For he ought to show first that the hypothetical excellence of this island exists as a real and indubitable fact, and in no wise as any unreal object, or one whose existence is uncertain, in my understanding.

Anselm's Reply to Gaunilon

But, you say, it is as if one should suppose an island in the ocean, which surpasses all lands in its fertility, and which, because of the difficulty, or the impossibility, of discovering what does not exist, is called a lost island; and should say that there can be no doubt that this island truly exists in reality, for this reason, that one who hears it described easily understands what he hears.

Now I promise confidently that if any man shall devise anything existing either in reality or in concept alone (except that than which a greater be conceived) to which he can adapt the sequence of my reasoning, I will discover that thing, and will give him his lost island, not to be lost again.

But it now appears that this being than which a greater is inconceivable cannot be conceived not to be, because it exists on so assured a ground of truth; for otherwise it would not exist at all.

Hence, if any one says that he conceives this being not to exist, I say that at the time when he conceives of this either he conceives of a being than which a greater is inconceivable, or he does not conceive at all. If he does not conceive, he does not conceive of the non-existence of that of which he does not conceive. But if he does conceive, he certainly conceives of a being which cannot be even conceived not to exist. For if it could be conceived not to exist, it could be conceived to have a beginning and an end. But this is impossible.

He, then, who conceives of this being conceives of a being which cannot be even conceived not to exist; but he who conceives of this being does not conceive that it does not exist; else he conceives what is inconceivable. The nonexistence, then, of that than which a greater cannot be conceived is inconceivable.

You say, moreover, that whereas I assert that this supreme being cannot be conceived not to exist, it might better be said that its non-existence, or even the possibility of its non-existence, cannot be understood.

But it was more proper to say, it cannot be conceived. For if I had said that the object itself cannot be understood not to exist, possibly you yourself, who say that in accordance with the true meaning of the term what is unreal cannot be understood, would offer the objection that nothing which is can be understood not to be, for the non-existence of what exists is unreal: hence God would not be the only being of which it could be said, it is impossible to understand its non-existence. For thus one of those beings which most certainly exist can be understood not to exist in the same way in which certain other real objects can be understood not to exist.

But this objection, assuredly, cannot be urged against the term conception, if one considers the matter well. For although no objects which exist can be understood not to exist, yet all objects, except that which exists in the highest degree, can be conceived not to exist. For all those objects, and those alone, can be conceived not to exist, which have a beginning or end or composition of parts: also, as I have already said, whatever at any place or at any time does not exist as a whole.

That being alone, on the other hand, cannot be conceived not to exist, in which any conception discovers neither beginning nor end nor composition of parts, and which any conception finds always and everywhere as a whole.

Be assured, then, that you can conceive of your own non-existence, although you are most certain that you exist. I am surprised that you should have admitted that you are ignorant of this. For we conceive of the non-existence of many objects which we know to exist, and of the existence of many which we know not to exist; not by forming the opinion that they so exist, but by imagining that they exist as we conceive of them.

And indeed, we can conceive of the non-existence of an object, although we know it to exist, because at the same time we can conceive of the former and know the latter. And we cannot conceive of the non-existence of an object, so long as we know it to exist, because we cannot conceive at the same time of existence and non-existence.

If, then, one will thus distinguish these two senses of this statement, he will understand that nothing, so long as it is known to exist, can be conceived not to exist; and that whatever exists, except that being than which a greater cannot be conceived, can be conceived not to exist, even when it is known to exist.

So, then, of God alone it can be said that it is impossible to conceive of his non-existence; and yet many objects, so long as they exist, in one sense cannot be conceived not to exist. But in what sense God is to be conceived not to exist, I think has been shown clearly enough in my book.

READING 7

Thomas Aquinas: God's Existence and Natural Law

From *Summa Theologica*

Born in what is now central Italy, Thomas Aquinas (1224–1274) was one of the great theologians and philosophers of medieval Christianity. In his masterpiece, Summa Theologica, *he presents five proofs for God's existence. Unlike Anselm's argument, which is based on the logical implications of a mental concept, Aquinas's arguments are based on information found in our actual experience. The first three of Aquinas's arguments rely on the notion of cause and effect, and today are referred to as cosmological*

Source: Thomas Aquinas, *Summa Theologica*, 1a, Q. 2.3, 46.2; 1a2ae, Q 90.1–2, 91.1–4, 93.3, 94.4, 95.1.

arguments for God's existence. Take, for example, his first argument, which is based on the motion that we see around us. There must be some being that is capable of moving other things but does not require to be moved, a being that actually is and that is capable of bringing others into being. That is, there must be a first mover, which is God. Although this argument is short and to the point, its brevity creates problems. We might think that Aquinas is simply saying that we cannot trace a causal sequence of motion back through infinity past. However, in another part of his Summa Theologica *(also contained herein), he states explicitly that there is nothing logically contradictory in the idea that the world existed from eternity past. That is, we might in theory trace the causal sequences of motion back to infinity. Aquinas then distinguishes between accidental causes (causes* per accidens*) that happen over a period of time, and essential causes (causes* per se*) that occur simultaneously. An example of accidental causes over time is Abraham begetting Isaac, who in turn begets Jacob. An example of simultaneous essential causes is a hand that moves a stick, which in turn moves a stone, all at the same time. Aquinas's point is that we can indeed trace accidental motion back to infinity past, but simultaneous essential motion—which occurs here and now—traces immediately back to a first mover. Aside from the three cosmological arguments that Aquinas offers, in his fifth proof he proposes an argument that in later years was dubbed the "design argument" or the "teleological argument" for God's existence. The central intuition behind this argument is clear: We see obvious signs of intelligent design in the natural world, and this implies that there must be an intelligent designer of the world. Aquinas observes that many things in nature are directed toward a purpose or final goal, and so we must conclude that an intelligent being orchestrates this purposeful direction.*

Also in his Summa Theologica, *Aquinas presents the classic statement of natural law theory—a position that emphasizes the moral dimension of the human laws that governments establish. He links the law of government to the moral law within human reason, which, in turn, is linked to the eternal law, which, according to Aquinas, is identical with God's reason. It follows in Aquinas's theory, therefore, that if a law of a government is contrary to the natural law known by human reason, then such a civil law does not even have the character of law and, presumably, does not have to be obeyed. Although the question of obedience to law is involved here, that was not Aquinas's chief concern. He appears to be more interested in clarifying what a law is and how necessary it is for a genuine law to conform to natural morality.*

FIVE WAYS TO PROVE GOD'S EXISTENCE

2.3. Whether God Exists?

Objection 1   It seems that God does not exist; because if one of two contraries be infinite, the other would be altogether destroyed. But the word "God" means that He is infinite goodness. If, therefore, God existed, there would be no evil discoverable; but there is evil in the world. Therefore God does not exist.

Objection 2   Further, it is superfluous to suppose that what can be accounted for by a few principles has been produced by many. But it seems that everything we see in the world can be accounted for by other principles, supposing

God did not exist. For all natural things can be reduced to one principle which is nature; and all voluntary things can be reduced to one principle which is human reason, or will. Therefore there is no need to suppose God's existence.

On the contrary, It is said in the person of God: "I am Who am." *I answer that*, The existence of God can be proved in five ways.

The first and more manifest way is the argument from motion. It is certain, and evident to our senses, that in the world some things are in motion. Now whatever is in motion is put in motion by another, for nothing can be in motion except it is in potentiality to that towards which it is in motion; whereas a thing moves inasmuch as it is in act. For motion is nothing else than the reduction of something from potentiality to actuality. But nothing can be reduced from potentiality to actuality, except by something in a state of actuality. Thus that which is actually hot, as fire, makes wood, which is potentially hot, to be actually hot, and thereby moves and changes it. Now it is not possible that the same thing should be at once in actuality and potentiality in the same respect, but only in different respects. For what is actually hot cannot simultaneously be potentially hot; but it is simultaneously potentially cold. It is therefore impossible that in the same respect and in the same way a thing should be both mover and moved, i.e., that it should move itself. Therefore, whatever is in motion must be put in motion by another. If that by which it is put in motion be itself put in motion, then this also must needs be put in motion by another, and that by another again. But this cannot go on to infinity, because then there would be no first mover, and, consequently, no other mover; seeing that subsequent movers move only inasmuch as they are put in motion by the first mover; as the staff moves only because it is put in motion by the hand. Therefore it is necessary to arrive at a first mover, put in motion by no other; and this everyone understands to be God.

The second way is from the nature of the efficient cause. In the world of sense we find there is an order of efficient causes. There is no case known (neither is it, indeed, possible) in which a thing is found to be the efficient cause of itself; for so it would be prior to itself, which is impossible. Now in efficient causes it is not possible to go on to infinity, because in all efficient causes following in order, the first is the cause of the intermediate cause, and the intermediate is the cause of the ultimate cause, whether the intermediate cause be several, or only one. Now to take away the cause is to take away the effect. Therefore, if there be no first cause among efficient causes, there will be no ultimate, nor any intermediate cause. But if in efficient causes it is possible to go on to infinity, there will be no first efficient cause, neither will there be an ultimate effect, nor any intermediate efficient causes; all of which is plainly false. Therefore it is necessary to admit a first efficient cause, to which everyone gives the name of God.

The third way is taken from possibility and necessity, and runs thus. We find in nature things that are possible to be and not to be, since they are found to be generated, and to corrupt, and consequently, they are possible to be and not to be. But it is impossible for these always to exist, for that which is possible not to be at some time is not. Therefore, if everything is possible not to be, then at one time there could have been nothing in existence. Now if this were true, even now there would be nothing in existence, because that which does not exist only begins to exist by something already existing. Therefore, if at one time nothing was in existence, it would have been impossible for anything to have begun to exist; and thus even now nothing would be in existence—which is absurd. Therefore, not all beings are merely possible, but there must exist something the existence of which is necessary. But every necessary thing either has its necessity caused by another, or not. Now it is impossible to go on to infinity in necessary things which have their necessity caused by another, as has been already proved in regard to efficient causes. Therefore we cannot but postulate the existence of some being having of itself its own necessity, and not receiving it from another, but rather causing in others their necessity. This all men speak of as God.

The fourth way is taken from the gradation to be found in things. Among beings there are some more and some less good, true, noble and the like. But "more" and "less" are predicated of different things, according as they resemble in their different ways something which is the maximum, as a thing is said to be hotter according as it more nearly resembles that which is hottest; so that there is something which is truest, something best, something noblest and, consequently, something which is uttermost being; for those things that are greatest in truth are greatest in being, as it is written in Metaphysics. ii. Now the maximum in any genus is the cause of all in that genus; as fire, which is the maximum heat, is the cause of all hot things. Therefore there must also be something which is to all beings the cause of their being, goodness, and every other perfection; and this we call God.

The fifth way is taken from the governance of the world. We see that things which lack intelligence, such as natural bodies, act for an end, and this is evident from their acting always, or nearly always, in the same way, so as to obtain the best result. Hence it is plain that not fortuitously, but designedly, do they achieve their end. Now whatever lacks intelligence cannot move towards an end, unless it be directed by some being endowed with knowledge and intelligence; as the arrow is shot to its mark by the archer. Therefore some intelligent being exists by whom all natural things are directed to their end; and this being we call God.

Reply to Objection 1   As Augustine says: "Since God is the highest good, He would not allow any evil to exist in His works, unless His omnipotence and goodness were such as to bring good even out of evil." This is part of the infinite goodness of God, that He should allow evil to exist, and out of it produce good.

Reply to Objection 2   Since nature works for a determinate end under the direction of a higher agent, whatever is done by nature must needs be traced back to God, as to its first cause. So also whatever is done voluntarily must also be traced back to some higher cause other than human reason or will, since these can change or fail; for all things that are changeable and capable of defect must be traced back to an immovable and self-necessary first principle, as was shown in the body of the Article.

46.2. Whether It Is an Article of Faith That the World Began?

Objection 1   It would seem that it is not an article of faith but a demonstrable conclusion that the world began. For everything that is made has a beginning of its duration. But it can be proved demonstratively that God is the effective cause of the world; indeed this is asserted by the more approved philosophers. Therefore it can be demonstratively proved that the world began. . . .

Objection 7   Further, if the world was eternal, generation also was eternal. Therefore one man was begotten of another in an infinite series. But the father is the efficient cause of the son. Therefore in efficient causes there could be an infinite series, which is disproved.

On the contrary, The articles of faith cannot be proved demonstratively, because faith is of things "that appear not." But that God is the Creator of the world: hence that the world began, is an article of faith; for we say, "I believe in one God," etc. And again, Gregory says, that Moses prophesied of the past, saying, "In the beginning God created heaven and earth": in which words the newness of the world is stated. Therefore the newness of the world is known only by revelation; and therefore it cannot be proved demonstratively.

I answer that, By faith alone do we hold, and by no demonstration can it be proved, that the world did not always exist, as was said above of the mystery of the Trinity. The reason of this is that the newness of the world cannot be demonstrated on the part of the world itself. For the principle of demonstration is the essence of a thing. Now everything according to its species is abstracted from "here" and "now"; whence it is said that universals are everywhere and always. Hence it cannot be demonstrated that man, or heaven, or a stone were not always. Likewise neither can it be demonstrated on the part of the efficient cause, which acts by will. For the will of God cannot be investigated by reason, except as regards those things which God must will of necessity; and what He wills about creatures is not among these, as was said above. But the divine will can be manifested by revelation, on which faith rests. Hence that the world began to exist is an object of faith, but not of demonstration or science. And it is useful to consider this, lest anyone, presuming to demonstrate what is of faith, should bring forward reasons that are not cogent, so as to give occasion to unbelievers to laugh, thinking that on such grounds we believe things that are of faith.

Reply to Objection 1   As Augustine says, the opinion of philosophers who asserted the eternity of the world was twofold. For some said that the substance of the world was not from God, which is an intolerable error; and therefore it is refuted by proofs that are cogent. Some, however, said that the world was eternal, although made by God. For they hold that the world has a beginning, not of time, but of creation, so that in a certain hardly intelligible way it was always made. "And they try to explain their meaning thus: for as, if the foot were always in the dust from eternity, there would always be a footprint which without doubt was caused by him who trod on it, so also the world always was, because its maker always existed." To understand this we must consider that the efficient cause, which acts by motion, of necessity precedes its effect in time; because the effect is only in the end of the action, and every agent must be the principle of action. But if the action is instantaneous and not successive, it is not necessary for the maker to be prior to the thing made in duration as appears in the case of illumination. Hence they say that it does not follow necessarily if God is the active cause of the world, that He should be prior to the world in duration; because creation, by which He produced the world, is not a successive change, as was said above. . . .

Reply to Objection 7 In efficient causes it is impossible to proceed to infinity *"per se"*—thus, there cannot be an infinite number of causes that are *"per se"* required for a certain effect; for instance, that a stone be moved by a stick, the stick by the hand, and so on to infinity. But it is not impossible to proceed to infinity "accidentally" as regards efficient causes; for instance, if all the causes thus infinitely multiplied should have the order of only one cause, their multiplication being accidental, as an artificer acts by means of many hammers accidentally, because one after the other may be broken. It is accidental, therefore, that one particular hammer acts after the action of another; and likewise it is accidental to this particular man as generator to be generated by another man; for he generates as a man, and not as the son of another man. For all men generating hold one grade in efficient causes—viz. the grade of a particular generator. Hence it is not impossible for a man to be generated by man to infinity; but such a thing would be impossible if the generation of this man depended upon this man, and on an elementary body, and on the sun, and so on to infinity . . .)

NATURAL LAW

90.1–2. The Essence of Law

Law is a rule and measure of acts, whereby man is induced to act or is restrained from acting: for *"lex"* [law] is derived from *"ligare"* [to bind], because it binds one to act. Now the rule and measure of human acts is the reason, which is the first principle of human acts, as is evident from what has been stated above; since it belongs to the reason to direct to the end, which is the first principle in all matters of action, according to the Philosopher. Now that which is the principle in any genus, is the rule and measure of that genus: for instance, unity in the genus of numbers, and the first movement in the genus of movements. Consequently it follows that law is something pertaining to reason. . . .

The law belongs to that which is a principle of human acts, because it is their rule and measure. Now as reason is a principle of human acts, so in reason itself there is something which is the principle in respect of all the rest: wherefore to this principle chiefly and mainly law must needs be referred. Now the first principle in practical matters, which are the object of the practical reason, is the last end: and the last end of human life is bliss or happiness, as stated above. Consequently the law must needs regard principally the relationship to happiness. Moreover, since every part is ordained to the whole, as imperfect to perfect; and since one man is a part of the perfect community, the law must needs regard properly the relationship to universal happiness. Wherefore the Philosopher, in the above definition of legal matters mentions both happiness and the body politic: for he says that we call those legal matters "just, which are adapted to produce and preserve happiness and its parts for the body politic": since the state is a perfect community.

91.1–4. The Various Kinds of Law

A law is nothing else but a dictate of practical reason emanating from the ruler who governs a perfect community. Now it is evident, granted that the world is ruled by Divine Providence, that the whole community of the universe is governed by Divine Reason. Wherefore the very Idea of the government of things in God the Ruler of the universe, has the nature of a law. And since the Divine Reason's conception of things is not subject to time but is eternal, according to Proverbs 8:23, therefore it is that this kind of law must be called eternal. . . .

Law, being a rule and measure, can be in a person in two ways: in one way, as in him that rules and measures; in another way, as in that which is ruled and measured, since a thing is ruled and measured, in so far as it partakes of the rule or measure. Wherefore, since all things subject to Divine providence are ruled and measured by the eternal law, as was stated above; it is evident that all things partake somewhat of the eternal law, in so far as, namely, from its being imprinted on them, they derive their respective inclinations to their proper acts and ends. Now among all others, the rational creature is subject to Divine providence in the most excellent way, in so far as it partakes of a share of providence, by being provident both for itself and for others. Wherefore it has a share of the Eternal Reason, whereby it has a natural inclination to its proper act and end: and this participation of the eternal law in the rational creature is called the natural law. Hence the Psalmist after saying: "Offer up the sacrifice of justice," as though someone asked what the works of justice are, adds: "Many say, Who showeth us good things?" in answer to which question he says: "The light of Thy countenance, O Lord, is signed upon us": thus implying that the light of natural reason, whereby we discern what is good and what is evil, which is the function of the natural law, is nothing else than an imprint on us of the Divine light. It is therefore evident that the natural law is nothing else than the rational creature's participation of the eternal law. . . .

A law is a dictate of the practical reason. Now it is to be observed that the same procedure takes place in the practical and in the speculative reason: for each proceeds from principles to conclusions. Accordingly we conclude that just as, in the speculative reason, from naturally known indemonstrable principles, we draw the conclusions of the various sciences, the knowledge of which is not imparted to us by nature, but acquired by the efforts of reason, so too it is from the precepts of the natural law, as from general and indemonstrable principles, that the human reason needs to proceed to the more particular determination of certain matters. These particular determinations, devised by human reason, are called human laws, provided the other essential conditions of law be observed. Wherefore Tully says in his *Rhetoric* that "justice has its source in nature; thence certain things came into custom by reason of their utility; afterwards these things which emanated from nature and were approved by custom, were sanctioned by fear and reverence for the law." . . .

I answer that, Besides the natural and the human law it was necessary for the directing of human conduct to have a Divine law. And this for four reasons. First, because it is by law that man is directed how to perform his proper acts in view of his last end. And indeed if man were ordained to no other end than that which is proportionate to his natural faculty, there would be no need for man to have any further direction of the part of his reason, besides the natural law and human law which is derived from it. But since man is ordained to an end of eternal happiness which is beyond man's natural faculty, therefore it was necessary that, besides the natural and the human law, man should be directed to his end by a law given by God.

Secondly, because, on account of the uncertainty of human judgment, especially on contingent and particular matters, different people form different judgments on human acts; whence also different and contrary laws result. In order, therefore, that man may know without any doubt what he ought to do and what he ought to avoid, it was necessary for man to be directed in his proper acts by a law given by God, for it is certain that such a law cannot err.

Thirdly, because man can make laws in those matters of which he is competent to judge. But man is not competent to judge of interior movements, that are hidden, but only of exterior acts which appear: and yet for the perfection of virtue it is necessary for man to conduct himself aright in both kinds of acts. Consequently human law could not sufficiently curb and direct interior acts; and it was necessary for this purpose that a Divine law should supervene.

Fourthly, because, as Augustine says, human law cannot punish or forbid all evil deeds: since while aiming at doing away with all evils, it would do away with many good things, and would hinder the advance of the common good, which is necessary for human intercourse. In order, therefore, that no evil might remain unforbidden and unpunished, it was necessary for the Divine law to supervene, whereby all sins are forbidden. . . .

93.3. The Eternal Law

The law denotes a kind of plan directing acts towards an end. Now wherever there are movers ordained to one another, the power of the second mover must needs be derived from the power of the first mover; since the second mover does not move except in so far as it is moved by the first. Wherefore we observe the same in all those who govern, so that the plan of government is derived by secondary governors from the governor in chief; thus the plan of what is to be done in a state flows from the king's command to his inferior administrators: and again in things of art the plan of whatever is to be done by art flows from the chief craftsman to the under-craftsmen, who work with their hands. Since then the eternal law is the plan of government in the Chief Governor, all the plans of government in the inferior governors must be derived from the eternal law. But these plans of inferior governors are all other laws besides the eternal law. Therefore all laws, in so far as they partake of right reason, are derived from the eternal law. Hence Augustine says that "in temporal law there is nothing just and lawful, but what man has drawn from the eternal law."

94.4. The Natural Law

To the natural law belongs those things to which a man is inclined naturally: and among these it is proper to man to be inclined to act according to reason. Now the process of reason is from the common to the proper, as stated in *Physics I*. The speculative reason, however, is differently situated in this matter, from the practical reason. For, since the speculative reason is busied chiefly with the necessary things, which cannot be otherwise than they are, its proper conclusions, like the universal principles, contain the truth without fail. The practical reason, on the other hand, is busied with contingent matters, about which human actions are concerned: and consequently, although there is necessity in the general principles, the more we descend to matters of detail, the more frequently we encounter defects. Accordingly then in speculative matters truth is the same in all men, both as to principles and as to conclusions: although the truth is not known to all as regards the conclusions, but only as regards the principles which are called common notions. But in matters of action, truth or practical rectitude is not the same for all, as to matters of detail, but only as to the general principles: and where there is the same rectitude in matters of detail, it is not equally known to all. . . .

Consequently we must say that the natural law, as to general principles, is the same for all, both as to rectitude and as to knowledge. But as to certain matters of detail, which are conclusions, as it were, of those general principles, it is the same for all in the majority of cases, both as to rectitude and as to knowledge; and yet in some few cases it may fail, both as to rectitude, by reason of certain obstacles (just as natures subject to generation and corruption fail in some few cases on account of some obstacle), and as to knowledge, since in some the reason is perverted by passion, or evil habit, or an evil disposition of nature; thus formerly, theft, although it is expressly contrary to the natural law, was not considered wrong among the Germans, as Julius Caesar relates.

95.1. Human Law

Man has a natural aptitude for virtue; but the perfection of virtue must be acquired by man by means of some kind of training. Thus we observe that man is helped by industry in his necessities, for instance, in food and clothing. Certain beginnings of these he has from nature, viz. his reason and his hands; but he has not the full complement, as other animals have, to whom nature has given sufficiency of clothing and food. Now it is difficult to see how man could suffice for himself in the matter of this training: since the perfection of virtue consists chiefly in withdrawing man from undue pleasures, to which above all man is inclined, and especially the young, who are more capable of being trained. Consequently a man needs to receive this training from another, whereby to arrive at the perfection of virtue. And as to those young people who are inclined to acts of virtue, by their good natural disposition, or by custom, or rather by the gift of God, paternal training suffices, which is by admonitions. But since some are found to be depraved, and prone to vice, and not easily amenable to words, it was necessary for such to be restrained from evil by force and fear, in order that, at least, they might desist from evil-doing, and leave others in peace, and that they themselves, by being habituated in this way, might be brought to do willingly what hitherto they did from fear, and thus become virtuous. Now this kind of training, which compels through fear of punishment, is the discipline of laws. Therefore in order that man might have peace and virtue, it was necessary for laws to be framed: for, as the Philosopher says, "as man is the most noble of animals if he be perfect in virtue, so is he the lowest of all, if he be severed from law and righteousness"; because man can use his reason to devise means of satisfying his lusts and evil passions, which other animals are unable to do.

As Augustine says "that which is not just seems to be no law at all": wherefore the force of a law depends on the extent of its justice. Now in human affairs a thing is said to be just, from being right, according to the rule of reason. But the first rule of reason is the law of nature, as is clear from what has been stated above. Consequently every human law has just so much of the nature of law, as it is derived from the law of nature. But if in any point it deflects from the law of nature, it is no longer a law but a perversion of law. But it must be noted that something may be derived from the natural law in two ways: first, as a conclusion from premises, secondly, by way of determination of certain generalities. The first way is like to that by which, in sciences, demonstrated conclusions are drawn from the principles: while the second mode is likened to that whereby, in the arts, general forms are particularized as to details: thus the craftsman needs to determine the general form of a house to some particular shape. Some things are therefore derived from the general principles of the natural law, by way of conclusions; e.g., that "one must not kill" may be derived as a conclusion from the principle that "one should do harm to no man": while some are derived therefrom by way of determination; e.g., the law of nature has it that the evil-doer should be punished; but that he be punished in this or that way, is a determination of the law of nature.

Accordingly both modes of derivation are found in the human law. But those things which are derived in the first way, are contained in human law not as emanating therefrom exclusively, but have some force from the natural law also. But those things which are derived in the second way, have no other force than that of human law.

PART THREE

Early Modern Philosophy

Blaise Pascal: Wagering on Belief in God
From *Thoughts*

Born in central France, Blaise Pascal (1623–1662) was a philosopher within a Catholic religious movement called Jansenism. He was well aware of previous efforts to prove God's existence, but he was not convinced of their success. In his Thoughts *he argues that reason is neutral on the whole matter of God's existence, and we cannot conclusively demonstrate that God does or does not exist. Where, then, does this leave us? According to Pascal, the issue of belief in God is purely a matter of faith, and our faith might only be sparked when we embrace a faith tradition, such as his own Catholicism. The issue, then, becomes one of psychologically motivating us to adopt a faith tradition. To this end, he proposes that we take a wager: consider the possible positive benefits of belief in God, and weigh them against the possible benefits of disbelief in God. His assessment is that, by affirming God's existence, we have everything to gain and nothing to lose. We should then enter into our faith tradition and have this initiate our faith.*

By faith we know God's existence. In the glorious state of heaven we will know his nature. Now, I have already shown that we may easily know the existence of a thing without knowing its nature. Let us speak now according to the light of nature. If there is a God he is infinitely incomprehensible, since, having neither parts nor limits, he has no proportion to us. We are then incapable of knowing either what he is, or whether he is. This being true, who will dare to undertake to resolve this question? It cannot be we who have no proportion to him.

Who, then, will blame those Christians who are not able to give a reason for their belief insofar as they profess a religion for which they can give no reason?

Source: Blaise Pascal, *Thoughts* (1670).

In exposing it to the world, they declare that it is a folly *stultitiam* (1 Corinthians 1:18). And then you complain that they do not prove it! If they proved it, they would not keep their word. It is in lacking proofs that they do not lack sense. Yes, but though this may excuse those who offer it such, and take away the blame for producing it without reason, this does not excuse those who receive it. Let us examine this point then, and say "God is, or he is not." But to which side shall we incline? Reason cannot decide it at all. There is an infinite chaos that separates us. A game is being played at the extremity of this infinite distance in which heads or tails must come up. Which will you take? By reason you can wager on neither. By reason you can hinder neither from winning.

Do not, then, charge those with falsehood who have made a choice. For you know nothing about it. "No. But I blame them for having made, not *this* choice, but *a* choice. For although he who takes heads, and the other, are in the same fault, they are both in fault. The proper way is simply not to wager." Yes, but you must wager. This is not voluntary. You have set sail. Which will you take? Let's see. Since a choice must be made, let's see which interests you the least. You have two things to lose: the true and the good. And you have two things to stake: your reason and your will; that is, your knowledge and your complete happiness. And your nature has two things to shun: error and misery. Your reason is not more wounded, since a choice must necessarily be made in choosing one rather than the other. Here a point is eliminated. But what about your happiness?

Let us weigh the gain and the loss in taking heads that God exists. Let us weigh these two cases. If you gain, you gain all. If you lose, you lose nothing. Wager without hesitation, then, that he is. "This is admirable. Yes, it is necessary to wager, but perhaps I wager too much." Let us see. Since there is equal risk of gaining or losing, if you had to gain but two lives for one, still you might wager. But if there were three lives to gain, it would be required to play (since you are under the necessity of playing). And, when you are forced to play, you would be imprudent not to risk your life in order to gain three in a play where there is equal hazard of loss and gain. But there is an eternity of life and happiness. And this being true, even if there were an infinity of chances (only one of which might be for you) you would still be right in wagering one in order to have two. And being obliged to play, if there was an infinity of life infinitely happy to gain, you would act foolishly to refuse to play one life against three in a game where among an infinity of chances there is one for you. But there is here an infinity of life infinitely happy to gain. And there is a chance of gain against a finite number of chances of loss, and what you play is finite. This [the balance of gain over loss] is quite settled. Wherever the infinite is, and where there is not an infinity of chances of loss against the chance of gain, there is nothing to weigh, and we must give all. And thus, when we are forced to play, we must renounce reason in order to keep life, rather than to risk it for the infinite gain, which is as likely to occur as the loss of nothingness.

For there is no use in saying that it is uncertain whether we shall gain, and that it is certain that we risk. And there is no use in saying that, [a] the infinite distance between the certainty of what we risk and, [b] the uncertainty of what we shall gain, raises the finite good which we certainly risk to a level of equality with the uncertain infinite gain. It is not so. Every player, without violating reason, risks a certainty to gain uncertainty, and nevertheless he risks a finite certainty to gain a finite uncertainty. The distance is not infinite between this certainty of what we risk, and the uncertainty of gain. This is false. There is, in truth, an infinity between the certainty of gaining and the certainty of losing. But the uncertainty of gaining is proportioned to the certainty of what we risk, according to the proportion of the chances of gain and loss. It follows from this that if there are as many chances on one side as there are on the other, the game is playing even. And then the certainty of what we risk is equal to the uncertainty of the gain. This is quite far from being infinitely distant. And thus our proposition [of infinite gain] is of infinite force when there is the finite to hazard in a play where the chances of gain and loss are equal, and the infinite to gain. This is demonstrative, and if people are capable of any truths, this is one of them.

"I confess it, I admit it. But, still, are there no means of seeing the truth behind the game?" Yes, the scriptures and the rest.

"Yes, but my hands are tied and my mouth is dumb. I am forced to wager, and I am not free. I am chained and so constituted that I cannot believe. What will you have me do then?" It is true. But at least learn your inability to believe, since reason brings you to such belief [given the above reasoning], and yet you cannot believe. Try then to convince yourself not by the addition of proofs for the existence of God, but by the reduction of your own passions. You would have recourse to faith, but don't know the ways. You wish to be cured of infidelity, and you ask for the remedy. Learn it from those who have been bound like yourself, and who would wager now all their goods. These know the road that you wish to follow, and are cured of a disease that you wish to be cured of. Follow their course, then, from its beginning. It consisted in doing all things *as if* they believed in them, in using holy water, in having masses said, etc. Naturally this will make you believe and stupefy you at the same time. "But this is what I fear." And why? What have you to lose?

But to show you that this leads to it [that is, belief], this will diminish the passions, which are your great obstacles. Now, what harm will come to you in taking this course? You would be faithful, virtuous, humble, grateful, beneficent, a sincere friend, truthful. Truly, you would not be given up to poisonous pleasures, to false glory, or false joys. But would you not have other pleasures?

I say to you that you will gain by it in this life. And, each step you take in this direction, you will see so much of the certainty of gain, and so much of the nothingness of what you hazard, that you will acknowledge in the end that you have wagered something certain, infinite for which you have given nothing.

Thomas Hobbes: The Social Contract
From *De Cive*

Born in Wiltshire, England, Thomas Hobbes (1588–1678) worked as a private tutor and late in life devoted himself to philosophy. In the seventeenth century, discussions of political philosophy focused heavily on the issue of the source of governmental authority. In his book De Cive *(1651), Hobbes argues that we obey the law primarily because of the prospect of anarchy if we do not. He describes what it would be like if each person were completely free to decide what it would take to preserve his or her own life. Under these circumstances each person would have a right to do anything and everything he or she considered necessary for this end. Because people frequently want the same thing (although only one person can have it), and because we have inconsistent ideas of what is just and right or even what religion requires, life thus becomes a continuous struggle and conflict, or a "war of all against all." In order, then, to overcome this anarchy, it is necessary for people to agree on one lawgiver, the sovereign, whose laws everyone must obey. Consequently, obedience to the laws is what creates and preserves a civil society. The alternative, says Hobbes, is for us to retain our former freedom in the state of nature to decide by ourselves what justice is and what our conduct should be.*

CHAPTER 1: OF THE STATE OF MEN WITHOUT CIVIL SOCIETY

1. The faculties of human nature may be reduced unto four kinds; bodily strength, experience, reason, passion. Taking the beginning of this following doctrine from these, we will declare in the first place what manner of inclinations men who are endued with these faculties bare towards each other, and whether, and by what faculty, they are born apt for society, and so preserve themselves against mutual violence; then proceeding, we will show what advice was necessary to be taken for this business, and what are the conditions of society, or of human peace; that is to say, (changing the words only) what are the fundamental laws of nature.

2. The greatest part of those men who have written aught concerning commonwealths, either suppose, or require us, or beg of us to believe, that man is a creature born fit for society. [Since we now see actually a constituted society among men, and none living out of it, since we discern all desirous of congress, and mutual correspondence, it may seem a wonderful kind of stupidity, to lay in the very threshold of this doctrine, such a stumbling block before the readers, as to deny man to be born fit for society. Therefore I must more plainly say, that it is true indeed, that to man, by nature (or *as* man, that is) as soon as he is born, solitude is an enemy. For infants have need of others to help them

Source: Thomas Hobbes, *De Cive* (1651), Chapters 1–3 and 5.

to live, and those of riper years to help them to live well, wherefore I deny not that men (even nature compelling) desire to come together. But civil societies are not mere meetings, but bonds, to the making whereof, faith and compacts are necessary. The virtue whereof to children, and fools, and the profit whereof to those who have not yet tasted the miseries which accompany its defects, is altogether unknown; whence it happens, that those, because they know not what society is, cannot enter into it; these, because ignorant of the benefit it brings, care not for it. Manifest therefore it is, that all men, because they are born in infancy, are born unapt for society. Many also (perhaps most men) either through defect of mind, or want of education remain unfit during the whole course of their lives; yet have infants, as well as those of riper years, an human nature. Wherefore man is made fit for society not by nature, but by education. Furthermore, although man were born in such a condition as to desire it, it follows not, that he therefore were born fit to enter into it. For it is one thing to desire, another to be in capacity fit for what we desire. For even they, who through their pride, will not stoop to equal conditions, without which there can be no society, do yet desire it.]

The Greeks call him *political animal*, and on this foundation they so build up the doctrine of civil society, as if for the preservation of peace, and the government of mankind there were nothing else necessary, than that men should agree to make curtain covenants and conditions together, which themselves should then call laws. Which axiom, though received by most, is yet certainly false, and an error proceeding from our too slight contemplation of human nature. For they who shall more narrowly look into the causes for which men come together, and delight in each other's company, shall easily find that this happens not because naturally it could happen no otherwise, but by accident. For if by nature one man should love another, that is as man, there could no reason be returned why every man should not equally love every man, as being equally man, or why he should rather frequent those whose society affords him honor or profit. We do not therefore by nature seek society for its own sake, but that we may receive some honor or profit from it; these we desire primarily, that secondarily: how by what advice men do meet, will be best known by observing those things which they do when they are met. For if they meet for traffic, it is plain every man regards not his fellow, but his business; if to discharge some office, a certain market-friendship is begotten, which has more of jealousy in it than true love, and whence factions sometimes may arise, but good will never. If for pleasure, and recreation of mind, every man is wont to please himself most with those things which stir up laughter, whence he may (according to the nature of that which is ridiculous) by comparison of another man's defects and infirmities, pass the more current in his own opinion; and although this be sometimes innocent, and without offence; yet it is manifest they are not so much delighted with the society, as their own vain glory. But for the most part, in these kind of meetings, we wound the absent; their whole life, sayings, actions are examined, judged, condemned; nay, it is very rare, but some present receive a fling before they part, so as his reason was not ill, who was wont always at parting to go out last. And these are indeed the true delights of society, unto which we are carried by nature; that is, by those passions which are incident to all creatures, until either by sad experience, or good precepts, it so fall out (which in many never happens) that the appetite, of present matters, be dulled with the memory of things past, without which, the discourse of most quick and nimble men, on this subject, is but cold and hungry.

But if it so happen, that being met, they pass their time in relating some stories, and one of them begins to tell one which concerns himself; instantly every one of the rest most greedily desires to speak of himself too. If one relate some wonder, the rest will tell you miracles, if they have them, if not, they will feign them: lastly, that I may say somewhat of them who pretend to be wiser than others; if they meet to talk of philosophy, look how many men, so many would be esteemed masters, or else they not only love not their fellows, but even persecute them with hatred: so clear is it by experience to all men who a little more narrowly consider human affairs, that all free congress arises either from mutual poverty, or from vain glory, whence the parties met, endeavor to carry with them either some benefit, or to leave behind them that same some esteem and honor with those, with whom they have been conversant: the same is also collected by reason out of the definitions themselves, of will, good, honor, profitable. For when we voluntarily contract society, in all manner of society we look after the object of the will; that is, that, which every one of those, who gather together, propounds to himself for good; now whatsoever seems good, is pleasant, and relates either to the senses, or the mind, but all the minds pleasure is either glory, (or to have a good opinion of oneself) or refers to glory in the end; the rest are sensual, or conducing to sensuality, which may be all comprehended under the word conveniences. All society therefore is either for gain, or for glory; that is, not so much for love of our fellows, as for love of ourselves: but no society can be great, or lasting, which begins from vain glory; because that glory is like honor, if all men have it, no man has it, for they consist in comparison and precellence neither does the society of others advance any whit the cause of my glorying in myself. For every man must account himself, such as he can make himself, without the help of others. But though the benefits of this life may be much furthered by mutual help, since yet those may be better attained to by dominion, than by the fear were removed, to obtain dominion, than to gain society. We must therefore resolve, that the original of all great, and lasting societies, consisted not in the mutual good will men had towards each other, but in the mutual fear they had of each other.

3. The cause of mutual fear consists partly in the natural equality of men, partly in their mutual will of hurting: whence it comes to pass that we can neither expect from others, nor promise to ourselves the least security. For if we look on men full-grown, and consider how brittle the frame of our human body is, (which perishing, all its strength, vigor, and wisdom itself perishes with it) and how easy a matter it is, even for the weakest man to kill the strongest, there is no reason why any man trusting to his own strength should conceive himself made by nature above others: they are equals who can do equal things one against the other; but they who can do the greatest things, (namely kill) can do equal things. All men therefore among themselves

are by nature equal; the inequality we now discern, has its spring from the civil law.

4. All men in the state of nature have a desire, and will to hurt, but not proceeding from the same cause, neither equally to be condemned. For one man according to that natural equality which is among us, permits as much to others, as he assumes to himself (which is an argument of a temperate man, and one that rightly values his power); another, supposing himself above others, will have a license to do what he lists, and challenges respect, and honor, as due to him before others, (which is an argument of a fiery spirit): this man's will to hurt arises from vainglory, and the false esteem he has of his own strength; the other's, from the necessity of defending himself, his liberty, and his goods against this man's violence.

5. Furthermore, since the combat of wits is the fiercest, the greatest discords which are, must necessarily arise from this contention. For in this case it is not only odious to contend against, but also not to consent. For not to approve of what a man says is no less than tacitly to accuse him of an error in that thing which he speaks; as in very many things to dissent, is as much as if you accounted him a fool whom you dissent from; which may appear hence, that there are no wars so sharply waged as between sects of the same religion, and factions of the same commonweal, where the contestation is either concerning doctrines, or politic prudence. And since all the pleasure, and jollity of the mind consists in this; even to get some, with whom comparing, it may find somewhat wherein to triumph, and vaunt itself; it's impossible but men must declare sometimes some mutual scorn and contempt either by laughter, or by words, or by gesture, or some sign or other; than which there is no greater vexation of mind; and than from which there cannot possibly arise a greater desire to do hurt.

6. But the most frequent reason why men desire to hurt each other, arises hence, that many men at the same time have an appetite to the same thing; which yet very often they can neither enjoy in common, nor yet divide it; whence it follows that the strongest must have it, and who is strongest must be decided by the sword.

7. Among so many dangers therefore, as the natural lusts of men do daily threaten each other withal, to have a care of ones self is not a matter so scornfully to be looked upon, as if so be there had not been a power and will left in one to have done otherwise. For every man is desirous of what is good for him, and shuns what is evil, but chiefly the chiefest of natural evils, which is death; and this he does, by a certain impulsion of nature, no less than that whereby a stone moves downward: it is therefore neither absurd, nor reprehensible; neither against the dictates of true reason for a man to use all his endeavors to preserve and defend his body, and the members thereof from death and sorrows; but that which is not contrary to right reason, that all men account to be done justly, and with right; neither by the word right is any thing else signified, than that liberty which every man has to make use of his natural faculties according to right reason: therefore the first foundation of natural right is this, that every man as much as in him lies endeavor to protect his life and members.

But because it is in vain for a man to have a right to the end, if the right to the necessary means be denied him; it follows, that since every man has a right to preserve himself, he must also be allowed a right to use all the means, and do all the actions, without which he cannot preserve himself.

9. Now whether the means which he is about to use, and the action he is performing, be necessary to the preservation of his life, and members, or not, he himself, by the right of nature, must be judge. For say another man, judge that it is contrary to right reason that I should judge of mine own peril: why now, because he judges of what concerns me, by the same reason, because we are equal by nature, will I judge also of things which do belong to him; therefore it agrees with right reason, that is, it is the right of nature that I judge of his opinion; that is, whether it conduce to my preservation, or not.

10. Nature has given to everyone a right to all. That is it was lawful for every man in the bare state of nature, or before such time as men had engaged themselves by any covenants, or bonds, to do what he would, and against whom he thought fit, and to possess, use, and enjoy all what he would, or could get. Now because whatsoever a man would, it therefore seems good to him because he wills it, and either it really does, or at least seems to him to contribute toward his preservation, (but we have already allowed him to be judge in the foregoing article whether it does or not, in so much as we are to hold all for necessary whatsoever he shall esteem so) and . . . it appears that by the right of nature those things may be done, and must be had, which necessarily conduce to the protection of life, and members, it follows, that in the state of nature, to have all, and do all is lawful for all. And this is that which is meant by that common saying, nature has given all to all, from whence we understand likewise, that in the state of nature, profit is the measure of right.

11. But it was the least benefit for men thus to have a common right to all things. For the effects of this right are the same, almost, as if there had been no right at all. For although any man might say of every thing, this is mine, yet could he not enjoy it, by reason of his neighbor, who having equal right, and equal power, would pretend the same thing to be his.

12. If now to this natural proclivity of men, to hurt each other, which they derive from their passions, but chiefly from a vain esteem of themselves: you add, the right of all to all, wherewith one by right invades, the other by right resists, and whence arise perpetual jealousies and suspicions on all hands, and how hard a thing it is to provide against an enemy invading us, with an intention to oppress, and ruin, though he come with a small number, and no great provision; it cannot be denied but that the natural state of men, before they entered into society, was a mere war, and that not simply, but a war of all men, against all men. For what is war, but that same time in which the will of contesting by force, is fully declared either by words, or deeds? The time remaining, is termed *peace*.

13. But it is easily judged how disagreeable a thing to the preservation either of mankind, or of each single man, a perpetual war is: but it is perpetual in its own nature, because in regard of the equality of those that strive, it cannot be ended by victory. For in this state the conqueror is subject to so much danger, as it were to be accounted a miracle, if any, even the most strong should close up his life with many years, and old age. They of America are examples hereof,

even in this present age: other nations have been in former ages, which now indeed are become civil, and flourishing, but were then few, fierce, short-lived, poor, nasty, and destroyed of all that pleasure, and beauty of life, which peace and society are wont to bring with them. Whoso-ever therefore holds, that it had been best to have continued in that state in which all things were lawful for all men, he contradicts himself. For every man, by natural necessity desires that which is good for him: nor is there any that esteems a war of all against all, which necessarily adheres to such a state, to be good for him. And so it happens that through fear of each other we think it fit to rid ourselves of this condition, and to get some fellows; that if there needs must be war, it may not yet be against all men, nor without some helps.

14. Fellows are gotten either by constraint, or by consent; by constraint, when after fight the conqueror makes the conquered serve him either through fear of death, or by laying fetters on him: by consent, when men enter into society to help each other, both parties consenting without any constraint. But the conqueror may by right compel the conquered, or the strongest the weaker, (as a man in health may one that is sick, or he that is of riper years a child) unless he will choose to die, to give caution of his future obedience. For since the right of protecting ourselves according to our own wills proceeded from our danger, and our danger from our equality, it's more consonant to reason, and more certain for our conservation, using the present advantage to secure ourselves by taking caution; than, when they shall be full grown and strong, and got out of our power, to endeavor to recover that power again by doubtful fight. And on the other side, nothing can be thought more absurd, than by discharging whom you already have weak in your power, to make him at once both an enemy, and a strong one. From whence we may understand likewise as a corollary in the natural state of men, that a sure and irresistible power confers the right of dominion, and ruling over those who cannot resist; insomuch, as the right of all things, that can be done, adheres essentially, and immediately unto this omnipotence hence arising.

15. Yet cannot men expect any lasting preservation continuing thus in the state of nature, that is, of war, by reason of that equality of power, and other human faculties they are endued withal. Wherefore to seek peace, where there is any hopes of obtaining it, and where there is none, to enquire out for auxiliaries of war, is the dictate of right reason; that is, the law of nature, as shall be showed in the next chapter.

CHAPTER 2: OF THE LAW OF NATURE CONCERNING CONTRACTS

1. All authors agree not concerning the definition of the natural law, who notwithstanding do very often make use of this term in their writings. The method therefore, wherein we begin from definitions, and exclusion of all equivocation, is only proper to them who leave no place for contrary disputes. For the rest, if any man say, that somewhat is done against the law of nature, one proves it

hence, because it was done against the general agreement of all the most wise, and learned nations: but this declares not who shall be the judge of the wisdom and learning of all nations: another hence, that it was done against the general consent of all mankind; which definition is by no means to be admitted. For then it were impossible for any but children, and fools, to offend against such a law. For sure, under the notion of mankind, they comprehend all men actually endued with reason. These therefore either do naught against it, or if they do aught, it is without their joint accord, and therefore ought to be excused; but to receive the laws of nature from the consents of them, who oftener break, than observe them, is in truth unreasonable: besides, men condemn the same things in others, which they approve in themselves; on the other side, they publicly commend what they privately condemn; and they deliver their opinions more by hearsay, than any speculation of their own; and they accord more through hatred of some object, through fear, hope, love, or some other perturbation of mind, than true reason. And therefore it comes to pass, that whole bodies of people often do those things by general accord, or contention, which those writers most willingly acknowledge to be against the law of nature. But since all do grant that is done by *right*, which is not done against reason, we ought to judge those actions only wrong, which are repugnant to right reason; that is, which contradict some certain truth collected by right reasoning from true principles; but that wrong which is done, we say it is done against some law: therefore true reason is a certain law, which (since it is no less a part of human nature, than any other faculty, or affection of the mind) is also termed natural. Therefore the law of nature, that I may define it, is the dictate of right reason, conversant about those things which are either to be done, or omitted for the constant preservation of life, and members, as much as in us lies.

2. But the first and fundamental law of nature is, that peace is to be sought after where it may be found; and where not, there to provide ourselves for helps of war. For we showed in the last article of the foregoing chapter, that this precept is the dictate of right reason; but that the dictates of right reason are natural laws, that has been newly proved above; but this is the first, because the rest are derived from this, and they direct the ways either to peace, or self-defense.

3. But one of the natural laws derived from this fundamental one is this, that the right of all men, to all things, ought not to be retained, but that some certain rights ought to be transferred, or relinquished. For if everyone should retain his right to all things, it must necessarily follow, that some by right might invade; and others, by the same right, might defend themselves against them, (for every man, by natural necessity, endeavors to defend his body, and the things which he judges necessary towards the protection of his body) therefore war would follow. He therefore acts against the reason of peace, that is, against the law of nature, whosoever he be, that does not part with his right to all things. . . .

18. No man is obliged by any contracts whatsoever not to resist him who shall offer to kill, wound, or any other way hurt his body. For there is in every man a certain high degree of fear through which he apprehends that evil which is done to him to be the greatest, and therefore by natural necessity he shuns

it all he can, and it is supposed he can do no otherwise: when a man is arrived to this degree of fear, we cannot expect but he will provide for himself either by flight, or fight. Since therefore no man is tied to impossibilities, they who are threatened either with death (which is the greatest evil to nature) or wounds, or some other bodily hurts, and are not stout enough to bear them, are not obliged to endure them. Furthermore, he that is tied by contract is trusted, (for faith only is the bond of contracts) but they who are brought to punishment, either capital, or more gentle, are fettered, or strongly guarded, which is a most certain sign that they seemed not sufficiently bound from nonresistance by their contracts. It's one thing if I promise thus: if I do it not at the day appointed, kill me. Another thing if thus: if I do it not, though you should offer to kill me, I will not resist: all men, if need be, contract the first way; but there is need sometimes. This second way, none, neither is it ever needful. For in the mere state of nature, if you have a mind to kill, that state itself affords you a right; insomuch as you need not first trust him, if for breach of trust you will afterward kill him. But in a civil state, where the right of life, and death, and of all corporal punishment is with the supreme; that same right of killing cannot be granted to any private person. Neither need the supreme himself contract with any man patiently to yield to his punishment, but only this, that no man offer to defend others from him. If in the state of nature, as between two cities, there should a contract be made, on condition of killing, if it were not performed, we must presuppose another contract of not killing before the appointed day. Wherefore on that day, if there be no performance, the right of war returns; that is, a hostile state, in which all things are lawful, and therefore resistance also. Lastly, by the contract of not resisting, we are obliged of two evils to make choice of that which seems the greater. For certain death is a greater evil than fighting; but of two evils it is impossible not to choose the least: by such a compact therefore we should be tied to impossibilities, which is contrary to the very nature of compacts.

19. Likewise no man is tied by any compacts whatsoever to accuse himself, or any other, by whose damage he is like to procure himself a bitter life; wherefore neither is a father obliged to bear witness against his son, nor a husband against his wife, nor a son against his father; nor any man against any one, by whose means he has his subsistence. For in vain is that testimony which is presumed to be corrupted from nature; but although no man be tied to accuse himself by any compact, yet in a public trial he may, by torture, be forced to make answer; but such answers are no testimony of the fact, but helps for the searching out of truth; insomuch as whether the party tortured his answer be true, or false, or whether he answer not at all, whatsoever he does, he does it by right.

CHAPTER 3: OF THE OTHER LAWS OF NATURE

14. As it was necessary to the conservation of each man, that he should part with some of his rights, so it is no less necessary to the same conservation, that he retain some others, to wit the right of bodily protection, of free enjoyment of air, water, and all necessaries for life. Since therefore many common rights are

retained by those who enter into a peaceable state, and that many peculiar ones are also acquired, hence arises this ninth dictate of the natural law, to wit, that what rights soever any man challenges to himself, he also grant the same as due to all the rest: otherwise he frustrates the equality acknowledged in the former article. For what is it else to acknowledge an equality of persons in the making up of society, but to attribute equal right and power to those whom no reason would else engage to enter into society? But to ascribe equal things to equals, is the same with giving things proportional to proportionals. The observation of this law is called *meekness,* the violation *pleonexia,* the breakers by the Latins are styled *immodici* and *immodesti.*

29. The laws of nature are immutable, and eternal; what they forbid, can never be lawful; what they command, can never be unlawful. For pride, ingratitude, breach of contracts (or injury), inhumanity, contumely, will never be lawful; nor the contrary virtues to these ever unlawful, as we take them for dispositions of the mind, that is, as they are considered in the court of conscience, where only they oblige, and are laws. Yet actions may be so diversified by circumstances, and the civil law, that what's done with equity at one time, is guilty of iniquity at another; and what suits with reason at one time, is contrary to it another. Yet reason is still the same, and changes not her end, which is peace, and defense; nor of the mind which the means to attain them, to wit, those virtues we have declared above, and which cannot be abrogated by any custom, or law whatsoever. . . .

31. All writers do agree that the natural law is the same with the moral. Let us see wherefore this is true. We must know therefore, that good and evil are names given to things to signify the inclination, or aversion of them by whom they were given. But the inclinations of men are diverse, according to their diverse constitutions, customs, opinions; as we may see in those things we apprehend by sense, as by tasting, touching, smelling; but much more in those which pertain to the common actions of life, where what this man commends, (that is to say, calls good) the other undervalues, as being evil; nay, very often the same man at diverse times, praises, and dispraises the same thing. While thus they do, necessary it is there should be discord, and strife: they are therefore so long in the state of war, as by reason of the diversity of the present appetites, they mete good and evil by diverse measures. All men easily acknowledge this state, as long as they are in it, to be evil, and by consequence that peace is good. They therefore who could not agree concerning a present, do agree concerning a future good, which indeed is a work of reason. For things present are obvious to the sense, things to come to our reason only. Reason declaring peace to be good, it follows by the same reason, that all the necessary means to peace be good also, and therefore, that modesty, equity, trust, humanity, mercy (which we have demonstrated to be necessary to peace) are good manners, or habits, that is, virtues. The law therefore, in the means to peace, commands also good manners, or the practice of virtue: and therefore it is called moral.

32. But because men cannot put off this same irrational appetite, whereby they greedily prefer the present good (to which, by strict consequence, many unforeseen evils do adhere) before the future, it happens, that though all men

do agree in the commendation of the foresaid virtues, yet they disagree still concerning their nature, to wit, in what each of them does consist. For as often as another's good action displeases any man, that action has the name given of some neighboring vice; likewise the bad actions, which please them, are ever entitled to some virtue; whence it comes to pass that the same action is praised by these, and called virtue, and dispraised by those, and termed vice. Neither is there as yet any remedy found by philosophers for this matter. For since they could not observe the goodness of actions to consist in this, that it was in order to peace, and the evil in this, that it related to discord, they built a moral philosophy wholly estranged from the moral law, and inconstant to itself. For they would have the nature of virtues seated in a certain kind of mediocrity between two extremes, and the vices in the extremes themselves; which is apparently false. For to dare is commended, and under the name of fortitude is taken for a virtue, although it be an extreme, if the cause be approved. Also the quantity of a thing given, whether it be great, or little, or between both, makes not liberality, but the cause of giving it. Neither is it injustice, if I give any man more, of what is mine own, than I owe him. The laws of nature therefore are the sum of moral philosophy, whereof I have only delivered such precepts in this place, as appertain to the preservation of ourselves against those dangers which arise from discord. But there are other precepts of rational nature, from whence spring other virtues. For temperance also is a precept of reason, because intemperance tends to sicknesses, and death. And so fortitude too, (that is) that same faculty of resisting stoutly in present dangers, (and which are more hardly declined than overcome) because it is a means tending to the preservation of him that resists.

CHAPTER 5: OF THE CAUSES, AND FIRST BEGINNING OF CIVIL GOVERNMENT

6. Since therefore the conspiring of many wills to the same end does not suffice to preserve peace, and to make a lasting defense, it is requisite that in those necessary matters which concern peace and self-defense, there be but one will of all men. But this cannot be done, unless every man will so subject his will to some other one, to wit, either man or counsel, that whatsoever his will is in those things which are necessary to the common peace, it be received for the wills of all men in general, and of every one in particular. Now the gathering together of many men who deliberate of what is to be done, or not to be done, for the common good of all men, is that which I call a *counsel*.

7. This submission of the wills of all those men to the will of one man, or one counsel, is then made, when each one of them obliges himself by contract to every one of the rest, not to resist the will of that one man, or counsel, to which he has submitted himself; that is, that he refuse him not the use of his wealth, and strength, against any others whatsoever (for he is supposed still to retain a right of defending himself against violence) and this is called *union*. But we understand that to be the will of the counsel, which is the will of the major part of those men of whom the counsel consists.

8. But though the will itself be not voluntary, but only the beginning of voluntary actions (for we will not to will, but to act) and therefore falls least of all under deliberation, and compact; yet he who submits his will to the will of another, conveys to that other the right of his strength, and faculties; insomuch as when the rest have done the same, he to whom they have submitted has so much power, as by the terror of it he can conform the wills of particular men unto unity, and concord.

9. Now union thus made is called a city, or civil society, and also a civil person. For when there is one will of all men, it is to be esteemed for one person, and by the word (one) it is to be known, and distinguished from all particular men, as having its own rights and properties; insomuch as neither any one citizen, nor all of them together (if we except him whose will stands for the will of all) is to be accounted the city. A *city* therefore (that we may define it) is one person, whose will, by the compact of many men, is to be received for the will of them all; so as he may use all the power and faculties of each particular person, to the maintenance of peace, and for common defense.

READING 3

René Descartes: Certainty and the Mind
From *Meditations* and *The Passions of the Soul*

René Descartes (1569–1650) was born in a city in western France which has since been renamed "Descartes" in his honor. Descartes was disturbed by a growing interest in ancient Greek skepticism in his day; he offers a more optimistic account of human knowledge in his book Meditations on First Philosophy *(1641). He opens this work by tentatively adopting a skeptical viewpoint and pushing it as far as he can. He asks himself whether he can, for example, ever be certain that he is sitting by his fireplace, or whether he is just dreaming it. After all, from time to time he had dreams in which he appeared to be doing things similar to his behavior during his waking moments. How can he now be certain that he is not dreaming? He finds it possible to doubt virtually everything and wonders whether he can ever discover anything that he cannot doubt. One thing he cannot doubt, says Descartes, is that he doubts. To doubt is to think, and "to think that I am something is necessarily true every time I propound it or mentally apprehend it even though I do not yet know in any adequate manner what I am." From this preliminary certainty, Descartes constructed his theory of knowledge, now called "rationalism," which emphasizes the ability of human reason to grasp fundamental truth about the world without the aid of sense impressions.*

Descartes also put forth a view that we now call "interactive dualism." As a dualist Descartes argues that a human being is composed of two distinct substances, namely,

Source: René Descartes, *Meditations on the First Philosophy* (1641), Meditation 1, 2 and 6; *The Passions of the Soul* (1649).

thought and extension, or mind and body. This distinction is intuitively understandable as a way of separating our various experiences, which alternately focus on physical things and our bodies, on the one hand, and on our ideas of thought and imagination, on the other. However, when we try to specify the exact nature of mind or thought as compared with body, many difficulties arise. The main problem is understanding how information transfers between our conscious spirit and our unconscious physical body. Even though my mind and body are distinct, the two must somehow interact. Suppose a mosquito bites my foot; that sensory information must eventually make its way up through my brain and out of my body into my spiritual mind. Similarly, if I decide to swat the mosquito with my hand, my spirit must issue a command that first flows back into my brain, then down through my hand. Descartes believed that the interactive gateway between these two realms is the pineal gland in the brain.

MEDITATION 1

It is now some years since I detected how many were the false beliefs that I had from my earliest youth admitted as true, and how doubtful was everything had since constructed on this basis; and from that time I was convinced that I must once for all seriously undertake to rid myself of all the opinions which I had formerly accepted, and commence to build a new from the foundation, if I wanted to establish any firm and permanent structure in the sciences. But as this enterprise appeared to be a very great one, I waited until I had attained an age so mature that I could not hope that at any later date I should be better fitted to execute my design. This reason caused me to delay so long that I should feel that I was doing wrong were I to occupy in deliberation the time that yet remains to me for action. Today, then, since very opportunely for the plan I have in view I have delivered my mind from every care and am happily agitated by no passions and since I have procured for myself an assured leisure in a peaceable retirement, I shall at last seriously and freely address myself to the general upheaval of all my former opinions.

Now for this object it is not necessary that I should show that all of these are false; I shall perhaps never arrive at this end. But inasmuch as reason already persuades me that I ought no less carefully to withhold my assent from matters which are not entirely certain and indubitable than from those which appear to me manifestly to be false, if I am able to find in each one some reason to doubt, this will suffice to justify my rejecting the whole. And for that end it will not be requisite that I should examine each in particular, which would be an endless undertaking; for owing to the fact that the destruction of the foundations of necessity brings with it the downfall of the rest of the edifice, I shall only in the first place attack those principles upon which all my former opinions rested.

All that up to the present time I have accepted as most true and certain I have learned either from the senses or through the senses; but it is sometimes proved to me that these senses are deceptive, and it is wiser not to trust entirely to anything by which we have once been deceived.

But it may be that although the senses sometimes deceive us concerning things which are hardly perceptible, or very far away, there are yet many others to be met with as to which we cannot reasonably have any doubt, although we recognize them by their means. For example, there is the fact that I am here, seated by the fire, attired in a dressing gown, having this paper in my hands and other similar matters. And how could I deny that these hands and this body are mine, were it not perhaps that I compare myself to certain persons, devoid of sense, whose cerebella are so troubled and clouded by the violent vapors of black bile, that they constantly assure us that they think they are kings when they are really quite poor, or that they are clothed in purple when they are really without covering, or who imagine that they have an earthenware head or are nothing but pumpkins or are made of glass. But they are mad, and I should not be any the less insane were I to follow examples so extravagant.

At the same time I must remember that I am a man, and that consequently I am in the habit of sleeping, and in my dreams representing to myself the same things or sometimes even less probable things, than do those who are insane in their waking moments. How often has it happened to me that in the night I dreamt that I found myself in this particular place, that I was dressed and seated near the fire, while in reality I was lying undressed in bed! At this moment it does indeed seem to me that it is with eyes awake that I am looking at this paper; that this head which I move is not asleep, that it is deliberately and of set purpose that I extend my hand and perceive it; what happens in sleep does not appear so clear nor so distinct as does all this. But in thinking over this I remind myself that on many occasions I have in sleep been deceived by similar illusions, and in dwelling carefully on this reflection I see so manifestly that there are no certain indications by which we may clearly distinguish wakefulness from sleep that I am lost in astonishment. And my astonishment is such that it is almost capable of persuading me that I now dream.

Now let us assume that we are asleep and that all these particulars, e.g., that we open our eyes, shake our head, extend our hands, and so on, are but false delusions; and let us reflect that possibly neither our hands nor our whole body are such as they appear to us to be. At the same time we must at least confess that the things which are represented to us in sleep are like painted representations which can only have been formed as the counterparts of something real and true, and that in this way those general things at least, i.e., eyes, a head, hands, and a whole body, are not imaginary things, but things really existent. For, as a matter of fact, painters, even when they study with the greatest skill to represent sirens and satyrs by forms the most strange and extraordinary, cannot give them natures which are entirely new, but merely make a certain medley of the members of different animals; or if their imagination is extravagant enough to invent something so novel that nothing similar has ever before been seen, and that then their work represents a thing purely fictitious and absolutely false, it is certain all the same that the colors of which this is composed are necessarily real. And for the same reason, although these general things, to wit, a body, eyes, a head, hands, and such like, may be imaginary, we are bound at the same time to confess that there are at least some other objects yet more simple and more universal, which are real and true; and of these just in the same way as with certain real colors, all these images of things which dwell in our thoughts, whether true and real or false and fantastic, are formed.

To such a class of things pertains corporeal nature in general, and its extension, the figure of extended things, their quantity or magnitude and number, as also the place in which they are, the time which measures their duration, and so on.

That is possibly why our reasoning is not unjust when we conclude from this that Physics, Astronomy, Medicine, and all other sciences which have as their end the consideration of composite things, are very dubious and uncertain; but that Arithmetic, Geometry, and other sciences of that kind which only treat of things that are very simple and very general, without taking great trouble to ascertain whether they are actually existent or not, contain some measure of certainty and an element of the indubitable. For whether I am awake or asleep, two and three together always form five, and the square can never have more than four sides, and it does not seem possible that truths so clear and apparent can be suspected of any falsity or uncertainty.

Nevertheless I have long had fixed in my mind the belief that an all-powerful God existed by whom I have been created such as I am. But how do I know that He has not brought it to pass that there is no earth, no heaven, no extended body, no magnitude, no place, and that nevertheless I possess the perceptions of all these things and that they seem to me to exist just exactly as I now see them? And, besides, as I sometimes imagine that others deceive themselves in the things which they think they know best, how do I know that I am not deceived every time that I add two and three, or count the sides of a square, or judge of things yet simpler, if anything simpler can be imagined? But possibly God has not desired that I should be thus deceived, for He is said to be supremely good. If, however, it is contrary to His goodness to have made me such that I constantly deceive myself, it would also appear to be contrary to His goodness to permit me to be sometimes deceived, and nevertheless I cannot doubt that He does permit this.

There may indeed be those who would prefer to deny the existence of a God so powerful, rather than believe that all other things are uncertain. But let us not oppose them for the present, and grant that all that is here said of a God is a fable; nevertheless in whatever way they suppose that I have arrived at the state of being that I have reached—whether they attribute it to fate or to accident, or make out that it is by a continual succession of antecedents, or by some other method—since to err and deceive oneself is a defect, it is clear that the greater will be the probability of my being so imperfect as to deceive myself ever, as is the Author to whom they assign my origin the less powerful. To these reasons I have certainly nothing to reply, but at the end I feel constrained to confess that there is nothing in all that I formerly believed to be true, of which I cannot in some measure doubt, and that not merely through want of thought or through levity, but for reasons which are very powerful and maturely considered; so that henceforth I ought not the less carefully to refrain from giving credence to these opinions than to that which is manifestly false, if I desire to arrive at any certainty in the sciences.

But it is not sufficient to have made these remarks, we must also be careful to keep them in mind. For these ancient and commonly held opinions still revert frequently to my mind, long and familiar custom having given them the right to occupy my mind against my inclination and rendered them almost masters of my belief; nor will I ever lose the habit of deferring to them or of placing my confidence in them, so long as I consider them as they really are, i.e., opinions in some measure doubtful, as I have just shown, and at the same time highly probable, so that there is much more reason to believe in than to deny them. That is why I consider that I shall not be acting amiss, if, taking of set purpose a contrary belief, I allow myself to be deceived, and for a certain time pretend that all these opinions are entirely false and imaginary, until at last, having thus balanced my former prejudices with my latter so that they cannot divert my opinions more to one side than to the other, my judgment will no longer be dominated by bad usage or turned away from the right knowledge of the truth. For I am assured that there can be neither peril nor error in this course, and that I cannot at present yield too much to distrust, since I am not considering the question of action, but only of knowledge.

I shall then suppose, not that God who is supremely good and the fountain of truth, but some evil genius not less powerful than deceitful, has employed his whole energies in deceiving me; I shall consider that the heavens, the earth, colors, figures, sound, and all other external things are nothing but the illusions and dreams of which this genius has availed himself in order to lay traps for my credulity; I shall consider myself as having no hands, no eyes, no flesh, no blood, nor any senses, yet falsely believing myself to possess all these things; I shall remain obstinately attached to this idea, and if by this means it is not in my power to arrive at the knowledge of any truth, I may at least do what is in my power, i.e., suspend my judgment, and with firm purpose avoid giving credence to any false thing, or being imposed upon by this arch deceiver, however powerful and deceptive he may be. But this task is a laborious one, and insensibly a certain lassitude leads me into the course of my ordinary life. And just as a captive who in sleep enjoys an imaginary liberty, when he begins to suspect that his liberty is but a dream, fears to awaken, and conspires with these agreeable illusions that the deception may be prolonged, so insensibly of my own accord I fall back into my former opinions, and I dread awakening from this slumber, lest the laborious wakefulness which would follow the tranquility of this repose should have to be spent not in daylight, but in the excessive darkness of the difficulties which have just been discussed.

MEDITATION 2

The Meditation of yesterday filled my mind with so many doubts that it is no longer in my power to forget them. And yet I do not see in what manner I can resolve them; and, just as if I had all of a sudden fallen into very deep water, I am so disconcerted that I can neither make certain of setting my feet on the bottom, nor can I swim and so support myself on the surface. I shall nevertheless make an effort and follow anew the same path as that on which I yesterday entered, i.e., I shall proceed by setting aside all that in which the least doubt could be supposed to exist, just as if I had discovered that it was absolutely false; and I shall ever follow in this road until I have met with something which is certain, or at least, if I can do nothing else, until I have learned for certain that there is nothing in the world that is certain. Archimedes, in order that he might draw the terrestrial globe out of its place, and transport it elsewhere, demanded only that one point should be fixed and immoveable; in the same way I shall have the right to conceive high hopes if I am happy enough to discover one thing only which is certain and indubitable.

I suppose, then, that all the things that I see are false; I persuade myself that nothing has ever existed of all that my fallacious memory represents to me. I consider that I possess no senses; I imagine that body, figure, extension, movement and place are but the fictions of my mind. What, then, can be esteemed as true? Perhaps nothing at all, unless that there is nothing in the world that is certain.

But how can I know there is not something different from those things that I have just considered, of which one cannot have the slightest doubt? Is there not some God, or some other being by whatever name we call it, who puts these reflections into my mind? That is not necessary, for is it not possible that I am capable of producing them myself? I myself, am I not at least something? But I have already denied that I had senses and body. Yet I hesitate, for what follows from that? Am I so dependent on body and senses that I cannot exist without these? But I was persuaded that there was nothing in all the world, that there was no heaven, no earth, that there were no minds, nor any bodies: was I not then likewise persuaded that I did not exist? Not at all; of a surety I myself did exist since I persuaded myself of something or merely because I thought of something. But there is some deceiver or other, very powerful and very cunning, who ever employs his ingenuity in deceiving me. Then without doubt I exist also if he deceives me, and let him deceive me as much as he will, he can never cause me to be nothing so long as I think that I am something. So that after having reflected well and carefully examined all things, we must come to the definite conclusion that this proposition: I am, I exist, is necessarily true each time that I pronounce it, or that I mentally conceive it.

But I do not yet know clearly enough what I am, I who am certain that I am; and hence I must be careful to see that I do not imprudently take some other object in place of myself, and thus that I do not go astray in respect of this knowledge that I hold to be the most certain and most evident of all that I have formerly learned. That is why I shall now consider anew what I believed myself to be before I embarked upon these last reflections; and of my former opinions I shall withdraw all that might even in a small degree be invalidated by the reasons which I have just brought forward, in order that there may be nothing at all left beyond what is absolutely certain and indubitable.

What then did I formerly believe myself to be? Undoubtedly I believed myself to be a man. But what is a man? Shall I say a reasonable animal? Certainly not; for then I should have to inquire what an animal is, and what is reasonable; and thus from a single question I should insensibly fall into an infinitude of others more difficult; and I should not wish to waste the little time and leisure remaining to me in trying to unravel subtleties like these. But I shall rather stop here to consider the thoughts which of themselves spring up in my mind, and which were not inspired by anything beyond my own nature alone when I applied myself to the consideration of my being. In the first place, then, I considered myself as having a face, hands, arms, and all that system of members composed of bones and flesh as seen in a corpse which I designated by the name of body. In addition to this I considered that I was nourished, that I walked, that I felt, and that I thought, and I referred all these actions to the soul: but I did not stop to consider what the soul was, or if I did stop, I imagined that it was something extremely rare and subtle like a wind, a flame, or an ether, which was spread throughout my grosser parts. As to body I had no manner of doubt about its nature, but thought I had a very clear knowledge of it; and if I had desired to explain it according to the notions that I had then formed of it, I should have described it thus: By the body I understand all that which can be defined by a certain figure: something which can be confined in a certain place, and which can fill a given space in such a way that every other body will be excluded from it; which can be perceived either by touch, or by sight, or by hearing, or by taste, or by smell: which can be moved in many ways not, in truth, by itself, but by something which is foreign to it, by which it is touched and from which it receives impressions: for to have the power of self-movement, as also of feeling or of thinking, I did not consider to appertain to the nature of body: on the contrary, I was rather astonished to find that faculties similar to them existed in some bodies.

But what am I, now that I suppose that there is a certain genius which is extremely powerful, and, if I may say so, malicious, who employs all his powers in deceiving me? Can I affirm that I possess the least of all those things which I have just said pertain to the nature of body? I pause to consider, I revolve all these things in my mind, and I find none of which I can say that it pertains to me. It would be tedious to stop to enumerate them. Let us pass to the attributes of soul and see if there is any one which is in me. What of nutrition or walking the first mentioned? But if it is so that I have no body it is also true that I can neither walk nor take nourishment. Another attribute is sensation. But one cannot feel without body, and besides I have thought I perceived many things during sleep that I recognized in my waking moments as not having been experienced at all. What of thinking? I find here that thought is an attribute that belongs to me; it alone cannot be separated from me. I am, I exist, that is certain. But how often? Just when I think; for it might possibly be the case if I ceased entirely to think, that I should likewise cease altogether to exist. I do not now admit anything which is not necessarily true: to speak accurately I am not more than a thing which thinks, that is to say a mind or a soul, or an understanding, or a reason, which are terms whose significance was formerly unknown to me. I am, however, a real thing and really exist; but what thing? I have answered: a thing which thinks.

And what more? I shall exercise my imagination in order to see if I am not something more. I am not a collection of members which we call the human body: I am not a subtle air distributed through these members, I am not a wind, a fire, a vapor, a breath, nor anything at all which I can imagine or conceive; because I have assumed that all these were nothing. Without changing that supposition I find that I only leave myself certain of the fact that I am somewhat. But perhaps it is true that these same things which I supposed were non-existent because they are unknown to me, are really not different from the self which I know. I am not sure about this, I shall not dispute about it now; I can only give judgment on things that are known to me. I know that I exist, and I inquire what I am, I whom I know to exist. But it is very certain that the knowledge of my existence taken in its precise significance does not depend on things whose existence is not yet known to me; consequently it does not depend on those which I can feign in imagination. And indeed the very term feign in imagination proves to me my error, for I really do this if I image myself a something, since to imagine is nothing else than to contemplate the figure or image of a corporeal thing. But I already know for certain that I am, and that it may be that all these images, and, speaking generally, all things that relate to the nature of body are nothing but dreams and chimeras. For this reason I see clearly that I have as little reason to say, "I shall stimulate my imagination in order to know more distinctly what I am," than if I were to say, "I am now awake, and I perceive somewhat that is real and true: but because I do not yet perceive it distinctly enough, I shall go to sleep of express purpose, so that my dreams may represent the perception with greatest truth and evidence." And, thus, I know for certain that nothing of all that I can understand by means of my imagination belongs to this knowledge which I have of myself, and that it is necessary to recall the mind from this mode of thought with the utmost diligence in order that it may be able to know its own nature with perfect distinctness.

But what then am I? A thing which thinks. What is a thing which thinks? It is a thing which doubts, understands, conceives, affirms, denies, wills, refuses, which also imagines and feels.

Certainly it is no small matter if all these things pertain to my nature. But why should they not so pertain? Am I not that being who now doubts nearly everything, who nevertheless understands certain things, who affirms that one only is true, who denies all the others, who desires to know more, is averse from being deceived, who imagines many things, sometimes indeed despite his will, and who perceives many likewise, as by the intervention of the bodily organs? Is there nothing in all this which is as true as it is certain that I exist, even though I should always sleep and though he who has given me being employed all his ingenuity in deceiving me? Is there likewise any one of these attributes which can be distinguished from my thought, or which might be said to be separated from myself? For it is so evident of itself that it is I who doubts, who understands, and who desires, that there is no reason here to add anything to explain it. And I have certainly the power of imagining likewise; for although it may happen (as I formerly supposed) that none of the things which I imagine are true, nevertheless this power of imagining does not cease to be really in use, and it forms part of my thought. Finally, I am the same who feels, that is to say, who perceives certain things, as by the organs of sense, since in truth

I see light, I hear noise, I feel heat. But it will be said that these phenomena are false and that I am dreaming. Let it be so; still it is at least quite certain that it seems to me that I see light, that I hear noise and that I feel heat. That cannot be false; properly speaking it is what is in me called feeling; and used in this precise sense that is no other thing than thinking.

From this time I begin to know what I am with a little more clearness and distinction than before; but nevertheless it still seems to me, and I cannot prevent myself from thinking, that corporeal things, whose images are framed by thought, which are tested by the senses, are much more distinctly known than that obscure part of me which does not come under the imagination. Although really it is very strange to say that I know and understand more distinctly these things whose existence seems to me dubious, which are unknown to me, and which do not belong to me, than others of the truth of which I am convinced, which are known to me and which pertain to my real nature, in a word, than myself. But I see clearly how the case stands: my mind loves to wander, and cannot yet suffer itself to be retained within the just limits of truth. Very good, let us once more give it the freest rein, so that, when afterwards we seize the proper occasion for pulling up, it may the more easily be regulated and controlled.

Let us begin by considering the commonest matters, those which we believe to be the most distinctly comprehended, to wit, the bodies which we touch and see; not indeed bodies in general, for these general ideas are usually a little more confused, but let us consider one body in particular. Let us take, for example, this piece of wax: it has been taken quite freshly from the hive, and it has not yet lost the sweetness of the honey which it contains; it still retains somewhat of the odor of the flowers from which it has been culled; its color, its figure, its size are apparent; it is hard, cold, easily handled, and if you strike it with the finger, it will emit a sound. Finally all the things which are requisite to cause us distinctly to recognize a body, are met with in it. But notice that while I speak and approach the fire what remained of the taste is exhaled, the smell evaporates, the color alters, the figure is destroyed, the size increases, it becomes liquid, it heats, scarcely can one handle it, and when one strikes it, now sound is emitted. Does the same wax remain after this change? We must confess that it remains; none would judge otherwise. What then did I know so distinctly in this piece of wax? It could certainly be nothing of all that the senses brought to my notice, since all these things which fall under taste, smell, sight, touch, and hearing, are found to be changed, and yet the same wax remains.

Perhaps it was what I now think, viz., that this wax was not that sweetness of honey, nor that agreeable scent of flowers, nor that particular whiteness, nor that figure, nor that sound, but simply a body which a little while before appeared to me as perceptible under these forms, and which is now perceptible under others. But what, precisely, is it that I imagine when I form such conceptions? Let us attentively consider this, and, abstracting from all that does not belong to the wax, let us see what remains. Certainly nothing remains excepting a certain extended thing which is flexible and movable. But what is the meaning of flexible and movable? Is it not that I imagine that this piece of wax being round is capable of becoming square and of passing from a square to a triangular figure? No, certainly it is not that, since I imagine it admits of an infinitude of similar changes, and I nevertheless do not know how to compass the infinitude by my imagination, and consequently this conception which I have of the wax is not brought about by the faculty of imagination. What now is this extension? Is it not also unknown? For it becomes greater when the wax is melted, greater when it is boiled, and greater still when the heat increases; and I should not conceive clearly according to truth what wax is, if I did not think that even this piece that we are considering is capable of receiving more variations in extension than I have ever imagined. We must then grant that I could not even understand through the imagination what this piece of wax is, and that it is my mind alone which perceives it. I say this piece of wax in particular, for as to wax in general it is yet clearer. But what is this piece of wax which cannot be understood excepting by the understanding or mind? It is certainly the same that I see, touch, imagine, and finally it is the same which I have always believed it to be from the beginning. But what must particularly be observed is that its perception is neither an act of vision, nor of touch, nor of imagination, and has never been such although it may have appeared formerly to be so, but only an intuition of the mind, which may be imperfect and confused as it was formerly, or clear and distinct as it is at present, according as my attention is more or less directed to the elements which are found in it, and of which it is composed.

Yet in the meantime I am greatly astonished when I consider the great feebleness of mind and its proneness to fall insensibly into error; for although without giving expression to my thought I consider all this in my own mind, words often impede me and I am almost deceived by the terms of ordinary language. For we say that we see the same wax, if it is present, and not that we simply judge that it is the same from its having the same color and figure. From this I should conclude that I knew the wax by means of vision and not simply by the intuition of the mind; unless by chance I remember that, when looking from a window and saying I see men who pass in the street, I really do not see them, but infer that what I see is men, just as I say that I see wax. And yet what do I see from the window but hats and coats which may cover automatic machines? Yet I judge these to be men. And similarly solely by the faculty of judgment which rests in my mind, I comprehend that which I believed I saw with my eyes. . . .

MEDITATION 6

. . . First of all, then, I perceived that I had a head, hands, feet, and all other members of which this body—which I considered as a part, or possibly even as the whole, of myself—is composed. Further I was sensible that this body was placed amidst many others, from which it was capable of being affected in many different ways, beneficial and hurtful, and I remarked that a certain feeling of pleasure accompanied those that were beneficial, and pain those which were harmful. And in addition to this pleasure and pain, I also experienced hunger, thirst, and other similar appetites, as also certain corporeal inclinations towards joy, sadness, anger, and other similar passions. And outside myself, in addition to extension, figure, and motions of bodies, I remarked in them hardness, heat, and all other tactile qualities, and, further, light and color, and scents and sounds, the variety of which gave me the means of distinguishing the sky, the earth, the sea, and generally all the other bodies, one from the other.

And certainly, considering the ideas of all these qualities which presented themselves to my mind, and which alone I perceived properly or immediately, it was not without reason that I believed myself to perceive objects quite different from my thought, to wit, bodies from which those ideas proceeded; for I found by experience that these ideas presented themselves to me without my consent being requisite, so that I could not perceive any object, however desirous I might be, unless it were present to the organs of sense; and it was not in my power not to perceive it, when it was present. . . .

Nor was it without some reason that I believed that this body (which be a certain special right I call my own) belonged to me more properly and more strictly than any other; for in fact I could never be separated from it as from other bodies; I experienced in it and on account of it all my appetites and affections, and finally I was touched by the feeling of pain and the titillation of pleasure in its parts, and not in the parts of other bodies which were separated from it.

But when I inquired, why, from some, I know not what, painful sensation, there follows sadness of mind, and from the pleasurable sensation there arises joy, or why this mysterious pinching of the stomach which I call hunger causes me to desire to eat, and dryness of throat causes a desire to drink, and so on, I could give no reason excepting that nature taught me so. . .

But there is nothing which this nature teaches me more expressly nor more sensibly than that I have a body which is adversely affected when I feel pain, which has need of food or drink when I experience the feelings of hunger and thirst, and so on; nor can I doubt there being some truth in all this.

Nature also teaches me by these sensations of pain, hunger, thirst, etc., that I am not only lodged in my body as a pilot in a vessel, but that I am not only lodged in my body as a pilot in a vessel, but that I am very closely united to it, and so to speak so intermingled with it that I seem to compose with it one whole. For if that were not the case, when my body is hurt, I, who am merely a thinking thing, should not feel pain, for I should perceive this wound by the understanding only, just as the sailor perceives by sight when something is damaged in his vessel; and when my body has need of drink or food, I should clearly understand the fact without being warned of it by confused feelings of hunger and thirst. For all these sensations of hunger, thirst, pain, etc., are in truth none other than certain confused modes of thought which are produced by the union and apparent intermingling of mind and body.

Moreover, nature teaches me that many other bodies exist around mine, of which some are to be avoided, and others sought after. And certainly from the fact that I am sensible of different sorts of colors, sounds, scents, tastes, heat, hardness, etc., I very easily conclude that there are in the bodies from which all these diverse sense-perceptions proceed certain variations which answer to them, although possibly these are not really at all similar to them. And also from the fact that amongst these different sense-perceptions some are very agreeable to me and others disagreeable, it is quite certain that my body (or rather myself in my entirety, inasmuch as I am formed of body and soul) may receive different impressions agreeable and disagreeable from the other bodies which surround it. . . .

In this sum [of my existence] many things are comprehended which only pertain to mind (and to these I do not refer in speaking of nature) such as the notion which I have of the fact that what has once been done cannot ever be undone and an infinitude of such things which I know by the light of nature without the help of the body; and seeing that it comprehends many other matters besides which only pertain to body, and are no longer here contained under the name of nature, such as the quality of weight which it possesses and the like, with which I also do not deal; for in talking of nature I only treat of those things given by God to me as a being composed of mind and body. But the nature here described truly teaches me to flee from things which cause the sensation of pain, and seek after the things which communicate to me the sentiment of pleasure and so forth; but I do not see that beyond this it teaches me that from those diverse sense-perceptions we should ever form any conclusion regarding things outside of us, without having carefully and maturely mentally examined them beforehand. For it seems to me that it is mind alone, and not mind and body in conjunction, that is requisite to a knowledge of the truth in regard to such things. . . .

In order to begin this examination, then, I here say, in the first place, that there is a great difference between mind and body, inasmuch as body is by nature always divisible, and the mind is entirely indivisible. For, as a matter of fact, when I consider the mind, that is to say, myself inasmuch as I am only a thinking thing, I cannot distinguish in myself any parts, but apprehend myself to be clearly one and entire; and although the whole mind seems to be united to the whole body, yet if a foot, or an arm, or some other part, is separated from my body, I am aware that nothing has been taken away from my mind. And the faculties of willing, feeling, conceiving, etc., cannot be properly speaking said to be its parts, for it is one and the same mind which employs itself in willing and in feeling and understanding. But it is quite otherwise with corporeal or extended objects, for there is not one of these imaginable by me which my mind cannot easily divide into parts, and which consequently I do not recognize as being divisible; this would be sufficient to teach me that the mind or soul of man is entirely different from the body, if I had not already learned it from other sources.

I further notice that the mind does not receive the impressions from all parts of the body immediately, but only from the brain, or perhaps even from one of its smallest parts, to wit, from that in which the common sense is said to reside, which, whenever it is disposed in the same particular way, conveys the same thing to the mind, although meanwhile the other portions of the body may be differently disposed, as is testified by innumerable experiments which it is unnecessary here to recount.

I notice, also, that the nature of body is such that none of its parts can be moved by another part a little way off which cannot also be moved in the same way by each one of the parts which are between the two, although this more remote part does not act at all. As, for example, in the cord ABCD which is in tension if we pull the last part D, the first part A will not be moved in any way differently from what would be the case if one of the intervening parts B or C were pulled, and the last part D were to remain unmoved. And in the same way, when I feel pain in my foot, my knowledge of physics teaches me that this sensation is communicated by means of nerves dispersed through the foot, which, being extended like cords from there to the brain, when they are contracted in the foot, at the same time contract the inmost portions of the brain which is their extremity and place of origin, and then excite a certain movement which nature has established in order to cause the mind to be affected by a sensation of pain represented as existing in the foot. But because these nerves must pass through the tibia, the thigh, the loins, the back and the neck, in order to reach from the leg to the brain, it may happen that although their extremities which are in the foot are not affected, but only certain ones of their intervening parts which pass by the loins or the neck, this action will excite the same movement in the brain that might have been excited there by a hurt received in the foot, in consequence of which the mind will necessarily feel in the foot the same pain as if it had received a hurt. And the same holds good of all the other perceptions of our senses. . . .

BODY, SOUL, AND THE PINEAL GLAND

31. That there is a small gland in the brain in which the soul exercises its function more particularly than in the other parts.   It is likewise necessary to know that although the soul is joined to the whole body, there is yet in that a certain part in which it exercises its functions more particularly than in all the others. And it is usually believed that this part is the brain, or possibly the heart. It is believed to be the brain because it is with it that the organs of sense are connected. And it is believed to be the heart because it is apparently in it that we experience the passions. But, in examining the matter with care, it seems as though I had clearly ascertained that the part of the body in which the soul exercises its functions immediately is in nowise the heart, nor the whole of the brain. Instead, it is merely the most inward of all its parts, namely, a certain very small gland which is situated in the middle of its substance and so suspended above the duct whereby the animal spirits in its anterior cavities have communication with those in the posterior. It is such that the slightest movements which take place in it may alter very greatly the course of these spirits. And, reciprocally, the smallest changes which occur in the course of the spirits may do much to change the movements of this gland.

32. How we know that this gland is the main seat of the soul.   The reason which persuades me that the soul cannot have any other seat in all the body than this gland wherein to exercise its functions immediately, is that I reflect that the other parts of our brain are all of them double, just as we have two eyes, two hands, two ears, and finally all the organs of our outside senses are double. And inasmuch as we have but one solitary and simple thought of one particular thing at one and the same moment, it must necessarily be the case that there must somewhere be a place where the two images which come to us by the two eyes, where the two other impressions which proceed from a single object by means of the double organs of the other senses, can unite before arriving at the soul, in order that they may not represent to it two objects instead of one. And it is easy to see how these images or other impressions might unite in this gland by the intermission of the spirits which fill the cavities of the brain. But there is no other place in the body where they can be thus united unless they are so in this gland.

33. How the soul and the body act on one another.   Let us then conceive here that the soul has its principal seat in the little gland which exists in the middle of the brain. For, from this spot it radiates forth through all the remainder of the body by means of the animal spirits, nerves, and even the blood, which, participating in the impressions of the spirits, can carry them by the arteries into all the members. Recall what has been said above about the machine of our body, that is, that the little filaments of our nerves are so distributed in all its parts, that on the occasion of the diverse movements which are there excited by sensible objects, they open in different ways the pores of the brain. This, in turn, causes the animal spirit contained in these cavities to enter in different ways into the muscles, by which means they can move the members in all the different ways in which they are capable of being moved. And also, recall all the other causes which are capable of moving the spirits in different ways and which suffice to conduct them into different muscles. Let us here add that the small gland which is the main seat of the soul is so suspended between the cavities which contain the spirits that it can be moved by them in as many different ways as there are sensible differences in the object. Further, it may also be moved in different ways by the soul, whose nature is such that it receives in itself as many different impressions, that is to say, that it possesses as many different perceptions as there are different movements in this gland. Reciprocally, likewise, the machine of the body is so formed that from the simple fact that this gland is differently moved by the soul (or by such other cause, whatever it is) it thrusts the spirits which surround it towards the pores of the brain, which conduct them by the nerves into the muscles, by which means it causes them to move the limbs.

Anne Conway: Blurring the Distinction between Mind and Body

From *Principles*

Born in London, Anne Conway (1631–1678) is one of the rare female philosophers of her time and is remembered for her posthumous work on the mind-body problem, Principles of the Most Ancient and Modern Philosophy *(1692). Descartes offered his pineal gland theory to explain how two radically different things—spirit and physical matter—could interact with each other. Conway was not impressed with Descartes's solution; she says that the entire mind-body problem rests on the mistaken assumption that mind and body are fundamentally different kinds of things. Conway suggests instead that matter and mind do not really differ in kind, but only in degree. That is, we should picture a graded spectrum of stuff, with the heaviest matter at one end and the lightest spirit at the other. In the middle of this spectrum there is light matter and heavy spirit. It is in this middle ground that heavy spirit, which is slightly physical itself, can physically push light matter such as air.*

BODY AND SOUL DIFFER ONLY IN DEGREE, NOT IN KIND

To prove that spirit and body differ not essentially, but gradually, I shall deduce my fourth argument from the intimate band or union, which intercedes between bodies and spirits. [It is] by means whereof the spirits have dominion over the bodies with which they are united, that they move them from one place to another, and use them as instruments in their various operations. For if spirit and body are so contrary one to another (so that a spirit is only life, or a living and sensible substance, but a body a certain mass merely dead; a spirit penetrable and indiscerptible [that is, indivisible into parts], which are all contrary attributes) what (I pray you) is that which does so join or unite them together? Or, what are those links or chains, whereby they have so firm a connection, and that for so long a space of time? Moreover also, when the spirit or soul is separated from the body, so that it has no longer dominion or power over it to move it as it had before, what is the cause of this separation?

If it be said, that the vital agreement ([which] the soul has to the body) is the cause of the said union, and that the body being corrupted that vital agreement ceases, I answer, we must first inquire in what this vital agreement does consist. For if they cannot tell us wherein it does consist, they only trifle with empty words, which give a sound, but want a signification. For certainly in the sense

Source: Anne Conway, *The Principles of the Most Ancient and Modern Philosophy* (1692), Chapters 8 and 9.

which they take body and spirit in, there is no agreement at all between them. For a body is always a dead thing, void of life and sense, no less when the spirit is in it, than when it is gone out of it. Hence there is no agreement at all between them. And if there is any agreement, that certainly will remain the same, both when the body is sound, and when it is corrupted.

If they deny this, because a spirit requires an organized body (by means whereof it performs its vital acts of the external senses—moves and transports the body from place to place, which organical action ceases when the body is corrupted) certainly by this the difficulty is never the better solved. For why does the spirit require such an organized body? For example, Why does it require a corporeal eye so wonderfully formed and organized, that I can see by it? Why does it need a corporeal light to see corporeal objects? Or, why is it requisite that the image of the object should be sent to it, through the eye, that I may see it? If the same were entirely nothing but a spirit, and no way corporeal, why does it need so many several corporeal organs, so far different from the nature of it?

Furthermore, how can a spirit move its body, or any of its members, if a spirit (as they affirm) is of such a nature, that no part of its body can in the least resist it, even as one body is wont to resist another, when it is moved by it, by reason of its impenetrability? For if a spirit could also easily penetrate all bodies, wherefore does it not leave the body behind it when it is moved from place to place, seeing it can so easily pass out without the least resistance? For certainly this is the cause of all motions which we see in the world, where one thing moves another, viz., because both are impenetrable in the sense aforesaid. For, were it not for this impenetrability, one creature could not move another, because this would not oppose that, nor at all resist it. An example whereof we have in the sails of a ship, by which the wind drives the ship, and that so much the more vehemently, by how much the fewer holes, vents, and passages, the same finds in the sails against which it drives. When on the contrary, if, instead of sails, nets were expanded, through which the wind would have a freer passage, certainly by these the ship would be but little moved, although it blew with great violence. Hence we see how this impenetrability causes resistance, and this makes motion. But if there were no impenetrability, as in the case of body and spirit, then there would be no resistance, and by consequence the spirit could make no motion in the body. . . .

For we may easily understand how one body is united with another, by that true agreement that one has with another in its own nature. And so the most subtle and spiritual body may be united with a body that is very gross and thick, namely, by means of certain bodies partaking of subtlety and grossness, according to diverse degrees consisting between two extremes. And these middle bodies are indeed the links and chains by which the soul, which is so subtle and spiritual, is conjoined with a body so gross—which middle spirits (if they cease, or are absent) the union is broken or dissolved. So from the same foundation we may easily understand how the soul moves the body, viz., as one subtle body can move another gross and thick body. And seeing body itself is a sensible life, or an intellectual substance, it is no less clearly conspicuous how one body can wound, or grieve, or gratify, or please another. [It is] because things of one, or alike nature can easily affect each other. . . .

I shall draw a fifth argument from what we observe in all visible bodies, as in earth, water, stones, wood, etc. What abundance of spirits is in all these things? For earth and water continually produce animals, as they have done from the beginning, so that a pool filled with water may produce fishes though none were ever put there to increase or breed. And seeing that all other things do more originally proceed from earth and water, it necessarily follows, that the spirits of all animals were in the water. And therefore it is said in Genesis, that the spirit of God moved upon the face of the waters, *viz.*, that from hence he might produce whatsoever was afterwards created.

But if it be said, this argument does not prove that all spirits are bodies, but that all bodies have in them the spirits of all animals (so that every body has a spirit in it, and likewise a spirit and body, and although they are thus united, yet they still remain different in nature one from another, and so cannot be changed one into another) to this I answer. If every body, even the least, has in it the spirits of all animals, and other things, even as matter is said to have in it all forms, now I demand, whether a body has actually all those spirits in it, or potentially only? If actually, how is it possible that so many spirits essentially distinct from body can actually exist in their distinct essences in so small a body (even in the least that can be conceived) unless it be by intrinsic presence, which is not communicable to any creature, as already proved. For if all kinds of spirits are in any, even the least body, how comes it to pass that such an animal is produced of this body and not another? Yea, how comes it to pass that all kinds of animals are not immediately produced out of one and the same body, which experience denies. For we see that nature keeps her order in all operations, whence one animal is formed of another, and one species proceeds from another, as well when it ascends to a farther perfection, as when it descends to a viler state and condition.

But if they say, all spirits are contained in any body, not actually in their distinct essences, but only potentially as they term it, then it must be granted, that the body and all those spirits are one and the same thing. That is, that a body may be turned into them, as when we say wood is potentially fire (that is, can be turned into fire), water is potentially air (that is, may be changed into air) . . .

AGAINST DESCARTES, HOBBES, AND SPINOZA

From what has been lately said, and from diverse reasons alleged, that spirit and body are originally in their first substance but one and the same thing, it evidently appears that the philosophers (so called) which have taught otherwise, whether ancient or modern, have generally erred . . .

And none can object, that all this philosophy is no other than that of Descartes or Hobbes under a new mask. For, first, as touching the Cartesian philosophy, this says that every body is a mere dead mass, not only void of all kind of life and sense, but utterly incapable thereof to all eternity. This grand error also is to be imputed to all those who affirm body and spirit to be contrary things, and inconvertible one into another, so as to deny a body all life and sense, but utterly incapable thereof to all eternity. This grand error also is to be imputed to all those who affirm body and spirit to be contrary things, and inconvertible one into another, so as to deny a body all life and sense, which is quite contrary to the grounds of this our philosophy. Wherefore it is so far from being a *Cartesian* principle, under a new mask, that it may be truly said it is *anti-Cartesian*, in regard of their fundamental principles—although, it cannot be denied that Descartes taught many excellent and ingenious things concerning the mechanical part of natural operations, and how all natural motions proceed according to rules and laws mechanical, even as indeed nature herself, i.e., the creature, as an excellent mechanical skill and wisdom in itself (given it from God, who is the fountain of all wisdom) by which it operates. But yet in nature, and her operations, they are far more than merely mechanical, and the same is not a mere organical body, like a clock, wherein there is not a vital principle of motion, but a living body, having life and sense, which body is far more sublime than a mere mechanism, or mechanical motion.

But, secondly, as to what pertains to Hobbes's opinion, this is more contrary to this our philosophy, than that of Descartes. For Descartes acknowledged God to be plainly immaterial, and an incorporeal spirit. Hobbes affirms God himself to be material and corporeal—yea, nothing else but matter and body—and so confounds God and the creatures in their essences, and denies that there is any essential distinction between them. These and many more the worst of consequences are the dictates of Hobbes's philosophy, to which may be added that of Spinoza, for this Spinoza also confounds God and the creatures together, and makes but one being of both, all which are diametrically opposite to the philosophy here delivered by us.

READING 5

John Locke: The Origin of All Our Ideas in Experience

From *Essay concerning Human Understanding*

Born near Bristol, England, John Locke (1632–1704) worked as a personal physician in private households and late in life authored some of philosophy's most influential works. In his Essay concerning Human Understanding *(1690), he argues that our knowledge is in fact based solely on our experiences—on the information supplied by our senses. Locke takes pains first of all to reject the notion that there are in our minds*

Source: John Locke, *Essay concerning Human Understanding* (1690), Books 1 and 2.

some "innate ideas or principles" as if implanted there at birth. Take, for example, how we know colors or taste. Locke says, "I would have anyone try to fancy any taste, which had never affected his palate; or frame the idea of a scent he had never smelt: and when he could do this, I will also conclude that a blind man hath ideas of colors, and a deaf man true distinct notions of sounds." The mind, says Locke, is originally "an empty cabinet," and "it is the senses that at first let in particular ideas." Using another metaphor, Locke asks us to "suppose the mind to be . . . white paper, void of all characters, without any ideas: how comes it to be furnished?" His answer to this question is the classic empiricist account of knowledge.

REJECTION OF INNATE IDEAS AND PRINCIPLES

1.1.1. The way shown how we come by any knowledge, sufficient to prove it not innate.   It is an established opinion amongst some men, that there are in the understanding certain innate principles; some primary notions, *koinai ennoiai,* characters, as it were stamped upon the mind of man; which the soul receives in its very first being, and brings into the world with it. It would be sufficient to convince unprejudiced readers of the falseness of this supposition, if I should only show (as I hope I shall in the following parts of this Discourse) how men, barely by the use of their natural faculties, may attain to all the knowledge they have, without the help of any innate impressions; and may arrive at certainty, without any such original notions or principles. For I imagine anyone will easily grant that it would be impertinent to suppose the ideas of colors innate in a creature to whom God has given sight, and a power to receive them by the eyes from external objects: and no less unreasonable would it be to attribute several truths to the impressions of nature, and innate characters, when we may observe in ourselves faculties fit to attain as easy and certain knowledge of them as if they were originally imprinted on the mind.

1.1.15. The steps by which the mind attains several truths.   The senses at first let in particular ideas, and furnish the yet empty cabinet, and the mind by degrees growing familiar with some of them, they are lodged in the memory, and names got to them. Afterwards, the mind proceeding further, abstracts them, and by degrees learns the use of general names. In this manner the mind comes to be furnished with ideas and language, the materials about which to exercise its discursive faculty. And the use of reason becomes daily more visible, as these materials that give it employment increase. But though the having of general ideas and the use of general words and reason usually grow together, yet I see not how this any way proves them innate. The knowledge of some truths, I confess, is very early in the mind but in a way that shows them not to be innate. For, if we will observe, we shall find it still to be about ideas, not innate, but acquired; it being about those first which are imprinted by external things, with which infants have earliest to do, which make the most frequent impressions on their senses. . . .

1.1.16. Assent to supposed innate truths depends on having clear and distinct ideas of what their terms mean, and not on their innateness.   A child knows not that three and four are equal to seven, till he comes to be able to count seven, and has got the name and idea of equality; and then, upon explaining those words, he presently assents to, or rather perceives the truth of that proposition. But neither does he then readily assent because it is an innate truth, nor was his assent wanting till then because he wanted the use of reason; but the truth of it appears to him as soon as he has settled in his mind the clear and distinct ideas that these names stand for. And then he knows the truth of that proposition upon the same grounds and by the same means, that he knew before that a rod and a cherry are not the same thing; and upon the same grounds also that he may come to know afterwards "That it is impossible for the same thing to be and not to be.". . .

THE ORIGIN OF ALL OUR IDEAS: SENSATION AND REFLECTION

2.1.2. All ideas come from sensation or reflection.   Let us then suppose the mind to be, as we say, white paper, void of all characters, without any ideas: How comes it to be furnished? Whence comes it by that vast store which the busy and boundless fancy of man has painted on it with an almost endless variety? Whence has it all the materials of reason and knowledge? To this I answer, in one word, from *experience*. In that all our knowledge is founded; and from that it ultimately derives itself. Our observation employed either, about external sensible objects, or about the internal operations of our minds perceived and reflected on by ourselves, is that which supplies our understandings with all the materials of thinking. These two are the fountains of knowledge, from whence all the ideas we have, or can naturally have, do spring.

2.1.3. The objects of sensation one source of ideas.   First, our Senses, conversant about particular sensible objects, do convey into the mind several distinct perceptions of things, according to those various ways wherein those objects do affect them. And thus we come by those ideas we have of yellow, white, heat, cold, soft, hard, bitter, sweet, and all those which we call sensible qualities; which when I say the senses convey into the mind, I mean, they from external objects convey into the mind what produces there those perceptions. This great source of most of the ideas we have, depending wholly upon our senses, and derived by them to the understanding, I call *sensation*.

2.1.4. The operations of our minds, the other source of them.   Secondly, the other fountain from which experience furnishes the understanding with ideas is the perception of the operations of our own mind within us, as it is employed about the ideas it has got; which operations, when the soul comes to reflect on and consider, do furnish the understanding with another set of ideas, which could not be had from things without. And such are perception, thinking, doubting, believing, reasoning, knowing, willing, and all the different actings of our own minds; which we being conscious of, and observing in ourselves, do from these receive into our understandings as distinct ideas as we do from bodies affecting our senses. This source of ideas every man has wholly in himself; and though it be not sense, as having nothing to do with external objects, yet it is very like it, and might properly enough be called internal sense. But as I call the other *sensation*, so I call this *reflection*, the ideas it affords being such only as the mind gets by reflecting on its own operations within itself. By reflection then, in the following part of this discourse, I would be understood to mean, that notice which the mind takes of its own operations, and the manner of them, by reason whereof there come to be ideas of these operations in the understanding. These two, I say, viz., external material things, as the objects of *sensation*, and the operations of our own minds within, as the objects of *reflection*, are to me the only originals from whence all our ideas take their beginnings.

SIMPLE IDEAS

2.2.1. Uncompounded appearances.   The better to understand the nature, manner, and extent of our knowledge, one thing is carefully to be observed concerning the ideas we have; and that is, that some of them are simple and some complex.

Though the qualities that affect our senses are, in the things themselves, so united and blended, that there is no separation, no distance between them, yet it is plain, the ideas they produce in the mind enter by the senses simple and un-mixed. For, though the sight and touch often take in from the same object, at the same time, different ideas—as a man sees at once motion and color; the hand feels softness and warmth in the same piece of wax. Yet, the simple ideas thus united in the same subject, are as perfectly distinct as those that come in by different senses. The coldness and hardness which a man feels in a piece of ice being as distinct ideas in the mind as the smell and whiteness of a lily; or as the taste of sugar, and smell of a rose. And there is nothing can be plainer to a man than the clear and distinct perception he has of those simple ideas; which, being each in itself uncompounded, contains in it nothing but one uniform appearance, or conception in the mind, and is not distinguishable into different ideas.

2.2.2. The mind can neither make nor destroy them.   These simple ideas, the materials of all our knowledge, are suggested and furnished to the mind only by those two ways above mentioned, viz., sensation and reflection. When the understanding is once stored with these simple ideas, it has the power to repeat, compare, and unite them, even to an almost infinite variety, and so can make at pleasure new complex ideas. But it is not in the power of the most exalted wit, or enlarged understanding, by any quickness or variety of thought, to invent or frame one new simple idea in the mind, not taken in by the ways before mentioned: nor can any force of the understanding destroy those that are there. The dominion of man, in this little world of his own understanding being much what the same as it is in the great world of visible things; wherein his power, however managed by art and skill, reaches no farther than to compound and divide the materials that are made to his hand; but can do nothing towards the making the least particle of new matter, or destroying one atom of what is already in being. The same inability will every one find in himself, who shall go about to fashion in his understanding one simple idea, not received in by his senses from external objects, or by reflection from the operations of his own mind about them. I would have any one try to fancy any taste which had never affected his palate; or frame the idea of a scent he had never smelt: and when he can do this, I will also conclude that a blind man has ideas of colors, and a deaf man true distinct notions of sounds.

PRIMARY AND SECONDARY QUALITIES OF BODIES

2.8.8. Our ideas and the qualities of bodies. Whatsoever the mind perceives in itself, or is the immediate object of perception, thought, or understanding, that I call idea; and the power to produce any idea in our mind, I call quality of the subject wherein that power is. Thus a snowball having the power to produce in us the ideas of white, cold, and round,—the power to produce those ideas in us, as they are in the snowball, I call qualities; and as they are sensations or perceptions in our understandings, I call them ideas; which ideas, if I speak of sometimes as in the things themselves, I would be understood to mean those qualities in the objects which produce them in us.

2.8.9. Primary qualities of bodies. Qualities thus considered in bodies are, first, such as are utterly inseparable from the body, in what state soever it be; and such as in all the alterations and changes it suffers, all the force can be used upon it, it constantly keeps; and such as sense constantly finds in every particle of matter which has bulk enough to be perceived; and the mind finds inseparable from every particle of matter, though less than to make itself singly be perceived by our senses: e.g., Take a grain of wheat, divide it into two parts; each part has still solidity, extension, figure, and mobility: divide it again, and it retains still the same qualities; and so divide it on, till the parts become insensible; they must retain still each of them all those qualities. For division (which is all that a mill, or pestle, or any other body, does upon another, in reducing it to insensible parts) can never take away either solidity, extension, figure, or mobility from anybody, but only makes two or more distinct separate masses of matter, of that which was but one before; all which distinct masses, reckoned as so many distinct bodies, after division, make a certain number. These I call original or *primary qualities* of body, which I think we may observe to produce simple ideas in us, viz., solidity, extension, figure, motion or rest, and number.

2.8.10. Secondary qualities of bodies. Secondly, such qualities which in truth are nothing in the objects themselves but power to produce various sensations in us by their primary qualities, i.e., by the bulk, figure, texture, and motion of their insensible parts, as colors, sounds, tastes, etc. These I call *secondary qualities*. To these might be added a third sort, which are allowed to be barely powers; though they are as much real qualities in the subject as those which I, to comply with the common way of speaking, call qualities, but for distinction, secondary qualities. For the power in fire to produce a new color, or consistency, in wax or clay, by its primary qualities, is as much a quality in fire, as the power it has to produce in me a new idea or sensation of warmth or burning, which I felt not before, by the same primary qualities, viz., the bulk, texture, and motion of its insensible parts.

COMPLEX IDEAS

2.12.1. Made by the mind out of simple ones.   We have hitherto considered those ideas, in the reception whereof the mind is only passive, which are those simple ones received from sensation and reflection before mentioned, whereof the mind cannot make one to itself, nor have any idea which does not wholly consist of them. But as the mind is wholly passive in the reception of all its simple ideas, so it exerts several acts of its own, whereby out of its simple ideas, as the materials and foundations of the rest, the others are framed. The acts of the mind, wherein it exerts its power over its simple ideas, are chiefly these three. (1) Combining several simple ideas into one compound one; and thus all complex ideas are made. (2) The second is bringing two ideas, whether simple or complex, together, and setting them by one another, so as to take a view of them at once, without uniting them into one; by which way it gets all its ideas of relations. (3) The third is separating them from all other ideas that accompany them in their real existence: this is called abstraction: and thus all its general ideas are made. This shows man's power, and its ways of operation, to be much the same in the material and intellectual world. For the materials in both being such as he has no power over, either to make or destroy, all that man can do is either to unite them together, or to set them by one another, or wholly separate them. I shall here begin with the first of these in the consideration of complex ideas, and come to the other two in their due places. As simple ideas are observed to exist in several combinations united together, so the mind has a power to consider several of them united together as one idea; and that not only as they are united in external objects, but as itself has joined them together. Ideas thus made up of several simple ones put together, I call complex—such as are beauty, gratitude, a man, an army, the universe; which, though complicated of various simple ideas, or complex ideas made up of simple ones, yet are, when the mind pleases, considered each by itself, as one entire thing, and signified by one name.

THE CONCEPT OF SUBSTANCE

2.23.1. Ideas of particular substances, how made.   The mind being, as I have declared, furnished with a great number of the simple ideas, conveyed in by the senses as they are found in exterior things, or by reflection on its own operations, takes notice also that a certain number of these simple ideas go constantly together; which being presumed to belong to one thing, and words being suited to common apprehensions, and made use of for quick dispatch, are called, so united in one subject, by one name; which, by inadvertency, we are apt afterward to talk of and consider as one simple idea, which indeed is a complication of many ideas together: because, as I have said, not imagining how these simple ideas can subsist by themselves, we accustom ourselves to suppose some substratum wherein they do subsist, and from which they do result, which therefore we call substance.

2.23.2. Our obscure idea of substance in general.   So that if anyone will examine himself concerning his notion of pure substance in general, he will find he has no other idea of it at all, but only a supposition of he knows not what support of such qualities which are capable of producing simple ideas in us; which qualities are commonly called accidents. If anyone should be asked, what is the subject wherein color or weight inheres, he would have nothing to say, but the solid extended parts; and if he were demanded, what is it that solidity and extension adhere in, he would not be in a much better case than the Indian . . . who, saying that the world was supported by a great elephant, was asked what the elephant rested on; to which his answer was, a great tortoise; but being again pressed to know what gave support to the broad-backed tortoise, replied, something he knew not what. And thus here, as in all other cases where we use words without having clear and distinct ideas, we talk like children: who, being questioned what such a thing is, which they know not, readily give this satisfactory answer, that it is something: which in truth signifies no more, when so used, either by children or men, but that they know not what; and that the thing they pretend to know, and talk of, is what they have no distinct idea of at all, and so are perfectly ignorant of it, and in the dark. The idea then we have, to which we give the general name substance, being nothing but the supposed, but unknown, support of those qualities we find existing, which we imagine cannot subsist *sine re substante,* without something to support them, we call that support *substantia;* which, according to the true import of the word, is, in plain English, standing under or upholding.

2.23.4. No clear or distinct idea of substance in general.   Hence, when we talk or think of any particular sort of corporeal substances, as horse, stone, etc., though the idea we have of either of them be but the complication or collection of those several simple ideas of sensible qualities, which we used to find united in the thing called horse or stone; yet, because we cannot conceive how they should subsist alone, nor one in another, we suppose them existing in and supported by some common subject; which support we denote by the name substance, though it be certain we have no clear or distinct idea of that thing we suppose a support.

READING 6

George Berkeley: Consciousness, Not Matter, the True Reality

From *Three Dialogues between Hylas and Philonous*

Born in southeastern Ireland, George Berkeley (1685–1753) was a minister and later a bishop in the Anglican Church. Berkeley famously defended the view that we now call "monistic idealism"—only spirit exists. In his Three Dialogues *(1713) he denies what seems obvious to most philosophers of his time, namely, that physical things have an external existence independent of our thoughts. There is no material world, he argues, and consequently, we have no physical bodies. The only things that exist are spiritual minds and the perceptions that these minds experience. And the perceptions that we have of external things—such as trees, other people, and our physical bodies—are injected into our minds by God. According to Berkeley, for something to be means simply that we have a perception. His formula is "To be is to be perceived" (in Latin,* esse est percipi*). Take the example of a cherry. We normally think that there is a cherry and that it has certain qualities. It is soft, red, round, sweet, and fragrant. All these qualities are ideas in our minds that the cherry has the power to produce through the senses, so that the softness is felt, the color is seen, the roundness is felt and seen, the sweetness is tasted, and the fragrance is smelled. The very existence of these qualities consists in their being perceived. However, apart from these qualities, there is no sensed something; in short, there is nothing else. The cherry, and everything else in our experience, consists of the qualities we perceive and, therefore, represents only a complex of sensations or ideas. In the selection included here, Berkeley defends his view that matter does not exist.*

HYLAS: You were represented, in last night's conversation, as one who maintained the most extravagant opinion that ever entered into the mind of man, to wit, that there is no such thing as *material substance* in the world.

PHILONOUS: That there is no such thing as what *philosophers call material substance,* I am seriously persuaded: but, if I were made to see anything absurd or skeptical in this, I should then have the same reason to renounce this that I imagine I have now to reject the contrary opinion.

HYLAS: What I can anything be more fantastical, more repugnant to Common Sense, or a more manifest piece of Skepticism, than to believe there is no such thing as *matter?*

PHILONOUS: Softly, good Hylas. What if it should prove that you, who hold there is, are, by virtue of that opinion, a greater skeptic, and maintain more paradoxes and repugnances to Common Sense, than I who believe no such thing?

HYLAS: You may as soon persuade me, the part is greater than the whole, as that, in order to avoid absurdity and Skepticism, I should ever be obliged to give up my opinion in this point.

Source: George Berkeley, *Three Dialogues between Hylas and Philonous* (1713), Dialogue 1.

PHILONOUS: Well then, are you content to admit that opinion for true, which upon examination shall appear most agreeable to Common Sense, and remote from Skepticism?

HYLAS: With all my heart. Since you are for raising disputes about the plainest things in nature, I am content for once to hear what you have to say. . . .

NO MATERIAL SUBSTRATUM

PHILONOUS: Make me to understand the difference between what is immediately perceived and a sensation.

HYLAS: The sensation I take to be an act of the mind perceiving; besides which, there is something perceived; and this I call the *object*. For example, there is red and yellow on that tulip. But then the act of perceiving those colors is in me only, and not in the tulip.

PHILONOUS: What tulip do you speak of? Is it that which you see?

HYLAS: The same.

PHILONOUS: And what do you see beside color, figure, and extension?. . .

HYLAS: I acknowledge, Philonous, that, upon a fair observation of what passes in my mind, I can discover nothing else but that I am a thinking being, affected with variety of sensations; neither is it possible to conceive how a sensation should exist in an unperceiving substance. But then, on the other hand, when I look on sensible things in a different view, considering them as so many modes and qualities, I find it necessary to suppose a *material substratum*, without which they cannot be conceived to exist.

PHILONOUS: *Material substratum* call you it? Pray, by which of your senses came you acquainted with that being?

HYLAS: It is not itself sensible; its modes and qualities only being perceived by the senses.

PHILONOUS: I presume then it was by reflection and reason you obtained the idea of it?

HYLAS: I do not pretend to any proper positive *idea* of it. However, I conclude it exists, because qualities cannot be conceived to exist without a support.

PHILONOUS: It seems then you have only a relative *notion* of it, or that you conceive it not otherwise than by conceiving the relation it bears to sensible qualities?

HYLAS: Right.

PHILONOUS: Be pleased therefore to let me know wherein that relation consists.

HYLAS: Is it not sufficiently expressed in the term *substratum*, or *substance*?

PHILONOUS: If so, the word *substratum* should import that it is spread under the sensible qualities or accidents?

HYLAS: True.

PHILONOUS: And consequently under extension?

HYLAS: I own it.

PHILONOUS: It is therefore somewhat in its own nature entirely distinct from extension?

HYLAS: I tell you, extension is only a mode, and matter is something that supports modes. And is it not evident the thing supported is different from the thing supporting?

PHILONOUS: So that something distinct from, and exclusive of, extension is supposed to be the *substratum* of extension?

HYLAS: Just so.

PHILONOUS: Answer me, Hylas. Can a thing be spread without extension? Or is not the idea of extension necessarily included in *spreading?*

HYLAS: It is.

PHILONOUS: Whatsoever therefore you suppose spread under anything must have in itself an extension distinct from the extension of that thing under which it is spread?

HYLAS: It must.

PHILONOUS: Consequently, every corporeal substance, being the *substratum* of extension, must have in itself another extension, by which it is qualified to be a *substratum:* and so on to infinity. And I ask whether this be not absurd in itself, and repugnant to what you granted just now, to wit, that the *substratum* was something distinct from and exclusive of extension?

NO MATERIAL SUBSTANCE WITH ACCIDENTS

HYLAS: Aye but, Philonous, you take me wrong. I do not mean that matter is *spread* in a gross literal sense under extension. The word *substratum* is used only to express in general the same thing with *substance.*

PHILONOUS: Well then, let us examine the relation implied in the term *substance.* Is it not that it stands under accidents?

HYLAS: The very same.

PHILONOUS: But, that one thing may stand under or support another, must it not be extended?

HYLAS: It must.

PHILONOUS: Is not therefore this supposition liable to the same absurdity with the former?

HYLAS: You still take things in a strict literal sense. That is not fair, Philonous.

PHILONOUS: I am not for imposing any sense on your words: you are at liberty to explain them as you please. Only, I beseech you, make me understand something by them. You tell me matter supports or stands under accidents. How! is it as your legs support your body?

HYLAS: No; that is the literal sense.

PHILONOUS: Pray let me know any sense, literal or not literal, that you under- stand it in.—How long must I wait for an answer, Hylas?

HYLAS: I declare I know not what to say. I once thought I understood well enough what was meant by matter's supporting accidents. But now, the more I think on it the less can I comprehend it: in short I find that I know nothing of it.

PHILONOUS: It seems then you have no idea at all, neither relative nor positive, of matter; you know neither what it is in itself, nor what relation it bears to accidents?

HYLAS: I acknowledge it.

PHILONOUS: And yet you asserted that you could not conceive how qualities or accidents should really exist, without conceiving at the same time a material support of them?

HYLAS: I did.

PHILONOUS: That is to say, when you conceive the real existence of qualities, you do withal conceive something which you cannot conceive?

HYLAS: It was wrong, I own. But still I fear there is some fallacy or other. Pray what think you of this? It is just come into my head that the ground of all our mistake lies in your treating of each quality by itself. Now, I grant that each quality cannot singly subsist without the mind. Color cannot without extension, neither can figure without some other sensible quality. But, as the several qualities united or blended together form entire sensible things, nothing hinders why such things may not be supposed to exist without the mind.

PHILONOUS: Either, Hylas, you are jesting, or have a very bad memory. Though indeed we went through all the qualities by name one after another, yet my arguments or rather your concessions, nowhere tended to prove that the Secondary Qualities did not subsist each alone by itself; but, that they were not *at all* without the mind. Indeed, in treating of figure and motion we concluded they could not exist without the mind, because it was impossible even in thought to separate them from all secondary qualities, so as to conceive them existing by themselves. But then this was not the only argument made use of upon that occasion. But (to pass by all that has been hitherto said, and reckon it for nothing, if you will have it so) I am content to put the whole upon this issue. If you can conceive it possible for any mixture or combination of qualities, or any sensible object whatever, to exist without the mind, then I will grant it actually to be so.

WE CANNOT CONCEIVE OF THINGS EXISTING INDEPENDENTLY OF MINDS

HYLAS: If it comes to that the point will soon be decided. What more easy than to conceive a tree or house existing by itself, independent of, and unperceived by, any mind whatsoever? I do at this present time conceive them existing after that manner.

PHILONOUS: How say you, Hylas, can you see a thing which is at the same time unseen?

HYLAS: No, that were a contradiction.

PHILONOUS: Is it not as great a contradiction to talk of *conceiving* a thing which is *unconceived*?

HYLAS: It is.

PHILONOUS: The tree or house therefore which you think of is conceived by you?

HYLAS: How should it be otherwise?

PHILONOUS: And what is conceived is surely in the mind?

HYLAS: Without question, that which is conceived is in the mind.

PHILONOUS: How then came you to say, you conceived a house or tree existing independent and out of all minds whatsoever?

HYLAS: That was I own an oversight; but stay, let me consider what led me into it.—It is a pleasant mistake enough. As I was thinking of a tree in a solitary place, where no one was present to see it, methought that was to conceive a tree as existing unperceived or unthought of; not considering that I myself conceived it all the while. But now I plainly see that all I can do is to frame ideas in my own mind. I may indeed conceive in my own thoughts the idea of a tree, or a house, or a mountain, but that is all. And this is far from proving that I can conceive them *existing out of the minds of all Spirits.*

PHILONOUS: You acknowledge then that you cannot possibly conceive how any one corporeal sensible thing should exist otherwise than in the mind?

HYLAS: I do.

PHILONOUS: And yet you will earnestly contend for the truth of that which you cannot so much as conceive?

HYLAS: I profess I know not what to think; but still there are some scruples remain with me. Is it not certain I *see things at* a distance? Do we not perceive the stars and moon, for example, to be a great way off? Is not this, I say, manifest to the senses?

PHILONOUS: Do you not in a dream too perceive those or the like objects?

HYLAS: I do.

PHILONOUS: And have they not then the same appearance of being distant?

HYLAS: They have.

PHILONOUS: But you do not thence conclude the apparitions in a dream to be without the mind?

HYLAS: By no means.

PHILONOUS: You ought not therefore to conclude that sensible objects are without the mind, from their appearance, or manner wherein they are perceived.

HYLAS: I acknowledge it. But does not my sense deceive me in those cases?

PHILONOUS: By no means. The idea or thing which you immediately perceive, neither sense nor reason informs you that it actually exists without the mind. By sense you only know that you are affected with such certain sensations of light and colors, etc. And these you will not say are without the mind.

HYLAS: True: but, beside all that, do you not think the sight suggests something of *outness or distance?*

PHILONOUS: Upon approaching a distant object, do the visible size and figure change perpetually, or do they appear the same at all distances?

HYLAS: They are in a continual change.

PHILONOUS: Sight therefore does not suggest, or any way inform you, that the visible object you immediately perceive exists at a distance, or will be perceived when you advance farther onward; there being a continued series of visible objects succeeding each other during the whole time of your approach.

HYLAS: It does not; but still I know, upon seeing an object, what object I shall perceive after having passed over a certain distance: no matter whether it be exactly the same or no: there is still something of distance suggested in the case.

PHILONOUS: Good Hylas, do but reflect a little on the point, and then tell me whether there be any more in it than this: from the ideas you actually perceive by sight, you have by experience learned to collect what other ideas you will (according to the standing order of nature) be affected with, after such a certain succession of time and motion.

HYLAS: Upon the whole, I take it to be nothing else.

PHILONOUS: Now, is it not plain that if we suppose a man born blind was on a sudden made to see, he could at first have no experience of what may be *suggested* by sight?

HYLAS: It is.

PHILONOUS: He would not then, according to you, have any notion of distance annexed to the things he saw; but would take them for a new set of sensations, existing only in his mind?

HYLAS: It is undeniable.

PHILONOUS: But, to make it still more plain: is not *distance* a line turned endwise to the eye?

HYLAS: It is.

PHILONOUS: And can a line so situated be perceived by sight?

HYLAS: It cannot.

PHILONOUS: Does it not therefore follow that distance is not properly and immediately perceived by sight?

HYLAS: It should seem so.

PHILONOUS: Again, is it your opinion that colors are at a distance?

HYLAS: It must be acknowledged they are only in the mind.

PHILONOUS: But do not colors appear to the eye as coexisting in the same place with extension and figures?

HYLAS: They do.

PHILONOUS: How can you then conclude from sight that figures exist without, when you acknowledge colors do not; the sensible appearance being the very same with regard to both?

HYLAS: I know not what to answer.

PHILONOUS: But, allowing that distance was truly and immediately perceived by the mind, yet it would not thence follow it existed out of the mind. For, whatever is immediately perceived is an idea: and can any idea exist out of the mind?

HYLAS: To suppose that were absurd: but, inform me, Philonous, can we perceive or know nothing beside our ideas?

PHILONOUS: As for the rational deducing of causes from effects, that is beside our inquiry. And, by the senses you can best tell whether you perceive anything which is not immediately perceived. And I ask you, whether the things immediately perceived are other than your own sensations or ideas? You have indeed more than once, in the course of this conversation, declared yourself on those points; but you seem, by this last question, to have departed from what you then thought.

NO MEDIATELY PERCEIVED OBJECTS

HYLAS: To speak the truth, Philonous, I think there are two kinds of objects:— the one perceived immediately, which are likewise called *ideas;* the other are real things or external objects, perceived by the mediation of ideas, which are their images and representations. Now, I own ideas do not exist without the mind; but the latter sort of objects do. I am sorry I did not think of this distinction sooner; it would probably have cut short your discourse.

PHILONOUS: Are those external objects perceived by sense or by some other faculty?

HYLAS: They are perceived by sense.

PHILONOUS: How! Is there anything perceived by sense which is not immediately perceived?

HYLAS: Yes, Philonous, in some sort there is. For example, when I look on a picture or statue of Julius Caesar, I may be said after a manner to perceive him (though not immediately) by my senses.

PHILONOUS: It seems then you will have our ideas, which alone are immediately perceived, to be pictures of external things: and that these also are perceived by sense, inasmuch as they have a conformity or resemblance to our ideas?

HYLAS: That is my meaning.

PHILONOUS: And, in the same way that Julius Caesar, in himself invisible, is nevertheless perceived by sight; real things, in themselves imperceptible, are perceived by sense.

HYLAS: In the very same.

PHILONOUS: Tell me, Hylas, when you behold the picture of Julius Caesar, do you see with your eyes any more than some colors and figures, with a certain symmetry and composition of the whole?

HYLAS: Nothing else.

PHILONOUS: And would not a man who had never known anything of Julius Caesar see as much?

HYLAS: He would.

PHILONOUS: Consequently he has his sight, and the use of it, in as perfect a degree as you?

HYLAS: I agree with you.

PHILONOUS: Whence comes it then that your thoughts are directed to the Roman emperor, and his are not? This cannot proceed from the sensations or ideas of sense by you then perceived; since you acknowledge you have no advantage over him in that respect. It should seem therefore to proceed from reason and memory: should it not?

HYLAS: It should.

PHILONOUS: Consequently, it will not follow from that instance that anything is perceived by sense which is not immediately perceived. Though I grant we may, in one acceptation, be said to perceive sensible things mediately by sense: that is, when, from a frequently perceived connection, the immediate perception of ideas by one sense *suggests* to the mind others, perhaps belonging to another sense, which are wont to be connected with them. For instance, when I hear a coach drive along the streets, immediately I perceive only the sound; but, from the experience I have had that such a sound is connected with a coach, I am said to hear the coach. It is nevertheless evident that, in truth and strictness, nothing can be heard but sound; and the coach is not then properly perceived by sense, but suggested from experience. So likewise when we are said to see a red-hot bar of iron; the solidity and heat of the iron are not the objects of sight, but suggested to the imagination by the color and figure which are properly perceived by that sense. In short, those things alone are actually and strictly perceived by any sense, which would have been perceived in case that same sense had then been first conferred on us. As for other things, it is plain they are only suggested to the mind by experience, grounded on former perceptions. But, to return to your comparison of Caesar's picture, it is plain, if you keep to that, you must hold the real things, or archetypes of our ideas, are not perceived by sense, but by some internal faculty of the soul, as reason or memory. I would therefore fain know what arguments you can draw from reason for the existence of what you call *real things* or *material objects*. Or, whether you remember to have seen them formerly as they are in themselves; or, if you have heard or read of any one that did.

HYLAS: I see, Philonous, you are disposed to raillery; but that will never convince me.

PHILONOUS: My aim is only to learn from you the way to come at the knowledge of *material beings*. Whatever we perceive is perceived immediately or mediately: by sense, or by reason and reflection. But, as you have excluded sense, pray show me what reason you have to believe their existence; or what *medium* you can possibly make use of to prove it, either to mine or your own understanding.

HYLAS: To deal ingenuously, Philonous, now I consider the point, I do not find I can give you any good reason for it. But, thus much seems pretty plain, that it is at least possible such things may really exist. And, as long as there is no absurdity in supposing them, I am resolved to believe as I did, till you bring good reasons to the contrary.

PHILONOUS: What! Is it come to this, that you only *believe* the existence of material objects, and that your belief is founded barely on the possibility of its being true? Then you will have me bring reasons against it: though another would think it reasonable the proof should lie on him who holds the affirmative. And, after all, this very point which you are now resolved to maintain, without any reason, is in effect what you have more than once during this discourse seen good reason to give up. But, to pass over all this; if I understand you rightly, you say our ideas do not exist without the mind, but that they are copies, images, or representations, of certain originals that do?

HYLAS: You take me right.

PHILONOUS: They are then like external things?

HYLAS: They are.

PHILONOUS: Have those things a stable and permanent nature, independent of our senses; or are they in a perpetual change, upon our producing any motions in our bodies—suspending, exerting, or altering, our faculties or organs of sense?

HYLAS: Real things, it is plain, have a fixed and real nature, which remains the same notwithstanding any change in our senses, or in the posture and motion of our bodies; which indeed may affect the ideas in our minds, but it were absurd to think they had the same effect on things existing without the mind.

PHILONOUS: How then is it possible that things perpetually fleeting and variable as our ideas should be copies or images of anything fixed and constant? Or, in other words, since all sensible qualities, as size, figure, color, etc., that is, our ideas, are continually changing, upon every alteration in the distance, medium, or instruments of sensation; how can any determinate material objects be properly represented or painted forth by several distinct things, each of which is so different from and unlike the rest? Or, if you say it resembles someone only of our ideas, how shall we be able to distinguish the true copy from all the false ones?

HYLAS: I profess, Philonous, I am at a loss. I know not what to say to this.

PHILONOUS: But neither is this all. Which are material objects in themselves—perceptible or imperceptible?

HYLAS: Properly and immediately nothing can be perceived but ideas. All material things, therefore, are in themselves insensible, and to be perceived only by our ideas.

PHILONOUS: Ideas then are sensible, and their archetypes or originals insensible?

HYLAS: Right.

PHILONOUS: But how can that which is sensible be like that which is insensible? Can a real thing, in itself *invisible*, be like a *color*; or a real thing, which is not *audible*, be like a *sound*? In a word, can anything be like a sensation or idea, but another sensation or idea?

HYLAS: I must own, I think not.

PHILONOUS: Is it possible there should be any doubt on the point? Do you not perfectly know your own ideas?

HYLAS: I know them perfectly; since what I do not perceive or know can be no part of my idea.

PHILONOUS: Consider, therefore, and examine them, and then tell me if there be anything in them which can exist without the mind: or if you can conceive anything like them existing without the mind.

HYLAS: Upon inquiry, I find it is impossible for me to conceive or understand how anything but an idea can be like an idea. And it is most evident that *no idea can exist without the mind*.

PHILONOUS: You are therefore, by your principles, forced to deny the *reality* of sensible things; since you made it to consist in an absolute existence exterior to the mind. That is to say, you are a downright skeptic. So I have gained my point, which was to show your principles led to Skepticism.

HYLAS: For the present I am, if not entirely convinced, at least silenced.

READING 7

David Hume: The Self, Experience, Determinism, Miracles, and God's Existence

From *Treatise of Human Nature, An Enquiry concerning Human Understanding,* and *Dialogues concerning Natural Religion*

Born in Edinburgh, Scotland, David Hume (1711–1776) worked as a librarian and governmental official and became infamous for his skeptical views on many philosophical issues. The first discussion below is his account of the foundation of knowledge from An Enquiry concerning Human Understanding *(1748). He argues that all factual knowledge about the world (i.e., "matters of fact") is grounded in cause and effect, which is in turn grounded in experience, rather than in a priori reasoning. This, though, raises another puzzle, which today is called the "problem of induction," namely, how do I know that my experiences in the past will hold true for my future experiences? Suppose that I take an aspirin and my headache goes away; it is logically possible that this sequence will not occur next time. Hume explores several possible explanations for inductive reasoning, and ultimately argues that it is based on instinctive abilities to form mental habits when we repeatedly see two things associated with each other. On the subject of personal identity, Hume rejects the common presumption that a person's mind is a unified thing that continues intact over time; instead, the self is just a bundle of mental experiences, one perception following another. Next, Hume defends the notion of determinism, that is, that all human actions are causally determined by prior motivations, and no act of our human will can override those prior motivations. Specific motives are constantly conjoined with specific actions, and, the presence of specific motives will prompt us to make an immediate mental inference*

Source: David Hume, An *Enquiry concerning Human Understanding* (1748), Sections 4, 5; *Treatise of Human Nature* (1739–40), 1.4.6; *An Enquiry concerning Human Understanding,* 7.1, and 10; *Dialogues concerning Natural Religion* (1779), Parts 2, 5, and 9.

regarding a specific human action. If free will (or "liberty" as he terms it) means an ability to act contrary to our motives, then, Hume argues, we simply have no free will. However, he offers a more watered-down notion of free will, namely, the ability to act in accord with our motivations. In this sense free will is compatible with his rigid view of determinism.

In the philosophy of religion, Hume attacks the belief in miracles on the grounds that uniform experience of natural law outweighs the testimony of any alleged miracle. On the one hand, we might amass the best evidence that we can in favor of a reported miraculous event, such as the credibility of the various witnesses. However, on the other hand, we have our lifelong and consistent experience of natural laws—laws that are unvarying. The strong evidence of natural laws, he argues, will always outweigh the weaker evidence in support of miraculous events. In his Dialogues concerning Natural Religion *(1779), he offers two key criticisms of the design argument for God's existence. First, he argues, it rests on a faulty analogy between objects of human design, such as watches, and the alleged order of the universe. Because the two are so dissimilar, we cannot reasonably draw a conclusion about a natural designer. Second, he argues that we must proportion the cause of a thing to the effects that we actually see; so, since the universe (as an effect) is limited, diverse, and imperfect, we cannot infer that the designer (the cause) is unlimited, single, and perfect. In the same work Hume attacks the cosmological argument, particularly a version articulated by British philosopher Samuel Clarke (1675–1729). Clarke grants that, in theory, we might trace the various causes of the world back to infinity past. We might envision an infinitely long sequence of dependent beings, each of which relies for its existence on the previous thing. Even though each thing in this sequence is adequately explained by its previous member, there is one huge fact that remains unexplained: why the entire infinite series exists to begin with. Clarke concludes that there must be a self-existent being to explain this huge fact. Against Clarke, Hume argues that once we adequately explain each individual item in an infinite series of dependent beings, we have thereby given a full explanation of the entire series.*

SCEPTICAL DOUBTS CONCERNING THE OPERATIONS OF THE UNDERSTANDING

The Source of Factual Reasoning

All the objects of human reason or enquiry may naturally be divided into two kinds, to wit, relations of ideas, and matters of fact. Of the first kind are the sciences of Geometry, Algebra, and Arithmetic; and in short, every affirmation which is either intuitively or demonstratively certain. That the square of the hypotenuse is equal to the square of the two sides, is a proposition which expresses a relation between these figures. That three times five is equal to the half of thirty, expresses a relation between these numbers. Propositions of this kind are discoverable by the mere operation of thought, without dependence on what is anywhere existent in the universe. Though there never were a circle or triangle in nature, the truths demonstrated by Euclid would forever retain their certainty and evidence.

Matters of fact, which are the second objects of human reason, are not ascertained in the same manner; nor is our evidence of their truth, however great, of a like nature with the foregoing. The contrary of every matter of fact is still possible; because it can never imply a contradiction, and is conceived by the mind with the same facility and distinctness, as if ever so conformable to reality. That the sun will not rise tomorrow is no less intelligible a proposition, and implies no more contradiction than the affirmation, that it will rise. We should in vain, therefore, attempt to demonstrate its falsehood. Were it demonstratively false, it would imply a contradiction, and could never be distinctly conceived by the mind.

It may, therefore, be a subject worthy of curiosity, to enquire what is the nature of that evidence which assures us of any real existence and matter of fact, beyond the present testimony of our senses, or the records of our memory. This part of philosophy, it is observable, has been little cultivated, either by the ancients or moderns; and therefore our doubts and errors, in the prosecution of so important an enquiry, may be the more excusable; while we march through such difficult paths without any guide or direction. They may even prove useful, by exciting curiosity, and destroying that implicit faith and security, which is the bane of all reasoning and free enquiry. The discovery of defects in the common philosophy, if any such there be, will not, I presume, be a discouragement, but rather an incitement, as is usual, to attempt something more full and satisfactory than has yet been proposed to the public.

All reasonings concerning matter of fact seem to be founded on the relation of cause and effect. By means of that relation alone we can go beyond the evidence of our memory and senses. If you were to ask a man, why he believes any matter of fact, which is absent; for instance, that his friend is in the country, or in France; he would give you a reason; and this reason would be some other fact; as a letter received from him, or the knowledge of his former resolutions and promises. A man finding a watch or any other machine in a desert island, would conclude that there had once been men in that island. All our reasonings concerning fact are of the same nature. And here it is constantly supposed that there is a connection between the present fact and that which is inferred from it. Were there nothing to bind them together, the inference would be entirely precarious. The hearing of an articulate voice and rational discourse in the dark assures us of the presence of some person: Why? Because these are the effects of the human make and fabric, and closely connected with it. If we anatomize all the other reasonings of this nature, we shall find that they are founded on the relation of cause and effect, and that this relation is either near or remote, direct or collateral. Heat and light are collateral effects of fire, and the one effect may justly be inferred from the other.

Cause and Effect Based on Experience

If we would satisfy ourselves, therefore, concerning the nature of that evidence, which assures us of matters of fact, we must enquire how we arrive at the knowledge of cause and effect.

I shall venture to affirm, as a general proposition, which admits of no exception, that the knowledge of this relation is not, in any instance, attained by reasonings a priori; but arises entirely from experience, when we find that any particular objects are constantly conjoined with each other. Let an object be presented to a man of ever so strong natural reason and abilities; if that object be entirely new to him, he will not be able, by the most accurate examination of its sensible qualities, to discover any of its causes or effects. Adam, though his rational faculties be supposed, at the very first, entirely perfect, could not have inferred from the fluidity and transparency of water that it would suffocate him, or from the light and warmth of fire that it would consume him. No object ever discovers, by the qualities which appear to the senses, either the causes which produced it, or the effects which will arise from it; nor can our reason, unassisted by experience, ever draw any inference concerning real existence and matter of fact.

This proposition, that causes and effects are discoverable, not by reason but by experience, will readily be admitted with regard to such objects, as we remember to have once been altogether unknown to us; since we must be conscious of the utter inability, which we then lay under, of foretelling what would arise from them. Present two smooth pieces of marble to a man who has no tincture of natural philosophy; he will never discover that they will adhere together in such a manner as to require great force to separate them in a direct line, while they make so small a resistance to a lateral pressure. Such events, as bear little analogy to the common course of nature, are also readily confessed to be known only by experience; nor does any man imagine that the explosion of gunpowder, or the attraction of a loadstone, could ever be discovered by arguments a priori. In like manner, when an effect is supposed to depend upon an intricate machinery or secret structure of parts, we make no difficulty in attributing all our knowledge of it to experience. Who will assert that he can give the ultimate reason, why milk or bread is proper nourishment for a man, not for a lion or a tiger?

But the same truth may not appear, at first sight, to have the same evidence with regard to events, which have become familiar to us from our first appearance in the world, which bear a close analogy to the whole course of nature, and which are supposed to depend on the simple qualities of objects, without any secret structure of parts. We are apt to imagine that we could discover these effects by the mere operation of our reason, without experience. We fancy, that were we brought on a sudden into this world, we could at first have inferred that one Billiard-ball would communicate motion to another upon impulse; and that we needed not to have waited for the event, in order to pronounce with certainty concerning it. Such is the influence of custom, that, where it is strongest, it not only covers our natural ignorance, but even conceals itself, and seems not to take place, merely because it is found in the highest degree.

But to convince us that all the laws of nature, and all the operations of bodies without exception, are known only by experience, the following reflections may, perhaps, suffice. Were any object presented to us, and were we required to pronounce concerning the effect, which will result from it, without consulting past observation; after what manner, I beseech you, must the mind proceed in this operation? It must invent or imagine some event, which it ascribes to the object as its effect; and it is plain that this invention must be entirely arbitrary. The mind can never possibly find the effect in the supposed cause, by the most accurate scrutiny and examination. For the effect is totally different from the cause, and consequently can never be discovered in it. Motion in the second Billiard-ball is a quite distinct event from motion in the first; nor is there any thing in the one to suggest the smallest hint of the other. A stone or piece of metal raised into the air, and left without any support, immediately falls: But to consider the matter a priori, is there any thing we discover in this situation which can beget the idea of a downward, rather than an upward, or any other motion, in the stone or metal?

And as the first imagination or invention of a particular effect, in all natural operations, is arbitrary, where we consult not experience; so must we also esteem the supposed tie or connection between the cause and effect, which binds them together, and renders it impossible that any other effect could result from the operation of that cause. When I see, for instance, a Billiard-ball moving in a straight line towards another; even suppose motion in the second ball should by accident be suggested to me, as the result of their contact or impulse; may I not conceive, that a hundred different events might as well follow from that cause? May not both these balls remain at absolute rest? May not the first ball return in a straight line, or leap off from the second in any line or direction? All these suppositions are consistent and conceivable. Why then should we give the preference to one, which is no more consistent or conceivable than the rest? All our reasonings a priori will never be able to show us any foundation for this preference.

In a word, then, every effect is a distinct event from its cause. It could not, therefore, be discovered in the cause, and the first invention or conception of it, a priori, must be entirely arbitrary. And even after it is suggested, the conjunction of it with the cause must appear equally arbitrary; since there are always many other effects, which, to reason, must seem fully as consistent and natural. In vain, therefore, should we pretend to determine any single event, or infer any cause or effect, without the assistance of observation and experience.

Hence we may discover the reason why no philosopher, who is rational and modest, has ever pretended to assign the ultimate cause of any natural operation, or to show distinctly the action of that power, which produces any single effect in the universe. It is confessed, that the utmost effort of human reason is to reduce the principles, productive of natural phenomena, to a greater simplicity, and to resolve the many particular effects into a few general causes, by means of reasonings from analogy, experience, and observation. But as to the causes of these general causes, we should in vain attempt their discovery; nor shall we ever be able to satisfy ourselves, by any particular explication of them. These ultimate springs and principles are totally shut up from human curiosity and enquiry. Elasticity, gravity, cohesion of parts, communication of motion by impulse; these are probably the ultimate causes and principles which we shall ever discover in nature; and we may esteem ourselves sufficiently happy, if, by accurate enquiry and reasoning, we can trace up the particular phenomena to, or near to, these general principles. The most perfect philosophy of the natural kind only staves off our ignorance a little longer: As perhaps the most perfect philosophy of the moral or metaphysical kind serves only to discover larger portions of it. Thus the observation of human blindness and weakness is the result of all philosophy, and meets us at every turn, in spite of our endeavors to elude or avoid it.

Nor is geometry, when taken into the assistance of natural philosophy, ever able to remedy this defect, or lead us into the knowledge of ultimate causes, by all that accuracy of reasoning for which it is so justly celebrated. Every part of mixed mathematics proceeds upon the supposition that certain laws are established by nature in her operations; and abstract reasonings are employed, either to assist experience in the discovery of these laws, or to determine their influence in particular instances, where it depends upon any precise degree of distance and quantity. Thus, it is a law of motion, discovered by experience, that the moment or force of any body in motion is in the compound ratio or proportion of its solid contents and its velocity; and consequently, that a small force may remove the greatest obstacle or raise the greatest weight, if, by any contrivance or machinery, we can increase the velocity of that force, so as to make it an overmatch for its antagonist. Geometry assists us in the application of this law, by giving us the just dimensions of all the parts and figures which can enter into any species of machine; but still the discovery of the law itself is owing merely to experience, and all the abstract reasonings in the world could never lead us one step towards the knowledge of it. When we reason a priori, and consider merely any object or cause, as it appears to the mind, independent of all observation, it never could suggest to us the notion of any distinct object, such as its effect; much less, show us the inseparable and inviolable connection between them. A man must be very sagacious who could discover by reasoning that crystal is the effect of heat, and ice of cold, without being previously acquainted with the operation of these qualities.

But we have not yet attained any tolerable satisfaction with regard to the question first proposed. Each solution still gives rise to a new question as difficult as the foregoing, and leads us on to further enquiries. When it is asked, What is the nature of all our reasonings concerning matter of fact? the proper answer seems to be, that they are founded on the relation of cause and effect. When again it is asked, What is the foundation of all our reasonings and conclusions concerning that relation? it may be replied in one word, experience. But if we still carry on our sifting humor, and ask, What is the foundation of all conclusions from experience? this implies a new question, which may be of more difficult solution and explication. Philosophers, that give themselves airs of superior wisdom and sufficiency, have a hard task when they encounter persons of inquisitive dispositions, who push them from every corner to which they retreat, and who are sure at last to bring them to some dangerous dilemma. The best expedient to prevent this confusion, is to be modest in our pretensions; and even to discover the difficulty ourselves before it is objected to us. By this means, we may make a kind of merit of our very ignorance.

The Problem of Induction

I shall content myself, in this section, with an easy task, and shall pretend only to give a negative answer to the question here proposed. I say then, that, even after we have experience of the operations of cause and effect, our conclusions from that experience are not founded on reasoning, or any process of the understanding. This answer we must endeavor both to explain and to defend.

It must certainly be allowed, that nature has kept us at a great distance from all her secrets, and has afforded us only the knowledge of a few superficial qualities of objects; while she conceals from us those powers and principles on which the influence of those objects entirely depends. Our senses inform us of the color, weight, and consistence of bread; but neither sense nor reason can ever inform us of those qualities which fit it for the nourishment and support of a human body. Sight or feeling conveys an idea of the actual motion of bodies; but as to that wonderful force or power, which would carry on a moving body for ever in a continued change of place, and which bodies never lose but by communicating it to others; of this we cannot form the most distant conception. But notwithstanding this ignorance of natural powers and principles, we always presume, when we see like sensible qualities, that they have like secret powers, and expect that effects, similar to those which we have experienced, will follow from them. If a body of like color and consistence with that bread, which we have formerly eat, be presented to us, we make no scruple of repeating the experiment, and foresee, with certainty, like nourishment and support. Now this is a process of the mind or thought, of which I would willingly know the foundation. It is allowed on all hands that there is no known connection between the sensible qualities and the secret powers; and consequently, that the mind is not led to form such a conclusion concerning their constant and regular conjunction, by any thing which it knows of their nature. As to past Experience, it can be allowed to give direct and certain information of those precise objects only, and that precise period of time, which fell under its cognizance: But why this experience should be extended to future times, and to other objects, which for aught we know, may be only in appearance similar; this is the main question on which I would insist. The bread, which I formerly eat, nourished me; that is, a body of such sensible qualities was, at that time, endued with such secret powers: But does it follow, that other bread must also nourish me at another time, and that like sensible qualities must always be attended with like secret powers? The consequence seems nowise necessary. At least, it must be acknowledged that there is here a consequence drawn by the mind; that there is a certain step taken; a process of thought, and an inference, which wants to be explained. These two propositions are far from being the same, I have found that such an object has always been attended with such an effect, and I foresee, that other objects, which are, in appearance, similar, will be attended with similar effects. I shall allow, if you please, that the one proposition may justly be inferred from the other: I know, in fact, that it always is inferred. But if you insist that the inference is made by a chain of reasoning, I desire you to produce that reasoning. The connection between these propositions is not intuitive. There is required a medium, which may enable the mind to draw such an inference, if indeed it be drawn by reasoning and argument. What that medium is, I must confess, passes my comprehension; and it is incumbent on those to produce it, who assert that it really exists, and is the origin of all our conclusions concerning matter of fact.

This negative argument must certainly, in process of time, become altogether convincing, if many penetrating and able philosophers shall turn their inquiries this way and no one be ever able to discover any connecting proposition or intermediate step, which supports the understanding in this conclusion. But as the question is yet new, every reader may not trust so far to his own penetration, as to conclude, because an argument escapes his inquiry, that therefore it does not really exist. For this reason it may be requisite to venture upon a more difficult task; and enumerating all the branches of human knowledge, endeavor to show that none of them can afford such an argument.

All reasonings may be divided into two kinds, namely, demonstrative reasoning, or that concerning relations of ideas, and moral reasoning, or that concerning matter of fact and existence. That there are no demonstrative arguments in the case seems evident; since it implies no contradiction that the course of nature may change, and that an object, seemingly like those which we have experienced, may be attended with different or contrary effects. May I not clearly and distinctly conceive that a body, falling from the clouds, and which, in all other respects, resembles snow, has yet the taste of salt or feeling of fire? Is there any more intelligible proposition than to affirm, that all the trees will flourish in December and January, and decay in May and June? Now whatever is intelligible, and can be distinctly conceived, implies no contradiction, and can never be proved false by any demonstrative argument or abstract reasoning a priori.

If we be, therefore, engaged by arguments to put trust in past experience, and make it the standard of our future judgment, these arguments must be probable only, or such as regard matter of fact and real existence according to the division above mentioned. But that there is no argument of this kind, must appear, if our explication of that species of reasoning be admitted as solid and satisfactory. We have said that all arguments concerning existence are founded on the relation of cause and effect; that our knowledge of that relation is derived entirely from experience; and that all our experimental conclusions proceed upon the supposition that the future will be conformable to the past. To endeavor, therefore, the proof of this last supposition by probable arguments, or arguments regarding existence, must be evidently going in a circle, and taking that for granted, which is the very point in question.

In reality, all arguments from experience are founded on the similarity which we discover among natural objects, and by which we are induced to expect effects similar to those which we have found to follow from such objects. And though none but a fool or madman will ever pretend to dispute the authority of experience, or to reject that great guide of human life, it may surely be allowed a philosopher to have so much curiosity at least as to examine the principle of human nature, which gives this mighty authority to experience, and makes us draw advantage from that similarity which nature has placed among different objects. From causes which, appear similar, we expect similar effects. This is the sum of all our experimental conclusions. Now it seems evident that, if this conclusion were formed by reason, it would be as perfect at first, and upon one instance, as after ever so long a course of experience. But the case is far otherwise. [There is] nothing so like as eggs. Yet no one, on account of this appearing similarity, expects the same taste and relish in all of them. It is only after a long course of uniform experiments in any kind, that we attain a firm reliance and security with regard to a particular event. Now where is that process of reasoning which, from one instance, draws a conclusion so different from that which it infers from a hundred instances that are nowise different from that single one? This question I propose as much for the sake of information, as with an intention of raising difficulties. I cannot find, I cannot imagine any such reasoning. But I keep my mind still open to instruction, if any one will vouchsafe to bestow it on me.

Should it be said that, from a number of uniform experiments, we infer a connection between the sensible qualities and the secret powers; this, I must confess, seems the same difficulty, couched in different terms. The question still recurs, on what process of argument this inference is founded? Where is the medium, the interposing ideas, which join propositions so very wide of each other? It is confessed that the color, consistence, and other sensible qualities of bread appear not, of themselves, to have any connection with the secret powers of nourishment and support. For otherwise we could infer these secret powers from the first appearance of these sensible qualities, without the aid of experience; contrary to the sentiment of all philosophers, and contrary to plain matter of fact. Here, then, is our natural state of ignorance with regard to the powers and influence of all objects. How is this remedied by experience? It only shows us a number of uniform effects, resulting from certain objects, and teaches us that those particular objects, at that particular time, were endowed with such powers and forces. When a new object, endowed with similar sensible qualities, is produced, we expect similar powers and forces, and look for a like effect. From a body of like color and consistence with bread we expect like nourishment and support. But this surely is a step or progress of the mind, which wants to be explained. When a man says, I have found, in all past instances, such sensible qualities conjoined with such secret powers: And when he says, similar sensible qualities will always be conjoined with similar secret powers; he is not guilty of a tautology, nor are these propositions in any respect the same. You say that the one proposition is an inference from the other. But you must confess that the inference is not intuitive; neither is it demonstrative: Of what nature is it, then? To say it is experimental, is begging the question. For all inferences from experience suppose, as their foundation, that the future will resemble the past, and that similar powers will be conjoined with similar sensible qualities. If there be any suspicion that the course of nature may change, and that the past may be no rule for the future, all experience becomes useless, and can give rise to no inference or conclusion. It is impossible, therefore, that any arguments from experience can prove this resemblance of the past to the future; since all these arguments are founded on the supposition of that resemblance.

Let the course of things be allowed hitherto ever so regular; that alone, without some new argument or inference, proves not that, for the future, it will continue so. In vain do you pretend to have learned the nature of bodies from your past experience. Their secret nature, and consequently all their effects and influence, may change, without any change in their sensible qualities. This happens sometimes, and with regard to some objects: Why may it not happen always, and with regard to all objects? What logic, what process or argument secures you against this supposition? My practice, you say, refutes my doubts. But you mistake the purport of my question. As an agent, I am quite satisfied in the point; but as a philosopher, who has some share of curiosity, I will not say skepticism, I want to learn the foundation of this inference. No reading, no enquiry has yet been able to remove my difficulty, or give me satisfaction in a matter of such importance. Can I do better than propose the difficulty to the public, even though, perhaps, I have small hopes of obtaining a solution? We shall at least, by this means, be sensible of our ignorance, if we do not augment our knowledge.

I must confess that a man is guilty of unpardonable arrogance who concludes, because an argument has escaped his own investigation, that therefore it does not really exist. I must also confess that, though all the learned, for several ages, should have employed themselves in fruitless search upon any subject, it may still, perhaps, be rash to conclude positively that the subject must, therefore, pass all human comprehension. Even though we examine all the sources of our knowledge, and conclude them unfit for such a subject, there may still remain a suspicion, that the enumeration is not complete, or the examination not accurate. But with regard to the present subject, there are some considerations which seem to remove all this accusation of arrogance or suspicion of mistake.

It is certain that the most ignorant and stupid peasants—nay infants, nay even brute beasts—improve by experience, and learn the qualities of natural objects, by observing the effects which result from them. When a child has felt the sensation of pain from touching the flame of a candle, he will be careful not to put his hand near any candle; but will expect a similar effect from a cause which is similar in its sensible qualities and appearance. If you assert, therefore, that the understanding of the child is led into this conclusion by any process of argument or ratiocination, I may justly require you to produce that argument; nor have you any pretence to refuse so equitable a demand. You cannot say that the argument is abstruse, and may possibly escape your enquiry; since you confess that it is obvious to the capacity of a mere infant. If you hesitate, therefore, a moment, or if, after reflection, you produce any intricate or profound argument, you, in a manner, give up the question, and confess that it is not reasoning which engages us to suppose the past resembling the future, and to expect similar effects from causes which are, to appearance, similar. This is the proposition which I intended to enforce in the present section. If I be right, I pretend not to have made any mighty discovery. And if I be wrong, I must acknowledge myself to be indeed a very backward scholar; since I cannot now discover an argument which, it seems, was perfectly familiar to me long before I was out of my cradle.

Inferences from Experience Based on Habit

. . . Suppose a person, though endowed with the strongest faculties of reason and reflection, to be brought on a sudden into this world; he would, indeed, immediately observe a continual succession of objects, and one event following another; but he would not be able to discover any thing farther. He would not, at first, by any reasoning, be able to reach the idea of cause and effect; since the particular powers, by which all natural operations are performed, never appear to the senses; nor is it reasonable to conclude, merely because one event, in one instance, precedes another, that therefore the one is the cause, the other the effect. Their conjunction may be arbitrary and casual. There may be no reason to infer the existence of one from the appearance of the other. And in a word, such a person, without more experience, could never employ his conjecture or reasoning concerning any matter of fact, or be assured of any thing beyond what was immediately present to his memory and senses.

Suppose, again, that he has acquired more experience, and has lived so long in the world as to have observed familiar objects or events to be constantly conjoined together; what is the consequence of this experience? He immediately infers the existence of one object from the appearance of the other. Yet he has not, by all his experience, acquired any idea or knowledge of the secret power by which the one object produces the other; nor is it by any process of reasoning, he is engaged to draw this inference. But still he finds himself determined to draw it: And though he should be convinced that his understanding has no part in the operation, he would nevertheless continue in the same course of thinking. There is some other principle which determines him to form such a conclusion.

This principle is custom or habit. For wherever the repetition of any particular act or operation produces a propensity to renew the same act or operation, without being impelled by any reasoning or process of the understanding, we always say, that this propensity is the effect of Custom. By employing that word, we pretend not to have given the ultimate reason of such a propensity. We only point out a principle of human nature, which is universally acknowledged, and which is well known by its effects. Perhaps we can push our enquiries no farther, or pretend to give the cause of this cause; but must rest contented with it as the ultimate principle, which we can assign, of all our conclusions from experience. It is sufficient satisfaction, that we can go so far, without repining at the narrowness of our faculties because they will carry us no farther. And it is certain we here advance a very intelligible proposition at least, if not a true one, when we assert that, after the constant conjunction of two objects—heat and flame, for instance, [or] weight and solidity—we are determined by custom alone to expect the one from the appearance of the other. This hypothesis seems even the only one which explains the difficulty, why we draw, from a thousand instances, an inference which we are not able to draw from one instance, that is, in no respect, different from them. Reason is incapable of any such variation. The conclusions which it draws from considering one circle are the same which it would form upon surveying all the circles in the universe. But no man, having seen only one body move after being impelled by another, could infer that every other body will move after a like impulse. All inferences from experience, therefore, are effects of custom, not of reasoning.

Custom, then, is the great guide of human life. It is that principle alone which renders our experience useful to us, and makes us expect, for the future, a similar train of events with those which have appeared in the past. Without the influence of custom, we should be entirely ignorant of every matter of fact beyond what is immediately present to the memory and senses. We should never know how to adjust means to ends, or to employ our natural powers in the production of any effect. There would be an end at once of all action, as well as of the chief part of speculation.

But here it may be proper to remark, that though our conclusions from experience carry us beyond our memory and senses, and assure us of matters of fact which happened in the most distant places and most remote ages, yet some fact must always be present to the senses or memory, from which we may first proceed in drawing these conclusions. A man, who should find in a desert country the remains of pompous buildings, would conclude that the country had, in ancient times, been cultivated by civilized inhabitants; but did nothing of this nature occur to him, he could never form such an inference. We learn the events of former ages from history; but then we must peruse the volumes in which this instruction is contained, and thence carry up our inferences from one testimony to another, till we arrive at the eyewitnesses and spectators of these distant events. In a word, if we proceed not upon some fact, present to the memory or senses, our reasonings would be merely hypothetical; and however the particular links might be connected with each other, the whole chain of inferences would have nothing to support it, nor could we ever, by its means, arrive at the knowledge of any real existence. If I ask why you believe any particular matter of fact, which you relate, you must tell me some reason; and this reason will be some other fact, connected with it. But as you cannot proceed after this manner, in infinitum, you must at last terminate in some fact, which is present to your memory or senses; or must allow that your belief is entirely without foundation. . . .

THE SELF AS A BUNDLE OF PERCEPTIONS

There are some philosophers who imagine we are every moment intimately conscious of what we call our self; that we feel its existence and its continuance in existence; and are certain, beyond the evidence of a demonstration, both of its perfect identity and simplicity. The strongest sensation, the most violent passion, say they, instead of distracting us from this view, only fix it the more intensely, and make us consider their influence on self either by their pain or pleasure. To attempt a further proof of this were to weaken its evidence; since no proof can be derived from any fact of which we are so intimately conscious; nor is there any thing of which we can be certain if we doubt of this.

Unluckily all these positive assertions are contrary to that very experience which is pleaded for them; nor have we any idea of self, after the manner it is here explained. For, from what impression could this idea be derived? This question it is impossible to answer without a manifest contradiction and absurdity; and yet it is a question which must necessarily be answered, if we would have the idea of self pass for clear and intelligible. It must be some one impression that gives rise to every real idea. But self or person is not any one impression, but that to which our several impressions and ideas are supposed to have a reference. If any impression gives rise to the idea of self, that impression must continue invariably the same, through the whole course of our lives; since self is supposed to exist after that manner. But there is no impression constant and invariable. Pain and pleasure, grief and joy, passions and sensations succeed each other, and never all exist at the same time. It cannot therefore be from any of these impressions, or from any other, that the idea of self is derived; and consequently there is no such idea.

But further, what must become of all our particular perceptions upon this hypothesis? All these are different, and distinguishable, and separable from each other, and may be separately considered, and may exist separately, and have no need of any thing to support their existence. After what manner therefore do they belong to self, and how are they connected with it? For my part, when I enter most intimately into what I call myself, I always stumble on some particular perception or other, of heat or cold, light or shade, love or hatred, pain or pleasure. I never can catch myself at any time without a perception, and never can observe any thing but the perception. When my perceptions are removed for any time, as by sound sleep, so long am I insensible of myself, and may truly be said not to exist. And were all my perceptions removed by death, and could I neither think, nor feel, nor see, nor love, nor hate, after the dissolution of my body, I should be entirely annihilated, nor do I conceive what is further requisite to make me a perfect nonentity. If any one, upon serious and unprejudiced reflection, thinks he has a different notion of himself, I must confess I can reason no longer with him. All I can allow him is, that he may be in the right as well as I, and that we are essentially different in this particular. He may, perhaps, perceive something simple and continued, which he calls himself; though I am certain there is no such principle in me.

But setting aside some metaphysicians of this kind, I may venture to affirm of the rest of mankind, that they are nothing but a bundle or collection of different perceptions, which succeed each other with an inconceivable rapidity, and are in a perpetual flux and movement. Our eyes cannot turn in their sockets without varying our perceptions. Our thought is still more variable than our sight; and all our other senses and faculties contribute to this change: nor is there any single power of the soul, which remains unalterably the same, perhaps for one moment. The mind is a kind of theatre, where several perceptions successively make their appearance; pass, repass, glide away, and mingle in an infinite variety of postures and situations. There is properly no simplicity in it at one time, nor identity in different, whatever natural propension we may have to imagine that simplicity and identity. The comparison of the theatre must not mislead us. They are the successive perceptions only, that constitute the mind; nor have we the most distant notion of the place where these scenes are represented, or of the materials of which it is composed.

OF LIBERTY AND NECESSITY

. . . It is universally allowed that matter, in all its operations, is actuated by a necessary force, and that every natural effect is so precisely determined by the energy of its cause that no other effect, in such particular circumstances, could possibly have resulted from it. The degree and direction of every motion is, by the laws of nature, prescribed with such exactness that a living creature may as soon arise from the shock of two bodies as motion in any other degree or direction than what is actually produced by it. Would we, therefore, form a just and precise idea of necessity, we must consider whence that idea arises when we apply it to the operation of bodies.

It seems evident that, if all the scenes of nature were continually shifted in such a manner that no two events bore any resemblance to each other, but every object was entirely new, without any similitude to whatever had been seen before, we should never, in that case, have attained the least idea of necessity, or of a connection among these objects. We might say, upon such a supposition, that one object or event has followed another; not that one was produced by the other. The relation of cause and effect must be utterly unknown to mankind. Inference and reasoning concerning the operations of nature would, from that moment, be at an end; and the memory and senses remain the only canals, by which the knowledge of any real existence could possibly have access to the mind. Our idea, therefore, of necessity and causation arises entirely from the uniformity observable in the operations of nature, where (1) similar objects are constantly conjoined together, and (2) the mind is determined by custom to infer the one from the appearance of the other. These two circumstances form the whole of that necessity, which we ascribe to matter. Beyond the constant conjunction of similar objects, and the consequent inference from one to the other, we have no notion of any necessity or connection.

If it appear, therefore, that all mankind have ever allowed, without any doubt or hesitation, that these two circumstances take place in the voluntary actions of men, and in the operations of mind; it must follow, that all mankind have ever agreed in the doctrine of necessity, and that they have hitherto disputed, merely for not understanding each other.

Constant Conjunction between Motives and Actions

As to the first circumstance, the constant and regular conjunction of similar events, we may possibly satisfy ourselves by the following considerations: It is universally acknowledged that there is a great uniformity among the actions of men, in all nations and ages, and that human nature remains still the same, in its principles and operations. The same motives always produce the same actions: The same events follow from the same causes. Ambition, avarice, self-love, vanity, friendship, generosity, public spirit: These passions, mixed in various degrees, and distributed through society, have been, from the beginning of the world, and still are, the source of all the actions and enterprises, which have ever been observed among mankind. Would you know the sentiments, inclinations, and course of life of the Greeks and Romans? Study well the temper and actions of the French and English: You cannot be much mistaken in transferring to the former most of the observations which you have made with regard to the latter. Mankind are so much the same, in all times and places, that history informs us of nothing new or strange in this particular. Its chief use is only to discover the constant and universal principles of human nature, by showing men in all varieties of circumstances and situations, and furnishing us with materials from which we may form our observations and become acquainted with the regular springs of human action and behavior. These records of wars, intrigues, factions, and revolutions, are so many collections of experiments, by which the politician or moral philosopher fixes the principles of his science, in the same manner as the physician or natural philosopher becomes acquainted with the nature of plants, minerals, and other external objects, by the experiments which he forms concerning them. Nor are the earth, water, and other elements, examined by Aristotle, and Hippocrates, more like to those which at present lie under our observation than the men described by Polybius and Tacitus are to those who now govern the world.

Should a traveler, returning from a far country, bring us an account of men, wholly different from any with whom we were ever acquainted; men, who were entirely divested of avarice, ambition, or revenge; who knew no pleasure but friendship, generosity, and public spirit; we should immediately, from these circumstances, detect the falsehood, and prove him a liar, with the same certainty as if he had stuffed his narration with stories of centaurs and dragons, miracles and prodigies. And if we would explode any forgery in history, we cannot make use of a more convincing argument, than to prove, that the actions ascribed to any person are directly contrary to the course of nature, and that no human motives, in such circumstances, could ever induce him to such a conduct. The veracity of Quintus Curtius is as much to be suspected, when he describes the supernatural courage of Alexander, by which he was hurried on singly to attack multitudes, as when he describes his supernatural force and activity, by which he was able to resist them. So readily and universally do we acknowledge a uniformity in human motives and actions as well as in the operations of body.

Hence likewise the benefit of that experience, acquired by long life and a variety of business and company, in order to instruct us in the principles of human nature, and regulate our future conduct, as well as speculation. By means of this guide, we mount up to the knowledge of men's inclinations and motives, from their actions, expressions, and even gestures; and again descend to the interpretation of their actions from our knowledge of their motives and inclinations. The general observations treasured up by a course of experience, give us the clue of human nature, and teach us to unravel all its intricacies. Pretexts and appearances no longer deceive us. Public declarations pass for the specious coloring of a cause. And though virtue and honor be allowed their proper weight and authority, that perfect disinterestedness, so often pretended to, is never expected in multitudes and parties; seldom in their leaders; and scarcely even in individuals of any rank or station. But were there no uniformity in human actions, and were every experiment which we could form of this kind irregular and anomalous, it were impossible to collect any general observations concerning mankind; and no experience, however accurately digested by reflection, would ever serve to any purpose. Why is the aged husbandman more skillful in his calling than the young beginner but because there is a certain uniformity in the operation of the sun, rain, and earth towards the production of vegetables; and experience teaches the old practitioner the rules by which this operation is governed and directed.

We must not, however, expect that this uniformity of human actions should be carried to such a length as that all men, in the same circumstances, will always act precisely in the same manner, without making any allowance for the diversity of characters, prejudices, and opinions. Such a uniformity in every particular, is found in no part of nature. On the contrary, from observing the variety of conduct in different men, we are enabled to form a greater variety of maxims, which still suppose a degree of uniformity and regularity.

Are the manners of men different in different ages and countries? We learn thence the great force of custom and education, which mould the human mind from its infancy and form it into a fixed and established character. Is the behavior and conduct of the one sex very unlike that of the other? Is it thence we become acquainted with the different characters which nature has impressed upon the sexes, and which she preserves with constancy and regularity? Are the actions of the same person much diversified in the different periods of his life, from infancy to old age? This affords room for many general observations concerning the gradual change of our sentiments and inclinations, and the different maxims which prevail in the different ages of human creatures. Even the characters, which are peculiar to each individual, have a uniformity in their influence; otherwise our acquaintance with the persons and our observation of their conduct could never teach us their dispositions, or serve to direct our behavior with regard to them.

I grant it possible to find some actions, which seem to have no regular connection with any known motives, and are exceptions to all the measures of conduct which have ever been established for the government of men. But if we would willingly know what judgment should be formed of such irregular and extraordinary actions, we may consider the sentiments commonly entertained with regard to those irregular events which appear in the course of nature, and the operations of external objects. All causes are not conjoined to their usual effects with like uniformity. An artificer, who handles only dead matter, may be disappointed of his aim, as well as the politician, who directs the conduct of sensible and intelligent agents.

The vulgar, who take things according to their first appearance, attribute the uncertainty of events to such an uncertainty in the causes as makes the latter often fail of their usual influence; though they meet with no impediment in their operation. But philosophers, observing that, almost in every part of nature, there is contained a vast variety of springs and principles, which are hid, by reason of their minuteness or remoteness, find, that it is at least possible the contrariety of events may not proceed from any contingency in the cause, but from the secret operation of contrary causes. This possibility is converted into certainty by farther observation, when they remark that, upon an exact scrutiny, a contrariety of effects always betrays a contrariety of causes, and proceeds from their mutual opposition. A peasant can give no better reason for the stopping of any clock or watch than to say that it does not commonly go right: But an artist easily perceives that the same force in the spring or pendulum has always the same influence on the wheels; but fails of its usual effects, perhaps by reason of a grain of dust, which puts a stop to the whole movement. From the observation of several parallel instances, philosophers form a maxim that the connection between all causes and effects is equally necessary, and that its seeming uncertainty in some instances proceeds from the secret opposition of contrary causes.

Thus, for instance, in the human body, when the usual symptoms of health or sickness disappoint our expectation; when medicines operate not with their wonted powers; when irregular events follow from any particular cause; the philosopher and physician are not surprised at the matter, nor are ever tempted to deny, in general, the necessity and uniformity of those principles by which the animal economy is conducted. They know that a human body is a mighty complicated machine: That many secret powers lurk in it, which are altogether beyond our comprehension: That to us it must often appear very uncertain in its operations: And that therefore the irregular events, which outwardly discover themselves, can be no proof that the laws of nature are not observed with the greatest regularity in its internal operations and government.

The philosopher, if he be consistent, must apply the same reasoning to the actions and volitions of intelligent agents. The most irregular and unexpected resolutions of men may frequently be accounted for by those who know every particular circumstance of their character and situation. A person of an obliging disposition gives a peevish answer: But he has the toothache, or has not dined. A stupid fellow discovers an uncommon alacrity in his carriage: But he has met with a sudden piece of good fortune. Or even when an action, as sometimes happens, cannot be particularly accounted for, either by the person himself or by others; we know, in general, that the characters of men are, to a certain degree, inconstant and irregular. This is, in a manner, the constant character of human nature; though it be applicable, in a more particular manner, to some persons who have no fixed rule for their conduct, but proceed in a continued course of caprice and inconstancy. The internal principles and motives may operate in a uniform manner, notwithstanding these seeming irregularities; in the same manner as the winds, rain, cloud, and other variations of the weather are supposed to be governed by steady principles; though not easily discoverable by human sagacity and enquiry.

Inferring Actions from Motives

Thus it appears, not only that the conjunction between motives and voluntary actions is as regular and uniform as that between the cause and effect in any part of nature; but also that this regular conjunction has been universally acknowledged among mankind, and has never been the subject of dispute, either in philosophy or common life. Now, as it is from past experience that we draw all inferences concerning the future, and as we conclude that objects will always be conjoined together which we find to have always been conjoined; it may seem superfluous to prove that this experienced uniformity in human actions is a source whence we draw inferences concerning them. But in order to throw the argument into a greater variety of lights we shall also insist, though briefly, on this latter topic.

The mutual dependence of men is so great in all societies that scarce any human action is entirely complete in itself, or is performed without some reference to the actions of others, which are requisite to make it answer fully the intention of the agent. The poorest artificer, who labors alone, expects at least the protection of the magistrate, to ensure him the enjoyment of the fruits of his labor. He also expects that, when he carries his goods to market, and offers them at a reasonable price, he shall find purchasers, and shall be able, by the money he acquires, to engage others to supply him with those commodities which are requisite for his subsistence. In proportion as men extend their dealings, and render their intercourse with others more complicated, they always comprehend, in their schemes of life, a greater variety of voluntary actions, which they expect, from the proper motives, to cooperate with their own. In all these conclusions they take their measures from past experience, in the same manner as in their reasonings concerning external objects; and firmly believe that men, as well as all the elements, are to continue, in their operations, the same that they have ever found them. A manufacturer reckons upon the labor of his servants for the execution of any work as much as upon the tools which he employs, and would be equally surprised were his expectations disappointed. In short, this experimental inference and reasoning concerning the actions of others enters so much into human life that no man, while awake, is ever a moment without employing it. Have we not reason, therefore, to affirm that all mankind have always agreed in the doctrine of necessity according to the foregoing definition and explication of it?

Nor have philosophers even entertained a different opinion from the people in this particular. For, not to mention that almost every action of their life supposes that opinion, there are even few of the speculative parts of learning to which it is not essential. What would become of history, had we not a dependence on the veracity of the historian according to the experience which we have had of mankind? How could politics be a science, if laws and forms of government had not a uniform influence upon society? Where would be the foundation of morals, if particular characters had no certain or determinate power to produce particular sentiments, and if these sentiments had no constant operation on actions? And with what pretence could we employ our criticism upon any poet or polite author, if we could not pronounce the conduct and sentiments of his actors either natural or unnatural to such characters, and in such circumstances? It seems almost impossible, therefore, to engage either in science or action of any kind without acknowledging the doctrine of necessity, and this inference from motive to voluntary actions, from characters to conduct.

And indeed, when we consider how aptly natural and moral evidence link together, and form only one chain of argument, we shall make no scruple to allow that they are of the same nature, and derived from the same principles. A prisoner who has neither money nor interest, discovers the impossibility of his escape, as well when he considers the obstinacy of the gaoler, as the walls and bars with which he is surrounded; and, in all attempts for his freedom, chooses rather to work upon the stone and iron of the one, than upon the inflexible nature of the other. The same prisoner, when conducted to the scaffold, foresees his death as certainly from the constancy and fidelity of his guards, as from the operation of the axe or wheel. His mind runs along a certain train of ideas: The refusal of the soldiers to consent to his escape; the action of the executioner; the separation of the head and body; bleeding, convulsive motions, and death. Here is a connected chain of natural causes and voluntary actions; but the mind feels no difference between them in passing from one link to another: Nor is it less certain of the future event than if it were connected with the objects present to the memory or senses, by a train of causes, cemented together by what we are pleased to call a physical necessity. The same experienced union has the same effect on the mind, whether the united objects be motives, volition, and actions; or figure and motion. We may change the name of things; but their nature and their operation on the understanding never change.

Were a man, whom I know to be honest and opulent, and with whom I live in intimate friendship, to come into my house, where I am surrounded with my servants, I rest assured that he is not to stab me before he leaves it in order to rob me of my silver standish; and I no more suspect this event than the falling of the house itself, which is new, and solidly built and founded.—But he may have been seized with a sudden and unknown frenzy.—So may a sudden earthquake arise, and shake and tumble my house about my ears. I shall therefore change the suppositions. I shall say that I know with certainty that he is not to put his hand into the fire and hold it there till it be consumed: And this event, I think I can foretell with the same assurance, as that, if he throw himself out at the window, and meet with no obstruction, he will not remain a moment suspended in the air. No suspicion of an unknown frenzy can give the least possibility to the former event, which is so contrary to all the known principles of human nature. A man who at noon leaves his purse full of gold on the pavement at Charing-Cross, may as well expect that it will fly away like a feather, as that he will find it untouched an hour after. Above one half of human reasonings contain inferences of a similar nature, attended with more or less degrees of certainty proportioned to our experience of the usual conduct of mankind in such particular situations.

Why People Oppose Necessity

I have frequently considered, what could possibly be the reason why all mankind, though they have ever, without hesitation, acknowledged the doctrine of necessity in their whole practice and reasoning, have yet discovered such a reluctance to acknowledge it in words, and have rather shown a propensity, in all ages, to profess the contrary opinion. The matter, I think, may be accounted for after the following manner. If we examine the operations of body, and the production of effects from their causes, we shall find that all our faculties can never carry us farther in our knowledge of this relation than barely to observe that particular objects are constantly conjoined together, and that the mind is carried, by a customary transition, from the appearance of one to the belief of the other. But though this conclusion concerning human ignorance be the result of the strictest scrutiny of this subject, men still entertain a strong propensity to believe that they penetrate farther into the powers of nature, and perceive something like a necessary connection between the cause and the effect. When again they turn their reflections towards the operations of their own minds, and feel no such connection of the motive and the action; they are thence apt to suppose, that there is a difference between the effects which result from material force, and those which arise from thought and intelligence. But being once convinced that we know nothing farther of causation of any kind than merely the constant conjunction of objects, and the consequent inference of the mind from one to another, and finding that these two circumstances are universally allowed to have place in voluntary actions; we may be more easily led to own the same necessity common to all causes. And though this reasoning may contradict the systems of many philosophers, in ascribing necessity to the determinations of the will, we shall find, upon reflection, that they dissent from it in words only, not in their real sentiment. Necessity, according to the sense in which it is here taken, has never yet been rejected, nor can ever, I think, be rejected by any philosopher. It may only, perhaps, be pretended that the mind can perceive, in the operations of matter, some farther connection between the cause and effect; and connection that has no place in voluntary actions of intelligent beings. Now whether it be so or not, can only appear upon examination; and it is incumbent on these philosophers to make good their assertion, by defining or describing that necessity, and pointing it out to us in the operations of material causes.

It would seem, indeed, that men begin at the wrong end of this question concerning liberty and necessity, when they enter upon it by examining the faculties of the soul, the influence of the understanding, and the operations of the will. Let them first discuss a more simple question, namely, the operations of body and of brute unintelligent matter; and try whether they can there form any idea of causation and necessity, except that of a constant conjunction of objects, and subsequent inference of the mind from one to another. If these circumstances form, in reality, the whole of that necessity, which we conceive in matter, and if these circumstances be also universally acknowledged to take place in the operations of the mind, the dispute is at an end; at least, must be owned to be thenceforth merely verbal. But as long as we will rashly suppose, that we have some farther idea of necessity and causation in the operations of external objects; at the same time, that we can find nothing farther in the voluntary actions of the mind; there is no possibility of bringing the question to any determinate issue, while we proceed upon so erroneous a supposition. The only method of undeceiving us is to mount up higher; to examine the narrow extent of science when applied to material causes; and to convince ourselves that all we know of them is the constant conjunction and inference above mentioned. We may, perhaps, find that it is with difficulty we are induced to fix such narrow limits to human understanding: But we can afterwards find no difficulty when we come to apply this doctrine to the actions of the will. For as it is evident that these have a regular conjunction with motives and circumstances and characters, and as we always draw inferences from one to the other, we must be obliged to acknowledge in words that necessity, which we have already avowed, in every deliberation of our lives, and in every step of our conduct and behavior.

The Notion of Liberty

But to proceed in this reconciling project with regard to the question of liberty and necessity; the most contentious question of metaphysics, the most contentious science; it will not require many words to prove, that all mankind have ever agreed in the doctrine of liberty as well as in that of necessity, and that the whole dispute, in this respect also, has been hitherto merely verbal. For what is meant by liberty, when applied to voluntary actions? We cannot surely mean that actions have so little connection with motives, inclinations, and circumstances, that one does not follow with a certain degree of uniformity from the other, and that one affords no inference by which we can conclude the existence of the other. For these are plain and acknowledged matters of fact. By liberty, then, we can only mean a power of acting or not acting, according to the determinations of the will; this is, if we choose to remain at rest, we may; if we choose to move, we also may. Now this hypothetical liberty is universally allowed to belong to every one who is not a prisoner and in chains. Here, then, is no subject of dispute.

Whatever definition we may give of liberty, we should be careful to observe two requisite circumstances; first, that it be consistent with plain matter of fact; secondly, that it be consistent with itself. If we observe these circumstances, and render our definition intelligible, I am persuaded that all mankind will be found of one opinion with regard to it.

It is universally allowed that nothing exists without a cause of its existence, and that chance, when strictly examined, is a mere negative word, and means not any real power which has anywhere a being in nature. But it is pretended that some causes are necessary, some not necessary. Here then is the advantage of definitions. Let any one define a cause, without comprehending, as a part of the definition, a necessary connection with its effect; and let him show distinctly the origin of the idea, expressed by the definition; and I shall readily give up the whole controversy. But if the foregoing explication of the matter be received, this must be absolutely impracticable. Had not objects a regular conjunction with each other, we should never have entertained any notion of cause and effect; and this regular conjunction produces that inference of the understanding, which is the only connection, that we can have any comprehension of. Whoever attempts a definition of cause, exclusive of these circumstances, will be obliged either to employ unintelligible terms or such as are synonymous to the term which he endeavors to define. And if the definition above mentioned be admitted; liberty, when opposed to necessity, not to constraint, is the same thing with chance; which is universally allowed to have no existence.

OF MIRACLES

Evidence from Nature versus Miracle Testimonies

Though experience be our only guide in reasoning concerning matters of fact; it must be acknowledged, that this guide is not altogether infallible, but in some cases is apt to lead us into errors. One, who in our climate, should expect better weather in any week of June than in one of December, would reason justly, and conformably to experience; but it is certain, that he may happen, in the event, to find himself mistaken. However, we may observe, that, in such a case, he would have no cause to complain of experience; because it commonly informs us beforehand of the uncertainty, by that contrariety of events, which we may learn from a diligent observation. All effects follow not with like certainty from their supposed causes. Some events are found, in all countries and all ages, to have been constantly conjoined together: Others are found to have been more variable, and sometimes to disappoint our expectations; so that, in our reasonings concerning matter of fact, there are all imaginable degrees of assurance, from the highest certainty to the lowest species of moral evidence.

A wise man, therefore, proportions his belief to the evidence. In such conclusions as are founded on an infallible experience, he expects the event with the last degree of assurance, and regards his past experience as a full proof of the future existence of that event. In other cases, he proceeds with more caution: He weighs the opposite experiments: He considers which side is supported by the greater number of experiments: To that side he inclines, with doubt and hesitation; and when at last he fixes his judgment, the evidence exceeds not what we properly call probability. All probability, then, supposes an opposition of experiments and observations, where the one side is found to overbalance the other, and to produce a degree of evidence, proportioned to the superiority. A hundred instances or experiments on one side, and fifty on another, afford a doubtful expectation of any event; though a hundred uniform experiments, with only one that is contradictory, reasonably beget a pretty strong degree of assurance. In all cases, we must balance the opposite experiments, where they are opposite, and deduct the smaller number from the greater, in order to know the exact force of the superior evidence.

To apply these principles to a particular instance; we may observe, that there is no species of reasoning more common, more useful, and even necessary to human life, than that which is derived from the testimony of men, and the reports of eye-witnesses and spectators. This species of reasoning, perhaps, one may deny to be founded on the relation of cause and effect. I shall not dispute about a word. It will be sufficient to observe that our assurance in any argument of this kind is derived from no other principle than our observation of the veracity of human testimony, and of the usual conformity of facts to the reports of witnesses. It being a general maxim, that no objects have any discoverable connection together, and that all the inferences, which we can draw from one to another, are founded merely on our experience of their constant and regular conjunction; it is evident, that we ought not to make an exception to this maxim in favor of human testimony, whose connection with any event seems, in itself, as little necessary as any other. Were not the memory tenacious to a certain degree; had not men commonly an inclination to truth and a principle of probity; were they not sensible to shame, when detected in a falsehood: Were not these, I say, discovered by experience to be qualities, inherent in human nature, we should never repose the least confidence in human testimony. A man delirious, or noted for falsehood and villainy, has no manner of authority with us.

And as the evidence, derived from witnesses and human testimony, is founded on past experience, so it varies with the experience, and is regarded either as a proof or a probability, according as the conjunction between any particular kind of report and any kind of object has been found to be constant or variable. There are a number of circumstances to be taken into consideration in all judgments of this kind; and the ultimate standard, by which we determine all disputes, that may arise concerning them, is always derived from experience and observation. Where this experience is not entirely uniform on any side, it is attended with an unavoidable contrariety in our judgments, and with the same opposition and mutual destruction of argument as in every other kind of evidence. We frequently hesitate concerning the reports of others. We balance the opposite circumstances, which cause any doubt or uncertainty; and when we discover a superiority on any side, we incline to it; but still with a diminution of assurance, in proportion to the force of its antagonist.

This contrariety of evidence, in the present case, may be derived from several different causes; from the opposition of contrary testimony; from the character or number of the witnesses; from the manner of their delivering their testimony; or from the union of all these circumstances. We entertain a suspicion concerning any matter of fact, when the witnesses contradict each other; when they are but few, or of a doubtful character; when they have an interest in what they affirm; when they deliver their testimony with hesitation, or on the contrary, with too violent asseverations. There are many other particulars of the same kind, which may diminish or destroy the force of any argument, derived from human testimony.

Suppose, for instance, that the fact, which the testimony endeavors to establish, partakes of the extraordinary and the marvelous; in that case, the evidence, resulting from the testimony, admits of a diminution, greater or less, in proportion as the fact is more or less unusual. The reason why we place any credit in witnesses and historians, is not derived from any connection, which we perceive a priori, between testimony and reality, but because we are accustomed to find a conformity between them. But when the fact attested is such a one as has seldom fallen under our observation, here is a contest of two opposite experiences; of which the one destroys the other, as far as its force goes, and the superior can only operate on the mind by the force, which remains. The very same principle of experience, which gives us a certain degree of assurance in the testimony of witnesses, gives us also, in this case, another degree of assurance against the fact, which they endeavor to establish; from which contradiction there necessarily arises a counterpoise, and mutual destruction of belief and authority.

I should not believe such a story were it told me by Cato; was a proverbial saying in Rome, even during the lifetime of that philosophical patriot. The incredibility of a fact, it was allowed, might invalidate so great an authority.

The Indian prince, who refused to believe the first relations concerning the effects of frost, reasoned justly; and it naturally required very strong testimony to engage his assent to facts, that arose from a state of nature, with which he was unacquainted, and which bore so little analogy to those events, of which he had had constant and uniform experience. Though they were not contrary to his experience, they were not conformable to it.

But in order to increase the probability against the testimony of witnesses, let us suppose, that the fact, which they affirm, instead of being only marvelous, is really miraculous; and suppose also, that the testimony considered apart and in itself, amounts to an entire proof; in that case, there is proof against proof, of which the strongest must prevail, but still with a diminution of its force, in proportion to that of its antagonist.

A miracle is a violation of the laws of nature; and as a firm and unalterable experience has established these laws, the proof against a miracle, from the very nature of the fact, is as entire as any argument from experience can possibly be imagined. Why is it more than probable, that all men must die; that lead cannot, of itself, remain suspended in the air; that fire consumes wood, and is extinguished by water; unless it be, that these events are found agreeable to the laws of nature, and there is required a violation of these laws, or in other words, a miracle to prevent them? Nothing is esteemed a miracle, if it ever happen in the common course of nature. It is no miracle that a man, seemingly in good health, should die on a sudden: Because such a kind of death, though more unusual than any other, has yet been frequently observed to happen. But it is a miracle, that a dead man should come to life; because that has never been observed in any age or country. There must, therefore, be a uniform experience against every miraculous event, otherwise the event would not merit that appellation. And as a uniform experience amounts to a proof, there is here a direct and full proof, from the nature of the fact, against the existence of any miracle; nor can such a proof be destroyed, or the miracle rendered credible, but by an opposite proof, which is superior.

The plain consequence is (and it is a general maxim worthy of our attention), "That no testimony is sufficient to establish a miracle, unless the testimony be of such a kind, that its falsehood would be more miraculous, than the fact, which it endeavors to establish: And even in that case there is a mutual destruction of arguments, and the superior only gives us an assurance suitable to that degree of force, which remains, after deducting the inferior." When any one tells me, that he saw a dead man restored to life, I immediately consider with myself, whether it be more probable, that this person should either deceive or be deceived, or that the fact, which he relates, should really have happened. I weigh the one miracle against the other; and according to the superiority, which I discover, I pronounce my decision, and always reject the greater miracle. If the falsehood of his testimony would be more miraculous, than the event which he relates; then, and not till then, can he pretend to command my belief or opinion.

Four Factors against Most Miracles

In the foregoing reasoning we have supposed, that the testimony, upon which a miracle is founded, may possibly amount to an entire proof, and that the falsehood of that testimony would be a real prodigy: But it is easy to shew, that we have been a great deal too liberal in our concession, and that there never was a miraculous event established on so full an evidence.

For first, there is not to be found, in all history, any miracle attested by a sufficient number of men, of such unquestioned good-sense, education, and learning, as to secure us against all delusion in themselves; of such undoubted integrity, as to place them beyond all suspicion of any design to deceive others; of such credit and reputation in the eyes of mankind, as to have a great deal to lose in case of their being detected in any falsehood; and at the same time, attesting facts performed in such a public manner and in so celebrated a part of the world, as to render the detection unavoidable: All which circumstances are requisite to give us a full assurance in the testimony of men.

Secondly. We may observe in human nature a principle which, if strictly examined, will be found to diminish extremely the assurance which we might, from human testimony, have in any kind of prodigy. The maxim by which we commonly conduct ourselves in our reasonings is that the objects, of which we have no experience, resembles those of which we have; that what we have found to be most usual is always most probable; and that where there is an opposition of arguments, we ought to give the preference to such as are founded on the greatest number of past observations. But though in proceeding by this rule we readily reject any fact which is unusual and incredible in an ordinary degree; yet in advancing farther, the mind observes not always the same rule; but when anything is affirmed utterly absurd and miraculous, it rather the more readily admits of such a fact, upon account of that very circumstance, which ought to destroy all its authority. The passion of surprise and wonder arising from miracles, being an agreeable emotion, gives a sensible tendency towards the belief of those events from which it is derived. And this goes so far, that even those who cannot enjoy this pleasure immediately, nor can believe those miraculous events, of which they are informed, yet love to partake of the satisfaction at second-hand or by rebound, and place a pride and delight in exciting the admiration of others.

With what greediness are the miraculous accounts of travelers received, their descriptions of sea and land monsters, their relations of wonderful adventures, strange men, and uncouth manners? But if the spirit of religion join itself to the love of wonder, there is an end of common sense; and human testimony, in these circumstances, loses all pretensions to authority. A religionist may be an enthusiast, and imagine he sees what has no reality: He may know his narrative to be false, and yet persevere in it, with the best intentions in the world, for the sake of promoting so holy a cause: Or even where this delusion has not place, vanity, excited by so strong a temptation, operates on him more powerfully than on the rest of mankind in any other circumstances; and self-interest with equal force. His auditors may not have, and commonly have not, sufficient judgment to canvass his evidence: What judgment they have, they renounce by principle, in these sublime and mysterious subjects: Or if they were ever so willing to employ it, passion and a heated imagination disturb the regularity of its operations. Their credulity increases his impudence: And his impudence overpowers their credulity. . . .

Thirdly. It forms a strong presumption against all supernatural and miraculous relations, that they are observed chiefly to abound among ignorant and barbarous nations; or if a civilized people has ever given admission to any of them, that people will be found to have received them from ignorant and barbarous ancestors, who transmitted them with that inviolable sanction and authority, which always attend received opinions. When we peruse the first histories of all nations, we are apt to imagine ourselves transported into some new world; where the whole frame of nature is disjointed, and every element performs its operations in a different manner, from what it does at present. Battles, revolutions, pestilence, famine and death, are never the effect of those natural causes, which we experience. Prodigies, omens, oracles, judgments, quite obscure the few natural events, that are intermingled with them. But as the former grow thinner every page, in proportion as we advance nearer the enlightened ages, we soon learn, that there is nothing mysterious or supernatural in the case, but that all proceeds from the usual propensity of mankind towards the marvelous, and that, though this inclination may at intervals receive a check from sense and learning, it can never be thoroughly extirpated from human nature. . . .

I may add as a fourth reason, which diminishes the authority of prodigies, that there is no testimony for any, even those which have not been expressly detected, that is not opposed by an infinite number of witnesses; so that not only the miracle destroys the credit of testimony, but the testimony destroys itself. To make this the better understood, let us consider, that, in matters of religion, whatever is different is contrary; and that it is impossible the religions of ancient Rome, of Turkey, of Siam, and of China should, all of them, be established on any solid foundation. Every miracle, therefore, pretended to have been wrought in any of these religions (and all of them abound in miracles), as its direct scope is to establish the particular system to which it is attributed; so has it the same force, though more indirectly, to overthrow every other system. In destroying a rival system, it likewise destroys the credit of those miracles, on which that system was established; so that all the prodigies of different religions are to be regarded as contrary facts, and the evidences of these prodigies, whether weak or strong, as opposite to each other. According to this method of reasoning, when we believe any miracle of Mahomet or his successors, we have for our warrant the testimony of a few barbarous Arabians: And on the other hand, we are to regard the authority of Titus Livius, Plutarch, Tacitus, and, in short, of all the authors and witnesses, Grecian, Chinese, and Roman Catholic, who have related any miracle in their particular religion; I say, we are to regard their testimony in the same light as if they had mentioned that Mahometan miracle, and had in express terms contradicted it, with the same certainty as they have for the miracle they relate. This argument may appear over subtle and refined; but is not in reality different from the reasoning of a judge, who supposes, that the credit of two witnesses, maintaining a crime against any one, is destroyed by the testimony of two others, who affirm him to have been two hundred leagues distant, at the same instant when the crime is said to have been committed . . .

Miracles and Christianity

Upon the whole, then, it appears, that no testimony for any kind of miracle has ever amounted to a probability, much less to a proof; and that, even supposing it amounted to a proof, it would be opposed by another proof; derived from the very nature of the fact, which it would endeavor to establish. It is experience only, which gives authority to human testimony; and it is the same experience, which assures us of the laws of nature. When, therefore, these two kinds of experience are contrary, we have nothing to do but subtract the one from the other, and embrace an opinion, either on one side or the other, with that assurance which arises from the remainder. But according to the principle here explained, this subtraction, with regard to all popular religions, amounts to an entire annihilation; and therefore we may establish it as a maxim, that no human testimony can have such force as to prove a miracle, and make it a just foundation for any such system of religion. . . .

I am the better pleased with the method of reasoning here delivered, as I think it may serve to confound those dangerous friends or disguised enemies to the Christian Religion, who have undertaken to defend it by the principles of human reason. Our most holy religion is founded on Faith, not on reason; and it is a sure method of exposing it to put it to such a trial as it is, by no means, fitted to endure. To make this more evident, let us examine those miracles, related in scripture; and not to lose ourselves in too wide a field, let us confine ourselves to such as we find in the Pentateuch, which we shall examine, according to the principles of these pretended Christians, not as the word or testimony of God himself, but as the production of a mere human writer and historian. Here then we are first to consider a book, presented to us by a barbarous and ignorant people, written in an age when they were still more barbarous, and in all probability long after the facts which it relates, corroborated by no concurring testimony, and resembling those fabulous accounts, which every nation gives of its origin. Upon reading this book, we find it full of prodigies and miracles. It gives an account of a state of the world and of human nature entirely different from the present: Of our fall from that state: Of the age of man, extended to near a thousand years: Of the destruction of the world by a deluge: Of the arbitrary choice of one people, as the favorites of heaven; and that people the countrymen of the author: Of their deliverance from bondage by prodigies the most astonishing imaginable: I desire any one to lay his hand upon his heart, and after a serious consideration declare, whether he thinks that the falsehood of such a book, supported by such a testimony, would be more extraordinary and miraculous than all the miracles it relates; which is, however, necessary to make it be received, according to the measures of probability above established.

What we have said of miracles may be applied, without any variation, to prophecies; and indeed, all prophecies are real miracles, and as such only, can be admitted as proofs of any revelation. If it did not exceed the capacity of human nature to foretell future events, it would be absurd to employ any prophecy as an argument for a divine mission or authority from heaven. So that, upon the whole, we may conclude, that the Christian Religion not only was at first attended with miracles, but even at this day cannot be believed by any reasonable person without one. Mere reason is insufficient to convince us of its veracity: And whoever is moved by Faith to assent to it, is conscious of a continued miracle in his own person, which subverts all the principles of his understanding, and gives him a determination to believe what is most contrary to custom and experience.

CRITICISM OF THE DESIGN ARGUMENT

The Design Argument Presented

CLEANTHES: . . . I shall briefly explain how I conceive this matter. Look round the world: contemplate the whole and every part of it: You will find it to be nothing but one great machine, subdivided into an infinite number of lesser machines, which again admit of subdivisions to a degree beyond what human senses and faculties can trace and explain. All these various machines, and even their most minute parts, are adjusted to each other with an accuracy which ravishes into admiration all men who have ever contemplated them. The curious adapting of means to ends, throughout all nature, resembles exactly, though it much exceeds, the productions of human contrivance; of human designs, thought, wisdom, and intelligence. Since, therefore, the effects resemble each other, we are led to infer, by all the rules of analogy, that the causes also resemble; and that the Author of Nature is somewhat similar to the mind of man, though possessed of much larger faculties, proportioned to the grandeur of the work which he has executed. By this argument a posteriori, and by this argument alone, do we prove at once the existence of a Deity, and his similarity to human mind and intelligence.

The Failure of the Analogy

PHILO: . . . That a stone will fall, that fire will burn, that the earth has solidity, we have observed a thousand and a thousand times; and when any new instance of this nature is presented, we draw without hesitation the accustomed inference. The exact similarity of the cases gives us a perfect assurance of a similar event; and a stronger evidence is never desired nor sought after. But wherever you depart, in the least, from the similarity of the cases, you diminish proportionably the evidence; and may at last bring it to a very weak analogy, which is confessedly liable to error and uncertainty. After having experienced the circulation of the blood in human creatures, we make no doubt that it takes place in Titius and Maevius. But from its circulation in frogs and fishes, it is only a presumption, though a strong one, from analogy, that it takes place in men and other animals. The analogical reasoning is much weaker, when we infer the circulation of the sap in vegetables from our experience that the blood circulates in animals; and those, who hastily followed that imperfect analogy, are found, by more accurate experiments, to have been mistaken.

    If we see a house, Cleanthes, we conclude, with the greatest certainty, that it had an architect or builder; because this is precisely that species of effect which we have experienced to proceed from that species of cause. But surely you will not affirm, that the universe bears such a resemblance to a house, that we can with the same certainty infer a similar cause, or that the analogy is here entire and perfect. The dissimilitude is so striking, that the utmost you can here pretend to is a guess, a conjecture, a presumption concerning a similar cause; and how that pretension will be received in the world, I leave you to consider.

CLEANTHES: It would surely be very ill received . . .; and I should be deservedly blamed and detested, did I allow, that the proofs of a Deity amounted to no more than a guess or conjecture. But is the whole adjustment of means to ends in a house and in the universe so slight a resemblance? The economy of final causes? The order, proportion, and arrangement of every part? Steps of a stair are plainly contrived, that human legs may use them in mounting; and this inference is certain and infallible. Human legs are also contrived for walking and mounting; and this inference, I allow, is not altogether so certain, because of the dissimilarity which you remark; but does it, therefore, deserve the name only of presumption or conjecture?

PHILO: That all inferences, Cleanthes, concerning fact, are founded on experience; and that all experimental reasonings are founded on the supposition that similar causes prove similar effects, and similar effects similar causes; I shall not at present much dispute with you. But observe, I entreat you, with what extreme caution all just reasoners proceed in the transferring of experiments to similar cases. Unless the cases be exactly similar, they repose no perfect confidence in applying their past observation to any particular phenomenon. Every alteration of circumstances occasions a doubt concerning the event; and it requires new experiments to prove certainly, that the new circumstances are of no moment or importance. A change in bulk, situation, arrangement, age, disposition of the air, or surrounding bodies; any of these particulars may be attended with the most unexpected consequences: And unless the objects be quite familiar to us, it is the highest temerity to expect with assurance, after any of these changes, an event similar to that which before fell under our observation. The slow and deliberate steps of philosophers here, if any where, are distinguished from the precipitate march of the vulgar, who, hurried on by the smallest similitude, are incapable of all discernment or consideration.

But can you think, Cleanthes, that your usual phlegm and philosophy have been preserved in so wide a step as you have taken, when you compared to the universe houses, ships, furniture, machines, and, from their similarity in some circumstances, inferred a similarity in their causes? Thought, design, intelligence, such as we discover in men and other animals, is no more than one of the springs and principles of the universe, as well as heat or cold, attraction or repulsion, and a hundred others, which fall under daily observation. It is an active cause, by which some particular parts of nature, we find, produce alterations on other parts. But can a conclusion, with any propriety, be transferred from parts to the whole? Does not the great disproportion bar all comparison and inference? From observing the growth of a hair, can we learn any thing concerning the generation of a man? Would the manner of a leaf's blowing, even though perfectly known, afford us any instruction concerning the vegetation of a tree?

But, allowing that we were to take the operations of one part of nature upon another, for the foundation of our judgment concerning the origin of the whole, (which never can be admitted,) yet why select so minute, so weak, so bounded a principle, as the reason and design of animals is found to be upon this planet? What peculiar privilege has this little agitation of the brain which we call thought, that we must thus make it the model of the whole universe? Our partiality in our own favor does indeed present it on all occasions; but sound philosophy ought carefully to guard against so natural an illusion.

So far from admitting . . . that the operations of a part can afford us any just conclusion concerning the origin of the whole, I will not allow any one part to form a rule for another part, if the latter be very remote from the former. Is there any reasonable ground to conclude, that the inhabitants of other planets possess thought, intelligence, reason, or any thing similar to these faculties in men? When nature has so extremely diversified her manner of operation in this small globe, can we imagine that she incessantly copies herself throughout so immense a universe? And if thought, as we may well suppose, be confined merely to this narrow corner, and has even there so limited a sphere of action, with what propriety can we assign it for the original cause of all things? The narrow views of a peasant, who makes his domestic economy the rule for the government of kingdoms, is in comparison a pardonable sophism.

But were we ever so much assured, that a thought and reason, resembling the human, were to be found throughout the whole universe, and were its activity elsewhere vastly greater and more commanding than it appears in this globe; yet I cannot see, why the operations of a world constituted, arranged, adjusted, can with any propriety be extended to a world which is in its embryo state, and is advancing towards that constitution and arrangement. By observation, we know somewhat of the economy, action, and nourishment of a finished animal; but we must transfer with great caution that observation to the growth of a fetus in the womb, and still more to the formation of an animalcule in the loins of its male parent. Nature, we find, even from our limited experience, possesses an infinite number of springs and principles, which incessantly discover themselves on every change of her position and situation. And what new and unknown principles would actuate her in so new and unknown a situation as that of the formation of a universe, we cannot, without the utmost temerity, pretend to determine.

A very small part of this great system, during a very short time, is very imperfectly discovered to us; and do we thence pronounce decisively concerning the origin of the whole?

Admirable conclusion! Stone, wood, brick, iron, brass, have not, at this time, in this minute globe of earth, an order or arrangement without human art and contrivance; therefore the universe could not originally attain its order and arrangement, without something similar to human art. But is a part of nature a rule for another part very wide of the former? Is it a rule for the whole? Is a very small part a rule for the universe? Is nature in one situation, a certain rule for nature in another situation vastly different from the former?

And can you blame me, Cleanthes, if I here imitate the prudent reserve of Simonides, who, according to the noted story, being asked by Hiero, What God was? desired a day to think of it, and then two days more; and after that manner continually prolonged the term, without ever bringing in his definition or description? Could you even blame me, if I had answered at first, that I did not know, and was sensible that this subject lay vastly beyond the reach of my faculties? You might cry out skeptic and railler, as much as you pleased: but having found, in so many other subjects much more familiar, the imperfections and even contradictions of human reason, I never should expect any success from its feeble conjectures, in a subject so sublime, and so remote from the sphere of our observation. When two species of objects have always been observed to be conjoined together, I can infer, by custom, the existence of one wherever I see the existence of the other; and this I call an argument from experience. But how this argument can have place, where the objects, as in the present case, are single, individual, without parallel, or specific resemblance, may be difficult to explain. And will any man tell me with a serious countenance, that an orderly universe must arise from some thought and art like the human, because we have experience of it? To ascertain this reasoning, it were requisite that we had experience of the origin of worlds; and it is not sufficient, surely, that we have seen ships and cities arise from human art and contrivance.

Concerning the Infinity, Perfection, and Unity of the Creator

PHILO: First, By this method of reasoning, you renounce all claim to infinity in any of the attributes of the Deity. For, as the cause ought only to be proportioned to the effect, and the effect, so far as it falls under our cognizance, is not infinite; what pretensions have we, upon your suppositions, to ascribe that attribute to the Divine Being? You will still insist, that, by removing him so much from all similarity to human creatures, we give in to the most arbitrary hypothesis, and at the same time weaken all proofs of his existence.

Secondly, You have no reason, on your theory, for ascribing perfection to the Deity, even in his finite capacity, or for supposing him free from every error, mistake, or incoherence, in his undertakings. There are many inexplicable difficulties in the works of Nature, which, if we allow a perfect author to be proved a priori, are easily solved, and become only seeming difficulties, from the narrow capacity of man, who cannot trace infinite relations. But according to your method of reasoning, these difficulties become all real; and perhaps will be insisted on, as new instances of likeness to human art and contrivance. At least, you must acknowledge, that it is impossible for us to tell, from our limited views, whether this system contains any great faults, or deserves any considerable praise, if compared to other possible, and even real systems. Could a peasant, if the Aeneid were read to him, pronounce that poem to be absolutely faultless, or even assign to it its proper rank among the productions of human wit, he, who had never seen any other production?

But were this world ever so perfect a production, it must still remain uncertain, whether all the excellences of the work can justly be ascribed to the workman. If we survey a ship, what an exalted idea must we form of the ingenuity of the carpenter who framed so complicated, useful, and beautiful a machine? And what surprise must we feel, when we find him a stupid mechanic, who imitated others, and copied an art, which, through a long succession of ages, after multiplied trials, mistakes, corrections, deliberations, and controversies, had been gradually improving? Many worlds might have been botched and bungled, throughout an eternity, ere this system was struck out; much labor lost, many fruitless trials made; and a slow, but continued improvement carried on during infinite ages in the art of world-making. In such subjects, who can determine, where the truth; nay, who can conjecture where the probability lies, amidst a great number of hypotheses which may be proposed, and a still greater which may be imagined?

And what shadow of an argument . . . can you produce, from your hypothesis, to prove the unity of the Deity? A great number of men join in building a house or ship, in rearing a city, in framing a commonwealth; why may not several deities combine in contriving and framing a world? This is only so much greater similarity to human affairs. By sharing the work among several, we may so much further limit the attributes of each, and get rid of that extensive power and knowledge, which must be supposed in one deity, and which, according to you, can only serve to weaken the proof of his existence. And if such foolish, such vicious creatures as man, can yet often unite in framing and executing one plan, how much more those deities or demons, whom we may suppose several degrees more perfect!

To multiply causes without necessity, is indeed contrary to true philosophy: but this principle applies not to the present case. Were one deity antecedently proved by your theory, who were possessed of every attribute requisite to the production of the universe; it would be needless, I own, (though not absurd,) to suppose any other deity existent. But while it is still a question, Whether all these attributes are united in one subject, or dispersed among several independent beings, by what phenomena in nature can we pretend to decide the controversy? Where we see a body raised in a scale, we are sure that there is in the opposite scale, however concealed from sight, some counterpoising weight equal to it; but it is still allowed to doubt, whether that weight be an aggregate of several distinct bodies, or one uniform united mass. And if the weight requisite very much exceeds any thing which we have ever seen conjoined in any single body, the former supposition becomes still more probable and natural. An intelligent being of such vast power and capacity as is necessary to produce the universe, or, to speak in the language of ancient philosophy, so prodigious an animal exceeds all analogy, and even comprehension.

But further, Cleanthes: men are mortal, and renew their species by generation; and this is common to all living creatures. The two great sexes of male and female, says Milton, animate the world. Why must this circumstance, so universal, so essential, be excluded from those numerous and limited deities? Behold, then, the theogony of ancient times brought back upon us.

And why not become a perfect Anthropomorphite? Why not assert the deity or deities to be corporeal, and to have eyes, a nose, mouth, ears, etc.? Epicurus maintained, that no man had ever seen reason but in a human figure; therefore the gods must have a human figure. And this argument, which is deservedly so much ridiculed by Cicero, becomes, according to you, solid and philosophical.

In a word, Cleanthes, a man who follows your hypothesis is able perhaps to assert, or conjecture, that the universe, sometime, arose from something like design: but beyond that position he cannot ascertain one single circumstance; and is left afterwards to fix every point of his theology by the utmost license of fancy and hypothesis. This world, for aught he knows, is very faulty and imperfect, compared to a superior standard; and was only the first rude essay of some infant deity, who afterwards abandoned it, ashamed of his lame performance: it is the work only of some dependent, inferior deity; and is the object of derision to his superiors: it is the production of old age and dotage in some superannuated deity; and ever since his death, has run on at adventures, from the first impulse and active force which it received from him.

CRITICISM OF THE COSMOLOGICAL ARGUMENT

The Cosmological Argument Presented

DEMEA: The argument . . . which I would insist on, is the common one. Whatever exists must have a cause or reason of its existence; it being absolutely
impossible for any thing to produce itself, or be the cause of its own existence. In mounting up, therefore, from effects to causes, we must either
go on in tracing an infinite succession, without any ultimate cause at all;
or must at last have recourse to some ultimate cause, that is necessarily
existent: Now, that the first supposition is absurd, may be thus proved. In
the infinite chain or succession of causes and effects, each single effect is
determined to exist by the power and efficacy of that cause which immediately preceded; but the whole eternal chain or succession, taken together, is
not determined or caused by any thing; and yet it is evident that it requires
a cause or reason, as much as any particular object which begins to exist
in time. The question is still reasonable, why this particular succession of
causes existed from eternity, and not any other succession, or no succession
at all. If there be no necessarily existent being, any supposition which can
be formed is equally possible; nor is there any more absurdity in Nothing's having existed from eternity, than there is in that succession of causes
which constitutes the universe. What was it, then, which determined Something to exist rather than Nothing, and bestowed being on a particular
possibility, exclusive of the rest? External causes, there are supposed to be
none. Chance is a word without a meaning. Was it Nothing? But that can
never produce any thing. We must, therefore, have recourse to a necessarily
existent Being, who carries the reason of his existence in himself, and who
cannot be supposed not to exist, without an express contradiction. There is,
consequently, such a Being; that is, there is a Deity.

The Failure of A Priori Arguments

CLEANTHES: I shall not leave it to Philo, . . . though I know that stating objections is his chief delight, to point out the weakness of this metaphysical
reasoning. It seems to me so obviously ill-grounded, and at the same time
of so little consequence to the cause of true piety and religion, that I shall
myself venture to show the fallacy of it.

I shall begin with observing, that there is an evident absurdity in pretending to demonstrate a matter of fact, or to prove it by any arguments a
priori. Nothing is demonstrable, unless the contrary implies a contradiction. Nothing, that is distinctly conceivable, implies a contradiction. Whatever we conceive as existent, we can also conceive as non-existent. There is
no being, therefore, whose non-existence implies a contradiction. Consequently there is no being, whose existence is demonstrable. I propose this
argument as entirely decisive, and am willing to rest the whole controversy
upon it.

It is pretended that the Deity is a necessarily existent being; and this necessity of his existence is attempted to be explained by asserting, that if we knew his whole essence or nature, we should perceive it to be as impossible for him not to exist, as for twice two not to be four. But it is evident that this can never happen, while our faculties remain the same as at present. It will still be possible for us, at any time, to conceive the non-existence of what we formerly conceived to exist; nor can the mind ever lie under a necessity of supposing any object to remain always in being; in the same manner as we lie under a necessity of always conceiving twice two to be four. The words, therefore, necessary existence, have no meaning; or, which is the same thing, none that is consistent.

But further, why may not the material universe be the necessarily existent Being, according to this pretended explication of necessity? We dare not affirm that we know all the qualities of matter; and for aught we can determine, it may contain some qualities, which, were they known, would make its non-existence appear as great a contradiction as that twice two is five. I find only one argument employed to prove, that the material world is not the necessarily existent Being: and this argument is derived from the contingency both of the matter and the form of the world. "Any particle of matter," it is said, "may be conceived to be annihilated; and any form may be conceived to be altered. Such an annihilation or alteration, therefore, is not impossible." But it seems a great partiality not to perceive, that the same argument extends equally to the Deity, so far as we have any conception of him; and that the mind can at least imagine him to be non-existent, or his attributes to be altered. It must be some unknown, inconceivable qualities, which can make his non-existence appear impossible, or his attributes unalterable: And no reason can be assigned, why these qualities may not belong to matter. As they are altogether unknown and inconceivable, they can never be proved incompatible with it.

Add to this, that in tracing an eternal succession of objects, it seems absurd to inquire for a general cause or first author. How can any thing, that exists from eternity, have a cause, since that relation implies a priority in time, and a beginning of existence?

In such a chain, too, or succession of objects, each part is caused by that which preceded it, and causes that which succeeds it. Where then is the difficulty? But the whole, you say, wants a cause. I answer, that the uniting of these parts into a whole, like the uniting of several distinct countries into one kingdom, or several distinct members into one body, is performed merely by an arbitrary act of the mind, and has no influence on the nature of things. Did I show you the particular causes of each individual in a collection of twenty particles of matter, I should think it very unreasonable, should you afterwards ask me, what was the cause of the whole twenty. This is sufficiently explained in explaining the cause of the parts.

READING 8

Voltaire: On the Best of All Possible Worlds

From *Philosophical Dictionary*

François Marie Arouet, better known by his pen name Voltaire (1694–1778), was one of France's most distinguished authors of the eighteenth century, and is most remembered in philosophy for his multivolume Philosophical Dictionary *(1764–9). One of the entries in that work is a discussion of what we now call "the problem of evil"— the relationship between God and human suffering. As in his famous novel* Candide, *Voltaire here attacks the view of Leibniz that God created the world in such a way that human suffering makes it a better place than it would have been otherwise. In response, Voltaire argues that common sense tells us that the enormous amount of suffering that we experience produces no obvious benefit for either God or humans. There is, then, an inconsistency between the presence of human suffering and the concept of an all-powerful and all-good God. Standard theological solutions to this problem include the Christian concept of original sin, and the non-Christian concept of two distinct deities, where one is good and the other evil. Voltaire rejects these and other attempted solutions and suggests that we plead ignorance on the entire issue.*

Please explain to me how everything is for the best, for I do not understand it. Does it mean that everything is arranged and ordered according to the laws of the impelling power? That I understand and acknowledge. Do you mean that everyone is well and possesses the means of living and that nobody suffers? You know that this is not the case. Are you of the opinion that the appalling tragedies that afflict the earth are good in reference to God, and that he takes pleasure in them? I do not give any credit to this horrible doctrine; neither do you.

Please have the goodness to explain how all is for the best. Plato, the dialectician, humbly allows to God the liberty of making five worlds; because, said Plato, there are five regular solids in geometry, the tetrahedron, the cube, the hexahedron, the dodecahedron, and the icosahedron. But why restrict divine power in this way? Why not permit the sphere, which is still more regular, and even the cone, the pyramid of many sides, the cylinder, etc.?

According to Plato, God necessarily chose the best of all possible worlds; and this system has been embraced by many Christian philosophers, although it appears opposed to the doctrine of original sin. After the disobedience of the first sin, our globe was no longer the best of all possible worlds. If it was ever so it might be so still, but many people believe it to be the worst of worlds instead of the best.

Leibniz takes the position of Plato. More readers than one complain of their inability to understand either of these writers, and for myself, having read both of them more than once, I confess my ignorance according to custom. Since

Source: Voltaire, "Optimism," *The Philosophical Dictionary* (1764).

the gospel has revealed nothing on the subject, we remain in darkness without remorse.

Leibniz, who writes on every subject, discusses original sin. Since every system-builder introduces into his plan something contradictory, Leibniz imagined that the disobedience towards God, with the frightful misfortunes which followed it, were integral parts of the best of worlds, and necessary ingredients of all possible happiness.

What! To be chased from a delightful place, where we might have lived forever only because of eating an apple? What! To produce unhappy children in misery who will suffer everything, and in return produce others to suffer after them? What! To experience all troubles, feel all pains, die in the midst of grief, and by way of compensation be burned to all eternity: is this fate the best possible? It certainly is not good for us, and in what manner can it be so for God? Leibniz felt that nothing could be said to these objections, but nevertheless he made great books in which he did not even understand himself.

[The Roman statesman] Lucullus, in good health, enjoying a good dinner with his friends and his mistress in the hall of Apollo, may jokingly deny the existence of evil. But let him put his head out of the window and he will see miserable people in abundance; let him be gripped with a fever, and he will be a miserable person himself.

I do not like to quote; it is typically a tricky matter. Nevertheless, what precedes and what follows the passage I just quoted is too frequently neglected; and thus a thousand objections may rise. I must, notwithstanding, quote Lactantius, one of the [early Christian] fathers, who, in the thirteenth chapter on *The Anger of God*, makes Epicurus speak as follows: "God can either take away evil from the world and will not; or being willing to do so, cannot; or he neither can nor will; or, lastly, he is both able and willing. If he is willing to remove evil and cannot, then he is not omnipotent. If he can, but will not remove it, then he is not benevolent; if he is neither able nor willing, then he is neither powerful nor benevolent; lastly, if he is both able and willing to eliminate evil, why does evil exist?"

The argument is weighty, and Lactantius replies to it very poorly by saying that God wills evil, but has given us wisdom to obtain the good. It must be confessed that this answer is very weak in comparison with the objection since it implies that God could bestow wisdom only by allowing evil—a pleasant wisdom truly! The origin of evil has always been an abyss, the depth of which no one has been able to measure. It was this difficulty that forced so many ancient philosophers and legislators to resort to two principles—the one good, the other evil. Typhon was the evil principle among the Egyptians, Arimanes among the Persians. The Manicheans, it is said, adopted this theory; but as these people have never spoken either of a good or of a bad principle, we have nothing to prove it.

Among the absurdities abounding in this world which may also be placed among the variety of our evils, here is a very considerable one. It presumes the existence of two all-powerful beings, fighting over which will succeed most in this world. They then make a treaty like the two physicians in Molière: "Allow me the vomit-inducer, and I will allow you the scalpel."

Along with the Platonists of the first century of the church, Basilides maintained that God assigned the task of making our world to his inferior angels, and these, being unskilled, have constructed it as we perceive. This theological fable is laid flat by the overwhelming objection that it is not in the nature of an all-powerful and all-wise deity to assign the construction of a world to incompetent architects.

Simon, who felt the force of this objection, sidesteps it by saying that the angel who presided over the workers is damned for having done his business so carelessly. But the roasting of this angel gives no compensation. The adventure of Pandora among the Greeks scarcely meets the objection better. The box in which every evil is enclosed, and at the bottom of which remains Hope, is indeed a charming allegory; but Pandora was made by Vulcan only to avenge himself on Prometheus, who had stolen fire to create a man of clay.

The Indians have succeeded no better. God having created man, gave him a drug which would insure him permanent bodily health. The man loaded his donkey with the drug; the donkey was thirsty, so the serpent directed him to a fountain, and while the donkey was drinking, the serpent stole the drug.

The Syrians said that man and woman were created in the fourth heaven; the couple decided to eat a cake instead of their natural food which was ambrosia; upon digestion, ambrosia was expelled through their pores. But after eating cake, they needed to relieve themselves in the usual manner. The man and the woman requested an angel to direct them to a toilet. The angel said "Observe that petty globe which is almost of no size at all; it is situated about 150 million miles from this place, and is the toilet of the universe; go there as quickly as you can. The man and woman obeyed the angel and came here, where they have ever since remained. Since that time the world has been as we now find it. The Syrians will forever be asked why God allowed man to eat the cake and experience such a multitude of dreadful evils.

I pass with speed from the fourth heaven to Lord Bolingbroke. This writer, who doubtless was a great genius, gave to the celebrated [poet Alexander] Pope his plan of "all for the best," as it is found word for word in the posthumous works of Lord Bolingbroke, and recorded by Lord Shaftesbury in his book *Characteristics*. We read in Shaftesbury's chapter on "The Moralists" the following passage:

> Much may be replied to these complaints of the defects of nature—How came it so powerless and defective from the hands of a perfect Being?—But I deny that it is defective. Beauty is the result of contrast, and universal concord springs out of a perpetual conflict. . . . It is necessary that everything be sacrificed to other things—vegetables to animals, and animals to the earth. . . . The laws of the central power of gravitation, which give to the celestial bodies their weight and motion, are not to be deranged in consideration of a pitiful animal, who, protected as he is by the same laws, will soon be reduced to dust.

Bolingbroke, Shaftesbury, and Pope, their working artisan, resolve their general question no better than the rest. Their motto "all for the best" says no more than that all is governed by unchanging laws; and who did not know that? We learn nothing when we remark, after the manner of little children, that flies are created to be eaten by spiders, spiders by swallows, swallows by hawks, hawks by eagles, eagles by men, men killed by one another, to provide food for worms—except about one in a thousand—by devils.

There is a constant and regular order established among animals of all kinds, a universal order. When a stone is formed in my bladder, the mechanical process is admirable. Sandy particles pass by small degrees into my blood; they are filtered by the veins; and passing the urethra, deposit themselves in my bladder; where, uniting delightfully according to Newton's theory of attraction, a stone is formed. It gradually increases, and I suffer pains a thousand times worse than death, all by means of the most admirable mechanism in the world. A surgeon who is an expert in the art of Tubalcain [i.e., metalworking], thrusts a sharp instrument into me. Cutting into the perineum, grabs hold of the stone with his pincers, which breaks during the event by the necessary laws of mechanics. Owing to the same mechanism, I die in frightful torments. All this is "for the best," being the evident result of unchanging physical principles, agreeably to which I know as well as you that I die.

If we were incapable of feeling, there would be nothing to say against this system of physics; but that is not the point here. I ask whether there are physical evils, and from where do they originate? There is no absolute evil, says Pope in his "Essay on Man"; and if there are particular evils, they are part of a general good. It is a singular general good that is composed of the kidney stone and the gout, of all sorts of crime and suffering, and of death and damnation.

The fall of man is our ointment for all these particular maladies of body and soul, which you call "the general health." But Shaftesbury and Bolingbroke have attacked original sin. Pope says nothing about it; but it is clear that their system undermines the foundations of the Christian religion, and explains nothing at all.

In the meantime, this system has been since accepted by many theologians, who willingly embrace contradictions. So be it. We ought to leave to everybody the privilege of reasoning in their own way upon the flood of suffering that overwhelm us. It would be as reasonable to prevent incurable patients from eating what they please. "God," says Pope, "beholds, with an equal eye, a hero perish or a sparrow fall; the destruction of an atom, or the ruin of a thousand planets; the bursting of a bubble, or the dissolution of a world."

This, I must confess, is a pleasant consolation! Who does not find a comfort in the declaration of Lord Shaftesbury who asserts "that God will not derange his general system for so miserable an animal as man?" It must be confessed at least that this pitiful creature has a right to cry out humbly, and, while moaning about himself, to try to understand why these eternal laws do not include the good of every individual.

This system of "all for the best" represents the author of nature as a powerful and malevolent monarch, who cares neither for the destruction of four or five hundred thousand men, nor for the many more who in consequence spend the rest of their days in poverty and tears, so long as he succeeds in his designs.

Thus, the view that "this is the best of all possible worlds" gives us no consolation, and is instead a hopeless doctrine to the philosophers who embrace it. The question of good and evil remains in permanent chaos for those who seek to understand it in reality. It is a mere mental sport to the disputants who are like prisoners that play with their chains. As to unreasoning people, they resemble the fish that are transported from a river to a reservoir, with no more suspicion that they are to be eaten during the approaching season of Lent, than we have ourselves of the facts which originate our destiny.

Let us place at the end of every chapter of metaphysics the two letters used by the Roman judges when they did not understand a pleading: N. L., *non liquet*, that is, "it is not clear." Let us, above all, silence the scoundrels who, overloaded like ourselves with the weight of human tragedy, add the injury of their slander. Let us refute their appalling dishonesty by turning instead to faith and providence.

Some reasoners hold the opinion that it is inconsistent with the nature of the Great Being of Beings for things to be otherwise than they are. It is a rough system, and I am too ignorant to attempt to examine it.

READING 9

Thomas Reid: The Argument for Free Will from Commonsense Beliefs

From *Essays on the Active Powers of Man*

Thomas Reid (1710–1796) was a philosophy professor at the University of Glasgow, and the most famous representative of what is called the Scottish commonsense school of philosophy. In the selection below, Reid attacks Hume's determinism and offers instead what he thinks is a more meaningful notion of free will. For Reid, we are free to the extent that we have power over the motivations of our will. All of us, he argues, have a natural commonsense conviction regarding the freedom of our wills, which we assume in any number of daily activities. Many defenses of free will after Reid make a similar point: If we abandon the notion of free will, then we sacrifice the notion of moral responsibility.

FIVE ARGUMENTS IN DEFENSE OF FREE WILL

We have, by our constitution, a natural conviction or belief that we act freely. A conviction so early, so universal, and so necessary in most of our rational operations, that it must be the result of our constitution, and the work of Him that made us.

Source: Thomas Reid, *Essays on the Active Powers of the Human Mind* (1788), Essay 4, Chapter 6, First Argument.

Some of the most strenuous advocates for the doctrine of necessity acknowledge, that it is impossible to act upon it. They say that we have a natural sense or conviction that we act freely, but that this is a fallacious sense.

This doctrine is dishonorable to our maker, and lays a foundation for universal skepticism. It supposes the Author of our being to have given us one faculty on purpose to deceive us, and another by which we may detect the fallacy, and find that be imposed upon us.

If any one of our natural faculties be fallacious, there can be no reason to trust to any of them; for he that made one made all.

The genuine dictate of our natural faculties is the voice of God, no less than what he reveals from heaven; and to say that it is fallacious, is to impute a lie to the God of truth.

If candor and veracity be not an essential part of moral excellence, there is no such thing as moral excellence, nor any reason to rely on the declarations and promises of the Almighty. A man may be tempted to lie, but not without being conscious of guilt and of meanness. Shall we impute to the Almighty what we cannot impute to a man without a heinous affront?

Passing this opinion, therefore, as shocking to an ingenuous minds and, in its consequences, subversive of all religion, all morals, and all knowledge, let us proceed to consider the evidence of our having a natural conviction that we have some degree of active power.

The very conception or idea of active power must be derived from something in our own constitution. It is impossible to account for it otherwise. We see events, but we see not the power that produces them. We perceive one event to follow another, but we perceive not the chain that binds them together. The notion of power and causation, therefore, cannot be got from external objects.

Yet the notion of causes, and the belief that every event must have a cause which had power to produce it, is found in every human mind so firmly established, that it cannot be rooted out.

This notion and this belief must have its origin from something in our constitution; and that it is natural to man, appears from the following observations.

First, we are conscious of many voluntary exertions, some easy, others more difficult, some requiring a great effort. These are exertions of power. And though a man may be unconscious of his power when he does not exert it, he must have both the conception and the belief of it when he knowingly and willingly exerts it, with intention to produce some effect.

Secondly, deliberation about an action of moment, whether we shall do it or not, implies a conviction that it is in our power. To deliberate about an end, we must be convinced that the means are in our power; and to deliberate about the means, we must be convinced that we have power to choose the most proper.

Thirdly, suppose our deliberation brought to an issue, and that we resolved to do what appeared proper, can we form such a resolution or purpose, without any conviction of power to execute it? No; it is impossible. A man cannot resolve to pay out a sum of money, which he neither has, nor hopes ever to have.

Fourthly, again, when I plight my faith in any promise or contract, I must believe that I shall have power to perform what I promise. Without this persuasion, a promise would be downright fraud.

There is a condition implied in every promise, *if we live*, and *if God continue with us the power which he has given us*. Our conviction, therefore, of this power derogates not in the least from our dependence upon God. The rudest savage is taught by nature to admit this condition in all promises, whether it be expressed or not. For it is a dictate of common sense, that we can be under no obligation to do what it is impossible for us to do.

If we act upon the system of necessity, there must be another condition implied in all deliberation, in every resolution, and in every promise; and that is, *if we shall be willing*. But the will not being in our power, we cannot engage for it.

If this condition be understood, as it must be understood if we act upon the system of necessity, there can be no deliberation or resolution, nor any obligation in a promise. A man might as well deliberate resolved and promise, upon the actions of other men as upon his own.

It is no less evident, that we have a conviction of power in other men, when we advise, or persuade, or command, or conceive them to be under obligation by their promises.

Fifthly, is it possible for any man to blame himself for yielding to necessity? Then he may blame himself for dying, or for being a man. Blame supposes a wrong use of power; and when a man does as well as it was possible for him to do, wherein is he to be blamed? Therefore all conviction of wrong conduct, all remorse, and self-condemnation, imply a conviction of our power to have done better. Take away this conviction, and there may be a sense of misery, or a dread of evil to come, but there can be no sense of guilt, or resolution to do better.

THE COMMON SENSE BELIEF IN FREE WILL

Many who hold the doctrine of necessity, disown these consequences of it, and think to evade them. To such they ought not to be imputed; but their inseparable connection with that doctrine appears self-evident; and therefore some late patrons of it have had the boldness to avow them. "They cannot accuse themselves of having done anything wrong in the ultimate sense of the words. In a strict sense, they have nothing to do with repentance, confession, and pardon, these being adapted to a fallacious view of things."

Those who can adopt these sentiments, may indeed celebrate, with high encomiums, *the great and glorious doctrine of necessity*. It restores them, in their own conceit, to the state of innocence. It delivers them from all the pangs of guilt and remorse, and from all fear about their future conduct, though not about their fate. They may be as secure that they shall do nothing wrong, as those who have finished their course. A doctrine so flattering to the mind of a sinner, is very apt to give strength to weak arguments.

After all, it is acknowledged by those who boast of this glorious doctrine, "That every man, let him use what efforts he can, will necessarily feel the sentiments of shame, remorse, and repentance, and, oppressed with a sense of guilt, will have recourse to that mercy of which he stands in need."

The meaning of this seems to me to be, that although the doctrine of necessity be supported by invincible arguments, and though it be the most consolatory doctrine in the world; yet no man in his most serious moments, when he sits himself before the throne of his maker, can possibly believe it, but must then necessarily lay aside this glorious doctrine, and all its flattering consequences, and return to the humiliating conviction of his having made a bad use of the power which God had given him.

If the belief of our having active power be necessarily implied in those rational operations we have mentioned, it must be coeval with our reason; it must be as universal among men, and as necessary in the conduct of life, as those operations are.

We cannot recollect by memory when it began. It cannot be a prejudice of education, or of false philosophy. It must be a part of our constitution, or the necessary result of our constitution, and therefore the work or God.

It resembles, in this respect, our belief of the existence of a material world; our belief that those we converse with are living and intelligent beings; our belief that those things did really happen which we distinctly remember, and our belief that we continue the same identical persons.

We find difficulty in accounting for our belief of these things; and some philosophers think, that they have discovered good reasons for throwing it off. But it sticks fast, and the greatest skeptic finds, that he must yield to it in his practice, while he wages war with it in speculation.

RESPONSES TO POSSIBLE OBJECTIONS

If it be objected to this argument, that the belief of our acting freely cannot be implied in the operations we have mentioned, because those operations are performed by them who believe that we are, in all our actions, governed by necessity; the answer to this objection is, that men in their practice may be governed by a belief which in speculation they reject.

However strange and unaccountable this may appear, there are many well-known instances of it.

I knew a man who was as much convinced as any man of the folly of the popular belief of apparitions in the dark, yet he could not sleep in a room alone, nor go alone into a room in the dark. Can it be said, that his fear did not imply a belief of danger? This is impossible. Yet his philosophy convinced him, that he was in no more danger in the dark when alone, than with company.

Here an unreasonable belief, which was merely a prejudice of the nursery, stuck so fast as to govern his conduct, in opposition to his speculative belief as a philosopher, and a man of sense.

There are few persons who can look down from the battlement of a very high tower without fear, while their reason convinces them that they are in no more danger than when standing upon the ground.

There have been persons who professed to believe that there is no distinction between virtue and vice, yet in their practice, they resented injuries, and esteemed noble and virtuous actions.

There have been skeptics who professed to disbelieve their senses, and every human faculty; but no skeptic was ever known, who did not, in practice, pay a regard to his senses and to his other faculties.

There are some points of belief so necessary, that, without them, a man would not be the being which God made him. These may be opposed in speculation, but it is impossible to root them out. In a speculative hour they seem to vanish, but in practice they resume their authority. This seems to be the case of those who hold the doctrine of necessity, and yet act as if they were free.

This natural conviction of some degree of power in ourselves and in other men, respects voluntary actions only. For as all our power is directed by our will, we can form no conception of power, properly so called, that is; not under the direction of will. And therefore our exertions, our deliberations, our purposes, our promises, are only in things that depend upon our will. Our advices, exhortations, and commands, are only in things that depend upon the will or those to whom they are addressed. We impute no guilt to ourselves, nor to others; in things where the will is not concerned.

But it deserves our notice, that we do not conceive everything, without exception to be in a man's power which depends upon his will. There are many exceptions to this general rule. The most obvious of these I shall mention, because they both serve to illustrate the rule, and are of importance in the question concerning the liberty of man.

In the rage of madness, men are absolutely deprived of the power of self-government. They act voluntarily, but their will is driven as by a tempest, which, in lucid intervals, they resolve to oppose with all their might, but are overcome when the fit of madness returns.

Idiots are like men walking in the dark, who cannot be said to have the power of choosing their way, because they cannot distinguish the good road from the bad. Having no light in their understanding, they must either sit still, or be carried on by some blind impulse.

Between the darkness of infancy, which is equal to that of idiots, and the maturity of reason, there is a long twilight which, by insensible degrees, advances to the perfect day.

In this period of life, man has but little of the power of self-government. His actions, by nature, as well as by the laws of society, are in the power of others more than in his own. His folly and indiscretion, his levity and inconstancy, are considered as the fault of youth, rather than of the man. We consider him as half a man and half a child, and expect that each by turns should play its part. He would be thought a severe and inequitable censor of manners, who required the same cool deliberation, the same steady conduct, and the same mastery over himself in a boy of thirteen, as in a man of thirty.

It is an old adage, that violent anger is a short fit of madness. If this be literally true in any case, a man in such a fit of passion, cannot be said to have the command of himself. If real madness could be proved, it must have the effect of madness while it lasts, whether it be for an hour or for life. But the madness of a short fit of passion, if it be really madness, is incapable of proof; and therefore is not admitted in human tribunals as an exculpation. And, I believe, there is no case where a man can satisfy his own mind that his passion, both in its beginning and in its progress, was irresistible. The Searcher of hearts alone knows infallibly what allowance is due in cases of this kind.

But a violent passion, though it may not be irresistible, is difficult to be resisted: and a man, surely, has not the same power over himself in passion, as when he is cool. On this account it is allowed by all men to alleviate, when it cannot exculpate; and has its weight in criminal courts, as well as in private judgment.

It ought likewise to be observed, that he who has accustomed himself to restrain his passions, enlarges by habit his power over them, and consequently over himself. When we consider that a Canadian savage can acquire the power of defying death, in its most dreadful forms, and of braving the most exquisite torment for many long hours, without losing the command of himself; we may learn from this, that, in the constitution of human natures there is ample scope for the enlargement of that power of self-command, without which there can be no virtue nor magnanimity.

There are cases, however, in which a man's voluntary actions are thought to be very little, if at all, in his power, on account of the violence of the motive that impels him. The magnanimity of a hero, or of a martyr, is not expected in every man, and on all occasions.

If a man trusted by the government with a secret, which it is high treason to disclose, be prevailed upon by a bribe, we have no mercy for him, and hardly allow the greatest bribe to be any alleviation of his crime.

But, on the other hand, if the secret be extorted by the rack, or by the dread of present death, we pity him more than we blame him, and would think it severe and unequitable to condemn him as a traitor.

What is the reason that all men agree in condemning this man as a traitor in the first case, and in the last, either exculpate him, or think his fault greatly alleviated? If he acted necessarily in both cases, compelled by an irresistible motive, I can see no reason why we should not pass the same judgment on both.

But the reason of these different judgments is evidently this, that the love of money, and of what is called a man's interest, is a cool motive, which leaves to a man the entire power over himself: but the torment of the rack, or the dread of present death, are so violent motives, that men who have not uncommon strength of mind, are not masters of themselves in such a situation, and therefore what they do is not imputed, or is thought less criminal.

If a man resist such motives, we admire his fortitude, and think his conduct heroical rather than human. If he yields, we impute it to human frailty, and think him rather to be pitied than severely censured.

Inveterate habits are acknowledged to diminish very considerably the power a man has over himself. Although we may think him highly blamable in acquiring them, yet when they are confirmed to a certain degree, we consider him as no longer master of himself, and hardly reclaimable without a miracle.

Thus we see, that the power which we are led by common sense to ascribe to man, respects his voluntary actions only, and that it has various limitations even with regard to them. Some actions that depend upon our will are easy, others very difficult, and some, perhaps, beyond our power. In different men, the power of self-government is different, and in the same man at different times. It may be diminished, or perhaps lost, by bad habits; it may be greatly increased by good habits.

These are facts attested by experience, and supported by the common judgment of mankind. Upon the system of liberty, they are perfectly intelligible; but, I think, irreconcilable to that of necessity; for, how can there be an easy and a difficult in actions equally subject to necessity? or, how can power be greater or less, increased or diminished, in those who have no power?

This natural conviction of our acting freely, which is acknowledged by many who hold the doctrine of necessity, ought to throw the whole burden of proof upon that side: for, by this, the side of liberty has what lawyers call *jus quæsitum,* or a right of ancient possession, which ought to stand good till it be overturned. If it cannot be proved that we always act from necessity, there is no need of arguments on the other side, to convince us that we are free agents.

To illustrate this by a similar case: if a philosopher would persuade me, that my fellow men with whom I converse, are not thinking intelligent beings, but mere machines; though I might be at a loss to find arguments against this strange opinion, I should think it reasonable to hold the belief which nature gave me before I was capable of weighing evidence, until convincing proof is brought against it.

READING 10
———

Mary Wollstonecraft: The Rights of Women

From *A Vindication of the Rights of Woman*

During the seventeenth and eighteenth centuries, political philosophers and political revolutionaries alike frequently emphasized the notion of natural rights, that is, rights that we are all born with and that are uncreated by governments. These writers frequently described these rights as the "rights of man." Although many writers used the term "man" in the gender-neutral sense of "human being," others believed that men were morally and intellectually superior to women, and, thus, the notion of the "rights of man" applied primarily to males. In her A Vindication of the Rights of Woman *(1792), British philosopher Mary Wollstonecraft (1759–1797) harshly attacked sexist philosophers of her day and defended the notion of women's rights.*

Source: Mary Wollstonecraft, *A Vindication of the Rights of Woman* (1792), Chapter 13, Section 6.

From a rational standpoint, she argues, men and women are essentially the same, and whatever differences there seem to be are only the consequence of sexist education, where women are raised to be little more than alluring sex objects of men. Once women are given a proper education as men are, then they will display all the signs of human reason and be contributing members of society.

It is not necessary to inform the sagacious reader, now I enter on my concluding reflections, that the discussion of this subject merely consists in opening a few simple principles, and clearing away the rubbish which obscured them. But, as all readers are not sagacious, I must be allowed to add some explanatory remarks to bring the subject home to reason—to that sluggish reason, which supinely takes opinions on trust, and obstinately supports them to spare itself the labor of thinking.

Moralists have unanimously agreed, that unless virtue be nursed by liberty, it will never attain due strength—and what they say of man I extend to mankind, insisting that in all cases morals must be fixed on immutable principles; and, that the being cannot be termed rational or virtuous, who obeys any authority, but that of reason.

To render women truly useful members of society, I argue that they should be led, by having their understandings cultivated on a large scale, to acquire a rational affection for their country, founded on knowledge, because it is obvious that we are little interested about what we do not understand. And to render this general knowledge of due importance, I have endeavored to show that private duties are never properly fulfilled unless the understanding enlarges the heart; and that public virtue is only an aggregate of private. But, the distinctions established in society undermine both, by beating out the solid gold of virtue, till it becomes only the tinsel-covering of vice; for while wealth renders a man more respectable than virtue, wealth will be sought before virtue; and, while women's persons are caressed, when a childish simper shows an absence of mind—the mind will lie fallow. Yet, true voluptuousness must proceed from the mind—for what can equal the sensations produced by mutual affection, supported by mutual respect? What are the cold, or feverish caresses of appetite, but sin embracing death, compared with the modest overflowings of a pure heart and exalted imagination? Yes, let me tell the libertine of fancy when he despises understanding in woman—that the mind, which he disregards, gives life to the enthusiastic affection from which rapture, short-lived as it is, alone can flow! And, that, without virtue, a sexual attachment must expire like a tallow candle in the socket, creating intolerable disgust. To prove this, I need only observe, that men who have wasted great part of their lives with women, and with whom they have sought for pleasure with eager thirst, entertain the meanest opinion of the sex. Virtue, true refiner of joy!—if foolish men were to fright thee from earth, in order to give loose to all their appetites without a check—some sensual wight of taste would scale the heavens to invite thee back, to give a zest to pleasure!

That women at present are by ignorance rendered vicious, is, I think, not to be disputed; and, that salutary effects tending to improve mankind might be expected from a *revolution* in female manners, appears, at least, with a face of probability, to rise out of the observation. For as marriage has been termed the parent of those endearing charities which draw man from the brutal herd, the corrupting intercourse that wealth, idleness, and folly, produce between the sexes, is more universally injurious to morality than all the other vices of mankind collectively considered. To adulterous lust the most sacred duties are sacrificed, because before marriage, men, by a promiscuous intimacy with women, learned to consider love as a selfish gratification—learned to separate it not only from esteem, but from the affection merely built on habit which mixes a little humanity with it. Justice and friendship are also set at defiance, and that purity of taste is vitiated which would naturally lead a man to relish an artless display of affection rather than affected airs. But that noble simplicity of affection, which dares to appear unadorned, has few attractions for the libertine, though it be the charm, which by cementing the matrimonial tie, secures to the pledges of a warmer passion the necessary parental attention; for children will never be properly educated till friendship subsists between parents. Virtue flies from a house divided against itself—and a whole legion of devils take up their residence there.

The affection of husbands and wives cannot be pure when they have so few sentiments in common, and when so little confidence is established at home, as must be the case when their pursuits are so different. That intimacy from which tenderness should flow, will not, cannot subsist between the vicious.

Contending, therefore, that the sexual distinction which men have so warmly insisted upon, is arbitrary, I have dwelt on an observation, that several sensible men, with whom I have conversed on the subject, allowed to be well founded; and it is simply this, that the little chastity to be found amongst men, and consequent disregard of modesty, tend to degrade both sexes; and further, that the modesty of women, characterized as such, will often be only the artful veil of wantonness instead of being the natural reflection of purity, till modesty be universally respected.

From the tyranny of man, I firmly believe, the greater number of female follies proceed; and the cunning, which I allow makes at present a part of their character, I likewise have repeatedly endeavored to prove, is produced by oppression.

Were not dissenters, for instance, a class of people, with strict truth, characterized as cunning? And may I not lay some stress on this fact to prove, that when any power but reason curbs the free spirit of man, dissimulation is practiced, and the various shifts of art are naturally called forth? Great attention to decorum, which was carried to a degree of scrupulosity, and all that puerile bustle about trifles and consequential solemnity, which Butler's caricature of a dissenter brings before the imagination, shaped their persons as well as their minds in the mould of prim littleness. I speak collectively, for I know how many ornaments in human nature have been enrolled amongst sectaries; yet, I assert, that the same narrow prejudice for their sect, which women have for their families, prevailed in the dissenting part of the community, however worthy in other respects; and also that the same timid prudence, or headstrong efforts, often disgraced the exertions of both. Oppression thus formed many of the features of their character perfectly to coincidence with that of the oppressed half of mankind; for is it not notorious that dissenters were, like women, fond of deliberating together, and asking advice of each other, till by a complication of little contrivances, some little end was brought about? A similar attention to preserve their reputation was conspicuous in the dissenting and female world, and was produced by a similar cause.

Asserting the rights which women in common with men ought to contend for, I have not attempted to extenuate their faults; but to prove them to be the natural consequence of their education and station in society. If so, it is reasonable to suppose that they will change their character, and correct their vices and follies, when they are allowed to be free in a physical, moral, and civil sense.

Let woman share the rights, and she will emulate the virtues of man; for she must grow more perfect when emancipated, or justify the authority that chains such a weak being to her duty. If the latter, it will be expedient to open a fresh trade with Russia for whips: a present which a father should always make to his son-in-law on his wedding day, that a husband may keep his whole family in order by the same means; and without any violation of justice reign, wielding this scepter, sole master of his house, because he is the only thing in it who has reason:—the divine, indefeasible earthly sovereignty breathed into man by the Master of the universe. Allowing this position, women have not any inherent rights to claim; and, by the same rule, their duties vanish, for rights and duties are inseparable.

Be just then, O ye men of understanding: and mark not more severely what women do amiss than the vicious tricks of the horse or the ass for whom ye provide provender—and allow her the privileges of ignorance, to whom ye deny the rights of reason, or ye will be worse than Egyptian task-masters expecting virtue where Nature has not given understanding.

READING 11

William Paley: The Design Argument from Analogy Defended

From *Natural Theology*

William Paley (1743–1805) was a minister in the Church of England and a prominent moral philosopher in his day. His most lasting contribution to philosophy is his book Natural Theology *(1802), in which he defends the design argument from analogy—specifically, with some of Hume's attacks in mind. The success of the argument from analogy rests on two key points. First, Paley argues that we are justified in inferring*

Source: William Paley, *Natural Theology: or, Evidences of the Existence and Attributes of the Deity* (1802), Chapters 1 and 2.

a watchmaker from a watch—even if we had never seen a watch before, or if the watch was broken. Second, he argues that the design of a watch sufficiently resembles the design that we see in many parts of the natural world. This is particularly so if we find a watch that is equipped with the capacity to automatically make other watches. Since we are justified in inferring a watchmaker from a watch, and a watch sufficiently resembles the world, then we are justified in concluding that the natural world is the product of a designing mind.

INFERRING A WATCHMAKER FROM A WATCH

In crossing a hearth, suppose I pitched my foot against a stone, and were asked how the stone came to be there; I might possibly answer, that, for any thing I knew to the contrary, it had lain there for ever: nor would it perhaps be very easy to show the absurdity of this answer. But suppose I had found a watch upon the ground, and it should be inquired how the watch happened to be in that place; I should hardly think of the answer which I had before given, that, for any thing I knew, the watch might have always been there. Yet why should not this answer serve for the watch as well as for the stone? Why is it not as admissible in the second case, as in the first? For this reason, and for no other, viz., that, when we come to inspect the watch, we perceive (what we could not discover in the stone) that its several parts are framed and put together for a purpose, e.g., that they are so formed and adjusted as to produce motion, and that motion so regulated as to point out the hour of the day; that, if the different parts had been differently shaped from what they are, of a different size from what they are, or placed after any other manner, or in any other order, than that in which they are placed, either no motion at all would have been carried on in the machine, or none which would have answered the use that is now served by it. To reckon up a few of the plainest of these parts, and of their offices, all tending to one result:

We see a cylindrical box containing a coiled elastic spring, which, by its endeavor to relax itself, turns round the box. We next observe a flexible chain (artificially wrought for the sake of flexure), communicating the action of the spring from the box to the fusee. We then find a series of wheels, the teeth of which catch in, and apply to, each other, conducting the motion from the fusee to the balance, and from the balance to the pointer; and at the same time, by the size and shape of those wheels, so regulating that motion, as to terminate in causing an index, by an equable and measured progression, to pass over a given space in a given time. We take notice that the wheels are made of brass in order to keep them from rust; the springs of steel, no other metal being so elastic; that over the face of the watch there is placed a glass, a material employed in no other part of the work, but in the room of which, if there had been any other than a transparent substance, the hour could not be seen without opening the case. This mechanism being observed (it requires indeed an examination of the instrument, and perhaps some previous knowledge of the subject, to perceive and understand it; but being once, as we have said, observed and understood), the inference, we think, is inevitable, that the watch must have had a maker: that there must have existed, at some time, and at some place or other, an artificer or artificers who formed it for the purpose which we find it actually to answer; who comprehended its construction, and designed its use.

1. Nor would it, I apprehend, weaken the conclusion, that we had never seen a watch made; that we had never known an artist capable of making one; that we were altogether incapable of executing such a piece of workmanship ourselves, or of understanding in what manner it was performed; all this being no more than what is true of some exquisite remains of ancient art, of some lost arts, and, to the generality of mankind, of the more curious productions of modern manufacture. Does one man in a million know how oval frames are turned? Ignorance of this kind exalts our opinion of the unseen and unknown artist's skill, if he be unseen and unknown, but raises no doubt in our minds of the existence and agency of such an artist, at some former time, and in some place or other. Nor can I perceive that it varies at all the inference, whether the question arise concerning a human agent, or concerning an agent of a different species, or an agent possessing, in some respects, a different nature.

2. Neither, secondly, would it invalidate our conclusion, that the watch sometimes went wrong, or that it seldom went exactly right. The purpose of the machinery, the design, and the designer, might be evident, and in the case supposed would be evident, in whatever way we accounted for the irregularity of the movement, or whether we could account for it or not. It is not necessary that a machine be perfect, in order to show with what design it was made: still less necessary, where the only question is, whether it were made with any design at all.

3. Nor, thirdly, would it bring any uncertainty into the argument, if there were a few parts of the watch, concerning which we could not discover, or had not yet discovered, in what manner they conduced to the general effect; or even some parts, concerning which we could not ascertain, whether they conduced to that effect in any manner whatever. For, as to the first branch of the case; if by the loss, or disorder, or decay of the parts in question, the movement of the watch were found in fact to be stopped, or disturbed, or retarded, no doubt would remain in our minds as to the utility or intention of these parts, although we should be unable to investigate the manner according to which, or the connection by which, the ultimate effect depended upon their action or assistance; and the more complex is the machine, the more likely is this obscurity to arise. Then, as to the second thing supposed, namely, that there were parts which might be spared, without prejudice to the movement of the watch, and that we had proved this by experiment—these superfluous parts, even if we were completely assured that they were such, would not vacate the reasoning which we had instituted concerning other parts. The indication of contrivance remained, with respect to them, nearly as it was before.

4. Nor, fourthly, would any man in his senses think the existence of the watch, with its various machinery, accounted for, by being told that it was one out of possible combinations of material forms; that whatever he had found in the place where he found the watch, must have contained some internal

configuration or other; and that this configuration might be the structure now exhibited, viz., of the works of a watch, as well as a different structure.

5. Nor, fifthly, would it yield his inquiry more satisfaction to be answered, that there existed in things a principle of order, which had disposed the parts of the watch into their present form and situation. He never knew a watch made by the principle of order; nor can he even form to himself an idea of what is meant by a principle of order, distinct from the intelligence of the watch-maker.

6. Sixthly, he would be surprised to hear that the mechanism of the watch was no proof of contrivance, only a motive to induce the mind to think so:

7. And not less surprised to be informed, that the watch in his hand was nothing more than the result of the laws of metallic nature. It is a perversion of language to assign any law, as the efficient, operative cause of anything. A law presupposes an agent; for it is only the mode, according to which an agent proceeds: it implies a power; for it is the order, according to which that power acts. Without this agent, without this power, which are both distinct from itself, the law does nothing; is nothing. The expression, the law of metallic nature, may sound strange and harsh to a philosophic ear; but it seems quite as justifiable as some others which are more familiar to him, such as the law of vegetable nature, the law of animal nature, or indeed as the law of nature in general, when assigned as the cause of phenomena, in exclusion of agency and power; or when it is substituted into the place of these.

8. Neither, lastly, would our observer be driven out of his conclusion, or from his confidence in its truth, by being told that he knew nothing at all about the matter. He knows enough for his argument: he knows the utility of the end: he knows the subserviency and adaptation of the means to the end. These points being known, his ignorance of other points, his doubts concerning other points, affect not the certainty of his reasoning. The consciousness of knowing little, need not beget a distrust of that which he does know.

A WATCH THAT MAKES A WATCH

Suppose, in the next place, that the person who found the watch, should, after some time, discover that, in addition to all the properties which he had hitherto observed in it, it possessed the unexpected property of producing, in the course of its movement, another watch like itself (the thing is conceivable); that it contained within it a mechanism, a system of parts, a mould for instance, or a complex adjustment of lathes, files, and other tools, evidently and separately calculated for this purpose; let us inquire, what effect ought such a discovery to have upon his former conclusion.

1. The first effect would be to increase his admiration of the contrivance, and his conviction of the consummate skill of the contriver. Whether he regarded the object of the contrivance, the distinct apparatus, the intricate, yet in many parts intelligible mechanism, by which it was carried on, he would perceive, in this new observation, nothing but an additional reason for doing what he had already done,—for referring the construction of the watch to design, and

to supreme art. If that construction without this property, or which is the same thing, before this property had been noticed, proved intention and art to have been employed about it; still more strong would the proof appear, when he came to the knowledge of this further property, the crown and perfection of all the rest.

2. He would reflect, that though the watch before him were, in some sense, the maker of the watch, which was fabricated in the course of its movements, yet it was in a very different sense from that, in which a carpenter, for instance, is the maker of a chair; the author of its contrivance, the cause of the relation of its parts to their use. With respect to these, the first watch was no cause at all to the second: in no such sense as this was it the author of the constitution and order, either of the parts which the new watch contained, or of the parts by the aid and instrumentality of which it was produced. We might possibly say, but with great latitude of expression, that a stream of water ground corn: but no latitude of expression would allow us to say, no stretch of conjecture could lead us to think, that the stream of water built the mill, though it were too ancient for us to know who the builder was. What the stream of water does in the affair, is neither more nor less than this; by the application of an unintelligent impulse to a mechanism previously arranged, arranged independently of it, and arranged by intelligence, an effect is produced, viz., the corn is ground. But the effect results from the arrangement. The force of the stream cannot be said to be the cause or author of the effect, still less of the arrangement. Understanding and plan in the formation of the mill were not the less necessary, for any share which the water has in grinding the corn: yet is this share the same, as that which the watch would have contributed to the production of the new watch, upon the supposition assumed in the last section. Therefore,

3. Though it be now no longer probable, that the individual watch, which our observer had found, was made immediately by the hand of an artificer, yet doth not this alteration in anywise affect the inference, that an artificer had been originally employed and concerned in the production. The argument from design remains as it was. Marks of design and contrivance are no more accounted for now, than they were before. In the same thing, we may ask for the cause of different properties. We may ask for the cause of the color of a body, of its hardness, of its head; and these causes may be all different. We are now asking for the cause of that subserviency to a use, that relation to an end, which we have remarked in the watch before us. No answer is given to this question, by telling us that a preceding watch produced it. There cannot be design without a designer; contrivance without a contriver; order without choice; arrangement, without any thing capable of arranging; subserviency and relation to a purpose, without that which could intend a purpose; means suitable to an end, and executing their office, in accomplishing that end, without the end ever having been contemplated, or the means accommodated to it. Arrangement, disposition of parts, subserviency of means to an end, relation of instruments to a use, imply the presence of intelligence and mind. No one, therefore, can rationally believe, that the insensible, inanimate watch, from which the watch before us issued, was the proper cause of the mechanism we so much admire in it;—could be

truly said to have constructed the instrument, disposed its parts, assigned their office, determined their order, action, and mutual dependency, combined their several motions into one result, and that also a result connected with the utilities of other beings. All these properties, therefore, are as much unaccounted for, as they were before.

4. Nor is anything gained by running the difficulty farther back, i.e., by supposing the watch before us to have been produced from another watch, that from a former, and so on indefinitely. Our going back ever so far, brings us no nearer to the least degree of satisfaction upon the subject. Contrivance is still unaccounted for. We still want a contriver. A designing mind is neither supplied by this supposition, nor dispensed with. If the difficulty were diminished the further we went back, by going back indefinitely we might exhaust it. And this is the only case to which this sort of reasoning applies. Where there is a tendency, or, as we increase the number of terms, a continual approach towards a limit, there, by supposing the number of terms to be what is called infinite, we may conceive the limit to be attained: but where there is no such tendency, or approach, nothing is effected by lengthening the series. There is no difference as to the point in question (whatever there may be as to many points), between one series and another; between a series which is finite, and a series which is infinite. A chain, composed of an infinite number of links, can no more support itself, than a chain composed of a finite number of links. And of this we are assured (though we never can have tried the experiment), because, by increasing the number of links, from ten for instance to a hundred, from a hundred to a thousand, etc., we make not the smallest approach, we observe not the smallest tendency, towards self-support. There is no difference in this respect (yet there may be a great difference in several respects) between a chain of a greater or less length, between one chain and another, between one that is finite and one that is infinite. This very much resembles the case before us. The machine which we are inspecting, demonstrates, by its construction, contrivance and design. Contrivance must have had a contriver; design, a designer; whether the machine immediately proceeded from another machine or not. That circumstance alters not the case. That other machine may, in like manner, have proceeded from a former machine: nor does that alter the case; contrivance must have had a contriver. That former one from one preceding it: no alteration still; a contriver is still necessary. No tendency is perceived, no approach towards a diminution of this necessity. It is the same with any and every succession of these machines; a succession of ten, of a hundred, of a thousand; with one series, as with another; a series which is finite, as with a series which is infinite. In whatever other respects they may differ, in this they do not. In all equally, contrivance and design are unaccounted for.

The question is not simply, How came the first watch into existence? which question, it may be pretended, is done away by supposing the series of watches thus produced from one another to have been infinite, and consequently to have had no such first, for which it was necessary to provide a cause. This, perhaps, would have been nearly the state of the question, if no thing had been before us but an unorganized, unmechanized substance, without mark or indication of contrivance. It might be difficult to show that such substance could not have existed from eternity, either in succession (if it were possible, which I think it is not, for unorganized bodies to spring from one another), or by individual perpetuity. But that is not the question now. To suppose it to be so, is to suppose that it made no difference whether we had found a watch or a stone. As it is, the metaphysics of that question have no place; for, in the watch which we are examining, are seen contrivance, design; an end, a purpose; means for the end, adaptation to the purpose. And the question which irresistibly presses upon our thoughts, is, whence this contrivance and design? The thing required is the intending mind, the adapting hand, the intelligence by which that hand was directed. This question, this demand, is not shaken off, by increasing a number or succession of substances, destitute of these properties; nor the more, by increasing that number to infinity. If it be said, that, upon the supposition of one watch being produced from another in the course of that other's movements, and by means of the mechanism within it, we have a cause for the watch in my hand, viz., the watch from which it proceeded. I deny, that for the design, the contrivance, the suitableness of means to an end, the adaptation of instruments to a use (all which we discover in the watch), we have any cause whatever. It is in vain, therefore, to assign a series of such causes, or to allege that a series may be carried back to infinity; for I do not admit that we have yet any cause at all of the phenomena, still less any series of causes either finite or infinite. Here is contrivance, but no contriver; proofs of design, but no designer.

5. Our observer would further also reflect, that the maker of the watch before him, was, in truth and reality, the maker of every watch produced from it; there being no difference (except that the latter manifests a more exquisite skill) between the making of another watch with his own hands, by the mediation of files, lathes, chisels, etc., and the disposing, fixing, and inserting of these instruments, or of others equivalent to them, in the body of the watch already made in such a manner, as to form a new watch in the course of the movements which he had given to the old one. It is only working by one set of tools, instead of another.

The conclusion of which the first examination of the watch, of its works, construction, and movement, suggested, was, that it must have had, for the cause and author of that construction, an artificer, who understood its mechanism, and designed its use. This conclusion is invincible. A second examination presents us with a new discovery. The watch is found, in the course of its movement, to produce another watch, similar to itself; and not only so, but we perceive in it a system or organization, separately calculated for that purpose. What effect would this discovery have, or ought it to have, upon our former inference? What, as hath already been said, but to increase, beyond measure, our admiration of the skill, which had been employed in the formation of such a machine? Or shall it, instead of this, all at once turn us round to an opposite conclusion, viz., that no art or skill whatever has been concerned in the business, although all other evidences of art and skill remain as they were, and this last and supreme piece of art be now added to the rest? Can this be maintained without absurdity? Yet this is atheism.

PART FOUR

Late Modern and Nineteenth Century

Immanuel Kant: Pure Reason and the Categorical Imperative

From *The Critique of Pure Reason* and *Groundwork of the Metaphysics of Morals*

German philosopher Immanuel Kant (1724–1804) is one of the most influential modern philosophers, impacting almost every area of the discipline. In epistemology, he forged a middle position between rationalists such as Descartes (who believed that knowledge is based on innate concepts) and empiricists such as Locke (who believed that knowledge comes from sensory experience). In his Critique of Pure Reason *(1781), Kant says, "There can be no doubt that all our knowledge begins with experience. . . . But although all our knowledge begins with experience, it does not follow that it all arises out of experience." Kant acknowledges that our faculty of knowledge is awakened into action by the objects affecting our senses. But having been awakened by sense impressions, our faculty of knowledge supplies from itself significant ingredients to the raw material of these impressions. The mind organizes the elements of our experiences by bringing to them its "ways of thinking." The human mind, he argues, is structured in such a way that as impressions enter it, the mind processes them. It is as though the mind possesses the capability of imposing its structure on the impressions received, just as a pair of colored lenses gives that particular color to the objects perceived. It is the mind's way of functioning that brings to experience the elements of cause and effect. Thus, we have some knowledge that is not immediately derived from experience, even though it is experience that triggers such knowledge.*

In moral philosophy, Kant objected to both the virtue theory of Aristotle and the pleasure-seeking theory of Epicurus. Like Aristotle, Kant believes that reason should be our guide in moral matters. However, in his Fundamental Principles of

Source: Immanuel Kant, *Critique of Pure Reason* (1781), Introduction; *Fundamental Principles of the Metaphysics of Morals* (1785), Sections 1 and 2.

the Metaphysics of Morals (1785), *he argues that human reason supplies us with a fundamental law of moral duty. The ethics of duty is sometimes called "deontological," based on the word deon, "that which is obligatory." Kant calls this law of duty the categorical imperative: "Act only on that maxim whereby you can at the same time will that it should become a universal law."*

PURE REASON

I. The Difference between Pure and Empirical Knowledge

That all our knowledge begins with experience there can be no doubt. For how is it possible that the faculty of knowledge should be awakened into action otherwise than by means of objects which affect our senses, and partly of themselves produce representations, partly rouse our powers of understanding into activity, to compare, to connect, or to separate these, and so to convert the raw material of our sensible impressions into a knowledge of objects, which is called experience? In respect of time, therefore, no knowledge of ours is antecedent to experience, but begins with it.

But, though all our knowledge begins with experience, it by no means follows that all arises out of experience. For, on the contrary, it is quite possible that our empirical knowledge is a compound of that which we receive through impressions, and that which the faculty of knowledge supplies from itself (sensible impressions giving merely the occasion), an addition which we cannot distinguish from the original element given by sense, till long practice has made us attentive to, and skillful in separating it.

It is, therefore, a question which requires close investigation, and not to be answered at first sight, whether there exists a knowledge altogether independent of experience, and even of all sensible impressions? Knowledge of this kind is called *a priori,* in contradistinction to empirical knowledge, which has its sources *a posteriori,* that is, in experience.

But the expression, "*a priori,*" is not as yet definite enough adequately to indicate the whole meaning of the question above stated. For, in speaking of knowledge which has its sources in experience, we are wont to say, that this or that may be known *a priori,* because we do not derive this knowledge immediately from experience, but from a general rule, which, however, we have itself borrowed from experience. Thus, if a man undermined his house, we say, "He might know *a priori* that it would have fallen"; that is, he needed not to have waited for the experience that it did actually fall. But still, *a priori,* he could not know even this much. For, that bodies are heavy, and, consequently, that they fall when their supports are taken away, must have been known to him previously, by means of experience.

By the term "knowledge *a priori,*" therefore, we shall in the following understand, not such as is independent of this or that kind of experience, but such as is absolutely so of all experience. Opposed to this is empirical knowledge, or that which is possible only *a posteriori,* that is, through experience. Knowledge *a priori* is either pure or impure. Pure knowledge *a priori* is that with which no empirical element is mixed up. For example, the proposition, "Every change has a cause," is a proposition *a priori*, but impure, because change is a conception which can only be derived from experience.

II. The Human Intellect, Even in an Unphilosophical State, Is in Possession of Certain Modes of Knowledge "*A Priori*"

The question now is as to a criterion, by which we may securely distinguish a pure from an empirical knowledge. Experience no doubt teaches us that this or that object is constituted in such and such a manner, but not that it could not possibly exist otherwise. Now, in the first place, if we have a proposition which contains the idea of necessity in its very conception, it is as if, moreover, it is not derived from any other proposition, unless from one equally involving the idea of necessity, it is absolutely *a priori*. Secondly, an empirical judgment never exhibits strict and absolute, but only assumed and comparative universality (by induction); therefore, the most we can say is—so far as we have hitherto observed, there is no exception to this or that rule. If, on the other hand, a judgment carries with it strict and absolute universality, that is, admits of no possible exception, it is not derived from experience, but is valid absolutely *a priori*.

Empirical universality is, therefore, only an arbitrary extension of validity, from that which may be predicated of a proposition valid in most cases, to that which is asserted of a proposition which holds good in all; as, for example, in the affirmation, "All bodies are heavy." When, on the contrary, strict universality characterizes a judgment, it necessarily indicates another peculiar source of knowledge, namely, a faculty of knowledge *a priori*. Necessity and strict universality, therefore, are infallible tests for distinguishing pure from empirical knowledge, and are inseparably connected with each other. But as in the use of these criteria the empirical limitation is sometimes more easily detected than the contingency of the judgment, or the unlimited universality which we attach to a judgment is often a more convincing proof than its necessity, it may be advisable to use the criteria separately, each being by itself infallible.

Now, that in the sphere of human knowledge we have judgments which are necessary, and in the strictest sense universal, consequently pure *a priori*, it will be an easy matter to show. If we desire an example from the sciences, we need only take any proposition in mathematics. If we cast our eyes upon the commonest operations of the understanding, the proposition, "Every change must have a cause," will amply serve our purpose. In the latter case, indeed, the conception of a cause so plainly involves the conception of a necessity of connection with an effect, and of a strict universality of the law, that the very notion of a cause would entirely disappear, were we to derive it, like Hume, from a frequent association of what happens with that which precedes; and the habit thence originating of connecting representations—the necessity inherent in the judgment being therefore merely subjective. Besides, without seeking for such examples of principles existing *a priori* in knowledge, we might easily show that such principles are the indispensable basis of the possibility of experience itself, and consequently prove their existence *a priori*. For whence could our experience itself acquire certainty, if all the rules on which it depends were themselves empirical, and consequently fortuitous? No one, therefore, can admit the validity of the use of such rules as first principles. But, for the present, we may content ourselves with having established the fact, that we do possess and exercise a faculty of pure *a priori* knowledge; and, secondly, with having pointed out the proper tests of such knowledge, namely, universality and necessity.

Not only in judgments, however, but even in conceptions, is an *a priori* origin manifest. For example, if we take away by degrees from our conceptions of a body all that can be referred to mere sensible experience—color, hardness or softness, weight, even impenetrability—the body will then vanish; but the space which it occupied still remains, and this it is utterly impossible to annihilate in thought. Again, if we take away, in like manner, from our empirical conception of any object, corporeal or incorporeal, all properties which mere experience has taught us to connect with it, still we cannot think away those through which we cogitate it as substance, or adhering to substance, although our conception of substance is more determined than that of an object. Compelled, therefore, by that necessity with which the conception of substance forces itself upon us, we must confess that it has its seat in our faculty of knowledge *a priori*.

III. Philosophy Stands in Need of a Science Which Shall Determine the Possibility, Principles, and Extent of Human Knowledge "*A Priori*"

Of far more importance than all that has been above said, is the consideration that certain modes of our knowledge rise completely above the sphere of all possible experience, and by means of conceptions, to which there exists in the whole extent of experience no corresponding object, seem to extend the range of our judgments beyond its bounds.

And just in this transcendental or supersensible sphere, where experience affords us neither instruction nor guidance, lie the investigations of reason, which, on account of their importance, we consider far preferable to, and as having a far more elevated aim than, all that the understanding can achieve within the sphere of sensible phenomena. So high a value do we set upon these investigations, that even at the risk of error, we persist in following them out, and permit neither doubt nor disregard nor indifference to restrain us from the pursuit. These unavoidable problems of mere pure reason are *God, freedom* (of will), and *immortality*. The science which, with all its preliminaries, has for its especial object the solution of these problems is named metaphysics—a science which is at the very outset dogmatical, that is, it confidently takes upon itself the execution of this task without any previous investigation of the ability or inability of reason for such an undertaking.

Now the safe ground of experience being thus abandoned, it seems nevertheless natural that we should hesitate to erect a building with the knowledge we possess, without knowing whence they come, and on the strength of principles, the origin of which is undiscovered. Instead of thus trying to build without a foundation, it is rather to be expected that we should long ago have put the question, how the understanding can arrive at this *a priori* knowledge, and what is the extent, validity, and worth which they may possess? We say, "This is natural enough," meaning by the word natural, that which is consistent with a just and reasonable way of thinking; but if we understand by the term, that, which usually happens, nothing indeed could be more natural and more comprehensible than that this investigation should be left long unattempted. For one part of our pure knowledge, the science of mathematics, has been long firmly established, and thus leads us to form flattering expectations with regard to others, though these may be of quite a different nature. Besides, when we get beyond the bounds of experience, we are of course safe from opposition in that quarter; and the charm of widening the range of our knowledge is so great that, unless we are brought to a standstill by some evident contradiction, we hurry on undoubtingly in our course. This, however, may be avoided, if we are sufficiently cautious in the construction of our fictions, which are not the less fictions on that account.

Mathematical science affords us a brilliant example, how far, independently of all experience, we may carry our *a priori* knowledge. It is true that the mathematician occupies himself with objects and knowledge only in so far as they can be represented by means of intuition. But this circumstance is easily overlooked, because the said intuition can itself be given *a priori,* and therefore is hardly to be distinguished from a mere pure conception. Deceived by such a proof of the power of reason, we can perceive no limits to the extension of our knowledge. The light dove cleaving in free flight the thin air, whose resistance it feels, might imagine that her movements would be far more free and rapid in airless space. Just in the same way did Plato, abandoning the world of sense because of the narrow limits it sets to the understanding, venture upon the wings of ideas beyond it, into the void space of pure intellect. He did not reflect that he made no real progress by all his efforts; for he met with no resistance which might serve him for a support, as it were, whereon to rest, and on which he might apply his powers, in order to let the intellect acquire momentum for its progress. It is, indeed, the common fate of human reason in speculation, to finish the imposing edifice of thought as rapidly as possible, and then for the first time to begin to examine whether the foundation is a solid one or no. Arrived at this point, all sorts of excuses are sought after, in order to console us for its want of stability, or rather, indeed, to enable us to dispense altogether with so late and dangerous an investigation. But what frees us during the process of building from all apprehension or suspicion, and flatters us into the belief of its solidity, is this. A great part, perhaps the greatest part, of the business of our reason consists in the analysis of the conceptions which we already possess of objects. By this means we gain a multitude of knowledge, which although really nothing more than elucidations or explanations of that which (though in a confused manner) was already thought in our conceptions, are, at least in respect of their form, prized as new introspections; while, so far as regards their matter or content, we have really made no addition to our conceptions, but only disinvolved them. But as this process does furnish real *a priori* knowledge, which has a sure progress and useful results, reason, deceived by this, slips in, without being itself aware of it, assertions of a quite different kind; in which, to given conceptions it adds others, *a priori* indeed, but entirely foreign to them, without our knowing how it arrives at these, and, indeed, without such a question ever suggesting itself. I shall therefore at once proceed to examine the difference between these two modes of knowledge.

IV. Of the Difference between Analytic and Synthetic Judgments

In all judgments wherein the relation of a subject to the predicate is cogitated (I mention affirmative judgments only here; the application to negative will be very easy), this relation is possible in two different ways. Either the predicate B belongs to the subject A, as somewhat which is contained (though covertly) in the conception A; or the predicate B lies completely out of the conception A, although it stands in connection with it. In the first instance, I term the judgment analytic, in the second, synthetic. Analytic judgments (affirmative) are therefore those in which the connection of the predicate with the subject is cogitated through identity; those in which this connection is cogitated without identity, are called synthetic judgments. The former may be called explicative, the latter augmentative judgments; because the former add in the predicate nothing to the conception of the subject, but only analyze it into its constituent conceptions, which were thought already in the subject, although in a confused manner; the latter add to our conceptions of the subject a predicate which was not contained in it, and which no analysis could ever have discovered therein. For example, when I say, "All bodies are extended," this is an analytic judgment. For I need not go beyond the conception of body in order to find extension connected with it, but merely analyze the conception, that is, become conscious of the manifold properties which I think in that conception, in order to discover this predicate in it: it is therefore an analytic judgment. On the other hand, when I say, "All bodies are heavy," the predicate is something totally different from that which I think in the mere conception of a body. By the addition of such a predicate, therefore, it becomes a synthetic judgment.

Judgments of experience, as such, are always synthetic. For it would be absurd to think of grounding an analytic judgment on experience, because in forming such a judgment I need not go out of the sphere of my conceptions, and therefore recourse to the testimony of experience is quite unnecessary. That "bodies are extended" is not an empirical judgment, but a proposition which stands firm *a priori*. For before addressing myself to experience, I already have in my conception all the requisite conditions for the judgment, and I have only to extract the predicate from the conception, according to the principle of contradiction, and thereby at the same time become conscious of the necessity of the judgment, a necessity which I could never learn from experience. On the other hand, though at first I do not at all include the predicate of weight in my conception of body in general, that conception still indicates an object of experience, a part of the totality of experience, to which I can still add other parts; and this I do when I recognize by observation that bodies are heavy. I can cognize beforehand by analysis the conception of body through the characteristics of extension, impenetrability, shape, etc., all which are cogitated in this conception. But now I extend my knowledge, and looking back on experience from which I had derived this conception of body, I find weight at all times connected with the above characteristics, and therefore I synthetically add to my conceptions this as a predicate, and say, "All bodies are heavy." Thus it is experience upon which rests the possibility of the synthesis of the predicate of weight with the conception of body, because both conceptions, although the one is not contained in the other, still belong to one another (only contingently, however), as parts of a whole, namely, of experience, which is itself a synthesis of intuitions.

But to synthetic judgments *a priori,* such aid is entirely wanting. If I go out of and beyond the conception A, in order to recognize another B as connected with it, what foundation have I to rest on, whereby to render the synthesis possible? I have here no longer the advantage of looking out in the sphere of experience for what I want. Let us take, for example, the proposition, "Everything that happens has a cause." In the conception of "something that happens," I indeed think an existence which a certain time antecedes, and from this I can derive analytic judgments. But the conception of a cause lies quite out of the above conception, and indicates something entirely different from "that which happens," and is consequently not contained in that conception. How then am I able to assert concerning the general conception—"that which happens"—something entirely different from that conception, and to recognize the conception of cause although not contained in it, yet as belonging to it, and even necessarily? What is here the unknown = X, upon which the understanding rests when it believes it has found, out of the conception A a foreign predicate B, which it nevertheless considers to be connected with it? It cannot be experience, because the principle adduced annexes the two representations, cause and effect, to the representation existence, not only with universality, which experience cannot give, but also with the expression of necessity, therefore completely *a priori* and from pure conceptions. Upon such synthetic, that is augmentative propositions, depends the whole aim of our speculative knowledge *a priori;* for although analytic judgments are indeed highly important and necessary, they are so, only to arrive at that clearness of conceptions which is requisite for a sure and extended synthesis, and this alone is a real acquisition.

V. In All Theoretical Sciences of Reason, Synthetic Judgments "*A Priori*" Are Contained as Principles

1. **Mathematical judgments are always synthetic.** Hitherto this fact, though incontestably true and very important in its consequences, seems to have escaped the analysts of the human mind, nay, to be in complete opposition to all their conjectures. For as it was found that mathematical conclusions all proceed according to the principle of contradiction (which the nature of every apodeictic certainty requires), people became persuaded that the fundamental principles of the science also were recognized and admitted in the same way. But the notion is fallacious; for although a synthetic proposition can certainly be

discerned by means of the principle of contradiction, this is possible only when another synthetic proposition precedes, from which the latter is deduced, but never in and of itself.

Before all, be it observed, that proper mathematical propositions are always judgments *a priori,* and not empirical, because they carry along with them the conception of necessity, which cannot be given by experience. If this be demurred to, it matters not; I will then limit my assertion to pure mathematics, the very conception of which implies that it consists of knowledge altogether non-empirical and *a priori.*

We might, indeed at first suppose that the proposition $7 + 5 = 12$ is a merely analytic proposition, following (according to the principle of contradiction) from the conception of a sum of seven and five. But if we regard it more narrowly, we find that our conception of the sum of seven and five contains nothing more than the uniting of both sums into one, whereby it cannot at all be cogitated what this single number is which embraces both. The conception of twelve is by no means obtained by merely cogitating the union of seven and five; and we may analyze our conception of such a possible sum as long as we will, still we shall never discover in it the notion of twelve. We must go beyond these conceptions, and have recourse to an intuition which corresponds to one of the two—our five fingers, for example, or like Segner in his Arithmetic five points, and so by degrees, add the units contained in the five given in the intuition, to the conception of seven. For I first take the number 7, and, for the conception of 5 calling in the aid of the fingers of my hand as objects of intuition, I add the units, which I before took together to make up the number 5, gradually now by means of the material image my hand, to the number 7, and by this process, I at length see the number 12 arise. That 7 should be added to 5, I have certainly cogitated in my conception of a sum $= 7 + 5$, but not that this sum was equal to 12. Arithmetical propositions are therefore always synthetic, of which we may become more clearly convinced by trying large numbers. For it will thus become quite evident that, turn and twist our conceptions as we may, it is impossible, without having recourse to intuition, to arrive at the sum total or product by means of the mere analysis of our conceptions. Just as little is any principle of pure geometry analytic. "A straight line between two points is the shortest," is a synthetic proposition. For my conception of straight contains no notion of quantity, but is merely qualitative. The conception of the shortest is therefore wholly an addition, and by no analysis can it be extracted from our conception of a straight line. Intuition must therefore here lend its aid, by means of which, and thus only, our synthesis is possible.

Some few principles preposited by geometricians are, indeed, really analytic, and depend on the principle of contradiction. They serve, however, like identical propositions, as links in the chain of method, not as principles—for example, $a = a$, the whole is equal to itself, or $(a + b) > a$, the whole is greater than its part. And yet even these principles themselves, though they derive their validity from pure conceptions, are only admitted in mathematics because they can be presented in intuition. What causes us here commonly to believe that the predicate of such apodeictic judgments is already contained in our conception, and that the judgment is therefore analytic, is merely the equivocal nature of the expression. We must join in thought a certain predicate to a given conception, and this necessity cleaves already to the conception. But the question is, not what we must join in thought to the given conception, but what we really think therein, though only obscurely, and then it becomes manifest that the predicate pertains to these conceptions, necessarily indeed, yet not as thought in the conception itself, but by virtue of an intuition, which must be added to the conception.

2. **The science of natural philosophy (physics) contains in itself synthetic judgments *a priori*, as principles.** I shall adduce two propositions. For instance, the proposition, "In all changes of the material world, the quantity of matter remains unchanged"; or, that, "In all communication of motion, action and reaction must always be equal." In both of these, not only is the necessity, and therefore their origin *a priori* clear, but also that they are synthetic propositions. For in the conception of matter, I do not cogitate its permanency, but merely its presence in space, which it fills. I therefore really go out of and beyond the conception of matter, in order to think on to it something *a priori*, which I did not think in it. The proposition is therefore not analytic, but synthetic, and nevertheless conceived *a priori*; and so it is with regard to the other propositions of the pure part of natural philosophy.

3. As to *metaphysics*, even if we look upon it merely as an attempted science, yet, from the nature of human reason, an indispensable one, we find that it must contain synthetic propositions *a priori*. It is not merely the duty of metaphysics to dissect, and thereby analytically to illustrate the conceptions which we form *a priori* of things; but we seek to widen the range of our *a priori* knowledge. For this purpose, we must avail ourselves of such principles as add something to the original conception—something not identical with, nor contained in it, and by means of synthetic judgments *a priori*, leave far behind us the limits of experience; for example, in the proposition, "The world must have a beginning," and such like. Thus metaphysics, according to the proper aim of the science, consists merely of synthetic propositions *a priori*.

VI. The Universal Problem of Pure Reason

It is extremely advantageous to be able to bring a number of investigations under the formula of a single problem. For in this manner, we not only facilitate our own labor, inasmuch as we define it clearly to ourselves, but also render it more easy for others to decide whether we have done justice to our undertaking. The proper problem of pure reason, then, is contained in the question: "How are synthetic judgments *a priori* possible?"

That metaphysical science has hitherto remained in so vacillating a state of uncertainty and contradiction, is only to be attributed to the fact that this great problem, and perhaps even the difference between analytic and synthetic judgments, did not sooner suggest itself to philosophers. Upon the solution of this problem, or upon sufficient proof of the impossibility of synthetic knowledge *a priori,* depends the existence or downfall of the science of metaphysics. Among philosophers, David Hume came the nearest of all to this problem; yet it never acquired in his mind sufficient precision, nor did he regard the question in its universality. On the contrary, he stopped short at the synthetic proposition of the connection of an effect with its cause (*principium causalitatis*), insisting that such proposition *a priori* was impossible.

According to his conclusions, then, all that we term metaphysical science is a mere delusion, arising from the fancied insight of reason into that which is in truth borrowed from experience, and to which habit has given the appearance of necessity. Against this assertion, destructive to all pure philosophy, he would have been guarded, had he had our problem before his eyes in its universality. For he would then have perceived that, according to his own argument, there likewise could not be any pure mathematical science, which assuredly cannot exist without synthetic propositions *a priori*—an absurdity from which his good understanding must have saved him.

In the solution of the above problem is at the same time comprehended the possibility of the use of pure reason in the foundation and construction of all sciences which contain theoretical knowledge *a priori* of objects, that is to say, the answer to the following questions:

How is pure mathematical science possible?

How is pure natural science possible?

Respecting these sciences, as they do certainly exist, it may with propriety be asked, how they are possible?—for that they must be possible is shown by the fact of their really existing. But as to metaphysics, the miserable progress it has hitherto made, and the fact that of no one system yet brought forward, far as regards its true aim, can it be said that this science really exists, leaves any one at liberty to doubt with reason the very possibility of its existence.

Yet, in a certain sense, this kind of knowledge must unquestionably be looked upon as given; in other words, metaphysics must be considered as really existing, if not as a science, nevertheless as a natural disposition of the human mind (*metaphysica naturalis*). For human reason, without any instigations imputable to the mere vanity of great knowledge, unceasingly progresses, urged on by its own feeling of need, towards such questions as cannot be answered by any empirical application of reason, or principles derived therefrom; and so there has ever really existed in every man some system of metaphysics. It will always exist, so soon as reason awakes to the action of its power of speculation. And now the question arises: "How is metaphysics, as a natural disposition, possible?" In other words, how, from the nature of universal human reason, do those questions arise which pure reason proposes to itself, and which it is impelled by its own feeling of need to answer as well as it can?

But as in all the attempts hitherto made to answer the questions which reason is prompted by its very nature to propose to itself, for example, whether the world had a beginning, or has existed from eternity, it has always met with unavoidable contradictions, we must not rest satisfied with the mere natural disposition of the mind to metaphysics, that is, with the existence of the faculty of pure reason, whence, indeed, some sort of metaphysical system always arises; but it must be possible to arrive at certainty in regard to the question whether we know or do not know the things of which metaphysics treats. We must be able to arrive at a decision on the subjects of its questions, or on the ability or inability of reason to form any judgment respecting them; and therefore either to extend with confidence the bounds of our pure reason, or to set strictly defined and safe limits to its action. This last question, which arises out of the above universal problem, would properly run thus: "How is metaphysics possible as a science?"

Thus, the critique of reason leads at last, naturally and necessarily, to science; and, on the other hand, the dogmatical use of reason without criticism leads to groundless assertions, against which others equally specious can always be set, thus ending unavoidably in skepticism.

Besides, this science cannot be of great and formidable prolixity, because it has not to do with objects of reason, the variety of which is inexhaustible, but merely with Reason herself and her problems; problems which arise out of her own bosom, and are not proposed to her by the nature of outward things, but by her own nature. And when once Reason has previously become able completely to understand her own power in regard to objects which she meets with in experience, it will be easy to determine securely the extent and limits of her attempted application to objects beyond the confines of experience.

We may and must, therefore, regard the attempts hitherto made to establish metaphysical science dogmatically as non-existent. For what if analysis, that is, mere dissection of conceptions, is contained in one or other, is not the aim of, but only a preparation for metaphysics proper, which has for its object the extension, by means of synthesis, of our *a priori* knowledge. And for this purpose, mere analysis is of course useless, because it only shows what is contained in these conceptions, but not how we arrive, *a priori*, at them; and this it is her duty to show, in order to be able afterwards to determine their valid use in regard to all objects of experience, to all knowledge in general. But little self-denial, indeed, is needed to give up these pretensions, seeing the undeniable, and in the dogmatic mode of procedure, inevitable contradictions of Reason with herself, have long since ruined the reputation of every system of metaphysics that has appeared up to this time. It will require more firmness to remain undeterred by difficulty from within, and opposition from without, from endeavoring, by a method quite opposed to all those hitherto followed, to further the growth and fruitfulness of a science indispensable to human reason—a science from which every branch it has borne may be cut away, but whose roots remain indestructible.

VII. Idea and Division of a Particular Science, under the Name of a Critique of Pure Reason

From all that has been said, there results the idea of a particular science, which may be called the Critique of Pure Reason. For reason is the faculty which furnishes us with the principles of knowledge *a priori*. Hence, pure reason is the faculty which contains the principles of cognizing anything absolutely *a priori*.

THE CATEORICAL IMPERATIVE

The Chief Good Is a Good Will

Nothing can possibly be conceived in the world, or even out of it, which can be called good, without qualification, except a *good will*. Intelligence, wit, judgment, and the other *talents* of the mind, however they may be named, or courage, resolution, perseverance, as qualities of temperament, are undoubtedly good and desirable in many respects; but these gifts of nature may also become extremely bad and mischievous if the will which is to make use of them, and which, therefore, constitutes what is called *character*, is not good. It is the same with the *gifts of fortune*. Power, riches, honor, even health, and the general well-being and contentment with one's condition which is called *happiness*, inspire pride, and often presumption, if there is not a good will to correct the influence of these on the mind, and with this also to rectify the whole principle of acting and adapt it to its end. The sight of a being who is not adorned with a single feature of a pure and good will, enjoying unbroken prosperity, can never give pleasure to an impartial rational spectator. Thus a good will appears to constitute the indispensable condition even of being worthy of happiness.

There are even some qualities which are of service to this good will itself and may facilitate its action, yet which have no intrinsic unconditional value, but always presuppose a good will, and this qualifies the esteem that we justly have for them and does not permit us to regard them as absolutely good. Moderation in the affections and passions, self-control, and calm deliberation are not only good in many respects, but even seem to constitute part of the intrinsic worth of the person; but they are far from deserving to be called good without qualification, although they have been so unconditionally praised by the ancients. For without the principles of a good will, they may become extremely bad, and the coolness of a villain not only makes him far more dangerous, but also directly makes him more abominable in our eyes than he would have been without it.

The Goodness of the Will Independent of Consequences

A good will is good not because of what it performs or effects, not by its aptness for the attainment of some proposed end, but simply by virtue of the volition; that is, it is good in itself, and considered by itself is to be esteemed much higher than all that can be brought about by it in favor of any inclination, nay even of the sum total of all inclinations. Even if it should happen that, owing to special disfavor of fortune, or the stingy provision of a step-motherly nature, this will should wholly lack power to accomplish its purpose, if with its greatest efforts it should yet achieve nothing, and there should remain only the good will (not, to be sure, a mere wish, but the summoning of all means in our power), then, like a jewel, it would still shine by its own light, as a thing which has its whole value in itself. Its usefulness or fruitfulness can neither add nor take away anything from this value. It would be, as it were, only the setting to enable us to handle it the more conveniently in common commerce, or to attract to it the attention of those who are not yet connoisseurs, but not to recommend it to true connoisseurs, or to determine its value. . . .

First Proposition: To Have Moral Worth, an Action Must Be Done from Duty

. . . We can readily distinguish whether the action which agrees with duty is done *from duty*, or from a selfish view. It is much harder to make this distinction when the action accords with duty and the subject has besides a *direct* inclination to it. For example, it is always a matter of duty that a dealer should not over charge an inexperienced purchaser; and wherever there is much commerce the prudent tradesman does not overcharge, but keeps a fixed price for everyone, so that a child buys of him as well as any other. Men are thus honestly served; but this is not enough to make us believe that the tradesman has so acted from duty and from principles of honesty: his own advantage required it; it is out of the question in this case to suppose that he might besides have a direct inclination in favor of the buyers, so that, as it were, from love he should give no advantage to one over another. Accordingly the action was done neither from duty nor from direct inclination, but merely with a selfish view.

On the other hand, it is a duty to maintain one's life; and, in addition, everyone has also a direct inclination to do so. But on this account the anxious care which most men take for it has no intrinsic worth, and their maxim has no moral import. They preserve their life *as duty requires,* no doubt, but not *because duty requires.* On the other hand, if adversity and hopeless sorrow have completely taken away the relish for life; if the unfortunate one, strong in mind, indignant at his fate rather than desponding or dejected, wishes for death, and yet preserves his life without loving it—not from inclination or fear, but from duty—then his maxim has a moral worth.

The Example of the Philanthropist

To be beneficent when we can is a duty; and besides this, there are many minds so sympathetically constituted that, without any other motive of vanity or self-interest, they find a pleasure in spreading joy around them and can take delight in the satisfaction of others so far as it is their own work. But I maintain that in such a case an action of this kind, however proper, however amiable it may be, has nevertheless no true moral worth, but is on a level with other inclinations, e.g., the inclination to honor, which, if it is happily directed to that which is in fact of public utility and accordant with duty and consequently honorable, deserves praise and encouragement, but not esteem. For the maxim lacks the moral import, namely, that such actions be done *from duty,* not from inclination. Put the case that the mind of that philanthropist were clouded by sorrow of his own, extinguishing all sympathy with the lot of others, and that, while he still has the power to benefit others in distress, he is not touched by their trouble because he is absorbed with his own; and now suppose that he tears himself out of this dead insensibility, and performs the action without any inclination to it, but simply from duty, then first has his action its genuine moral worth. . . .

Second Proposition: The Moral Worth of an Action Derives Not from Results but Because It Was Based on Principle

The second proposition is: That an action done from duty derives its moral worth, *not from the purpose* which is to be attained by it, but from the maxim by which it is determined, and therefore does not depend on the realization of the object of the action, but merely on the principle of volition by which the action has taken place, without regard to any object of desire. It is clear from what precedes that the purposes which we may have in view in our actions, or their effects regarded as ends and springs of the will, cannot give to actions any unconditional or moral worth. In what, then, can their worth lie, if it is not to consist in the will and in reference to its expected effect? It cannot lie anywhere but in the *principle of the will* without regard to the ends which can be attained by the action. For the will stands between its *a priori* principle, which is formal, and its *a posteriori* spring, which is material, as between two roads, and as it must be determined by something, in that it must be determined by the formal principle of volition when an action is done from duty, in which case every material principle has been withdrawn from it.

Third Proposition: Duty Is the Necessity of Acting from Respect of the Moral Law

The third proposition, which is a consequence of the two preceding, I would express thus *Duty is the necessity of acting from respect for the law.* I may have inclination for an object as the effect of my proposed action, but I cannot have respect for it, just for this reason, that it is an effect and not an energy of will. Similarly I cannot have respect for inclination, whether my own or another's; I can at most, if my own, approve it; if another's, sometimes even love it; i.e., look on it as favorable to my own interest. It is only what is connected with my will as a principle, by no means as an effect—what does not subserve my inclination, but overpowers it, or at least in case of choice excludes it from its calculation—in other words, simply the law of itself, which can be an object of respect, and hence a command. Now an action done from duty must wholly exclude the influence of inclination and with it every object of the will, so that nothing remains which can determine the will except objectively the *law*, and subjectively *pure respect* for this practical law, and consequently the maxim that I should follow this law even to the thwarting of all my inclinations.

Thus the moral worth of an action does not lie in the effect expected from it, nor in any principle of action which requires to borrow its motive from this expected effect. For all these effects—agreeableness of one's condition and even the promotion of the happiness of others—could have been also brought about by other causes, so that for this there would have been no need of the will of a rational being; whereas it is in this alone that the supreme and unconditional good can be found. The pre-eminent good which we call moral can therefore consist in nothing else than *the conception of law* in itself, *which certainly is only possible in a rational being*, in so far as this conception, and not the expected effect, determines the will. This is a good which is already present in the person who acts accordingly, and we have not to wait for it to appear first in the result.

Promise: An Example of Moral Law

But what sort of law can that be, the conception of which must determine the will, even without paying any regard to the effect expected from it, in order that this will may be called good absolutely and without qualification? As I have deprived the will of every impulse which could arise to it from obedience to any law, there remains nothing but the universal conformity of its actions to law in general, which alone is to serve the will as a principle, i.e., I am never to act otherwise than *so that I could also will that my maxim should become a universal law.* Here, now, it is the simple conformity to law in general, without assuming any particular law applicable to certain actions, that serves the will as its principle and must so serve it, if duty is not to be a vain delusion and a chimerical notion. The common reason of men in its practical judgments perfectly coincides with this and always has in view the principle here suggested. Let the question be, for example: May I when in distress make a promise with the intention not to keep it? I readily distinguish here between the two significations which the question may have: Whether it is prudent, or whether it is right, to make a false promise. The former may undoubtedly be the case. I see clearly indeed that it is not enough to extricate myself from a present difficulty by means of this subterfuge, but it must be well considered whether there may not hereafter spring from this lie much greater inconvenience than that from which I now free myself, and as, with all my supposed *cunning,* the consequences cannot be so easily foreseen but that credit once lost may be much more injurious to me than any mischief which I seek to avoid at present, it should be considered whether it would not be more *prudent* to act herein according to a universal maxim and to make it a habit to promise nothing except with the intention of keeping it. But it is soon clear to me that such a maxim will still only be based on the fear of consequences. Now it is a wholly different thing to be truthful from duty and to be so from apprehension of injurious consequences. In the first case, the very notion of the action already implies a law for me; in the second case, I must first look about elsewhere to see what results may be combined with it which would affect myself. For to deviate from the principle of duty is beyond all doubt wicked; but to be unfaithful to my maxim of prudence may often be very advantageous to me, although to abide by it is certainly safer. The shortest way, however, and an unerring one, to discover the answer to this question whether a lying promise is consistent with duty, is to ask myself, Should I be content that my maxim (to extricate myself from difficulty by a false promise) should hold good as a universal law, for myself as well as for others? and should I be able to say to myself, "Every one may make a deceitful promise when he finds himself in a difficulty from which he cannot otherwise extricate himself"? Then I presently become aware that while I can will the lie, I can by no means will that lying should be a universal law. For with such a law there would be no promises at all, since it would be in vain to allege my intention in regard to my future actions to those who would not believe this allegation, or if they over hastily did so would pay me back in my own coin. Hence my maxim, as soon as it should be made a universal law, would necessarily destroy itself.

Imperatives: Hypothetical and Categorical

Everything in nature works according to laws. Rational beings alone have the faculty of acting according to *the conception* of laws, that is according to principles, i.e., have a will. . . .

Now all imperatives command either *hypothetically* or *categorically*. The former represent the practical necessity of a possible action as means to *something else* that is willed (or at least which one might possibly will). The categorical imperative would be that which represented an action as necessary of itself without reference to another end, i.e., as objectively necessary.

Since every practical law represents a possible action as good and, on this account, for a subject who is practically determinable by reason, necessary, all imperatives are formula determining an action which is necessary according to the principle of a will good in some respects. If now the action is good only as a means to something else, then the imperative is *hypothetical;* if it is conceived as good *in itself* and consequently as being necessarily the principle of a will which of itself conforms to reason, then it is *categorical.* . . .

There is therefore but one categorical imperative, namely, this: *Act only on that maxim whereby you can at the same time will that it should become a universal law.* . . .

The Formula of the Law of Nature

Since the universality of the law according to which effects are produced constitutes what is properly called nature in the most general sense (as to form), that is the existence of things so far as it is determined by general laws, the imperative of duty may be expressed thus: *Act as if the maxim of your action were to become by your will a universal law of nature.*

We will now enumerate a few duties, adopting the usual division of them into duties to ourselves and to others, and into perfect and imperfect duties.

1. A man reduced to despair by a series of misfortunes feels wearied of life, but is still so far in possession of his reason that he can ask himself whether it would not be contrary to his duty to himself to take his own life. Now he inquires whether the maxim of his action could become a universal law of nature. His maxim is: "From self-love I adopt it as a principle to shorten my life when its longer duration is likely to bring more evil than satisfaction." It is asked then simply whether this principle founded on self-love can become a universal law of nature. Now we see at once that a system of nature of which it should be a law to destroy life by means of the very feeling whose special nature it is to impel to the improvement of life would contradict itself and, therefore, could not exist as a system of nature; hence that

maxim cannot possibly exist as a universal law of nature and, consequently, would be wholly inconsistent with the supreme principle of all duty.

2. Another finds himself forced by necessity to borrow money. He knows that he will not be able to repay it, but sees also that nothing will be lent to him unless he promises stoutly to repay it in a definite time. He desires to make this promise, but he has still so much conscience as to ask himself: "Is it not unlawful and inconsistent with duty to get out of a difficulty in this way?" Suppose however that he resolves to do so: then the maxim of his action would be expressed thus: "When I think myself in want of money, I will borrow money and promise to repay it, although I know that I never can do so." Now this principle of self-love or of one's own advantage may perhaps be consistent with my whole future welfare; but the question now is, "Is it right?" I change then the suggestion of self-love into a universal law, and state the question thus: "How would it be if my maxim were a universal law?" Then I see at once that it could never hold as a universal law of nature, but would necessarily contradict itself. For supposing it to be a universal law that everyone when he thinks himself in a difficulty should be able to promise whatever he pleases, with the purpose of not keeping his promise, the promise itself would become impossible, as well as the end that one might have in view in it, since no one would consider that anything was promised to him, but would ridicule all such statements as vain pretences.

3. A third finds in himself a talent which with the help of some culture might make him a useful man in many respects. But he finds himself in comfortable circumstances and prefers to indulge in pleasure rather than to take pains in enlarging and improving his happy natural capacities. He asks, however, whether his maxim of neglect of his natural gifts, besides agreeing with his inclination to indulgence, agrees also with what is called duty. He sees then that a system of nature could indeed subsist with such a universal law although men (like the South Sea islanders) should let their talents rest and resolve to devote their lives merely to idleness, amusement, and propagation of their species—in a word, to enjoyment; but he cannot possibly *will* that this should be a universal law of nature, or be implanted in us as such by a natural instinct. For, as a rational being, he necessarily wills that his faculties be developed, since they serve him and have been given him, for all sorts of possible purposes.

4. A fourth, who is in prosperity, while he sees that others have to contend with great wretchedness and that he could help them, thinks: "What concern is it of mine? Let everyone be as happy as Heaven pleases, or as he can make himself; I will take nothing from him nor even envy him, only I do not wish to contribute anything to his welfare or to his assistance in distress!" Now no doubt if such a mode of thinking were a universal law, the human race might very well subsist and doubtless even better than in a state in which everyone talks of sympathy and good will, or even takes care occasionally to put it into practice, but, on the other side, also cheats when he can, betrays the rights of men, or otherwise violates them. But although it is possible that a universal law of nature might exist in accordance with

that maxim, it is impossible to *will* that such a principle should have the universal validity of a law of nature. For a will which resolved this would contradict itself, inasmuch as many cases might occur in which one would have need of the love and sympathy of others, and in which, by such a law of nature, sprung from his own will, he would deprive himself of all hope of the aid he desires. . . .

The Formula of the End Itself

Supposing, however, that there were something *whose existence* has *in itself* an absolute worth, something which, being *an end in itself*, could be a source of definite laws; then in this and this alone would lie the source of a possible categorical imperative, i.e., a practical law.

Now I say: man and generally any rational being *exists* as an end in himself, *not merely as a means* to be arbitrarily used by this or that will, but in all his actions, whether they concern himself or other rational beings, must be always regarded at the same time as an end. All objects of the inclinations have only a conditional worth, for if the inclinations and the wants founded on them did not exist, then their object would be without value. But the inclinations, themselves being sources of want, are so far from having an absolute worth for which they should be desired that on the contrary it must be the universal wish of every rational being to be wholly free from them. Thus the worth of any object which is *to be acquired* by our action is always conditional. Beings whose existence depends not on our will but on nature's, have nevertheless, if they are irrational beings, only a relative value as means, and are therefore called *things*; rational beings, on the contrary, are called *persons*, because their very nature points them out as ends in themselves, that is as something which must not be used merely as means, and so far therefore restricts freedom of action (and is an object of respect). These, therefore, are not merely subjective ends whose existence has a worth *for us* as an effect of our action, but *objective ends*, that is, things whose existence is an end in itself; an end moreover for which no other can be substituted, which they should subserve *merely* as means, for otherwise nothing whatever would possess *absolute worth*; but if all worth were conditioned and therefore contingent, then there would be no supreme practical principle of reason whatever.

If then there is a supreme practical principle or, in respect of the human will, a categorical imperative, it must be one which, being drawn from the conception of that which is necessarily an end for everyone because it is *an end in itself*, constitutes an *objective* principle of will, and can therefore serve as a universal practical law. The foundation of this principle is: rational nature exists as an end in itself. Man necessarily conceives his own existence as being so; so far then this is a *subjective* principle of human actions. But every other rational being regards its existence similarly, just on the same rational principle that holds for me: so that it is at the same time an objective principle, from which as a supreme practical law all laws of the will must be capable of being deduced. Accordingly the practical imperative will be as follows: *So act as to treat humanity, whether in your own person or in that of any other, in every case as an end withal, never as means only.* . . .

READING 2

Georg Wilhelm Friedrich Hegel: Lordship-Bondage and World History

From *Phenomenology of Spirit* and *The Philosophy of Right*

Born in Stuttgard, Germany, Georg Wilhelm Friedrich Hegel (1770–1831) was the foremost philosopher in the nineteenth-century school of German idealism. Below are the two most famous portions of his writings. In the first, titled "Lordship and Bondage" from his Phenomenology of Spirit *(1807), Hegel describes how individual consciousness develops into universal self-consciousness. Individual consciousness first emerges when it is recognized by another self. When this happens, the first consciousness is inclined to assert its own existence over that of the second self—even to the point of annihilating it. It cannot do that, though, since its very existence as an individual consciousness depends upon being recognized by the second self. So it does the next best thing, which is to enslave the second self. But this master-slave (or lordship-bondage) relationship is also unsatisfactory. For, the first self needs to be recognized as free, but this cannot happen as long as the first self does not recognize the enslaved second self as a real person. By lacking freedom, the first self thereby lacks an essential condition of self-consciousness and personhood. In the meantime, the second self turns itself into a material thing by engaging in the material world. The tension between the two selves develops to the point that they exist in the same self, and the tension resolves only when that self ascends to universal self-consciousness. In the second selection, titled "World History" from* The Philosophy of Right *(1821), Hegel describes how the universal mind develops over time through actions of individuals, collections of people, and governments. He notes four specific periods of historic development: Oriental, Greek, Roman, and Germanic. In the earlier ones, individuals have no self-consciousness of personality, and, in the last one, the modern nation-state becomes self-conscious of its own nature.*

LORDSHIP AND BONDAGE

Self-consciousness exists in itself and for itself, in that, and by the fact that it exists for another self-consciousness; that is to say, it is only by being acknowledged or "recognized." The conception of this its unity in its duplication, of infinitude realizing itself in self-consciousness, has many sides to it and encloses within it elements of varied significance. Thus its moments must on the one hand be strictly kept apart in detailed distinctiveness, and, on the other, in this distinction must, at the same time, also be taken as not distinguished, or must always be accepted and understood in their opposite sense. This double meaning of what is distinguished lies in the nature of self-consciousness:—of its being infinite, or directly the opposite of the determinateness in which it is

Source: Georg Wilhelm Friedrich Hegel, *Phenomenology of Spirit* (1807), B.4.A, tr. J. B. Baillie, and *The Philosophy of Right* (1821), 341–360, tr. Samuel Walters Dyde.

fixed. The detailed exposition of the notion of this spiritual unity in its duplication will bring before us the process of Recognition.

Self-consciousness has before it another self-consciousness; it has come outside itself. This has a double significance. First it has lost its own self, since it finds itself as an other being; secondly, it has thereby sublated that other, for it does not regard the other as essentially real, but sees its own self in the other.

It must cancel this its other. To do so is the sublation of that first double meaning, and is therefore a second double meaning. First, it must set itself to sublate the other independent being, in order thereby to become certain of itself as true being, secondly, it thereupon proceeds to sublate its own self, for this other is itself.

This sublation in a double sense of its otherness in a double sense is at the same time a return in a double sense into its self. For, firstly, through sublation, it gets back itself, because it becomes one with itself again through the cancelling of its otherness; but secondly, it likewise gives otherness back again to the other self-consciousness, for it was aware of being in the other, it cancels this its own being in the other and thus lets the other again go free.

This process of self-consciousness in relation to another self-consciousness has in this manner been represented as the action of one alone. But this action on the part of the one has itself the double significance of being at once its own action and the action of that other as well. For the other is likewise independent, shut up within itself, and there is nothing in it which is not there through itself. The first does not have the object before it only in the passive form characteristic primarily of the object of desire, but as an object existing independently for itself, over which therefore it has no power to do anything for its own behalf, if that object does not per se do what the first does to it. The process then is absolutely the double process of both self-consciousnesses. Each sees the other do the same as itself; each itself does what it demands on the part of the other, and for that reason does what it does, only so far as the other does the same. Action from one side only would be useless, because what is to happen can only be brought about by means of both.

The action has then a double entente not only in the sense that it is an act done to itself as well as to the other, but also in the sense that the act simpliciter is the act of the one as well as of the other regardless of their distinction.

In this movement we see the process repeated which came before us as the play of forces; in the present case, however, it is found in consciousness. What in the former had effect only for us [contemplating experience], holds here for the terms themselves. The middle term is self-consciousness which breaks itself up into the extremes; and each extreme is this interchange of its own determinateness, and complete transition into the opposite. While qua consciousness, it no doubt comes outside itself, still, in being outside itself, it is at the same time restrained within itself, it exists for itself, and its self-externalization is for consciousness. Consciousness finds that it immediately is and is not another consciousness, as also that this other is for itself only when it cancels itself as existing for itself, and has self-existence only in the self-existence of the other. Each is the mediating term to the other, through which each mediates and unites itself with itself; and each is to itself and to the other an immediate self existing reality, which, at the same time, exists thus for itself only through this mediation. They recognize themselves as mutually recognizing one another.

This pure conception of recognition, of duplication of self-consciousness within its unity, we must now consider in the way its process appears for self-consciousness. It will, in the first place, present the aspect of the disparity of the two, or the break-up of the middle term into the extremes, which, qua extremes, are opposed to one another, and of which one is merely recognized, while the other only recognizes.

Self-consciousness is primarily simple existence for self, self-identity by exclusion of every other from itself. It takes its essential nature and absolute object to be Ego; and in this immediacy, in this bare fact of its self-existence, it is individual. That which for it is other stands as unessential object, as object with the impress and character of negation. But the other is also a self-consciousness; an individual makes its appearance in antithesis to an individual. Appearing thus in their immediacy, they are for each other in the manner of ordinary objects. They are independent individual forms, modes of Consciousness that have not risen above the bare level of life (for the existent object here has been determined as life). They are, moreover, forms of consciousness which have not yet accomplished for one another the process of absolute abstraction, of uprooting all immediate existence, and of being merely the bare, negative fact of self-identical consciousness; or, in other words, have not yet revealed themselves to each other as existing purely for themselves, i.e., as self-consciousness. Each is indeed certain of its own self, but not of the other, and hence its own certainty of itself is still without truth. For its truth would be merely that its own individual existence for itself would be shown to it to be an independent object, or, which is the same thing, that the object would be exhibited as this pure certainty of itself. By the notion of recognition, however, this is not possible, except in the form that as the other is for it, so it is for the other; each in its self through its own action and again through the action of the other achieves this pure abstraction of existence for self.

The presentation of itself, however, as pure abstraction of self-consciousness consists in showing itself as a pure negation of its objective form, or in showing that it is fettered to no determinate existence, that it is not bound at all by the particularity everywhere characteristic of existence as such, and is not tied up with life. The process of bringing all this out involves a twofold action—action on the part of the other and action on the part of itself. In so far as it is the other's action, each aims at the destruction and death of the other. But in this there is implicated also the second kind of action, self-activity; for the former implies that it risks its own life. The relation of both self-consciousnesses is in this way so constituted that they prove themselves and each other through a life-and-death struggle. They must enter into this struggle, for they must bring their certainty of themselves, the certainty of being for themselves, to the level of objective truth, and make this a fact both in the case of the other and in their own case as well. And it is solely by risking life that freedom is obtained; only thus is it tried and proved that the essential nature of self-consciousness is not bare existence, is not the merely immediate form in which it at first makes its appearance, is not its mere absorption in the expanse of life. Rather it is thereby guaranteed that there is nothing present but what might be taken as a vanishing moment—that self-consciousness is merely pure self-existence, being-for-self. The individual, who has not staked his life, may, no doubt, be recognized as a Person; but he has not attained the truth of this recognition as an independent self-consciousness. In the same way each must aim at the death of the other, as it risks its own life thereby; for that other is to it of no more worth than itself the other's reality is presented to the former as an external other, as outside itself; it must cancel that externality. The other is a purely existent consciousness and entangled in manifold ways; it must view its otherness as pure existence for itself or as absolute negation.

This trial by death, however, cancels both the truth which was to result from it, and therewith the certainty of self altogether. For just as life is the natural "position" consciousness, independence without absolute negativity, so death is the natural "negation" of consciousness, negation without independence, which thus remains without the requisite significance of actual recognition. Through death, doubtless, there has arisen the certainty that both did stake their life, and held it lightly both in their own case and in the case of the other; but that is not for those who underwent this struggle. They cancel their consciousness which had its place in this alien element of natural existence; in other words, they cancel themselves and are sublated as terms or extremes seeking to have existence on their own account. But along with this there vanishes from the play of change the essential moment, viz., that of breaking up into extremes with opposite characteristics; and the middle term collapses into a lifeless unity which is broken up into lifeless extremes, merely existent and not opposed. And the two do not mutually give and receive one another back from each other through consciousness; they let one another go quite indifferently, like things. Their act is abstract negation, not the negation characteristic of consciousness, which cancels in such a way that it preserves and maintains what is sublated, and thereby survives its being sublated.

In this experience self-consciousness becomes aware that life is as essential to it as pure self-consciousness. In immediate self-consciousness the simple ego is absolute object, which, however, is for us or in itself absolute mediation, and has as its essential moment substantial and solid independence. The dissolution of that simple unity is the result of the first experience; through this there is posited a pure self-consciousness, and a consciousness which is not purely for itself, but for another, i.e., as an existent consciousness, consciousness in the form and shape of thinghood. Both moments are essential, since, in the first instance, they are unlike and opposed, and their reflection into unity has not yet come to light, they stand as two opposed forms or modes of consciousness. The one is independent, and its essential nature is to be for itself; the other is dependent, and its essence is life or existence for another. The former is the Master, or Lord, the latter the Bondsman.

The master is the consciousness that exists for itself; but no longer merely the general notion of existence for self. Rather, it is a consciousness existing on its own account which is mediated with itself through an other consciousness, i.e., through an other whose very nature implies that it is bound up with an independent being or with thinghood in general. The master brings himself into relation to both these moments, to a thing as such, the object of desire, and to the consciousness whose essential character is thinghood. And since the master, is (a) qua notion of self-consciousness, an immediate relation of self-existence, but (b) is now moreover at the same time mediation, or a being-for-self which is for itself only through an other—he [the master] stands in relation (a) immediately to both (b) mediately to each through the other. The master relates himself to the bondsman mediately through independent existence, for that is precisely what keeps the bondsman in thrall; it is his chain, from which he could not in the struggle get away, and for that reason lie proved himself to be dependent, to have his independence in the shape of thinghood. The master, however, is the power controlling this state of existence, for he has shown in the struggle that lie holds it to be merely something negative. Since he is the power dominating existence, while this existence again is the power controlling the other [the bondsman], the master holds, par consequence, this other in subordination. In the same way the master relates himself to the thing mediately through the bondsman. The bondsman being a self-consciousness in the broad sense, also takes up a negative attitude to things and cancels them; but the thing is, at the same time, independent for him and, in consequence, he cannot, with all his negating, get so far as to annihilate it outright and be done with it; that is to say, lie merely works on it. To the master, on the other hand, by means of this mediating process, belongs the immediate relation, in the sense of the pure negation of it, in other words he gets the enjoyment. What mere desire did not attain, he now succeeds in attaining, viz., to have done with the thing, and find satisfaction in enjoyment. Desire alone did not get the length of this, because of the independence of the thing. The master, however, who has interposed the bondsman between it and himself, thereby relates himself merely to tile dependence of the thing, and enjoys it without qualification and without reserve. The aspect of its independence he leaves to the bondsman, who labors upon it.

In these two moments, the master gets his recognition through an other consciousness, for in them the latter affirms itself as unessential, both by working upon the thing, and, on the other hand, by the fact of being dependent on a determinate existence; in neither case can this other get the mastery over existence, and succeed in absolutely negating it. We have thus here this moment of recognition, viz., that the other consciousness cancels itself as self-existent, and, ipso facto, itself does what the first does to it. In the same way we have the other moment, that this action on the part of the second is the action proper of the first; for what is done by the bondsman is properly an action on the part of the master. The latter exists only for himself, that is his essential nature; he is the negative power without qualification, a power to which the thing is naught. And he is thus the absolutely essential act in this situation, while the bondsman is not so, he is an unessential activity. But for recognition proper there is needed the moment that what the master does to the other he should also do to himself, and what the bondsman does to himself, he should do to the other also. On that account a form of recognition has arisen that is one sided and unequal.

In all this, the unessential consciousness is, for the master, the object which embodies the truth of his certainty of himself. But it is evident that this object does not correspond to its notion; for, just where the master has effectively achieved lordship, he really finds that something has come about quite different from an independent consciousness. It is not an independent, but rather a dependent consciousness that he has achieved. He is thus not assured of self-existence as his truth; he finds that his truth is rather the unessential consciousness, and the fortuitous unessential action of that consciousness.

The truth of the independent consciousness is accordingly the consciousness of the bondsman. This doubtless appears in the first instance outside itself, and not as the truth of self-consciousness. But just as lordship showed its essential nature to be the reverse of what it wants to be, so, too, bondage will, when completed, pass into the opposite of what it immediately is: being a consciousness repressed within itself, it will enter into itself, and change round into real and true independence.

We have seen what bondage is only in relation to lordship. But it is a self-consciousness, and we have now to consider what it is, in this regard, in and for itself. In the first instance, the master is taken to be the essential reality for the state of bondage; hence, for it, the truth is the independent consciousness existing for itself, although this truth is not taken yet as inherent in bondage itself. Still, it does in fact contain within itself this truth of pure negativity and self-existence, because it has experienced this reality within it. For this consciousness was not in peril and fear for this element or that, nor for this or that moment of time, it was afraid for its entire being; it felt the fear of death, the sovereign master. It has been in that experience melted to its inmost soul, has trembled throughout its every fiber, and all that was fixed and steadfast has quaked within it. This complete perturbation of its entire substance, this absolute dissolution of all its stability into fluent continuity, is, however, the simple, ultimate nature of self-consciousness, absolute negativity, pure self-referent existence, which consequently is involved in this type of consciousness. This moment of pure self-existence is moreover a fact for it; for in the master it finds this as its object. Further, this bondsman's consciousness is not only this total dissolution in a general way; in serving and toiling the bondsman actually carries this out. By serving he cancels in every particular aspect his dependence on and attachment to natural existence, and by his work removes this existence away.

The feeling of absolute power, however, realized both in general and in the particular form of service, is only dissolution implicitly; and albeit the fear of the lord is the beginning of wisdom, consciousness is not therein aware of being self-existent. Through work and labor, however, this consciousness of the bondsman comes to itself. In the moment which corresponds to desire in the case of the master's consciousness, the aspect of the non-essential relation to the thing seemed to fall to the lot of the servant, since the thing there retained its independence. Desire has reserved to itself the pure negating of the object and thereby unalloyed feeling of self. This satisfaction, however, just for that reason is itself only a state of evanescence, for it lacks objectivity or subsistence. Labor, on the other hand, is desire restrained and checked, evanescence delayed and postponed; in other words, labor shapes and fashions the thing. The negative relation to the object passes into the form of the object, into something that is permanent and remains; because it is just for the laborer that the object has independence. This negative mediating agency, this activity giving shape and form, is at the same time the individual existence, the pure self-existence of that consciousness, which now in the work it does is externalized and passes into the condition of permanence. The consciousness that toils and serves accordingly attains by this means the direct apprehension of that independent being as its self.

But again, shaping or forming the object has not only the positive significance that the bondsman becomes thereby aware of himself as factually and objectively self-existent; this type of consciousness has also a negative import, in contrast with its moment, the element of fear. For in shaping the thing it only becomes aware of its own proper negativity, existence on its own account, as an object, through the fact that it cancels the actual form confronting it. But this objective negative element is precisely alien, external reality, before which it trembled. Now, however, it destroys this extraneous alien negative, affirms and sets itself up as a negative in the element of permanence, and thereby becomes for itself a self-existent being. In the master, the bondsman feels self-existence to be something external, an objective fact; in fear self-existence is present within himself; in fashioning the thing, self-existence comes to be felt explicitly as his own proper being, and he attains the consciousness that he himself exists in its own right and on its own account. By the fact that the form is objectified, it does not become something other than the consciousness molding the thing through work; for just that form is his pure self existence, which therein becomes truly realized. Thus precisely in labor where there seemed to be merely some outsider's mind and ideas involved, the bondsman becomes aware, through this rediscovery of himself by himself, of having and being a "mind of his own."

For this reflection of self into self the two moments, fear and service in general, as also that of formative activity, are necessary: and at the same time both must exist in a universal manner. Without the discipline of service and obedience, fear remains formal and does not spread over the whole known reality of existence. Without the formative activity shaping the thing, fear remains inward and mute, and consciousness does not become objective for itself. Should consciousness shape and form the thing without the initial state of absolute fear, then it has a merely vain and futile "mind of its own"; for its form or negativity is not negativity per se, and hence its formative activity cannot furnish the consciousness of itself as essentially real. If it has endured not absolute fear, but merely some slight anxiety, the negative reality has remained external to it, its substance has not been through and through infected thereby. Since the entire content of its natural consciousness has not tottered and shaken, it is still inherently a determinate mode of being; having a "mind of its own" is simply stubbornness, a type of freedom which does not get beyond the attitude of bondage. As little as the pure form can become its essential nature, so little is that form, considered as extending over particulars, a universal formative activity, an absolute notion; it is rather a piece of cleverness which has mastery within a certain range, but not over the universal power nor over the entire objective reality.

WORLD HISTORY

341. World history is a court of judgment. The universal spirit exists concretely in art in the form of perception and image, in religion in the form of feeling and pictorial imaginative thinking, and in philosophy in the form of pure free thought. In world-history this concrete existence of spirit is the spiritual actuality in the total range of its internality and externality. It is a court of judgment because in its absolute universality the particular, namely, the Penates, the civic community, and the national spirit in their many-colored reality are all merely ideal. The movement of spirit in this case consists in visibly presenting these spheres as merely ideal.

342. World history is not the verdict of mere might, but actualization of the universal mind. Moreover, world-history is not a court of judgment, whose principle is force, nor is it the abstract and irrational necessity of a blind fate. It is self-caused and self-realized reason, and its actualized existence in spirit is knowledge. Hence, its development issuing solely out of the conception of its freedom is a necessary development of the elements of reason. It is, therefore, an unfolding of the spirit's self-consciousness and freedom. It is the exhibition and actualization of the universal spirit.

343. The history of mind is its own act. The history of spirit is its overt deeds, for only what it does it is, and its deed is to make itself as a spirit the object of its consciousness, to explain and lay hold upon itself by reference to itself. To lay hold upon itself is its being and principle, and the completion of this act is at the same time self-renunciation and transition. To express the matter formally, the spirit which again apprehends what has already been grasped and actualized, or, what is the same thing, passes through self-renunciation into itself, is the spirit of a higher stage.

Note: Here occurs the question of the perfection and education of humanity. They who have argued in favor of this idea, have surmised something of the nature of spirit. They have understood that spirit has "known itself" as a law of its being, and that when it lays hold upon what it itself is, it assumes a higher form. To those who have rejected this idea, spirit has remained an empty word and history a superficial play of accidental and so-called mere human strife and passion. Though in their use of the words "providence" and "design of providence," they express their belief in a higher control, they do not fill up the notion, but announce that the design of providence is for them unknowable and inconceivable.

344. States, nations, and individuals are all the time the unconscious tools of the world mind at work within them. States, peoples, and individuals are established upon their own particular definite principle, which has systematized reality in their constitutions and in the entire compass of their surroundings. Of this systematized reality they are aware, and in its interests are absorbed. Yet are they the unconscious tools and organs of the world-spirit, through whose inner activity the lower forms pass away. Thus the spirit by its own motion and for its own end makes ready and works out the transition into its next higher stage.

345. Each stage of world-history is a necessary moment in the Idea of the world mind.   Justice and virtue, wrong, force, and crime, talents and their results, small and great passions, innocence and guilt, the splendor of individuals, national life, independence, the fortune and misfortune of states and individuals, have in the sphere of conscious reality their definite meaning and value, and find in that sphere judgment and their due. This due is, however, as yet incomplete. In world-history, which lies beyond this range of vision, the idea of the world-spirit, in that necessary phase of it which constitutes at any time its actual stage, is given its absolute right. The nation, then really flourishing, attains to happiness and renown, and its deeds receive completion.

346. History is mind clothing itself with the form of events.   Since history is the embodiment of spirit in the form of events, that is, of direct natural reality, the stages of development are present as direct natural principles. Because they are natural, they conform to the nature of a multiplicity, and exist one outside the other. Hence, to each nation is to be ascribed a single principle, comprised under its geographical and anthropological existence.

347. The nation ascribed a moment of the Idea is entrusted with giving complete effect to it.   To the nation, whose natural principle is one of these stages, is assigned the accomplishment of it through the process characteristic of the self-developing self-consciousness of the world-spirit. In the history of the world this nation is for a given epoch dominant, although it can make an epoch but once (§ 346). In contrast with the absolute right of this nation to be the bearer of the current phase in the development of the world-spirit, the spirits of other existing nations are void of right, and they, like those 'whose epochs are gone, count no longer in the history of the world.

Note: The special history of a world-historic nation contains the unfolding of its principle from its undeveloped infancy up to the time when, in the full manhood of free ethical self-consciousness, it presses in upon universal history. It contains, moreover, the period of decline and destruction, the rise of a higher principle being marked in it simply as the negative of its own. Hence, the spirit passes over into that higher principle, and thus indicates to world-history another nation. From that time onward the first nation has lost absolute interest, absorbs the higher principle positively, it may be, and fashions itself in accordance with it, but is, after all, only a recipient, and has no indwelling vitality and freshness. Perhaps it loses its independence, perhaps continues to drag itself on as a particular state or circle of states, and spends itself in various random civil enterprises and foreign broils.

348. World-historical actions culminate with individuals as subjects—living instruments of the world mind.   At the summit of all actions, including world-historical actions, stand individuals. Each of these individuals is a subjectivity who realizes what is substantive (§ 279, note). He is a living embodiment of the substantive deed of the world-spirit, and is, therefore, directly identical with this deed. It is concealed even from himself, and is not his object and end (§ 344). Thus they do not receive honor and thanks for their acts either from their contemporaries (§ 344), or from the public opinion of posterity. By this opinion they are viewed merely as formal subjectivities, and, as such, are simply given their part in immortal fame.

349. The transition from a family, a horde, &c., to political conditions is the realization of the Idea as that nation.   A people is not as yet a state. The transition from the family, horde, clan, or multitude into a state constitutes the formal realization in it of the idea. If the ethical substance, which every people has implicitly, lacks this form, it is without that objectivity which comes from laws and thought-out regulations. It has neither for itself nor for others any universal or generally admitted reality. It will not be recognized. Its independence, being devoid of objective law or secure realized rationality, is formal only and not a sovereignty.

Note: From the ordinary point of view we do not call the patriarchal condition a constitution, or a people in this condition a state, or its independence sovereignty. Before the beginning of actual history there are found uninteresting stupid innocence and the bravery arising out of the formal struggle for recognition and out of revenge (§§ 331, 57, note).

350. The right of heroes to found states.   It is the absolute right of the idea to come visibly forth, and proceeding from marriage and agriculture (§ 203, note) realize itself in laws and objective institutions. This is true whether its realization appears in the form of divine law and beneficence or in the form of force and wrong. This right is the right of heroes to found states.

351. Civilized nations are justified in regarding as barbarians those who lag behind them in institutions.   In the same way civilized nations may treat as barbarians the peoples who are behind them in the essential elements of the state. Thus, the rights of mere herdsmen, hunters, and tillers of the soil are inferior, and their independence is merely formal.

Note: Wars and contests arising under such circumstances are struggles for recognition in behalf of a certain definite content. It is this feature of them which is significant in world-history.

352. Four world-historical realms.   The concrete ideas, which embody the national minds or spirits, has its truth in the concrete idea in its absolute universality. This is the spirit of the world, around whose throne stand the other spirits as perfecters of its actuality, and witnesses and ornaments of its splendor. Since it is, as spirit, only the movement of its activity in order to know itself absolutely, to free its consciousness from mere direct naturalness, and to come to itself, the principles of the different forms of its self-consciousness, as they appear in the process of liberation, are four. They are the principles of the four world-historic kingdoms.

353. The substantive spirit, ethical individuality as beauty, mind-forsaken and actual laws.   In its first and direct revelation the world-spirit has as its principle the form of the substantive spirit, in whose identity individuality is in its essence submerged and without explicit justification.

In the second principle the substantive spirit is aware of itself. Here spirit is the positive content and filling, and is also at the same time the living form, which is in its nature self-referred.

The third principle is the retreat into itself of this conscious self-referred existence. There thus arises an abstract universality, and with it an infinite opposition to objectivity, which is regarded as deprived of spirit.

In the fourth principle this opposition of the spirit is overturned in order that spirit may receive into its inner self its truth and concrete essence. It thus becomes at home with objectivity, and the two are reconciled. Because the spirit has come back to its formal substantive reality by returning out of this infinite opposition, it seeks to produce and know its truth as thought, and as a world of established reality.

354. Four World-Historic empires.   In accordance with these four principles the four world-historic empires are (1) the Oriental, (2) the Greek, (3) the Roman, and (4) the Germanic.

355. The Oriental Empire.   (1) The Oriental Empire:—The first empire is the substantive world-intuition, which proceeds from the natural whole of patriarchal times. It has no internal divisions. Its worldly government is theocracy, its ruler a high priest or God, its constitution and legislation are at the same time its religion, and its civic and legal regulations are religious and moral commands or usages. In the splendor of this totality the individual personality sinks without rights; external nature is directly divine or an ornament of God, and the history of reality is poetry. The distinctions, which develop themselves in customs, government, and the state, serve instead of laws, being converted by mere social usage into clumsy, diffuse, and superstitious ceremonies, the accidents of personal power and arbitrary rule. The division into classes becomes a caste fixed as the laws of nature. Since in the Oriental empire there is nothing stable, or rather what is firm is petrified, it has life only in a movement, which goes on from the outside, and becomes an elemental violence and desolation. Internal repose is merely a private life, which is sunk in feebleness and lassitude.

Note: The element of substantive natural spirituality is present in the first forming of every state, and constitutes the absolute starting-point of its history. This assertion is presented and historically established by Dr. Stuhr in his well-reasoned and scholarly treatise "Vom Untergange der Naturstaaten" (Berlin, 1812), who, moreover, suggests in this work a rational method of viewing constitutional history and history in general. The principle of subjectivity and self-conscious freedom he ascribes to the German nation. But since the treatise is wholly taken up with the decline of the nature-states, it simply leads to the point at which this modern principle makes its appearance. At that time it assumed in part the guise of restless movement, human caprice, and corruption, in part the particular guise of feeling, not having as yet developed itself into the objectivity of self-conscious substantivity or the condition of organized law.

356. The Greek Empire.   (2) The Greek Empire:—This empire still contains the earlier substantive unity of the finite and infinite, but only as a mysterious background, suppressed and kept down in gloomy reminiscence, in caves and in traditional imagery. This background under the influence of the self-distinguishing spirit is recreated into individual spirituality, and exalted into the daylight of consciousness, where it is tempered and clarified into beauty and a free and cheerful ethical life. Here arises the principle of personal individuality, although it is not as yet self-centered, but held in its ideal unity. One result of this incompleteness is that the whole is broken up into a number of particular national minds or spirits. Further, the final decision of will is not as yet entrusted to the subjectivity of the independent self-consciousness, but resides in a power, which is higher than, and lies beyond it (§ 279, note). Moreover, the particularity, which is found in wants, is not yet taken up into freedom, but segregated in a class of slaves.

357. The Roman Empire.   (3) The Roman Empire:—In this empire the distinctions of spirit are carried to the length of an infinite rupture of the ethical life into two extremes, personal private self-consciousness, and abstract universality. The antagonism, arising between the substantive intuition of an aristocracy and the principle of free personality in democratic form, developed on the side of the aristocracy into superstition and the retention of cold self-seeking power, and on the side of the democracy into the corrupt mass. The dissolution of the whole culminates in universal misfortune, ethical life dies, national individualities, having merely the bond of union of a Pantheon, perish, and individuals are degraded to the level of that equality, in which they are merely private persons and have only formal rights.

358. The German Empire.   (4) The German Empire:—Owing to the loss of itself and its world, and to the infinite pain caused by it, a loss of which the Jewish people were already held to be the type, spirit is pressed back into itself, and finds itself in the extreme of absolute negativity. But this extreme is the absolute turning-point, and in it spirit finds the infinite and yet positive nature of its own inner being. This new discovery is the unity of the divine and the human. By means of it objective truth is reconciled with freedom, and that, too, inside of self-consciousness and subjectivity. This new basis, infinite and yet positive, it has been charged upon the northern principle of the Germanic nations to bring to completion.

359. The power of mind over the ordinary heart acts against the heart as a compulsive and frightful force.   The internal aspect of this northern principle exists in feeling as faith, love, and hope. Although it is in this form still abstract, it is the reconciliation and solution of all contradiction. It proceeds to unfold its content in order to raise it to reality and self-conscious rationality. It thus constructs a kingdom of this world, based upon the feeling, trust, and fellowship of free men. This kingdom in this its subjectivity is an actual kingdom of rude caprice and barbarism in contrast with the world beyond. It is an intellectual empire, whose content is indeed the truth of its spirit. But as it is yet not thought out, and still is veiled in the barbarism of picture-thinking, it exists as a spiritual force, which exercises over the actual mind a despotic and tyrannical influence.

360. The realm of mind lowers itself to an earthly here and now and the ordinary realm builds up into thought.   These kingdoms are based upon the distinction, which has now won the form of absolute antagonism, and yet at the same time are rooted in a single unity and idea. In the obdurate struggle, which thus ensues, the spiritual has to lower its heaven to the level of an earthly and temporal condition, to common worldliness, and to ordinary life and thought. On the other hand the abstract actuality of the worldly is exalted to thought, to the principle of rational being and knowing, and to the rationality of right and law. As a result of these two tendencies, the contradiction has become a marrowless phantasm. The present has stripped off its barbarism and its lawless caprice, and truth has stripped off its beyond and its casualness. The true atonement and reconciliation has become objective, and unfolds the state as the image and reality of reason. In the state, self-consciousness finds the organic development of its real substantive knowing and will, in religion it finds in the form of ideal essence the feeling and the vision of this its truth, and in science it finds the free conceived knowledge of this truth, seeing it to be one and the same in all its mutually completing manifestations, namely, the state, nature, and the ideal world.

READING 3
———

Søren Kierkegaard: Faith and Paradox
From *Fear and Trembling*

Born in Copenhagen, Søren Kierkegaard (1813–1855) was Denmark's most influential philosopher. Reacting against the overly abstract and formal philosophical system of Hegel, Kierkegaard instead emphasized more practical concerns of individual choice and faith commitment. In the selection below, from his work Fear and Trembling *(1843), he uses the Old Testament story of Abraham and Isaac as a way to show the difficulty of acting on the basis of faith. In the story, God commands Abraham to sacrifice Isaac his son, and, in an act of faith, Abraham prepares to do so, and nearly succeeds, until at the last moment God calls it off. For Kierkegaard, Abraham was justified in abandoning*

Source: Søren Kierkegaard, *Fear and Trembling* (1843), tr. L.M. Hollander.

his ordinary ethical duty in response to God's command, but the choice was one of intense anguish. Further, Abraham's only ground for doing so was his faith, which, considering what was at stake, produced fear and trembling.

PREPARATION

There lived a man who, when a child, had heard the beautiful Bible story of how God tempted Abraham and how he stood the test, how he maintained his faith and, against his expectations, received his son back again. As this man grew older he read this same story with ever greater admiration. For now life had separated what had been united in the reverent simplicity of the child. And the older he grew, the more frequently his thoughts returned to that story. His enthusiasm intensified more and more, and yet the story grew less and less clear to him. Finally he forgot everything else in thinking about it, and his soul contained but one wish, which was, to behold Abraham: and but one longing, which was, to have been witness to that event. His desire was, not to see the beautiful lands of the Orient, and not the splendor of the Promised Land, and not the reverent couple whose old age the Lord had blessed with children, and not the venerable figure of the aged patriarch, and not the god-given vigorous youth of Isaac; it would have been the same to him if the event had come to pass on some barren heath. But his wish was, to have been with Abraham on the three days' journey, when he rode with sorrow before him and with Isaac at his side. His wish was, to have been present at the moment when Abraham lifted up his eyes and saw Mount Moriah afar off; to have been present at the moment when he left his donkeys behind and wended his way up to the mountain alone with Isaac. For the mind of this man was busy, not with the delicate and fanciful thoughts of the imagination, but rather with his shuddering thought.

The man we speak of was no thinker, he felt no desire to go beyond his faith. it seemed to him the most glorious fate to be remembered as the Father of Faith, and a most enviable lot to be possessed of that faith, even if no one knew it.

The man we speak of was no learned theologian, he did not even understand Hebrew—who knows but a knowledge of Hebrew might have helped him to understand readily both the story and Abraham.

The Story of Abraham

And God tempted Abraham and said to him: take Isaac, your only son, whom you love and go to the land Moriah and sacrifice him there on a mountain which I shall show you.

It was in the early morning, Abraham arose and had his donkeys saddled. He departed from his tent, and Isaac with him; but Sarah looked out of the window after them until they were out of sight. Silently they rode for three days; but on the fourth morning Abraham did not say a word, but lifted up his eyes and beheld Mount Moriah in the distance. He left his servants behind and, leading Isaac by the hand, he approached the mountain. But Abraham said to himself: "I shall surely conceal from Isaac where he is going." He stood still, he laid his hand on Isaac's head to bless him, and Isaac bowed down to receive his blessing. Abraham's appearance was fatherly, his glance was mild, his speech admonishing. But Isaac did not understand him, his soul would not rise to him; he embraced Abraham's knees, he begged him at his feet, he begged for his young life, for his beautiful hopes, he recalled the joy in Abraham's house when he was born, he reminded him of the sorrow and the loneliness that would be after him. Then Abraham raised up the youth and led him by his hand, and his words were full of consolation and admonishment. But Isaac did not understand him. He ascended Mount Moriah, but Isaac did not understand him. Abraham then hid his face for a moment. But when Isaac looked again, his father's expression was changed, his glance wild, his aspect terrible, he seized Isaac and threw him to the ground and said: "You foolish boy, do you believe I am your father? An idol-worshipper am I. Do you believe it is God's command? No, it is but my pleasure." Then Isaac trembled and cried out in his fear: "God in heaven, have pity on me, God of Abraham, show mercy to me, I have no father on earth, be you then my father!" But Abraham said softly to himself: "Father in heaven, I thank you. Better is it that he believes that I am inhuman than that he should lose his faith in you.". . .

PRELIMINARY EXPECTORATION

Different Ways of Understanding Abraham's Story

An old saying, derived from the world of experience, has it that "he who will not work shall not eat." But, strange to say, this does not hold true in the world where it is thought applicable. For in the world of matter the law of imperfection prevails, and we see, again and again, that he also who will not work has bread to eat—indeed, that he who sleeps has a greater abundance of it than he who works. In the world of matter everything belongs to whosoever happens to possess it. It is slave to the law of indifference, and he who happens to possess the Ring also has the Spirit of the Ring at his beck and call, whether now he be Noureddin or Aladdin, and he who controls the treasures of this world, controls them, howsoever he managed to do so. It is different in the world of spirit. There, an eternal and divine order obtains, there the rain does not fall on the just and the unjust alike, nor does the sun shine on the good and the evil alike. But there the saying does hold true that he who will not work shall not eat, and only he who was troubled shall find rest, and only he who descends into the nether world shall rescue his beloved, and only he who unsheathes his knife shall be given Isaac again. There, he who will not work shall not eat, but shall be deceived, as the gods deceived Orpheus with an immaterial figure instead of his beloved Euridice, deceived him because he was love-sick and not courageous, deceived him because he was a player on the cithara rather than a man. There, it is of no use to have an Abraham for one's father, or to have seventeen ancestors. But in that world the saying about Israel's maidens will hold true of him who will not work: he shall bring forth wind; but he who will work shall give birth to his own father.

There is a kind of learning which would presumptuously introduce into the world of spirit the same law of indifference under which the world of matter groans. It is thought that to know about great men and great deeds is quite sufficient, and that other exertion is not necessary. And therefore this learning shall not eat, but shall perish of hunger while seeing all things transformed into gold by its touch. And what, in fact, does this learning really know? There were many thousands of contemporaries, and countless men in after times, who knew all about the triumphs of Miltiades; but there was only one whom they made sleepless. There have existed countless generations that knew by heart, word for word, the story of Abraham; but how many has it made sleepless?

Now the story of Abraham has the remarkable property of always being glorious, in however limited a sense it is understood. Still, here also the point is whether one means to labor and exert oneself. Now people do not care to labor and exert themselves, but wish nevertheless to understand the story. They praise Abraham, but how? By expressing the matter in the most general terms and saying: "the great thing about him was that he loved God so passionately that he was willing to sacrifice to Him his most precious possession." That is very true; but "the most precious possession" is an indefinite expression. As one's thoughts, and one's mouth, run on one assumes, in a very easy fashion, the identity of Isaac and "the most precious possession"—and meanwhile he who is meditating may smoke his pipe, and his audience comfortably stretch out their legs. If the rich youth whom Christ met on his way had sold all his possessions and given all to the poor, we would praise him as we praise all which is great—aye, would not understand even him without labor; and yet would he never have become an Abraham, notwithstanding his sacrificing the most precious possessions he had. That which people generally forget in the story of Abraham is his fear and anxiety. For as regards money, one is not ethically responsible for it, whereas for his son a father has the highest and most sacred responsibility. However, fear is a dreadful thing for cowardly spirits, so they omit it. And yet they wish to speak of Abraham.

Example of a Man Who Emulates Abraham

So they keep on speaking, and in the course of their speech the two terms "Isaac" and "the most precious thing" are used alternately, and everything is in the best order. But now suppose that among the audience there was a man who suffered with sleeplessness; and then the most terrible and profound, the most tragic, and at the same time the most comic, misunderstanding is within the range of possibility. That is, suppose this man goes home and wishes to do as did Abraham; for his son is his most precious possession. If a certain preacher learned of this he would, perhaps, go to him, he would gather up all his spiritual dignity and exclaim: "You abominable creature, you scum of humanity, what devil possessed you to wish to murder your son?" And this preacher, who had not felt any particular warmth, nor perspired while speaking about Abraham, this preacher would be astonished himself at the earnest wrath with which he poured forth his thunders against that poor wretch; indeed, he would rejoice over himself, for never had he spoken with such power and unction, and he would have said to his wife: "I am a preacher, the only thing I have lacked so far was the occasion. Last Sunday, when speaking about Abraham, I did not feel thrilled in the least."

Now, if this same preacher had just a bit of sense to spare, I believe he would lose it if the sinner would reply, in a quiet and dignified manner: "Why, it was on this very same matter you preached, last Sunday!" But however could the preacher have entertained such thoughts? Still, such was the case, and the preacher's mistake was merely not knowing what he was talking about. Ah, would that some poet might see his way clear to prefer such a situation to the stuff and nonsense of which novels and comedies are full! For the comic and the tragic here run parallel to infinity. The sermon probably was ridiculous enough in itself, but it became infinitely ridiculous through the very natural consequence it had. Or, suppose now the sinner was converted by this lecture without daring to raise any objection, and this zealous divine now went home elated, glad in the consciousness of being effective, not only in the pulpit, but chiefly, and with irresistible power, as a spiritual guide, inspiring his congregation on Sunday, while on Monday he would place himself like a cherub with flaming sword before the man who by his actions tried to give the lie to the old saying that "the course of the world follows not the priest's word."

If, on the other hand, the sinner were not convinced of his error his position would become tragic. He would probably be executed, or else sent to the lunatic asylum—at any rate, he would become a sufferer in this world; but in another sense I should think that Abraham made him happy; for he who labors, he shall not perish.

Now how shall we explain the contradiction contained in that sermon? Is it due to Abraham's having the reputation of being a great man—so that whatever he does is great, but if another should undertake to do the same it is a sin, a heinous sin? If this is the case, I prefer not to participate in such thoughtless laudations. If faith cannot make it a sacred thing to wish to sacrifice one's son, then let the same judgment be visited on Abraham as on any other man. And if we possibly lack the courage to drive our thoughts to the logical conclusion and to say that Abraham was a murderer, then it were better to acquire that courage, rather than to waste one's time on undeserved praise. The fact is, the ethical expression for what Abraham did is that he wanted to murder Isaac. The religious expression is that he wanted to sacrifice him. But precisely in this contradiction is contained the fear which may well rob one of one's sleep. Yet Abraham were not Abraham without this fear. Or, again, supposing Abraham did not do what is attributed to him, if his action was an entirely different one, based on conditions of those times, then let us forget him; for what is the use of calling to mind that past which can no longer become a present reality?—Or, the speaker had perhaps forgotten the essential fact that Isaac was the son. For if faith is eliminated, having been reduced to a mere nothing, then only the brutal fact remains that Abraham wanted to murder Isaac—which is easy for everybody to imitate who has not the faith—the faith, that is, which renders it most difficult for him. . . .

The Absurdity of Faith

Love has its priests in the poets, and one hears at times a poet's voice which worthily praises it. But not a word does one hear of faith. Who is there to speak in honor of that passion? Philosophy "goes right on." Theology sits at the window with a painted appearance and sues for philosophy's favor, offering it her charms. It is said to be difficult to understand the philosophy of Hegel; but to understand Abraham, why, that is an easy matter! To proceed further than Hegel is a wonderful feat, but to proceed further than Abraham, why, nothing is easier! Personally, I have devoted a considerable amount of time to a study of Hegelian philosophy and believe I understand it fairly well; in fact, I am rash enough to say that when, notwithstanding an effort, I am not able to understand him in some passages, it is because he is not entirely clear about the matter himself. All this intellectual effort I perform easily and naturally, and it does not cause my head to ache. On the other hand, whenever I attempt to think about Abraham I am, as it were, overwhelmed. At every moment I am aware of the enormous paradox which forms the content of Abraham's life, at every moment I am repulsed, and my thought, notwithstanding its passionate attempts, cannot penetrate into it, cannot forge on the breadth of a hair. I strain every muscle in order to contemplate the problem—and become a paralytic in the same moment.

I am by no means unacquainted with what has been admired as great and noble. My soul feels kinship with it, being satisfied, in all humility, that it was also my that cause the hero espoused. And when contemplating his deed I say to myself: "your cause too is at stake." I am able to identify myself with the hero; but I cannot do so with Abraham, for whenever I have reached his height I fall down again, since he confronts me as the paradox. It is by no means my intention to maintain that faith is something inferior, but, on the contrary, that it is the highest of all things; also that it is dishonest in philosophy to offer something else instead, and to pour scorn on faith; but it ought to understand its own nature in order to know what it can offer. It should take away nothing; least of all, fool people out of something as if it were of no value. I am not unacquainted with the sufferings and dangers of life, but I do not fear them, and cheerfully go forth to meet them. . . . But my courage is not, for all that, the courage of faith, and is as nothing compared with it. I cannot carry out the movement of faith: I cannot close my eyes and confidently plunge into the absurd—it is impossible for me; but neither do I boast of it. . . .

Now I wonder if everyone of my contemporaries is really able to perform the movements of faith. Unless I am much mistaken they are, rather, inclined to be proud of making what they perhaps think me unable to do, namely, the imperfect movement. It is repugnant to my soul to do what is so often done, to speak inhumanly about great deeds, as if a few thousands of years were an immense space of time. I prefer to speak about them in a human way and as though they had been done but yesterday, to let the great deed itself be the distance which either inspires or condemns me. Now if I, in the capacity of tragic hero—for a higher flight I am unable to take—if I had been summoned to such an extraordinary royal progress as was the one to Mount Moriah, I know very well what I would have done. I would not have been cowardly enough to remain at home. Neither would I have dawdled on the way. Nor would I have forgot my knife—just to draw out the end a bit. But I am rather sure that I would have been promptly on the spot, with everything in order. In fact, I would probably have been there before the appointed time, so as to have the business soon over with. But I know also what I would have done besides. In the moment I mounted my horse I would have said to myself: "Now all is lost, God demands Isaac, I shall sacrifice him, and with him all my joy. But for all that, God is love and will remain so for me. For in this world God and I cannot speak together, we have no language in common."

The Infinite Resignation of Faith

Possibly, one or the other of my contemporaries will be stupid enough, and jealous enough of great deeds, to wish to persuade himself and me that if I had acted in this way I should have done something even greater than what Abraham did. For my sublime resignation was (he thinks) by far more ideal and poetic than Abraham's literal-minded action. And yet this is absolutely not so, for my sublime resignation was only a substitute for faith. I could not have made more than the infinite movement (of resignation) to find myself and again peace in myself. Nor would I have loved Isaac as Abraham loved him. The fact that I was resolute enough to resign is sufficient to prove my courage in a human sense, and the fact that I loved him with my whole heart is the very presupposition without which my action would be a crime; but still I did not love as did Abraham, for else I would have hesitated even in the last minute, without, for that matter, arriving too late on Mount Moriah. Also, I would have spoiled the whole business by my behavior; for if I had had Isaac restored to me I would have been embarrassed. That which was an easy matter for Abraham would have been difficult for me, I mean, to rejoice again in Isaac; for he who with all the energy of his soul "by his own impulse and on his own responsibility" has made the infinite movement of resignation and can do no more, he will retain possession of Isaac only in his sorrow.

But what did Abraham do? He arrived neither too early nor too late. He mounted his donkey and rode slowly on his way. All the while he had faith, believing that God would not demand Isaac of him, though ready all the while to sacrifice him, should it be demanded of him. He believed this on the strength of the absurd; for there was no question of human calculation any longer. And the absurdity consisted in God's, who yet made this demand of him, recalling his demand the very next moment. Abraham ascended the mountain and while the knife already gleamed in his hand he believed—that God would not demand Isaac of him. He was, to be sure, surprised at the outcome; but by a double movement he had returned at his first state of mind and therefore received Isaac back more gladly than the first time. . . .

On this height, then, stands Abraham. The last stage he loses sight of is that of infinite resignation. He does really proceed further, he arrives at faith. For consider all these caricatures of faith. Wretched lukewarm sloth thinks: "Oh, there is no hurry, it is not necessary to worry before the time comes." Miserable hopefulness says: "One cannot know what will happen, there might perhaps—" All these caricatures belong to the degraded view of life and have already fallen under the infinite scorn of infinite resignation.

I am not able to understand Abraham, and in a certain sense I can learn nothing from him without being struck with wonder. They who flatter themselves that by merely considering the outcome of Abraham's story they will necessarily arrive at faith, only deceive themselves and wish to cheat God out of the first movement of faith. It is equivalent to deriving worldly wisdom from the paradox. But who knows, one or the other of them may succeed in doing this. For our times are not satisfied with faith, and not even with the miracle of changing water into wine: they "go right on" changing wine into water.

Is it not preferable to remain satisfied with faith, and is it not outrageous that everyone wishes to "go right on"? If people in our times decline to be satisfied with love, as is proclaimed from various sides, where will we finally land? In worldly shrewdness, in mean calculation, in paltriness and baseness, in all that which makes man's divine origin doubtful. Were it not better to stand fast in the faith, and better that he that stands beware for fear that he fall. For the movement of faith must ever be made by virtue of the absurd, but, note well, in such wise that one does not lose the things of this world but wholly and entirely regains them.

Going through the Motions of Faith

As far as I am concerned, I am able to describe most excellently the movements of faith. But I cannot make them myself. When a person wishes to learn how to swim he has himself suspended in a swimming-belt and then goes through the motions; but that does not mean that he can swim. In the same fashion I too can go through the motions of faith; but when I am thrown into the water I swim; to be sure (for I am not a wader in the shallows), but I go through a different set of movements, to-wit, those of infinity; whereas faith does the opposite, namely, makes the movements to regain the finite after having made those of infinite resignation. Blessed is he who can make these movements, for he performs a marvelous feat, and I shall never weary of admiring him, whether now it be Abraham himself or the slave in Abraham's house, whether it be a professor of philosophy or a poor servant-girl: it is all the same to me, for I have regard only to the movements. But these movements I watch closely, and I will not be deceived, whether by myself or by anyone else. The knights of infinite resignation are easily recognized, for their gait is dancing and bold. But they who possess the jewel of faith frequently deceive one because their bearing is curiously like that of a class of people heartily despised by infinite resignation as well as by faith—the philistines.

Let me admit frankly that I have not in my experience encountered any certain example of this type. But I do not refuse to admit that as far as I know, every other person may be such a example. At the same time I will say that

I have searched vainly for years. It is the custom of scientists to travel around the globe to see rivers and mountains, new stars, gay-colored birds, misshapen fish, ridiculous races of men. They abandon themselves to a sluggish state of unconsciousness which stares at existence and believe they have seen something worthwhile. All this does not interest me; but if I knew where there lived such a knight of faith I would journey to him on foot, for that marvel occupies my thoughts exclusively. Not a moment would I leave him out of sight, but would watch how he makes the movements, and I would consider myself provided for life, and would divide my time between watching him and myself practicing the movements, and would thus use all my time in admiring him.

The Knight of Faith

As I said, I have not met with such a one; but I can easily imagine him. Here he is. I make his acquaintance and am introduced to him. The first moment I lay my eyes on him I push him back, leaping back myself, I hold up my hands in amazement and say to myself: "Good Lord! that person? Is it really he— why, he looks like a parish-beadle!" But it is really he. I become more closely acquainted with him, watching his every movement to see whether some insignificant incongruous movement of his has escaped me, some trace, perchance, of a signaling from the infinite, a glance, a look, a gesture, a melancholy air, or a smile, which might betray the presence of infinite resignation contrasting with the finite.

But no! I examine his figure from top to toe to discover whether there is anywhere a chink through which the infinite might be seen to peer forth. But no! he is of one piece, all through. . . . Thus he shows as much unconcern as any worthless happy-go-lucky fellow; and yet, every moment he lives he purchases his leisure at the highest price, for he makes not the least movement except by virtue of the absurd; and yet, yet—indeed, I might become furious with anger, if for no other reason than that of envy—and yet, this man has performed, and is performing every moment, the movement of infinity . . . He has resigned everything absolutely, and then again seized hold of it all on the strength of the absurd. . . .

The Paradoxical Moment of Faith

This last movement, the paradoxical movement of faith, I cannot make, whether or not it is my duty, although I desire nothing more passionately than to be able to make it. It must be left to a person's discretion whether he cares to make this confession. And at any rate, it is a matter between him and the Eternal Being, who is the object of his faith, whether an amicable adjustment can be affected. But what every person can do is to make the movement of absolute resignation, and I for my part would not hesitate to declare him a coward who imagines he cannot perform it. It is a different matter with faith. But what no person has a right to, is to delude others into the belief that faith is something of no great significance, or that it is an easy matter, whereas it is the greatest and most difficult of all things.

But the story of Abraham is generally interpreted in a different way. God's mercy is praised which restored Isaac to him—it was but a trial! A trial. This word may mean much or little, and yet the whole of it passes off as quickly as the story is told: one mounts a winged horse, in the same instant one arrives on Mount Moriah, and presto one sees the ram. It is not remembered that Abraham only rode on an ass which travels but slowly, that it was a three day journey for him, and that he required some additional time to collect the firewood, to bind Isaac, and to sharpen his knife.

And yet one praises Abraham. He who is to preach the sermon may sleep comfortably until a quarter of an hour before he is to preach it, and the listener may comfortably sleep during the sermon, for everything is made easy enough, without much exertion either to preacher or listener. But now suppose a man was present who suffered with sleeplessness and who went home and sat in a corner and reflected as follows: "The whole lasted but a minute, you need only wait a little while, and then the ram will be shown and the trial will be over." Now if the preacher should find him in this frame of mind, I believe he would confront him in all his dignity and say to him: "Wretch that you are, to let your soul lapse into such foolishness; miracles do not happen, all life is a trial." And as he proceeded he would grow more and more passionate, and would become ever more satisfied with himself; and whereas he had not noticed any congestion in his head whilst preaching about Abraham, he now feels the veins on his forehead swell. Yet who knows but he would stand aghast if the sinner should answer him in a quiet and dignified manner that it was precisely this about which he preached the Sunday before.

Let us then either waive the whole story of Abraham, or else learn to stand in awe of the enormous paradox which constitutes his significance for us, so that we may learn to understand that our age, like every age, may rejoice if it has faith. If the story of Abraham is not a mere nothing, an illusion, or if it is just used for show and as a pastime, the mistake cannot by any means be in the sinner's wishing to do likewise. But it is necessary to find out how great was the deed which Abraham performed, in order that the man may judge for himself whether he has the courage and the mission to do likewise. The comical contradiction in the procedure of the preacher was his reduction of the story of Abraham to insignificance whereas he rebuked the other man for doing the very same thing.

But should we then cease to speak about Abraham? I certainly think not. But if I were to speak about him I would first of all describe the terrors of his trial. To that end, like a leech I would suck all the suffering and distress out of the anguish of a father, in order to be able to describe what Abraham suffered while yet preserving his faith. I would remind the hearer that the journey lasted three days and a major part of the fourth—in fact, these three and a half days ought to become infinitely longer than the few thousand years which separate me from Abraham. I would remind him, as I think right, that every person is still permitted to turn about before trying his strength on this formidable task;

in fact, that he may return every instant in repentance. Provided this is done, I fear for nothing. Nor do I fear to awaken great desire among people to attempt to emulate Abraham. But to put forward a cheap version of Abraham and yet forbid everyone to do as he did, that I call ridiculous.

John Stuart Mill: Liberty and Utilitarianism
From *On Liberty* and *Utilitarianism*

Born in London, England, John Stuart Mill (1818–1883) was one of Britain's most influential moral and political philosophers, and for a short time served in the British parliament. In his book On Liberty *(1859) Mill defends the notion of individual freedom: as long as others are not harmed by our conduct, then we should be free to engage in almost any activity we please, without governmental interference. He argues that there are four benefits to the freedom of opinion, even when one's idea is unpopular and the public would like to censor it. First, a view may turn out to be true; second, even a view that is erroneous may contain some truth; third, even a true view will be viewed with prejudice unless it is vigorously defended against opposing views; and fourth, the substance and meaning behind the truth will become lost if it is not vigorously defended. In his book* Utilitarianism *(1861), Mill defends the utilitarian moral theory that right actions are ones that produce the most general happiness, that is, pleasure and the avoidance of pain. The heart of Mill's version of utilitarianism is his distinction between higher and lower pleasures. The lower ones appeal to basic bodily desires, such as the desire for food, whereas the higher ones are mental in nature and involve the cultivation of one's mind. The higher ones are qualitatively superior to the lower ones, and thus cannot be tallied into a strict utilitarian calculus as Jeremy Bentham had suggested. For, while lower bodily pleasures can be quantified (for example, two slices of apple pie are better than one), we cannot quantify the value of pleasures that are qualitatively superior.*

ON LIBERTY

1. Introductory

. . . The object of this Essay is to assert one very simple principle, as entitled to govern absolutely the dealings of society with the individual in the way of compulsion and control, whether the means used be physical force in the form

Source: John Stuart Mill, *On Liberty* (1859), Chapters 1–4; *Utilitarianism* (1861), Chapters 2 and 3.

of legal penalties, or the moral coercion of public opinion. That principle is, that the sole end for which mankind are warranted, individually or collectively in interfering with the liberty of action of any of their number, is self-protection. That the only purpose for which power can be rightfully exercised over any member of a civilized community, against his will, is to prevent harm to others. His own good, either physical or moral, is not a sufficient warrant. He cannot rightfully be compelled to do or forbear because it will be better for him to do so, because it will make him happier, because, in the opinions of others, to do so would be wise, or even right. These are good reasons for remonstrating with him, or reasoning with him, or persuading him, or entreating him, but not for compelling him, or visiting him with any evil, in case he do otherwise. To jus-tify that, the conduct from which it is desired to deter him must be calculated to produce evil to someone else. The only part of the conduct of any one, for which he is amenable to society, is that which concerns others. In the part which merely concerns himself, his independence is, of right, absolute. Over himself, over his own body and mind, the individual is sovereign. . . .

It is proper to state that I forego any advantage which could be derived to my argument from the idea of abstract right as a thing independent of utility. I regard utility as the ultimate appeal on all ethical questions; but it must be utility in the largest sense, grounded on the permanent interests of man as a progressive being. Those interests, I contend, authorize the subjection of indi-vidual spontaneity to external control, only in respect to those actions of each, which concern the interest of other people. . . .

. . . This, then, is the appropriate region of human liberty. It comprises, first, the inward domain of consciousness; demanding liberty of conscience, in the most comprehensive sense; liberty of thought and feeling; absolute free-dom of opinion and sentiment on all subjects, practical or speculative, scien-tific, moral, or theological. The liberty of expressing and publishing opinions may seem to fall under a different principle, since it belongs to that part of the conduct of an individual which concerns other people; but, being almost of as much importance as the liberty of thought itself, and resting in great part on the same reasons, is practically inseparable from it. Secondly, the principle requires liberty of tastes and pursuits; of framing the plan of our life to suit our own character; of doing as we like, subject to such consequences as may follow; without impediment from our fellow-creatures, so long as what we do does not harm them even though they should think our conduct foolish, perverse, or wrong. Thirdly, from this liberty of each individual, follows the liberty, within the same limits, of combination among individuals; freedom to unite, for any purpose not involving harm to others: the persons combining being supposed to be of full age, and not forced or deceived.

No society in which these liberties are not, on the whole, respected, is free, whatever may be its form of government; and none is completely free in which they do not exist absolute and unqualified. The only freedom which deserves the name, is that of pursuing our own good in our own way, so long as we do not attempt to deprive others of theirs, or impede their efforts to obtain it. Each is the proper guardian of his own health, whether bodily, or mental or spiritual.

Mankind are greater gainers by suffering each other to live as seems good to themselves, than by compelling each to live as seems good to the rest. . . .

2. Of the Liberty of Thought and Discussion

. . . If all mankind minus one, were of one opinion, and only one person were of the contrary opinion, mankind would be no more justified in silencing that one person, than he, if he had the power, would be justified in silencing mankind. Were an opinion a personal possession of no value except to the owner; if to be obstructed in the enjoyment of it were simply a private injury, it would make some difference whether the injury was inflicted only on a few persons or on many. But the peculiar evil of silencing the expression of an opinion is, that it is robbing the human race; posterity as well as the existing generation; those who dissent from the opinion, still more than those who hold it. If the opinion is right, they are deprived of the opportunity of exchanging error for truth: if wrong, they lose, what is almost as great a benefit, the clearer perception and livelier impression of truth, produced by its collision with error. . . .

. . . But it is not the minds of heretics that are deteriorated most, by the ban placed on all inquiry which does not end in the orthodox conclusions. The greatest harm done is to those who are not heretics, and whose whole mental development is cramped, and their reason cowed, by the fear of heresy. Who can compute what the world loses in the multitude of promising intellects combined with timid characters, who dare not follow out any bold, vigorous, independent train of thought, lest it should land them in something which would admit of being considered irreligious or immoral? Among them we may occasionally see some man of deep conscientiousness, and subtile and refined understanding, who spends a life in sophisticating with an intellect which he cannot silence, and exhausts the resources of ingenuity in attempting to reconcile the promptings of his conscience and reason with orthodoxy, which yet he does not, perhaps, to the end succeed in doing. No one can be a great thinker who does not recognize, that as a thinker it is his first duty to follow his intellect to whatever conclusions it may lead. . . .

We have now recognized the necessity to the mental well-being of mankind (on which all their other well-being depends) of freedom of opinion, and freedom of the expression of opinion, on four distinct grounds; which we will now briefly recapitulate.

First, if any opinion is compelled to silence, that opinion may, for aught we can certainly know, be true. To deny this is to assume our own infallibility.

Secondly, though the silenced opinion be an error, it may, and very commonly does, contain a portion of truth; and since the general or prevailing opinion on any object is rarely or never the whole truth, it is only by the collision of adverse opinions that the remainder of the truth has any chance of being supplied.

Thirdly, even if the received opinion be not only true, but the whole truth; unless it is suffered to be, and actually is, vigorously and earnestly contested, it will, by most of those who receive it, be held in the manner of a prejudice, with little comprehension or feeling of its rational grounds. And not only this, but, fourthly, the meaning of the doctrine itself will be in danger of being lost, or enfeebled, and deprived of its vital effect on the character and conduct: the dogma becoming a mere formal profession, inefficacious for good, but cumbering the ground, and preventing the growth of any real and heartfelt conviction, from reason or personal experience. . . .

3. On Individuality, as One of the Elements of Well-Being

Such being the reasons which make it imperative that human beings should be free to form opinions, and to express their opinions without reserve; and such the baneful consequences to the intellectual, and through that to the moral nature of man, unless this liberty is either conceded, or asserted in spite of prohibition; let us next examine whether the same reasons do not require that men should be free to act upon their opinions—to carry these out in their lives, without hindrance, either physical or moral, from their fellow-men, so long as it is at their own risk and peril. This last proviso is of course indispensable. No one pretends that actions should be as free as opinions. On the contrary, even opinions lose their immunity, when the circumstances in which they are expressed are such as to constitute their expression a positive instigation to some mischievous act. An opinion that corn-dealers are starvers of the poor, or that private property is robbery, ought to be unmolested when simply circulated through the press, but may justly incur punishment when delivered orally to an excited mob assembled before the house of a corn-dealer, or when handed about among the same mob in the form of a placard. Acts of whatever kind, which, without justifiable cause, do harm to others, may be, and in the more important cases absolutely require to be, controlled by the unfavorable sentiments, and, when needful, by the active interference of mankind. The liberty of the individual must be thus far limited; he must not make himself a nuisance to other people. But if he refrains from molesting others in what concerns them, and merely acts according to his own inclination and judgment in things which concern himself, the same reasons which show that opinion should be free, prove also that he should be allowed, without molestation, to carry his opinions into practice at his own cost. That mankind are not infallible; that their truths, for the most part, are only half-truths; that unity of opinion, unless resulting from the fullest and freest comparison of opposite opinions, is not desirable, and diversity not an evil, but a good, until mankind are much more capable than at present of recognizing all sides of the truth, are principles applicable to men's modes of action not less than to their opinions. As it is useful that while mankind are imperfect there should be different opinions, so is it that there should be different experiments of living; that free scope should be given to varieties of character, short of injury to others; and that the worth of different modes of life should be proved practically, when anyone thinks fit to try them. It is desirable, in short, that in things which do not primarily concern others, individuality should assert itself. Where, not the person's own character, but the traditions of customs of other people are the rule of conduct, there is wanting one of the principal ingredients of human happiness, and quite the chief ingredient of individual and social progress. . . .

4. Of the Limits to the Authority of Society over the Individual

What, then, is the rightful limit to the sovereignty of the individual over himself? Where does the authority of society begin? How much of human life should be assigned to individuality, and how much to society?

Each will receive its proper share, if each has that which more particularly concerns it. To individuality should belong the part of life in which it is chiefly the individual that is interested; to society, the part which chiefly interests society.

Though society is not founded on a contract, and though no good purpose is answered by inventing a contract in order to deduce social obligations from it, everyone who receives the protection of society owes a return for the benefit, and the fact of living in society renders it indispensable that each should be bound to observe a certain line of conduct towards the rest. This conduct consists, first, in not injuring the interests of one another; or rather certain interests, which, either by express legal provision or by tacit understanding, ought to be considered as rights; and secondly, in each person's bearing his share (to be fixed on some equitable principle) of the labors and sacrifices incurred for defending the society or its members from injury and molestation. These conditions society is justified in enforcing, at all costs to those who endeavor to withhold fulfillment. Nor is this all that society may do. The acts of an individual may be hurtful to others, or wanting in due consideration for their welfare, without going the length of violating any of their constituted rights. The offender may then be justly punished by opinion, though not by law. As soon as any part of a person's conduct affects prejudicially the interests of others, society has jurisdiction over it, and the question whether the general welfare will or will not be promoted by interfering with it, becomes open to discussion. But there is no room for entertaining any such question when a person's conduct affects the interests of no persons besides himself, or needs not affect them unless they like (all the persons concerned being of full age, and the ordinary amount of understanding). In all such cases there should be perfect freedom, legal and social, to do the action and stand the consequences.

It would be a great misunderstanding of this doctrine, to suppose that it is one of selfish indifference, which pretends that human beings have no business with each other's conduct in life, and that they should not concern themselves about the well-doing or well-being of one another, unless their own interest is involved. Instead of any diminution, there is need of a great increase of disinterested exertion to promote the good of others. But disinterested benevolence can find other instruments to persuade people to their good, than whips and scourges, either of the literal or the metaphorical sort. . . . But neither one person, nor any number of persons, is warranted in saying to another human creature of ripe years, that he shall not do with his life for his own benefit what he chooses to do with it. . . .

What I contend for is, that the inconveniences which are strictly inseparable from the unfavorable judgment of others, are the only ones to which a person should ever be subjected for that portion of his conduct and character which concerns his own good, but which does not affect the interests of others in their relations with him. Acts injurious to others require a totally different treatment. Encroachment on their rights; infliction on them of any loss or damage not justified by his own rights; falsehood or duplicity in dealing with them; unfair or ungenerous use of advantages over them; even selfish abstinence from defending them against injury—these are fit objects of moral reprobation, and, in grave cases, of moral retribution and punishment.

UTILITARIANISM

Pleasure and the Greatest Happiness Principle

The creed which accepts as the foundation of morals, Utility, or the Greatest Happiness Principle, holds that actions are right in proportion as they tend to promote happiness, wrong as they tend to produce the reverse of happiness. By happiness is intended pleasure, and the absence of pain; by unhappiness, pain, and the privation of pleasure. To give a clear view of the moral standard set up by the theory, much more requires to be said; in particular, what things it includes in the ideas of pain and pleasure; and to what extent this is left an open question. But these supplementary explanations do not affect the theory of life on which this theory of morality is grounded—namely, that pleasure, and freedom from pain, are the only things desirable as ends; and that all desirable things (which are as numerous in the utilitarian as in any other scheme) are desirable either for the pleasure inherent in themselves, or as means to the promotion of pleasure and the prevention of pain.

Now, such a theory of life excites in many minds, and among them in some of the most estimable in feeling and purpose, inveterate dislike. To suppose that life has (as they express it) no higher end than pleasure—no better and nobler object of desire and pursuit—they designate as utterly mean and groveling; as a doctrine worthy only of swine, to whom the followers of Epicurus were, at a very early period, contemptuously likened; and modern holders of the doctrine are occasionally made the subject of equally polite comparisons by its German, French, and English assailants.

When thus attacked, the Epicureans have always answered, that it is not they, but their accusers, who represent human nature in a degrading light; since the accusation supposes human beings to be capable of no pleasures except those of which swine are capable. If this supposition were true, the charge could not be gainsaid, but would then be no longer an imputation; for if the sources of pleasure were precisely the same to human beings and to swine, the rule of life which is good enough for the one would be good enough for the other. The comparison of the Epicurean life to that of beasts is felt as degrading, precisely because a beast's pleasures do not satisfy a human being's conceptions of happiness. Human beings have faculties more elevated than the animal appetites, and when once made conscious of them, do not regard anything as happiness which does not include their gratification. I do not, indeed, consider the Epicureans to have been by any means faultless in drawing out their scheme of consequences from the utilitarian principle. To do this in any sufficient manner, many Stoic, as well as Christian elements require to be included. But there is no known Epicurean theory of life which does not assign to the pleasures of the intellect, of the feelings and imagination, and of the moral sentiments, a much higher value as pleasures than to those of mere sensation. It must be admitted, however, that utilitarian writers in general have placed the superiority of mental over bodily pleasures chiefly in the greater permanency, safety, uncostliness, etc., of the former—that is, in their circumstantial advantages rather than in their intrinsic nature. And on all these points utilitarians have fully proved their case; but they might have taken the other, and, as it may be called, higher ground, with entire consistency. It is quite compatible with the principle of utility to recognize the fact, that some kinds of pleasure are more desirable and more valuable than others. It would be absurd that while, in estimating all other things, quality is considered as well as quantity, the estimation of pleasures should be supposed to depend on quantity alone.

Some Pleasures Are Qualitatively Better Than Others

If I am asked, what I mean by difference of quality in pleasures, or what makes one pleasure more valuable than another, merely as a pleasure, except its being greater in amount, there is but one possible answer. Of two pleasures, if there be one to which all or almost all who have experience of both give a decided preference, irrespective of any feeling of moral obligation to prefer it, that is the more desirable pleasure. If one of the two is, by those who are competently acquainted with both, placed so far above the other that they prefer it, even though knowing it to be attended with a greater amount of discontent, and would not resign it for any quantity of the other pleasure which their nature is capable of, we are justified in ascribing to the preferred enjoyment a superiority in quality, so far outweighing quantity as to render it, in comparison, of small account.

Now it is an unquestionable fact that those who are equally acquainted with, and equally capable of appreciating and enjoying, both, do give a most marked preference to the manner of existence which employs their higher faculties. Few human creatures would consent to be changed into any of the lower animals, for a promise of the fullest allowance of a beast's pleasures; no intelligent human being would consent to be a fool, no instructed person would be an ignoramus, no person of feeling and conscience would be selfish and base, even though they should be persuaded that the fool, the dunce, or the rascal is better satisfied with his lot than they are with theirs. They would not resign what they possess more than he for the most complete satisfaction of all the desires which they have in common with him. If they ever fancy they would, it is only in cases of unhappiness so extreme, that to escape from it they would exchange their lot for almost any other, however undesirable in their own eyes. A being of higher faculties requires more to make him happy, is capable probably of more acute suffering, and certainly accessible to it at more points, than one of an inferior type; but in spite of these liabilities, he can never really wish to sink into what he feels to be a lower grade of existence. We may give what explanation we please of this unwillingness; we may attribute it to pride, a name which is given indiscriminately to some of the most and to some of the least estimable feelings of which mankind are capable: we may refer it to the love of liberty and personal independence, an appeal to which was with the Stoics one of the most effective means for the inculcation of it; to the love of power, or to the love of excitement, both of which do really enter into and contribute to it: but its most appropriate appellation is a sense of dignity, which all human beings possess in one form or other, and in some, though by no means in exact, proportion to their higher faculties, and which is so essential a part of the happiness of those in whom it is strong, that nothing which conflicts with it could be, otherwise than momentarily, an object of desire to them.

Whoever supposes that this preference takes place at a sacrifice of happiness—that the superior being, in anything like equal circumstances, is not happier than the inferior—confounds the two very different ideas, of happiness, and content. It is indisputable that the being whose capacities of enjoyment are low, has the greatest chance of having them fully satisfied; and a highly endowed being will always feel that any happiness which he can look for, as the world is constituted, is imperfect. But he can learn to bear its imperfections, if they are at all bearable; and they will not make him envy the being who is indeed unconscious of the imperfections, but only because he feels not at all the good which those imperfections qualify. It is better to be a human being dissatisfied than a pig satisfied; better to be Socrates dissatisfied than a fool satisfied. And if the fool, or the pig, are [of] a different opinion, it is because they only know their own side of the question. The other party to the comparison knows both sides.

Preferring Higher Pleasures to Lower Pleasures

It may be objected, that many who are capable of the higher pleasures, occasionally, under the influence of temptation, postpone them to the lower. But this is quite compatible with a full appreciation of the intrinsic superiority of the higher. Men often, from infirmity of character, make their election for the nearer good, though they know it to be the less valuable; and this no less when the choice is between two bodily pleasures, than when it is between bodily and mental. They pursue sensual indulgences to the injury of health, though perfectly aware that health is the greater good.

It may be further objected, that many who begin with youthful enthusiasm for everything noble, as they advance in years sink into indolence and selfishness. But I do not believe that those who undergo this very common change, voluntarily choose the lower description of pleasures in preference to the higher. I believe that before they devote themselves exclusively to the one, they have already become incapable of the other. Capacity for the nobler feelings is in most natures a very tender plant, easily killed, not only by hostile influences, but by mere want of sustenance; and in the majority of young persons it speedily dies away if the occupations to which their position in life has devoted them, and the society into which it has thrown them, are not favorable to keeping that higher capacity in exercise. Men lose their high aspirations as they lose their intellectual tastes, because they have not time or opportunity for indulging them; and they addict themselves to inferior pleasures, not because they deliberately prefer them, but because they are either the only ones to which they have access, or the only ones which they are any longer capable of enjoying. It may be questioned whether anyone who has remained equally susceptible to both classes of pleasures, ever knowingly and calmly preferred the lower; though many, in all ages, have broken down in an ineffectual attempt to combine both.

From this verdict of the only competent judges, I apprehend there can be no appeal. On a question which is the best worth having of two pleasures, or which of two modes of existence is the most grateful to the feelings, apart from its moral attributes and from its consequences, the judgment of those who are qualified by knowledge of both, or, if they differ, that of the majority among them, must be admitted as final. And there needs be the less hesitation to accept this judgment respecting the quality of pleasures, since there is no other tribunal to be referred to even on the question of quantity. What means are there of determining which is the acutest of two pains, or the intensest of two pleasurable sensations, except the general suffrage of those who are familiar with both? Neither pains nor pleasures are homogeneous, and pain is always heterogeneous with pleasure. What is there to decide whether a particular pleasure is worth purchasing at the cost of a particular pain, except the feelings and judgment of the experienced? When, therefore, those feelings and judgment declare the pleasures derived from the higher faculties to be preferable in kind, apart from the question of intensity, to those of which the animal nature, disjoined from the higher faculties, is susceptible, they are entitled on this subject to the same regard.

According to the Greatest Happiness Principle, as above explained, the ultimate end, with reference to and for the sake of which all other things are desirable (whether we are considering our own good or that of other people), is an existence exempt as far as possible from pain, and as rich as possible in enjoyments, both in point of quantity and quality; the test of quality, and the rule for measuring it against quantity, being the preference felt by those who in their opportunities of experience, to which must be added their habits of self-consciousness and self-observation, are best furnished with the means of comparison. This, being, according to the utilitarian opinion, the end of human action, is necessarily also the standard of morality; which may accordingly be defined, the rules and precepts for human conduct, by the observance of which an existence such as has been described might be, to the greatest extent possible, secured to all mankind; and not to them only, but, so far as the nature of things admits, to the whole sentient creation.

Pleasure and Self-Sacrifice

. . . The utilitarian morality does recognize in human beings the power of sacrificing their own greatest good for the good of others. It only refuses to admit that the sacrifice is itself a good. A sacrifice which does not increase, or tend to increase, the sum total of happiness, it considers as wasted. The only self-renunciation which it applauds, is devotion to the happiness, or to some of the means of happiness, of others; either of mankind collectively, or of individuals within the limits imposed by the collective interests of mankind.

I must again repeat, what the assailants of utilitarianism seldom have the justice to acknowledge, that the happiness which forms the utilitarian standard of what is right in conduct, is not the agent's own happiness, but that of all concerned. As between his own happiness and that of others, utilitarianism requires him to be as strictly impartial as a disinterested and benevolent specta-tor. In the golden rule of Jesus of Nazareth, we read the complete spirit of the ethics of utility. To do as you would be done by, and to love your neighbor as yourself, constitute the ideal perfection of utilitarian morality. . . .

Whether There Is Enough Time to Calculate the Effects of Our Conduct

Again, defenders of utility often find themselves called upon to reply to such objections as this—that there is not time, previous to action, for calculating and weighing the effects of any line of conduct on the general happiness. This is exactly as if any one were to say that it is impossible to guide our conduct by Christianity, because there is not time, on every occasion on which anything has to be done, to read through the Old and New Testaments. The answer to the objection is, that there has been ample time, namely, the whole past duration of the human species. During all that time, mankind have been learning by experience the tendencies of actions; on which experience all the prudence, as well as all the morality of life, are dependent. People talk as if the commencement of this course of experience had hitherto been put off, and as if, at the moment when some man feels tempted to meddle with the property or life of another, he had to begin considering for the first time whether murder and theft are injurious to human happiness. . . .

Whether We Are Born with the Feeling of Moral Duty

It is not necessary, for the present purpose, to decide whether the feeling of duty is innate or implanted. Assuming it to be innate, it is an open question to what objects it naturally attaches itself; for the philosophic supporters of that theory are now agreed that the intuitive perception is of principles of morality and not of the details. If there be anything innate in the matter, I see no reason why the feeling which is innate should not be that of regard to the pleasures and pains of others. If there is any principle of morals which is intuitively oblig-atory, I should say it must be that. If so, the intuitive ethics would coincide with the utilitarian, and there would be no further quarrel between them. Even as it is, the intuitive moralists, though they believe that there are other intuitive moral obligations, do already believe this to one; for they unanimously hold that a large portion of morality turns upon the consideration due to the inter-ests of our fellow-creatures. Therefore, if the belief in the transcendental ori-gin of moral obligation gives any additional efficacy to the internal sanction, it appears to me that the utilitarian principle has already the benefit of it.

On the other hand, if, as is my own belief, the moral feelings are not innate, but acquired, they are not for that reason the less natural. It is natural to man to speak, to reason, to build cities, to cultivate the ground, though these are acquired faculties. The moral feelings are not indeed a part of our nature, in the sense of being in any perceptible degree present in all of us; but this, unhappily, is a fact admitted by those who believe the most strenuously in their transcendental origin. Like the other acquired capacities above referred to, the moral faculty, if not a part of our nature, is a natural outgrowth from it; capable, like them, in a certain small degree, of springing up spontaneously; and susceptible of being brought by cultivation to a high degree of development. Unhappily it is also susceptible, by a sufficient use of the external sanctions and of the force of early impressions, of being cultivated in almost any direction: so that there is hardly anything so absurd or so mischievous that it may not, by means of these influences, be made to act on the human mind with all the authority of conscience. To doubt that the same potency might be given by the same means to the principle of utility, even if it had no foundation in human nature, would be flying in the face of all experience.

READING 5

Karl Marx: The Clash of Class Interests
From *Manifesto of the Communist Party*

Born in Trier, Germany, Karl Marx (1818–1883) was the principal founder of the communist political theory and became one of the most influential political philosophers of the modern era. Though Marx was a voluminous writer, he lays out the basic elements of the communist vision in a short work titled the Manifesto of the Communist Party *(1848). In this, Marx describes a series of conflicts throughout history between the upper ruling classes who have economic power and the lower working classes who are oppressed by the rulers. These include the masters and slaves, feudal lords and serfs, and, in Marx's own day, an economic system in which the ruling middle class of capitalists (the bourgeoisie) exploit the working class (the proletariat). The solution to this class conflict, according to Marx, is an all-out revolution of the working class, by which they would take control of the country's economic system.*

HISTORY AND CLASS STRUGGLE

The history of all hitherto existing societies is the history of class struggles.

Freeman and slave, patrician and plebeian, lord and serf, guild-master and journeyman, in a word, oppressor and oppressed, stood in constant opposition to one another, carried on an uninterrupted, now hidden, now open fight, a fight

Source: Karl Marx, *Manifesto of the Communist Party* (1848), Chapter 1.

that each time ended, either in a revolutionary re-constitution of society at large, or in the common ruin of the contending classes. In the earlier epochs of history, we find almost everywhere a complicated arrangement of society into various orders, a manifold gradation of social rank. In ancient Rome we have patricians, knights, plebeians, slaves; in the Middle Ages, feudal lords, vassals, guild-masters, journeymen, apprentices, serfs; in almost all of these classes, again, subordinate gradations.

The modern bourgeois society that has sprouted from the ruins of feudal society has not done away with class antagonisms. It has but established new classes, new conditions of oppression, new forms of struggle in place of the old ones. Our epoch, the epoch of the bourgeoisie, possesses, however, this distinctive feature: it has simplified the class antagonisms: Society as a whole is more and more splitting up into two great hostile camps, into two great classes, directly facing each other: Bourgeoisie and Proletariat.

From the serfs of the Middle Ages sprang the chartered burghers of the earliest towns. From these burgesses the first elements of the bourgeoisie were developed.

The discovery of America, the rounding of the Cape, opened up fresh ground for the rising bourgeoisie. The East-Indian and Chinese markets, the colonization of America, trade with the colonies, the increase in the means of exchange and in commodities generally, gave to commerce, to navigation, to industry, an impulse never before known, and thereby, to the revolutionary element in the tottering feudal society, a rapid development.

The feudal system of industry, under which industrial production was monopolized by closed guilds, now no longer sufficed for the growing wants of the new markets. The manufacturing system took its place. The guild-masters were pushed on one side by the manufacturing middle class; division of labor between the different corporate guilds vanished in the face of division of labor in each single workshop.

Meantime the markets kept ever growing, the demand ever rising. Even manufacture no longer sufficed. Thereupon, steam and machinery revolutionized industrial production. The place of manufacture was taken by the giant, Modern Industry, the place of the industrial middle class, by industrial millionaires, the leaders of whole industrial armies, the modern bourgeois.

Modern industry has established the world-market, for which the discovery of America paved the way. This market has given an immense development to commerce, to navigation, to communication by land. This development has, in its time, reacted on the extension of industry; and in proportion as industry, commerce, navigation, railways extended, in the same proportion the bourgeoisie developed, increased its capital, and pushed into the background every class handed down from the Middle Ages.

BOURGEOISIE EXPLOITATION OF LABORERS

We see, therefore, how the modern bourgeoisie is itself the product of a long course of development, of a series of revolutions in the modes of production and of exchange.

Each step in the development of the bourgeoisie was accompanied by a corresponding political advance of that class. An oppressed class under the sway of the feudal nobility, an armed and self-governing association in the medieval commune; here independent urban republic (as in Italy and Germany), there taxable "third estate" of the monarchy (as in France), afterwards, in the period of manufacture proper, serving either the semi-feudal or the absolute monarchy as a counterpoise against the nobility, and, in fact, cornerstone of the great monarchies in general, the bourgeoisie has at last, since the establishment of Modern Industry and of the world-market, conquered for itself, in the modern representative State, exclusive political sway. The executive of the modern State is but a committee for managing the common affairs of the whole bourgeoisie.

The bourgeoisie, historically, has played a most revolutionary part.

The bourgeoisie, wherever it has got the upper hand, has put an end to all feudal, patriarchal, idyllic relations. It has pitilessly torn asunder the motley feudal ties that bound man to his "natural superiors," and has left remaining no other nexus between man and man than naked self-interest, than callous "cash payment." It has drowned the most heavenly ecstasies of religious fervor, of chivalrous enthusiasm, of philistine sentimentalism, in the icy water of egotistical calculation. It has resolved personal worth into exchange value. And in place of the numberless and feasible chartered freedoms, has set up that single, unconscionable freedom—Free Trade. In one word, for exploitation, veiled by religious and political illusions, naked, shameless, direct, brutal exploitation.

The bourgeoisie has stripped of its halo every occupation hitherto honored and looked up to with reverent awe. It has converted the physician, the lawyer, the priest, the poet, the man of science, into its paid wage laborers.

The bourgeoisie has torn away from the family its sentimental veil, and has reduced the family relation to a mere money relation.

The bourgeoisie has disclosed how it came to pass that the brutal display of vigor in the Middle Ages, which Reactionists so much admire, found its fitting complement in the most slothful indolence. It has been the first to show what man's activity can bring about. It has accomplished wonders far surpassing Egyptian pyramids, Roman aqueducts, and Gothic cathedrals; it has conducted expeditions that put in the shade all former Exoduses of nations and crusades.

BOURGEOISIE EXPANSION

The bourgeoisie cannot exist without constantly revolutionizing the instruments of production, and thereby the relations of production, and with them the whole relations of society. Conservation of the old modes of production in unaltered form, was, on the contrary, the first condition of existence for all earlier industrial classes. Constant revolutionizing of production, uninterrupted disturbance of all social conditions, everlasting uncertainty and agitation distinguish the bourgeois epoch from all earlier ones. All fixed, fast-frozen relations, with their train of ancient and venerable prejudices and opinions, are swept away, all new-formed ones become antiquated before they can ossify. All that is solid melts into air, all that is holy is profaned, and man is at last compelled to face with sober senses, his real conditions of life, and his relations with his kind.

The need of a constantly expanding market for its products chases the bourgeoisie over the whole surface of the globe. It must nestle everywhere, settle everywhere, establish connections everywhere.

The bourgeoisie has through its exploitation of the world-market given a cosmopolitan character to production and consumption in every country. To the great chagrin of Reactionists, it has drawn from under the feet of industry the national ground on which it stood. All old-established national industries have been destroyed or are daily being destroyed. They are dislodged by new industries, whose introduction becomes a life and death question for all civilized nations, by industries that no longer work up indigenous raw material, but raw material drawn from the remotest zones; industries whose products are consumed, not only at home, but in every quarter of the globe. In place of the old wants, satisfied by the productions of the country, we find new wants, requiring for their satisfaction the products of distant lands and climes. In place of the old local and national seclusion and self-sufficiency, we have intercourse in every direction, universal interdependence of nations. And as in material, so also in intellectual production. The intellectual creations of individual nations become common property. National one-sidedness and narrow-mindedness become more and more impossible, and from the numerous national and local literatures, there arises a world literature.

The bourgeoisie, by the rapid improvement of all instruments of production, by the immensely facilitated means of communication, draws all, even the most barbarian, nations into civilization. The cheap prices of its commodities are the heavy artillery with which it batters down all Chinese walls, with which it forces the barbarians' intensely obstinate hatred of foreigners to capitulate. It compels all nations, on pain of extinction, to adopt the bourgeois mode of production; it compels them to introduce what it calls civilization into their midst, i.e., to become bourgeois themselves. In one word, it creates a world after its own image.

The bourgeoisie has subjected the country to the rule of the towns. It has created enormous cities, has greatly increased the urban population as compared with the rural, and has thus rescued a considerable part of the population from the idiocy of rural life. Just as it has made the country dependent on the towns, so it has made barbarian and semi-barbarian countries dependent on the civilized ones, nations of peasants on nations of bourgeois, the East on the West.

The bourgeoisie keeps more and more doing away with the scattered state of the population, of the means of production, and of property. It has agglomerated production, and has concentrated property in a few hands. The necessary consequence of this was political centralizations. Independent, or but loosely connected provinces, with separate interests, laws, governments and systems of taxation, became lumped together into one nation, with one government, one code of laws, one national class-interest, one frontier and one customs-tariff. The bourgeoisie, during its rule of scarce one hundred years, has created more massive and more colossal productive forces than have all preceding generations together. Subjection of Nature's forces to man, machinery, application of chemistry to industry and agriculture, steam-navigation, railways, electric telegraphs, clearing of whole continents for cultivation, canalization of rivers, whole populations conjured out of the ground—what earlier century had even a presentiment that such productive forces slumbered in the lap of social labor?

We see then: the means of production and of exchange, on whose foundation the bourgeoisie built itself up, were generated in feudal society. At a certain stage in the development of these means of production and of exchange, the conditions under which feudal society produced and exchanged, the feudal organization of agriculture and manufacturing industry, in one word, the feudal relations of property became no longer compatible with the already developed productive forces; they became so many fetters. They had to be burst asunder; they were burst asunder.

Into their place stepped free competition, accompanied by a social and political constitution adapted to it, and by the economical and political sway of the bourgeois class.

A similar movement is going on before our own eyes. Modern bourgeois society with its relations of production, of exchange and of property, a society that has conjured up such gigantic means of production and of exchange, is like the sorcerer, who is no longer able to control the powers of the nether world whom he has called up by his spells. For many a decade past the history of industry and commerce is but the history of the revolt of modern productive forces against modern conditions of production, against the property relations that are the conditions for the existence of the bourgeoisie and of its rule. It is enough to mention the commercial crises that by their periodical return put on its trial, each time more threateningly, the existence of the entire bourgeois society. In these crises a great part not only of the existing products, but also of the previously created productive forces, are periodically destroyed. In these crises there breaks out an epidemic that, in all earlier epochs, would have seemed an absurdity—the epidemic of over-production. Society suddenly finds itself put back into a state of momentary barbarism; it appears as if a famine, a universal war of devastation had cut off the supply of every means of subsistence; industry and commerce seem to be destroyed; and why? Because there is too much civilization, too much means of subsistence, too much industry, too much commerce. The productive forces at the disposal of society no longer tend to further the development of the conditions of bourgeois property; on the contrary, they have become too powerful for these conditions, by which they are fettered, and so soon as they overcome these fetters, they bring disorder into the whole of bourgeois society, endanger the existence of bourgeois property. The conditions of bourgeois society are too narrow to comprise the wealth created by them. And how does the bourgeoisie get over these crises? On the one hand enforced destruction of a mass of productive forces; on the other, by the conquest of new markets, and by the more thorough exploitation of the old ones. That is to say, by paving the way for more extensive and more destructive crises, and by diminishing the means whereby crises are prevented.

SELF-DESTRUCTION OF THE BOURGEOISIE

The weapons with which the bourgeoisie felled feudalism to the ground are now turned against the bourgeoisie itself.

But not only has the bourgeoisie forged the weapons that bring death to itself; it has also called into existence the men who are to wield those weapons—the modern working class—the proletarians.

In proportion as the bourgeoisie, i.e., capital, is developed, in the same proportion is the proletariat, the modern working class, developed—a class of laborers, who live only so long as they find work, and who find work only so long as their labor increases capital. These laborers, who must sell themselves piece-meal, are a commodity, like every other article of commerce, and are consequently exposed to all the vicissitudes of competition, to all the fluctuations of the market.

Owing to the extensive use of machinery and to division of labor, the work of the proletarians has lost all individual character, and consequently, all charm for the workman. He becomes an appendage of the machine, and it is only the most simple, most monotonous, and most easily acquired knack, that is required of him. Hence, the cost of production of a workman is restricted, almost entirely, to the means of subsistence that he requires for his maintenance, and for the propagation of his race. But the price of a commodity, and therefore also of labor, is equal to its cost of production. In proportion therefore, as the repulsiveness of the work increases, the wage decreases. Nay more, in proportion as the use of-machinery and division of labor increases, in the same proportion the burden of toil also increases, whether by prolongation of the working hours, by increase of the work exacted in a given time or by increased speed of the machinery, etc.

Modern industry has converted the little workshop of the patriarchal master into the great factory of the industrial capitalist. Masses of laborers, crowded into the factory, are organized like soldiers. As privates of the industrial army they are placed under the command of a perfect hierarchy of officers and sergeants. Not only are they slaves of the bourgeois class, and of the bourgeois State; they are daily and hourly enslaved by the machine, by the over-looker, and, above all, by the individual bourgeois manufacturer himself. The more openly this despotism proclaims gain to be its end and aim, the more petty, the more hateful and the more embittering it is.

The less the skill and exertion of strength implied in manual labor, in other words, the more modern industry becomes developed, the more is the labor of men superseded by that of women. Differences of age and sex have no longer any distinctive social validity for the working class. All are instruments of labor, more or less expensive to use, according to their age and sex.

No sooner is the exploitation of the laborer by the manufacturer, so far, at an end, that he receives his wages in cash, than he is set upon by the other portions of the bourgeoisie, the landlord, the shopkeeper, the pawnbroker, etc.

The lower strata of the middle class—the small tradespeople, shopkeepers, retired tradesmen generally, the handicraftsmen and peasants—all these sink gradually into the proletariat, partly because their diminutive capital does not suffice for the scale on which Modern Industry is carried on, and is swamped in the competition with the large capitalists, partly because their specialized skill is rendered worthless by the new methods of production. Thus the proletariat is recruited from all classes of the population.

The proletariat goes through various stages of development. With its birth begins its struggle with the bourgeoisie. At first the contest is carried on by individual laborers, then by the workpeople of a factory, then by the operatives of one trade, in one locality, against the individual bourgeois who directly exploits them. They direct their attacks not against the bourgeois conditions of production, but against the instruments of production themselves; they destroy imported wares that compete with their labor, they smash to pieces machinery, they set factories ablaze, they seek to restore by force the vanished status of the workman of the Middle Ages.

At this stage the laborers still form an incoherent mass scattered over the whole country, and broken up by their mutual competition. If anywhere they unite to form more compact bodies, this is not yet the consequence of their own active union, but of the union of the bourgeoisie, which class, in order to attain its own political ends, is compelled to set the whole proletariat in motion, and is moreover yet, for a time, able to do so. At this stage, therefore, the proletarians do not fight their enemies, but the enemies of their enemies, the remnants of absolute monarchy, the landowners, the non-industrial bourgeois, the petty bourgeoisie. Thus the whole historical movement is concentrated in the hands of the bourgeoisie; every victory so obtained is a victory for the bourgeoisie.

COLLISION BETWEEN THE PROLETARIAT AND THE BOURGEOISIE

But with the development of industry the proletariat not only increases in number; it becomes concentrated in greater masses, its strength grows, and it feels that strength more. The various interests and conditions of life within the ranks of the proletariat are more and more equalized, in proportion as machinery obliterates all distinctions of labor, and nearly everywhere reduces wages to the same low level. The growing competition among the bourgeois, and the resulting commercial crises, make the wages of the workers ever more fluctuating. The unceasing improvement of machinery, ever more rapidly developing, makes their livelihood more and more precarious; the collisions between individual workmen and individual bourgeois take more and more the character of collisions between two classes. Thereupon the workers begin to form combinations (Trades Unions) against the bourgeois; they club together in order to keep up the rate of wages; they found permanent associations in order to make provision beforehand for these occasional revolts. Here and there the contest breaks out into riots.

Now and then the workers are victorious, but only for a time. The real fruit of their battles lies, not in the immediate result, but in the ever-expanding union of the workers. This union is helped on by the improved means of communication that are created by modern industry and that place the workers of different localities in contact with one another. It was just this contact that was needed to centralize the numerous local struggles, all of the same character, into one national struggle between classes. But every class struggle is a political struggle. And that union, to attain which the burghers of the Middle Ages, with their miserable highways, required centuries, the modern proletarians, thanks to railways, achieve in a few years.

This organization of the proletarians into a class, and consequently into a political party, is continually being upset again by the competition between the workers themselves. But it ever rises up again, stronger, firmer, mightier. It compels legislative recognition of particular interests of the workers, by taking advantage of the divisions among the bourgeoisie itself. Thus the ten-hours' bill in England was carried.

Altogether collisions between the classes of the old society further, in many ways, the course of development of the proletariat. The bourgeoisie finds itself involved in a constant battle. At first with the aristocracy; later on, with those portions of the bourgeoisie itself, whose interests have become antagonistic to the progress of industry; at all times, with the bourgeoisie of foreign countries. In all these battles it sees itself compelled to appeal to the proletariat, to ask for its help, and thus, to drag it into the political arena. The bourgeoisie itself, therefore, supplies the proletariat with its own instruments of political and general education, in other words, it furnishes the proletariat with weapons for fighting the bourgeoisie.

Further, as we have already seen, entire sections of the ruling classes are, by the advance of industry, precipitated into the proletariat, or are at least threatened in their conditions of existence. These also supply the proletariat with fresh elements of enlightenment and progress.

Finally, in times when the class struggle nears the decisive hour, the process of dissolution going on within the ruling class, in fact within the whole range of society, assumes such a violent, glaring character, that a small section of the ruling class cuts itself adrift, and joins the revolutionary class, the class that holds the future in its hands. Just as, therefore, at an earlier period, a section of the nobility went over to the bourgeoisie, so now a portion of the bourgeoisie goes over to the proletariat, and in particular, a portion of the bourgeois ideologists, who have raised themselves to the level of comprehending theoretically the historical movement as a whole. . . .

Friedrich Nietzsche: Turning Values Upside Down

From Beyond Good and Evil, The Twilight of the Idols, and The Will to Power

Born in a small village in what is now central Germany, Friedrich Nietzsche (1844–1900) was a professor of philology at the University of Basel. Chronic health problems forced him to resign while in his mid-30s, and he lived out his remaining years with his mother and sister. Reacting against the entire tradition of Western moral theories, Nietzsche expresses the view that there are no preexisting rules of good and evil. His philosophy calls for a person's fullest expression of all intrinsic vital powers and passions, although he urges a balance between the Dionysian (passionate) element in human nature and the Apollonian (rational) element. He is especially critical of the Christian value system for destroying the natural origin of morality and replacing it with weak notions of God, last judgment, truth, love, wisdom, and the Holy Spirit.

BEYOND GOOD AND EVIL

I hope to be forgiven for discovering that all moral philosophy hitherto has been tedious and has belonged to the soporific appliances—and that "virtue," in my opinion, has been more injured by the *tediousness* of its advocates than by anything else; at the same time, however, I would not wish to overlook their general usefulness. It is desirable that as few people as possible should reflect upon morals, and consequently it is *very* desirable that morals should not some day become interesting! But let us not be afraid! Things still remain today as they have always been: I see no one in Europe who has (or discloses) an idea of the fact that philosophizing concerning morals might be conducted in a dangerous, captious, and ensnaring manner—that *calamity* might be involved therein. Observe, for example, the indefatigable, inevitable English utilitarians: how ponderously and respectably they stalk on, stalk along (a Homeric metaphor expresses it better) in the footsteps of Bentham, just as he had already stalked in the footsteps of the respectable Helvétius! (no, he was not a dangerous man, Helvétius, *ce senateur Pococurante*, to use an expression of Galiani). No new thought, nothing of the nature of a finer turning or better expression of an old thought, not even a proper history of what has been previously thought on the subject: an *impossible* literature, taking it all in all unless one knows how to leaven it with some mischief. In effect, the old English vice called cant, which is *moral Tartuffism*, has insinuated itself also into these

Source: Friedrich Nietzsche, *Beyond Good and Evil* (1886), *The Twilight of the Idols* (1888), and *The Will to Power* (1906).

moralists (whom one must certainly read with an eye to their motives if one *must* read them), concealed this time under the new form of the scientific spirit; moreover, there is not absent from them a secret struggle with the pangs of conscience, from which a race of former Puritans must naturally suffer, in all their scientific tinkering with morals. (Is not a moralist the opposite of a Puritan? That is to say, as a thinker who regards morality as questionable, as worthy of interrogation, in short, as a problem? Is moralizing not—immoral?) In the end, they all want English morality to be recognized as authoritative, inasmuch as mankind, or the "general utility," or "the happiness of the greatest number,"— no! the happiness of *England,* will be best served thereby. They would like, by all means, to convince themselves that the striving after *English* happiness, I mean after *comfort and fashion* (and in the highest instance, a seat in Parliament), is at the same time the true path of virtue; in fact, that in so far as there has been virtue in the world hitherto, it has just consisted in such striving. Not one of those ponderous, conscience-stricken herding-animals (who undertake to advocate the cause of egoism as conducive to the general welfare) wants to have any knowledge or inkling of the facts that the "general welfare" is no ideal, no goal, no notion that can be at all grasped, but is only a nostrum,—that what is fair to one *may not* at all be fair to another, that the requirement of one morality for all is really a detriment to higher men, in short, that there is a *distinction of* rank between man and man, and consequently between morality and morality. They are an unassuming and fundamentally mediocre species of men, these utilitarian Englishmen, and, as already remarked, in so far as they are tedious, one cannot think highly enough of their utility. One ought even to *encourage* them, as has been partially attempted in the following rhymes:

> Hail, ye worthies, barrow-wheeling, "Longer—better,"
> aye revealing,
> Stiffer aye in head and knee;
> Unenraptured, never jesting,
> Mediocre everlasting, *Sans genie et sans esprit!*

Every elevation of the type "man," has hitherto been the work of an aristocratic society—and so will it always be—a society believing in a long scale of gradations of rank and differences of worth among human beings, and requiring slavery in some form or other. Without the *pathos of distance,* such as grows out of the incarnated difference of classes, out of the constant out-looking and down-looking of the ruling caste on subordinates and instruments, and out of their equally constant practice of obeying and commanding, of keeping down and keeping at a distance—that other more mysterious pathos could never have arisen, the longing for an ever new widening of distance within the soul itself, the formation of ever higher, rarer, further, more extended, more comprehensive states, in short, just the elevation of the type "man," the continued "self-surmounting of man," to use a moral formula in a super-moral sense. To be sure, one must not resign oneself to any humanitarian illusions about the history of the origin of an aristocratic society (that is to say, of the preliminary condition for the elevation of the type "man"): the truth is hard. Let us acknowledge unprejudicedly how every higher civilization hitherto has *originated!* Men with a still natural nature, barbarians in every terrible sense of the word, men of prey, still in possession of unbroken strength of will and desire for power, threw themselves upon weaker, more moral, more peaceful races (perhaps trading or cattle-rearing communities), or upon old mellow civilizations in which the final vital force was flickering out in brilliant fireworks of wit and depravity. At the commencement, the noble caste was always the barbarian caste: their superiority did not consist first of all in their physical, but in their Psychical power—they were more *complete* men (which at every point also implies the same as "more complete beasts").

To refrain mutually from injury, from violence, from exploitation, and put one's will on a par with that of others: this may result in a certain rough sense in good conduct among individuals when the necessary conditions are given (namely, the actual similarity of the individuals in amount of force and degree of worth, and their co-relation within one Organization). As soon, however, as one wished to take this principle more generally, and if possible even as *the fundamental principle of society*, it would immediately disclose what it really is— namely, a Will to the *denial* of life, a principle of dissolution and decay. Here one must think profoundly to the very basis and resist all sentimental weakness: life itself is essentially appropriation, injury, conquest of the strange and weak, suppression, severity, obtrusion of peculiar forms, incorporation, and at the least, putting it mildest, exploitation;—but why should one for ever use precisely these words on which for ages a disparaging purpose has been stamped? Even the Organization within which, as was previously supposed, the individuals treat each other as equal—it takes place in every healthy aristocracy—must itself, if it be a living and not a dying Organization, do all that towards other bodies, which the individuals within it refrain from doing to each other: it will have to be the incarnated Will to Power, it will endeavor to grow, to gain ground, attract to itself and acquire ascendency—not owing to any morality or immorality, but because it *lives,* and because life is precisely Will to Power. On no point, however, is the ordinary consciousness of Europeans more unwilling to be corrected than on this matter; people now rave everywhere, even under the guise of science, about coming conditions of society in which "the exploiting character" is to be absent:—that sounds to my ears as if they promised to invent a mode of life which should refrain from all organic functions. "Exploitation" does not belong to a depraved, or imperfect and primitive society: it belongs to the *nature* of the living being as a primary organic function; it is a consequence of the intrinsic Will to Power, which is precisely the Will to Life.—Granting that as a theory this is a novelty—as a reality it is the *fundamental fact* of all history: let us be so far honest towards ourselves!

In a tour through the many finer and coarser moralities which have hitherto prevailed or still prevail on the earth, I found certain traits recurring regularly together and connected with one another, until finally two primary types revealed themselves to me, and a radical distinction was brought to light. There is *master*-morality and *slave*-morality;—I would at once add, however, that in all higher and mixed civilizations, there are also attempts at the reconciliation of the two moralities; but one finds still oftener the confusion and mutual misunderstanding of them, indeed, sometimes their close juxtaposition—even in the same man, within one soul. The distinctions of moral values have either originated in a ruling caste, pleasantly conscious of being different from the ruled—or among the ruled class, the slaves and dependents of all sorts. In the first case, when it is the rulers who determine the conception "good," it is the exalted, proud disposition which is regarded as the distinguishing feature, and that which determines the order of rank. The noble type of man separates from himself the beings in whom the opposite of this exalted, proud disposition displays itself: he despises them. Let it at once be noted that in this first kind of morality the antithesis "good" and "bad" means practically the same as "noble" and "despicable";—the antithesis "good" and "*evil*" is of a different origin. The cowardly, the timid, the insignificant, and those thinking merely of narrow utility are despised; moreover, also, the distrustful, with their constrained glances, the self-abasing, the dog-like kind of men who let themselves be abused, the mendicant flatterers, and above all the liars:—it is a fundamental belief of all aristocrats that the common people are untruthful. "We truthful ones"—the nobility in ancient Greece called themselves. It is obvious that everywhere the designations of moral value were at first applied to *men,* and were only derivatively and at a later period applied to *actions;* it is a gross mistake, therefore, when historians of morals start with questions like, "Why have sympathetic actions been praised?" The noble type of man regards himself as a determiner of values; he does not require to be approved of; he passes the judgment: "What is injurious to me is injurious in itself"; he knows that it is he himself only who confers honor on things; he is a creator of values. He honors whatever he recognizes in himself: such morality is self-glorification. In the foreground there is the feeling of plenitude, of power, which seeks to overflow, the happiness of high tension, the consciousness of a wealth which would fain give and bestow:— the noble man also helps the unfortunate, but not—or scarcely—out of pity, but rather from an impulse generated by the superabundance of power. The noble man honors in himself the powerful one, him also who has power over himself, who knows how to speak and how to keep silence, who takes pleasure in subjecting himself to severity and hardness, and has reverence for all that is severe and hard. "Wotan placed a hard heart in my breast," says an old Scandinavian Saga: it is thus rightly expressed from the soul of a proud Viking. Such a type of man is even proud of *not* being made for sympathy; the hero of the Saga therefore adds warningly: "He who has not a hard heart when young, will never have one." The noble and brave who think thus are the furthest removed from the morality which sees precisely in sympathy, or in acting for the good of others, or in *désintéressement,* the characteristic of the moral; faith in oneself, pride in oneself, a radical enmity and irony towards "selflessness," belong as definitely to noble morality, as do a careless scorn and precaution in presence of sympathy and the "warm heart."—It is the powerful who *know* how to honor, it is their art, their domain for invention. The profound reverence for age and for tradition— all law rests on this double reverence,—the belief and prejudice in favor of ancestors and unfavorable to newcomers, is typical in the morality of the powerful; and if, reversely, men of "modern ideas" believe almost instinctively in "progress" and the "future," and are more and more lacking in respect for old age, the ignoble origin of these "ideas" has complacently betrayed itself thereby. A morality of the ruling class, however, is more especially foreign and irritating to present-day taste in the sternness of its principle that one has duties only to one's equals; that one may act towards beings of a lower rank, towards all that is foreign, just as seems good to one, or "as the heart desires," and in any case "beyond good and evil": it is here that sympathy and similar sentiments can have a place. The ability and obligation to exercise prolonged gratitude and prolonged revenge—both only within the circle of equals,—artfulness in retaliation, *raffinement* of the idea in friendship, a certain necessity to have enemies (as outlets for the emotions of envy, quarrelsomeness, arrogance—in fact, in order to be a good *friend*): all these are typical characteristics of the noble morality, which, as has been pointed out, is not the morality of "modern ideas," and is therefore at present difficult to realize, and also to unearth and disclose.— It is otherwise with the second type of morality, *slave-morality.* Supposing that the abused, the oppressed, the suffering, the unemancipated, the weary, and those uncertain of themselves, should moralize, what will be the common element in their moral estimates? Probably a pessimistic suspicion with regard to the entire situation of man will find expression, perhaps a condemnation of man, together with his situation. The slave has an unfavorable eye for the virtues of the powerful; he has a skepticism and distrust, a *refinement* of distrust of everything "good" that is there honored—he would fain persuade himself that the very happiness there is not genuine. On the other hand, *those* qualities which serve to alleviate the existence of sufferers are brought into prominence and flooded with light; it is here that sympathy, the kind, helping hand, the warm heart, patience, diligence, humility, and friendliness attain to honor; for here these are the most useful qualities, and almost the only means of supporting the burden of existence. Slave-morality is essentially the morality of utility. Here is the seat of the origin of the famous antithesis "good" and "evil":—power and dangerousness are assumed to reside in the evil, a certain dreadfulness, subtlety, and strength, which do not admit of being despised. According to slave-morality, therefore, the "evil" man arouses fear: according to master-morality, it is precisely the "good" man who arouses fear and seeks to arouse it, while the bad man is regarded as the despicable being. The contrast attains its maximum when, in accordance with the logical consequences of slave-morality, a shade of depreciation—it may be slight and well-intentioned—at last attaches itself even to the "good" man of this morality; because, according to the servile mode of thought, the good man must in any case be the *safe* man: he is good-natured, easily deceived, perhaps a little stupid, *un bonhomme.* Everywhere that slave-morality gains the ascendency, language shows a tendency to approximate the significations of the words "good" and "stupid."—A last fundamental difference: the desire for *freedom*, the instinct for happiness and the refinements of the feeling of liberty belong as necessarily to slave-morals and morality, as artifice and enthusiasm in reverence and devotion are the regular symptoms of an aristocratic mode of thinking and estimating.—Hence we can understand without further detail why love as *a passion*—it is our European speciality—must absolutely be of noble origin; as is well known, its invention is due to the Provençal poet-cavaliers, those brilliant ingenious men of the "gai saber," to whom Europe owes so much, and almost owes itself.

THE TWILIGHT OF THE IDOLS

What then, alone, can our teaching be?—That no one gives man his qualities, either God, society, his parents, his ancestors, nor himself (this nonsensical idea, which is at last refuted here, was taught as "intelligible freedom" [by] Kant, and perhaps even as early as Plato himself). No one is responsible for the fact that he exists at all, that he is constituted as he is, and that he happens to be in certain circumstances and in a particular environment. The fatality of his being cannot be divorced from the fatality of all that which has been and will be. This is not the result of an individual attention, of a will, of an aim, there is no attempt at attaining to any "ideal man," or "ideal happiness" or "ideal morality" with him—it is absurd to wish him to be careering towards some sort of purpose. We invented the concept "purpose"; in reality purpose is altogether lacking. One is necessary, one is a piece of fate, one belongs to the whole, one is in the whole—there is nothing that could judge, measure, compare, and condemn our existence, for that would mean judging, measuring, comparing and condemning the whole. *But there is nothing outside the whole!* The fact that no one shall any longer be made responsible, that the nature of existence may not be traced to a *causa prima,* that the world is an entity neither as a sensorium nor as a spirit—this alone is the great deliverance—*thus alone is the innocence of Becoming restored.* . . . The concept "God" has been the greatest objection to existence hitherto. . . . We deny God, we deny responsibility in God: thus alone do we save the world.

THE WILL TO POWER

I regard Christianity as the most fatal and seductive lie that has ever existed—as the greatest and most *impious* lie: I can discern the last sprouts [and] branches of its ideal beneath every form of disguise, I decline to enter into compromise or false position in reference to it—I urge people to declare open war with it.

   The morality of paltry people as the measure of all things: this is the most repugnant kind of degeneracy that civilization has ever yet brought into existence. And this *kind of ideal* is hanging still, under the name of "God," over men's heads!!

   However modest one's demands may be concerning intellectual cleanliness, when one touches the New Testament one cannot help experiencing a sort of inexpressible feeling of discomfort; for the unbounded cheek with which the least qualified people will have their say in its pages, in regard to the greatest problems of existence, and claim to sit in judgment on such matters, exceeds all limits. The impudent levity with which the most unwieldy problems are spoken of here (life, the world, God, the purpose of life), as if they were not problems at all, but the most simple things which these little bigots *know all about!!!*

This was the most fatal form of insanity that has ever yet existed on earth:—when these little lying abortions of bigotry begin laying claim to the words "God," "last judgment," "truth," "love," "wisdom," "Holy Spirit," and thereby distinguishing themselves from the rest of the world; when such men begin to transvalue values to suit themselves, as though they were the sense, the salt, the standard, and the measure of all things; then all that one should do is this: build lunatic asylums for their incarceration. To *persecute* them was an egregious act of antique folly: this was taking them too seriously; it was making them serious.

The whole fatality was made possible by the fact that a similar form of megalomania was already *in existence*, the *Jewish* form (once the gulf separating the Jews from the Christian-Jews was bridged, the Christian-Jews were *compelled* to employ those self-preservative measures afresh which were discovered by the Jewish instinct, for their own self-preservation, after having accentuated them); and again through the fact that Greek moral philosophy had done everything that could be done to prepare the way for moral-fanaticism, even among Greeks and Romans, and to render it palatable. . . . Plato, the great importer of corruption, who was the first who refused to see Nature in morality, and who had already deprived the Greek gods of all their worth by his notion *"good,"* was already tainted with *Jewish bigotry* (in Egypt?). . . .

The *law,* which is the fundamentally realistic formula of certain self-preservative measures of a community, forbids certain actions that have a definite tendency to jeopardize the welfare of that community: it does *not* forbid the attitude of mind which gives rise to these actions—for in the pursuit of other ends the community requires these forbidden actions, namely, when it is a matter of opposing its *enemies.* The moral idealist now steps forward and says: "God sees into men's hearts: the action itself counts for nothing; the reprehensible attitude of mind from which it proceeds must be extirpated. . . ." In normal conditions men laugh at such things; it is only in exceptional cases, when a community lives *quite* beyond the need of waging war in order to maintain itself, that an ear is lent to such things. Any attitude of mind is abandoned, the utility of which cannot be conceived.

This was the case, for example, when Buddha appeared among a people that was both peaceable and afflicted with great intellectual weariness.

This was also the case in regard to the first Christian community (as also the Jewish), the primary condition of which was the absolutely *unpolitical* Jewish society. Christianity could grow only upon the soil of Judaism—that is to say, among a people that had already renounced the political life, and which led a sort of parasitic existence within the Roman sphere of government. Christianity goes a step *farther;* it allows men to "emasculate" themselves even more; the circumstances actually favor their doing so.—*Nature* is *expelled* from morality when it is said, "Love ye your enemies": for *Nature's* injunction, "Ye shall *love* your neighbor and *hate* your enemy," has now become senseless in the law (in instinct); now, even *the love a man feels for his neighbor* must first be based upon something (*a sort of love of God*). *God* is introduced everywhere, and *utility* is withdrawn; the natural *origin* of morality is denied everywhere: the *veneration of Nature,* which lies in *acknowledging a natural morality, is destroyed* to the roots. . . .

Whence comes the *seductive charm* of this emasculate ideal of man? Why are we not *disgusted* by it, just as we are disgusted at the thought of a eunuch? . . . The answer is obvious: it is not the voice of the eunuch that revolts us, despite the cruel mutilation of which it is the result; for, as a matter of fact, it has grown sweeter. . . . And owing to the very fact that the "male organ" has been amputated from virtue, its voice now has a feminine ring, which, formerly, was not to be discerned.

On the other hand, we have only to think of the terrible hardness, dangers, and accidents to which a life of manly virtues leads—the life of a Corsican, even at the present day, or that of a heathen Arab (which resembles the Corsican's life even to the smallest detail: the Arab's songs might have been written by Corsicans)—in order to perceive how the most robust type of man was fascinated and moved by the voluptuous ring of this "goodness" and "purity. . . . A pastoral melody . . . an idyll . . . the "good man": such things have most effect in ages when tragedy is abroad.

The Astuteness of moral castration.—How is war waged against the virile passions and valuations? No violent physical means are available; the war must therefore be one of ruses, spells, and lies—in short, a "spiritual war."

First recipe: One appropriates virtue in general, and makes it the main feature of one's ideal; the older ideal is denied and declared to be *the reverse of all ideals.* Slander has to be carried to a fine art for this purpose.

Second recipe: One's own type is set up as a general *standard;* and this is projected into all things, behind all things, and behind the destiny of all things—as God.

Third recipe: The opponents of one's ideal are declared to be the opponents of God; one arrogates to oneself a *right* to great pathos, to power, and a right to curse and to bless.

Fourth recipe: All suffering, all gruesome, terrible, and fatal things are declared to be the results of opposition to *one's* ideal—all suffering is *punishment* even in the case of one's adherents (except it be a trial, etc.).

Fifth recipe: One goes so far as to regard Nature as the reverse of one's ideal, and the lengthy sojourn amid natural conditions is considered a great trial of patience—a sort of martyrdom; one studies contempt, both in one's attitudes and one's looks towards all "natural things."

Sixth recipe: The triumph of anti-naturalism and ideal castration, the triumph of the world of the pure, good, sinless, and blessed, is projected into the future as the consummation, the finale, the great hope, and the "Coming of the Kingdom of God."

I hope that one may still be allowed to laugh at this artificial hoisting up of a small species of man to the position of an absolute standard of all things?

To what extent psychologists have been corrupted by the moral idiosyncrasy!—Not one of the ancient philosophers had the courage to advance the theory of the non-free will (that is to say, the theory that denies morality);—not one had the courage to identify the typical feature of happiness, of every kind of happiness ("pleasure"), with the will to power: for the pleasure of power was considered immoral;—not one had the courage to regard virtue as a *result of immorality* (as a result of a will to power) in the service of a species (or of a race, or of a *polis);* for the will to power was considered immoral.

In the whole of moral evolution, there is no sign of truth: all the conceptual elements which come into play are fictions; all the psychological tenets are false; all the forms of logic employed in this department of prevarication are sophisms. The chief feature of all moral philosophers is their total lack of intellectual cleanliness and self-control: they regard "fine feelings" as arguments: their heaving breasts seem to them the bellows of godliness. . . . Moral philosophy is the most suspicious period in the history of the human intellect.

The first great example: in the name of morality and under its patronage, a great wrong was committed, which as a matter of fact was in every respect an act of decadence. Sufficient stress cannot be laid upon this fact, that the great Greek philosophers not only represented the decadence of *every kind of Greek ability,* but also made it *contagious.* . . . This "virtue" made wholly abstract was the highest form of seduction; to make oneself abstract means to *turn one's back on the world.*

The moment is a very remarkable one: the Sophists are within sight of the first *criticism* of morality, the first *knowledge* of morality:—they classify the majority of moral valuations (in view of their dependence upon local conditions) together;—they lead one to understand that every form of morality is capable of being upheld dialectically: that is to say, they guessed that all the fundamental principles of a morality must be *sophistical*—a proposition which was afterwards proved in the grandest possible style by the ancient philosophers from Plato onwards (up to Kant);—they postulate the primary truth that there is no such thing as a "moral *per se,"* a "good *per se,"* and that it is madness to talk of "truth" in this respect.

Wherever was *intellectual uprightness* to be found in those days?

The Greek culture of the Sophists had grown out of all the Greek instincts; it belongs to the culture of the age of Pericles as necessarily as Plato does not: it has its predecessors in Heraclitus, Democritus, and in the scientific types of the old philosophy; it finds expression in the elevated culture of Thucydides, for instance. And—it has ultimately shown itself to be right: every step in the science of epistemology and morality has *confirmed the attitude of* the Sophists. . . . Our modern attitude of mind is, to a great extent, Heraclitean, Democritean, and Protagorean. . . to say that it is *Protagorean* is even sufficient: because Protagoras was in himself a synthesis of the two men Heraclitus and Democritus.

(*Plato: a great Cagliostro,*—let us think of how Epicurus judged him; how Timon, Pyrrho's friend, judged him—Is Plato's integrity by any chance beyond question?. . . But we at least know what he wished to have *taught as* absolute truth—namely, things which were to him not even relative truths: the separate and immortal life of "souls.")

Leo Tolstoy: The Aim of Life
From *My Confession*

Born into a wealthy family near the Russian city of Tula, Leo Tolstoy (1828–1910) was one of that country's most important authors, and is best remembered for his novels War and Peace, *and* Anna Karenina. *In his autobiography titled* My Confession *(1882), he describes his personal history, in which he discovered that no amount of achievement, wealth, or fame can prevent a person from being concerned about the meaning of life. Tolstoy describes how he found a meaning for himself in religious faith—although he does not describe in any detail the elements of that faith.*

I was baptized and educated in the Orthodox Christian faith. I was taught it from childhood and through the whole time of my boyhood and youth. But when I, at eighteen years of age, left the second year's course of the university, I no longer believed any of the things I had been taught. . . .

My defection from faith took place in the same manner as it has taken place and still takes place in people of our cultivated class. . . .

I wished with all my heart to be good; but I was young, I had passions, and I was alone, completely alone, when I was trying to find the good. Every time I endeavored to give utterance to what formed my most intimate wishes, namely, that I wished to be morally good, I met with contempt and ridicule; and the moment I surrendered myself to the abominable passions, I was praised and encouraged.

Ambition, lust of power, selfishness, voluptuousness, pride, anger, revenge—all that was respected. By abandoning myself to these passions I became like a grown person, and I felt that people were satisfied with me. A good aunt of mine, a pure soul, with whom I was living, kept telling me that there was nothing she wished so much for me as that I should have a liaison with a married woman. . . . I . . . fornicated, and cheated. Lying, stealing, acts of lust of every description, drunkenness, violence, murder—there was not a crime which I did not commit, and for all that I was praised, and my contemporaries regarded me as a comparatively moral man.

Thus I lived for ten years. . . .

When I came back [from St. Petersburg], I got married. The new conditions of my happy family life completely drew me away from all search for the general meaning of life. All my life during that time was centered in my family, my wife, my children, and, therefore, in cares for the increase of the means of existence. The striving after perfection. . . now gave way simply to the striving after making it as comfortable as possible for me and my family.

Thus another fifteen years passed.

Leo Tolstoy, from *My Confession* (1882).

Although I regarded authorship as a waste of time, I continued to write during those fifteen years. I had talked of the seduction of authorship, of the seduction of enormous monetary remunerations and applauses for my insignificant labor, and so I submitted to it, as being a means for improving my material condition and for stifling in my soul all questions about the meaning of my life and life in general.

In my writings I advocated, what to me was the only truth, that it was necessary to live in such a way as to derive the greatest comfort for oneself and one's family.

Thus I proceeded to live, but five years ago something very strange began to happen with me: I was overcome by minutes at first of perplexity and then of an arrest of life, as though I did not know how to live or what to do, and I lost myself and was dejected. But that passed, and I continued to live as before. Then those minutes of perplexity were repeated oftener and oftener, and always in one and the same form. These arrests of life found their expression in ever the same questions: "Why? Well, and then?"

At first I thought that those were simply aimless, inappropriate questions. It seemed to me that that was all well known and that if I ever wanted to busy myself with their solution, it would not cost me much labor—that now I had no time to attend to them, but that if I wanted to I should find the proper answers. But the questions began to repeat themselves oftener and oftener, answers were demanded more and more persistently, and, like dots that fall on the same spot, these questions, without any answers, thickened into one black blotch. . . .

My life came to a standstill. . . . The truth was that life was meaningless. It was as though I had just been living and walking along, and had come to an abyss, where I saw clearly that there was nothing ahead but perdition. . . .

. . . I did not know myself what it was I wanted: I was afraid of life, strove to get away from it, and, at the same time, expected something from it.

All that happened with me when I was on every side surrounded by what is considered to be complete happiness. I had a good, loving, and beloved wife, good children, and a large estate, which grew and increased without any labor on my part. I was respected by my neighbors and friends, more than ever before, was praised by strangers, and, without any self-deception, could consider my name famous. With all that, I was not deranged or mentally unsound—on the contrary, I was in full command of my mental and physical powers, such as I had rarely met with in people of my age: physically I could work in a field, mowing, without falling behind a peasant; mentally I could work from eight to ten hours in succession, without experiencing any consequences from the strain. And while in such condition I arrived at the conclusion that I could not live, and, fearing death, I had to use cunning against myself, in order that I might not take my life. . . .

Long ago has been told the Eastern story about the traveler who in the steppe is overtaken by an infuriated beast. Trying to save himself from the animal, the traveler jumps into a waterless well, but at its bottom he sees a dragon who opens his jaws in order to swallow him. And the unfortunate man does not dare climb out, lest he perish from the infuriated beast, and does not dare jump down to the bottom of the well, lest he be devoured by the dragon, and so clutches the twig of a wild bush growing in a cleft of the well and holds on to it. His hands grow weak and he feels that soon he shall have to surrender to the peril which awaits him at either side; but he still holds on and sees two mice, one white, the other black, in even measure making a circle around the main trunk of the bush to which he is clinging, and nibbling at it on all sides. Now, at any moment, the bush will break and tear off, and he will fall into the dragon's jaws. The traveler sees that and knows that he will inevitably perish; but while he is still clinging, he sees some drops of honey hanging on the leaves of the bush, and so reaches out for them with his tongue and licks the leaves. Just so I hold on to the branch of life, knowing that the dragon of death is waiting inevitably for me, ready to tear me to pieces, and I cannot understand why I have fallen on such suffering. And I try to lick that honey which used to give me pleasure; but now it no longer gives me joy, and the white and the black mouse day and night nibble at the branch to which I am holding on. I clearly see the dragon, and the honey is no longer sweet to me. I see only the inevitable dragon and the mice, and am unable to turn my glance away from them. That is not a fable, but a veritable, indisputable, comprehensible truth.

The former deception of the pleasures of life, which stifled the terror of the dragon, no longer deceives me. No matter how much one should say to me, "You cannot understand the meaning of life, do not think, live!" I am unable to do so, because I have been doing it too long before. Now I cannot help seeing day and night, which run and lead me up to death. I see that alone, because that alone is the truth. Everything else is a lie.

The two drops of honey that have longest turned my eyes away from the cruel truth, the love of family and of authorship, which I have called an art, are no longer sweet to me.

"My family," I said to myself, "but my family, my wife and children, they are also human beings. They are in precisely the same condition that I am in: they must either live in the lie or see the terrible truth. Why should they live? Why should I love them, why guard, raise, and watch them? Is it for the same despair which is in me, or for dullness of perception? Since I love them, I cannot conceal the truth from them,—every step in cognition leads them up to this truth. And the truth is death."

"Art, poetry?" For a long time, under the influence of the success of human praise, I tried to persuade myself that that was a thing which could be done, even though death should come and destroy everything, my deeds, as well as my memory of them; but soon I came to see that that, too, was a deception. It was clear to me that art was an adornment of life, a decoy of life. But life lost all its attractiveness for me. How, then, could I entrap others? So long as I did not live my own life, and a strange life bore me on its waves; so long as I believed that life had some sense, although I was not able to express it,—the reflections of life of every description in poetry and in the arts afforded me pleasure, and I was delighted to look at life through this little mirror of art; but when I began to look for the meaning of life, when I experienced the necessity of living myself, that little mirror became either useless, superfluous, and ridiculous, or painful to me. I could no longer console myself with what I saw in the mirror, namely, that my situation was stupid and desperate. It was all right for me to rejoice so long as I believed in the depth of my soul that life had some sense. At that time the play of lights—of the comical, the tragical, the touching, the beautiful, the terrible in life—afforded me amusement. But when I knew that life was meaningless and terrible, the play in the little mirror could no longer amuse me. No sweetness of honey could be sweet to me, when I saw the dragon and the mice that were nibbling down my support.

That was not all. If I had simply comprehended that life had no meaning, I might have known that calmly, I might have known that that was my fate. But I could not be soothed by that. . . . I was like a man who had lost his way in the forest, who was overcome by terror because he had lost his way, who kept tossing about in his desire to come out on the road, knowing that every step got him only more entangled, and who could not help tossing. . . .

"But, perhaps, I overlooked something, or did not understand something right?" I said to myself several times. "It is impossible that this condition of despair should be characteristic of men!" And I tried to find an explanation for these questions in all those branches of knowledge which men had acquired . . . and I found nothing.

For a long time I could not believe that science had no answer to give to the questions of life. . . .

. . . If you turn to the branch of knowledge which does not busy itself with the solution of the problems of life, but answers only its special, scientific questions, you are delighted at the power of the human mind, but know in advance that there will be no answers there to the questions of life. These sciences directly ignore the question of life. They say: "We have no answers to what you are and why you live, and we do not busy ourselves with that; but if you want to know the laws of light, of chemical combinations, the laws of the development of organisms, if you want to know the laws of the bodies, their forms, and the relation of numbers and quantities, if you want to know the laws of your mind, we shall give you clear, definite, incontrovertible answers to all that.". . .

No matter how strange, how incredibly incomprehensible it now seems to me that I, discussing life, should have been able to overlook all those who surrounded me on all sides, the life of humanity, that I should have been able to err in such a ridiculous manner as to think that my life, and the life of a Solomon and a Schopenhauer, was the real, the normal life, while the life of billions was a circumstance that did not deserve consideration . . .

I lived for a long time in this madness, which, not in words, but in deeds, is particularly characteristic of us, the most liberal and learned of men. But, thanks either to my strange, physical love for the real working class, which made me understand it and see that it is not so stupid as we suppose, or to the sincerity of my conviction, which was that I could know nothing and that the best that I could do was to hang myself,—I felt that if I wanted to live and understand the meaning of life, I ought naturally to look for it, not among those who had lost the meaning of life and wanted to kill themselves, but among those billions departed and living men who had been carrying their own lives and ours upon their shoulders. And I looked around at the enormous masses of deceased and living men,—not learned and wealthy, but simple men,—and I saw something quite different. I saw that all these billions of men that lived or had lived, all, with rare exceptions, did not fit into my subdivisions, and that I could not recognize them as not understanding the question, because they themselves put it and answered it with surprising clearness. Nor could I recognize them as Epicureans, because their lives were composed rather of privations and suffering than of enjoyment. Still less could I recognize them as senselessly living out their meaningless lives, because every act of theirs and death itself was explained by them. They regarded it as the greatest evil to kill themselves. It appeared, then, that all humanity was in possession of a knowledge of the meaning of life, which I did not recognize and which I contemned. It turned out that rational knowledge did not give any meaning to life, excluded life, while the meaning which by billions of people, by all humanity, was ascribed to life was based on some despised, false knowledge.

The rational knowledge in the person of the learned and the wise denied the meaning of life, but the enormous masses of men, all humanity, recognized this meaning in an irrational knowledge. This irrational knowledge was faith, the same that I could not help but reject. That was God as one and three, the creation in six days, devils and angels, and all that which I could not accept so long as I had not lost my senses.

My situation was a terrible one. I knew that I should not find anything on the path of rational knowledge but the negation of life, and there, in faith, nothing but the negation of reason, which was still more impossible than the negation of life. From the rational knowledge it followed that life was an evil and men knew it,—it depended on men whether they should cease living, and yet they lived and continued to live, and I myself lived, though I had known long ago that life was meaningless and an evil. From faith it followed that, in order to understand life, I must renounce reason, for which alone a meaning was needed.

There resulted a contradiction, from which there were two ways out: either what I called rational was not so rational as I had thought; or that which to me appeared irrational was not so irrational as I had thought. And I began to verify the train of thoughts of my rational knowledge.

In verifying the train of thoughts of my rational knowledge, I found that it was quite correct. The deduction that life was nothing was inevitable; but I saw a mistake. The mistake was that I had not reasoned in conformity with the question put by me. The question was, "Why should I live?" that is, "What real, indestructible essence will come from my phantasmal, destructible life? What meaning has my finite existence in this infinite world?" And in order to answer this question, I studied life.

The solutions of all possible questions of life apparently could not satisfy me, because my question, no matter how simple it appeared in the beginning, included the necessity of explaining the finite through the infinite, and vice versa.

I asked, "What is the extra-temporal, extra-causal, extra-spatial meaning of life?" But I gave an answer to the question, "What is the temporal, causal, spatial meaning of my life?" The result was that after a long labor of mind I answered, "None."

In my reflections I constantly equated, nor could I do otherwise, the finite with the finite, the infinite with the infinite, and so from that resulted precisely what had to result: force was force, matter was matter, will was will, infinity was infinity, nothing was nothing,—and nothing else could come from it.

There happened something like what at times takes place in mathematics: you think you are solving an equation, when you have only an identity. The reasoning is correct, but you receive as a result the answer: $a = a$, or $x = x$, or $0 = 0$. The same happened with my reflection in respect to the question about the meaning of my life. The answers given by all science to that question are only identities.

Indeed, the strictly scientific knowledge, that knowledge which, as Descartes did, begins with a full doubt in everything, rejects all knowledge which has been taken on trust, and builds everything anew on the laws of reason and experience, cannot give any other answer to the question of life than what I received,—an indefinite answer. . . . Thus the philosophical knowledge does not negate anything, but only answers that the question cannot be solved by it, that for philosophy the solution remains insoluble.

When I saw that, I understood that it was not right for me to look for an answer to my question in rational knowledge, and that the answer given by rational knowledge was only an indication that the answer might be got if the question were differently put, but only when into the discussion of the question should be introduced the question of the relation of the finite to the infinite. I also understood that, no matter how irrational and monstrous the answers might be that faith gave, they had this advantage that they introduced into each answer the relation of the finite to the infinite, without which there could be no answer.

No matter how I may put the question, "How must I live?" the answer is, "According to God's law." "What real result will there be from my life?" "Eternal torment or eternal bliss." "What is the meaning which is not destroyed by death?"—"The union with infinite God, paradise." Thus, outside the rational knowledge, which had to me appeared as the only one, I was inevitably led to recognize that all living humanity had a certain other irrational knowledge, faith, which made it possible to live.

All the irrationality of faith remained the same for me, but I could not help recognizing that it alone gave to humanity answers to the questions of life, and, in consequence of them, the possibility of living.

The rational knowledge brought me to the recognition that life was meaningless,—my life stopped, and I wanted to destroy myself. When I looked around at people, at all humanity, I saw that people lived and asserted that they knew the meaning of life. I looked back at myself: I lived so long as I knew the meaning of life. As to other people, so even to me, did faith give the meaning of life and the possibility of living.

Looking again at the people of other countries, contemporaries of mine and those passed away, I saw again the same. Where life had been, there faith, ever since humanity had existed, had given the possibility of living, and the chief features of faith were everywhere one and the same.

No matter what answers faith may give, its every answer gives to the finite existence of man the sense of the infinite,—a sense which is not destroyed by suffering, privation, and death. Consequently in faith alone could we find the meaning and possibility of life. What, then, was faith? I understood that faith was not merely an evidence of things not seen, and so forth, not revelation (that is only the description of one of the symptoms of faith), not the relation of man to man (faith has to be defined, and then God, and not first God, and faith through him), not merely an agreement with what a man was told, as faith was generally understood,—that faith was the knowledge of the meaning of human life, in consequence of which man did not destroy himself, but lived. Faith is the power of life. If a man lives he believes in something. If he did not believe that he ought to live for some purpose, he would not live. If he does not see and understand the phantasm of the finite, he believes in that finite; if he understands the phantasm of the finite, he must believe in the infinite. Without faith one cannot live.

I was prepared now to accept any faith, so long as it did not demand from me a direct denial of reason, which would have been a lie. . . .

In order that all humanity may be able to live, in order that they may continue living, giving a meaning to life, they, those billions, must have another, a real knowledge of faith, for not the fact that I, with Solomon and Schopenhauer, did not kill myself convinced me of the existence of faith, but that these billions had lived and had borne us, me and Solomon, on the waves of life.

Then I began to cultivate the acquaintance of the believers from among the poor, the simple and unlettered folk, of pilgrims, monks, dissenters, peasants. The doctrine of these people from among the masses was also the Christian doctrine that the quasi-believers of our circle professed. With the Christian truths were also mixed in very many superstitions, but there was this difference: the superstitions of our circle were quite unnecessary to them, had no connection with their lives, were only a kind of an Epicurean amusement, while the superstitions of the believers from among the laboring classes were to such an extent blended with their life that it would have been impossible to imagine it without these superstitions,—it was a necessary condition of that life. I began to examine closely the lives and beliefs of these people, and the more I examined them, the more did I become convinced that they had the real faith, that their faith was necessary for them, and that it alone gave them a meaning and possibility of life. In contradistinction to what I saw in our circle, where life without faith was possible, and where hardly one in a thousand professed to be a believer, among them there was hardly one in a thousand who was not a believer. In contradistinction to what I saw in our circle, where all life passed in idleness, amusements, and tedium of life, I saw that the whole life of these people was passed in hard work, and that they were satisfied with life. In contradistinction to the people of our circle, who struggled and murmured against fate because of their privations and their suffering, these people accepted diseases and sorrows without any perplexity or opposition, but with the calm and firm conviction that it was all for good. In contradistinction to the fact that the more intelligent we are, the less do we understand the meaning of life and the more do we see a kind of a bad joke in our suffering and death, these people live, suffer, and approach death, and suffer in peace and more often in joy. In contradistinction to the fact that a calm death, a death without terror or despair, is the greatest exception in our circle, a restless, insubmissive, joyless death is one of the greatest exceptions among the masses. And of such people, who are deprived of everything which for Solomon and for me constitutes the only good of life, and who withal experience the greatest happiness, there is an enormous number. I cast a broader glance about me. I examined the life of past and present vast masses of men, and I saw people who in like manner had understood the meaning of life, who had known how to live and die, not two, not three, not ten, but hundreds, thousands, millions. All of them, infinitely diversified as to habits, intellect, culture, situation, all equally and quite contrary to my ignorance knew the meaning of life and of death, worked calmly, bore privations and suffering, lived and died, seeing in that not vanity, but good.

I began to love those people. The more I penetrated into their life, the life of the men now living, and the life of men departed, of whom I had read and heard, the more did I love them, and the easier it became for me to live. Thus I lived for about two years, and within me took place a transformation, which has long been working within me, and the germ of which had always been in me. What happened with me was that the life of our circle—of the rich and the learned—not only disgusted me, but even lost all its meaning. All our acts, reflections, sciences, arts—all that appeared to me in a new light. I saw that all that was mere pampering of the appetites, and that no meaning could be found in it; but the life of all the working masses, of all humanity, which created life, presented itself to me in its real significance. I saw that that was life itself and that the meaning given to this life was truth, and I accepted it.

PART FIVE

Twentieth Century and Contemporary

William James:
Free Will and Pragmatism

From *The Dilemma of Determinism* and *Pragmatism*

Born in New York City, William James (1842–1919) made significant contributions in the fields of both philosophy and psychology. He was one of the chief proponents of a distinctively American approach to philosophy called "pragmatism," which emerged in the late nineteenth and early twentieth centuries, and selections from two of his works are below. In The Dilemma of Determinism *(1884), James asks how it is possible to explain our judgments of regret if we could never have behaved differently. This problem, he believes, should prompt us to reject determinism. In* Pragmatism: A New Name for Some Old Ways of Thinking *(1907), James presents the radical view that "truth is made," that is, that "truth is what happens to an idea." What was so radical about this was that James rejected the conventional definition of truth—now called the "correspondence theory of truth"—that truth is the agreement of an idea with "reality." On this view a true idea is something like a mental copy of an external thing. James found fault with this notion of truth because he did not know with any clarity what it means for an idea to "agree with" or "copy" reality, and he certainly could not be sure what in every case was meant by "reality." For him the essential question was this: What practical value is there in saying that something is true? He asks, "What concrete difference will [an idea's] being true make in one's actual life?" Or, "What experience will be different from those which would obtain if the belief were false?" Finally, "What, in short, is the truth's cash-value in experiential terms?" An idea is true "if it works." Truth is made true by events. And, says James, "True ideas are those that we can assimilate, validate, corroborate, and verify."*

Source: William James, "The Dilemma of Determinism," in *Unitarian Review* (September 1884); *Pragmatism* (1907), Lecture 6.

HOW CAN WE EXPLAIN JUDGMENTS OF REGRET?

The Dispute between Determinism and Indeterminism

What does determinism profess?

It professes that those parts of the universe already laid down absolutely appoint and decree what the other parts shall be. The future has no ambiguous possibilities hidden in its womb: the part we call the present is compatible with only one totality. Any other future complement than the one fixed from eternity is impossible. The whole is in each and every part, and welds it with the rest into an absolute unity, an iron block, in which there can be no equivocation or shadow of turning.

> With earth's first clay they did the last man knead,
> And there of the last harvest sowed the seed.
> And the first morning of creation wrote
> What the last dawn of reckoning shall read.

Indeterminism, on the contrary, says that the parts have a certain amount of loose play on one another, so that the laying down of one of them does not necessarily determine what the others shall be. It admits that possibilities may be in excess of actualities, and that things not yet revealed to our knowledge may really in themselves be ambiguous. Of two alternative futures which we conceive, both may now be really possible; and the one become impossible only at the very moment when the other excludes it by becoming real itself.

Indeterminism thus denies the world to be one unbending unit of fact. It says there is a certain ultimate pluralism in it; and, so saying, it corroborates our ordinary unsophisticated view of things. To that view, actualities seem to float in a wider sea of possibilities from out of which they are chosen; and, *somewhere*, indeterminism says, such possibilities exist, and form a part of truth.

Determinism, on the contrary, says they exist *nowhere*, and that necessity on the one hand and impossibility on the other are the sole categories of the real. Possibilities that fail to get realized are, for determinism, pure illusions: they never were possibilities at all. There is nothing inchoate, it says, about this universe of ours, all that was or is or shall be actual in it having been from eternity virtually there. The cloud of alternatives our minds escort this mass of actuality withal is a cloud of sheer deceptions, to which "impossibilities" is the only name that rightfully belongs.

The issue, it will be seen, is a perfectly sharp one, which no eulogistic terminology can smear over or wipe out. The truth *must* lie with one side or the other, and its lying with one side makes the other false.

The question relates solely to the existence of possibilities, in the strict sense of the term, as things that may, but need not, be. Both sides admit that a volition, for instance, has occurred. The indeterminists say another volition might have occurred in its place: the determinists swear that nothing could possibly have occurred in its place. Now, can science be called in to tell us which of these two point-blank contradicters of each other is right? Science professes to draw no conclusions but such as are based on matters of fact, things that have actually happened; but how can any amount of assurance that something actually happened give us the least grain of information as to whether another thing might or might not have happened in its place? Only facts can be proved by other facts. With things that are possibilities and not facts, facts have no concern. If we have no other evidence than the evidence of existing facts, the possibility-question must remain a mystery never to be cleared up.

And the truth is that facts practically have hardly anything to do with making us either determinists or indeterminists. Sure enough, we make a flourish of quoting facts this way or that; and if we are determinists, we talk about the infallibility with which we can predict one another's conduct; while if we are indeterminists, we lay great stress on the fact that it is just because we cannot foretell one another's conduct, either in war or statecraft or in any of the great and small intrigues and businesses of men, that life is so intensely anxious and hazardous a game. But who does not see the wretched insufficiency of this so-called objective testimony on both sides? What fills up the gaps in our minds is something not objective, not external. What divides us into *possibility* men and *anti-possibility* men is different faiths or postulates—postulates of rationality. To this man the world seems more rational with possibilities in it—to that man more rational with possibilities excluded; and talk as we will about having to yield to evidence, what makes us monists or pluralists, determinists or indeterminists, is at bottom always some sentiment like this.

The stronghold of the deterministic sentiment is the antipathy to the idea of chance. As soon as we begin to talk indeterminism to our friends, we find a number of them shaking their heads. This notion of alternative possibility, they say, this admission that any one of several things may come to pass, is, after all, only a round-about name for chance; and chance is something the notion of which no sane mind can for an instant tolerate in the world. What is it, they ask, but barefaced crazy unreason, the negation of intelligibility and law? And if the slightest particle of it exists anywhere, what is to prevent the whole fabric from failing together, the stars from going out, and chaos from recommencing her topsy-turvy reign?

Remarks of this sort about chance will put an end to discussion as quickly as anything one can find. I have already told you that "chance" was a word I wished to keep and use. Let us then examine exactly what it means, and see whether it ought to be such a terrible bugbear to us. I fancy that squeezing the thistle boldly will rob it of its sting.

The sting of the word "chance" seems to lie in the assumption that it means something positive, and that if anything happens by chance, it must needs be something of an intrinsically irrational and preposterous sort. Now, chance means nothing of the kind. It is a purely negative and relative term, giving us no information about that of which it is predicated, except that it happens to be disconnected with something else—not controlled, secured, or necessitated by other things in advance of its own actual presence.

As this point is the most subtle one of the whole lecture, and at the same time the point on which all the rest hinges, I beg you to pay particular attention to it. What I say is that it tells us nothing about what a thing may be in itself to call it "chance." It may be a bad thing, it may be a good thing. It may be lucidity, transparency, fitness incarnate, matching the whole system of other things, when it has once befallen, in an unimaginably perfect way. All you mean by calling it "chance" is that this is not guaranteed, that it may also fall out otherwise. For the system of other things has no positive hold on the chance-thing. Its origin is in a certain fashion negative: it escapes, and says, Hands off! coming, when it comes, as a free gift, or not at all. . . .

Nevertheless, many persons talk as if the minutest dose of disconnectedness of one part with another, the smallest modicum of independence, the faintest tremor of ambiguity about the future, for example, would ruin everything, and turn this goodly universe into a sort of insane sand-heap or nulliverse—no universe at all. Since future human volitions are as a matter of fact the only ambiguous things we are tempted to believe in, let us stop for a moment to make ourselves sure whether their independent and accidental character need be fraught with such direful consequences to the universe as these.

What is meant by saying that my choice of which way to walk home after the lecture is ambiguous and a matter of chance as far as the present moment is concerned? It means that both Divinity Avenue and Oxford Street are called; but that only one, and that only *either* one, shall be chosen. Now, I ask you seriously to suppose that this ambiguity of my choice is real; and then to make the impossible hypothesis that the choice is made twice over, and each time falls on a different street. In other words, imagine that I first walk through Divinity Avenue, and then imagine that the powers governing the universe annihilate ten minutes of time with all that it contained, and set me back at the door of this hall just as I was before the choice was made. Imagine then that, everything else being the same, I now make a different choice and traverse Oxford Street. You, as passive spectators, look on and see the two alternative universes—one of them with me walking through Divinity Avenue in it, the other with the same me walking through Oxford Street. Now, if you are determinists you believe one of these universes to have been from eternity impossible: you believe it to have been impossible because of the intrinsic irrationality or accidentality somewhere involved in it. But looking outwardly at these universes, can you say which is the impossible and accidental one, and which the rational and necessary one? I doubt if the most iron-clad determinist among you could have the slightest glimmer of light on this point. In other words, either universe *after the fact* and once there would, to our means of observation and understanding, appear just as rational as the other. . . .

We have seen what determinism means: we have seen that indeterminism is rightly described as meaning chance; and we have seen that chance, the very name of which we are urged to shrink from as from a metaphysical pestilence, means only the negative fact that no part of the world, however big, can claim to control absolutely the destinies of the whole. But although, in discussing the word "chance," I may at moments have seemed to be arguing for its real existence, I have not meant to do so yet. We have not yet ascertained whether this be a world of chance or no; at most, we have agreed that it seems so. And I now repeat what I said at the outset, that, from any strict theoretical point of view, the question is insoluble. To deepen our theoretic sense of the *difference* between a world with chances in it and a deterministic world is the most I can hope to do; and this I may now at last begin upon, after all our tedious clearing of the way.

Implications of a Deterministic World

I wish first of all to show you just what the notion that this is a deterministic world implies. The implications I call your attention to are all bound up with the fact that it is a world in which we constantly have to make what I shall, with your permission, call judgments of regret. Hardly an hour passes in which we do not wish that something might be otherwise. . . . Even from the point of view of our own ends, we should probably make a botch of remodeling the universe. How much more then from the point of view of ends we cannot see! Wise men therefore regret as little as they can. But still some regrets are pretty obstinate and hard to stifle—regrets for acts of wanton cruelty or treachery, for example, whether performed by others or by ourselves. Hardly any one can remain *entirely* optimistic after reading the confession of the murderer at Brockton the other day: how, to get rid of the wife whose continued existence bored him, he inveigled her into a desert spot, shot her four times, and then, as she lay on the ground and said to him, "You didn't do it on purpose, did you, dear?" replied, "No, I didn't do it on purpose," as he raised a rock and smashed her skull. Such an occurrence, with the mild sentence and self-satisfaction of the prisoner, is a field for a crop of regrets, which one need not take up in detail. We feel that, although a perfect mechanical fit to the rest of the universe, it is a bad moral fit, and that something else would really have been better in its place.

But for the deterministic philosophy the murder, the sentence, and the prisoner's optimism were all necessary from eternity; and nothing else for a moment had a ghost of a chance of being put into their place. To admit such a chance, the determinists tell us, would be to make a suicide of reason; so we must steel our hearts against the thought. And here our plot thickens, for we see the first of all those difficult implications of determinism and monism which it is my purpose to make you feel. If this Brockton murder was called for by the rest of the universe, if it had to come at its pre-appointed hour, and if nothing else would have been consistent with the sense of the whole, what are we to think of the universe? Are we stubbornly to stick to our judgment of regret, and say, though it *couldn't* be, yet it *would* have been a better universe with something different from this Brockton murder in it? That, of course, seems the natural and spontaneous thing for us to do; and yet it is nothing short of deliberately espousing a kind of pessimism. The judgment of regret calls the murder bad. Calling a thing bad means, if it mean anything at all, that the thing ought not to be, that something else ought to be in its stead. Determinism, in denying that anything else can be in its stead, virtually defines the universe as a place in which what ought to be is impossible—in other words, as an organism whose constitution is afflicted with an incurable taint, an irremediable flaw. The pessimism of a Schopenhauer says no more than this—that the murder is a symptom; and that it is a vicious symptom because it belongs to a vicious whole, which can express its nature no otherwise than by bringing forth just such a symptom as that at this particular spot. Regret for the murder must transform itself, if we are determinists and wise, into a larger regret. It is absurd to regret the murder alone. Other things being what they are, *it* could not be different. What we should regret is that whole frame of things of which the murder is one member. I see no escape whatever from this pessimistic conclusion if, being determinists, our judgment of regret is to be allowed to stand at all.

The only deterministic escape from pessimism is everywhere to abandon the judgment of regret. That this can be done, history shows to be not impossible. The devil, *quoad existentiam,* may be good. That is, although he be a *principle* of evil, yet the universe, with such a principle in it, may practically be a better universe than it could have been without. On every hand, in a small way, we find that a certain amount of evil is a condition by which a higher form of good is brought. There is nothing to prevent anybody from generalizing this view, and trusting that if we could but see things in the largest of all ways, even such matters as this Brockton murder would appear to be paid for by the uses that follow in their train. An optimism *quand même,* a systematic and infatuated optimism like that ridiculed by Voltaire in his *Candide,* is one of the possible ideal ways in which a man may train himself to look on life. Bereft of dogmatic hardness and lit up with the expression of a tender and pathetic hope, such an optimism has been the grace of some of the most religious characters that ever lived.

> Throb thine with Nature's throbbing breast,
> And all is clear from east to west.

Even cruelty and treachery may be among the absolutely blessed fruits of time, and to quarrel with any of their details may be blasphemy. The only real blasphemy, in short, may be that pessimistic temper of the soul which lets it give way to such things as regrets, remorse, and grief.

Thus, our deterministic pessimism may become a deterministic optimism at the price of extinguishing our judgments of regret.

But does not this immediately bring us into a curious logical predicament? Our determinism leads us to call our judgments of regret wrong, because they are pessimistic in implying that what is impossible yet ought to be. But how then about the judgments of regret themselves? If they are wrong, other judgments, judgments of approval presumably, ought to be in their place. But as they are necessitated, nothing else *can* be in their place; and the universe is just what it was before—namely, a place in which what ought to be appears impossible. We have got one foot out of the pessimistic bog, but the other one sinks all the deeper. We have rescued our actions from the bonds of evil, but our judgments are now held fast. When murders and treacheries cease to be sins, regrets are theoretic absurdities and errors. The theoretic and the active life thus play a kind of see-saw with each other on the ground of evil. The rise of either sends the other down. Murder and treachery cannot be good without regret being bad: regret cannot be good without treachery and murder being bad. Both, however, are supposed to have been foredoomed; so something must be fatally unreasonable, absurd, and wrong in the world. It must be a place of which either sin or error forms a necessary part. From this dilemma there seems at first sight no escape. Are we then so soon to fall back into the pessimism from which we thought we had emerged? And is there no possible way by which we may, with good intellectual consciences, call the cruelties and the treacheries, the reluctances and the regrets, all good together? . . .

The only consistent way of representing a pluralism and a world whose parts may affect one another through their conduct being either good or bad is the indeterministic way. What interest, zest, or excitement can there be in achieving the right way, unless we are enabled to feel that the wrong way is also a possible and a natural way—nay, more, a menacing and an imminent way? And what sense can there be in condemning ourselves for taking the wrong way, unless we need have done nothing of the sort, unless the right way was open to us as well? I cannot understand the willingness to act, no matter how we feel, without the belief that acts are really good and bad. I cannot understand the belief that an act is bad, without regret at its happening. I cannot understand regret without the admission of real, genuine possibilities in the world. Only *then* is it other than a mockery to feel, after we have failed to do our best, that an irreparable opportunity is gone from the universe, the loss of which it must forever after mourn. . . .

PRAGMATISM'S CONCEPTION OF TRUTH

When Clerk Maxwell was a child it is written that he had a mania for having everything explained to him, and that when people put him off with vague verbal accounts of any phenomenon he would interrupt them impatiently by saying, "Yes; but I want you to tell me the *particular* go of it!" Had his question been about truth, only a pragmatist could have told him the particular go of it. I believe that our contemporary pragmatists, especially Messrs. Schiller and Dewey, have given the only tenable account of this subject. It is a very ticklish subject, sending subtle rootlets into all kinds of crannies, and hard to treat in the sketchy way that alone befits a public lecture. But the Schiller-Dewey view of truth has been so ferociously attacked by rationalistic philosophers, and so abominably misunderstood, that here, if anywhere, is the point where a clear and simple statement should be made.

I fully expect to see the pragmatist view of truth run through the classic stages of a theory's career. First, you know, a new theory is attacked as absurd; then it is admitted to be true, but obvious and insignificant; finally it is seen to be so important that its adversaries claim that they themselves discovered it. Our doctrine of truth is at present in the first of these three stages, with symptoms of the second stage having begun in certain quarters. I wish that this lecture might help it beyond the first stage in the eyes of many of you.

Correspondence versus a Pragmatic Theory of Truth

Truth, as any dictionary will tell you, is a property of certain of our ideas. It means their "agreement," as falsity means their disagreement, with "reality." Pragmatists and intellectualists both accept this definition as a matter of course. They begin to quarrel only after the question is raised as to what may precisely be meant by the term "agreement," and what by the term "reality," when reality is taken as something for our ideas to agree with.

In answering these questions the pragmatists are more analytic and painstaking, the intellectualists more offhand and irreflective. The popular notion is that a true idea must copy its reality. Like other popular views, this one follows the analogy of the most usual experience. Our true ideas of sensible things do indeed copy them. Shut your eyes and think of yonder clock on the wall, and you get just such a true picture or copy of its dial. But your idea of its "works" (unless you are a clock-maker) is much less of a copy, yet it passes muster, for it in no way clashes with the reality. Even though it should shrink to the mere word "works," that word still serves you truly; and when you speak of the "time-keeping function" of the clock, or of its spring's "elasticity," it is hard to see exactly what your ideas can copy.

You perceive that there is a problem here. Where our ideas cannot copy definitely their object, what does agreement with that object mean? Some idealists seem to say that they are true whenever they are what God means that we ought to think about that object. Others hold the copy-view all through, and speak as if our ideas possessed truth just in proportion as they approach to being copies of the Absolute's eternal way of thinking.

These views, you see, invite pragmatistic discussion. But the great assumption of the intellectualists is that truth means essentially an inert static relation. When you've got your true idea of anything, there's an end of the matter. You're in possession; you *know;* you have fulfilled your thinking destiny. You are where you ought to be mentally; you have obeyed your categorical imperative; and nothing more need follow on that climax of your rational destiny. Epistemologically you are in stable equilibrium.

Pragmatism, on the other hand, asks its usual question. "Grant an idea or belief to be true," it says, "what concrete difference will its being true make in anyone's actual life? How will the truth be realized? What experiences will be different from those which would obtain if the belief were false? What, in short, is the truth's cash-value in experiential terms?"

The moment pragmatism asks this question, it sees the answer: *True ideas are those that we can assimilate, validate, corroborate, and verify. False ideas are those that we cannot.* That is the practical difference it makes to us to have true ideas; that, therefore, is the meaning of truth, for it is all that truth is known-as.

This thesis is what I have to defend. The truth of an idea is not a stagnant property inherent in it. Truth *happens* to an idea. It *becomes* true, is *made* true by events. Its verity *is* in fact an event, a process: the process namely of its verifying itself, its veri-*fication.* Its validity is the process of its valid-*ation.*

The Process of Verifying Truth

But what do the words verification and validation themselv
mean? They again signify certain practical consequences of
validated idea. It is hard to find any one phrase that characteriz
quences better than the ordinary agreement-formula—just such
being what we have in mind whenever we say that our ideas "agree
ity. They lead us, namely, through the acts and other ideas which they i
into or up to, or towards, other parts of experience with which we feel a
while—such feeling being among our potentialities—that the original ide
remain in agreement. The connections and transitions come to us from point to
point as being progressive, harmonious, satisfactory. This function of agreeable
leading is what we mean by an idea's verification. Such an account is vague and
it sounds at first quite trivial, but it has results which it will take the rest of my
hour to explain.

Let me begin by reminding you of the fact that the possession of true
thoughts means everywhere the possession of invaluable instruments of
action; and that our duty to gain truth, so far from being a blank command
from out of the blue, or a "stunt" self-imposed by our intellect, can account
for itself by excellent practical reasons.

The importance to human life of having true beliefs about matters of fact
is a thing too notorious. We live in a world of realities that can be infinitely
useful or infinitely harmful. Ideas that tell us which of them to expect count as
the true ideas in all this primary sphere of verification, and the pursuit of such
ideas is a primary human duty. The possession of truth, so far from being here
an end in itself, is only a preliminary means towards other vital satisfactions.
If I am lost in the woods and starved, and find what looks like a cow-path,
it is of the utmost importance that I should think of a human habitation at the
end of it, for if I do so and follow it, I save myself. The true thought is useful
here because the house which is its object is useful. The practical value of true
ideas is thus primarily derived from the practical importance of their objects
to us. Their objects are, indeed, not important at all times. I may on another
occasion have no use for the house; and then my idea of it, however verifiable,
will be practically irrelevant, and had better remain latent. Yet since almost any
object may some day become temporarily important, the advantage of having
a general stock of *extra* truths, of ideas that shall be true of merely possible
situations, is obvious. We store such extra truths away in our memories, and
with the overflow we fill our books of reference. Whenever such an extra truth
becomes practically relevant to one of our emergencies, it passes from cold-
storage to do work in the world, and our belief in it grows active. You can say
of it then either that "it is useful because it is true" or that "it is true because it is
useful." Both these phrases mean exactly the same thing, namely that here is an
idea that gets fulfilled and can be verified. True is the name for whatever idea
starts the verification-process, useful is the name for its completed function in
experience. True ideas would never have been singled out as such, would never

e acquired a class-name, least of all a name suggesting value, unless they
d been useful from the outset in this way.

From this simple cue pragmatism gets her general notion of truth as
something essentially bound up with the way in which one moment in our
experience may lead us towards other moments which it will be worthwhile
to have been led to. Primarily, and on the common-sense level, the truth of
a state of mind means this function of *a leading that is worthwhile*. When a
moment in our experience, of any kind whatever, inspires us with a thought
that is true, that means that sooner or later we dip by that thought's guidance
into the particulars of experience again and make advantageous connection
with them. This is a vague enough statement, but I beg you to retain it, for it
is essential.

Our experience meanwhile is all shot through with regularities. One bit
of it can warn us to get ready for another bit, can "intend" or be significant
of that remoter object. The object's advent is the significance's verification.
Truth, in these cases, meaning nothing but eventual verification, is manifestly
incompatible with waywardness on our part. Woe to him whose beliefs play
fast and loose with the order which realities follow in his experience: they will
lead him nowhere or else make false connections.

By "realities" or "objects" here, we mean either things of common sense,
sensibly present, or else common-sense relations, such as dates, places, distances, kinds, activities. Following our mental image of a house along the cow-
path, we actually come to see the house; we get the image's full verification.
*Such simply and fully verified leadings are certainly the originals and prototypes of
the truth-process.* Experience offers indeed other forms of truth-process, but
they are all conceivable as being primary verifications arrested, multiplied or
substituted one for another.

Take, for instance, yonder object on the wall. You and I consider it to be
a "clock," although no one of us has seen the hidden works that make it one.
We let our notion pass for true without attempting to verify. If truths mean
verification-process essentially, ought we then to call such unverified truths as
this abortive? No, for they form the overwhelmingly large number of the truths
we live by. Indirect as well as direct verifications pass muster. Where circumstantial evidence is sufficient, we can go without eye-witnessing. Just as we here
assume Japan to exist without ever having been there, because it *works* to do so,
everything we know conspiring with the belief, and nothing interfering, so we
assume that thing to be a clock. We *use* it as a clock, regulating the length of our
lecture by it. The verification of the assumption here means its leading to no
frustration or contradiction. Verif*iability* of wheels and weights and pendulum
is as good as verification. For one truth-process completed there are a million
in our lives that function in this state of nascency. They turn us *towards* direct
verification; lead us into the *surroundings* of the objects they envisage; and then,
if everything runs on harmoniously, we are so sure that verification is possible
that we omit it, and are usually justified by all that happens.

Truth lives, in fact, for the most part on a credit system. Our thoughts and
beliefs "pass," so long as nothing challenges them, just as bank-notes pass so

long as nobody refuses them. But this all points to direct face-to-face verifications somewhere, without which the fabric of truth collapses like a financial system with no cash-basis whatever. You accept my verification of one thing, I yours of another. We trade on each other's truth. But beliefs verified concretely by *somebody* are the posts of the whole superstructure.

Another great reason—beside economy of time—for waiving complete verification in the usual business of life is that all things exist in kinds and not singly. Our world is found once for all to have that peculiarity. So that when we have once directly verified our ideas about one specimen of a kind, we consider ourselves free to apply them to other specimens without verification. A mind that habitually discerns the kind of thing before it, and acts by the law of the kind immediately, without pausing to verify, will be a "true" mind in ninety-nine out of a hundred emergencies, proved so by its conduct fitting everything it meets, and getting no refutation.

Indirectly or only potentially verifying processes may thus be true as well as full verification processes. They work as true processes would work, give us the same advantages, and claim our recognition for the same reasons. All this on the common-sense level of matters of fact, which we are alone considering.

Verifying Mental Relations among Ideas

But matters of fact are not our only stock in trade. *Relations among purely mental ideas* form another sphere where true and false beliefs obtain, and here the beliefs are absolute, or unconditional. When they are true they bear the name either of definitions or of principles. It is either a principle or a definition that 1 and 1 make 2, that 2 and 1 make 3, and so on; that white differs less from gray than it does from black; that when the cause begins to act the effect also commences. Such propositions hold of all possible "ones," of all conceivable "whites" and "grays" and "causes." The objects here are mental objects. Their relations are perceptually obvious at a glance, and no sense-verification is necessary. Moreover, once true, always true, of those same mental objects. Truth here has an "eternal" character. If you can find a concrete thing anywhere that is "one" or "white" or "gray," or an "effect," then your principles will everlastingly apply to it. It is but a case of ascertaining the kind, and then applying the law of its kind to the particular object. You are sure to get truth if you can but name the kind rightly, for your mental relations hold good of everything of that kind without exception. If you then, nevertheless, failed to get truth concretely, you would say that you had classed your real objects wrongly.

In this realm of mental relations, truth again is an affair of leading. We relate one abstract idea with another, framing in the end great systems of logical and mathematical truth, under the respective terms of which the sensible facts of experience eventually arrange themselves, so that our eternal truths hold good of realities also. This marriage of fact and theory is endlessly fertile. What we say is here already true in advance of special verification, *if we have subsumed our objects rightly.* Our ready-made ideal framework for all sorts of possible objects follows from the very structure of our thinking. We can no more play fast and loose with these abstract relations than we can do so with our sense-experiences. They coerce us; we must treat them consistently, whether or not we like the results. The rules of addition apply to our debts as rigorously as to our assets. The hundredth decimal of pi, the ratio of the circumference to its diameter, is predetermined ideally now, though no one may have computed it. If we should ever need the figure in our dealings with an actual circle we should need to have it given rightly, calculated by the usual rules; for it is the same kind of truth that those rules elsewhere calculate.

Between the coercions of the sensible order and those of the ideal order, our mind is thus wedged tightly. Our ideas must agree with realities, be such realities concrete or abstract, be they facts or be they principles, under penalty of endless inconsistency and frustration.

So far, intellectualists can raise no protest. They can only say that we have barely touched the skin of the matter.

Realities mean, then, either concrete facts, or abstract kinds of things and relations perceived intuitively between them. They furthermore and thirdly mean, as things that new ideas of ours must no less take account of, the whole body of other truths already in our possession. But what now does "agreement" with such threefold realities mean?—to use again the definition that is current.

"Agreement" as Useful Leading

Here it is that pragmatism and intellectualism begin to part company. Primarily, no doubt, to agree means to copy, but we saw that the mere word "clock" would do instead of a mental picture of its works, and that of many realities our ideas can only be symbols and not copies. "Past time," "power," "spontaneity"—how can our mind copy such realities?

To "agree" in the widest sense with a reality, *can only mean to be guided either straight up to it or into its surroundings, or to be put into such working touch with it as to handle either it or something connected with it better than if we disagreed.* Better either intellectually or practically! And often agreement will only mean the negative fact that nothing contradictory from the quarter of that reality comes to interfere with the way in which our ideas guide us elsewhere. To copy a reality is, indeed, one very important way of agreeing with it, but it is far from being essential. The essential thing is the process of being guided. Any idea that helps us to *deal*, whether practically or intellectually, with either the reality or its belongings, that doesn't entangle our progress in frustrations, that *fits*, in fact, and adapts our life to the reality's whole setting, will agree sufficiently to meet the requirement. It will hold true of that reality.

Thus, *names* are just as "true" or "false" as definite mental pictures are. They set up similar verification-processes, and lead to fully equivalent practical results.

All human thinking gets discursified; we exchange ideas; we lend and borrow verifications, get them from one another by means of social intercourse. All truth thus gets verbally built out, stored up, and made available for everyone. Hence, we must *talk* consistently just as we must *think* consistently: for both in talk and thought we deal with kinds. Names are arbitrary, but once understood they must be kept to. We mustn't now call Abel "Cain" or Cain "Abel." If we do, we ungear ourselves from the whole book of Genesis, and from all its connections with the universe of speech and fact down to the present time. We throw ourselves out of whatever truth that entire system of speech and fact may embody.

The overwhelming majority of our true ideas admit of no direct or face-to-face verification—those of past history, for example, as of Cain and Abel. The stream of time can be remounted only verbally, or verified indirectly by the present prolongations or effects of what the past harbored. Yet if they agree with these verbalities and effects, we can know that our ideas of the past are true. *As true as past time itself was,* so true was Julius Caesar, so true were antediluvian monsters, all in their proper dates and settings. That past time itself was, is guaranteed by its coherence with everything that's present. True as the present *is,* the past *was* also.

Agreement thus turns out to be essentially an affair of leading—leading that is useful because it is into quarters that contain objects that are important. True ideas lead us into useful verbal and conceptual quarters as well as directly up to useful sensible termini. They lead to consistency, stability, and flowing human intercourse. They lead away from eccentricity and isolation, from foiled and barren thinking. The untrammeled flowing of the leading-process, its general freedom from clash and contradiction, passes for its indirect verification; but all roads lead to Rome, and in the end and eventually, all true processes must lead to the face of directly verifying sensible experiences *somewhere,* which somebody's ideas have copied.

Such is the large loose way in which the pragmatist interprets the word agreement. He treats it altogether practically. He lets it cover any process of conduction from a present idea to a future terminus, provided only it run prosperously. It is only thus that "scientific" ideas, flying as they do beyond common sense, can be said to agree with their realities. It is, as I have already said, *as if* reality were made of ether, atoms or electrons, but we mustn't think so literally. The term "energy" doesn't even pretend to stand for anything "objective." It is only a way of measuring the surface of phenomena so as to string their changes on a simple formula.

Yet in the choice of these man-made formulas we cannot be capricious with impunity any more than we can be capricious on the common-sense practical level. We must find a theory that will *work;* and that means something extremely difficult; for our theory must mediate between all previous truths and certain new experiences. It must derange common sense and previous belief as little as possible, and it must lead to some sensible terminus or other that can be verified exactly. To "work" means both these things; and the squeeze is so tight that there is little loose play for any hypothesis. Our theories are wedged and controlled as nothing else is. Yet sometimes alternative theoretic formulas are equally compatible with all the truths we know, and then we choose between them for subjective reasons. We choose the kind of theory to which we are already partial; we follow "elegance" or "economy." Clerk Maxwell somewhere says it would be "poor scientific taste" to choose the more complicated of two equally well-evidenced conceptions; and you will all agree with him. Truth in science is what gives us the maximum possible sum of satisfactions, taste included, but consistency both with previous truth and with novel fact is always the most imperious claimant. . . .

READING 2
—————

Bertrand Russell: Appearance and Reality

From Problems of Philosophy

Bertrand Russell (1872–1970) was born in the Welsh village of Trellech, and over his long life became one of Britain's most important philosophers of the twentieth century. He is one of the founders of what we now call the "Anglo-American analytic philosophical tradition." In his short book Problems of Philosophy *(1912), he addresses the problem of distinguishing between appearance and reality. He uses the example of a table to demonstrate that almost every appearance produced by the table turns out to raise questions about the table's true reality. To our eyes it is oblong, brown, shiny, hard, smooth, and cool. Each of us looking at the table will agree with these appearances of the shape, size, color, and texture—but only if each of us looks at it from the same position. But when viewed from a different point of view, the shape and color will appear different. This raises the question of whether we can ever see the real shape or color. Russell concludes that "the real table, if there is one, is not immediately known to us at all, but must be an inference from what is immediately known."*

Is there any knowledge in the world which is so certain that no reasonable man could doubt it? This question, which at first sight might not seem difficult, is really one of the most difficult that can be asked. When we have realized the obstacles in the way of a straightforward and confident answer, we shall be well launched on the study of philosophy—for philosophy is merely the attempt to answer such ultimate questions, not carelessly and dogmatically, as we do in ordinary life and even in the sciences, but critically after exploring all that makes such questions puzzling, and after realizing all the vagueness and confusion that underlie our ordinary ideas.

In daily life, we assume as certain many things which, on a closer scrutiny, are found to be so full of apparent contradictions that only a great amount of thought enables us to know what it is that we really may believe. In the search for certainty, it is natural to begin with our present experiences, and in some sense, no doubt, knowledge is to be derived from them. But any statement as

Source: Bertrand Russell, *The Problems of Philosophy* (1912), Chapter 1.

to what it is that our immediate experiences make us know is very likely to be wrong. It seems to me that I am now sitting in a chair, at a table of a certain shape, on which I see sheets of paper with writing or print. By turning my head I see out of the window buildings and clouds and the sun. I believe that the sun is about ninety-three million miles from the earth; that it is a hot globe many times bigger than the earth; that, owing to the earth's rotation, it rises every morning, and will continue to do so for an indefinite time in the future. I believe that, if any other normal person comes into my room, he will see the same chairs and tables and books and papers as I see, and that the table which I see is the same as the table which I feel pressing against my arm. All this seems to be so evident as to be hardly worth stating, except in answer to a man who doubts whether I know anything. Yet all this may be reasonably doubted, and all of it requires much careful discussion before we can be sure that we have stated it in a form that is wholly true.

PROBLEMS DISCOVERING THE REAL TABLE

To make our difficulties plain, let us concentrate attention on the table. To the eye it is oblong, brown and shiny, to the touch it is smooth and cool and hard; when I tap it, it gives out a wooden sound. Any one else who sees and feels and hears the table will agree with this description, so that it might seem as if no difficulty would arise; but as soon as we try to be more precise our troubles begin. Although I believe that the table is "really" of the same color all over, the parts that reflect the light look much brighter than the other parts, and some parts look white because of reflected light. I know that, if I move, the parts that reflect the light will be different, so that the apparent distribution of colors on the table will change. It follows that if several people are looking at the table at the same moment, no two of them will see exactly the same distribution of colors, because no two can see it from exactly the same point of view, and any change in the point of view makes some change in the way the light is reflected.

For most practical purposes these differences are unimportant, but to the painter they are all-important: the painter has to unlearn the habit of thinking that things seem to have the color which common sense says they "really" have, and to learn the habit of seeing things as they appear. Here we have already the beginning of one of the distinctions that cause most trouble in philosophy—the distinction between "appearance" and "reality," between what things seem to be and what they are. The painter wants to know what things seem to be, the practical man and the philosopher want to know what they are; but the philosopher's wish to know this is stronger than the practical man's, and is more troubled by knowledge as to the difficulties of answering the question.

To return to the table. It is evident from what we have found, that there is no color which preeminently appears to be *the* color of the table, or even of any one particular part of the table—it appears to be of different colors from different points of view, and there is no reason for regarding some of these as more really its color than others. And we know that even from a given point of view the color will seem different by artificial light, or to a color-blind man, or to a man wearing blue spectacles, while in the dark there will be no color at all, though to touch and hearing the table will be unchanged. This color is not something which is inherent in the table, but something depending upon the table and the spectator and the way the light falls on the table. When, in ordinary life, we speak of *the* color of the table, we only mean the sort of color which it will seem to have to a normal spectator from an ordinary point of view under usual conditions of light. But the other colors which appear under other conditions have just as good a right to be considered real; and therefore, to avoid favoritism, we are compelled to deny that, in itself, the table has any one particular color.

The same thing applies to the texture. With the naked eye one can see the grain, but otherwise the table looks smooth and even. If we looked at it through a microscope, we should see roughnesses and hills and valleys, and all sorts of differences that are imperceptible to the naked eye. Which of these is the "real" table? We are naturally tempted to say that what we see through the microscope is more real, but that in turn would be changed by a still more powerful microscope. If, then, we cannot trust what we see with the naked eye, why should we trust what we see through a microscope? Thus, again, the confidence in our senses with which we began deserts us.

The *shape* of the table is no better. We are all in the habit of judging as to the "real" shapes of things, and we do this so unreflectingly that we come to think we actually see the real shapes. But, in fact, as we all have to learn if we try to draw, a given thing looks different in shape from every different point of view. If our table is "really" rectangular, it will look, from almost all points of view, as if it had two acute angles and two obtuse angles. If opposite sides are parallel, they will look as if they converged to a point away from the spectator; if they are of equal length, they will look as if the nearer side were longer. All these things are not commonly noticed in looking at a table, because experience has taught us to construct the "real" shape from the apparent shape, and the "real" shape is what interests us as practical men. But the "real" shape is not what we see; it is something inferred from what we see. And what we see is constantly changing in shape as we move about the room; so that here again the senses seem not to give us the truth about the table itself, but only about the appearance of the table.

Similar difficulties arise when we consider the sense of touch. It is true that the table always gives us a sensation of hardness, and we feel that it resists pressure. But the sensation we obtain depends upon how hard we press the table and also upon what part of the body we press with; thus the various sensations due to various pressures or various parts of the body cannot be supposed to reveal *directly* any definite property of the table, but at most to be signs of some property which perhaps *causes* all the sensations, but is not actually apparent in any of them. And the same applies still more obviously to the sounds which can be elicited by rapping the table.

Thus it becomes evident that the real table, if there is one, is not the same as what we immediately experience by sight or touch or hearing. The real table, if there is one, is not *immediately* known to us at all, but must be an inference from what is immediately known. Hence, two very difficult questions at once arise; namely, (1) Is there a real table at all? (2) If so, what sort of object can it be?

THE IDEALIST'S SOLUTION

It will help us in considering these questions to have a few simple terms of which the meaning is definite and clear. Let us give the name of "sense-data" to the things that are immediately known in sensation: such things as colors, sounds, smells, hardnesses, roughnesses, and so on. We shall give the name "sensation" to the experience of being immediately aware of these things. Thus, whenever we see a color, we have a sensation *of* the color, but the color itself is a sense-datum, not a sensation. The color is that *of* which we are immediately aware, and the awareness itself is the sensation. It is plain that if we are to know anything about the table, it must be by means of the sense-data—brown color, oblong shape, smoothness, etc.—which we associate with the table; but, for the reasons which have been given, we cannot say that the table is the sense-data, or even that the sense-data are directly properties of the table. Thus a problem arises as to the relation of the sense-data to the real table, supposing there is such a thing.

The real table, if it exists, we will call a "physical object." Thus we have to consider the relation of sense-data to physical objects. The collection of all physical objects is called "matter." Thus our two questions may be re-stated as follows: (1) Is there any such thing as matter? (2) If so, what is its nature?

The philosopher who first brought prominently forward the reasons for regarding the immediate objects of our senses as not existing independently of us was Bishop Berkeley (1685–1753). His *Three Dialogues between Hylas and Philonous, in Opposition to Sceptics and Atheists,* undertake to prove that there is no such thing as matter at all, and that the world consists of nothing but minds and their ideas. Hylas has hitherto believed in matter, but he is no match for Philonous, who mercilessly drives him into contradictions and paradoxes, and makes his own denial of matter seem, in the end, as if it were almost common sense. The arguments employed are of very different value: some are important and sound, others are confused or quibbling. But Berkeley retains the merit of having shown that the existence of matter is capable of being denied without absurdity, and that if there are any things that exist independently of us they cannot be the immediate objects of our sensations.

There are two different questions involved when we ask whether matter exists, and it is important to keep them clear. We commonly mean by "matter" something which is opposed to "mind," something which we think of as occupying space and as radically incapable of any sort of thought or consciousness. It is chiefly in this sense that Berkeley denies matter; that is to say, he does not deny that the sense-data which we commonly take as signs of the existence of the table are really signs of the existence of *something* independent of us, but he does deny that this something is nonmental, that it is neither mind nor ideas entertained by some mind. He admits that there must be something which continues to exist when we go out of the room or shut our eyes, and that what we call seeing the table does really give us reason for believing in something which persists even when we are not seeing it. But he thinks that this something cannot be radically different in nature from what we see, and cannot be independent of seeing altogether, though it must be independent of *our* seeing. He is thus led to regard the "real" table as an idea in the mind of God. Such an idea has the required permanence and independence of ourselves, without being—as matter would otherwise be—something quite unknowable, in the sense that we can only infer it, and can never be directly and immediately aware of it.

. . . It will be well to consider for a moment what it is that we have discovered so far. It has appeared that, if we take any common object of the sort that is supposed to be known by the senses, what the senses *immediately* tell us is not the truth about the object as it is apart from us, but only the truth about certain sense-data which, so far as we can see, depend upon the relations between us and the object. Thus what we directly see and feel is merely "appearance," which we believe to be a sign of some "reality" behind. . . .

READING 3

Arthur Eddington: Commonsense Knowledge and Scientific Knowledge
From *The Nature of the Physical World*

Arthur Eddington (1882–1944) was a British astrophysicist and philosopher of science who worked in the area of the theory of relativity. In The Nature of the Physical World *(1928) he addresses the philosophical problem of appearance and reality, and argues that we must distinguish between commonsense knowledge and scientific knowledge. On the one hand, there is a commonsense table before my eyes that I see and understand. On the other, there is the scientific table of electric charges, quanta, or electrons.*

I have settled down to the task of writing these lectures and have drawn up my chairs to my two tables. Two tables! Yes; there are duplicates of every object about me—two tables, two chairs, two pens.

This is not a very profound beginning to a course which ought to reach transcendent levels of scientific philosophy. But we cannot touch bedrock

Source: Arthur Eddington, *The Nature of the Physical World* (1928).

immediately; we must scratch a bit at the surface of things first. And whenever I begin to scratch; the first thing I strike is—my two tables.

One of them has been familiar to me from earliest years. It is a commonplace object of that environment which I call the world. How shall I describe it? It has extension; it is comparatively permanent; it is colored; above all it is substantial. By substantial I do not merely mean that it does not collapse when I lean up on it; I mean that it is constituted of "substance," and by that word I am trying to convey to you some conception of its intrinsic nature. It is a thing; not like space, which is a mere negation; nor like time, which is—Heaven knows what! But that will not help you to my meaning because it is the distinctive characteristic of a "thing" to have this substantiality, and I do not think substantiality can be described better than by saying that it is the kind of nature exemplified by an ordinary table. And so we go round in circles. After all if you are a plain common-sense man, not too much worried with scientific scruples, you will be confident that you understand the nature of an ordinary table. I have even heard of plain men who had the idea that they could better understand the mystery of their own nature if scientists would discover a way of explaining it in terms of the easily comprehensible nature of a table. Table no. 2 is my scientific table. It is a more recent acquaintance and I do not feel so familiar with it. It does not belong to the world previously mentioned—that world which spontaneously appears around me when I open my eyes, though how much of it is objective and how much subjective I do not here consider. It is part of a world which in more devious ways has forced itself on my attention. My scientific table is mostly emptiness. Sparsely scattered in that emptiness are numerous electric charges rushing about with great speed; but their combined bulk amounts to less than a billionth of the bulk of the table itself. Notwithstanding its strange construction it turns out to be an entirely efficient table. It supports my writing paper as satisfactorily as table no. 1; for when I lay the paper on it the little electric particles with their headlong speed keep on hitting the underside, so that the paper is maintained in shuttlecock fashion at a nearly steady level. If I lean upon this table I shall not go through; or, to be strictly accurate, the chance of my scientific elbow going through my scientific table is so excessively small that it can be neglected in practical life. Reviewing their properties one by one, there seems to be nothing to choose between the two tables for ordinary purposes; but when abnormal circumstances befall, then my scientific table shows to advantage. If the house catches fire my scientific table will dissolve quite naturally into scientific smoke, whereas my familiar table undergoes a metamorphosis of its substantial nature which I can only regard as miraculous.

There is nothing substantial about my second table. It is nearly all empty space—space pervaded, it is true, by fields of force, but these are assigned to the category of "influences," not of "things." Even in the minute part which is not empty we must not transfer the old notion of substance. In dissecting matter into electric charges we have traveled far from that picture of it which first gave rise to the conception of substance, and the meaning of that conception—if it ever had any—has been lost by the way. The whole trend of modern scientific views is to break down the separate categories of "things," "influences," "forms," etc., and to substitute a common background of all experience. Whether we are studying a material object, a magnetic field, a geometrical figure, or a duration of time, our scientific information is summed up in measures; neither the apparatus of measurement nor the mode of using it suggests that there is anything essentially different in these problems. The measures themselves afford no ground for a classification by categories. We feel it necessary to concede some background to the measures—an external world; but the attributes of this world, except insofar as they are reflected in the measures, are outside scientific scrutiny. Science has at last revolted against attaching the exact knowledge contained in these measurements to a traditional picture—gallery of conceptions which convey no authentic information of the background and obtrude irrelevancies into the scheme of knowledge.

I will not here stress further the nonsubstantiality of electrons, since it is scarcely necessary to the present line of thought. Conceive them as substantially as you will, there is a vast difference between my scientific table with its substance (if any) thinly scattered in specks in a region mostly empty and the table of everyday conception which we regard as the type of solid reality—an incarnate protest against Berkeleian subjectivism. It makes all the difference in the world whether the paper before me is poised as it were on a swarm of flies and sustained in shuttlecock fashion by a series of tiny blows from the swarm underneath, or whether it is supported because there is substance below it, it being the intrinsic nature of substance to occupy space to the exclusion of other substance; all the difference in conception at least, but no difference to my practical task of writing on the paper.

I need not tell you that modern physics has by delicate test and remorseless logic assured me that my second scientific table is the only one which is really there—wherever "there" may be. On the other hand I need not tell you that modern physics will never succeed in exorcising that first table—strange compound of external nature, mental imagery, and inherited prejudice—which lies visible to my eyes and tangible to my grasp. We must bid good-bye to it for the present, for we are about to turn from the familiar world to the scientific world revealed by physics. This is, or is intended to be, a wholly external world.

"You speak paradoxically of two worlds. Are they not really two aspects or two interpretations of one and the same world?"

Yes, no doubt they are ultimately to be identified after some fashion. But the process by which the external world of physics is transformed into a world of familiar acquaintance in human consciousness is outside the scope of physics. And so the world studied according to the methods of physics remains detached from the world familiar to consciousness, until after the physicist has finished his labors upon it. Provisionally, therefore, we regard the table which is the subject of physical research as altogether separate from the familiar table, without prejudging the question of their ultimate identification. It is true that the whole scientific inquiry starts from the familiar world and in the end it must return to the familiar world; but the part of the journey over which the physicist has charge is in foreign territory.

READING 4

Jean-Paul Sartre: Existentialism and Humanism

From *Existentialism Is a Humanism*

Jean-Paul Sartre (1905–1980) was born in Paris, and, as one of the founders of the existentialist movement, became one of France's most influential philosophers of the twentieth century. In his essay Existentialism Is a Humanism *(1946) he expresses the point of view of atheistic existentialism. He argues here that we have a duty to create our own values and meanings, but not just any values. Rather, those values should be the ones that would be consistent with everyone's behaving according to them. In spite of his atheism, Sartre's prescription for behavior, if it is to be authentic, requires virtually as much choice and commitment as religion itself.*

. . . There are two kinds of existentialists; first, those who are Christian, among whom I would include Jaspers and Gabriel Marcel, both Catholic; and on the other hand the atheistic existentialists among whom I class Heidegger, and then the French existentialists and myself. What they have in common is that they think that existence precedes essence, or, if you prefer, that subjectivity must be the starting point.

Just what does that mean? Let us consider some object that is manufactured, for example, a book or a paper-cutter: here is an object which has been made by an artisan whose inspiration came from a concept. He referred to the concept of what a paper-cutter is and likewise to a known method of production, which is part of the concept, something which is, by and large, a routine. Thus, the paper-cutter is at once an object produced in a certain way and, on the other hand, one having a specific use; and one cannot postulate a man who produces a paper-cutter but does not know what it is used for. Therefore, let us say that, for the paper-cutter, essence—that is, the ensemble of both the production routines and the properties which enable it to be both produced and defined—precedes existence. Thus, the presence of the paper-cutter or book in front of me is determined. Therefore, we have here a technical view of the world whereby it can be said that production precedes existence.

When we conceive God as the Creator, He is generally thought of as a superior sort of artisan. Whatever doctrine we may be considering, whether one like that of Descartes or that of Leibniz, we always grant that will more or less follows understanding or, at the very least, accompanies it, and that when God creates He knows exactly what He is creating. Thus, the concept of man in the

Source: Jean-Paul Sartre, "Existentialism Is a Humanism" (1946). From *The Philosophy of Existentialism*, ed., Wade Baskin (New York: Philosophical Library, 1965), reprinted by permission of Philosophical Library.

mind of God is comparable to the concept of a paper-cutter in the mind of the manufacturer, and, following certain techniques and a conception, God produces man, just as the artisan, following a definition and a technique, makes a paper-cutter. Thus, the individual man is the realization of a certain concept in the divine intelligence.

In the eighteenth century, the atheism of the philosophers discarded the idea of God, but not so much for the notion that essence precedes existence. To a certain extent, this idea is found everywhere; we find it in Diderot, in Voltaire, and even in Kant. Man has a human nature; this human nature, which is the concept of the human, is found in all men, which means that each man is a particular example of a universal concept, man. In Kant, the result of this universality is that the wild-man, the natural man, as well as the bourgeois, are circumscribed by the same definition and have the same basic qualities. Thus, here too the essence of man precedes the historical existence that we find in nature.

Atheistic existentialism, which I represent, is more coherent. It states that if God does not exist, there is at least one being in whom existence precedes essence, a being who exists before he can be defined by any concept, and that this being is man, or, as Heidegger says, human reality. What is meant here by saying that existence precedes essence? It means that, first of all, man exists, turns up, appears on the scene, and, only afterwards, defines himself. If man, as the existentialist conceives him, is indefinable, it is because at first he is nothing. Only afterward will he be something, and he himself will have made what he will be. Thus, there is no human nature, since there is no God to conceive it. Not only is man what he conceives himself to be, but he is also only what he wills himself to be after his thrust toward existence.

Man is nothing else but what he makes of himself. Such is the first principle of existentialism. It is also what is called subjectivity, the name we are labeled with when charges are brought against us. But what do we mean by this, if not that man has a greater dignity than a stone or table? For we mean that man first exists, that is, that man first of all is the being who hurls himself toward a future and who is conscious of imagining himself as being in the future. Man is at the start a plan which is aware of itself, rather than a patch of moss, a piece of garbage, or a cauliflower; nothing exists prior to this plan; there is nothing in heaven; man will be what he will have planned to be. Not what he will want to be. Because by the word "will" we generally mean a conscious decision, which is subsequent to what we have already made of ourselves. I may want to belong to a political party, write a book, get married; but all that is only a manifestation of an earlier, more spontaneous choice that is called "will." But if existence really does precede essence, man is responsible for what he is. Thus, existentialism's first move is to make every man aware of what he is and to make the full responsibility of his existence rest on him. And when we say that a man is responsible for himself, we do not only mean that he is responsible for his own individuality, but that he is responsible for all men.

The word subjectivism means, on the one hand, that an individual chooses and makes himself; and, on the other, that it is impossible for man to transcend human subjectivity. The second of these is the essential meaning of existentialism. When we say that man chooses his own self, we mean that every one of us does likewise; but we also mean by that that in making this choice he also chooses all men. In fact, in creating the man that we want to be, there is not a single one of our acts which does not at the same time create an image of man as we think he ought to be. To choose to be this or that is to affirm at the same time the value of what we choose, because we can never choose evil. We always choose the good, and nothing can be good for us without being good for all.

If, on the other hand, existence precedes essence, and if we grant that we exist and fashion our image at one and the same time, the image is valid for everybody and for our whole age. Thus, our responsibility is much greater than we might have supposed, because it involves all mankind. If I am a working-man and choose to join a Christian trade-union rather than be a communist, and if by being a member I want to show that the best thing for man is resignation, that the kingdom of man is not of this world, I am not only involving my own case—I want to be resigned for everyone. As a result, my action has involved all humanity. To take a more individual matter, if I want to marry, to have children; even if this marriage depends solely on my own circumstances or passion or wish, I am involving all humanity in monogamy and not merely myself. Therefore, I am responsible for myself and for everyone else. I am creating a certain image of man of my own choosing. In choosing myself, I choose man.

This helps us understand what the actual content is of such rather grandiloquent words as anguish, forlornness, despair. As you will see, it's all quite simple.

First, what is meant by anguish? The existentialists say at once that man is anguish. What that means is this: the man who involves himself and who realizes that he is not only the person he chooses to be, but also a lawmaker who is, at the same time, choosing all mankind as well as himself, cannot help escape the feeling of his total and deep responsibility. Of course, there are many people who are not anxious; but we claim that they are hiding their anxiety, that they are fleeing from it. Certainly, many people believe that when they do something, they themselves are the only ones involved, and when someone says to them, "What if everyone acted that way?" they shrug their shoulders and answer, "Everyone doesn't act that way." But really, one should always ask himself, "What would happen if everybody looked at things that way?" There is no escaping this disturbing thought except by a kind of double-dealing. A man who lies and makes excuses for himself by saying "Not everybody does that," is someone with an uneasy conscience, because the act of lying implies that a universal value is conferred upon the lie.

Anguish is evident even when it conceals itself. This is the anguish that Kierkegaard called the anguish of Abraham. You know the story: an angel has ordered Abraham to sacrifice his son; if it really were an angel who has come and said, "You are Abraham, you shall sacrifice your son," everything would be all right. But everyone might first wonder, "Is it really an angel, and am I really Abraham? What proof do I have?"

There was a madwoman who had hallucinations; someone used to speak to her on the telephone and give her orders. Her doctor asked her, "Who is it who talks to you?" She answered, "He says it's God." What proof did she really have that it was God? If an angel comes to me, what proof is there that it's an angel? And if I hear voices, what proof is there that they come from heaven and not from hell, or from the subconscious, or a pathological condition? What proves that they are addressed to me? What proof is there that I have been appointed to impose my choice and my conception of man on humanity? I'll never find any proof or sign to convince me of that. If a voice addresses me, it is always for me to decide that this is the angel's voice; if I consider that such an act is a good one, it is I who will choose to say that it is good rather than bad.

Now, I'm not being singled out as an Abraham, and yet at every moment I'm obliged to perform exemplary acts. For every man, everything happens as if all mankind had its eyes fixed on him and were guiding itself by what he does. And every man ought to say to himself, "Am I really the kind of man who has the right to act in such a way that humanity might guide itself by my actions?" And if he does not say that to himself, he is masking his anguish.

There is no question here of the kind of anguish which would lead to quietism, to inaction. It is a matter of a simple sort of anguish that anybody who has had responsibilities is familiar with. For example, when a military officer takes the responsibility for an attack and sends a certain number of men to death, he chooses to do so, and in the main he alone makes the choice. Doubtless, orders come from above, but they are too broad; he interprets them, and on this interpretation depend the lives of ten or fourteen or twenty men. In making a decision he can not help having a certain anguish. All leaders know this anguish. That doesn't keep them from acting; on the contrary, it is the very condition of their action. For it implies that they envisage a number of possibilities, and when they choose one, they realize that it has value only because it is chosen. We shall see that this kind of anguish, which is the kind that existentialism describes, is explained, in addition, by a direct responsibility to the other men whom it involves. It is not a curtain separating us from action, but is part of action itself.

When we speak of forlornness, a term Heidegger was fond of, we mean only that God does not exist and that we have to face all the consequences of this. The existentialist is strongly opposed to a certain kind of secular ethics which would like to abolish God with the least possible expense. About 1880, some French teachers tried to set up a secular ethics which went something like this: God is a useless and costly hypothesis; we are discarding it; but, meanwhile, in order for there to be an ethics, a society, a civilization, it is essential that certain values be taken seriously and that they be considered as having an a priori existence. It must be obligatory, a priori, to be honest, not to lie, not to beat your wife, to have children, etc., etc. So we're going to try a little device which will make it possible to show that values exist all the same, inscribed in a heaven of ideas, though otherwise God does not exist. In other words—and this, I believe, is the tendency of everything called reformism in France—nothing will be changed if God does not exist. We shall find ourselves with the same norms of honesty, progress, and humanism, and we shall have made of God an outdated hypothesis which will peacefully die off by itself.

The existentialist, on the contrary, thinks it very distressing that God does not exist, because all possibility of finding values in a heaven of ideas disappears along with Him; there can no longer be an a priori Good, since there is no infinite and perfect consciousness to think it. Nowhere is it written that the Good exists, that we must be honest, that we must not lie; because the fact is we are on a plane where there are only men. Dostoyevsky said, "If God didn't exist, everything would be permitted." That is the very starting point of existentialism. Indeed, everything is permissible if God does not exist, and as a result man is forlorn, because neither within him nor without does he find anything to cling to. He can't start making excuses for himself.

If existence really does precede essence, there is no explaining things away by reference to a fixed and given human nature. In other words, there is no determinism, man is free, man is freedom. On the other hand, if God does not exist, we find no values or commands to turn to which legitimize our conduct. So, in the bright realm of values, we have no excuse behind us, nor justification before us. We are alone, with no excuses.

That is the idea I shall try to convey when I say that man is condemned to be free. Condemned, because he did not create himself, yet, in other respects is free; because, once thrown into the world, he is responsible for everything he does. The existentialist does not believe in the power of passion. He will never agree that a sweeping passion is a ravaging torrent which fatally leads a man to certain acts and is therefore an excuse. He thinks that man is responsible for his passion.

The existentialist does not think that man is going to help himself by finding in the world some omen by which to orient himself. Because he thinks that man will interpret the omen to suit himself. Therefore, he thinks that man, with no support and no aid, is condemned every moment to invent man. Ponge, in a very fine article, has said, "Man is the future of man." That's exactly it. But if it is taken to mean that this future is recorded in heaven, that God sees it, then it is false, because it would really no longer be a future. If it is taken to mean that, whatever a man may be, there is a future to be forged, a virgin future before him, then this remark is sound. But then we are forlorn. . . .

Actually, things will be as man will have decided they are to be. Does that mean that I should abandon myself to quietism? No. First, I should involve myself; then, act on the old saw, "Nothing ventured, nothing gained." Nor does it mean that I shouldn't belong to a party, but rather that I shall have no illusions and shall do what I can. For example, suppose I ask myself, "Will socialization, as such, ever come about?" I know nothing about it. All I know is that I'm going to do everything in my power to bring it about. Beyond that, I can't count on anything. Quietism is the attitude of people who say, "Let others do what I can't do." The doctrine I am presenting is the very opposite of quietism, since it declares, "There is no reality except in action." Moreover, it goes further, since it adds, "Man is nothing else than his plan; he exists only to the extent that he fulfills himself; he is therefore nothing else than the ensemble of his acts, nothing else than his life."

According to this, we can understand why our doctrine horrifies certain people. Because often the only way they can bear their wretchedness is to think, "Circumstances have been against me. What I've been and done doesn't show my true worth. To be sure, I've had no great love, no great friendship, but that's because I haven't met a man or woman who was worthy. The books I've written haven't been very good because I haven't had the proper leisure. I haven't had children to devote myself to because I didn't find a man with whom I could have spent my life. So there remains within me, unused and quite viable, a host of propensities, inclinations, possibilities, that one wouldn't guess from the mere series of things I've done."

Now, for the existentialist there is really no love other than one which manifests itself in a person's being in love. There is no genius other than one which is expressed in works of art; the genius of Proust is the sum of Proust's works; the genius of Racine is his series of tragedies. Outside of that, there is nothing. Why say that Racine could have written another tragedy, when he didn't write it? A man is involved in life, leaves his impress on it, and outside of that there is nothing. To be sure, this may seem a harsh thought to someone whose life hasn't been a success. But, on the other hand, it prompts people to understand that reality alone is what counts, that dreams, expectations, and hopes warrant no more than to define a man as a disappointed dream, as miscarried hopes, as vain expectations. In other words, to define him negatively and not positively. However, when we say, "You are nothing else than your life," that does not imply that the artist will be judged solely on the basis of his works of art; a thousand other things will contribute toward summing him up. What we mean is that a man is nothing else than a series of undertakings, that he is the sum, the organization, the ensemble of the relationships which make up these undertakings.

When all is said and done, what we are accused of, at bottom, is not our pessimism, but an optimistic toughness. If people throw up to us our works of fiction in which we write about people who are soft, weak, cowardly, and sometimes even downright bad, it's not because these people are soft, weak, cowardly, or bad; because if we were to say, as Zola did, that they are that way because of heredity, the workings of environment, society, because of biological or psychological determinism, people would be reassured. They would say, "Well, that's what we're like, no one can do anything about it." But when the existentialist writes about a coward, he says that this coward is responsible for his cowardice. He's not like that because he has a cowardly heart or lung or brain; he's not like that on account of his physiological make-up; but he's like that because he has made himself a coward by his acts. There's no such thing as a cowardly constitution; there are nervous constitutions; there is poor blood, as the common people say, or there are strong constitutions. But the man whose blood is poor is not a coward on that account, for what makes cowardice is the act of renouncing or yielding. A constitution is not an act; the coward is defined on the basis of the acts he performs. People feel, in a vague sort of way, that this coward we're talking about is guilty of being a coward, and the thought frightens them. What people would like is that a coward or a hero be born that way.

One of the complaints most frequently made about The Ways of Freedom can be summed up as follows: "After all, these people are so spineless, how are you going to make heroes out of them?" This objection almost makes me laugh, for it assumes that people are born heroes. That's what people really want to think. If you're born cowardly, you may set your mind perfectly at rest; there's nothing you can do about it; you'll be cowardly all your life, whatever you may do. If you're born a hero, you may set your mind just as much at rest; you'll be a hero all your life; you'll drink like a hero and eat like a hero. What the existentialist says is that the coward makes himself cowardly, that the hero makes himself heroic. There's always a possibility for the coward not to be cowardly anymore and for the hero to stop being heroic. What counts is total involvement; some one particular action or set of circumstances is not total involvement.

. . . [Because existentialism] defines man in terms of action there is no doctrine more optimistic, since man's destiny is within himself; it tells him that the only hope is in his acting and that action is the only thing that enables a man to live.

READING 5

Willard Van Orman Quine: Two Dogmas of Empiricism

From "Two Dogmas of Empiricism"

Born in Akron, Ohio, American philosopher Willard Van Orman Quine (1908–2000) was one of the twentieth-century's leading proponents of the analytic approach to philosophy. One of his most influential works is his essay "Two Dogmas of Empiricism" (1951) in which he criticizes the two key assumptions held by empiricist philosophy, particularly logical positivism in his time. The first is the distinction between analytic and synthetic propositions, that is, analytic statements are true by virtue of the meaning of their terms (e.g., all bachelors are unmarried men), while synthetic propositions are not (e.g., the sun will rise tomorrow). Quine criticizes that the concept of an analytic proposition hinges on the notion of synonymy, but "synonymy", in turn, is dependent on the concept of "analytic." Thus, there is no way of understanding the concept of "analytic" that is noncircular. The second dogma of empiricism is reductionism, the view that statements derive their meaning from terms that rest entirely on immediate experience. Quine criticizes that empiricists have no acceptable proof for the notion of reductionism, and thus it is something that is only an article

Source: Willard Van Orman Quine, "Two Dogmas of Empiricism," *The Philosophical Review* 60 (1951): 20–43.

of faith for them. In place of these two dogmas, Quine offers a holistic theory of meaning. That is, we should reject the empiricists' effort to verify statements individually to find their meaning; instead, we should see that all scientific statements are interconnected and thus verify the whole field of science.

Modern empiricism has been conditioned in large part by two dogmas. One is a belief in some fundamental cleavage between truths which are *analytic*, or grounded in meanings independently of matters of fact and truths which are *synthetic*, or grounded in fact. The other dogma is *reductionism*: the belief that each meaningful statement is equivalent to some logical construct upon terms which refer to immediate experience. Both dogmas, I shall argue, are ill founded. One effect of abandoning them is, as we shall see, a blurring of the supposed boundary between speculative metaphysics and natural science. Another effect is a shift toward pragmatism.

I. BACKGROUND FOR ANALYTICITY

Kant's cleavage between analytic and synthetic truths was foreshadowed in Hume's distinction between relations of ideas and matters of fact, and in Leibniz's distinction between truths of reason and truths of fact. Leibniz spoke of the truths of reason as true in all possible worlds. Picturesqueness aside, this is to say that the truths of reason are those which could not possibly be false. In the same vein we hear analytic statements defined as statements whose denials are self-contradictory. But this definition has small explanatory value; for the notion of self-contradictoriness, in the quite broad sense needed for this definition of analyticity, stands in exactly the same need of clarification as does the notion of analyticity itself. The two notions are the two sides of a single dubious coin.

Kant conceived of an analytic statement as one that attributes to its subject no more than is already conceptually contained in the subject. This formulation has two shortcomings: it limits itself to statements of subject-predicate form, and it appeals to a notion of containment which is left at a metaphorical level. But Kant's intent, evident more from the use he makes of the notion of analyticity than from his definition of it, can be restated thus: a statement is analytic when it is true by virtue of meanings and independently of fact. Pursuing this line, let us examine the concept of *meaning* which is presupposed.

We must observe to begin with that meaning is not to be identified with naming or reference. Consider Frege's example of "Evening Star" and "Morning Star." Understood not merely as a recurrent evening apparition but as a body, the Evening Star is the planet Venus, and the Morning Star is the same. The two singular terms name the same thing. But the meanings must be treated as distinct, since the identity "Evening Star = Morning Star" is a statement of fact established by astronomical observation. If "Evening Star" and "Morning Star" were alike in meaning, the identity "Evening Star = Morning Star" would be analytic.

Again there is Russell's example of "Scott" and "the author of Waverly." Analysis of the meanings of words was by no means sufficient to reveal to George IV that the person named by these two singular terms was one and the same.

The distinction between meaning and naming is no less important at the level of abstract terms. The terms "9" and "the number of planets" name one and the same abstract entity but presumably must be regarded as unlike in meaning; for astronomical observation was needed, and not mere reflection on meanings, to determine the sameness of the entity in question.

Thus far we have been considering singular terms.

With general terms, or predicates, the situation is somewhat different but parallel. Whereas a singular term purports to name an entity, abstract or concrete, a general term does not; but a general term is *true of* an entity, or of each of many, or of none. The class of all entities of which a general term is true is called the *extension* of the term. Now paralleling the contrast between the meaning of a singular term and the entity named, we must distinguish equally between the meaning of a general term and its extension. The general terms "creature with a heart" and "creature with a kidney," e.g., are perhaps alike in extension but unlike in meaning.

Confusion of meaning with extension, in the case of general terms, is less common than confusion of meaning with naming in the case of singular terms. It is indeed a commonplace in philosophy to oppose intention (or meaning) to extension, or, in a variant vocabulary, connotation to denotation.

The Aristotelian notion of essence was the forerunner, no doubt, of the modern notion of intension or meaning. For Aristotle it was essential in men to be rational, accidental to be two-legged. But there is an important difference between this attitude and the doctrine of meaning. From the latter point of view it may indeed be conceded (if only for the sake of argument) that rationality is involved in the meaning of the word "man" while two-leggedness is not; but two-leggedness may at the same time be viewed as involved in the meaning of "biped" while rationality is not. Thus from the point of view of the doctrine of meaning it makes no sense to say of the actual individual, who is at once a man and a biped, that his rationality is essential and his two-leggedness accidental or vice versa. Things had essences, for Aristotle, but only linguistic forms have meanings. Meaning is what essence becomes when it is divorced from the object of reference and wedded to the word.

For the theory of meaning the most conspicuous question is as to the nature of its objects: what sort of things are meanings?

They are evidently intended to be ideas, somehow—mental ideas for some semanticists, Platonic ideas for others. Objects of either sort are so elusive, not to say debatable, that there seems little hope of erecting a fruitful science about them. It is not even clear, granted meanings, when we have two and when we have one; it is not clear when linguistic forms should be regarded as *synonymous*, or alike in meaning, and when they should not. If a standard of synonymy should be arrived at, we may reasonably expect that the appeal to meanings as entities will not have played a very useful part in the enterprise.

A felt need for meant entities may derive from an earlier failure to appreciate that meaning and reference are distinct. Once the theory of meaning is sharply separated from the theory of reference, it is a short step to recognizing as the business of the theory of meaning simply the synonymy of linguistic forms and the analyticity of statements; meanings themselves, as obscure intermediary entities, may well be abandoned.

The description of analyticity as truth by virtue of meanings started us off in pursuit of a concept of meaning. But now we have abandoned the thought of any special realm of entities called meanings. So the problem of analyticity confronts us anew.

Statements which are analytic by general philosophical acclaim are not, indeed, far to seek. They fall into two classes. Those of the first class, which may be called logically true, are typified by:

1. No unmarried man is married.

The relevant feature of this example is that it is not merely true as it stands, but remains true under any and all reinterpretations of "man" and "married." If we suppose a prior inventory of *logical* particles, comprising "no," "un-" "if," "then," "and," etc., then in general a logical truth is a statement which is true and remains true under all reinterpretations of its components other than the logical particles.

But there is also a second class of analytic statements, typified by:

2. No bachelor is married.

The characteristic of such a statement is that it can be turned into a logical truth by putting synonyms for synonyms; thus (2) can be turned into (1) by putting "unmarried man" for its synonym "bachelor." We still lack a proper characterization of this second class of analytic statements, and therewith of analyticity generally, inasmuch as we have had in the above description to lean on a notion of "synonymy" which is no less in need of clarification than analyticity itself. . . .

II. DEFINITION

There are those who find it soothing to say that the analytic statements of the second class reduce to those of the first class, the logical truths, by *definition*; "bachelor," for example, is *defined* as "unmarried man." But how do we find that "bachelor" is defined as "unmarried man"? Who defined it thus, and when? Are we to appeal to the nearest dictionary, and accept the lexicographer's formulation as law? Clearly this would be to put the cart before the horse. The lexicographer is an empirical scientist, whose business is the recording of antecedent facts; and if he glosses "bachelor" as "unmarried man" it is because of his belief that there is a relation of synonymy between these forms, implicit in general or preferred usage prior to his own work. The notion of synonymy presupposed here has still to be clarified, presumably in terms relating to linguistic behavior. Certainly the "definition" which is the lexicographer's report of an observed synonymy cannot be taken as the ground of the synonymy.

Definition is not, indeed, an activity exclusively of philologists. Philosophers and scientists frequently have occasions to "define" a recondite term by paraphrasing it into terms of a more familiar vocabulary. But ordinarily such a definition, like the philologist's, is pure lexicography, affirming a relationship of synonymy antecedent to the exposition in hand.

Just what it means to affirm synonymy, just what the interconnections may be which are necessary and sufficient in order that two linguistic forms be properly describable as synonymous, is far from clear; but, whatever these interconnections may be, ordinarily they are grounded in usage. Definitions reporting selected instances of synonymy come then as reports upon usage. . . .

In formal and informal work alike, thus, we find that definition—except in the extreme case of the explicitly conventional introduction of new notation—hinges on prior relationships of synonymy. Recognizing then that the notation of definition does not hold the key to synonymy and analyticity, let us look further into synonymy and say no more of definition.

III. INTERCHANGEABILITY

A natural suggestion, deserving close examination, is that the synonymy of two linguistic forms consists simply in their interchangeability in all contexts without change of truth value; interchangeability, in Leibniz's phrase, *salva veritate*. Note that synonyms so conceived need not even be free from vagueness, as long as the vaguenesses match. . . .

The question remains whether interchangeability *salva veritate* (apart from occurrences within words) is a strong enough condition for synonymy, or whether, on the contrary, some non-synonymous expressions might be thus interchangeable. Now let us be clear that we are not concerned here with synonymy in the sense of complete identity in psychological associations or poetic quality; indeed no two expressions are synonymous in such a sense. We are concerned only with what may be called *cognitive synonymy*. Just what this is cannot be said without successfully finishing the present study. . . .

Interchangeability *salva veritate* is meaningless until relativized to a language whose extent is specified in relevant respects. Suppose now we consider a language containing just the following materials. There is an indefinitely large stock of one- and many-place predicates, mostly having to do with extralogical subject matter. The rest of the language is logical. The atomic sentences consist each of a predicate followed by one or more variables "x", "y", etc.; and the complex sentences are built up of atomic ones by truth functions ("not", "and", "or", etc.) and quantification. In effect such a language enjoys the benefits also of descriptions and class names and indeed singular terms generally, these being contextually definable in known ways.

Such a language can be adequate to classical mathematics and indeed to scientific discourse generally, except in so far as the latter involves debatable devices such as modal adverbs and contrary-to-fact conditionals.

Now a language of this type is *extensional*, in this sense: any two predicates which *agree extensionally* (i.e., are true of the same objects) are interchangeable *salva veritate*.

In an extensional language, therefore, interchangeability *salva veritate* is no assurance of cognitive synonymy of the desired type. That "bachelor" and "unmarried man" are interchangeable *salva veritate* in an extensional language assures us of no more than that (3) is true. There is no assurance here that the extensional agreement of "bachelor" and "unmarried man" rests on meaning rather than merely on accidental matters of fact, as does extensional agreement of "creature with a heart" and "creature with a kidney."

For most purposes extensional agreement is the nearest approximation to synonymy we need care about. But the fact remains that extensional agreement falls far short of cognitive synonymy of the type required for explaining analyticity in the manner of Section I. The type of cognitive synonymy required there is such as to equate the synonymy of "bachelor" and "unmarried man" with the analyticity of (3), not merely with the truth of (3).

So we must recognize that interchangeability *salva veritate*, if construed in relation to an extensional language, is not a sufficient condition of cognitive synonymy in the sense needed for deriving analyticity in the manner of Section I. If a language contains an intensional adverb "necessarily" in the sense lately noted, or other particles to the same effect, then interchangeability *salva veritate* in such a language does afford a sufficient condition of cognitive synonymy; but such a language is intelligible only if the notion of analyticity is already clearly understood in advance.

The effort to explain cognitive synonymy first, for the sake of deriving analyticity from it afterward as in Section I, is perhaps the wrong approach. Instead we might try explaining analyticity somehow without appeal to cognitive synonymy. Afterward we could doubtless derive cognitive synonymy from analyticity satisfactorily enough if desired. We have seen that cognitive synonymy of "bachelor" and "unmarried man" can be explained as analyticity of (3). The same explanation works for any pair of one-place predicates, of course, and it can be extended in obvious fashion to many-place predicates. Other syntactical categories can also he accommodated in fairly parallel fashion. Singular terms may be said to be cognitively synonymous when the statement of identity formed by putting "=" between them is analytic. Statements may be said simply to be cognitively synonymous when their biconditional (the result of joining them by "if and only if") is analytic. If we care to lump all categories into a single formulation, at the expense of assuming again the notion of "word" which was appealed to early in this section, we can describe any two linguistic forms as cognitively synonymous when the two forms are interchangeable (apart from occurrences within "words") *salva* (no longer *veritate* but) *analyticitate*. Certain technical questions arise, indeed, over cases of ambiguity or homonymy; let us not pause for them, however, for we are already digressing. Let us rather turn our backs on the problem of synonymy and address ourselves anew to that of analyticity. . . .

V. THE VERIFICATION THEORY
AND REDUCTIONISM

In the course of these somber reflections we have taken a dim view first of the notion of meaning, then of the notion of cognitive synonymy: and finally of the notion of analyticity. But what, it may be asked, of the verification theory of meaning? This phrase has established itself so firmly as a catchword of empiricism that we should be very unscientific indeed not to look beneath it for a possible key to the problem of meaning and the associated problems.

The verification theory of meaning, which has been conspicuous in the literature from Peirce onward, is that the meaning of a statement is the method of empirically confirming or infirming it. An analytic statement is that limiting case which is confirmed no matter what.

As urged in Section I, we can as well pass over the question of meanings as entities and move straight to sameness of meaning, or synonymy. Then what the verification theory says is that statements are synonymous if and only if they are alike in point of method of empirical confirmation or infirmation.

This is an account of cognitive synonymy not of linguistic forms generally, but of statements. However, from the concept of synonymy of statements we could derive the concept of synonymy for other linguistic forms, by considerations somewhat similar to those at the end of Section III. Assuming the notion of "word," indeed, we could explain any two forms as synonymous when the putting of the one form for an occurrence of the other in any statement (apart from occurrences within "words") yields a synonymous statement. Finally, given the concept of synonymy thus for linguistic forms generally, we could define analyticity in terms of synonymy and logical truth as in Section I. For that matter, we could define analyticity more simply in terms of just synonymy of statements together with logical truth; it is not necessary to appeal to synonymy of linguistic forms other than statements. For a statement may be described as analytic simply when it is synonymous with a logically true statement.

So, if the verification theory can be accepted as an adequate account of statement synonymy, the notion of analyticity is saved after all. However, let us reflect. Statement synonymy is said to be likeness of method of empirical confirmation or infirmation. Just what are these methods which are to be compared for likeness? What, in other words, is the nature of the relationship between a statement and the experiences which contribute to or detract from its confirmation?

The most naive view of the relationship is that it is one of direct report. This is *radical reductionism*. Every meaningful statement is held to be translatable into a statement (true or false) about immediate experience. Radical reductionism, in one form or another, well antedates the verification theory of meaning explicitly so called. Thus Locke and Hume held that every idea must either originate directly in sense experience or else be compounded of ideas thus originating; and taking a hint from Tooke we might rephrase this doctrine in semantical jargon by saying that a term, to be significant at all, must be either a name of a sense datum or a compound of such names or an abbreviation of such a compound. So stated, the doctrine remains ambiguous as between sense data as sensory events and sense data as sensory qualities; and it remains vague as to the admissible ways of compounding. Moreover, the doctrine is unnecessarily and intolerably restrictive in the term-by-term critique which it imposes. More reasonably, and without yet exceeding the limits of what I have called radical reductionism, we may take full statements as our significant units— thus demanding that our statements as wholes be translatable into sense-datum language, but not that they be translatable term by term.

This emendation would unquestionably have been welcome to Locke and Hume and Tooke, but historically it had to await two intermediate developments. One of these developments was the increasing emphasis on verification or confirmation, which came with the explicitly so-called verification theory of meaning. The objects of verification or confirmation being statements, this emphasis gave the statement an ascendancy over the word or term as unit of significant discourse. The other development, consequent upon the first, was Russell's discovery of the concept of incomplete symbols defined in use.

Radical reductionism, conceived now with statements as units, sets itself the task of specifying a sense-datum language and showing how to translate the rest of significant discourse, statement by statement, into it. . . .

But the dogma of reductionism has, in a subtler and more tenuous form, continued to influence the thought of empiricists. The notion lingers that to each statement, or each synthetic statement, there is associated a unique range of possible sensory events such that the occurrence of any of them would add to the likelihood of truth of the statement, and that there is associated also another unique range of possible sensory events whose occurrence would detract from that likelihood. This notion is of course implicit in the verification theory of meaning.

The dogma of reductionism survives in the supposition that each statement, taken in isolation from its fellows, can admit of confirmation or infirmation at all. My countersuggestion, issuing essentially from Carnap's doctrine of the physical world in the *Aufbau*, is that our statements about the external world face the tribunal of sense experience not individually but only as a corporate body.

The dogma of reductionism, even in its attenuated form, is intimately connected with the other dogma: that there is a cleavage between the analytic and the synthetic. We have found ourselves led, indeed, from the latter problem to the former through the verification theory of meaning. More directly, the one dogma clearly supports the other in this way: as long as it is taken to be significant in general to speak of the confirmation and infirmation of a statement, it seems significant to speak also of a limiting kind of statement which is vacuously confirmed, *ipso facto*, come what may; and such a statement is analytic.

The two dogmas are, indeed, at root identical. We lately reflected that in general the truth of statements does obviously depend both upon extra-linguistic fact; and we noted that this obvious circumstance carries in its train, not logically but all too naturally, a feeling that the truth of a statement is somehow analyzable into a linguistic component and a factual component. The factual component must, if we are empiricists, boil down to a range of confirmatory experiences.

In the extreme case where the linguistic component is all that matters, a true statement is analytic. But I hope we are now impressed with how stubbornly the distinction between analytic and synthetic has resisted any straightforward drawing. I am impressed also, apart from prefabricated examples of black and white balls in an urn, with how baffling the problem has always been of arriving at any explicit theory of the empirical confirmation of a synthetic statement. My present suggestion is that it is nonsense, and the root of much nonsense, to speak of a linguistic component and a factual component in the truth of any individual statement. Taken collectively, science has its double dependence upon language and experience; but this duality is not significantly traceable into the statements of science taken one by one.

Russell's concept of definition in use was, as remarked, an advance over the impossible term-by-term empiricism of Locke and Hume. The statement, rather than the term, came with Russell to be recognized as the unit accountable to an empiricist critique.

But what I am now urging is that even in taking the statement as unit we have drawn our grid too finely. The unit of empirical significance is the whole of science.

VI. EMPIRICISM WITHOUT THE DOGMAS

The totality of our so-called knowledge or beliefs, from the most casual matters of geography and history to the profoundest laws of atomic physics or even of pure mathematics and logic, is a man-made fabric which impinges on experience only along the edges. Or, to change the figure, total science is like a field of force whose boundary conditions are experience. A conflict with experience at the periphery occasions readjustments in the interior of the field. Truth values have to be redistributed over some of our statements. Re-evaluation of some statements entails re-evaluation of others, because of their logical interconnections—the logical laws being in turn simply certain further statements of the system, certain further elements of the field. Having re-evaluated one statement we must re-evaluate some others, whether they be statements logically connected with the first or whether they be the statements of logical connections themselves. But the total field is so undetermined by its boundary conditions, experience, that there is much latitude of choice as to what statements to re-evaluate in the light of any single contrary experience. No particular experiences are linked with any particular statements in the interior of the field, except indirectly through considerations of equilibrium affecting the field as a whole.

If this view is right, it is misleading to speak of the empirical content of an individual statement—especially if it be a statement at all remote from the experiential periphery of the field. Furthermore it becomes folly to seek a boundary between synthetic statements, which hold contingently on experience, and analytic statements which hold come what may. Any statement can be held true come what may, if we make drastic enough adjustments elsewhere in the system. Even a statement very close to the periphery can be held true in the face of recalcitrant experience by pleading hallucination or by amending certain statements of the kind called logical laws. Conversely, by the same token, no statement is immune to revision. Revision even of the logical law of the excluded middle has been proposed as a means of simplifying quantum mechanics; and what difference is there in principle between such a shift and the shift whereby Kepler superseded Ptolemy, or Einstein Newton, or Darwin Aristotle?

For vividness I have been speaking in terms of varying distances from a sensory periphery. Let me try now to clarify this notion without metaphor. Certain statements, though about physical objects and not sense experience, seem peculiarly germane to sense experience—and in a selective way: some statements to some experiences, others to others. Such statements, especially germane to particular experiences, I picture as near the periphery. But in this relation of "germaneness" I envisage nothing more than a loose association reflecting the relative likelihood, in practice, of our choosing one statement rather than another for revision in the event of recalcitrant experience. For example, we can imagine recalcitrant experiences to which we would surely be inclined to accommodate our system by re-evaluating just the statement that there are brick houses on Elm Street, together with related statements on the same topic. We can imagine other recalcitrant experiences to which we would be inclined to accommodate our system by re-evaluating just the statement that there are no centaurs, along with kindred statements. A recalcitrant experience can, I have already urged, be accommodated by any of various alternative re-evaluations in various alternative quarters of the total system; but, in the cases which we are now imagining, our natural tendency to disturb the total system as little as possible would lead us to focus our revisions upon these specific statements concerning brick houses or centaurs. These statements are felt, therefore, to have a sharper empirical reference than highly theoretical statements of physics or logic or ontology. The latter statements may be thought of as relatively centrally located within the total network, meaning merely that little preferential connection with any particular sense data obtrudes itself.

As an empiricist I continue to think of the conceptual scheme of science as a tool, ultimately, for predicting future experience in the light of past experience. Physical objects are conceptually imported into the situation as convenient intermediaries—not by definition in terms of experience, but simply as irreducible posits comparable, epistemologically, to the gods of Homer. Let me interject that for my part I do, qua lay physicist, believe in physical objects and not in Homer's gods; and I consider it a scientific error to believe otherwise. But in point of epistemological footing the physical objects and the gods differ only in degree and not in kind. Both sorts of entities enter our conception only as cultural posits. The myth of physical objects is epistemologically superior to most in that it has proved more efficacious than other myths as a device for working a manageable structure into the flux of experience.

Imagine, for the sake of analogy, that we are given the rational numbers. We develop an algebraic theory for reasoning about them, but we find it inconveniently complex, because certain functions such as square root lack values for some arguments. Then it is discovered that the rules of our algebra can be much simplified by conceptually augmenting our ontology with some mythical entities, to be called irrational numbers. All we continue to be really interested in, first and last, are rational numbers; but we find that we can commonly get from one law about rational numbers to another much more quickly and simply by pretending that the irrational numbers are there too. . . .

Positing does not stop with macroscopic physical objects. Objects at the atomic level and beyond are posited to make the laws of macroscopic objects, and ultimately the laws of experience, simpler and more manageable; and we need not expect or demand full definition of atomic and subatomic entities in terms of macroscopic ones, any more than definition of macroscopic things in terms of sense data. Science is a continuation of common sense, and it continues the common-sense expedient of swelling ontology to simplify theory.

Physical objects, small and large, are not the only posits. Forces are another example; and indeed we are told nowadays that the boundary between energy and matter is obsolete. Moreover, the abstract entities which are the substance of mathematics—ultimately classes and classes of classes and so on up—are another posit in the same spirit. Epistemologically these are myths on the same footing with physical objects and gods, neither better nor worse except for differences in the degree to which they expedite our dealings with sense experiences.

The over-all algebra of rational and irrational numbers is underdetermined by the algebra of rational numbers, but is smoother and more convenient; and it includes the algebra of rational numbers as a jagged or gerrymandered part. Total science, mathematical and natural and human, is similarly but more extremely underdetermined by experience. The edge of the system must be kept squared with experience; the rest, with all its elaborate myths or fictions, has as its objective the simplicity of laws.

Ontological questions, under this view, are on a par with questions of natural science. Consider the question whether to countenance classes as entities. This, as I have argued elsewhere, is the question whether to quantify with respect to variables which take classes as values. Now Carnap has maintained that this is a question not of matters of fact but of choosing a convenient language form, a convenient conceptual scheme or framework for science. With this I agree, but only on the proviso that the same be conceded regarding scientific hypotheses generally. Carnap has recognized that he is able to preserve a double standard for ontological questions and scientific hypotheses only by assuming an absolute distinction between the analytic and the synthetic; and I need not say again that this is a distinction which I reject.

Some issues do, I grant, seem more a question of convenient conceptual scheme and others more a question of brute fact.

The issue over there being classes seems more a question of convenient conceptual scheme; the issue over there being centaurs, or brick houses on Elm Street, seems more a question of fact. But I have been urging that this difference is only one of degree, and that it turns upon our vaguely pragmatic inclination to adjust one strand of the fabric of science rather than another in accommodating some particular recalcitrant experience. Conservatism figures in such choices, and so does the quest for simplicity.

Carnap, Lewis, and others take a pragmatic stand on the question of choosing between language forms, scientific frameworks; but their pragmatism leaves off at the imagined boundary between the analytic and the synthetic. In repudiating such a boundary I espouse a more thorough pragmatism. Each man is given a scientific heritage plus a continuing barrage of sensory stimulation; and the considerations which guide him in warping his scientific heritage to fit his continuing sensory promptings are, where rational, pragmatic.

READING 6

John Rawls: Justice as Fairness
From "Justice as Fairness"

Born in Baltimore, Maryland, John Rawls (1921–2002) was one of the most important American political philosophers in recent times, particularly as his views appear in his book A Theory of Justice *(1971). Rawls fashions a conception of justice that balances the values of both freedom and equality. Whereas justice requires political equality for all, Rawls argues that economic inequality is consistent with justice, provided that as a result of the unequal distribution of economic resources all people, especially the disadvantaged, are better off. The heart of his theory is found in two principles of justice: (1) Each person is to have an equal right to the most extensive basic liberty compatible with a similar liberty for others, and (2) social and economic inequalities are to be arranged so that they are both reasonably expected to be to everyone's advantage, and attached to positions and offices open to all. According to Rawls, everyone benefits if political power is concentrated in the hands of a few, as with representative democracies. However, inequalities are permitted only when each person benefits from that inequality. How do we arrive at these two principles of justice? According to Rawls we do so in what he calls an "original position" in which people negotiate the basic rules of society without consideration of their own actual position of wealth and power. As a negotiator in this social contract setting, if I set aside considerations of my actual social status, I will thereby prefer a plan of justice that is fair for everyone, and not one that shows special favor to me.*

INTRODUCTION

1. It might seem at first sight that the concepts of justice and fairness are the same, and that there is no reason to distinguish them, or to say that one is more fundamental than the other. I think that this impression is mistaken. In this paper I wish to show that the fundamental idea in the concept of justice is fairness; and I wish to

Source: John Rawls, "Justice as Fairness," *Philosophical Review,* Vol. 67, 1958, pp. 164–194.

offer an analysis of the concept of justice from this point of view. To bring out the force of this claim, and the analysis based upon it, I shall then argue that it is this aspect of justice for which utilitarianism, in its classical form, is unable to account, but which is expressed, even if misleadingly, by the idea of the social contract.

To start with I shall develop a particular conception of justice by stating and commenting upon two principles which specify it, and by considering the circumstances and conditions under which they may be thought to arise. The principles defining this conception, and the conception itself, are, of course, familiar. It may be possible, however, by using the notion of fairness as a framework, to assemble and to look at them in a new way. Before stating this conception, however, the following preliminary matters should be kept in mind.

Throughout I consider justice only as a virtue of social institutions, or what I shall call practices. The principles of justice are regarded as formulating restrictions as to how practices may define positions and offices, and assign thereto powers and liabilities, rights and duties. Justice as a virtue of particular actions or of persons I do not take up at all. It is important to distinguish these various subjects of justice, since the meaning of the concept varies according to whether it is applied to practices, particular actions, or persons. These meanings are, indeed, connected, but they are not identical. I shall confine my discussion to the sense of justice as applied to practices, since this sense is the basic one. Once it is understood, the other senses should go quite easily.

Justice is to be understood in its customary sense as representing but *one* of the many virtues of social institutions, for these may be antiquated, inefficient, degrading, or any number of other things, without being unjust. Justice is not to be confused with an all-inclusive vision of a good society; it is only one part of any such conception. It is important, for example, to distinguish that sense of equality which is an aspect of the concept of justice from that sense of equality which belongs to a more comprehensive social ideal. There may well be inequalities which one concedes are just, or at least not unjust, but which, nevertheless, one wishes, on other grounds, to do away with. I shall focus attention, then, on the usual sense of justice in which it is essentially the elimination of arbitrary distinctions and the establishment, within the structure of a practice, of a proper balance between competing claims.

Finally, there is no need to consider the principles discussed below as *the* principles of justice. For the moment it is sufficient that they are typical of a family of principles normally associated with the concept of justice. The way in which the principles of this family resemble one another, as shown by the background against which they may be thought to arise, will be made clear by the whole of the subsequent argument.

TWO PRINCIPLES OF JUSTICE

2. The conception of justice which I want to develop may be stated in the form of two principles as follows: first, each person participating in a practice, or affected by it, has an equal right to the most extensive liberty compatible with

a like liberty for all; and second, inequalities are arbitrary unless it is reasonable to expect that they will work out for everyone's advantage, and provided the positions and offices to which they attach, or from which they may be gained, are open to all. These principles express justice as a complex of three ideas: liberty, equality, and reward for services contributing to the common good.

The term "person" is to be construed variously depending on the circumstances. On some occasions it will mean human individuals, but in others it may refer to nations, provinces, business firms, churches, teams, and so on. The principles of justice apply in all these instances, although there is a certain logical priority to the case of human individuals. As I shall use the term "person," it will be ambiguous in the manner indicated.

The first principle holds, of course, only if other things are equal: that is, while there must always be a justification for departing from the initial position of equal liberty (which is defined by the pattern of rights and duties, powers and liabilities, established by a practice), and the burden of proof is placed on him who would depart from it, nevertheless, there can be, and often there is, a justification for doing so. Now, that similar particular cases, as defined by a practice, should be treated similarly as they arise, is part of the very concept of a practice; it is involved in the notion of an activity in accordance with rules. The first principle expresses an analogous conception, but as applied to the structure of practices themselves. It holds, for example, that there is a presumption against the distinctions and classifications made by legal systems and other practices to the extent that they infringe on the original and equal liberty of the persons participating in them. The second principle defines how this presumption may be rebutted.

[It might be argued at this point that justice requires only an equal liberty. If, however, a greater liberty were possible for all without loss or conflict, then it would be irrational to settle on a lesser liberty. There is no reason for circumscribing rights unless their exercise would be incompatible, or would render the practice defining them less effective. Therefore no serious distortion of the concept of justice is likely to follow from including within it the concept of the greatest equal liberty.]

The second principle defines what sorts of inequalities are permissible; it specifies how the presumption laid down by the first principle may be put aside. Now by inequalities it is best to understand not *any* differences between offices and positions, but differences in the benefits and burdens attached to them either directly or indirectly, such as prestige and wealth, or liability to taxation and compulsory services. Players in a game do not protest against there being different positions, such as batter, pitcher, catcher, and the like, nor to there being various privileges and powers as specified by the rules; nor do the citizens of a country object to there being the different offices of government such as president, senator, governor, judge, and so on, each with their special rights and duties. It is not differences of this kind that are normally thought of as inequalities, but differences in the resulting distribution established by a practice, or made possible by it, of the things men strive to attain or avoid.

Thus they may complain about the pattern of honors and rewards set up by a practice (e.g., the privileges and salaries of government officials) or they may object to the distribution of power and wealth which results from the various ways in which men avail themselves of the opportunities allowed by it (e.g., the concentration of wealth which may develop in a free price system allowing large entrepreneurial or speculative gains).

It should be noted that the second principle holds that an inequality is allowed only if there is reason to believe that the practice with the inequality, or resulting in it, will work for the advantage of *every* party engaging in it. Here it is important to stress that *every* party must gain from the inequality. Since the principle applies to practices, it implies that the representative man in every office or position defined by a practice, when he views it as a going concern, must find it reasonable to prefer his condition and prospects with the inequality to what they would be under the practice without it. The principle excludes, therefore, the justification of inequalities on the grounds that the disadvantages of those in one position are outweighed by the greater advantages of those in another position. This rather simple restriction is the main modification I wish to make in the utilitarian principle as usually understood. When coupled with the notion of a practice, it is a restriction of consequence, and one which some utilitarians, e.g., Hume and Mill, have used in their discussions of justice without realizing apparently its significance, or at least without calling attention to it. Why it is a significant modification of principle, changing one's conception of justice entirely, the whole of my argument will show.

Further, it is also necessary that the various offices to which special benefits or burdens attach are open to all. It may be, for example, to the common advantage, as just defined, to attach special benefits to certain offices. Perhaps by doing so the requisite talent can be attracted to them and encouraged to give its best efforts. But any offices having special benefits must be won in a fair competition in which contestants are judged on their merits. If some offices were not open, those excluded would normally be justified in feeling unjustly treated, even if they benefited from the greater efforts of those who were allowed to compete for them. Now if one can assume that offices are open, it is necessary only to consider the design of practices themselves and how they jointly, as a system, work together. It will be a mistake to focus attention on the varying relative positions of particular persons, who may be known to us by their proper names, and to require that each such change, as a once for all transaction viewed in isolation, must be in itself just. It is the system of practices which is to be judged, and judged from a general point of view: unless one is prepared to criticize it from the standpoint of a representative man holding some particular office, one has no complaint against it.

THE ORIGINAL POSITION

3. Given these principles one might try to derive them from a priori principles of reason, or claim that they were known by intuition. These are familiar enough steps and, at least in the case of the first principle, might be made with some

success. Usually, however, such arguments, made at this point, are unconvincing. They are not likely to lead to an understanding of the basis of the principles of justice, not at least as principles of justice. I wish, therefore, to look at the principles in a different way.

Imagine a society of persons amongst whom a certain system of practices is *already* well established. Now suppose that by and large they are mutually self-interested; their allegiance to their established practices is normally founded on the prospect of self-advantage. One need not assume that, in all senses of the term "person," the persons in this society are mutually self-interested. If the characterization as mutually self-interested applies when the line of division is the family, it may still be true that members of families are bound by ties of sentiment and affection and willingly acknowledge duties in contradiction to self-interest. Mutual self-interestedness in the relations between families, nations, churches, and the like, is commonly associated with intense loyalty and devotion on the part of individual members. Therefore, one can form a more realistic conception of this society if one thinks of it as consisting of mutually self-interested families, or some other association. Further, it is not necessary to suppose that these persons are mutually self-interested under all circumstances, but only in the usual situations in which they participate in their common practices.

Now suppose also that these persons are rational: they know their own interests more or less accurately; they are capable of tracing out the likely consequences of adopting one practice rather than another; they are capable of adhering to a course of action once they have decided upon it; they can resist present temptations and the enticements of immediate gain; and the bare knowledge or perception of the difference between their condition and that of others is not, within certain limits and in itself, a source of great dissatisfaction. Only the last point adds anything to the usual definition of rationality. This definition should allow, I think, for the idea that a rational man would not be greatly downcast from knowing, or seeing, that others are in a better position than himself, unless he thought their being so was the result of injustice, or the consequence of letting chance work itself out for no useful common purpose, and so on. So if these persons strike us as unpleasantly egoistic, they are at least free in some degree from the fault of envy.

Finally, assume that these persons have roughly similar needs and interests, or needs and interests in various ways complementary, so that fruitful cooperation amongst them is possible; and suppose that they are sufficiently equal in power and ability to guarantee that in normal circumstances none is able to dominate the others.

This condition (as well as the others) may seem excessively vague; but in view of the conception of justice to which the argument leads, there seems no reason for making it more exact here.

Since these persons are conceived as engaging in their common practices, which are already established, there is no question of our supposing them to come together to deliberate as to how they will set these practices up for the first time. Yet we can imagine that from time to time they discuss with one another whether any of them has a legitimate complaint against their established institutions. Such discussions are perfectly natural in any normal society. Now suppose that they have settled on doing this in the following way. They first try to arrive at the principles by which complaints, and so practices themselves, are to be judged. Their procedure for this is to let each person propose the principles upon which he wishes his complaints to be tried with the understanding that, if acknowledged, the complaints of others will be similarly tried, and that no complaints will be heard at all until everyone is roughly of one mind as to how complaints are to be judged. They each understand further that the principles proposed and acknowledged on this occasion are binding on future occasions. Thus each will be wary of proposing a principle which would give him a peculiar advantage, in his present circumstances, supposing it to be accepted. Each person knows that he will be bound by it in future circumstances the peculiarities of which cannot be known, and which might well be such that the principle is then to his disadvantage. The idea is that everyone should be required to make in advance a firm commitment, which others also may reasonably be expected to make, and that no one be given the opportunity to tailor the canons of a legitimate complaint to fit his own special conditions, and then to discard them when they no longer suit his purpose. Hence each person will propose principles of a general kind which will, to a large degree, gain their sense from the various applications to be made of them, the particular circumstances of which being as yet unknown. These principles will express the conditions in accordance with which each is the least unwilling to have his interests limited in the design of practices, given the competing interests of the others, on the supposition that the interests of others will be limited likewise. The restrictions which would so arise might be thought of as those a person would keep in mind if he were designing a practice in which his enemy were to assign him his place.

The two main parts of this conjectural account have a definite significance. The character and respective situations of the parties reflect the typical circumstances in which questions of justice arise. The procedure whereby principles are proposed and acknowledged represents constraints, analogous to those of having a morality, whereby rational and mutually self-interested persons are brought to act reasonably. Thus the first part reflects the fact that questions of justice arise when conflicting claims are made upon the design of a practice and where it is taken for granted that each person will insist, as far as possible, on what he considers his rights. It is typical of cases of justice to involve persons who are pressing on one another their claims, between which a fair balance or equilibrium must be found. On the other hand, as expressed by the second part, having a morality must at least imply the acknowledgment of principles as impartially applying to one's own conduct as well as to another's, and moreover principles which may constitute a constraint, or limitation, upon the pursuit of one's own interests. There are, of course, other aspects of having a morality: the acknowledgment of moral principles must show itself in accepting a reference to them as reasons for limiting one's claims, in acknowledging the burden of providing a special explanation, or excuse, when one acts contrary to them, or else in showing shame and remorse and a desire to make amends, and so on. It is sufficient to remark here that having a morality is analogous to having made a firm commitment in advance; for one must acknowledge the principles of morality even when to one's disadvantage. A man whose moral judgments always coincided with his interests could be suspected of having no morality at all.

Thus the two parts of the foregoing account are intended to mirror the kinds of circumstances in which questions of justice arise and the constraints which having a morality would impose upon persons so situated. In this way one can see how the acceptance of the principles of justice might come about, for given all these conditions as described, it would be natural if the two principles of justice were to be acknowledged. Since there is no way for anyone to win special advantages for himself, each might consider it reasonable to acknowledge equality as an initial principle. There is, however, no reason why they should regard this position as final; for if there are inequalities which satisfy the second principle, the immediate gain which equality would allow can be considered as intelligently invested in view of its future return. If, as is quite likely, these inequalities work as incentives to draw out better efforts, the members of this society may look upon them as concessions to human nature: they, like us, may think that people ideally should want to serve one another. But as they are mutually self-interested, their acceptance of these inequalities is merely the acceptance of the relations in which they actually stand, and a recognition of the motives which lead them to engage in their common practices. They have no title to complain of one another. And so provided that the conditions of the principle are met, there is no reason why they should not allow such inequalities. Indeed, it would be short-sighted of them to do so, and could result, in most cases, only from their being dejected by the bare knowledge, or perception, that others are better situated. Each person will, however, insist on an advantage to himself, and so on a common advantage, for none is willing to sacrifice anything for the others.

These remarks are not offered as a proof that persons so conceived and circumstanced would settle on the two principles, but only to show that these principles could have such a background, and so can be viewed as those principles which mutually self-interested and rational persons, when similarly situated and required to make in advance a firm commitment, could acknowledge as restrictions governing the assignment of rights and duties in their common practices, and thereby accept as limiting their rights against one another. The principles of justice may, then, be regarded as those principles which arise when the constraints of having a morality are imposed upon parties in the typical circumstances of justice.

CLARIFICATION

4. These ideas are, of course, connected with a familiar way of thinking about justice which goes back at least to the Greek Sophists, and which regards the acceptance of the principles of justice as a compromise between persons of roughly equal power who would enforce their will on each other if they could,

but who, in view of the equality of forces amongst them and for the sake of their own peace and security, acknowledge certain forms of conduct insofar as prudence seems to require. Justice is thought of as a pact between rational egoists the stability of which is dependent on a balance of power and a similarity of circumstances. While the previous account is connected with this tradition, and with its most recent variant, the theory of games, it differs from it in several important respects which, to forestall misinterpretations, I will set out here.

First, I wish to use the previous conjectural account of the background of justice as a way of analyzing the concept. I do not want, therefore, to be interpreted as assuming a general theory of human motivation: when I suppose that the parties are mutually self-interested, and are not willing to have their (substantial) interests sacrificed to others, I am referring to their conduct and motives as they are taken for granted in cases where questions of justice ordinarily arise. Justice is the virtue of practices where there are assumed to be competing interests and conflicting claims, and where it is supposed that persons will press their rights on each other. That persons are mutually self-interested in certain situations and for certain purposes is what gives rise to the question of justice in practices covering those circumstances. Amongst an association of saints, if such a community could really exist, the disputes about justice could hardly occur; for they would all work selflessly together for one end, the glory of God as defined by their common religion, and reference to this end would settle every question of right. The justice of practices does not come up until there are several different parties (whether we think of these as individuals, associations, or nations and so on, is irrelevant) who do press their claims on one another, and who do regard themselves as representatives of interests which deserve to be considered. Thus the previous account involves no general theory of human motivation. Its intent is simply to incorporate into the conception of justice the relations of men to one another which set the stage for questions of justice. It makes no difference how wide or general these relations are, as this matter does not bear on the analysis of the concept.

Again, in contrast to the various conceptions of the social contract, the several parties do not establish any particular society or practice; they do not covenant to obey a particular sovereign body or to accept a given constitution. Nor do they, as in the theory of games (in certain respects a marvelously sophisticated development of this tradition), decide on individual strategies adjusted to their respective circumstances in the game. What the parties do is to jointly acknowledge certain principles of appraisal relating to their common practices either as already established or merely proposed. They accede to standards of judgment, not to a given practice; they do not make any specific agreement, or bargain, or adopt a particular strategy. The subject of their acknowledgment is, therefore, very general indeed; it is simply the acknowledgment of certain principles of judgment, fulfilling certain general conditions, to be used in criticizing the arrangement of their common affairs. The relations of mutual self-interest between the parties who are similarly circumstanced mirror the conditions under which questions of justice arise, and the procedure by which the principles of judgment are proposed and acknowledged reflects the constraints of having a morality. Each aspect, then, of the preceding hypothetical account serves the purpose of bringing out a feature of the notion of justice. One could, if one liked, view the principles of justice as the "solution" of this highest order "game" of adopting, subject to the procedure described, principles of argument for all coming particular "games" whose peculiarities one can in no way foresee. But this comparison, while no doubt helpful, must not obscure the fact that this highest order "game" is of a special sort. Its significance is that its various pieces represent aspects of the concept of justice.

Finally, I do not, of course, conceive the several parties as necessarily coming together to establish their common practices for the first time. Some institutions may, indeed, be set up de novo; but I have framed the preceding account so that it will apply when the full complement of social institutions already exists and represents the result of a long period of development. Nor is the account in any way fictitious. In any society where people reflect on their institutions they will have an idea of what principles of justice would be acknowledged under the conditions described, and there will be occasions when questions of justice are actually discussed in this way. Therefore if their practices do not accord with these principles, this will affect the quality of their social relations. For in this case there will be some recognized situations wherein the parties are mutually aware that one of them is being forced to accept what the other would concede is unjust. The foregoing analysis may then be thought of as representing the actual quality of relations between persons as defined by practices accepted as just. In such practices the parties will acknowledge the principles on which it is constructed, and the general recognition of this fact shows itself in the absence of resentment and in the sense of being justly treated. Thus one common objection to the theory of the social contract, its apparently historical and fictitious character, is avoided.

FAIRNESS

5. That the principles of justice may be regarded as arising in the manner described illustrates an important fact about them. Not only does it bring out the idea that justice is a primitive moral notion in that it arises once the concept of morality is imposed on mutually self-interested agents similarly circumstanced, but it emphasizes that, fundamental to justice, is the concept of fairness which relates to right dealing between persons who are cooperating with or competing against one another, as when one speaks of fair games, fair competition, and fair bargains. The question of fairness arises when free persons, who have no authority over one another, are engaging in a joint activity and amongst themselves settling or acknowledging the rules which define it and which determine the respective shares in its benefits and burdens. A practice will strike the parties as fair if none feels that, by participating in it, they or any of the others are taken advantage of, or forced to give in to claims which they do not regard as legitimate. This implies that each has a conception of legitimate claims which he thinks it reasonable for others as well as himself to

acknowledge. If one thinks of the principles of justice as arising in the manner described, then they do define this sort of conception. A practice is just or fair, then, when it satisfies the principles which those who participate in it could propose to one another for mutual acceptance under the aforementioned circumstances. Persons engaged in a just, or fair, practice can face one another openly and support their respective positions, should they appear questionable, by reference to principles which it is reasonable to expect each to accept.

It is this notion of the possibility of mutual acknowledgment of principles by free persons who have no authority over one another which makes the concept of fairness fundamental to justice. Only if such acknowledgment is possible can there be true community between persons in their common practices; otherwise their relations will appear to them as founded to some extent on force. If, in ordinary speech, fairness applies more particularly to practices in which there is a choice whether to engage or not (e.g., in games, business competition), and justice to practices in which there is no choice (e.g., in slavery), the element of necessity does not render the conception of mutual acknowledgment inapplicable, although it may make it much more urgent to change unjust than unfair institutions. For one activity in which one can always engage is that of proposing and acknowledging principles to one another supposing each to be similarly circumstanced; and to judge practices by the principles so arrived at is to apply the standard of fairness to them. . . .

READING 7

Thomas Nagel:
What Is It Like to Be a Bat?
From "What Is It Like to Be a Bat?"

Thomas Nagel (b. 1937) was born in Belgrade, in what is now Serbia, and spent much of his career teaching at universities in the United States. In his influential essay "What Is It Like to Be a Bat?" (1974), Nagel criticizes efforts to reduce mental consciousness to explanations about physical brain activity. While we may have good reason for believing that consciousness is, indeed, a function of brain activity, theories of reductionalist physicalism are inadequate since they cannot account for the subjective character of conscious experience. Suppose we try to imagine what it is like for a bat to perceive things through sonar; we cannot even form the conception since there are limits to our conceptual schemes that prevent us from expressing truths about a bat's experience in human language. We have the same problem when attempting to explain human conscious experience: There is no physicalist conceptual scheme that adequately describes subjective consciousness.

Source: Thomas Nagel, *The Philosophical Review* 83 (October 1974).

REDUCTIONIST PHYSICALISM
AND THE SUBJECTIVE CHARACTER OF EXPERIENCE

Consciousness is what makes the mind-body problem really intractable. Perhaps that is why current discussions of the problem give it little attention or get it obviously wrong. The recent wave of reductionist euphoria has produced several analyses of mental phenomena and mental concepts designed to explain the possibility of some variety of materialism, psychophysical identification, or reduction. But the problems dealt with are those common to this type of reduction and other types, and what makes the mind-body problem unique, and unlike the water-H_2O problem or the Turing machine–IBM machine problem or the lightning–electrical discharge problem or the gene-DNA problem or the oak tree–hydrocarbon problem, is ignored.

Every reductionist has his favorite analogy from modern science. It is most unlikely that any of these unrelated examples of successful reduction will shed light on the relation of mind to brain. But philosophers share the general human weakness for explanations of what is incomprehensible in terms suited for what is familiar and well understood, though entirely different. This has led to the acceptance of implausible accounts of the mental largely because they would permit familiar kinds of reduction. I shall try to explain why the usual examples do not help us to understand the relation between mind and body—why, indeed, we have at present no conception of what an explanation of the physical nature of a mental phenomenon would be. Without consciousness the mind-body problem would be much less interesting. With consciousness it seems hopeless. The most important and characteristic feature of conscious mental phenomena is very poorly understood. Most reductionist theories do not even try to explain it. And careful examination will show that no currently available concept of reduction is applicable to it. Perhaps a new theoretical form can be devised for the purpose, but such a solution, if it exists, lies in the distant intellectual future.

Conscious experience is a widespread phenomenon. It occurs at many levels of animal life, though we cannot be sure of its presence in the simpler organisms, and it is very difficult to say in general what provides evidence of it. (Some extremists have been prepared to deny it even of mammals other than man.) No doubt it occurs in countless forms totally unimaginable to us, on other planets in other solar systems throughout the universe. But no matter how the form may vary, the fact that an organism has conscious experience at all means, basically, that there is something it is like to be that organism. There may be further implications about the form of the experience; there may even (though I doubt it) be implications about the behavior of the organism. But fundamentally an organism has conscious mental states if and only if there is something that it is to be that organism—something it is like for the organism.

We may call this the subjective character of experience. It is not captured by any of the familiar, recently devised reductive analyses of the mental, for all of them are logically compatible with its absence. It is not analyzable in terms of any explanatory system of functional states, or intentional states, since these could be ascribed to robots or automata that behaved like people though they experienced nothing. It is not analyzable in terms of the causal role of experiences in relation to typical human behavior—for similar reasons. I do not deny that conscious mental states and events cause behavior, nor that they may be given functional characterizations. I deny only that this kind of thing exhausts their analysis. Any reductionist program has to be based on an analysis of what is to be reduced. If the analysis leaves something out, the problem will be falsely posed. It is useless to base the defense of materialism on any analysis of mental phenomena that fails to deal explicitly with their subjective character. For there is no reason to suppose that a reduction which seems plausible when no attempt is made to account for consciousness can be extended to include consciousness. Without some idea, therefore, of what the subjective character of experience is, we cannot know what is required of a physicalist theory.

While an account of the physical basis of mind must explain many things, this appears to be the most difficult. It is impossible to exclude the phenomenological features of experience from a reduction in the same way that one excludes the phenomenal features of an ordinary substance from a physical or chemical reduction of it—namely, by explaining them as effects on the minds of human observers. If physicalism is to be defended, the phenomenological features must themselves be given a physical account. But when we examine their subjective character it seems that such a result is impossible. The reason is that every subjective phenomenon is essentially connected with a single point of view, and it seems inevitable that an objective, physical theory will abandon that point of view.

Let me first try to state the issue somewhat more fully than by referring to the relation between the subjective and the objective, or between the pour-soi and the en-soi. This is far from easy. Facts about what it is like to be an X are very peculiar, so peculiar that some may be inclined to doubt their reality, or the significance of claims about them. To illustrate the connection between subjectivity and a point of view, and to make evident the importance of subjective features, it will help to explore the matter in relation to an example that brings out clearly the divergence between the two types of conception, subjective and objective.

THE SUBJECTIVE EXPERIENCE OF BATS

I assume we all believe that bats have experience. After all, they are mammals, and there is no more doubt that they have experience than that mice or pigeons or whales have experience. I have chosen bats instead of wasps or flounders because if one travels too far down the phylogenetic tree, people gradually shed their faith that there is experience there at all. Bats, although more closely related to us than those other species, nevertheless present a range of activity and a sensory apparatus so different from ours that the problem I want to pose is exceptionally vivid (though it certainly could be raised with other species). Even without the benefit of philosophical reflection, anyone who has spent some time in an enclosed space with an excited bat knows what it is to encounter a fundamentally alien form of life.

I have said that the essence of the belief that bats have experience is that there is something that it is like to be a bat. Now we know that most bats (the microchiroptera, to be precise) perceive the external world primarily by sonar, or echolocation, detecting the reflections, from objects within range, of their own rapid, subtly modulated, high-frequency shrieks. Their brains are designed to correlate the outgoing impulses with the subsequent echoes, and the information thus acquired enables bats to make precise discriminations of distance, size, shape, motion, and texture comparable to those we make by vision. But bat sonar, though clearly a form of perception, is not similar in its operation to any sense that we possess, and there is no reason to suppose that it is subjectively like anything we can experience or imagine. This appears to create difficulties for the notion of what it is like to be a bat. We must consider whether any method will permit us to extrapolate to the inner life of the bat from our own case, and if not, what alternative methods there may be for understanding the notion.

Our own experience provides the basic material for our imagination, whose range is therefore limited. It will not help to try to imagine that one has webbing on one's arms, which enables one to fly around at dusk and dawn catching insects in one's mouth; that one has very poor vision, and perceives the surrounding world by a system of reflected high-frequency sound signals; and that one spends the day hanging upside down by one's feet in an attic. In so far as I can imagine this (which is not very far), it tells me only what it would be like for me to behave as a bat behaves. But that is not the question. I want to know what it is like for a bat to be a bat. Yet if I try to imagine this, I am restricted to the resources of my own mind, and those resources are inadequate to the task. I cannot perform it either by imagining additions to my present experience, or by imagining segments gradually subtracted from it, or by imagining some combination of additions, subtractions, and modifications.

To the extent that I could look and behave like a wasp or a bat without changing my fundamental structure, my experiences would not be anything like the experiences of those animals. On the other hand, it is doubtful that any meaning can be attached to the supposition that I should possess the internal neurophysiological constitution of a bat. Even if I could by gradual degrees be transformed into a bat, nothing in my present constitution enables me to imagine what the experiences of such a future stage of myself thus metamorphosed would be like. The best evidence would come from the experiences of bats, if we only knew what they were like.

So if extrapolation from our own case is involved in the idea of what it is like to be a bat, the extrapolation must be incompletable. We cannot form more than a schematic conception of what it is like. For example, we may ascribe general types of experience on the basis of the animal's structure and behavior. Thus we describe bat sonar as a form of three-dimensional forward perception; we believe that bats feel some versions of pain, fear, hunger, and lust, and that they have other, more familiar types of perception besides sonar. But we believe that these experiences also have in each case a specific subjective character, which it is beyond our ability to conceive. And if there's conscious life elsewhere in the universe, it is likely that some of it will not be describable even in the most general experiential terms available to us. (The problem is not confined to exotic cases, however, for it exists between one person and another. The subjective character of the experience of a person deaf and blind from birth is not accessible to me, for example, nor presumably is mine to him. This does not prevent us each from believing that the other's experience has such a subjective character.)

If anyone is inclined to deny that we can believe in the existence of facts like this whose exact nature we cannot possibly conceive, he should reflect that in contemplating the bats we are in much the same position that intelligent bats or Martians would occupy if they tried to form a conception of what it was like to be us. The structure of their own minds might make it impossible for them to succeed, but we know they would be wrong to conclude that there is not anything precise that it is like to be us: that only certain general types of mental state could be ascribed to us (perhaps perception and appetite would be concepts common to us both; perhaps not). We know they would be wrong to draw such a skeptical conclusion because we know what it is like to be us. And we know that while it includes an enormous amount of variation and complexity, and while we do not possess the vocabulary to describe it adequately, its subjective character is highly specific, and in some respects describable in terms that can be understood only by creatures like us. The fact that we cannot expect ever to accommodate in our language a detailed description of Martian or bat phenomenology should not lead us to dismiss as meaningless the claim that bats and Martians have experiences fully comparable in richness of detail to our own. It would be fine if someone were to develop concepts and a theory that enabled us to think about those things; but such an understanding may be permanently denied to us by the limits of our nature. And to deny the reality or logical significance of what we can never describe or understand is the crudest form of cognitive dissonance.

LIMITS TO OUR CONCEPTUAL SCHEMES

This brings us to the edge of a topic that requires much more discussion than I can give it here: namely, the relation between facts on the one hand and conceptual schemes or systems of representation on the other. My realism about the subjective domain in all its forms implies a belief in the existence of facts beyond the reach of human concepts. Certainly it is possible for a human being to believe that there are facts which humans never will possess the requisite concepts to represent or comprehend. Indeed, it would be foolish to doubt this, given the finiteness of humanity's expectations. After all there would have been transfinite numbers even if everyone had been wiped out by the Black Death before Cantor discovered them. But one might also believe that there are facts which could not ever be represented or comprehended by human beings, even if the species lasted for ever—simply because our structure does not permit us to operate with concepts of the requisite type. This impossibility might even be observed by other beings, but it is not clear that the existence of such beings, or the possibility of their existence, is a precondition of the significance of the hypothesis that there are humanly inaccessible facts. (After all, the nature of beings with access to humanly inaccessible facts is presumably itself a humanly inaccessible fact.) Reflection on what it is like to be a bat seems to lead us, therefore, to the conclusion that there are facts that do not consist in the truth of propositions expressible in a human language. We can be compelled to recognize the existence of such facts without being able to state or comprehend them.

    I shall not pursue this subject, however. Its bearing on the topic before us (namely, the mind-body problem) is that it enables us to make a general observation about the subjective character of experience. Whatever may be the status of facts about what it is like to be a human being, or a bat, or a Martian, these appear to be facts that embody a particular point of view.

    I am not adverting here to the alleged privacy of experience to its possessor. The point of view in question is not one accessible only to a single individual. Rather it is a type. It is often possible to take up a point of view other than one's own, so the comprehension of such facts is not limited to one's own case. There is a sense in which phenomenological facts are perfectly objective: one person can know or say of another what the quality of the other's experience is. They are subjective, however, in the sense that even this objective ascription of experience is possible only for someone sufficiently similar to the object of ascription to be able to adopt his point of view—to understand the ascription in the first person as well as in the third, so to speak. The more different from oneself the other experiencer is, the less success one can expect with this enterprise. In our own case we occupy the relevant point of view, but we will have as much difficulty understanding our own experience properly if we approach it from another point of view as we would if we tried to understand the experience of another species without taking up its point of view.

    This bears directly on the mind-body problem. For if the facts of experience—facts about what it is like for the experiencing organism—are accessible only from one point of view, then it is a mystery how the true character of experiences could be revealed in the physical operation of that organism. The latter is a domain of objective facts par excellence—the kind that can be observed and understood from many points of view and by individuals with differing perceptual systems. There are no comparable imaginative obstacles to the acquisition of knowledge about bat neurophysiology by human scientists, and intelligent bats or Martians might learn more about the human brain than we ever will.

    This is not by itself an argument against reduction. A Martian scientist with no understanding of visual perception could understand the rainbow, or lightning, or clouds as physical phenomena, though he would never be able to understand the human concepts of rainbow, lightning, or cloud, or the place these things occupy in our phenomenal world. The objective nature of the things picked out by these concepts could be apprehended by him because, although the concepts themselves are connected with a particular point of view and a particular visual phenomenology, the things apprehended from that point of view are not: they are observable from the point of view but external to it; hence they can be comprehended from other points of view also, either by the same organisms or by others. Lightning has an objective character that is not exhausted by its visual appearance, and this can be investigated by a Martian without vision. To be precise, it has a more objective character than is revealed in its visual appearance. In speaking of the move from subjective to objective characterization, I wish to remain noncommittal about the existence of an end point, the completely objective intrinsic nature of the thing, which one might or might not be able to reach. It may be more accurate to think of objectivity as a direction in which the understanding can travel. And in understanding a phenomenon like lightning, it is legitimate to go as far away as one can from a strictly human viewpoint.

In the case of experience, on the other hand, the connection with a particular point of view seems much closer. It is difficult to understand what could be meant by the objective character of an experience, apart from the particular point of view from which its subject apprehends it. After all, what would be left of what it was like to be a bat if one removed the viewpoint of the bat? But if experience does not have, in addition to its subjective character, an objective nature that can be apprehended from many different points of view, then how can it be supposed that a Martian investigating my brain might be observing physical processes which were my mental processes (as he might observe physical processes which were bolts of lightning), only from a different point of view? How, for that matter, could a human physiologist observe them from another point of view?

We appear to be faced with a general difficulty about psychophysical reduction. In other areas the process of reduction is a move in the direction of greater objectivity, toward a more accurate view of the real nature of things. This is accomplished by reducing our dependence on individual or species-specific points of view toward the object of investigation. We describe it not in terms of the impressions it makes on our senses, but in terms of its more general effects and of properties detectable by means other than the human senses. The less it depends on a specifically human viewpoint, the more objective is our description. It is possible to follow this path because although the concepts and ideas we employ in thinking about the external world are initially applied from a point of view that involves our perceptual apparatus, they are used by us to refer to things beyond themselves—toward which we have the phenomenal point of view. Therefore we can abandon it in favor of another, and still be thinking about the same things.

Experience itself, however, does not seem to fit the pattern. The idea of moving from appearance to reality seems to make no sense here. What is the analogue in this case to pursuing a more objective understanding of the same phenomena by abandoning the initial subjective viewpoint toward them in favor of another that is more objective but concerns the same thing? Certainly it appears unlikely that we will get closer to the real nature of human experience by leaving behind the particularity of our human point of view and striving for a description in terms accessible to beings that could not imagine what it was like to be us. If the subjective character of experience is fully comprehensible only from one point of view, then any shift to greater objectivity—that is, less attachment to a specific viewpoint—does not take us nearer to the real nature of the phenomenon: it takes us farther away from it.

In a sense, the seeds of this objection to the reducibility of experience are already detectable in successful cases of reduction; for in discovering sound to be, in reality, a wave phenomenon in air or other media, we leave behind one viewpoint to take up another, and the auditory, human or animal view-point that we leave behind remains unreduced. Members of radically different species may both understand the same physical events in objective terms, and this does not require that they understand the phenomenal forms in which those events appear to the senses of members of the other species. Thus it is a condition of their referring to a common reality that their more particular viewpoints are not part of the common reality that they both apprehend. The reduction can succeed only if the species-specific viewpoint is omitted from what is to be reduced.

But while we are right to leave this point of view aside in seeking a fuller understanding of the external world, we cannot ignore it permanently, since it is the essence of the internal world, and not merely a point of view on it. Most of the neobehaviorism of recent philosophical psychology results from the effort to substitute an objective concept of mind for the real thing, in order to have nothing left over which cannot be reduced. If we acknowledge that a physical theory of mind must account for the subjective character of experience, we must admit that no presently available conception gives us a clue how this could be done. The problem is unique. If mental processes are indeed physical processes, then there is something it is like, intrinsically, to undergo certain physical pro-cesses. What it is for such a thing to be the case remains a mystery.

THE STATUS OF PHYSICALISM

What moral should be drawn from these reflections, and what should be done next? It would be a mistake to conclude that physicalism must be false. Noth-ing is proved by the inadequacy of physicalist hypotheses that assume a faulty objective analysis of mind. It would be truer to say that physicalism is a posi-tion we cannot understand because we do not at present have any conception of how it might be true. Perhaps it will be thought unreasonable to require such a conception as a condition of understanding. After all, it might be said, the meaning of physicalism is clear enough: mental states are states of the body; mental events are physical events. We do not know which physical states and events they are, but that should not prevent us from understanding the hypoth-esis. What could be clearer than the words "is" and "are"?

But I believe it is precisely this apparent clarity of the word "is" that is deceptive. Usually, when we are told that X is Y we know how it is supposed to be true, but that depends on a conceptual or theoretical background and is not conveyed by the "is" alone. We know how both "X" and "Y" refer, and the kinds of things to which they refer, and we have a rough idea how the two referential paths might converge on a single thing, be it an object, a person, a process, an event or whatever. But when the two terms of the identification are very disparate it may not be so clear how it could be true. We may not have even a rough idea of how the two referential paths could converge, or what kind of things they might converge on, and a theoretical framework may have to be supplied to enable us to understand this. Without the framework, an air of mysticism surrounds the identification.

This explains the magical flavor of popular presentations of fundamental scientific discoveries, given out as propositions to which one must subscribe without really understanding them. For example, people are now told at an early age that all matter is really energy. But despite the fact that they know what "is" means, most of them never form a conception of what makes this claim true, because they lack the theoretical background.

At the present time the status of physicalism is similar to that which the hypothesis that matter is energy would have had if uttered by a pre-Socratic philosopher. We do not have the beginnings of a conception of how it might be true. In order to understand the hypothesis that a mental event is a physical event, we require more than an understanding of the word "is." The idea of how a mental and a physical term might refer to the same thing is lacking, and the usual analogies with theoretical identification in other fields fail to supply it. They fail because if we construe the reference of mental terms to physical events on the usual model, we either get a reappearance of separate subjective events as the effects through which mental reference to physical events is secured, or else we get a false account of how mental terms refer (for example, a causal behaviorist one).

Strangely enough, we may have evidence for the truth of something we cannot really understand. Suppose a caterpillar is locked in a sterile safe by someone unfamiliar with insect metamorphosis, and weeks later the safe is reopened, revealing a butterfly. If the person knows that the safe has been shut the whole time, he has reason to believe that the butterfly is or was once the caterpillar, without having any idea in what sense this might be so. (One possibility is that the caterpillar contained a tiny winged parasite that devoured it and grew into the butterfly.)

It is conceivable that we are in such a position with regard to physicalism. Donald Davidson has argued that if mental events have physical causes and effects, they must have physical descriptions. He holds that we have reason to believe this even though we do not—and in fact could not—have a general psychophysical theory. His argument applies to intentional mental events, but I think we also have some reason to believe that sensations are physical processes, without being in a position to understand how. Davidson's position is that certain physical events have irreducibly mental properties, and perhaps some view describable in this way is correct. But nothing of which we can now form a conception corresponds to it; nor have we any idea what a theory would be like that enabled us to conceive of it.

Very little work has been done on the basic question (from which mention of the brain can be entirely omitted) whether any sense can be made of experiences' having an objective character at all. Does it make sense, in other words, to ask what my experiences are really like, as opposed to how they appear to me? We cannot genuinely understand the hypothesis that their nature is captured in a physical description unless we understand the more fundamental idea that they have an objective nature (or that objective processes can have a subjective nature).

I should like to close with a speculative proposal. It may be possible to approach the gap between subjective and objective from another direction. Setting aside temporarily the relation between the mind and the brain, we can pursue a more objective understanding of the mental in its own right. At present we are completely unequipped to think about the subjective character of experience without relying on the imagination—without taking up the point of view of the experiential subject. This should be regarded as a challenge to form new concepts and devise a new method—an objective phenomenology not dependent on empathy or the imagination. Though presumably it would not capture everything, its goal would be to describe, at least in part, the subjective character of experiences in a form comprehensible to beings incapable of having those experiences.

We would have to develop such a phenomenology to describe the sonar experiences of bats; but it would also be possible to begin with humans. One might try, for example, to develop concepts that could be used to explain to a person blind from birth what it was like to see. One would reach a blank wall eventually, but it should be possible to devise a method of expressing in objective terms much more than we can at present, and with much greater precision. The loose intermodal analogies—for example, "Red is like the sound of a trumpet"—which crop up in discussions of this subject are of little use. That should be clear to anyone who has both heard a trumpet and seen red. But structural features of perception might be more accessible to objective description, even though something would be left out. And concepts alternative to those we learn in the first person may enable us to arrive at a kind of understanding even of our own experience which is denied us by the very ease of description and lack of distance that subjective concepts afford.

Apart from its own interest, a phenomenology that is in this sense objective may permit questions about the physical basis of experience to assume a more intelligible form. Aspects of subjective experience that admitted this kind of objective description might be better candidates for objective explanations of a more familiar sort. But whether or not this guess is correct, it seems unlikely that any physical theory of mind can be contemplated until more thought has been given to the general problem of subjective and objective. Otherwise we cannot even pose the mind-body problem without sidestepping it.

Carol Gilligan: Is There a Characteristically Feminine Voice Defining Morality?

From "In a Different Voice"

Born in New York City, Carol Gilligan (b. 1936) is a leading social psychologist and one of the founders of the theory of female care ethics. In her essay "In a Different Voice" (1977), Gilligan criticizes male-oriented notions of moral reasoning, particularly as represented by Lawrence Kohlberg's six stages of moral development, which emphasizes strict adherence to moral rules and concepts of justice. Instead, she argues, morality should emphasize the female value of caring for others who are in a position of need and vulnerability.

The men whose theories have largely informed [the] understanding of [human] development have all been plagued by the same problem, the problem of women, whose sexuality remains more diffuse, whose perception of self is so much more tenaciously embedded in relationships with others and whose moral dilemmas hold them in a mode of judgment that is insistently contextual. The solution has been to consider women either as deviant or deficient in their development.

That there is a discrepancy between concepts of womanhood and adulthood is nowhere more clearly evident than in the series of studies on sex-role stereotypes. . . . The repeated finding of these studies is that the qualities deemed necessary for adulthood—the capacity for autonomous thinking, clear decision making, and responsible action—are those associated with masculinity but, considered undesirable as attributes of the feminine self. The stereotypes suggest a splitting of love and work that relegates the expressive capacities requisite for the former to women while the instrumental abilities necessary for the latter reside in the masculine domain. Yet, looked at from a different perspective, these stereotypes reflect a conception of adulthood that is itself out of balance, favoring the separateness of the individual self over its connection to others and leaning more toward an autonomous life of work than toward the interdependence of love and care. . . .

The revolutionary contribution of Piaget's work is the experimental confirmation and refinement of Kant's assertion that knowledge is actively constructed rather than passively received. Time, space, self, and other, as well as the categories of developmental theory, all arise out of the active interchange

Source: Carol Gilligan, "In a Different Voice: Women's Conception of Self and of Morality," in *Harvard Educational Review* 47 (1977). Copyright 1977 by the President and Fellows of Harvard College. All rights reserved.

between the individual and the physical and social world in which he lives and of which he strives to make sense. . . .

Kohlberg (1969), in his extension of the early work of Piaget, discovered six stages of moral judgment, which he claimed formed an invariant sequence, each successive stage representing a more adequate construction of the moral problem, which in turn provides the basis for its more just resolution. The stages divide into three levels, each of which denotes a significant expansion of the moral point of view from an egocentric through a societal to a universal ethical conception. With this expansion in perspective comes the capacity to free moral judgment from the individual needs and social conventions with which it had earlier been confused and anchor it instead in principles of justice that are universal in application. These principles provide criteria upon which both individual and societal claims can be impartially assessed. In Kohlberg's view, at the highest stages of development morality is freed from both psychological and historical constraints, and the individual can judge independently of his own particular needs and of the values of those around him.

That the moral sensibility of women differs from that of men was noted by Freud (1925/1961) in the following by now well-quoted statement:

> I cannot evade the notion (though I hesitate to give it expression) that for women the level of what is ethically normal is different from what it is in man. Their superego is never so inexorable, so impersonal, so independent of its emotional origins as we require it to be in men. Character-traits which critics of every epoch have brought up against women—that they show less sense of justice than men, that they are less ready to submit to the great exigencies of life, that they are more often influenced in their judgments by feelings of affection or hostility—all these would be amply accounted for by the modification in the formation of their superego.

While Freud's explanation lies in the deviation of female from male development around the construction and resolution of the Oedipal problem, the same observations about the nature of morality in women emerge from the work of Piaget and Kohlberg. Piaget (1932/1965), in his study of the rules of children's games, observed that, in the games they played, girls were "less explicit about agreement [than boys] and less concerned with legal elaboration." In contrast to the boys' interest in the codification of rules, the girls adopted a more pragmatic attitude, regarding "a rule as good so long as the game repays it." As a result, in comparison to boys, girls were found to be more tolerant and more easily reconciled to innovations.

Kohlberg (1971) also identifies a strong interpersonal bias in the moral judgments of women, which leads them to be considered as typically at the third of his six-stage developmental sequence. At that stage, the good is identified with "what pleases or helps others and is approved of by them." This mode of judgment is conventional in its conformity to generally held notions of the good but also psychological in its concern with intention and consequences as the basis for judging the morality of action.

That women fall largely into this level of moral-judgment is hardly surprising when we read from the Broverman et al. (1972) list that prominent among the twelve attributes considered to be desirable for women are tact, gentleness, awareness of the feelings of others, strong need for security, and easy expression of tender feelings. And yet, herein lies the paradox, for the very traits that have traditionally defined the "goodness" of women, their care for and sensitivity to the needs of others, are those that mark them as deficient in moral development. The infusion of feeling into their judgments keeps them from developing a more independent and abstract ethical conception in which concern for others derives from principles of justice rather than from compassion and care. Kohlberg, however, is less pessimistic than Freud in his assessment, for he sees the development of women as extending beyond the interpersonal level, following the same path toward independent, principled judgment that he discovered in the research on men from which his stages were derived. In Kohlberg's view, women's development will proceed beyond Stage Three when they are challenged to solve moral problems that require them to see beyond the relationships that have in the past generally bound their moral experience.

What then do women say when asked to construct the moral domain; how do we identify the characteristically "feminine" voice? A Radcliffe undergraduate, responding to the question, "If you had to say what morality meant to you, how would you sum it up," replies:

> When I think of the word morality, I think of obligations. I usually think of it as conflicts between personal desires and social things, social considerations, or personal desires of yourself versus personal desires of another person or people or whatever. Morality is that whole realm of how you decide these conflicts. A moral person is one who would decide, like by placing themselves more often than not as equals, a truly moral person would always consider another person as their equal . . . in a situation of social interaction, something is morally wrong where the individual ends up screwing a lot of people. And it is morally right when everyone comes out better off.

Yet when asked if she can think of someone whom she would consider a genuinely moral person, she replies, "Well, immediately I think of Albert Schweitzer because he has obviously given his life to help others." Obligation and sacrifice override the ideal of equality, setting up a basic contradiction in her thinking.

Another undergraduate responds to the question, "What does it mean to say something is morally right or wrong?" by also speaking first of responsibilities and obligations:

> Just what it has to do with responsibilities and obligations and values, mainly values. . . . In my life situation I relate morality and interpersonal relationships that have to do with respect for the other person and myself. [Why respect other people?] Because they have a consciousness or feelings that can be hurt, an awareness that can be hurt.

The concern about hurting others persists as a major theme in the responses of two other Radcliffe students:

> [Why be moral?] Millions of people have to live together peacefully. I personally don't want to hurt other people. That's a real criterion, a main criterion for me.

It underlies my sense of justice. It isn't nice to inflict pain. I empathize with anyone in pain. Not hurting others is important in my own private morals. Years ago, I would have jumped out of a window not to hurt my boyfriend. That was pathological. Even today though, I want approval and love and I don't want enemies. Maybe that's why there is morality—so people can win approval, love and friendship.

My main moral principle is not hurting other people as long as you aren't going against your own conscience and as long as you remain true to yourself. . . . There are many moral issues such as abortion, the draft, killing, stealing, monogamy, etc. If something is a controversial issue like these, then I always say it is up to the individual. The individual has to decide and then follow his own conscience. There are no moral absolutes. . . . Laws are pragmatic instruments, but they are not absolutes. A viable society can't make exceptions all the time, but I would personally. . . . I'm afraid I'm heading for some big crisis with my boyfriend someday, and someone will get hurt, and he'll get more hurt than I will. I feel an obligation to not hurt him, but also an obligation to not lie. I don't know if it is possible to not lie and not hurt.

The common thread that runs through these statements, the wish not to hurt others and the hope that in morality lies a way of solving conflicts so that no one will get hurt, is striking in that it is independently introduced by each of the four women as the most specific item in their response to a most general question. The moral person is one who helps others; goodness is service, meeting one's obligations and responsibilities to others, if possible, without sacrificing oneself. While the first of the four women ends by denying the conflict she initially introduced, the last woman anticipates a conflict between remaining true to herself and adhering to her principle of not hurting others. The dilemma that would test the limits of this judgment would be one where helping others is seen to be at the price of hurting the self.

The reticence about taking stands on "controversial issues," the willingness to "make exceptions all the time" expressed in the final example above, is echoed repeatedly by other Radcliffe students, as in the following two examples:

I never feel that I can condemn anyone else. I have a very relativistic position. The basic idea that I cling to is the sanctity of human life. I am inhibited about impressing my beliefs on others.

I could never argue that my belief on a moral question is anything that another person should accept. I don't believe in absolutes. . . . If there is an absolute for moral decisions, it is human life. . . .

When women feel excluded from direct participation in society, they see themselves as subject to a consensus or judgment made and enforced by the men on whose protection and support they depend and by whose names they are known. A divorced middle-aged woman, mother of adolescent daughters, resident of a sophisticated university community, tells the story as follows:

As a woman, I feel I never understood that I was a person, that I can make decisions and I have a right to make decisions. I always felt that that belonged to my father or my husband in some way or church which was always represented by a male clergyman. They were the three men in my life: father, husband, and clergyman, and they had much more to say about what I should or shouldn't do. They were really authority figures which I accepted. I didn't rebel against that. It only has lately occurred to me that I never even rebelled against it, and my girls are much more conscious of this, not in the militant sense, but just in the recognizing sense. . . . I still let things happen to me rather than make them happen, than to make choices, although I know all about choices. I know the procedures and the steps and all. [Do you have any clues about why this might be true?] Well, I think in one sense, there is less responsibility involved. Because if you make a dumb decision, you have to take the rap. If it happens to you, well, you can complain about it. I think that if you don't grow up feeling that you ever had any choices, you don't either have the sense that you have emotional responsibility. With this sense of choice comes this sense of responsibility.

The essence of the moral decision is the exercise of choice and the willingness to accept responsibility for that choice. To the extent that women perceive themselves as having no choice, they correspondingly excuse themselves from the responsibility that decision entails. Childlike in the vulnerability of their dependence and consequent fear of abandonment, they claim to wish only to please but in return for their goodness they expect to be loved and cared for. This, then, is an "altruism" always at risk, for it presupposes an innocence constantly in danger of being compromised by an awareness of the trade-off that has been made. Asked to describe herself, a Radcliffe senior responds:

I have heard of the onion skin theory. I see myself as an onion, as a block of different layers, the external layers for people that I don't know that well, the agreeable, the social, and as you go inward there are more sides for people I know that I show. I am not sure about the innermost, whether there is a core, or whether I have just picked up everything as I was growing up, these different influences. I think I have a neutral attitude towards myself, but I do think in terms of good and bad. Good—I try to be considerate and thoughtful of other people and I try to be fair in situations and be tolerant. I use the words but I try and work them out practically. Bad things—I am not sure if they are bad, if they are altruistic or I am doing them basically for approval of other people. [Which things are these?] The values I have when I try to act them out. They deal mostly with interpersonal type relations. If I were doing it for approval, it would be a very tenuous thing. If I didn't get the right feedback, there might go all my values.

. . . Women have traditionally deferred to the judgment of men, although often while intimating a sensibility of their own which is at variance with that judgment. Maggie Tulliver, in *The Mill on the Floss* (Eliot, 1860/1965), responds to the accusations that ensue from the discovery of her secretly continued relationship with Philip Wakem by acceding to her brother's moral judgment while at the same time asserting a different set of standards by which she attests her own superiority:

I don't want to defend myself. . . . I know I've been wrong—often continually. But yet, sometimes when I have done wrong, it has been because I have feelings that you would be the better for if you had them. If *you* were in fault ever, if you

had done anything very wrong, I should be sorry for the pain it brought you;
I should not want punishment to be heaped on you.

The morality of responsibility which women describe stands apart from the morality of rights which underlies Kohlberg's conception of the highest stages of moral judgment. Kohlberg . . . sees the progression toward these stages as resulting from the generalization of the self-centered adolescent rejection of societal morality into a principled conception of individual natural rights. To illustrate this progression, he cites an example . . . of a male college senior whose moral judgment also was scored by Kohlberg as at Stage Five or Six:

> [Morality] is a prescription, it is a thing to follow, and the idea of having a concept of morality is to try to figure out what it is that people can do in order to make life with each other livable, make for a kind of balance, a kind of equilibrium, a harmony in which everybody feels he has a place and an equal share in things, and it's doing that—doing that is kind of contributing to a state of affairs that go beyond the individual in the absence of which, the individual has no chance for self-fulfillment of any kind. Fairness; morality is kind of essential, it seems to me, for creating the kind of environment, interaction between people, that is prerequisite to this fulfillment of most individual goals and so on. If you want other people to not interfere with your pursuit of whatever you are into, you have to play the game.

In contrast, a woman in her late twenties responds to a similar question by defining a morality not of rights but of responsibility:

> [What makes something a moral issue?] Some sense of trying to uncover a right path in which to live, and always in my mind is that the world is full of real and recognizable trouble, and is it heading for some sort of doom and is it right to bring children into this world when we currently have an overpopulation problem, and is it right to spend money on a pair of shoes when I have a pair of shoes and other people are shoeless. . . . It is part of a self-critical view, part of saying, how am I spending my time and in what sense am I working? I think I have a real drive to, I have a real maternal drive to take care of someone. To take care of my mother, to take care of children, to take care of other people's children, to take care of my own children, to take care of the world. I think that goes back to your other question, and when I am dealing with moral issues, I am sort of saying to myself constantly, are you taking care of all the things that you think are important and in what ways are you wasting yourself and wasting those issues?

. . . From another perspective, however, this judgment represents a different moral conception, disentangled from societal conventions and raised to the principled level. In this conception, moral judgment is oriented toward issues of responsibility. The way in which the responsibility orientation guides moral decision at the post-conventional level is described by the following woman in her thirties:

> [Is there a right way to make moral decisions?] The only way I know is to try to be as awake as possible, to try to know the range of what you feel, to try to consider all that's involved, to be as aware as you can be to what's going on,

as conscious as you can of where you're walking. [Are there principles that guide you?] The principle would have something to do with responsibility, responsibility and caring about yourself and others. . . . But it's not that on the one hand you choose to be responsible and on the other hand you choose to be irresponsible—both ways you can be responsible. That's why there's not just a principle that once you take hold of you settle—the principle put into practice here is still going to leave you with conflict.

The moral imperative that emerges repeatedly in the women's interviews is an injunction to care, a responsibility to discern and alleviate the "real and recognizable trouble" of this world. For the men Kohlberg studied, the moral imperative appeared rather as an injunction to respect the rights of others and thus to protect from interference the right to life and self-fulfillment. Women's insistence on care is at first self-critical rather than self-protective, while men initially conceive obligation to others negatively in terms of noninterference. Development for both sexes then would seem to entail an integration of rights and responsibilities through the discovery of the complementarity of these disparate views. For the women I have studied, this integration between rights and responsibilities appears to take place through a principled understanding of equity and reciprocity. This understanding tempers the self-destructive potential of a self-critical morality by asserting the equal right of all persons to care.

READING 9

James Rachels: The Challenge of Cultural Relativism

From *Elements of Moral Philosophy*

Born in Columbus, Georgia, James Rachels (1941–2003) was an influential American moral philosopher, and is most remembered for his Elements of Moral Philosophy *(1986). One of Rachels's key contributions was his criticism of the moral theory of cultural relativism—the view that moral values are creations of society. According to Rachels, the theory leads to absurd consequences; for example, we could no longer say that the customs of other societies are morally inferior to our own. Further, he argues, when surveying the cultures around the world, we find that they have three core values in common: care for children, truth telling, and prohibition against murder. While the theory of cultural relativism exaggerates the differences in moral values in different cultures, he argues, it nevertheless teaches us the important lesson that we should keep an open mind.*

"Morality differs in every society, and is a convenient term for socially approved habits." Ruth Benedict, *Patterns of Culture* (1934).

Source: James Rachels, *Elements of Moral Philosophy* (1999).

HOW DIFFERENT CULTURES HAVE
DIFFERENT MORAL CODES

Darius, a king of ancient Persia, was intrigued by the variety of cultures he encountered in his travels. He had found, for example, that the Callatians (a tribe of Indians) customarily ate the bodies of their dead fathers. The Greeks, of course, did not do that—the Greeks practiced cremation and regarded the funeral pyre as the natural and fitting way to dispose of the dead. Darius thought that a sophisticated understanding of the world must include an appreciation of such differences between cultures. One day, to teach this lesson, he summoned some Greeks who happened to be present at his court and asked them what they would take to eat the bodies of their dead fathers. They were shocked, as Darius knew they would be, and replied that no amount of money could persuade them to do such a thing. Then Darius called in some Callatians, and while the Greeks listened asked them what they would take to burn their dead fathers' bodies. The Callatians were horrified and told Darius not even to mention such a dreadful thing.

This story, recounted by Herodotus in his *History*, illustrates a recurring theme in the literature of social science: Different cultures have different moral codes. What is thought right within one group may be utterly abhorrent to the members of another group, and vice versa. Should we eat the bodies of the dead or burn them? If you were a Greek, one answer would seem obviously correct; but if you were a Callatian, the opposite would seem equally certain.

It is easy to give additional examples of the same kind. Consider the Eskimos. They are a remote and inaccessible people. Numbering only about 25,000, they live in small, isolated settlements scattered mostly along the northern fringes of North America and Greenland. Until the beginning of the 20th century, the outside world knew little about them. Then explorers began to bring back strange tales.

Eskimo customs turned out to be very different from our own. The men often had more than one wife, and they would share their wives with guests, lending them for the night as a sign of hospitality. Moreover, within a community, a dominant male might demand and get regular sexual access to other men's wives. The women, however, were free to break these arrangements simply by leaving their husbands and taking up with new partners—free, that is, so long as their former husbands chose not to make trouble. All in all, the Eskimo practice was a volatile scheme that bore little resemblance to what we call marriage.

But it was not only their marriage and sexual practices that were different. The Eskimos also seemed to have less regard for human life. Infanticide, for example, was common. Knud Rasmussen, one of the most famous early explorers, reported that he met one woman who had borne 20 children but had killed 10 of them at birth. Female babies, he found, were especially liable to be destroyed, and this was permitted simply at the parents' discretion, with no social stigma attached to it. Old people also, when they became too feeble to contribute to the family, were left out in the snow to die. So there seemed to be, in this society, remarkably little respect for life.

To the general public, these were disturbing revelations. Our own way of living seems so natural and right that for many of us it is hard to conceive of others living so differently. And when we do hear of such things, we tend immediately to categorize those other peoples as "backward" or "primitive." But to anthropologists and sociologists, there was nothing particularly surprising about the Eskimos. Since the time of Herodotus, enlightened observers have been accustomed to the idea that conceptions of right and wrong differ from culture to culture. If we assume that our ideas of right and wrong will be shared by all peoples at all times, we are merely naive.

To many thinkers, this observation—"Different cultures have different moral codes"—has seemed to be the key to understanding morality. The idea of universal truth in ethics, they say, is a myth. The customs of different societies are all that exist. These customs cannot be said to be "correct" or "incorrect," for that implies we have an independent standard of right and wrong by which they may be judged. But there is no such independent standard; every standard is culture-bound. The great pioneering sociologist William Graham Sumner, writing in 1906, put the point like this:

The "right" way is the way which the ancestors used and which has been handed down. The tradition is its own warrant. It is not held subject to verification by experience. The notion of right is in the folkways. It is not outside of them, of independent origin, and brought to test them. In the folkways, whatever is, is right. This is because they are traditional, and therefore contain in themselves the authority of the ancestral ghosts. When we come to the folk-ways we are at the end of our analysis.

This line of thought has probably persuaded more people to be skeptical about ethics than any other single thing. Cultural Relativism, as it has been called, challenges our ordinary belief in the objectivity and universality of moral truth. It says, in effect, that there is no such thing as universal truth in ethics; there are only the various cultural codes, and nothing more. Moreover, our own code has no special status; it is merely one among many.

As we shall see, this basic idea is really a compound of several different thoughts. It is important to separate the various elements of the theory because, on analysis, some parts turn out to be correct, while others seem to be mistaken. As a beginning, we may distinguish the following claims, all of which have been made by cultural relativists:

1. Different societies have different moral codes.
2. There is no objective standard that can be used to judge one societal code better than another.
3. The moral code of our own society has no special status; it is merely one among many.
4. There is no "universal truth" in ethics; that is, there are no moral truths that hold for all peoples at all times.
5. The moral code of a society determines what is right within that society; that is, if the moral code of a society says that a certain action is right, then that action is right, at least within that society.
6. It is mere arrogance for us to try to judge the conduct of other peoples. We should adopt an attitude of tolerance toward the practices of other cultures.

Although it may seem that these six propositions go naturally together, they are independent of one another, in the sense that some of them might be false even if others are true. In what follows, we will try to identify what is correct in Cultural Relativism, but we will also be concerned to expose what is mistaken about it.

THE CULTURAL DIFFERENCES ARGUMENT

Cultural Relativism is a theory about the nature of morality. At first blush it seems quite plausible. However, like all such theories, it may be evaluated by subjecting it to rational analysis; and when we analyze Cultural Relativism we find that it is not so plausible as it first appears to be.

The first thing we need to notice is that at the heart of Cultural Relativism there is a certain *form of argument*. The strategy used by cultural relativists is to argue from facts about the differences between cultural outlooks to a conclusion about the status of morality. Thus we are invited to accept this reasoning:

1. The Greeks believed it was wrong to eat the dead, whereas the Callatians believed it was right to eat the dead.
2. Therefore, eating the dead is neither objectively right nor objectively wrong. It is merely a matter of opinion, which varies from culture to culture.

Or, alternatively:

1. The Eskimos see nothing wrong with infanticide, whereas Americans believe infanticide is immoral.
2. Therefore, infanticide is neither objectively right nor objectively wrong. It is merely a matter of opinion, which varies from culture to culture.

Clearly, these arguments are variations of one fundamental idea. They are both special cases of a more general argument, which says:

1. Different cultures have different moral codes.
2. Therefore, there is no objective "truth" in morality. Right and wrong are only matters of opinion, and opinions vary from culture to culture.

We may call this the Cultural Differences Argument. To many people, it is persuasive. But from a logical point of view, is it sound?

It is not sound. The trouble is that the conclusion does not follow from the premise—that is, even if the premise is true, the conclusion still might be false. The premise concerns what people *believe*: In some societies, people believe one thing; in other societies, people believe differently. The conclusion, however, concerns *what really is the case*. The trouble is that this sort of conclusion does not follow logically from this sort of premise.

Consider again the example of the Greeks and Callatians. The Greeks believed it was wrong to eat the dead; the Callatians believed it was right. Does it follow, *from the mere fact that they disagreed,* that there is no objective truth in the matter? No, it does not follow; for it could be that the practice was objectively right (or wrong) and that one or the other of them was simply mistaken.

To make the point clearer, consider a different matter. In some societies, people believe the earth is flat. In other societies, such as our own, people believe the earth is (roughly) spherical. Does it follow, *from the mere fact that people disagree,* that there is no "objective truth" in geography? Of course not; we would never draw such a conclusion because we realize that, in their beliefs about the world, the members of some societies might simply be wrong. There is no reason to think that if the world is round everyone must know it. Similarly, there is no reason to think that if there is moral truth everyone must know it. The fundamental mistake in the Cultural Differences Argument is that it attempts to derive a substantive conclusion about a subject from the mere fact that people disagree about it.

This is a simple point of logic, and it is important not to misunderstand it. We are not saying (not yet, anyway) that the conclusion of the argument is false. It is still an open question whether the conclusion is true or false. The logical point is just that the conclusion does not *follow from* the premise. This is important, because in order to determine whether the conclusion is true, we need arguments in its support. Cultural Relativism proposes this argument, but unfortunately the argument turns out to be fallacious. So it proves nothing.

THE CONSEQUENCES OF TAKING CULTURAL RELATIVISM SERIOUSLY

Even if the Cultural Differences Argument is invalid, Cultural Relativism might still be true. What would it be like if it were true?

In the passage quoted above, William Graham Sumner summarizes the essence of Cultural Relativism. He says that there is no measure of right and wrong other than the standards of one's society: "The notion of right is in the folkways. It is not outside of them, of independent origin, and brought to test them. In the folkways, whatever is, is right."

Suppose we took this seriously. What would be some of the consequences?

1. **We could no longer say that the customs of other societies are morally inferior to our own.** This, of course, is one of the main points stressed by Cultural Relativism. We would have to stop condemning other societies merely because they are "different." So long as we concentrate on certain examples, such as the funerary practices of the Greeks and Callatians, this may seem to be a sophisticated, enlightened attitude.

   However, we would also be stopped from criticizing other, less benign practices. Suppose a society waged war on its neighbors for the purpose of taking slaves. Or suppose a society was violently anti-Semitic and its leaders set out to destroy the Jews. Cultural Relativism would preclude us from saying that either of these practices was wrong. We would not even be able to say that a society tolerant of Jews is *better* than the anti-Semitic society, for that would imply some sort of transcultural standard of comparison. The failure to condemn *these* practices does not seem enlightened; on the contrary, slavery and anti-Semitism seem wrong wherever they occur.

Nevertheless, if we took Cultural Relativism seriously, we would have to regard these social practices as also immune from criticism.

2. **We could decide whether actions are right or wrong just by consulting the standards of our society.** Cultural Relativism suggests a simple test for determining what is right and what is wrong: All one need do is ask whether the action is in accordance with the code of one's society. Suppose in 1975 a resident of South Africa was wondering whether his country's policy of *apartheid*—a rigidly racist system—was morally correct. All he had to do was ask whether this policy conformed to his society's moral code. If it did, there would have been nothing to worry about, at least from a moral point of view.

   This implication of Cultural Relativism is disturbing because few of us think that our society's code is perfect; we can think of ways it might be improved. Yet Cultural Relativism would not only forbid us from criticizing the codes of other societies; it would stop us from criticizing our own. After all, if right and wrong are relative to culture, this must be true for our own culture just as much as for other cultures.

3. **The idea of moral progress is called into doubt.** Usually, we think that at least some social changes are for the better. (Although, of course, other changes may be for the worse.) Throughout most of Western history the place of women in society was narrowly circumscribed. They could not own property; they could not vote or hold political office; and generally they were under the almost absolute control of their husbands. Recently much of this has changed, and most people think of it as progress.

   If Cultural Relativism is correct, can we legitimately think of this as progress? Progress means replacing a way of doing things with a better way. But by what standard do we judge the new ways as better? If the old ways were in accordance with the social standards of their time, then Cultural Relativism would say it is a mistake to judge them by the standards of a different time. Eighteenth-century society was, in effect, a different society from the one we have now. To say that we have made progress implies a judgment that present-day society is better, and that is just the sort of transcultural judgment that, according to Cultural Relativism, is impermissible.

   Our idea of social reform will also have to be reconsidered. Reformers such as Martin Luther King, Jr., have sought to change their societies for the better. Within the constraints imposed by Cultural Relativism, there is one way this might be done. If a society is not living up to its own ideals, the reformer may be regarded as acting for the best: The ideals of the society are the standard by which we judge his or her proposals as worthwhile. But the "reformer" may not challenge the ideals themselves, for those ideals are by definition correct. According to Cultural Relativism, then, the idea of social reform makes sense only in this limited way.

These three consequences of Cultural Relativism have led many thinkers to reject it as implausible on its face. It does make sense, they say, to condemn some practices, such as slavery and anti-Semitism, wherever they occur. It makes sense to think that our own society has made some moral progress, while admitting that it is still imperfect and in need of reform. Because Cultural Relativism says that these judgments make no sense, the argument goes, it cannot be right.

WHY THERE IS LESS DISAGREEMENT THAN IT SEEMS

The original impetus for Cultural Relativism comes from the observation that cultures differ dramatically in their views of right and wrong. But just how much do they differ? It is true that there are differences. However, it is easy to overestimate the extent of those differences. Often, when we examine what seems to be a dramatic difference, we find that the cultures do not differ nearly as much as it appears.

Consider a culture in which people believe it is wrong to eat cows. This may even be a poor culture, in which there is not enough food; still, the cows are not to be touched. Such a society would appear to have values very different from our own. But does it? We have not yet asked why these people will not eat cows. Suppose it is because they believe that after death the souls of humans inhabit the bodies of animals, especially cows, so that a cow may be someone's grandmother. Now do we want to say that their values are different from ours? No; the difference lies elsewhere. The difference is in our belief systems, not in our values. We agree that we shouldn't eat Grandma; we simply disagree about whether the cow is (or could be) Grandma.

The point is that many factors work together to produce the customs of a society. The society's values are only one of them. Other matters, such as the religious and factual beliefs held by its members, and the physical circumstances in which they must live, are also important. We cannot conclude, then, merely because customs differ, that there is a disagreement about values. The difference in customs may be attributable to some other aspect of social life. Thus there may be less disagreement about values than there appears to be.

Consider again the Eskimos, who often kill perfectly normal infants, especially girls. We do not approve of such things; a parent who killed a baby in our society would be locked up. Thus there appears to be a great difference in the values of our two cultures. But suppose we ask why the Eskimos do this. The explanation is not that they have less affection for their children or less respect for human life. An Eskimo family will always protect its babies if conditions permit. But they live in a harsh environment, where food is in short supply. A fundamental postulate of Eskimo thought is: "Life is hard, and the margin of safety small." A family may want to nourish its babies but be unable to do so.

As in many "primitive" societies, Eskimo mothers will nurse their infants over a much longer period of time than mothers in our culture. The child will take nourishment from its mother's breast for four years, perhaps even longer. So even in the best of times there are limits to the number of infants that one mother can sustain. Moreover, the Eskimos are a nomadic people—unable to farm, they must move about in search of food. Infants must be carried, and a mother can carry only one baby in her parka as she travels and goes about her outdoor work. Other family members help whenever they can.

Infant girls are more readily disposed of because, first, in this society the males are the primary food providers—they are the hunters, according to the traditional division of labor—and it is obviously important to maintain a sufficient number of food providers. But there is an important second reason as well. Because the hunters suffer a high casualty rate, the adult men who die prematurely far outnumber the women who die early. Thus, if male and female infants survived in equal numbers, the female adult population would greatly outnumber the male adult population. Examining the available statistics, one writer concluded that "were it not for female infanticide. . . there would be approximately one-and-a-half times as many females in the average Eskimo local group as there are food-producing males."

So among the Eskimos, infanticide does not signal a fundamentally different attitude toward children. Instead, it is a recognition that drastic measures are sometimes needed to ensure the family's survival. Even then, however, killing the baby is not the first option considered. Adoption is common; childless couples are especially happy to take a more fertile couple's "surplus." Killing is only the last resort. I emphasize this in order to show that the raw data of the anthropologists can be misleading; it can make the differences in values between cultures appear greater than they are. The Eskimos' values are not all that different from our values. It is only that life forces upon them choices that we do not have to make.

HOW ALL CULTURES HAVE SOME VALUES IN COMMON

It should not be surprising that, despite appearances, the Eskimos are protective of their children. How could it be otherwise? How could a group survive that did not value its young? It is easy to see that, in fact, all cultural groups must protect their infants:

1. Human infants are helpless and cannot survive if they are not given extensive care for a period of years.
2. Therefore, if a group did not care for its young, the young would not survive, and the older members of the group would not be replaced. After a while the group would die out.
3. Therefore, any cultural group that continues to exist must care for its young. Infants that are not cared for must be the exception rather than the rule.

Similar reasoning shows that other values must be more or less universal. Imagine what it would be like for a society to place no value at all on truth telling. When one person spoke to another, there would be no presumption at all that he was telling the truth for he could just as easily be speaking falsely. Within that society, there would be no reason to pay attention to what anyone says. (I ask you what time it is, and you say, "Four o'clock." But there is no presumption that you are speaking truly; you could just as easily have said the first thing that came into your head. So I have no reason to pay attention to your answer; in fact, there was no point in my asking you in the first place.) Communication would then be extremely difficult, if not impossible. And because complex societies cannot exist without communication among their members, society would become impossible. It follows that in any complex society there must be a presumption in favor of truthfulness. There may of course be exceptions to this rule: There may be situations in which it is thought to be permissible to lie. Nevertheless, these will be exceptions to a rule that is in force in the society.

Here is one further example of the same type. Could a society exist in which there was no prohibition on murder? What would this be like? Suppose people were free to kill other people at will, and no one thought there was anything wrong with it. In such a "society," no one could feel secure. Everyone would have to be constantly on guard. People who wanted to survive would have to avoid other people as much as possible. This would inevitably result in individuals trying to become as self-sufficient as possible—after all, associating with others would be dangerous. Society on any large scale would collapse. Of course, people might band together in smaller groups with others that they could trust not to harm them. But notice what this means: They would be forming smaller societies that did acknowledge a rule against murder. The prohibition of murder, then, is a necessary feature of all societies.

There is a general theoretical point here, namely, that *there are some moral rules that all societies will have in common, because those rules are necessary for society to exist.* The rules against lying and murder are two examples. And in fact, we do find these rules in force in all viable cultures. Cultures may differ in what they regard as legitimate exceptions to the rules, but this disagreement exists against a background of agreement on the larger issues. Therefore, it is a mistake to overestimate the amount of difference between cultures. Not every moral rule can vary from society to society.

JUDGING A CULTURAL PRACTICE
TO BE UNDESIRABLE

In 1996, a 17-year-old girl named Fauziya Kassindja arrived at Newark International Airport and asked for asylum. She had fled her native country of Togo, a small West African nation, to escape what people there call "excision."

Excision is a permanently disfiguring procedure that is sometimes called "female circumcision," although it bears little resemblance to the Jewish ritual. More commonly, at least in Western newspapers, it is referred to as "genital mutilation." According to the World Health Organization, the practice is widespread in 26 African nations, and two million girls each year are "excised." In some instances, excision is part of an elaborate tribal ritual, performed in small traditional villages, and girls look forward to it because it signals their acceptance into the adult world. In other instances, the practice is carried out by families living in cities on young women who desperately resist.

Fauziya Kassindja was the youngest of five daughters in a devoutly Muslim family. Her father, who owned a successful trucking business, was opposed to excision, and he was able to defy the tradition because of his wealth. His first four daughters were married without being mutilated. But when Fauziya was 16, he suddenly died. Fauziya then came under the authority of his father, who arranged a marriage for her and prepared to have her excised. Fauziya was terrified, and her mother and oldest sister helped her to escape. Her mother, left without resources, eventually had to formally apologize and submit to the authority of the patriarch she had offended.

Meanwhile, in America, Fauziya was imprisoned for two years while the authorities decided what to do with her. She was finally granted asylum, but not before she became the center of a controversy about how foreigners should regard the cultural practices of other peoples. A series of articles in the *New York Times* encouraged the idea that excision is a barbaric practice that should be condemned. Other observers were reluctant to be so judgmental—live and let live, they said; after all, our practices probably seem just as strange to them.

Suppose we are inclined to say that excision is bad. Would we merely be applying the standards of our own culture? If Cultural Relativism is correct, that is all we can do, for there is no culture-neutral moral standard to which we may appeal. Is that true?

Is There a Culture-Neutral Standard of Right and Wrong?

There is, of course, a lot that can be said against the practice of excision. Excision is painful and it results in the permanent loss of sexual pleasure. Its short-term effects include hemorrhage, tetanus, and septicemia. Sometimes the woman dies. Long-term effects include chronic infection, scars that hinder walking, and continuing pain.

Why, then, has it become a widespread social practice? It is not easy to say. Excision has no obvious social benefits. Unlike Eskimo infanticide, it is not necessary for the group's survival. Nor is it a matter of religion. Excision is practiced by groups with various religions, including Islam and Christianity, neither of which commend it.

Nevertheless, a number of reasons are given in its defense. Women who are incapable of sexual pleasure are said to be less likely to be promiscuous; thus there will be fewer unwanted pregnancies in unmarried women. Moreover, wives for whom sex is only a duty are less likely to be unfaithful to their husbands; and because they will not be thinking about sex, they will be more attentive to the needs of their husbands and children. Husbands, for their part, are said to enjoy sex more with wives who have been excised. (The women's own lack of enjoyment is said to be unimportant.) Men will not want unexcised women, as they are unclean and immature. And above all, it has been done since antiquity, and we may not change the ancient ways.

It would be easy, and perhaps a bit arrogant, to ridicule these arguments. But we may notice an important feature of this whole line of reasoning: it attempts to justify excision by showing that excision is beneficial—men, women, and their families are all said to be better off when women are excised. Thus we might approach this reasoning, and excision itself, by asking which is true: Is excision, on the whole, helpful or harmful?

Here, then, is the standard that might most reasonably be used in thinking about excision: We may ask *whether the practice promotes or hinders the welfare of the people whose lives are affected by it*. And, as a corollary, we may ask if there is an alternative set of social arrangements that would do a better job of promoting their welfare. If so, we may conclude that the existing practice is deficient.

But this looks like just the sort of independent moral standard that Cultural Relativism says cannot exist. It is a single standard that may be brought to bear in judging the practices of any culture, at any time, including our own. Of course, people will not usually see this principle as being "brought in from the outside" to judge them, because, like the rules against lying and homicide, the welfare of its members is a value internal to all viable cultures.

Why Thoughtful People May Nevertheless Be Reluctant to Criticize Other Cultures

Although they are personally horrified by excision, many thoughtful people are reluctant to say it is wrong, for at least three reasons.

First, there is an understandable nervousness about "interfering in the social customs of other peoples." Europeans and their cultural descendents in America have a shabby history of destroying native cultures in the name of Christianity and enlightenment, not to mention self-interest. Recoiling from this record, some people refuse to make any negative judgments about other cultures, especially cultures that resemble those that have been wronged in the past. We should notice, however, that there is a difference between (a) judging a cultural practice to be morally deficient and (b) thinking that we should announce the fact, conduct a campaign, apply diplomatic pressure, or send in the army to do something about it. The first is just a matter of trying to see the world clearly, from a moral point of view. The second is another matter altogether. Sometimes it may be right to "do something about it," but often it will not be.

People also feel, rightly enough, that they should be tolerant of other cultures. Tolerance is, no doubt, a virtue—a tolerant person is willing to live in peaceful cooperation with those who see things differently. But there is nothing in the nature of tolerance that requires you to say that all beliefs, all religions, and all social practices are equally admirable. On the contrary, if you did not think that some were better than others, there would be nothing for you to tolerate.

Finally, people may be reluctant to judge because they do not want to express contempt for the society being criticized. But again, this is misguided: To condemn a particular practice is not to say that the culture is on the whole contemptible or that it is generally inferior to any other culture, including one's own. It could have many admirable features. In fact, we should expect this to be true of most human societies—they are mixes of good and bad practices. Excision happens to be one of the bad ones.

WHAT CAN BE LEARNED FROM
CULTURAL RELATIVISM

At the outset, I said that we were going to identify both what is right and what is wrong in Cultural Relativism. Thus far I have mentioned only its mistakes: I have said that it rests on an invalid argument, that it has consequences that make it implausible on its face, and that the extent of moral disagreement is far less than it implies. This all adds up to a pretty thorough repudiation of the theory. Nevertheless, it is still a very appealing idea, and the reader may have the feeling that all this is a little unfair. The theory must have something going for it, or else why has it been so influential? In fact, I think there is something right about Cultural Relativism, and now I want to say what that is. There are two lessons we should learn from the theory, even if we ultimately reject it.

1. Cultural Relativism warns us, quite rightly, about the danger of assuming that all our preferences are based on some absolute rational standard. They are not. Many (but not all) of our practices are merely peculiar to our society, and it is easy to lose sight of that fact. In reminding us of it, the theory does a service.

Funerary practices are one example. The Callatians, according to Herodo-tus, were "men who eat their fathers"—a shocking idea, to us at least. But eating the flesh of the dead could be understood as a sign of respect. It could be taken as a symbolic act that says: We wish this person's spirit to dwell within us. Per-haps this was the understanding of the Callatians. On such a way of thinking, burying the dead could be seen as an act of rejection, and burning the corpse as positively scornful. If this is hard to imagine, then we may need to have our imaginations stretched. Of course we may feel a visceral repugnance at the idea of eating human flesh in any circumstances. But what of it? This repugnance may be, as the relativists say, only a matter of what is customary in our particu-lar society.

There are many other matters that we tend to think of in terms of objective right and wrong that are really nothing more than social conventions. Should women cover their breasts? A publicly exposed breast is scandalous in our society, whereas in other cultures it is unremarkable. Objectively speaking, it is neither right nor wrong—there is no objective reason why either custom is better. Cultural Relativism begins with the valuable insight that many of our practices are like this; they are only cultural products. Then it goes wrong by inferring that, because some practices are like this, all must be.

2. The second lesson has to do with keeping an open mind. In the course of growing up, each of us has acquired some strong feelings: We have learned to think of some types of conduct as acceptable, and others we have learned to reject. Occasionally, we may find those feelings challenged. We may encounter someone who claims that our feelings are mistaken. For example, we may have been taught that homosexuality is immoral, and we may feel quite uncomfort-able around gay people and see them as alien and "different." Now someone suggests that this may be a mere prejudice; that there is nothing evil about homosexuality; that gay people are just people, like anyone else, who happen, through no choice of their own, to be attracted to others of the same sex. But

because we feel so strongly about the matter, we may find it hard to take this seriously. Even after we listen to the arguments, we may still have the unshakable feeling that homosexuals must, somehow, be an unsavory lot.

Cultural Relativism, by stressing that our moral views can reflect the prejudices of our society, provides an antidote for this kind of dogmatism. When he tells the story of the Greeks and Callatians, Herodotus adds:

> For if anyone, no matter who, were given the opportunity of choosing from amongst all the nations of the world the set of beliefs which he thought best, he would inevitably, after careful consideration of their relative merits, choose that of his own country. Everyone without exception believes his own native customs, and the religion he was brought up in, to be the best.

Realizing this can result in our having more open minds. We can come to understand that our feelings are not necessarily perceptions of the truth—they may be nothing more than the result of cultural conditioning. Thus, when we hear it suggested that some element of our social code is not really the best, and we find ourselves instinctively resisting the suggestion, we might stop and remember this. Then we may be more open to discovering the truth, whatever that might be.

We can understand the appeal of Cultural Relativism, then, even though the theory has serious shortcomings. It is an attractive theory because it is based on a genuine insight that many of the practices and attitudes we think so natural are really only cultural products. Moreover, keeping this insight firmly in view is important if we want to avoid arrogance and have open minds. These are important points, not to be taken lightly. But we can accept these points without going on to accept the whole theory.

READING 10

Daniel C. Dennett: How to Protect Human Dignity from Science

From "How to Protect Human Dignity from Science"

American philosopher Daniel Dennett (b. 1942) is a leading voice in the philosophy of mind, and in the essay below, "How to Protect Human Dignity from Science" (2008), he discusses the threat that science and technology pose to traditional values. The starting point is our conviction that human life is uniquely valuable, yet modern science and technology risk viewing humans as just one more biological specimen to be scientifically manipulated. This, in turn, might eventually undermine our long-standing moral value systems. Dennett rejects traditional religious answers to this problem,

Source: Daniel C. Dennett, "How to Protect Human Dignity from Science," *Human Dignity and Bioethics* (Washington D.C.: President's Council on Bioethics, 2008).

*particularly the concept of an immortal soul. A better solution, he argues, is to seek out
the values that we already hold, which are grounded in life here and now, apart from
considerations of an afterlife.*

Many people fear that science and technology are encroaching on domains
of life in a way that undermines human dignity, and they see this as a threat
that needs to be resisted vigorously. They are right. There is a real crisis, and it
needs our attention now, before irreparable damage is done to the fragile environment of mutually shared beliefs and attitudes on which a precious conception of human dignity does indeed depend for its existence. I will try to show
both that the problem is real and that the most widely favored responses to the
problem are deeply misguided and bound to fail. There is a solution that has
a good chance of success, however, and it employs principles that we already
understand and accept in less momentous roles. The solution is natural, reasonable, and robust instead of fragile, and it does not require us to try to put the
genie of science back in the bottle—a good thing, since that is almost certainly
impossible. Science and technology can flourish open-endedly while abiding
by restrictive principles that are powerful enough to reassure the anxious and
mild enough to secure the unqualified endorsement of all but the most reckless
investigators. We can have dignity and science too, but only if we face the conflict with open minds and a sense of common cause.

THE PROBLEM

Human life, tradition says, is infinitely valuable, and even sacred: not to be
tampered with, not to be subjected to "unnatural" procedures, and of course
not to be terminated deliberately, except (perhaps) in special cases such as
capital punishment or in the waging of a just war: "Thou shalt not kill." Human
life, science says, is a complex phenomenon admitting of countless degrees and
variations, not markedly different from animal life or plant life or bacterial life
in most regards, and amenable to countless varieties of extensions, redirections,
divisions, and terminations. The questions of when (human) life begins and ends,
and of which possible variants "count" as (sacred) human lives in the first place
are, according to science, more like the question of the area of a mountain than
of its altitude above sea level: it all depends on what can only be conventional
definitions of the boundary conditions. Science promises—or threatens—to
replace the traditional absolutes about the conditions of human life with a host
of relativistic complications and the denial of any sharp boundaries on which
to hang tradition.

Plato spoke of seeking the universals that "carve Nature at its joints," and
science has given us wonderful taxonomies that do just that. It has identified
electrons and protons (which have the mass of 1,836 electrons and a positive
charge), distinguished the chemical elements from each other, and articulated
and largely confirmed a Tree of Life that shows why "creature with a backbone"
carves Nature better than "creature with wings." But the crisp, logical boundaries

that science gives us don't include any joints where tradition demands them. In particular, there is no moment of *ensoulment* to be discovered in the breathtakingly complicated processes that ensue after sperm meets egg and they begin producing an embryo (or maybe twins or triplets—when do *they get* their individual souls?), and there is no moment at which the soul leaves the body and human life ends. Moreover, the more we understand, scientifically, about these complexities, the more practical it becomes, technologically, to exploit them in entirely novel ways for which tradition is utterly unprepared: *in vitro* fertilization and cloning, organ harvest and transplant, and, at the end of life, the artificial prolongation of life—of one sort or another—after most if not all the sacred aspects of life have ceased. When we start treating living bodies as motherboards on which to assemble cyborgs, or as spare parts collections to be sold to the highest bidder, where will it all end? It is not as if we could halt the slide by just prohibiting (some of) the technology. Technology may provide the *faits accomplis* that demonstrate beyond all controversy that the science is on the right track, but long before the technology is available, science provides the huge changes in conceptualization, the new vistas on possibility, that will flavor our imaginations henceforth whether or not the possibilities become practical. We are entering a new conceptual world, thanks to science, and it does not harmonize comfortably with our traditional conceptions of our lives and what they mean.

In particular, those who fear this swiftly growing scientific vista think that it will destroy something precious and irreplaceable in our traditional scheme, subverting the last presumptions of human specialness which ground—they believe—our world of morality. Oddly enough, not much attention has been paid to the question of exactly how the rise of the scientific vista would subvert these cherished principles—in this regard, it is a close kin to the widespread belief that homosexual marriage would somehow subvert traditional "family values"—but in fact there is a good explanation for this gap in the analysis. The psychologist Philip Tetlock identifies values as *sacred* when they are so important to those who hold them that the very act of considering them is offensive. The comedian Jack Benny was famously stingy—or so he presented himself on radio and television—and one of his best bits was the skit in which a mugger puts a gun in his back and barks "Your money or your life!" Benny just stands there silently. "Your money or your life!" repeats the mugger, with mounting impatience. "I'm thinking, I'm thinking," Benny replies. This is funny because most of us think that nobody should even think about such a trade-off. Nobody should have to think about such a trade-off. It should be unthinkable, a "no-brainer." Life is sacred, and no amount of money would be a fair exchange for a life, and if you don't already know that, what's wrong with you? "To transgress this boundary, to attach a monetary value, to one's friendships, children, or loyalty to one's country, is to disqualify oneself from the accompanying social roles." That is what makes life a sacred value.

Tetlock and his colleagues have conducted ingenious (and sometimes troubling) experiments in which subjects are obliged to consider "taboo trade-offs," such as whether or not to purchase live human body parts for some worthy end, or whether or not to pay somebody to have a baby that you then raise, or pay somebody to perform your military service. As their model predicts, many subjects exhibit a strong "mere contemplation effect": they feel guilty and sometimes get angry about being lured into even thinking about such dire choices, even when they make all the right choices. When given the opportunity by the experimenters to engage in "moral cleansing" (by volunteering for some relevant community service, for instance) subjects who have had to think about taboo trade-offs are significantly more likely than control subjects to volunteer— for real—for such good deeds. (Control subjects had been asked to think about purely non-sacred trade-offs, such as whether to hire a house-cleaner or buy food instead of something else.)

So it is not surprising that relatively little attention has been paid to charting the paths by which science and technology might subvert the value of life. If you feel the force of the admonition, "Don't even think about it!", you will shun the topic by distracting your own attention from it, if at all possible. I know from experience that some readers of this essay will already be feeling some discomfort and even guilt for allowing themselves to broach these topics at all, so strong is the taboo against thinking the unthinkable, but I urge them to bear with me, since the policy that I will propose may have more going for it than their own.

The fact that the threat has not been well articulated does not mean it is not real and important. Let me try to make it plain by drawing some parallels. Like climate change, the threat is environmental and *global* (which means you can't just move to a different place where the environment hasn't yet been damaged), and time is running out. While global warming threatens to affect many aspects of the *physical* environment—the atmosphere, the flora and fauna, the ice caps and ocean levels—and hence alter our geography in catastrophic ways from which recovery may be difficult or impossible, the threat to human dignity affects many aspects of what we may call the *belief environment*, the manifold of ambient attitudes, presumptions, common expectations—the things that are "taken for granted" by just about everybody, and that just about everybody expects just about everybody to take for granted.

The belief environment plays just as potent a role in human welfare as the physical environment, and in some regards it is both more important and more fragile. Much of this has been well-known for centuries, particularly to economists, who have long appreciated the way a currency can become worthless almost overnight, for example, and the way public trust in financial institutions needs to be preserved as a condition for economic activity in general. Today we confront the appalling societal black holes known as failed states, where the breakdown of law and order makes the restoration of decent life all but impossible. (If you have to pay off the warlords and bribe the judges and tolerate the drug traffic, just to keep enough power and water and sanitation going to make life bearable, let alone permit agriculture and commerce to thrive, your chances of long-term success are minimal.) What matters in these terrible conditions is what people in general assume *whether they are right or wrong*. It might in fact be safe for them to venture out and go shopping, or to invest in a clothing factory, or plant their crops, but if they don't, in general, believe that, they cannot resume anything like normal life and rekindle a working society. This creates a belief environment in which there is a powerful incentive for the most virtuous and civic-minded to lie, vigorously, just to preserve what remains of the belief environment. Faced with a deteriorating situation, admitting the truth may only accelerate the decline, while a little creative myth-making might—*might*—save the day. Not a happy situation.

And this is what people fear might happen if we pursue our current scientific and technological exploration of the boundaries of human life: we will soon find ourselves in a deteriorating situation where people—rightly or wrongly— start jumping to conclusions about the non-sanctity of life, the commodification of all aspects of life, and it will be too late to salvage the prevailing attitudes that protect us all from something rather like a failed state, a society in which the sheer security needed for normal interpersonal relations has dissolved, making trust, and respect, and even love, all but impossible. Faced with that dire prospect, it becomes tempting indeed to think of promulgating a holy lie, a myth that might carry us along for long enough to shore up our flagging confidence until we can restore "law and order."

That is where the doctrine of the soul comes in. People have immortal souls, according to tradition, and that is what makes them so special. Let me put the problem unequivocally: the traditional concept of the soul as an immaterial thinking thing, Descartes's *res cogitans*, the internal locus in each human body of all suffering, and meaning, and decisions, both moral and immoral, has been utterly discredited. Science has banished the soul as firmly as it has banished mermaids, unicorns, and perpetual motion machines. There are no such things. There is no more scientific justification for believing in an immaterial immortal soul than there is for believing that each of your kidneys has a tap-dancing poltergeist living in it. The latter idea is clearly preposterous. Why are we so reluctant to dismiss the former idea? It is obvious that there must be some non-scientific motivation for believing in it. It is seen as being needed to play a crucial role in preserving our self-image, our dignity. If we don't have souls, we are *just animals*! (And how could you love, or respect, or grant responsibility to something that was just an animal?)

Doesn't the very meaning of our lives depend on the reality of our immaterial souls? No. We don't need to be made of two fundamentally different kinds of substance, matter and mind-stuff, to have morally meaningful lives. On the face of it, the idea that all our striving and loving, our yearning and regretting, our hopes and fears, depend on some secret ingredient, some science-proof nugget of specialness that defies the laws of nature, is an almost childish ploy: "Let's gather up all the wonderfulness of human life and sweep it into the special hidey-hole where science can never get at it!" Although this fortress mentality has a certain medieval charm, looked at in the cold light of day, this idea is transparently desperate, implausible, and risky: putting all your eggs in one basket, and a remarkably vulnerable basket at that. It is vulnerable because it must declare science to be unable to shed any light on the various aspects of human consciousness and human morality at a time when exciting progress is being made on these very issues. One of Aristotle's few major mistakes was declaring "the heavens" to be made of a different kind of stuff, entirely unlike the matter here on Earth—a tactical error whose brittleness became obvious once Galileo and company began their still-expanding campaign to understand the physics of the cosmos. Clinging similarly to an immaterial concept of a soul at a time when every day brings more understanding of how the material basis of the mind has evolved (and goes on evolving within each brain) is a likely path to obsolescence and extinction.

The alternative is to look to the life sciences for an understanding of what does in fact make us different from other animals, in morally relevant ways. We are the only species with language, and art, and music, and religion, and humor, and the ability to imagine the time before our birth and after our death, and the ability to plan projects that take centuries to unfold, and the ability to create, defend, revise, and live by codes of conduct, and—sad to say—to wage war on a global scale. The ability of our brains to help us see into the future, thanks to the culture we impart to our young, so far surpasses that of any other species, that it gives us the powers that in turn give us the responsibilities of moral agents. *Noblesse oblige*. We are the only species that can know enough about the world to be reasonably held responsible for protecting its precious treasures. And who on earth could hold us responsible? Only ourselves. Some other species—the dolphins and the other great apes—exhibit fascinating signs of protomorality, a capacity to cooperate and to care about others, but we persons are the only animals that can conceive of *the project of leading a good life*. This is not a mysterious talent; it can be explained.

Here I will not attempt to survey the many threads of that still unfolding explanation, but rather to construct and defend a perspective and a set of policies that could protect what needs to be protected as we scramble, with many false steps, towards an appreciation of the foundations of human dignity. Scientists make their mistakes in public, but mostly only other scientists notice them. This topic has such momentous consequences, however, that we can anticipate that public attention—and reaction—will be intense, and could engender runaway misconstruals that could do serious harm to the delicate belief environment in which we (almost) all would like to live.

I have mentioned the analogy with the ominous slide into a failed state; here is a less dire example of the importance of the belief environment, and the way small changes in society can engender unwanted changes in it. In many parts of rural America people feel comfortable leaving their cars and homes unlocked, day and night, but any country mouse who tries to live this way in the big city soon learns how foolish that amiably trusting policy is. City life is not intolerable, but it is certainly different. Wouldn't it be fine if we could somehow re-engineer the belief environment of cities so that people seldom felt the need to lock up! An all but impossible dream. At the same time, rural America is far from utopia and is sliding toward urbanity. The felicitous folkways of the countryside can absorb a modest amount of theft and trespass without collapse, but it wouldn't take much to extinguish them forever. Those of us who get to live in this blissfully secure world cherish it, for good reason, and would hate to abandon it, but we also must recognize that any day could be the last day of unlocked doors in our neighborhood, and once the change happened, it would be very hard to change back. That too is like global climate change; these changes are apt to be irreversible. And unlike global climate change, drawing attention to the prospect may actually hasten it, by kindling and spreading what Douglas Hofstadter once called "reverberant doubt." The day that our local newspaper begins running a series about what percentage of local people lock their doors under what circumstances is the day that door-locking is apt to become the norm. So those who are in favor of diverting attention from too exhaustive an examination of these delicate topics might have the right idea. This is the chief reason, I think, for the taboo against thinking about sacred values: it can sometimes jeopardize their protected status. But in this case, I think it is already too late to follow the tip-toe approach. There is already a tidal wave of interest in the ways in which the life sciences are illuminating the nature of "the soul," so we had better shift from distraction to concentration and see what we can make of the belief environment for human dignity and its vulnerabilities.

THE SOLUTION

How are we to protect the ideal of human dignity from the various incursions of science and technology? The first step in the solution is to notice that the *grounds* for our practices regarding this are not going to be *local* features of particular human lives, but rather more *distributed* in space and time. There is already a clear precedent in our attitude toward human corpses. Even people who believe in immortal immaterial souls don't believe that human "remains" harbor a soul. They think that the soul has departed, and what is left behind is just a body, just unfeeling matter. A corpse can't feel pain, can't suffer, can't be aware of any indignities—and yet still we feel a powerful obligation to handle a corpse with respect, and even with ceremony, and even when nobody else is watching. Why? Because we appreciate, whether acutely or dimly, that how we handle *this* corpse *now* has repercussions for how other people, still alive, will be able to imagine their own demise and its aftermath. Our capacity to imagine the future is both the source of our moral power and a condition of our vulnerability. We cannot help but see all the events in our lives against the backdrop of what Hofstadter calls the *implicosphere* of readily imaginable alternatives—and the great amplifier of human suffering (and human joy) is our irresistible tendency to anticipate, with dread or delight, what is in store for us.

We live not just in the moment, but in the past and the future as well. Consider the well-known advice given to golfers: *keep your head down* through the whole swing. "Wait a minute," comes the objection: "that's got to be voodoo superstition! Once the ball leaves the club head, the position of my head couldn't possibly affect the trajectory of the ball. This has to be scientifically unsound advice!" Not at all. Since we plan and execute all our actions in an anticipatory belief environment, and have only limited and indirect control over our time-pressured skeletal actions, it can well be the case that the only way to get the part of the golf swing that does affect the trajectory of the ball to have the desirable properties is to concentrate on making the later part of it, which indeed could not affect the trajectory, take on a certain shape. Far from being superstitious, the advice can be seen to follow quite logically from facts we can discover from a careful analysis of the way our nervous systems guide our muscles.

Our respect for corpses provides us with a clear case of a wise practice that does not at all depend on finding, locally, a special (even supernatural) ingredient that justifies or demands this treatment. There are other examples that have the same feature. Nobody has to endorse magical thinking about the gold in Fort Knox to recognize the effect of its (believed-in) presence there on the stability of currencies. Symbols play an important role in helping to maintain social equilibria, and we tamper with them at our peril. If we began to adopt the "efficient" policy of disposing of human corpses by putting them in large biodegradable plastic bags to be taken to the landfill along with the rest of the "garbage," this would flavor our imaginations in ways that would be hard to ignore, and hard to tolerate. No doubt we could get used to it, the same way city folk get used to locking their doors, but we have good reasons for avoiding that path. (Medical schools have learned to be diligent in their maintenance of respect and decorum in the handling of bodies in their teaching and research, for while those who decide to donate their bodies to medicine presumably have come to terms with the imagined prospect of students dissecting and discussing their innards, they have limits on what they find tolerable.)

The same policy and rationale apply to end-of-life decisions. We handle a corpse with decorum even though we *know* it cannot suffer, so we can appreciate the wisdom of extending the same practice to cases where we don't know. For instance, a person in a persistent vegetative state might be suffering, or might not, but in either case, we have plenty of grounds for adopting a policy that creates a comforting buffer zone that errs on the side of concern. And, once again, the long-range effect on community beliefs is just as important as, or even more important than, any locally measurable symptoms of suffering. (In a similar spirit, it is important that wolves and grizzly bears still survive in the wilder regions of our world even if we almost never see them. Just knowing that they are there is a source of wonder and delight and makes the world a better place. Given our invincible curiosity and penchant for skepticism, we have to keep checking up on their continued existence, of course, and could not countenance an official myth of their continued presence if they had in fact gone extinct. This too has its implications for our topic.)

What happens when we apply the same principle to the other boundary of human life, its inception? The scientific fact is that there is no good candidate, and there will almost certainly never be a good candidate, for a moment of *ensoulment*, when a mere bundle of living human tissue becomes a person with all the rights and privileges pertaining thereunto. This should not be seen as a sign of the weakness of scientific insight, but rather as a familiar implication of what science has already discovered. One of the fascinating facts about living things is the way they thrive on gradualism. Consider speciation: there are uncounted millions of different species, and each of them had its inception "at some point" in the nearly four billion year history of life on this planet, but there is literally no telling exactly when any species came into existence because what counts as speciation is something that only gradually and cumulatively emerges over very many generations. Speciation can emerge only *in the aftermath*. Consider dogs, the millions of members of hundreds of varieties of *Canis familiaris* that populate the world today. As different as these varieties are—think of St. Bernards and Pekinese—they all count as a single species, cross-fertile (with a little mechanical help from their human caretakers) and all readily identifiable as belonging to the same species, descended from wolves, by their highly similar DNA. Might one or more of these varieties or subspecies become a species of its own some day? Absolutely. In fact, every puppy born is a potential founder of a new species, but nothing about that puppy on the day of its birth (or for that matter on any day of its life) could be singled out as the special feature that marked it as the Adam or Eve of a new species. If it dies without issue, it definitely won't found a new species, but as long as it has offspring that have offspring, it might turn out, in the fullness of time, to be a good candidate for the first member of a new species.

Or consider our own species, *Homo sapiens*. Might it divide in two some day? Yes it might, and in fact, it might, in a certain sense, already have happened. Consider two human groups alive today that probably haven't had any common ancestors in the last thirty thousand years: the Inuit of Cornwallis Island in the Arctic, and the Andaman Islanders living in remarkable isolation in the Indian Ocean. Suppose some global plague sweeps the planet sometime in the next hundred years (far from an impossibility, sad to say), leaving behind only these two small populations. Suppose that over the next five hundred or a thousand years, say, they flourish and come to reinhabit the parts of the world vacated by us—and discover that they are not cross-fertile with the other group! Two species, remarkably similar in appearance, physiology and ancestry, but nevertheless as reproductively isolated as lions are from tigers. When, then, did the speciation occur? Before the dawn of agriculture about ten thousand years ago, or after the birth of the Internet? There would be no principled way of saying. We can presume that today, Inuits and Andaman Islanders are cross-fertile, but who knows? The difference between "in principle" reproductive isolation (because of the accumulation of genetic and behavioral differences that make offspring "impossible") and *de facto* reproductive isolation, which has already been the case for many thousands of years, is not itself a principled distinction.

A less striking instance of the same phenomenon of gradualism is *coming of age*, in the sense of being mature enough and well enough informed to be suitable for marriage, or—to take a particularly clear case—to drive a car. It will come as no surprise, I take it, that there is no special moment of *driver-edment*, when a teenager crisply crossed the boundary between being too immature to have the right to apply for a driver's license, and being adult enough to be allowed the freedom of the highway behind the wheel. Some youngsters are manifestly mature enough at fourteen to be reasonable candidates for a driver's license, and others are still so heedless and impulsive at eighteen that one trembles at the prospect of letting them on the road. We have settled (in most jurisdictions) on the policy that age sixteen is a suitable threshold, and what this means is that we simply refuse to consider special pleading on behalf of unusually mature younger people, and also refrain from imposing extra hurdles on those sixteen-year-olds who manage to pass their driving test fair and square in spite of our misgivings about the safety of letting them on the road. In short, we settle on a conventional threshold which we know does not mark any special internal mark (brain myelination, IQ, factual knowledge, onset of puberty) but strikes us as a good-enough compromise between freedom and public safety. *And once we settle on it, we stop treating the location of the threshold as a suitable subject for debate.* There are many important controversies to consider and explore, and this isn't one of them. Not as a general rule. Surprising new discoveries may in principle trigger a reconsideration at any time, but we foster a sort of inertia that puts boundary disputes out of bounds for the time being.

Why isn't there constant pressure from fifteen-year-olds to lower the legal driving age? It is not just that they tend not to be a particularly well-organized or articulate constituency. Even they can recognize that soon enough they will be sixteen, and there are better ways to spend their energy than trying to adjust a policy that is, all things considered, quite reasonable. Moreover, there are useful features of the social dynamics that make it systematically difficult for them to mount a campaign for changing the age. We adults have created a tacit scaffolding of presumption, *holding* teenagers responsible before many of them have actually achieved the requisite competence, thereby encouraging them to try to grow into the status we purport to grant them and discouraging any behavior—any action that could be interpreted as throwing a tantrum, for instance—that would undercut their claim to maturity. They are caught in a bind: the more vehemently they protest, the more they cast doubt on the wisdom of their cause. In the vast array of projects that confront them, this is not an appealing choice.

The minimum driving age is not quite a sacred value, then, but it shares with sacred values the interesting feature of being considered best left unexamined, by common consensus among a sizable portion of the community. And there is a readily accessible reason for this inertia. We human beings lead lives that cast long beams of anticipation into the foggy future, and we appreciate—implicitly or explicitly—almost any fixed points that can reduce our uncertainty. Sometimes this is so obvious as to be trivial. Why save money for your children's education if money may not be worth anything in the future? How could you justify going to all the trouble of building a house if you couldn't count on the presumption that you will be able to occupy it without challenge? Law and order are preconditions for the sorts of ambitious life-planning we want to engage in. But we want more than just a strong state apparatus that can be counted on not to be vacillating in its legislation, or whimsical in enforcement. We, as a society, do need to draw some lines—"bright" lines in legalistic jargon—and stick with them. That means not just promulgating them and voting on them, but putting an unequal burden on any second-guessing, so that people can organize their life projects with the reasonable expectation that these are fixed points that aren't going to shift constantly under the pressure of one faction or another. We want there to be an ambient attitude of mutual recognition of the stability of the moral—not legal—presumptions that can be taken for granted, something approximating a meta-consensus among those who achieve the initial consensus about the threshold: let's leave well enough alone now that we've fixed it. In a world where every candidate for a bright line of morality is constantly under siege from partisans who would like to change it, one's confidence is shaken that one's everyday conduct is going to be above reproach. Consider that nowadays, in many parts of the world, women simply cannot wear fur coats in public with the attitudes their mothers could adopt. Today, wearing a fur coat is making a political statement, and one cannot escape that by simply disavowing the intent. Driving a gas-guzzling SUV carries a similar burden. People may resent the activities of the partisans who have achieved these shifts in opinion even though they may share many of their attitudes about animal rights or energy policy; they have made investments—in all innocence, let us suppose—that now are being disvalued. Had they been able to anticipate this shift in public opinion, they could have spent their money better.

These observations are not contentious, I think. How, though, can we apply this familiar understanding to the vexing issues surrounding the inception—and manipulation and termination—of human life, and the special status it is supposed to enjoy? By recognizing, first, that we are going to have to walk away from the traditional means of securing these boundaries, which are not going to keep on working. They are just too brittle for the 21st century.

We know too much. Unlike traditional sacred values that depend on wide-spread acceptance of myths (which, even if true, are manifestly unjustifiable—that's why we call them myths rather than common knowledge), we need to foster values that can withstand scrutiny about their own creation. That is to say, we have to become self-conscious about our reliance on such policies, without in the process destroying our faith in them.

BELIEF IN BELIEF

We need to appreciate the importance in general of the phenomenon of *belief in belief*. Consider a few cases that are potent today. Because many of us believe in democracy and recognize that the security of democracy in the future depends critically on maintaining the belief in democracy, we are eager to quote (and quote and quote) Winston Churchill's famous line: "Democracy is the worst form of government except for all the others that have been tried." As stewards of democracy, we are often conflicted, eager to point to flaws that ought to be repaired, while just as eager to reassure people that the flaws are not that bad, that democracy can police itself, so their faith in it is not misplaced.

The same point can be made about science. Since the belief in the integrity of scientific procedures is almost as important as the actual integrity, there is always a tension between a whistle-blower and the authorities, even when they know that they have mistakenly conferred scientific respectability on a fraudulently obtained result. Should they quietly reject the offending work and discreetly dismiss the perpetrator, or make a big stink?

And certainly some of the intense public fascination with celebrity trials is to be explained by the fact that belief in the rule of law is considered to be a vital ingredient in our society, so if famous people are seen to be above the law, this jeopardizes the general trust in the rule of law. Hence we are not just interested in the trial, but in the public reactions to the trial, and the reactions to those reactions, creating a spiraling inflation of media coverage. We who live in democracies have become somewhat obsessed with gauging public opinion on all manner of topics, and for good reason: in a democracy it really matters what the people believe. If the public cannot be mobilized into extended periods of outrage by reports of corruption, or of the torturing of prisoners by our agents, for instance, our democratic checks and balances are in jeopardy. In his hopeful book, *Development as Freedom* and elsewhere, the Nobel laureate economist Amartya Sen makes the important point that you don't have to win an election to achieve your political aims. Even in shaky democracies, what the leaders believe about the beliefs that prevail in their countries influences what they take their realistic options to be, so belief-maintenance is an important political goal in its own right.

Even more important than political beliefs, in the eyes of many, are what we might call metaphysical beliefs. Nihilism—the belief in nothing—has been seen by many to be a deeply dangerous virus, for obvious reasons. When Friedrich Nietzsche hit upon his idea of the Eternal Recurrence—he thought he had proved that we relive our lives infinitely many times—his first inclination (according to some stories) was that he should kill himself without revealing the proof, in order to spare others from this life-destroying belief. Belief in the *belief that something matters* is understandably strong and widespread. Belief in free will is another vigorously protected vision, for the same reasons, and those whose investigations seem to others to jeopardize it are sometimes deliberately misrepresented in order to discredit what is seen as a dangerous trend. The physicist Paul Davies has recently defended the view that belief in free will is so important that it may be "a fiction worth maintaining." It is interesting that he doesn't seem to think that his own discovery of the awful truth (what he takes to be the awful truth) incapacitates him morally, but that others, more fragile than he, will need to be protected from it.

This illustrates the ever-present risk of paternalism when belief in belief encounters a threat: we must keep these facts from "the children," who cannot be expected to deal with them safely. And so people often become systematically disingenuous when defending a value. Being the unwitting or uncaring bearer of good news or bad news is one thing; being the self-appointed champion of an idea is something quite different. Once people start committing themselves (in public, or just in their "hearts") to particular ideas, a strange dynamic process is brought into being, in which the original commitment gets buried in pearly layers of defensive reaction and meta-reaction. "Personal rules are a recursive mechanism; they continually take their own pulse, and if they feel it falter, that very fact will cause further faltering," the psychiatrist George Ainslie observes in his remarkable book, *Breakdown of Will*. He describes the dynamic of these processes in terms of competing strategic commitments that can contest for control in an organization—or an individual. Once you start living by a set of explicit rules, the stakes are raised: when you lapse, what should you do? Punish yourself? Forgive yourself? Pretend you didn't notice?

> After a lapse, the long-range interest is in the awkward position of a country that has threatened to go to war in a particular circumstance that has then occurred. The country wants to avoid war without destroying the credibility of its threat and may therefore look for ways to be seen as not having detected the circumstance. Your long-range interest will suffer if you catch yourself ignoring a lapse, but perhaps not if you can arrange to ignore it without catching yourself. This arrangement, too, must go undetected, which means that a successful process of ignoring must be among the many mental expedients that arise by trial and error—the ones you keep simply because they make you feel better without your realizing why.

This idea that there are myths we live by, myths that must not be disturbed at any cost, is always in conflict with our ideal of truth-seeking and truth-telling, sometimes with lamentable results. For example, racism is at long last widely recognized as a great social evil, so many reflective people have come to endorse the second-order belief that *belief in the equality of all people* regardless of their race is to be vigorously fostered. How vigorously? Here people of good will differ sharply. Some believe that belief in racial differences is so pernicious that *even when it is true* it is to be squelched. This has led to some truly unfortunate excesses. For instance, there are clear clinical data about how people of different ethnicity are differently susceptible to disease, or respond differently to various drugs, but such data are considered off-limits by some researchers, and by some funders of research. This has the perverse effect that strongly indicated avenues of research are deliberately avoided, much to the detriment of the health of the ethnic groups involved.

Ainslie uncovers strategic belief-maintenance in a wide variety of cherished human practices:

> Activities that are spoiled by counting them, or counting on them, have to be undertaken through indirection if they are to stay valuable. For instance, romance undertaken for sex or even "to be loved" is thought of as crass, as are some of the most lucrative professions if undertaken for money, or performance art if done for effect. Too great an awareness of the motivational contingencies for sex, affection, money, or applause spoils the effort, and not only because it undeceives the other people involved. Beliefs about the intrinsic worth of these activities are valued beyond whatever accuracy these beliefs might have, because they promote the needed indirection.

So what sort of equilibrium can we reach? If we want to maintain the momentousness of all decisions about life and death, and take the steps that elevate the decision beyond the practicalities of the moment, we need to secure the appreciation of this very fact and enliven the imaginations of people so that they can recognize, and avoid wherever possible, and condemn, activities that would tend to erode the public trust in the presuppositions about what is—and should be—unthinkable. A striking instance of failure to appreciate this is the proposal by President Bush to reconsider and unilaterally refine the Geneva

Convention's deliberately vague characterization of torture as "outrages on personal dignity." By declaring that the United States is eager to be a pioneer in the adjustment of what has heretofore been mutually agreed to be unthinkable, this policy is deeply subversive of international trust, and of national integrity. We as a nation can no longer be plausibly viewed as above thinking of arguable exceptions to the sacred value of not torturing people, and this diminishes us in ways that will be difficult if not impossible to repair.

What forces can we hope to direct in our desire to preserve respect for human dignity? Laws prohibit; traditions encourage and discourage, and in the long run, laws are powerless to hold the line unless they are supported by a tradition, by the mutual recognition of most of the people that they preserve conditions that deserve preservation. Global opinion, as we have just seen, cannot be counted on to discourage all acts of degradation of the belief environment, but it can be enhanced by more local traditions. Doctors, for instance, have their proprietary code of ethics, and most of them rightly covet the continuing respect of their colleagues, a motivation intensified by the system of legal liability and by the insurance that has become a prerequisite for practice. Then there are strict liability laws, which target particularly sensitive occupations such as pharmacist and doctor, preemptively removing the excuse of ignorance and thereby putting all who occupy these positions on notice that they will be held accountable whether or not they have what otherwise would be a reasonable claim of innocent ignorance. So forewarned, they adjust their standards and projects accordingly, erring on the side of extreme caution and keeping a healthy distance between themselves and legal consequences. Anyone who attempts to erect such a network of flexible and mutually supporting discouragements of further tampering with traditional ideas about human dignity will fail unless they attend to the carrot as well as the stick. How can we kindle and preserve a sincere allegiance to the ideals of human dignity? The same way we foster the love of a democratic and free society: by ensuring that the lives one can live in such a regime are so manifestly better than the available alternatives.

And what of those who are frankly impatient with tradition, and even with the values that tradition endorses? We must recognize that there are a vocal minority of people who profess unworried acceptance of an entirely practical and matter-of-fact approach to life, who scoff at romantic concerns with Frankensteinian visions. Given the presence and articulateness of these proponents, we do well to have a home base that can withstand scrutiny and that is prepared to defend, in terms other than nostalgia, the particular values that we are trying to protect. That is the germ of truth in multiculturalism. We need to articulate these values in open forum. When we attempt this, we need to resist the strong temptation to resort to the old myths, since they are increasingly incredible, and will only foster incredulity and cynicism in those we need to persuade. Tantrums in support of traditional myths will backfire, in other words. Our only chance of preserving a respectable remnant of the tradition is to ensure that the values we defend deserve the respect of all.

Appendix

Classical Eastern Philosophy: Hinduism, Buddhism, Confucianism, Daoism
From Selected Primary Texts

The philosophical traditions covered in this book are the ones that emerged in Western civilization, from ancient Greece on through the present. This is largely a history of philosophers from European countries and countries that have European colonial roots. There are, however, other philosophical traditions of the world that emerged within their own distinct cultural environments, often with little or no contact with the ideas of Western civilization. Classical Eastern philosophy is a case in point, particularly the philosophies that developed in ancient India and China, which are as elaborate and varied as those from Western civilization. Below are selections from a few of the more influential classics in Hindu, Buddhist, Confucian, and Daoist philosophy. Most of these texts were composed within the religious traditions of Eastern cultures, often anonymously written. Much like medieval philosophy in the Western tradition, they express the symbiotic relation that philosophical and religious thought had at the time. But while Eastern philosophy is grounded in religion, it draws on assumptions about God and ultimate reality that have largely been rejected by mainstream religions in Western civilization. More precisely, Eastern religion—and philosophy—draw heavily on the concept of an ultimate reality that encompasses all existing things, including human existence. On this view, our individual human identities are really just an aspect of larger existence and, according to some Eastern philosophers, our experience of individual consciousness is just an illusion. Some Western philosophers had similar convictions about an all-pervading reality, such as Parmenides, Plotinus, Spinoza, Hegel, and Schopenhauer. The common term for this in Western philosophy is "pantheism," the view that God is identical with nature as a whole. However, just as Parmenides's theory differs from Spinoza's, for example, so too do the particular elements of Eastern philosophies differ from their Western pantheistic counterparts, as well as they do from each other.

HINDU PHILOSOPHY

The Self-God

Bees make honey by collecting the juices of distant trees and reducing the juices into one form. These juices have no discrimination and do not say "I am the juice of this tree or that tree." In the same manner, when all these creatures merge with Being [either in deep sleep or in death], they do not know that they merged with Being. Whatever these creatures are here—whether a lion, a wolf, a boar, a worm, a fly, a gnat, or a mosquito—they become that again and again. Everything that exists has as its soul that which is the finest essence. It is Reality. It is the Atman, and *you are that*, my son. . . . The eastern rivers [like the Ganges] flow toward the east, and the western rivers [like the Sindhu] flow toward the west. They go from sea to sea. They become the sea. When those rivers are in the sea, they do not say "I am this or that river." In the same manner, when all these creatures come forth from Being, they do not know that they have come forth from Being. Whatever these creatures are here—whether a lion, a wolf, a boar, a worm, a fly, a gnat, or a mosquito—they become that again and again. Everything that exists has as its soul that which is the finest essence. It is Reality. It is the Atman, and *you are that*, my son. [*Chandogya Upanishad*, 6:9–11]

We may understand that the Atman is sitting in the chariot, the body is the chariot, the intellect (*buddhi*) is the charioteer, and the mind is the reins. The senses are the horses, the objects of the senses are their roads. When he [i.e., the highest Atman] is in union with the body, the senses, and the mind, then wise people call him the Enjoyer. If someone has no understanding and his mind [i.e., the reins] is never firmly held, then his senses, like vicious horses, are unmanageable. But if someone has understanding and his mind is always firmly held, then his senses are under control, like good horses of a charioteer. If someone has no understanding and is unmindful and always impure, then he never reaches that place, but enters into the cycle of births. But if someone has understanding and is mindful and always pure, then he indeed reaches that place, and from there he is not born again. And if someone has understanding for his charioteer, and who holds the reins of the mind, then he reaches the end of his journey, and that is the highest place of Vishnu. [*Katha Upanishad*]

Release and Reincarnation

As a person throws off worn-out garments and takes new ones, so too the dweller in the body throws off worn-out bodies and enters into others that are new. Weapons do not pierce him, fire does not burn him, water does not make him wet, and wind does not dry him away. He cannot be pierced, burned, made wet, or dried. He is perpetual, all pervasive, stable, immovable, and ancient. He is called unmanifest, unthinkable, and immutable. Therefore, knowing him as such, you should not grieve. Or if you think of him as being constantly born and constantly dying, even then, you should not grieve. For death is certain for those who are born, and birth is certain for those who are dead. Therefore, you should not grieve over the inevitable. [*Bhagavad Gita*, 2]

Action Yoga

The foolish utter flowery speech, and rejoice in the letter of the Vedas [i.e., Hindu scriptures]. For them there is nothing but a desire for the self with only the intent on reaching heaven. They prescribe many ceremonies to attain pleasure and power, but rebirth is the fruit of their actions. . . .

Your business is with actions only, and never with the fruits of your actions. So do not let the fruit of your actions motivate you, and do not be attached to inaction. Perform action, Arjuna, dwelling in the union of the divine. Renounce attachments, and balance yourself evenly between success and failure. Equilibrium is called Yoga. Action is inferior to discrimination; so, take refuge in the intellect. People are pitiable who work only for its fruits. By disciplining one's intellect, one abandons both good and evil deeds. Therefore you should cling to [*karma*] Yoga, which is skill in action. The wise disciplined their intellect, renounced the fruits of their actions, released themselves from the bonds of birth, and attained a state of bliss. When your intellect escapes from the tangle of delusion, then you too will be indifferent about what you had heard and will hear [in the Vedas]. . . .

When a person abandons all the desires of his heart and is satisfied in the Self and by the Self, then he is called "stable in mind." A sage of stable mind is free from anxiety when surrounded by pains, is indifferent when surrounded by pleasures, and is freed from passion, fear and anger. He is without attachments on every side, whether desirable or undesirable, and neither likes nor dislikes. The person of understanding is well poised. Just as a tortoise pulls in all its limbs, the sage withdraws his senses from the objects, and his understanding is well poised. [*Bhagavad Gita*, 2]

Meditation Yoga

KRISHNA: He who performs his actions as a duty, independently of the fruit of the action, is an ascetic. He is a Yogi, and not the person who intentionally avoids actions such as lighting the sacred fire and performing the sacred rites. Understand that "Yoga" is renunciation, and no one becomes a Yogi without renouncing his will. . . . The Yogi should constantly engage himself in Yoga, staying in a secret place by himself, subduing his thoughts and self, and freeing himself from hope and greed. He should set up a fixed seat for himself in a pure place, which is neither too high, nor too low, made of a cloth, a black deerskin, and kusa grass, one over the other. Once there he should practice Yoga for the purification of the self; he should make his mind one-pointed, subduing his thoughts and the functions of his senses. He should hold his body, head and neck erect, immovably steady, looking at the point of his nose with an unseeing gaze.

His heart should be serene, fearless and firm in the vow of renunciation. His mind should be controlled as he sits in harmony. In this manner he will think on me and aspire after me. Thus, always keeping the mind balanced, the Yogi, with the mind controlled, attains to the peace abiding in me, which culminates in release.

Yoga is not for the person who eats too much or too little, or who sleeps too much or too little. Yoga kills all pain for the person who is moderate in eating, amusement, performing actions, sleeping, and waking. When his subdued thought is fixed on the Atman and free from desiring things, then we can say that he is harmonized. Just as a lamp in a windless place does not flicker, so too will the subdued thought of the Yogi be absorbed in the Yoga of the self. . . . The Yogi who harmonizes the self and puts away evil, will enjoy the infinite bliss of unity with the eternal Brahman. The self, harmonized by Yoga, sees the Atman abiding in all beings, and all beings in the Atman. Everywhere he sees the same thing. I will never lose hold of the person who sees me everywhere, and sees everything in me, and that person will never lose hold of me. Regardless of how else he may live, the Yogi lives in me who is established in unity and worships me abiding in all things. The perfect Yogi is the one who, established in unity, sees equality in everything, whether pleasant or painful.

ARJUNA: You describe this Yoga as a unity. However, Krishna, I see no basis for it given the impermanence of thought. The mind is very restless. Indeed, it is impetuous, strong, and difficult to bend. Perhaps it is as hard to control as the wind.

KRISHNA: Undoubtedly, Arjuna, the mind is restless and hard to control. But it may be controlled with constant practice and dispassion. I think Yoga is hard to attain by an uncontrolled self. But for a controlled Atman, it is attainable by properly directing energy.

ARJUNA: Suppose that a person has faith, but his mind is still uncontrolled and wanders away from Yoga, thus failing to attain perfection in Yoga. What is in store for him? He fails in his quest from Brahman, and thus fails both his earthy and spiritual quest. Please dispel my doubts, since only you are able to do this.

KRISHNA: No, he will not be lost in this life or the next. No one who does what is right will walk the path of destruction. Even if he fell from Yoga, by virtue of his good actions, he will be reborn in a pure and house, and may even be born into a family of wise Yogis. But this kind of birth is difficult to obtain in this world. In this reborn state, he retains the characteristics belonging to his previous body, and with these he again works for perfection. . . . [*Bhagavad Gita*, 6]

Vedanta: Sankara

When accepted as the doctrine of the Vedas, this doctrine of the individual soul having its Self in Brahman does away with the independent existence of the individual soul. This is just as the idea of the rope does away with the idea of the snake [for which the rope had been mistaken]. And if the doctrine of the independent existence of the individual soul has to be set aside, then the view of the entire phenomenal world having an independent existence must likewise be set aside insofar as it is based on the individual soul. But in addition to the element of unity, an element of manifoldness would have to be [falsely] assumed in Brahman only for the purpose of establishing the phenomenal world. . . .

Scriptural passages also declare that for people who see that everything has its Self in Brahman, [they also see that] the whole phenomenal world is non-existent, including actions, agents, and consequences of actions. Nor can it be said that this non-existence of the phenomenal world is declared by Scripture to be limited to certain states. For the passage "You are that" shows that the general fact of Brahman being the Self of all is not limited by any particular state.

. . . By quoting parallel instances of clay (and its various modifications), it may be objected that Scripture itself endorses a Brahman which is capable of modification. For we know from experience that clay and similar things do undergo modifications. In reply, this objection is without force. A number of scriptural passages deny all modifications of Brahman and thereby teach that it is absolutely changeless. Such passages are, "Indeed, Brahman is this great unborn Self, undecaying, undying, immortal, fearless." . . . For we cannot ascribe to one Brahman the two qualities of (a) being subject to modification and (b) being free from modification. And if you say, "Why should they not be both predicated of Brahman?" we reply that the qualification "absolutely changeless" precludes this. For the changeless Brahman cannot be the substratum of varying attributes.

. . . In this manner the Vedanta texts declare that, for those who have reached the state of truth and reality, the whole apparent world does not exist. The *Bhagavad Gita* also declares that in reality the relation of Ruler and ruled does not exist. Scripture as well as the *Bhagavad Gita* says that, on the other hand, all those distinctions are valid [only] as far as the phenomenal world is concerned. . . . Further, the view of Brahman as undergoing modifications will be of use [only] when closely reflecting on the Brahman-with-attributes (*saguna*). [Sankara, *Commentary on the Vedanta Sutra* 2:1:14]

Vedanta: Ramanuja

We cannot admit the claim that Scripture teaches that the cessation of ignorance springs only from the cognition of a Brahman devoid of all difference. Such a view is clearly denied by other scripture passages such. . . . Because Brahman is characterized by difference, all Vedic texts declare that final release results from the cognition of a qualified Brahman. And even those texts that describe Brahman by way of negation really aim at setting forth a Brahman that possesses attributes.

In texts such as "You are that" (*tat tvam asi*), the relation of the constituent parts is not meant to convey the idea of the absolute unity of an undifferentiated substance. On the contrary, the words "that" and "you" denote a Brahman distinguished by difference. The word "that" refers to Brahman as omniscient, etc., which had been introduced as the general topic of consideration in previous passages of the same section, such as "It thought, may I be many." The word "you," which stands in relation to "that," conveys the idea of Brahman insofar as its body consists of the individual souls connected with non-intelligent matter. . . .

Moreover, it is not possible for ignorance to belong to Brahman, whose essential nature is knowledge, which is free from all imperfections, omniscient, comprising within itself all favorable qualities. However, ignorance would result from the absolute oneness of "that" and "you." It [i.e., Brahman] would be the underlying strata of all those defects and afflictions which spring from ignorance. . . .

If, on the other hand, the text is understood to refer to Brahman as having the individual souls for its body, both words ("that" and "you") keep their primary meaning. Thus, by making a declaration about one substance distinguished by two aspects, the text preserves the fundamental principle of "relation." On this interpretation the text further implies that Brahman (free from all imperfection and comprising within itself all favorable qualities) is the internal ruler of the individual souls and possesses lordly power. [Ramanuja, *Commentary on the Vedanta Sutra*, 1.1.1]

BUDDHIST PHILOSOPHY

Four Noble Truths

Now this is the noble truth concerning suffering. Birth is attended with pain, decay is painful, disease is painful, and death is painful. Union with the unpleasant is painful, and separation from the pleasant is painful. Any craving that is unsatisfied is also painful. In brief, the five components which spring from attachment are painful. This then is the noble truth concerning suffering.

Now this is the noble truth concerning the origin of suffering. It is that thirst or craving which causes the renewal of existence, accompanied by sensual delight, and the seeking of satisfaction first here, then there. That is to say, it is the craving for the gratification of the passions, or the craving for a future life, or the craving for success in this present life. This then is the noble truth concerning the origin of suffering.

Now this is the noble truth concerning the elimination of suffering [i.e., the attainment of Nirvana]. It is the destruction of this very thirst, in which no passion remains. It is the laying aside of, the getting rid of, the being free from, and the harboring no longer of this thirst. This, then, is the noble truth concerning the destruction of suffering.

Now this is the noble truth concerning the *path* that leads to the elimination of suffering. It is the noble eightfold path.

There are two extremes, fellow monks, which a holy person should avoid: the habitual practice of . . . self-indulgence, which is vulgar and profitless . . . and the habitual practice of self-mortification, which is painful and equally profitless. There is a middle path discovered by the Tathagata [i.e., the Buddha]—a path which opens the eyes and bestows understanding which leads to peace of mind, to the higher wisdom, to full enlightenment, and to Nirvana. Truly, it is the noble eightfold path consisting of the following: Right views [free from superstition or delusion]; Right aims [high and worthy of the intelligent, earnest person]; Right Speech [kindly, open, and truthful]; Right Conduct [peaceful, honest, and pure]; Right livelihood [bringing no hurt or danger to living things]; Right effort [in self-training and self-control]; Right mindfulness [the active, watchful mind]; Right contemplation [earnest thought on the mysteries of life] This is the middle path, avoiding these two extremes. [*Samyutta-nikaya 56:2*]

Questions That Do Not Lead to Enlightenment

MALUNKYAPUTTA: Reverend sir, I was just now in seclusion and plunged in meditation, when a thought occurred to my mind. There are theories that the Blessed One has left unexplained, and has set aside and rejected. They are, that the world is eternal, that the world is not eternal, . . . that the saint neither exists nor does not exist after death. The Blessed One does not explain these to me. . . .

BUDDHA: Suppose that a man had been wounded by an arrow thickly smeared with poison. When friends and relatives went to procure for him a physician, suppose the sick man said, "I will not have this arrow taken out until I have learned whether the man who wounded me belonged to the warrior caste, priestly caste, worker caste, or servant caste." Or again, suppose he said, "I will not have this arrow taken out until I have learned the name of the man who wounded me, and to what clan he belongs." Or again, suppose he said, "I will not have this arrow taken out until I have learned the whether the man who wounded me was tall, short, or middle height . . . or was black, white, or yellow skinned . . . or from this or that village, town or city. . . ." That man would die without ever having learned these things. Suppose similarly someone said "I will not lead the religious life under the Blessed One [i.e., the Buddha] until the Blessed One explained to me that the world is eternal or not eternal . . . or that the saint exists or does not exist after death." That person too would die before the Tathagata [i.e, the Buddha] ever explained this to him.

The religious life does not depend on the dogma that the world is eternal, nor on the dogma that the world is not eternal. Whether the dogma obtains that the world is eternal or that the world is not eternal, there still remains birth, old age, death, sorrow, lamentation, misery, grief, and despair; and I prescribe the extinction of these in the present life. So, always bear in mind what it is that I have not explained, and what it is that I have explained. And what have I not explained? I have not explained that the world is eternal, . . . that the world is not eternal, . . . and that the saint neither exists nor does not exist after death. And why have I not explained this? Because this does not profit us, it has nothing to do with the fundamentals of religion, and does not tend to aversion, absence of passion, cessation, calm, the supernatural faculties, supreme wisdom, and nirvana. . . . And what have I explained? Misery, the origin of misery, the cessation of misery, and the path leading to the cessation of misery. And why have I explained this? Because this does profit and concerns the fundamentals of religion . . . [*Majjhima-Nikaya*, 63]

No Self

BUDDHA: In regard to the self, Ananda, what are the views held concerning it? One holds the view that (1) sensation is the self, saying, "sensation is my self," or one holds the view that, (2) truly, sensation is not my self insofar as my self has no sensation. Or one holds the view that (3) truly, neither is sensation my self, nor does my self have no sensation; my self *has* sensation and my self *possesses* the faculty of sensation.

In the first case above where it is said, "sensation is my self," one should reply as follows. Brother, there are three sensations, namely, the pleasant sensation, the unpleasant sensation, and the indifferent sensation. Which of these three sensations do you hold to be the self? Whenever a person experiences a pleasant sensation, he does not at the same time experience an unpleasant sensation, nor does he experience an indifferent sensation. At that time, he only feels the pleasant sensation. Whenever a person experiences an unpleasant sensation, he does not at the same time experience a pleasant sensation, nor does he experience an indifferent sensation. He only feels the unpleasant sensation. Whenever a person experiences an indifferent sensation, he does not at the same time experience a pleasant sensation, nor does he experience an unpleasant sensation. He only feels the indifferent sensation.

Now, pleasant sensations are transitory, are due to causes, originate by dependence, and are subject to decay, disappearance, effacement, and cessation. Unpleasant sensations are transitory, are due to causes, originate by dependence, and are subject to decay, disappearance, effacement, and cessation. Finally, indifferent sensations are transitory, due to causes, originate by dependence, and are subject to decay, disappearance, effacement, and cessation. While this person is experiencing a pleasant sensation, he thinks, "this is my self." And after the cessation of this same pleasant sensation, he thinks, "my self has passed away." While he is experiencing an unpleasant sensation, he thinks, "this is my self." And after the cessation of this same unpleasant sensation, he thinks, "my self has passed away." And while he is experiencing an indifferent sensation, he thinks, "this is my self." And after the cessation of this same indifferent sensation, he thinks, "my self has passed away." So that he who says, "sensation is my self," holds the view that even during his lifetime his self is transitory, that it is pleasant, unpleasant, or mixed, and that it is subject to rise and disappearance.

BUDDHA: So, Ananda, it is not possible to hold the view that sensation is my self. In the second case above where it is said that truly sensation is not my self insofar as my self has no sensation, one should reply as follows. Brother, where there is no sensation, is there any "I am"?

ANANDA: No, truly, Reverend Sir.

BUDDHA: So, Ananda, it is not possible to hold the view that, truly sensation is not my self insofar as my self has no sensation. In the third case above, one states that truly neither is sensation my self, nor does my self have no sensation. My self *has* sensation and my self *possesses* the faculty of sensation. One should reply to this as follows. Suppose, brother, all sensation were to cease, utterly, completely, and without remainder. If there were nowhere any sensation, would there be anything after the cessation of sensation of which you could say "this is me?"

ANANDA: No, truly, Reverend Sir.

BUDDHA: So, Ananda, it is not possible to hold the view that truly neither is sensation my self, nor does my self have no sensation. My self *has* sensation and my self *possesses* the faculty of sensation.

BUDDHA: From the time a monk rejects the above three views (namely that sensation is the self, that the self has no sensation, and that the self has sensation insofar as it possesses the faculty of sensation) he ceases to attach himself to anything in the world, and is free from attachment. He is never agitated, and being never agitated, he attains nirvana in his own person. He knows that rebirth is all gone, that he has lived a holy life, that he has done what it obligated him to do, and that he is no more for this world. [*Digha-nikaya* 256, *Mahanidana sutta*]

Doctrine of Dependent Origin

ANANDA: Revered sir, how wonderful, marvelous and complex is dependent origin, and how complicated it appears to be. Nevertheless, to me it is as clear as clear can be.

BUDDHA: Don't say that, Ananda, please don't say that. Dependent origin appears complicated and is complex. It is through not understanding and penetrating this doctrine that humankind is accordingly like an entangled twist, an ensnared web, or like jumbled munja grass and pabbaja grass. It fails to disengage itself from punishment, suffering, destruction, and rebirth. If one asks whether old age and death depend on anything, the reply should be that old age and death depend on birth. If one asks whether birth depends on anything, the reply should be that birth depends on existence. If one asks whether existence depends on anything, the reply should be that existence depends on attachment. If one asks whether attachment depends on anything, the reply should be that attachment depends on desire. If one asks whether desire depends on anything, the reply should be that desire depends on sensation. If one asks whether sensation depends on anything, the reply should be that sensation depends on contact. If one asks whether contact depends on anything, the reply should be that contact depends on mental and physical phenomena. If one asks whether mental and physical phenomena depend on anything, the reply should be that they depend on consciousness. If one asks whether consciousness depends on anything, the reply should be that consciousness depends on mental and physical phenomena.

Thus, consciousness depends on mental and physical phenomena; mental and physical phenomena depend on consciousness; contact depends on mental and physical phenomena; sensation depends on contact; desire depends on sensation; attachment depends on desire; existence depends on attachment; birth depends on existence; old age, death, sorrow, lamentation, misery, grief and despair all depend on birth. This is how the entire aggregate of misery arises. [*Digha-nikaya 256, Mahanidana sutta*]

Emptiness

The venerable *Bodhisattva* Avalokitesvara was studying in the deep Perfection of Wisdom. He reflected that there are the five components (*skandhas*) [of our phenomenal nature], and he considered these to be empty by their nature. [Speaking to Sariputra,] he said, "Oh Sariputra, form here is emptiness and emptiness is indeed form. Emptiness is not different from form, and form is not different from emptiness. Whatever is form is emptiness, and whatever is emptiness is form. The same applies to perception, name, conception and knowledge. Here, Sariputra, all things have the character of emptiness. They have no beginning, no end, they are faultless and not faultless, they are perfect and they are imperfect. Therefore, Sariputra, there is no form in this emptiness, no perception, no name, no concepts, no knowledge. There is no eye, ear, nose, tongue, body, or mind. There is no form, sound, smell, taste, touch, or objects. There is no eye, ear, nose, tongue, body, and mind, no objects, no mind-knowledge.

There is no knowledge, no ignorance, or no destruction of knowledge. There is no decay and death, or no destruction of decay and death. There are no [four noble truths, namely,] that there is pain, the origin of pain, the elimination of pain, and the path to it. There is no knowledge, no obtaining, no not obtain of nirvana. Therefore, Sariputra, as there is no obtaining of nirvana, a man who has approached the Perfection of Wisdom of the *Bodhisattvas* dwells for a time enveloped in consciousness. But when the envelopment of consciousness has been annihilated, then he becomes free of all fear, beyond the reach of change, enjoying final nirvana.

All Buddhas of the past, present, and future, after approaching the Perfection of Wisdom, have awaken to the highest perfect knowledge. Therefore we ought to know the great verse of the Perfection of Wisdom. It is the verse of the great wisdom, the unsurpassed verse, the verse that appeases all pain. It is truth, not falsehood. It is the verse fit for obtaining the Perfection of Wisdom: 'Oh wisdom gone; gone, gone to the other shore, landed at the other shore; it is offered (*svaha*)!' In this way, Sariputra, should a *Bodhisattva* teach in the study of the deep Perfection of Wisdom." [*Heart Sutra*]

If everything is relative, and there is no [real] origination and no [real] annihilation, how, then is nirvana conceived? Through what deliverance and through what annihilation [would this take place]? If everything is real in substance, and there is no [new] creation and no [new] destruction, how, then, would nirvana be reached? Through what deliverance and through what annihilation [would this take place]? [Nirvana is] what is neither released, nor ever reached; what is neither annihilated nor is eternal; what neither disappears nor has been created. This is nirvana. It escapes precision. . . . There is no difference at all between nirvana and the realm of life/death (*samsara*). There is no difference at all between the realm of life/death and nirvana. What makes the limit of nirvana is also then the limit of the realm of life/death. Between the two we cannot find the slightest shade of difference. [Nagarjuna, *Treatise*, Ch. 25]

CONFUCIAN PHILOSOPHY

Ritual Conduct

7:17. The Master's frequent themes of discourse were—the Odes, the History, and the maintenance of the rules of social custom. On all these he frequently discoursed.

8:2. The Master said, "Respectfulness without the rules of social custom becomes laborious bustle. Carefulness without the rules of social custom becomes timidity. Boldness without the rules of social custom becomes insubordination. Straightforwardness without the rules of social custom becomes rudeness. When those who are in high stations properly perform all their duties to their relations, the people are inspired towards virtue. When old friends are not neglected by them, the people are preserved from meanness."

8:8. The Master said, "It is by the Odes that the mind is aroused. It is by the rules of social custom that the character is established. It is from Music that the finish is received."

12:1. Yen Yuan asked about perfect virtue. The Master said, "To subdue one's self and return to social custom is perfect virtue. If a person can for one day subdue himself and return to social custom, all under heaven will attribute perfect virtue to him. Is the practice of perfect virtue from a person himself, or is it from others?" Yen Yuan said, "I beg to ask the steps of that process." The Master replied, "Do not look at what is contrary to social custom; do not listen to what is contrary to social custom; do not speak what is contrary to social custom; do not make movements which are contrary to social custom." Yen Yuan then said, "Though I am deficient in intelligence and vigor, I will make it my business to practice this lesson."

16:13. Another day he was in the same way standing alone, when I passed by below the hall with hasty steps. He said to me, "Have you learned the rules of social custom?" On my replying "Not yet," he added, "If you do not learn the rules of social custom, your character cannot be established." I then retired, and learned the rules of social custom. [*Analects*]

Humanity

1:3. The Master said, "Fine words and an insinuating appearance are seldom associated with true humanity."

4:1–4. The Master said, "It is humane manners that constitute the excellence of a neighborhood. If a person in selecting a residence does not fix on one where such prevail, how can he be wise?" The Master said, "Those who are without humanity cannot abide long either in a condition of poverty and hardship, or in a condition of enjoyment. The virtuous rest in humanity; the wise desire humanity." The Master said, "It is only the truly humane person who can love, or who can hate, others." The Master said, "If one's will is set on humanity, there will be no practice of wickedness."

4:6–7. The Master said, "I have not seen a person who really loved humane attitudes, or one who really hated inhumane attitudes. One who loved humanity would value nothing above it. One who hated inhumanity would practice virtue in such a way that he would not allow anything that is not humane to approach his person. Is anyone able to apply his strength to humanity for even a single day? I have not seen the case in which his strength would be insufficient to do so. Should there possibly be any such case, I have not seen it." The Master said, "The faults of people are characteristic of the class to which they belong. By observing a person's faults, it may be known that he is virtuous."

5:11. Tzu-kung said, "What I do not wish people to do to me, I also wish not to do to people." The Master said, "Ts'ze, you have not attained to that."

12:1–2. Chung-kung asked about perfect virtue. The Master said, "It is, when you go abroad, to behave to everyone as if you were receiving a great guest; to employ the people as if you were assisting at a great sacrifice; not to do to others as you would not wish done to yourself; to have no murmuring against you in the country, and none in the family." Chung-kung said, "Though I am deficient in intelligence and vigor, I will make it my business to practice this lesson." Sze-ma Niu asked about perfect virtue. The Master said, "The person of perfect virtue is cautious and slow in his speech."

15:23. Tzu-kung asked, saying, "Is there one word that may serve as a rule of practice for all one's life?" The Master said, "Is not reciprocity such a word? What you do not want done to yourself, do not do to others." [*Analects*]

Superior Person

2:9. The Master said, "The superior person is universal and not partisan. The inferior person is partisan and not universal."

4:10. The Master said, "The superior person in the world does not set his mind either for anything, or against anything. What is right he will follow."

4:11. The Master said, "The superior person thinks of virtue; the small person thinks of comfort. The superior person thinks of the sanctions of law; the small person thinks of favors which he may receive."

4:24. The Master said, "The superior person wishes to be slow in his speech and earnest in his conduct."

5:15. The Master said of Tzu-ch'an that he had four of the characteristics of a superior person: in his conduct of himself, he was humble; in serving his superior, he was respectful; in nourishing the people, he was kind; in ordering the people, he was just."

15:17–22. The Master said, "The superior person in everything considers righteousness to be essential. He performs it according to the rules of social custom. He brings it forth in humility. He completes it with sincerity. This is indeed a superior person." The Master said, "The superior person is distressed by his want of ability. He is not distressed by people not knowing him." The Master said, "The superior person dislikes the thought of his name not being mentioned after his death." The Master said, "What the superior person seeks is in himself. What the inferior person seeks is in others." The Master said, "The superior person is dignified, but does not wrangle. He is sociable, but not a partisan." The Master said, "The superior person does not promote someone simply on account of his words, nor does he put aside good words because of the person."

7:32. The Master said, "The sage and the person of perfect virtue; how dare I rank myself with them? It may simply be said of me, that I strive to become such without being filled, and teach others without weariness." Kung-hsi Hwa said, "This is just what we, the disciples, cannot imitate you in."

7:33. The Master said, "In letters I am perhaps equal to other people, but the character of the superior person, carrying out in his conduct what he professes, is what I have not yet attained to."

7:36. The Master said, "The superior person is satisfied and composed; the inferior person is always full of distress."

11:4–5. Sze-ma Niu asked about the superior person. The Master said, "The superior person has neither anxiety nor fear." Nui said, "Being without anxiety or fear! Does this constitute what we call the superior person?" The Master said, "When internal examination discovers nothing wrong, what is there to be anxious about? What is there to fear?" Sze-ma Niu anxiously replied, "Other people all have their brothers, I'm the only one who doesn't." Confucius said to him, "There is a saying which I have heard: 'Death and life have their determined appointment; riches and honors depend upon Heaven.' Let the superior person never fail in reverence to order his own conduct, and let him be respectful to others and observant of social custom. Then everyone within the four seas will be his brothers. What has the superior person to do with being distressed because he has no brothers?" [*Analects*]

Filial Obedience

1:2. The philosopher Yu [i.e., Confucius's pupil] said, "Few people who are filial and fraternal are also fond of offending superiors. No one who is respectful to superiors is fond of stirring up confusion. The superior person bends his attention to what is fundamental. When that root is established, moral law (*Dao*) naturally grow. Filial obedience and fraternal submission, are the root of all humane action (*jen*).

1:6. The Master said, "When at home, a youth should be filial [to his parents], and when abroad he should be respectful to his elders. He should be earnest and truthful. He should overflow in love to all, and cultivate the friendship good people. When he has time and opportunity, after the performance of these things, he should study art and literature (*wen*)."

2:7. Tzu-yu asked what filial obedience was. The Master said, "Filial obedience nowadays means to support one's parents. But dogs and horses also are able to do something in the way of support. Without reverence, what is there to distinguish the one support given from the other?"

4:10. The Master said, "If the son for three years does not alter from the way of his father, he may be called filial."

2:5. Meng-I-tzu asked what filial obedience was. The Master said, "It is not being disobedient." Soon after, as Fan Ch'ih was driving him, the Master told him, "Meng-sun asked me what filial obedience was, and I answered him, 'not being disobedient.'" Fan Ch'ih said, "What did you mean?" The Master replied, "That parents, when alive, be served according to social custom; that, when dead, they should be buried according to social custom; and that they should be sacrificed to according to social custom." [*Analects*]

Good Government

2:1. The Master said, "He who exercises government by means of his virtue may be compared to the north polar star, which keeps its place and all the stars turn towards it."

2:3. The Master said, "If the people are led by laws, and uniformity imposed through punishments, then they will try to avoid the punishment, but have no sense of shame. If they are led by virtue, and uniformity imposed through the rules of social custom, then they will have the sense of shame, and moreover will become good."

13:16. The Duke of Sheh asked about government. The Master said, "Good government obtains when those who are near are made happy, and those who are far off are attracted to come."

13:17. Tzu-hsia, being governor of Chu-fu, asked about government. The Master said, "Do not desire to have things done quickly and do not look at small advantages. If you desire to have things done quickly, this prevents them being done thoroughly. If you look at small advantages, this prevents great affairs from being accomplished."

16:2. Confucius said, "When good government prevails in the empire, ceremonies, music, and military expeditions proceed from the son of Heaven. When bad government prevails in the empire, ceremonies, music, and military expeditions proceed from the princes. . . ."

20:2. Tzu-chang asked Confucius, saying, "In what way should a person in authority act in order that he may conduct government properly?" The Master replied, "Let him honor the five excellent things, and banish away the four bad, things; then may he conduct government properly." Tzu-chang said, "What are meant by the five excellent things?" The Master said, "When the person in authority is beneficent without great expense; when he lays tasks on the people without their grieving; when he pursues what he desires without being selfish; when he maintains a dignified ease without being proud; when he is majestic without being cruel."

Tzu-chang said, "What is meant by being beneficent without great expenditure?" The Master replied, "When the person in authority makes those things more beneficial to the people from which they naturally derive benefit; is not this being beneficent without great expense? When he chooses the labors which are proper, and makes them labor on them, who will grieve? When his desires are set on benevolent government, and he secures it, who will accuse him of greed? Whether he has to do with many people or few, or with things great or small, he does not dare to indicate any disrespect. Isn't this maintaining a dignified ease without any pride? He adjusts his clothes and cap, and throws a dignity into his looks, so that, thus dignified, he is looked at with awe. Isn't this being majestic without being fierce?"

Tzu-chang then asked, "What is meant by the four bad things?" The Master said, "To put the people to death without having instructed them; this is called cruelty. To suddenly require from them a full load of work, without having given them warning; this is called oppression. To issue orders as if without urgency, at first, and, when the time comes, to insist on them with severity; this is called injury. And, generally, in the giving pay or rewards to people, to do it in a stingy way; this is called acting the part of a mere official." [*Analects*]

Mencius

KAO: Human nature is like a tree, and righteousness (*i*) is like a wooden cup or a bowl. The fashioning of benevolence and righteousness out of a person's nature is like the making of cups and bowls from the tree.

MENCIUS: Without touching the nature of the tree, can you make it into cups and bowls? You must do violence and injury to the tree before you can make cups and bowls with it. If you must do violence and injury to the tree in order to make cups and bowls with it, on your principles you must in the same way do violence and injury to humanity in order to fashion from it benevolence and righteousness. Thus, your words would certainly lead all people on to consider benevolence and righteousness to be calamities.

KAO: Human nature is like water whirling around in a corner. Open a passage for it to the east, and it will flow to the east. Open a passage for it to the west, and it will flow to the west. Human nature is indifferent to good and evil, just as water is indifferent to the east and west.

MENCIUS: Water indeed will flow indifferently to the east or west, but will it flow indifferently up or down? The tendency of human nature to do good is like the tendency of water to flow downwards. All people have this tendency to good, just as all water flows downwards. Now, by striking water and causing it to leap up, you may make it go over your forehead, and, by damming and leading it, you may force it up a hill. But are such movements according to the nature of water? It is the force applied which causes them. When people are made to do what is not good, their nature is dealt with in this way. [*Mencius*, 6a1, 2]

DAOIST PHILOSOPHY

The Dao

1. The Dao that can be named is not the eternal and unchanging Dao. The name that can be spoken is not the eternal and unchanging name. The nameless is the source of heaven and earth. The named is the mother of all things. Always be without desires and you will see mystery. Always be with desire, and you will see only its effects. These two are really the same, although, as development takes place, they receive the different names. They are both a mystery, and where mystery is the deepest we find the gate of all that is subtle and wonderful.

4. The Dao is like the emptiness of a vessel; and in our employment of it we must be on our guard against all fullness. How deep and unfathomable it is, as if it were the honored ancestor of all things. We should blunt our sharp points, and unravel the complications of things; we should dim our brightness, and bring ourselves into agreement with the obscurity of others. How pure and still the Dao is, as if it would continue forever. I do not know whose son it is. It might appear to have been before God.

10 . . . The Dao produces all things and nourishes them; it produces them and does not claim them as its own; it does all, and yet does not boast of it; it presides over all, and yet does not control them. This is what is called "the mysterious quality" of the Dao.

14. We look at it, and we do not see it, and we name it "the Equable." We listen to it, and we do not hear it, and we name it "the Inaudible." We try to grasp it, and do not get hold of it, and we name it "the Subtle." With these three qualities, it cannot be made the subject of description; and hence we blend them together and obtain The One. Its upper part is not bright, and its lower part is not obscure. Ceaseless in its action, it yet cannot be named, and then it again returns and becomes nothing. This is called the Form of the Formless, and the Appearance of the Invisible; this is called the Fleeting and Indeterminable. We meet it and do not see its front; we follow it, and do not see its back. When we can lay hold of the Dao of old to direct the things of the present day, and are able to know it as it was of old in the beginning, this is called unwinding the clue of Dao.

18. When the Great Dao ceased to be observed, benevolence and righteousness came into fashion. Then appeared wisdom and shrewdness, and there arose great hypocrisy. When harmony no longer prevailed throughout the six kinships, filial sons found their manifestation; when the states and clans fell into disorder, loyal ministers appeared.

25. There was something undefined and complete, coming into existence before Heaven and Earth. How still and formless it was, standing alone, and undergoing no change, reaching everywhere and in no danger of being exhausted. It may be regarded as the Mother of all things. I do not know its name, and I give it the designation of the Dao, the Way or Course. Making an effort further to give it a name I call it "the Great." Great, it passes on in constant flow. Passing on, it becomes remote. Having become remote, it returns.

Therefore the Dao is great; Heaven is great; Earth is great; and the sage king is also great. In the universe there are four that are great, and the sage king is one of them. People take their law from the Earth; the Earth takes its law from Heaven; Heaven takes its law from the Dao. The law of the Dao is its being what it is.

32. The Dao, considered as unchanging, has no name. Though in its primordial simplicity it may be small, the whole world dares not deal with one embodying it as a government minister. If a feudal prince or the king could guard and hold it, all would spontaneously submit themselves to him. Heaven and Earth under its guidance unite together and send down the sweet dew, which, without the directions of people, reaches equally everywhere as of its own accord. As soon as it moves on to action, it has a name. When it once has that name, people can know to rest in it. When they know to rest in it, they can be free from all risk of failure and error. The relation of the Dao to all the world is like that of the great rivers and seas to the streams from the valleys. [*Dao De Jing*]

Return

16. The state of vacancy should be brought to the utmost degree, and that of stillness guarded with unwearying vigor. All things alike go through their processes of activity, and then we see them return to their original state. When things in the vegetable world have displayed their luxuriant growth, we see each of them return to its root. This returning to their root is what we call the state of stillness; and that stillness may be called a reporting that they have fulfilled their appointed end.

58. When the government is unwise, the people are good. When the government is alert, the people meddle with everything. Happiness rests on misery, misery lurks beneath happiness. Who knows what either will come to in the end? Should we give up on correcting things? The method of correction will in turn become a distortion, and the good in it will in turn become evil. The delusion of the people on this point has indeed subsisted for a long time. [*Dao De Jing*]

Non-Action

43. The softest thing in the world dashes against and overcomes the hardest; that which has no substantial existence enters where there is no crevice. I know by this what advantage there is to doing nothing with a purpose. There are few in the world who attain to the teaching without words, and the advantage arising from non-action.

57. A state may be ruled by measures of correction; weapons of war may be used with crafty dexterity; but the kingdom is made one's own only by freedom from action and purpose. How do I know that it is so? By these facts: growth of restrictive laws in kingdoms increases the poverty of the people; the more devices that the people have to add to their profit, the greater disorder there is

in the state and clan; the more acts of crafty dexterity that people possess, the more do strange contrivances appear; the more display there is of legislation, the more thieves and robbers there are. Therefore a sage has said, "I will do nothing with purpose, and the people will transform themselves; I will keep still, and the people will correct themselves. I will not trouble with them, and the people will become rich by themselves; I will show no ambition, and the people will arrive at primitive simplicity by themselves."

63. It is the way of the Dao to act without thinking of acting; to conduct affairs without feeling the trouble of them; to taste without discerning any flavor; to consider what is small as great, and a few as many; and to recompense injury with kindness. . . .

76. Man at his birth is supple and weak; at his death, firm and strong. So it is with all things. In their early growth, trees and plants are soft and brittle; at their death they are dry and withered. In this manner, firmness and strength are the accompaniments of death, whereas softness and weakness are the accompaniments of life. Hence the person who relies on the strength of his forces does not conquer; and a tree that is strong will fill out-stretched arms, and thereby invites the lumberjack. Therefore the place of what is firm and strong is below, and that of what is soft and weak is above.

78. There is nothing in the world more soft and weak than water, and yet for attacking things that are firm and strong there is nothing that can outrank it. For, there is nothing so effective for which it can be changed. Everyone in the world knows that the soft overcomes the hard, and the weak overcomes the strong, but no one is able to carry it out in practice. Therefore a sage said, "Those who accept the humiliation of the state are worthy of offering sacrifices. Those who accept the state's woes are worthy of ruling an empire." Words that are strictly true seem to be paradoxical. [*Dao De Jing*]

Non-Mind

47. Without going outside his door, one understands all that takes place under the sky; without looking out from his window, one sees the Dao of Heaven. The further that one goes out from himself, the less he knows. Therefore the sages got their knowledge without traveling, gave their right names to things without seeing them, and accomplished their ends without any purpose of doing so.

48. He who devotes himself to learning seeks from day to day to increase his knowledge. He who devotes himself to the Dao seeks from day to day to diminish his doing. He diminishes it and again diminishes it, until he arrives at doing nothing on purpose. Having arrived at this point of non-action, there is nothing that he does not do. He who gets as his own all under heaven does so by giving himself no trouble with that end. If one take trouble with that end, he is not equal to getting as his own all under heaven.

81. Sincere words are not fine, and fine words are not sincere. Those who are skilled in the Dao do not dispute about it, and those who dispute are not skilled in it. Those who know the Dao are not extensively learned, and the extensively learned do not know it. The sage does not accumulate for himself.

The more that he expends for others, the more does he possess of his own. The more that he gives to others, the more does he have himself. With all the sharpness of the Way of Heaven, it injures not; with all the doing in the way of the sage he does not strive.

3. Not to value and employ people of superior ability is the way to keep the people from rivalry among themselves. Not to prize articles which are difficult to procure is the way to keep them from becoming thieves. Not to show them what is likely to excite their desires is the way to keep their minds from disorder. Therefore, in exercising his government, the sage empties the people's minds, fills their bellies, weaken their wills, and strengthen their bones. He constantly tries to keep them without knowledge and without desire, and where there are those who have knowledge, to keep them from acting on it. When there is this abstinence from action, good order is universal. [*Dao De Jing*]

Story of the Cook

Prince Hui's cook was cutting up a bull. Every blow of his hand, every heave of his shoulders, every tread of his foot, every thrust of his knee, every whshh of cut flesh, every chhk of the knife, was in perfect harmony, rhythmical like the dance of the Mulberry Grove, simultaneous like the chords of the Ching Shou.

The prince said, "Ah! It is indeed admirable that your art has become so perfect!"

[Having finished his task], the cook laid down his knife, and replied to the remark. "I am devoted to the method of the Dao, which is superior to any skill. When I first began to cut up bulls, I saw nothing but the [entire] carcass. After three years I ceased to see it as a whole. Now I deal with it in a spirit-like manner, and do not look at it with my eyes. I discarded the use of my senses, and my spirit acts as it wills. Observing the natural lines, [my knife] slips through the great crevices and slides through the great cavities, taking advantage of the accommodations thus presented. My skill avoids the ligaments, and much more the large bones.

A good cook changes his knife every year because he cleanly *cuts*. An ordinary cook changes his every month because he *hacks*. Now I have used my knife for nineteen years. It has cut up several thousand bulls, and yet its edge is as sharp as if it came right from the whetstone. There are crevices in the joints, and the edge of the knife has no appreciable thickness. When that which is so thin enters the crevice, how easily it moves along! The blade has more than enough room. However, whenever I come to a complicated joint and see that there will be some difficulty, I proceed with caution. I do not allow my eyes to wander from the place, and move my hand slowly. Then by a very slight movement of the knife, the part is quickly separated, and drops like a clod of earth to the ground. Then standing up with the knife in my hand, I leisurely look all round, and with an air of satisfaction, wipe it clean, and put it in its sheath."

"Excellent!" said the Prince. "I have heard the words of my cook, and learned how to care for life." [*Chuang-Tzu*, 3]

Transformation and the Story of the Dying Man

Masters Ssu, Yu, Li, and Lai were all four conversing together. They asked, "Who can make non-action his head, life his backbone, and death the tail of his existence? Who knows how birth and death, existence and annihilation comprise one single body? The person who understands this will be admitted to friendship with us." The four men looked at one another and laughed, but no one seized with his mind the drift of the questions. All, however, were friends together.

Not long after, Yu fell ill, and Ssu went to see him. "How great is the Creator!" said the sufferer. "He made me the deformed object that I am!" Yu was a crooked hunchback; his five viscera were squeezed into the upper part of his body; his chin bent over his navel; his shoulder was higher than his crown; on his crown was an ulcer pointing to the sky; his breath came and went in gasps. Nevertheless, he was easy in his mind, and made no trouble of his condition. He limped to a well, looked at himself in it, and said, "I can't believe that the Creator would have made me the deformed object that I am!" Ssu said, "Do you dislike your condition?" He replied, "No, why should I dislike it? If the creator transformed my left arm into a rooster, I would watch the time of the night. If he transformed my right arm into a cross-bow, I would then be looking for a duck to shoot for roasting. If he transformed my rump-bone into a wheel and my spirit into a horse, I would then be able to ride in my own chariot. I'd never have to change horses. I obtained life because it was my time. I am now parting with it in accordance with the same law. When we rest in what the time requires, and manifest that submission, neither joy nor sorrow can enter. This is what the ancients called 'loosening the rope.' Some, though, are hung up and cannot loosen themselves. They are held fast by the bonds of material existence. But it is a long-acknowledged fact that no creatures can overcome Heaven. Why, then, should I hate my condition?" [*Chuang-Tzu*, 6]

Freedom from Society's Constraints

With their hoofs horses can tread on ice and snow, and with their hair withstand the wind and cold; they feed on the grass and drink water; they prance with their legs and leap. This is the true nature of horses. Even if grand towers and large dormitories were made for them, they would prefer not to use them. One day Poh Loh [i.e., the original mythical tamer of horses] said, "I know well how to manage horses." Accordingly, he clipped them, pared their hoofs, haltered their heads, bridled them and shackled their legs, and confined them in stables and corrals. [With this treatment] two or three in every ten of them died. Still, he subjected them to hunger and thirst; he galloped them and raced them, and made them prance in regular order. In front of the horses were the evils of the bit and ornamented breast bands, and behind were the terrors of the whip and switch. With this treatment more than half of them died. . . .

According to my idea, those who know how to properly govern humankind would not act so. People had their regular and constant nature. They originally wove and made themselves clothes; they tilled the ground for food. These are common to humanity. They all agreed on this, and did not form themselves into separate classes. In this way they were constituted and left to their natural tendencies. Therefore in the age of perfect virtue people walked along quietly, steadily looking forward. At that time, on the hills there were no footpaths or excavated passages. On the lakes there were no boats or dams. All creatures lived in groups, and the places of their settlement were made close to one another. Birds and beasts multiplied to flocks and herds. The grass and trees grew luxuriant and long. In this condition the birds and beasts could be led about without feeling the constrained. One could climb up to the nest of the raven and peep into it. Yes, in the age of perfect virtue, people lived in common with birds and beasts, and were on equal terms with all creatures, forming one family. How could they have distinctions between superior and inferior people? As they were all without knowledge, they did not leave their condition of natural virtue. Equally free from evil desires, they were in the state of natural integrity. In that state of natural integrity, the nature of the people was what it ought to be.

But when sages appeared, tripping people up with charity and constraining people with the duty to one's neighbor, then people universally began to be perplexed. The sages went to excess in performing music and fussed over the practice of ceremonies. Then people began to be separated from each other. If raw materials were not cut and hacked, who could have made a sacrificial vase from them? If natural jade was not broken, who could have made the handles for the ceremonial drinking cups? If the Dao was not abandoned, who could have introduced charity and duty to one's neighbor? If they did not depart from natural instincts, how could ceremonies and music have come into use? If the five colors were not confused, who would practice decoration? If the five notes were not confused, who would adopt the six pitched-pipes? The cutting and hacking of the raw materials to form vessels was the crime of the artisans. The injury done to the Dao in order to practice charity and duty to one's neighbor was the error of the sages. [*Chuang-Tzu*, 9]

Lieh-Tzu

The longest life span is 100 years, although not even one person in a thousand lives that long. Even if there is someone who lives out his span, infancy and incapacitating old age consume almost half of it. Sleeping at night and wasted days consume nearly half of what remains. Suffering and illness, sadness and drudgery, loss of loved ones, distress and fear consume almost half of that. During the remaining ten or so years, I suppose that there is less than an hour during which time we are comfortable, satisfied and carefree.

What, then, are we to live for? Where do we find happiness? It is only found in beautiful things and good food, music and sex. However, we cannot always have beautiful things and good food. We are not always in a position to enjoy music and sex. Further, we are inhibited by punishments and motivated by rewards. We are urge on by fame and restrained by the law. We busily compete for a moment of empty praise and strategize for fame that will last beyond our deaths. Even when we are alone we conform to what others do and say, and deny our own preferences. We thus deny ourselves happiness in our best years, and we cannot live freely for a moment. Are we any different than prisoners bound in chains and bondage?

People of long ago understood that in life we are here temporarily and in death we are gone temporarily. Accordingly they behaved as they pleased and they did not resist their natural desires. . . . Some die in ten years, and others in a hundred. Saints and sages both die. The wicked and foolish both die. While alive they were the virtuous emperors Yao and Shun. When dead they are rotten bones. While alive they were the evil emperors Chieh and Chou. When dead they are rotten bones. In either case, they are rotten bones. Can anyone tell them apart? Enjoy your life right now while you still have it. Why bother with what happens to you after you die? [*Lieh-Tzu*, 7]

Source: The sources of above selections are indicated within brackets at the close of the relevant paragraphs. The selections were edited and adapted by Alan Smithee, and reprinted by permission.

Glossary of Key Concepts

Aesthetics   The branch of philosophy concerned with the analysis of concepts such as beauty or beautiful as standards for judging works of art.

Agnostic   One who neither believes nor disbelieves that God exists since there is no conclusive evidence either way.

Analytic statement   A statement that is necessarily true because the predicate is already in the subject—for example, "all dogs are animals," where the word *dogs* already contains the concept "animal."

A posteriori   Literally, "after experience"; *a posteriori* knowledge is that derived from experience. This is in contrast to *a priori* knowledge (see below).

Appearance   How something presents itself to our senses as compared with its true reality. For example, the oar appears bent in the water, but it really is not bent.

A priori   Literally, "before experience"; *a priori* knowledge is before or independent of experience. For example, according to some philosophers, we know that "every event has a cause" even though we have not experienced every event.

Artificial intelligence   A contemporary theory that attempts to duplicate human cognitive mental states in computing machinery.

Authority   A source of our theological knowledge, specifically for philosophers and theologians who hold that the mysteries of faith surpass the reach of human reason.

Autonomy   Literally, self-rule; independence from external authority; freedom of the will to make its own law or rule of conduct, in contrast to *heteronomy* (being subject to someone else's rules).

Becoming   In Hegelian thought, refers to the world in which everything in our daily experience—persons and things—comes into being and passes away.

Behaviorism, logical   A contemporary theory of the mind-body problem associated with Ryle that reduces mental events to sensory input and behavioral output.

Being A general term in metaphysics referring to ultimate reality or existence. True being, for Plato, is the realm of the eternal Forms.

Categorical imperative In Kant's moral theory the absolute moral law understood as a duty by any rational creature. This is compared with *hypothetical imperatives*, which permit exceptions.

Categories A term used by Aristotle and Kant, for the concepts that the human mind brings to knowing—for example, cause and effect, or space and time.

Causality The relation of cause and effect, in which one event necessarily follows another.

Cause Something that has the power to produce a change, motion, or action in another thing; this change (*effect*) can be explained in terms of the behavior of the cause.

Change The alteration of anything, the rearrangement of something's parts, the coming into being of something that did not exist before, and the decline and dissolution of something.

Chinese Room Argument A thought experiment offered by Searle to refute the claims of strong artificial intelligence advocates that suitably programmed machines are capable of cognitive mental states.

Cogitatum The content of what is thought; hence, to think (*cogito*) is to think something (*cogitatum*).

Cogito Literally, in Latin, "I think." Used by Descartes to describe the self as a thinking thing.

Cognition In the broadest sense, knowledge, or the act of knowing.

Cognitive meaning A term used by logical positivists and analytical philosophers in reference to statements that are either true by definition or empirically verifiable (see *verification principle*).

Contingent An event that is not necessary; that is, it may or may not be, depending on other events that also may or may not be.

Cosmological argument A proof for the existence of God based on the idea that there had to be a first cause for the existence of the universe.

Deconstruction A post-structuralist theory associated with Derrida that attempts to show that all pairs of opposite concepts in philosophical systems are in fact self-refuting.

Deduction A process of reasoning by which the mind relates the truth of one proposition to the truth of another by inferring that the truth of the second proposition is involved in and therefore derived from the first (see *induction*).

Determinism The theory that every fact, or even the universe, is determined or caused by previous facts or events; human behavior and the events of history follow strict laws of causation or necessary connection. Accordingly, on this view, human beings do not possess freedom of the will or the power to originate independent or genuine choices.

Dialectic As in dialogue (Socrates), or debate over opposites (Hegel), or a clash of material forces (Marx) producing dynamic change. Or, a process of reasoning based on the analysis of opposing propositions. Socrates used the dialectic method of teaching by distinguishing between opinion and knowledge. Hegel and Marx developed dialectic conceptions of history in which for Hegel opposing ideas were the key while for Marx history was explained as the conflict of material forces.

Dionysian A concept in Nietzsche's philosophy referring to the forces of life. For Nietzsche true culture was a unity of the Dionysian and Apollonian elements, the latter of which is the love of form and beauty.

Dogmatism The act of making a positive assertion without demonstration by either rational argument or experience.

Dualism A theory holding that there are two independent and irreducible substances, such as mind and body, the intelligible world of ideas and the visible world of things, or the forces of good and evil. Dualism is in contrast to monism and pluralism.

Empiricism The theory that experience is the source of all knowledge, which thereby denies that human beings possess inborn knowledge or that they can derive knowledge through the exercise of reason alone.

Epistemology The branch of philosophy that studies the nature, origin, scope, and validity of knowledge.

Essence The chief characteristic, quality, or necessary function that makes a thing what it uniquely is.

Ethics (1) A set of rules for human behavior; (2) a study of judgments of value—of good and evil, right and wrong, or desirable and undesirable; (3) theories of obligation or duty or why we "ought" to behave in a certain way.

Existentialism A movement in twentieth-century philosophy, the leading exponents of which were Sartre and Merleau-Ponty. For Sartre the central thesis of existentialism is that *existence* precedes *essence;* that is, people have no given identity until they have made specific decisions and have chosen their work and have thereby defined themselves.

Extension For Descartes the character of physical things as having dimension in space and time.

Finitude Having definable limits.

Form, theory of Plato's view that ultimate reality is located in a spirit-realm containing archetypes of things, such as *triangularity, humanity,* or *justice.*

Free will The theory that in some cases the will makes decisions or choices independent of prior physiological or psychological causes.

Functionalism A contemporary theory of the mind-body problem that mental events depend on networks, pathways, and the interconnection of mental processes, but not on any specific material stuff that the brain is composed of, such as neurons. Functionalism holds open the possibility that mental events can occur in nonbiological systems, such as silicon chips.

Gestalt theory   The twentieth-century psychological theory that our perceptual experience consists of a full range of characteristics—form, structure,
sense, meaning, and value—all simultaneously.

Herd-mentality   A view in Nietzsche's philosophy that people are often
reduced to a common level of mediocrity.

Idealism   The view that mind is the ultimate reality in the world, as opposed
to *materialism*, the view that all reality is composed of material things.

Identity theory   A contemporary theory of the mind-body problem associated
with Armstrong and Smart that reduces mental events to brain activity.

Illusion   An erroneous impression, such as an optical illusion, or, for Freud, a
false belief growing out of a deep wish.

Impression   Hume's term for experience consisting of sensations and mental
reflections.

Indeterminism   The theory that in some cases the will makes decisions or
choices independent of prior physiological or psychological causes.

Induction   Proceeding from the observation of some particular facts to a
generalization (or conclusion) concerning all such facts (see *deduction*).

Innate ideas   Inborn notions that we know without requiring proof from
experience.

Instrumental   Refers to a thing, quality, or act that is a means for achieving
something else; compare *intrinsic*, which describes a thing, quality, or act as
existing for its own sake.

Instrumentalism   Dewey's theory that thought is instrumental insofar as it
produces practical consequences.

Intrinsic   Refers to a thing, quality, or act that exists for its own sake; compare
instrumental, which describes a thing, quality, or act as a means to some
other end.

Intuition   Direct and immediate knowledge of the self, the external world,
values, or other metaphysical truths, without the need to define the notions,
to justify a conclusion, or to build up inferences.

Logical positivism   The twentieth-century movement in the analytical tradition that rests on the verification principle.

Materialism   The view that matter constitutes the basis of all that exists in the
universe. Hence, combinations of matter and material forces account for
every aspect of reality, including the nature of thought, the process of historical and economic events, and the standard of values based on sensuous
bodily pleasures and the abundance of things; the notion of the primacy of
spirit or mind and rational purpose in nature is rejected.

Metaphysics   The branch of philosophy concerned with the question of the
ultimate nature of reality. Unlike the sciences, which focus on various
aspects of nature, metaphysics goes beyond particular things to inquire
about more general questions, such as what lies beyond nature, how things
come into being, what it means for something to be, and whether there is a

realm of being that is not subject to change and that is, therefore, the basis of certainty in knowledge.

Monism   The view that there is only one substance in the universe; idealism and materialism are monistic theories. Monism is in contrast to *dualism* and *pluralism*.

Nihilism   The view that there are no values. According to Nietzsche, "death of God" will be followed by the rejection of absolute values and the rejection of the idea of an objective and universal moral law.

Noumenal world   The real world as opposed to the world of appearance. According to Kant, the noumenal world cannot be known.

Ontological Argument   A proof for God's existence devised by Anselm, such that God is defined as the greatest possible being, which necessarily entails existence.

Ontology   The study of being, from the Greek *ontos*, "being," and *logos*, "science"; related to the field of metaphysics.

Participation   A central notion in Plato's theory that things in this world are modeled after ideal archetypes in the realm of the Forms.

Perception   The sensory vehicle by which we obtain knowledge about the world.

Phenomenal world   In Kant's theory the world of appearance versus the noumenal world beyond our knowledge.

Phenomenology   A twentieth-century philosophical movement founded by Husserl; in accounting for knowledge, we should not go beyond the data available to consciousness derived from appearances.

Pluralism   The view that there are more than one or two separate substances making up the world. This stands in contrast to both *monism* and *dualism*.

Positivism   A nineteenth-century philosophical movement founded by Comte; asserts that we should reject any investigation that does not rest on direct observation.

Postmodernism   The theory in contemporary Continental philosophy that rejects the Renaissance and Enlightenment assumption that the world can be explained in a unified system.

Post-structuralism   The radical extension of the structuralist position contending that novels and philosophical texts are completely closed systems whose meanings derive from what individual readers bring to the texts.

Postulate   In Kant's theory a practical or moral principle that cannot be proved, such as the existence of God, the freedom of the will, or immortality, which must be believed to make possible our moral duty.

Pragmatism   A twentieth-century movement associated with Peirce, James, and Dewey contending that there is little value in philosophical theories that do not somehow make a difference in daily life.

Prime mover   A view in Aristotelian thought that there is a first cause of everything and does not itself require a cause.

Rationalism   The philosophical view that emphasizes the ability of human reason to grasp fundamental truths about the world without the aid of sense impressions.

Relativism   The view that there is no absolute knowledge, that truth is different for each individual, social group, or historical period and is, therefore, relative to the circumstances of the knowing subject.

Scholasticism   The theological and philosophical method of learning in medieval schools that emphasized deductive logic and the authority of key figures such as Plato, Aristotle, and Augustine.

Sense-data   The elements of information that we receive through our senses.

Skepticism   (1) The tendency to doubt some fundamental component of knowledge. (2) The ancient Greek school of thought associated with Plato's Academy, Pyrrho, and Sextus Empiricus.

Solipsism   From the Latin *solus*, "alone" and *ipse*, "self"; the view that the self alone is the source of all knowledge of existence, which sometimes leads to the conclusion that the self is the only reality.

Sophists   Wandering teachers in fifth-century Athens who especially prepared young men for political careers, who hence emphasized rhetoric and the ability to persuade audiences and win debates, and who were less concerned with pursuing truth.

Sovereign   A person or state independent of any other authority or jurisdiction.

Structuralism   The theory in contemporary Continental philosophy associated with Saussure and Lévi-Strauss that the meaning of a thing is defined by its surrounding cultural structures, which in turn rely on pairs of opposite concepts, such as light and dark.

Substance   A separate and distinct thing; that which underlies phenomena; the essence of a thing that underlies the other qualities of a thing.

Syllogism   A form of reasoning. For example, All humans are mortal (major premise); Socrates is a human (minor premise); therefore, Socrates is mortal (conclusion).

Synthetic statement   In Kant's theory a statement that adds an idea to the subject that the subject does not already contain—for example, "a dog will help catch foxes,"—but that is not true of all dogs. This is in contrast to *analytic* sentences, in which the subject contains the predicate.

Teleology   From the Greek *telos*, "purpose"; the study of purpose in human nature and in the events of history.

Utilitarianism   An ethical theory associated with Bentham and Mill that an action is morally good if it produces as much good as or more good than any alternative behavior.

Verification   Demonstrating or proving something to be true either by means of evidence or by formal rules of reasoning.

Verification principle   A principle in logical positivism contending that a statement is meaningful if (1) it asserts something that is true simply because the words used necessarily and always require the statement to be true (as in mathematics) or (2) it asserts something that can be judged as true or false by verifying it in experience.

Virtue epistemology   An epistemological theory that focuses on the character traits of a person, rather than on the properties of a person's belief.

Virtue theory   A moral theory that focuses on the development of good character traits, or virtues, rather than on rules for solving moral dilemmas.

Wager, Pascal's   A contention by Pascal that, when reason is neutral on the issue of God's existence, we should be psychologically compelled to believe based on the benefits of such belief.

Index